american democracy in theory and practice

---

the national government

Robert K. Carr

Joel Parker Professor of Law and Political Science, Dartmouth College

Donald H. Morrison

Dean of the Faculty and Professor of Government, Dartmouth College

Marver H. Bernstein

Assistant Professor of Politics, Princeton University

Richard C. Snyder

Associate Professor of Politics, Princeton University

american democracy

in theory and practice

---

the national government

Rinehart & Company, Inc., New York and Toronto

$\mathcal{T}$EXT BOOKS for use in introductory political science courses traditionally have been of two types. They describe the structure and operation of American government, on the theory that students should know the facts about the political system of their own country if they are to become good citizens. Or they analyze the general principles of political science on the equally valid theory that a satisfactory understanding of the function and work of a present-day government can be acquired only if the student is familiar with the basic concepts of political theory.

We have attempted to bridge the gap between these two alternative approaches to the study of political science. Our main purpose is to cover the traditional ground concerning the organization and functioning of American National Government; we have tried also to make factual information more meaningful by placing it in the context of the general principles and problems of political science. Two methods have been used to accomplish this latter purpose. First, each of the nine sections of the book contains one or more introductory chapters setting forth principles, theories, and problems that are pertinent to the more specific material on American government found in subsequent chapters. Second, throughout all of the chapters an attempt is made to relate the details of government structure and procedures to the underlying and ever-present problems of American society that government exists to solve. We have tried at all times to keep in mind the student's "what of it?" reaction to the traditional emphasis in textbooks upon facts. The book supplies factual information about American government essential to informed and intelligent citizenship; it also tries to give the student a basis for judging the adequacy of our governmental structures and processes in light of current problems.

A continuous effort has been made to view the American political system as an experiment in democracy. The case for the democratic way of life is set forth in the opening chapters and thereafter an attempt has been made to keep the reader's attention fixed constantly upon the question of the effectiveness of the American political record as tested by democratic principles.

Attention may be called to certain other features of this book that depart somewhat from the traditions of writing in this area. Extended treatment is

43146   *v*

given to problems of foreign policy, national defense, and civil rights. These matters loom so large in contemporary life that it has seemed to us they should receive careful and detailed examination in a book designed for use in introductory political science courses. Several chapters are also devoted to the personnel factor in American government. It is our conviction that an understanding of government must include awareness of the quality of men and women who staff the government and of the personal contributions that they make.

The frequent use of questions—questions that are often left unanswered—particularly in the chapters on government in action calls for comment. This device is used as a means of emphasizing the extent to which the American people are faced with issues and problems that remain unsolved, with respect to government structure, procedures, and substantive policy.

Bibliographic material has been cast in the form of brief notes attempting to describe and evaluate some of the literature relevant to the subject matter of the separate chapters. It should be emphasized that these notes are highly selective in character and that no effort has been made to call attention to all of the *good* books and articles on a subject, let alone to list the entire literature of an area. An attempt has been made to hold the footnotes throughout the text to an absolute minimum. It is our belief that an unrestrained use of such notes in a book of this character is confusing and distracting to the student and does not encourage him to make use of the sources indicated. Accordingly, we have used footnotes primarily to indicate the source of quotations, specific data, court opinions, and the like, and in the main have placed suggestions for further reading in the bibliographic notes.

In the preparation of this book, individual authors were responsible in the first instance for the drafting of the separate chapters. But in the final analysis all four men have participated in the writing of the entire book and each man assumes responsibility for it. At different stages in its preparation the manuscript was read in its entirety by Professor Royden J. Dangerfield of the University of Illinois and by Professor E. E. Schattschneider of Wesleyan University. Both men offered valuable aid and counsel, but neither has thereby accepted any responsibility for factual errors or questionable judgments that may still remain. We desire also to indicate our deep sense of appreciation for the aid and encouragement given by Olive Carr, Elizabeth Morrison, Sheva Bernstein, and Marjorie Snyder.

Hanover, N.H.
Princeton, N.J.
March, 1951

ROBERT K. CARR
DONALD H. MORRISON
MARVER H. BERNSTEIN
RICHARD C. SNYDER

1. the problem

2. the American constitutional system

3. government of the people

4. the formulation of policy

5. the administration of justice

6. securing the blessings of liberty

7. the implementation of policy

8. promoting the general welfare

9. national security and foreign policy

list of tables

part 1

_____

the problem

---

the meaning of government:

the regulatory and service functions of the state

The government of the United States is the largest and most difficult task undertaken by the American people, and at the same time the most important and the noblest. Our Government does more for more men, women, and children than any other institution; it employs more persons in its work than any other employer. It covers a wider range of aims and activities than any other enterprise; it sustains the frame of our national and our community life, our economic system, our individual rights and liberties. . . . Our goal is the constant raising of the level of the happiness and dignity of human life, the steady sharing of the gains of our Nation, whether material or spiritual, among those who make the Nation what it is.[1]

*T*ODAY, when there are so many fears about the threat of totalitarianism and so much controversy about the dangers of the welfare state, these sensible words from one of the great public documents of our time make a good starting point for the study of American government. It is a truism that almost every moment in the life of every American is somehow affected by what government does. Although there is no inevitability about the particular policies followed by government at any given moment, its general role in society is an inescapable one. Accordingly, we do well to seek to see its meaning and its role in proper perspective.

Even a cursory reading of the history of mankind makes it clear that gov-

---

[1] The quotation is from the opening passage of the Report of the President's Committee on Administrative Management, submitted to President Roosevelt in 1937. The commission's membership consisted of three eminent political scientists, Louis Brownlow, Charles E. Merriam, and Luther Gulick. This report, entitled *Administrative Management in the United States,* served as a starting point for modern discussion and action with respect to administrative reorganization of the national government of the United States.

3

ernment is an inextricable part of man's story. To begin with, government is a man-made institution which reflects the existence of social problems and man's need to take action with respect to them. Government is both the chief means by which man has climbed from a state of nature to civilization and the most important institution through which he copes with the complexities which civilization entails. It is the chief means by which he resolves conflicts with his fellow men, gains protection against his enemies, maintains a just social order, and satisfies certain material wants.

the role of government

Abraham Lincoln once said: "The legitimate object of government is to do for the community of people whatever they need to have done, but cannot do so well, for themselves in their separate and individual capacities." More recently Justice William O. Douglas of the United States Supreme Court has written, "Government is the most advanced art of human relations. It dispenses the various services that the complexities of civilization require or make desirable. It is designed to keep in balance the various competing forces present in any society and to satisfy the dominant, contemporary demands made upon it. As a result it serves a high purpose; it is the cohesive quality in civilization." [2]

From the observations of these men it will be seen that government has two primary functions to perform—service and regulation. In the first place, government exists to render some of those services which civilized man expects and demands but cannot obtain by his own individual efforts. As will shortly be seen, government is by no means the only social agency through which man seeks to satisfy his need for services, but it is one of the most important. Second, government has a regulatory function. The continuous clash of man against man, as all men seek to adance their interests in a complex society, makes necessary a considerable measure of regulation if individual and collective rights and interests are to be safeguarded, or, as Justice Douglas puts it, kept in balance. Again, government is not the sole regulatory force in society, for so great is man's need to live in peace that he has found many means of adjusting his conflicts with other men. But government is perhaps the chief of these regulatory forces.

distrust of governments' role is perennial

Distrust of government is a continuous theme in history. This may seem surprising in view of the two great functions, each logical and inevitable, that government exists to perform. But the reason for man's perennial apprehensions about government is not hard to find. Government can do, and throughout history has done, much harm to men. At one extreme it can through weakness fall

---

[2] William O. Douglas, *Being An American* (New York: The John Day Company, 1948), p. 51.

short of satisfactory performance of the functions assigned to it. It can bungle the job of rendering services by supplying them inadequately or, if adequately, at too high a cost. It can fail in its regulatory function and allow the conflict of interests to lead to social disorder and violence. At the other extreme, government can, through the possession and exercise of too much power, become a threat to freedom. It can be captured by individuals or groups motivated by that lust for power which seems at all times to be one of the components of human nature. It can be used to advance the interests of the few at the expense of the interests of the many. Its importance may be magnified to a point where it is viewed as an end in itself rather than a mere means for the advancement of human interests.

At whichever extreme the erring tendencies appear it is clear that government can make mistakes which will cause all members of society to suffer. This is true because government undertakes nothing less than the most difficult task known to history: the development and ordering of a society in which the individual can thrive. Since government can make serious mistakes, a moderate distrust of its policies and tendencies is a healthy thing.

Distrust of government manifests itself in various ways. Throughout much of American history it has shown itself in the popular acceptance of the Jeffersonian concept of government: dislike for "big" government, for central government; and a strong preference for local government, for that government which governs least. Today, the existence of a "big" society, the growing power of "big" business and "big" labor, the emergence of "big" problems in a "big" age and a "big" world force us inevitably to accept more and more "big" government. But always the Jeffersonian tradition has served as a brake upon the expansionist tendencies of government in the United States.

Again distrust of government expresses itself in the continued popularity of nineteenth-century liberalism, in the belief in a self-regulating economic order, in the conviction that governmental attempts to interfere with the inexorable working out of natural economic laws are likely to do more harm than good. Actually, we have also come to distrust laissez-faire economics and to conclude that man would not be rational were he not to make strong efforts to rise above environmental forces and to control his social destiny by pursuing carefully calculated and consciously designed policies. At the same time, the old notion that nature is good and government bad never quite dies and there remains an instinctive resistance to the further expansion of public power and collective action.

Finally, the fact that the cost of government is sooner or later reflected in taxation serves as a restraining influence upon expanding government and as a basis for distrust of government. Throughout all history the tax collector has been a detested individual, and admittedly the avarice of government at times seems to be without limit. And yet, citizens in a democratic society come slowly to recognize that their government does render valued services for the charges it exacts in taxes. Perhaps the reality of the taxation process was never better expressed than in the famous anecdote about the late Justice Holmes. The story runs that he was asked the question one day by a young law clerk, "Don't you hate to pay taxes, Mr. Justice Holmes?" The answer came back, "No, young man, I like to pay taxes. With taxes I buy civilization."

There is increasing realization that private enterprise also collects taxes, either in the open and readily recognized form of "prices," or in such "hidden" forms as excess charges by business monopolies or tributes exacted by powerful labor unions through such practices as "featherbedding." In the end there is increasing awareness that income and money exist to be spent, and that what is bought from government compares favorably in price and quality with what is bought from private enterprise. Nonetheless, dislike for taxes remains strong and serves as a powerful force slowing down the tendency of government to expand its sphere of activity.

The restraining forces upon government which exist in American society are basically sound and healthy. But the spirit of distrust can be pushed too far. "Government is not something that is invented by the cunning or the strong and imposed on the rest." [3] Accordingly, a spirit of sympathy and understanding toward government is also needed. Learning to see government in its proper perspective is not easy. At one extreme it is clearly necessary to avoid any tendency toward viewing government as an end in itself, as the agency of an authoritarian state whose citizens are swallowed up in some mystical "totality," with the result that the interests of the state take precedence over those of the individual. And lest this tendency seem to be more characteristic of ancient philosophies and states than of the enlightened thought and practices of modern times, only a gentle reminder is needed that twentieth-century governments have in many parts of the world shown as strong totalitarian tendencies as did ever any ancient governments.

At the other extreme it is just as important to avoid the too easy view of government as a necessary evil entitled only to suspicion and distrust. Government is a necessity, but it can be viewed as a necessary evil only if man's march from the state of nature to a civilized society itself be viewed as an evil turn of events in human history. Too much suspicion of government, like too much worship of government, can frustrate the great purposes of society by rendering it difficult for government to make that contribution to man's forward march which is its reason for existence.

A proper understanding of government, then, necessitates that the reasons for government's existence be grasped, that its social role be understood, and that the dangers inherent in all governments be appreciated but not exaggerated.

[3] R. M. MacIver, *The Web of Government* (New York: The Macmillan Company, 1947), p. 22.

A people must be not afraid of their government; yet they must seek ever to control it.

government and the nature of man

The role of government as so far described is based upon certain assumptions concerning the nature of man. It has been suggested that man is selfish and that he lusts for power and wealth. Accordingly, society is characterized by a continuous conflict of interests and a struggle for power. Unless some means is found to reconcile or compromise the conflict of interests and to maintain a wide distribution of power among the diverse elements of society, man's selfish nature threatens to make life unbearable. Thus, from earliest times one of the reasons for government's existence has been to referee the perennial battles caused by man's selfish and acquisitive nature.

But in a modern democracy it is also assumed that man is rational, that he has an innate goodness, and that he is motivated by a sense of justice in his dealings with other men and in his search for solutions to problems he shares with other men. Above all, it is assumed that each man has a basic integrity and importance, that it is desirable that each man be given a fair chance to realize his potentiality, and that all social institutions have as their chief and ultimate end the providing of a favorable environment for the enjoyment of life by the individual.

All of these assumptions about the nature of man are, of course, controversial. From the beginnings of history philosophers and religious leaders have held many views concerning man and his relation to the material world. Obviously, there is irrationality as well as rationality in man's conduct, there is evil as well as good in the world, and injustice seems often to outweigh justice. It is far from true that all governmental experiments throughout political history have been predicated upon rationality, goodness, and justice as innate qualities of human nature. Nonetheless, the student of political institutions today assumes that behind all man's fears, irrationalities, and uncertainties, behind his greediness, his animosities, his conflicts, and his evil tendencies, lies a basic human integrity. Consciously or unconsciously, man seeks to do good, to make progress. His motives are honorable, his ideas sensible. Whatever the crudities and vagaries of particular political adventures and undertakings, government in the long run of history is part of a rational and moral man's effort to give meaning to life and to bring order and direction to human society.

government's place among social institutions

A proper understanding of the role of government necessitates a recognition that government is one among many social institutions man has created to meet the two needs of service and regulation. There are at least three institutions which have had an importance throughout history comparable to that of government. They are the family, the church, and the business enterprise. Not only do they rival government in importance; they closely resemble it in their purposes and functions. In particular, they all serve, and they all regulate. For example, the church performs an exceedingly important regulatory function through formulating and enforcing the moral law which is the regulatory basis of much human conduct. It also performs a service function through ministering to man's spiritual needs, as well as by providing such material services as education and charity —services that often parallel those supplied by government. Business enterprise is perhaps more interested in service than in regulation, since, in capitalist countries at least, it is the chief purveyor of the material goods which play such an important part in the enjoyment of civilization. But business also regulates; it has a great deal to say about the kind, quality, and price of goods; and in good part it controls the distribution of earnings between shareholders and labor— thereby affecting the purchasing power of each. In both of these respects it influences and controls the kind of society in which we live, and it resolves conflicts between individuals and between groups.

The analogy between the family and the government is an obvious one. Professor Robert M. MacIver points out that "the family is everywhere the matrix of government." And he adds, "Wherever the family exists—and it exists everywhere in human society—government already exists." [4] The role of the family as a service agency is indicated by the material values which it gives its members—protection, shelter, food, love, and care for the young and the old. True, these services are made possible not by the family as an inanimate object but by the labor and contributions of the individuals who make up the family. But the same is true of the services rendered by all other social institutions, including government. That the family has an important regulatory function is seen in the way it governs such matters as sex relations, the inheritance and use of property, and the training and behavior of youth.

the difference between public and private government

It is helpful, in seeking an understanding of the varying roles played by different social institutions in determining the kind of life men enjoy, to refer to *public* government and *private* government. By public government is meant the state and its machinery, and in particular the services rendered by the state and the control it exercises over the lives of its citizens. By private government is meant all other social institutions save the state, and the services and controls through which they, too, profoundly affect the lives of people. That public government and private government are but different phases of the same social phenomenon is an imperfectly understood condition. The role of private government has not

---

[4] MacIver, *Web of Government*, pp. 24, 26.

been adequately studied, nor have its failures and successes been properly evaluated. In particular, the way in which these two kinds of government divide the business of rendering service and of regulating society needs attention if the nature of the social order is to be fully understood. Frequently, insufficient attention is given to the fact that the rendering of new services or the establishment of new regulations by government may not involve an increase in the total services available or in the total measure of regulation in society. Instead, there may be a mere transfer of service rendering or of regulating from private government to public government.

It has been pointed out that "more government by the state does not necessarily result in less freedom. The control exercised over an individual by a private agency may be far more tyrannical than anything the state imposes." [5] For example, there is almost always more democracy in the way in which government in America fulfills its functions of serving and regulating than there is in the performance of these same functions by the family, the business corporation, or the church. The family is largely an autocratic institution, and even the most enthusiastic advocates of democracy do not suggest that all members of the family should have equal voting rights when decisions are being made with respect to services and regulations. Much the same is true of the church. There is a strongly dogmatic quality about the religious doctrines and moral laws of most churches, and this means that by its very nature the regulatory function of the church cannot be subject to democratic control. Most business enterprise is operated as an autocracy, although it is likely that business will in the future be democratized far more than will the family or the church. This is not to say that democracy is the only quality to look for in social institutions, for there are other qualities such as cohesion, efficiency, adaptability, and continuity which determine the worth of institutions. But the fact remains that if it is more democracy which is desired in the rendering of a service or in the devising and enforcing of a regulation, such a result can perhaps be more easily obtained through governmental activity than it can through the activity of private social agencies.

Civilization means government. Accordingly, the central issue of our political life is not so much whether we shall have more government or less government as it is whether we shall have more public government and less private government, or vice versa. To be more specific, the issue with respect to the meeting of any particular human need is whether the necessary services or regulations can best be undertaken by public or private agencies. In making such a determination many factors need consideration. Democratic control of the enterprise, already referred to, is an important factor but by no means the only one to be considered. Traditional ways of doing things, the nature of the times, the amount of

---

[5] Pendleton Herring, *The Politics of Democracy* (New York: Rinehart & Company, 1940), p. 46.

social pressure for change, relative costs and efficiency, the degree of interference with the freedom of individuals, and other similar factors must be taken
into account.

the great ends of government

Service and regulation are the two great functions of government. The meaning
of government is better understood if attention is also given to the specific ends
which government seeks to promote through these functions. There are many
ways in which these ends may be enumerated or described. Moreover, the ends
of government have seemingly varied greatly from one period in history to another. However, it is a reasonably satisfactory analysis of ends to say that government tries to preserve the peace, safeguard individual freedom, ensure justice,
and promote the general welfare. These four ends might be differently worded.
Moreover, they are not in all ways separate ends, for there is often considerable
overlapping among them.

1. preserving the peace

The first end of government is to preserve the peace and to maintain order. In
the state of nature, man found that violence and warfare were the inevitable
methods used to resolve the conflicts which continuously arise between men and
between groups. Desiring an orderly and peaceful way of settling these conflicts,
man turned to government. Government is expected to preserve the peace by
preventing violence and crime within the society and war between societies, and
by providing machinery for settlement of disputes without resort to violence or
war. It is probable that man's desire for internal order in society and security
against external threats to the peace was the earliest of all forces leading to the
establishment of government.

Government has been more successful in maintaining domestic order than
it has been in preserving peace. Today, when well over half of the expenditures of the federal government of the United States are made to meet the costs
of past wars and to safeguard the nation's present and future security, it is apparent that preserving the peace is the greatest unsolved problem confronting
government. Obviously, government has enjoyed only a limited success in achieving this end. Often in the past all efforts to preserve the peace have failed, and
warfare, civil or international, has resulted. Paradoxically, the fighting of a war
by government may still be viewed as a means of preserving the peace. For the
moment peace has been lost, but, whatever a people's motivation in fighting a
war may be, the ultimate goal is the restoration of peace, and usually the hope
is that the resulting peace will provide more security than did the preceding peace.

By and large it is not governments which create internal disorder or international warfare but individuals and peoples. There have been disorders and wars which were deliberately instigated by governmental officers as means of gratifying their lust for power. There have been others caused by the incompetence of these officers. But the great social disorders of history have more often grown out of the conflicting interests of peoples and nations. Here it has been the end of government to resolve these conflicts in a peaceful manner wherever possible (and it should not be forgotten that throughout history much disorder—domestic and international—has unquestionably been avoided by governmental efforts). When war comes it is the end of government to resolve the conflict through a speedy and successful prosecution of the war and a restoration of peace.

2. safeguarding individual freedom

A second great end of government is encouraging and safeguarding the freedom of its individual citizens. In the state of nature, man discovers that he is a slave to necessity and environment and that he has little opportunity to develop his individuality. Thus he turns to government as a means of bringing about a favorable social climate in which the individual may thrive. Conscious recognition of this purpose of government has not been present in all societies or in all times. For one thing this end of government assumes that the state exists to serve the individual and not vice versa. As will be seen in a later chapter, *"Liberty vs. Authority,"* conscious and persistent assertion of this belief has been limited pretty much to the democratic states of the Western world in the last two centuries. But the integrity and importance of individual man is an idea which is as old as human history and one which has profoundly affected the growth of social institutions. "It was a great day for the human race . . . when the idea dawned that every man is a human being, an end in himself, with a claim for the development of his own personality, and that human beings had a dignity and a worth, respect for which is the firm basis of human association."[6] The ways in which human associations, including government, have their basis in respect for the dignity and worth of the individual make a complex and confusing story. The story is filled with many false starts and contradictory subplots. Often government has been used for the aggrandizement of a few men or a particular social class, and other men and classes have been denied full opportunity to advance their interests, or have even been reduced to a condition of slavery. But in the long run of history it is proper to say that government does exist to advance the freedom of all men by providing an orderly environment in which individuals may give expression to their personal interests without thereby encroaching unreasonably upon the interests of other individuals.

It is difficult to grasp the truth that there is no irreconcilable conflict be-

[6] Charles E. Merriam, *Systematic Politics* (Chicago: The University of Chicago Press, 1945), p. 59.

tween governmental activity and individual liberty. Governments have so often by their activities encroached upon the sphere of human freedoms that it is easy to draw the conclusion that government and freedom are mortal enemies. The truth is that freedom for the individual who wishes to live in an organized society and to enjoy the benefits of civilization is vitally dependent upon government activity, and that this is indeed a chief end of government. This truth is recognized in such a defense of individualism as our own Declaration of Independence. There the statement that "life, liberty, and the pursuit of happiness" are man's unalienable rights is followed by the assertion that "it was to secure these rights that governments are instituted among men."

The regulation of the affairs of men by government often seems to be in conflict with the wish of the individual to do as he pleases subject to no restraint. This conflict is often real, for it is perfectly possible for government to push its activities so far that the individual's freedom is curtailed to an unnecessary and unreasonable extent. But often, too, the interference with freedom is largely illusory. The man who drives his automobile upon the public highways finds his freedom limited by the necessity of obeying traffic regulations. Actually, his freedom in the sense of mobility is enhanced by these regulations. Without them he would find it utterly impossible to move from place to place as his needs or his fancy might dictate.

Professor Charles E. Merriam has illustrated this truth by suggesting that whereas government regulation may have increased tenfold in modern times, the average man has probably increased his range of activities, his freedom, by a hundredfold. Thus, at the same time that the scope of governmental activity has been enormously broadened percentagewise, governmental interference with the individual's freedom has been greatly reduced. Merriam concludes: ". . . there is much ground for believing that the continuing extension of governmental regulation as such is really an illusion. It is just as possible to assert that what is in store is the diminution of governmental regulation."[7]

It is also true that some forms of governmental regulation do come to an end. Within the life span of our own American political system such practices as Negro slavery, subjugation of women, and entail and primogeniture with respect to the transfer of land, have all been discontinued. All of these practices depended for their existence upon law enforced by government. All of them interfered with human freedom to a far greater extent than do many present-day governmental controls against which we are accustomed to complain.

It is important to recognize that the freedom of the individual is often affected as much by what private institutions do as by what government does. Freedom of the press in a community may be as readily threatened by a profit-seeking, monopolistic publishing company as by a power-mad politician.

[7] *Ibid.,* p. 73.

The right to vote has been encroached upon as much by vigilante groups, such as the Ku Klux Klan, as it has by public officers acting under law. Freedom to engage in gainful employment is as readily endangered by the reluctance of investors to risk their capital in business ventures, or by the efforts of a professional trade association or a labor union to restrict job opportunities in a particular area to a chosen few, as it is by unwise tax policies or restrictive regulatory activities on the part of government. Indeed, it is to government that the people usually turn for relief when they discover that their freedom is being unduly curbed because of private institutional arrangements or practices.

The sweep of history seems to lead inevitably to more and more government, but it is far from clear that in a nation such as the United States there is today less freedom than there was in the past. Indeed, it can with truth be said that much, if not all, of the increased governmental activity has served to advance individual freedom.

3. ensuring justice

One of the oldest ends of government is to so regulate the affairs of men, to so resolve human conflicts, that life will be marked by a sense of fairness and decency, by a degree of predictability, by a quality called justice. Justice is a concept that has interested philosophers from the time of Plato and Aristotle to the present, but it is not easily defined or explained. However, an understanding of the role of justice in society and of government's part in promoting justice can be furthered by examining "legal justice" and "social justice."

Legal justice is the justice administered by courts under law. Government undertakes to provide a means for the settlement of conflicts between individuals in such a way that justice is done to the parties. This is done by first providing a frame of reference so that justice may be discovered or measured, and by then providing formal machinery through which justice may be applied. The frame of reference is law, and the machinery is the court.

There is much talk about absolute justice, by which is meant a justice measured by immutable rules of law eternally valid in all lands. "Natural law" is one way of referring to such fixed rules which are valid *in the nature of things*. Actually, most law is man-made and consists of a set of value judgments that reflect the customs and attitudes of a particular people at a particular time. In any case the ideal of legal justice is that human disputes may be settled under fixed, fair rules by impartial judges. In practice, legal justice always falls short of this ideal, but government has succeeded in introducing a considerable amount of "fairness" into the settlement of conflicts among men.

Social justice is concerned with the sharing of the gains of civilization in a manner which will be fair to all men. Again there are different value judgments by which such a distribution of goods may be measured. A capitalist society believes that men shall be differently rewarded for their labors in the light of the

quantity and quality of their output, and that these different rewards shall measure each man's power to claim his share of society's goods. A socialist society
takes as its value judgment in this respect the rule that each man shall contribute
to the production of social wealth according to his ability, and share in that
wealth according to his need. But in either case government has a part to play in
promoting social justice. In times past this part was not so significant a reason
for the existence of government as was government's part in promoting legal
justice, but it has become increasingly important in modern times. Such contemporary governmental activities as those dealing with old-age assistance, unemployment insurance, the wages and hours of labor, and subsidies to agriculture are evidence of an increased concern with social justice—with giving to all
men a just share of the nation's produce.

4. promoting the general welfare.

Finally, government is concerned with the end of promoting the material well-
being of society and its members. Again nations have been built upon different
economic philosophies, but always, even if in varying ways and degrees, government has been expected to encourage a healthy social economy. To use present-
day language, it has been expected to encourage "full production" so that society
might enjoy the highest possible standard of living; to promote "full employment" so that every man might have a sense of participation in the collective
effort and a right to share in the fruits of society; and to iron out the peaks and
valleys of the business cycle so that unemployment and fluctuations in production might be avoided. All of this sounds highly contemporary in its application.
Moreover, there is even today much controversy over the degree of responsibility
which government should assume in attempting to guarantee such things as full
production or full employment. Nonetheless, a concern for the material well-being of society is one of the oldest ends of government, and consciously or unconsciously people have looked to government to foster their economic needs.

The mistake is sometimes made of supposing that the economic philosophy
of *laissez faire*, which denies to government any positive role in promoting the
material well-being of society, dominated political history until the second quarter of the present century. Actually, laissez faire is a nineteenth-century phenomenon. The careful examination of political history of the ancient world, the Middle Ages, and modern times shows that government has always been expected to
take positive steps to promote the material well-being of the people. Such measures to this end as protective tariffs, subsidies to private enterprise, publicly operated enterprise, manipulation of prices and currency to produce specific results
are as old as history. Even the nineteenth century, carefully studied, reveals far
more governmental concern for economic welfare than one would suppose existed under laissez faire. One of the wisest of American historians has said: "It is
far too late to ask whether government should interfere in business enterprise. It

always has interfered in business enterprise. The only relevant question is in what ways and to what extent it should so interfere."[8]

"the withering away of the state" is a delusion

The delusion must be avoided that government as a force in man's existence can somehow be minimized. "The withering away of the state" is an enchanting possibility which man wistfully contemplates as his struggles to solve social problems through government meet at best with limited success. Yet common sense suggests that in dealing with many of life's problems through government man is at least on the right road. For what is government but a man-made institution through which—to refer again to Lincoln's words—the community of people tries to do what needs to be done but which obviously cannot be done by individuals acting separately?

Much of the current controversy in the United States about the "welfare state" is misleading and even dangerous because it suggests that the American people have a choice of alternatives between using government to advance their welfare and not using it. No such choice exists. Of course, individual proposals for new or expanded governmental services looking toward the promotion of the general welfare should always be carefully and thoroughly examined and debated on their merits before they are approved. In the course of such debate many proposals will be, and should be, rejected. But the idea that government should properly be concerned with advancing the general welfare, that it can render specific and positive services to people, is an inescapable one.

the continuous search for better governmental forms

The history of government is a history of experimentation. Nowhere has a people ever been permanently satisfied with existing governmental forms. Always the tendency has been to try some new plan in the hope that the ends of government can be better realized than they have under some past arrangement. It is significant that the American constitutional system, although not yet two centuries old, is already one of the longest-lived major political experiments in history.

Change in governmental institutions is due not only to efforts to find better means of solving existing problems. It is due also to the fact that civilization itself is constantly changing. If there is one obvious fact about man's history on earth it is that great changes in the nature of his existence have taken place through the centuries. It is true that for limited periods in history—such as the Middle Ages—life, for the most part, stood still, and human institutions and customs adhered to fixed patterns. But in the longer run of history, change has

---

[t] Carl Becker, *Modern Democracy* (New Haven: Yale University Press, 1941), p. 71.

been the dominant rule. Moreover, change has been particularly strong in modern times. It is a truism that since the close of the eighteenth century, civilization has moved forward in a dynamic, breath-taking fashion.

It is important to recognize that throughout history government has had to be constantly adapted to the changing environment which man's ambition and inventiveness have produced. Where political institutions have remained static, sooner or later they have become obsolete and unworkable. Ultimately, they have had to be altered, usually by revolutionary means. In general, man has had to pay a heavy price for these revolutionary changes, since they have often been accompanied by force and violence. As he has grown more experienced and sophisticated in the field of politics, he has searched for peaceful, scientific means of altering his governmental institutions and processes so as to keep them abreast of the times. Thus, a fundamental test of a nation's political system is the ease with which it lends itself to change and adaptation as human history moves inexorably forward.

This is not to say that change and reform are to be looked upon favorably whatever their character. Any political system which has been moderately successful over a period of years has become a delicately balanced mechanism entitled to a good deal of respect. To tamper recklessly with such a mechanism would be highly irresponsible. And yet the conclusion is unavoidable that unless efforts are made more or less constantly to improve a government, to adapt it to the needs of changing times and new problems, it will in the end prove unsatisfactory.

The maintenance of an experimental spirit in the attack upon social problems is well illustrated by the presidency of Franklin D. Roosevelt, and undoubtedly explains much of the political appeal which his administration enjoyed. Shortly before he was nominated for the presidency in 1932, Roosevelt stated in an address at Oglethorpe University: "The country needs and, unless I mistake its temper, the country demands bold, persistent experimentation. It is common sense to take a method and try it. If it fails, admit it frankly and try another. But above all, try something."[9]

Again in 1937, after four years in the presidency, Roosevelt reaffirmed his belief in the importance of experimentation:

> We know it takes time to adjust government to the needs of society. But modern history proves that reforms too long delayed or denied have jeopardized peace, undermined democracy and swept away civil and religious liberties.

> Yes, time more than ever before is vital in statesmanship and in government, in all three branches of it.

---

[9] *The Public Papers and Addresses of Franklin D. Roosevelt* (New York: Random House, 1938), I, 646.

We will no longer be permitted to sacrifice each generation in turn while the law catches up with life.[10]

The history of government is a history of limited successes and notable failures. In trying to evolve satisfactory political institutions as a means of furthering the development of orderly, civilized societies, men have been attempting one of the most difficult feats in human history. In view of the tremendous ends which government is expected to serve it is not surprising that absolute success has not yet been achieved in the search for satisfactory political forms. Moreover, life grows steadily more complex and the problems of civilization grow more difficult to solve. Thus, if anything, modern man seems further away from the final solution to political problems than were some of his predecessors.

The fact that government is forever in a state of flux does not indicate there is anything basically wrong about man's efforts to make his existence on earth more satisfactory and more meaningful by the establishment of government and by political experimentation. On the other hand, it becomes increasingly apparent that government must fulfill its purposes ever more effectively if man is even to hold his own in his efforts to cope with the problems of a changing world. History is indeed a race between civilization and catastrophe. The success or failure of government will profoundly affect the outcome of the race. Without government the race would surely be lost, but with government it may still be lost unless government can be made more and more adequate to the needs it must serve.

Gunnar Myrdal points out in *An American Dilemma,* one of the monumental studies of contemporary social science, that the shortcomings of present-day society are not the result of the fact that men have tried to solve problems through institutions such as government, but rather of the fact that those institutions are not better than they are. He writes:

> Social study is concerned with explaining why . . . potentially and intentionally good people so often make life a hell for themselves and each other when they live together, whether in a family, a community, a nation or a world. The fault is certainly not with becoming organized *per se.* In their formal organizations . . . people invest their highest ideals. These institutions regularly direct the individual toward more cooperation and justice than he would be inclined to observe as an isolated private person. The fault is, rather, that our structures of organizations are too imperfect, each by itself, and badly integrated into a social whole.

And he points the way ahead in these words: "The rationalism and moralism which is the driving force behind social study . . . is the faith that institutions can be improved and strengthened and that people are good enough to live a

---

[10] *The Public Papers and Addresses of Franklin D. Roosevelt* (New York: The Macmillan Company, 1941), VI, 365-366.

happier life. . . . To find the practical formulas for this never-ending reconstruction of society is the supreme task of social science." [11]

In the end, it is clear that the governmental arrangements through which the difficult problems of contemporary society are dealt with must produce ever more satisfactory results if man is even to hold his own in his struggle to make himself the master of his environment. As American government is examined in this book an effort should be made to determine the extent to which its organization and its procedures have proved themselves effective in advancing the ends which they exist to serve, and have proved themselves adaptable to the needs of a constantly changing social order. The questions may properly be asked of American government: Was it soundly conceived to serve the great ends for which governments exist? As shortcomings in the original plan have been discovered, have they been corrected? Have its agencies and operations been altered and improved as times have changed and social problems grown more complex? Is it today properly organized to perform in reasonably effective fashion the great functions assigned to it?

bibliographic note

From the time of Plato and Aristotle to the present day there has been no shortage of books examining the science of government systematically or philosophically. Curiously, however, there are few such contemporary works by American political scientists. Two notable titles in the short list are Robert M. MacIver's *The Web of Government* (New York: The Macmillan Company, 1947) and Charles E. Merriam's *Systematic Politics* (Chicago: The University of Chicago Press, 1945). An earlier work of Professor Merriam, *Political Power: Its Composition and Incidence* (New York: McGraw-Hill Book Company, 1934), deals in more limited fashion with the nature of political power in modern society. William Ernest Hocking's *Man and the State* (New Haven: Yale University Press, 1926) examines political concepts from the point of view of the philosopher. Herman Finer's *Theory and Practice of Modern Government* (New York: Henry Holt and Company, 1949) is a systematic work examining contemporary political institutions from both a philosophical and a descriptive point of view. A stimulating, highly sophisticated essay on political science is Thurman Arnold's *The Symbols of Government* (New Haven: Yale University Press, 1935).

Among the systematic studies of American government, James Bryce's *The*

---

[11] Gunnar Myrdal, *An American Dilemma* (New York: Harper & Brothers, 1944), pp. 1023–1024. Reprinted by permission of Harper & Brothers, publishers.

American Commonwealth (New York: The Macmillan Company, 1888) is still a significant book. Bryce had many remarkable insights into the American political system, although present-day political science has developed techniques and theories unknown to him. A more recent publication is Charles A. Beard's *The Republic* (New York: The Viking Press, 1943). In this brief, readable book one of the greatest of American social scientists set down in the form of dialogues between himself and his friends his thoughts concerning the American political system. Two excellent collections of readings dealing with government and politics are *Man and the State,* edited by William Ebenstein (New York: Rinehart & Company, 1947) and *Roots of Political Behavior,* edited by Richard C. Snyder and H. Hubert Wilson (New York: American Book Company, 1949).

In recent years numerous books have dealt with the question of whether there is a basic conflict between a planned society and the democratic tradition. Among those which see in planning and the welfare state a threat to democracy are Friedrich A. Hayek, *The Road to Serfdom* (Chicago: The University of Chicago Press, 1944); Ludwig von Mises, *Omnipotent Government* (New Haven: Yale University Press, 1944); and Henry M. Wriston, *Challenge to Freedom* (New York: Harper & Brothers, 1943). The compatibility of planning and democracy is asserted in Herman Finer, *Road to Reaction* (Boston: Little, Brown & Company, 1945); Barbara Wootton, *Freedom under Planning* (Chapel Hill: University of North Carolina Press, 1945); and John M. Clark, *Alternative to Serfdom* (New York: Alfred A. Knopf, Inc., 1948). The important role that reform and political experimentation have played in the development of American government and the adaptability of democracy to a changing environment is admirably described in a recent work by Arthur M. Schlesinger, *The American as Reformer* (Cambridge: Harvard University Press, 1950).

The student's attention should be called to certain general sources of information on political subjects. The *Encyclopaedia of the Social Sciences* (New York: The Macmillan Company, 1930–1935) is an excellent source of signed articles by leading authorities on almost all topics within the field of political science. There are a number of learned journals in the political science field to which the student may profitably turn in a search for articles on subjects of interest to him. The *American Political Science Review* (450 Ahnaip St., Menasha, Wisconsin) is published by the American Political Science Association, which is the national association of the political science profession. Several regional political science associations also publish journals. These associations and their journals are as follows: Academy of Political Science (sponsored by Columbia University)—*Political Science Quarterly* (Fayerweather Hall, Columbia University, New York City); The American Academy of Political and Social Science (sponsored by the University of Pennsylvania)—*The Annals* (University of Pennsylvania, Philadelphia); Southern Political Science Association—*Journal of Politics* (University of Florida, Gainesville); Southwestern Social Science

Association—*Southwestern Social Science Quarterly* (University of Oklahoma, Norman) ; Western Political Science Association and Pacific Northwest Political Science Association—*Western Political Science Quarterly* (Institute of Government, University of Utah, Salt Lake City) ; and *Review of Politics* (University of Notre Dame, Notre Dame, Indiana).

the meaning of democracy:

the importance of compromise in society

*W*HAT exactly do we mean by democracy? No other term is more common to the language of present-day American politics; no other concept is considered to be more basic to our national ideals. Yet the word is not an easy one to define. Like such words as progress, justice, or welfare, its connotation is vague and nebulous. It has no "referent"—that is, it does not call to mind a tangible or precise object or picture.[1] Moreover, democracy has clearly meant different things to different peoples and different times. It has been said: "Democracy has a context in every sphere of life; and in each of those spheres it raises its special problems which do not admit of satisfactory or universal generalization." [2] The present quarrel with the Soviet Union over the proper use of the word is merely the latest indication of this difficulty of definition. The Soviet Union on the one hand, and the Western nations, such as France, Great Britain, and the United States, on the other, all claim that their systems are democratic. Obviously they are not using the word in the same way.

Even if attention be confined solely to the political experience of the United States it is clear that there has been much confusion among Americans concerning the meaning of democracy. Ours has been one of the great democratic experiments of all time; yet there is doubt as to the extent to which it was consciously intended to be such by the makers of the Constitution. Throughout much of our history many people have failed to grasp the implications of democracy, and those who have understood these implications have sometimes opposed them. There has always been opposition to the democratic element in our way of life. For example, people often insist that ours is a republic, not a democracy. Those who make such a distinction are seldom able to give a coherent explanation of

---

[1] See Carl Becker, *Modern Democracy* (New Haven: Yale University Press, 1941), p. 4.
[2] Harold J. Laski, "Democracy," *Encyclopaedia of the Social Sciences* (New York: The Macmillan Company, 1931), V, 76. Excerpts reprinted from the *Encyclopaedia of the Social Sciences* are used by permission of The Macmillan Company, publishers.

what they mean by it, but it is usually clear that they are motivated by a distaste for what they regard to be too much popular influence in the affairs of government.

Finally, an understanding of democracy is made difficult by the gap which always exists between principle and reality: here the gap between theoretical democracy and democracy in action. The American political system today in practice falls far short of perfect democracy. It is easy to point to many forms, procedures, or conditions which are characterized by something less than complete democracy. And yet our national traditions and ideals have been and are as nearly democratic as those of any people known to history. Thus it is necessary to distinguish between creed and practice in discussing the meaning of democracy.

There is no description or definition of democracy which readily tells the full story. The concept of democracy can best be understood by examining its historical origins, the theoretical arguments men have put forth in its favor, the experiences encountered by people who have tried to live a democratic way of life, and the difficulties and controversies growing out of contemporary experiments in democracy. Such a systematic analysis is beyond the scope and purpose of this early chapter. But some preliminary attention must be given to the meaning of democracy if American political institutions are to be properly examined and evaluated.

modern democracy a product of the Age of Reason

Although the modern world has seen dictatorships and tyrannies as powerful and widespread as any known to history, the American is inclined to take democracy for granted. To him the democratic way of life seems so reasonable and desirable he finds it hard to understand that there is no inevitability about it. He is surprised to learn that most present-day democratic systems were worked out only during the last century or so. The Greek city-states of the ancient world enjoyed a brief period in which democracy—as we understand the term today— found considerable expression. Similarly, the word may perhaps be used to characterize a few decades in the life of ancient Rome. Democracy was also known to certain of the city governments of the medieval and early modern world, as well as to one or two small nations like Switzerland and Holland. But the great democracies of today—Great Britain, France, and the United States— began to emerge only at the close of the eighteenth century and are very largely the end product of the Age of Reason, a philosophic and cultural movement which came into full flowering in that century. Many men, such as Locke, Montesquieu, Voltaire, and Rousseau, made contributions to the philosophy of the Age of Reason, and many events—in particular, the revolutions in England, America, and France—are part of the history of the movement. The important thing is that with the Age of Reason there came into being a climate of opinion favorable to the use of democratic political institutions as the best means of meeting those human needs which are the responsibility of government.

Among the ideas which were widely held by the philosophers of the Age of Reason and which were joined together in a systematic body of political thought are the following:

1. man's integrity

The individual rather than the group is viewed as the central and important unit of life. Each man has a dignity and personality which society must recognize and respect. All social institutions should have as their ultimate goal the furtherance of the aspirations and potentialities of the individuals who make up society. This does not mean that individual interests must never be subordinated to group interests. But the group is not important *per se*; it is not the end of life, but only a means. Group interests may sometimes properly override the interests of some individuals, because more people—as individuals—are thereby helped than are hindered.

2. man's equality

As a corollary to his belief in the dignity and importance of the individual there is asserted the doctrine of the equality of men. It is not necessarily claimed that all men are biologically equal, but it is argued that all men should enjoy equality of opportunity and equal status under the law. There must be no aristocracy of birth, wealth, race, or creed which would deny to any man a fair chance to express his personality and develop and use his talents.

3. man's rationality

Man is a reasoning being who can use his mind to understand and solve the practical problems which he encounters in life. There is no compulsion about the direction of human history. Man does possess a freedom of choice in selecting the paths he follows. Thus progress toward a better way of life is at all times possible and should be the constant aim of men.

4. man's goodness

There is a basic goodness in man. Although the individual inevitably seeks to advance his own interests and put his talents to good use, he has also a humanitarian instinct; there are in him a sense of kindness, a measure of unselfishness. This indicates that man is more than a mere animal. He has a soul, and thus life can be lived in accordance with moral principles.

5. man's practicality

Because man is both a reasoning and a moral being he is prepared to discipline himself so that the collective interests of society may be safeguarded and promoted. Democratic thought rejects the argument that social progress requires the subjection of men, but it assumes that men are capable of self-discipline. In particular it assumes that each man sees that conflicting interests must be reconciled if he and his neighbors are to live together in peace. It assumes that man accepts the need for a good deal of compromise in human affairs. There may be ultimate principles by which life should be ordered, and man should seek ever to live by principles. But since men are certain to disagree in their adherence to principles, it is only common sense that they should adjust themselves to one another's views, giving such ground to each other as may be necessary for the maintenance of harmony.

Democracy, then, may be defined informally both as a way of life and as a mechanism—as an ideology, and as a political system. As an ideology it emphasizes the importance of individuals and the right of each man to express his personality, to have an equal voice with other men in the making of group decisions and social policy, and to have equal opportunity with his fellow men to take advantage of the benefits of life. As a political system it is the mechanism through which people govern themselves so as to enhance the enjoyment of life's benefits by individuals, and also to provide compromise and reconciliation in those areas of human activity where the conflict of individual and group interests is great.

the case for democracy

the case in logic

The philosophy of the Age of Reason provided a strong logical argument in support of democracy as a way of life. Man is a rational being who has it within his power to establish a highly civilized social order which will give all individuals a chance to express their talents and to enjoy a high standard of living. But the way ahead to this goal is not clearly indicated, and society must decide which routes to follow. To do this necessitates the maintenance of a free market place of thought in which rival ideas may be presented and debated and the search for the best way of doing things constantly pressed. Since men are not likely to be unanimous in preferring one idea over another, the most sensible thing to do is to ask all men to speak their minds with respect to those matters that are of concern to the collective interests of society, and then follow the paths favored by the majority.

Democracy clearly puts its faith in majority judgments and majority action. Since there is no one clear way ahead, guesses must be hazarded as to the best paths to follow. The majority's guesses will more often be right than wrong. The majority will more often be right than will any minority. In a society of free and equal citizens the experience and judgment of the many are superior to the experience and judgment of the few.

men are the best judges of their own interests

The case for democracy is also seen in the argument that since men have conflicting interests which ought to be recognized in the making of social decisions, no one can better express and reconcile these interests than the men who hold them. "He who wears the shoe knows best where it pinches." By popular control of the government the people can do a better job of advancing their own interests than can any philosopher-king or benevolent despot who may claim to know better than do the masses what is good for them. In some ways the strongest argument for democracy is a negative one: whatever its shortcomings, government by the many is better than government by the few, for no government of the latter type has ever in the long run recognized or safeguarded the interests of the mass of the people. Sooner or later, even in the benevolent despotisms, the interests of the ruling class are preferred to those of the people. Winston Churchill has put the negative argument for democracy in the following terms: "It has been said that democracy is the worst form of government except all those other forms that have been tried from time to time."[3]   And Abraham Lincoln recognized that only the people can see to it that their interests are safeguarded by the state when he praised "government of the people, by the people, and for the people."

democracy is psychologically sound

The traditional defense of democracy depends heavily upon the use of logical reasoning. Certain premises are accepted concerning the nature of man and the goals of life. Logical argument is then used to prove that democracy is the soundest method by which to govern human affairs. As modern psychology has thrown new light upon man, this traditional case for democracy has been reinforced. The democratic process gives the individual a sense that he is wanted, that his membership in the group is prized, that his point of view is respected and carries weight. He participates in the group effort, his voice influences the selection of the group's leaders and the making of social policy. Thus his sense of satisfaction is deepened; his sense of frustration is lessened. The individual becomes a healthier being and society itself is thereby strengthened.

the case against democracy

No one has ever developed a single, systematic case against democracy. Democracy is but one political system which has competed historically and ideologically with a variety of other systems. Accordingly, the arguments used against democracy have depended in any given place or time on the facts of the particular situation, on the nature of the rival political system available as an alternative to

---

[3] Remarks in the House of Commons, November 11, 1947.

democracy. Nonetheless, antidemocratic thought, ancient and modern, conforms in a general way to the same pattern, and there are certain common characteristics of all arguments against democracy that can be noted.

To begin with, almost all opponents of democracy have denied the assertion that all men are entitled to enjoy a measure of equality—be it equality of birth, equality of opportunity, or equality under the law. In one form or another the antidemocrat believes in the existence of an elite class in society. A privileged few are entitled to enter an aristocracy of wealth and power through birth or by demonstrating superior intellectual ability or wealth-getting power. In any case society should be governed by members of the elite class, for they know better than does the common man what policies are socially wise. Some advocates of rule by an elite class acknowledge that all members of society are entitled to share the fruits of economic progress and social development, but they insist that such progress and such sharing can result only where the control of society is placed in the hands of a wise and just minority. Other proponents of rule by the few take the more extreme position that since the members of the elite know better than do the members of the herd how to savor and enjoy the subtle pleasures and the finer things of life, they are entitled to claim the lion's share of the world's goods and services. Democracy is attacked as a vulgarizing process which threatens to overwhelm the high aspirations and deep potentialities of the privileged few. The world belongs not to the common man but to the uncommon man.

Second, many antidemocrats reject the notion that the individual is more important than the group. Man's destiny is found not in the expression of his own personality or the realization of his individual talents but rather in the achievements and glory of the group—or more particularly of the state, the church, the elite, or the culture. Since the individual's progress and well-being are not the end of society, society need not be governed by the will of a majority of the individuals which make it up. Society is better governed by those few men who understand and appreciate the heritage and destiny of the culture, and who have demonstrated their right to govern by the acquisition of wealth, power, and prestige.

Third, many of those who attack democracy sooner or later reject the path of logic and rationality as the best way of arriving at a sound social order and fall back upon mysticism and irrationality in defending an undemocratic social organization. Thus kings have claimed a divine (i.e., mystical) right to rule; tyrants have asserted that might makes right; dictators have insisted that the people accept their leadership on a hero-worship basis. Or again, a common characteristic of authoritarian institutions has been their claim to absolutism—their dogmatic insistence that the truth has been discovered, or revealed, and that any opposition doctrine is heresy—an essentially irrational claim, for man's reason tells him that there is no one truth, no one way of doing things, no one path ahead when it comes to such human problems as organizing a society for harmonious and satisfying relations among men, stimulating the production of goods and services, and arranging for a fair and equitable distribution of the products of the economy.

Finally, many antidemocrats make no pretense of developing a systematic philosophic defense of their actions or positions, but are content to point to the defects of democracy and to assert that it is unworkable. It is said the people are not able or willing to maintain the careful and continuous interest in public affairs which democracy postulates. Legislative assemblies inevitably become corrupt, inefficient, or subservient to vicious interests. Democracy stands in the way of the "great men" of history who have an inevitable and infallible role to play in human affairs. For these and other reasons it is argued that rule by a few men or by one man is most natural and practicable.

environmental factors essential to democracy

The eighteenth century saw the development of democratic theory; the nineteenth century was largely concerned with putting democracy into practice—with finding workable institutions through which democratic government might become a fact. The Age of Reason optimistically assumed that democracy would soon encompass the world. Experience has shown that successful experiments in self-government have thus far been few in number. Something more than enthusiasm for the democratic creed is necessary. Certain favorable environmental factors are seemingly essential if democracy is to be made to work in practice. Moreover, institutionalizing democracy calls for the invention of actual governmental machinery which will be consistent with democratic principles at the same time that it proves workable. Four environmental factors favorable to democracy should be noted:

1. an educated citizenry

In the first place, democracy places upon the citizens of a country the burden of understanding the facts pertaining to social problems, of evaluating the arguments for alternative courses of action, of determining the direction to be taken in the attack upon these problems, and above all, of approving wise and fair plans for compromising the conflicts of human relations. Considerable educational training and experience are necessary if this burden is to be successfully carried. It is not enough that citizens should be potentially intelligent. They must have a present body of knowledge and experience if they are to exercise wise control of government. Such a man as Thomas Jefferson, who was a close student of the philosophers of the Age of Reason, saw this clearly, and strongly urged the development of a broad program of public education as a sure bulwark of democracy. Indeed, all exponents of democracy have urged the importance of educating the masses. It is a fact that democracy's successes have been limited to countries in which the people are reasonably well educated to begin with, and in which there is continuous further education of citizens as life and its problems grow ever more complex.

2. ease of communication and mobility

Democracy assumes a free and complete exchange of ideas and factual information concerning affairs of state. Rival candidates for public office must have easy access to the ear of the voter if the latter is to make an intelligent choice between them. Alternative solutions to public problems must be thoroughly debated if men are to have confidence in the belief that majority decisions are generally wiser than minority decisions. In other words, the concept of the free market place of thought, by its very nature, assumes that all citizens have ready access to that market both for the purpose of being active participants in the debate over an issue and for the purpose of being passive listeners to such debate.

Only in the last century or so have the means of communication and transportation improved to a point where it is physically possible for the population of a large area to share the common experience of studying and debating a particular set of social issues. This, as much as any other single factor, explains why the democracies of the ancient and medieval world were confined almost without exception to city-states. On the other hand, the miracle of the radio and the airplane explains why contemporary discussion of a world-state organized along democratic lines is for the first time in history something more than wild and impossible fantasy.

3. a measure of economic security

The history of democratic experiments also seems to show that efforts at self-government have enjoyed even modest success only in areas where the mass of the people enjoy a reasonable measure of economic security. Where people are poor and the struggle for existence consumes all their energies and colors all their thoughts, a society is apt to be without that degree of stability which makes possible the calm, dispassionate discussion of political issues and candidates which the logic of democracy calls for. If a large number of citizens are without that fair share of a nation's wealth and produce which they think is their due, they are not likely to give the state or its government that loyalty which is essential to success. Impoverished people are unstable people. They are the ready victims of demagogues and, worse, of despots. Democratic political institutions, then, must have firm economic underpinnings.

4. a measure of consensus

Finally, and perhaps most important of all, there must be a considerable measure of consensus among the members of a society if it is to make successful use of democratic institutions in governing itself. The Age of Reason taught that men's personalities differ and that in civilization men develop different interests. It is part of the meaning of a democratic society that men should be free to express these differences and to advance their several interests. But a democratic society must remain a peaceful society. If men push the expression of their personalities or their interests to extremes, violence results.

The violent solution of human conflicts is an ever-present threat in history. Where the conflict is between individual and individual, the threat is that one individual may try murder, theft, embezzlement, or other crime as a solution of the difficulty. Where the conflict is between groups of individuals, class strife or civil warfare may be resorted to as a solution. Where the conflict is between nations, the threat is international warfare. Although the use of violence to settle disputes has never been eliminated from society, it is the constant aim of men to find peaceful methods of resolving conflicts. It is part of the theory of democracy that the conflict of interests in society should be brought out into the open, that the facts concerning a conflict should be ascertained and studied, and that people are then capable, by majority action, of reconciling their differing interests and opinions in an orderly, law-abiding way. However, it is clear that the strain placed upon a democratic society's mechanism for the peaceful settlement of disputes must be held within limits lest the machinery break down. Carl Becker, one of the wisest students of American history, has written: "By and large, democratic government, being government by discussion and majority vote, works best when there is nothing of profound importance to discuss, when the rival party programs involve the superficial aspects rather than the fundamental structure of the social system, and when for that reason the minority can meet defeat at the polls in good temper since it need not regard the decision as either a fatal or a permanent surrender of its vital interests." [4]

Thus, people in a democracy must be reasonably homogeneous. Men may differ in their beliefs and interests, but their differences must not exceed certain limits. The stakes for which men compete must not be too high, lest the loser in the game feel that his losses are more than he can stand, and refuse accordingly to accept defeat gracefully. In other words, all men in a democratic society must hold some interests and beliefs in common. In particular, they cannot be widely separated in their acceptance of fundamental principles if the political mechanism is to function smoothly. They may, however, differ greatly in the small things of life.

To put it more specifically, men may properly develop a complex economy and a rich, varied culture in a democracy. They may engage in different occupations, prefer business or farming, live in the city or the country, in the East or the West, raise large families or small families, practice whatever religions

---

[4] Becker, *Modern Democracy*, pp. 87–88.

they choose, join such clubs, fraternities, and societies as they will, and spend their leisure as they see fit. These different interests and activities will produce conflicts that will have to be continuously reconciled by the people themselves through their democratic institutions. Often the process of compromise will be difficult, and solutions will not come easily. But rival interests will never be so far apart that a settlement of differences in an orderly, peaceful way becomes impossible.

But where men differ concerning fundamentals, the ability of a democratic system to show these men how they can live together harmoniously in the same society becomes doubtful.

In a recent Supreme Court opinion Justice Jackson warned against "goals" that would "set up a cleavage among us too fundamental to be composed by democratic processes." And he added: "Our constitutional scheme of elections will not settle issues between large groups when the price of losing is to suffer extinction. When dissensions cut too deeply, men will fight, even hopelessly, before they will submit." [5] In American history the Civil War illustrates what happens when such a condition comes about. Widely separated sections of a large, sprawling nation grew apart economically and culturally to such an extent that the central government was finally unable to formulate national policies acceptable to all sections. In particular, the moral issue of slavery was one which bitterly divided men at the level of fundamental principle. On both sides people came increasingly to feel that they could not compromise their principles. They could only insist upon following the truth, as they saw it, to a point of violence and warfare if need be.

It is never easy to say where the line is to be drawn between the conflicts which are a normal and necessary characteristic of a rich and diversified society of free citizens and those conflicts of basic principle and material interest which cut so deeply as to indicate the absence of consensus in society. Today, there are those who question whether a democratic nation can be divided down the middle between citizens who favor an essentially capitalist economy and those who favor an essentially socialist economy. It is argued that it would be mechanically difficult for the political parties representing the interests of these two groups to succeed each other in controlling the government in the normal manner characteristic of democracies. A fear is expressed that two such groups would become increasingly antagonistic and that sooner or later one or the other group would refuse to accept the result of an election it had lost, and would resort to violence to protect its interests.

Walter Lippmann has pointed to the importance of consensus in a democratic society:

---

[5] *American Communications Association* v. *Douds,* 339 U.S. 382, 426 (1950).

. . . in a sound democracy the central mass of the voters who decide the result are not doctrinaires and ideologues but moderate and pragmatically-minded men and women. Without these middle people, who hold the balance of power, democracy is unworkable, as we can readily see in all the countries where the middle people do not exist. For a nation, divided irreconcilably on "principle," each party believing it is pure white and the other pitch black, cannot govern itself. The sharp division of parties will first paralyze the government, and then when conditions become bad enough, men will feel they must achieve by violence what they cannot achieve by the normal processes of law.

And he adds that it is through "solidarity" that "free societies survive through storm and stress. They never allow their differences to divide them, their debates to become battles, and they push their leaders on to that common ground where all can live together in the same community." [6]

There is some reason to fear that scientific and cultural progress is rapidly bringing mankind to a point where the enormous variations present in a highly complex civilization will make consensus in society exceedingly difficult to obtain. Paradoxically, man may build a world in which all individuals are at last given full opportunity to express their personalities and to satisfy their wants, only to discover that the resulting gaps between individual interests and group interests cannot be bridged by democratic means. But as yet there is no reason to despair of the result. Life grows richer and more varied, interests become more difficult to reconcile. But scientific progress eases some problems as it creates others. The vast improvements in the means of transportation and communication are bringing people closer together and making it easier for them to see how the other half lives, to understand the other man's point of view. Moreover, the steady increase in the production of goods and services made possible by technological progress makes it easier to meet the wants of all people and reduces the strain upon the social mechanism in arranging for a fair distribution of an economy's output.

The ultimate effect of scientific progress upon consensus in society is still far from clear. There are those who fear that democracy may be destroyed because of an increase in centrifugal forces to a point where society can no longer hold together. But there are those who fear mechanical progress may produce a world peopled by robots who will have no need for democracy as a means of settling social conflicts, since all differences among men will have been destroyed.

It is impossible to foretell the future. It can only be said that seemingly there must be a proper measure of consensus among a people who seek to govern

---

[6] Walter Lippmann, "Today and Tomorrow," *The Washington Post*, January 26, 1950. Reprinted by permission of Walter Lippmann.

themselves: let consensus be insufficient, and a democratic government cannot settle human conflicts by peaceful means; let there be too much consensus, and a society ceases to be democratic.

problems encountered in institutionalizing democracy

1. direct and representative democracy

The first difficulty encountered in applying democracy to practical situations is the necessity of making a choice between a mechanism in which the people by direct action govern themselves, and one in which the power to govern is delegated by the people to a limited number of representatives. Actually the difficulty is more seeming than real. At no time in the history of modern democracy has any real measure of direct democracy been practically possible. The New England town meeting, in which the citizens of a community gathered together and determined public policy, is always cited as a form of direct democracy. But even in its heyday, long since past, a good deal of power to formulate and execute the governmental program was necessarily delegated by the voters to town selectmen and other representatives.

The use today by a number of American states and cities of the initiative and referendum to enact laws or pass upon laws made by the legislature is a form of direct democracy. By these devices the mass of the voters is given an opportunity to pass directly upon certain issues of public policy. But at best this can be done for only a small percentage of the policy decisions which are being made at one time. Moreover, there can in the nature of things be very little participation by the general citizenry in the administrative aspects of government. Since administrators necessarily exercise a good deal of discretionary power to add details to policy as they enforce legislation, even policy making cannot be subjected completely to direct popular control. It is true that the initiative and the referendum are often accompanied by the recall—a means whereby the voters may remove a public officer before his term is up, presumably because of popular dissatisfaction with his policies or with his record as an administrator. But this is a negative check and hardly results in participation in the direct governmental process by the people.

The facts of life compel a democratic people to delegate a vast measure of power to agents. Indeed it may be said that the development of representative institutions was the key to modern democracy. All contemporary democracies are in one degree or another representative democracies. Specifically this means that provision is made for the voters at regular intervals in free elections to choose the legislators, and even certain administrators—in particular, the chief executive. Implicit in the arrangement is the idea that a representative shall have a limited period in which to carry out the promises he has made the people and to fulfill the responsibility which he has accepted, and that he must then go back to the voters, account for his stewardship, and either be returned to office for a new period of power or be replaced by someone else.

2. absolute and limited democracy

One of the most difficult problems in the application of democracy is to determine where the line shall be drawn between absolute and limited democracy. Absolute democracy involves complete acceptance of the logic of the democratic principle. The people are to govern themselves in all matters of importance. But since unanimity of opinion is not to be expected on controversial issues, decisions are made by majority vote. Therefore government should be so arranged that a majority of the people have it within their power to make any decisions they please, to commit the entire population to any course of action which they deem wise or desirable. One of the strongest advocates of such an arrangement in our own history was Thomas Jefferson. He had tremendous confidence in the infinite wisdom of the people and felt that there was no satisfactory alternative to majority rule. Either the majority has absolute power, or its will can be frustrated by minorities. There is no middle ground. Accordingly, Jefferson opposed arranging the machinery of government so as to allow minorities to interfere with action along lines preferred by the majority. For example, he attacked, as an instrument of minority rule, the power of the Supreme Court to invalidate legislation enacted by Congress as an agency representing the people.

Other men have been troubled by the thought that a majority can become a tyranny which may ruthlessly destroy the rights of minorities temporarily at its mercy, or which may try to perpetuate itself in power by denying to minorities the opportunity to become at a later time the majority. To meet these possibilities it is argued that the governmental mechanism must be constructed along the lines of limited rather than absolute democracy. The power given into the hands of the majority must be limited and checked so that it may not do violence to the rights of minorities. There must be a balancing of majority power and minority rights.

There is a certain logical dilemma about limited democracy. The very idea of democracy, whatever its degree may be, supposes that ultimate power resides in the people. Inevitably this means that the power of decision must belong to a simple majority of the people. Any other arrangement, whether it be a requirement of approval by a larger majority—such as two thirds—before action can be taken, or an arrangement that permits a minority to veto a proposed course of action, means in the final analysis that a smaller number of people has the power to outvote a larger number of people.

In practice, most democracies are limited rather than absolute, in spite of the logical dilemma referred to. As will be seen when we turn to an analysis of the American political system, the placing of a limitation upon the power which would theoretically belong to the majority in a pure democracy is effected by compelling governmental agencies to operate under a constitution. In other words, constitutional government results in limited democracy, for the most important characteristic of a constitution is that it limits majority power. This it does by drawing a line between the power of government and the rights of individuals. Insofar as a constitution reserves certain rights to individuals, it forbids a majority through its control of the government to pursue policies which would result in an abridgment of these rights. This is not in all ways a satisfactory situation from the point of view of logic even though it provides a practical means of safeguarding basic civil rights. However slight the constitutional restraints placed upon the majority, sooner or later there is bound to be some interference with society's efforts to solve its problems.

No philosophy has ever been evolved which quite succeeds in providing a rational justification for the placing of limitations upon the majority in a democracy. The most persistent explanatory theory has been the doctrine of natural rights. This doctrine asserts that men hold certain rights not because they are recognized in any constitution, granted by the majority, or protected by the government, but because they are a natural consequence of the nature of man and of life. Sometimes these rights are said to have been sanctified by divine authority; sometimes they are said to have had their origin in the state of nature. In any case, natural rights can never be surrendered by individuals, and any encroachment upon them, even as an indirect consequence of governmental action desired by a majority of the people, is a violation of natural law and cannot be condoned by any man-made arrangement.

The trouble with this theory is that there is no permanent list of rights which all men agree should enjoy the preferred status of natural rights. Inclusion or exclusion of specific rights has varied from time to time. The assertion of a specific right as natural tends in practice to be a mere rationalization designed to place a certain interest beyond the control of majority rule. A good example is to be seen in the status of private property. Private property is a man-made institution which society has found useful. That it has any divine inspiration or that it is identified with nature is impossible to prove. Yet there is a strong tradition in American history that property is, in certain ways at least, beyond the control of governments and majorities, however strong the factual case for control may be.

Because there is no satisfactory rational defense of limited democracy it does not follow that the nations of the West, such as the United States, have necessarily been wrong in not building their political systems in conformity with the theory of absolute democracy. Here as elsewhere in human progress it has been necessary for man to feel his way ahead. Because modern life is complex, adherence to the rule of compromise in the affairs of men seems an absolute necessity. Because the majority cannot always be trusted to give adequate recognition to minority interests in the making of compromises, special safeguards for these minority interests and some measure of restraint of majorities have seemed in practice desirable. By and large, in the nations that are known as democratic these safeguards and restraints have not thwarted government by majority in important ways. Sooner or later, vigorous and persistent majorities have had their way and have left their mark upon history. But interferences there have been, some slight, some consequential, some fleeting, some chronic. The student of political institutions cannot evade the question whether a nation committed to democracy must not in the long sweep of history move forward toward the ultimate goal of unrestrained majority rule.

3. political and economic democracy

In ordinary usage "democracy" refers to a form of government. But "democracy" is a word that is often used more broadly. It is said that the democratic spirit must pervade not only man's political life but his nonpolitical institutions and relations as well. There is much talk about the need for more democracy in labor unions, more democracy in business corporations, more democracy on the campus. And it is said that all tendencies toward caste or class must be eliminated from a truly democratic society, and that even though individuals enjoy differing economic or cultural advantages they should all be imbued with a sense of social equality.

In particular, there has been much talk in modern times about the importance of economic democracy. It is said that political democracy is not enough, that such things as free elections, rival political parties, freedom of speech, and democratic procedures in the legislature are desirable, but they are inadequate and perhaps even meaningless unless a nation's economy is also democratic. There has even been a tendency to point to the Soviet Union as a nation which may not have democratic political institutions but one in which this shortcoming is more than offset by the democracy that is found in its economic system.

Advocates of economic democracy have had an even harder time than have the supporters of the more traditional political democracy making clear just what it is they are talking about. Many people who talk about economic democracy seem to have in mind little more than a desire for more economic security or economic justice in society. They believe it is not fair, or necessary, that there should be great disparities of income and wealth in a democracy, and they think a democratic government can and should insure the individual against the hazards of life that threaten his economic security, such as physical disability, unemployment, and old age.

Other people use the phrase "economic democracy" in a more systematic way and refer to the extension of democratic machinery and controls into the area of private economic enterprise. There are widely differing notions of the extent to which such a democratization should be pushed. The more moderate advocates of this policy have in mind such changes as the broader use of collective bargaining as a means of settling disputes between business and labor. They feel that in the past labor has not had that voice in the making of decisions concerning economic problems which it ought to have if these problems are to be attacked by democratic procedures. It is also asserted that there is room for more democracy in the internal structure of labor unions and business corporations, that the workers should have greater control over their union leaders and policies, and that stockholders should have a greater voice in corporation affairs.

Other advocates of economic democracy would go further and subject such private agencies as corporations and unions to a greater measure of government control, and thus of democratic control. They would leave "business" for the most part private in character, but they would provide for public supervision of the many aspects of business activity which vitally affect the general welfare: supervision of decisions as to the kind and quantity of goods to be produced, the marketing or distribution of these goods, and the disposition of profits. For example, there was a good deal of discussion following World War II concerning the need for expansion of the steel industry in the United States. Traditionally, the decision to expand or not to expand such an industry has been made privately by the officers and, to a certain extent, the stockholders of the business organizations immediately affected. But it was argued that both the external security and the internal prosperity of the nation were vitally dependent upon a steel industry with adequate capacity, and that accordingly the government, representing all of the complex economic and social forces which make up the nation, should have a voice in making the very difficult decision as to what constitutes "adequate capacity."

Finally, still other people take the position that economic democracy can be secured only through socialism. It is pointed out that government is the one social institution that is in a position to advance the general welfare, the one institution that can be and has been subjected to control by a majority of all the people. Thus, it is said, if there are important decisions respecting the production and distribution of goods that ought to be made in the light of the general welfare and along lines that the majority of the people thinks wise, the only way to bring this about is by making government responsible for such production and distribution. Only in this way, say the socialists, can an economy be made completely democratic. Socialism, say its advocates, is the natural and logical outcome of the democratic principle.

The extension of the democratic spirit into the operation of an economy is a very real problem. Indeed, if it was the task of the nineteenth century to implement democracy politically, it may properly be said that it is the task of the present century to implement democracy economically. But the contrast between so-called political democracy and economic democracy can easily be exaggerated. Any suggestion that economic democracy is more important than political democracy is at best misleading and at worst dangerous. The governmental mechanism which enables people to control the main currents of their nation's political development has a fundamental value which certainly takes precedence over such lesser arrangements as democratic organization of corporations or labor unions. Political democracy is *the* central manifestation of the democratic spirit in an organized society; economic democracy refers to the logical extension of the democratic spirit into the everyday activities of life. In commenting upon the distinction between political and economic democracy Professor Sidney Hook has written: "Those who speak of two *kinds* of democracy make the fundamental mistake of separating what cannot be separated. Democracy is a matter of degree, not of kind. Political democracy without economic democracy is incomplete: but economic democracy without political democracy is impossible. As well say that there are two kinds of life: life with oxygen and life with any quality you please but without oxygen. *Political* democracy is the oxygen of the democratic body politic." [7]

In any case the conclusion is inescapable that democracy is not irrevocably identified with a capitalist economy. If it be assumed that the masses of the people know better than do a few individuals how to govern themselves wisely and what is for the common good, this hypothesis must have some validity in the economic sphere too. Whether the extension of democracy into this sphere can best be achieved through government regulation or even operation of economic enterprise, or by broadening the influence of the masses in such private, voluntary associations as cooperative societies, business corporations, and labor unions is an issue which is not yet decided.

the challenge to democracy

The student of history quickly discovers that there is no inevitability about the democratic way of life. However persuasive the logic of democracy may be, it is a fact that democratic institutions are found to have existed only in brief periods of history and in limited parts of the world. Moreover, today democracy is challenged both in principle and in practice by alternative systems which have a dynamic quality that makes them dangerous rivals. One system is fascism, another is communism. Like democracy, fascism and communism are hard to define. Both, however, reject certain of the most fundamental tenets of democracy. Both reject the notion that the happiness and satisfaction of the individual man are the goal of life; both reject the idea that the best way ahead is always to be found through debating alternative routes in a free market place of thought and by counting votes to determine the path preferred by the majority. Both systems are essentially authoritarian; each believes that it has found the truth and that no dissent or opposition should be tolerated. Communism perhaps differs from fascism in that it has as its ultimate goal the advancement of the interests of

[7] "What Exactly Do We Mean by 'Democracy'?" *The New York Times Magazine*, March 16, 1947, p. 48.

all the people, whereas fascism is a bald effort to promote the interests of an elite class. But both revert to the mystical and irrational idea widely held in the past that the group is more important than the individual, that the latter can find his complete meaning in life only by submerging his personality in the collective undertaking.

For the moment fascism lies defeated. It has no powerful home state from which to operate on the world scene; its philosophers are silent. Fascism continues, however, to have a powerful appeal, particularly to individuals and groups who through the accident of birth or through exploitation of the inequalities of the social process have gained a privileged status and who regard themselves as members of an elite. That such individuals and groups will find new opportunities in the future to reassert their interests and to challenge democratic institutions seems certain.

Communism is today an aggressive force throughout much of the world. Its challenge to democracy is found perhaps not so much in its ideological appeal as in its use of naked force and violence. But the appeal to reason plays a part, too, and there is no question that communism has an ideological attraction for people in many parts of the world—for people to whom the case for democracy has never been properly presented, and for others, who while knowing democracy, have been impressed by its failures and imperfections.

Both fascism and communism have a powerful appeal for the very reason that they are dogmatic systems. Both insist that the individual accept on faith all policies prescribed by the state, and both thereby relieve him of any necessity to use his intellectual powers in seeking answers to the difficult problems of modern society. Democracy, on the other hand, places a heavy burden upon the individual by asking him to express informed judgments concerning these problems. Francis Biddle, onetime Attorney General of the United States, has recently pointed to the fact that the democratic way of life is a difficult way of life: "The democratic faith is the hardest faith there is, for it is necessarily skeptical, opposed to fanaticism, based on compromise, turned toward tolerance, hopeful for variety and diversity. Its nature is scientific rather than dogmatic." [8]

In the contemporary world, torn by ideological and physical dissension, the fate of democracy is inextricably associated with the fate of the United States of America. The heritage of the Age of Reason is ours to lose or to preserve. If we still have faith in the promise of democracy, it is clear that never before in our history has it been so important to put democracy into practice as it is today. Thus, as the American political system is studied and evaluated, two questions that should never be far from mind are these: How democratic have we succeeded in making our institutions, our processes, and our policies? How democratic is the result—the way of life, the society, the economy—produced by these institutions, processes, and policies?

---

[8] From a work now in manuscript.

A word of warning is necessary. In its fullest sense democracy is an ideal which has never been fully achieved by any people or any state. Students of American government must not make the mistake of condemning the nation's political system in its totality merely because it is not a perfect democracy. The American people have felt their way ahead through nearly two centuries of political experimentation, and the progress which has been made is both real and great. Yet, the times in which we live grow more difficult and troubled; the challenge to our way of life becomes more insistent. If we believe that democracy offers the best hope that man can live a happy and rewarding life, the best means by which man can solve his social problems, we cannot be complacent about the shortcomings of our own democratic experiment.

bibliographic note

Books and articles on democracy are so varied in their approach to the subject it is almost impossible to list them in orderly fashion. Although written over one hundred years ago, Alexis de Tocqueville's *Democracy in America* (Phillips Bradley, ed.; New York: Alfred A. Knopf, Inc., 1945) is still a perceptive, stimulating analysis of American democracy. James B. Bryce's *Modern Democracies* (New York: The Macmillan Company, 1921) is an attempt to compare the great democracies of the Western world. A less successful book than his *American Commonwealth,* it nevertheless provides a useful means of comparing democratic institutions in different countries.

James H. Randall's *The Making of the Modern Mind* (Boston: Houghton Mifflin Company, 1940) is an excellent account of the forces and conditions that have influenced the emergence of Western democracy during the last three or four centuries. Jerome Kerwin's *The Great Tradition: The Democratic Idea* (New York: Declan X. McMullen, 1948) is an essay showing the contribution of early Greek and Christian values to democratic ideology.

Two world wars and the great economic depression of the present century have stimulated social scientists to a re-examination of the theory and practice of democracy. Three excellent collections of readings which stress particularly the historic rise of democratic principles and institutions and which contain many of the most famous formulations of democratic ideas are William Y. Elliott and Neil A. McDonald, *Western Political Heritage* (New York: Prentice-Hall, Inc., 1949); Irwin Edman, *Fountainheads of Freedom: The Growth of the Democratic Idea* (New York: Harcourt, Brace and Company, 1941); and Francis W. Coker, *Democracy, Liberty, and Property* (New York: The Macmillan Company, 1942). A number of recent publications on the history and meaning of democracy are noted without comment: Carl Becker, *Modern Democracy* (New

Haven: Yale University Press, 1941); Crane Brinton, *Ideas and Men* (New York: Prentice-Hall, Inc., 1950); David Bryn-Jones, *Toward a Democratic New Order* (Minneapolis: University of Minnesota Press, 1945); Herman Finer, *America's Destiny* (New York: The Macmillan Company, 1947); George W. Gobles, *The Design of Democracy* (Norman: University of Oklahoma Press, 1946); Harold F. Gosnell, *Democracy—The Threshold of Freedom* (New York: The Ronald Press Company, 1948); A. D. Lindsay, *The Modern Democratic State* (New York: Oxford University Press, 1947); Charles E. Merriam, *What Is Democracy?* (Chicago: The University of Chicago Press, 1941); J. Roland Pennock, *Liberal Democracy: Its Merits and Prospects* (New York: Rinehart & Company, 1950); and Laurence Stapleton, *The Design of Democracy* (New York: Oxford University Press, 1949).

The case for absolute democracy as against limited democracy is set forth in Henry Steele Commager's *Majority Rule and Minority Rights* (New York: Oxford University Press, 1944) and Willmoore Kendall, *John Locke and the Doctrine of Majority Rule* (Urbana: University of Illinois Press, 1941). A recent article discussing the case against absolute democracy is Herbert McClosky's "The Fallacy of Absolute Majority Rule," *Journal of Politics*, XI (November, 1949), 638.

David Spitz, *Patterns of Anti-Democratic Thought* (New York: The Macmillan Company, 1949), is a useful attempt to describe in an orderly fashion some of the antidemocratic movements and writings of the present century with particular reference to the United States.

part 2

---

the American constitutional system

constitutionalism and the rule of law

THE quest for certainty has been one of the great motivating forces in human history. From his earliest beginnings, man has sought to fathom the unknown, to see into the outer darkness surrounding him, to discover the hidden meaning of life. From the beginning, man has learned to distrust capricious nature and has tried to gain an upper hand over the irrational and mysterious forces in his environment by establishing fixed ways of life. Over many aspects of nature's power man found it possible to establish little or no control. But one thing man could and did do, and that was to fight against the uncertainty that depended upon his own erratic nature; he could and did seek to force his neighbors to abide by certain rules of the game, to respect established customs so that he might know where he stood and thereby enjoy a measure of stability and security. Against storms and earthquakes man might find himself helpless, but against the threat to his welfare resulting from the selfish, brutal, or merely unthinking conduct of other men he could fight with some hope of victory.

There is much disagreement among historians and anthropologists as to the exact ways in which or the reasons why men first banded together into a political society and recognized the advantages of living under government. But without reference to any specific historical data it seems likely that two motivating forces were at work. One of these forces contributing to the emergence of governmental institutions was the desire to cope more effectively with group problems; the other was the desire for power that is always strong in many men. Government was from the start highly useful to man in the way in which it made it easier for him to deal with his local social problems or to obtain protection against enemies outside his own group. But unfortunately, because of the individual's lust for power, the control of government was from the beginning all too likely to fall into the hands of tyrants and dictators, and therefore to become uncertain and undependable in its policies—that is to say, to become *arbitrary* government.

Accordingly, it early became desirable to minimize the human factor in government and to avoid the threat of dictatorial, monarchial, aristocratic, totalitarian, or authoritarian (the terminology varies through the years but the implicit threat remains the same) government by providing some higher force than bare, uncontrolled human power in political affairs. There resulted a quest for a superior force, certain in character, just and impersonal in outlook, under which a few men might safely be permitted to exercise political power over many men. This search for a higher force has long been present in human history and its rationalization has taken many forms. But almost always it has culminated in the creation of law—rules by which man must live. Not all of these rules are identified with government. Some of the most important rules by which men live find their origins in such social institutions as the family or the church and depend for their observance upon sanctions that are largely nonpolitical. But almost always the most striking illustration of the attempt to make life more certain by establishing rules which all men must obey is seen in *law* as enforced by government.

At times these rules are claimed to have a divine origin and to depend upon God's ordinance. Again, advocates of a law-controlled society have been content to argue that society is governed by *natural law*, inevitably and immutably derived from the nature of the world in which man finds himself. Still others have avoided claiming any superhuman origin for this legal force in society and have justified the rule of law as a rational product of man's intellect. The pages of religion, philosophy, and history are filled with phrases which describe this search for certainty in law or which seek to justify it. One of the most famous phrases, attributed to the thirteenth-century English writer of legal treatises, Bracton, is found inscribed over the entrance to the great library of the Harvard Law School—"Not under Man, but under God and Law." [1] Or again the visitor to the United States Supreme Court reads as he enters the marbled home of that tribunal in Washington—"Equal Justice under Law." Equal justice under *law*; not equal justice under *man!* And all such aphorisms have been joined together in the oft-repeated phrase that what is needed is a government of laws and not of men.

The search for a rule of law is centuries old. The process by which man finds a superior law in a formal *constitution* is a much more recent phenomenon which had its origin in the eighteenth century. Beginning, perhaps with the American Declaration of Independence in 1776 and continuing through such events as the American Revolution, the French Revolution, the European revolutionary movements of 1830 and 1848, and the political upheavals and rearrangements

---

[1] Bracton's phrase has been removed from its original context and its meaning thereby somewhat changed, but it is the altered meaning, suggested above, that has had significance through the centuries.

that have followed the wars of the present century, national peoples have shown a tendency to supplement the main body of ordinary law with a still higher, central, formal document, known as a constitution, in which political power is organized, described, and delimited. There were constitutions before the eighteenth century, but it is the attempt of many peoples to find in the last two centuries a superlegal basis for their governmental systems which the word "constitutionalism" attempts to describe.

Let us examine further the meaning of constitutional government and the rule of law, and thereby prepare ourselves for a better understanding of the character of the American Constitution and of the success it has enjoyed. In this respect we will do well to seek answers to questions such as the following: How may a constitution properly be defined? What is the difference between so-called rigid and flexible constitutions? How important is the distinction? How important is the distinction between written and unwritten constitutions? What is the relationship between a constitution and ordinary law?

the meaning of constitutionalism

Constitutionalism may be described as the use of fundamental, superior law to keep a government in order. Or again it may be said to be the means by which the people of a nation organize for political action, while retaining for themselves some degree of freedom, of independence from government control. More specifically a constitution defines the political system of a country: it describes the machinery of government, enumerates the powers granted to specific agencies of government, and lists the powers or rights reserved to the people.

It may be asked whether any independent nation can ever be without a constitution. In the sense that a constitution, whatever form it may take, is merely a description of the governmental machinery and political system that exists in a land, no country can be without one, for in modern times every civilized country has some type of formal, organized government, reasonably stable, at least for limited periods of time. But the most important single factor in the meaning of constitutionalism is the concept of *limited government*. That is, a constitution, to be worthy of the name, is one that both establishes governmental power to act and reserves certain rights and freedoms to the people. A constitution can be defined very briefly as the means whereby authority and liberty are balanced in a state. In a large sense the success or failure of any specific constitution depends upon the way in which the constitutional settlement establishes a satisfactory equilibrium between these two inevitable, but opposite, forces in society. Thus a constitution that merely describes the machinery of government, and makes no attempt to reconcile group authority and personal liberty by delimiting the areas of each, is not worthy of the name. Germany under Hitler had a political system,

a very specific and carefully organized one, but the Nazi regime wielded un-
checked power. There was a complete absence of any sense of restraint. In
short, Nazi Germany had authoritarian government, not constitutional government.

the difference between rigid and flexible constitutions

Modern constitutions can be classified in many different ways. One distinction
sometimes said to be of great importance is that between constitutions
easily changed and those changed only with relative difficulty. The former are
called flexible and the latter rigid. The American Constitution is often cited as an
example of the rigid variety and the English Constitution as an example of the
flexible type. The formal amending procedure set forth in the American Constitution is admittedly very complex, and is seldom successfully invoked because
of the requirements of two-thirds and three-fourths majorities to complete the
process. It is this that is said to make the system a rigid one. On the other hand,
the British Parliament is free to alter the British Constitution at any time by the
mere enactment of a statute; hence it is asserted that the system is a flexible one.

In truth this alleged distinction between rigid and flexible constitutions is
far less important than it is said to be, for it may be argued with much justification that any modern constitution must have a high degree of flexibility or it cannot long survive. Here we encounter one of the paradoxes of constitutionalism.
It has been said that a constitution "offers exact and enduring language as a test
for official conduct," but at the same time creates "the risk of imposing outworn
standards upon current activities." [2] If a constitution is to prove successful, it
would seem that it must offer a reasonably exact "test for official conduct," yet be
sufficiently flexible to meet the needs of changing times.

Inasmuch as the American Constitution and the British Constitution have
been highly successful, it may safely be assumed that both have shown a high
degree of flexibility through the years. In actual practice the British Constitution has been somewhat less flexible than one might suppose, for although
Parliament has had the power to amend it very readily, it has seldom exercised
this power. "In the realism of history the British constitution is not flexible. It
changes very slowly." [3] On the other hand, the American Constitution has been
more flexible than one might guess from a reading of its amendment clause, for
it has proved possible to adapt the Constitution to the needs of changed conditions without adding formal amendments to it. In other words, a constitution can
have the necessary degree of flexibility either by having a formal amending pro-

[2] Walton H. Hamilton, "Constitutionalism," *Encyclopaedia of the Social Sciences*, IV, 255.
[3] Howard Lee McBain, "Constitutions," *Encyclopaedia of the Social Sciences*, IV, 259, 260.

cedure that is easily invoked, or by being so worded that new problems can be met without changing its language. The British Constitution is of the first type; the American Constitution is of the second.

To be flexible within its original terms without the necessity of formal amendment, a constitution must be general and it must be brief. By being general its terms are sufficiently broad to lend themselves to periodic redefinition or reinterpretation. By being brief it necessarily leaves many of the exact details of governmental organization and procedure to be filled in by statutes and other means. One cannot do better in illustrating these observations than to quote from the famous opinion of Chief Justice Marshall in the great case of *McCulloch* v. *Maryland*. In giving consideration to the general nature of constitutions, and of the American Constitution in particular, he said:

> A constitution, to contain an accurate detail of all the subdivisions of which its great powers will admit, and of all the means by which they may be carried into execution, would partake of the prolixity of a legal code, and could scarcely be embraced by the human mind. It would probably never be understood by the public. Its nature, therefore, requires, that only its great outlines should be marked, its important objects designated, and the minor ingredients which compose those objects be deduced from the nature of the objects themselves.

And again, he speaks of ours as

> . . . . a constitution intended to endure for ages to come, and consequently, to be adapted to the various crises of human affairs. To have prescribed the means by which government should, in all future time, execute its powers, would have been to change, entirely, the character of the instrument, and give it the properties of a legal code. It would have been an unwise attempt to provide, by immutable rules, for exigencies which, if foreseen at all, must have been seen dimly, and which can best be provided for as they occur.[4]

A century later another great judge, Benjamin N. Cardozo, said:

> A *constitution* states or ought to state not rules for the passing hour, but principles for an expanding future. In so far as it deviates from that standard, and descends into details and particulars, it loses its flexibility, the scope of interpretation contracts, the meaning hardens. While it is true to its function, it maintains its power of adaptation, its suppleness, its play.[5]

We have in our American political experience forty-eight examples of constitutions that in general have proved less flexible within their original terms

---

[4] *McCulloch* v. *Maryland*, 4 Wheaton, 316, 407, 415 (1819).
[5] Benjamin N. Cardozo, *The Nature of the Judicial Process* (New Haven: Yale University Press, 1921), p. 83. Reprinted by permission of Yale University Press, publishers.

than has the federal Constitution. The reference is, of course, to our state constitutions. Most of our state constitutions are easier to change by formal amendment than is the federal Constitution. Every one of them is longer than the federal Constitution, largely because these documents contain so much descriptive material concerning governmental machinery and procedure. These two observations concerning the nature of our state constitutions are not unrelated. Because most state constitutions are easily changed there has been no continuing necessity to keep their language brief, broad, and flexible. Instead there has been a natural tendency to load them down with lengthy provisions descriptive of the political system of the moment. And to complete the circle, because they are so loaded down with technical detail, their language soon becomes obsolete and frequent amendments are necessary.

Each of these two types of constitution has its advantages and disadvantages. The type illustrated by our state constitutions is not without merit in that the exact language of the constitution is kept up to date and reflects the specific character of current conditions and problems. Moreover, the document is by its nature a more exact constitutional settlement and there is perhaps less danger that the men who exercise political power under it will distort its terms or abuse their powers to suit their own selfish or power-seeking ends. On the other hand, this type of constitution is apt to be long and filled with technical terms. As Chief Justice Marshall suggested, it tends to take on the prolixity of a legal code and is little understood by the people.

Contrariwise, the shorter, general, difficult-to-amend constitution, so well illustrated by our federal Constitution, offers the advantage of permanency in the constitutional settlement, and of building a long-lived constitutional tradition. It is easily read, if not always understood, and over a period of years it comes to enjoy the respect of the people, a condition which is highly conducive to stability in the political system. Under this type of constitution, however, the risk is run that the limitations upon power which it provides will be so vaguely and broadly stated that they will not in fact limit, and the chief purpose of a constitution will be lost. Similarly, there is a risk that even though the language be broad, the men to whom power is given to interpret such a constitution will fail to adapt it "to the various crises of human affairs."

In trying to evaluate the advantages and disadvantages of these two types of constitution we cannot avoid paying great attention to the actual records of our American constitutions in the federal and state fields. The long life of our national Constitution, the stability and continuity it has given to our politics, its high degree of flexibility, its preservation of a reasonable balance between liberty and authority—as contrasted with the limited life of the average state constitution, and the somewhat less satisfactory character of our state political systems—argue strongly in favor of the constitution that is brief, general, and stable, yet flexible.

the difference between written and
unwritten constitutions

A further classification of constitutions which is sometimes said to be important is that which draws a line between written and unwritten constitutions. The great English student of political institutions, Lord Bryce, emphasized this distinction and also identified it closely with the distinction between rigid and flexible constitutions,[6] his thesis being that written constitutions tend to be rigid and unwritten constitutions flexible.

The distinction between written and unwritten constitutions may be a convenient one for purposes of classifying constitutions, but it has little value otherwise. It is natural to suppose that the writing down of a constitution makes it more secure and discourages change, but the experience of nations shows that there are far more important considerations determining the stability enjoyed by any particular constitutional system. It has been said, "The genius of constitutions, written and unwritten alike, lies in usage." [7] The Weimar Constitution of the German Republic, which was adopted soon after the close of World War I, was one of the most remarkable written constitutions in the history of political institutions; yet circumstances combined to bring about its early death. When the Nazis were ready to overthrow it, the fact that it was written made little if any difference. On the other hand, the British Constitution, which is always cited as the great example of an unwritten constitution, has had a long life and, as we have seen, has even shown a strong tendency toward rigidity.

A second reason why it is of little importance to distinguish between written and unwritten constitutions is that the distinction seldom exists in practice. The difficulty lies in supposing that the presence or absence of a central, written document tells the story of a country's constitution. The United States has such a document, and England does not; but in each country the ultimate character of the constitutional system is a much broader thing, dependent on many other factors. It is entirely proper to use the word "constitution" to refer to our central, written document. But if by "constitution" is meant a complete description of the essentials of a nation's political system, it is obvious that we must look beyond the formal American Constitution for the full story in the United States. To give just one illustration, it is clear that the political party plays a vital part in American government, and that its nature, its organization, and its control are part of the American constitutional system. Yet there is not a word in our written Constitution about the political party, and one must look beyond the confines of that document to find a description of the party system.

---

[6] James Bryce, *The American Commonwealth* (New York: The Macmillan Company, new ed., 1919), I, 360 ff.

[7] Hamilton, "Constitutionalism," p. 258.

If we turn away from formal constitutional documents to an examination of broader constitutional systems, the written-unwritten distinction ceases to have any meaning at all, for such constitutional systems are always partly written and partly unwritten. There is no central, written constitution in England, but there is much about the British constitutional system that is written. Insofar as the Magna Carta, the Petition of Right, and the Bill of Rights still have life today and help determine the nature of the British political system, the constitutional determination is in writing, for these are all formal, written documents. Again, insofar as the British political system is determined by acts of Parliament, such as the Parliamentary Act of 1911 by which the power of the House of Lords was greatly curtailed, the British Constitution is written. On the other hand, there is much about the American political system that is unwritten. The process by which department heads serve the President as an advisory council, known as the cabinet, is entirely a development in the field of custom, and is not controlled by written rule. Likewise, although our party system is today controlled at many points by statutes, federal and state, its early development was entirely in the field of custom. Even now there is much about the party system that remains governed by custom and is not controlled by statute.

Moreover, it by no means follows that those aspects of a constitutional system which depend upon mere usage or custom are lacking in stability or are susceptible of easy change. In the history of human institutions nothing has shown greater permanency than have many customs which have never been reduced to formal writing. Indeed, the political customs of a people sometimes show greater rigidity than do their written rules. In the final analysis the lasting quality of a constitutional system depends upon a vast number of considerations, such as the presence of a satisfactory social and economic environment in which to carry on a political program; a high degree of satisfaction on the part of an overwhelming majority of the people with the nature of the constitutional settlement and the results it achieves; and an adequate measure of protection against enemies, foreign and domestic, who may attempt aggression or a *coup d'état* against the system. This is not to say that reducing the most important aspects of a constitutional system to writing may not contribute to its strength or help give it a lasting quality, but by itself it is not nearly enough to produce such results.

the distinction between a constitution and ordinary law

"Constitutionalism" and "the rule of law" are terms that are frequently used interchangeably. Both are concerned with the attempt to maintain a social order in which life is lived in accordance with known, fixed rules. In a broad sense it may be said that constitutionalism has to do with placing government under the restraining influence of fixed rules, and that the rule of law has to do with placing individuals under similar controls in their dealings with one another. Moreover, the rule of law suggests a recognition on the part of the government of an obligation to make a formal announcement by statute, court decision, or some similar method, of the policies and the rules which it intends to enforce with respect to the ordinary, everyday relations between man and man. In this way the individual is given fair warning of the rules he must obey in the course of his personal economic and social relations with other individuals. In other words, there can be no bills of attainder where a rule of law prevails. In times past, legislative bodies sometimes dragged individuals before them, declared these individuals guilty of previously undefined offenses against society, and ordered them punished. Under a rule of law, the legislature is expected to enact laws governing social conduct and defining crimes in advance of their application to cases involving particular individuals. The application of these general laws to specific situations and individuals then becomes the task of administrators and judges.

Constitutionalism refers more particularly to a higher law above statutory law or court law. It is a superior law which is concerned with the main lines of the political settlement in a country. It determines the form of government, provides for governmental machinery, specifies the political procedures to be followed in the performance of governmental tasks, and, above all, reserves certain rights to the people. Ordinary law deals with social policies which are stated and prescribed by the government operating under the terms of the constitution. This is quite an important distinction, and one of the factors that may determine the success or failure of a constitution is the extent to which it is confined to a statement of *higher* law. Ordinary law should be rigidly excluded, for the latter has no place in a constitution. A constitution should be impartial as to the everyday social and economic conflicts in which the citizens of a modern democratic state are bound to engage. In the words and phrases it uses it should be neutral as to the quarrels between capital and labor, producer and consumer, industrialist and farmer, section and section, and one racial or religious group and another. It must provide the means—the governmental machinery and the political power —by which such conflicts can be reconciled, but it is a dangerous thing for the constitution itself to take sides in such disputes. It may perhaps properly restate certain social policies which have enjoyed wide acceptance for such long periods of time that few if any people deny their validity. An example would be a constitutional statement of the right of people to hold private property and to enjoy legal protection in their possession of it against individuals who would take it from them. On the other hand, the Eighteenth Amendment is an example of a statement of policy concerning a social problem which had had no such acceptance for a long period of time. Consequently it was out of place in the American Constitution. It would have been a proper thing for such an amendment to have given Congress power by statute to establish prohibition as a national policy if the people wished such a law. But the Eighteenth Amendment gave Congress no such discretionary power; it wrote a rigid statment of social policy into the Constitution itself.

If this distinction between constitutional and ordinary law is carefully observed, it is possible to keep a constitution relatively brief. Contrariwise, where a constitution is inordinately long, as is true of many of the constitutions of the American states, chances are that statements as to ordinary social policy have been permitted to creep into fundamental law. On the other hand, it must be admitted that the national Constitution could be a great deal longer than it is and still be confined to proper constitutional subject matter. For example, a more complete description of the administrative and judicial machinery of government would not be out of place in the Constitution, although it by no means follows that the decision of our constitutional fathers to leave such details to be covered in statutory enactments was an unwise one.

has constitutionalism been successful?

To what extent has the quest for certainty in the attempt to establish limited constitutional government met with success? Is it possible in the statement of higher law to define the fundamental rules of the game with sufficient preciseness and clarity to establish a real and lasting control over the acts of public officers? The most successful constitutions have been those which tended toward vagueness in their language and which have proved quite flexible and adaptable over a period of time. Accordingly, it may be asked whether this does not suggest that the successful constitution is one that ceases to have exact meaning, one that may mean all things to all men? And if this be so, does not such a constitution fail to function as a controlling and limiting force in a nation's political life? These are questions not easily answered. In particular, any attempt to answer them in the light of the experience of the United States under its Constitution must await the detailed examination of the American political system which follows in this volume. But it is proper to note at this point two extreme answers that have been given to these questions, and to suggest that there is also a middle view that may have more validity than the answer at either extreme.

One view of the nature of law, whether it be higher constitutional law or ordinary statutory law, is that it has an exact meaning which absolutely binds those who are affected by it to one course of action, and one course only, in any given situation. By this view it is thought that the human factor in government is reduced virtually to the vanishing point, all aspects of the governmental program being carried on in strict accordance with the provisions of law. In the field of constitutional law those who adhere to this theory believe that there can be little argument as to what is permissible and what is forbidden under the higher law. In the United States, particularly, where the Supreme Court of the nation has come to act as a watchdog of the Constitution which calls a halt when legislative or

administrative officials exceed the limits of their constitutional powers, it is asserted that the Court's duty and decisions are always clearly indicated. If, for example, an act of Congress is challenged as to constitutionality, those who hold to
this position assert that all the Court has to do is to lay the statute alongside the
Constitution to see whether one squares with the other.

In the field of ordinary law the advocates of this view believe that all human relations whether between the citizen and his government, or between citizen and citizen, are governed by precise rules, crystal-clear as to meaning and
purpose. Under such a system there is no uncertainty, no mere whim or caprice,
no arbitrary edict by man over man. Instead, there is an unchanging, beneficent
rule of law, and the judge who is called upon to apply law and decide a case between two persons who have come into conflict with each other always follows
certain fixed legal principles which permit one decision and one only.

At the other extreme is the opinion that constitutions and laws have little to
do with the control of human conduct. It is argued that constitutions are necessarily vague and general or that there are so many competing and conflicting
rules of law that their application to specific situations and problems calls the
human factor into play to such an extent that the resulting action depends far
more upon the personal whims and prejudices of administrators and judges than
it does upon any fixed legal principles. When it is a matter of the United States
Supreme Court testing the constitutionality of acts of Congress, those who hold
this view insist that the Court can decide a case either way it wishes. When it is a
matter of the use of ordinary law to settle the social and economic conflicts of individuals, it is argued that administrators and judges follow their own personal
judgment or prejudices rather than any guiding legal principles.

Those who believe that the human factor supplants the legal factor in the
control of the affairs of men regard this as an inevitable condition. It is not
merely the result of badly drafted laws, or of selfish and ambitious men deliberately ignoring the law or distorting its meaning. Instead it is said that laws are always necessarily so general or so conflicting that political officers, whether they
like it or not, must make their own decisions as they govern—decisions that grow
out of the realities of a given situation or problem rather than being dictated by
the compelling force of law.

This is not the place to attempt a final evaluation of these rival theories, but
it is appropriate to note the existence of a middle view between the two extreme
positions. Admittedly life in the modern world is so complex that any rule which
is devised to meet a given social problem must be worded rather broadly lest its
applicability prove too limited. Moreover, rules of law are a bit like proverbs: one
rule is almost always offset by another rule which, if it does not flatly contradict
the first rule, at least faces in the opposite direction. As will be seen in a later chapter, the judicial process is in good part one by which judges decide which of two
more or less contradictory rules shall determine a given case. But it hardly follows

that because a legal rule is broadly worded or is offset by an opposing rule, the law must lose all its meaning or have no binding character whatsoever. Indeed, the records of such countries as England and the United States, which have operated in a definite and fixed political pattern for a century and more, prove that this is not so. A comparison of their records with the highly arbitrary, erratic, and unstable records of the modern authoritarian states illustrates the fallacy of the argument that constitutionalism has little or no meaning. But it is perhaps just as unsound to assume that because a country operates under a constitution all life is lived in compliance with the fixed requirements of law, or that the human factor plays a completely negligible role. Certainly, repeated references to such aphorisms as the one that proclaims ours to be a government of laws rather than of men can have an unfortunate effect in producing a distorted and unsound impression concerning the meaning of constitutionalism and the fundamental nature of government. Nearly three centuries ago William Penn wrote: "Governments, like clocks, go from the motion men give them; and as governments are made and moved by men, so by them they are ruined too. Wherefore governments rather depend upon men than men upon governments." [8] And in a provocative little book of recent times, Professor Howard Lee McBain writes:

> The difference . . . between a government of laws and a government of men (to the extent that these phrases have any real meaning) is not a difference in kind but a difference of degree only. It is nevertheless a difference of high and important degree; for it bespeaks a difference in spirit; and in government as in most other human institutions the spirit is often the essence.
>
> In the limited sense just defined the American government is of a certainty a government of laws. No other people on earth is or ever has been governed under so many and such elaborate laws as we acquiesce in and apparently rejoice in. [9]

Constitutionalism is one of the noblest ideals to which man can aspire. Moreover, it has had real meaning, as the political history of the world since 1776 so clearly reveals. Once more the words of Benjamin Cardozo help us to understand the value of a constitution:

> The great ideals of liberty and equality are preserved against the assaults of opportunism, the expediency of the passing hour, the erosion of small encroachments, the scorn and derision of those who have no patience with general principles, by enshrining them in constitutions, and consecrating to the task of their protection a body of defenders. By conscious or subconscious influence, the presence of this restraining power, aloof in the back-

---

[8] *Frame of Government of Pensilvania,* quoted in Max Farrand, *The Framing of the Constitution of the United States* (New Haven: Yale University Press, 1926), pp. 209–210.
[9] Howard Lee McBain, *The Living Constitution* (New York: The Macmillan Company, 1928), p. 5.

ground, but none the less always in reserve, tends to stabilize and rationalize the legislative judgment, to infuse it with the glow of principle, to hold the standard aloft and visible for those who must run the race and keep the faith.[10]

Whenever and wherever a liberal democratic people undertake to make a new constitutional settlement, man's continuous search for more and more satisfactory political institutions is advanced, be it ever so little. Few of the new constitutions of the last century and a half have enjoyed any very considerable measure of success, but it does not follow that we have accordingly been on the wrong track. Man has made much political progress in four thousand years of recorded history; yet at the same time far more political experiments have ended in failure than in success. Thus the failure of a particular constitutional experiment does not discredit constitutionalism itself. In estimating the degree of political certainty that man has finally been able to achieve, or in evaluating the constitutional systems of modern nations, we need to maintain a relative point of view. We must see history in perspective, always remembering what a stupendous and precarious undertaking it is for a people to endeavor to set up a new political system, particularly where the attempt proceeds along democratic constitutional lines. Such an undertaking is never easy. It means finding a balance between the old and the new, avoiding both the extreme of wiping the slate completely clean and the extreme of adhering too closely to outworn and unsatisfactory institutions. It means finding a balance between authority and liberty, avoiding both the evil of too much power in government and the evil of too much emphasis upon individual freedom. It means finding a balance between rigidity and flexibility, realizing that a too complete attempt to provide precise rules of law dooms a political system to a short life, and that a too vague and general enunciation of fundamental principles endangers the rule of law and encourages arbitrary government. Truly the task of successful constitution makers is a formidable one! If we are to achieve an adequate understanding and appreciation of the product of their labors, the American Constitution, we will do well to keep such thoughts in mind as we turn to the work of the Founding Fathers who labored at Philadelphia in 1787.

bibliographic note

A good starting point for further reading by the student interested in the general problem of constitutional government will be found in three articles in the *Encyclopaedia of the Social Sciences*. They are "Constitutionalism" by Walton H.

---

[10] Cardozo, *The Nature of the Judicial Process*, pp. 92–93. Reprinted by permission of Yale University Press, publishers.

Hamilton, Vol. IV; "Constitutions" by Howard Lee McBain in Vol. IV; and "Rule of Law" by Roscoe Pound in Vol. VIII. Howard Lee McBain's *The Living Constitution* (New York: The Macmillan Company, 1928) is an excellent, easily read account of general constitutional concepts and of the American Constitution in particular. One of the greatest authorities on the rise of constitutional government is Charles H. McIlwain, who has published two collections of essays on this subject: *Constitutionalism and the Changing World* (New York: The Macmillan Company, 1939) and *Constitutionalism, Ancient and Modern* (Ithaca: Cornell University Press, 1947). A recent book that examines the development of such constitutional principles as separation of powers, checks and balances, and judicial review is Francis D. Wormuth's *The Origins of Modern Constitutionalism* (New York: Harper & Brothers, 1949). Frederick Watkins's *The Political Tradition of the West; A Study in the Development of Modern Liberalism* (Cambridge: Harvard University Press, 1948) is an informative account of the rise of liberalism, a concept which has been closely associated with modern constitutionalism. Carl J. Friedrich's *Constitutional Government and Democracy* (Boston: Ginn and Company, 1946) is a systematic analysis of present-day democratic, constitutional institutions.

The development and nature of the Anglo-American system of law is admirably set forth in two books now regarded as classics: Oliver Wendell Holmes, *The Common Law* (Boston: Little, Brown & Company, 1881), and Roscoe Pound, *The Spirit of the Common Law* (Boston: Marshall Jones Company, 1931). William Seagle's *The Quest For Law* (New York: Alfred A. Knopf, Inc., 1941) is a provocative, frequently controversial study of law as a basis for certainty in human institutions. Willard Hurst's *The Growth of American Law: The Law Makers* (Boston: Little, Brown & Company, 1950) considers the development of law by focusing attention upon lawmaking agencies.

the formation of a more perfect union

*N*O EVENT in the entire history of political institutions is of greater interest to the student of government than the American Constitutional Convention held at Philadelphia in the summer of 1787. This meeting, the men who attended it, and the Constitution they produced have at times been eulogized to an extent that goes well beyond any respect for fact or logic. Nonetheless, it is almost impossible to exaggerate the historical importance of this convention or the success the American Constitution has enjoyed in the more than century and a half of its existence. As we have seen, man's attempts through thousands of years to establish satisfactory and lasting political arrangements have not always been conspicuously successful. This has been particularly true of attempts to establish political systems upon a *constitutional* basis. The pages of history tell the stories of wrecked constitutions, many of which represented promising political experiments made by nations whose historical traditions and social wisdom were not markedly inferior to our own. Thus no student can fail to be interested in the making of the American Constitution or in the reasons why it was destined to enjoy such a long life.

There are other reasons for giving attention to the work of the Philadelphia convention. For one thing, present-day supporters of an international federation find much encouragement in this remarkable step by which thirteen states were welded together into a close political union. The parallel is obviously not a complete one. The thirteen original states had a more or less common social background, they had had quite similar histories, and they were contiguous to one another geographically. Similarly, the thirty-five states subsequently added to the Union, having with few exceptions been settled and developed under American auspices, were absorbed without too much difficulty. On the other hand, in 1787 New Hampshire and Georgia were perhaps as far away from each other in terms of transportation, communication, trade, and exchange of ideas as are England

and China today. The purpose of such an observation is not to minimize the almost insurmountable practical difficulties that stand in the way of an international federation that would include England and China, but rather to emphasize what a remarkable feat it was to bring New Hampshire and Georgia together in a close political union.

In the second place, a knowledge of the work of the framers of the American Constitution is essential to a complete understanding of our present political system. That the American people must have such an understanding goes almost without saying; yet there is widespread ignorance of the nature of our constitutional system. There are those people who are only too ready to invoke the Constitution in support of, or in opposition to, some proposed step, but who have little or no knowledge of the language of the Constitution, or understanding of its clauses in the light of the purposes of the men who wrote them. This is not to say that the intent of the framers should be the sole or even the primary consideration governing twentieth-century decisions on great political issues. For one thing, the language of the Constitution is on the whole broad and general, and can have no precise application to many contemporary problems which could not possibly have been present in the minds of the framers. Yet if the spirit of constitutionalism is to be fully accepted, there is an obligation to ascertain the meaning the framers intended their document to convey. It is perhaps fair to say that an understanding of the purposes of the framers ought to be the starting point in any attempt to determine the nature and extent of the political power that can properly be used in coping with a specific problem.

why the Philadelphia convention was held

Why did the Founding Fathers produce the Constitution that they did? What practical considerations influenced them? To what extent were they guided by fundamental political principles? Why were they dissatisfied with the existing governmental arrangement? What were they trying to achieve in the new system that they established? These and many other similar questions which come readily to mind must be answered if we are to have a better understanding of the American Constitution. To begin with, it is important to remember that the Constitution of 1787 was *constitution Number* 2 in the political history of the United States of America as a sovereign, independent nation. Our first constitution was known as the Articles of Confederation and was in formal effect from 1781 to 1789, at the end of which period the present constitutional system went into operation. Actually our emergence as a sovereign state dates back to the Declaration of Independence, July 4, 1776, but for several years during the early part of the Revolutionary War the national government was a provisional one consisting of the Continental Congress, which governed without benefit of any constitutional charter.

the weaknesses of the Articles of Confederation

Although the Articles of Confederation had been in effect only six years when the Philadelphia Convention met, this was long enough to have demonstrated certain basic weaknesses in the governmental system for which they provided. The Articles had been found to be seriously defective with respect both to the form of government and to the power of government, the essential difficulty being one of deficiency. The sole agency of national government described in the Articles was a unicameral Congress. There was no reference to a chief executive or to administrative machinery, although certain powers granted to Congress implied that it might create some such machinery. There were no national courts save those that Congress was authorized to establish for the limited purposes of trying piracy and prize cases or settling disputes between the states. The Congress was not so much a legislative assembly as it was a conference of state ambassadors. Each state was authorized to send from two to seven delegates, but, regardless of its population, was to have but one vote in the Congress. Important public laws could be voted only on the approval of the delegates from nine states; amendments to the Articles could be proposed in the Congress only by the unanimous vote of thirteen states. Thus the Articles provided for very little machinery of government, and also made it difficult to turn the wheels of the little that was provided.

On the side of power, the Congress under the Articles had little lawmaking authority. It had no direct taxing power, and could only ask the states' governments to make contributions to the national treasury. It had no power to regulate interstate commerce. It could, however, coin money, borrow money, establish a postal system, fix standards of weights and measures, and regulate Indian affairs. Only in the field of foreign relations and national defense did the Congress have powers that might be regarded as commensurate with the role and duties of the central government of a nation. Here the Congress was authorized to make treaties, to send and receive ambassadors, to raise and equip an army and a navy, and to declare war.

The Articles expressly provided that each state was to retain its sovereignty, and in contrast to the "more perfect Union" established by the later Constitution, the Articles spoke of "a firm league of friendship" among the states. In the final analysis, the weakness of the central government under the Articles is best seen in the fact that it had no direct authority over the people of the United States. Instead, its laws and policies bore directly only upon the states, and it was only as it received the cooperation of the states that its laws or policies could ultimately affect the citizen.

the convention's place in the pattern of revolution

It is interesting to correlate the rapidly changing events of the fifteen-year period in American history between 1775 and 1790 with the so-called "pattern of revolution" which historians assert may be seen in most, if not all, of the great revolutionary movements of the last two or three centuries. The assertion is that every revolution proceeds through a somewhat similar sequence of events: that the movement begins with a long period of unrest and discontent, occasioned by the growing decadence of "the old regime," in which the intellectuals take the lead in stimulating action; that the revolution proper begins with a moderate phase but proceeds into a period of violence or "reign of terror," in which the radicals have the upper hand; that there follows a period of uncertainty and threatened anarchy after the revolution is won, in which no group is in complete control and in which there is much experimentation with governmental forms; that the revolution finally culminates in a conservative reaction, in which the less hotheaded among the revolutionaries obtain control, the gains of the revolution are consolidated, and a more or less permanent political system is established.[1] Some historians have concluded that the years in which we were governed under the Articles of Confederation represented our uncertain period in which experimentation was the order of the day, and that the Convention of 1787 was the conservative reaction by which control passed from the radicals into the hands of the propertied, law-abiding class, which proceeded to set up a stable, lasting government.[2] Although such an attempt to explain so readily and so simply the events of a very complex period in American history is bound to leave a great many questions unanswered, there is much about it that is valid.

the fortunate timing of the Constitutional Convention

A somewhat different way of putting much this same point is to say that the Founding Fathers met at just the right moment for the performance of their task. This is true not only with respect to internal conditions within the United States, to the experience that had been gained under the Continental Congresses and the Articles of Confederation, or to the possibility that somewhat later the several states might have gone their separate ways to such an extent that they would have been unwilling to be swallowed up in a federal union. It is true also of external forces and the state of the world. In 1787 there were certain historical forces operating in the world which were conducive to the building of a powerful new nation organized along democratic lines. The philosophy of the Age of Reason had reached its full development and was at the peak of its influence. Perhaps even so short a time as a generation earlier it would have been impossible to undertake a national political experiment characterized by the faith in reason, the belief in progress, and the confidence in the importance of the individual which were so

---

[1] See Crane Brinton, *The Anatomy of Revolution* (New York: W. W. Norton & Company, 1938), and S. E. Morison and H. S. Commager, *The Growth of the American Republic* (New York: Oxford University Press, 1937), I, 162.
[2] See Charles A. and Mary R. Beard, *The Rise of American Civilization* (New York: The Macmillan Company, 1927), Vol. I, chap. 7, "Populism and Reaction."

strong at the close of the eighteenth century. On the other hand, a little later the Western world had been plunged into the horrors of the wars of the French Revolution and the Napoleonic period. That a successful constitutional experiment could have been initiated in the United States in such an atmosphere of military and ideological conflict is exceedingly doubtful.

the economic motives of the framers

It is clear that there was a high degree of cohesion and unity among the fifty-five men who made the Constitution, both as to their social and economic backgrounds and as to the practical reasons that led them to take the step they did. In the first place, the delegates to the convention were, by and large, wealthy individuals with varying property and commercial interests. In a careful analysis of the economic interests of these men, Charles A. Beard has shown the very considerable extent to which they were the important people of the day—the holders of government securities, the owners of plantations and large areas of western lands, the creditors, the slaveowners, and the men with mercantile, manufacturing, and trading interests.[3] The radicals who had played important roles at various stages of the Revolution, and with whom the conservatives had joined hands during that period, were absent. Samuel Adams and John Hancock were missing. Patrick Henry could have been a delegate, but declined to serve, as did several other men. His laconic explanation for this conduct was "I smelt a rat!" Thomas Jefferson and Thomas Paine were in Europe. In fact, only eight of the fifty-six men who had signed the Declaration of Independence eleven years earlier were numbered among the fifty-five delegates to the Philadelphia convention. Furthermore, "not one member represented in his immediate personal economic interests the small farming or mechanic classes."[4]

In the second place, it is clear that extreme dissatisfaction with the existing system of government under the Articles of Confederation was the great driving force that motivated the work of the Philadelphia convention. In particular, the Founding Fathers were troubled by the lack of a positive governmental program for the protection of property, for the encouragement of economic enterprise, and for the preservation of law and order. The security holders were concerned about the growing inability or unwillingness of both state and national governments to meet the interest and principal payments on the public debt. The western landowners wanted a more vigorous governmental program providing roads into the West and protection against the Indians. Creditors were worried about the increasing tendency of debtors to support proposals to inflate the currency, and even to seek legislation from their state governments freeing them from part

---

[3] Charles A. Beard, *An Economic Interpretation of the Constitution of the United States* (New York: The Macmillan Company, 1913), Chap. 5, "The Economic Interests of the Members of the Convention."

[4] *Ibid.*, p. 149.

or all of their obligations. Merchants and manufacturers were handicapped by the lack of a uniform national currency, and were suffering because of the disruption of our foreign trade which followed the break with the British imperial system. They were also disturbed at the growing stagnation in interstate trade caused by the numerous trade barriers established by the individual states. In short, these groups of men deplored the absence of a central, coercive power in the land. George Washington stated the common view of such men when he wrote: "I do not conceive we can exist long as a nation without having lodged somewhere a power, which will pervade the whole Union in as energetic a manner as the authority of the State governments extends over the several States." [5] and with reference to existing disorder and threatened anarchy throughout the nation, he likewise expressed the grave concern of the Fathers when he wrote in 1786: "I feel, my dear General Knox, infinitely more than I can express to you, for the disorders which have arisen in these States. Good God! Who, besides a Tory, could have foreseen, or a Briton predicted them? . . . There are combustibles in every State, which a spark might set fire to."[6]

Above all, it is certain that the fathers of the constitution, whatever else may or may not have been true of them, were not advocates of the laissez-faire doctrine. As they saw it the country was passing through a "critical period" in which the gravest threat to the national welfare lay in too little rather than too much government, in too little rather than too much political activity designed to protect property and to stimulate economic enterprise. In one sense it is misleading to use such terms as "conservative" and "radical" to describe the contending forces of the period. The so-called conservatives of the constitutional period unquestionably favored a great increase in governmental activity and a considerable strengthening of the power of the national government. The radicals of the period, on the other hand, looked upon government as a necessary evil. They were the states' rights people of their time in that they felt that such political power as was necessary should be largely centered in the state governments.

It should be noted that not all, or perhaps not even a majority, of the American people regarded the times as "critical" in character. Nor were they sufficiently dissatisfied with the government under the Articles of Confederation to favor any increase in central power. The small farmers in the rural areas and the mechanics, small traders, and shopkeepers in the towns and cities were reasonably well satisfied with the existing political system even though they had their social and economic grievances. Certainly there was no overwhelming public demand for a new constitution, or, as Beard has put it, there is no evidence

[5] George Washington, *Writings* (W. C. Ford, ed.; New York: G. P. Putnam's Sons, 1891), XI, 53–54.

[6] *Ibid.*, pp. 103–104.

"that the entire country was seized with a poignant sense of impending calamity."

There are many historians who have placed far less stress upon the extent to which the delegates to the Philadelphia convention were motivated by personal economic considerations than have Beard and his followers. Such an eminent historian of the constitutional period as Max Farrand advances a "good government" theory of the writing of the Constitution. He emphasizes the extent to which the delegates sought a better political system by following fundamental political principles. As he saw it,

> The thirteen united states of America had renounced their allegiance to Great Britain, because the latter country no longer governed them well, and it now appeared as if they were unable to govern themselves. If the people of the United States were to prove their right "to assume among the Powers of the earth, the separate and equal station to which the Laws of Nature and of Nature's God entitle them," they must show themselves capable of establishing and maintaining an efficient government. To justify themselves before the world and to justify themselves in their own eyes, an effective union was essential.[7]

Actually, both points of view are correct. Certainly the Fathers, as true statesmen, were ambitious for their country, eager that it should succeed as an independent nation, and, aware of the impermanency of most political institutions, anxious to build carefully and wisely so that the new government might prove successful. On the other hand, it is impossible for any impartial student to overlook the very close relationship between the personal economic interests of the Fathers and the decisions they made in reorganizing the nation's political system. One reason why there has perhaps been reluctance to admit the existence of this relationship is that it is felt such a recognition would belittle the character of the Founding Fathers or destroy the tradition of the high statesmanship which was shown in the Philadelphia convention. Such a feeling is unfortunate. Professor Arthur Schlesinger, who, like Charles Beard, stresses the economic motivation in the writing of the Constitution, points out: "No discriminating reader need feel that such a presentation carries with it the imputation of ignoble or unworthy motives to the Fathers of the Constitution; rather, it forms an illuminating commentary on the fact that intelligent self-interest, whether conscious or instinctive, is one of the motive forces of human progress." [8]

Beard himself has observed, ". . . never in the history of assemblies has there been a convention of men richer in political experience and in practical

---

[7] Max Farrand, *The Framing of the Constitution of the United States* (New Haven: Yale University Press, 1926), pp. 1–2.

[8] Arthur M. Schlesinger, *New Viewpoints in American History* (New York: The Macmillan Company, 1925), p. 189.

knowledge, or endowed with a profounder insight into the springs of human ac
tion and the intimate essence of government." [9]

In other words, one sees an indication here of the close and important connection between politics and economics in the affairs of men. We need to remind ourselves over and over again that government is a means to an end, and
that furthering their economic well-being is one of the chief purposes men expect government to serve. Moreover, in our society, which places so much emphasis upon the importance of the individual, men are bound to try to influence
government in such a way as to advance their separate and individual economic
interests. This is not to say that the Marxists, with their theory of economic de-
terminism, are correct in arguing that man's desire for material well-being is the
sole, all-important motivating force in political affairs. Man is often capable of
minimizing his own personal economic desires as he seeks to advance the well-
being of all. Moreover, he quite obviously seeks other services from government
than the mere advancement of his economic interests. Nonetheless, there is a
widespread tendency either to ignore the extent to which politics finds its motivation in economics, or to deplore the relationship when it is brought out into
the open. This tendency should be overcome, for it does not lead to an intelligent
understanding of the true character of the political process. There is no better
illustration of the importance of economics to politics in all American history
than the undeniable economic motivation that lay behind the work of the Philadelphia convention.

mechanics of the convention

The secret of the Constitution's greatness is an elusive thing. We can only speculate as to what were the most important factors in the fortuitous combination of
circumstances that made possible the highly successful conclusion of the convention's labors. Many a similar constitutional assembly has met throughout the
world during the last century and a half under circumstances seemingly not much
less favorable than those that marked the Philadelphia meeting, and yet more
often than not the results have been disappointing. In seeking an explanation of
the brilliant outcome of the American constitutional assembly, the mechanics
of the convention should first be noted. How was it organized and how did it
proceed?

The convention, meeting in the famous State House in Philadelphia, was in
session from the end of May to the middle of September, throughout the hot
summer months of 1787. In all, fifty-five delegates attended, but many of these
were late in arriving; only forty-two stayed until the end, and only thirty-nine
signed the finished Constitution. Twelve states were represented, Rhode Island

---

[9] Charles A. Beard, *The Supreme Court and the Constitution* (New York: The Macmillan
Company, 1912), p. 86.

refusing to send any delegates. It is estimated that the average attendance was about thirty, so it seems probable that a high degree of intimacy and even informality in the proceedings and debates must have been the rule. The usual hours of the meetings were from ten in the morning until three in the afternoon. The cobblestones in the street outside the State House were covered with earth so as to deaden the sound of passing vehicles and thereby provide a more favorable environment for a successful undertaking.

The delegates to the convention were generally appointed by the state legislatures; in no instance was a delegate elected by the voters. The states sent varying numbers of delegates, but, although the large states would have preferred a weighted system of voting based on population, a decision was early made in the convention that the voting on each issue should be by states. Thus there was a maximum of twelve votes that might be cast on any question. A simple majority was agreed upon as sufficient to carry any proposal.

the record of the convention

There is no official or formal record of the proceedings of the convention. The meeting appointed a secretary, one William Jackson, but he kept very sparse and inadequate minutes of the sessions. Fortunately, it has proved possible for historians to piece together a quite complete record by drawing upon the personal papers, diaries, and memoranda of the delegates. Far and away the most valuable source of information has proved to be a very complete diary kept by James Madison, in which he reported the story of the convention in great detail, even including lengthy and seemingly accurate résumés of the remarks and speeches made by the delegates on the floor of the assembly. Although the importance in a democracy of preserving a careful, complete record of such an important event as a constitutional assembly had not yet come to be formally recognized, one man, at least, sensed the need for such a report and himself assumed the responsibility of providing it.

the convention met in secret sessions

The convention saw no need of opening its meetings to the public or of permitting any daily accounts in the press of its labors, so it early decided upon a rule of rigid secrecy in its proceedings. Although the issue of giving publicity to the deliberations of such an assembly has been a troublesome one in modern times, more often than not the decision has been that in a democratic society there is no alternative to the principle of "open covenants openly arrived at." Nonetheless, it is clear that in the light of the troubled times, and in the face of the bitter disagreement over the propriety and wisdom of thoroughgoing constitutional reform, the labors of the Philadelphia convention were greatly simplified because they took place behind closed doors. The evidence seems convincing that public sessions would have greatly handicapped the convention and would even have seriously endangered the remarkable opportunity to write a new constitution. From start to finish the work of the convention had a dubious legal basis. The convention's formal call clearly limited it to a mere revision of the Articles of Confederation. Had it been known publicly that a new constitution was being drafted, the convention might have found it difficult to complete its labors. Moreover, there would have been strong opposition to many of the specific principles and proposals that proved popular within the convention, opposition which would almost certainly have brought down upon the assembly a torrent of abuse and criticism had its work been reported from day to day.

the submission of the Virginia and New Jersey plans

Because of the small size of the group, and because the modern dependence of parliamentary and constituent assemblies upon the committee system of procedure is a much later development, most of the work was performed on the floor of the convention. George Washington was quickly and unanimously chosen presiding officer, and the sessions got under way in an interesting and significant manner. A group of delegates who in general favored a considerable strengthening of the power of the national government, and an extensive rewriting of the Articles of Confederation amounting virtually to an entirely new constitution, sponsored a concrete program for consideration known as the Virginia Plan. It was also known as the Randolph Plan, since it was presented by Governor Edmund Randolph, one of Virginia's delegates, but much of its authorship has been attributed to James Madison. Having received this proposal, the convention thereupon for two weeks devoted its entire attention to it. To give the plan consideration the convention went into the committee of the whole so that its deliberations might be informal and tentative.

Two weeks after the submission of the Virginia Plan, those delegates who advocated a mere revision of the Articles of Confederation, with a modest increase in the powers of the central government, rallied their forces and presented their proposals to the convention in the form of the New Jersey or Paterson Plan. This plan, too, was considered by the delegates as a committee of the whole. But from the point of view of the mild revisionists, the damage had been done, for when the committee of the whole finally chose between the two plans, the vote was seven to three for accepting the Virginia Plan as a basis for further deliberations. Historians seem to be agreed that this presentation of a scheme for drastic constitutional reform at the very beginning of the convention was significant in that it accustomed the delegates to the thought of radical revision of the constitutional system from the start. It is possible that if the two plans had been presented simultaneously, the New Jersey Plan would have been preferred as being more in line with the purpose for which the convention had been called.[10]

---

[10] Farrand, *Framing of the Constitution*, p. 89.

the use of committees by the convention

Although the convention did not make use of permanent standing committees, it did employ certain substitutes. For one thing, since the delegates lived and ate in close proximity to one another during the months the convention was in session, there were many opportunities for informal discussion. By this means small groups were able to meet in caucus sessions for the discussion of troublesome points. Furthermore, upon occasion the convention did make important use of special committees. When the question of representation in the proposed Congress threatened to wreck the convention, a committee consisting of one delegate from each state was appointed. It made a recommendation that was accepted by the convention. Again, about halfway through the sessions, the convention found that it had made enough progress on issues of fundamental principle and on the main outlines of a new governmental system to warrant setting up a committee of five men to prepare a detailed and formal constitution based upon these decisions. Such a committee of detail was created, and the convention adjourned for ten days to allow the committee time to complete its assignment. At the end of this period the committee reported; thereafter for five weeks the convention went over the committee's proposed constitution with great care, debating it section by section, and attempting to make final decisions on each point.

Early in September, this work being completed, the convention was once more ready to use the services of a committee. Accordingly, a committee of five was appointed "to revise the style of and arrange the articles which had been agreed to by the house." This committee finished its labors in three days, and in a very important sense the final arrangement and exact language of the finished Constitution were determined by it. The convention then spent three days scrutinizing the recommendations of this committee on style, a few last-minute changes were made, and the Constitution was ready to be signed.

So far as the mechanics of the convention's organization and procedure are concerned, then, it is difficult to point to any specific features which obviously contributed to the writing of a great constitution. But it seems reasonably clear that in the convention's small and intimate sessions, its proceedings behind closed doors, its judicious use of the committee of the whole and of two or three special committees, and its acceptance of a specific "plan" early in its labors as a basis for further discussions are to be seen features which help to explain the successful result.

personalities in the convention

Historians who have praised the Fathers in such unrestrained terms as to suggest that they were demigods have not contributed to a better understanding of the writing of the American Constitution. Nonetheless the fifty-five delegates were a remarkable array of men. There can be no doubt that the presence of these particular fifty-five men had a profound influence upon the exact language of the Constitution that emerged from the Philadelphia meeting. There was nothing predestined or inevitable about our Constitution. It is very definitely the product of the men who wrote it. Again and again, specific individuals left their mark upon the Constitution, and in their absence the Constitution must have been otherwise than it is.

That the convention was a gathering of scholarly men who had intellectual as well as economic interests is very clear. Thirty-one of the delegates had had college educations and many others had had private tutors. Two college presidents and three professors were present. Many individuals were famous for their scholarship and learning. James Madison, particularly, was known as a remarkably thorough student of political theory and of governments of the past. Indeed, the fifty-five men have been called "the first American 'brain trust.' " [11] Although the Fathers were in many instances students of history and political philosophers, they had also had much practical experience in politics. Thirty-nine of the fifty-five delegates had been members of Congress; eight had served in state constitutional conventions; seven had been state governors; twenty-one had fought in the Revolutionary War. Thus the advice given the convention by John Dickinson, a delegate from Delaware—"Experience must be our only guide. Reason may mislead us"—was more than an empty platitude. A further general characteristic worthy of note is the relative youth of the delegates. Several men were under thirty, many were under forty, and the average age was but little more than forty-two.

George Washington was easily the most eminent and respected member of the convention. As presiding officer he maintained an austere demeanor and seldom made any remarks on an issue before the assembly, but his opinions were frequently strongly held and generally known. It is the belief of historians that he exercised a very considerable influence on many of the delegates at numerous points along the way. James Madison, like Washington a Virginia delegate, has often been called "the Father of the Constitution." There is considerable exaggeration in such a title, but as the partial author of the Randolph Plan, as an active participant in the convention's deliberations, as its real if not official secretary, and as a member of the final committee on style, his influence was of a very high order. Only thirty-six years old and later to fill several important public offices, including the presidency, he was at his greatest in the convention.

Benjamin Franklin, representing Pennsylvania, was the oldest and certainly the most experienced and worldly-wise of the delegates, but at eighty-one he was past his prime, and there is no evidence that his contribution to the writing of the Constitution was in proportion to his fame or his past achievements. Two other Pennsylvania delegates played very important roles. James Wilson's con-

[11] Morison and Commager, *Growth of the American Republic*, I, 165.

tribution was second only to that of Madison, whose able assistant he was. He was, perhaps, the strongest advocate among the delegates of the democratic principle. In favoring popular election of all congressmen and the President, he went well beyond what a majority of the delegates were willing to accept in the direction of democracy. Gouverneur Morris should be mentioned because it is generally agreed that as one of the five members of the committee on style it was he who actually gave the Constitution much of its final language. Since the exact arrangement and language of the clauses of the Constitution have proved again and again to be of great importance, Morris's role must not be overlooked.

Alexander Hamilton, only thirty years old at this time, was one of the most famous of the delegates, but his contribution to the drafting of the Constitution was not a substantial one. His own personal ideas were far too reactionary and undemocratic even for his conservative colleagues. Moreover, he was frequently outvoted by the other two delegates representing New York. In fact, his influence was so slight that he spent little time in attendance at the convention's sessions, although he was present to sign the finished document. Hamilton's great service was to come a little later, when he helped so much to secure ratification of the Constitution by the state of New York.

Professor Farrand mentions fifteen other men who stood out above their colleagues and made important contributions to the work of the convention. Among this group were Charles Pinckney of South Carolina; George Mason of Virginia; Oliver Ellsworth, William Johnson, and Roger Sherman of Connecticut; and Rufus King and Elbridge Gerry of Massachusetts. Moreover, it seems clear that while a few of the delegates were obstructionists, and a few were mediocre men of little talent, the contribution made by the average delegate was considerably higher than has frequently been true in similar assemblies.

the role of compromise in the convention

Historians have vacillated in their views of the difficulty experienced by the Fathers in securing agreement among themselves as the writing of the Constitution progressed. For a long while it was fashionable to stress the disagreements that were encountered, and the resulting extent to which the finished Constitution was "a bundle of compromises." In recent years the pendulum has swung back, and historians have emphasized the unanimity which existed among the delegates on many points.[12] In differing senses each interpretation is correct. As has been seen, the fifty-five men who attended the Philadelphia meeting came for the most part from the same walks of life. Most of them were members of the elite class—socially, economically, and intellectually. The great gulf that existed between the common people of the day—the small farmers, the artisans, and the debtors—and the more privileged classes was not apparent at Philadelphia for

---

[12] Beard and Beard, *Rise of American Civilization*, I, 314.

the simple reason that the lower classes were almost totally without representation. Accordingly, the overwhelming majority of the delegates who were present saw eye to eye on many of the basic issues of the day. Particularly, there was quite general accord on such propositions as (1) the need for a much stronger government to cope with the nation's economic and social problems, (2) the wisdom of providing such increased power in the central government rather than in the states, and (3) the desirability of incorporating the principles of separation of powers and checks and balances into the new governmental system so as to prevent the abuse of these increased political powers.

Nonetheless, there were important differences of opinion among the delegates, and writing a constitution that all could agree upon was far from an easy task. Although the delegates did have a common social background, they came from twelve different states, many of which were widely separated geographically and economically. It was only natural that the delegates should reflect these varying practical interests. All tended to be agreed as to the necessity of providing a stronger, national government; yet each was at the same time concerned about the use that might be made of this increased central power. Here in the Philadelphia convention may be noted the appearance of an issue that has troubled our nation throughout its entire history. Granting the wisdom of bringing together the American people in one great national state, how can each part of that nation, possessed of economic and social interests peculiar to its own locale, be assured that these interests will receive fair and reasonable consideration from the national government? The delegates to the convention found their sectional interests differing at several crucial points, and compromise played a very important role in their efforts to resolve these conflicts. Two or three and the manner in which they were compromised will now be noted.

1. the compromise between the large and the small states

The most famous of the conflicts in the Philadelphia convention was that between the large and the small states. The dividing line was not a precise one, but in general there was a large-state group led by Virginia, Pennsylvania, and Massachusetts that preferred a substantial increase in the power of the national government and that supported the Virginia Plan. This group was opposed by a small-state faction, including New Jersey, Delaware, and Maryland, that backed the New Jersey Plan and was inclined to take a states' rights position. Actually, there is little evidence to show that the issue of states' rights was advanced by many of the delegates on the level of principle alone. Instead, most of the delegates at heart desired a strengthening of national power. The large states expected to dominate the new national government and thus had little cause to fear its increased power. The small states, afraid that they might be outvoted in the councils of the new government, were inclined for this very practical reason to think twice before they agreed to the proposed increase in its powers. John Dickinson, a small-state delegate, told Madison: "Some of the members from the small States wish for two branches in the General Legislature, *and are friends to a good National Government;* but we would sooner submit to a foreign power, than submit to be deprived of an equality of suffrage, in both branches of the legislature, and thereby be thrown under the domination of the large States." [13]

As Dickinson's comment indicates, the crux of the problem concerned no conflict in principle between centralized power and states' rights but was found in the matter of representation in the new Congress. The large states, in the Virginia Plan, proposed giving each state representation proportional to its population in both houses; the small states, in the New Jersey Plan, proposed keeping the plan of equal representation for each state found in the Articles of Confederation. When it came to a showdown, it was apparent that the large states were in the majority, for it was voted that in the lower house proportional representation should prevail. But when it was time to vote on representation in the upper house, the adamant attitude of the smaller states had its effect. Aware that this was a rock upon which the ship of the convention might founder, a few of the delegates began to waver and showed a tendency to compromise. The first vote on a proposal that each state have equal representation in the Senate resulted in a tie, but after a special committee had studied and reported on the problem, the convention voted by a narrow majority to approve such a proposal. Thus, the small states had their way in the upper house, and the large states had their way in the lower house. The genesis of this compromise plan apparently occurred within the Connecticut delegation, so the arrangement is often described as the "Connecticut Compromise," although it is also known merely as the "Great Compromise." Although many of the large-state delegates, including such leaders as Madison and Wilson, voted against the compromise, there were men in the convention who saw the necessity of compromising this disagreement if a finished constitution was to be produced. Moreover, it was already apparent that unless virtual unanimity prevailed among the delegates in accepting the final constitution its ratification would be impossible. No constitution that emerged from the convention with the approval of a bare majority of the delegates would have had any chance whatsoever of being ratified and of providing the basis for a new national system encompassing all thirteen states.

2. the compromise between the North and the South

Almost as serious as the conflict between the large and the small states was one between the northern and the southern states. Behind this conflict was the fact, already evident in 1787, that the two sections were going their separate ways economically. On the eve of the industrial revolution the northern states, which al-

---

[13] James Madison, *The Debates in the Federal Convention of 1787 Which Framed the Constitution of the United States of America* (G. Hunt and J. B. Scott, eds.; New York: Oxford University Press, 1920), p. 102. Italics added.

ready had important interests in commerce, trade, and shipping, stood ready for the development of the factory system and a manufacturing economy which the next half century would bring. The South, on the other hand, was already witnessing the beginnings of a large-scale plantation system of agriculture. It was producing increasingly large surpluses which it was eager to exchange in outside markets for the finished goods and mechanical products that were unavailable in its own economy. The slave labor system of operating such plantations was already well developed, and, just ahead, the invention of the cotton gin in 1792 was to accentuate these developments, bringing about a large-scale, one-crop agricultural economy that would dominate the South for a century.

Accordingly, each section was apprehensive lest the increased power of the new national government be used to advance the economic interests of the other section at the expense of its own. The southern delegates in particular harbored such fears, and it was necessary to make many concessions before these fears could be calmed. In the first place, whereas many of the northern delegates who represented trading and shipping interests would have preferred complete power in the federal government to regulate interstate and foreign commerce, it was necessary to place an absolute prohibition upon export taxes. In this way the fear of the South was quieted that Congress might try to tax both the flow of the agricultural surplus out of and the flow of finished goods into its territory, thereby placing most of the burden of financing the new federal government upon it. Similarly, the South was troubled about lack of adequate representation in the national Congress. Although it had expected that three fifths of its slaves would be counted as population in determining the number of representatives to which a southern state would be entitled in the lower house, some Southerners were inclined to demand that representation be based upon all the slaves. Northern extremists among the delegates, on the other hand, argued that none of the slaves should be counted. But the compromise spirit prevailing, the three-fifths plan was incorporated in the Constitution. As a further aspect of this compromise, it was decided that direct taxes should be levied among the states on the basis of population and that at this point, too, three fifths of the slaves would be counted in determining a southern state's tax quota.

A third compromise between North and South was arranged on the question of the slave trade. Delegates from the Deep South were anxious to see the importation of slaves from Africa continue without restraint. The Middle states, particularly Virginia, which bred their own slaves and even had a surplus for sale, were willing to see the importation of slaves brought to an end, as were also some of the northern delegates for moral reasons. A compromise decision finally allowed the slave trade to continue until 1808, when Congress might forbid further importation—which it promptly did when that year arrived. In the meantime imported slaves were not to be taxed by the national government at a figure in excess of ten dollars a head. A fourth compromise between North and

South is to be seen in the provision for the ratification of treaties. The South was fearful that the new government would enter into commercial agreements with foreign nations detrimental to its interests, such as a treaty with Spain that might sacrifice American interests in the Gulf of Mexico and Mississippi River areas. Thus, the requirement of a two-thirds majority in the Senate for the ratification of treaties assured the South of a veto power over agreements with foreign nations that might prove distasteful to it.

These compromises between the North and the South were of tremendous importance to the making of our constitutional settlement, for they made it possible to bring together within the framework of a relatively close political union two regions not in close proximity to each other and with widely differing economic systems. Whether they could be kept together within such a union was a question which only the events of the next century could answer.

3. *the compromise between the East and the West*

A less obvious geographic conflict in the convention existed between the East and the West. Reflecting the more conservative propertied and financial interests of the eastern seaboard, the delegates from this area were frightened by the specter of the admission of new states that might be carved out of the western wilderness. They felt they had good reason to believe that these states would almost certainly reflect the radical interests of the debtor and small-farmer classes that they had learned to distrust so much during the Confederation period. Accordingly, there was pressure that a clause be inserted in the Constitution restricting the admission of new states and providing for their membership in the Union on an inferior basis. Fortunately, although the West itself was not well represented in the convention, there were enough delegates who saw the wisdom of permitting the free development of the West to insist upon compromise. It proved impossible to put into the Constitution a clause guaranteeing the right of new states to come into the Union "on the same terms with the original States," but neither was any express language placed in the Constitution condemning new states to an inferior position. Instead, the power to decide finally the terms upon which new states might be accepted was delegated to Congress. Ultimately the doctrine of complete equality was fully accepted by that body.

4. *the compromise on the issue of democracy*

A conflict which never assumed serious proportions but which was nonetheless present in the convention was one that brought those delegates who favored a rather complete following of the democratic principle in the new political system into disagreement with those who were less enthusiastic about democracy. The conflict never became acute because the great majority of the delegates adhered to the latter position. When George Mason commented in the convention that permitting the people to elect the President would be as "unnatural" as "to refer a trial of colors to a blind man," he expressed a sentiment that most of the delegates approved. Nevertheless, there were a few delegates, led by James Wilson, who argued for the election of the President and of the members of both houses of Congress by the people.

The compromise between these opposing factions is not an obvious one, and was perhaps in a very considerable degree unconscious. Those who opposed too direct a participation of the people in governmental affairs certainly carried the day, for only the House of Representatives was made directly responsible to the voters, whereas the Senate, the Presidency, and the federal judiciary were all placed at least one step beyond the immediate control of the electorate. But the best evidence of the compromise character of the Constitution on this all-important issue of democracy is to be seen in the fact that these initial undemocratic features of the document were not made irrevocable or inflexible. Subsequently, it proved possible to make the election of the President quite democratic within the framework of the original system without changing a single word of the written Constitution. The direct election of senators did require alteration of the Constitution, but in the amending clause of the Constitution its framers invited formal change.

Finally, the Constitution left to the states the power to determine the extent of the suffrage. Thus, through changes in state requirements, it proved possible to establish the universal right of all white men to vote without altering a word of the national Constitution. Formal amendments were utilized, however, to extend the suffrage to Negroes and to women.

Although the Founding Fathers showed no pronounced enthusiasm for democracy, they did write a constitution that had tremendous potentialities for development in that direction. Moreover, it should be remembered that for their time the Fathers went relatively far in the direction of democracy. There was no political and social system in any foreign land in 1787 in which the spirit of democracy was stronger. No other government of the day was more directly responsible to the people or better designed to serve the public interest.

Lest this discussion of the conflicts and compromises of the convention lead one to overlook the ease with which many issues were settled, the unanimity that prevailed at many points should once more be recalled. The fifty-five delegates were the end product of a generation of political turmoil and experimentation. The American people had been learning the lessons of self-government and good government the hard way, but by 1787 they were ready to demonstrate that their perspicacity and ingenuity in devising workable, efficient political institutions were of a very high order. Accordingly, such crucial issues as giving increased powers to the national legislature, providing for a much-needed federal judiciary, and placing certain specific prohibitions upon the central and state governments were settled with little debate and a minimum of dissension.

Nonetheless, in the spirit of compromise that prevailed in the convention is to be seen what is perhaps the most important single factor explaining the success that crowned the labors of the meeting. Even though the moment was right for the drafting of the new Constitution, even though the thirteen states were at last ready for a close union, it was still necessary to compromise many troublesome issues if any substantial progress toward these goals was to be made. Moreover, the extent to which the delegates saw the wisdom of a compromise policy that would include some concessions at least to the divergent elements of American society is all the more remarkable in the light of the absence of the extreme conflicts and contrasts among their own ranks which were to be found in society at large. Settling their own differences of opinion would have been an easier matter than settling the differences that existed throughout the thirteen states, but they recognized that they must give some ground to the absent forces. It must not be supposed that all of these wider conflicts were compromised, for, as we have seen, certain interests were pretty largely ignored. Yet in their realization of the complexity of life and in their awareness of the need for compromise if men with varying interests were to live together peacefully, the Fathers proved their claim to greatness.

the struggle over ratification

Three points should be made concerning the process by which the Constitution was ratified and put into operation. One concerns the unlawful and even revolutionary character of the mechanics of the process itself; a second reveals the extremely narrow margin by which the ratification of the Constitution was achieved; and the third deals with the very high order of statesmanship which the supporters of the Constitution showed in their efforts to win support for the document during the long months late in 1787 and in 1788 when it was before the states for consideration.

the revolutionary character of the mechanics of ratification

The work of the convention was done. The great talents and ingenuity of the framers and the spirit of compromise that pervaded the convention's sessions had made possible the fashioning of a document which thirty-nine of the forty-two delegates who were present at the end were able to sign.[14] Virtual unanimity among the delegates had thus been achieved. But the final issue was still in doubt, and there was good reason for the grave fears of the delegates that their Constitution would never be ratified by the states. As has been noted, although most of the delegates to the convention viewed the years under the Articles of Confederation as a "critical period," their opinions were not shared by all per-

---

[14] The three who refused to sign were Edmund Randolph and George Mason of Virginia and Elbridge Gerry of Massachusetts. However, Randolph later changed his mind about the Constitution and argued in its favor in the Virginia ratifying convention.

sons. It seems probable that a majority of the people were in no sense so dissatisfied with government under the Articles that they were anxious for a completely new constitutional settlement. Moreover, in scrapping the Articles of Confederation and devising a new constitution, the framers had clearly exceeded the authority which had been conferred upon them by the Congress under the Articles to meet "for the sole and express purpose of revising the Articles of Confederation, and reporting to Congress and the several Legislatures, such alterations and provisions therein, as shall, when agreed to in Congress, and confirmed by the States, render the federal Constitution adequate to the exigencies of Government, and the preservation of the Union." Furthermore, when the convention came to an end and the thoroughgoing extent of its labors became evident, the fact that it had met in secret sessions did not serve to render the new Constitution any more acceptable.

The Fathers were well aware that drastic action was called for. Accordingly, in the wording of that section of the Constitution that prescribed the manner in which it was to be considered and ratified they did not hesitate to violate the express command of the Articles in three specific ways. The Articles of Confederation were still in effect as the supreme law of the land and, by the terms of its amending clause, revision of the fundamental law could take place only by a unanimous vote of Congress and the approval of the legislatures in all thirteen states. Ignoring this command, the Philadelphia convention directed the Congress to send the Constitution on to the several states without stopping to give the document its own consideration or approval; secondly, it ordered that consideration in the states be by special conventions rather than by the state legislatures; and thirdly, it provided that approval by nine rather than thirteen states should be sufficient to put the new Constitution into operation. In other words, the Fathers did not dare run the risk of complying with the rigid requirements of the amending clause of the Articles. Approval of an amendment by Congress under the Articles required a unanimous vote, which would have been impossible to secure. The state legislatures were almost certain to be antagonistic to a document that would subordinate the state governments to the national government to the extent that the new Constitution did; moreover, it was unthinkable that all thirteen states, including Rhode Island, which had even refused to send delegates to the Philadelphia convention, would ratify.

Viewed legalistically, the action of the supporters of the Constitution in easing its way to ratification can only be regarded as a *coup d'état*. Viewed realistically, their action showed high statesmanship. The requirement in the Articles of Confederation of two kinds of unanimous approval of amendments was an exceedingly unwise one. It is a serious and potentially dangerous error for a democracy to make its fundamental law too difficult to change. Faced with the virtual impossibility of securing a new constitution by lawful methods, the Fathers did the only thing intelligent men can do under the circumstances—they resorted to the method of bloodless revolution. Moreover, their action was justifiable from the point of view of the democratic principle, for democracy does not mean that action shall be had only where the people are unanimous. In voting to submit the Constitution to state conventions rather than to state legislatures it is probably true that the delegates reasoned the document would get more favorable treatment from the former than from the latter. Nonetheless, several delegates argued that this method was the more democratic one in that approval of the Constitution by delegates to state conventions chosen by the voters for that one purpose alone would much more nearly approximate popular ratification of the Constitution than would approval by the state legislatures.

the close margin of ratification

That the fears of the Fathers were not unfounded is proved by the exceedingly close margin by which the Constitution was accepted. In several crucial states the margin of success was almost unbelievably narrow. In the Massachusetts convention the vote was 187 to 168; in Virginia it was 89 to 79; and in New York it was 30 to 27. It is true that all of the states, even Rhode Island, finally ratified, but it seems clear that one or two die-hard states did so only because they realized that the new system was going into operation and that they could not very well remain outside the Union. Had Rhode Island's consent been necessary before the Constitution could take effect there is reason to believe it would never have approved the change.

Not only was the margin in favor of ratification close in several of the state conventions. There is further evidence that the voters who supported the Constitution in the elections in which delegates to the state conventions were chosen were at best only a small minority of the adult white male population. Either because of the severe restrictions upon suffrage that prevailed in many of the states, or because of disinterest or disaffection, it is estimated that not more than one fourth of the adult white males voted either way, and that the actual voters favoring the Constitution did not exceed one hundred thousand in a population of four million.[15]

efforts in support of ratification

The statesmanship of the Fathers did not stop with their action easing the requirements for the Constitution's ratification. There remained the task of securing a favorable vote in at least nine of the state conventions, a task of no mean character, as the very close vote that actually occurred in several of these conventions so conclusively shows. Accordingly, the Fathers kept up their labors. They served in the state conventions, working long and hard for favorable action, and they were active on the platform and in the press in endeavoring to shape a positive public opinion in support of the Constitution.

---

[15] Beard and Beard, *Rise of American Civilization*, I, 332.

Perhaps the most notable effort on behalf of the Constitution during the ratification struggle was made in New York. There, Alexander Hamilton, James Madison, and John Jay joined forces to write a series of letters analyzing the Constitution and extolling its merits. These letters, widely printed in the newspapers of the day, have been gathered together and preserved under the title of *The Federalist*. It is significant that this, America's greatest single contribution to the literature of political thought, should have been called forth by the practical necessity of winning support for the proposed Constitution.

Not all of the methods used by the supporters of the Constitution deserve to be characterized as acts of high statesmanship. For example, in the Pennsylvania legislature the opponents of the Constitution tried to delay the calling of a state ratifying convention by leaving their seats so as to prevent action by a nec essary quorum of members. Faced with this tactic the Constitution's supporters took drastic action against the absentees. In the words of the Beards, "a federalist mob invaded their lodgings, dragged them through the streets, and pushed them back into the assembly room," where the legislature then proceeded to issue a call for a convention.[16]

The opposition to the new Constitution during the ratification period was extensive and vociferous. Almost everywhere, the small farmers, the debtors, the poorer classes in the towns and cities, and the state politicians were opposed to ratification. Moreover, opposition was strongly entrenched in many of the state conventions. The following comment by a rural member of the Massachusetts convention reveals the strong feeling of these opponents:

These lawyers, and men of learning, and moneyed men, that talk so finely, and gloss over matters so smoothly, to make us poor illiterate people swallow down the pill, expect to get into Congress themselves; they expect to be the managers of this Constitution, and get all the power and all the money into their own hands, and then they will swallow up all us little folks, like the great *Leviathan*, Mr. President; yes, just as the whale swallowed up *Jonah*.[17]

To the last the Fathers showed their willingness to compromise. As the struggle over ratification proceeded it became evident that the decision of the Philadelphia convention to exclude a bill of rights from the Constitution had been a strategic mistake. To win for the Constitution the support of those numerous persons who were vigorous in their demands for the inclusion of such a bill of rights, an informal promise was soon given that the first Congress under the new Constitution would draw up a series of amendments which would provide a fundamental guarantee of a free people's traditional liberties.

---

[16] *Ibid.*, p. 331.
[17] Jonathan Elliot, *The Debates in the Several State Conventions on the Adoption of the Federal Constitution* (Philadelphia: J. B. Lippincott Company, 1888), II, 102.

Considering all aspects of the ratification struggle, the use of unlawful methods to secure final approval of the Constitution remains most significant. Herein is to be seen one of the great lessons of American political experience. The events of 1787 and 1788 are entirely comparable to the situation that would exist were a constitutional convention to be called at some future time in the city of Chicago with the approval of Congress, and were this convention to submit to the nation a new constitution with the proviso that it should go into effect when ratified by a majority of the voters in a national referendum election. Such action would clearly violate the terms of the amending clause of our present Constitution; yet who can say that it would not be action of high statesmanship were the nation to be confronted on one hand with a severe economic and social crisis requiring drastic revision of our political system and on the other hand with an inability to secure the two-thirds and three-fourths majorities necessary under our present Constitution for such revision?

The task of the Founding Fathers was a double one: to the writing of the Constitution they had to bring great wisdom based both upon reason and upon experience; to secure ratification of the Constitution they had to show high courage and great boldness. How well they performed this double task is an issue to which history has given one of its most decisive responses.

In this chapter attention has been given to one of the greatest political problems a free people ever faces—the mechanics of devising a new constitutional system. In the next two chapters attention will be turned to the content of this Constitution, including the varying purposes of its articles and the nature of its fundamental principles.

bibliographic note

Documentary sources bearing upon the work of the Philadelphia convention, including Madison's diary, have been gathered together by Max Farrand in a four-volume work, *The Records of the Federal Convention of 1787* (New Haven: Yale University Press, 1911). Madison's diary is also available in separate editions, of which one of the most authoritative is G. Hunt and J. B. Scott, *The Debates in the Federal Convention of 1787 Which Framed the Constitution of the United States of America* (New York: Oxford University Press, 1920). This edition presents Madison's notes in chronological order. Arthur T. Prescott has supplied a useful edition in which Madison's notes are regrouped to show the consecutive development of each part of the Constitution. The title of this edition is *Drafting the Federal Constitution* (University: Louisiana State University Press, 1941). For the debates in the state conventions that ratified the federal Constitution, the standard source is Jonathan Elliot, *The Debates in the Several*

State Conventions on the Adoption of the Federal Constitution (Philadelphia: J. B. Lippincott Company, 1888).

There are several accounts of the work of the Philadelphia convention designed for the general reader. Perhaps the most authoritative of these is Max Farrand's *The Framing of the Constitution* (New Haven: Yale University Press, 1926). Others are Burton J. Hendrick, *Bulwark of the Republic* (Boston: Little, Brown & Company, 1937); Fred Rodell, *Fifty-five Men* (New York: The Telegraph Press, 1936); and Carl Van Doren, *The Great Rehearsal* (New York: The Viking Press, 1948). There is an excellent chapter on the Philadelphia convention in Charles A. and Mary R. Beard, *The Rise of American Civilization* (New York: The Macmillan Company, 1927), entitled "Populism and Reaction."

Attention should also be called to Charles A. Beard's *An Economic Interpretation of the Constitution of the United States* (New York: The Macmillan Company, 1913). This pioneer study of the economic motives which influenced the delegates to the Philadelphia convention is a remarkable illustration of historical research. Although there has been a tendency in recent years to re-emphasize the fact that the Founding Fathers were influenced by principles and ideals as well as by material considerations, this study profoundly affected all subsequent examinations of the work of the convention by political scientists and historians.

the Constitution distributes power:

the great principles

ONE OF the chief purposes of the framers of the Constitution was to provide for a considerable increase in governmental power in the United States. Having provided for such an increase, it was necessary to arrange for the distribution or allocation of the new power. Indeed, distribution of this power was one of the central problems that confronted the Founding Fathers. It is quickly apparent from a reading of the Constitution that in attacking this problem the Convention was governed by a belief that a widespread diffusion of power was highly desirable.

Why did the Fathers favor a wide distribution of power? In the first place, at certain points they were compelled by the force of circumstances to follow such a path. For example, in making provision for a division of power between the national government and the state governments, the Philadelphia convention could have followed no other policy. An absolute concentration of power in a central government would have been utterly unacceptable to the states and to the people, even if a majority of the framers had preferred such a course. The political realities of the day dictated a sharing of power between two kinds of government; the element of discretion lay in the degree of power that each government was to possess.

In the second place, the Fathers believed that a wide distribution of governmental power had positive merit in its own right as a means of preventing the abuse of power by tyrannical officers—especially by legislators. The Fathers had created a much stronger national government because they were convinced that the solution of the social and economic problems confronting the country called for vigorous governmental action. And yet in distributing power widely they ran the risk of hamstringing the government and preventing such action. At this point the framers were merely facing the age-old dilemma which has always confronted those makers of government who have had the public interest at heart, the dilemma of how to create a government strong enough to cope with a nation's problems, yet one that will not use its power in arbitrary or tyrannical fashion. For example, in providing for a separation of powers among three branches of government, there is evidence that the framers were aware that some such arrangement had long been counseled by political theorists, both those of antiquity and of more recent times, as a way of preventing the abuse of political power by those to whom it is entrusted. Madison expressed this belief when he wrote in *The Federalist*: "The accumulation of all powers, legislative, executive, and judiciary, in the same hands, whether of one, a few, or many, and whether hereditary, self-appointed, or elective, may justly be pronounced the very definition of tyranny." [1]

Some students of American government have argued that the Philadelphia convention had a much more pointed reason for favoring a wide distribution of political power. It is said, and with some justification, that the framers had a profound distrust of the democratic process and particularly feared that the increased power of the national government might become an effective instrument for carrying the desires of a popular majority of the people into effect. One authority states that the Constitution makers "constructed a government of balances devised to prevent the majority from ever dominating 'the minority of the opulent.'" He adds: "This scheme of balances, with its different methods and time-schedules of election, rendered the new government virtually safe from the dangers of popular, agrarian domination." [2] It is possible to point to numerous statements of the delegates themselves in which the antidemocratic motive seems at least partly to explain the decision to diffuse power on a wide basis. The following remark of Edmund Randolph in the opening speech of the convention is a typical one: "Our chief danger arises from the democratic parts of our constitutions. It is a maxim which I hold incontrovertible, that the powers of government exercised by the people swallows [sic] up the other branches. None of the constitutions have provided sufficient checks against the democracy." [3]

We may now examine the exact manner in which power is distributed by the Constitution, noting the accompanying principles which serve to explain and justify the result. The distribution is a threefold one: (1) a division of power between the national and the state governments, arranged in accordance with the principle of *federalism*; (2) a division of power among three branches within the national government, in accordance with the principle of *separation of powers*; and (3) a less obvious division of power between the government and the people, in accordance with the principle of *limited government*. Related to these major principles of the Constitution are certain secondary principles which

---

[1] *The Federalist*, No. 47.

[2] J. M. Jacobson, *The Development of American Political Thought: A Documentary History* (New York: Appleton-Century-Crofts, Inc., 1932), pp. 174–175.

[3] Max Farrand, ed., *The Records of the Federal Convention of 1787* (New Haven: Yale University Press, 1911), I, 26–27.

will be examined in their proper places. These are the principle of *the supremacy of federal law*, the principle of *implied powers*, and the principle of *checks and balances*.

the principle of federalism

the nature of federalism

Perhaps the most striking and unique aspect of the American constitutional system is its federal character. Federalism may be defined as the division of political power between a central government, with authority over the entire territory of a nation, and a series of local governments, called "states" in America, which individually include only limited portions of a country but which collectively cover the entire area. Each of these two kinds of government must be more or less independent of the other in a true federal system. Neither may be dependent upon the other for its grant of power. It may be argued that in 1789 the American states actually granted or surrendered to the national government a part of their political power. But in the legal sense both the national government and the state governments derived their powers directly from the Constitution.

Federalism may be contrasted with unitary government. The latter is found in Great Britain. In that country there are, to be sure, divisional units of government in addition to the central government in London. But these divisions are created by and subject to the constant control of the central government. Therein lies the distinction between federal and unitary governments.

Federalism is nowhere specifically explained or defined in the Constitution. But the principle pervades almost every article of the document. It is clear that the national government whose organization and powers are being defined is only part of the total governmental system; "states" are referred to repeatedly, limitations are placed upon them, and powers not granted to the national government are reserved to them. Perhaps the Constitution comes closest to defining federalism in the Tenth Amendment, where it is stated that the powers not delegated to the central government are reserved to the states or to the people.

the acceptance of federalism in 1787

The reasons for the acceptance of the federal principle in 1787 have already been touched upon. Such an extremist as Alexander Hamilton would have abolished the states as independent governments altogether, concentrating all power in a national government, but such a policy was in no sense a possible one in the year of the Philadelphia convention. The states already existed as sovereign units, they were jealous of their powers, and the only real possibility was to persuade them to surrender enough of their power to make possible the creation of a new national government with vigorous, albeit limited, power to govern.

In this respect the contrast between a *confederation* and a *federation* may be noted. The former existed in this country during the seventeen eighties. Under the Articles of Confederation the states retained the lion's share of power and were said to be *sovereign* states. The national government was a weak agency possessed of little power. Moreover, it did not govern the people directly, but was a mere council or league of states. In 1789 the union of states progressed into a true federal stage in which the national government as well as the state governments became a fully organized political agency with executive and judicial machinery as well as a legislative council. Most important of all, it gained power to govern the people directly, not only as to matters pertaining to foreign policy but with respect to many matters of purely domestic concern. The individual states surrendered their sovereignty, which thereafter resided in a single, *national* state—the United States of America.

In the light of the difficulties that have been encountered in modern times in trying to set up any international council of nations, with a central governing agency that plays anything more than the very weak role assigned to such a government in a *confederation*, the decision of the delegates representing the American states to establish a truly federal union is a remarkable one. That they should have gone even further and have created a unitary system of government in America was unthinkable.

the advantages of federalism

In the long run of history there has been a trend toward larger political states and stronger central governments. In many countries this trend has resulted in the growth of large and powerful unitary states. But in other countries conditions have seemed to favor the emergence of federal institutions. For example, a federal arrangement has proved to be a natural means of satisfying a desire for a common government in a large geographical area, or on the part of peoples of differing racial, cultural, or historical backgrounds. Or again where two or more areas that have previously enjoyed a high degree of political independence seek political union, a federal state has been found to be a logical way of effecting it. Federalism is an obvious compromise between extremists who argue for a complete union and those who, prizing the local traditions of the hitherto separate states, are reluctant to see these states disappear into a new and greater state.

It is important to remember this compromise character of any federal plan of government. All compromises are necessarily in some ways illogical and unsatisfactory. Thus, if we are inclined at times to grow weary of the continuous attempts over a period of a century and a half to perfect a federal system of government in the United States, we do well to recall the compromise character of our government. Justice Frankfurter has observed: "Federal governments are not the offspring of political science; they are the product of economic and social pressure."

Although the less than ideal character of any federal system is recognized, it would be wrong to minimize the merits of the particular scheme of federalism that emerged from the Philadelphia convention. In referring to the difficult task which faced the Founding Fathers in their attempt to balance the powers of a national government with the powers of a group of independent local governments, one eminent American historian has observed:

> That was a question that might well have confused the clearest brain of the
> .time; no more delicate and intricate problem in practical politics and state-
> craft ever confronted a thinking people. If a system could be found which
> did not involve the destruction of the states, which preserved an equitable
> distribution of authority between the centre and the parts, the great problem
> of imperial organization had found a solution. If this could be done, Amer-
> ica would make one of the greatest contributions ever made by a nation
> to the theory and practice of government.[4]

division of power between the federal and state governments

Since federalism entails a delicate balancing of power between two independent governments, it is clear that there must be a careful and reasonably specific allocation of specific powers to each government. Faced with this need to make a clear-cut division of power between central and state governments, the framers of the American Constitution hit upon a very clever and ingenious plan. They proceeded to enumerate in precise fashion the powers of the national government, leaving it to be inferred that all remaining powers were reserved to the states. However, this latter point was not long to depend on inference, for almost at once, as a part of the Bill of Rights, the Tenth Amendment was added to the Constitution, which expressly provides that all powers not granted to the government of the United States, nor actually forbidden to the states, are reserved to the state governments or to the people. This scheme of enumerated and reserved powers is a remarkable one, but it should be noted that the grant of power to each type of government under this plan can be reversed. For example, in Canada's federal system the constitutional arrangement assigns certain delegated powers to the Canadian provinces and leaves all of the residual powers with the central government in Ottawa.

The bare outline of national and state powers under the American Constitution is a straightforward one. Certain powers are delegated to the national government. For example, Congress is expressly authorized to declare war, to provide a system of post offices and post roads, and to regulate interstate commerce. Certain other powers are quite clearly reserved to the state governments by infer-

---

[4] A. C. McLaughlin, *The Confederation and the Constitution* (New York: Harper & Brothers, 1905), pp. 176–177.

ence. Congress is granted no authority to maintain a system of public schools, or to regulate such human relations as marriage and divorce. So it may well be supposed that these are powers reserved to the states. Finally, there are powers which belong to neither government, being specifically prohibited to both. For example, both Congress and the state legislatures are expressly forbidden to pass ex post facto laws or bills of attainder.

some powers are shared by both governments

Unfortunately, the distribution of power between the national and state governments is not as simple as this outline would indicate. In the first place, the powers possessed by each government are not necessarily *exclusive* with that government. Instead, many powers are definitely shared in *concurrent* fashion by both governments. Congress is granted the power to tax, but this does not deny the exercise of this power by the states. It was certainly the expectation of the framers that both governments would use such a power. It is true that a few powers are expressly granted to the national government and expressly denied to the states. Examples are the power to make treaties and the power to coin money. On the other hand, many powers commonly associated with the national government, such as the power to regulate interstate commerce, or even the power to wage war, are not necessarily exclusive with that government, and may upon occasion be exercised by the states.

The fact that certain powers may be exercised concurrently by both central and state governments results in a blurring of the principle of federalism and creates confusion as to the dividing line between the two governments. Fortunately, this particular difficulty is solved, in part at least, by a subsidiary constitutional principle which provides for the *supremacy of federal law*. This principle is clearly stated in Article Six of the Constitution, where it is provided that the laws of the United States which are made in pursuance of the Constitution shall be the supreme law of the land, anything in the constitutions or laws of the states to the contrary notwithstanding. In other words, a state may under certain circumstances regulate interstate commerce but only insofar as such regulations are consistent with, or permissible under, the policy Congress has chosen to establish. Federal law is supreme, then, in those fields where both governments may be active. Moreover, the Constitution places a duty upon all judges, federal and state, to observe this principle by giving preference to a federal statute wherever there is a conflict between federal and state law.

the effect of the principle of implied powers upon federalism

In the second place, the powers of the national government are not in fact limited to those *expressly* enumerated in the Constitution. It might be supposed, and indeed it was first argued by many people, that the specific enumeration of the powers of the national government limits this government absolutely to the exercise of express powers only. But it was early argued that the grant of express powers necessarily carries with it certain further, resultant, or *implied* powers. There is good reason to believe that the framers of the Constitution held this latter point of view, one indication of this being the wording they gave to the so-called eighteenth grant of power to Congress in Article One, which provides that Congress shall have power "To make all laws which shall be necessary and proper for carrying into execution the foregoing powers, and all other powers vested by this Constitution in the government of the United States, or in any department or officer thereof."

The question whether the doctrine of implied powers was to be accepted as valid was answered in the affirmative by the Supreme Court of the United States in the famous case of *McCulloch* v. *Maryland*, decided in 1819. In its decision the Court, speaking through Chief Justice Marshall, passed upon the constitutionality of an act of Congress creating a Bank of the United States as a quasi-governmental corporation. Congress had been granted no power which in so many words authorized it to take such action. But the defenders of Congress's position asserted that such express powers as those to lay and collect taxes, to borrow money, to regulate commerce, to declare and conduct a war, and to raise and support armies and navies, when combined with the eighteenth grant of power, justified creation of a bank by Congress as a convenient means of facilitating the exercise of express powers. This reasoning met with the Court's approval:

> We admit, as all must admit, that the powers of the government are limited, and that its limits are not to be transcended. But we think the sound construction of the constitution must allow to the national legislature that discretion, with respect to the means by which the powers it confers are to be carried into execution, which will enable that body to perform the high duties assigned to it, in the manner most beneficial to the people. Let the end be legitimate, let it be within the scope of the constitution, and all means which are appropriate, which are plainly adapted to that end, which are not prohibited, but consist with the letter and spirit of the constitution, are constitutional.[5]

Thus it was that Congress ventured to assert, and the Supreme Court agreed, that the powers of the national government are not limited solely to the ones expressly enumerated in the Constitution, but include all those that may reasonably be implied from those expressly stated.

The far-reaching effects of the principle of implied powers have long been evident. On the basis of its express powers to regulate interstate commerce, to

---

[5] 4 Wheaton 316, 421 (1819).

establish a postal system, to lay and collect taxes, and to support an army and a navy, Congress has passed a whole host of measures which invade the realm of power that might have seemed to be reserved to the states. The great majority of these laws have been sustained by the courts as constitutional. To take an example, it might seem as though the power to enact criminal statutes providing for the punishment of those persons who commit unlawful acts was reserved by the Constitution to the state governments. As a matter of fact, most of our criminal laws have been, and remain today, state laws. But Congress early began to supplement these state laws with federal laws by utilizing its implied powers. Today the theft of an automobile or the kidnaping of a person has been made a federal crime where the thief or the kidnaper crosses a state line, the commerce power having been held to justify such a federal statute. Or the criminal who embezzles money or starts a fraudulent business enterprise runs afoul of federal criminal law if he uses the mails in furthering his ventures, the postal power being said to justify this type of federal criminal statute. Again, if a notorious operator of a gambling establishment evades prosecution under state law he may find himself being prosecuted under federal criminal law on the ground that he has failed to declare his ill-gotten gains and to pay an income tax to the federal government upon them. This time the taxing power is said to justify such a federal criminal prosecution.

It is clear that the idea of federal implied power is itself a constitutional principle which is not in all ways consistent with the principle of federalism. Had federalism found expression in the Constitution in pure form, it is theoretically possible that a precise formula for the separation of federal and state powers might have been worked out through the years. But once it was conceded that the national government possessed implied as well as express power, the limits of national authority became extremely difficult to fix. How far could implied power be stretched? What laws could Congress pass upon this basis without invading the realm of state power, and where did it have to stop? The difficulty was, and is, that such questions have no fixed or certain answers. The process of implication is a limitless one. So it is that for a century and a half we have had under our Constitution only a broad, general dividing line between federal and state government.

Actually, the doctrine of implied powers was a natural development brought about by irresistible social and historical forces. No absolutely fixed or precise division of power between a central government and local governments is ever possible. There must always be a good deal of play in the constitutional machinery to make it possible to adjust to the needs of changing times. The last century and a half have seen the development of relentless pressures upon the national government of the United States for the undertaking of new and increased activities. The principle of implied powers has been the chief rationalization by which these changes have been justified. Had it not been this rationalization, another would have been provided, for it was inevitable that the federal system should prove dynamic in character if it was to endure.

intergovernmental obligations

The pattern of federalism is completed in the Constitution by the prescription of certain intergovernmental obligations. The federal government is directed (1) to guarantee the states a republican form of government, (2) to protect the states against invasion and domestic violence, (3) to refrain from changing the boundaries of a state without its consent, and (4) to maintain equality of state representation in the Senate. Upon the states, in turn, is placed the duty of conducting elections for federal offices. Specifically, they are directed to make provision for the election of United States senators and representatives (allowing all persons qualified to vote for members of the most numerous branch of a state legislature to participate in such elections) and presidential electors. Finally the states are ordered to meet certain obligations to one another. These are (1) to give full faith and credit to each other's official acts, (2) to extend all privileges and immunities to visitor-citizens from other states that they extend to their own citizens, and (3) to deliver up fugitives from justice at the demand of the executive authority of the states where the crimes occurred.

The actual development and usage of these obligations have varied considerably since 1789. Some, such as the obligation of the federal government to honor state boundaries, have been quietly and consistently observed. Others have required considerable interpretation by the courts or other government agencies, and their actual meaning has depended greatly upon usage. For example, the United States Supreme Court has ruled that it is up to the President and Congress to determine when to intervene in the affairs of a state in order that a republican form of government may be maintained. Instances of such intervention have been so few in number that no body of precedent exists as to where the line runs between a condition of state government that is republican in form and one that is not. On the other hand, the federal courts have had much to say about the meaning of the requirement that the states give full faith and credit to each other's acts and a considerable body of judge-made law on this point has developed. But the law is confusing. For example, in general one state must recognize a decree of divorce granted by another state, but this rule has been qualified in its application by the development of rules as to what constitutes a bona fide residence of persons in the state granting a divorce.[6]

Similarly, the obligation as to the extradition of criminals from one state to another has been substantially affected by usage. Although the obligation as prescribed in the Constitution seems rigid and binding, in practice it has established

---

[6] See the two cases entitled *Williams* v. *North Carolina*, 317 U.S. 287 (1942) and 325 U.S. 226 (1945), which involved the obligation of North Carolina to recognize a Nevada divorce.

only a moral, as against a mandatory or enforceable, duty upon states to sur-render fugitives at the request of other states.

the principle of separation of powers

separation of powers and the governmental process

The principle of federalism calls for a *geographic* distribution of power between federal and state government. Under the principle of *separation of powers* a further distribution of power is made within the national government itself along *functional* lines. According to this principle government is viewed as a threefold process and is divided into three separate branches, one for each process. The total governmental process is said to run somewhat as follows: First, certain policies must be selected as a means of coping with social problems. This is the legislative process. Second, it is necessary to interpret such general policies as they are applied to particular individuals and situations. This is the judicial process. Finally, the completion of the total governmental process requires that policies as adopted by a legislative body and as interpreted and applied by a judicial body be enforced or carried out by an administrative authority. This is the executive or administrative process. Lawmaking, law interpretation, law en-forcement—these are the three aspects of government.

separation of powers and governmental machinery

The three *processes* are inevitably present in any form of government. But the framers of our Constitution had in mind something more than this threefold character of the governmental process. They provided that the actual exercise of each of the three powers of government should be entrusted to a separate agency more or less independent of the other two. The legislative power is ex-ercised by an independent Congress, the judicial power by an independent judiciary, and the executive power by an independent President.

contrast between the American and British governments

Separation of powers may be contrasted with centralized authority. For example, in Great Britain government is divided into three branches, but the system is said to be one of *legislative supremacy* because the administrative and judicial branches are subject to complete control by Parliament. They themselves have no legal or constitutional independence, although they may in practice, partic-ularly in the case of the courts, enjoy a large degree of independence.

The contrast between the American and British governments in this regard may be put somewhat differently by saying that ours is a "presidential" system of government, whereas the British is a "parliamentary" system. The great dif-ference between the two systems is that in the United States the chief executive is chosen by the voters rather than by the legislature, whereas in Great Britain the chief executive is a "prime minister" who is chosen by the House of Commons from among its own membership and who can be forced from office by an adverse vote of that chamber on a major issue. It is significant that although the principle of separation of powers is an old one which can be traced back through the writings of such great political philosophers as Montesquieu, Locke, and even Aristotle, it has not been widely followed by modern democracies, most of which have chosen to pattern their governments after the parliamentary system.

The principle of separation of powers, like the principle of federalism, is not formally set forth or defined at any one place in the Constitution. But the very first sections of each of the first three articles make it clear that the organization of the national government is based upon such a principle. Article One opens with the statement: *"All legislative powers* herein granted shall be vested in a Congress of the United States. . . ."* The first sentence of Article Two is, *"The executive power* shall be vested in a President of the United States of America."* And Article Three begins: *"The judicial power* of the United States shall be vested in one Supreme Court, and in such inferior courts as the Congress may from time to time ordain and establish." [7] It may be noted that under the Constitution the principle of separation of powers applies only to the national government, there being nothing in the Constitution that requires the states to organize their own governments along such threefold lines. Nonetheless, all of our states have voluntarily observed this principle to a very considerable degree and have incorporated it in their own constitutions. But if one of our states should desire to experiment with parliamentary government, it would be free to do so under the national Constitution.

separation of powers offset by checks and balances

Separation of powers in American government is one of the most widely misunderstood aspects of our political system. The most common mistake lies in the easy assumption that the principle is found in the Constitution in pure form, and that participation by one branch of government in the affairs of the other two branches is improper. As was true of federalism, separation of powers is a principle that has its counterpart in a supplementary principle. In this case, the latter is the principle of *checks and balances.* Having divided government into a threefold process and having assigned each process to a supposedly independent branch, the Philadelphia convention proceeded to authorize a very considerable amount of participation in, or "checking" of, the affairs of each branch by the other two. The checks are very numerous. To the Congress, the Fathers gave several powers enabling it to interfere with the President's conduct of the affairs of the executive branch. Executive appointments of all superior officers are subject to confirmation by the Senate, and members of the executive

---

[7] The italics have been added.

branch, from the President down, are subject to impeachment and removal from office by Congress. Perhaps the most striking illustration of the way the Constitution enables Congress to check the executive branch is to be seen in the amazing fact that, apart from the offices of the Presidency and the Vice-Presidency, all of the nine executive departments, and the several score independent administrative commissions and agencies, have been created by act of Congress.[8] What is more, they are subject at any moment to revision, alteration, or even outright abolition by Congress.

President and Congress are given many checks over the federal judiciary. The President exercises a measure of control over the courts through his power to name all federal judges. A legislative check of both the executive and the judiciary is found in the power of the Senate to confirm these judicial appointments made by the President. The very existence of all federal courts, save one—the Supreme Court—depends upon congressional legislation. In the case of the Supreme Court the number of justices who serve on that tribunal is subject to complete congressional control. Further, the very power of the federal courts to hear cases is subject in many ways to the will of Congress. Finally, Congress may impeach and remove federal judges from office, and it has done so more than once.

The checks are not all one-sided by any means. Lest the conclusion be reached that our federal judges are hardly more than helpless pawns in the game of government, we need but note the power of the judiciary to check the other two branches by declaring acts of Congress and policies of the President null and void as contrary to the Constitution. It is true that this check of *judicial review* is not provided for in the Constitution in so many words, but it was exercised by the Supreme Court as early as 1803. Its existence as a valid and powerful check has long been recognized by the other two branches of government.

The principle of checks and balances does more than enable each of the branches to interfere with or check the activities of the other two. At certain points it actually enables one branch to participate directly in the process that is supposedly the exclusive concern of one of the other two. A good example of this is to be seen in the President's active and direct concern with legislation. In the exercise of his constitutional powers to recommend measures to the consideration of Congress and to approve or reject congressional bills before they become law, the President does more than "check" Congress. He actually takes part in the legislative process and virtually functions as a third house of the national legislature. Much the same thing is true of the President's power in the field of foreign affairs. When he negotiates a treaty with a foreign nation he is making policy. Although he is subject to a Senate check in that a treaty must be ratified

---

[8] Some administrative agencies have been created by executive order of the President, but generally under authority granted to him by Congress.

by a two-thirds vote in that body, nonetheless his is the power to initiate our foreign policy.

Again, when the Senate tries an impeachment case it sits as a high court of justice, employs many of the traditional forms of judicial procedure, and is definitely participating in the judicial process. The power to try impeachment cases might well have been assigned to the courts, as indeed it has been in certain of the states. But the framers chose to vest this judicial power in the Senate. Congress also has the judicial power to punish persons for contempt in certain situations.

It should now be clear that there is not a hard and fast separation between the three branches of the national government or the three processes of government. Just as the supplementary principle of implied powers is not in all ways consistent with the principle of federalism, so it is difficult to reconcile completely the supplementary principle of checks and balances with the principle of separation of powers. The national government of the United States consists of three independent branches, each more or less concerned with a particular governmental process. But this concern is neither complete nor exclusive. Congress has undoubted constitutional power to check the President and the courts in the executive and judicial fields. Similarly, the President checks the legislative and judicial processes, and the courts check legislature and executive. Moreover, there are many uncertainties about such checks and balances. How far may Congress properly go in interfering with the judicial process by altering the jurisdiction of a particular court or by changing the size of the Supreme Court? How far may the President properly go in trying to influence Congress in the enactment of certain laws? Or how readily may the courts substitute their judgment for the judgment of Congress as to whether it is constitutional to enact a certain law? Again the difficulty is that these are questions to which there are no fixed or certain answers. The process of checking, like the process of implying, has no precise limits. So it is that for a century and a half we have had under our Constitution only an approximate separation of powers. Great extremes of independence and interference have been possible, and from time to time one department or another has seemed to dominate our national government.

the principle of limited government

The distribution of political power under the American Constitution is further determined by a third principle, that of *limited government*. According to this principle the Constitution makes a delegation of political power to governmental agencies, in the name of the people. But this delegation is not complete, for there are certain potential political powers which no government in our political system has any authority to exercise and which the people have chosen to retain. Power is thus in a sense divided between the government and the people.

Actually, while the Tenth Amendment to the Constitution speaks of "powers" reserved to the people, it is not so much *powers* that are possessed by the people as *rights*.

As is true of the principles of federalism and separation of powers, this principle of limited government is not set forth in the Constitution in any one place in detailed fashion. Nonetheless it permeates the Constitution in a thoroughgoing way. In fact, as has been seen in the consideration of *constitutionalism*, it is perhaps the prime purpose of any constitution to place substantial restraints upon the exercise of political power by agencies of government. Accordingly it may well be doubted whether any constitution worthy of the name can fail either expressly or by implication to incorporate the principle of limited government. Nonetheless, it is important to note the extent to which the principle is followed in our own Constitution.

evidences of limited government in the Constitution

In the first place, the national government is drastically limited in that it is granted certain delegated powers only, all other powers being reserved to the states or the people. This idea finds clear expression in the Tenth Amendment, and at this point the principle of limited government is closely identified with the principle of federalism.

In the second place, the principle is to be seen in the numerous express limitations or prohibitions which the Constitution places on both national and state governments. For example, the national government is forbidden to levy export taxes, the state governments are forbidden to pass laws impairing the obligation of contracts, and both governments are forbidden to deprive persons of their lives, liberty, or property, without due process of law. The long list of civil liberties enumerated in the Bill of Rights amounts to a prohibition upon national power, and insofar as the Supreme Court has ruled that the Fourteenth Amendment re-enacts these prohibitions and applies them to state government, the limitation of both governments is thus effected.

In the third place, the Supreme Court has declared that in addition to the express prohibitions contained in the Constitution there are certain other prohibitions which are to be implied from the Constitution but which are no less effective because they are of an implied character. For example, the Court once ruled that Congress might not use its taxing power for such a regulatory purpose as the discouragement of child labor.[9] Moreover, at the same time that the Supreme Court formulated the doctrine of *implied power* in *McCulloch* v. *Maryland* as a basis for upholding the law creating the Bank of the United States, it denied a state government power to tax this bank on the theory that there is an *implied prohibition* against the taxation of agencies of the federal government by

---

[9] *Bailey* v. *Drexel Furniture Co.*, 259 U.S. 20 (1922). It may be doubted whether this decision has continuing validity today.

the states. Later this reasoning was extended to forbid the taxation of certain state agencies by the federal government.

the relative character of limited government

As was true of the principles of federalism and separation of powers, the principle of limited government is also offset at many points by certain countertendencies or principles. In the first place, the principle of implied power offsets the principle of limited government much as it offsets the principle of federalism. Once it is admitted that the national government may exercise implied as well as express powers, the concept that its total authority is limited to those powers actually delegated to it loses much of its meaning.

In the second place, numerous Supreme Court decisions make it clear that virtually all of the express prohibitions which operate upon the national and state governments are to be regarded as relative rather than absolute. For example, the power of the national government to declare and conduct a war has been used to justify the placing of relatively drastic restrictions upon freedom of speech and freedom of the press even though the First Amendment states that Congress shall pass *no* law abridging these rights. In such cases the Supreme Court is called upon to weigh the positive exercise of an undeniable power of government against the restrictive force of just as undeniable a prohibition. Power and prohibition are often evenly matched contenders in such a conflict, and the decision may well go in either direction.

The failure of the Constitution to enumerate state powers, and its suggestion instead, that the great residue of political power is reserved to the states, considerably upsets the concept that they are governments of limited powers only. Moreover, the express limitations that are placed on the states, like those that are placed on the national government, are relative rather than absolute. For example, one of the powers reserved to the states is the so-called *police power*, which authorizes a state to take any reasonable step necessary to foster and protect the general welfare of its people. Yet there is an express prohibition upon the states forbidding them to deprive persons of life, liberty, or property, without due process of law. The exercise of the police power and the limitation of the due process clause have often been in conflict. The courts have invalidated many state statutes as contrary to the requirement of due process, but many others have been upheld. Accordingly, this limitation must be regarded as a relative one insofar as some measures pertaining to the police power are upheld, for any such measure is almost certain to deprive certain persons of a portion of their liberty if not their property. A state statute providing for compulsory vaccination might well be regarded as a necessary police power measure in the interest of public health. Yet some people might argue that such a regulation was unconstitutional because it deprived them of their liberty to decide not to be vaccinated. As a matter of fact, the Supreme Court was once called upon to decide just such a case.

and there was disagreement among the justices as to whether to hold that there had been a proper exercise of a valid constitutional power, or a definite violation of an express constitutional prohibition.[10]

the conflict of constitutional principles

From our discussion it will be seen that the principles of the Constitution group themselves in pairs, and that within each pair one principle tends to offset the other. This conflict between principles leads one to question the extent to which our American Constitution has a fixed meaning or purpose. We have seen that it is the purpose of a constitution to establish a particular form of government, to grant that government limited powers, and to safeguard the people against the dangers of tyrannical or arbitrary exercise of political power. If the clauses of a constitution, because of the way they seem to face in opposite directions, tend to cancel each other out, it may be doubted whether a constitution has much meaning. On the other hand, it has also been seen that two prime requirements of a successful constitution are that it have a tendency toward generality, and even ambiguity in its clauses, and that it possess a high degree of adaptability to the needs of changing times. A high degree of detail and precision in constitutional language is not necessarily a virtue. Enough has been said about the American Constitution to show that it does not err in the direction of detail or precision. Admittedly, it is a constitution that seems to contradict itself at certain points. The extent to which this is true and the way in which this condition has affected the growth of our American political system, perhaps depriving it of a requisite degree of precision, are matters that require additional study. Further attention will be given to them in the next chapter.

bibliographic note

A starting point for the analysis of constitutional principles is necessarily *The Federalist*, the title given to the collection of letters written by Hamilton, Madison, and Jay in support of the proposed constitution during the ratification period. *The Federalist* is generally regarded as America's greatest work of political theory. It is available in countless editions. Two good recent ones have been edited by Max Beloff (New York: The Macmillan Company, 1950) and by Henry Steele Commager (New York: Appleton-Century-Crofts, Inc., 1949). The Commager edition is abridged for student use. The constitutional doctrines and rules of law that have been applied by the Supreme Court under the Constitution are set forth in Charles K. Burdick's *The Law of the American Constitution* (New York: G. P. Putnam's Sons, 1922) and at greater length in the

---

[10] *Jacobson* v. *Massachusetts,* 197 U.S. 11 (1905).

three-volume study by Westel W. Willoughby, *The Constitutional Law of the United States* (New York: Baker, Voorhis and Company, 2d ed., 1929). Two handbooks of constitutional law designed for use by students are Edward S. Corwin and Jack W. Peltason, *Understanding the Constitution* (New York: William Sloane Associates, Inc., 1949) and Edward S. Corwin, *The Constitution and What It Means Today* (Princeton: Princeton University Press, 9th ed., 1947). There are any number of analytical studies of specific constitutional principles, such as the works of Edward S. Corwin. For example, notice may be taken here of his *The Commerce Power Versus States Rights* (Princeton: Princeton University Press, 1936). The introductory notes to the Supreme Court decisions reprinted in Robert E. Cushman's *Leading Constitutional Decisions* (New York: Appleton-Century-Crofts, Inc., 9th ed., 1950) are an excellent source of data concerning the development of specific doctrines of constitutional law. Similar notes are found in Charles Fairman's *American Constitutional Decisions* (New York: Henry Holt and Company, 1948) and in *Basic Constitutional Cases* (New York: Oxford University Press, 1948), edited by C. Gordon Post, Frances P. DeLancy, and Fredryc R. Darby.

The historical approach to the American Constitution is illustrated by such texts as Alfred H. Kelly and Winfred A. Harbison, *The American Constitution: Its Origins and Development* (New York: W. W. Norton & Company, 1948); Andrew C. McLaughlin, *A Constitutional History of the United States* (New York: Appleton-Century-Crofts, Inc., 1935); and Carl B. Swisher, *American Constitutional Development* (Boston: Houghton Mifflin Company, 1943). These volumes set forth the entire story of constitutional development in the United States from colonial beginnings to the present day. Other historical studies, somewhat more limited as to the ground covered or point of view expressed, are Woodrow Wilson, *Constitutional Government in the United States* (New York: Columbia University Press, 1908); Arthur N. Holcombe, *Our More Perfect Union* (Cambridge: Harvard University Press, 1950); and Benjamin F. Wright, *The Growth of American Constitutional Law* (New York: Reynal & Hitchcock, Inc., 1942).

There are numerous studies or texts dealing with American political ideas which contain material on the development of constitutional principles. Charles E. Merriam's *American Political Ideas* (New York: The Macmillan Company, 1920) is a series of "studies in the development of American political thought, 1865–1917" by an eminent political scientist. Vernon L. Parrington's *Main Currents in American Thought* (New York: Harcourt, Brace and Company, 1927–1930) is a classic in this field. Francis G. Wilson's *The American Political Mind* (New York: McGraw-Hill Book Company, 1948) is a standard political theory text of recent date, and Alpheus T. Mason's *Free Government in the Making: Readings in American Political Thought* (New York: Oxford University Press, 1949) is an excellent collection of readings.

the dual Constitution:

instrument of power and symbol of restraint

$\mathcal{O}$NE OF the most striking developments in American history is the way in which the violent opposition to the Constitution, expressed during the ratification period in 1787 and 1788, disappeared after the Constitution went into operation.[1] There have always been serious differences of opinion concerning the proper interpretation of this or that clause of the Constitution. Moreover, there was during the first three quarters of a century following the Philadelphia convention a bitter conflict concerning the kind of federation established by the Constitution. In the end, the American people found it necessary to fight a great civil war to determine whether the union of states under the Constitution was to endure. Nonetheless, at no time since 1789 has any very large number of Americans attacked the Constitution itself. Federalist, Antifederalist, Whig, Republican, Democrat, conservative, liberal, Northerner, Southerner, and Westerner, have all held the Constitution in high esteem, however violent the clash of interests among such factions has been. Moreover, all such groups have taken their stands upon the rock of the Constitution; no one of them has ever admitted the existence of conflict between the Constitution and its political program.

How is it that all forces in American politics have been able to claim constitutional justification for their very different ideas and policies? Have some of these factions been guilty of insincerity in paying their respects to the Constitution? Or is it possible that the Constitution itself provides an explanation of this situation?

The American Constitution faces in two directions. Even a casual reading of the document makes it clear that the Constitution both grants power and restrains the exercise of power. Certain sections are obviously concerned with the first of these purposes. For example, section eight of Article One is a long enumeration of some eighteen express powers that are bestowed upon Congress. The second

---

[1] Woodrow Wilson, *Congressional Government* (Boston: Houghton Mifflin Company, 1885), pp. 2 ff.

and third sections of Article Two enumerate in a similar manner the powers of the President, and Article Three is largely concerned with vesting certain judicial powers in the federal courts. Other sections of the Constitution are just as obviously concerned with the opposite purpose of restraining power. For example, the enumeration of congressional powers in section eight of Article One is followed immediately by a listing in section nine of prohibitions upon Congress. This in turn is followed by section ten, in which certain restraints are placed upon the state governments.

The arrangement of these successive articles dealing on the one hand with power and on the other hand with restraints upon power is neither very orderly nor logical. But there is no missing the fact that the Constitution has a dual character, one aspect of which is concerned with the creation of a vast, central governmental authority in the United States, and the other with curbing the exercise of this same authority.

the Constitution viewed as instrument and as symbol

In a paper read at the Harvard University Tercentenary celebration in 1936, Professor Edward S. Corwin made an interesting analysis of this dual character of the Constitution, employing the words "instrument" and "symbol" to suggest its two phases. To Corwin, the Constitution as an *instrument* serves as a basis for the exercise of positive political power; it is an agency for getting things done:

> . . . the word "instrument" connotes the future and things needing to be done in the future. It assumes that man is the master of his fate, able to impart a desired shape to things and events. And regarded from this point of view a constitution is *an instrument of popular power—sovereignty*, if you will—*for the achievement of progress.*[2]

In speaking of its *symbolic* aspect, Corwin has in mind a constitution of negative restraint, a document of limitations and prohibitions which holds government within well-defined and narrow limits. The Constitution as a *symbol* is a

> consecration of an *already established order of things.* [It] harks back to primitive man's terror of a chaotic universe, and his struggle toward security and significance behind a slowly erected barrier of custom, magic, fetish, tabu. While, therefore, the constitutional instrument exists to energize and canalize *public power*, it is the function of the constitutional symbol to protect and tranquilize *private interest or advantage as against public power.* . . .[3]

---

[2] Edward S. Corwin, "The Constitution as Instrument and as Symbol," *American Political Science Review*, XXX (December, 1936), 1071. The italics are Corwin's. Reprinted by permission of *The American Political Science Review.*

[3] *Ibid.*, p. 1072.

Although the original American Constitution has both strong *instrumental* and strong *symbolic* aspects, as these words are used by Corwin, it is clear that the framers were first of all interested in the Constitution as a source of positive power. Corwin observes:

> That the attitude of the members of the Federal Convention toward their task was predominantly instrumentalist and practical is clear at a glance. They had not gone to Philadelphia merely to ratify the past . . . but with *reform* in mind, and specifically the creation of *a strong, effective national government.*[4]

It is significant that the most strongly *symbolic* section of the Constitution, the Bill of Rights, was not the work of the Philadelphia convention but became part of the supreme law of the land at the insistence of those who distrusted the powerful central government provided for by the Founding Fathers.

the principles of the Constitution viewed as instruments or as symbols

federalism as symbol

The principles of the Constitution may now be reviewed to determine the instrumental or symbolic value of each one. Federalism appears at once to be a principle which has a strong symbolic significance, one that has lent itself to use by those groups in American history that have sought to curtail governmental activity. It is a principle that has often been used by the courts to curb the expansive tendencies of both Congress and the state legislatures. In the overwhelming majority of the cases in which legislative acts of Congress have been declared unconstitutional, it is the principle of federalism which the courts have said has been violated. When it has come to declaring state legislation unconstitutional the courts have based their decisions upon a variety of grounds, but a goodly number of state laws have been set aside as contrary to that principle. In other words, this principle of federalism has led the courts to hold a number of federal statutes unconstitutional because they encroach upon areas of action supposedly reserved to the states; contrariwise, many state statutes have been set aside as invading the realm of national power.

implied power as instrument

On the other hand, the principle of *implied power* has strong instrumental potentialities and has often proved a more than adequate basis upon which to sanction increased national governmental activity. Many a national statute that might have seemed at first thought to be of doubtful constitutionality because of

---

[4] *Ibid.*, p. 1073.

encroachment upon state power has finally been approved by the fortuitous discovery of an implied power justifying such congressional action.

An excellent example of contrasting uses of these two principles is to be found in the attitude of the Supreme Court as to the propriety of attempts of Congress to control agricultural production along national lines. It is of course clear that Congress possesses no express power to deal with agriculture. Although Congress long ago began passing statutes pertaining to agriculture, such as the Homestead Act of 1862, it has generally been supposed that governmental power to control agricultural production, if it existed at all, was reserved to the states. Nonetheless, Congress in 1933 passed the Agricultural Adjustment Act, which provided for federal regulation of agricultural production. As a basis for this action it was asserted that Congress possessed implied power, derived from its express power to collect taxes to provide for the general welfare. But the Supreme Court, by a divided vote, rejected this defense. In a decision invalidating the act as contrary to the principle of federalism, the Court asserted that Congress was exceeding the scope of national authority and invading the realm of power reserved to the states.[5] In 1938 Congress passed a second Agricultural Adjustment Act having objectives similar to those of the first act. In this instance the implied power for the act was said to be derived from Congress's express power to regulate interstate commerce. Once more the justices of the Supreme Court divided, but this time the majority chose to stress the doctrine of implied power and the law was upheld.[6] In other words, although the regulation of agriculture had hitherto seemed by the principle of federalism to be a power reserved to the states, it now appeared that congressional authority to accomplish such a purpose could be supported on the basis of implied power.

separation of powers as symbol: checks and balances as instrument

Turning to the principle of *separation of powers* we find that, like the principle of federalism, it has a strong symbolic value. It is a principle that seemingly places each of the agencies of the national government in an airtight compartment of its own, and invites court action invalidating any attempt by one of these agencies to encroach upon the powers of the others. But again, the rival principle of checks and balances has a strong instrumental value sufficient to justify an occasional invasion of one department's realm by another.

There is no illustration of the contradictory use of these two principles by the Supreme Court to sustain or invalidate action by a governmental agency as clear-cut as the one given with respect to the conflict between federalism and implied power. But, although less straightforward, an excellent illustration is found in the Supreme Court's varying attitude toward congressional delegation of discretionary power to the President to fill in the details of legislation. In invalidat-

---

[5] *United States* v. *Butler*, 297 U.S. 1 (1936).

[6] *Mulford* v. *Smith*, 307 U.S. 38 (1939).

ing the National Industrial Recovery Act in 1935 the Supreme Court held that Congress, by delegating *legislative* power to the President to determine the content of industrial codes of fair competition, had violated the principle of separation of powers.[7] But there are other cases in which the Court has upheld very substantial delegations of discretionary power by Congress to the President or other executive agencies. For example, in 1939 the Court upheld a sweeping grant of power which Congress made in the Agricultural Marketing Agreement Act·of 1937 to the Secretary of Agriculture to fix the price of milk.[8] In decisions of this latter type upholding delegation of power, the Court has not used the principle of checks and balances to sanction the exercise of legislative power by an executive officer. Indeed, it has consistently maintained that no *legislative* power has been delegated to such an officer. But this is little more than a fiction, for it is quite clear in fact, if not in legal theory, that in some of these cases the Court is permitting executive officers to use legislative power.

limited government as symbol

The principle of limited government is highly symbolic in its operation. References to this principle are made almost exclusively for the purpose of challenging the validity of some sort of governmental activity. But many of the prohibitions upon government, particularly those that are designed to safeguard the rights of the individual, have been held to be relative rather than absolute, with strong instrumental results. Likewise, the use of the principle of implied power to offset the force of a prohibition upon government has sometimes meant that the instrument has triumphed over the symbol.

Several times in our history Congress has passed espionage and sedition acts that have placed substantial restraints upon speech and press, particularly in time of war. When these acts have been challenged in the Supreme Court that tribunal has always upheld such legislation. Preferring the Constitution in its instrumental phase, the Court has pointed to the power of Congress to raise and support an army, arguing that the successful exercise of this power may well necessitate curbing seditious utterances against the government or its policy.[9] On the other hand, the prohibition against interferences with speech or the press is a powerful one, and it cannot be assumed that the courts will never use this symbolic phase of the Constitution to strike down legislation. Up to now the Supreme Court has never been persuaded that Congress has gone too far, although the language of the First Amendment dealing with freedom of speech and press has been violated in its literal sense again and again. It may be noted that the Supreme Court has upon occasion held state laws pertaining to speech and press invalid as contrary

---

[7] *Schechter* v. *United States*, 295 U.S. 495 (1935).

[8] *United States* v. *Rock Royal Co-operative*, 307 U.S. 533 (1939).

[9] See *Schenck* v. *United States*, 249 U.S. 47 (1919).

to the prohibitions of the Constitution, although here too the Court has more often preferred the instrument to the symbol.[10]

The analysis of the symbolic and instrumental character of the principles of the Constitution may now be summarized. As a symbol of restraint the Constitution contains certain principles which can be employed by those who are opposed to particular uses of public power to hold agencies of government within narrow limits of activity. Thus federalism may be used to restrict activities of the national government which are said to encroach upon areas reserved to the states. Vice versa, state activities may be challenged on the ground that national power is being endangered. Second, the principle of separation of powers is primarily useful as a means of restricting governmental activity whenever it appears that the threefold character of the governmental process is being threatened. And finally, the principle of limited government is of great value as a means of curbing the exercise of power.

But when circumstances or the strongest political pressures of the moment seem to call for increased governmental activity, advocates of such activity are able to point the way down the ample instrumental thoroughfares of the Constitution. Thus the doctrine of implied powers has a strong instrumental value sufficient upon occasion to offset any seeming barrier imposed by federalism. Likewise, the same principle is often capable of overcoming any negative restraint offered by the principle of limited government. Finally, the principle of checks and balances has an instrumental value which sometimes proves stronger than the restrictive force of the principle of separation of powers.

the varying history of American political institutions under the dual Constitution: nationalism vs. states' rights

It will be helpful at this point to turn to American history for material showing some of the contradictory lines of political development which our dual Constitution has made possible. First, the contrasting tendencies toward centralized and decentralized government may be noted. The conflict between these rival tendencies has been a perennial one dating back to the time of the writing of the Constitution and the struggle over its ratification. There is no missing the fact that our history has witnessed many periods in which the emphasis has been upon increased use of power by the national government, and other periods in which the cause of states' rights seemed to be gaining ground. It is not quite accurate to use the pendulum figure of speech to describe these changes, for the contrasting periods have not followed one another in any orderly or regular

---

[10] Compare *Gitlow* v. *New York*, 268 U.S. 652 (1925), with *Near* v. *Minnesota*, 283 U.S. 697 (1931).

fashion, and in the long run there has been a tendency for the federal periods to prove longer and their effects more lasting than the state periods and the effects thereof. Nonetheless, it is possible to point to certain chapters in American history when one or the other force seemed for the moment to dominate our political life. It is generally agreed that the first years after the adoption of the new Constitution were marked by a strong nationalist development. When in 1801 the Federalist party surrendered the executive and legislative departments to the Antifederalists under Jefferson, the latter continued a vigorous and positive program of federal activity. In particular, the movement toward centralized power was kept alive by the Supreme Court under the influence of John Marshall. Following Marshall's death in 1835, the Supreme Court, as well as the presidency and Congress, tended to reflect for the most part states' rights sentiment, which persisted until the beginning of the Civil War. After 1861 the pendulum motion grows more confused. The three great periods of war—1861–1865, 1914–1918, and 1939–1945—were all marked by an extreme use of centralized power. In addition to the wartime administrations of Lincoln, Wilson, and Franklin Roosevelt, the presidency of Theodore Roosevelt was also characterized by nationalist policies. On the other hand, under such Presidents as Hayes, McKinley, Taft, and Coolidge, the activity of the national government was held at a minimum and the country seemed to turn toward decentralized government.

flexibility of the Constitution as to federalism

Two comments may be made concerning this vacillation between centralized and decentralized government. The first of these is that the Constitution establishes no fixed pattern with respect to federalism. Thus the advocates of all political points of view have found it possible to claim the support of the Constitution for their policies and programs. It is true that the framing of the Constitution represented a substantial step toward centralized government. Nonetheless, the pattern of federalism established by the Constitution has always been a flexible one which has permitted wide fluctuations between nationalism and states' rights. Accordingly, interpretation of the principle of federalism has ranged all the way from Chief Justice Marshall's theory of nationalism to John Calhoun's belief that under the Constitution the state governments retained so much power that they could even nullify national laws or withdraw from the Union.

Up to the actual outbreak of the Civil War both sides in the great conflict over slavery and secession based their arguments upon the Constitution, each claiming that it was properly interpreting that document. The ultimate ruling that ours is a centralized system in which the member states possess no rights to nullify federal laws or to withdraw from the Union was established through force and the shedding of blood, rather than by any mere reference to uncontrovertible language or logic in the Constitution.

inconsistency of parties as to federalism

The second comment is that the advocates of nationalism and of states' rights have often been inconsistent in their arguments and policies and have shown little adherence to principle for principle's sake alone. The opinions which people hold in this field are seldom nothing more than the result of a desire to find the "correct" meaning of federalism in any abstract sense. Practical considerations have always been important motivating forces in determining the attitudes of people toward centralized or decentralized government. In making up his mind the individual has usually asked himself such questions as: For what purposes is national or state power being used at the moment? Who is likely to benefit and who is likely to suffer if the balance shifts from state activity toward national activity, or vice versa? What particular social or economic interests are likely to be advanced or retarded by such shifts?

Few persons have ever been consciously or unconsciously so naïve as to turn first of all to the Constitution to determine the stand they ought to take on states' rights or nationalism. For example, no man in American history ever worked out a more careful and systematic set of political principles than did John Calhoun. Yet his biographer in the *Encyclopaedia of the Social Sciences* says of him: "Calhoun's political career was closely tied up with the economic interests of his state, South Carolina, and of the entire South; his principal significance in American history lies in the cogency with which he framed syllogisms of political theory which rationalized these interests." [11]

The vacillating positions which our great political parties have taken from time to time on the issue of nationalism vs. states' rights are a significant indication of the way in which positions in principle reflect practical forces. At the time of the adoption of the Constitution and in the first years of the new government, the lines were drawn between the two parties somewhat as follows: On the one side were the members of the Federalist party, friends of the new Constitution, who favored the nationalization of political power. On the other side were the Antifederalists, who, while accepting the Constitution once it went into operation, continued to work for a federal system in which state power would be dominant. But the triumph of the Antifederalists in the election of 1800 by no means resulted in a withering away of the national state. It is true that this political upheaval, which saw the Federalists driven from power permanently, did result in a general enhancement of the position and power of the states in the Union. But under such Presidents as Jefferson and Jackson the groups which had distrusted and opposed centralized government found it possible to make vigorous use of federal power to further ends which they supported.

If it be assumed that first the Whig party and then the Republican party took

---

[11] William S. Carpenter, "John Caldwell Calhoun," *Encyclopaedia of the Social Sciences,* III, 144.

the place of the Federalist party, and that the Democratic party was the direct descendant of the Antifederalist party, the original contrast between the theories of the parties as to the nature of the federal system persisted into the present century. The position of the Republican party during much of its existence may be characterized as follows: Born to fight the cause of the Union against that of the states, it usually favored the enhancement of national power as a superior means of protecting property, stimulating commerce and business enterprise, and serving conservative interests generally. State power, on the other hand, was often distrusted by the Republicans because of its greater usefulness to local interests having "radical" aims.

The Democratic party's position may be characterized in these words: First as the representative of the unique social and economic interests of the South, and later as the representative of the interests of the small farmer, the immigrant, and the worker in other parts of the country, it tended to view with grave distrust the exercise of national power because of the traditional use of this power to serve conservative interests. The use of the power of the states was viewed much more favorably because the interests the party represented seemed on the whole to have much more influence at the state level than they did at the national level.

Whatever its position in principle, each party has always shown a tendency to deplore the exercise of national power when its rival was in office, only to make extensive use of this power when in office itself. This has been strikingly illustrated in the period since 1900. The Democratic party was in power nationally during the two great wars of this century. That in itself was sufficient to compel the party to pursue much more highly centralized programs of governmental activity than its rival had ever dreamed of undertaking. But the change of heart was not alone the result of international developments over which the party had no control. With Woodrow Wilson and his New Freedom program, and with Franklin Roosevelt and his New Deal program, the Democratic party abandoned its historic battle cry of states' rights, and deliberately chose to make vigorous use of national power to put into effect two great reform programs in domestic policy. It is one of the great ironies of American history that the states' rights party of the last century became the agency through which a modern "welfare state" was established in the United States along national lines.

Needless to say, the Republican party did not view with equanimity these two attempts to use national power for purposes other than those it had traditionally favored. Federal legislation providing for social security, public works, full employment, collective bargaining, wage and hour control, reciprocal trade agreements, rural electrification, rehabilitation of tenant farmers, and other similar purposes was inevitably viewed as endangering the interests of property and business. Accordingly, in recent decades Republicans have found themselves denouncing centralization of governmental activity in Washington and arguing for a return of political power to the state capitals, "where it belongs."

There is no intent here to pass judgment on the use any party has made of national power when it was in office. The important point is that sooner or later all parties have made extensive use of such power, thereby contributing greatly to the growth of centralized government in America. Accordingly, the repeated and continuous invocation of the Constitution by political parties to denounce the policies of their rivals must be viewed with suspicion. It is probable that no extreme in policy, favored by any major party up to now, whether in the direction of states' rights or nationalism, has exceeded the flexible limits of the federal system established by the Constitution. This is not to say that there are no limits; nor does it say that because we have stayed within constitutional limits all our policies have been wise ones. Honest men can disagree as to the proper balance that should exist in the use of national and state power in the United States today. But there can be no denying the wideness of the choice that the Constitution allows us in this respect.

the varying history of American political institutions under the dual Constitution: the struggle of the legislature, executive, and judiciary for supremacy

A second illustration of the contrasting political developments that have taken place within the framework of our Constitution is to be seen in the area of separation of powers. Here there has been a more or less continuous struggle by the President, Congress, and, to a lesser degree, the Supreme Court to achieve a dominant position in our political system. Here, too, there have been repeated references to the Constitution to prove that this or that relationship among the three agencies is or is not the proper one. The Constitution of 1787 provided that there should be three independent branches of government, and it dealt specifically with the interaction of these branches at many points. But it did not freeze the relationship into any one mold; neither did it establish a clear pattern as to precedence among these three branches. Whether we were to have a form of "legislative government," "presidential government," or one marked by "judicial supremacy" was not indicated. Accordingly the way was clear for much experimentation with varying relationships, and for a prolonged struggle for power by the agencies themselves.

Again it is somewhat misleading to use the pendulum figure of speech in telling the story of this development, although the changes in the relationship of the departments have been somewhat cyclical in character. For example, without too much distortion of the facts of history it can be argued that the first twenty-year period, from 1789 to 1809, was marked by executive supremacy, with Presidents Washington and Jefferson dominating the political scene. Thereafter, for half a century our Presidents were, more often than not, second-rate men, and the spotlight shifted to Congress, where the giants of the period, men like Calhoun, Clay, and Webster, were striding across the stage. For the brief period of the Lincoln administration the executive was once again very powerful. Then until the close of the nineteenth century the center of power seemed to return to Congress. On the whole, since 1900 Congress has lost ground and the presidency has reached new heights of power and importance.

legislative supremacy

To put the matter in somewhat different terms, from time to time in our history we have appeared to be on the verge of evolving differing forms of government as the institutional relations between the President and Congress have changed. At times in the nineteenth century there seemed to be a real likelihood that the balance of power would finally be centered in Congress so strongly that we would come close to having a parliamentary system of government. At the beginning of the century two developments threatened to make the President a mere servant of the legislature. One was the congressional caucus by which nominees for the presidency were selected by members of Congress. The other was the exercise by Congress of its power to select a President in case of a tie vote or the absence of a majority vote in the electoral college. This power was exercised in 1800 and again in 1824.

In the end the threat did not materialize. The congressional caucus gave place to the national nominating convention in which congressmen had to share power with other party leaders, and 1824 proved to be the last election in which Congress made the final selection of a President. On the other hand, the impeachment and near conviction of Andrew Johnson in 1868 once again threatened to subordinate the executive to the legislature. Had Johnson been convicted, Congress might thereafter have used the threat of impeachment to curb initiative and independence in the office of the chief executive. Such a use of the power of impeachment would have been of more than dubious constitutionality, but had Congress made repeated attempts to use impeachment as a means of asserting its control over the President, it might have succeeded. At any rate, the power and the prestige of Congress were once more so high in the eighteen eighties that Woodrow Wilson, writing his early study of American government, chose to give it the title *Congressional Government*. In it he observes:

> It is said that there is no single or central force in our federal scheme; and so there is not in the federal *scheme*, but only a balance of powers and a nice adjustment of interactive checks, as all the books say. How is it, however, in the practical conduct of the federal government? In that, unquestionably, the predominant and controlling force, the centre and source of all motive and of all regulative power, is Congress.[12]

---

[12] Woodrow Wilson, *Congressional Government* (Boston: Houghton Mifflin Company, 15th ed., 1913), p. 11.

executive supremacy

At other times in American history there have been indications that sufficient power and prestige were being centered in the presidency to makes ours a truly "executive government," with the legislature reduced to the role of a mere sounding board possessing advisory but little deliberative power. In the last century, Jefferson, Jackson, and Lincoln all challenged Congress on various issues and, in winning their way, asserted the superiority of executive over legislature. In the present century, Wilson and the two Roosevelts brought the presidency to a new high level. In fact, the movement toward executive government is perhaps proving to be a more persistent tendency than the earlier one toward legislative supremacy. Two powerful forces have been, and are, contributing to this result. One is the growing political strength of the President with the people, which has reached a point where the nation expects and demands vigorous leadership from that officer in both the formulation and the execution of the governmental program. The other is a world-wide force, the growing number and complexity of the social problems with which all nations must deal. This development has tended to compel all legislatures to confine lawmaking to broad declarations of policy and to leave to executive officers wide discretionary power to determine the details of policy.

judicial supremacy

The Supreme Court has at many points in our history enjoyed great prestige and has wielded much influence in the conduct of public affairs in America. As early as 1803 the Supreme Court asserted its right to invalidate acts of Congress, and during the Marshall period the Court rendered many decisions that were profoundly important in shaping both the character of the American government and that of public policies. On the eve of the Civil War, when the executive and legislative branches were trying to find a solution to the slavery problem, the Court attempted in the ill-fated *Dred Scott* decision to prescribe the solution itself. Again, at the close of the last century, the Court reached one of its peaks of power, and in a long series of decisions began to challenge the policies of the executive and legislative branches.[13] In the present century the Court has on numerous occasions, notably in the early twenties and the middle thirties, asserted its power in vigorous fashion. But although the Supreme Court has thus challenged the authority of both President and Congress, it has never really bid for the role of the *dominant governing* agency in the land. In the final analysis the Court has no political power, no powerful weapons, no position of great strategic strength comparable to those of either of the other great agencies of government. Accordingly, it is particularly vulnerable to counterattack when it does

---

[13] See, for example, two decisions rendered in 1895, *Pollock* v. *Farmers' Loan and Trust Co.*, 158 U.S. 601, and *United States* v. *E. C. Knight Co.*, 156 U.S. 1, in which the Court invalidated a federal income tax law and emasculated the Sherman Antitrust Act.

assert itself. It has sometimes brought about a temporary halt in the exercise of power in certain directions by President and Congress, but where they have chosen to fight back they have never been permanently stopped. In the final mixture of powers, forces, and influences that determines governmental policy in the United States, the contribution made by the Supreme Court cannot be ignored. But although we talk at times of "government by judiciary" or of "judicial supremacy" in American government,[14] referring thereby to the exercise of power by the judiciary to declare null and void the acts of the other agencies of government, there has never been any real likelihood that the Supreme Court would actually dominate these agencies in the business of government.

In these struggles between President and Congress, or between these two branches and the Supreme Court, for power and prestige the exact language of the Constitution has been an almost irrelevant factor. Had Congress succeeded in asserting its superior power over that of the President, barring only improper use of the impeachment power, the resulting near-parliamentary system of government could have been encompassed by the Constitution. Woodrow Wilson believed that the "congressional government" of which he wrote in 1885 did "violence to none of the principles of self-government contained in the Constitution." Similarly the powerful presidency of today does no violence to constitutional principles, for there is language in the Constitution providing an ample basis for occupancy by the executive of a dominant position in the government. Finally, the Constitution is particularly vague about the position of the judiciary in the government. The power of the courts to invalidate the acts of the other two branches of government is not provided for in so many words. Neither is it expressly forbidden. Thus almost any result that might have come to prevail as to the power and prestige of the judiciary could have been justified under the language of the Constitution.

the varying history of American political institutions under the dual Constitution: contractions and expansions of governmental activity

A third illustration of contradictory lines of political development within our constitutional system may be seen in the history of the principle of limited government. There have been great variations in the amount of governmental activity in the United States. At times the scope of the governmental program has been quite narrow, and at other times it has been broad. Upon occasion a Theodore Roosevelt who believes in a vigorous and extensive use of governmental power is succeeded in the presidency by a William Howard Taft whose admin-

---

[14] See, for example, Charles G. Haines, *The American Doctrine of Judicial Supremacy* (Berkeley: University of California Press, 2d ed., 1932), and L. B. Boudin, *Government by Judiciary* (New York: William Godwin, Inc., 2 vols., 1932).

istration is controlled by the principle that that government is best that governs least. Then again a Herbert Hoover who obviously regards an active government as a dangerous government is succeeded by a Franklin D. Roosevelt who pushes the governmental program to new limits. Here, too, there is perennial argument about the intention of the Constitution, with strong assertions that it limits government to a minimum role, and equally strong assertions that there is little if any governmental activity that it forbids, provided only that passing attention is paid to its vague limiting clauses.

Many illustrations are available of the extremes of broad and narrow governmental activity which have been possible under the Constitution. For example, at times Congress has made a vigorous use of the commerce power in extending into new fields federal regulation of private enterprise; at other times Congress has refrained from exercising such a power, or its activity has been restrained by the Supreme Court on the ground that the constitutional limits of power have been reached and exceeded.

police power vs. due process of law

A further conflict between power and limitation which has had varying outcomes is that involving the police power and due process of law. The police power enables government to foster and protect the health, safety, morals, and welfare of its citizens. Under the Constitution it is a power reserved primarily to the state governments, although by indirect means the national government may properly exercise a similar power. The due process of law clauses of the Fifth and Fourteenth Amendments forbid all governments—national, state, and local alike—to deprive persons of their life, liberty, or property "without due process of law." In the face of the rapid urbanization and industrialization of the United States which took place in the decades following the Civil War, and confronted with increasingly serious social problems, the state governments began passing numerous police power measures establishing safety and health standards, providing special protection to women and children, fixing minimum-wage and maximum-hour standards for labor, and generally extending government regulation of private enterprise as a means of promoting the public welfare. At about the turn of the century the national government also undertook a somewhat similar program of social legislation. This program of increased governmental activity might have seemed to be in compliance with constitutional principles. But such legislation had the inevitable effect of curbing the freedom of some individuals, and, in particular, of business organizations, in very substantial ways. Accordingly, it was not long before the contention was heard that these interferences with freedom amounted to deprivations of liberty and property without due process of law, and were thus contrary to the Constitution. Although such an interpretation of the due process clauses of the Constitution had almost never before been suggested in the century that had elapsed since 1789, the Supreme Court was asked to accept it as a means of striking down progressive legislation, thereby limiting the scope of the governmental program. The Court at first resisted this pressure, but in the eighteen nineties its resistance came to an end and it began using the due process clauses to invalidate both federal and state statutes. For forty years a conservatively minded Court continued to interpret the Constitution so as to curb police power activity by government.[15] In 1936, in one of the last decisions of this type, the Court, by five-to-four vote, invalidated a statute of the state of New York prescribing minimum wages for women and children.[16] In the very next year, however, in a decision upholding a Washington State minimum-wage law, the Supreme Court not only reversed its decision of the year before but also pretty generally repudiated the whole theory that the due process clauses of the Constitution could properly be used to curb legislation of the social welfare type.[17] Since 1937 no federal, and relatively few state, laws of this type have been declared unconstitutional.

Thus we see how during our history, and particularly during the last half century, there has been a conflict between the rival ideas that American government is free to take positive action to promote the general welfare, and that its actions must not interfere with the rights of individuals or organizations. Here again, in spite of the Supreme Court decisions to the contrary,[18] the position of the Constitution with respect to this conflict was a largely neutral one. The Constitution does forbid the use of governmental power in such a way as to deprive persons of liberty or property without due process of law. But this is a relative and not an absolute prohibition upon governmental activity, since deprivations of liberty or property that are *with* due process of law are not forbidden. Moreover, the phrase "due process of law" is one that has no exact definition, either in terms of the intrinsic meaning of words or in the connotations of history.

the mechanics of constitutional development

Enough has now been said to indicate why a Constitution written for an age very different from our own is still serving as a satisfactory basis for the present-day American political system. The explanation is, of course, found in the high degree of flexibility which the Constitution has shown from the very beginning of its history. Wholly apart from the momentous historical forces that influenced and made essential the institutional growth of our government, and also apart

---

[15] See, for example, *Chicago, Milwaukee and St. Paul Ry. Co.* v. *Minnesota*, 134 U.S. 418 (1890); *Lochner* v. *New York*, 198 U.S. 45 (1905); *Adair* v. *United States*, 208 U.S. 161 (1908); *Adkins* v. *Children's Hospital*, 261 U.S. 525 (1923); *Tyson* v. *Banton*, 273 U.S. 418 (1927); and *Railroad Retirement Board* v. *Alton Rr. Co.*, 295 U.S. 330 (1935).

[16] *Morehead* v. *Tipaldo*, 298 U.S. 587 (1936).

[17] *West Coast Hotel Co.* v. *Parrish*, 300 U.S. 379 (1937).

[18] In these cases in which federal and state legislation was held to violate the due process requirement there were almost always justices who dissented from this conclusion.

from questions as to the wisdom of the directions in which our political system has moved, is the important matter of the *mechanics* of change. Just *how* has the American constitutional system lent itself to the changes, formal and informal, which have enabled it to survive through one of the most dynamic periods in man's history? This question may be answered in two different ways. First, there are three different ways in which the constitutional system has grown; and, second, the growth has manifested itself in four forms. The three ways have been (1) growth outside the specific language of the written Constitution; (2) interpretation of the language of the Constitution; and (3) formal changes in the language of the Constitution. The forms in which constitutional changes have revealed themselves have been (1) statutes; (2) executive actions and judicial rulings; (3) customs and usages; and (4) amendments to the Constitution. Growth in each of the three ways has led to changes in one or more of the four forms, but it is neither necessary nor possible to keep these ways and forms separate from each other as the mechanics of constitutional development are analyzed. Accordingly, the ways will be examined one by one and the forms noted wherever appropriate.

1. constitutional development outside the words of the written Constitution
By all odds the most extensive and significant changes in the American political system have taken place outside the language of the written Constitution. This result has been possible because of the extent to which the Constitution either is entirely silent concerning many aspects of government and politics, or provides that they shall be controlled by statute. A good example of the latter situation is seen with respect to the conduct of elections. The Constitution does mention the conduct of elections, but it does so only to provide that the times, places, and manner of conducting elections shall be determined by federal and state laws. Thus, the very important issue of the way in which elections are to be run in the United States has been subject to the determination of the federal and state legislatures, and, what is more, to a more or less continuously changing determination.

An example of a matter concerning which the Constitution is entirely silent is the nomination of candidates for public office. There is not a word in the Constitution about the manner in which candidates for the Presidency or for Congress shall be chosen, and no provision is made for control of this matter by statute. Thus the way has been left open for the development of nomination procedures partly as a matter of custom and partly by statute. For example, the nomination of presidential candidates by national party conventions has been very largely a matter of custom, although there are today statutes which have a bearing upon these conventions. On the other hand, the selection of congressional candidates in each state either by a state convention or by a party primary is very largely controlled by state statutes.

An example of a change outside the Constitution which has depended largely upon executive action is seen in the cabinet system. Although the Constitution expressly authorizes the President to require the opinions in writing of the heads of departments, it says nothing at all that even vaguely suggests the creation of an executive council to act as the President's adviser in the making of administrative decisions. The cabinet has nonetheless become an important part of the American governmental mechanism, and the fact that it consists of the heads of nine executive departments—indeed, the fact that it exists at all—has been exclusively determined by presidential action.

2. growth through interpretation of the language of the Constitution

There are many aspects of the existing political system in the United States which can be traced back to specific clauses in the written Constitution, but which can be derived from these clauses only by a process of interpretation. In other words, it is not possible to say that these aspects have developed entirely outside the language of the Constitution, but neither have they been provided for in the document in so many words. A good example is found in the practice of judicial review. The Constitution certainly does not expressly provide that the Supreme Court shall have the power to declare acts of Congress null and void. Yet when the Supreme Court in 1803 in the case of *Marbury* v. *Madison* ruled that the courts do possess such a power it did so by the process of constitutional interpretation—that is, it read the idea into certain vague clauses of the Constitution, such as the one providing that judicial officers shall take an oath to support the Constitution (the reasoning being that in being required to take such an oath a judge is in effect ordered to refuse to enforce a statute which in his opinion is in conflict with the Constitution). Here it may be said that constitutional development takes the form of a court opinion.

Constitutional development by interpretation has not been the exclusive work of the courts. At times, Congress, the President, and even lesser public officers have taken part in this process. For example, the actual clauses of the Constitution on the matter of the removal from office of public officers of varying types are exceedingly vague and ambiguous. May a President be impeached and removed from office for political reasons? May the President remove a member of the civil service without seeking the consent of the Senate? May Congress by law limit the power of the President to remove a member of one of the so-called independent administrative commissions? This is not the place to try to indicate the actual answers that have been given to these questions, insofar as they have been *finally* answered. The point to be noted is that in the process of finding answers it has been necessary to interpret the Constitution, and many agencies of government have participated in this business of interpretation. Or, to put it differently, the interpretations have taken the form of statutes, court decisions, and executive action.

3. growth through formal changes in the language of the Constitution

Somewhat surprisingly, formal change of the language of the Constitution has proved to be the least important method by which the constitutional system has grown. This is undoubtedly due, first, to the ease by which constitutional growth has been achieved through the other means which have already been examined; and, second, to the mechanical difficulties that stand in the way of the successful use of the formal amending procedure described in Article Five of the Constitution.

The difficulties of the amendment procedures are quickly realized from an analysis of the system set forth in the Constitution. The procedure is divided into two parts: proposing an amendment, and ratifying an amendment. Moreover, there are two ways in which an amendment may be proposed, and two ways in which it may be ratified. It may be proposed (1) by a two-thirds vote of both houses of Congress, or (2) by a national constitutional convention called by Congress on the application of the legislatures of two thirds of the states. It may be ratified by the legislatures of three fourths of the states, or by special conventions in three fourths of the states.

Of the two methods of proposing amendments, only one, proposal by Congress, has ever been used. The way is open in the express language of the Constitution to the calling of a national convention to propose amendments or even a new constitution. But although various state legislatures have at one time or another petitioned Congress to call a convention, such a petition has not yet come from two thirds of the states with respect to any issue at the same time. Congress has never regarded the filing of such petitions as a cumulative matter. Thus petitions filed in the past do not have a continuing vitality. There are many technical questions pertaining to the calling of a national convention which Congress presumably would have to answer, since Article Five is silent as to details. One can only speculate on such interesting issues as where such a convention would be held, how many delegates would attend, how they would be chosen, and so forth.

Of the two methods of ratifying amendments, ratification by state legislatures has been used twenty times, ratification by conventions once—in the instance of the Twenty-first Amendment. There is much to be said in favor of the latter method on the score that it is more democratic, for in electing delegates to a ratifying convention the voters would enjoy an opportunity to pass more or less directly upon an amendment itself. There was reason to hope that in having selected this method of ratification in the case of the controversial proposal for the repeal of prohibition, Congress would specify its use in the case of subsequent amendments. Unfortunately, it has not done so, having reverted, in the case of the pending amendment that prescribes a two-term limit to the presidency, to ratification by the state legislatures.

There are many technical questions concerning the amending procedure which the Constitution does not answer. May the President veto a proposed amendment? How long a time may be allowed to secure ratification by three fourths of the states? May a state, having ratified or rejected an amendment, change its mind? It has fallen to the lot of the Supreme Court to answer some of these questions, although in its latest decision on the subject the Court has indicated a strong belief that Congress is the proper agency to answer such questions with finality.[19] Actually all of the questions suggested above have been answered by one means or another. The President does not pass upon an amendment, having authority neither to approve nor to veto it. Congress may fix a time limit of seven years in which the necessary number of states must ratify an amendment if it is to go into effect, and it has done so. If Congress fails to specify a time limit, the Supreme Court has said Congress itself must determine whether an amendment ratified in a period longer than seven years should be put into effect. A state having approved an amendment may not reconsider its action, but a rejection is not regarded as final action and can be reversed.

The language of the Constitution suggests there are two types of amendment that require the approval of more than three fourths of the states. Article Four provides that no state shall be divided or combined with another state without the consent of its legislature, and Article Five provides that no state, without its consent, shall be deprived of its equal representation in the Senate. Thus amendments proposing such changes would presumably have to be ratified by the states affected as an additional requirement beyond the approval of three fourths of the states.[20]

The difficulty of changing the Constitution through the formal amending procedure is also realized when the twenty-one amendments that have been adopted over a period of more than a century and a half are analyzed and it is seen how little they have actually changed the American political system. To begin with, the first ten amendments, which make up the Bill of Rights, should properly be regarded as part of the original Constitution. It was agreed during the struggle over the ratification of the Constitution that a bill of rights would promptly be added once the new government had been set up. The amendments were proposed by the First Congress in 1789, and, having been quickly ratified by the necessary number of states, went into effect in 1791. That means that between 1791 and 1951 the Constitution has been formally amended only eleven times. Moreover, two of the eleven cancel each other out. The Eighteenth Amendment gave Congress the power to establish national prohibition, and the Twenty-first Amendment withdrew that power.

---

[19] See *Hawke* v. *Smith*, 253 U.S. 221 (1920) ; *Dillon* v. *Gloss*, 256 U.S. 368 (1921) ; and, in particular, *Coleman* v. *Miller*, 307 U.S. 433 (1939).

[20] This point is clear as to representation in the Senate, since the proviso is found in Article Five, the amendment article. The effect of the proviso of Article Four as to the union or division of states upon the amendment situation is perhaps debatable.

What of the other nine amendments? Two make relatively minor changes in the mechanics of government, the Eleventh correcting the manner in which members of the electoral college cast their two votes for a President and a Vice-President, and the Twentieth changing the calendar of the government so as to eliminate the lameduck sessions of Congress and to provide for the earlier inauguration of the President. One amendment, the Eleventh, withdrew a bit of the jurisdiction originally granted the federal courts in Article Three by forbidding them to hear cases in which a state is sued by a citizen of another state. Three amendments, the Thirteenth, Fourteenth, and Fifteenth, were in effect the treaty of peace which ended the Civil War. The Thirteenth abolished slavery and involuntary servitude in all forms, the Fourteenth defined United States citizenship and placed certain prohibitions upon the states to prevent them from encroaching upon civil rights, and the Fifteenth outlawed all interferences with the right to vote based upon race, color, or previous condition of servitude. Another amendment, the Nineteenth, followed the pattern of the Fifteenth Amendment closely and outlawed interferences with the right to vote based upon sex. The Sixteenth Amendment granted Congress the power to levy federal income taxes without apportioning them among the states on the basis of population. And, finally, the Seventeenth Amendment provided for the direct election of United States senators by the people.

Obviously a number of these amendments have been far-reaching in their consequences. For example, the Fourteenth Amendment substantially altered the balance of power between national and state governments and gave the federal courts a vastly increased power to check the constitutionality of state activity. And yet it is very clear that the amendments added since 1791 hardly even begin to tell the story of the tremendous changes that have taken place in the American system of government in the one hundred and sixty years since that date. The story of those changes is very largely told either outside the language of the written Constitution or through the interpretation and reinterpretation of its clauses.

the importance of the Constitution

It may well seem from the discussion of the conflicts and changes that have taken place under our Constitution that the document has had little or no meaning. Such a conclusion would be an unfounded one. We Americans do have a Constitution. It does contain certain ideas that are very meaningful. There *is* something to the principle of federalism. It is far from being meaningless. In addition to the national government there are today forty-eight more or less vigorous state governments carrying on very substantial and reasonably independent programs. The dividing line between the powers of these two types of government has been relatively clear in many respects. Such things as public education, road building, protection against crime, and the control of local governments have been primarily, if not exclusively, concerns of the state governments. On the other hand, military activity, control of foreign affairs, and operation of a postal system have been almost exclusively functions of the national government. Moreover, it should be remembered that in spite of the vast increase in the program of the national government in recent decades, the state governments have also expanded their programs. It is a fact that the state governments today spend more money, engage in more activities, and have more workers in their employ than at any previous point in their history. Thus the enhancement of federal power and prestige has not taken place at the expense of state power and prestige.

Likewise, there is something to the principle of separation of powers. It cannot be denied that the courts have enjoyed a high degree of independence and freedom from political control which, although not complete in every respect, has been the equal of that to be found in any other land. Or it cannot be denied that the chief executive has come to enjoy greater freedom from legislative control than is true of the chief executive under parliamentary government.

"We must never forget that it is a *constitution* we are expounding." Thus spoke Chief Justice Marshall more than a century ago in his famous opinion in *McCulloch* v. *Maryland*.[21] Removed from its context in this way, the phrase might seem to suggest that Marshall was warning against the threat of governmental activities which violate the Constitution. The Chief Justice might have been thinking of the Constitution as a symbol of restraint—to recall Professor Corwin's figure of speech once more. A careful reading of the rest of Marshall's opinion in the *McCulloch* case, in which the Court upheld the power of Congress to establish a Bank of the United States, makes it clear that the Chief Justice was referring to the Constitution as an instrument rather than as a symbol. In effect, he was arguing that our Constitution—indeed, any *good* constitution—must be regarded as a broad essay on the essential character of a government, deliberately written in words general in meaning and capable of interpretation and expansion to meet changing needs. For ours is a "constitution intended to endure for ages to come, and, consequently, to be adapted to the various crises of human affairs."

Such is the essence of our dual Constitution; as we will, it is a symbol, or an instrument, capable of being used to justify policies in many different directions. The Constitution clearly places the nation in no strait jacket. Under the Constitution Americans enjoy great freedom to advance both their personal interests and the public welfare through government action. In the long run the Constitution has not prevented the people from undertaking any social experiment they have strongly desired to make. But it has served at times to slow things down, and it has meant that we have been willing to bind ourselves by a legal tradition. This

---

[21] *McCulloch* v. *Maryland*, 4 Wheaton 316, 407 (1819). Emphasis added.

tradition has often beeen stretched, and it has constantly moved forward with the times. But it remains a tradition, and it has served as a limiting factor in American politics.

bibliographic note

As has been indicated, this chapter is largely suggested by Edward S. Corwin's famous article "The Constitution as Instrument and as Symbol," originally presented at the Harvard Tercentenary celebration and then published in *American Political Science Review*, XXX (December, 1936), 1071. Many of the readings in the bibliographic note for Chapter 5 have a bearing upon this subject. Attention may also be called to Carl Swisher's *The Growth of Constitutional Power in the United States* (Chicago: The University of Chicago Press, 1946). This is a collection of lectures in which one of the leading contemporary constitutional historians describes the development of the American Constitution from both the power and the restraint points of view.

part 3

_____

government of the people

the political process

*I*T IS fitting and proper that a democracy should enshrine its principles in a constitution. Moreover, it is desirable that the people should give frequent voice to their highest aspirations by repeating such phrases as "government of the people, by the people, and for the people." But to achieve the reality of democracy something more than principles and aspirations is required. A living, working governmental mechanism must be established in which these principles and aspirations actually find expression. Accordingly, having agreed upon its constitutional principles, a democratic nation is constantly confronted with the practical problem of making the will of the people effective in the actual operation of government. The means whereby this is done may be referred to as the political process, a process that is concerned with the methods, agencies, and techniques by which the people are enabled to control the government, both in the sense of choosing the officers who fix the main lines of public policy, and in the sense of keeping those officers sensitive to public opinion after they are chosen.

the role of politics in a democracy

The word "politics" may properly be employed as an abbreviation for the phrase "political process," for politics deals with such things as elections, political parties, pressure groups, and the operation of legislatures and other agencies of government. If the state be thought of as a body and the government the vital organs through which the body functions, then politics is the lifeblood which keeps the body mechanism alive.

Politics is a word which is often used in different ways. The word is sometimes used very broadly as though it were synonymous with political science. The dictionary definition of politics as "the science and art of government" illustrates this usage. At the other extreme, the word is often used in a very narrow sense to describe the intrigues and maneuvers of political machines and politicians. In this latter sense politics is, unfortunately, a word which carries a bad connotation. It has come to suggest both unworthy aims and improper activities. Actually the word should be one of the most respected in our vocabulary, for it describes the process by which man seeks to realize one of his highest aspirations and to solve one of his most difficult practical problems. The aspiration is that each man should have a chance to develop his personality, to use his talents, to express his individuality, to realize fully the potentialities with which he is endowed. The problem is to create a favorable social environment in which it will be possible for man to realize such an aspiration. In other words, politics and democracy are inseparable terms, for politics is the means by which a free society copes with its problems in a democratic manner.

politics and the selection of public officers

Since politics is such an elusive word it is helpful to note some of the uses to which it is customarily put. Perhaps politics is most commonly associated with elections. In a democracy the first step in the process of setting up and operating a government in accordance with the will of the people is the selection of public officers who have substantial popular support. This means that a great deal of popular attention is certain to be paid to elections, and that a vast electoral mechanism will inevitably emerge in a nation like our own. Accordingly, it is not surprising that the word "politics" should first call to mind the organizations and tactics that have become part of the all-important business of conducting campaigns and winning elections.

politics as the making of public policy

Many definitions of politics stress its concern with the making of public policy. And in a democracy this means the making of policy in such a way as to give expression to the wishes of the people. Professors P. H. Odegard and E. A. Helms, in their study entitled *American Politics*, assert that "politics involves the translation of social pressures into public policies." [1] and Pendleton Herring in his *Politics of Democracy* puts much the same idea into these words: "The task of democratic politics is to evolve and execute a policy reflecting the desires of the community and capable of meeting current demands for security and prosperity." [2] Since the formation of public policy is concerned with issues which are frequently exceedingly controversial, it should not be surprising that politics often becomes a very vigorous process.

politics as the means of operating the government

Politics is also concerned with the mechanics of running the government. Professor V. O. Key, in his *Politics, Parties, and Pressure Groups*, says that "broadly,

---

[1] P. H. Odegard and E. A. Helms, *American Politics* (New York: Harper & Brothers, 1938), p. 1.

[2] Pendleton Herring, *Politics of Democracy* (New York: Rinehart & Company, 1940), p. 24.

the study of politics is concerned with the institutions and processes of govern-ance," and then he speaks more narrowly of "the dynamics that make the wheels of government turn." [3] A modern government is a complex mechanism, a cum-bersome machine, which constantly threatens to break down. Often it is difficult to get the machine started in the first place, especially in the direction that has been indicated by constitutional principles.

In the United States, government at the national level has from the start presented many organizational and procedural difficulties. It has been necessary to man a large and unwieldy bicameral legislature and to keep it running so that policy formulation might take place. It has been necessary to establish and main-tain working relations between an independent legislature and an independent executive so that the former might have the benefit of leadership in evolving policy and the latter might administer policy in a way that would satisfy its mak-ers. It has been the business of politics to meet such needs as these and thereby to make our system of government a workable one.

politics as who gets what, when, and how

One of the most stimulating books on the political process which has appeared in recent years bears the provocative title *Politics, Who Gets What, When, How.* The author of this book, Professor Harold D. Lasswell, makes clear the mean-ing of his title when he says: "The study of politics is the study of influence and the influential. . . . The influential are those who get the most of what there is to get." [4] This is admittedly cynical language to use in describing politics. But it points, nonetheless, to an inevitable aspect of the social process—the strug-gle for power and the search for rewards in which all men seem to engage. Since government has much to do with controlling the economic order and determin-ing social status, it is not surprising that politics should become concerned with the struggle over the division of society's goods and services, and with deter-mining the position and prestige which each segment of the population is to have in society.

Here is a further reason why politics has acquired a bad name. We somehow hesitate to admit that men have a selfish side to their nature, and that one of the motivating forces in the political process is the desire of men to get ahead. Charles A. Beard has pointed this out: "The average American, if there is such a person, appears to think that when anybody, except himself, follows a special interest, the operation is corrupt." And he adds: "The notion is false and the public is led astray by this conception of business and politics." [5] In any case, whatever the moral judgment which may be pronounced upon the competitive

[3] V. O. Key, *Politics, Parties, and Pressure Groups* (New York: Thomas Y. Crowell Com-pany, 2d ed., 1947), pp. 1, 2.
[4] Harold D. Lasswell, *Politics, Who Gets What, When, How* (New York: Whittlesey House, 1936), p. 3.
[5] Charles A. Beard, *The Republic* (New York: The Viking Press, 1943), p. 202.

aspect of life, the fact remains that men do compete with each other for wealth, power, and prestige. Politics cannot very well ignore this reality and must accordingly concern itself with the way in which wealth and power are distributed.

politics as the "art of the possible"

The observation is often made that "politics is the art of the possible." Like all aphorisms, this phrase tells something less than the whole truth, but it does emphasize an important aspect of the political process. It suggests that when man moves from the area of aspiration and principle into the realm of action he must be prepared to give ground to other men and to accept something less than he started out to seek. Not all men hold the same principles, not all men seek the same goals. On the other hand, as Lasswell points out, men do seek to carve up the limited wealth and power that the world holds.

Whether it is a matter of conflicting principles or a scramble for a share of the good things of life, it is clear that if men are to live together in a reasonable state of harmony there must be a good deal of give-and-take in their daily relations with one another. Politics, then, is inevitably concerned with finding the means by which men with different aims and conflicting interests can live together in peace. This is true of the local scene, of the national scene, and of the world scene. Philosophers, theologians, and economists may argue at the level of principle as to what is the "best" social order, the "true" religion, or the "soundest" business system. In action men find themselves in violent disagreement on many of the issues of life and locked in combat over the ownership of the world's wealth. Accordingly, in the short run, differences of opinion must be compromised and conflicting interests must be adjusted if life is to be made livable. This is one of the greatest needs which politics tries to meet. And yet in serving such a worthy purpose politics opens itself to attack, for the business of arranging compromises is bound to be, in part at least, an unprincipled one. In the long run, however, politics must also concern itself with principle. Opportunism and compromise are permissible, even necessary, means of resolving the conflicts of the current scene. But because man is both a moral and a rational being it is inevitable that he should seek to solve his larger problems in accordance with positive principles which, as he sees it, express the truth. Moreover, whatever compromising of principles is necessary if men are to live together in peace should take place in a responsible, democratic manner. Politics, then, requires the use of practical methods to settle the petty, but often acute, crises of everyday life, but it also necessitates the following of high ideals if a just and enduring social order is ever to be established.

the mechanism of politics

To approach the problem from a different angle, the political process is concerned with evolving and putting into successful operation institutional devices which will keep the wheels of government turning and which will make for the responsible formation of public policy by a government which can and does act in the interest of all the people at the direction of a majority of the people. To begin with, a democratic framework must be provided. Public officers who determine the main lines of public policy, or who hold the major responsibility for the broad course which government is to follow, must be chosen by the people in free elections. Citizenship must be enjoyed almost automatically by all responsible members of the society, and the right to vote must be the almost automatic accompaniment of citizenship. To support this framework ways and means must be found of creating an intelligent and informed public opinion, and such institutional devices as political parties and pressure groups must be established and put to work if elective officers are to be chosen in a democratic way and if they are to be kept continuously responsive to public opinion during their terms of office.

The Founding Fathers of the United States were content for varying reasons to lay down a few fundamental political principles, to provide a rough framework of government, and to leave it to the people in their day to day experience under the Constitution to devise and control the dynamics that would make the wheels of government turn in a democratic way. To a limited extent it was found necessary thereafter to deal with some aspects of the political process in amendments to the Constitution, but it is still true that the machinery of American politics rests largely upon an extraconstitutional basis.

role of public opinion in the political process

public opinion and democracy

Public opinion is an essential and integral part of the democratic process. Indeed, democracy has even been described as "government by public opinion." [6] The existence of an intelligent and informed citizenry is one of the basic assumptions of democracy. It is assumed that controversial public problems will be discussed by an educated population, that differing opinions will take shape as to how best to deal with these problems, and that finally majority sentiment will be ascertained and followed, on the theory that the majority is more likely to have arrived at a wise or sound judgment than is any minority.

Between such assumptions and the reality of democracy in action there is apt to be a wide gap. Seldom is the evidence available to show that governmental

---

[6] J. A. Corry, *Elements of Democratic Government* (New York: Oxford University Press, 1947), p. 257.

policy on specific issues is determined by public opinion intelligently arrived at by a majority of the people. This does not mean that the assumptions of democracy are invalid. But it does mean that the actual role played by public opinion in a democracy is not easy to describe. There are many difficult questions to answer. What is public opinion? How is it formed? What factors or influences help shape public opinion? Is it influenced unduly by propaganda or is it the result of impartial consideration of facts? By what means can the necessary information concerning a problem be communicated to the public? Is there such a thing as majority public opinion? Should the government influence public opinion, or should public opinion influence the government? How does public opinion express itself and how can it be accurately measured?

what is public opinion?

There is no one accepted definition of public opinion. The concept is as vague and elusive as any that is encountered in the study of the social process. Any definition of public opinion is bound to be a highly personal formulation which emphasizes some points and ignores others. It may be simply defined as a point of view held by two or more people on any subject. But such a definition is too broad and is obviously not very helpful in bringing about a better understanding of the relationship between public opinion and government in a democracy. On the other hand, some authorities have gone to such an extreme in defining the term in precise, technical language that it is difficult to follow their meaning. It is perhaps well to avoid any attempt at precise definition and to be content with noting certain component parts of public opinion as the term is used in the study of government. In this context public opinion consists of views held by a considerable number of people which have some basis in rational thinking, and which concern problems that are open to controversy and are subject to governmental action.[7] Public opinion is seldom used to describe views on which there is unanimity of opinion—murder is evil; which are narrowly held—the equality of the states in the Senate should be abolished; which have no political significance—jazz music is unpleasant; and which have a completely emotional basis—all congressmen are fools. There is a good deal of room for disagreement as to the inclusion or exclusion of factors in this description of public opinion, but in many ways this description will be found to be a useful one.

how is public opinion formed?

According to the theory of an ideal democratic society, public opinion should take shape solely as the result of educational influences. In practice it is obvious that public opinion is much influenced by what we call "propaganda." This latter term, like public opinion, is an exceedingly hazy one. It may be described

---

[7] This description of public opinion is suggested by the discussion in Corry's excellent study, *Elements of Democratic Government*, pp. 260–261.

as the deliberate use of data or arguments, which may or may not have a rational basis, to influence public opinion in the particular direction favored by the user. Propaganda is sometimes contrasted with education, which is said to be a process by which facts and theories having a strictly rational basis are presented more or less impartially with no intention of influencing public opinion one way or the other. In practice, this distinction between education and propaganda is only partially valid, for education often necessarily stresses a point of view. The difference between education and propaganda is one of degree rather than of kind.

Whether the means by which public opinion is formed are primarily educational or propagandist in character, a further determining factor in the making of public opinion is the nature of the system of communications which exists in a society. In a modern democracy the means of communicating ideas are certain to be numerous and varied. The roles played by newspapers, magazines, books, the radio, the motion picture, literature in the mails, lectures, forums, and schools, in making available factual information and in suggesting points of view have long been obvious, if imperfectly understood. In fact we have become so aware of the great variety of efforts which are constantly being made to influence the public mind and of the ease with which certain means of communicating facts and ideas can be manipulated to produce desired results, that we have tended to become rather cynical about public opinion.

It is easy to persuade oneself that public opinion cannot possibly remain intelligent or honest in the face of the conflicting and confusing barrages of propaganda which are sent up on almost every controversial issue of any importance. Moreover, the faults of our communications system can easily lead to discouragement. The press has become a "big business" enterprise largely inclined to look with favor upon the conservative side of all issues. The number of newspapers has declined steadily in modern times. The cost of starting a new paper has increased so greatly that it is a rare event when such a paper makes an appearance, and an even rarer thing when it survives for any length of time. The day when every important social and economic faction had a journal of its own, or had easy access to one, is gone, and the day of the "one-newspaper town" is here. The radio and the motion picture oversimplify all matters, emphasize the sentimental and romantic, the cheap and vulgar. The public lecture and forum have lost much of the vitality they enjoyed half a century ago. The mails are loaded with slick, high-pressure propaganda leaflets which are all too infrequently a source of detailed, accurate information about a problem. How can an intelligent public opinion possibly take shape in the face of such shortcomings in our communications system?

But the cynicism and discouragement can be overdone. There is much evidence to support a conclusion that no society has ever been able to come closer to an approximation of the democratic ideal of an informed and intelligent citizenry than has our own. Granted the unprecedented use which is now made of

propaganda in the United States today, and granted the shortcomings of our devices for communicating information, there are many saving features to our situation. In particular, there is the saving feature of competition—competition in
propaganda and competition among the agencies of communication. One private
pressure group offsets another in its efforts to influence the public mind. The
number of newspapers has declined and the lecture hall has lost much of its power
to interest. But the radio, the motion picture, the increased publication of books,
and the expansion of our educational system more than compensate for the lost
ground. Moreover, the government itself has become increasingly interested, by
one means or another, in disseminating information about public issues
and problems. There is, of course, the perennial danger that all of these freely
competing agencies will merely confuse the public mind rather than be conducive to the formation of enlightened public opinion. Nonetheless, it seems fair
to conclude that "the free market place of thought" has never been freer and
never broader, and that the public has never followed public problems with
greater interest or formed opinions on a more intelligent basis than is true in
America today.

what forces or factors influence the formation of public opinion?

It is difficult to describe in systematic fashion the forces or factors that may influence or condition the formation of public opinion in the United States at any
given time or with respect to any particular topic or problem. Public opinion is
itself a nebulous concept. Moreover, it takes shape in such uncertain ways and is
so obviously the result of a variety of confusing, complex forces that it would
be misleading to discuss the formation of public opinion as though the process
could be logically and scientifically described. It is also impossible in a brief
discussion to do more than suggest some of the factors that play a part in the
process.

It is helpful at the beginning to recognize that the forces influencing public
opinion are partly rational or intellectual in character, and partly irrational or
emotional in character. The rationale of democracy assumes that the former will
dominate the latter, and in the long run one of the tests by which a nation's experience under democracy can be measured for success or failure is the extent
to which people are influenced by rational forces in their thinking about public
affairs. On the other hand, it is clear that emotions do enter into the making of
public opinion and it is important that the emotional factor in public opinion
be recognized if the rational factor is ultimately to be safeguarded and strengthened.

The first force influencing public opinion may be labeled ideology. All men
come finally to have a general point of view, a general scheme of life, or a set of
values or morals. Such an ideological outlook is the result of a variety of conditions and influences. For example, most men belong to a formal church which

prescribes a set of religious dogmas for them to accept. Most men belong to a political party and accept certain political principles and traditions, vague though they may be. All men have ancestral and nationality allegiances. These and other influences produce in each man an ideological outlook against which he tests his thinking concerning political issues and problems. The testing is sometimes conscious, sometimes unconscious, and the ideological influence with respect to a particular issue may be weak or strong. But there is no escaping the fact that with respect to most issues the individual's general ideology plays a significant part in influencing his stand.

Second, public opinion is governed in a most important way by economic or material considerations. In a capitalist society every person is interested sooner or later in making his way ahead so far as the acquisition or enjoyment of material goods and wealth is concerned. Accordingly, he becomes identified with an economic class. He regards himself as a businessman, as a worker, or as a farmer, and thereby acquires specific interests and loyalties. Similarly, he lives in a certain section of the country and recognizes that he is identified with the very real material interests of that section. In these and other ways, he comes to feel that he is a member of a competitive system. His bread seems to him to be buttered on one side or the other and he is very likely to take this into account in lining up with respect to the issues of the day.

Third, public opinion is affected by a psychological factor. Each individual has a personality which is the result of a variety of complex drives and forces. He is a mixture of satisfactions, frustrations, and inhibitions. He may be relatively well adjusted to life; he may be badly adjusted. The person who is relatively normal, well adjusted, and happy is certain to react differently to many social problems than will an embittered, frustrated, and unhappy person, even though the two may have identical ideological outlooks and material interests. The influence of the psychological factor, more than that of the ideological or economic factor, is apt to be both irrational and unconscious. It does not follow that because a man is influenced by his emotions as well as his intellect in the views he holds concerning public issues those views will necessarily be erroneous. Neither will they necessarily be bad because he is not entirely conscious of the reasons for which he holds them. There are times when men must trust their instincts or emotions in arriving at judgments. Nonetheless, democracy assumes the existence of an educated, reasoning citizenry, and unless the rational and conscious forces in the long run dominate the irrational and unconscious forces in the making of public opinion democracy will surely be endangered. Thus, it is important that increasing attention be paid to the operation of the psychological factor in public opinion and that the influence of the emotions be recognized and subjected to intelligent control.

Fourth, public opinion is conditioned in a variety of ways by the progress of science and technology. For one thing, the formation of public opinion in a nation as large and as populous as the United States is today possible only because of the existence of satisfactory means of communication and transportation. At the same time, the highly technological character of our society produces issues and problems that are unknown to a rural, agrarian society, and it allows less time for the finding of satisfactory solutions to such issues and problems. Moreover, many of the issues are exceedingly difficult to understand because of the highly technical character of the information pertaining to them. At times, it may even prove impossible to make such information generally available to the public. For example, one of the greatest issues of our time—finding a satisfactory system for the social control of atomic energy—is made almost impossibly difficult because of the secrecy seemingly required by security interests. When it is impossible to inform even the members of Congress on such a vital point as the number of atomic bombs that have been stockpiled by the United States, how can the American people do the intelligent thinking necessary if social control of atomic energy is to be democratic in character?

In other words, the highly technological character of American civilization makes it possible through the mass-circulation newspaper and magazine, and the magic of radio and television, to bring essential information concerning social problems to every citizen and thereby to encourage the formation of intelligent public opinion. At the same time, it renders the problems themselves so complex and difficult that there arises a question concerning the ability of even an educated and informed citizenry to think about them intelligently and rationally. The machine age is placing a strain upon the democratic process in this respect. There is no reason to despair completely concerning the outcome, but it is clear that if the democratic system is to survive, increasing attention must be paid to such a basic point as bringing essential information concerning the social problems of a technological age to the people so that the process of forming public opinion may be carried forward.

should government influence public opinion?

The question whether government officers should influence public opinion or only be influenced by it is an old one which has long interested political theorists. Fortunately, it is not as difficult a question to answer as many others pertaining to public opinion. Public officers in a democracy must show a high sensitivity to public opinion. But it is also clear that they must often provide strong leadership as public opinion takes shape on a difficult issue. For example, where the President possesses expert information concerning such matters as the international situation or economic trends within the country, which information in his judgment more or less necessitates the following of particular policies, he must do his best to shape a favorable public opinion in support of these policies.

A closely related question is whether a legislator in a representative democracy should follow the wishes of his constituents or use his own judgment in voting on important issues. Although this question has intrigued students of government since the time of Burke's famous statement to his constituents in Bristol, in which he argued that a legislator should follow his own unbiased and mature judgment, practice indicates that a legislator must follow both courses. In the main, legislators should seek to give expression to the wishes of the voters. But in a representative democracy there are many decisions that must often be made without direct reference to the wishes of the people. Many issues, although important, are so technical that there is little or no public opinion concerning them. Other issues must be decided quickly, and there is insufficient time to wait for public opinion to take shape or be ascertained. And even where public opinion does exist, there are times when legislators will feel compelled to follow their own judgment in voting on bills, even at great risk to their careers. As long as the voters finally have an opportunity to pass upon the record of the legislator who has occasionally used his own judgment, and to accept or reject him for further service, it cannot be said that his independent action is improper in a democracy. On the other hand, the officer who regularly and consistently flouts public opinion is likely to be defeated when he comes up for re-election. Actually, discussion of this problem of the duty of the legislator to follow public opinion is meaningless unless attention is also given to the role he should play as a loyal member of a responsible party group. It may be argued that in a democracy the individual legislator seldom functions as a free agent, and that his *first* duty is to serve public opinion by adhering to the platform of the party under whose auspices he has won his office.

how does public opinion make itself felt?

How does public opinion influence the political process? How do public officers find out what the public wants? How is public opinion measured? These questions all point to one of the most crucial aspects of the democratic process—the means by which government is made responsive to the people.

It may be noted at once that too much can be expected of democracy at this point. A nation may have an informed and intelligent citizenry and in the broad sense public opinion may play the role democracy assigns to it; yet on many a specific issue opinion may be but vaguely formed, held by only a minority of the people, and weakly held by them. "Like fog or smoke, public opinion is obvious in its larger manifestations, but intangible at closer view." [8]

But some public opinion is bound to exist on most major issues, and it is desirable that public officers should know what that public opinion is, by how many people it is held, and how intensely it is held. What, then, are the methods by which it is practical to measure public opinion?

[8] Herring, *Politics of Democracy*, p. 305.

the measurement of public opinion through elections

The traditional way in which public opinion has been measured in a democracy is through the ballot box. In their selection of public officers it is presumed that the voters pass judgment upon differing platforms offered by rival candidates and political parties and give a mandate to the victorious candidates and parties to carry out their campaign promises. In practice there has been much argument about the kind and extent of mandate which the American people give in a national election. It is difficult, for example, to prove that in the 1920 presidential election, the voters, in preferring Harding to Cox, indicated their disapproval of the League of Nations; that in 1928, in preferring Hoover to Smith, the voters indicated continuing approval of the prohibition experiment; or that, in preferring Roosevelt to Hoover in 1932, they gave advance approval to the New Deal program. More recently there has been much argument as to the nature of the mandate given to President Truman in his surprising re-election in 1948. For example, it cannot be proved that the voters thereby indicated profound dissatisfaction with the Taft-Hartley Act and called for its repeal or substantial revision. On the other hand, the voters certainly did not call for a revival of conservative policies, as the opponents of the Truman "Fair Deal" program have seemed to imply in arguing that the President received no liberal mandate.

The plain truth of the matter is that our national parties are such heterogeneous collections of diverse factions, the platforms of these parties are often so evasive, and so many extraneous and irrational factors play a part in influencing the choice of the voters, that a national election seldom produces a clear-cut mandate on the issues of the day. But the meaninglessness of national elections can be exaggerated, for if no mandate is indicated, such an election can and usually does at least indicate which way the wind is blowing. Moreover, in a two-party system the victorious party usually holds office on the strength of majority support of the people, and however imperfect an instrument it may be for the reflection of public opinion, it does at least qualify as such an instrument.

A further difficulty with the measurement of public opinion through the selection of federal officers is that our national elections occur at fixed intervals of two and four years. Only at the four-year intervals in presidential elections do the candidates and parties make their stands definite enough to provide the voters with a reasonably clear opportunity to make known their wishes with respect to issues. At best an "off-year" congressional election gives the voters a chance to show their approval or disapproval of what the party in power has been doing, for the parties seldom try to clarify their stands upon the issues in such an election. In any case there are long intervals between these rigidly fixed elections during which new problems arise and public opinion takes shape concerning them. How is this opinion to be measured during the many months, and even years, that may remain before the next election?

the measurement of public opinion between elections

Many traditional methods of measuring public opinion between elections have been used. Congressmen learn much from the mail they receive from their constituents, although they know that only those who have strong personal interests in the outcome of an issue and who have learned to be vocal about such matters are likely to write to them. Similarly, they learn from the witnesses before the committees of Congress, and administrators learn from those who come to their offices and make known their problems or their wishes. It is the organized pressure group which is responsible for much of this activity. Indeed, it may be said that if the party is the chief institutional means by which public opinion can be measured at election time, the pressure group has become the most important institutional means for the measurement of public opinion between elections. There are, however, other means. President and congressmen alike follow the editorial columns of the press and are able thereby to sense some of the trends of public opinion. But they have learned that there is often a wide gap between these columns and the sentiment of the majority of the people. Again, legislators and administrators alike frequently go directly to the people to sound out public opinion. The President makes a swing around the circle and both tells the people about his program and tries to gauge public sentiment. The congressman goes back home and talks on Main Street with the voters. Indeed, it was the intention of the Legislative Reorganization Act of 1946 that Congress should adjourn its regular session not later than July of each year so that our national legislators might spend part of the year at home and thereby keep in touch with their constituents.

There has long been a feeling that these methods are not enough, and that there is needed a more formal, or highly institutionalized device for the measurement of public opinion between elections. Two attempts to supply such a device are to be seen in the initiative, referendum, and recall, and in the public opinion poll.

the initiative, referendum, and recall as means of measuring public opinion

The *initiative* is a formal means whereby the voters themselves are enabled to legislate. A proposed statute or constitutional amendment is placed upon the ballot by securing the signatures of a required number of voters, and if it is approved by the voters it goes into effect. The *referendum* is a means whereby a bill or constitutional amendment which has been voted by the legislature is submitted to the electorate for its approval before going into effect. Finally, the *recall* is a means whereby the voters may remove a public officer before his regular term is up, presumably because of disapproval of his policies.

All three of these devices have been widely used in state and local governments. But there is no provision for their use in the federal government, and it would take constitutional amendments to make them part of federal procedure. At one time or another specific proposals have been made for the recall of federal judges, for popular ratification of constitutional amendments, and for submitting declarations of war to a referendum vote of the people, but there has been little agitation for the general use of these devices at the national level. Indeed, many authorities assert that their use in state and local government has not been conspicuously successful. It is argued that they tend to lengthen the ballot unduly and to place upon the voters an intolerable burden. In a sense the initiative, referendum, and recall represent an attempt to return to *direct* democracy. Any such attempt is almost certainly doomed to failure, for the complexity of modern life and the technical difficulty of most of the policy decisions we must make today commit us inevitably to the use of *indirect* or *representative* democracy.

public opinion polling

In the last generation efforts have been made to measure public opinion by scientific polling devices. The taking of "straw votes" is an ancient pastime. Newspapers have long quizzed voters so as to be able to predict the outcome of elections, and party organizations have always tried to gauge sentiment by various measuring devices. In the 1920's and early 1930's the *Literary Digest* gained fame for its successful polling of the national electorate during presidential campaigns. Almost without exception these early polls sought for accuracy by polling large numbers of persons, hoping thereby to obtain a true cross section of the electorate more or less automatically. For example, in the 1936 campaign the *Literary Digest* mailed out ballots to some ten million persons, more than two million of which were marked and returned. In spite of the size of this sample, the faulty character of the method was exposed when the count of the ballots indicated a Landon victory in an election which was actually won by Roosevelt by a ten-million majority that gave him the electoral vote of all but two of the states.

This 1936 polling fiasco all but destroyed confidence in unscientific "mass" polling of the electorate. Thereafter attention shifted to the Gallup, Roper, and Crossley polls, which claimed to achieve a scientific result by controlling the sample for quality rather than by striving for mere quantity. Polls of this type try to achieve accuracy by giving proper attention in their cross section of persons quizzed to such variables as place of residence, age, sex, religion, professional interests, and economic status. By such means experts assert that it is theoretically possible to secure a highly accurate indication of public opinion through the polling of a remarkably small but carefully chosen group of people. For example, the size of the Gallup Poll sample is sometimes as small as 3,000 and is always well below 100,000.

The scientific polls have been used not only to predict the results of elections but to measure opinion on the controversial issues which confront Congress and other government agencies between elections. It is in this latter respect that the public opinion poll offers a possible means for the strenthening of democracy. It is probable that the sampling of opinion on issues by the privately controlled polls has already profoundly affected government policy. There is evidence, for example, that polls on international issues encouraged both the President and Congress in the years and months before the attack upon Pearl Harbor to break sharply with the American tradition of isolationism and to give the Allied Powers every aid short of war. Accordingly, it seems probable that an increased and more systematic use by both public and private agencies of scientific polling as a means of measuring public opinion with respect to pending governmental decisions is both desirable and inevitable. It has been seen that elections are an inadequate means of determining where the public stands on issues. Similarly, the testimony of witnesses, the trend of newspaper editorials, and letters from voters are unsatisfactory indications of public sentiment. Indeed, it is likely that public opinion polls would frequently show that the most vocal pressure groups speak only for minorities. If such polls enabled public officers to resist these minority pressures more effectively than they do today, their use would be an important step toward a more perfect democracy.

criticism of public opinion polls

An initial criticism of public opinion polls is that they are still bothered by scientific shortcomings. The spectacular failure of all the leading polls to predict the victory of President Truman in the 1948 election led many people to assert that they were no better than the old *Literary Digest* Poll and served momentarily to discredit polling. But it is unlikely that this setback will prove to be more than temporary. Admittedly the leading polls have not solved all of their technical problems. Seemingly they still have much to learn about the preparation of accurate and representative samples. Likewise, in polling people on complex issues rather than on candidates there are unsolved difficulties about the wording of questions so as to achieve strict impartiality and avoid prejudging a person's answer. Finally, a better job must be done in measuring the intensity of opinion. It is true that a halfhearted vote counts just as much as does an enthusiastic vote in an election. But in ascertaining public opinion on issues, it is important to differentiate between a well-thought-out conclusion which is firmly held, and an emotional or superficial view which may give way to the first argument heard the other way.

Second, it is argued that polls which try to predict the outcome of elections serve no socially useful purpose. At best, so the argument runs, where they correctly predict the result they merely provide information that will shortly be known anyway. At the worst, they are said to be dangerous because they may actually alter the outcome of an election, either by encouraging a band wagon movement for the predicted winner or by lulling the leading party into a sense of false security that may lead to relaxation and defeat. Obviously, both of these last results cannot prevail at one time. Although there is no way of telling whether any one of these arguments has any basis in fact or not, it seems doubtful whether election polls, by merely predicting the outcome, have actually influenced election results in either direction. If it be granted that election polls do not cause any positive harm, can it be said that they do any good? One argument in their favor is that they encourage efficiency in party organization and campaign tactics by measuring the success and failure of methods as a campaign proceeds. Another argument is that although the polling of public opinion on issues is more socially useful than the use of polls to predict the outcome of elections, the latter is important to polling organizations, because it provides them with their only opportunity to measure the accuracy of their work, and thus enables them to perfect their methods and do a better job of measuring opinion on issues.

A third criticism of the polls is that they seek to measure opinion on issues concerning which the public cannot possibly have an informed judgment. Professor Lindsay Rogers writes:

> What questions could be put to an electorate? In an age when 531 representatives and senators who are paid so well for their time that they do not have to have other means of livelihood, and who are staffed for the investigation of the merits of proposed legislation, have to throw up their hands and say there are many details on which they cannot pass and which they must leave to administrative determination, it is absurd to suggest that counting the public pulse can give any light or leading save on the simplest kind of a proposition.[9]

This is, in effect, the same argument that is made against the initiative and referendum: that the poll is an attempt to move toward direct democracy in the face of the fact that the nature of our times forces us inevitably to make use of representative democracy. On many issues public opinion can only be superficial. For legislators to follow such opinion blindly would make it difficult to preserve the deliberative and compromise aspects of policy making. On the other hand, in a democracy there are surely many major issues on which it is important to determine the dominant public opinion. Dr. George Gallup puts the case for the polling of public opinion on issues as follows: "To the extent that a political leader does take public opinion into account in making his decisions, he should have an accurate and objective measure of that opinion rather than mere guesswork. What polls endeavor to supply is a more systematic and more objective measure of opinions." [10]

Finally, there is a more basic objection to public opinion polling which is be-

---

[9] Lindsay Rogers, *The Pollsters* (New York: Alfred A. Knopf, Inc., 1949), p. 78.
[10] "The Case for the Public Opinion Polls," *New York Times Magazine*, February 27, 1949, pp. 11, 55.

ing increasingly voiced. The objection is nothing less than the assertion that such polling offers a fundamental threat to the very existence of a progressive, intelligent society. The fear is that through the use of these devices the American people will be turned into a disciplined, monotonous army of robots in whom the last spark of individuality will have been stamped out. The poll will be used by both private business and government to discover the dead center of thought on any issue, candidate, consumer's item, or amusement, and then a propaganda campaign will follow to sell the entire country a standardized idea or product. The result will be a society in which the lowest common denominator of public taste, morality, and intelligence will prevail.

Admittedly, there is much basis for this fear. In politics, some public officers have shown signs of being governed by polls which seem to show that public opinion supports this issue or opposes that one. They lose their inclination to lead and become satisfied to follow. The use of the poll by private enterprise to ascertain public wants seems in some instances, as for example when used by the motion-picture industry, to result in a cheapened, vulgarized product.

Fortunately, the picture is not as dark as it seems. For one thing, a knowledge of where the majority of the people stand on an issue can have the effect of encouraging public officers to follow a bold and imaginative course, for the people do not always or necessarily prefer a "safe" or middle-of-the-road policy. It has already been suggested that this was true of our policy before World War II. As the international crisis deepened in the late 1930's the American people came to recognize the threat of fascism and to favor strong support for England and France. Public opinion polls showed the strength of this trend, and although Congress and the President still had cause in 1939 and 1940 to follow at times a cautious international policy lest they incur the displeasure of the people—particularly in the 1940 election—it seems certain that slowly but surely our government's hand was strengthened as the polls revealed the true character of public opinion. Again there is evidence that from time to time a poll makes it easier for public officials to resist the vigorous pressure of an organized minority by showing up its lack of support among the people generally. For example, there is reason to believe that a Gallup Poll which showed less than 4 per cent of the people supporting the Townsend Plan had such an effect.[11]

Admittedly there is the danger that public opinion polling will result in the long run in public officers, like motion-picture producers, trying to find out what the people want, and, having found out, being satisfied to give it to them. But there is just as much reason to suppose that the capable public officer, who understands that in a democracy he must lead as well as follow, will utilize the knowledge supplied by polls to undertake with better understanding of the exact nature of his task the difficult but necessary business of overcoming an unfriendly

---

[11] G. H. Gallup and S. F. Rae, *The Pulse of Democracy* (New York: Simon and Schuster, 1940), pp. 145–147.

public opinion and of persuading the people to accept the wisdom of the policies he seeks to pursue.

Moreover, as against the threat that through propaganda public opinion can be manipulated to produce any desired result, there is the saving grace of the continuing good judgment of the American people. It is significant that the professional pollers of public opinion have been impressed in their work by the intelligence of the American people. In their book, *The Pulse of Democracy*, Dr. George Gallup and his assistant, S. F. Rae, conclude:

> The serious observer of public opinion on scores of issues cannot fail to come away with a feeling of intense admiration for the honesty and common sense with which an enormous number of ordinary people in all walks of life and at all levels of the economic scale have continued to meet their responsibilities as citizens. He will be profoundly impressed with the grasp of broad principles which voters of all types possess, and with their capacity to adjust themselves to the ever-changing movement of events.[12]

And Elmo Roper has written that "six years of sampling public opinion has given me a profound respect for the wisdom of the American people as a whole and with it a firm conviction that if we keep the power in the hands of the people and further develop techniques for making them vocal, we need never have fear that this country will ever face the situation now being faced in certain countries of Europe."[13]

And finally, the 1948 presidential election showed that the voters are still capable of independence of thought and action. In the face of the power of the press, which was used to an overwhelming extent to support the losing candidate, and in the face of the polls which predicted a Republican victory, they dared to vote as they pleased.

bibliographic note

A stimulating treatment of the political process, philosophical as well as descriptive in character, is found in Pendleton Herring's *The Politics of Democracy* (New York: Rinehart & Company, 1940). Arthur F. Bentley's *The Process of Government* (Bloomington: The Principia Press, Inc., new ed., 1949), originally published in 1908, is a remarkable pioneer study of social pressures and their effect upon the political process. V. O. Key's *Southern Politics in State and Nation* (New York: Alfred A. Knopf, Inc., 1949) is a brilliant work that describes in systematic fashion the politics of one section of the United States. This study is a superb example of research in political science.

---

[12] *Ibid.*, p. 287.
[13] "Sampling Public Opinion," *Journal of the American Statistical Association*, XXXV (June, 1940), 325, 334.

There are numerous texts on the subject of public opinion. Two pioneer studies are Abbott Lawrence Lowell's *Public Opinion and Popular Government* (New York: Longmans, Green & Co., 1913), and Walter Lippmann's *The Phantom Public* (New York: Harcourt, Brace and Company, 1925). Among the more recent texts are A. Hadley Cantril, *Gauging Public Opinion* (Princeton: Princeton University Press, 1944); Harwood L. Childs, *An Introduction to Public Opinion* (New York: John Wiley & Sons, Inc., 1940); Leonard W. Doob, *Public Opinion and Propaganda* (New York: Henry Holt and Company, 1948); and Marbury B. Ogle, *Public Opinion and Political Dynamics* (Boston: Houghton Mifflin Company, 1950). *The Public Opinion Quarterly*, published under the auspices of Princeton University, is an excellent source of articles about public opinion, propaganda, and, in particular, public opinion polls.

The development of public opinion polls in the last generation, the *Literary Digest* fiasco in 1936, and the failure of all the polls accurately to predict the outcome of the 1948 election have resulted in the publication of a number of studies of polling. Louis H. Bean's *How to Predict Elections* (New York: Alfred A. Knopf, Inc., 1948) is a statement by a man who has been remarkably successful in analyzing the record of past elections and in predicting future trends. Two books that examine the 1948 failure of the polls are Morris L. Ernst and David Loth, *The People Know Best: The Ballots Vs. the Polls* (Washington: Public Affairs Press, 1949), and Lindsay Rogers, *The Pollsters* (New York: Alfred A. Knopf, Inc., 1949). The findings of a committee of experts established by the Social Science Research Council to analyze the 1948 fiasco have been published under the title *Election Polls of 1948* (New York: Social Science Research Council, 1949). A general collection of papers read at a recent conference on polling is found in Norman C. Meier and Harold W. Saunders, eds., *The Polls and Public Opinion* (New York: Henry Holt and Company, 1949).

The literature dealing with the roles of press, radio, and motion picture as mass communications media in a democratic society is extensive. Attention may be called to the report of the Commission on Freedom of the Press, published in 1947 under the title *A Free and Responsible Press*. This report was accompanied by a series of monographs prepared by outstanding authorities. Among these are Zechariah Chafee, *Government and Mass Communications*; William E. Hocking, *Freedom of the Press: A Framework of Principle;* Ruth A. Inglis, *Freedom of the Movies;* and Llewellyn White, *The American Radio*. All of these volumes were published by The University of Chicago Press in 1947.

"The Motion Picture Industry" was examined in the 254th volume of *The Annals* of The American Academy of Political and Social Science (November, 1947) under the editorship of Gordon S. Watkins.

Many of the items in the bibliographic notes for Chapter 1 and 2 are also concerned with the political process.

citizenship and the right to vote

$\mathscr{S}$INCE it is a purpose of government in a democracy to regulate the activity of each man in the interest of all men, it follows that every mature and responsible person must be able to enjoy full citizenship and have an equal voice in his government. Because the right to participate in the political process is customarily limited to citizens there can be no denial of access to citizenship based upon race, color, creed, or national origin." [1] In these words, the President's Committee on Civil Rights expressed its view of the importance of citizenship to the democratic process. It is citizenship which gives the "mature and responsible person" his standing in a free society. In the United States today one is nowhere allowed to vote unless he is a citizen. Only citizens may be elected to national office or to most state offices. In many states only citizens may own land, enter the professions, or engage in certain businesses.

Accordingly, the way in which citizenship is achieved by the individual is one of the most important points to be settled in evolving a governmental system. Moreover, this point is apt to prove a troublesome one for constitution makers. Certainly, it has been one of the most difficult constitutional problems that the United States has had to face, and there are aspects of the problem which to this day remain unsolved.

There are two reasons why citizenship is not an easy status to define or regulate. In the first place, it is a problem which has many technical complications. For example, there are two kinds of citizenship to keep track of—that kind which a man acquires by birth, and that which he may acquire in his later life by changing his residence from one country to another. There is also the age-old problem of drawing the line between that native citizenship which is determined by the place of a man's birth, and that which is determined by the nationality of his parents.

Second, because citizenship always carries with it certain valuable privileges or rights, the status itself has been an exceedingly controversial one. Up to now

---

[1] *To Secure These Rights* (Washington: Government Printing Office, 1947), pp. 6–7.

mankind has not succeeded in distributing all of life's advantages on a basis that satisfies all persons. There has always been rivalry between the privileged and the underprivileged members of society. Moreover, conflicts over the enjoyment of privilege have often been colored by emotion and prejudice rather than by reason. Arguments as to the enjoyment of citizenship have not been free from emotion and prejudice, and to the extent that that is so, the finding of a satisfactory constitutional and legal definition of citizenship has been made more difficult.

native citizenship

Although the original Constitution as it came from the Philadelphia convention several times mentioned "citizens," it nowhere defined the status itself. Although they required, for instance, that the President of the United States be a "natural born citizen," the Founding Fathers did not lay down any rules to determine which persons fell into this category. Many questions were left unanswered. Did one become an American citizen merely by being born within the United States? Did one's racial ancestry or national origin make a difference? Were children born to American citizens anywhere in the world "natural born citizens" of this country? Was national citizenship or state citizenship the dominant status, and what was the proper relationship between the two kinds of citizenship?

The constitutional definition of citizenship remained in doubt for nearly a century until, in 1868, the Fourteenth Amendment in its very first words provided for the first time a formal, constitutional description of citizenship: "All persons born or naturalized in the United States, and subject to the jurisdiction thereof, are citizens of the United States and of the State wherein they reside." In this one sentence the amendment went far toward removing the uncertainties pertaining to American citizenship.

the rule of jus soli

The Fourteenth Amendment makes it clear that the basic consideration in determining native citizenship is *place* of birth. In thus providing that *all* persons born in the United States are to be American citizens, the makers of the amendment wrote into the Constitution the ancient rule of *jus soli* (the law or right of place), a rule closely identified with English legal traditions. The adoption of this rule has meant that there can be no discrimination in the acquisition of citizenship against anyone who is born in this country. Regardless of his race, color, creed, ancestry, or of the fact that his parents may themselves be aliens, such a person *automatically* becomes an American citizen by being born in the United States. The Fourteenth Amendment seems clear enough on this point, but whatever doubt might still have existed in the minds of some people was removed by the Supreme Court in 1898 in its decision in *United States* v. *Wong Kim Ark* in which it emphasized that the amendment means what it says. In this case the Court held that a man of Chinese ancestry born in San Francisco to alien parents, who under American law were ineligible to become citizens of this country by naturalization, was nonetheless an American citizen by birth.[2]

Once this doubt was cleared up, our practice has coincided closely with constitutional principle. In the words of the Civil Rights Committee, "we have in fact followed the ideal very closely. American-born children of aliens have encountered no barriers to citizenship." [3]

There are certain minor exceptions to the application of *jus soli*. In common with international practice on this point, children born in the United States of foreign diplomatic agents are not regarded as American citizens. Neither are children born on foreign public ships in American waters so regarded. Technically, these persons are not viewed as being "subject to the jurisdiction" of the United States.

the rule of jus sanguinis

By the Roman civil law of *jus sanguinis* (the right of blood), native citizenship was acquired through the blood relationship between parent and child, and the place of birth was irrelevant. This rule of citizenship has been followed in modern times by many nations on the continent of Europe. The Fourteenth Amendment does not follow the rule of *jus sanguinis* by expressly recognizing as American citizens children born of American parents outside the United States. But Congress since 1802 has extended citizenship to such children by law, subject to certain technical qualifications and conditions.[4] Whether such a child is a "natural born citizen" in the sense that he might become President of the United States has not been determined. But otherwise he is certainly a native citizen possessed of all the rights and privileges enjoyed by those born in the United States.

the relationship between federal and state citizenship

The Fourteenth Amendment also removed the confusion which had existed between national citizenship and state citizenship. Although before 1868 it was not clear whether the two types of citizenship were related or entirely distinct, the amendment expressly makes national citizenship the dominant status and state citizenship a secondary status. In other words, an American citizen automatically becomes a state citizen merely by taking up residence in a state, and no state may deny such a person the right of state citizenship. It seems clear also that no state may grant state citizenship to any person who is not a national citizen. It may,

---

[2] *United States* v. *Wong Kim Ark*, 169 U.S. 649 (1898).
[3] *To Secure These Rights*, p. 32.
[4] See § 601 of Title 8 (Aliens and Nationality) of the United States Code. The latest restatement by Congress of the statutory law of nationality was made in 1940.

of course, grant aliens such privileges as it chooses, including even the right to vote, so that for all practical purposes an alien might enjoy the same privileges as a "state" citizen. But *citizenship* itself is determined nationally, and no state may by positive action grant or withhold state citizenship.

citizenship by naturalization

The Founding Fathers recognized that persons leaving their native lands and coming to this country to take up permanent residence might wish to acquire American citizenship. Accordingly, they gave Congress express power "to establish a uniform rule of naturalization." Naturalization has been defined by Congress as "the conferring of nationality of a state upon a person after birth." The power to establish a naturalization system was immediately exercised by Congress in 1790, and throughout our history we have had federal legislation prescribing the conditions under and procedures by which aliens may become naturalized citizens of the United States.

collective naturalization

Upon occasion provision has been made by Congress for the collective naturalization of a large number of people—usually the inhabitants of a newly acquired territory. This was done by treaty in the case of the inhabitants of the Louisiana Territory and of Alaska. It was done by statute in the case of the inhabitants of Texas, Hawaii, Puerto Rico, and the Virgin Islands. There are still certain American possessions, notably Guam and Samoa, whose inhabitants have not been collectively naturalized. Since we presumably intend to hold these islands permanently, there is no good reason for withholding citizenship from their residents. The President's Committee on Civil Rights recommended in 1947 that this step be taken at once.

individual naturalization

The millions of aliens who have emigrated to the United States from their native lands have for the most part been able to become American citizens individually by meeting requirements set forth in federal statutes. It is clear that the Constitution gives to Congress power to set any conditions it may wish the naturalization candidate to meet, and to prescribe any sort of naturalization procedure that it considers desirable. During much of our history citizenship by naturalization was limited to white persons and persons of African descent. But in the last decade racial and nationality barriers have been eliminated, until in 1949 the only remaining ineligible groups were the Japanese, Koreans, and certain Pacific Islanders. A bill to eliminate these last-remaining exceptions was passed by Congress in 1950 but was vetoed by the President because he felt it prescribed a discriminatory requirement.

Further statutory conditions require an applicant for citizenship to be eighteen years old, to provide proof of lawful entry into the United States, and to swear that he is not an anarchist or a disbeliever in organized government. Before citizenship is finally granted, the individual must meet such further tests as ability to speak English, continuous residence of five years in the United States, indication that he does not believe in or advocate overthrow of government by force or violence; that he is attached to the principles of the Constitution of the United States and well disposed to the good order and happiness of the United States; and that he is of good moral character. Finally, the law requires him to renounce all allegiance and fidelity to a foreign state or ruler and to take an oath that he will support and defend the Constitution and laws of the United States against all enemies, foreign and domestic, and bear true faith and allegiance to the same.

The naturalization procedure prescribed by the present statutes is an elaborate one taking at least two years for an individual applicant to complete and consisting of three distinct steps—the declaration of intention, the filing of a petition, and a final hearing in an open court before a judge. In part the naturalization system is administered by the Immigration and Naturalization Service, a unit in the Department of Justice, and in part by the courts, federal and state.

citizenship of women

The citizenship, both native and naturalized, of women has long been a troublesome matter. The difficulty results from the problem as to whether an adult woman is an independent person whose citizenship status is determined by her own actions and intentions, or whether she is a dependent person whose citizenship is governed by her husband's actions and intentions. In general up to 1922 American law and practice placed married women in the second category. But in the Cable Act of that year Congress reversed a long-standing policy and declared that an alien woman did not automatically gain citizenship by marrying an American, nor did an American woman lose her citizenship by marrying an alien. Later acts have further developed the principle that women enjoy the same status as men in acquiring and losing citizenship.

criticism of the present naturalization system

To many of the conditions imposed by Congress upon would-be citizens there can be no objection. It is reasonable to require an applicant to be able to speak English, and to indicate that he regards himself as a permanent resident of the United States. But there has been much criticism of the statutory exclusion of certain racial groups from citizenship by naturalization. Although this problem is now well on the way to a final solution, the underlying difficulties should be noted. As recently as 1943 virtually all persons indigenous to Asia were excluded.

The argument had long been made that exclusion of such groups was based on dangerous and unwarranted racial and national prejudices which had no place in a democracy. It was further argued that the policy was a foolish one in any case since it denied citizenship to thousands of persons legally resident within the United States who in many instances had lived here a quarter of a century or more and who might remain here until they died. To confine such legal and permanent residents to the status of aliens created a sort of "second-class citizenship" which was quite incompatible with the principle that all persons in a democratic society should enjoy a free and equal legal status.

Further criticism has been directed against the denial of citizenship to certain persons because of their political or religious beliefs. A notable controversy has occurred over the issue of granting citizenship to pacifists. The naturalization laws do not in so many words provide for the exclusion of pacifists. But administrative officers charged with the enforcement of these laws held during the 1920's that a congressional intent to exclude pacifists was to be inferred from the express requirement that applicants must swear to support and defend the Constitution and laws against all enemies, foreign and domestic. This ruling was followed by judges conducting citizenship hearings and was held to be correct as a matter of statutory interpretation by the Supreme Court in *United States* v. *Schwimmer*, decided by a six-to-three vote in 1929.[5] In this case the Court upheld action by naturalization officials and the lower courts, denying citizenship to an applicant, Rosika Schwimmer, well known as a lecturer and writer on public problems, who refused to promise specifically that she would take up arms in defense of the nation even though she was a woman of middle age. At her hearing Miss Schwimmer had stated: "I am willing to do everything that an American citizen has to do except fighting. . . . I am an uncompromising pacifist. . . . I am not willing to bear arms. In every other single way I am ready to follow the law and do everything that the law compels American citizens to do."

In one of the most eloquent dissenting opinions he ever wrote, Justice Holmes protested against the majority's interpretation of the statute: " . . . if there is any principle of the Constitution that more imperatively calls for attachment than any other it is the principle of free thought—not free thought for those who agree with us but freedom for the thought that we hate. I think that we should adhere to that principle with regard to admission into, as well as life within, this country."

The Court adhered to the same position in later cases in 1931. Finally, however, in 1946 in *Girouard* v. *United States*, the Court by a five-to-three vote reversed itself, and held that, in the absence of specific congressional instructions that applicants must indicate a willingness to serve in the armed forces

---

[5] *United States* v. *Schwimmer*, 279 U.S. 644 (1929). See also *United States* v. *Macintosh*, 283 U.S. 605 (1931) and *United States* v. *Bland*, 283 U.S. 636 (1931).

in defense of the nation, such a requirement cannot be inferred by naturalization officials.[6]

Congress has expressly excluded from naturalization persons believing in anarchism, and those who advocate the overthrow of government by force and violence. Some persons argue that this is unfortunate because it creates a distinction between the views which any native citizen can hold without prejudice to his citizenship and those which a naturalized citizen is permitted to hold—at least at the moment of his naturalization. It is part of the meaning of democracy that any member of the body politic is entitled to hold, and advocate, any political or social views that he pleases, subject only to the operation of general statutes, such as a sedition law, which properly limit the freedom of expression and action of all persons—citizens and aliens alike. In other words, since it is possible to control conduct that is truly dangerous to the public welfare by means of criminal statutes, it is asked whether it is proper or desirable to deny applicants for citizenship the same freedom of thought and expression which native citizens possess. If it is said that the moment of naturalization is a good one at which to make certain that potential citizens do not hold radical views which are contrary to majority public opinion the reply may be made that such a policy is based upon a misconception as to the meaning of democracy. In a democratic society there can be no requirement that the individual, who stays within the limits of conduct permissive to all persons under criminal statutes, must "conform" by accepting the beliefs or habits of the majority of the poeple.

the loss of citizenship

The Constitution is silent on the loss of citizenship, and there has been considerable controversy in our history as to the conditions under which an American may voluntarily or involuntarily surrender or be deprived of his citizenship. In 1868 Congress formally recognized the right of expatriation, so that there is no doubt that an American may voluntarily give up his citizenship, for example, by leaving the country and being naturalized in a foreign state.

Whether Congress may by law provide for the involuntary loss of citizenship by a natural-born American is not entirely clear. It has provided that members of the armed forces convicted for desertion automatically forfeit their citizenship. Likewise, under laws prevailing up until 1922 a native American woman who married an alien also lost her citizenship. However, in these cases, Congress and the courts have used the fiction that citizenship is being voluntarily relinquished by the individual because he consciously acts in a way which he knows will mean loss of citizenship.[7]

A person born abroad who claims American citizenship under the rule of *jus*

---

[6] *Girouard* v. *United States*, 328 U.S. 61 (1946).

[7] See *Mackenzie* v. *Hare*, 239 U.S. 299 (1915).

sanguinis may properly be required to meet certain statutory conditions, such as continued residence in the United States, in gaining and retaining his citizenship, since this kind of citizenship by birth is not expressly recognized by the Constitution but depends rather upon congressional action. It is also true that, because of conviction for crime or because of mental incompetence, a native citizen may be deprived of certain of the rights usually associated with citizenship, such as the right to vote, but he does not thereby lose citizenship itself.

The power of Congress to rescind the citizenship of naturalized citizens likewise remains uncertain. Congress has specified certain conditions under which such a citizen may be denaturalized, such as by residing in a foreign state for five years, or by being shown to have obtained his citizenship in a fraudulent or illegal manner. In recent years there has been a tendency for administrative officials to use denaturalization as a political weapon against persons holding radical views, but the courts have checked this tendency by construing the denaturalization laws narrowly.[8]

Wholly apart from the constitutional consideration, it seems clear that the power of Congress or administrative officials to provide for what amounts to involuntary loss of citizenship should be used very sparingly, if at all. Citizens of all kinds and aliens alike are subject to the operation of the ordinary laws governing the conduct of individuals, and it seems clear that the traditional punishments imposed for crime are sufficient to provide society with all the protection it needs against antisocial or disloyal conduct. In the troubled world of the present, loss of citizenship is a fearful threat to hold over the head of an individual. Moreover, power to threaten this loss is one that is peculiarly subject to abuse. It is to be hoped that all branches of the government will be slow to use this power.

the right to vote

One of the basic conditions of democracy is the participation of all mature and responsible citizens in the political process. Second only to the right of the individual to use his freedom of expression to take part in public discussion of social issues is his right to vote.

> To deny qualified citizens the right to vote while others exercise it is to do violence to the principle of freedom and equality. Without the right to vote, the individual loses his voice in the group effort and is subjected to rule by a body from which he has been excluded. Likewise, the right of the individual to vote is important to the group itself. Democracy assumes that the majority is more likely as a general rule to make decisions which are wise and desirable from the point of view of the interests of the whole society than is any minority. Every time a qualified person is denied a

---

[8] See *Schneiderman* v. *United States*, 320 U.S. 118 (1943).

voice in public affairs, one of the components of a potential majority is lost, and the formation of a sound public policy is endangered.[9]

suffrage in the Constitutional Convention

In the words of one of the delegates to the Constitutional Convention, "the right of suffrage was a tender point" to the Founding Fathers. In the end the convention dodged a clear-cut constitutional guarantee of the right to vote and instead provided that qualifications for voting in national elections should be fixed by each state. However, a careful reading of *Madison's Notes* on the convention shows that this was a victory for the pro-democracy forces, for by a seven-to-one vote the convention rejected a proposal that would have limited voting to property holders. George Mason of Virginia is reported by Madison as having made this assertion on the convention floor: "The true idea . . . was that every man having evidence of attachment to, and permanent common interest with, the society, ought to share in all its rights and privileges." [10] In referring the matter to the states, the majority of the delegates obviously believed that this would result in the broadening of the right to vote, since they were well aware of the strong democratic tendencies already evident in many of the states.

the Constitution on suffrage

The Constitution is relatively silent on the matter of voting. The only provision in the original Constitution is that in Article One, section two, which says that "the electors in each State [voting for members of the House of Representatives— originally the only federal officers chosen by the people] shall have the qualifications requisite for electors of the most numerous branch of the State legislature." Four amendments to the Constitution also have a bearing on the right to vote. The Seventeenth Amendment, in providing for the direct popular election of United States senators, repeats the language of Article One, that the qualifications for voting shall be the same as those used in each state in the election of the most numerous branch of the state legislature. The Fifteenth and Nineteenth Amendments, although leaving the fixing of voting qualifications with the states, provide that no citizen shall be denied the right to vote *in a national or state election* on account of race, color, previous condition of servitude, or sex. And the Fourteenth Amendment, in forbidding the states to deny to persons the equal protection of the laws, prohibits unreasonable classifications or discriminations affecting the right to vote. The Fourteenth Amendment also contains a so-called penalty clause which was designed to give Congress a weapon to use against states abridging the right to vote. It provides that "when the right to vote at any election for the choice of electors for President and Vice-President of the United

[9] *To Secure These Rights*, p. 8.
[10] A. T. Prescott, *Drafting the Federal Constitution* (University: Louisiana State University Press, 1941), p. 215. The full debate on the suffrage issue is reported by Prescott in pp. 212–218.

States, representatives in Congress, the executive and judicial officers of a State, or the members of the legislature thereof, is denied to any of the male inhabitants of such State, being twenty-one years of age, and citizens of the United States, or in any way abridged, except for participation in rebellion, or other crime, the basis of representation [in the House of Representatives] therein shall be reduced in the proportion which the number of such male citizens shall bear to the whole number of male citizens twenty-one years of age in such State." Except for these constitutional provisions, whose protective devices are almost wholly negative in character, the states are today free to fix the qualifications for voting in national elections as they see fit.

the growth of the suffrage

If it be true the Founding Fathers believed that in turning control of the suffrage over to the states they were opening the way to a broader exercise of the right to vote, history has supported their judgment. From 1789 on, the story of the suffrage is one of more or less continuous extension of the right until, with the adoption of the Nineteenth Amendment in 1920, the ultimate goal was reached: a society in which all mature and responsible adults, in theory, at least, were allowed access to the ballot box.

The story divides itself into three parts: (1) the gaining of universal, white, manhood suffrage; (2) extension of the right to vote to male Negroes; (3) the extension of the suffrage to women. Universal suffrage for all white men necessitated action by the states in dropping their property holding, taxpaying, and religious qualifications. Such action was widely taken during the "age of Jackson" in the 1830's and was largely completed by 1850. In theory, suffrage for Negro males was won in 1870 with the adoption of the Fifteenth Amendment; in practice, the fight to implement the amendment has been a continuous one and to this day has not been finally won. The struggle to extend the right to vote to women occupied nearly a century. As early as 1838 Kentucky established a limited right of women to vote in school elections. Wyoming, while still a territory, granted complete suffrage to women in 1869. But the movement as a whole made slow progress until the second decade of the present century, when a more vigorous campaign resulted in favorable action in many states, and the final adoption of the national amendment in 1920. Since the extension of the suffrage to Negroes has been the most difficult part of the story, and has even now not been finally achieved, the details of this struggle will be examined at greater length.

the Negro and the right to vote

It is the verdict of the President's Committee on Civil Rights that "the denial of the suffrage on account of race is the most serious present interference with the right to vote." The history of Negro disfranchisement has been marked by the use of an almost endless series of devices to deny to the Negro the right which the Fifteenth Amendment presumably established more than three quarters of a century ago. These devices fall into two categories: those that have had a presumed basis in law, and those that have been frankly beyond the law. It is probable that intimidation, force, and even violence—and the *threat* of these—have always been the most influential factor in keeping the Negro away from the polls on Election Day. But from the beginning of the story efforts have been made to find a regular, or lawful, method of getting around the constitutional guarantee of suffrage to the Negro. As one method has been held unconstitutional, another has taken its place; and up to now the ingenuity of the dozen or more states in which the Negro has been generally disfranchised has enabled them to keep pace with adverse Supreme Court decisions. Four "legal" methods that have been widely used to prevent the Negro from voting will be examined. They are (1) discriminatory administration of literacy tests, (2) the "grandfather clause," (3) the poll tax, and (4) the "white primary."

discriminatory administration of literacy tests

One of the earliest devices used to disfranchise the Negro was the literacy test. For example, a provision in the Constitution of Mississippi which became effective in 1892 required a voter to be able to read any section of the constitution, or to understand and give a reasonable interpretation of a section read to him. There was no discrimination against the Negro on the face of this provision, but it was relatively easy to administer the test in such a way as to allow whites, but not blacks, to qualify. This device met the test of constitutionality when in 1898 in *Williams* v. *Mississippi*[11] the Supreme Court held that it had not been shown that the actual administration of the test was discriminatory, but only that discrimination was possible under it.

That this device has persisted to present times is illustrated by an amendment added to the Alabama Constitution in 1946 by which voters were required "to understand and explain" provisions of the federal Constitution. Some of the sponsors of this amendment were frank to admit that it could be used to discriminate against potential Negro voters. Actually the 1946 Alabama amendment was declared invalid by the federal courts.[12]

the "grandfather clause"

Whether constitutional or not, the device was early discovered to have practical limitations, for it was not always easy to distinguish in its use between illiterate

---

[11] *Williams* v. *Mississippi*, 170 U.S. 213 (1898).
[12] Early in 1949 the Supreme Court without opinion affirmed a federal district court judgment to this effect. *Schnell* v. *Davis*, 336 U.S. 933.

whites and illiterate Negroes. Accordingly, a number of states soon went a step further than had Mississippi in 1892 and developed the so-called "grandfather clause," which provided that persons could qualify as voters either by showing that they or their ancestors were eligible to vote before the adoption of the Fifteenth Amendment, or by passing a literacy test. In general, whites could qualify under the first alternative and thus avoid the ofttimes embarrassing need to pass a literacy test, whereas the only course open to most Negroes was to pass the literacy test. In 1915 the grandfather clause in the Constitution of Oklahoma was declared unconstitutional by the Supreme Court in *Guinn* v. *United States*.[13] However, during the years the clause had been in effect in Oklahoma it had served its purpose by enabling whites to get their names on permanent registration lists, leaving Negroes still faced with the necessity of passing at the very least a nondiscriminatory literacy test.

the poll tax as a means of discriminating against Negro voters

At one time or another many states have required the payment of a poll, or head tax, and often this has been made a prerequisite to voting. In some states the tax is cumulative, and the taxpayer who has fallen behind must pay more than one year's tax before he can vote. The poll tax has effectively disfranchised large numbers of whites as well as blacks,[14] but because of the poor economic status of the average Negro in the South, the tax, even where administered without discrimination, has been particularly effective in keeping the latter from voting. In 1948 there were still seven states—all in the South—which used the tax as a prerequisite to voting. No successful constitutional attack upon the tax has been made, or probably can be made.[15] Instead, the opponents of the poll tax have concentrated their efforts upon securing its repeal in the states using it or have tried to secure the enactment of a federal statute outlawing the tax as restricting the right to vote in national elections. In 1949 the House of Representatives passed such a bill for the fifth time, but these bills have always been defeated in the Senate, usually by means of the filibuster.

the white primary

The most effective, modern, "legal" device for disfranchising Negroes was, for many years, the white primary. This device was based upon the assumption that the Negro might safely be allowed to vote in the final election in southern states (subject to other forces which tended to hold down his numbers there) if he

---

[13] *Guinn* v. *United States*, 238 U.S. 347 (1915).

[14] On this much overlooked point of the disfranchisement of whites through the poll tax requirement see Donald S. Strong, "The Poll Tax: The Case of Texas," *American Political Science Review*, XXXVIII (August, 1944), 693, 696-697, 701-707.

[15] As early as 1898 in its decision in the *Williams* case the Supreme Court upheld the poll tax as a prerequisite to voting.

SUFFRAGE IN POLL TAX STATES

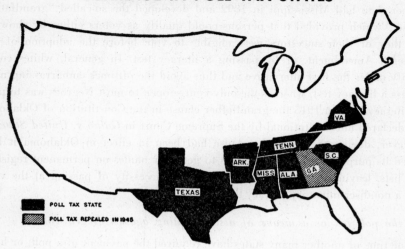

POLL TAX STATE
POLL TAX REPEALED IN 1945

POTENTIAL VOTERS WHO VOTED IN
THE 1944 PRESIDENTIAL ELECTIONS

**8 POLL TAX
STATES ---- 18.31%**

**40 NON-POLL
TAX STATES-- 68.74%**

This chart, which is taken from the Report of the President's Committee on Civil Rights, is perhaps misleading in that it suggests that the poll tax alone was responsible for reducing the size of the electorate in these eight states in the 1944 election. Actually many forces contributed to the result. However, the fact remains that the electorate is much smaller in poll tax states than in states with no poll tax. (*Source: The Report of the President's Committee on Civil Rights,* To Secure These Rights. *Government Printing Office, 1947. Data taken from U.S. Bureau of the Census.*)

were prevented from participating in the primary election of the Democratic party, where the real choice of public officers is made. The constitutionality of the white primary has been the subject of four highly controversial cases decided by the Supreme Court between 1927 and 1944, all four of which involved the Texas white primary. In the first two the Court held the Texas device invalid on the ground that it rested on state statutes which operated to deny Negroes the equal protection of the laws contrary to the Fourteenth Amendment.[16] In the third case, *Grovey* v. *Townsend*,[17] decided in 1935, the Court upheld a revised white primary, which rested solely on a party regulation, on the ground that in the absence of statutory action there was no violation of the Fourteenth or Fifteenth Amendments, which are directed against improper *state* action only.

However, in one of the most sensational reversals of position ever made by the Supreme Court, the white primary was once more outlawed in 1944 in *Smith* v. *Allwright*.[18] In this case the Court held that even though the Texas white primary rested upon a party resolution rather than a state law, the Democratic party acted as the agent of the state in conducting the primary and thus party exclusion of Negroes was *state* action within the meaning of the Fifteenth Amendment. The Court said: " . . . when, as here, [the] privilege [of membership in a party] is . . . the essential qualification for voting in a primary to select nominees for a general election, the State makes the action of the party the action of the State." [19]

One last loophole remained to be plugged before the legal basis of the white primary was finally destroyed. In the *Allwright* case the Court stressed the fact that although Texas did not by law fix the conditions of membership in the Democratic party, the Democratic primary election was otherwise conducted along lines indicated in state statutes. Accordingly, South Carolina tried to get around the Court's ruling by repealing all of its laws which in any way touched upon primary elections, hoping thereby that the Court might find it necessary to rule that the Democratic primary as limited by party action to whites was a "private" undertaking, beyond the scope of the Fourteenth or Fifteenth Amendments. But the South Carolina system was also declared unconstitutional by the federal courts.[20]

the future of Negro suffrage

The President's Committee on Civil Rights in 1947 found "reports of increased voting by Negroes in many southern states, both in primary and general elec-

---

[16] *Nixon* v. *Herndon*, 273 U.S. 536 (1927), and *Nixon* v. *Condon*, 286 U.S. 73 (1932).

[17] *Grovey* v. *Townsend*, 295 U.S. 45 (1935).

[18] *Smith* v. *Allwright*, 321 U.S. 649 (1944).

[19] *Ibid.*, pp. 664–665.

[20] *Rice* v. *Elmore*, 165 F. 2d 387 (1947). The Supreme Court refused to review the case, thereby affirming the lower court's action.

tions," to be "particularly encouraging." Nonetheless, it also felt compelled to call the extension of Negro suffrage "limited and precarious." The precarious character of the gains in this field is illustrated by recent developments in Georgia. Within the last decade Georgia has dropped its poll tax requirement for voting and abandoned its efforts to maintain a white primary in the Democratic party. But in 1949 the Georgia legislature enacted a statute establishing a new registration system deliberately designed to make it difficult for Negroes to meet its requirements. Thus it is clear that the efforts of southern states to find a method of disfranchising Negroes that will meet the test of constitutionality are by no means at an end. There is good reason to believe that only the enactment and vigorous enforcement of a federal statute safeguarding the right of qualified persons to vote can bring an end to Negro disfranchisement. Congress is given ample power to enact such a statute by the Fifteenth Amendment.

denial of the suffrage to the Indian

It may be noted that a number of states have in the past refused to allow Indians to vote. As long as the tribal Indian remained in the curious position, recognized in the original Constitution, of enjoying a semi-independent status, there was some justification for such state action. But this status long ago ceased to exist in fact, and in 1924 Congress granted full citizenship to all Indians, including those who remained on tribal reservations. Nonetheless, New Mexico and Arizona continued to disfranchise Indians as late as 1947, when the President's Committee on Civil Rights surveyed the situation as to voting. Subsequent to the Committee's Report, both states acted to correct this situation and as a result Indians voted freely in the 1948 presidential election.

the penalty clause of the Fourteenth Amendment

It is frequently asked why Congress has never invoked the penalty clause of the Fourteenth Amendment against the states that have denied the right to vote to male citizens being twenty-one years of age. Undoubtedly the failure of Congress to apply the penalty in a single case is to be largely explained on political grounds. No party group in Congress could sponsor such action without inviting the kind of political reprisal which a *national* political party is always anxious to avoid. But there is a further difficulty about the clause. Although it was clearly intended as a means of protecting the Negro's right to vote, its language does not indicate such a purpose in so many words. Instead it provides for the disciplining of any state which denies *any* male adult citizen the right to vote for *any* reason other than "participation in rebellion, or other crime." Thus a state with a perfectly reasonable nondiscriminatory residence requirement, or literacy test, is technically just as much an offender against the amendment as a state which uses flagrantly discriminatory methods of disfranchising voters.

traditional voting requirements

In exercising the power granted to them by the Constitution, American states have at one time or another made use of some seven qualifications for voting. Two of these have been generally abandoned. These are property holding or tax-paying, and religious qualifications. The latter disappeared soon after the Constitution went into effect, and it is reasonably certain that a religious test for voting would today be held by the courts to violate the equal protection clause of the Fourteenth Amendment. Taxpaying or property holding qualifications had generally been dropped by 1850, although it should be remembered that seven states still make payment of a poll tax a prerequisite to voting. In some states participation in bond issue elections is limited to taxpayers. From time to time proposals are made that persons receiving public charity or employed on relief projects should be disfranchised. Such proposals ignore the fact that there are other ways in which individuals make contributions to the public good than through direct tax payments, and thus earn the right to be full voting members of society. Moreover, they overlook the truth that in a democracy all groups must have a voice in government regardless of eonomic status.

present-day prerequisites for voting

There are five general conditions which voters are required to meet today. These have to do with citizenship, residence, age, literacy, and registration. There is nothing in the Constitution which requires the states to limit voting to citizens, and in the past many states have granted the suffrage to aliens under varying conditions. However, citizenship is now an absolute requirement for voting in every state. This is a desirable limitation, provided no mature and responsible permanent residents of the country are denied the right to become citizens.

A residence requirement is maintained by every state, although the specific period of residence required by law varies from six months to two years. Some sort of minimum residence requirement is certainly defensible as a means of compelling persons to prove their good faith as residents of particular states, and also to prevent double voting. But in view of the increasing mobility of our population, a requirement which goes beyond the minimum needs of the situation— say six months—may well disqualify in an unfair manner otherwise competent voters.

Twenty-one has long been the minimum voting age in state law, and indeed this figure is given negative recognition in the "penalty" clause of the Fourteenth Amendment. However, in 1944 Georgia reduced the requirement to eighteen. In so doing it recognized that our improved systems of public education now give the high school graduate a considerable understanding of the governmental process and of public affairs, and it accepted as valid the argument that a person who is old enough to fight in defense of his country is old enough to vote. Other states have not followed Georgia's lead, and twenty-one remains for the present firmly entrenched as the minimum voting age.[21]

Something less than half of the states employ literacy tests in granting the right to vote. This generally means that the would-be voter must prove his ability to read and write. Such a requirement is legitimate if voters are to be equal to the requirements imposed by the secret, written ballot. However, the percentage of illiteracy among citizens in the United States is not large in most states. Only in states where there are still substantial numbers of naturalized citizens who have learned to speak English but not to read or write it, or in backward areas where compulsory public education is not yet a fact does the literacy test disqualify many persons. Occasionally it is suggested that the literacy test should be stiffened to the point where it would become an "intelligence" test. In fact it is so used in some states, particularly to disqualify Negroes. However attractive the ideal of an intelligent electorate may be, any attempt in practice to measure the intelligence of voters is almost certain to encourage discrimination. The possibility that an otherwise desirable policy may result in administrative abuses is not in itself enough to discredit the policy. But a proposal which seems likely to involve a high measure of administrative difficulty, if not dishonesty, should be avoided.

Most states also disqualify mental incompetents and persons who have been convicted of certain crimes. Voters are also in effect partly or wholly disfranchised where there is a dishonest count of ballots, where the apportionment of legislative seats is not based upon districts of equal population, or where district lines are drawn so as to produce unfair political results. Political manipulation of the boundaries of congressional or state legislative districts is known as *gerrymandering*. Often the gerrymander is used to secure an advantage for one party over another which is not warranted by the actual division of voting strength between them. Again it is employed to safeguard the traditional dominance in Congress and the state legislatures of rural over urban areas. In either case the result is to deny the right of equal suffrage to large numbers of voters.

Qualifications for voting are almost everywhere administered through a registration system. Persons desiring to become voters are required by state law to appear before election officials, indicate their ability to meet legal requirements, and have their names placed upon the voting list. This registration of voters in advance of elections is necessary and desirable as a means of avoiding fraud, but it obviously provides no automatic check against such a result, since the registration process itself may be marked by dishonesty. Some states maintain permanent registration lists; once a person qualifies as a voter his name remains on the list until he dies, moves away, or becomes otherwise disqualified.

---

[21] Persons eighteen years old are allowed to participate in the Democratic primary in South Carolina by party regulations.

Other states employ periodic registration systems by which voters are required to register anew every year or at some longer interval. Periodic registration perhaps holds down the possibilities of fraud by ensuring the elimination of inactive names at regular intervals, but it has the disadvantage of discouraging voting because of the annoyance of reregistration. Probably the wisest policy is to maintain permanent registration lists with ample safeguards for the regular erasure of obsolete names, and a majority of the states have moved in that direction.

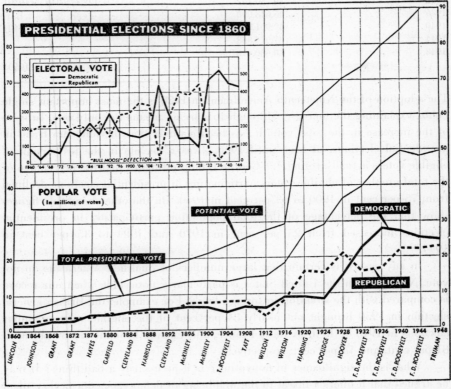

Nonvoting in Presidential Elections. (*Source: Adapted from the New York* Times, *October 31, 1948.*)

the problem of nonvoting

It has been estimated that more than one third of the people legally eligible to vote regularly fail to participate in presidential elections. The percentage of nonvoters in congressional and state and local elections is much higher. It is difficult to be accurate about such generalizations, for voting statistics are not easy to obtain. Once beyond the known data as to the number of votes actually cast in an election, increasing difficulties are encountered in trying to obtain figures showing the number of persons on registration lists, or the number of persons qualified to go on such lists.

There has been a very striking increase in the size of the presidential vote since World War I, as the following figures indicate:

Total	Presidential Vote	Population
1920	26,746,878	105,710,620 (1920)
1924	29,090,926	
1928	36,818,081	
1932	39,750,162	122,775,046 (1930)
1936	45,648,090	
1940	49,901,835	131,669,275 (1940)
1944	47,974,868	
1948	48,680,416	
		150,697,361 (1950)

The adoption of the Nineteenth Amendment in 1920 is the most important single factor explaining the increase, although it is by no means the only one. In spite of the increase in the total vote, it has been claimed that the long-run trend in presidential elections, at least until 1936, "was a decline in the proportion of eligible voters actually voting." [22] George Gallup estimates that the percentage of the total number of eligible voters participating in presidential elections declined from 75 per cent in 1900 to 63 per cent in 1940. On the other hand, his figures show that the percentage of the total population participating in presidential elections increased from 25 per cent in 1920 and 1924 to 35 per cent in 1944.[23]

In any case it is certain that large numbers of qualified Americans do not vote. Nonvoting in the United States is particularly noticeable when our record is compared with the situation in foreign lands. For example, the British general election in 1950 brought out nearly 84 per cent of the eligible voters. Similar elections in 1945 or 1946 in Italy, France, and Canada brought out 89 per cent, 81 per cent, and 74 per cent, respectively.

What is the significance of nonvoting? Is it necessarily a bad thing? It may be argued that it offers a threat to the well-being of democracy, since every silent voice is one of the potential components of a majority which might well differ from the actual majority. However, it is difficult to demonstrate the extent to which the vote actually cast produces a result different from the one that would prevail if 100 per cent of the eligible voters went to the polls. For example, it has been observed that nonvoting is greater among low-income groups than among

[22] V. O. Key, *Politics, Parties, and Pressure Groups* (New York: Thomas Y. Crowell Company, 1st. ed., 1942), p. 607. All references to this book are to the 2d edition, published in 1947, unless the 1st edition is specifically indicated, as here.

[23] *The Gallup Political Almanac for 1948* (Princeton: American Institute of Public Opinion, 1948), p. 13.

high-income groups. Since the Democratic party is seemingly stronger among the former it has been said that a large turnout of voters favors it, and a small turnout favors the Republicans. But this theory seemed to fail in 1948, when the Democratic party won a totally unexpected victory, and won it in the face of a smaller total vote in the presidential election than had been predicted.

Nonetheless, it seems probable that the pattern of nonvoting is such that the votes actually cast in a national election do not constitute an accurate cross section of the total electorate. Professor V. O. Key has raised the question, for example, as to whether the larger vote cast in presidential elections as opposed to congressional elections does not tend to place in office a President who is more liberal than the members of Congress, with the result that friction within the government is accentuated.[24]

efforts to increase voting

It has been traditional for candidates, newspaper editorial writers, and civic organizations to urge voters to turn out on Election Day, and sporadic efforts are made in each election by nonpartisan groups to get voters to the polls. In principle, such efforts are commendatory, but it is doubtful whether they make much sense in practice. In the first place, it is likely that only the party organizations or closely affiliated agencies, such as labor unions, enjoy much success in turning out the vote, since they alone have a practical argument to use with the reluctant voter. The argument of the civic group that voting is important, regardless of the way the ballot is cast, is not apt to carry much weight with the indifferent voter. In the second place, if he is finally persuaded to go to the polls may not his participation in an election do real injury to the public good? If he votes blindly he may well give his vote to the poorer candidate. If he votes his sectional, economic, or religious loyalties he may well strengthen a particular election bloc to the point where it gains additional power.

bibliographic note

The standard work on American citizenship is Luella Gettys, *The Law of Citizenship in the United States* (Chicago: The University of Chicago Press, 1934). A more specialized work that examines the status of the alien in the United States, and particularly of Asiatic aliens who have been ineligible for citizenship, is Milton R. Konvitz, *The Alien and the Asiatic in American Law* (Ithaca: Cornell University Press, 1946). An article by James A. Gathings entitled "Loss of Citizenship and Civil Rights for Conviction of Crime," *American Political Sci-*

---

[24] Key, *Politics, Parties, and Pressure Groups,* p. 588.

ence Review, XLIII (December, 1949), 1228, considers the difficult issue in American law of loss of citizenship.

A good historical account of the development of the suffrage in this country is Kirk H. Porter's *A History of Suffrage in the United States* (Chicago: The University of Chicago Press, 1918). The preparation of voting lists is examined in Joseph P. Harris, *Registration of Voters in the United States* (Washington: The Brookings Institution, 1929). An article that considers the problem of setting up a satisfactory registration system in a great city is J. P. Horlacher, "The Administration of Permanent Registration in Philadelphia," *American Political Science Review*, XXXVII (October, 1943), 829. The extension of the vote to Negroes has been one of the major chapters in the history of the suffrage. Aspects of this problem are considered in Henry L. Moon, *Balance of Power: The Negro Vote* (Garden City: Doubleday & Company, 1948); O. Douglas Weeks, "The White Primary: 1944–1948," *American Political Science Review*, XLII (June, 1948), 500; Donald S. Strong, "The Rise of Negro Voting in Texas," *American Political Science Review*, XLII (June, 1948), 510.

the role of the political party

$\mathscr{T}$HE American political party is perhaps the best illustration of the development of the American governmental system outside the realm of the written Constitution. There is not a word in that document about the role played by political parties in the operation of American government. Such all-important matters as nominating conventions, caucuses, party committees and chairmen, and other details of party machinery and procedure are conspicuous by their absence. For that matter, the Constitution is either silent or nearly silent on related matters of politics. There is, of course, no mention of pressure groups and pressure politics. Very little is said about the conduct of elections and the right to vote.

It must not be supposed from this that political parties were unknown to the men who drafted the Constitution in 1787. Political parties were even at that time a common enough phenomenon, and the decision of the Philadelphia convention was a conscious one to establish a governmental system which might be kept free of party factionalism. Although political parties were not debated in the Convention, Washington well expressed the attitude of many of the Founding Fathers when in his Farewell Address at the end of his presidency he warned against the "baneful effects of the spirit of party."

On the other hand, the language of the Constitution did not preclude the development of a party system in the United States on an extraconstitutional basis. Indeed, it is possible that some members of the convention expected such a development. James Madison, in Number 10 of *The Federalist*, which was originally published in November, 1787, stated: "A landed interest, a manufacturing interest, a mercantile interest, a monied interest, with many lesser interests, grow up of necessity in civilized nations, and divide them into different classes, actuated by different sentiments and views. The regulation of these various and interfering interests forms the principal task of modern legislation, and involves the spirit of party and faction in the necessary and ordinary operations of government."

In any case, rival political parties appeared upon the national scene before the end of Washington's administration, and they have been with us ever since. This suggests that there is an inevitability about political parties in a modern democracy; it suggests that they perform necessary functions. Moreover, we should not allow the fact that the party system has developed outside the realm of the written Constitution to lead us to the conclusion that parties are merely a supplementary aspect of our system of government. Professor E. E. Schattschneider has pointed out that parties are not "merely appendages of modern government; they are in the center of it and play a determinative and creative role in it." [1]

the value of party government in a democracy

In theory, political parties come into being in a governmental system such as our own to meet two strongly felt needs. In the first place, the party provides an agency through which people who have certain interests in common and who wish to influence the course of public policy in the light of those interests may express themselves. The party is a simple and obvious means by which such people are enabled to organize their strength and to try to win control of the government. It may be said at once that at many points in American history political parties have failed to function in such a responsible manner, for they have not always enabled voters who think alike to work collectively to control the government. But this failure of political parties at all times to live up to the ideals that men hold for them does not alter the fact that such ideals have been responsible for the appearance and continued existence of political parties.

In the second place, the party, more than any other agency or force, tends to keep the wheels of government in a democracy turning. There is always the danger that government, confronted with the enormity of the tasks it is expected to perform, and with conflicting judgments as to the best way ahead, will become ineffective and inactive. Government is a great leviathan, but there is a danger that its own size and strength will make it as ineffective as were certain of the prehistoric monsters. Professors P. H. Odegard and E. A. Helms have pointed out that "unless the numerous and conflicting interests in the community can somehow be united upon some basis to allow for effective governmental action the result will be deadlock, impotence and ultimate disaster. To bring about this unity is the major contribution of political parties to the process of government."[2] By the phrase "party government" is meant, then, a system whereby political parties actually undertake to run the government—to run it smoothly and effi-

---

[1] E. E. Schattschneider, *Party Government* (New York: Rinehart & Company, Inc., 1942), p. 1.
[2] P. H. Odegard and E. A. Helms, *American Politics* (New York: Harper & Brothers, 1938), p. 8.

ciently, and to run it in a *responsible* manner. Professor James M. Burns describes party government as "a condition where centralized and disciplined parties formulate national policy on key issues and use government machinery to carry out that policy." And he adds: "Ideally, party government works as follows: As a result of winning a majority of the votes, one of two rival political parties wins power. Its platform is attuned to national needs. Its leaders are responsible to a majority of the people. The head of the party becomes President, and other high-ranking party officials assume key positions in Congress, in the Cabinet, and in state governments. A group of national politicians tries to translate majority will into majority rule, and in doing so puts the general interest above special interest."[3] Thereafter, if things go badly, the voters can blame the party in power, turn to the opposition party in the next election, and give it control of the government.

the functions of the political party

The functions of the political party in a democracy may be stated in a variety of ways. A list of functions may be prepared which stresses the practical, everyday activities of the party, such as getting the voters to the polls on Election Day, or holding legislative caucuses to select the officials and committee members of a legislature. Or it is possible to discuss the role of the party in general, theoretical terms, stressing, for example, the way in which parties serve to implement democracy. Striking a middle ground, it may be said that the party should serve three purposes: (1) it should define the political issues of the day and sharpen the choice between the alternative paths which may be followed by government; (2) it should present to the voters, and strive to elect, candidates who are committed to announced positions with respect to the issues of the day; and (3) it should accept responsibility for the actual operation of government. With respect to the third function of the party, a distinction should be made between the roles played by the majority and the minority parties. It is the function of the majority party to organize the government, both in the legislative and in the executive branches, and to carry out its announced policies during the period that it holds power. It is the function of the minority party to engage in constant criticism of the governmental policies which are formulated by the majority, to scrutinize carefully the manner in which these policies are administered, and to keep the possibility of alternative legislative policies and administrative practices constantly in the view of the electorate.

An important aspect of the party's role in operating the government is the way in which parties serve to minimize the force of the principle of the separation of powers and to bridge the gaps which the Constitution establishes between

---

[3] James M. Burns, *Congress on Trial* (New York: Harper & Brothers, 1949), pp. 193, 194. Reprinted by permission of Harper & Brothers, publishers.

the branches of government. Where one party wins control of the presidency, the Senate, and the House of Representatives—which is the normal result of a national election—these three agencies tend to reflect their common party control and to cooperate in the achievement of common goals. Of course, it must be said at once that where an election results in divided control of the government by two or more parties, the separation between branches provided by the Constitution is accentuated, and the party system may for the period following such an election bring the wheels of government to a complete stop in a way which even the most staunch advocate of separation of powers could not have contemplated.

This threefold description of the functions of the party partially, at least, emphasizes the theoretical, and it may readily be observed that practice does not always coincide with theory in the world of politics. In practice our parties never fail to go through the business of seeming to take a stand on the issues of the day, presenting candidates for public office, and operating the government when successful at the polls. But it often seems as though a party is more interested in advancing the desires of men for personal power and prestige, or in controlling the distribution of patronage to its faithful followers than it is in electing candidates to office who will carry out announced policies. But here we should realize that the failure of political parties to perform at all times the functions assigned to them by political theory does not prove that the theoretical analysis is false or even misleading. There is much evidence in American history to show that parties have, in their imperfect way, played the role which theory assigns to them. Schattschneider has stated:

> It is doubtless true that the victors rarely understand fully the value of the powers they have won and that they do not use as effectively as they might the powers resulting from their success, but it is a misconception of the truth to imagine that they do not look beyond the public payroll. The power which results from the winning of a Presidential election is so great that even the refusal to do something about it is a significant exercise of power. Recent history proves how great the stakes of an election may be—in 1932 the Democratic Party, perhaps in spite of itself, was used by the nation to produce a reversal of public policy so great that it is difficult even now to estimate its consequences.[4]

the American two-party system

There is no inevitability about a two-party system—even in a democracy. In France the parliamentary system has long seen half a dozen or more major

---

[4] "Pressure Groups Versus Political Parties," *The Annals* of the American Academy of Political and Social Science, CCLIX (September, 1948), 17, 21. Reprinted by permission of the publisher.

parties competing with one another for control of the government. Likewise, in most of the European republics which enjoyed a brief life between the two world wars the multiparty system was present. This system has the obvious advantage of providing a more adequate basis for the representation of the many groups into which a modern society is divided. On the other hand, British parliamentary government has for a century and more used the two-party system. For a brief period in recent English history it appeared that the rise of the Labour party would result in a three-party system, but the Labour party has now all but supplanted the Liberal party, and it is likely that it alone will henceforth oppose the Conservative party in a traditional two-party conflict.

At the other extreme, notice should be taken of the one-party systems of the Soviet Union, of Germany under Hitler, and of Italy under Mussolini. But the Communist, Nazi, and Fascist parties are characteristic of totalitarian states, and it is difficult to imagine a democracy (at least in the sense in which the Western world uses this word) in which there is for any length of time but one party. The democratic alternatives are the two-party and the multiparty systems.

why we have a two-party system in America

One can only speculate as to the reasons why the two-party system has gained such a strong foothold in the United States. Presumably chance has played an important part, as it frequently does in the evolution of political institutions. But there are three factors which have certainly influenced this result. The first is the early tendency of the American people to divide into two, and only two, groups over a political issue—a tendency that may well have been inherited from our English forebears, who had resolved most of their political issues into conflicts between a Tory and a Whig position.[5] In this country, the conflict over the Constitution and the new, centralized government which it established divided people into pro and con groups which quickly became the nuclei of the Federalist and Antifederalist parties. Behind this two-way political alignment and perhaps largely responsible for it was a twofold economic division of the people into an agrarian class and a mercantilist or business class. The former provided much of the initial opposition to the Constitution and strong, central government, and the latter provided most of the support. This original division into two political groupings set a pattern for the American party system which unquestionably had a lasting influence.

A second factor explaining America's two-party system is the use of the presidential rather than the parliamentary form of democratic government. The election by the voters of a single chief executive as opposed to his selection by the legislature from among its own membership has always strongly encouraged

---

[5] V. O. Key calls this tendency a "dualism of interest." *Politics, Parties, and Pressure Groups* (New York: Thomas Y. Crowell Company, 2d ed., 1947), p. 220. See also Arthur W. Macmahon, "Parties, Political; United States," *Encyclopaedia of the Social Sciences*, XI, 596–601.

a two-way division within the electorate so as to permit an effective majority choice. It is easier for a majority of multiparty representatives in a legislature to compromise their differences and to pick a Prime Minister than it is for
the masses of voters, owing allegiance to a variety of parties, to agree finally
upon a President. Moreover, the specific language of the American Constitution
requiring majority agreement if a President is to be chosen by the electoral college has provided a further force limiting the number of presidential candidates
to two—and thus political parties to two. It is true that the Founding Fathers
contemplated elections in which there would be numerous candidates at the electoral college stage, and expected that the final choice would often be made by
the House of Representatives from among "the five highest on the list." But this
expectation existed in the absence of any thought that separate political parties
would have their respective candidates for the presidency which they
would strive mightily to elect to office. Once that condition came into being, as
it promptly did, the number of major parties could not exceed two without creating the strong possibility of ineffective voting by the electoral college. Of course,
parties could still strive to win the election in the House, as they did in 1800 and
again in 1824, when it became necessary for the House to complete the electoral
process. But the addition of this extra step was certain to confuse the situation
in a presidential election and to lessen the influence of the voters in controlling
the result. And even in the House of Representatives the requirement of the Constitution is that "a majority of all the states shall be necessary to a choice." Hence
the voters had a good reason to limit their differing political views to those supported by two-party groupings. Moreover, the election of single chief executives
at the state and local levels has served further to strengthen the two-party system.

The third factor which has operated to bring about a two-party system is
the use of single-member districts for the election of members of Congress and of
most state and local legislative bodies. The presence of three or more candidates
in such an election creates a strong possibility that a plurality rather than a majority of the voters will control the result. Where three or more legislative seats
are to be filled by the voters of a single district, it is possible to use an electoral
system known as *proportional representation*, which enables three or more parties to divide the seats in direct proportion to the percentage of the total vote won
by each party. But obviously in a single-member district one party only can win,
and under such circumstances it is not surprising that the voters should prefer
that the winning party be a majority party rather than just the strongest of a
number of minority parties. It should be pointed out that the Constitution does
not require the election of members of the House of Representatives from single-
member districts. But throughout most of our history Congress has by law required the use of the district system. Moreover, the election of senators is in

effect a single-member district undertaking since a state does not normally elect more than one senator at a time.

consequences of the two-party system

There are two important consequences of the two-party system in the United States. In the first place, our elections are usually decisive, and one party receives a mandate to govern which is given by a majority of the voters. In general this has been true, even though it is possible for one party to win the presidency and the second party to win control of one or both houses of Congress. In no presidential election since 1884 has the winning party failed to gain control of both the presidency and Congress. It should be noted, however, that in five out of sixteen off-year congressional elections the opposition party has gained control of one or both houses. In the 160-year period from 1789 to 1949 one party controlled all three political agencies of the government for 94 of these years.

Offsetting this first consequence is a second one which looks in the opposite direction. In a two-party system the choice of party membership available to the voters is often such a narrow one that each of the parties inevitably becomes the home of many diverse factions. This puts strong pressure upon each party to become a compromise agency which appeals to different blocs of voters—indeed to all voters across the entire political spectrum. This can only be done by making the party's stand on the most controversial issues of the day open to many interpretations. It does not follow that the two parties must become identical or that the price a party must pay for the support of a majority of the voters is necessarily an evasion of all of the issues. But it is clear that a successful appeal to the twenty-five million or more voters whose support is necessary for the capture of the presidency can only be made by promising many things to many people to an extent that often means flatly contradictory positions. Thus, a political victory in a two-party country provides the winning party with a majority mandate, but the party may have purchased its victory by making an appeal so broad and universal that it does not have an orderly, systematic program to put into effect.

the Democratic and Republican parties

An examination of the present-day Democratic and Republican parties is obviously the best way of determining the character of the parties produced by a two-party system. It is at once apparent that the two parties are both like and unlike each other. Since the days of the Civil War, the Republican party has found the core of its strength in an East-West coalition which has brought it the support of the businessman and the farmer. The Democratic party has depended upon a North-South coalition which has given it the support of the agrarian South and that of the urban proletariat in the North. Needless to say, both of these coalitions have been exceedingly tenuous. The two constants have been the continuing loyalty of the South to the Democratic party and that of the businessman to the Republican party. But for the Republican party to win the presidency it has had to receive some support from labor, and the Democratic victories beginning in 1932 have all depended in part upon the support of western farmers.

Traditionally, the Republican party is said to stand for sound money, a protective tariff, and strong national government; the Democratic party, to stand for cheap money, free trade, and states' rights. But an analysis of national elections since the Civil War shows at once that neither party has been consistent about these policies. The banking and creditor classes of the East have favored a strong currency and conservative fiscal policies; the farmer and debtor classes have favored government subsidies, public works, and a cheap currency. Insofar as each party has appealed to all of these classes it has had to vacillate on the currency issue. For example, the 1896 and 1900 presidential campaigns saw the Democratic party under William Jennings Bryan take a strong stand for cheap money in an attempt to carry the West. But in 1904 the party nominated a "gold Democrat," Alton B. Parker, and shifted its appeal to the conservative East.

From Abraham Lincoln to Herbert Hoover, the Republican party, although frequently conservative, was always the "nationalist party" in Washington and prone to favor central rather than local power in resolving the equilibrium of our federal system. But with the advent of the New Deal in 1933 the Democratic party discovered that national power could be used to advance the interests of its supporters, and the Republicans began to assert a philosophy of decentralization and states' rights.

The truth of the matter is that sooner or later both parties have been on all sides of most of the issues that have been important in American politics since the Civil War. And yet it will not do to characterize the two parties as Tweedledee and Tweedledum. Certainly in the national elections of the last twenty years the Democratic party, in spite of its conservative southern wing, has been oriented toward strong national government, prolabor and profarmer policies, the welfare state, and internationalism. On the other hand, the Republican party, in spite of many liberals in its midst, has had a states' rights orientation and has been probusiness, laissez faire, and isolationist in its policies.

role of the third party

No nation in modern times has adhered more closely to the two-party system than has the United States. In the century and a half from 1800 to 1948 there have been but two presidential elections in which there were more than two major candidates who had any real chance of victory. In 1824 in the midst of the so-called "era of good feeling," the one period in our history when we seemed to be moving in the direction of a one-party system, the Democratic party was unable to agree upon a single candidate (these were the days before the national convention), and there were four candidates in the race, all of whom received votes in the electoral college. In 1912, the split in the Republican party resulted in two strong Republican candidates, Taft and Roosevelt, making the race against the Democratic candidate, Wilson. But although these are the only two elections out of thirty-eight in which there has been any striking departure from the two-party system, in almost all of the other elections "third-party" candidates have been in the race. The list of such parties is a long one. The Know-Nothing party, the Greenback party, the Populist party, the Prohibition party, the Farmer-Labor party, the Socialist party, and various progressive parties all have well-known places in the pages of American history. But no one of these has ever shown any signs of breaking out of the category of *minority* parties. Seldom has the presidential candidate of such a party received as much as 10 per cent of the popular vote, and only rarely has he obtained any vote in the electoral college. Only a handful of men have ever been elected to Congress by these parties. One of the strongest third-party races in our entire history was that made by the elder Senator La Follette in 1924 on the Progressive party ticket. La Follette received 4,822,856 popular votes, or 16.6 per cent of the total vote cast in that year, but he won the electoral vote of only one state, his own Wisconsin. La Follette died before the next presidential race in 1928, and with his death the Progressive party disappeared from the national political scene.

Other third parties, although not attaining the strength of La Follette's party, have shown a greater persistency. But in only two instances in our entire history have new parties been able to climb out of the third-party category and become major parties in a two-party system. The first of these was the Whig party, which in the 1830's succeeded in filling the vacuum left by the death of the Federalist party. The second was the Republican party, which supplanted the Whig party in the 1850's. In each case, the new party served no long apprenticeship as a third party. In other words, the parties whose places they took were already well on the way to disappearance, and new parties came into being to fill the vacuum left in the two-party system by these disappearances.

Although virtually all of the third parties in American history have thus remained third parties throughout their lives, it does not follow that the contribution of the third party to American politics has been inconsequential. The success enjoyed by the Whig and Republican parties in becoming major parties has always kept alive the possibility that some new party might one day do the same thing. This has not happened now for almost a century, but many third parties have won enough support among the voters to threaten the major parties with the possibility that they would at least gain the balance of power. This situation has forced the major parties to pay constant attention to the pressures exerted by third parties. Often the third party in American history has taken a more decisive, and generally more progressive, stand upon the issues than has either of the major parties. Because of its small size the third party has generally been a cohesive organization which has been able to present a consistent, systematic political program to the voters. Whenever it has appeared that any large number of voters were being attracted by such a program, sooner or later one (or both) of the major parties has been sufficiently impressed by these gains to take over at least a part of the third party's program, thus cutting the ground from beneath it. For example, in 1932, when it appeared that the Socialist party, under Norman Thomas's leadership, might well make considerable headway because of the economic depression, the Democratic party itself turned to the left, and the resulting New Deal program under Roosevelt quickly brought to an end any Socialist party growth. The small vote polled by Henry A. Wallace's Progressive party in 1948 is in part to be explained by the extent to which the Democratic party under President Truman moved to the left on such issues as civil rights and labor-management relations to meet the threat offered by the new third party. Thus it can be said that it has been the chief function of the third party to make American politics more progressive.

the legal status of parties

Although political parties have developed outside the realm of the written Constitution, they have come to have a formal, legal basis in our political system. There is no systematic description of the organization and procedure of parties in law, and much party machinery and activity still have only a traditional or customary basis. Nonetheless, many aspects of the party system are governed by statute, both federal and state—particularly the latter. Needless to say, there is a considerable lack of uniformity in the laws of the forty-eight states on the subject of political parties.

the legal definition of political parties

In most states, political parties are now defined by law in the sense that the right of a party to appear on the printed ballot is subject to statutory control. The usual requirement is that a party must have polled a certain percentage of the total vote in the last state election if it is to continue to be recognized as a party. If the party is a new one, or if it failed to poll the necessary vote, legal recognition is usually made dependent upon the filing of petitions containing the signatures of a prescribed number of legal voters. There has been much controversy about state laws on this subject. In particular, it has been argued that standards established by certain states are altogether too rigid. For example, the Wallace party failed to get on the ballot in Illinois in 1948 because of inability to meet a requirement that 200 voters in each of 50 counties must sign petitions in sup port of a new party. We are confronted here with one of the dilemmas of modern politics. In a democracy the way to the formation of new political parties must always remain open lest the dynamic quality of a democratic society be destroyed. Moreover, any substantial minority group is seemingly entitled to legal recognition even though it may show no signs of winning majority support. And yet it is clear that the democratic process can be frustrated if the voter is asked to choose from among a myriad of competing political groups. In particular the placing of control of the government in the hands of a reasonably cohesive majority is threatened. Likewise such minor but important consequences as a large and unwieldy ballot may result from a too generous policy with respect to the formation of new parties. It seems necessary, then, that the formation and recognition of political parties must to some extent be limited by law.

In addition to the statutory definition of parties, almost all states now subject to legal control such aspects of the party system as the organization and control of party machinery, conditions of party membership, the selection of candidates for public office, and expenditures in campaigns.

the party as an agency of government

Although the political party has long been subject to a considerable measure of statutory control, it has been customary until recently to regard the party as a private association of citizens which was not in any sense an official agency of the government. As recently as 1935 the Supreme Court of the United States, in the case of *Grovey* v. *Townsend*,[6] said in essence that the Democratic party in Texas was not to be regarded as an agency of the state government. However, in 1944 in the all-important case of *Smith* v. *Allwright*[7] the Court repudiated its ruling in the earlier case and held that the state, in permitting the party to conduct a primary election and select nominees for public office, makes the party's action its action.

Following the decision in the *Allwright* case, South Carolina, as noted above, tried to strengthen the argument that the political party is a private agency by repealing all state laws pertaining to the organization of parties and the conduct of primary elections. But this move found no favor with the courts. In a decision holding that action by the Democratic party in South Carolina excluding Negroes from membership in its ranks was still *state* action (and thus forbidden by the Fourteenth and Fifteenth Amendments) the federal Court of Appeals for the Fourth Circuit stated:

> The fundamental error in defendant's position consists in the premise that a political party is a mere private aggregation of individuals like a country club and that the primary is a mere piece of party machinery. The party may, indeed, have been a mere private aggregation of individuals in the

---

[6] *Grovey* v. *Townsend*, 295 U. S. 45 (1935).
[7] *Smith* v. *Allwright*, 321 U.S. 649 (1944).

early days of the Republic, but with the passage of years, political parties have become in effect state institutions, governmental agencies through which sovereign power is exercised by the people.[8]

the organization of party machinery

The organization of party machinery closely parallels the two main activities of the party: winning elections and running the government. Each of these activities has an elaborate but more or less independent machinery. To take care of the first there is the traditional party organization, hierarchal in form, consisting of a convention or caucus at the base, a central committee in the middle, and a chairman at the top. The convention is made up of a relatively large number of delegates who are chosen in varying ways and represent the rank and file of party members. It meets in election years to determine party policy, largely through the preparation of a *platform* in which the party, in theory if not in practice, takes its stand on the issues of the day; and to select the party's nominees for public office where that is not done through a direct primary participated in by all party members. The central committee is a much smaller agency, usually selected at the time of the convention and serving as the party's governing body during the period between conventions. Heading this committee is the chairman, who is the party's executive officer. There are certain other committee officers, such as the treasurer, some of which may be full-time salaried workers. Finally, the central committee, the chairman, and the non-salaried officers are usually served by a secretariat or paid staff, which may be large or small depending on the size of the party unit and the condition of its treasury.

At the level of national government the party machinery thus far described has little to do with running the government. Instead, the party there makes its presence felt through independent agencies existing within the government. This is particularly true of Congress, where the party groups in Senate and House alike organize party machinery which parallels congressional structure. This machinery is described in the chapters on Congress. Ordinarily the national chairman and the national committee have little to do directly with the exercise of legislative power by members of the party who are serving in Congress. To a lesser degree this is also true of the presidency and the executive branch of the government. In a strong sense the President's cabinet serves as the agency of the party in power so far as party control of the executive aspects of the governmental process is needed or exists.

In the area of state and local government the central committee and the chairman often have more to do with running the government than is true on the national scene. More often than not, where a city or a state has a party "boss"

---

[8] *Rice* v. *Elmore*, 165 F. 2d 387, 389 (1947). The Supreme Court refused certiorari.

he is the chairman of the central committee. Public officers entrusted with the operation of the government frequently turn to him for an indication of party authority and policy rather than to party agencies which they themselves have organized within the government.

national party machinery

We may now examine the party machinery at the national level, keeping in mind that state and local party machinery follows the national pattern rather closely. The national convention is described in detail in the chapter on presidential elections. It may be observed here that, apart from the selection of the party's nominees and the adoption of the platform, the convention has little authority, and none at all of a continuous nature. In theory, during the four-year period between conventions the party is run by the national chairman and the national committee. The latter consists of about one hundred members—one man and one woman from each state and territory—who serve without compensation. Ordinarily the committee meets only on call by the chairman, and such calls are infrequent. Apart from offering advice and help during the campaign and meeting early in presidential years to issue the call for the convention and to select the city in which it is to be held, a national committee more often than not exercises no further authority. If a party is passing through a trying period and there is rivalry among prominent figures in the party for its control, resolving such a conflict may become the responsibility of the national committee. But the committee never actually runs the party, and it seldom determines party policy except in the sense of ratifying proposals laid before it by the chairman or party members holding public office. Individual members of the committee, known as national committeemen, frequently wield considerable power within their several states, but, everything considered, their collective power is not great.

The national chairman is chosen by the national committee at the presidential convention every four years. In practice the chairman is the personal choice of the presidential nominee, and the committee merely ratifies the name suggested. The first task confronting the new chairman is to organize and conduct the party's campaign for the presidency, and in the long run this is his most important function. He is also active in the biennial congressional campaigns occurring between presidential elections, but here he and the national committee share power and responsibility with the Senate and House campaign committees organized by the party groups in Congress. Frequently a national chairman fails to serve through the four-year period. If a vacancy develops between conventions, the national committee selects a new chairman. If the party is in power the President will almost certainly tell the committee whom to select. If the party is out of power and there are rival candidates for the job as well as a struggle for control of the party, the national committee may for the moment wield great power in making a choice.

Perhaps the outstanding characteristic of the office of national chairman is its general lack of power and prestige. Seldom, if ever, has a national chairman become a "boss" in the sense that state and local chairmen often have. In the words of Professor V. O. Key, "The national chairman is, in effect, a technician, a specialist in campaign management and machine tending, who exercises his power only so long as he enjoys the confidence of the presidential nominee." [9]

the fluid character of party machinery

Party machinery, whether within or outside the government, is seldom "set" in any formal or permanent sense. Almost always it operates erratically and informally. The resting place of power is frequently hard to determine. The varying interests of different party agencies and their rivalry for power may bring them into serious conflicts, with first one agency dominating the scene and then another. For example, the possibility of a clash within a state between the state chairman (of the state central committee) and the national committeeman (the male member of the national committee from the state) is always present. There is no formal or permanent division of power and responsibility between these two party officers, and the relationship between them and the national organization at any given moment is strongly affected by personalities and the condition of the national and the local organizations.

Similarly, particularly when it controls the presidency, there are frequent clashes within a national party between the machinery under the control of the national chairman and the party machine in Congress. The former largely reflects the power and wishes of the President. Thus the President's quarrels with Congress—particularly with congressmen of his own party—are apt to bring national party headquarters into conflict with the congressional party organization. To avoid such intraparty bickering both parties have sometimes named a member of Congress to the position of national chairman. For example, in the 1948 presidential campaign, the Republican national chairman was Hugh D. Scott, a member of the House of Representatives, and the Democratic chairman was J. Howard McGrath, United States Senator from Rhode Island.

the dominant position of state and local party organizations

One of the reasons why the national chairman almost never becomes a national "boss", and why, in fact, a national party agency seldom dominates the political life of the country is that the balance of power within a party definitely rests in the state and local organizations. It has been repeatedly observed by virtually all students of the American political process that our national parties are lit-

---

[9] *Politics, Parties, and Pressure Groups*, p. 285.

tle more than loose alliances of state and local parties joined together every four years for the purpose of winning a presidential election.

reasons for party decentralization

Several reasons explain the high degree of decentralization which has almost always prevailed in the major parties of the American political system. Perhaps the most important force contributing to the relative weakness of our national parties is the enormous size and diversity of the country. In a nation of 150 million people, three thousand miles broad, and containing every social and economic diversity known to modern civilization, it is inevitable that the force of localism should be a strong one in politics. This is not to say that strong national parties are inconceivable in a democracy. But, in the main, people think first of their local sectional or economic interests, and, following the path of least resistance, parties tend to reflect these interests. This makes for strong local party organizations.

This primary reason for party decentralization is strengthened in the American political system by the ways in which we elect our President and congressmen. In both cases the state is the all-important unit of the electoral process. Moreover, each state is allowed its say without regard to the stands taken by the other states, individually or collectively. Thus local interests, local personalities, *and local political machines* tend to dominate a national election. There is no strong institutional reason for a party to be closely knit nationally. True, a party wishes to win the presidency, and this necessitates collective national action. Moreover, majority and minority parties alike are under strong social pressures to provide the nation at large with responsible democratic government. Nonetheless, social and economic interests are local more often than they are national, and each member of Congress owes his power and his position, and thus his responsibility in any immediate sense, only to the people in his own state or in his own district. He can, if he wishes, come into conflict with a President who belongs to his own party, and with the national leaders of his party, and still retain his seat in Congress if his standing with his state organization and his constituents remains strong.

The dominance of local parties is further explained by our use of the federal system of government. The forces which have already been mentioned as being conducive to party decentralization might not in themselves bring about such a result were it not for the fact that state and local party organizations are bound to be strong because of the needs of state and local politics. Since these local party units exist to run state and local governments, it is natural that a national party should be built upon them. Thus the decentralizing forces that exist in national politics find ready machinery through which to express themselves because strong local party units already exist for reasons apart from these national forces.

party members

Membership in the Democratic or Republican parties is on the whole easily acquired and is a largely informal status. Such membership is not at all comparable to membership in the single party of a totalitarian state or in certain minor parties in the United States, such as the Communist party. Membership in a totalitarian party is usually limited to a small elite group which is thoroughly indoctrinated in party policy. Persons accepted into this group must first meet strict requirements imposed by the party itself and must thereafter observe a rigid discipline. Membership in one of the major American parties is acquired by the qualified voter almost for the asking; its acquisition is determined in good part by state law rather than by party rules, and once acquired it imposes no responsibilities upon the voter and is readily sloughed off.

In a recent case in which the Supreme Court found it necessary to pass upon the difficult issue as to whether the Communist party is an ordinary party in the American tradition, Justice Jackson made an interesting attempt to describe membership in our regular parties which is worth quoting in full:

> What constitutes a party? Major political parties in the United States have never been closely knit or secret organizations. Anyone who usually votes the party ticket is reckoned a member, although he has not applied for or been admitted to membership, pays no dues, has taken no pledge, and is free to vote, speak and act as he wills. Followers are held together by rather casual acceptance of general principles, the influence of leaders, and sometimes by the cohesive power of patronage. Membership in the party carries with it little assurance that the member understands or believes in its principles and none at all that he will take orders from its leaders. One may quarrel with the party and bolt its candidates and return again as much a member as those who were regular. And it is often a source of grief to those who have labored long in the vineyard that late arrivals are taken into the party councils from other parties without scrutiny. Of course, when party organization is of this character, there is little ground for inference that all members are committed to party plans or that they are agents for their execution.[10]

Insofar as being a member of the Republican or Democratic parties means voting for Republican or Democratic candidates in a final election, the status is entirely subject to the voter's discretion, and indeed the party itself cannot even know for certain who its members are! If it means participating in a party primary and helping nominate a party's candidates for public office, membership may be made subject to certain conditions. To participate in a *closed* party primary, a voter is required by law to declare his allegiance to a party and often to indicate that he voted for the party's candidates in the last election. Such a declaration may be challenged by party watchers at the primary, in which case a

---

[10] *American Communications Association* v. *Douds*, 339 U.S. 382, 431–432 (1950).

decision is ordinarily rendered by election officials. Moreover, party membership in such a system is not easily abandoned, for once having participated in the primary of a party the voter is frequently required by state law to wait a period of years before he can shift his allegiance to another party, or to appear before election officials and ask permission to make such a change. Some states employ the *open* primary system in which ballots containing the lists of all parties are readily available to the voter and he makes his selection of a party list in the privacy of the polling place. Under such circumstances party membership is not only to be had for the asking but may be readily surrendered at the next primary in favor of membership in another party.

Where the convention rather than the primary is used to nominate candidates, the right to participate in the selection process, i.e., the right to become a party member, is apt to be more strictly controlled not only by state law but by party regulations. Attendance at such a convention as a delegate is almost certain to be limited to party "regulars." The right to vote for such delegates, if they are chosen in a primary, is apt to be subject to the same conditions as the right to party membership indicated above. If they are chosen in local conventions or caucuses, the right, as a party member, to vote for such delegates may be more rigidly controlled.

the party's dual personality

In the light of what has been said about rival agencies within a party organization and about the informal character of party membership, it appears that a political party is a somewhat nebulous thing. To explain just what the Republican or the Democratic party is, of what it consists, where one can find it, or what it does, is not easy. However, the true nature of an American political party is perhaps suggested when it is observed that a party has two beings. One is the voters; the other is the officeholders and the organization leaders. In one sense the 25 million persons, more or less, who vote for a party's presidential candidate are *the party*. They give it its strength; in the final analysis they determine its personality and its policies. But in a more practical sense the men who hold public office or who run the party organization are the party. They determine party policy in the more immediate sense, and they, rather than the voters, actually make use of the power the party holds in the American governmental system. Key has observed: "In the major political parties the sense of group membership felt by the party followers is so slight that for all practical purposes the party machine is the party." [11]

the independent voter

In spite of the informality of party membership, there are many people who reject even this vague status and who insist upon being known as independent vot-

---

[11] *Politics, Parties, and Pressure Groups*, (1st ed., 1942), p. 294.

ers. Presumably these are the voters who split their ballots in an election and who move back and forth between the parties from election to election. Their number is difficult to determine accurately. Gallup has estimated that they constitute about 20 per cent of the total electorate, and his figure is probably a reasonably good one. In any case the number of voters who do not regard themselves as either Republicans or Democrats is considerable, and the problem they pose is thus an important one to our political life. Generally speaking, independence in politics is regarded as a virtue; it is a sign of the intelligent voter who weighs the issues, evaluates the candidates, and then votes as wisely as he can in an attempt to advance the general welfare.

Actually there is good reason to question whether the independent voter is as good a citizen as the party member. There is no need to pass moral judgment on the independent, but in the light of purely practical considerations he perhaps leaves something to be desired. For one thing, the true independent cannot very well participate in party primaries or conventions, and thus, in effect, he washes his hands of the all-important business of nominating candidates for public office. Furthermore, insofar as the political party more than any other single force has been responsible for the increasingly democratic character of the American political system, the independent voter has failed to play a direct part in this important development. In other words, if all voters insisted upon being independents, there would be no parties, and responsible government would be an impossibility.

The most important practical contribution which the independent voter makes to American politics is the competition for his support which he stimulates. The parties do not know which way he will vote, so they must do their best to win his support by offering able candidates and an attractive stand on the issues. But in view of the ease with which even so-called party members may desert the party in any given election, it may be asked whether the party is not compelled to put its best foot forward without paying any particular attention to the independents. If this is so, does not independence in politics cease to be a virtue? Does it not gain little for the individual voter while denying to society the benefit of his voice in the selection of candidates and the making of party policy? However, if by independence in politics is meant simply the tendency of a substantial number of party members to regard their party allegiance as free from traditional influences, such as family or sectional loyalties, and thus temporary only, then independence in politics is not only virtuous morally but a practical asset to good government.

continuing controversy as to the party system

There are two aspects of the present party system in the United States which are the subject of much controversy. One is the compromise character of our two major parties; the other is their high degree of decentralization. Although each of these conditions is the result of deep-seated and complex forces, neither is necessarily inevitable. If change in either respect seemed wise, pressures to move in new directions could be brought.

the compromise character of the political party

The extent to which the major parties in American politics duplicate each other's candidates and policies in appealing to all classes of voters has already been noted. It is easy to argue against this situation. Since it is the purpose of parties to make democratic government responsible to the voters, then it is desirable that parties sharpen the choice between alternative policies in attacking the great issues of the day, and present rival candidates for office who stand for different programs. It has been traditional to condemn our parties because they fail to do this, thus forcing the voter to choose between highly similar candidates and policies. Insofar as the facts support such condemnation the case of the critic is a persuasive one. It is hard not to agree, for example, with Professor Clarence A. Berdahl, a careful student of American politics, when he concludes: "It ought to be possible, as it would seem to be desirable, to make our major party organizations somewhat more closely knit and responsible than they now are, in order that their declarations of platform and principle may be something better than glittering generalities, may represent something like the actual views of the respective groups, and may offer some fairly clear alternative programs to the voter. [12]

And yet a strong argument can be advanced in support of the compromise character of our parties, and many keen students of American politics have advanced such an argument. For example, in *The Politics of Democracy*, Pendleton Herring develops the thesis that a democratic society can survive only where there is a constant reconciliation of conflicting economic and social interests. One of the most powerful forces working for such reconciliation is the political party which appeals to a wide variety of groups and wins their support by offering something to each. Herring says: "The accomplishment of party government lies in its demonstrated ability for reducing warring interests and conflicting classes to cooperative terms." [13]

This means that party platforms, although frequently inconsistent and evasive, make it possible for people who have clashing interests to live together in peace. In other words, opposing groups which are contending for power must keep their quarrels within narrow limits. Once the lines of conflict are too clearly drawn, once the stakes in politics are set too high, there is danger that the de-

---

[12] "Party Membership in the United States," *American Political Science Review*, XXXVI (April, 1942), 241, 262.

[13] Pendleton Herring, *The Politics of Democracy* (New York: Rinehart & Company, Inc., 1940), p. 132.

feated faction in an election will refuse to accept the result in a peaceful manner. It may conclude that too much has been lost and that it is better to oppose the result with force and violence than to permit the government to pursue policies antagonistic to its interests.

Harold Laski, the famous British political scientist, raised the question whether the day may not come in England when the Labour or the Conservative party will find itself compelled to refuse to accept the result of an election in which the other party has triumphed. Up to now the Labour party has stopped short of advocating or attempting to put into operation a program of complete socialism, and the Conservative party has stopped far short of insisting upon pure capitalism. In other words, it seems probable that the two English parties are still offering the voters sufficiently similar programs that no important bloc of voters need regard the defeat of the party it is supporting as sheer disaster. And yet it is clear that the two English parties do face in opposite directions and do give the voter a choice of alternatives that is meaningful.

Herring has pointed out that "compromise need not be sheer opportunism." [14] It has also been said: "Compromise among interests is compatible with the aims of a free society only when the terms of reference reflect an openly acknowledged concept of the public interest." [15] In the end it is perhaps fortunate that the Democratic and Republican parties should provide a cohesive rather than a divisive force in a nation as complex as our own; yet it is also desirable that they should offer the voter a substantial choice between them. If the compromise tendency is pushed too far, issues and policies may be obscured to a point where politics becomes irrational. Democracy assumes that an educated citizenry will engage in an intelligent debate of issues and that a conscious, rational choice will be made between alternative policies. Unless the political party facilitates the making of such choices it fails to play the primary role for which it exists in a democracy.

the decentralized character of the political party

A further criticism of the American party system is that the extreme measure of decentralization and the resulting lack of discipline that prevail in each of the major parties threaten the element of responsibility which the party provides in a democracy. As we have seen, the strong position occupied by state and local party organizations in American politics and the dominance of local personalities and local issues in national elections make it difficult for the national party to carry out its platform even when it wins control of both the presidency and Congress by substantial majorities. In its report, "Toward a More Responsible Two-

---

[14] *Ibid.*, p. 167.
[15] "Toward a More Responsible Two-Party System," Report of the Committee on Political Parties, American Political Science Association. Printed as a Supplement to the *American Political Science Review*, Vol. XLIV (September, 1950), p. 20.

Party System," the American Political Science Association's Committee on Political Parties states the situation in these words:

> Historical and other factors have caused the American two-party system to operate as two loose associations of state and local organizations, with very little national machinery and very little national cohesion. As a result, either major party, when in power, is ill-equipped to organize its members in the legislative and the executive branches into a government held together and guided by the party program. Party responsibility at the polls thus tends to vanish. This is a very serious matter, for it affects the very heartbeat of American democracy. It also poses grave problems of domestic and foreign policy in an era when it is no longer safe for the nation to deal piecemeal with issues that can be disposed of only on the basis of coherent programs.[16]

In favoring a strengthening of the national party it will not do to ignore the forces which are responsible for the power wielded by local party units. These forces are real, and their effect will not be overcome by moral arguments to the effect that our parties and our politicians should be more nationally minded and seek to advance the general welfare of the American people rather than the particular welfare of local groups. The general welfare always consists in good part of a mingling of local interests, and any attempt to suppress these interests completely not only is doomed to defeat but would be most unwise in principle.

It seems probable, however, that even if proper recognition be given to the force of localism in politics, a good deal might be done to give our national parties a stronger *esprit de corps*, to make them more unified and thus more responsible agencies. The steps that might be taken in this direction are exceedingly numerous, ranging all the way from the thoroughgoing reform of the American political system to minor alterations in the existing arrangement. An example of the former would be the adoption of the parliamentary system and the accompanying abandonment of separation of powers. Such a drastic alteration in our government would unquestionably heighten the discipline of the national party, for one thing because it would eliminate the present rivalry between the congressional and presidential factions in the party. The power to dissolve Congress and to call a new election possessed by the chief executive and his close associates in the national party would give them far greater prestige and authority than is now enjoyed by national party leaders. In the face of such a threat, the individual congressman, torn as he often would be between the wishes of his national leaders and the demands of his local constituents, would have to weigh the former much more heavily than he now does.

A more moderate way of achieving greater party unity would be the adoption of a national primary for the nomination of congressmen. If all Democratic

---

[16] *Ibid.*, p. v.

and Republican candidates for Congress were selected by the party voters throughout the country on a single day it seems certain that greater attention would be paid to national issues, and that national party leaders would find it easier to influence the selection of nominees in the different states and districts.

Failing such drastic or even moderate reform in the American government, there are many minor steps that might in their limited ways result in a lessening of the spirit of localism in party politics. For example, abandonment of the rule of seniority in the selection of committee chairmen and committee personnel would almost certainly strengthen the party organizations in Congress. If the individual congressman knew that his advancement to an important committee post or ultimately to a chairmanship depended not so much upon his constituents returning him to office as it did upon winning the approval of his party colleagues and leaders he would necessarily give more attention to the latter in resolving the balance between the conflicting wishes of his local district and his national leaders on a given issue.

"toward a more responsible two-party system"

A series of specific proposals looking toward the strengthening of the major political parties in the United States to make them more highly centralized and disciplined bodies is set forth in the report of the American Political Science Association's Committee on Political Parties. Several of the committee's recommendations are noted briefly at this point, although some of them pertain to electoral reform rather than to changes in party organization and procedure. Those recommendations pertaining to Congress are noted at the end of the chapter entitled "Congress at Work: Lawmaking."

1. Each party should have a national *party council* of fifty members so selected as to constitute a representative cross section of the party's leaders in federal and state public office and also of the rank-and-file party members. The council would have power to "consider and settle the larger problems of party management" including preparation of a preliminary draft of the party platform for submission to the national convention. interpretation of the platform between elections, suggestion of suitable congressional candidates to the states and districts, and preliminary screening of presidential candidates before the national convention meets.

2. National party platforms should be formulated at least every two years. They should be drawn with greater care than in the past, and should state national principles and policies to which party members in Congress and state and local party agencies would be expected to adhere.

3. National conventions should consist of about five to six hundred delegates (half the present number), more than half of whom should be elected directly by party voters on a representative basis, the others to consist of prominent party leaders in the national and state organizations and in Congress, who

would serve ex officio. Conventions should be held every two years and should serve as the parties' representative and deliberative organs in fixing the main lines of party principles and policies to which all party agencies, members, and public officers would be expected to adhere.

4. Electoral and suffrage reforms should be effected to strengthen the lines of party responsibility These would include lengthening the term of representatives to four years, establishment of congressional districts of equal population, nomination of congressional candidates in closed primaries, ultimate nomination of presidential candidates in national primaries and abolition of the electoral college and development of a system of electing Presidents that would encourage the growth of a strong two-party system in all of the states.

Whether this particular set of recommendations, or any other similar set, will actually produce the desired result of stronger, more responsible parties can be proved only in practice. In general the Political Science Association's committee has avoided spectacular recommendations whose adoption would require amendment of the Constitution. Its modest program might almost be said to constitute an absolute minimum of steps that must be taken if American democracy is to be strengthened. If the party is to fulfill its functions as an agency making for responsibility in politics and as an agency facilitating the smooth operation of government, we must move in the direction of stronger, better-disciplined national parties, and we must move toward parties that take stronger stands on issues and do a better job of fulfilling their promises when they are given power.

bibliographic note

A good introduction to the American party system is found in Arthur W. Macmahon's article, "Parties, Political: United States," in *Encyclopaedia of the Social Sciences*, XI, 591. Wilfred E. Binkley's *American Political Parties: Their Natural History* (New York: Alfred A. Knopf, Inc., 1943) provides an excellent historical background for the present-day party system. Herbert Agar's *The Price of Union* (Boston: Houghton Mifflin Company, 1950) is a detailed account of the role political parties have played in American history, stressing what the author believes to have been their great contribution, furtherance of compromise. Somewhat in contrast to the Agar volume are E. E. Schattschneider's *Party Government* (New York: Rinehart & Company, 1942) and his *The Struggle for Party Government* (College Park: University of Maryland Press, 1948), in which a plea is made for stronger and more highly disciplined parties that would take definitive stands upon the issues of the day, be less prone to compromise, and show more resistance to pressure groups. An article by Samuel P.

Huntington entitled "A Revised Theory of American Party Politics," *American Political Science Review,* XLIV (September, 1950), 669, develops the interesting thesis that the growing urbanization of the United States is resulting in a sharper contrast between the two major parties. Charles C. Rohlfring and James C. Charlesworth have edited an excellent collection of articles on the party system in the 259th volume of *The Annals* of the American Academy of Political and Social Science (September, 1948) entitled "Parties and Politics: 1948."

There are a number of excellent textbooks on the American party system, most of which also cover pressure groups. Recently published texts are Hugh A. Bone, *American Politics and the Party System* (New York: McGraw-Hill Book Company, 1949); V. O. Key, *Politics, Parties and Pressure Groups* (New York: Thomas Y. Crowell Company, 2d ed., 1947); Dayton D. McKean, *Party and Pressure Politics* (Boston: Houghton Mifflin Company, 1949) Charles E. Merriam and Harold F. Gosnell, *The American Party System* (New York: The Macmillan Company, 1929); and Peter H. Odegard and E. Allen Helms, *American Politics: A Study in Political Dynamics* (New York: Harper & Brothers, 2d ed., 1947). Harold F. Gosnell's *Machine Politics: Chicago Model* (Chicago: The University of Chicago Press, 1937) is an informative account of a local political organization.

Joseph R. Starr's long article, "The Legal Status of American Political Parties," *American Political Science Review,* XXXIV (June, August, 1940), 439, 685, examines the uncertain and somewhat anomalous position of the political party in law. Clarence A. Berdahl has written two long articles that deal systematically with the equally difficult problem of the status and character of party membership: "Party Membership in the United States," *American Political Science Review,* XXXVI (February, April, 1942), 16, 241, and "Some Notes on Party Membership in Congress," *American Political Science Review,* XLIII (April, June, August, 1949), 30, 492, 721.

"Toward a More Responsible Two-Party System," the report of the Committee on Political Parties, was published just before the national election in 1950. This committee of sixteen experts in public and academic life was appointed by the American Political Science Association in 1946 to survey the American party system. The report was published as a supplement to the September, 1950, issue of the *American Political Science Review.* It has also been published as a book by Rinehart & Company. The report contains a series of specific proposals for change looking toward the strengthening of the major national parties in the United States. In general the committee believes that our national parties should be made more highly centralized and disciplined bodies.

the role of the pressure group

*T*HE pressure group is the second formal agency which enables people with common interests to try to influence government in a democracy. No provision is made for it in the Constitution, but, like the political party, it has taken shape as the result of strong social forces which were certain to become institutionalized in one way or another.

The pressure group, like the party, took shape very early in our history. There is a tendency to think of the pressure group as a twentieth-century phenomenon, and it is true that the present-day diversification of group interests and group organizations largely reflects the complexity of modern life in an industrial civilization. Nonetheless, as we have become more aware of the important role played by pressure groups, historians have found early examples of strong organizations that functioned much as do those of today. In particular, the farmers have long been organized into pressure groups. The Grange, for example, was founded nearly one hundred years ago and was more important as a pressure group in the closing decades of the last century than it is today. Few of the famous pressure groups of today can trace their origins back to the early days of the country. But many of them had early forerunners. For example, the American Legion was preceded by the Grand Army of the Republic, an organization of Union soldiers who served in the Civil War, which for fifty years was a dominant force in national politics.

The pressure group is constantly under fire as the instrument of a selfish minority which seeks to use the government to advance its own interests rather than those of the whole people. And yet the pressure group, like the party, provides a vital missing link in our political system without which government in America could not function—at least in a democratic manner.

the difference between parties and pressure groups

Although parties and pressure groups are both agencies through which people try to influence the governmental program, they are quite unlike one another in most ways. The party is a large agency which seeks to win the active support of as many as 25 million people. Consequently its appeal must be broad and its program must deal with many problems. The pressure group consists of a varying number of people, never more than a minority of the population, who have the same specific interests. Consequently its appeal is narrow and its program limited. It is sometimes said that in actual practice the party is primarily interested in winning and holding public office; the pressure group is primarily interested in shaping public policy. The party's greatest moment comes on Election Day; the pressure group's greatest activity comes after the election is over. It is said that we have a two-party system in the United States for purposes of winning elections, and a multiparty system for purposes of determining public policy. The Republicans and Democrats are the parties that contest elections; the National Association of Manufacturers, the American Federation of Labor, the American Farm Bureau Federation, and scores of similar organizations are the parties that determine public policy.

why pressure groups do not become parties

It may be asked why a pressure group, particularly if it is a large and important one, does not run candidates of its own for public office and seek direct control of government, thereby becoming a political party. If its purpose is to bring about the enactment of laws favorable to its cause and to kill those that it views as unfavorable, how can it better achieve this purpose than by electing its own men to office? As a matter of fact, many pressure groups are subject to a strong temptation to do just that. But almost always the temptation is resisted. No pressure group, least of all a specific organization, ever has the support of anything more than a minority of the voters. Consequently, a direct attempt to take control of the government could not ordinarily hope to enjoy more than a very limited success. On the other hand, if a well-organized minority sells its support as dearly as it can to one or the other of the major parties in an election, or remains neutral in the election and then brings its pressure to bear upon the victorious party, threatening opposition in the next election, it has a far better chance of influencing the course of government.

The experience of the American Federation of Labor illustrates why even a large and well-organized minority sometimes prefers to use pressure politics rather than party politics to secure its ends. In foreign countries, such as England, and in a few American states, labor has organized its own parties. These attempts have met with some success, for labor in a highly industrialized area is a sufficiently numerous pressure group to have some chance of winning an election. But at best that chance is less than even unless a labor party is able and willing to broaden its appeal to include farmers, consumers, professional men, trades people, or other numerous groups. In fact, to become one of England's two major parties the Labour party there has had to pursue such a policy, and in so doing it has ceased to be a pure labor party. In the United States the AFL, following the lead set by its famous president, Samuel Gompers, has steadfastly refused to organize a party and has instead followed a policy of supporting its friends and opposing its enemies in public office without regard to party affiliations. In that way both Republicans and Democrats have been put on notice that the labor vote is for sale and can be had by the highest bidder. It is a rare congressman and an even rarer President who can afford to ignore entirely labor's desires with respect to government policy. The AFL has not gotten everything it has wanted through the years, but it has gotten a great deal from government, and whether it could have gotten more by direct action through its own political party may be doubted. Much the same thing can be said of the other large pressure groups—the farmers, the businessmen, the war veterans, and the religious and racial groups.

the reconciliation of parties and pressure groups

Party and pressure groups have to a large extent become integral parts of the total political process. The line between the two is not in all ways clear, and at times each gets in the way of the other. But in the main they occupy different positions, serve different functions, and complement one another. It may be said that our system of pressure politics is superimposed on our system of party politics. At the base of our national political life is the party. Its effect is cohesive; it enables the voters to forget their differences sufficiently to join together for purposes of organizing a government that has the support of a majority of the people. But this is done at the expense of blurring the issues and of ignoring the valid differences that separate interest groups. The government having been organized and a working majority placed in office through party politics, the pressure group appears upon the scene and enables its members to bring specific and direct pressure upon the government. The effect of the pressure group is divisive and, accordingly, may become dangerous. But if it does no more than enable the people to give expression to their reasonable differences, the danger to the national well-being or unity should not be too great since the expression is made through the agency of the parties.

In other words, it is possible for a congressman to be a good party member but also to show sensitivity to the demands of pressure groups. His two-way allegiance may at times prove an embarrassment to him, and the maintenance of a satisfactory equilibrium between party and pressure group is never an easy matter. Yet their relationship is a fundamentally harmonious rather than inharmonious one.

However, some critics of the pressure group are inclined to see a high degree of antagonism between the party and the pressure group. Moreover, they are apprehensive lest the latter undermine the former, for they regard the party as a more desirable agency for achieving responsible representation of the popular will than they do the pressure group. For example, Professor James M. Burns asserts: "The pressure politicians and their allies hamstring action by the majority, and to the extent that popular government rests on majority rule, they are a threat to democracy." [1] And Professor E. E. Schattschneider points out that parties and pressure groups compete with each other for the loyalty of legislators. He deplores the fact that congressmen often seem more sensitive to the influences that are brought to bear by the pressure groups than they are to the appeals of their party leaders for loyalty to the party's position on pending issues.[2] Schattschneider does not believe that there is a fundamental inconsistency between the party and the pressure group but he does argue strongly that the party should become a more highly centralized and strongly disciplined agency and that this change would automatically cut the pressure groups down to their proper size. He concludes:

> If the pressure groups are to be controlled the job must be done by the political parties. That is, the pressure groups can be made harmless by the use of a superior form of political organization. If the parties are made strong enough to take a firm grip on the policymaking machinery of the government they will be able to defend the public interest against the excesses of the organized minorities. The battle with the pressure groups will be won as soon as the parties learn to exploit their position in the government. Party government is, therefore, the liberal democratic solution of the problem.[3]

types of pressure groups

the spectrum of pressure politics

One is tempted in this day of hyperorganizational activity to say that every conceivable kind of pressure group is to be found in national politics. In terms of sheer numbers this statement does not seem to be an exaggerated one. It is difficult to make an accurate count of pressure groups, but in any case their number is very great. For example, under the Regulation of Lobbying Act of 1946 some 1,650 lobbyists and organizations had registered by the end of 1949. Moreover, the kinds of lobbies represented in the list range so widely that one is tempted to say that no group is missing. Business, labor, agriculture, the professions, consumer, the region, racial, religious, and nationality groupings, war veterans—every type of loyalty or allegiance known to man seems to be present.

And yet even a superficial analysis of these pressure groups and their activities makes it clear that there are certain areas in the spectrum of pressure politics where organizational activity is weak or nonexistent. The mere fact that

---

[1] James M. Burns, *Congress on Trial* (New York: Harper & Brothers, 1949), p. 31.

[2] See his *Party Government* (New York: Rinehart & Company, Inc., 1942), Chap. 8.

[3] "Pressure Groups Versus Political Parties," *The Annals* of The American Academy of Political and Social Science, CCLIX (September, 1948), 17, 22. Reprinted by permission of the publisher.

a group is seemingly organized and represented by a lobbyist in Washington does not prove that its influence upon the government is equal to that of other pressure groups.

There are many forces that explain the uneven character of the pressure group spectrum. Some social groupings are more nebulous than others and the individual members are either not sufficiently aware of their common interests to band together for effective political action, or they find the task of organizing difficult. This is particularly true of consumer pressure groups. Although every person is a consumer, and complaints about high prices and shortages of goods are perennial, it has always been difficult to persuade large numbers of people to support consumer pressure groups.

Other handicaps under which some pressure groups labor are lack of education and understanding among members, inadequate financial resources, and lack of social prestige. Money is by no means the only essential resource in lobbying, but it is probably the most important single factor contributing to success. Obviously, some groups are much stronger in this respect than are others. The National Association of Manufacturers can spend more money fighting for the kind of labor legislation it desires than can the American Federation of Labor, even taking into account the large lobbying funds that labor has been able to raise in recent years. Social prestige is likewise a varying factor. Professional groups, such as doctors and engineers, are in general highly respected. Thus the stand of the American Medical Association in opposition to any government policy which looks in the direction of "socialized medicine" has often carried more weight with public opinion and the makers of public policy than has the contrary stand of organizations numerically much stronger.

A further condition which makes for uneven results in pressure politics is the varying ability of pressure groups to reach the general public with their messages. Business usually has more direct access to the pages of newspapers and magazines with a general circulation and to the airwaves than has labor or agriculture. The latter groups publish their own journals but to a considerable extent circulation is confined to their own members and does not include the general public.

The mistake should not be made, then, of concluding that the American people have pushed their talent for organization to a point where all possible pressure groups exist and function with maximum effectiveness. The number of pressure groups and the variety and persistency of their activity tempt one to such a conclusion, but actual data will not support any such easy generalization.

economic groupings

The strongest and most effective pressure groups are without any doubt those which are based upon man's economic interests. There are enough noneconomic

groups which play important roles in politics to lead one to question the soundness of the *economic determinist's* assertion that all social conflicts and groupings have an economic motivation, but the facts show that the organizations that
have influenced government most through the years have been the business,
labor, and farmer groups.

Business has two great organizations which purport to speak its interests
on a general and nation-wide basis. These are the Chamber of Commerce of
the United States, and the National Association of Manufacturers. Each has an
elaborate office in Washington, and the strong influence of each in national politics has long been relatively easy to follow. In addition, there are scores of
smaller organizations representing the more specific interests of particular segments of business. Each area of business activity has a "trade association"
which zealously promotes the interests of the area, often to the point where it
is in conflict with other business groups. Such industries as steel, oil, railroads,
building construction, motion pictures, sugar, electric power, banking, shipping,
and aviation, to mention only a few of the most obvious examples, have exceedingly strong trade associations which engage in continuous and vigorous lobbying. The political paths of these organizations are often less easy to trace than
those of the two large business groups. This is particularly true of lobbying activity with respect to a specific and technical legislative proposal such as the
quota for Cuban sugar, or the ownership of oil tidelands, as opposed to lobbying
concerning a general measure such as one providing for collective bargaining
between business and labor on a national scale. Nonetheless, the available facts
show that these smaller groups in their collective activity have at the very least
as substantial an effect upon government policy and practice as do the two large
business groups.

Labor is more dependent than is business upon its two general organizations, the American Federation of Labor and the Congress of Industrial Organizations. Some of the larger affiliated unions, such as the United Automobile
Workers, as well as such large, independent organizations as the railroad brotherhoods and the United Mine Workers, also maintain strong and active lobbies.

Three national organizations represent the farmer's interests in politics.
The oldest and most conservative is the Grange, or Patrons of Husbandry. It
enjoyed its greatest influence in the closing decades of the nineteenth century,
but it is still an active pressure group. Its members are most numerous today
in the older rural areas which have been traditionally Republican. In general,
the Grange opposes government efforts to regulate or "plan" the agricultural
economy. Much the most powerful of the farm groups is the American Farm
Bureau Federation. Only slightly less conservative than the Grange, it represents the interests of the great middle-class farm population and also those of
the big commercial farmers. It has close ties to the state agricultural extension
services and it is at its strongest in the corn belt area from Ohio to Kansas. It

is not so adverse as is the Grange to government planning, and it supported the Agricultural Adjustment Acts of the 1930's. In recent years, however, it has vigorously opposed such legislation as the Employment Act of 1946 and the Missouri Valley Authority bill. The third and most liberal farm group is the National Farmers Union, which is smaller than either of its rivals. Its members come in good part from the states west of the Mississippi, and particularly from the Dust Bowl area. The Union favors extensive legislation designed to promote balanced agricultural production and to guarantee the farmer a fair annual return. Like the businessman and the worker, the farmer has also organized many smaller agencies which promote specific regional or functional interests. For example, the dairy farmers have a Milk Producers Federation, and the poorer farmers of the South are represented by the Southern Tenant Farmers Union.

A striking characteristic of economic pressure groups is the very large extent to which they represent the interests of producers rather than those of consumers. There has never been an effective national consumer organization. During the years of the depression and World War II sporadic efforts were made to establish formal agencies to represent the consumer, and there are today a few small consumer groups in existence. But their influence in national politics has never been great. Almost certainly this condition reflects the tendency of the individual man to evaluate his producer interests more highly than he does his consumer interests. In other words, we are all earners as well as spenders and we seem to be much more concerned about government policy which touches our incomes than that which affects our expenditures. Although the sharp rise in prices which followed World War II produced a powerful political reaction, it did not bring about a strengthening of consumer organizations. Farmer and worker alike continued to be more interested in increasing their incomes and wages than in organizing for lower prices.

noneconomic groupings

The organizational loyalties of the American people along noneconomic lines are so extensive that it is impossible to present a brief but inclusive analysis of pressure groups of this kind. Moreover, some organizations that appear to be primarily noneconomic in character often show a very strong interest in economic issues. Some idea of the nature and complexity of these groups can be gained by noting their number and activity under such headings as race, religion, the professions, and the military.

Many strong organizations represent the interests of racial and religious groups on the national scene. Two Negro organizations, for example, the National Association for the Advancement of Colored People and the National Urban League, keep a constant watch over government policy as it affects the interests of the Negro. Protestants frequently seek to influence government through such an organization as the Federal Council of Churches; Catholics, through the National Catholic Welfare Council; and Jews, through the American Jewish Committee, the American Jewish Congress, and the Anti-Defamation League.

All of the professions have strong organizations which are active from time to time in pressure politics in promoting their noneconomic as well as economic interests. This is particularly true of the doctors and lawyers, who through the American Medical Association and the American Bar Association have sought to influence many aspects of the governmental program ranging all the way from court organization and public health to administration of the antitrust laws. In general, the pressure groups of the professions are exceedingly conservative, and their main concern seems to be to protect the vested interests of their members. On the other hand, each profession almost always has a liberal or even radical minority within its ranks. For example, the conservative American Bar Association is somewhat offset in its political activity by that of the radical National Lawyers Guild.

Organizations representing the veterans of the wars in which America has participated have always been among the strongest of pressure groups. Such groups find an immediate and powerful incentive for political activity in such issues as pensions for veterans and their dependents, and relief and rehabilitation for the disabled. But their interest has also encompassed such issues as national defense and foreign policy. By all odds the largest veterans' organization today is the American Legion. Smaller organizations are the Veterans of Foreign Wars and the American Veterans Committee.

pressure groups within the government

In the heat of battle over a legislative proposal, references are sometimes made to the President and his cabinet, or to government employees, as pressure groups which are actively seeking to influence the result. In general this is not a sound use of terminology. Under the Constitution the President has both the power and the duty to influence the making of public policy by Congress, and many Presidents have used this power in a vigorous manner. Although the President may find himself fighting with or against particular pressure groups in the struggle over a bill, his motivation is usually quite different from that of the latter. Concern for the general welfare is usually a much more powerful influence upon the President than it is upon the typical pressure group. Presidential activity is very definitely a force which will affect congressional action, but, as we shall see at a later point, it is a force which is in contrast with, rather than a part of, the force of pressure politics. To a large extent the same thing is true of the pressure which is brought upon Congress by the administrative agencies. These agencies are bound to be interested in the formation of policies which they will be called upon to enforce, but their attempts to influence congressional action are apt to be motivated by very different considerations from those that explain pressure group activity. In general the pressures they exert reflect their experience and their knowledge rather than selfish personal interests. An exception to this is found where administrative agencies have been "captured" by private groups with whom the agencies have come in contact during their work. For example, the Interstate Commerce Commission sometimes shows a pro-railroad bias; the National Labor Relations Board, a pro-labor bias; and the Department of Agriculture, a pro-farmer bias. Another exception is found in those situations where Congress is considering the abolition of government jobs or where government employees are seeking pay increases or other job improvements. Here government employees, through their numbers and their organizational strength, are able to bring pressure upon the legislature in much the same way as do pressure groups of private citizens.

the techniques of pressure politics

Pressure groups have two main purposes. One is to influence directly the formation and administration of the government program. The other is to influence the making and expression of public opinion, and thereby to gain an indirect influence upon government, since government in a democracy is ultimately controlled by public opinion. For the achievement of each of these purposes separate techniques are used by pressure groups. Those techniques which are used in direct dealings with the government may be examined generally under the heading of *lobbying;* those which are aimed at the public mind may be considered under the heading of *propaganda.* To be sure, in the active business of pressure politics there is a good deal of overlapping in the use of lobbying and propaganda techniques. Nevertheless, as often as not, a pressure group is aware that it has two quite different jobs to do, and separate techniques have been developed for each job.

the range of lobbying activity

Lobbying may be defined as the pressure which is brought to bear directly upon public officers, usually by paid professionals, in an effort to influence and control governmental decisions and actions. Traditionally, lobbying has been thought of as directed at members of the legislature, and we have developed a stereotype of the lobbyist who wines and dines a congressman, buttonholes him in the corridors and cloakrooms of the Capitol, or who testifies before congressional committees. It should be emphasized that although the legislative arena is admittedly at the center of the lobbyist's interest, his activity is frequently directed toward administrative agencies and, upon occasion, even toward the courts. That this is so should not be difficult to understand. The making of a public law by Congress which is certain to affect the interests of farmers,

businessmen, or workers will, of course, be the occasion of vigorous and conflicting activity by pressure groups. But the influence of government upon individual interests depends upon a great deal more than the words of statutes. It
depends also upon the way in which a general policy as defined by the legislature takes on detailed meaning as it is applied to specific situations in the course
of law enforcement. For example, a statute subjecting labor-management relations to government control will inevitably be subject to interpretation and elaboration as it is enforced through court decision and administrative ruling. Accordingly, business and labor pressure groups cannot limit their activity to the
legislative arena when they know that important decisions affecting government
policy remain to be made in the executive and judicial arenas.

lobbying techniques

Lobbying techniques are extremely varied, ranging from bribery and blackmail
at one extreme, through such in-between methods as entertainment, flattery, and
offers of campaign contributions, to the use of logical arguments and the presentation of detailed and systematic information, at the other extreme. Moreover, the techniques employed by pressure groups in their lobbying activities
vary from one area of government to another. An approach that is effective
with a congressman is almost certain to give way to different methods in dealing
with an agency head or a judge. Generally speaking, the informal contacts
which a lobbyist may use in his relations with a legislator are inappropriate in
his dealings with administrators and judges.

In dealing with a congressman a lobbyist, in general, can use two techniques. He can wine and dine the congressman in an effort to establish a reservoir of good will and perhaps even a sense of obligation in the legislator's
mind. And he can present technical data or logical argument in an effort to
persuade the congressman that the course of action favored by the lobbyist is
sound or, better yet, that it will promote the interests of the congressman's constituents and win him their gratitude and support.

In dealing with an administrative agency, such as the Federal Trade Commission, the lobbyist may have to depend almost entirely upon the formal opportunity to be "heard" while the commission is contemplating the issuance of
regulations or rulings under a statute. In the case of the Supreme Court, the
pressure group's opportunity may come only in the submission of a written brief
in a case, perhaps as *amicus curiae* (friend of the court), in which brief a lobby-
ist-lawyer uses his detailed knowledge of a problem to make a telling argument
which even judges will find persuasive.

In spite of the formality of the approaches which a lobbyist must often use
in dealing with an administrator or a judge, it is important to recognize that
their utilization is part of the total process of pressure politics. The submission
of a brief to the Supreme Court by the National Association for the Advance-

ment of Colored People in a case in which the constitutionality of restrictive covenants is being determined is much more limited and circumscribed than are the methods the Association's lobbyist can employ in trying to persuade the chairman of a congressional committee to give an FEPC bill his vigorous support. But the decision of the Supreme Court may have as profound an effect upon the course of public policy as will the enactment of a statute. The interest of the NAACP in securing a favorable restrictive covenant decision is just as much that of a pressure group as is the interest of the American Farm Bureau Federation in bringing about the enactment of a congressional statute supporting corn prices.

the range of propaganda activity

A pressure group seldom dares limit its campaign for favored governmental treatment to lobbying alone. A direct-action approach through public officers is often an uphill struggle, and success is unlikely unless it can be shown that the demands of a pressure group have considerable public support. Occasionally in an area of policy making where the public is disinterested or where the issues are exceedingly technical, an organization will concentrate all of its energies in a frontal attack at the point where policy is to be made. But more often than not a pressure group mounts simultaneous assaults upon government agencies and the public mind in an effort to win its way. A good illustration is to be seen in the activities of industry and labor in the months preceding the enactment of the Taft-Hartley Act by the Eightieth Congress in 1947. Neither group left any stone unturned in its efforts to persuade Congress to follow one line of policy or the other. But both groups also carried their cases to the people through elaborate and costly "campaigns of education." Business told the public that the proposed legislation would merely restore a proper balance between labor and business in the national economy, whereas labor argued that it would establish "slave labor" in the United States.

Political parties are as much interested as are pressure groups in influencing public opinion. But where the latter are primarily interested in selling ideas, the party's first problem is to sell its candidates. Moreover, the stage is set regularly for the party by our biennial national elections, and although there may be considerable apathy among voters, the general public is prepared to listen more or less automatically to the arguments advanced by each party. This is frequently not true of the situation that confronts a pressure group. If the oil industry wants to persuade public opinion that federal ownership of the tideland oil reserves is undesirable, if the teaching profession wants to win public backing for its inclusion in the social security program, or if the American Medical Association wants to arouse public opinion against "socialized medicine," it must first convince the people that its message is worth listening to. Accordingly, although parties and pressure groups are both interested in the use of propaganda, the latter, having the more difficult task, has done more to develop effective propaganda techniques.

propaganda techniques

In spite of the fact that a great deal has been written about propaganda and its use, the term remains a vague and inexact one. Propaganda may be good or bad. It may be designed to further the general welfare; it may have a narrow, selfish motivation. It may be aimed at reason; it may play upon emotion. It may try to persuade through fact and logical argument; it may seek to sway men through an appeal to their prejudices. But in any case propaganda has an end in view; it seeks to influence the public mind with respect to certain issues, specific or general, short-term or long-term. In this, propaganda differs from education, for the latter seeks primarily to give man factual information, to train his mind to effective thinking, and to give him valuable skills, leaving it to the individual to make his own decisions concerning controversial issues.

Such means as the newspaper, the magazine, the radio and television, the motion picture, the mailing piece, the lecture hall, and, when its use is perverted, the classroom, have all been employed by the modern propagandist in attempts to influence public opinion. Moreover, the fields of psychology and sociology have been carefully studied for the light they can throw on human nature. Such methods as name calling, abuse of scapegoats, repetition of ideas, and the calculated use of words with a "good" connotation, such as "home," "country," "patriot," "tradition," "the American way of life," or with a "bad" connotation, such as "government regulation," "regimentation," "bureaucrat," "high taxes," and "monopoly" have become commonplace attempts to influence public opinion.

Much progress has been made by the specialists who have been seeking an understanding of public opinion and of the forces that influence its formation. And yet there is good cause to be skeptical about the effects of propaganda. Obviously public opinion is affected in very substantial ways by the deliberately contrived pressures which are brought to bear upon it all the time. To ignore or deny the extent to which men's thoughts are molded, and often corrupted, by the propagandist is to miss one of the most important realities of modern life. At the same time one cannot avoid the feeling that many specific propaganda campaigns fall far short of the goals that have been set for them. For one thing, there is almost no controversial issue of public policy today which fails to stimulate conflicting propaganda efforts. This in itself does much to protect the integrity of the public mind against the emotional or misleading assertions of any one set of propagandists. Second, it is clear that present-day mass media for the communication of information and ideas do not always have the overpowering effect upon the mind of the individual that is sometimes claimed for them. The motion picture has certainly had a limited usefulness for propaganda purposes. It has undoubtedly encouraged *general* patterns of thought and conduct with respect to romance, success, style, standards of beauty, and the like, but it has had little to do with the shaping of public opinion upon controversial social and political issues. Similarly, such a powerful and vociferous newspaper as the *Chicago Tribune* has seemingly had a limited success as an organ of propaganda. What other conclusion can one draw in the light of its repeated failures to influence the political thinking of the area it dominates?

Finally, as Professor V. O. Key has pointed out, "propaganda of the word" is frequently offset by "propaganda of the event or deed."[4] In influencing the formation of public opinion it seems clear that mere talk is not enough. When people come to make up their minds concerning a controversial social issue they are inevitably influenced by deeds, actions, and events which have touched their lives. The voter may be momentarily disturbed by talk about "regimentation," but if social security has meant unemployment insurance for him when he lost a job, his vote is more apt to be cast in the light of the latter than the former. The specter of "socialized medicine" may frighten many people, but the man whose health needs are being inadequately met will not be permanently deterred from supporting some change in the traditional pattern of medical practice by the force of mere words, however clever their presentation may be.

pressure group organization

Whether a pressure group is interested in lobbying, or propaganda, or both, the effectiveness of its work depends in large part upon the efficiency of its organization. An efficient organization in turn depends upon the vigor and cohesiveness of the membership and the ability and energy of its leaders. Most of the pressure groups that are active in national politics have relatively large numbers of people identified with them. Unless the rank and file of the group's membership is reasonably well disciplined, understands the goals for which the group is fighting, and is prepared to provide necessary financial support and to give its leaders firm backing, the group's gains are likely to be disappointing. An example of a pressure group which has enjoyed considerable success in national politics, in good part because of superior organization and the excellent *esprit de corps* of its membership, is the United Mine Workers. Its leader, John L. Lewis, is an experienced lobbyist, but the concessions he has wrung from Presidents and Congresses would never have been granted were it not for the care with which his union has been organized. On the other hand, the ineffectiveness of virtually all lobbyists who have claimed to speak for the consumer has unquestionably been due to the disorganization which prevails among consumers.

But a well-organized rank and file is not enough. Lobbying has become a

---

[4] V. O. Key, *Politics, Parties, and Pressure Groups* (New York: Thomas Y. Crowell Company, 2d ed., 1947), p. 447.

highly developed profession, and unless a group is able to command the services of wise and experienced operators its success is apt to be limited. Here as elsewhere in the study of institutional organization and procedure, not enough attention has been paid to the role of the secretariat. The paid employees into whose hands the actual operation of an organization is placed inevitably acquire great power and much independence. In the long run it is they who determine the success or failure of the organization's efforts. In view of the high stakes for which pressure groups contend, it is not surprising that the stereotype of the paid lobbyist as a cigar-smoking, back-slapping individual is pretty much obsolete. The modern lobbyist is more likely to be a highly intelligent, technically competent individual who is an able student of the field in which he works and who can command a high salary. It is not surprising that some of the most successful lobbyists are men who once served in Congress or in the administrative branch of the government and who there attracted the attention of their present employees through the high caliber of their work in the public service and were lured into private employment by higher salaries.

the attack upon pressure politics

No aspect of our political system has been the subject of more violent and persistent criticism than has the pressure group. On every hand one hears condemnation of these groups as selfish, antisocial agencies which seek to advance the interests of small numbers of people at the expense of the general welfare. It is argued that democracy can only be achieved when men overcome their individual desires and seek to advance the national interest. Businessmen, farmers, workers, veterans are successively singled out and denounced for their self-seeking activities and for the way in which they feed at the public trough or use public power to promote their own narrow interests.

In particular, there is a tendency these days to suggest that in the present state of world affairs, pressure groups are a luxury which our democratic society can no longer afford. The question is asked whether, as America is compelled by the force of circumstances to show one face to the world, she can continue to allow argument and disunity at home. Probably the deepening world crisis of our times does indicate that the *general, national welfare* must receive greater attention than it has been accorded in the past as pressure groups have fought each other bitterly over some purely domestic issue. Surely American interests on the international scene are endangered when such a thing as the ECA program is subjected to pulling and hauling by selfish pressure groups which want to use the opportunity to exploit their own interests. At the same time, the international crisis does not warrant the total suppression of pressure groups upon the American scene. It may well be that we cannot afford quite so many domestic rivalries and conflicts as we once did when our national security seemed more assured than it does today. But to doubt whether there remains any place at all for pressure groups is much the same thing as doubting whether America can continue to practice democracy in the face of the foreign dangers which beset it.

Beyond this broad condemnation of pressure politics as evil in principle there are two specific criticisms which are frequently made. One is directed at the unequal influence which is achieved by different groups. At one moment it is big business which is said to outweigh all other groups and to dominate the government. At another moment it is labor which is depicted as the leviathan about to swallow everything in sight. At other moments it has been the veteran, or the elderly person who is said to be sweeping all others aside as he moves irresistibly forward in his selfish search for personal gain.

It is easy enough to point to groups in our society who are poorly organized and whose welfare is insufficiently considered in the making and enforcement of public policy. The consumer has already been mentioned in this respect. Some of the smaller racial groups, such as the Indians, and persons of Mexican or Oriental ancestry, and certain underprivileged groups, such as share croppers and itinerant farm workers, have tended to slip from sight partly because of their own lack of organization.

The other specific criticism is directed against the improper means which pressure groups employ. The lobbyist is pointed out as a low-principled person who does not hesitate to use bribery and other corrupt methods to achieve his ends. The propagandist is referred to as a cynical individual who caters to man's lowest instincts and exploits his emotional and irrational nature to achieve a public opinion which has no basis in a calm and intelligent understanding of social problems. It is easy enough to supply specific illustrations which seemingly support the critic's contention. It is not difficult to prove that cynicism and selfishness, as well as downright corruption and dishonesty, are present in our society. It is much more difficult to prove that these qualities and conditions are present in larger degree in pressure politics than they are in other parts of the social process. Moreover, there are several positive arguments advanced by the defenders of pressure groups which must be set alongside of the arguments of the critics if one is to see this problem in proper perspective.

the defense of pressure groups

At the level of principle a strong argument can be made in defense of pressure groups. Life in a modern democratic state, particularly one that is highly industrialized, is exceedingly complex and diversified. Moreover, democracy emphasizes the importance of the individual man—his right to develop a distinct personality, to make full use of his personal talents, and to express his unique interests and desires. Accordingly, it is not surprising that there should exist in

a democratic society a variety of different, and often conflicting interests, based
on economic, professional, sectional, racial, religious, and age factors. To be
sure, there is a *general welfare*. Particularly in its international relations does
our nation tend to have a single or united interest. But it is argued that the
general welfare by and large is made up of particular interests, that it consists
merely of a piecing together of these interests, or of a merging of them into
a middle or compromise position. It is said that it is not realistic to talk of the
general good of all the people—apart from the expression of such vague hopes
as that all men desire peace and prosperity—unless the general good takes
cognizance of, and is built upon, the specific interests and desires of particular
groups of people.

This idea of the general welfare as the sum of many group interests can be
pushed too far. One able critic of pressure groups, E. E. Schattschneider, asserts:
"The notion that public policy can ever be the mere resultant of the blind
pressures of a multitude of special interests each working for its selfish advantage is fantastic." [5] But less scholarly critics of pressure groups often talk glibly
about advancing the national welfare and ignore the valid individual differences which are ever-present in a free society. In fact, to refuse to recognize these
differences and to insist upon the need for "individuals" to be absorbed into a
"people" or "society" even for such a worthy purpose as advancing the general
welfare is to repudiate democracy and to agitate unconsciously for a totalitarian
social organization.

ours is a pluralistic society

Having made this general defense of a diversified society as a natural manifestation of democracy, the defender of pressure groups goes on to point out that
the continuing expression of diverse interests does not lead inevitably to confusion, conflict, or civil war. Instead, the very existence of conflicting interests
and demands tends to result in a pluralistic society, one in which there is no
single, dominant, motivating force or institution. In such a society many divergent forces find expression through a variety of social institutions, through government, church, family, corporation, labor union, and professional and fra-
ternal societies. In an authoritarian society, the state suppresses all independent
institutions—the church and the labor union, for example—and insists upon a
singleness of purpose and policy. In a democracy, rival social interests and
groupings make compromise an ever-present aspect of the social process. As a
result society achieves a balance or equilibrium within itself. No group or institution can set the policy for all the people, establish a single pattern of life,
or seek total power.

To put the matter in somewhat different words, a democracy which permits

[5] "Pressure Groups Versus Political Parties," p. 19.

its citizens to express their varying interests and desires is saved from serious trouble by the existence of conflicting claims and divergent loyalties. Businessmen, workers, farmers, racial groups, churchmen, and veterans are powerful and often self-seeking groups, but they compete with one another and are compelled to modify their demands and to form shifting alliances in their struggles for power and prestige. This, in itself, saves society from the threat of the winning of a total victory by any one force or faction.

Moreover, such groups as labor, business, and agriculture are often badly divided within themselves. Labor is torn between the rival aims of craft and industrial unions, of skilled and unskilled workers. The dairy farmer of Wisconsin finds himself pitted against the cotton farmer of Texas over the issue of oleomargarine taxation. The automobile manufacturer and the pottery manufacturer are in total disagreement on the tariff; one wants to develop foreign markets for American automobiles, the other seeks to make headway against the competition of popular and traditional imported china. These examples only begin to suggest the extent to which the supposedly loyal and unified members of a single grouping can come into conflict with one another even in the total absence of conflict with a different group.

Finally, the individuals who give their allegiance to particular pressure groups have divided personal loyalties. One man may be a loyal, even fanatical, member of the labor group. But he is also, shall we say, a man of Swedish ancestry, a resident of California, a white, a Protestant, a war veteran, and the father of a family. Each of these conditions exerts a powerful pull upon him. Often these forces conflict, particularly as they relate to any specific issue. At times one force may dominate his thinking and his action. In the midst of a strike he will be a loyal union man; when discriminatory freight rates are being attacked he will react strongly as a resident of the Far West; when Congress proposes to reduce the appropriation for national defense he will add his voice to the veterans' chorus of protest. Again this simple illustration hardly begins to suggest the variety of loyalties which the average American holds; nor does it adequately suggest the extent to which these loyalties may be in conflict. Professor Harold Lasswell has said:

> John Citizen may pay his dues to a veterans' organization which seeks to raise the cost of government by demanding higher bonus rates, and he may also support a business association which tries to lower the cost of government by reducing payments from the public treasury. He may belong to an association of bondholders which strives to prevent the liquidation of fixed claims, and he may contribute to a trade association which urges inflation in order to reduce the burden of fixed charges on business enterprise. He may contribute to a civic league to improve the honesty and efficiency of government, and also pay the local bosses to protect his franchise. Hence the person may in effect argue against himself in the press, lobby against himself at

the capital, vote against himself in Congress, and defeat in administration what he supported as legislation.[6]

pressure groups are constitutional

A practical argument advanced in support of pressure groups is that they are protected under the Constitution and that any real effort to outlaw them would certainly be declared null and void by the courts. The argument is based upon the language of the First Amendment, which forbids Congress to make any law abridging the right of the people to assemble, and to petition the government for a redress of grievances. There is no Supreme Court decision specifically applying this language to pressure groups, but it seems likely that any federal statute which on a broad basis denied interest groups the right to influence government agencies would be held to violate this amendment. Moreover, it is probable that the Court would hold that the Fourteenth Amendment offers the same kind of protection against state laws prohibiting pressure group activity.

pressure groups render service

A more specific argument in support of pressure groups stresses the practical contributions which they make to the successful operation of democratic government. In the first place, it is argued, they supply the public with needed information concerning specific problems, thereby making possible the emergence of an informed public opinion. True, the propagandist role of many pressure groups involves distortion of the truth and raises the danger that public opinion will be misinformed. Nonetheless, the record shows that certain pressure groups have at times brought information to the general public which was not being made available by disinterested groups or by news sources. For example, organizations representing underprivileged racial and nationality groups—the Negro, the Indian, the Mexican-American, the Japanese-American, to name a few— have performed a valuable public service in bringing the details of the plight and problems of these people to the light of day. Even the highly colored and biased statements of such organizations as the National Association of Manufacturers and the Congress of Industrial Organizations, made in the heat of battle over the Taft-Hartley Act, probably had an educational value in stimulating debate and even in providing some measure of accurate data to the general public.

In the second place, pressure groups are said to supply government agencies with valuable and necessary data. Information is provided by lobbyists testifying before congressional committees which enables Congress to legislate more

---

[6] Harold Lasswell, "The Person: Subject and Object of Propaganda," *The Annals* of The American Academy of Political and Social Science, CLXXIX (May, 1935), 187. Reprinted by permission of the publisher.

wisely than would otherwise be the case. Similarly, technical data are often supplied administrative agencies by interested persons and make possible the following of sound administrative practices. Moreover, much of this information supplied government officers is necessarily more complete and accurate than that used by pressure groups for general propaganda purposes, for here the lobbyist is dealing with public officers who already enjoy some familiarity with the problems under consideration. This is not to say that there is no biased testimony or plain "hot air" in the information submitted by representatives of special interests to congressional committees. But the average lobbyist quickly learns that one of the surest ways to win influence with a congressman is to show the latter that he can supply him with detailed, accurate data. Again this is not to suggest that congressmen should depend exclusively, or even primarily, upon such private sources for the information necessary to the enactment of satisfactory laws. Congress has two other very important sources of information. One is the executive branch of the government which, through such devices as presidential messages, annual and special reports, and the testimony of administrative officers before the committees of Congress, is engaged in a continuous process of feeding information to Congress. The other is Congress's own staff, which has been greatly expanded under the Legislative Reorganization Act of 1946. Through the facilities of the Legislative Reference Service of the Library of Congress and the expert staffs which many of the standing committees have built up, congressmen are able to obtain much detailed information without going outside the legislative branch. Belle Zeller, one of the ablest students of pressure politics, has pointed out that "by placing greater professional expert and clerical assistance at the disposal of legislative committees and members, Congress has made itself less dependent on unofficial sources of information than ever before." And she adds, "Strengthening the ability of government to formulate legislative policy will go a long way toward providing effective regulation of pressure groups." [7]

And yet the intricacies of many a modern governmental problem are so difficult to fathom, and the wise course to take in attacking the problem is so difficult to determine, that Congress needs and can make effective use of every possible bit of information that can be supplied it. The fact that a pressure group such as the American Legion or the American Civil Liberties Union is interested in influencing Congress in a particular direction does not mean that all of the information it supplies is necessarily suspect. Indeed, it is clear that these agencies can upon occasion supply Congress with data pertaining to the problems of veterans or civil rights that would be difficult to secure elsewhere.

---

[7] Belle Zeller, "The Federal Regulation of Lobbying Act," *American Political Science Review*, XLII (April, 1948), 239, 271.

President versus pressure groups

The relationship between President and Congress is examined elsewhere. But it is important to note here that the President, and to a lesser extent subordinate administrative officers, tends to offset the influence of lobbyists upon Congress. This is due to the fact that the President is responsible to the national electorate and owes his office to the support of 25 million or more voters. The President is by no means totally unconcerned about the interests of such large groups as the farmers, the businessmen, the workers, or the veterans. But his sensitivity to particular interests is usually much less strong than that of congressmen, who represent much smaller constituencies. It is easier for the President to give adequate consideration to the national welfare, particularly in those situations where the latter is something more than the mere projection of local or special interests upon a broader screen. Congress is thus in the fortunate position of being able not only to listen to "both sides" before enacting an important statute, but to listen to those who are concerned about the effect of the statute upon particular interests, and to the man (or his assistants) who, more than any other American, has the responsibility of watching over the general welfare. Moreover, both the President and the pressure groups, for institutional and political reasons, have a good deal of influence with Congress and are assured at the very least of getting a respectful hearing. Since pressure groups and the national administration are often on opposite sides of a controversial issue and are more or less evenly matched in their influence upon the formation of national policy, the tendency toward compromise is further enhanced.

the regulation of pressure groups

Whether pressure groups be viewed finally as an asset or a liability in a democratic society it is hard to avoid the conclusion that they are prone to abuse their position and their power. There is general agreement that this is one aspect of our private institutional arrangement in America which should be subjected to a measure of legal control by government in the interest of the general good. Unfortunately, to regulate pressure groups effectively is not easy. The primary difficulty is that the placing of any substantial legal restraints upon lobbies or their agents is apt to go beyond mere regulation and end in suppression. Nonetheless, more than half of the states, and finally the national government in 1946, have enacted general laws for the regulation of lobbying. By and large these laws make use of the two devices of *registration* and *disclosure*. Organizations, as well as their agents, that seek to influence government policy and practice are compelled to register with some public agency and to disclose certain information about themselves. The latter usually includes data as to the identity of officers (in some cases, membership), sources of income, and the extent and purposes of expenditures. The theory behind such regulation is that if vital information concerning lobbies is made a matter of public knowledge, the people will be able to evaluate the propriety of the pressures which are brought to bear upon government officers. In particular it is hoped that legislators will thereby be able to resist pressures which in the past they have submitted to because of fears that public opinion would not support them if they stood their ground.

A serious practical difficulty in this approach to the regulation of pressure groups is finding a way to give wide publicity to the information submitted by lobbies. The typical lobbying statute provides for the filing of data with a public officer and their publication in some official journal such as the *Congressional Record*. Beyond that it is necessary for the public to show an interest if the data are to become widely known. Experience under the federal Regulation of Lobbying Act of 1946 may be noted.

federal lobby regulation

The federal lobby control law was enacted in 1946 as a separate title in the Legislative Reorganization Act. It requires each *person* hired to influence the passage or defeat of legislation by Congress to register with the clerk of the House of Representatives and the secretary of the Senate, and to disclose such information as "the name and address of the person by whom he is employed, and in whose interest he appears or works, the duration of such employment, how much he is paid and is to receive, by whom he is paid or is to be paid, how much he is to be paid for expenses, and what expenses are to be included." Moreover, every three months he must file a further statement as to moneys actually received and expended, "and the names of any papers, periodicals, magazines, or other publications in which he has caused to be published any articles or editorials; and the proposed legislation he is employed to support or oppose." Exempted from this requirement are persons who do no more than appear as witnesses before congressional committees and public officers who act in their official capacity. Likewise regularly published newspapers or periodicals which in the ordinary course of business publish news items, editorials, or paid advertisements urging the passage or defeat of legislation are exempted if they engage in no further lobbying activities.

The act also requires every *organization* whose "principal purpose" is to influence the passage or defeat of congressional legislation to keep a detailed record of its receipts and expenditures for lobbying purposes (including the names and addresses of all persons contributing more than $500, or to whom more than $10 was paid) and to file this information with the clerk of the House of Representatives every three months. All statements required by the law are to be preserved by the clerk of the House for two years and shall be open to public inspection. Moreover, the data as to paid lobbyists are to be compiled and printed in the *Congressional Record* every three months. Severe penalties, ranging up to a $10,000 fine and a five-year prison term, for violations of the act are provided.[8]

The act itself is badly drawn. In the words of one authority, "a literal reading of the provisions of the lobbying title [of the Legislative Reorganization Act] presents a mass of contradictions and ambiguities."[9] By and large, the administration of the act has been uneventful and results under it have been disappointing. Some 1,650 organizations and lobbyists had registered by the end of 1949, and slightly more than 250 organizations were filing quarterly statements on receipts and expenditures. The resulting data have been placed on public file and printed at regular intervals in the *Congressional Record*. But the public has shown little interest in these data, and it is doubtful whether the pattern of lobbying has been affected very much by the law. Several large organizations, well known for their active interest in governmental affairs, either have been slow to register or have failed to register at all, asserting that they are not lobbies as defined by the act. Moreover, the information filed is often exceedingly scanty and fails to give the public a real basis for determining the extent and significance of an organization's or a lobbyist's political activity. Although as of late 1948, three individuals (including a former congressman) had been indicted for failure to register as lobbyists, a further weakness in the act is its failure to make any agency of the government specifically responsible for its enforcement.

It should also be noted that the investigating power of Congress has been used as a means of regulating pressure groups and lobbying in particular. At regular intervals inquiries into lobbying practices and evils have been undertaken, and the findings of the committees making these probes have been widely publicized. The lobby investigation of the middle 1930's made under the direction of Senator Hugo Black was a noteworthy one, and its spectacular findings made a tremendous impression upon the nation. At the time of writing in 1950 another congressional investigation of lobbies was getting under way. This time the inquiry was being made by a special House committee under the chairmanship of Representative Frank Buchanan. For the most part these investigations have not resulted in the enactment of any regulatory legislation by Congress. But they have unquestionably served to hold down to a minimum the more flagrant lobbying practices.

continuing controversy as to pressure politics

Pressure groups play a legitimate, and even necessary, role in the democratic process. Any thought of their complete elimination from American politics must be rejected. Nonetheless, their activity does present certain problems for which

[8] 60 Stat. 839.
[9] Zeller, "The Federal Regulation of Lobbying Act," pp. 239, 245.

adequate solutions have not yet been found. Insofar as one of the central tasks in a free and diversified society is to find a proper balance between the interests of individuals and the interests of the whole people, it is probably true that pressure groups have tended to weigh the balance too much in favor of selfish group interests. In particular, two difficulties need to be corrected if the theoretical defense of pressure groups as a proper means by which the people are able to express themselves and to control their government is to be valid in practice.

inadequate coverage by pressure groups

The first of these difficulties is the failure of the pressure group system to provide adequate coverage of all segments of the population which have group interests that will be affected by government policies. As we have seen, certain underprivileged groups, such as unskilled labor or small racial minorities, have not been able to organize very effectively for political activity. The same is true of other groups, such as consumers, which have not come to realize the unity of their interests. It may be argued as to the former that society as a whole cannot very well force them to organize or provide them with organizations; and as to the latter that if they do not see the benefits to be derived from unified action, that is their own fault. Nonetheless, it is true that the lack of organization among these groups undermines the theory that pressure groups collectively represent all the people. If certain existing interests are not reflected as real pressures upon government, then to that extent government ceases to be "of the people." To put it differently, if the general welfare is but a merging of particular interests, the absence of certain components from the mixture means that the result is not truly "general." Thus, if we are to make democracy work in practice, and enjoy that security offered by a society that is in fact one in which all components are "balanced," some way must be found to strengthen the power and organization of groups now weak but potentially strong and important.

the lack of democracy within pressure groups

The second difficulty is the absence of democracy within the internal organization of many a pressure group. The fact is that many groups are dominated by a few men at the top who are often arrogant, selfish, and shortsighted in the way they view the interests of their groups. Many "spokesmen" of businessmen, workers, farmers, veterans, and other groups of people are not responsible to the people they claim to represent. There is little or no democracy in the structure of the organization. Leaders have held office for years and manage to perpetuate their power by manipulating to their advantage the machinery of the formal organization. Far from the leader being controlled by the rank and file, where there is any contact at all between a group's officers and its members, the latter are dictated to by the former. In other words, much of the propaganda that issues from central headquarters is intended to keep a group's followers loyal to the "party line" as much as it is calculated to sway public opinion generally.

Here, as elsewhere, one of the things that must be done, if American democracy is to be perfected, is to find ways and means of strengthening the role played by the people in the institutional aspects of our pluralistic society. We have succeeded reasonably well in establishing democratic control within government itself. But in many of our nongovernmental social organizations the voice of the people is heard but faintly.

bibliographic note

There are a number of general studies of the role of pressure groups in the American political system. Harwood L. Childs has edited an issue of *The Annals* of the American Academy of Political and Social Science, CLXXIX (May, 1935), entitled "Pressure Groups and Propaganda," that provides an excellent starting point for further reading. Pendleton Herring's *Group Representation before Congress* (Baltimore: The Johns Hopkins Press, 1929) is an early, and still highly useful, analysis of pressure politics at the national level. Donald C. Blaisdell's *Government under Pressure* (New York: Public Affairs Committee, 1942), a reprint of a monograph prepared for the Temporary National Economic Committee in the late thirties, has become a classic statement of the pressure group system. Stuart Chase's *Democracy under Pressure* (New York: The Twentieth Century Fund, 1945) contains a popular and rather critical description of pressure groups. Another popular and easily read study of pressure groups, from the point of view of a Washington newspaperman, is Kenneth G. Crawford's *The Pressure Boys; The Inside Story of Lobbying in America* (New York: Julian Messner, Inc., 1939). An excellent brief article which takes a rather friendly view of pressure groups is Mary E. Dillon's *"Pressure Groups,"* *American Political Science Review*, XXXVI (June, 1942), 471.

There are a number of excellent studies of regional pressure politics and of specific pressure groups. Two informative regional studies by political scientists who have specialized in the field of politics are Dayton D. McKean's *Pressures on the Legislature of New Jersey* (New York: Columbia University Press, 1938) and Belle Zeller's *Pressure Politics in New York* (New York: Prentice-Hall, Inc., 1937). Among the studies of particular pressure groups or of specific pressure campaigns are the following: Oliver Garceau, *The Political Life of the American Medical Association* (Cambridge: Harvard University Press, 1941); Louis C. Kesselman, *The Social Politics of FEPC; A Study in Reform Pressure Movements* (Chapel Hill: University of North Carolina Press, 1948); V. O. Key,

"The Veterans and the House of Representatives: A Study of a Pressure Group and Electoral Mortality," *Journal of Politics*, V (February, 1943), 27; Peter H. Odegard, *Pressure Politics; The Story of the Anti-Saloon League* (New York: Columbia University Press, 1928); and E. E. Schattschneider, *Politics, Pressures, and the Tariff* (New York: Prentice-Hall, Inc., 1935).

Arthur N. Holcombe's *The Middle Classes in American Politics* (Cambridge: Harvard University Press, 1940) provides a revealing account of the way in which the middle class has dominated American politics. An article by Avery Leiserson, "Problems of Representation in the Government of Private Groups," *Journal of Politics*, XI (August, 1949), 566, deals briefly with the important problem of the internal government of pressure groups.

electing the Congress

$\mathcal{I}$N A very important sense there are no national elections in the United States. It is true that on the first Tuesday after the first Monday of November in even-numbered years millions of voters go to the polls all over the country to choose the elective officers of the national government. But although this step is taken simultaneously by the voters of all the states (Maine excepted), it is not a collective step in the sense that the voters of the nation thereby select their national officers in one central election. Instead the conduct of these elections in which Presidents and congressmen are chosen is very much in the hands of the state governments. Apart from the common date, there is little if any exaggeration in the statement that our national officers are chosen in a series of local elections which are conducted by local governments and in which local personalities, local issues, and local politics are dominant forces.

The decision to decentralize, as it were, our national election system was not one that occasioned much debate or disagreement in the Constitutional Convention. The decision undoubtedly reflected the belief of the delegates that under the federal plan of government which they were establishing the elective officers of the national government were to be representatives of the states and that accordingly their selection should be entrusted to the states. The possibility that the American people might elect their national officers from the nation at large with state lines ignored was alien to the thought of the Founding Fathers.

The decision of the convention to give the dominant role in the selection of national officers to the states has only been accentuated as the President and senators have been added to the list of popularly elected officers, which originally included only representatives. Even today any suggestion that our laws or Constitution be changed to provide for the conduct, or even control, of elections by the national government raises an immediate cry of dictatorship and a call to protect the states against the threat of centralized power. Nonetheless, as we shall see, many of the shortcomings of our electoral system can be attributed directly to this decentralization of the electoral process. Any thoroughgoing effort to correct the defects of our presidential and congressional elections will almost certainly necessitate some measure of increased federal control.

election of public officers a twofold process

In the second place, it is important to recognize that the selection of those public officers chosen by the people has become a twofold process consisting of a nomination stage and a final election stage. These two stages are quite distinct from each other, and each has been institutionalized in elaborate, highly formalized procedures. It should be noted that the nomination of national officers is nowhere expressly referred to in the federal Constitution. Accordingly its development has largely taken place outside the range of the written Constitution. For this reason, and for others, the importance of this first stage in the total electoral process has not been sufficiently recognized by either the general public or students of government. In a two-party system, such as our own, the formal nomination of candidates for public offices by the parties limits the choice of the voters to just two possibilities—a very substantial limitation indeed!

Moreover, the decentralized character of national elections is particularly pronounced at the nomination stage. It may be argued that the final selection by the voters of a President and of congressmen in a November election comes very close to being a *national* election in which control of the process by the states is merely incidental. But if this point be conceded for the sake of argument, it is at once clear that no such claim can be made concerning the nomination of federal officers. For, as will later be demonstrated in this chapter, this is a highly decentralized operation. It is almost exclusively the concern of the separate states, and we shall discover that not all of them even use the same method of nominating candidates. Moreover, they do not all take the step at the same time. Instead, the operation is a staggered one, with some five months elapsing between the nomination by the first state of its congressional candidates and similar action by the last state.

It is true that the nomination of presidential candidates necessarily becomes a nation-wide operation since in the end each party can select only one person to make the final race. But, as will be shown in the next chapter, the selection of the delegates to the national party conventions who have the power to nominate the presidential candidates is just as decentralized an operation as the nomination of congressional candidates, both with respect to the method and the time of selection.

constitutional provisions concerning congressional elections

Every two years, 435 representatives, the entire membership of the lower house, and 32 senators, one third of the members of the upper house, are chosen by the voters of the states in a November election. To what extent does the Constitution by its express language control or limit the method by which these national legislators are selected? To begin with, it fixes the qualifications and terms of senators and representatives and provides that they shall be popularly elected. Senators must be thirty years of age, and citizens of the United States for nine years; they serve for six years. Representatives must be twenty-five years of age and citizens for seven years; they serve for two years. Both senators and representatives are required to be inhabitants of their states at the time of their choice.

The Constitution of 1787 provided that representatives should be "chosen . . . by the people of the several States." The Seventeenth Amendment, added to the Constitution in 1913, makes the same provision for the election of senators, the original Constitution having provided for their choice by the state legislatures. The Constitution further provides for the division of the Senate's members into three groups so that one third of the seats become vacant every two years. These staggered terms are so distributed among the states that each state elects a senator in two out of three biennial elections, no state ever electing both of its senators at the same time (except where death or resignation makes necessary a special election to choose a senator to fill out a part of a term).

With respect to the House the Constitution further provides that representatives shall be apportioned among the states on the basis of population, and although it does not say so in so many words, the implication is that Congress shall make a new apportionment every ten years following the taking of the census.

the "times, places, and manner" clause

The most important provision in the federal Constitution concerning the conduct of congressional elections is the paragraph in Article One, section four, which states: "The times, places, and manner of holding elections for Senators and Representatives shall be prescribed in each State by the legislature thereof; but the Congress may at any time by law make or alter such regulations. . . ." It is this provision which has served as the basis for the conduct of congressional elections by the states. It is clear that Congress might, if it wished under this paragraph, take the control of congressional elections completely out of the hands of the states and provide for their direct operation by the national government itself. But, with the exception of the program of federal supervision of elections in the southern states during the Reconstruction era following the Civil War, Congress has taken no step in that direction.

power of Congress to determine the qualifications of its members

Notice should also be taken of the clause in Article One, section five, of the Constitution, which says, "Each House shall be the judge of the elections, returns, and qualifications of its own members." It is the clear implication of this provision that the two houses possess the exclusive power to determine whether newly elected members have been properly chosen or have the qualifications set forth in the Constitution. Presumably failure by either house to seat a member-elect should rest either upon proof of election irregularities or on inability to meet the constitutional qualifications. Actually, the two houses have, upon occasion, refused to seat members for other reasons. The House has refused to seat a polygamist, and also a Socialist who had been convicted under the sedition laws during World War I. The Senate has refused to seat members-elect because of the expenditure of allegedly improper sums of money in winning senatorial primary elections. Such action by the two houses amounts to the establishment of additional qualifications for members of Congress beyond those set forth in the Constitution. But because Congress is made the exclusive judge of the qualifications of its members, no argument concerning the unconstitutionality of such action can be carried beyond Congress itself.

statutory control of congressional elections

Although Congress has not exercised its constitutional power to "nationalize" congressional elections, it has enacted several statutes establishing a limited measure of federal supervision of these elections. An act of 1842 provided that representatives should be chosen in each state by districts rather than at large, and an act of 1872 provided that each state should hold its election of federal officers on the first Tuesday after the first Monday in November. For a period Congress required that the districts from which representatives are chosen were to be so arranged by the states as to be compact, contiguous, and equal in population, but this requirement was dropped from the Reapportionment Act of 1929. Congress has also enacted legislation protecting qualified voters in congressional elections against interference by violence or intimidation, and it has also provided penalties against fraud and corruption in these elections. The Supreme Court has held that such legislation is valid under section four, as well as under section two, of Article One.[1] Finally, Congress has enacted so-called corrupt practices legislation which limits campaign expenditures by candidates for federal office. This legislation will be examined in detail later in this chapter.

the nomination of congressmen

congressional control of the nominating process

Whether or not the "times, places, and manner" clause gives Congress power to control the process by which congressmen are nominated is a question that has

---

[1] *Ex parte Siebold*, 100 U.S. 371 (1880); *Ex parte Yarbrough*, 110 U.S. 651 (1884); and *United States* v. *Mosley*, 238 U.S. 383 (1915).

not been easily answered. The difficulty of interpretation has been whether the word "elections" as used in the clause is broad enough to include the nomination stage or is limited solely to the final step by which the voters choose a congressman from among the nominees. In 1920 a closely divided Supreme Court seemingly held in *Newberry* v. *United States*[2] that congressional power over "elections" did not extend to the control of nominating primaries. However, this position was reversed in 1941 when in *United States* v. *Classic*[3] the Court held that Congress might regulate congressional primaries by federal law if it so wished. Congress has made sparing use of this power to the present time, and the nomination of congressmen is still controlled almost exclusively by the states.

The caucus system and nomination by personal declaration were briefly used in the early days of the nation, and nomination by convention was the common method in the nineteenth century. Almost all of the states now provide for the nomination of United States senators and representatives by party primaries. As has been indicated, the primary election is a state affair and there is little or no uniformity in state practice. Certain important differences may be noted.

the staggering of primaries minimizes the role of national parties

First, the time of holding primary elections varies greatly. The first states nominate their congressional candidates as early as April in election years, whereas, the last states do not take this step until September. This staggering of congressional primaries has a pronounced decentralizing effect upon the selection of national legislators. Because of the long primary "season" it is extremely difficult to focus the attention of voters upon national issues. National party organizations and leaders are ordinarily unable to exert much influence upon the selection of their congressional candidates in the several states. Instead, local organizations and leaders play a dominant role in the process, and the voters are very much inclined to make their selections on the basis of local personalities and local issues.

The extent to which the staggered congressional primaries serve to weaken the influence of national parties in the selection of congressional personnel is emphasized if one examines the British system of nominating candidates for the House of Commons. In Great Britain the system used is that of nomination by declaration. Any person may declare his candidacy for the House of Commons in one of the parliamentary districts, although he must post a deposit of £150, which he forfeits if he fails to poll one eighth of the vote in his district. But running as the nominee of one of the major parties is another matter. The designation of the party candidates in each district is subject to the approval of the national organizations. A would-be candidate who is denied the party designation may run as an independent, but unless he enjoys unusual personal strength in

---

[2] *Newberry* v. *United States,* 256 U.S. 232 (1921).

[3] *United States* v. *Classic,* 313 U.S. 299 (1941). The holding on this point was unanimous.

his district the loss of the official party label is almost certain to be fatal to his cause.

In the United States there is no institutional arrangement which compels a candidate for Congress to seek the endorsement of a national party organization. He is free to enter the primary of his party in his state provided only that he can meet the very easy requirement found in most states that he be a "member" of the party. If his local prestige is sufficient, he may even win the nomination in the face of active opposition by the national leaders of the party. In particular because of the staggering of the primaries, the latter are apt to be frustrated in their attempts to influence the outcome of the nominating process in the states. For example, when President Roosevelt attempted in 1938 to purge certain Democrats in Congress who had failed to support his legislative program, he found that he could not limit his campaign to one or two radio talks directed at the entire country at the proper moment. Instead he had to take to the road and go from state to state, making his appeal to local electorates as the state primaries occurred one by one. Under such circumstances the President was seriously handicapped in his attempts to persuade local Democrats that they ought to pick their candidates for the national legislature in the light of national problems and issues. Indeed, his attempts came to naught, for, with one lone exception, all of the Democrats whom he opposed won renomination.

open and closed primaries; runoff primaries

The congressional primaries in most of the states are of the so-called closed type. Participation in a closed primary is limited in the case of each party to those persons who have formally declared their affiliation with the party and who remain members in good standing. The open primary allows each qualified voter to make up his mind in the polling place on the day of the primary election which party primary he will participate in, and, whatever his choice, he is not subject to challenge. The open primary has the advantage of letting the individual voter decide anew at each election the party in which he desires to influence the selection of candidates; it has the disadvantage of permitting the "raiding" of a party primary by members of the opposite party to bring about the nomination of a weak candidate. This latter is a speculative conclusion, for very few actual data are available on this point. Some authorities are of the opinion that where the voters cross party lines in a primary their desire, more often than not, is to bring about the nomination of a strong candidate in a vigorously contested race.[4]

Closely related to the situation existing in an open primary race is the "cross-filing" that is permitted in a few states, notably New York and California. In such states congressional candidates can file in two or more parties and try to

---

[4] See V. O. Key, *Politics, Parties, and Pressure Groups* (New York: Thomas Y. Crowell Company, 2d ed., 1947), p. 367.

win more than one nomination. In California, particularly, candidates for Congress have sometimes managed to win both the Republican and the Democratic nomination.

A number of southern states make use of a runoff primary system. Under this system, if the leading candidate in the first primary fails to poll a majority of the vote, a second, or runoff, primary is held in which the choice is narrowed to the two highest candidates in the first primary. In one-party states this system has the advantage of guaranteeing that the person who wins the nomination—and thereby the election—shall have the support of something more than the small plurality that is often enough to win in a race in which three or more strong candidates are seeking nomination.

financing elections

It is not surprising that political campaigns in the United States should be costly undertakings. It has been estimated, for example, that the total expenditures on behalf of the two major party tickets in a presidential election range somewhere between twenty-five and thirty million dollars.[5] When one realizes that the cost of such a simple step in a national campaign as sending a single postcard to each eligible voter would be more than $1,000,000 for postage alone, the wonder is that the total expenditures can be anything like as low as the figure given. In a democracy there must be persistent and intensive efforts on the part of candidates for public office to reach the voters with their campaign stories if the voters are to make an intelligent choice among them. Furthermore, in a nation of 150 million people spread out over a tremendous expanse of territory, the cost of such campaign efforts is bound to be great.

On the other hand, the American people have always had a healthy distrust of "money in politics." The threat that certain candidates will "buy" their way into public office, or that certain interests will "buy" public policies from the government favorable to their cause is an ever-present one. The result is one of the most difficult dilemmas of American politics: parties and candidates must be allowed to spend money in campaigns so that the voters may acquire necessary information; yet constant vigilance is necessary lest the democratic process be corrupted by the dollar sign.

why money is needed for campaigns

Professor V. O. Key states that campaign funds are needed for five purposes: (1) "general overhead," for party headquarters, including the salaries of the secretariat of the national, state, and local organizations, and such expenses as

---

[5] John W. Lederle, "Party Finance in a Presidential Election Year," *The Annals* of The American Academy of Political and Social Science, CCLIX (September, 1948), 64.

office rent, postage, and telephone; (2) "field activities," covering the costs of the speaking trips of the candidates and of campaign rallies and meetings; (3) "publicity," covering the costs of radio broadcasts, newspaper advertisements, campaign literature, and the like; (4) "grants to subsidiary committees," which takes care of transfers of funds from national organizations to state and local organizations and to special committees and groups; (5) "Election Day expenses," covering payments to party workers who try to bring out the vote, to watchers at the polls, and to others who are active on Election Day.[6] This listing of campaign expenses may not be complete, but it certainly suggests very readily the numerous ways in which a party organization can quickly and legitimately spend large sums of money in the course of an election campaign.

where the money comes from

Apart from the size of the sums raised to meet campaign expenses, the most striking thing about party finances is the narrow range of donors. One student of party finance concludes: "As far as the two major parties are concerned, it can be said categorically that neither of them has a broad and democratic financial basis. . . . Out of the millions of party cohorts, comparatively few see fit to furnish the financial wherewithal with which to conduct the party battle." [7] Professor Louise Overacker, perhaps the leading authority on campaign finances, points out that in the 1944 campaign the national committees of both major parties received more than half of their total funds from donors who gave $1,000 or more.[8] Because of this narrow basis of support, the business of raising campaign funds has become highly specialized and is made the responsibility of a small number of experienced party workers.

federal control of party finances

The ever-present danger that the fiscal activities of parties and candidates will be marked by corruption long ago resulted in a demand for the enactment of laws to ward off this threat. Congress began to respond to this demand early in the present century and has enacted a series of corrupt practices laws. These federal laws establish the following limitations: (1) Certain contribution sources are prohibited. As early as 1907 Congress forbade corporations chartered under federal law, such as national banks, to make contributions in *any* political campaign, federal or local, and it forbade all corporations to make contributions in *national* campaigns. Labor unions were subjected to a similar ban by the Smith-Connally Act in 1943. When this act expired at the end of the war, the

---

[6] Key, *Politics, Parties, and Pressure Groups,* p. 458.
[7] Lederle, "Party Finance in a Presidential Election Year," pp. 71–72.
[8] Louise Overacker, "Presidential Campaign Funds, 1944," *American Political Science Review,* XXXIX (October, 1945), 899, 908.

Taft-Hartley Act of 1947 renewed the ban on labor union contributions and also extended it to cover direct *expenditures* by unions themselves as well as business corporations on behalf of candidates for federal office. In the 1944 campaign the CIO had refrained from making any contributions to the Roosevelt campaign fund, but it *spent* over $1,000,000 on direct aid to the Roosevelt ticket through its own "Political Action Committee." The Taft-Hartley Act was obviously designed to outlaw such direct expenditures in addition to contributions to party organizations. There is grave doubt about the constitutionality of such a ban upon direct expenditures by labor unions and business corporations.[9] From 1883 on, Congress has tried to protect government employees from requests for contributions to campaign funds. However, this protection extends only to the solicitation of funds by one government employee from another. It does not extend to solicitation by private persons. (2) Size of contributions is limited. The Hatch Act of 1940 limits to $5,000 a person individual contributions to national party organizations in a national campaign, and also limits to $3 million the total contributions that may be made to any one political committee.[10] (3) Expenditures by parties and candidates are limited. The Hatch Act of 1940 also limits expenditures by a political committee to a maximum of $3 million in any one year. In 1925 Congress also placed limitations on the amounts that may be spent by candidates for Congress. These amounts are fixed at $10,000 for senatorial candidates and at $2,500 for candidates for the House. However, recognizing that candidates in the populous states may legitimately incur greater expenses, Congress approved an alternative formula which allows a candidate to exceed these limits by spending three cents for every vote cast in the last general election, although in no event may this exceed $25,000 for senatorial candidates and $5,000 for candidates for the House. (4) Public disclosure of the fiscal record is required. Beginning in 1910 Congress has enacted laws requiring political committees and candidates for Congress to file statements at certain intervals with the clerk of the House of Representatives concerning contributions received and expenditures made. Among the required data are the name and address of each person contributing more than $100, and the names of persons to whom more than $10 is paid. Such information is then available for public inspection, and a certain amount of it is usually reported by the press in rather sketchy fashion.

---

[9] See *United States* v. *Congress of Industrial Organizations,* 335 U.S. 106 (1948) in which five justices held that the Taft-Hartley Act was not intended to prevent a labor organization from supporting a congressional candidate in a newspaper which it publishes. However, four justices felt that the act was intended to ban such activity and that, so construed, it was unconstitutional.

[10] A "political committee" is defined by the Federal Corrupt Practices Act as "any committee, association, or organization which accepts contributions or makes expenditures for the purpose of influencing the election of candidates . . . in two or more states . . . ." 2 U.S.C. § 241.

constitutionality of corrupt practices legislation

The "times, places, and manner" clause of Article One of the Constitution quite clearly provides a basis for federal legislation restricting and controlling contributions and expenditures in congressional elections. The power of Congress to regulate the finances of presidential elections is less explicit. However, the Supreme Court has held that Congress has the implied power to safeguard such an election against the improper use of money.[11] On the other hand, much of the federal corrupt practices legislation does not apply to fiscal activities in congressional and presidential *primaries*. In 1921 a closely divided Supreme Court cast doubt upon the constitutional power of Congress to regulate primary election finances. This ruling was expressly repudiated by the Court in 1941,[12] and in the Taft-Hartley Act of 1947 Congress extended the ban on contributions and expenditures made by business and labor to cover the nomination of candidates as well as the election of public officers. But the limitation on expenditures by candidates and political committees has not yet been extended by Congress to primaries or nominating conventions.

ineffectiveness of corrupt practices legislation

In the end most of the corrupt practices legislation now in existence fails to achieve the specific purposes for which it was enacted. Several examples of this failure may be noted. The Hatch Act limitation of $3 million on the total expenditure of a political committee is meaningless, because it does not prevent two or more separate committees from spending up to $3 million each in support of the same party ticket. Thus in addition to the Republican National Committee, the Republican Senatorial Campaign Committee, the Republican Congressional Campaign Committee, each of the forty-eight state Republican committees and an endless number of "independent" committees committed to the support of Republican candidates may spend up to the $3 million maximum in each campaign. There is no evidence that the Hatch Act has brought about a reduction in the total amount of money spent by the major parties in presidential elections. About all it has done is to encourage a decentralization of expenditures, a change of doubtful value to the public good. Second, the limitations upon the expenditures of individual candidates for Congress are apt to be meaningless because of the absolute impossibility of making any check upon the vast sums that may be and are spent by private persons on behalf of a candidate, without the candidate receiving the money or even knowing that it is being used to aid him. Third, the $5,000 limitation on the contributions of a single person is rendered meaningless by the fact that each of several members of a family can give such an amount. Inspection of the contribution lists filed with the

---

[11] *Burroughs* v. *United States,* 290 U.S. 534 (1934).

[12] *Newberry* v. *United States,* 256 U.S. 232 (1921); *United States* v. *Classic,* 313 U.S. 299 (1941).

House clerk reveals the presence of long lists of donors bearing the same family name, so that the total contribution of a family may run to many times $5,000. Moreover, this limit applies only to the total contributions made by a person to national organizations. The same person can make as many additional $5,000 gifts to state and local committees of the same party as he wishes. For example, in the 1944 campaign, one member of the Du Pont family gave more than $39,000 to organizations supporting the Republican ticket, and the total contribution of the Du Pont family exceeded $125,000.[13]

However, it would be a mistake to conclude that because legislative efforts to curb the use of money in politics have failed to achieve specific purposes they have had no value at all. It seems probable that the presence of such laws on the statute books has a healthy effect in reminding parties, candidates, and voters alike that the proper use of money in campaigns is to provide the public with necessary information, and not to "buy" public office. It is likely that these laws have restrained individuals and organizations from the bold and corrupt use of money which characterized certain earlier periods in American politics.

inadequacies of congressional elections

One of the most surprising things about the American electoral system is the way in which our elections fail to resolve conflicts in our political life. In particular, it is difficult to understand why a November election in a presidential year, in which one of the major parties appears to sweep the nation and win large majorities in House and Senate in addition to the presidency, can in the end prove so indecisive. In good part the inability of a President and the party majorities in the two houses to work together in the formulation and administration of a program is the result of our constitutional system of checks and balances. No group of party members, however solidly knit they might be, could possibly hope to bridge all the gulfs established by the Constitution between Congress and President, and between House and Senate.

And yet part of the trouble lies with our congressional election system, which has failed to bring about the selection of national legislators in strict accordance with the democratic principle. The election of a President, as will be seen in the next chapter, is by no means pure democracy in operation. But in the way we go about selecting a President we come much closer to achieving the democratic ideal than we do in selecting our congressmen. It is not too much to say, then, that the inability of President and Congress to cooperate, even where the same party dominates the national political scene, is in part due to the fact that these three agencies represent the people in varying degrees. It seems clear that the President represents majority public opinion much more closely than does

---

[13] Overacker, "Presidential Campaign Funds, 1944," p. 912.

Congress. In good part the failure of Congress to function more satisfactorily as a democratic agency reflecting the will of the people can be traced to defects in the election system.

the inadequate size of the electorate

The failure of large numbers of people to vote in national elections seriously prejudices the result in an antidemocratic direction. Moreover, it is clear that the situation is more serious with respect to participation in congressional elections than it is in presidential elections. In each of the last three presidential elections, nearly 50 million voters have gone to the polls and voted. But in the intervening congressional elections of 1942 and 1946, the vote dropped alarmingly to 28 million and 34 million. This drop indicates that our congressmen often represent a narrower electorate than does the President, and to that extent are less perfect instrumentalities of democratic rule.

	Total Vote	Midterm vote as percentage of vote in preceding Presidential election
1928	34,109,460	
1930	24,772,663	(72.6)
1932	37,254,016	
1934	32,487,865	(87.2)
1936	43,068,434	
1938	36,224,428	(84.1)
1940	46,918,351	
1942	28,043,748	(59.8)
1944	45,070,787	
1946	34,400,742	(76.3)

Source: Gallup Political Almanac for 1948

In part, the failure of persons to vote in national elections is involuntary—the result of restrictions, often unfair and undemocratic, placed by the states upon the suffrage. The correction of this situation requires continued pressure upon the states to alter their policies. But in good part nonvoting is voluntary, and it would appear that this is particularly serious in congressional elections. It is proper to attack the individual voter for his apathy, and efforts to stimulate more widespread voting are certainly commendatory. But it is probable that the apathy of the voter depends on something more than mere carelessness or absent-mindedness. There is reason to believe that the size of the congressional vote in other than presidential elections will remain alarmingly small in spite of all efforts to bring out larger numbers of voters. Accordingly, the question may well be asked whether this condition does not suggest the need for a thoroughgoing reform of our consititutional system, particularly as to terms of office, so as to synchronize the election of President, senators, and representatives, thereby stimulating voter interest and enhancing the possibility that the persons elected to these offices will all tend to represent the same public will.

imperfect congressional representation of the popular will

Second, there are certain mechanical difficulties that stand in the way of the democratic representation of the popular will in Congress even where the voters do turn out to the polls on Election Day in large numbers. First and foremost among these difficulties is the rigid equality of representation enjoyed by all of the states in the Senate without regard to population. This means today that the number of people represented by a senator ranges all the way from 14,830,192 in the case of a senator from New York, to 160,083 in the case of a senator from Nevada.

As we have seen, the equality of the states in the Senate was an integral part of the most important compromise made in the Philadelphia convention of 1787, and it has become as firmly established as any aspect of the American constitutional system. Moreover, any alteration of this arrangement would require not only a constitutional amendment but one that would in effect have to be ratified by all forty-eight states, since the Constitution in so many words provides that no state shall be deprived of its equal representation in the Senate without its consent. Thus any suggestion that the system might be altered is a purely academic one. Nonetheless the fact remains that the Senate is a most imperfect legislative body for the representation of the popular will.

A second mechanical difficulty is found in the unequal representation of people by the members of the House of Representatives. The apportionment every ten years by Congress of the total number of seats in the House among the forty-eight states has provided a reasonably close approximation of representation based strictly upon population. Bitter battles have been waged over the use by Congress of differing mathematical formulas for the determination of each state's quota of seats in the House. But these need not concern us here, for in any case the assignment of seats has always shown fairly close adherence to the basic notion that a state's representation in the House should be proportional to its population. The trouble has come with the determination of the congressional districts within the states by the state legislatures. As has been seen, Congress since 1842 has required the states to elect their representatives by districts rather than at large, and in varying degree it has required the states to draw the district lines so as to produce districts equal in population and compact in shape. But these congressional directions have not been sufficient to prevent the state legislatures from doing great violence to the democratic principle in the performance of this task. Two practices have contributed to this unfortunate condition.

The first practice is the failure of many state legislatures to redraw district lines every ten years after each new census. Even where a state's quota of seats in the House remains the same, the movement of people within the state may create inequalities in the population of districts which can be corrected only by redistricting. Yet the legislatures are often slow to act. Sometimes the old arrangement is allowed to prevail well into the new decade before being changed, and occasionally a legislature fails to make any change within the ten-year period. For example, the present district lines in Ohio were drawn in 1911, and the districts in Illinois were not changed between 1901 and 1947. Needless to say, this produced great inequalities in the size of districts in both states. In Illinois, before the latest redistricting, one district had as few as 112,000 people and one as many as 914,000. The range in Ohio runs from a low of 163,500 to a high of 698,600. Writing in 1949, Professor James M. Burns estimated that in fourteen of the forty-four states having more than one representative, the population of the largest district was more than double that of the smallest.[14] In general these discrepancies favor rural areas over urban areas, since the population shifts of the present century have been from the country to the city.

The second practice is the gerrymander. Gerrymandering may be defined as the drawing of the lines of legislative districts in such a way as to give an advantage to one party over another. In other words, a state legislature that is controlled by one party almost always tries to draw congressional district lines in such a way as to enhance that party's chances of carrying a maximum of the districts in subsequent congressional elections. Gerrymandering is made possible because of the fact that the same ratio between Republicans and Democrats does not prevail through all parts of a state. The two major parties are heterogeneous in their make-up and include members from all walks of life. Yet there tend to be concentrations of party strength on a geographic basis. For example, in the northeastern states Democratic strength is greatest in the cities, whereas rural areas are often strongly Republican.

In any case the existence of gerrymanders in certain states is apparent. For example, the fourteen districts in Massachusetts represent at the present time a very effective Republican gerrymander. In state-wide elections in Massachusetts in the last generation the Democratic party has more often than not received a majority of the vote. Yet in no election since 1932 have the Democrats won a majority of the state's seats in the national House of Representatives. In the 1948 election, in spite of the fact that President Truman's majority in the state was almost a quarter of a million and that the Democratic candidate for governor won by a margin of nearly four hundred thousand votes, the Republicans won eight of the fourteen House seats.

It need hardly be said that there are other states in which a gerrymander operates very effectively to the advantage of the Democratic party. Indeed, it is probable that many of the most flagrant party advantages dependent upon gerrymanders in the different states tend to cancel each other out. But there

---

[14] James M. Burns, *Congress on Trial* (New York: Harper & Brothers, 1949), p. 51.

is obviously no guarantee that this is so, and at best the practice of gerry-mandering means that the democratic representation of the varying political desires of equal numbers of people is interfered with in greater or less degree.

inadequate lines of democratic control

Finally, to repeat the point once more, the decentralized and undisciplined character of our political parties makes it difficult for the voters to hold their congressmen accountable for their conduct in office—much more difficult than it is to hold a President accountable. Even where there is no interference with the right of all qualified voters to help select a state's congressmen, and even where bad districting does not put barriers in the way of democratic representation, the voter is frequently frustrated in his efforts to make his congressmen represent his will.

To take just one manifestation of this difficulty, it is clear that the average congressman feels much less responsible for the implementation of his party's platform than does the President. Moreover, he is seldom called to account on this score because of the extent to which the complexities of congressional organization and procedure, combined with weak party discipline in Congress, make it exceedingly difficult for the average voter to learn what goes on in Congress or to evaluate the record of his senators and representatives in an intelligent way. The congressman finds it particularly easy in nonpresidential years to seek re-election on the basis of his personality and his local political connections, without bothering to discuss national issues with the voter, to defend his own voting record in Congress, or to make clear his own stand on impending issues.

proposed changes in congressional elections

Many changes in the American system of electing congressmen have been proposed at one time or another. As has been indicated, no mere alteration of the electoral system will make the government completely democratic. Certain of the difficulties about the present political arrangement are the result of forces or conditions that have little or nothing to do with elections, one of these conditions being our system of checks and balances. We must not make the mistake of supposing that all of the ills of government can be cured by procedural reforms. Some such hope has been held for almost every change that has been made in the electoral system. A good example is found in the Seventeenth Amendment providing for popular election of United States senators. It was widely believed that this change would make the Senate a hardly less than perfect instrument for the representation of the popular will.[15]

That the amendment produced no such result should not, however, discredit

---

[15] Similar high hopes have been held for other electoral reforms such as the initiative and referendum, the recall, proportional representation, and the short ballot.

electoral reform, for if one does not make the mistake of expecting too much, there are weaknesses in our methods of electing public officers that it ought to be possible to correct. Three proposed changes in congressional elections will be noted.

a uniform congressional primary

Reference has already been made to the fact that Congress could, if it wished, use its power under the "times, places, and manner" clause of Article One of the Constitution to require all the states to nominate their candidates for both the House and the Senate by primary election, and, furthermore, to require that this be done throughout the country on the same day. There is little doubt that such a change would greatly strengthen the power of the national party organizations to influence the choice of candidates. It is likely that it would also make congressmen more responsible public officers by making it easier for the voters in each party to check the records of their national legislators. As it is, the Republican or the Democrat who is displeased with his congressmen and who perhaps feels that they have been unfaithful to the party's platform often finds it extremely difficult to express his displeasure when these legislators seek renomination. They may encounter no opposition in the primary, or at best the outcome of a primary contest may depend upon local issues and personalities. A national, uniform primary would almost certainly force candidates to make clear their identification with, or opposition to, the national platform of their parties.

uniform terms for President, senators, and representatives

One of the things that makes it difficult to preserve the lines of party responsibility in the American democracy is the fact that the President, senators, and representatives have varying terms of office. Where one party is given complete control of the national government by the voters in a presidential election, as were the Democrats in 1948, the President and the party majorities in Senate and House have a collective responsibility to fulfill their party's promises to the electorate. Where, as is so often the case, that responsibility is repudiated by some members of the majority, the voter's efforts to hold someone accountable are apt to be frustrated because of the differing two-year, four-year, and six-year terms of the men who have repudiated their promises.

To correct this defect it has been proposed that all three types of officer be elected for a coterminous period, say four years or six years. One of the latest advocates of this reform is Thomas K. Finletter, who in his little volume, *Can Representative Government Do the Job?*[16] suggests that President, senators, and

---

[16] Thomas K. Finletter, *Can Representative Government Do the Job?* (New York: Harcourt, Brace and Company, 1945). Finletter combines this proposal with the further suggestion that the President be authorized, in case of a deadlock between him and the Congress within the six-year period, to dissolve the government and order a new national election in which he and all members of Congress would have to stand for re-election.

representatives all be elected at one time for six-year terms. Needless to say, this change would involve a constitutional amendment. Moreover, favorable action on such an amendment would require persistent and vigorous backing. But the argument in favor of the change is nonetheless a very persuasive one.

proportional representation

A third reform proposal is that the members of the House of Representatives be chosen by proportional representation. P.R. is a complicated electoral system whereby three or more legislators are chosen from a single voting district more or less in strict proportion to the voting strength of each party group or other faction making up the electorate in the district. The system has been used in several American cities in selecting municipal councils but it has never been tried at the state or national level. Under the "times, places, and manner" clause it seems clear again that Congress could order the system used in the election of representatives. It would be necessary to order the states to elect their representatives at large (or at least by districts from which three or more representatives would be chosen). Moreover, the system could be expected to work properly only in those states having three or more seats in the House. Actually a close ratio between the percentage of the total vote won by a party and the number of seats it secured could be expected only where a state had five or more seats to fill. The use of proportional representation in the election of senators would be impossible unless the Constitution were amended to provide for the election of senators in groups of three or more.

Where proportional representation has been used in American cities its advocates have argued that its greatest merit lies in the strictly democratic result which it produces—each party or group receiving exactly the number of seats to which its vote entitles it. Its opponents, however, have attacked its divisive tendency, arguing that it encourages factionalism and thereby reduces the chances that one party will win majority control of the government. Insofar as this result has prevailed, the argument against proportional representation is a sound one, for it would seem more important in a democracy that a unified and cohesive majority win control of the government in an election than that minority groups be guaranteed representation in strict proportion to their voting strength.[17] These arguments become rather academic when applied to the national scene, for in the realities of present-day politics the possibility that Congress might order the election of representatives by proportional representation is exceedingly remote.

---

[17] New York City made use of proportional representation in the election of its council between 1937 and 1947. For an article which argues that the system worked well during this period, and did not encourage undue factionalism, see Belle Zeller and Hugh A. Bone, "The Repeal of P.R. in New York City—Ten Years in Retrospect," *American Political Science Review*, XLII (December, 1948), 1127.

THE RESULTS PRODUCED BY PROPORTIONAL REPRESENTATION IN THE ELECTION OF THE NEW YORK CITY COUNCIL, 1937–1945.

VOTER STRENGTH AND REPRESENTATION BY PARTIES*

	1937			1939			1941			1943			1945		
	No. Seats	% Seats	% Votes	No. Seats	% Seats	% Votes	No. Seats	% Seats	% Votes	No. Seats	% Seats	% Votes	No. Seats	% Seats	% Votes
DEMOCRATIC	13	50.0	47.0	14	66.5	65.5	17	65.5	64.0	10	59.0	53.0	14	60.0	59.0
REPUBLICAN	3	11.5	8.5	2	9.5	8.0	2	7.5	6.5	3	17.0	22.0	3	13.0	15.0
INSURGENT DEMOCRATIC	2	8.0	7.0	1	5.0	4.0	—	—	—	—	—	—	—	—	—
AMERICAN LABOR	5	19.0	21.0	2	9.5	11.5	3	11.5	11.5	2	12.0	11.0	2	9.0	10.0
FUSION	3	11.5	10.5	2	9.5	11.0	3	11.5	12.5	—	—	—	—	—	—
LIBERAL	—	—	2.5	—	—	—	—	—	—	—	—	—	2	9.0	7.0
COMMUNIST	—	—	3.5	—	—	—	1	4.0	5.5	2	12.0	14.0	2	9.0	9.0
OTHER	—	—	—	—	—	—	—	—	—	—	—	—	—	—	—
TOTAL	26			21			26			17			23		

* The figures used in the third column for each election represent the votes cast for persons on the deciding count, i.e., after the elimination of hopeless candidates and the transfer of their votes. (*Source:* Belle Zeller and Hugh A. Bone, "The Repeal of P. R. in New York City—Ten Years in Retrospect," *American Political Science Review,* XLII (December, 1948) 1127, 1132.)

bibliographic note

There are a number of excellent studies of general aspects of the American electoral system. Joseph P. Harris's *Election Administration in the United States* (Washington: The Brookings Institution, 1934) is a careful study of the way in which elections are conducted. Spencer D. Albright's *The American Ballot* (Washington: American Council on Public Affairs, 1942) examines ballot types and practices. The conduct of primary elections is subjected to systematic examination in Charles E. Merriam and Louise Overacker, *Primary Elections* (Chicago: The University of Chicago Press, 1924). Professor Overacker has devoted many years to the study of the raising and spending of money in election campaigns. Her volume *Money in Elections* (New York: The Macmillan Company, 1932) is an early discussion of the problem. This has been supplemented by numerous articles dealing with expenditures in specific campaigns, several of which will be found in the *American Political Science Review*. James K. Pollock's *Party Campaign Funds* (New York: Alfred A. Knopf, Inc., 1926) is another study of this same problem. The problem of *Non-Voting, Causes and Methods of Control* is dealt with in a volume bearing that title by Charles E. Merriam and Harold F. Gosnell (Chicago: The University of Chicago Press, 1924).

Cortez A. M. Ewing's *Congressional Elections, 1896–1944* (Norman: University of Oklahoma Press, 1947) is a statistical study of congressional elections during the last fifty years that brings to light many interesting facts and trends. Volta Torrey's *You and Your Congress* (New York: William Morrow & Company, 1944) is largely concerned with, and highly critical of, the process by which congressmen are elected. The history and practice of apportionment of seats in the House of Representatives among the several states is examined critically in Laurence F. Schmeckebier's *Congressional Apportionment* (Washington: The Brookings Institution, 1941). An interesting study of the apportionment problem in a single state is found in Henry N. Williams's "Congressional Apportionment in Tennessee," *Journal of Politics*, IV (November, 1942), 507. The problem of "Contested Congressional Elections" is considered in a scholarly article by Vincent Barnett, *Political Science Quarterly*, LIV (June, 1939), 187.

Proportional representation as a means of electing members of a legislative body has been examined in a variety of publications. A sympathetic treatment is found in George H. Hallett's *Proportional Representation—The Key to Democracy* (New York: The Macmillan Company, 2d ed., 1940). Unfavorable views of proportional representation are found in F. A. Herman's *Democracy or Anarchy? A Study of Proportional Representation* (Notre Dame: Review of Politics, 1941) and Dankwart A. Rustow's "Some Observations on Proportional Representation," *Journal of Politics*, XII (February, 1950), 107.

electing the President

*T*HE election of a president of the United States every four years is unquestionably the outstanding illustration in the modern world of a free people choosing their chief executive in democratic fashion. A presidential election is not pure democracy, and, as we shall see, it is not without its technical faults. But it is, nonetheless, unique. In no other great nation is there found any system of nominating candidates for the highest executive post that offers the spectacle and interest of the national convention or that shows as much sensitivity to public opinion. In no other nation is there so prolonged or intense a campaign in which rival candidates make every effort to carry their cases to the far corners of the land. In no other nation do fifty million voters go to the polls on Election Day and freely choose between two leading candidates for so powerful a post of national leadership.

Only in Great Britain, in the election of the 600-odd members of the House of Commons, usually at five-year intervals, is there found an election which rivals the American one in its democratic quality, its spectacular aspects, and its important stakes. But in a British election the Prime Minister—which officer in power and prestige does compare favorably with the President—is not chosen directly by the British voters. Instead, each voter in England participates only in the selection of a member of Parliament to represent his district. After the election is over, the party which has won a majority of the seats in the House of Commons chooses one of its leaders to serve as Prime Minister, much as the majority party in our House of Representatives chooses one of its leaders to serve as Speaker. Only the voters in the district which sends a Chamberlain, a Churchill, or an Attlee to represent them in the House of Commons ever pass directly upon the man who is to become Prime Minister.

It is true that in a British election the voters usually know pretty well who the Prime Minister will be in the event of a Labour or a Conservative victory. In the 1950 election a vote for the Labour candidate in a parliamentary district

was a vote for Attlee for Prime Minister, and a vote for the Conservative candidate was a vote for Churchill for Prime Minister. Moreover, in casting his
ballot for a single member of the House of Commons the British voter is also
consciously choosing between two party programs which are usually more
precisely defined than are the programs of American parties. It may even be
said that he votes for a party and not a mere candidate, and that accordingly the
choice he makes is more meaningful from the point of view of democracy than
is the choice made by the American voter. It is also true that American voters
do not vote directly for presidential candidates but rather for "electors" who
make the official choice of a chief executive. Nonetheless, for all practical purposes the American people have for a century and more chosen their President
at the moment of the national, popular election, whereas the British people have
chosen rather the party that is to govern them, leaving to that party the selection
of the chief executive. There is much to be said in favor of the British system as
against the American, but it is probably true that a British parliamentary election is not as colorful or dramatic as an American presidential election.

the original method of electing the President

The democratic character of a present-day presidential election seems all the
more remarkable when the undemocratic method provided for in the Constitution in 1789 is examined. The fact is that the Founding Fathers did not wish
to have the chief executive chosen by the people. The method of his selection was
one of the most difficult issues which confronted the Philadelphia convention,
and at one time or another election of the President by Congress or by the people
was proposed. But the former plan was rejected because of the fears of the
Founding Fathers that it would have made the President subservient to Congress
and thereby have undermined the principle of separation of powers. The latter
plan was opposed because the majority of the delegates did not feel that the
selection of so powerful a public officer could wisely be entrusted to the people.
Not all of the delegates may have felt so strongly as did George Mason, a delegate from Virginia, who said on the floor of the convention that "it would be as
unnatural to refer the choice of a . . . chief magistrate to the people as it would
be to refer a trial of colors to a blind man." [1] But when the question of the election of the President by the people was put to a vote only one state voted aye.

how the original system was expected to work

The plan finally approved by the convention for the selection of a chief executive was an ingenious one, and it is clear that the Fathers expected it to work

---

[1] A. T. Prescott, *Drafting the Federal Constitution* (University: Louisiana State University
Press, 1941), p. 563.

along very different lines from those that ultimately prevailed. In Article Two of the Constitution it was provided that the President and the Vice-President were to be chosen by the members of an *electoral college*. This college was to be a small body in which each state would have as many members as it had senators and representatives combined. Members of the college were to be chosen every four years in each state in such manner as the legislature thereof might direct, and were to meet in their respective states at a time designated by Congress and vote by ballot for two persons. These ballots were then to be forwarded to Congress to be opened and counted in the presence of the two houses. The person having the greatest number of votes, provided such number was a majority of the whole number of electors, was to be declared President, and the person standing second was to be declared Vice-President. If no person had a majority, then the House of Representatives was to choose immediately one of the five highest on the list to serve as President, the representatives from each state having one collective vote, and a majority of all the states being necessary to a choice. Likewise in case of a tie vote in the electoral college the House was to choose one of the tied candidates to serve as President; if there was a tie for second place the Senate would break the tie and choose a Vice-President.

Several significant points about the original system should be noted. In the first place, not a word was said in the Constitution about the nomination of presidential candidates. It was regarded as a foregone conclusion that Washington would be chosen as the first President. But thereafter the Convention seems to have expected that in each election the members of the electoral college would have a free hand in canvassing a wide list of possible candidates and that there would be no "nominees" in any formal sense. Second, the electors were never to meet in any one place as a single unit, but were to meet only as small groups in their respective states. In the absence of a *nomination* process by which the number of active candidates for the presidency would be greatly reduced, this was almost certain to mean that the electoral vote would be widely distributed. Accordingly, it is clear the convention expected that in many elections the electoral vote would be ineffective and the House of Representatives would have to choose the President. In fact, there were predictions in the convention that this would happen quite regularly. In other words, the convention seemingly viewed the electoral college as an agency that would *nominate* five candidates for the presidency, and it intended to place in the House of Representatives the true power to *elect* the President. Moreover, there is evidence that this arrangement was intended to serve as a compromise between the large and the small states. In the nomination process the large states would enjoy an advantage, since in good part the size of each state's electoral vote depended on population. At the election stage the small states would have the advantage, since the voting in the House was to be by states rather than by members, each state having one vote.

the development of the present system
of electing the President

As the Founding Fathers had expected, Washington was unanimously elected the first President of the United States. But thereafter the expectations of the Fathers were realized less and less. As early as the election of 1800 the system began to operate along quite different lines from those laid down by the convention. During the first third of the nineteenth century the system remained in a state of flux, until in the Jackson era the method of electing the President, as we know it today, became more or less crystallized.

In examining the way the revised system works in practice we will do well to keep certain questions in mind. To what extent has the system taken shape within the bounds of the Constitution? To what extent does it operate outside the framework of the written Constitution? What role have political parties played in altering our presidential elections? What degree of democracy finally pervades these elections?

The business of choosing a President today is divided into two stages of about equal importance: nomination and election. The importance of the first stage should not be minimized. In a two-party system like our own, as a presidential election draws near there may be as many as twenty-five men who are real possibilities to fill the office. But when the parties have selected their nominees for the presidency the race has been narrowed to a point where only two candidates remain. In other words, by the time the nominations are made the nation has moved forward *at least halfway* toward the final goal.

the nomination of presidential candidates

The process by which presidential candidates are nominated is a development that lies completely outside the scope of the written Constitution, for there is still not a word in that document about this aspect of the election system. It is at this point that the political parties have made an all-important contribution to our electoral system. It is not too much to say that the means by which the choice of the voters is narrowed to two candidates are almost completely controlled by the parties.

nomination by convention

For something over a century presidential candidates have been nominated by the political parties in national conventions consisting of a rather large number of delegates chosen along state lines to represent the total party membership. However, there is nothing inevitable about the convention system. Indeed, until the time of Jackson the parties nominated their presidential candidates by means of congressional caucuses. In other words, the right to participate in a party's selection of its presidential candidate was limited to those party members who held seats in Congress. However, in the eighteen thirties nomination by convention replaced nomination by caucus as a means of bringing to an end domination of a party by its congressional members. In particular the change was made to give a greater voice to the party leaders in the states.

the convention system rests largely on a customary basis

Not only is the Constitution utterly silent concerning the nomination of presidential candidates by party conventions; there is also little statutory control over this phase of the election system. A small body of state law deals with some of the details of convention organization and procedure, such as the method of selecting the delegates from the several states and the manner in which some of the state delegates cast their votes in the convention, but the larger aspects of the convention system—the total number of delegates, the time and place of the meeting, the vote required for nomination—have not been made the subject of legal control by either federal or state statute. Instead the organization and the control of a national convention are largely the responsibility of the party and rest for the most part upon a customary basis only. This party control finds expression in regulations formulated every four years by the convention itself serving as the legislative body of the party. It is also expressed through the decisions of the national committee, which functions as an executive committee during the long four-year stretches between conventions. For example, the selection of the city in which the nominating convention is to be held and the fixing of the time of such a meeting are decisions made by the national committee. On the other hand, the number of delegates who attend a convention and the method of voting used by them in selecting a nominee are fixed by the conventions themselves.

the size of a convention

In modern times the Democratic and the Republican national conventions have consisted of about one thousand delegates, with each state's representation being roughly equal to twice the size of its congressional delegation. Actually both parties now use modified formulas by which the size of a state delegation may be larger or smaller than this automatic figure.[2] This element of flexibility allows states which give a party substantial election support to enjoy increased voting power in that party's conventions, and, vice versa, it makes it possible to

---

[2] The size of the 1948 conventions was determined as follows:

Democratic: Each state was allowed two delegates for each seat in Congress, plus four additional delegates if it went Democratic in 1944. This produced a total of 1,234 delegates entitled to cast one vote each.

Republican: Each state was allowed four delegates plus three additional delegates if the state went Republican in 1944 or 1946, plus one additional delegate for each congressional district that cast a minimum of 1,000 Republican votes plus a second additional delegate for each congressional district that cast more than 10,000 Republican votes. This produced a total of 1,094 delegates entitled to cast one vote each.

reduce the convention influence of those states which give a party little support at election time. Both parties were reluctant to adopt a flexible system of determining the size of state delegations, for in taking this step they were admitting that their strength was not evenly distributed through the nation and that they were not true *national* parties. But the anomaly of the states in the Deep South sending two hundred or more delegates to the Republican convention, although they seldom gave the party a single electoral vote, was bound to be corrected sooner or later. In the 1912 convention, these delegates were largely controlled by President Taft, who was seeking renomination. This was not surprising, since a Republican President easily controls the weak party organizations in the South by means of the patronage power. The irritation which this condition caused in the party faction backing Theodore Roosevelt, the split that followed the Taft nomination, and the repair of the break in 1916 finally led to the adoption of a formula allowing a state maximum representation in the Republican convention only if it gave the party's presidential candidate its electoral vote in the last preceding election and only if each congressional district cast 10,000 or more votes for Republican electors. Operation of the formula in 1916 resulted in loss by the southern states of 76 votes in the Republican convention.

election of convention delegates

Once a state's quota of delegates to either party convention has been assigned to it, the manner of the selection of these delegates is left largely to the state to decide. Obviously this is an exceedingly important stage in the total process of selecting a president, for by the time the delegates to the convention are chosen, various candidates for its presidential nomination are waging active campaigns and the character of a state delegation usually determines how that state will vote in the convention. Two methods are now in use for the selection of delegates —the convention system and the primary system.

Throughout the nineteenth century, delegates were chosen by state and local conventions or caucuses. Early in the present century the desire to make the presidential election system more democratic led to the appearance of the presidential primary, in which the rank and file of party members in a state were not only allowed to choose the state's delegates to the national convention but were often given an opportunity to express their preferences for a presidential candidate. At first it appeared that the primary would soon entirely replace the state convention as a means of choosing delegates, but after 1916 a reaction set in, and today less than one third of the states make use of presidential primaries. Moreover, in many of these states the primary has become a mere formality. For example, in the 1948 preconvention campaign there was not a single state in which a crucial Democratic presidential primary election was held, and not more than five or six states held important Republican primaries in which leading candidates for the Republican nomination figured.

Thus it would seem that the attempt to democratize the business of nominating presidential candidates by giving the masses of party voters control over the selection of convention delegates has ended in failure. Today the selection of the one thousand or more delegates to the national conventions is largely determined by the party leaders and organizations in the states and local communities. Moreover, the roster of convention delegates consists in good part of loyal party workers and even of colorless party hacks who are easily dictated to by the small group of party leaders who dominate most national conventions.

"availability" of presidential candidates

Unless it is clear that a party is committed to the renomination of a President in office, anywhere from two or three to a dozen or more candidates for the nomination may be expected to be active in the preconvention campaign. Who are these men and what factors determine their "availability"? To begin with, most of them will be men with well-known records in politics. Occasionally a businessman can step directly into the role of a party's standard-bearer with little or no previous experience in politics, as did Wendell Willkie in 1940. Somewhat more frequently a military hero makes the same transition. But the overwhelming majority of the men who have received the nominations of the major parties throughout our history have been active in politics.

Moreover, state rather than national politics has been the great training ground for presidential candidates. Seventeen of the twenty-eight candidates nominated by the two major parties between 1900 and 1948 were state governors or former governors. In particular, the governors of such states as New York, Ohio, and Illinois, whether Republicans or Democrats, are almost always highly available candidates for their parties' nominations. These states have large electoral votes, and their location and their social and economic interests also make them "key" states. Only rarely does a member of Congress, such as Harding, Borah, Taft, or Vandenberg, or a national administrative officer, such as Hoover, become an active candidate.

This preference for men with successful careers in state politics is to be explained on two grounds. First, a national convention is usually dominated by state party leaders rather than by congressional party leaders. There is almost always an element of distrust, however slight, between these two groups within a party, and this leads the larger group to prefer one of its own kind for the party's highest honor. Second, men who have been active in national politics are in a sense too well known. They have inevitably made enemies and antagonized many voters by their stands on national issues. The governor of a large state, on the other hand, may be a well-known national figure, but his political quarrels and difficulties within his state are not apt to have been widely advertised in the rest of the country.

Up to now virtually all candidates for the presidency have been of "American stock," and Protestant in religion. Beyond that, if a candidate has a large and attractive family, a pleasing appearance and personality, and, above all, a knack for campaign oratory, he will have no difficulty about qualifying as an available candidate. Whether the lightning will finally strike him depends upon a further complex of forces and circumstances which defy any systematic analysis and in which luck is by no means the least important factor.

are presidential nominees chosen in "smoked-filled hotel rooms"?

In spite of the failure of the American people to evolve a formal procedure for the democratic selection of convention delegates and thus of presidential candidates, it is possible to exaggerate the absence of democracy in the work and decisions of conventions. Certainly the notion that at a well-timed moment a small group of party leaders get together in a smoke-filled hotel room and agree upon a candidate, who is then meekly accepted by the delegates, is not a valid one. Such meetings do occur and there are instances in the present century in which presidential candidates have been selected in this fashion. Nonetheless even the most arrogant of party leaders are ordinarily anxious to have their party win a national election. Accordingly they are inclined to give considerable attention to a potential candidate's acceptability to the voters. Occasionally these leaders may persuade themselves that the party can "win with a Chinaman" and attempt to force upon the delegates the nomination of a candidate whose popular backing is not strong. But far more often than not the outcome of the election seems uncertain and the leaders are persuaded that the convention should nominate the party's strongest candidate.

Two forces operate in the present-day national convention to bring about the nomination of a candidate who has strong backing among the rank-and-file party members. One is the influence of the public opinion poll. The leading polling agencies have in recent presidential election years conducted elaborate straw votes of party opinion during the months and weeks preceding the conventions which unquestionably carry great weight with both convention leaders and delegates. In fact, in the three or four presidential elections since polling has come to occupy such a prominent place on the American scene, neither major party has failed to nominate the candidate who stood at the top of the polls.[3]

To a limited extent it may even be said that the poll has taken the place of

---

[3] The final prenomination Gallup Polls were as follows:

1936	Republican	Landon	55%
		Borah	18%
	Democratic	No poll. Roosevelt virtually the unanimous choice of Democrats for renomination.	
1940	Republican	Willkie	44%
		Dewey	29%
	Democratic	Roosevelt	92%

the presidential primary as a means of enabling the masses of voters to influence the selection of presidential nominees. The failure of the polls to predict accurately the outcome of the 1948 election may in 1952 and thereafter lessen the influence of preconvention analyses of public opinion, but that remains to be seen.

Second, the presidential primary, in spite of its declining use, continues to have some value as an indicator of public opinion. For example, Wendell Willkie withdrew from the race for the Republican nomination in 1944 after his disastrous defeat in the early Wisconsin primary, concluding, probably correctly, that the vote in this single state indicated that his strength with Republicans in the Middle West generally had declined very considerably. Again in 1948 the last-minute Republican primary in Oregon in which Dewey won a close victory over Stassen was unquestionably regarded as a strong indication that the Stassen tide, which had been running strong, was definitely beginning to ebb, and that Dewey was the preferred candidate among Republicans everywhere. In other words, the Oregon primary in a sense served as a national primary and profoundly influenced the action of the Republican Convention in nominating Dewey.

However one evaluates the influence of the poll and the primary upon the making of presidential nominations, it is clear that since 1928 the convention system has operated in reasonably democratic fashion. In the twelve conventions held during this period the presidential nominees were in every instance selected from among the two or three leading candidates for the nomination, and, more often than not, the victor had been the leading candidate in the preconvention polls and presidential primaries.

procedure in the convention

It is not necessary to describe in detail the procedure which is followed during the four- or five-day period that a national convention is in session, for much of the activity at a convention is "full of sound and fury, signifying nothing." There are two important items of business to be transacted: the drafting and adoption of a party platform, and the nomination of candidates for the presidency and vice-presidency.

The platform is today drafted and approved before the formal selection of candidates occurs, a fact which sometimes produces an incongruous situation in which presidential nominee and platform do not fit each other too well. But

1944	Republican	Dewey	58%
		MacArthur	13%
		Bricker	12%
	Democratic	Roosevelt	90%
1948	Republican	Dewey	33%
		Stassen	26%
		Vandenberg	13%
	Democratic	Truman	67%
		Marshall	12%

where the successful candidate is pretty well indicated in advance, as where a President in office is seeking renomination and re-election, the platform is usually tailored to fit the wishes of this candidate. And in any case a party platform is usually sufficiently vague and ambiguous that almost any man a party is likely to nominate finds it possible to give it his approval. Occasionally in the subsequent campaign a candidate tends to ignore the platform and proceeds to make his position clear in a series of speeches. In fact, in nearly all campaigns the platforms are more or less lost sight of as public interest becomes centered in the rival speeches and campaign tactics of the two candidates.

The platform is drafted by a committee on resolutions on which sit one man and one woman from each state and territory selected by their own delegations. This committee usually holds public hearings at which representatives of pressure groups are given a chance to urge their views. However, much of the platform is often prepared in advance by a small group of party leaders or, in the case of the party in power, by the President and his advisers. On the other hand, the party's stand on certain controversial issues may remain in doubt until the end, so that the leading pressure groups seem to feel that it is worth their time and effort to be active at this stage of the political process. The platform is submitted to the delegates on the floor of the convention on the second or third day, usually being approved with a minimum of debate or controversy. Occasionally an effort is made to amend the platform from the floor, and once in a while such a move succeeds, as, for example, when a group of liberal "rebels" in the 1948 Democratic Convention succeeded in strengthening the civil rights plank prepared by the resolutions committee.

It is difficult to determine the exact role played by the party platform in American politics. It is easy enough to ridicule the average platform, for as one expert says, it "speaks with boldness and forthrightness on issues that are already well settled; it is likely to be ambiguous on contentious questions." [4] But such criticism frequently overlooks the importance of compromise in politics. The national convention brings together the diverse and all-important state and local factions which make up our national parties. If these agencies are to function effectively on the national political scene certain cohesive forces are necessary to offset the divisive tendencies always present in our American parties. The strongest of these forces is the desire of local political leaders and organizations to see their party win control of the presidency and of the national government. But often the individual who finally emerges as the party's standard-bearer is not overly popular with certain factions within his own party, and if, in addition to him, these factions are also asked to accept an unequivocal platform which dodges none of the issues and whose planks run counter to their own attitudes

[4] V. O. Key, *Politics, Parties, and Pressure Groups* (New York: Thomas Y. Crowell Company, 2d ed., 1947), pp. 404–405.

and policies, they may well balk. Thus the evasive platform is one of the forces that makes it possible for our parties to hold together at least long enough to carry through the business of electing a President every four years who has the backing of 25 million voters. This is an achievement whose importance should not be minimized. It is true that the price paid for it is sometimes a heavy one in terms of the confusing of issues which ought rationally to be brought out in the open and intelligently discussed.

On the other hand, the evasive quality of the platform can be exaggerated. From time to time bitter intraparty fights have been fought over such issues as sound currency, prohibition, isolationism, civil rights, and labor relations, with one or another faction winning the battle and committing its party to a forthright stand on such an issue. Moreover, at least some of these party stands were ultimately reflected in the adoption of positive governmental policies.

Both major party conventions now employ much the same method of nominating candidates. First the roll of the states is called so that the contending candidates for the presidential nomination may be placed before the convention in formal nominating speeches. Then the balloting begins, each state casting its votes orally as the roll is called from Alabama to Wyoming. A majority of all votes cast is necessary to a choice, and successive ballots are taken until a majority is obtained by one of the candidates. The first ballot frequently proves effective; in fact, in the present century ten Republican candidates and eight Democratic candidates have been chosen on the first ballot.

Following the selection of a presidential candidate, the convention proceeds, usually in short order, to the selection of a vice-presidential candidate. The presidential nominee's advice is sought, and as often as not only one name is placed before the convention, and only one ballot is necessary for a choice. Often the vice-presidential candidate is one of the disappointed seekers of the presidential nomination, and he is almost always someone who will give the party ticket geographical balance. Sometimes an effort is made to give the ticket a liberal-conservative combination. This may prove to be expedient politically, but it has little or no logical justification.

For many years the nominating practices of the two major parties differed in that the Democrats made use of the so-called unit rule and required a two-thirds majority for the nomination of its candidates. These two practices were not unrelated. The unit rule meant that the vote of each state delegation be cast unanimously for some one candidate. This rule was not (and is not) imposed by the Democratic party upon the states; instead the national convention recognized the right of the state party to direct its delegation to the national convention to vote as a unit. In times past this was the usual practice of the states, and inasmuch as some of the state delegations which appeared to be voting solidly for a candidate might well contain delegates who as individuals favored other candidates, there was always the possibility that a candidate who received a bare majority of the total vote in the convention would actually be a minority nominee. To prevent such a result was one of the purposes of the two-thirds rule.

A further explanation for the use of the two-thirds rule was the belief of southern Democrats, always jealous of their prestige and power, that it gave them a veto power which could be used to prevent the nomination of a candidate unacceptable to them. In any case the 1936 Democratic Convention abandoned the two-thirds rule and provided for nomination by simple majority. This step was helped by the fact that the use of the unit rule, although never formally abandoned, had declined to a point where it was no longer necessary to require a two-thirds majority in order to ensure that a victorious candidate be the choice of at least a majority of the delegates.

the national convention evaluated

No aspect of the American political system is easier to criticize or has been more vigorously condemned than the national convention. Its vulgar demonstrations, its cheap and emotional speechmaking, the contemptuous position to which its delegates are frequently reduced, and the utter lack, to outward appearances at least, of dignity and high purpose are difficult to explain or defend to a rational person.

It has been suggested that if the American people want to get away from the crudities of the convention system and desire to pick their presidential candidates in a more democratic manner the way is open. Let Congress provide by law (or if there be doubt about its power in this respect, let it propose an amendment to the Constitution) that the parties shall nominate their presidential candidates in national primary elections held sometime in the late summer of presidential years.[5] In this way the great masses of Republican and Democratic voters throughout the nation would go to the polls on a single day and select their nominees.

The suggestion is an intriguing one, for its acceptance would represent a logical and, in the final analysis, desirable extension of the democratic principle in the actual workings of American government. At the same time, apart from the fact that its adoption is totally unlikely, there are practical objections that can be advanced against it. For one thing, many troublesome technical questions would have to be answered. For example, what if three or more strong candidates for the presidential nomination of one of the parties so divided the popular vote that the top man had less than a majority of the votes cast? Would it be wise to provide in such a case that a mere plurality be sufficient for a choice, or would it be better to provide for a second runoff primary in which the two highest candidates would compete against each other? If the former alternative was

---

[5] President Wilson advanced such a proposal in his first message to Congress in 1913. Again in 1924 the Progressive party's platform advocated a national primary system of nominating presidential candidates. See Key, *Politics, Parties, and Pressure Groups*, p. 393.

preferred, would the selection of a candidate be any more "democratic" than it is under the convention system? If the latter alternative was followed, would not the result be too complex and unwieldy, requiring as it would *three* national elections before a President could be chosen?

In any case it is doubtful whether the convention system has failed to such an extent as to warrant any radical change in the American system of nominating presidential candidates. In the first place, the record of the last quarter of a century indicates that the conventions have not been unmindful of public opinion in selecting the nominees. It is a fair guess that the public opinion poll and the continued use of the presidential primary make it unlikely that a major party convention will force upon the party members a candidate who does not stand near the top in the preconvention campaign, particularly so long as the two parties remain anything like equal in strength.

Second, the opportunity which a national convention provides to further the compromise spirit in American politics is not something that should be idly rejected. In the selection of a presidential candidate from among the three or four leading contenders, in the balancing of the ticket through the selection of contrasting presidential and vice-presidential candidates, and in the balancing of candidates and platform, the convention system makes it possible to reconcile opposing forces within a party. As has already been indicated, this kind of compromise has its bad side as well as its good. But insofar as there must be some measure of give-and-take in the control of a national party, it is doubtful whether any other system of nominating presidential candidates would offer so good an opportunity for compromise or hold to a minimum the possibility of one party faction so dominating the nominating process as to alienate other groups within the party. In the end it is possible to conclude that the convention system of nominating presidential candidates has served American democracy reasonably well, and that to correct its defects the wisest policy to follow is to continue the exertion of constant pressure upon the parties to prevent the recurrence of incidents of the "smoke-filled hotel room" type and to strengthen the sensitivity of the convention to opinion among the rank-and-file party members.

the presidential campaign

The national conventions are usually over by the middle of July in presidential years. Thereafter, until some time in September, the political scene remains relatively quiet until the active campaigning begins. Then for a period of some eight weeks before Election Day in November the candidates campaign vigorously, and the country is treated to one of the most exciting and colorful spectacles in its political life. Different candidates for the presidency have used so many forms of campaign strategy and tactics that it is almost impossible to generalize about this subject. Indeed, there is much disagreement as to whether a presidential campaign has any important effect upon the outcome of an election. In recent years such diverse authorities as James Farley and poll takers Gallup and Roper have all asserted that campaigning has a limited value since most voters have made up their minds at the beginning of a campaign. V. O. Key comes to the conclusion that "campaigns mainly renew the loyalties of the faithful, bring the apathetic out to the polls for the expression of their predispositions, and effect the conversion of a very few electors." [6]

The unexpected victory of President Truman in the 1948 elections suggests that this tendency to minimize the importance of campaigning has been carried much too far, for it seems clear that the particular kinds of campaign waged by Dewey and Truman in 1948 profoundly affected the outcome of the election— Dewey having lost votes by the glib generalizing which marked his "high-level" campaign speeches, and Truman having won votes by carrying his down-to-earth message to the common man who came out to welcome the President at the whistle stops across the land.

organizing the party machinery

Organizing a presidential campaign includes three substantial tasks. The first is to make certain that the party machinery is in good repair and well oiled for the intensive September-October drive preceding the November election. Meeting this responsibility is the biggest job that comes to the national chairman during his four-year term and is, indeed, the main reason for that officer's existence. In general his problem is to be sure that party organizations are prepared for action at national, state, and local levels, for party workers must not only carry the burden of campaigning but also be ready to bring out the millions of voters on Election Day. It might be supposed that the voter who has paid any attention to a presidential campaign, and who has even a mild interest in seeing one candidate win, could almost certainly be counted upon to go to the polls on Election Day under his own initiative. Although this is probably true of the majority of voters, experience has shown it is not true of the many millions of others who seem to need personal encouragement and assistance if they are to manage to vote on Election Day. If it be assumed, for example, that one in ten of the voters who supported Truman in 1948 would not have gone to the polls except as a result of organization activity and pressure, the resulting two and a half million votes which they cast were more than enough to account for Truman's margin of victory.

In recent elections the activity of the old-line party organizations has been supplemented by the work of "independent committees" and even of pressure groups and labor unions. Indeed, there is reason to believe that in 1948 the regular Democratic party machinery was in many parts of the country poorly organized and grossly inefficient, and that its work was taken over in effective fashion

---

[6] Key, *Politics, Parties, and Pressure Groups*, p. 449.

by labor unions and other nonparty groups who were anxious to see President Truman re-elected.

financing the campaign

The second task is to raise sufficient money to meet the heavy costs of a presidential campaign. This highly specialized undertaking is usually assigned to a small number of party professionals who use well-tested methods of raising money from a relatively small number of people who are persuaded to contribute to the cause in large amounts. The Wallace campaign in 1948 was financed, in part at least, by charging admission to the Wallace speeches and by seeking small contributions from large numbers of people almost on a dues-paying basis. The major parties sometimes make similar efforts to raise money, but in the end they usually find themselves dependent upon large donors for most of their support.

determining the strategy

The third task is to determine the main lines of strategy which are to govern a presidential campaign. Here the possibilities are almost infinite, and the record of the past is so confusing as almost to defy any scientific analysis. The line between successful and unsuccessful strategy is so elusive and subtle that it is virtually impossible to draw any final conclusions or to present any systematic treatment of the subject. Nonetheless, every presidential candidate for better or worse must make certain basic decisions early in a campaign and then proceed accordingly. He and his advisers must decide whether he is to take the offense or play it safe; whether to stay at home and wage what in McKinley's time was called a "front-porch" campaign or make a "swing around the circle" and take his campaign to every whistle stop in America, as Harry S. Truman attempted to do in 1948. He must decide whether to ignore his opponent (as Franklin Roosevelt did so effectively in 1936, 1940, and 1944) or attack him continuously and vigorously (as did Roosevelt's opponents in the same years). He must choose the issues with care, doing his best to emphasize those which will enable him and his party to show to advantage, and to sidetrack or obscure whatever will cause embarrassment. He must have a good sense of timing, starting his campaign not too early and not too late, and bringing it to a climax at the proper moment.

There are so many crucial decisions to make and so many possibilities of error in judgment and action that a candidate might well despair of ever bringing a campaign to a successful conclusion. A sense of discouragement results also from the famous stories that are told of campaign "blunders"—for example, of how Charles Evans Hughes lost the presidency in 1916 by failing to shake hands with Hiram Johnson on his visit to California during the campaign.[7] But most

---

[7] See the interesting article by F. M. Davenport, "Did Hughes Snub Johnson?—An Inside Story," *American Political Science Review*, XLIII (April, 1949), 321.

candidates soon throw off any sense of discouragement and early in the campaign do their best to create and maintain an "illusion of victory." After all, each candidate runs much the same risks, and in the end it is unlikely that the presidency will be won or lost on any one tactical error or even strategic mistake. And yet a campaign must be planned with care and shrewdness, the decisions to be made are numerous, and the balance between opposing policies is always difficult to maintain.

the final election of a President

selection of the electoral college

On the first Tuesday after the first Monday in November, a date fixed by federal law, some fifty million voters in the forty-eight states go to the polls and select the 531 members of the electoral college. The legislatures of all the states long ago provided that the presidential electors should be chosen by the voters, but it should be remembered that under the Constitution the state legislatures retain the right to prescribe the selection of the electors in whatever manner they choose.[8]

Before Election Day each of the parties selects a full slate of candidates for the seats to which a state is entitled in the electoral college. The identity of these candidates and the manner of their selection is of no consequence whatsoever, provided there is no question of a revolt on the part of a state's electors against their party's candidate for the presidency. Indeed, in nearly half the states the names of the candidates for the electoral college no longer appear upon the ballot. Instead, even though the voters are technically voting for electors and not for a President, the ballots in these states carry only the names of the party candidates for President and Vice-President, and a phrase for each party column indicating that the proper number of candidates for the electoral college are pledged to vote for the party's nominees.

In all the states the electors are chosen at large, which means, of course, that the entire slate of the party receiving the most votes in the state-wide election is elected and the electoral vote of the state is thereafter cast as a unit. There is nothing in the Constitution to prevent a state legislature from providing for the choosing of electors by single-member districts, an arrangement which would make possible a divided state electoral vote. No state has followed such a plan since 1891 (and few before that date) because the dominant party in each state naturally opposes any plan which would give the minority party a chance to win a few electoral votes. Moreover, the state legislatures have reasoned that the possibility of a divided electoral vote would lessen a state's influence and prestige in national politics.

---

[8] See *McPherson* v. *Blacker*, 146 U.S. 1 (1892).

selection of a President by the electors

By midnight of Election Day, as the returns come in, it is usually possible to determine which party has elected a majority of the 531 members of the electoral college and thus to know who will be the new President. But technically the voting for President and Vice-President occurs in December when, on a day fixed by federal law, the victorious electors meet in their respective state capitals and formally cast their ballots. Under the terms of the Twelfth Amendment each elector casts one vote for President and one for Vice-President. Under the original Constitution each elector in effect cast two votes for President, and the candidate receiving the most votes became President and the candidate standing second became Vice-President. But in the election of 1800, the first to be dominated by political parties, all of the electors pledged to the Republican party cast their two votes for Jefferson and Burr, intending the first to be President and the latter Vice-President. But since both men had the same number of electoral votes there was no legal way of carrying out the intention of the electors, and it was necessary for the House of Representatives to break the tie. It was clear that the same result would prevail in subsequent elections if political parties continued to be active. Accordingly the Twelfth Amendment was added to the Constitution in 1804, directing the electors to cast one of their votes specifically for President and one for Vice-President.

The outcome of the balloting of the electoral college is not officially known until the new Congress assembles on January 3, counts the ballots of the electors in a joint House-Senate session, and proclaims the result. It is at this point that the House would proceed to elect a President in case of a tie vote or in case no candidate had a clear majority of electoral votes, the Senate electing a Vice-President under similar conditions. Since the Twentieth Amendment fixes January 20 as Inauguration Day, Congress would have to act promptly were the electoral vote to prove ineffective.

is the electoral college system democratic?

The system of the electoral college has functioned reasonably well through the years, so well in fact, that its potential shortcomings are generally overlooked. Actually the system has three serious weaknesses, each of which offers a threat to the democratic character of presidential elections

electors may break their pledges

In the first place, as has been indicated, there is no provision in the federal Constitution or law to prevent electors from repudiating their pledges. Unless a state itself prohibits such conduct, there is nothing to prevent an elector from voting in December for someone other than his party's candidates. Only two states expressly compel electors to fulfill their pledges, although several others have laws which make an incidental recognition of this obligation. The possibility of such highhanded action by electors has long been discussed, and from time to time its imminency in particular elections rumored. Not until the election of 1948 did it become an actuality in modern times. In the election of that year the Dixiecrat movement presented a real threat to the integrity of the presidential election system. In Louisiana and Alabama the Dixiecrats took control of the local Democratic organizations, and the Democratic electors chosen by those states refused to cast their votes for the presidential and vice-presidential candidates nominated by the Democratic National Convention. However, they announced their intentions in advance of the November election, and in Louisiana a separate slate of electors pledged to Truman and Barkley was placed in the running. In Tennessee one Democratic elector voted for Thurmond although the state went for Truman and he was presumably committed to vote for his party's official candidate.

a candidate may win the presidency with a minority of the popular vote

The second weakness in the system is the ever-present possibility that the popular vote and the electoral vote will get out of line and that the victor in the electoral vote will actually receive fewer popular votes than his opponent. This possibility is the direct result of the fact that the electoral vote of each state is cast as a unit. To take an extreme example, it would become a reality if winning candidate A carried by a narrow margin in the popular vote a sufficient number of states to give him an electoral majority but lost the other states by a wide margin in the popular vote. Candidate B's popular vote, being almost as great as A's in the states which A carried and considerably greater in the states B carried, would under these circumstances reach a higher total. Actually, this condition has prevailed in two elections since the Civil War, as follows:

Year	Candidates	Popular Vote	Electoral Vote
1876	Hayes (Rep.)	4,033,768	185
	Tilden (Dem.)	4,285,992	184
1888	Harrison (Rep.)	5,439,853	233
	Cleveland (Dem.)	5,540,329	168

Moreover, as commentators are fond of pointing out, the same result could have prevailed in many other elections had small blocs of popular votes been cast the other way in certain states. For example, in the 1948 election, in spite of the fact that Truman's popular majority exceeded two million votes, if some 40,-000 voters had cast their votes the other way in Ohio, Illinois, and California, Dewey would have had a majority in the electoral college. The mere possibility that such a result might have prevailed is a disturbing thought—whatever one's politics. For Mr. Dewey to have become President in spite of the fact that he would have had nearly two million fewer popular votes than his opponent, and to have found himself confronted by large Democratic majorities in Congress, which presumably would not have been altered by the reversal of a mere 40,000 votes, would have been highly unfortunate. A dangerous situation would have existed in which the national welfare might have suffered grave damage.

"Don't Expect Me To Get This Real Accurate, Bub"

(Reprinted with permission of Herblock and the Washington Post Co.)

an election thrown into the House may produce untoward results

The third weakness is the possibility that the electoral college may fail to give a majority to any candidate and that the election of a President will be thrown into the House of Representatives. This has happened only once in our history, when in 1824 four presidential candidates divided the electoral vote in such a way that no one of them had a majority. As long as only two candidates receive electoral votes, one is bound to have a majority. But there have been frequent elections in the last century in which strong third-party candidates threatened in advance to win enough electoral votes to throw the election into the House. The 1948 election provides a good illustration. As events turned out, Thurmond, the Dixiecrat candidate, carried four states and received 39 electoral votes.[9] Had Dewey rather than Truman carried Ohio and Illinois (Truman's combined popu-

---

[9] Thurmond carried Alabama, Louisiana, Mississippi, and South Carolina and also received 1 electoral vote in Tennessee.

lar majority in these states was only 50,000), Dewey's electoral vote would have been 242 and Truman's 250. Both men would have been short of a majority and the House would have been called upon to pick a President.

It may be asked why there should be any misfortune about having a presidential election thrown into the House of Representatives. Two difficulties should be mentioned. In the first place the voting in the House for President is by states and not by members. It is entirely possible mathematically for the minority party in the House to have control of a majority of the state delegations and thereby to be in a position to elect its candidate to the presidency even though he stood second in both the popular and the electoral votes. Second, an even more serious difficulty results from the constitutional requirement that the winning candidate must receive the support of a majority of all the states. It is possible for the party control of state delegations to be so scrambled that the House would be unable to elect a President. Indeed such a result might well have prevailed had the 1948 election been thrown into the House in spite of the fact that the Democrats held 263 out of the 435 seats, and controlled 25 state delegations while the Republicans controlled only 20. Had the representatives from the four states carried by Thurmond continued to vote for him (and as one of the "three" candidates receiving the highest number of electoral votes he would, under the Twelfth Amendment, have been an eligible candidate in the House voting), the Democrats would have been unable to control the delegation votes of a majority of the states since three delegations consisted of an equal number of Democrats and Republicans, leaving the Democrats with outright control of only 21 delegations. Had the House been unable to make a decision by January 20, 1949, the Twentieth Amendment provides that the Vice-President should act as President. In the meantime the Senate presumably would have been choosing a Vice-President from among the three candidates with the highest number of votes in the electoral college. Conceivably the Democratic majority of 54 would have resulted in the election of Alben Barkley as Vice-President and he would have become "acting" President on January 20. Continuing inability on the part of the House thereafter to resolve its dilemma could have meant that Barkley would have served as President indefinitely—perhaps even for two or four years.

An even more fantastic situation would have come into being had the eight senators from the four states carried by Thurmond refused to vote for either Barkley or Warren for Vice-President. Since the Twelfth Amendment provides that " a majority of the whole number shall be necessary to a choice," the Senate would under those circumstances have also been unable to make a choice by January 20. In that case the Twentieth Amendment seems to provide that Congress may by law declare who shall act as President or specify the manner in which one who is to act as President shall be selected. What Congress would have done with this power under such unusual circumstances is anyone's guess. And lest it seem that the fantastic situation just described is not worthy of consideration as a real possibility, it need only be recalled that 25,000 votes cast the other way would have given Dewey Ohio and Illinois and thereby have set in motion the chain of events that might have led to the final incredible result.

proposals for change

The three difficulties described above have long been recognized, and although they have not come to pass very often many proposals for correcting the situation have been made. The threat or actual presence of each one of the three difficulties in the 1948 election has led to a recent renewal of demands for change.

popular election of the President

The most extreme proposal that has been made to change our system of presidential elections is that the electoral college and vote be abolished entirely and Presidents chosen in straight popular elections along national lines. From the point of view of the democratic principle there is much to be said for this proposal. An election in which fifty million or more Americans may go to the polls and choose a President without regard to state lines or without the interposition of an artificial "electoral vote" between the people and the winning candidate has much to commend it in logic, and it offers no serious mechanical difficulties.

But for the present such a change is beyond the realm of the politically possible. The difficulty about this proposal is that it would entirely eliminate the states as factors in a presidential election. In particular the less populous states would oppose such a constitutional amendment because of fears that the voters in the Northeast would dominate a popular election. The southern states (or at least the present leaders of these states) would also oppose such a method because it would force them to broaden the suffrage and let Negroes and "poor whites" vote if they were to enjoy the influence in a national popular election to which they would be entitled on the basis of their populations.

eliminating the electors but preserving the electoral vote

A generation ago Senator George Norris of Nebraska proposed an amendment to the Constitution which would have abolished the office of elector while preserving the electoral vote of each state and providing that it be cast as a unit automatically on the basis of the popular vote. This relatively mild proposal would have met only one objection to the existing system—the fact that there is nothing to prevent the electors from repudiating their pledges. However, even such a mild proposal as this failed to win necessary support in Congress. Because it would accomplish so little, present-day advocates of reform have urged a more drastic change in presidential elections.

eliminating the electors and dividing the electoral vote proportionally

Following the 1948 election Senator Henry C. Lodge, Jr., of Massachusetts and Representative Ed Gossett of Texas renewed a proposal which has gained support in recent years: that the Constitution be amended to eliminate the office of elector and to provide for the division of the electoral vote of each state in direct proportion to the popular vote. For example, had such a plan been in effect in 1948, New York State's 47 electoral votes would have been divided as follows: Dewey, who received 2,841,163 popular votes or 46 per cent of the total, would have obtained 21.8 electoral votes; Truman, with 2,780,204 popular votes (45 per cent of the total), would have obtained 21.3 electoral votes; and Wallace with 509,559 popular votes (8.2 per cent of the total) would have obtained 3.8 electoral votes. In the nation at large the use of this system would have altered the distribution of the electoral vote as follows:

	Actual Distribution of Electoral Vote	Distribution under the Proposed Amendment
TRUMAN	303	261.2
DEWEY	189	222.5
THURMOND	39	36.8
WALLACE	0	9.9
	531	530.4 [a]

[a] Norman Thomas, the Socialist candidate, and other minor party candidates would presumably have divided the remaining 0.6 of an electoral vote.

The Lodge-Gossett proposal would go a long way toward correcting all three of the defects in the present system. The abolition of the office of elector would take care of the threat of arbitrary exercise of voting power by the members of the electoral college. Second, the dividing of each state's electoral vote in proportion to the popular vote would reduce to a minimum the possibility that the electoral vote and popular vote might get out of line nationally to a point where the candidate with an electoral majority had fewer popular votes than did his opponent. The threat of such a result would not be eliminated completely, and cannot be, as long as the electoral vote is preserved in whatever altered form. This is due to the fact that the electoral vote of each state has an imperfect correlation with population. Insofar as it is dependent upon the number of seats a state has in the House of Representatives the correlation is almost (but not quite) complete. But insofar as each state has two electoral votes because of its representation in the Senate, population is ignored. For example, New York's 47 electoral votes and Nevada's 3 electoral votes do not accurately reflect the difference in population between the two states, for New York's population is much more than fifteen times as large as Nevada's. Thus, even though the electoral vote be divided among presidential candidates in proportion to the popular vote cast in each state, the resulting totals of the national electoral vote cannot correspond exactly with the totals of the national popular vote. But the chance that a discrepancy would develop which would permit the election of a minority President would be greatly reduced by the Lodge-Gossett proposal.

Third, this proposed amendment contains a clause providing that a 40 per cent plurality of the electoral vote shall be sufficient to elect a President. Assuming the continuation of anything like our present two-party system, this would eliminate the necessity of having the House of Representatives choose a President in the absence of a majority of the electoral votes.

The Lodge-Gossett amendment passed the Senate by the necessary two-thirds majority in the Eighty-first Congress, but it died in the House. Many criticisms were directed against it. It was argued that the split-state electoral vote would encourage third parties because they would be assured of their fair share of the electoral vote. This in turn, the argument continued, would increase the number of minority Presidents and might even result in the development of a true multiparty system in the United States which would make it virtually impossible to pick a single chief executive identified with one party only.

Admittedly this result might come to pass, although the amendment's sponsors argued that this country is so firmly committed to the two-party tradition that there is no real danger that a multiparty system, with its attendant evils, would come into being. A fair evaluation of the situation perhaps suggests that this risk is one worth taking, in view of the undeniable gains which the amendment would produce.

Senator Robert A. Taft of Ohio also vigorously opposed the amendment on the ground that it would prejudice Republican chances of winning the presidency. His argument was that dividing the electoral vote in proportion to the popular vote would mean a fairly even division between the two parties in most nothern states but a heavy Democratic electoral vote in the South sufficient to give that party victory in close elections. It should be noted that a statistical analysis of the effect the amendment would have had in past elections does not provide much support for the Taft thesis. In the thirteen presidential elections between 1900 and 1948 the Republican candidate would, under the Lodge-Gossett plan, have received more electoral votes than he actually did in six instances, and fewer votes in seven instances. As shown on the accompanying chart, the outcome of no one of these thirteen elections would have been altered, although under the proposed amendment Bryan would have come within a hair's breadth of beating McKinley in 1900. Moreover, the Taft argument overlooks the likely possibility that the amendment would encourage an increase in Republican voting in the South.

The reform was also opposed by some liberals and by representatives of so-called minority groups, such as Negroes and Jews, on the ground that it would

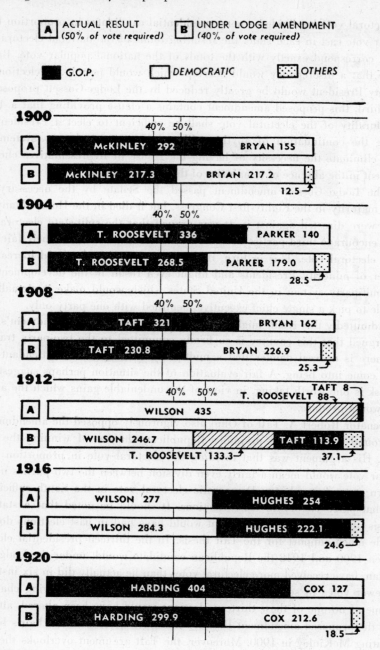

A ACTUAL RESULT (50% of vote required)   B UNDER LODGE AMENDMENT (40% of vote required)

■ G.O.P.   □ DEMOCRATIC   ▨ OTHERS

1900
40% 50%

A McKINLEY 292   BRYAN 155

B McKINLEY 217.3   BRYAN 217.2   12.5→

1904
40% 50%

A T. ROOSEVELT 336   PARKER 140

B T. ROOSEVELT 268.5   PARKER 179.0   28.5→

1908
40% 50%

A TAFT 321   BRYAN 162

B TAFT 230.8   BRYAN 226.9   25.3→

1912
40% 50%   T. ROOSEVELT 88→   TAFT 8→

A WILSON 435

B WILSON 246.7   TAFT 113.9
T. ROOSEVELT 133.3→   37.1→

1916

A WILSON 277   HUGHES 254

B WILSON 284.3   HUGHES 222.1   24.6→

1920

A HARDING 404   COX 127

B HARDING 299.9   COX 212.6   18.5→

Electoral Possibilities. How Lodge amendment would have affected electoral votes for President if it had been in effect since 1900. Hypothetical votes were computed by the Legislative Reference Service of the Library of Congress. The 1900 compilation differs slightly from

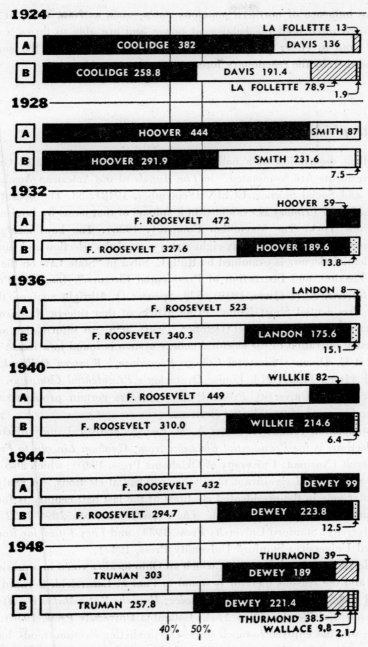

1924

A   COOLIDGE 382   DAVIS 136   LA FOLLETTE 13

B   COOLIDGE 258.8   DAVIS 191.4   LA FOLLETTE 78.9   1.9

1928

A   HOOVER 444   SMITH 87

B   HOOVER 291.9   SMITH 231.6   7.5

1932

A   F. ROOSEVELT 472   HOOVER 59

B   F. ROOSEVELT 327.6   HOOVER 189.6   13.8

1936

A   F. ROOSEVELT 523   LANDON 8

B   F. ROOSEVELT 340.3   LANDON 175.6   15.1

1940

A   F. ROOSEVELT 449   WILLKIE 82

B   F. ROOSEVELT 310.0   WILLKIE 214.6   6.4

1944

A   F. ROOSEVELT 432   DEWEY 99

B   F. ROOSEVELT 294.7   DEWEY 223.8   12.5

1948

A   TRUMAN 303   DEWEY 189   THURMOND 39

B   TRUMAN 257.8   DEWEY 221.4   THURMOND 38.5   WALLACE 9.8   2.1

40%   50%

others, particularly with respect to a table introduced in debate by Senator Taft, who contended that Bryan would have defeated McKinley. (*Source: The New York* Times, *February 12, 1950.*)

lessen the influence of northern populous states—such as New York, in which these groups often hold the balance of power and are able to throw a state's electoral vote to either party—and strengthen the influence of the southern states and thereby the reactionary forces in the Democratic party.

bibliographic note

An excellent description of a national convention is found in E. D. Graper's "How Presidents Are Nominated," in *The Annals* of the American Academy of Political and Social Science, CCLIX (September, 1948), 53. The operation of *The Presidential Primary* is examined in a volume of that name by Louise Overacker (New York: The Macmillan Company, 1926). The bewildering, conflicting manner in which the forty-eight states control the selection and functions of presidential electors is examined by Ruth C. Silva in "State Law on the Nomination, Election, and Instruction of Presidential Electors," *American Political Science Review*, XLII (June, 1948), 523. Spencer D. Albright analyzes the use of "The Presidential Short Ballot" in an article of that title in *American Political Science Review*, XXXIV (October, 1940), 955. An informative account of the actual operation of the electoral college system is found in a recent article by Robert G. Dixon—"Electoral College Procedure," *Western Political Quarterly*, III (June, 1950), 214. Louise Overacker's *Presidential Campaign Funds* (Boston: Boston University Press, 1946) considers certain problems arising out of the financing of presidential elections.

A companion volume to Cortez A. M. Ewing's statistical study of congressional elections is his *Presidential Elections from Abraham Lincoln to Franklin D. Roosevelt* (Norman: University of Oklahoma Press, 1940), which also brings to light a number of significant trends in presidential elections. An analysis of the popular vote in the presidential elections of the last half century is found in two volumes by Edgar E. Robinson: *The Presidential Vote, 1896–1932* (Stanford University: Stanford University Press, 1934) and *They Voted for Roosevelt* (Stanford University: Stanford University Press, 1947).

A detailed study of the way in which an Ohio locality voted in a presidential election and the reasons therefor is found in Paul F. Lazarsfeld, Bernard Berelson, and Hazel Gaudet, *The People's Choice; How the Voter Makes Up His Mind in a Presidential Election* (New York: Columbia University Press, 1948). Louis H. Bean, who has enjoyed so much success in predicting election trends, has published a study of presidential elections under the title *Ballot Behavior* (Washington: American Council on Public Affairs, 1940). The extent to which the urban vote determines the outcome of presidential elections is examined in an article by Samuel J. Eldersveld, "The Influence of Metropolitan Party Pluralities in

Presidential Elections since 1920," *American Political Science Review*, XLIII (December, 1949), 1189.

The two recently proposed constitutional amendments affecting the office of the presidency are examined in articles by Everett S. Brown, "The Term of Office of the President," *American Political Science Review*, XLI (June, 1947), 447 and Ruth C. Silva, "The Lodge-Gossett Resolution: A Critical Analysis," *American Political Science Review*, XLIV (March, 1950), 86.

government personnel:

the politician

$\mathscr{P}$OLITICIAN," like "politics," is a term of opprobrium to the average American. There are several different stereotypes of the politician. To many people the term calls to mind the picture of a gross and corrupt "boss" who presides like a dictator over a political organization and whose hand despoils everything it touches. To others it suggests a smooth and cynical legislator who decides every issue of policy making by a carefully calculated evaluation of narrow partisan interests or by reference to the selfish demands of pressure groups. At times it suggests an appointive bureaucrat who delights in the use of red tape and the regulation of private enterprise. But whatever the picture conjured up by the term, the politician is viewed by most people as a parasite upon society, a manipulator who uses government as an easy means of enriching himself and advancing his own interests while other men earn their way through hard work and a job well done.

There can be no denying the fact that this view of the politician has much validity and that it has come to be widely held because the politician through the years has committed most of the offenses with which he is charged. Many American cities, large and small, and not a few states have suffered throughout much of their histories from the corrupt rule of a boss or a machine. Many a congressman or head of a federal department has sought first and last to advance the interests of party or pressure group or, of course, his own.

People also view the politician unfavorably because of the strong American tradition of individualism which looks upon government as at best a necessary evil. The politician is on the side of the state, and he seeks to curb and to regulate. Like the tax collector of old, he is an evil force in life because he interferes with personal freedom and makes a living for himself as an agent of the government by exploiting the people.

In good part, however, the low estimate which most people have of the politician results from a failure to understand the exact nature of the role he plays in the social process. It represents a failure to see the positive and unique contribution which he makes to the public good. In an even more fundamental sense it reflects the unhealthy distrust many people hold of government itself, for the politician is, after all, the agent of government. Since government is an exceedingly useful social mechanism, the politician cannot be wholly bad.

the definition of a politician

The fact that "politician" is a term very difficult to define is part of the trouble. In the narrowest sense in which the term is used a politician is synonymous with a "boss." He is the head of a political machine, the leader of a more or less "invisible" organization which makes it its business to "operate" the formal, visible machinery of government. The boss has been defined as "a political leader whose authority extends beyond the office, if any, that he holds. His real power does not come from any mandate of the people, but from his control of party machinery." [1]

In the broadest sense any person on the public payroll is a politician, for politics is his business, i.e., in some measure, great or small, he keeps the wheels of government turning and helps to perform one of the functions or to render one of the services of government.

Obviously, the term is one that can be defined almost at will. Perhaps as helpful a definition as any is one which views the politician as a man who is peculiarly and particularly concerned with making government work, with seeing to it that government serves the ends for which it exists. This definition is obviously broad enough to include both officeholders and private citizens. It is broad enough to include the persons who man and operate the party machinery from the lowly precinct worker at the bottom to the national chairman at the top. It is also broad enough to include many of the people who man and operate the machinery of government: administrators—President, governors, and mayors; legislators; and even judges.

It is not so broad, however, as to include the great army of civil servants. There is probably no public servant, however small and insignificant his post, who does not at some time or other perform the true function of the politician by helping make the machinery of government work. But this is not his usual role; his daily activity consists rather in the performance of routine, ministerial duties. In other words, we may limit our examination of the politician to those persons who accept the responsibility of leadership in seeing to it that government operates smoothly and serves the purposes that men expect of it.

The politician's profession, admittedly a hard one to define or describe, is

---

[1] Charles Edison, "How to Get Rid of the Bosses," *New York Times Magazine*, June 4, 1944, p. 14.

somewhat more clearly characterized if the peculiar contribution which the politician makes is carefully examined.

the contribution of the politician

the politician is the mechanic who keeps the government running

The politician's contribution is a twofold one. In the first place, he is the able mechanic who keeps the government machine well oiled and its wheels turning. He may not be a profound student of the history or theory of political institutions, but he knows the machine's weaknesses and, by tinkering with its parts, he prevents it from breaking down. For example, the politician, through his close identification with the political party, is in good part responsible for the actual conduct of nominations and elections. He has also had much to do with the successful bridging of the gaps between the agencies of government created by separation of powers, and the gaps between the geographic levels of government created by federalism. Alan Valentine, former President of the University of Rochester, and more recently head of the Economic Stabilization Agency, has described this first contribution of the politician in somewhat unique terms in an article entitled "The Politician as Housekeeper for the Nation." [2] As he sees it, "politicians are the domestic servants who do the nation's political housekeeping. They perform the daily chores which the average citizen ignores and does not even understand." And he adds: "These domestic workers may be inefficient, neglecting to dust the corners of our political house, and occasionally taking a nip of the master's sherry, but could we do without them?"

the politician mediates group conflicts

In the second place, it is the politician who seeks to discover the terms upon which men can live together. Pendleton Herring, one of the ablest students of American politics, has described this contribution of the politician as follows:[3] Modern industrial society is a complex organization in which men have widely varying interests and desires. These different interests and desires threaten constantly to bring men into conflict. It is the function of the politician, by using or promoting the power of government, to adjust or mediate the conflicting interests of men so that society may remain peaceful. It is "the task of leadership . . . to bring the diversity of our society into a working harmony." And we are told that the politician's "function is to stand for relativity in the struggle of absolute values and thus to promote continuity and cohesion in social relations." [4]

Briefly stated, this second contribution of the politician to the social good is

---

[2] Alan Valentine, "The Politician as Housekeeper for the Nation," *Saturday Review of Literature,* April 12, 1947, p. 21.

[3] See particularly his wise and profound volume, *The Politics of Democracy* (New York: Rinehart & Company, 1940). This chapter draws heavily upon Herring's theories.

[4] *Ibid.,* pp. 64, 136.

that he serves as a compromiser. He is a specialist in human nature who likes people and understands why they get into trouble with one another. His desire is to get along with people himself and to help people to get along with one another.

Admittedly the contribution of the politician as an adjuster or compromiser is not enough by itself to ensure social progress. Compromise in the affairs of men is both necessary and desirable, but society must have vision and principles even though the goal is never quite reached, and it must have expertness so that it may try to make efficient and maximum use of its opportunities. Thus the role of the politician as a mediator may be contrasted with the role of the reformer, who provides the vision in politics; and with the role of the administrator, who provides the technical ability, or expertness, in the use of governmental power. Were it not for the contributions of the reformer and the administrative expert, the politician's unique service to society would soon prove inadequate. But, similarly, without the politician, the reformer and the expert would also be inadequate. In Herring's words, "Neither the vision of the reformer nor the expertness of the technician can displace the peculiar contribution of the specialist in human relations." [5] And up to now, at least, it is the politician who has been that specialist. The contributions of the reformer and the technician have long been recognized and appreciated; that of the politician has not.

criticism of the view of the politician as mediator

It goes almost without saying that if the view of the politician as a friend of all mankind and a mediator of conflicts is pushed too far it becomes ludicrous. Any close observer of the political scene can point at once to "politicians" who seem by their actions much more enamored with themselves than with other men, and whose efforts to resolve social conflicts make only sorrier messes of those conflicts.

Without necessarily disagreeing with Herring's central thesis, other students of politics have chosen to emphasize the inadequate fashion in which the politician serves his social function and the high price he charges for his contribution. In particular the political "boss" has been the object of bitter attacks. A penetrating critic of the boss has been Professor E. E. Schattschneider, who compares the local boss with a feudal lord.[6]

> He thrives on the same kind of breakdown of central authority as that in which the feudal system flourished. He bears an interesting relation to racketeers, gangsters, strong-arm squads, and the like, which on occasion enable him to employ violent direct action. Like the medieval baron, he is effectively responsible to no one. He levies tribute on all sorts of people and

---

[5] *Ibid.*, p. 135.

[6] See *Party Government* (New York: Rinehart & Company, Inc., 1942), particularly Chap. 7, "The Local Bosses: The Politicians versus the Public."

sells "protection" to his victims. He is likely to form leagues with other bosses for the purpose of overthrowing or subordinating the central authorities and may make "treaties" with the central authorities. That is, he negotiates with the central authorities as a sovereign power. Like his feudal predecessors he has learned that the perverted administration of public policy can be made to yield a revenue.[7]

In particular, Schattschneider deplores the power wielded by the "unofficial, professional" politician. By the "unofficial" politician he means the man who holds no office but who controls a party organization and thereby is in a position to manipulate governmental agencies from behind the scenes. By the "professional" politician he refers to the man who is in politics more or less permanently on a basis that is profitable to him personally—to the man to whom issues mean little, and money and power mean much. Schattschneider does not deny that the politician renders a much-needed service to society which other men seem unable to supply, but he would like to see this need met by the "official amateur politician," i.e., by the officeholder himself who is an "amateur" in the sense that he is motivated by a desire to do good and to solve issues and problems, rather than to enrich himself by means of a political career.[8]

ethics of the politician

It is easy enough to point to evidence showing that many a politician has been inefficient, venal, or corrupt. From the days of the "muckrakers" to the present, the literature of American politics has been full of case studies of bosses who have waxed rich practicing the profession of the politician. But there has been a sound tendency on the part of the modern student of politics to argue that placing too much emphasis on the politician's less-than-perfect ethics can prove misleading. Without denying the case against the politician in this respect, and while agreeing that there is much room for improvement, some observers insist that when the politician is viewed as part of the larger scene he does not seem quite so bad. In particular, two points are made in his favor.

the politician reflects his environment

In the first place, it is argued that the politician in his habits reflects the character of the society in which he operates. He is "of the people," and if his methods are sometimes crude or dishonest it is because prevailing social standards permit, and even encourage, crudity and dishonesty. Many students of politics have made this point. Professors P. H. Odegard and E. A. Helms in *American Politics* observe: "The methods which the machine employs and the purposes it serves depend basically upon its economic, political and cultural *milieu*.

[7] *Ibid.*, pp. 185–186.
[8] *Ibid.*, pp. 109–110.

. . . Moral standards in politics tend to reflect those of the social and economic world which the politician serves." [9] J. T. Salter, one of the leading students of the boss as a social phenomenon, asserts, "The politician in our democracy is like the people, only more so." [10] And Herring says: "The experienced politician is not disturbed by . . . inconsistencies. He takes life as he finds it. This is his value and his limitation." [11]

The politician also reflects the character of the American political system. Insofar as we have followed a politics of expediency and compromise rather than a politics of reason and principle, it is hardly surprising that the agent of politics—the politician—should be better known for his ability as a mediator and his interests in compromise than for his consistent and intelligent stands upon issues or his zest for principle. This is not to say that a politics of expediency is in all ways a bad thing, but only to suggest that the politician is limited by the nature of the political system in which he must work. For the politician to become the statesman, politics itself must make some progress away from the grosser crudities of expediency toward the methods and goals of intelligence and principle.

the politician is no worse than the businessman

Bringing the argument as to the politician's ethics down to the comparative level, it is asserted, second, that his standards are no worse than those of other groups in the social process. It is pointed out that the politician is watched rather closely by the public for wrongdoing, and we are asked how many other professions would enjoy a better reputation if subjected to the same close examination. Claude Bowers, an eminent historian and onetime ambassador to Spain, has written: "When we reflect that in the case of men engaged politically in the public service the spotlight is constantly thrown upon them and the microscope used in eager search of evidence of wrongdoing, we tremble to think what might be the result if all the other elements of society were subjected to the same constant and intensive scrutiny." [12]

In particular, it is argued that the politician's record compares favorably with that of the businessman. There is much truth in this assertion. The average politician is much more like the average businessman than we are inclined to admit, or even to see. In appearance, manner of dress, personal habits, professional techniques, "operating" methods, and standards of loyalty and morality, the two are apt to resemble each other much more closely than our stereotypes

---

[9] P. H. Odegard and E. A. Helms, *American Politics* (New York: Harper & Brothers, 1938), p. 483.

[10] J. T. Salter, *The Pattern of Politics* (New York: The Macmillan Company, 1940), p. 109.

[11] *Politics of Democracy*, pp. 64–65.

[12] Claude Bowers, "In Defense of Politicians," *Virginia Quarterly Review*, XXI (April, 1945), 219, 220.

of the politician and the businessman have allowed us to realize. There are many indications that this is so.

First of all, many individuals are active in both fields and actually qualify both as politicians and as businessmen. Few politicians are content to confine their talents and energies to the field of government alone. If they have not established business enterprises before entering politics, they soon discover that the abilities and techniques which make for success in politics—knowing how to manage a complex, bureaucratic organization, how to get along with people, how to sense public tastes and wants—are often the same qualities that take a man far in the field of business enterprise. Similarly, many a businessman has made the same discovery in reverse order. If it be asserted that a career in either business or politics is enough to occupy one man's full time and that there are not many men who are simultaneously active in both fields, the reply can be made that many men have found it easy and convenient to move back and forth from one career to the other in the course of a lifetime. Moreover, they have not changed very much in the process; their abilities and their ethics remain much the same whether they are active for the moment as businessmen or as politicians.

Many examples can be given of men who have had simultaneous interests in business and politics, or who earlier or later in their careers have been conspicuously successful in both fields. In national government many names come readily to mind. Herbert Hoover indicates in his *Who's Who* biography that he was active in "professional work in mines, railroads and metallurgical works" in more than ten countries between 1895 and 1913. Wendell Willkie gave up the presidency of a great public utility, Commonwealth & Southern Company, to run for President in 1940. After Alfred E. Smith retired from politics he served as head of the Empire State Building Corporation and as a director of several of the country's greatest corporations. John J. Raskob in 1928 resigned as an officer of the General Motors Corporation to become the national chairman of the Democratic party. James A. Farley resigned that post in 1940 to become chairman of the board of the Coca-Cola Export Corporation. James Forrestal, who listed himself in *Who's Who* as an "investment banker," gave up the presidency of Dillon, Read & Co., to embark upon a decade of service in national administration, most of the time as a cabinet officer. W. A. Harriman, long active in the Roosevelt and Truman administrations as a cabinet officer and in other important government posts, was once chairman of the board of the Union Pacific Railroad Company. Many members of Congress have had, or still retain, important business connections. Among present or recent members of the Senate, to mention just a few illustrations, Homer E. Capehart of Indiana was once president of the Capehart Corporation; Ralph E. Flanders of Vermont was president of the Jones and Lamson Machine Company; Herbert H. Lehman of New York was an investment banker; Theodore F. Green of

Rhode Island had numerous business connections in banking and transportation; J. Howard McGrath of Rhode Island had similar connections in real estate, insurance, and banking; and James E. Murray of Montana was prominent in banking. Many congressmen, of course, have had successful careers in the law which brought them in close touch with business enterprise of all types. Indeed, the very high prevalence of lawyers in many areas of the public service that are also thought of as staffed by politicians is in itself an indication of the fact that politicians are often men with much the same professional background and outlook as are found in the area of private enterprise.

In the second place, a careful examination of the record makes it apparent that businessmen have not been conspicuously more honest or ethical than politicians. From Boss Tweed to Boss Pendergast, politics has had its corrupt figures whose wrongdoings have become a matter of public record, and who have gone to prison. But from Jay Gould to Richard Whitney,[13] business, too, has had its corrupt figures.

If we move from the area of criminal wrongdoing into the area of the merely unethical or unsocial practice, it is doubtful whether the businessman's record is any better than that of the politician. A good basis for comparison is found in the degree to which nepotism is practiced in business and politics. Admittedly the congressman occasionally puts his wife or his son on the public payroll as a member of his office force, or an administrative officer takes care of an uncle or a cousin by finding him a job with some public agency. But such action is certainly widely prevalent in business. Indeed, the very fact that nepotism is frowned upon in politics and taken for granted in private business suggests that in this regard politics may have the higher standards.

The objection may be made to this last observation that a mayor has no right to give his son a public job, whereas it is fitting and proper for a businessman to bring his son into his office since, after all, the business is his to run as he sees fit. But is it not a valid reply to say that in a completely "ethical" society every individual should make his way, whether in private or public enterprise, solely on the basis of personal merit? More than one business has failed because the members of the second and subsequent generations who took it over from its founders through nepotism did not have the necessary talents or energy to keep it running on a successful basis. Moreover, the enterprise, although a private one, was not necessarily theirs to run into the ground as they saw fit. The social cost of such a business failure, although partly hidden, may be high. Large numbers of stockholders may suffer, and, even more important, an entire community, dependent for its economic well-being on the continued success of a single business enterprise, may suffer bitterly because of nepotism.

---

[13] A former president of the New York Stock Exchange who went to prison in 1938 because of fraudulent dealings in securities.

what standards should the politician be required to meet?

It is not the purpose of this comparison of the relative ethics of the businessman and the politician to argue that the former is more unethical than people realize or to suggest that because he does sometimes engage in questionable or even dishonest practices the latter should be allowed to do the same thing. Actually, it is reasonable to demand that the politician meet higher standards than the businessman does since, after all, government is everyone's business. It is true that business (as "private government") has a greater social responsibility than has yet been recognized by many businessmen or by much of the public. And yet in a capitalist society there is a distinction of degree between government and private business in the way in which they render service to the people. The very fact of competition provides some public protection against inefficiency and wrongdoing in business that is usually not present as a safeguard in public enterprise. Accordingly, it would be a tragic mistake to condone the politician's inadequacies merely by saying that he is only reflecting his environment or that he is no worse than the businessman.

Nonetheless, it is possible to hold the politician up to impossibly high standards and thereby to refuse to recognize, or utilize, his peculiar talents for certain kinds of jobs. A good illustration is to be seen in the storm of criticism which greeted President Roosevelt's effort to name "Ed" Flynn, boss of the Bronx, as ambassador to Australia during World War II. The public was indignant (or at least the press was) that the President should consider a municipal boss—a man inevitably tarnished a bit as the result of a long, well-advertised career in New York City politics—worthy of such an important international assignment, and the President was compelled to withdraw the appointment lest the Senate reject it. It may be queried whether a local boss—assuming that he is honest and able—through his long association with people, through placating individuals who have been wronged, in real or fancied ways, and through resolving the conflicts that are forever dividing people into camps, has not gained experience which peculiarly fits him for the difficult and exacting role of diplomatic agent. It is not as though diplomacy had (or should) become an exclusive field for the careerists or professionals. Many a businessman with no training in international relations whatever has been appointed to a diplomatic post in modern times, and although the record is a mixed one, some of these men, at least, have rendered valuable service. It is likely that the same qualities—in particular the quality to understand people and to work harmoniously with them—that explain the successful careers of certain businessmen in diplomacy are also possessed by the politician. Indeed, President Roosevelt did subsequently give Mr. Flynn certain diplomatic assignments as his personal agent, including a mission to the Vatican, and although the record of Flynn's activity is not readily available, there is some cause to believe that he fulfilled his diplomatic duties in a reasonably competent manner.

the decline of the boss

An unmistakable trend in the political life of the nation during the last generation or so has been the decline of the "boss." There is nothing inconsistent between this observation and the assertion that the politician plays a necessary and
valuable role in the political process. It is not the politician who has lost ground,
but only that particular type known specifically as the boss, or the type that
Schattschneider has in mind when he uses the phrase "unofficial professional
politician." The "official, amateur politician" must always be with us as long
as our democracy is capable of political action. It was the "boss" Fiorello La
Guardia had in mind when he made a statement that otherwise would be ludicrous: "I am in a position to say, from actual experience, that it is possible to
administer a great city without the benefit of politicians." [14] In the broader
sense in which the term is used, La Guardia was one of the most masterly politicians of the modern era.

The waning power of the boss has been particularly noticeable in municipal
government. Such things as the successful attack upon Boss Pendergast in Kansas City, the unmistakable decline, at long last, of Tammany Hall, and the recent defeats suffered by Boss Frank Hague in Jersey City and James Curley in
Boston, are more than the mere ups and downs of politics. They are sympto-
matic of a substantial change that is being felt throughout the nation. Of course,
the change can be exaggerated. Often an old and well-known boss gives way to a
man who is not so well known but who nonetheless has many of the characteristics of the boss. But the day when every city had its machine, and every machine had its boss is gone.

The change is evident at the state and national levels, too. Boss Ed Crump
still hangs on in Tennessee, although the victory of Estes Kefauver in the Democratic senatorial primary in 1948 was a sign that even Crump has become vulnerable. But many a state, once famed for its domination by a particular machine or boss, seems now free from this kind of political control. In national
government, as we have seen, there has been no continuous tradition of bossism.
But even the national chairman, who in times past came closer than did any
other unofficial, professional politician to serving as a national boss, has declined in power and importance. Most of the recent holders of this post, the
Walkers, Hannegans, McGraths, Spanglers, Scotts, and Gabrielsons have been
singularly innocuous and ineffectual.

factors leading to the decline of the boss

Many factors have played a part in contributing to the decline of the boss. The
following may be noted:

1. THE CHANGE IN THE COMPOSITION OF THE ELECTORATE.   In times

---

[14] "Bosses Are Bunk," *Atlantic Monthly*, July, 1947, p. 21.

past the boss frequently depended for his continued power upon the control and manipulation of large numbers of underprivileged and unsophisticated voters. Many of these were newly arrived immigrants who were grateful to a political machine for favors and kindnesses, which they found all too rare in a new and strange land. But as immigration has declined and virtually disappeared in the last quarter-century, as voters have become more literate, wiser, and secure, and as the total electorate has increased greatly in size, the influence of the boss with certain segments of the electorate has declined both quantitatively and relatively.

2. THE RISE OF THE LABOR UNION. As labor unions have gained in number, membership, and power, they have usurped some of the functions of the boss and his machine, particularly at the level of local government. Specifically, they have brought a higher standard of living and greater security to the working people, who once were dependent upon the boss for help. The union has made it possible for the laborer to claim his rightful voice in the operation of the nation's economy and his fair share of its produce, making it unnecessary for him to look to a political machine for material assistance or help when he gets into trouble.

3. THE BROADENING OF FEDERAL SERVICES. As the federal government has undertaken, slowly and incompletely to be sure, to protect the individual against the economic risks of sickness, unemployment, and old age, to guarantee full employment, and to provide suitable housing, the position of the boss has been weakened. In times past it was the local boss who offered help to the sick and aged, who maintained an unemployment insurance system of sorts, and who through picnics, boat rides, and the like, provided some slight relief from the dreary routine of life. But today the national government provides all these services and more in such a way as to cut the ground right out from under the local machine and all but destroy its most effective method of winning and keeping the loyalty of the downtrodden masses. It has not only provided these new services; it has provided them on a systematic and efficient basis. Schattschneider has said, "the boss lives by bad administration." [15] Unquestionably, the great advances in public administration which have occurred simultaneously with the widening of the services rendered by the federal government have had much to do with the growing obsolescence of the boss.

4. THE CONSOLIDATION OF LOCAL GOVERNMENTS. Herring has pointed out that among the local boss's most important contributions to the social process were his understanding of the confused labyrinth of overlapping and conflicting units of government that marked many a community and his ability to make such a system work. In the last two or three decades real progress has been made in reducing this confusion and in providing at least a semblance of

---

[15] Schattschneider, *Party Government*, p. 176.

orderly governmental organization in urban areas. Where such progress has occurred, again one of the boss's reasons for being has ceased to exist.

   5. THE REFORMER AND THE EXPERT HAVE LEARNED TO BE POLITICIANS,
TOO.   The varying contributions which the politician, the reformer, and the expert make to social progress have been noted. In a real sense the period of the
1930's and 1940's has seen these three professions grow closer and closer together. The reformer and the technician have learned how to be politicians, too,
and the politician has acquired a zeal for reform and a measure of expertness
in certain fields of public administration. Many illustrations can be cited. In
New York City, Fiorello La Guardia, as the latest of the long line of reform
mayors, succeeded where virtually all of his predecessors had failed, because in good part he matched his sincerity as a reformer with a consummate
ability as a politician. The New Deal was full of men who in varying ways combined the qualities of the three professions. In no small degree the success of
the New Deal was due to this condition. Such men, for example, as Harold Ickes
and Harry Hopkins came into the New Deal as experts, as men who had a
technical competence in some area of public administration. But they will be
remembered longest for the ability they showed in mastering the art of politics
and in functioning in the politician's role of mediator, fixer, and compromiser.

   It is ironical that the effectiveness with which certain of the politician-re-
formers or politician-technicians of the New Deal operated had much to do with
the undermining of local Democratic bosses and machines. It was even a frontal
attack by the national Democratic administration that sent such local Democratic
bosses as Pendergast and Curley to prison, and which had much to do with the
downfall of such Democratic organizations as Tammany Hall. On the other hand,
this tendency of the federal welfare state to undermine the position of the local
boss has had its exceptions. Professor D. D. McKean, a careful student of the
Hague machine in Jersey City, wrote in 1940 that "the Hague organization, far
from being injured by the New Deal, has flourished under it, been preserved by
it." [16] This result is explained in part by the effectiveness with which Hague
used federal public works and federal grants-in-aid to broaden the services seemingly rendered by his local machine. Herring has also noted this countertend-
ency. He points out that the inability of the federal government under the
Constitution to render certain services directly to the people and its need to
work through state and local agencies has given the local boss and machine a
new function to perform.[17] In some areas a clever boss has used this means to
regain some of his lost power and prestige. But it seems doubtful whether this
condition can offset the powerful forces that are working for his downfall.

---

[16] D. D. McKean, *The Boss: The Hague Machine in Action* (Boston: Houghton Mifflin Company, 1940), p. xiv.
[17] Herring, *Politics of Democracy*, p. 141.

the politician's future

Municipal bosses may become obsolete, the expert and the reformer may gain greater know-how in working with people, but the politician will always be with us. He is as inevitable to the democratic process as is the political party; indeed, it is he who makes the party system work. To think that government in a complex nation like our own can somehow be made to operate satisfactorily without the services of specialists in politics is to be an impractical visionary.

We must persuade ourselves that the politician's profession is a necessary and legitimate one and eliminate from our thinking the notion that politics is, per se, an unworthy, parasitical field of human endeavor. We must also stop holding the politician up to impossible standards that we do not demand of men in other professions. There is no need to wink at the politician's inadequacies, or to condone his wrongdoing, but an attitude of perfectionism in the evaluation of any aspect of human relations can be a dangerous thing insofar as it means loss of ability to see things in their proper perspective. It would be a mistake to measure the politician's usefulness and success by purely pragmatic standards, but obsession with his failure to meet the highest theoretical standards can lead to dangerous ignorance of the important contribution that he makes to a democratic society. Indeed, Claude Bowers goes so far as to argue that the traditional contempt which Americans hold for the politician represents unconscious fascism. He sums up his argument as follows:

> Democracies operate best through political parties.
> Political parties function only through politicians.
> Eliminate politicians and you wipe out parties.
> Wipe out parties and you throw democracies into a state of unorganized,
> undisciplined chaos.
> And when in a democracy the people are unorganized, undirected, undisciplined, the Fascist has his excuse and the tyrant appears to dominate the nation by brute force.[18]

Admittedly, we should do everything in our power to encourage able men to embark upon political careers. There is no doubt that the low esteem which many people have for politics as a profession has deterred a great many individuals from entering the public service. W. W. Waymack, when he was editor of the Des Moines *Register and Tribune,* wrote, "Politics as a career is rated lower in America than in any other country that is really devoted to democratic ways."[19]

In particular, college and university students have not viewed careers in politics with favor. Unfortunately, we have little or none of the British tradition

---

[18] Bowers, "In Defense of Politicians," p. 233.
[19] W. W. Waymack, "In Defense of Politicians," *New York Times Magazine,* October 29, 1944, p. 13.

whereby students at Oxford, Cambridge, and other universities early in their undergraduate days give earnest and favorable thought to entering the government, and by which the political parties welcome the young graduate and give him every opportunity to make a start in politics. It is true that we have developed organizations of "Young Republicans" and "Young Democrats" and that there is much talk about interesting young people in politics. But we have done little to *institutionalize* the training of our youth for political careers or to open doors into the politics profession. Valentine points out, "The party which first makes easier the entrance of able young men into politics will strengthen its position." And he complains, "Although new recruits to the party organization are welcome in theory, they are often repelled in practice." [20]

At the same time we need to avoid the naïve thought that if "college people" can be persuaded to become politicians, all the crudities and shortcomings of the profession will soon disappear. There can be no denying the need to give the politician a technical competence which the fearfully complex problems of present-day government require of him and which only specialized training in institutions of higher learning can provide. But there is a sort of snobbishness in supposing that somehow the college graduate is wiser, more honest, or more anxious to serve the public good than is the individual who has entered politics from a more humble background. The latter lacks the technical skills and a detailed, if largely theoretical, knowledge of the social process which education can provide, and today that is a handicap for which society may pay dearly if he rises to the top. But his ability to work with people, his understanding, gained through experience, of the conflicts that separate men, and his concept of what constitutes fair and reasonable compromise in the making of public policies are not necessarily inferior to those of the well-educated man. The college graduate is needed in politics, but he should approach this worthiest of professions with a proper sense of humility.

bibliographic note

The literature dealing with the politician in the traditional sense of a boss or a person identified with party organizations or elections is enormous. Lincoln Steffens's *Autobiography* (New York: Harcourt, Brace and Company, 1931) contains many excellent, highly interesting descriptions of well-known politicians of a generation or two ago. Raymond Moley's *27 Masters of Politics* (New York: Funk & Wagnalls Company, 1949) is a collection of essays on a number of different types of practicing politicians. John T. Salter has long been interested in the human side of politics and has published a number of volumes describing

---

[20] Valentine, "The Politician As Housekeeper for the Nation," p. 21.

the careers of politicians of all types. Attention may be called to two symposia he has edited: *Public Men In and Out of Office* (Chapel Hill: University of North Carolina Press, 1946) and *The American Politician* (Chapel Hill: University of North Carolina Press, 1938). Harold Zink's *City Bosses in the United States* (Durham: Duke University Press, 1930) is an early but now classic study of local politicians. Dayton McKean's *The Boss* (Boston: Houghton Mifflin Company, 1940) is a detailed study of former Mayor Frank Hague of Jersey City and his machine. A study of a famous boss of the past is found in Harold F. Gosnell's *Boss Platt and His New York Machine* (Chicago: The University of Chicago Press, 1924). An amusing but informative account of the career of a minor Tammany Hall politician which has recently been republished is William L. Riordan's *Plunkitt of Tammany Hall* (New York: Alfred A. Knopf, Inc., 1948).

Two recent autobiographical volumes by men who served with great success as national chairmen of the Democratic party are James A. Farley's *Behind the Ballots: The Personal History of a Politician* (New York: Harcourt, Brace and Company, 1938) and Edward J. Flynn's *You're the Boss* (New York: The Viking Press, 1947). These books should be read with caution, for they tell something less than the whole story of the master politicians who wrote them. In some respects, however, they are more revealing than their authors intended them to be.

In addition to the short essays defending the politician, referred to in the text of the chapter, attention may be called to Chester C. Maxey's "A Plea for the Politician," *Western Political Science Quarterly*, I (September, 1948), 271.

part 4

---

the formulation of policy

the legislative process

 OVERNMENT in action may be said to begin with the making of public
policy. A modern nation is beset on every side with innumerable problems, extremely complex and technical in character, which it must try to solve. The
country's rivers and streams periodically overflow their banks, with great loss
of life and property alike, and a demand arises that the government create a
flood control agency with authority to condemn property, build dams, and maintain reservoirs. Continued strife between labor and management makes serious
inroads upon production, and the people, threatened with the loss of goods and
services, demand that government set up machinery for the prompt settlement
of labor disputes. Juvenile delinquency shows an alarming tendency to increase,
and pressure is brought upon the government to expand its program of education and recreation so as to direct the energies of the nation's young people into
healthy and useful channels. The threat of war remains ever-present on world
horizons, and the advocates of military preparedness grow more insistent in their
arguments. On the other hand, peace lovers, alarmed at the mounting tide of
armaments, bend all their efforts to persuade their country to work for a stronger
international federation of states as the best means of averting war.

Such are the problems of this modern age, problems that concern government since man cannot hope to solve them by his own resources or even through
his lesser social groupings—the family, the church, the professional society,
the labor union, or the business corporation. It may be admitted at once that
men will disagree profoundly as to what is a wise or feasible policy to pursue in
attacking a particular problem. It is part of the meaning of democracy that men
should hold differing views, and debate the wisdom of pursuing alternative
policies. But the need finally for a society to make up its mind and follow particular paths in attacking its problems can be denied by no rational man. At
times we may be tempted by the illusion that we can escape life and its problems; the religious mystic withdraws from the world of reality, the philosophic
anarchist retires into the woods, or the social misfit shuns the company of his

fellow men. That there is perhaps a primordial instinct in all of us to rebel against the discipline of civilization is to be seen in the success that candidates for public office enjoy in winning votes by suggesting that we have too many laws and that our crying need is for less government. But such attitudes toward life seldom prove attractive to any great number of people for any length of time. For the most part we accept the premise of the need for positive action, and spend our energies searching for satisfactory policies and devising modes of administering them.

Let us now turn to American political experience and note in greater detail the emergence of a specific national problem which called finally for the determination of a formal, national, public policy.

an illustration of the need for policy formulation by government

In 1890 the Congress of the United States, coming finally to grips with a problem that had long been of increasing concern to the nation, passed the Sherman Antitrust Act, one of the most famous national statutes in the history of the country. The problem may be stated in the form of a question: What was the nation to do about the growing tendency of American business to become monopolistic in form?

During the greater part of the nineteenth century the nation tried to build an economy based on the doctrine of free enterprise. There has been much controversy about the true meaning of *laissez faire*. There are those who doubt whether such a system ever really existed in England or the United States and who argue that its achievement anywhere, anytime, is impossible. But there is no doubt that for better or worse we placed our hopes during the last century in the unfettered market, in free competition, and in the law of supply and demand to give us a fair price structure and a satisfactory distribution of man's productive energies over the entire range of enterprise. Following the Civil War this scheme of things was seriously threatened by the rapid growth of the "trust." In certain of the nation's most basic industries, such as steel, oil, tobacco, farm machinery, and railway transportation, there seemed to be an irresistible tendency toward consolidation into ever-larger units. Where outright consolidation did not occur, competing business units within the same field frequently entered into agreements providing for price fixing, limitation of production, centralized selling, or quota systems of doing business. These practices were designed to provide greater profits for business by enabling it to escape from the restrictive effects of free competition. Thus there was a clearly defined conflict between a national economic system which presupposed free competition, and a practical development in the economic life of the nation that was tending to make free competition largely illusory. A *problem* had come into being which sooner or later had to receive the attention of Congress as the supreme agency with power to define national public policy.

There were available, of course, many alternative ways of attacking the problem. These will be noted later in the chapter. The point to be emphasized here is that the problem, itself, was inescapable. In the course of our national life a condition had come into being which could not be ignored. Some sort of decision had to be made. Once again, as had been true more or less continuously in the past, there was a need for conscious formation of a national policy on a point of considerable concern to the public interest.

the dominant role played by the legislature in policy formulation

What agencies of government determine policy in a modern democratic state? The natural inclination is to reply at once to such a question that the legislature determines policy. Certainly every American immediately thinks of Congress as the maker of national policies in the country. There is nothing fundamentally incorrect about such an answer, for the Constitution specifically provides: "All legislative powers herein granted shall be vested in a Congress of the United States. . . ."

And yet it has not always been true that public policy has been determined in a nation by a *legislative assembly*. There were assemblies as far back as the times of ancient Greece and Rome, but these bodies were seldom *representative* in character and their *legislative* powers were usually slight. The origins of what may be called *legislative government* are obscured in the vague and often contradictory histories of many countries in different eras, yet it seems clear that the democratic legislature of today has been largely an Anglo-American development of the last three or four centuries. Moreover, it appears that the most important motivating force in the initial development of the modern legislature was the necessity of providing representation for the diverse groups in society, which began to appear as the feudalism of the Middle Ages gave way to a freer and more complex way of life. These new groups found themselves confronted with a monolithic governmental arrangement in which public policy was determined by kings, priests, or judges. King, priest, and judge, although never completely insensitive to the needs or wishes of the people, were imperfect *representative* agencies, and in making laws often tended to reflect their own interests or the interests of the social groups to which they belonged. At best their commendable efforts to advance the general welfare, or to render the administration of governmental affairs more satisfactory, were inadequate because of their inability to understand or represent the new interests which were appearing in society. In the long run these interests were bound to make themselves felt, and ultimately there came into being our modern English and American political systems in which administrators and judges, as historic and necessary parts of government, are subordinated to a legislative body representing and controlled by the citizenry in all its diverse character.

three motives for the appearance of modern legislatures

Of course, it must not be supposed that the legislature appeared suddenly, in Minerva-like fashion, fully developed in any one country or at any one time. The motivation for the emergence of legislative bodies was always complex and was only imperfectly understood at the time. Here it was a matter of the rising commercial or business class discovering the inadequacy of governmental policies formulated by an aristocratic class with agrarian interests, and demanding new lawmaking machinery by which its own interests would receive increased attention. At another point it was a matter of a king needing additional revenues and finding his more powerful subjects unwilling to provide further financial assistance except by the formal action of a body representing their own interests. Or again as the *administration* of governmental policies grew ever more complex there appeared a need to set a watch over kings, judges, and other public officers, lest the public interest as expressed in the law be dissipated in the process of law enforcement. And where could such a watch be better set than in the representative assembly?

In these three suggestions as to the varying motives that were responsible for the development of legislatures may be seen the germs of the three great powers a legislature today exercises in a democracy. The first of these is the lawmaking or policy determining power itself. The second is the power to control the purse strings, for in democratic states it is now a general principle that only the legislature possesses authority to levy taxes or authorize the expenditure of funds from the public treasury. The third is the power to supervise the administrative process and to hold law enforcement officials to a more or less constant and strict accountability for their conduct.

the union of democracy and representative government

Just as the development of the legislature was a slow historical process, so the close identification of representative government with the democratic principle did not occur overnight. The first assemblies were far from being democratically organized or elected in any modern sense. Moreover, many interest groups did not at once obtain representation. In their earliest beginnings, legislatures usually gave representation to the clergy and the nobility, the two powerful social classes of the late Middle Ages. With the decline of feudalism and the coming of the Protestant Reformation, a middle class, or bourgeoisie, appeared and made great gains in power. As a result of the seventeenth-century revolutions in England and the eighteenth-century revolutions in America and France this middle class secured representation in legislative bodies. However, even in the nineteenth century the legislative assemblies of England, France, and America were only partly democratic in the representation they gave to interest groups. The present century has witnessed the growing importance and recognition of labor and certain minority groups, such as the Negro, and the final identification of the representative and democratic principles seems not far off.

But almost as the perfecting of *representative government* as a democratic means of determining policy is being achieved, doubts begin to be expressed as to the legislature's continuing importance as a policy determining body. In the United States talk is heard on every side about the decline of Congress, about the extent to which it has become a mere hollow shell of the great body the Founding Fathers created. It is not only that Congress as the legislative body seems to have declined in relative importance as the judicial and particularly the executive branches have gained in prestige and power. It is also argued that even in the field of lawmaking, Congress has largely surrendered its powers to other agencies of government and now serves as a rubber stamp, automatically approving legislative proposals submitted to it by these other agencies. Indeed, one commentator speaks of the possibility that Congress is becoming little more than "a badly tarnished pageant." And what is being said of the American congress merely reflects a widespread attitude as to the decline of legislative assemblies all over the world.

What is the true position of the legislature in respect to the legislative process? Does it by passing laws determine the policies of a nation? Or is it merely a mirror in which policies that have originated elsewhere are reflected? These are not easy questions to answer, and many of the hasty judgments that have been pronounced upon the modern legislative assembly by both its supporters and its detractors are clearly erroneous. A calm consideration of such questions will, however, throw much light upon the true character of the process by which national policy is formed as well as reveal the continuing importance of the legislature today.

the legislature does not have complete control of policy formulation

Much of the present talk about the decline of the legislature reveals considerable ignorance as to the actual role that such assemblies have played in the past, even in the recent past. It has never been true even when the powers of representative assemblies were supposedly at flood tide that legislative halls alone witnessed the making of "law." There have always been both a prestatutory phase and a poststatutory phase in the formulation of policy. To begin with, long before a legislature gives formal voice to a new policy by the enactment of a statute, this policy is almost certain to have received tentative expression and recognition in a variety of ways. Often a rule of society which men obey has its first beginnings as a mere custom which comes to find widespread acceptance. Somewhat later a rule of custom may find expression in judicial decisions or administrative orders, as judges and administrators find it necessary to make decisions in the absence of any statutory directions from the legislature. Needless to say, these earlier rulings may often be in conflict with one another, thereby reflecting different approaches to a problem or conclusions concerning it. The importance of such prestatutory activity may be noted by a further examination of the American formulation of an antitrust policy.

prestatutory development of American antitrust policy

Although the modern trust developed largely after the Civil War, the threat of monopolistic or unfair competitive practices to a system of free enterprise had long been recognized in England and America, and for scores of years before the Sherman Act, governmental policy had been taking shape. In fact, for centuries the common law had been concerned with the problem, and in both England and America judges, in deciding cases between private litigants, had established and followed rules which came to have the force of law. For example, it was early recognized that contracts between private persons might restrain free trade and competition. Accordingly, judge-made rules were laid down outlawing certain types of contract, such as one by which an apprentice worker agreed not to compete with his former employer. In all, the common law came to outlaw six business practices, and a sixfold test as to what constituted a valid contract was subsequently applied.[1] In addition to these rules outlawing certain types of contracts, the common law developed principles as to conspiracy and illegal combinations which upon occasion were employed to curb monopolistic business practices.

It is important to note the element of flexibility that early appeared in the use of these rules of common law in the field of monopoly, for almost at once conflicting tendencies in public policy were apparent. As long as people adhered to the fundamental notion of a society in which economic enterprises would compete freely with one another, monopolistic tendencies constituted a grave threat to the public welfare. But monopolies persisted in appearing, nonetheless, and sooner or later the argument was bound to be made that certain types of monopolies, at least, were the inevitable result of economic progress and were by no means opposed to the public interest. The development of the common law soon reflected such counterarguments, and early in the eighteenth century there came into being the famous "rule of reason," which recognized that certain monopolies, combinations, or agreements in restraint of trade might be reasonable and thus lawful. For example, although the general rule of common law outlawing contracts by which an apprentice agreed not to compete

---

[1] Milton Handler, "Restraint of Trade," *Encyclopaedia of the Social Sciences*, XIII, 339.

with his first employer remained in effect, it was recognized that such contracts might be reasonable if the agreement applied only to a limited geographic area— say the confines of the town in which the employer had his business. Had not the common law been so modified, tradesmen and craftsmen might have refrained from training apprentices for fear of the competition they would thereby encourage, and such a state of affairs would not have advanced the public interest.

So it may be seen that when, as recently as 1890, the American Congress enacted a formal statute dealing with monopoly control, it was by no means establishing the first public policy in this field. Much experimentation had already taken place, and a considerable body of law, or *policy*, had already come into being. Congress was well aware of the law this experimentation had produced. On the other hand, Congress's decision was not thereby predestined, for certain alternative policies were clearly available. In the first place, a basic decision had to be made as to whether to permit the state governments to continue the experiments at monopoly control which they had been making, thereby encouraging a decentralized and diverse law of monopoly for the United States, or whether to undertake the development of a uniform national policy. In the second place, some sort of choice had to be made between rival theories, each of which had gained some support in the earlier development: one, that the trust was an inevitable economic development which had come to stay and which called for regulation and control ·rather than abolition; and the other, that the trust was an evil and dangerous threat to the still sound theory of free enterprise, and should thus be outlawed completely.

In choosing between these various alternatives Congress determined upon the development of a single national policy as against many state policies, and it expressed its faith in free enterprise and free competition by deciding that the trust was basically evil and should be abolished. Accordingly, it provided in the first two sections of the Sherman Act:

1. Every contract, combination in the form of trust or otherwise, or conspiracy, in restraint of trade or commerce among the several States, or with foreign nations, is hereby declared to be illegal. . . . .
2. Every person who shall monopolize, or attempt to monopolize or combine or conspire with any other person or persons, to monopolize any part of the trade or commerce among the several states, or with foreign nations, shall be deemed guilty of a misdemeanor. . . .[2]

It is clear that in so legislating, Congress did not initiate any new or completely original policy but, instead, selected from or ratified certain tendencies which had long been taking shape. It is for this reason that one authority on the legislative process has declared, "The term *making the law* does not imply

---

[2] 26 Stat. 209.

that any legislature originates legislation. They are law-declaring rather than law-making bodies." [3]

This particular discussion of the development of our antitrust policy has emphasized the extent to which courts participate in policy determination before the statutory stage is reached. In a somewhat similar way members of the administrative department of government also participate in this earlier work of policy formation. Just as in the absence of a pertinent statute a judge may find it necessary to make his own law in deciding a dispute between opposing parties, so an administrator in his dealings with the people may frequently find that he must evolve rules of his own to cover certain problems where there is no statute to guide him. These rules, too, may later be given statutory dignity by act of the legislature.

policy determination does not end with action by the legislature

The process of policy formation is usually underway long before the legislature enacts a statute. Likewise, the process by no means comes to an end when the legislature has acted. No matter what the character of a statute, a certain measure of policy refinement and extension is inevitable through the years that a statute is being enforced. It is a truism that the complex problems of modern society compel legislatures to adopt statutes in more and more general terms. Many problems have become so technically complex and difficult that the legislature does not dare to attempt to deal with detail, but instead contents itself with indicating the broad lines of policy, leaving the elaboration of the policy to other governmental agencies. This is an aspect of the governmental process that has always existed. Although the condition may perhaps have become more striking in recent decades, the change is one of degree and not of kind. The enforcement of the Sherman Act reveals the extent to which both administrator and judge have been called upon to interpret and extend a congressional policy dating back to 1890.

poststatutory development of American antitrust policy

The Sherman Act, as passed by Congress, enunciated policy in exceedingly broad fashion and was singularly lacking in detail. Congress consciously determined that the trust was basically evil and should be destroyed, and that the attack should be made by the federal government along national lines. Beyond that it left an immense measure of discretion to other agencies of government to formulate a practical and detailed antitrust program. The enforcement of

---

[3] Joseph P. Chamberlain, *Legislative Processes: National and State* (New York: Appleton-Century-Crofts, Inc., 1936), p. 3.

the act was turned over to the Department of Justice, and the very use of the law in any situation has always depended upon the initiative shown by that agency. It is a well-known fact that under certain Presidents the act has remained idle on the statute books, whereas other Presidents have directed the department to prosecute suits under the law in a vigorous manner. It may be argued that this matter of prosecuting or not prosecuting under a law is a typically *adminis-trative* decision, but it is true that such discretionary conduct by an adminis-trator also profoundly affects *policy*.

Moreover, it was not solely a matter of deciding whether to enforce or not to enforce; many important issues of detail had to be settled in administering the statute. Two of these details may be noted here. The first of these con-cerned the over-all scope of the act. In spite of the fact that by its words the Sherman Act seemed designed to outlaw *all* contracts and combinations in re-straint of interstate trade, it was early argued that Congress had nonetheless in-tended to incorporate the old common-law "rule of reason" into its antitrust pol-icy and that, accordingly, the statute was to be applied in a discriminating fash-ion only to those situations where there existed unreasonable restraint of trade. The second issue concerned the possible application of the law's prohibitions to labor unions and labor practices. Might a labor union be held in violation of the act because of the way in which a strike brought about a stoppage in the flow of goods across state lines? Or had Congress intended to limit the application of the act's provisions strictly to business and industry?

This is not the place to trace out the long controversy that has existed as to the Sherman Act's meaning in these two respects. The significant thing to be noted here is that it inevitably fell to the lot of the administrators charged with the enforcement of the act, and the judges who were compelled to interpret it in the process of deciding cases, to make decisions in both respects. In other words, an Attorney General might, as some have done, conclude that labor union ac-tivity was within the province of the act and file suit against an offending union. Thereupon it would become necessary for courts, and the Supreme Court in par-ticular, to determine finally whether such a conclusion was sound and whether a union might properly be proceeded against under the Sherman Act. Over a period of more than fifty years the Department of Justice and the Supreme Court have shown a great deal of vacillation in their attempts to settle these two issues, but it seems fair to say that the ultimate decisions have been that the rule of reason is to be followed in applying the Sherman Act, and that labor unions are largely excluded from its operation.[4]

It may be asked, is not the legislature aware of the administrative and

---

[4] See the *Standard Oil Company* and *American Tobacco Company* cases, 221 U.S. 1, and 221 U.S. 106 (1911); *Apex Hosiery Company* v. *Leader*, 310 U.S. 469 (1940); and *United States* v. *Hutcheson*, 312 U.S. 219 (1941).

judicial rulings that are made in the enforcement of its statutes, and does it not retain the power at any time to veto these rulings by the enactment of amending statutes superseding the administrative and judicial rulings? The answer is, of course, in the affirmative, and, in the case of the Sherman Act, Congress has repeatedly passed such amending laws, notably in the Clayton and Federal Trade Commission Acts of 1914, the Norris-La Guardia Act of 1932, and the Robinson-Patman Act of 1936. Nonetheless, it must be remembered that the way in which the Sherman Act is enforced is not the only problem demanding the attention of Congress. Moreover, Congress does not legislate easily. We have deliberately chosen to make our national legislative process an exceedingly difficult and complex one. Occasionally, sufficient public opinion takes shape, and congressional majorities can be organized to put through such a great piece of legislation as the Sherman Act. But once such a statute is passed, it is apt to be a case of the "moving finger" of legislation, "having writ, moves on." The moment is gone, public opinion is diverted elsewhere, legislative coalitions dissolve, and new ones take their place. It is only rarely that the scene can be reconstructed, the actors returned to their places on the stage, and the members of an applauding audience returned to their seats. Once in a while this can be done, and a great amending statute to an original piece of legislation is adopted. But to assume that the legislature is capable of following on a regular and intimate basis the work of innumerable courts and administrative agencies to which it may have entrusted the interpretation and enforcement of a wide variety of statutes, and capable, furthermore, of ratifying or repudiating the more or less continuous legislative rulings of these bodies, is to assume the impossible.

influences upon policy formulation:
forces existing within the government

Attention should now be given to the forces and influences that tend to bring about the shaping of the particular policies favored by a nation. Although policy formulation has both a prestatutory and a poststatutory phase, we may at this point confine our attention to the pressures which are brought to bear upon the legislature when it enacts a statute. At other points we will note the extent to which judges and administrators are subject to similar pressures when they go about the business of poststatutory policy making and implementation.

The forces influencing a legislature have two sources: one set of pressures to which it is subject is found within the government itself; the other is found outside the government. This contrast between governmental and nongovernmental forces is in some ways a formal or artificial one, for the forces within government are often allied with, or tend to reflect, the forces outside government. Nonetheless, the means whereby the pressures upon the legislature have become institutionalized do emphasize this contrast.

influence of the President upon Congress

In passing laws the legislature, whether it likes it or not—indeed, whether it is even conscious of this influence—is always swayed by the desires of the chief executive and members of the administrative agencies of government. This is not difficult to understand, for the chief executive in a modern democracy, whether he be a President or a Prime Minister, must inevitably play the role of a leader. The evil of modern totalitarianism has led the American people to distrust the leadership principle and to be apprehensive about the appearance of a *Führer* or a *Duce* upon the scene. Nonetheless, the force of circumstances in this highly mechanized and war-torn age compels even a democratic people to turn to their chief executive for a very considerable measure of inspiration and guidance in the formulation of national policy. The American President has become the leader of a great nation, for the prestige and power that have always been associated with the office, combined with the consequences of the two-party system of politics, have persuaded the people that they may look to the President for national leadership. There can be no doubt that the people hold a President responsible for the course of the nation's destiny during his four-year term of office. Congressmen, too, are inevitably aware of the extent to which they must look to the President for guidance. Presidents may be reluctant to lead, and congressmen may rebel against whatever presidential leadership is forthcoming, but the fact remains that in their chief executive Americans do not have, and have never had, a mere administrator, but an officer compelled by the Constitution, by the nature of the American party system, and by the realities of history to guide the nation into paths which he thinks it should follow.

influence of administrative agencies upon Congress

The influence which lesser administrative officers inevitably exercise upon the legislature must not be overlooked. An illustration of administrative influence upon Congress can be found in such an agency as the Federal Trade Commission. This agency was created by Congress in 1914 as a further means of enforcing the national antitrust program. Among other things it was given the responsibility and power to develop and enforce a code of fair-trade regulations. As a result of thirty-five years of experience, the commission, in its collective membership, is unquestionably possessed of extensive knowledge concerning the problems with which it deals. The hope that an agency possessed of just such knowledge would develop was one of the reasons that led Congress to create the commission in the first place. Aware of the information that would ultimately come to the agency, and the plans and ideas that would emerge from its experience, Congress provided that the commission should report regularly to it. Accordingly, it is safe to say that Congress would not make any change in our national policy as to fair-trade practices without giving careful thought to the advice and recommendations offered by this commission. It does not follow that any such change in law would reflect only the recommendations or wishes of the commission, for Congress is subject to other, and possibly conflicting, pressures which might well in a given case outweigh the influence of the commission. Actually, Congress, since 1914, has passed a long series of acts, some of which deal directly with the commission and its work, and others of which are concerned with closely related monopoly problems. Everything considered, these statutes probably reflect less sensitivity by Congress to the Federal Trade Commission than might be expected, for this particular administrative agency has not enjoyed the prestige with Congress that certain other agencies have, and in the controversial field in which it operates, its influence with Congress has sometimes been less strong than has that of certain other forces, chiefly nongovernmental.

Nonetheless, a legislature can hardly fail to be influenced by the recommendations of administrative agencies of government. The illustration that has been offered in the work of the Federal Trade Commission can be duplicated many times over in the field of national government. There are particular agencies which, because of shortcomings of personnel, or because of the exceptionally controversial character of the fields in which they operate, seem to be *persona non grata* to the legislature. For example, in the years since its creation in 1935, the National Labor Relations Board has had an extremely stormy and controversial career in an unusually difficult field of public administration, and it is perhaps true that Congress has shown little inclination to follow the recommendations of this agency in the enactment of subsequent labor laws. Other agencies, such as the Federal Bureau of Investigation or the Interstate Commerce Commission, for one reason or another have become immensely popular with Congress, and it has followed their wishes closely in the enactment of new laws in the areas in which they are interested. If one may generalize, a legislature is bound to show much sensitivity to the findings and recommendations of the agencies to which it has given law enforcement responsibilities, as from time to time these laws need modification, extension, or replacement. Moreover, it seems clear that much of a legislature's need for accurate, technical information in a difficult field of government policy can be satisfied, perhaps better than in any other way, in the advice it receives from the administrators of the statutes it has enacted.

influence of courts upon Congress

In the discussion earlier in this chapter of the prestatutory development of an antitrust policy an illustration was provided of judicial influence upon the legislature. The part which courts play in influencing the enactment of statutes is less direct and less comprehensive than the part played by the executive branch of government, for courts are not in continuous touch with the legislature, and their opinion concerning a proposed law is not ordinarily sought in any formal fashion. Yet by their work in developing prestatutory common law in an area of public policy, the courts almost always exert an influence upon the legislature, be it indirect and unconscious. The legislature is almost certain to use this judge-made law as a starting point in devising a statute, and even though significant changes may be made on particular points, large portions of the common law are apt to find their way into the act of the legislature. A. V. Dicey, the great English legal historian, has noted that this was true in the late nineteenth century in England when Parliament was engaged in the process of translating much English social policy into a statutory form. He points out that "many Acts of Parliament . . . such as the Sale of Goods Act, 1893, or the Bills of Exchange Act, 1882, are little less than the reproduction in a statutory shape of rules originally established by the Courts. Judge-made law has in such cases passed into statute law." [5]

influences upon policy formulation: forces outside the government

influence of the political party

It need hardly be said that the legislature is affected by forces outside the government as it makes use of its lawmaking powers. One can take the existence of such influence in a democracy for granted. What is not so obvious is the manner in which the popular influence upon the legislature is institutionalized. Attention has been given in earlier chapters to this problem, but we may note again the roles of the political party and the pressure group in reflecting the desires of the people as to legislation. The influence which the political party has upon the formulation of policy in the United States is easily exaggerated. It is commonly believed that congressional consideration of important bills is marked by voting along straight party lines, but any analysis of the work of Congress reveals the extent to which party influences are often secondary in importance. For example, an analysis of the voting in Congress during the years of the Roosevelt administration, in which the Democratic party continuously controlled Congress, shows that a majority of the Democrats usually voted for administration measures and a majority of the Republicans against, but that almost always there were some members voting contrary to the majority faction in their own party. Frequently, enough Democrats deserted an administration measure so that its enactment was possible only because of Republican support; or vice versa, the Republican minority was joined by enough dissident Democrats to form a legislative majority, which thereupon controlled the outcome of the voting on a measure.

[5] A. V. Dicey, *Law and Public Opinion in England* (New York: The Macmillan Company, 1905), p. 360. Used by permission of The Macmillan Company, publishers.

However, the role of the party as an agency through which interest groups make their wishes known to the legislature should not be unduly minimized. By the force of its platform, vague though it often is, and by its organization and discipline, however incomplete, the party unquestionably has much influence upon the voting of congressmen. For example, those segments of our population which have favored social policies advantageous to business have in the main in recent years sought to impose their will upon Congress by working through the agency of the Republican party. Similarly, those which have sought legislation favorable to labor have found the Democratic party a reasonably receptive and effective agency through which to influence the result in Congress. In each instance, the party has welcomed the allegiance of such members and has made varying efforts to secure the adoption of national policies reflecting the desires of its supporters.

influence of the pressure group

The pressure group has nonetheless been much more effective than the party in serving as an instrumentality through which groups of people may influence the course of the legislative process. The party, as has been seen, is much more complex in its organization and its purposes, whereas the pressure group, by its very nature, exists primarily to influence either the making of governmental policy or its enforcement, and unless it serves in some such capacity a particular pressure group loses any reason for being and usually disappears from the political scene. It is not surprising that pressure groups should show a particular interest in the determination of governmental policies concerning important social problems. How can an organization of farmers fail to be interested in a legislative proposal that crop limitation be adopted as a means of coping with a national agricultural surplus, or how can businessmen ignore a proposal that corporation taxes be raised? Is it logical to expect that the South will show no interest in a statutory system of freight rates that favors traffic between the West and the Northeast, or that New England will fail to support a minimum-wage policy that might offset the low-wage advantage enjoyed by the southern textile industry? Is it not inevitable that Negroes should lend their support to a proposed federal statute making it unlawful for employers to show racial discrimination in hiring workers, or that war veterans should favor a more generous pension policy for ex-soldiers, or that elderly people should be enthusiastic about extension of the old-age insurance program? Such reactions are natural and reasonable; they are deeply rooted in the realities of civilization; they are the inevitable products of man's intelligence. If such reactions are natural, it follows that men who hold these views will organize for action and set up pressure groups which will be continuously interested in the making of policy by a legislative body.

the complexity of influences upon the legislator

Influences in voting can be, and ordinarily are, exceedingly complex, for the legislator may find himself affected by diverse factors, sectional, economic, and social in character, each of which seeks to dominate his voting. Take, for example, the plight of a Republican congressman from an urban district in New England when he is confronted with the necessity of making up his mind concerning the proposal of a Democratic President that the minimum-wage level be raised. Party considerations would argue that he oppose the measure; his own personal economic philosophy might well incline him to vote against such a bill as a further instance of "government regulation"; the heavy labor vote in his urban district would suggest the wisdom of voting for the bill; and finally, the strong possibility that such a law might help the New England textile industry to recover some of the ground it has lost to the textile industry of the South would also argue in favor of his support of the bill. Torn in both directions though the congressman may be, he must finally make up his mind to vote one way or the other. In the end it will probably be a combination of influences rather than one isolated force that will control his decision.

We see in this situation an illustration of the way in which the pressures, organized and otherwise, that are brought to bear upon a phase of the governmental process often offset one another. This conflict of interests tends to bring about a balance or equilibrium in social forces which is desirable in a democratic society. The balance is largely achieved by the introduction of a strong element of compromise in legislation. This is not to say that the general will can never be anything more than a collection of, or compromise between, particular wills, for at times the formulation of national policy on such a basis is a dangerous thing. This is frequently true of the making of a nation's foreign policy. But, more often than not, the determination of domestic policies in a democratic society must reflect a variety of conflicting interests and proceed along compromise lines even at the price of a failure to pursue a more rational, logical, and systematic program.

On the other hand there is always a danger that the formulation of public policy in a democracy will be rendered difficult or even be completely frustrated by the numerous and conflicting forces that are certain to be brought to bear on any crucial legislative issue. In a very careful study of the steps by which the Employment Act of 1946 became law, Professor Stephen Bailey comes to a rather pessimistic conclusion concerning the ability of our society to evolve positive public policies which reflect the desires of majorities. He writes:

> Put in its baldest form, the story of S. 380 adds up to the fact that majority sentiment expressed in popular elections for a particular economic policy can be, and frequently is, almost hopelessly splintered by the power struggles of

competing political, administrative, and private interests, and is finally pieced together, if at all, only by the most laborious, complicated, and frequently covert coalition strategies.[6]

influences upon our antitrust policy

We may turn once more to the Sherman Act, this time to note the diverse pressures, both within and outside the government, which were brought to bear upon Congress to secure the passage of this law. Within the government, President Cleveland in messages to Congress in 1887 and 1888 asked for the enactment of an antitrust law, and President Harrison repeated the request in his annual message in 1889, in which he stated that trusts were often "dangerous conspiracies against the public good, and should be made the subject of prohibitory and even penal legislation." Outside the government, agitation for legislation against trusts was extensive even though the issue was seemingly not a burning one. Third parties had long been demanding that government take action to prevent monopolies, and in 1888 both major parties included planks in their platforms calling for such action. Although pressure groups were not in this period as highly organized as they are today, many factions were demanding that the government act. The writings of such men as Henry George, Edward Bellamy, and Henry Demarest Lloyd contained attacks upon monopolies and had wide circulation and influence. In particular, labor and agricultural groups and independent manufacturers and businessmen took up the cry and asked for congressional legislation.

Of course, it should not be supposed that congressmen were necessarily reluctant to legislate against trusts or that Congress was finally compelled, against its own desire in the matter, to pass such a law. In noting both congressional sensitivity to pressures that are brought to bear upon it, and the extent to which executive and judicial agencies participate in the lawmaking process in prestatutory and poststatutory ways, the error of underestimating the continuing importance of the independent judgment of the legislature must not be made. However vigorous the pressures for or against the enactment of a law, and however general the terms a legislature finds it necessary to give a statute, it is still that body that weighs the pressures that are brought to bear upon it and decides the direction of the fundamental policy to be followed.

two criteria for satisfactory policy determination

Before we turn our attention to the actual operation of the legislative process in American government, it will be well to recall the two criteria by which it was earlier suggested that American government might properly be evaluated. The

---

[6] Stephen Kemp Bailey, *Congress Makes a Law* (New York: Columbia University Press, 1950), p. 237.

first of these criteria is the democratic principle. To what extent does legislative policy take shape along democratic lines? We are committed to the ideal of democratic government, and it seems clear that, unless the determination of policies reflects the wishes of the people, democracy is failing at a very crucial point. The second criterion is technical efficiency. Is our legislative system so organized and does it operate in such a manner that laws are enacted efficiently and with a minimum of unnecessary delay or disturbance? After all, the problems presented for solution by a modern, industrial civilization are themselves apt to be so complex in the technical sense that, unless the machinery for the formation of policy operates readily and smoothly, the policies finally selected may very well be unsatisfactory. So we have the two tests of democracy and efficiency to apply to our legislative system. Both are necessary. Neither by itself is enough. Failing either test a free nation invites disaster.

bibliographic note

There are relatively few works which are concerned with the *theory* of the legislative process. In the *Encyclopaedia of the Social Sciences*, there is an article on "Legislation" by Ernest Freund, as well as a series of articles on "Legislative Assemblies" by well-known authors. "The History and Theory of Legislative Assemblies" is examined by W. J. Shepard and the "United States Congress" by Lindsay Rogers (IX, 347, 355, 361). T. V. Smith has published a collection of essays called *The Legislative Way of Life* (Chicago: The University of Chicago Press, 1940), in which the legislative process is examined from the point of view of a man who is both a philosopher and a political scientist and who has served as a member of the Illinois legislature and the national House of Representatives. Robert Luce's *Legislative Principles* (Boston: Houghton Mifflin Company, 1930), one of several volumes in this field by a former member of Congress, examines the theory of the legislative process. The same author's *Legislative Procedure* (Boston: Houghton Mifflin Company, 1922) may also be noted, although it is largely concerned with describing the means by which legislative assemblies go about their work. Joseph P. Chamberlain's *Legislative Processes: National and State* (New York: Appleton-Century-Crofts, Inc., 1936) is in form a textbook on legislative organization and procedure, but it gives considerable attention to the theory of the legislative process. The same is true of Harvey Walker's *The Legislative Process* (New York: The Ronald Press, 1948).

W. F. Willoughby's *Principles of Legislative Organization and Administration* (Washington: The Brookings Institution, 1934) is a systematic work which contains essays on a variety of subjects, such as relations between legislatures and the electorate, relations between legislatures and the executive and judicial branches of the government, legislative organization and procedure, and legislative leadership.

Woodrow Wilson's *Congressional Government: A Study in American Politics* (Boston: Houghton Mifflin Company, 1885) is a classic study of our national legislature. It is amazing how well Wilson's insights and judgments stand up nearly three quarters of a century after this book was published. In particular, Wilson's analysis of the lack of responsible leadership in Congress remains significant today.

Sidney P. Simpson, Julius Stone, and M. M. Schoch, *Cases and Readings on Law and Society* (in three volumes: *Law and Society in Evolution; Law in Modern Democratic Society; Law, Totalitarianism and Democracy;* St. Paul: West Publishing Company, 1948–1949), is a recent publication providing case studies on the making of public policy.

For further readings on the legislative process, see also the bibliographic note to Chapter 16, "Congress at Work: Lawmaking."

the organization of Congress

$\mathcal{T}$HE most obvious thing about the organization of the American Congress is that it is a bicameral body. Bicameral legislative bodies are so common in political history that one is inclined to take the two houses of Congress almost for granted. This is a mistake, for it was by no means inevitable that our Congress should be bicameral. Its parent legislative body, the Congress under the Articles of Confederation, consisted of a single house, as did all of the *national* assemblies of the American colonial and revolutionary periods. On the other hand, it should be remembered that although these earlier national assemblies had all been unicameral, the Founding Fathers were well aware of the bicameral arrangement. Practically all of the assemblies in the thirteen American colonies and the legislatures set up in the American states after 1776 had consisted of two houses. And the English Parliament, with which every American was familiar, was, of course, a bicameral body.

Faced as they were with definite precedents in either direction, why did the Fathers prefer a bicameral Congress? Of course, the Connecticut Compromise, which resolved the most serious conflict that troubled the delegates, necessitated a bicameral arrangement. By having two houses, it was possible to satisfy the more populous states by providing for proportional representation in one house, and at the same time satisfy the smaller states by guaranteeing them equal representation in a second house. However, it seems likely that the convention would have preferred a bicameral legislature even if there had been no need for one as a convenient means of compromising between the large-state and small-state groups. The convention decided very early in its sessions that the legislature should consist of two houses. After all, bicameralism was consistent with the principle of checks and balances, one of the strongest forces that motivated the work of the convention. A historian of the constitutional period relates that when Thomas Jefferson returned from France after the Philadelphia convention had completed its labors, he objected to the bicameral feature of the national legislature and asked Washington why the convention had taken such a step.

The conversation occurred at breakfast, and Washington is said to have asked Jefferson, "Why did you pour that coffee into your saucer?" "To cool it," was Jefferson's reply. "Even so," answered Washington, "we pour legislation into the senatorial saucer to cool it." [1]

the nature of American bicameralism

There is nothing novel about the fact that Congress is a bicameral body, but its particular form of bicameralism has been somewhat unusual, in that its two houses, for all of their surface differences, have been remarkably similar in the power they possess, and in their modes of organization and procedure. More often than not, bicameralism in other countries has meant two legislative bodies, highly dissimilar in character and power. This has been particularly true of the British Parliament, with its extreme contrast between the House of Commons and the House of Lords. Actually, the men who made the American Constitution had in mind two legislative bodies that were to differ from one another far more than they do today. Under the original plan the Senate was to be a small body of twenty-six members chosen by the state legislatures. These features, plus the fact that the qualifications for membership were to be somewhat stricter than those for the House, were expected to result in a strongly conservative body that would serve to restrain the more democratic and radical lower chamber. There is no need to be concerned here with the long evolutionary history of the two bodies, or to seek to discover whether the Senate was in fact in the early days a conservative body, for it is clear that this original contrast between the two houses has long ceased to exist. One significant force that has heightened the similarity between the two houses has been the system of political parties, which has provided for a common system of partisan control and responsibility for legislation in both House and Senate. Likewise, the adoption of the Seventeenth Amendment in 1913, providing for the direct popular election of senators, increased the similarity of the houses.

Today it is not possible, at least for any length of time, to say that one house is more conservative or liberal than the other. Certainly, the Senate has long since ceased to function primarily as a "check" upon the House. Legislation, with very few exceptions, originates as readily in one house as in the other, and at any given moment either house may seem to be the more conservatively minded of the two. During the years of the New Deal, at times it was the House that proved to be a thorn in the side of the administration; again in notable instances it was the Senate that refused to go along with the President after the House had accepted his recommendations.

Senators still represent states, whereas representatives are chosen from

[1] Max Farrand, *The Framing of the Constitution* (New Haven: Yale University Press, 1926), p. 74.

smaller districts. Occasionally, this distinction leads to important differences in the sensitivity of the two houses to the demands of pressure groups. Likewise, members of the House are elected on a population basis, and the average member represents in the neighborhood of 300,000 persons. Senators are elected without regard to population, and the range of persons represented runs all the way from 160,083 in the case of the Nevada senators to 14,830,192 in the case of the senators from New York. Because of its smaller size, the Senate has the more exclusive air of a gentlemen's club, and the individual senator has more influence and prestige than does the average representative. Moreover, there are some important differences of organization and procedure in the two houses which will be discussed at a later point. Yet the two houses have become evenly matched partners in the legislative process. The passage of a bill through Congress is pretty much a matter of securing the approval of two chambers which have no fundamental reason for disagreeing with one another. A bill may be accepted by one house and rejected by the other, but such contrasting action is not usually the result of any profound difference in the character of the two houses. The element of timing, the influence of the different personalities who may dominate the scene in either house, and the fact that no legislative proposal ever receives identical treatment from two legislative bodies—all these factors have far more to do with variations in the action of House and Senate than do their differing characters.

Because the House and the Senate have grown through the years to resemble each other so closely, there is good reason to question the continuing validity of the bicameral principle in national legislation. It is not logical to submit legislative proposals to two essentially identical bodies for their approval, and the result is inevitably to make it more difficult to formulate positive national policies of any kind. Bicameralism of the type found in the American Congress is an invitation to deadlock and frustration. In recent years such legislative proposals as federal aid to education, a fair-employment practices program, statehood for Hawaii and Alaska, and abolition of the electoral college have passed one house but failed to win the approval of the other. The first two proposals died in the House, the latter two in the Senate; in fact, honors are not far from even between the two houses when it comes to responsibility for killing bills already passed by one house. If the filibuster has proved to be a weapon which a minority of senators can use to prevent favorable action on a bill in the upper house, pigeonholing a bill in committee or refusal of the Rules Committee to give it the right of way to the floor are weapons which enable small groups of representatives to kill bills in the House.

Whatever the logic of the situation may be, bicameralism in our national government is firmly established as a practical arrangement, and change at this point is extremely unlikely. Serious consideration of the much larger issue of the entire system of checks and balances in all of its ramifications is, however, necessary and feasible. It is entirely possible that the day will come when it will seem wise to make the American government more straightforward—to streamline it for democratic action. Out of some such intelligent consideration of the over-all character of our system of checks and balances may ultimately come a decision by the American people to alter the historic two-house organization of the Congress at the same time that other changes are being made. But any isolated, frontal attack upon the bicameral character of Congress is almost certain to fail.

congressional organization and procedure under the Constitution

The organization and procedure of the two houses of Congress are dependent upon the words of the Constitution in small degree only. The Constitution provides that there shall be two houses of Congress; it prescribes in certain ways the manner of electing senators and representatives; and it fixes the size of the Senate by providing that each state shall have two seats. For all practical purposes it leaves the size of the House of Representatives to be freely determined by Congress itself. The only congressional officers that are mentioned in the Constitution are the Speaker of the House of Representatives; the Vice-President, who is directed to preside over the Senate; and the President pro tempore of the Senate. All other congressional offices may be freely created and controlled by each house. There is not a word in the Constitution about the committee structure of Congress. Neither the standing committees that consider legislation, the conference committees that determine the final versions of bills, nor the spectacular investigating committees are in any way controlled by the Constitution, either as to organization or as to procedure. Almost the same thing is true of the rules of procedure by which the two houses legislate. A few are prescribed. The quorum for each house is fixed at one more than half of the total membership. One fifth of the members present are guaranteed the right to demand a record vote on any question. Each house may punish its members for disorderly behavior, or by a two-thirds vote expel a member. Each house is directed to keep a journal of its proceedings, and neither house may adjourn for more than three days without the consent of the other. And that is about all the Constitution prescribes by way of rules. All of the elaborate procedure in each house by which bills are referred to and considered by committees, debate is controlled on the floor, amendments to bills are offered and disposed of, and voting procedure is determined—all these depend upon rules formulated by each house.

As a result of the relative silence of the Constitution on congressional organization and procedure, Congress has been largely free over a period of a century and a half to develop a system of legislative procedure unfettered by constitutional restraints. Accordingly, there has been much experimentation, frequent changes have been made, and the cumulative result is one of the great examples of the development of the American system of government outside the words of the written Constitution. Moreover, further reform or reorganization of Congress can be accomplished in large degree without any necessity of formal amendment of the Constitution.

the sessions of Congress

the two-year life of a Congress

Congress operates on a two-year cycle. The Congress that convened early in January, 1949, was known formally as "The Eighty-first Congress," there having been eighty previous "Congresses" in one hundred and sixty years. The Constitution does not clearly prescribe this two-year cycle, but its use is the inevitable result of our election system whereby all the seats in the House and one third of the seats in the Senate become vacant every two years. Accordingly, the Congress that meets in January of an odd-numbered year is a new body, many of its members having just been elected to their offices two months before, in the November election held in each even-numbered year. The meeting in the odd-numbered year is thus the "first" session, and assuming that no special session is called, the meeting in the following even-numbered year is the "second" and final session of a Congress. Very early in a first session the two houses proceed to organize, and the resulting arrangements prevail for the two-year period. Any bill introduced in the first session of a Congress, but not finally disposed of when the session ends, may be taken up at the beginning of the second session at whatever stage had been reached when the first session adjourned. But when the final session in the two-year cycle comes to an end, all unfinished business automatically dies. Thus a bill introduced early in the first session of a Congress has a two-year period in which to become law.

regular sessions

Under the Twentieth Amendment which went into effect in 1933 Congress meets every year on the third day of January, unless by law it appoints a different day.[2] It may then remain in session as long as it pleases right up to the following January 3. In normal times adjournment may be expected anywhere from

---

[2] A two-year congressional period after the adoption of the Twentieth Amendment ran as follows:

  November, 1942—Biennial election—78th Congress is chosen.
  January 3, 1943—Life of the 78th Congress legally begins.
  January 6, 1943—78th Congress meets for the first time.
  December 21, 1943—First session of the 78th Congress ends.
  January 10, 1944—78th Congress meets for its second and last session.
  December 19, 1944—Second session of the 78th Congress ends.
  November, 1944—Biennial election—79th Congress is chosen.

June to August. During the period of the international crisis which began in the late nineteen thirties, Congress remained virtually in continuous session. It is interesting to note that the 1940 session of Congress actually lasted 367 days, since 1940 was a leap year and the session began at noon on January 3, 1940, and extended into the early hours of January 3, 1941. This was, of course, the longest session in congressional history and it can hardly be exceeded!

The Constitution authorizes either or both houses to take recesses in the midst of a session, although both houses must agree to any recess that is to last for more than three days. During the protracted sessions that have occurred since 1939 this recess arrangement has been utilized to provide long breaks in a session. For example, the 1944 Congress took two long vacations, one of five weeks' and the other of seven weeks' duration. There is some evidence to indicate that Congress chose this method of obtaining relief from its arduous labors, so as to avoid an adjournment sine die, which would have left it to the President to call a special session if the need arose.

The Legislative Reorganization Act of 1946 provides that except in time of war or during a national emergency proclaimed by the President, Congress shall adjourn each year by the end of July. But this is an advisory admonition only, and any particular Congress may remain in session beyond July if it so desires. The chief argument advanced in favor of the July adjournment clause of the Reorganization Act was that the members of a *representative* assembly ought to spend some time each year at home among their constituents so that they might know the temper and wishes of the people.

the influence of party in congressional organization

the organizing of House and Senate at the beginning of each Congress

Organization of each house is the first order of business when a new Congress meets. This is ordinarily a more important task for the House than it is for the Senate. At most, only one third of the seats in the Senate can be occupied by new men. Consequently, the Senate customarily makes no attempt to rebuild its organization anew every two years. New members are fitted into committee vacancies, and Senate and party officers are reappointed more or less automatically, provided there has been no change in the majority-minority status of the two great parties. Moreover, the Senate never reaffirms its rules, it being assumed that the old rules remain in effect automatically. Indeed, the Senate regards itself as a continuous body.

In the House (and in the Senate, too, subject to the tendency just noted) the opening days of a first session are marked by an atmosphere of activity and excitement as the business of organizing is carried out. Officers are elected, committee personnel designated, and the rules adopted or, more accurately, reaffirmed. It is at this point in the work of Congress that party politics is at its peak, for organizing Congress is a party responsibility. It is assumed that the majority party in each house will elect all the formal congressional officers, receive a majority of the seats on each of the committees, and designate the chairman of each committee. But the minority party has work to do, too, for it must go through the form of putting up its leading members as candidates for the congressional offices, it must select its own unofficial party officers, such as the floor leaders and whips, and it must determine the assignment of its members to the seats to which the minority is entitled on every committee. No matter how much party lines may break down later, when Congress turns its attention to controversial legislative problems, in the work of organization they hold fast. Even the most independent senator or representative is apt to be a loyal Democrat or Republican at this moment. In noting this tendency one authority refers to "the paradox of all Congresses . . . partisanship in building the machine; eclectic voting or bipartisan combinations in the actual passing of bills." [3]

the party committee on committees

In this partisan business of organizing the houses, two types of party agency are of importance—the Committee on Committees and the caucus. As the name indicates, it is the function of the first of these to select the congressmen who are to serve on the standing committees. In both houses each party group sets up its own Committee on Committees. These four committees, functioning independently, then proceed to give party members standing committee assignments. The only exception to this procedure is that in the House of Representatives the Democrats, instead of creating a special committee on committees, first select their members to serve on the House Ways and Means Committee and this group then functions automatically as the Democratic Committee on Committees.

Before the Committees on Committees can perform their work, the majority party in each house must decide the ratio that is to prevail between Democrats and Republicans on each standing committee. Occasionally there is controversy over this decision as in 1949, when the Senate Democrats cut the Republican membership on the Foreign Relations Committee to a lower point than the Republicans considered fair. But usually the ratio tends to reflect fairly accurately the division between the two parties in the houses; furthermore, it is governed by traditions which both parties have long accepted. The slates that have been prepared by the party Committees on Committees must be ratified by the party caucuses and the two houses, but this action is almost without exception a mere formality. Actually, in the House as well as in the Senate, the standing committees are reasonably continuous bodies, and the party task every two years is merely one of filling vacancies. This usually involves allowing some of

---

[3] A. W. Macmahon, "First Session of the Seventieth Congress," *American Political Science Review*, XXII (August, 1928), 650. Much of the statistical material in this and the next chapter is derived from this valuable series of annual articles on the sessions of Congress.

the older congressmen to move up to the vacancies on the more important committees and filling the vacancies at the bottom with the freshman members of Congress. This is one aspect of the famous rule of seniority; the other aspect provides for the automatic selection as chairman of that majority member of each committee who has served longest on the committee. The controversial character of this rule of seniority will be discussed later in the chapter.

the party caucus

The caucus (or "conference," the word preferred by the Republicans in recent years) is an agency of declining importance. At the height of its power it was a meeting of all members of a party in the House or the Senate called to determine party position on a controversial issue. Although the rules of the Republican or the Democratic caucus varied from time to time, the essential feature was the obligation of the individual congressman to cast his vote on the floor of the house in accordance with a party decision made in the caucus. Today, this binding character of the caucus decision has pretty well disappeared, except in the case of the organization meetings in the early days of a new Congress when each party chooses its candidate for Speaker, President pro tempore, or other congressional officers, and ratifies the committee slates prepared by its Committee on Committees. Party caucuses are still held from time to time during the session to discuss legislative strategy from the point of view of the party's interest, but almost no attempt is now made by either party caucus to dictate how its members shall vote in the House or the Senate on a bill. This is not to say that party leaders do not frequently exert all the pressure they can in an effort to influence the votes of party members on important legislative issues, but insistence upon party regularity stops short of the attempt to bind members by caucus action.

House and Senate rules

the difficulty of evolving satisfactory rules

It is difficult to exaggerate the importance of an adequate system of rules to a modern legislative body. Obviously the success that the legislature of any country enjoys in coping with the difficult problems which are inescapable in our present civilization is dependent upon a great many other factors than its mere rules of organization and procedure. Yet it seems fair to say that even where many of these other factors are reasonably favorable to the finding of satisfactory solutions, faulty rules can seriously handicap the attack upon a nation's problems. For example, many observers have commented on the part played by the unworkable rules of the Chamber of Deputies and the Senate in the failure of the French parliamentary system and the fall of France in 1940.

It is easy to remark on the necessity of a system of rules which will be conducive to the efficient and democratic operation of a legislative system; it is difficult actually to devise workable rules. The rules of any modern legislative body are bound to be the result of a slow, evolutionary development in which conflicting forces contribute to the final result. For example, not the least serious difficulty in formulating a satisfactory system of House or Senate rules has been the necessity of protecting the legitimate interests of both the majority and the minority. The democratic principle requires that in the business of governing a nation an organized majority must be permitted to take shape, and thereafter for some limited period of time allowed to formulate and put into effect a legislative program. But democracy also requires that the interests of the minority be protected during such a period and that the minority have the opportunity to state and discuss its position on the controversial issues of the day before any legislative decisions are made. To be more specific, all legislative bodies have great difficulty in formulating a rule on freedom of debate that adequately protects the interests of both majority and minority. It is clearly desirable to permit expression of all points of view during debate, and yet it is also necessary that a matter be finally brought to a vote and disposed of by majority action.

formal and informal rules

This difficulty of finding a satisfactory rule on freedom of debate is in a certain sense illustrative of a much more fundamental dilemma in the formulation of a system of rules for a legislative body. The rules of the House or the Senate must necessarily as a whole be exact, detailed, and formal. The business of legislating for a country as great and as complex as the United States is a tremendous responsibility, and, inevitably, technical procedures concerning the order of business, the length of debate, the amending of bills, the methods of voting, and the reconciliation of House and Senate differences must be carefully prescribed. Yet there is the constant danger that procedure will become so detailed and circumscribed that business can be transacted only with difficulty. Again and again, episodes occur in Congress in which members who are clever parliamentarians are able to tie the business of House or Senate into knots merely by insisting upon the following of the letter of the rules. But although this is often possible, both houses have in part solved this dilemma by the creation of two entirely different sets of rules: one a formal set that recognizes each distinct problem of parliamentary procedure by providing a prescribed and official mode of action; the other an informal, and largely unwritten set that makes it possible for the legislative body to transact much of its business in disregard of prescribed procedures.

The existence of these rival sets of rules has not been sufficiently appreciated, although careful observers of the congressional scene have long been aware of them and their significance. For example, in commenting on the 1938 session of Congress, one observer said: "The Senate has operated so long as a gentlemen's club that two sets of rules have developed, one written and the other based on custom. Only after specific warning is it considered fair to enforce the written rules." [4]

One manifestation of informal procedure in both houses is the extensive transaction of business on a basis of unanimous consent. Either house can violate its formal rules at any time so long as no member objects. Since, however, any single member can prevent the use of such informal procedures by voicing objection and insisting upon the following of the formal rules, it has always been difficult for the layman to understand how both houses succeed in transacting so much business, much of it controversial, without encountering such objections. The answer is that, even though there are 96 senators and 435 representatives, with widely varying interests and points of view, congressmen, for the most part, recognize the necessity of preferring the informal to the formal rules in the transaction of much congressional business. Yet they know that the formal rules are there, ready to be invoked when the issues at stake are serious, or when the conflict of interests is not being compromised.

There is a second reason why it is not enough to read the formal rules of the House and the Senate if one is to have an understanding of the procedure that is actually followed in Congress. The difficulty is that a rule itself is apt to be meaningless unless it is considered in the light of the extensive precedents that have been developed and followed as the rule has been applied. These precedents bear much the same relation to the rule that the decisions of a court do to a statute; they are the flesh and skin which added to the bones produce the living body. Moreover, like court decisions, these precedents have been formally collected, set down in writing, and are carefully studied when any new question as to the meaning or application of a rule arises.[5]

the officers of the House and the Senate: congressional and party

Legislative officers are of two types—those that are formal or official in character, such as the Speaker; and those that are related to the parties, such as the floor leaders. In practice, there is a great deal of overlapping between the two types of office. For example, although the Speaker presides over the House as a formal, nonpartisan officer, his office has its political side, too, and much of the power and influence that he wields as a congressional leader depends upon his position as one of the outstanding figures of the majority party. On the other

[4] O. R. Altman, "Second and Third Sessions of the Seventy-fifth Congress, 1937–38," *American Political Science Review*, XXXII (December, 1938), 1099, 1116.

[5] See Asher C. Hinds, *Precedents of the House of Representatives* (Washington: Government Printing Office, 1907, 8 vols.) ; Clarence Cannon, *Precedents of the House of Representatives* (Washington: Government Printing Office, 1936–1941, 11 vols., the first five of which are a reprint of Hind's *Precedents*) ; H. H. Gilfrey, *Precedents, Decisions on Points of Order with Phraseology, in the Senate* (Washington: Government Printing Office, 1914).

hand, the floor leader, although strictly a party officer, plays an important role in keeping business moving along; indeed, were it not for his existence, the Senate and the House might have to make some more formal provision for such an official. Nonetheless, in spite of the vagueness that sometimes separates the work of a house officer from that of a party officer, the distinction is a significant one. For one thing it illustrates the difference between the visible and invisible governments of the House and the Senate. Both houses have formal offices and procedures, but the actual resting place of power and the actual modes employed in enacting legislation are profoundly influenced by the political situation in Congress.

the presiding officers of House and Senate

The most important formal officers are those who preside over the two houses. In the House this is the Speaker; in the Senate, the Vice-President. The latter is, of course, not really a member of the Senate, but that is also true of certain other congressional officers such as the clerks and parliamentarians. Each house has a second presiding officer. In the Senate this is the President pro tempore, a constitutional officer, who presides in the absence of the Vice-President. In the House it is the chairman of the Committee of the Whole. Technically speaking, the latter is not a House officer but a committee officer. Nonetheless, he is the officer who actually presides while the House is transacting much of its important business. However, he is not a permanent officer but is appointed from time to time by the Speaker as the House rises and goes into the Committee of the Whole. Even when the Senate or the House is in formal session almost any member of either body may be found in the chair, for the Speaker, the Vice-President, or the President pro tempore frequently leaves the chair and designates some representative or senator to preside in his absence.

the power of recognition

The powers of the Speaker and the Vice-President as presiding officers may be considered simultaneously, although certain differences must be noted. Both exercise the usual powers of presiding officers in preserving order, recognizing members seeking the floor, and putting matters to a vote. The Speaker may ask a representative who seeks recognition the question, "For what purpose does the Gentleman rise?" If he is not satisfied with the reply, he may refuse to extend recognition. The Vice-President must extend the floor to senators without first ascertaining their business. Actually, there is a tendency to exaggerate the extent to which either officer may exercise the power of recognition in partisan fashion or so as to favor particular legislative proposals. From time to time situations do arise in which the course of legislation may be profoundly affected by the recognition of a certain member at a particular moment, and the Speaker and Vice-President sometimes consciously give the floor to members with such considerations in mind. But far more often than not, recognition is a completely impersonal, nonpartisan procedure, and very often in the course of debate on a controversial measure, schedules of speakers are prepared on the floor by party leaders and are followed more or less automatically by the presiding officer.

the power to interpret the rules

Both Speaker and Vice-President have the power to interpret and apply the rules when any question of proper procedure is raised. Here, too, the routine use of this power is rather unspectacular and noncontroversial, for mere reference to the precedents is often enough to indicate the proper interpretation. Every textbook cites the famous exercise of this power made by Speaker Thomas B. Reed in 1890 when he changed the interpretation of the quorum rule so as to include in the quorum count those members present but not voting yea or nay on a bill, and thereby frustrated the attempts of the Democratic minority to prevent the transaction of business by not voting. But the opportunity to make a new and significant interpretation of the rules is a rare event. Because Senate rules are less numerous and detailed, and because the Senate tradition is one of very informal procedure, the Vice-President has even less power than the Speaker in the interpretation of the rules. In both houses any ruling of the presiding officer may be appealed to the floor and reversed by a majority of the members present, but such reversals seldom occur.

the powers to refer bills and appoint special committees

Two further powers of the presiding officers should be noted. In each house it is his duty to refer all bills to committees for consideration. Although such reference is made in conformance with certain fixed traditions, occasionally the presiding officer can make a significant choice between two or more committees. Both presiding officers also exercise the power of naming the members of special committees, such as conference committees and investigating committees. However, this action is usually so controlled by tradition as to leave very little freedom of choice. For example, it is the almost unvarying tradition in both houses to name the members of conference committees in order of seniority from the standing committees that originally considered a bill.

the lost powers of the Speaker

Before the famed parliamentary revolution of 1910 against Speaker Joseph G. Cannon in the House of Representatives, the Speaker possessed certain additional powers which unquestionably made the office one of vastly greater importance than it is today. At that time the rules of the House were changed and the Speaker was deprived of the power to name the personnel of all standing committees, which power he had previously exercised in such a way as to gain great influence over the House membership. He was also denied membership on the all-important Rules Committee of the House.

other powers of presiding officers

As a regular member of the House, the Speaker retains the right to vote and to speak on any proposal, whereas the Vice-President has no regular right to participate in debate, and may vote only to break a tie. More often than not, the Speaker does not exercise these powers. Upon occasion the Speaker does leave the chair to enter the debate. One of these rare speeches by the Speaker is apt to carry much weight with other members. By this device the Speaker wields much influence, but he must be careful not to overuse it. Needless to say, if the Speaker has already voted, he cannot vote again to break a tie.

In the final analysis, the power and influence of the presiding officer depends upon political considerations. Ordinarily this means that the actual power of the Speaker goes well beyond his formal power, since he is almost always one of the two or three outstanding members of the majority party. On the other hand, it means that, more often than not, the Vice-President is a colorless and powerless presiding officer, since he is not the choice of the majority senators, and indeed may even upon occasion belong to the party of the Senate minority. There are exceptions to these generalizations in both houses. Once in a while the majority party in the House finds it desirable, for reasons of party policy, to give the speakership to one of its lesser leaders. This was true in 1933, when the Democratic majority, to offset the assignment of so many committee chairmanships to southern Democrats, elected as Speaker a northern Democrat, Henry T. Rainey, who lacked sufficient prestige and standing within his own party group to become a powerful or influential Speaker. Conversely, Vice-President Barkley has made a relatively influential presiding officer in the Senate, no doubt because of his status as a former Senator and because of his high standing in Democratic party circles.

committee chairmen

Next to the presiding officers of House and Senate, the most important formal, congressional officers are the standing committee chairmen. A very considerable part of the total business of Congress is today performed in committee. Moreover, since the chairmen are something more than mere titular heads of their committees, their offices are of greater importance. To the chairman usually fall such duties and powers as arranging the meetings of his committee, determining the order in which bills are considered by it, deciding whether public hearings shall be held on a bill, arranging to have a bill, which the committee has reported favorably, brought to the floor of the House, managing the floor debate on the bill, warding off unwanted amendments, and serving as a member of the conference committee on a particular bill, should one be necessary. Not all committees are of major importance, but there are perhaps eight or ten committee chairmen in each house whose power and work are sufficiently important to place them among the influential leaders of Congress. The extent to which these chairmen function independently of one another should be noted. The following statement on this point by Woodrow Wilson was made a great many years ago, but it is still a valid judgment: "The chairmen of the Standing Committees do not constitute a cooperative body like a ministry. They do not consult and concur in the adoption of homogeneous and mutually helpful measures; there is no thought of acting in concert." [6]

the floor leaders

Of first importance among the *party* officers in Congress are the majority floor leader and the minority floor leader in each house. These men are chosen by the party caucuses, and, as their titles indicate, their main duty is to watch over and control business on the floor of the House or Senate from a strictly party point of view. A floor leader keeps in touch with party members, tries to persuade them to vote in accordance with the wishes of party leaders, supervises debate, directs the activity of the party whips, and is in general the party's chief strategist. This is a tremendous responsibility and, because of the extent to which party lines are apt to break down in the course of debate and action on a specific measure, a somewhat thankless one. The success the party whip enjoys in these activities is certain to vary from time to time. Although the office is not a formal congressional one, it is of great institutional importance in the actual operation of the legislative department.

other party officers

The floor leader, as a party official, shares power with such other party officers as the whips, the chairman of the party caucus, and the chairman of the party steering or policy committee. In practice, these agencies vary from time to time in importance, for the two party groups in each house are more or less constantly experimenting with congressional party machinery. For example, following the death of Senate minority Floor Leader Charles McNary in 1944, the Republicans in the Senate proceeded to curtail the power of this office and to expand the power of the chief whip, that of the chairman of the Republican Conference (or caucus), and that of the chairman of the Republican Policy Committee. The Republican senators then appointed four prominent members of their group to these offices, and it was expected that they would function as

---

[6] Woodrow Wilson, *Congressional Government* (Boston: Houghton Mifflin Company, 1885), p. 61.

a team of four in directing party strategy. On the other hand, there have been instances in which a powerful floor leader has fought off attempts to make him share power with other party officers, and has succeeded in retaining top influence in the direction of party affairs.

An additional word may be said about the steering committees, somewhat vague groups of a dozen or more men maintained by each party in both houses. The members of these committees are designated by the party caucuses, or by the floor leaders, and are usually prominent party figures. Presumably these committees function as central executive committees making party decisions, planning strategy, determining the order of House and Senate business, exerting pressure upon wavering party members, and controlling party policy and action generally. However, it is difficult to evaluate the importance of these committees because of the ups and downs of their duties and powers in recent years. It seems fair to say that party leadership and power have not become institutionalized in the steering committee to any great extent.

Two aspects of the officer system of the American Congress call for further comment. One is the use of the seniority rule in the selection of officers; the other is the extent to which power of leadership is diffused through a large number of officers.

the rule of seniority

the meaning of the rule

The rule of seniority is not susceptible of precise definition. In general it means that all important congressional offices, both official and party, are given automatically to those congressmen who have the longest tenure, without regard for the individual congressman's background, his special interests, his skills, or his experience. The rule is followed most rigidly in the selection of committee chairmen, for the designation as chairman of any one but that member of the majority party with the longest period of continuous service on a committee is so rare as to be a sensation when it does occur. The selection of the Speaker of the House, the President pro tempore of the Senate and the floor leaders and the assignment of congressmen to committee vacancies are not so rigidly controlled in accordance with seniority. The senior majority member of the House is by no means certain to be chosen as Speaker, but there is a definite congressional ladder that junior congressmen are expected to climb in reaching these offices. Seniority is not the sole consideration in the naming of these officers, but it is unquestionably the most important single factor. The days when a Henry Clay could be elected Speaker in his first term as a member of the House of Representatives are so distant from the practice of the present as to be all but forgotten.

the attack upon the rule

The attack upon the rule of seniority by observers outside Congress is vigorous and continuing. The case against the rule is a strong one. The seniority rule ignores ability; it puts a premium upon mere continuous service; it discourages any attempt to achieve recognition and high office by hard work and demonstration of interest or skill; and it sentences junior congressmen to a long period of apprenticeship which is said to deter able and mature men in public life from seeking election to Congress. It is further argued that the seniority rule is undemocratic in that it tends to place in office, particularly as committee chairmen, men who come from so-called "safe" congressional districts. Because of the certainty of their election to Congress these men are said to be insensitive to changing public opinion and to represent a point of view current at the time of their original election to Congress. For example, the coming to office of the Democratic administration in 1933, with a mandate for action and change, automatically resulted in the naming of a score or more southern Democrats to committee chairmanships in Congress. Many of these men, as conservatives of long standing, were quite out of sympathy with the national feeling which had made possible their party's majority in Congress.

Likewise, the seniority rule makes it difficult to provide for effective and responsible party government in Congress. A committee chairman can safely ignore the legislative wishes of his party organization in Congress, for as long as he enjoys the support of a majority of the voters in his state or district his seat in Congress is safe, and under the seniority rule so, too, is his chairmanship of a committee. One of the most effective ways of providing for increased party discipline and regularity in Congress would be to assign committee chairmanships on the basis of service and loyalty to the party, and to insist upon such continued service and loyalty as the price of retention of a chairmanship over a period of years. Professor James M. Burns has stated this argument against the seniority rule in very effective fashion:

> The seniority system stacks the cards against those areas where competition for votes is the keenest, where the two-party system is the liveliest, where political currents run fresh and free. It stacks them in favor of the politically stagnant districts—those made "safe" for the incumbent by the poll tax and other restrictions on voting, by the monopolistic position of one party, by the ascendancy of a major interest group, by city or rural machines.[7]

the defense of the rule

The strongest argument in favor of the seniority rule, and the one that seemingly carries most weight with Congress itself, is a negative one: the system may

---

[7] James M. Burns, *Congress on Trial* (New York: Harper & Brothers, 1949), p. 59. Reprinted by permission of Harper & Brothers, publishers.

have its faults but any change would be for the worse. This argument is based upon the belief that any attempt to get away from a purely automatic method of selecting party officers, through paying greater attention to the qualifications of individual congressmen for particular offices, would result in an unfortunate increase of intraparty bickering and intrigue. It is contended that each congressman, as a member of either the majority party or the minority party, in order to secure satisfactory committee appointments, would have to engage in all sorts of wire pulling and logrolling with his fellow party members. Admittedly, such a result is possible. Intrigue is particularly strong in a decentralized party, where vigorous leadership and discipline at the top are missing, a condition that is quite pronounced in the present-day American political party. But putting the selection of congressional officers on a merit basis would itself provide a powerful impetus for the development of a stronger and more intelligent party organization with sufficient power to enable it to control the assignment of its members to posts on a merit basis without undue bickering and intrigue. Moreover, a certain amount of intraparty quarreling over the making of these assignments could hardly be more demoralizing to party organization than is the seniority rule itself, under which party members know that party regularity has absolutely nothing to do with receiving the important posts which the party has to bestow upon its members.

In a report published in 1945, the Committee on Congress of the American Political Science Association, after carefully weighing the arguments for and against the seniority rule, recommends its abandonment.[8] Two alternatives to the present system are suggested: that the selection of committee chairmen be made at the beginning of each Congress by a committee on committees of the majority party on a merit basis; or, if seniority is to remain the dominant consideration, that an automatic time limit of six years be placed upon the term of all chairmen, thereby forcing a reasonably regular rotation of office. It is also recommended that the power of a chairman be lessened somewhat, particularly with respect to the calling of committee meetings, and the reporting of bills upon which the committee has taken favorable action.

the committee system in Congress

alternative committee systems

Both the House and the Senate maintain elaborate systems of committees, to which bodies all proposed legislation is referred for study, revision, and recommendations. There is little about the present committee system in Congress that is inevitable. The Constitution certainly does not prescribe it. Other famous legislatures have developed quite different systems. For example, the British Parliament makes use of a much smaller number of committees, and it is not

---

[8] *The Reorganization of Congress* (Washington: Public Affairs Press, 1945), pp. 37, 80.

the custom to give each committee permanent jurisdiction over all bills falling into particular categories, such as taxation or foreign affairs. Similarly, many of our state legislatures make use of committee arrangements that are different from those used by Congress. In particular, some of them have gone much further than has Congress in developing joint committees which cut across the membership of the two houses. The one thing that is perhaps inevitable about the organization of any modern legislative body is that it shall employ some sort of committee system so that a division of labor can be made in dealing with the numerous and difficult proposals for legislation that are bound to confront it. The only development in government that may offset this need is the assignment to administrative agencies of the task of preparing statutory proposals. Such a policy is followed under parliamentary government, and that is the chief reason why the English Parliament is able to function with far fewer committees than is the American Congress.

the committee system under the Legislative Reorganization Act

The House and the Senate have very similar committee systems. The number of permanent or so-called "standing" committees has varied considerably through the years, but the modern tendency has been to reduce the number. The Legislative Reorganization Act of 1946 reduced the number of Senate committees from thirty-three to fifteen, and the number of House committees from forty-eight to nineteen. This act in general also limits senators to service on two committees and representatives to service on one committee. In part the drastic reduction in the number of committees has been offset by the creation of numerous subcommittees, some of which, at least, have functioned quite independently of their parent committees.

A very important result of the change effected by the 1946 act was the creation in the two houses of largely parallel committee systems. Thus there are in each house committees on agriculture, appropriations, the armed services, banking and currency, civil service, the District of Columbia, expenditures in the executive departments, public lands, public works, rules, labor, taxation, foreign relations, the judiciary, and interstate and foreign commerce. For the most part, House and Senate committees still function independently of each other, but the new arrangement is conducive to joint House-Senate committee hearings and deliberations, and may one day lead to that result.

joint committees

The two houses have established a few joint committees. Among these are the joint committees on Printing, the Library of Congress, Atomic Energy, Internal Revenue Taxation, and the Economic Report. The next to the last consists of five members of the Senate and five members of the House, and was created in 1926 to provide a much-needed liaison agency between the House Ways and

Means Committee and the Senate Finance Committee in the formulation of tax policy. It has functioned imperfectly, inasmuch as the two parent committees, particularly the Ways and Means Committee, have jealously guarded their separate prerogatives.

special committees

Last but not least are the select or special committees. These are temporary bodies usually created to conduct some extraordinary investigation into a matter which, for one reason or another, the House or the Senate does not choose to assign to one of its standing committees. In the 1944 session of Congress, in addition to the regular standing committees, the House made use of thirty-one, and the Senate, twenty, special committees. However, since 1946 the number of *special* investigating committees has declined greatly. Although the Legislative Reorganization Act does not expressly ban the making of investigations by special committees, it was the understanding that investigations would thereafter be made by the standing committees.

Conference committees are also a form of special committee, since a separate committee is created for each bill that goes to conference. Such a committee consists of a group of senators and representatives who are appointed to iron out the differences between the House and Senate versions of a bill. When it has prepared a compromise version it reports that version to the two houses and goes out of existence.

committees not accurate cross sections of House and Senate

All of the standing committees in both houses are bipartisan in character. Because of the large size of a committee (most Senate committees have thirteen members and House committees twenty-five members) and its bipartisan membership, it inevitably possesses a certain cross-sectional character, but it would be a mistake to think of each committee as constituting a House or a Senate in miniature, at least so far as the interests and voting inclinations of the members are concerned. Each of the committees is apt to have a somewhat larger percentage of its membership favorably inclined toward positive action in its sphere of interest than is true of Congress as a whole. For example, in both houses the committees on agriculture and on labor are usually more proagriculture and prolabor, respectively, than is the House or the Senate. Many authorities on Congress have recognized the existence of this condition. In the words of one observer:

> There is a tendency for committees to represent special interests, leaving the guardianship of the general welfare to the full houses and the Executive. Ex-soldiers seek places on the committee dealing with veterans; members from the farm states control the committees on Agriculture. . . . Similarly, a large majority on Finance, the tax and tariff committee, represent industrial states

of the North and East. Naval Affairs committeemen are usually delegates from shipyard or steel areas.[9]

lawyers on the Senate Judiciary Committee

A special study of the Senate Judiciary Committee has shown the extent to which that body has been dominated by the legal profession. Every one of its 219 members between 1816 and 1943 was a lawyer! About one third of these men had had previous experience as judges, 38 having served on the highest court in their states. About half of the group had served as county or state attorneys.[10] In view of the conservative traditions of the legal profession it is not surprising that this committee has usually been quite prone to resist changes in court organization and procedure and in the criminal law—areas over which it has jurisdiction.

bibliographic note

The publications of the Joint Committee on the Organization of Congress (the La Follette-Monroney Committee) provide a good starting point for further reading on the organization of Congress. The committee's public hearings (March 13—June 20, 1945) have been published in a 1,200-page volume bearing the title *Organization of Congress*. The final report, dated March 4, 1946, is a 35-page document outlining the committee's recommendations. Some, but not all, of these recommendations were incorporated in the Legislative Reorganization Act of 1946 (Public Law 601, 79th Congress) found in the 60th volume (Part 1) of the *Statutes at Large*, p. 812. Attention may be called to two other government publications, the House and Senate *Manuals*, which give the rules of the two houses and a certain amount of supplementary material on the precedents that are followed in enforcing them.

There are several textbooks and monographs that describe the organization of Congress. The most encyclopedic of these is Floyd M. Riddick's *The United States Congress: Organization and Procedure* (Washington: National Capitol Publishers, 1949). George B. Galloway's *Congress at the Crossroads* (New York: Thomas Y. Crowell Company, 1946) is a more readable volume that goes beyond mere description of the organization of Congress and raises many questions concerning the adequacy of the present congressional system. Mr. Galloway was the head of the staff of the La Follette-Monroney Committee. *A Twentieth Century Congress* by Estes Kefauver and Jack Levin (New York: Duell, Sloan

---

[9] O. R. Altman, "First Session of the Seventy-fifth Congress," *American Political Science Review*, XXXI (December, 1937), 1071, 1076.

[10] David G. Farrelly, "The Senate Judiciary Committee: Qualifications of Members," *American Political Science Review*, XXXVII (June, 1943), 469.

and Pearce, 1947) is a more personal and critical account of the organization of Congress. Mr. Kefauver is now a senator from Tennessee and has long been interested in the problem of congressional reform. Robert Luce's *Congress: An Explanation* (Cambridge: Harvard University Press, 1926) is an older volume by a former member of Congress who has published several volumes on legislative bodies. In these essays Mr. Luce has set down some of his central ideas.

There are two excellent volumes on the United States Senate. Lindsay Rogers's *The American Senate* (New York: Alfred A. Knopf, Inc., 1926), although published twenty-five years ago, contains a number of lively, provocative essays on problems, such as the filibuster, that are still with us today. George H. Haynes's two-volume *The Senate of the United States* (Boston: Houghton Mifflin Company, 1938) is a monumental study based upon a lifetime of work. It is an excellent example of first-class research in political science.

An interesting article on the effects of the La Follette-Monroney reorganization bill has been written by Elbert D. Thomas, a former senator from Utah, under the title, "How Congress Functions under Its Reorganization Act," *American Political Science Review*, XLIII (December, 1949), 1179.

chapter 16

Congress at work:

lawmaking

THE visitor to the House or Senate galleries is almost invariably disillusioned by the experience. In looking forward to a glimpse of Congress in action, he has perhaps anticipated an impressive parliamentary scene, with traditional ceremony in the procedure, dignity in the debate, and high drama in the clash of great political personalities. Instead, the scene that meets his eye is apt to be one of confusion confounded; or at the other extreme, one of dullness and inactivity. More often than not the latter condition prevails. Where are the members of Congress? Of the 435 representatives, or 96 senators, perhaps 30 or 40 of the former and a dozen of the latter will be present on the floor of House or Senate. What of ceremony in the procedure or dignity of debate? A lone figure has the floor, and while he drones along in an unexciting monologue his inattentive colleagues read newspapers, work at their desks, or sit in rear rows engaged in personal conversation. Congress in session—the supreme legislature in a great land determining policies of momentous import and authorizing the expenditure of unbelievable billions of dollars—is a spectacle that often stimulates contempt, or at best, amusement. At the close of a particularly futile and disappointing session of the Senate a number of years ago the gallery broke into laughter, and the Vice-President, whether with his tongue in his cheek or in a sincere attempt to regain the lost dignity of the body over which he presided, solemnly proclaimed, "No one in the gallery has a right to laugh."

Such is the seeming picture of Congress at work, somewhat exaggerated, to be sure, but a picture that troubles most congressional visitors. It is a picture which has led to much criticism of Congress, as a body that is either careless, lazy, and indifferent to the weighty matters of state demanding its attention, or one that has lost or abdicated its powers and remains but a hollow shell of its former self. Woodrow Wilson once said: "Like a vast picture thronged with figures of equal prominence and crowded with elaborate and obtrusive details, Congress is hard to see satisfactorily and appreciatively at a single view and from a single stand-point." [1] It is unfortunately true that understanding and appreciating Congress at work is not an easy matter. We witness in our national assembly a form that is a century and a half old, but the substance has changed. Today Congress is a curious mixture of the ancient and the modern, of precedent and expediency, of tradition and improvisation, of the formal and the informal. As we have seen, both houses have formal rules which are the equal of any yet devised by the mind and purpose of man, yet much business is transacted under suspension of these rules or with a deliberate and unanimous disregard of them. The American Congress is unquestionably one of the most successful legislative bodies of all time; one that gets its work done by means of a most remarkable institutional system, only part of which has been formalized in written rule, or falls within the gaze of the casual visitor to the gallery.

the scope of congressional work

It is often said that Congress has three historic functions, all of which are related, but each of which is nonetheless separate and distinct. The first of these functions is to determine policy, the second is to control the purse strings, and the third is to supervise the administrative and judicial departments of government. In performing these three functions Congress makes use of two great methods: the enactment of statutes, and the making of investigations. The lawmaking power is used to declare policy, as is illustrated by the passing of the Sherman Antitrust Act; it is used to control the purse, as is shown by the enactment of numerous annual appropriation laws and an occasional revenue measure; and it is constantly employed to create and revise judicial and administrative machinery, to prescribe the powers and duties of these agencies, and to indicate administrative or judicial procedures for them to follow.

Similarly, the investigating power of Congress is used as a means of gathering information which will enable Congress to formulate policy more wisely; it is used to supervise the expenditure of public funds in accordance with the intentions indicated in congressional statutes; and it is used to keep in touch with the activities of judicial and administrative agencies and to bring pressure upon them.

the introduction of bills

the volume of proposed legislation

With but two exceptions any member of either house of Congress may introduce a bill or resolution dealing with any subject over which Congress has power. What is more, he can introduce as many of them as he pleases. The

---

[1] Woodrow Wilson, *Congressional Government* (Boston: Houghton Mifflin Company, 1885), p. 58.

first exception is that all fiscal bills must be introduced in the House: revenue bills because the Constitution requires that they originate in the lower house, and appropriation bills because of custom. The second exception is that a resolution proposing the impeachment of a federal official may be introduced only in the House.

Because of the ease with which bills are introduced, the biennial total for the life of a Congress usually reaches a very high figure. For example, during the life of the Eightieth Congress 8,561 bills and resolutions were introduced in the House and 3,529 in the Senate, or 12,090 in all.[2] One might conclude that this volume of proposed legislation would clog the legislative channels at the very start, and, indeed, this criticism is often made. It is left to the standing committees to weed out the overwhelming majority of these bills and to report back only a small percentage of them to the House or Senate for consideration. Insofar as there are many duplicates or near duplicates among the bills referred to committee, the weeding-out process is an easy one. But this takes care of only part of the huge tide of bills introduced by congressmen, and the fact remains that the system is an irresponsible one so far as numbers are concerned.

the sources of proposed legislation

Much more important than the number of bills introduced is the divided responsibility that exists for the originating of legislation in the national government. The birth of a legislative idea may occur in three different ways. The introduction of a bill may reflect personal labors and conclusions on the part of the man or the men introducing the bill. A good example is to be seen in the National Labor Relations Act of 1935, which was introduced by Senator Robert Wagner and represented a proposal for which he assumed most of the original responsibility. Or again, a bill may have had its birth in the deliberations of a standing committee which has given much time and consideration to the need for new legislation in a particular field. The formal introduction of such a bill is made in the usual way by some member of the House or the Senate, but the writing of the bill has been a committee labor. Most new tax bills are so prepared by the House Ways and Means Committee. And, finally, many bills are prepared by the President and his administrative subordinates and are sent from the executive agencies to Capitol Hill to be introduced. There are no "Government" measures in Congress in the sense in which they are found in the British Parliament—bills that bear the formal approval of the cabinet as the policy committee of the majority party, and rejection of which would create a parliamentary "crisis." Nonetheless, the situation sometimes closely approaches this British practice. There is always some senator or representative who is willing to introduce a measure which has been prepared at the executive end of Pennsylvania

---

[2] 94 *Congressional Record* (Part 14) D537.

Avenue. The presidential authorship or sponsorship of such a bill is usually clearly known and is often a powerful factor tending to bring about its adoption. There have, of course, been many such bills in recent years. The Economic Cooperation Act (ECA) of 1948 is a good example of a law which had such an origin.

This divided responsibility for the formulation of legislative policy is obviously a matter of serious consequence and is closely related to the problem of legislative leadership, which will receive further examination in the chapter on the President and Congress.

committee action

reference of bills

With exceptions that are so rare as to require no attention, every bill or resolution introduced in House or Senate is referred to a standing committee for study and a recommendation. This reference is made by the presiding officer, usually in accordance with the wishes of the member introducing a bill. Occasionally there is a controversy at this point. In 1941 the Speaker referred the Lend-Lease Bill to the House Foreign Affairs Committee, an entirely proper reference. But the House Military Affairs Committee, which was regarded as being somewhat less enthusiastic about the bill, might also have received it. This latter committee exercised its right to challenge the Speaker's reference of the bill, but the House sustained the Speaker's action.

the importance of committee procedure

No matter who has been responsible for the drafting and introduction of a bill, its careful study and probable revision in the committee stage are foregone conclusions. Too much emphasis cannot be given to the work of these standing committees, and to the extent to which the content of national legislation is shaped by their labors. Over half a century ago Woodrow Wilson observed that "Congress in session is Congress on public exhibition, whilst Congress in its committee-rooms is Congress at work." [3] More recent congressional observers have seen no cause to revise this opinion. One authority, who has had the opportunity to observe the work of Congress closely, goes so far as to say: "Officially the House and Senate legislate, but in reality they do little more than approve or disapprove what the committees respectively report to them." [4] Or again, it has been said: "Through the committee system we are ruled by a score and a half of 'little legislatures,' each of which goes its own way regardless of the others, and each of which is headed by a chairman who has got his position by seniority,

---

[3] Wilson, *Congressional Government*, p. 79.

[4] Floyd M. Riddick, *Congressional Procedure* (Boston: Chapman and Grimes, 1941), p. 112.

and neither by merit nor because he represents the views of Congress as a whole." [5] The soundness of these observations is undeniable.

The mere physical extent of committee labors may be indicated by an estimate that in the 1940 session of Congress the printed record of the formal *hearings* of all the committees ran to between 65,000 and 75,000 pages. Moreover, it should be remembered that the public hearing is but part of the story of the labors of a committee, for a great deal of hard work in studying a bill and determining its final wording is done in executive session or by individual members informally. Accordingly, it is the time and energy that the member of Congress must bring to his committee tasks which in good part explains his seeming indifference to the formal sessions of the House or the Senate.

Every member is aware of the extent to which the most important work of Congress is done in committee, and his first interest is in his committee tasks. Since each committee customarily has jurisdiction over all bills falling within a particular area, the opportunity for the individual congressman to become a specialist in certain types of legislation is pronounced. Over a period of years the average senator or representative, through his committee labors, becomes something of an expert in national defense, interstate commerce, taxation, agriculture, labor, or some similar field. Thus it is not surprising that the House and the Senate should be prone to accept the findings of their committees. The extent to which both houses pass bills in versions closely resembling those reported by the committees is not sufficiently realized. Even where important amendments are added to a bill on the floor of the House or the Senate, more often than not such changes are sponsored by members of the committee reporting the bill.

committee procedure

There is a great deal of variation in committee procedure. Some committees are kept very busy, some have little to do, and others have occasional periods of activity. In the case of important public bills it may be assumed that public hearings will be held by the committees to which these bills have been referred, but such hearings are far from uniform. At best they are calm, dignified sessions at which committee members honestly seek the advice and assistance of informed persons who are interested in the proposed legislation. At the worst they sometimes become whitewash or witch-hunt proceedings in which a committee seeks publicity for its own prejudices. In the light of the tendency of the average committee to be heavily weighted in the direction of a special interest, and because of the recognized practice of the two houses in accepting so many committee recommendations without change, it is not surprising that pressure groups are as active at committee hearings as they are at any other point in the entire governmental process.

---

[5] From an editorial in *The New York Times,* June 17, 1942, p. 22.

Committees frequently assign to a subcommittee the task of studying a particular bill, and more often than not the full committee accepts the subcommittee's recommendations with little or no change. Under the Legislative Reorganization Act of 1946 many committees have set up permanent subcommittees to handle all bills falling into particular categories. Thus, much that has been said about the full committee—the opportunity that it affords congressmen to specialize, the time and energy that its sessions consume, the extent to which pressure groups are active before it—may also be said of the subcommittee.

committee reports

The overwhelming majority of all the bills referred to committees are never heard from again, for it is at the committee stage that the highest mortality rate exists. Perhaps 80 per cent of all the bills introduced in Congress are killed in committee. The remaining bills are reported back to the House or the Senate, usually with a recommendation that they pass, although occasionally a committee may report a bill with no recommendation, or even with a recommendation that it be rejected. Although a committee seldom splits on a strictly partisan basis, there is frequently some sort of minority report on a major bill. Both majority and minority reports are often lengthy, detailed documents. They are always printed and, together with copies of the bill in question, are made available to all members of the House or Senate.

order of business on the floor

When a committee has reported a bill, the proposed legislation, depending on its subject matter, is placed on one of several calendars. In theory these bills are then taken in order from the calendars for consideration on the floor of the House or the Senate. This theory is borne out in practice only as to private bills or unimportant public bills, which are passed with little or no debate by what amounts to unanimous consent. The position on the calendar of an important public bill has little to do with the order in which it is considered. Instead, both houses have developed further procedures for determining the order of business. This is due to the fact that, in spite of the high mortality rate among bills in the committee stage, the committees report more bills to the floor than can conveniently be considered, so that further weeding out is necessary. Moreover, the element of timing is often of great importance in the passing of a particular bill, and it is frequently desirable or necessary to take up a bill considerably ahead of the time that it would normally have been reached on the calendar.

selection of bills for consideration in the Senate

The system in the Senate for the consideration of bills is relatively simple. Under the Senate rules any senator may gain the floor and move to take a specific bill from the calendar for consideration. If the motion is adopted by a majority vote, the Senate turns to the bill in question. In practice, the order of business is largely determined by the majority floor leader in consultation with his party's steering committee. Occasionally, a bipartisan majority takes shape which desires to give consideration to a certain measure. The majority leader will often cooperate with such a group in preparing the Senate program of business. In any case, an informal weekly calendar is prepared and announced in advance to members of the Senate.

selection of bills for consideration in the House

The House system of determining the order of business is much more complex. Although some six or eight different devices are used for bringing bills to the floor of the House, only the most important need be noted. In the first place, certain legislative proposals are privileged, and the committees reporting them may call them up on the floor of the House at any time. Only two or three committees make frequent use of this privilege—chiefly the Ways and Means Committee, which can report a tax bill whenever it wishes; and the Appropriations Committee, which has the same privilege as to all general appropriation bills.

Second, virtually all important public bills are now brought to the floor of the House by means of a special rule or order prepared by the Rules Committee. This is a development of the last quarter century. It has now become standard procedure for the chairman of the standing committee reporting a bill to go to the Rules Committee to ask for such a rule. Usually the Rules Committee provides a rule, but the action is not always automatic, for it keeps in touch with party leaders and tries to sense the wishes of the House. In any case, with several bills usually awaiting such rules at any one time, the Rules Committee necessarily exercises discretion in determining the order in which they will be taken up. Increasingly in late years this committee has assumed arbitrary power and has refused to give bills supported by standing committees and by the majority party leadership a special rule. Early in 1949 the House amended its rules so as to make it possible for chairmen of standing committees to move to bring bills to the floor if the Rules Committee has withheld a special rule for a bill for a period of twenty-one days. In 1951 this change was rescinded.

The special rule usually fixes the time that consideration of a bill by the House shall begin, limits the period of general debate, and guarantees the bringing of the bill to a final vote. Most special rules are "open," but a few are "closed" or "gag" rules which limit or forbid the offering of amendments to a bill from the floor. For example, tax bills are usually considered under a rule which forbids all amendments from the floor and permits amendments to be offered only at the direction of the Ways and Means Committee. Needless to say, a minority of the House members can always be depended upon to protest the adoption of such a gag rule, but the majority is often willing to accept dictation and to permit a standing committee to insist that its bill be passed or rejected without change. Whether open or closed, these special rules reported by the Rules Committee must be adopted by a majority vote in the House.

The importance of the special rule as a means of determining the order of business in the House may be seen by an examination of statistics concerning the 1947 session of the House. In all, 1,029 bills and resolutions were passed by the House, approximately 900 of which were noncontroversial and disposed of under unanimous consent. With respect to the more controversial bills, the Rules Committee reported 70 special rules; 58 of these were adopted by the House, and 52 bills were passed under these rules.[6]

Brief reference should also be made to the bringing of a bill to the floor of the House by motion to suspend the rules, or by discharging a standing committee from further consideration of a bill when it appears that the committee is unlikely to report the bill at its own initiative. The motion to suspend is in order only two days each month and takes a two-thirds vote for adoption. In 1947, thirteen bills passed the House by this method. Discharging a committee from further consideration of a bill requires that 218 members of the House sign a petition to that effect and that the House then approve by a majority vote the motion to discharge. Such action takes a bill away from a committee and brings it to the floor of the House. In 1947, no such petition obtained the necessary 218 signatures, but in recent years the House has used this method of bringing certain matters to the floor. This was true of the Wages and Hours bill and the Anti-Poll Tax bill.

It should be noted finally that in both houses power rests largely in the collective hands of majority party leaders to prepare the program of business. In the House particularly, the Speaker, the majority floor leader, the standing committee chairmen, and the Rules Committee share in the exercise of this responsibility, and the wishes of each may play a part in the preparation of the final program. However, in both houses bipartisan majorities sometimes take shape and succeed in forcing consideration of measures over the objections of party leaders.

procedure on the floor of the House and Senate

the quorum rule

We come now to that limited portion of the business of Congress that the visitor to the House or Senate galleries actually witnesses. The requirement of the

---

[6] Floyd M. Riddick, "The First Session of the Eightieth Congress," *American Political Science Review*, XLII (August, 1948), 677, 683–684.

presence of a quorum, fixed by the Constitution at a majority of the members of each house, may first be noted. This means that at least 49 members of the Senate and 218 members of the House must be present if business is to be transacted. Nonetheless, attendance at any moment is usually far below these figures. It is in order for a member to doubt the presence of a quorum, and frequent quorum calls are had in both houses by this device. But it is standard procedure for congressmen to come onto the floor to answer the quorum call and then leave. By this method the two houses maintain the fiction that a quorum is present while business is being transacted. Needless to say, when a record vote is had on the final passage of a bill a majority of the members must participate in the action; otherwise the absence of a quorum would render the action ineffective.

the Committee of the Whole

The House has a further method of circumventing the quorum rule—and many other rules as well—by one of the most interesting fictions in the entire congressional system. The method is the use of a device known as the *Committee of the Whole*. This is a committee made up of the entire membership of the House. At the proper moment a motion is made and adopted that the House rise and go into the Committee of the Whole. The business of the House then goes on, but technically it is sitting as a committee rather than as the House. Eventually, the Committee of the Whole rises and the House resumes its session and proceeds to take action upon the recommendations of the Committee of the Whole. But while the House is sitting as the Committee of the Whole, it need not follow House rules. Instead, it employs a special set of Committee-of-the-Whole rules. In general, the rules of the Committee of the Whole are less rigid and detailed than those of the House and permit of more rapid and informal transaction of business. For example, the quorum is fixed at one hundred members for the Committee of the Whole.

Traditionally the Committee of the Whole has been employed by parliamentary bodies to permit preliminary and tentative consideration of, and action on, business, with the possibility that the body may change its mind later when it gives final, official consideration to a matter. In practice, however, the House of Representatives actually debates and amends virtually all important public bills while sitting as the Committee of the Whole. Of course, the House itself may and sometimes does reject the recommendation of this committee, but no further debate or amendments are in order when the committee rises and the members resume business as the House.

It may be noted that the Senate has not since 1930 made use of the committee of the whole. The Senate is a much smaller body and, since its formal rules provide for much simpler procedure than do those of the House, it has not had continuing need to use this device.

debate in the House and Senate

the quality of congressional debate

In no other way, argue the critics of the American Congress, is the deterioration of our national legislature more pronounced than in the decline of its debate. By recalling the great days of Webster, Hayne, Clay, Calhoun, Sumner, and other famous orators it is easy enough to argue that present debate fails to measure up to the standards of the past. But in good part such criticism is merely another evidence of failure to recognize the changed character of the congressional system.

Because of the great increase in the size of the House and the Senate, because of the tremendous increase in the volume of business, and because of the constantly changing character of modern life which frequently necessitates prompt legislative action, the center of business has inevitably shifted from the floors of Congress to committee chambers, and the quality of congressional debate has necessarily suffered. And yet it is possible to exaggerate the poor quality of present-day debate. In particular, there is a tendency to underestimate the importance and quality of debate in the House of Representatives. Great oratory in the tradition of the past is gone from the halls of Congress, just as it has largely disappeared from the pulpit, the lecture hall, and the courtroom. But the congressional speech, briefer and less dramatic though it has become, is not without its impressiveness and its effect. Far more often than most people realize, debate in Congress is lively, intelligent, relevant, and informed. It is, of course, all too easy to find examples in the *Congressional Record* of debate that is ludicrous and stupid. But if one takes the trouble to turn to the pages in which are found the House and Senate debates on a major legislative proposal, one is almost certain to find an extensive amount of pertinent and detailed information bearing upon the subject.

limitation of debate in the House

Both houses have rules limiting debate. In the House a member is theoretically entitled to gain the floor and to speak for one hour on the subject under consideration. But this right means little in practice, because of the fact that it is usually in order for the member who has the floor, even though he be the first speaker on the subject, to move the previous question. This motion must be voted on immediately. If it is supported by a majority, debate ends at once, and the bill or proposal, whatever it may be, is brought to a final vote. Of course, if a majority of the members can be persuaded to reject the previous question, debate may go on; but a majority in the House definitely has it within its power to prevent minority members from further discussion and to bring an issue to a vote. Moreover, it must be remembered that the House debates virtually all important measures while sitting as the Committee of the Whole. Here debate is divided into two sections; a first period of general debate on a bill, and a second period when the bill is read section by section for amendment. In the first period the duration of the general debate is fixed in advance, and the control of the time is divided between two members, one in favor of and one in opposition to the bill. Other members who wish to speak must persuade one of these two men to grant them portions of the time at their disposal. In the second period, debate occurs under the so-called "five-minute rule," by which five-minute speeches are in order for or against proposed amendments. Debate in the House is thus apt to be brief and lively. But a bill may, nonetheless, be before the House for a considerable period. It is not unusual to allow two or three days for the period of general debate on an important bill. Further debate under the five-minute rule may, upon occasion, lengthen House consideration of a bill to a period of a week or more.

freedom of debate in the Senate

In the Senate it is not in order to move the previous question. Senators may gain the floor and speak as long as they please on the matter under consideration. In theory, and usually in practice, as long as members wish to continue speaking, the Senate must delay taking a final vote on a bill. It is this situation which makes possible the Senate tradition of freedom of debate and the specific practice of filibustering. It is somewhat difficult to define filibustering, because of the many forms it may take, but it usually means prolonged debate by a minority in an attempt to prevent the majority from taking some action, such as passing a bill.

From the point of view of the democratic principle and the right of the majority to rule, logic is all against the filibuster, for it enables a minority to frustrate the will of the majority. But the defenders of the Senate's unlimited debate argue that it protects the right of the minority to present its views and to prevent hasty action. We are reminded that the majority point of view today was always a minority point of view yesterday or the day before. Silence a minority opinion, the argument runs, and you may unknowingly be undermining tomorrow's majority position.

Moreover, some congressional observers argue, a factual analysis of the work of the Senate shows that, more often than not, filibusters are waged against unwise and undesirable measures. Writing in 1926, Professor Lindsay Rogers claimed, ". . . it is a remarkable fact that practically every proposal defeated by a filibuster has been unregretted by the country and rarely readvocated by its supporters." [7] There are those today who would challenge this judgment by arguing that in permitting filibusters over a period of years against such meas-

---

[7] Lindsay Rogers, *The American Senate* (New York: Alfred A. Knopf, Inc., 1926), p. 168.

ures as the Boulder Dam bill, antilynching bills, fair employment practices bills, and anti-poll tax bills, the Senate has allowed the majority will to be frustrated by well-organized, persistent minorities. In the final analysis the argument against the filibuster has never been better put than it was by the elder Senator Henry Cabot Lodge as far back as 1893. He said that "there is another right more sacred in a legislative body than the right of debate, and that is the right to vote." [8]

curtailment of debate

1. THE TWO-SPEECH RULE Freedom of debate is not absolutely unlimited in the Senate. In the first place, the Senate has a long series of rules and precedents which, either in piecemeal or in wholesale fashion, can be invoked to limit debate or curtail a filibuster, if the Senate wishes. For example, there is a Senate rule that no member can speak more than twice on a single subject on the same legislative day. By recessing, rather than adjourning, at the end of a day's session the Senate can prolong a "legislative day" indefinitely, and thereby limit the amount of speaking that can be done on a single item of business.

2. THE CLOTURE RULE In the second place, the Senate has a specific cloture rule adopted in 1917 following a particularly unpopular filibuster against the Armed Ship bill. Under the original version of the rule, sixteen senators might petition the Senate to close debate upon a pending measure. If such a petition was approved by a two-thirds vote of the Senate, the measure became the unfinished business of the Senate to the exclusion of all other matters, and thereafter no senator might speak for more than one hour on the measure and amendments pending thereto. In practice it proved virtually impossible to invoke this rule. Only nineteen cloture petitions were brought to a vote between 1917 and 1946. In only four instances, all of which occurred in the first decade after the rule's adoption, did the Senate vote by the necessary two-thirds margin to close debate—in 1919 to close debate on the Versailles Treaty, in 1926 to bring the World Court Treaty to a vote, and twice in 1927 to bring ordinary legislative proposals to a vote. After 1927 all attempts to invoke the rule failed, and even in the case of the very obnoxious and unpopular one-man filibusters conducted by Huey Long, the members of the Senate refused to enforce cloture against him. In 1948 a further weakness in the cloture rule developed. In the course of a filibuster against an anti-poll tax bill, the President pro tempore of the Senate, Senator Arthur H. Vandenberg, ruled that cloture was not applicable to debate on a motion to call up a bill but could only be invoked during debate on a bill itself. This ruling meant that if a group of minority senators started a filibuster on a motion to call up a bill, the cloture rule was of no use in trying to

---

[8] Quoted by James M. Burns, *Congress on Trial* (New York: Harper & Brothers, 1949), p. 63.

break such a filibuster. In the following year the Senate amended its cloture rule to make cloture applicable to debate on motions to call up measures as well as to debate on measures themselves. But the price of this reform was a change in the rule as to the vote necessary to invoke cloture. The original requirement that two thirds of the members present must vote to approve cloture was changed to provide that two thirds of the entire membership—sixty-four senators— must vote to support cloture. It seems unlikely that this drastic requirement will often, if ever, be met, and the United States Senate remains today a legislative body in which a determined minority can prevent indefinitely the enactment of legislation strongly favored by a majority.

3. CURTAILMENT OF DEBATE BY UNANIMOUS CONSENT AGREEMENTS In the third place, senators frequently agree by unanimous consent that further debate on an amendment to a bill be limited to a fixed period of time, or that the final vote on the passage of a bill be taken at a set hour. Somewhat surprisingly, it is much easier to persuade the Senate to make such an agreement than it is to obtain a two-thirds majority for invoking the cloture rule. The explanation of this seeming anomaly is that attempts are made to invoke the cloture rule only in the face of an existing filibuster against a highly controversial bill, whereas the hour of a final vote on a less controversial bill is fixed by unanimous consent as a matter of convenience where there is no real opposition to letting the debate come to a close.

number of bills debated at length in Congress

One final observation concerning debate in the House and the Senate should be made as to the number of measures which are debated at any length. A series of studies reveals that during recent years the number of bills debated for more than three pages of the *Congressional Record* (perhaps thirty minutes in actual time) has ranged from 60 to 80 a year in the Senate and from 100 to 125 in the House. In the 1947 session, of the 841 measures passed by the Senate, only 71 occupied more than three pages of debate, and of the 1,029 measures passed by the House, only 108 were debated at similar length.[9] In the Senate, bills debated over a period of several days now number no more than a dozen or so a session; certainly the total of such bills is no greater in the House.

Thus it is clear that most of the business brought up on the floors of Congress is transacted in routine fashion with great dispatch, and it is a safe conclusion that less than 10 per cent of the business requires any substantial debate. This indicates, first, that many legislative proposals are noncontroversial, and, second, that the controversial issues are often thrashed out elsewhere than on the floor of the House or the Senate—in other words, at the time a bill is being drafted, or at the time of committee consideration.

---

[9]Riddick, "The First Session of the Eightieth Congress," pp. 677, 679.

methods of voting

Both House and Senate employ several methods of voting. The simplest and most common form is a viva-voce vote in which the members in turn call out the yeas and nays, and the presiding officer judges which side has prevailed. Any member who doubts the result can ask for a rising, or division, vote, in which the two groups rise alternately and are counted. In the House, one fifth of a quorum (44 members when the members sit as the House; 20 members when they sit as the Committee of the Whole) may request a teller vote by which the two groups leave their seats, pass between tellers, and are counted. Finally, in both houses, as prescribed in the Constitution, one fifth of the members present may demand a record vote in which the roll is called and members are recorded by name as voting yea or nay.

A roll-call vote is a tedious affair in both houses. In the House it takes anywhere from thirty to forty-five minutes to complete, and in the Senate about six minutes. Both houses have refused to authorize the use of any mechanical or electrical voting device as a timesaver. It is notable how often both houses dodge record votes on measures of great consequence, although the House is the more serious offender in this respect. When the House is sitting as the Committee of the Whole, record votes are not even in order, so that many controversial amendments are frequently disposed of without individual members going on record. Admittedly, on many noncontroversial bills no record vote is necessary, but if the people of a democratic nation are to formulate intelligent views on legislation and legislators, it seems reasonable to demand that representatives go on record in their votes on important measures.

conference committees

When a bill has been passed by the house in which it was introduced, it goes to the second house, where virtually all of the steps thus far described must be repeated. Consideration of a bill in the second house may sometimes be less detailed or protracted than it was in the first house, but, as often as not, the second house insists upon giving a bill its most careful attention, as though the favorable judgment of the first house was an irrelevant factor. The result is that many important public bills are apt to pass the two houses in versions that differ from one another in some degree, small or great. At this point these differences must be compromised if any further progress in the enactment of a law is to take place. Such compromise may come in either of two ways.

In the first place, one house may vote to give way and accept the version approved by the other. If the differences are slight, if time is an important factor, or if the bill is an unimportant one, this frequently occurs. Otherwise, both houses, as a matter of traditional policy, will stand fast, and it then becomes necessary to make use of the conference committee as a means of effecting a compromise between the two versions of the bill. It has been estimated that about 10 per cent of all bills passed by both houses are sent to conference. In the 1947 session of Congress in which 526 laws were enacted, 66 measures were sent to conference, of which 59 were reported back.[10]

The members of conference committees are chosen by the Speaker and the Vice-President, but in practice there is little discretion in the choice they make, for almost without exception the members of a conference committee are chosen in order of seniority and in bipartisan fashion from the standing committee in each house that originally considered the bill. In theory, a conference committee must produce a compromise version of a bill that ranges somewhere between the extremes of the House and Senate versions. But since these versions are often quite far apart, the discretionary power of such a committee may be very great. When the conference committee reports a compromise version, it must be accepted or rejected as it stands by both houses, and no amendments may be proposed at that point on the floor of either house. However, either house may reject a conference report and send a bill back to conference a second time, making it clear that it desires a particular change before it will accept the bill.

Careful examination of the work of conference committees in recent years makes it very evident that these bodies are of great importance. There is little exaggeration in the frequent description of them as "third houses" of the national legislature. Many an important measure has been substantially rewritten in conference. Because of this very significant role of the conference committee there is some reason for criticism of the conference procedure as lacking in democracy, inasmuch as membership in these all-powerful committees is somewhat a matter of accident. Furthermore, the meetings of conference committees are informal and always secret, so that it is difficult to bring any public pressure upon them. It is true that a conference committee is always influenced by the realization that it must produce a compromise bill that will be acceptable to both houses of Congress. On the other hand, the need for certain legislation is sometimes so acute that the rank-and-file members of Congress have little choice at this point but to accept the report of a conference committee. It is a rare bill that is ever defeated at the conference stage, and circumstances usually make it fairly certain that whatever bill comes out of conference will ultimately be approved by both houses.

the volume of legislation

The total number of laws passed by the Eightieth Congress (1947–1948) was 1,364. Of this number, 526 were passed in the first session, and 838 in the second session. There were 906 public laws and 458 private laws in the total of 1,364.

---

[10] *Ibid.*, p. 685.

These figures are not dissimilar to those for other Congresses; hence it is clear that a considerable volume of new legislation is enacted each year. On the other hand, only a small percentage of these new laws are of major public importance. In the past the total volume of legislation has been swelled by private claims bills in which Congress authorized payments to private persons having claims against the government, by bills authorizing the construction of bridges across navigable streams and other bodies of water, and by bills dealing with the municipal problems of the District of Columbia. In the Legislative Reorganization Act of 1946 Congress made provision for the handling of claims and the authorizing of bridges without the necessity of passing laws on these matters. Private bills have not disappeared entirely since 1946, but their number has declined. If Congress should eventually grant home-rule powers to the city of Washington, a further decrease in the number of laws passed each year might be expected.

evaluation of lawmaking in Congress

the mechanics of lawmaking are unduly complex and difficult

The most striking characteristic of the national lawmaking process is its complex nature. Leaving aside for the present the approval or rejection of bills by the President, there are usually five major steps in the adoption of a major law by Congress. These are the consideration of the bill by standing committees in two houses, the passage of the bill on the floor of two houses, and the final perfecting of a bill at the hands of a conference committee. The inevitable result of this situation is that it is ordinarily very difficult to persuade Congress to enact legislation. To put the matter in slightly different words, it is usually far easier to kill a bill in Congress than it is to secure its adoption. The organization and procedures of Congress are such that the cards are stacked against action. Unless one assumes that it is wise in modern society to pursue a do-nothing policy, this situation is most unfortunate, particularly from the point of view of the democratic principle. It ought to be easier than it is for majority public opinion in the United States to take shape and find positive expression in the adoption of national legislation. As things are, it is a long, uphill struggle to obtain legislative action in Congress on the average issue of major importance. An outstanding example of the slowness of Congress in enacting legislation, presumably favored by a majority of the American people, is to be seen in the legislative story of the 1938 Fair Labor Standards Act. It is worth while to record here the successive steps in the long process by which that act was finally adopted. (1) In May, 1937, a message from President Roosevelt called upon Congress "to extend the frontiers of social progress" by enacting a wages and hours bill. (2) The Senate and House Labor Committees held joint hearings on the bill during the first two weeks of June. (3) Thereafter these committees held separate hearings, the Senate committee reporting the bill in July, the House committee, in August.

(4) The Senate debated the bill for five days and passed it on July 31. (5) The bill failed to get to the floor of the House because of the refusal of the Committee on Rules to give it a special rule, and Congress adjourned without further action. (6) The President called Congress in special session in November, 1937, one purpose of the special session being to secure action on the bill. (7) When the Rules Committee still balked, a petition to discharge it from further consideration of a rule by which to bring the bill to the floor of the House was filed, the last of 218 signatures being obtained on December 2. (8) The bill was brought to the floor of the House, but on December 17 the House voted 216–198 to recommit it to the Labor Committee, and the session came to an end with no further action. (9) The President's "state of the Union" message to Congress in January, 1938, again urged enactment of the bill. (10) A subcommittee of the House Labor Committee held new hearings and ultimately a revised bill was reported to the House. (11) The Rules Committee once more balked, and in May, 1938, for the second time, 218 signatures were obtained to a discharge petition. (12) On May 13 the House passed the bill and it was sent to conference. (13) The Conference Committee met for two weeks in June and wrote what was essentially a new bill. (14) On June 14, 1938, the conference report was accepted by both houses. (15) On June 28, President Roosevelt signed the bill and it became law.

It may be admitted that the legislative history of the Fair Labor Standards Act provides an extreme illustration of the complexities of the national legislative process, but even making allowance for this, it seems valid to conclude that the route of a bill through Congress is beset with an altogether unreasonable number of pitfalls and barriers. From the point of view of efficiency in the process by which laws are enacted, our congressional system is in need of substantial simplification.

lawmaking in Congress is an imperfect democratic process

Closely associated with the issue of the organizational and procedural complexities of the congressional system, and hardly less serious, is the issue of Congress's deficiencies as a democratic body. Professor James M. Burns concludes that "Congress . . . is fatally defective as a means of expressing the majority will of the nation." [11] This conclusion is simply the latest in a long line of similar observations made by students of Congress. Many of the conditions conducive to the weakness of Congress as a democratic body will be difficult to correct. Those that depend upon the faulty system of state representation in the Senate and district representation in the House and upon the defects of the election system are not at all easy to get at. Correction in many instances would require constitutional amendments. Similarly, insofar as it is the weakness of the

---

[11] Burns, *Congress on Trial*, p. 152.

party system that explains Congress's inability to function more satisfactorily as a democratic body, the cure will not be an easy one, and no amount of tinkering with congressional organization and procedure will get at the fundamental difficulty. At the same time, internal weaknesses in Congress accentuate this difficulty and could be corrected. Among the organizational arrangements and procedures which are basically *undemocratic* are the committee system whereby laws are largely written by small groups of congressmen who in each instance represent not a cross section of the people, but a concentration of sectional and special interests; the seniority rule in the selection of committee chairmen; the power of the Rules Committee in the House to determine the order of business; the rule permitting unlimited debate in the Senate; the conference committee system of determining the final language of bills. Every one of these conditions tends to frustrate the majority will; every one of them has been brought into being by Congress itself; every one of them could be corrected by Congress through the simple expedient of changing the internal rules of the House and the Senate.

toward more responsible party government in Congress

Brief notice is here taken of those recommendations of the American Political Science Association's Committee on Political Parties which pertain to Congress. The committee's general point of view is expressed in the following words: "A general structure of congressional party organization already exists. It should be tightened up. . . . If such action were taken, it would not mean that every issue would become a party issue. It would not eliminate the need for or the possibility of nonpartisan and bipartisan policies. But it would result in a more responsible approach to party programs and a more orderly handling of *all* congressional activities." [12]

The committee's recommendations are:

1. "Leadership Committees" should be created by each party in House and Senate. Powers now scattered through such agencies as the steering committees, the Committees on Committees, and the House Rules Committee would be concentrated in these new agencies. They would draw up the slates of committee assignments, issue calls for party caucuses, and, in the case of the majority party leadership committees, control the legislative schedule in House and Senate.

2. The party caucus should be revived and strengthened as a means of allowing democratic discussion of the party program by all of a party's members in each house, and of providing for a *binding* decision on important legislative proposals that would force all party members to vote in accordance with the party's established principles and platform.

3. Assignment of committee posts and distribution of patronage should

---

[12] "Toward a More Responsible Two-Party System," Report of the Committee on Political Parties, American Political Science Association. Printed as a Supplement to the *American Political Science Review*, XLIV (September, 1950), 57.

deliberately be used to encourage loyalty in congressmen to the established party platform.

4. The seniority rule should be modified to permit the party leadership to name as committee chairmen only those senior members who are loyal to the party program.

5. Control of the legislative schedule in the House of Representatives should be transferred from the Rules Committee to the majority party leadership committee.

6. The Senate rule on freedom of debate should be modified to permit debate to be closed by a simple majority vote.

bibliographic note

Attention may first be called to the government publications which provide an excellent record of the work of Congress. The work of the congressional committees is to be found recorded in documents known as *Hearings*, which contain the verbatim testimony given by witnesses at the public hearings of each committee, and as *Reports*, which give the complete formal reports of each committee to the House or the Senate.

The official record of the work of the two houses themselves is to be found in the *House* and *Senate Journals*, which the Constitution directs shall be kept. These publications include no debate and provide only the bare record as to the putting of formal motions, the vote on bills, and similar matters. Because of their outline character they are far less widely known or used than the *Congressional Record*, which provides a nearly verbatim reporting of everything that is said or done on the floor of each house. The *Record* is a government publication, but as such it dates back only to 1873. The record of congressional debate for the years before 1873 is to be found in three privately printed publications: the *Annals of Congress*, for the period 1789–1824; the *Register of Debates*, for the period 1824–1837; and the *Congressional Globe*, covering the period 1833–1873. The present-day *Record* is published in two editions: a daily issue which appears within twenty-four hours of a meeting of Congress, and a permanent edition consisting of half a dozen or more bound volumes appearing at the close of a year's session. Needless to say, the *Record* is a voluminous publication, and in recent years each annual edition has contained 10,000 to 20,000 pages.

The statutes enacted by Congress are available in three forms. Immediately following its enactment, a statute is published in the *Slip Law* format, a pamphlet providing the text of the single law. At the end of the year's session (or, previous to 1938, at the end of the two-year life of a Congress) bound volumes of the *United States Statutes at Large* are published. These contain in chronological order the text of all laws passed during the one- or two-year period. There are now about sixty volumes in this series. (Actually a "volume" usually consists of two books: a "Part One" containing the text of "Public Laws," and a "Part Two" containing the text of "Private Laws.") The *Statutes at Large* citation of a law is usually given in this form: 60 Stat. 812 (the sixtieth volume of the *Statutes at Large* at page 812). Third, the laws of the United States are to be found in various codified collections. A "code" represents an attempt to do two things: (1) to weed out statutes that have been repealed or superseded, and to present only the law that is actually in effect at the time the code is published; and (2) to arrange the laws topically, rather than chronologically, so that all statutory provisions dealing with a single subject, such as immigration, agriculture, or internal revenue, may be found in one place. Mention should be made of the *United States Code*, published by the federal government in 1941 in four volumes, to which yearly supplements have been added, and of the *United States Code Annotated*, in fifty-six volumes, published originally in 1927 by two private publishing houses and brought up to date each year by the publication of supplements. The Code citation of a provision of law is given as follows: 18 U.S.C. § 51 (the 18th "Title" of the *United States Code*, "Section" 51).

A valuable documentary source of information concerning the procedures employed by the House of Representatives is the eleven-volume *Precedents of the House of Representatives* (Washington: Government Printing Office, 1907–1941) by Clarence A. Cannon and Asher C. Hinds. These precedents were originally collected by Asher C. Hinds in six volumes early in the present century. A decade ago they were brought up to date by Clarence A. Cannon, a longtime member of the House of Representatives.

A private organization, the Congressional Quarterly News Features (732 17th Street, N.W., Washington. D.C.), issues a weekly publication known as the *Congressional Quarterly*. The *Quarterly* is designed primarily for use by newspapers and contains a remarkably detailed and accurate summary of congressional activities. Roll-call votes on important issues are reproduced, substantive analyses of pending bills are provided, and the work of pressure groups is examined. At the end of the year this material is presented systematically in a single volume. The *Congressional Quarterly* is available for purchase by libraries. It is a truly remarkable effort to tell the detailed story of the activities of the legislative branch of the national government.

The texts by Robert Luce, Joseph P. Chamberlain, Floyd M. Riddick, Harvey Walker, and George B. Galloway mentioned in the bibliographic notes to the two preceding chapters contain chapters on the lawmaking process.

Roland A. Young's *This is Congress* (New York: Alfred A. Knopf, Inc.,

1943) is a sprightly volume that examines Congress in action. It contains a number of cogent observations as to both the strengths and the weaknesses of our national legislature.

Many publications deal with specific aspects of the legislative process. Paul D. Hasbrouck's *Party Government in the House of Representatives* (New York: The Macmillan Company, 1927) is a classic account of the influence political parties have on the conduct of the business of the House of Representatives. Franklin L. Burdette's *Filibustering in the Senate* (Princeton: Princeton University Press, 1940) is an exhaustive account of the use and abuse of freedom of speech in the Senate, a problem of great current importance. Two informative accounts of the organization and work of congressional committees are Eleanor E. Dennison's *The Senate Foreign Relations Committee* (Stanford University: Stanford University Press, 1942) and Albert C. F. Westphal's *The House Committee on Foreign Affairs* (New York: Columbia University Press, 1942). Ada C. McCown's *The Congressional Conference Committee* (New York: Columbia University Press, 1927) examines in systematic fashion the organization and work of the all-important conference committees.

Stephen K. Bailey's *Congress Makes a Law* (New York: Columbia University Press, 1950) is a unique study of the enactment of a single statute, the Employment Act of 1946. It gives a detailed account of the procedural stages by which this law was enacted and of the social and political forces and influences that were present in the congressional arena as the bill was considered.

chapter 17

Congress at work:

investigations

$\mathcal{T}$HE scene of routine activity that greets the visitor to the House or the Senate gallery often leads him to express a sense of disappointment; the spectator at a public hearing of a congressional investigating committee infrequently voices such a complaint. Let the committee be a well-known one, let the subject it is investigating be both important and controversial, and the public will follow its sessions with close interest. The most ample room in the office building of the House or the Senate will be none too large for its place of meeting, for hundreds of people and dozens of press and radio representatives will seek admission to watch and listen as, amid the glare of klieg lights and the grinding and clicking of cameras, some prominent figure in public life or private business takes the witness chair and testifies concerning an allegation of great public interest—"subversive" activity in Hollywood, the flotation of worthless bonds by Wall Street bankers and brokers, the infiltration of Communists in federal offices, or the "truth" about Pearl Harbor.

continued use of the investigating power by Congress

There is no need to exaggerate the extent to which Congress investigating rivals Congress legislating, for it is clear that the congressional investigation has become an activity of major significance. Almost continuously since the close of World War I Congress has conducted a series of spectacular investigations which have thrown light upon a variety of subjects of great interest to the public. The nineteen twenties witnessed the sensational inquiries into the scandals of the Harding administration, chief among which were the Teapot Dome and Justice Department investigations. Then in the nineteen thirties, under the New Deal, came the famous investigations of Wall Street, the munitions industry, the TVA, lobbying, and civil liberties. In the nineteen forties the activities of such groups as the respected Truman-Mead Committee, which investigated the wartime defense program, the notorious Un-American Activities Committee, and the politics-torn Pearl Harbor Committee were closely followed by millions of Americans.

As a matter of fact, the congressional investigation is much older than these facts suggest. It is generally agreed that the first of the long line of investigations was conducted just three years after Congress was established, when in 1792 the House of Representatives appointed a committee to look into the disaster that befell the St. Clair expedition against the Indians. Since that early year there has been no period long without some spectacular use of the investigating technique. It is, however, somewhat difficult to present statistics showing the total number of investigations conducted by Congress since 1792. The chief difficulty lies in defining an "investigation." Ordinarily the term is used in a somewhat limited sense to refer to a special study of a particular problem which Congress formally orders made, as opposed to the routine investigations into a wide variety of subjects which the standing committees constantly make at their own initiative. So defined, it would appear that Congress conducted somewhere in the neighborhood of 300 such formal investigations from 1789 to 1925.[1] In more recent years there has unquestionably been a substantial increase in the number of investigations. One study shows that during the first four years of the Roosevelt administration, 165 investigations were authorized or conducted, of which 104 were made in the Senate, 47 were made in the House, and 14 were conducted jointly by the two houses.[2]

controversy over investigations

If further proof of the great importance of this congressional activity is needed, it is to be seen in the continuing controversy that is waged over the use of the investigating power by Congress. Hardly a major investigation is conducted that does not call forth both extreme criticism and unrestrained praise. As early as 1860 there occurred a famous debate in the Senate over the use of the investigating power to look into John Brown's raid on Harpers Ferry. The power of inquiry was both vigorously defended and bitterly attacked. The vehemence of the attack is indicated by the remarks of Senator Charles Sumner:

> I know it is said this power is necessary *in aid of legislation.* I deny the necessity. *Convenient,* at times, it may be; but *necessary, never.* . . . Such a power as this—which, without sanction of law, and merely at the will of a partisan majority, may be employed to ransack the most distant States, and

---

[1] M. E. Dimock, *Congressional Investigating Committees* (Baltimore: Johns Hopkins Press, 1929), p. 57. See also E. J. Eberling, *Congressional Investigations* (New York: Columbia University Press, 1928).

[2] M. N. McGeary, "Congressional Investigations during Franklin Roosevelt's First Term," *American Political Science Review,* XXXI (August, 1937), 680.

to drag citizens before the Senate all the way from Wisconsin or from South Carolina—may be convenient, and, to certain persons, may seem to be necessary. An alleged necessity has, throughout all time, been the apology for wrong. "So spoke the Fiend, and with *necessity*, the tyrant's plea excused his devilish deeds." [3]

The investigations of the nineteen-twenties led Walter Lippmann to refer to "that legalized atrocity, the Congressional investigation, where Congressmen, starved of their legitimate food for thought, go on a wild and feverish manhunt, and do not stop at cannibalism." [4] Writing in 1924, Dean John H. Wigmore, an eminent legal scholar, used vigorous language in condemning congressional inquiries:

> The Senatorial debauch of investigations—poking into political garbage cans and dragging the sewers of political intrigue—filled the winter of 1923–24 with a stench which has not yet passed away. . . . As a prosecutor the Senate presented a spectacle which cannot even be dignified by a comparison with the prosecutive scoldings of Coke and Scroggs and Jeffreys, but fell rather in popular estimate to the level of professional searchers of municipal dunghills.[5]

One member of Congress has asserted: "Out of practically every investigation there comes legislation improving the security of the Government and the people against selfishness and greed." Another disagrees: "In my opinion 95 per cent of these investigations are absolutely worthless and nothing has been accomplished by them." [6]

The range of criticism of congressional investigations has been extremely wide. If the congressmen conducting an investigation are too vigorous and thorough in their methods, they are sure to be accused of carrying on a "witch hunt." On the other hand, if they go about their inquiries in calm and unspectacular fashion, sooner or later their efforts will be belittled as amounting to a "whitewash." Moreover, the same critics do not hesitate to use both arguments. In recent years the Communists have attacked all inquiries into subversive activity as witch hunts, whereas inquiries into business irregularities are to them never sufficiently vigorous and are accordingly denounced as whitewashes. On the other hand, conservatives called the Wall Street investigation a witch hunt and never tired of attacking inquiries into such New Deal undertakings as the TVA as whitewash affairs.

---

[3] *Congressional Globe*, 36 Cong., 1 Sess., Pt. 4, p. 3007.

[4] Walter Lippmann, *Public Opinion* (New York: Harcourt, Brace and Company, 1922), p. 289.

[5] John H. Wigmore, "Legislative Power to Compel Testimonial Disclosure," *Illinois Law Review*, XIX (1925), 452–453.

[6] M. N. McGeary, *The Developments of Congressional Investigative Power* (New York: Columbia University Press, 1940), p. 7.

purposes of congressional investigations

The perennial criticism of the investigation, and the specific proposals for reform which such criticism has stimulated, can properly be evaluated only if the purposes for which Congress employs its inquisitorial power are kept in mind. Some five purposes have influenced the making of investigations. First is the obvious need of Congress to obtain detailed and accurate information if it is to take intelligent action in legislating. A good illustration of this motivation at work is seen in the Wall Street Investigation in 1933, where Congress sought and obtained information about banking and stock exchange practices which led to the enactment of a series of statutes, notably those establishing the Securities and Exchange Commission. A second purpose, only slightly less important than the first, is the use of the investigation by Congress to supervise or check the work of administrative agencies charged with the enforcement of laws. The House Committee to Investigate Acts of Executive Agencies Beyond the Scope of Their Authority, created in 1943, by its very title illustrates this motive for investigation. A third motive for investigations is the desire to influence public opinion by giving circulation to certain facts or ideas. The Committee on Un-American Activities and the La Follette Civil Liberties Committee are good examples of investigating groups that were motivated primarily by this desire to publicize information. A fourth motive that has sometimes figured in the undertaking of investigations is the desire for personal publicity on the part of the chairman or the members of the committee making the investigation. More than one congressman has achieved fame or enjoyed advancement in public life because of the reputation he made as an investigator. It is not surprising that congressmen should show awareness of this possibility in seeking authorization for new investigations. Certainly, in his unceasing attempts to keep the Committee on Un-American Activities alive, Representative Martin Dies, an otherwise obscure member of the House of Representatives, was strongly motivated by the fame and notoriety that he gained as its chairman. Fifth, and by no means least important, has been the undeniable partisan motivation that has been present in many an investigation. Desire of a political party to advance its own interests or to embarrass its adversary is not infrequently apparent in the work of an investigating committee. It need hardly be said that two or more of these motives in combination are often responsible for the making of one investigation.

subjects of investigations

Examination of the subject matter of congressional investigations, past and present, almost makes it seem as though, sooner or later, everything under the sun has been the object of congressional scrutiny. Actually, Congress is subject to rigid constitutional restrictions as to the scope of its inquiries. Hence a limited number of topics have accounted for the majority of all investigations. Heading the list is the executive agency, for at one time or another every cabinet department and practically every independent administrative agency of any consequence has been investigated. For example, the Department of State and the Department of Justice, the Tennessee Valley Authority, the Federal Communications Commission, and the National Labor Relations Board have all been the objects of thoroughgoing investigations in recent years. War and the aftermath of war have also occasioned numerous investigations throughout our history. But the wide range of congressional investigations can readily be seen by merely noting the subjects of some of the fifty-one investigations which were authorized by the Seventy-eighth Congress in 1943 and 1944. Among the matters investigated were Small Business, Conservation of Wild Life, Grade Labeling, Conditions in Puerto Rico, Air Commerce, Administration of Civil Service Laws, Gasoline and Fuel Oil Shortage, Postwar Economic Policy, Seizure of Montgomery Ward and Company, Campaign Expenditures, War Effects on Education in Colleges and Universities, Centralization of Heavy Industry, Censorship, and Adjustment of Veterans into Civil Life.[7]

types of investigating committees

Our examination of congressional investigations will be limited to those situations where Congress formally authorizes an inquiry into a particular subject, calls upon some specific committee to make this study, votes an appropriation to meet the costs of the inquiry, and grants the committee power to subpoena witnesses and to compel the production of papers. So limited, there are still many different types of investigations, depending primarily upon what kind of committee is designated to make the inquiry. The overwhelming majority of investigations are conducted by the House or the Senate acting independently of one another. Accordingly, either house in authorizing an investigation may specify the agency by which it shall be made. The most obvious possibility is to turn an investigation over to a regular standing committee, or to a subcommittee of such a committee. Thirteen of the twenty investigations ordered by the 1944 session of Congress were made by standing committees, and in each instance the chairman of the standing committee appointed a subcommittee to conduct the actual investigation. The Senate Civil Liberties Investigation in the nineteen thirties was made by a subcommittee of the standing Senate Committee on Education and Labor. A second possibility is to turn an investigation over to a special committee. In the past many famous investigations have been made by such special committees created for this one purpose. The original Dies Un-American Activi-

[7] For the complete list see the articles on the sessions of the Seventy-eighth Congress by Floyd M. Riddick in *American Political Science Review*, XXXVIII (April, 1944), 301, 311, and XXXIX (April, 1945), 317, 332–333.

ties and the Truman Defense investigations illustrate the use of such special committees. A third possibility is the creation of a special joint House and Senate committee to conduct an investigation authorized simultaneously by both houses. The investigation of the TVA in 1938 was made by a committee consisting of five senators and five representatives. The Pearl Harbor Investigation in 1945 was made by a similar joint committee. A fourth type of committee involves a natural step beyond the joint committee, one which adds members of the executive branch of government to the members of the two houses. The best recent example of this type is to be seen in the famous Hoover Commission on the Organization of the Executive Branch of the Government created by Congress in 1947. Its twelve members consisted of senators, representatives, officers of the executive branch, and private citizens. Finally, there is a type of investigation that is made by a committee consisting entirely of members from outside Congress. If Congress has authorized the investigation, it is nonetheless proper to speak of this type as a congressional investigation, even though no congressmen may figure in the actual inquiry. The spectacular investigation of the electric and gas public-utility companies, which was authorized by Congress in 1928, was turned over to the Federal Trade Commission, which carried on the inquiry for Congress.

procedure in conducting an investigation

authorization of an investigation

A formal congressional investigation is always authorized by a specific resolution. The Senate resolution which authorized the Lobby Investigation in 1935 directed the President of the Senate to appoint five men to a special committee which was "authorized and directed to make a full and complete investigation of all lobbying activities and all efforts to influence, encourage, promote, or retard legislation, directly or indirectly, in connection with the so-called 'holding company bill,' or any other matter or proposal affecting legislation." The committee was further authorized to hold hearings during the sessions or recesses of the Seventy-fourth and succeeding Congresses, to call upon the executive departments for clerical and other assistance, "to send for persons and papers"; moreover, an initial fund of $50,000 was appropriated for the committee's use.

personnel of an investigating committee and staff

The appointment of the members of a special investigating committee is usually made by the presiding officer in either house, the members of a special subcommittee being appointed by the chairman of a standing committee, but freedom of choice is limited by certain traditions. Virtually all investigating committees must have a bipartisan membership. The chairman and to a lesser degree the other members of such a committee are customarily named because of the personal interest they have shown in proposing the investigation and in supporting the resolution authorizing it. Obviously, the success or failure of an investigation depends to a very considerable degree upon the personnel of a committee. Unfortunately, the personnel of these committees is not always good. The Dies Committee was notorious for the narrow, petty, and vindictive outlook of many of its members. On the other hand, the Truman-Mead National Defense Committee was famous for the high quality of its personnel. It was universally admitted that only able, intelligent, and vigorous members of the Senate, in both party groups, were able to secure appointment to it.

Following the appointment of the congressional members of a committee, the next step is to engage the services of expert investigators and clerical assistants from outside the ranks of Congress. At this point, too, an investigation's ultimate success or failure may well be determined. Almost any investigation into a difficult and technical problem necessitates a considerable amount of preliminary, laborious spadework in searching through documentary material and ferreting out pertinent facts. Unless a committee is able to secure the talented assistance of capable workers in making these all-important but unpublicized preliminary studies, its later activity is apt to be of little value. The matter of limited funds constitutes an immediate difficulty. For lack of adequate financial aid, a committee is often frustrated in hiring the workers it needs or in conducting the studies that are necessary to its success. Hugo Black, who as senator from Alabama was chairman of the famous Lobby Investigation, has spoken of the fact that

> . . . all investigations are crippled from the start unless able and public-spirited counsel can be found to make the sacrifice. . . . It was an interesting spectacle to see Judge Pecora during the Senate Banking Committee investigation of Wall Street, sitting at the committee table facing eminent financiers who were surrounded by high-priced accountants and assistants and guarded on both sides by lawyers whose fees must have run into the hundreds of thousands, while he was working for around $60 a week for nearly two years.[8]

procedure at public hearings

After a committee and its investigators have spent weeks and perhaps months conducting preliminary explorations into its subject, the usual procedure is to hold public hearings at which interested persons are allowed to testify and are questioned. Not all committees follow this plan, and in its last stages the Dies Committee, through its chairman, acting in highly dubious fashion, merely released from time to time statements and reports concerning work which had been carried on behind the scenes. The public hearing is of tremendous value

[8] Hugo Black, "Inside a Senate Investigation," *Harper's Magazine*, CLXXII (February, 1936), 275, 278.

both from the point of view of giving interested and informed witnesses, who may well disagree with one another, an opportunity to thresh out the problems pertinent to the inquiry, and also from the point of view of resultant publicity and educational effect. Nonetheless, it has become increasingly clear that a public hearing will not be particularly fruitful unless it has been preceded by careful and thorough preliminary research. Aimless testimony by any private person who wishes to appear or random cross-examination based on no previous analysis is apt to be of little consequence.

Testimony at the public hearings of an investigation is usually reported at some length in the press, and is published verbatim by the Government Printing Office. These hearings and the printed Committee *Reports*, made at the completion of investigations, are available for distribution and careful study by congressmen and private citizens. Thereafter, further action depends upon the particular situation. It is impossible to generalize about all investigations.

legal and constitutional difficulties
in conducting investigations

For more than a century the Supreme Court of the United States has concerned itself with legal and constitutional questions growing out of congressional investigations, the result being one of the most interesting chapters in American constitutional law. What subjects may Congress properly investigate? How far may a committee go in subpoenaing witnesses or seizing documentary evidence? May private persons be punished for contempt because of their refusal to appear as witnesses or to answer certain questions? These and similar issues have come to the Supreme Court in a series of notable cases growing out of the highly controversial conduct of certain investigating committees.

It is significant that the Court has chosen to consider such questions at all. It was early argued that the independent position of the legislative branch under the principle of separation of powers placed it beyond judicial scrutiny of the purely procedural aspects of congressional activity. A congressional statute might properly be declared null and void by the Court, so the argument ran, but Congress was answerable to no one as to the procedural methods it used in obtaining information and enacting laws. But others argued that, since a congressional investigation frequently involved a forcible invasion of the privacy of individuals, the courts might properly intervene to enforce the legal and constitutional rights of private persons as against the action of Congress. The Supreme Court agreed with the latter argument and as early as 1821 it asserted its rights to review congressional procedure.

Most of the decisions of the Supreme Court in this field of law have been favorable to the congressional point of view; a few have served, at least temporarily, to restrict congressional activity. The favorable decisions may be summarized as follows: The right of Congress to conduct an investigation into a subject that may properly result in legislation is established as an implied one, derived from the express power to legislate. In making such investigations Congress may authorize its committees to compel the attendance of witnesses and the production of documentary evidence, and it may punish, by fine and imprisonment, persons who place themselves in contempt of Congress by failing to obey the orders of an investigating committee, provided always that the inquiry deals with a subject of proper concern to Congress or that the questions a witness refuses to answer are pertinent to the investigation.[9] Decisions unfavorable to Congress have stressed the limited subject-matter areas in which Congress is free to make investigations, and limit punishment for contempt to situations where a witness deliberately flouts the authority of a committee. For example, the Supreme Court set aside a citation of contempt by the House of Representatives of a person who had inspired a newspaper article impugning the motives of an investigating committee. The Court held that there had been no serious interference with a proper congressional function warranting such a limitation of the individual's freedom to criticize the government.[10]

criticism of congressional investigations

As has already been indicated, no aspect of congressional activity has been the subject of such bitter, persistent condemnation as has the investigation. At times such criticism has certainly been warranted; but at other times it has been based upon a narrow, unimaginative view of the proper scope of the legislative process. Certain of the perennial criticisms should be considered.

prying into private affairs

Perhaps the oldest criticism is the one used by Senator Charles Sumner in 1860: the congressional investigation involves too much prying into the lives of private citizens. The spectacle of a committee dragging a man across the country to Washington, putting him on the witness stand, and compelling him to testify as to his private affairs is condemned as worthy only of the methods of a totalitarian state. This criticism has been used by both liberals and conservatives. The inquisitorial tactics of congressional liberals a dozen years ago infuriated conservatives. When J. P. Morgan was photographed holding a midget in his lap, this was said to show the supreme indignity to which private citizens were being subjected, even though the committee before which he was appearing was

---

[9] See *Anderson* v. *Dunn*, 6 Wheaton 204 (1821); *In re Chapman*, 166 U.S. 661 (1897); *McGrain* v. *Daugherty*, 273 U.S. 135 (1927); *Sinclair* v. *United States*, 279 U.S. 263 (1929); *Jurney* v. *MacCracken*, 294 U.S. 125 (1935).

[10] *Marshall* v. *Gordon*, 243 U.S. 521 (1917). See also *Kilbourn* v. *Thompson*, 103 U.S. 168 (1880).

not responsible for the episode. More recently the cry of unwarranted interference with the citizen's right of privacy has been heard on the left as conservative congressmen have prodded witnesses to reveal their membership in the Communist party or in radical organizations.

Woodrow Wilson has provided an answer to this type of objection. He once said, "If there is nothing to conceal then why conceal it? . . . Everybody knows that corruption thrives in secret places, and avoids public places, and we believe it a fair presumption that secrecy means impropriety. So, our honest politicians, and our honorable corporation heads owe it to their reputations to bring their activities out into the open." [11] In other words, it is unfortunately true in modern society that the furtherance of the general welfare sometimes necessitates a limited invasion of the individual's privacy. Where a person possesses information that is vital to the making of an intelligent decision by a legislative body, it seems reasonable to compel this individual to tell what he knows if he is unwilling to cooperate on a voluntary basis. On the other hand, it is indefensible for a committee to allow irresponsible witnesses to indulge in irrelevant gossip about other persons, or to compel a witness to reveal private information which is not necessary to the solution of a legislative problem affecting the public welfare.

criticism of investigation procedures

A second criticism has centered about the procedural methods employed by investigating committees. It is argued that committees bully their witnesses, or encourage them to attack the reputations of private citizens and then refuse the latter a decent opportunity to defend themselves. More specifically, the complaints are that committees do not allow witnesses to read prepared statements, to enjoy the assistance of legal counsel, to face their accusers or cross-examine other witnesses; that questions are deliberately worded so as to compel answers that reveal the witness in a bad light; that unfair use is made of search warrants in the seizure of documentary evidence. Such criticism has often seemed justifiable. It is certainly true that a committee should treat its witnesses fairly, show them ordinary courtesy, and permit them a decent opportunity to tell what they know in their own words. And yet the witness is not standing trial on criminal charges, and to give him the benefit of all the protective devices associated with Anglo-American criminal procedure would gravely hamper many investigations. Investigating committees frequently run into recalcitrant witnesses who must sometimes be handled quite sternly if any testimony is to be obtained from them. Or again, to permit each witness to read a prepared statement or to permit his lawyer to cross-examine other witnesses would often so

---

[11] Quoted by Black in "Inside a Senate Investigation," p. 275.

hamper a committee and delay its proceedings as seriously to restrict its effectiveness.

On the other hand, the committee ordinarily has the advantage over the witness, and if it insists upon asking him unfair or irrelevant questions or is determined to put him in a bad light, the resulting publicity can do him grave personal harm. In effect this criticism raises much the same problem as does the first criticism. In the modern democratic state the citizen must enjoy protection against arbitrary and unjust procedure. But he has a duty to society to cooperate in those undertakings that are designed to further the general welfare. Admittedly some citizens are derelict in the meeting of such an obligation, and upon occasion it becomes necessary to compel the necessary cooperation.

cost and futility of investigations

A third criticism is that congressional investigations cost a lot of money, waste the time of inquisitor and witness alike, and seldom prove anything in the end. Admittedly, certain investigations have cost a great deal of money. It is estimated, for example, that the investigation of the American Telephone and Telegraph Company, conducted by the Federal Communications Commission at the request of Congress during the years from 1935 to 1939, cost more than one million dollars. But even if investigations are responsible for only a small percentage of the benefits that have been attributed to them, their cost, being such an infinitesimal part of the total expense of government, is readily justifiable. The argument as to waste of time is a relative one. Some committees have admittedly wasted the time of their witnesses or have compelled busy public administrators and businessmen to make repeated appearances on the witness stand. But, again, the potentialities for gain in an investigation are ordinarily great enough to warrant a reasonable sacrifice of time on the part of those whose duty it is to cooperate with such a proceeding.

The argument about the futility of investigations is clearly false if pushed to an extreme. Admittedly there have been many investigations which have not resulted in legislation or had any other tangible consequences. But many investigations have resulted in positive legislative action. The La Follette-Monroney Investigation produced the Legislative Reorganization Act, many of the Hoover Commission recommendations have been put into effect, the Pecora investigation resulted in the SEC program, the Nye Munitions Investigation was largely responsible for the Neutrality Acts of the nineteen thirties, and the investigations into the wrongdoings of the Harding administration resulted in the resignation of cabinet members, successful criminal prosecutions, and the recovery of government property. There may well be disagreement about the wisdom of these results. Certainly the fruits of the Nye inquiry did not stand the test of time. But there can be no denying that action was taken in these instances.

In addition to such tangible results, investigations have sometimes had more subtle, but nonetheless equally important, consequences. It has often been possible to trace to the work of congressional committees, trends in public opinion, changes in administrative practices in government, and revision of business policies.

partisan and personal motivation of investigations

A fourth argument is that too many congressional inquiries are motivated by partisan considerations or the personal ambitions of the inquisitors. For example, when the Republicans took control of the Eightieth Congress in 1947 while the executive branch remained in the hands of the Democrats, it was facetiously reported that the former planned "to open each session with a prayer and close it with a probe." One careful student of congressional investigations has said: "Few, if any . . . of the investigations carried on between the First and the Sixty-ninth Congresses were devoid of personal strife or partisan purpose." Nonetheless, he is inclined to conclude: "If . . . the itch for power and partisan malice have been at the bottom of most Congressional investigations, they have also been both a salutary force in the direction of good government and a strong support of the investigative function." [12] In general this is a sound conclusion. Certainly it is part of the theory of our system of party government that one party should seek to expose the shortcomings of the other, and there is nothing wrong in principle with partisan motivation of criticism in government. It is the right and the duty of the opposition party to criticize the party in power, and it remains for public opinion to evaluate such criticism. Of course, it goes almost without saying that if an investigation is unduly marked by personality or partisanship, the search for impartial information will in all likelihood not be conspicuously successful.

improvement of congressional investigations

In the democratic state the citizen must enjoy protection against arbitrary and unjust governmental procedures. Moreover, it is clear that some of the abuses of certain investigating committees have tended to bring Congress itself into disrepute. Any condition which serves to discredit the legislative process cannot be viewed with equanimity in a democracy. It is highly important, then, that steps be taken to protect our national legislature against its own worst practices.

What can be done to correct the faults of the congressional investigation? It must be recognized at once that there is no easy solution to the problem. There is no simple blueprint by which the conduct of an investigation can be so ordered that furtherance of the search for information and protection of the

---

[12] George B. Galloway, "The Investigative Function of Congress," *American Political Science Review*, XXI (February, 1927), 47.

rights of witnesses will result automatically. Nonetheless, two lines of improvement can be suggested.

use of substitutes

First of all it is often argued that Congress should delegate the making of its investigations to administrative agencies and other bodies of experts which would report their findings and recommendations back to Congress. As we have seen, this is sometimes done. Mention has been made of the excellent study of the gas and electric public-utility industry that was made for Congress by the Federal Trade Commission. In support of the further use of this technique reference is frequently made to the practice in Great Britain where Parliament directs that investigations be made by so-called Royal Commissions, consisting of experts outside Parliament, usually in the administrative offices. One study compares the congressional investigation unfavorably with the Royal Commission and asserts that the former is "blatant and vulgar." In contrast with the impartiality of the Royal Commission in its search for information it is said that congressional "investigations are conducted on the plane of propaganda." [13] Nonetheless, the same study points to shortcomings in the Royal Commission device and concludes that its golden age is past. In the United States, when investigations are undertaken by experts, it is difficult to obtain sufficient publicity for their findings, or subsequent action upon their recommendations. For example, the United States Coal Commission, which was created during the Harding administration, made a thoroughgoing study and filed a monumental report on the coal problem, but it was only with difficulty that Congress was persuaded even to finance the printing of the report, and the study resulted in no legislation. [14]

It has been suggested that the mixed commission, consisting of congressmen, administrators, and private citizens as well, provides a means of meeting both the objection that the purely congressional committee is apt to be prejudiced and incompetent and the objection that the purely administrative commission has too little influence or publicity-getting power. For example, the Temporary National Economic Committee, a mixed commission which investigated monopoly conditions in the late thirties, was generally considered to have been one of the most successful inquiries of modern times, although the coming of the international crisis diverted attention from its findings, and very little was accomplished by way of resulting action. Reference has already been made to the Hoover Commission on the Organization of the Executive Branch of the Government. It seems likely that its final record with respect to action taken on the basis of its recommendations will be an excellent one.

---

[13] Hugh M. Clokie and J. William Robinson, *Royal Commissions of Inquiry* (Stanford University: Stanford University Press, 1937), p. 21.

[14] Joseph P. Chamberlain, *Legislative Processes: National and State* (New York: Appleton-Century-Crofts, Inc., 1936), p. 101.

a code of fair procedures

Second, a good deal of attention has been given in recent years to the development of a code of fair procedures which all investigating committees would be expected to follow. Numerous law review articles and newspaper editorials have been written on the subject, and bills have been introduced in Congress providing for such procedures. Certain specific committees have voluntarily adopted some of those recommended, but no general limitation has yet been put into effect by either house. One difficulty lies in securing agreement among the experts as to which procedures should be prescribed, for virtually all students of the subject agree that Congress must be careful not to go so far that it hamstrings its committees. However, there is fairly general agreement in support of the inclusion of the following procedures in a code: no specific hearings to be held by a committee unless authorized by a majority of its members; similarly, no reports or statements to be issued which do not carry the approval of a committee majority; witnesses to enjoy assistance of counsel with respect to their legal rights and duties; witnesses to enjoy a limited right to read or file prepared statements, and also some sort of opportunity to reply to other witnesses who have attacked them personally.

Unquestionably some improvement in congressional investigations can be achieved through procedural reform. But whatever changes in procedure are made, in the end much will still depend upon the wisdom, the integrity, the sense of fair play, and the understanding of national needs which our legislators bring to the actual conduct of investigations. When he retired in 1944 as chairman of one of the most successful investigating committees in congressional history, Senator Harry S. Truman said on the floor of the Senate:

> The work of this committee has demonstrated what can be accomplished through investigation by committees of the Congress. Our industrial economy has become so complex and the necessary changes so numerous that it is impossible for the Congress in legislating to provide all the safeguards which are necessary for proper administration. If an attempt were made to do so, great delays would ensue, and in many cases the detailed requirements of specific legislation would be harmful rather than beneficial. For these reasons, it is important that Congress not only continue but enlarge its work of investigation. In my opinion, the power of investigation is one of the most important powers of Congress. The manner in which that power is exercised will largely determine the position and prestige of the Congress in the future. An informed Congress is a wise Congress; an uninformed Congress surely will forfeit a large portion of the respect and confidence of the people.[15]

---

[15] 90 *Congressional Record* (August 7, 1944); 6747.

bibliographic note

Two definitive treatments of congressional investigations published some twenty years ago are Marshall E. Dimock's *Congressional Investigating Committees* (Baltimore: The Johns Hopkins Press, 1929) and Ernest J. Eberling's *Congressional Investigations* (New York: Columbia University Press, 1928). These volumes are rich sources of information on the history of the investigating power of Congress and on the constitutional law that has resulted from Supreme Court examination of particular investigations.

Martin N. McGeary's *The Developments of Congressional Investigative Power* (New York: Columbia University Press, 1940) is a more recent publication which supplements the two earlier volumes by reviewing the numerous investigations that took place during the 1930's.

Relatively few volumes describe in any detail the work of single investigating committees. An exception to this statement is August R. Ogden's *The Dies Committee* (Washington: Catholic University of America Press, 1943), which examines in careful, dispassionate fashion the work of one of the most controversial congressional investigating committees of our time. Morris R. Werner's *Privileged Characters* (New York: R. M. McBride & Company, 1933) describes a number of famous investigations of the 1920's. There are separate chapters on the Teapot Dome, Justice Department, and other inquiries. *War Madness*, by Stephen and Joan Raushenbush (Washington: National Home Library Foundation, 1937), is based upon the work of the Senate Munitions Investigating Committee which was active in the 1930's under Senator Gerald P. Nye's chairmanship.

the President and Congress:

legislative leadership

$\mathcal{T}$HE proper relationship between the President and Congress is a dynamic problem that is never solved. We have failed after a century and a half of political experimentation and development under our Constitution to establish any fixed pattern as to this relationship. Striking evidence of the uncertainty of attitudes toward our political system at this point is to be seen in the criticism that was directed at the Roosevelt administration during the twelve years of its existence. No President in history was ever subjected to more bitter criticism than Franklin D. Roosevelt on the score that he tried to dominate Congress by insisting upon the passage of bills bearing administration approval. Yet, at times, the criticism of Mr. Roosevelt was of a contrary character to the effect that he was failing to provide Congress with necessary advice and leadership in its treatment of certain difficult problems. For example, in the President's third term, when upon occasion he adopted the position toward such matters as manpower control and price fixing that it was up to Congress to formulate policies in these respects, his critics argued that it was his duty to use all of the prestige and power of his office to persuade Congress to take necessary action. Moreover, in many instances these critics were the same people who had earlier argued that the President exercised too much influence over Congress. This illustration is given not with any purpose of defending Mr. Roosevelt or of attacking his critics, but merely to show the great difficulty that intelligent observers of American government always have in maintaining a consistent attitude as to the President's relations with Congress.

history of President-Congress relations

Although the Constitution has a good deal to say about the President's relations with Congress, it does not fix the pattern of government at this point with any degree of certainty or finality. Accordingly, great extremes have been possible

350

in our history. Mention has already been made of Franklin Roosevelt's active participation in the legislative process. He clearly followed in a great tradition, for such Presidents as Jackson, Lincoln, Theodore Roosevelt, and Wilson all assumed that theirs was the duty and power to provide Congress with active and positive leadership in the performance of its legislative tasks. Differences in the policies of these men toward Congress were those of degree only and largely reflected the varying problems and the severity of the crises that confronted their administrations. Up until the time of World War II the peak had been reached

"Gotcha Either Way"

(Reprinted with permission of Herblock and the Washington Post Co.)

in 1933, when, during the famous "hundred-day session" of Congress in that year, the President functioned virtually as a Prime Minister in his dealings with Congress. Almost all of the major bills enacted by Congress in that session originated within the executive branch of government, and circumstances gave Congress little choice but to accept them. President Roosevelt was not able to use the power of a Prime Minister in threatening dissolution of Congress should it refuse to accept his measures, but the knowledge that the people stood behind him and that he might well appeal to them if Congress proved recalcitrant was sufficient to give the President his way.

At the other extreme is found such a President as Calvin Coolidge, who, content to function as "chief *executive*," seldom made any serious effort to provide Congress with leadership in the formulation of national policy. Of course, his was a relatively quiet period in the White House, and it may be asserted that there was no need for him to lead Congress and the country down new paths. On the other hand, had there been another man in the White House during the middle twenties, a man temperamentally inclined to follow in the "strong" President tradition, he might well have anticipated the fearful domestic and international crises that lay just ahead and have sought to persuade Congress to adopt a more positive program of legislation. But whatever the verdict of history as to Coolidge and the other Presidents of the twenties, they, too, followed in an old tradition, that of the "weak" President who is content to play the role of the nation's business manager, concerning himself with technical improvements looking toward greater administrative efficiency and leaving to Congress the responsibility of originating new policies.

Although there has been a certain periodicity in the relations between President and Congress, with alternate periods of strong and weak executive leadership succeeding each other with more or less regularity, the fact remains that each returning swing of the pendulum in the direction of executive domination of Congress has been more pronounced. This tendency is an old one in American political history, and there is little in the character of present-day government that suggests any lessening of it. Three reasons for this situation will now be examined.

the Constitution gives the President legislative power

There is one powerful reason for presidential concern with the work of Congress which has operated from the very beginning of our present government. The Constitution, itself, gives the President express legislative powers. This it does in line with the decision of the Fathers not to accept a rigid principle of separation of powers but instead to incorporate a very considerable element of checking and balancing in the government. There are three express powers granted by the Constitution to the President which are more concerned with legislation than with administration.

presidential control of the sessions of Congress

The first of these three powers gives the President a certain measure of control over the sessions of Congress. The Constitution provides for an automatic beginning of the regular sessions of Congress. But the President alone has power to call Congress in special session. The President may suggest legislative business to Congress in the call for a special session, but he cannot compel Congress to act on his proposals, nor can he prevent it from taking up other business not mentioned in the call. In the past some of the most notable sessions of Congress have been special ones. For example, the hundred-day session in 1933 was a special session called by President Roosevelt in March immediately after he took office. However, the Twentieth Amendment has brought an end to the short, three-month regular sessions which used to occur every other year, and it is unlikely that the future will witness as many special sessions as has the past. But the special session called by President Truman in the summer of 1948 just before the national election of that year proves that a President can still make spectacular use of this power.

The Constitution provides that the two houses of Congress must agree before either house can adjourn or recess for more than three days, and then adds the provision that, in case of the inability of the two houses to so agree, the President may order an adjournment of Congress, "to such time as he shall think proper." This is a power which might conceivably have developed and been used in such a way as to give the President a very substantial control over the business of Congress. Actually, there is not a single instance of its use in our entire history. It seems clear today that the political repercussions which might well follow the use of this power would serve to dissuade a President from exercising it in any but an extreme situation.

presidential messages to Congress

A second express constitutional power is the power of the President to send messages to Congress. The Constitution is quite specific at this point, for it authorizes the President both to "give to the Congress information of the state of the Union," and to "recommend to their consideration such measures as he shall judge necessary and expedient." There can be little argument about the meaning of this power. It is clear that the Founding Fathers intended the President to exercise the power and responsibility of presenting programs of legislation to Congress for consideration by it. And lest there be any doubt about the situation, they authorized him to make these programs as general, or as specific, as he might choose.

In practice, there has been considerable variation in the exercise of this power by different Presidents, although certain traditions concerning its use have emerged. For example, although the Constitution does not make this a requirement, all Presidents have used the opening of each regular session of Congress as the occasion for so-called State of the Union messages. But there the uniformity ends. Recent Presidents have delivered this message in person before a joint session of the two houses, although for a century the practice was to send the message in writing to be read by clerks. Some Presidents have chosen to make their annual messages fairly detailed, covering miscellaneous subjects and presenting numerous specific requests for legislative action. Others, such as Franklin Roosevelt, have chosen rather to make the State of the Union message a general speech addressed perhaps as much to the people as to Congress.

These general speeches have then been followed by a series of special messages making recommendations concerning specific measures.

The Constitution, of course, does not require Congress to accept any of the President's recommendations, and the influence which particular messages have had with Congress has obviously depended upon a variety of circumstances and influences. One thing is certain, however: there can be no objection under the Constitution to the action of a President who sends a carefully prepared and fully detailed bill to Congress and respectfully invites Congress to give it favorable consideration.

the veto power

The third constitutional power of the President which may be said to be legislative in character is the power to veto bills passed by Congress. Here, too, the Constitution is specific in its provisions: "Every order, resolution, or vote to which the concurrence of the Senate and the House of Representatives may be necessary (except on a question of adjournment) shall be presented to the President of the United States. . . ." Although the specific wording of this clause seems to permit of but one exception to the requirement, others have been added. Concurrent resolutions need not be submitted to the President, and the same is true of proposed constitutional amendments.[1] In recent years, moreover, Congress has written into certain statutes a proviso to the effect that they may be suspended from operation by joint action. Some authorities have been inclined to question the constitutionality of this device, but its use is increasing.[2]

In any case, all "bills" passed by Congress are submitted to the President in accordance with the constitutional requirement mentioned above. Under the further provisions of the Constitution, four alternatives may be available to the President when he receives a bill. The first and most obvious is to sign the bill, in which case it becomes law. If the President disapproves the bill he may return it without his signature to the house where it originated, together with his objections to it. Thereupon, if the bill is repassed by each house with a two-thirds majority, it becomes law without the President's approval; otherwise the veto holds and the bill dies. The third possibility is for the President to let a bill remain on his desk ten days without either signing it or returning it to Congress, in which case the bill becomes law without his signature. Presumably this third alternative may be chosen by a President who does not wish to put his personal stamp of approval upon a bill but, on the other hand, is unwilling to take the responsibility of killing it. In practice, Presidents have seldom selected this alternative. President Roosevelt in 1938 allowed an important tax bill to become law without his signature, but he was severely criticized for this action, particu-

---

[1] See *Hollingsworth* v. *Virginia*, 3 Dallas 378 (1798).

[2] For a discussion of this problem, see Howard White, "Executive Responsibility to Congress via Concurrent Resolution," *American Political Science Review*, XXXVI (October, 1942), 895.

larly in Congress. Nonetheless, he followed this policy again in 1944 when he let the Soldiers' Vote Bill, which he regarded as inadequate, become law without his signature. The fourth possibility is a variation of the third: if during the ten-day period that the President holds a bill without signing it Congress ends its session and adjourns the bill automatically dies instead of becoming law. This is the so-called "pocket" veto. It is unquestionably the most effective veto from the President's point of view, for adjournment of Congress makes it absolute, there being no possibility of its being overridden. Moreover, since Congress tends to pass a great many bills during the closing days and even closing hours of a session, the opportunity of a President to use the pocket veto is apt to be extensive.

The veto has had a long, varied, and controversial history. Two Presidents, Grover Cleveland and Franklin Roosevelt, account for two thirds of all the vetoes since George Washington. Each man vetoed more than five hundred bills. On the other hand, eight Presidents vetoed no bills at all during their terms of office. Early Presidents made very sparing use of the veto power, and up until the time of the Civil War most of the vetoes were justified on the ground of a bill's doubtful constitutionality. In fact, it was even contended by some that this was the only reason for which a President should exercise the power. Since the Civil War, far more often than not, Presidents have based their objection to a bill on its lack of wisdom or on its inexpediency rather than on its alleged unconstitutionality.

Messages accompanying a vetoed bill on its return to Congress vary considerably. If the bill is a major one and the President is anxious that Congress sustain his veto, the message may well be elaborate, and even upon rare occasion be delivered in person. Cleveland and Roosevelt both vetoed many private claims bills, and the messages accompanying such vetoes were usually very short and specific. Ordinarily, pocket vetoes are not accompanied by messages, since the bill is not returned to Congress. However, a President may choose to make a public statement giving the reasons for his objection to a bill that is being vetoed through this device.

Relatively few bills are ever repassed over the President's veto. The Constitution makes reconsideration mandatory, but this requirement is fullfilled by mere reference of the bill and the veto message to the standing committee that reported the bill to the house in which it originated. In the first eight years of Franklin Roosevelt's presidency 505 bills were vetoed and only 7 of these vetoes were overridden.[3] This is probably not far from the average experience in this respect. In the first one hundred years of our present government there were

---

[3] Much of this statistical data is taken from Katherine A. Towle, "The Presidential Veto since 1889," *American Political Science Review*, XXXI (February, 1937), 51, and from George C. Robinson, "The Veto Record of Franklin D. Roosevelt," *American Political Science Review*, XXXVI (February, 1942), 75. By the end of 1944 Mr. Roosevelt's veto total had risen to 624.

451 vetoes, 29 of which were overridden. But of these 29, over half occurred in Andrew Johnson's administration. One of the most notable instances in which Congress has overridden a veto occurred in 1944 when, for the first time in history, the President vetoed a tax bill. Congress took offense at the very strongly worded veto message in which the President seemed to question the good motives of Congress. In a sensational break with the President, Alben Barkley, the Senate majority floor leader, urged that "if the Congress of the United States has any self-respect yet left, it will override the veto of the President and enact this tax bill into law, his objections to the contrary notwithstanding." [4] Both houses accepted Senator Barkley's advice and repassed the bill over the veto. A President is seldom so rebuked, and the incident clearly illustrates the rapidity with which Congress takes offense if it feels that the President is not showing proper respect for the legislative branch of government.

The President does not possess an item veto power, as do certain American state governors. Accordingly, he must accept or reject a bill in its entirety. It has often been argued that because of the detailed or omnibus character of much modern congressional legislation the President should have the power to veto items to which he objects and accept the remainder of a bill. In particular, this is urged concerning appropriation bills. As it is, the President has little choice but to accept the great annual appropriation bills. They are apt to come to him so close to the beginning of the new fiscal year, and to represent so many months of planning and activity, that he can entertain little or no thought of vetoing them, however much he may object to certain items. Admittedly, to give the President an item veto power would strengthen his hand in his dealings with Congress. Moreover, it is possible that the President might use such a power to bully individual congressmen by threatening to veto items in which they were interested. Any sweeping grant of an item veto power would require a constitutional amendment, although it seems permissible for Congress to write into each appropriation bill a clause authorizing the President to suspend items from operation if he wishes. But Congress has shown little inclination to give the President any such discretionary power.

The veto power is of far greater importance than the mere mechanics of its operation would indicate. Its frequent and increasing use by modern Presidents has unquestionably led Congress to have greater respect for this power, the result being that the mere threat of its exercise frequently influences congressional action during the stages when legislation is being formulated. In other words, the veto power has served to put the President into the very midst of the legislative process. Consequently the average President no longer takes the attitude that under the veto power he should make no statement concerning his position until Congress has completed action on a bill. Nor does Congress in general expect him to maintain any such aloof position. Instead, the knowledge

[4] 90 *Congressional Record* (February 23, 1944), 1966.

that the President, through the exercise of the veto power, can pronounce a life-or-death sentence upon a bill has inevitably resulted in the development of a very great measure of presidential influence at all stages of the legislative process.

evaluation of the President's legislative power under the Constitution

Recent Presidents have not hesitated to seek informal contact with Congress at almost any point in the legislative process, whether it be when a bill is in committee, is being debated on the floor of the House or the Senate, or is in conference. In 1932 President Hoover invited the members of a conference committee to come to the White House to talk with him lest he be forced to veto a relief bill it was putting into final shape. The meeting with the President took place, but it came to naught, and Mr. Hoover had to carry through with his threat to veto the bill. In 1935, Mr. Roosevelt wrote a famous letter to the chairman of a subcommittee of the House Ways and Means Committee, which was considering the Guffey Coal Bill, in which he said, "I hope your committee will not permit doubt as to the constitutionality, however reasonable, to block the suggested legislation." Again in 1938, he sent a telegram to the chairman of the House Labor Committee urging that a discharge petition be filed to force the Committee on Rules to report the Wages and Hours bill to the floor of the House. In 1943, he sent a letter to the Vice-President urging renewal of the Reciprocal Trade Agreements Act, which letter was read to the Senate. Such communications are fairly common, as is also the congressional resentment they produce if they are not tactfully worded. For example, Senator Gillette once protested against a letter from President Roosevelt to Vice-President Henry A. Wallace which the latter laid before the Senate, on the ground that it should have been addressed to the members of the Senate and should have been read to the Senate by a member of that body. Moreover, he objected to any effort by the President "to influence the course of pending legislation by unsought advice, threat of disapproval, or by any other type of pressure." [5]

Such protests are unrealistic, whatever validity they may have in theory. There is no formal institutional device by which a President may establish contact with a congressional committee. If a President, in an attempt to influence the final version of a bill, gives a conference committee the impression that the bill is in danger of a veto unless it is finally passed in a version acceptable to him, it is difficult to find in such action any violation of the letter or the spirit of the Constitution. So far as the language of the Constitution is concerned, the message and veto powers go far toward justifying the influence that even our strongest Presidents have endeavored to exercise over Congress and the process of law-making. Of course, under any President, Congress has always retained the final authority to ignore messages or to override vetoes. Nearly every President has

[5] 89 *Congressional Record* (June 2, 1943), 5192.

sooner or later discovered this, ofttimes to his sorrow. It is true that many Presidents, and in particular certain of the early ones, made but a slight attempt to
influence the course of legislative policy. Yet there is no denying that the Constitution itself has always invited such influence, and from the very beginning
compelled Congress to share a certain measure of the lawmaking power with
the President.

absence of leadership within Congress encourages presidential leadership

no institutional basis for leadership within Congress

A second reason for the positive role which the President plays in the legislative
process is the absence of any institutional arrangement within Congress which
produces a strong measure of internal leadership on a continuous, or systematic basis. It is an inescapable fact that there is insufficient power in any one office
or combination of offices within Congress to produce vigorous, powerful leaders from among the 531 members of that body. It is true that considerable
power and prestige is associated with certain congressional offices, and occasionally individual congressmen, by the force of their own personalities and ability,
come to possess influence over their colleagues. This power is sufficient to provide Congress with a form of "commission leadership." At times the Speaker of
the House, the Vice-President or the President pro tempore of the Senate, the
majority floor leaders, the committee chairmen, and the dominant figures on the
House Committee on Rules or on the steering committees are welded together
so as to provide a reasonably positive and vigorous measure of legislative leadership. But such commission leadership is apt to be extremely unstable, and there
is no continuing force that guarantees cooperation on the part of these different
officers. If one of these men finds himself in disagreement with his colleagues
on a legislative issue, and if he feels that his position will prove acceptable to
his own constituents back home, there is little to deter him from dissociating
himself from the small group of leaders who are endeavoring to control Congress. Much the same reasoning leads the ordinary member of Congress to
feel that he can accept or reject the advice of his party leaders as he sees fit.

This inability of congressional officers to provide vigorous leadership for
the national legislature is closely associated with the weakness of the national
parties. The average member of Congress has little reason to respect his party
leaders in Congress because he knows that they have relatively little to offer him,
and, contrariwise, that they can do him little harm. In other words, if the party
system were more highly centralized and included, for example, some measure
of control by national party headquarters over nominations in the states and the
congressional districts, then the officers and party leaders in Congress would automatically gain power and prestige. However, the difficulty inherent in commis-

sion leadership would not necessarily be corrected by this change in the party system.

Some measure of reasonably vigorous leadership of Congress is an absolute necessity in modern government. The absence of such leadership within Congress has inevitably resulted in the encouragement of presidential leadership over that body. Of course, the President finds his position as a legislative leader threatened by some of the same forces that prevent the leaders in Congress from exercising more influence. For example, the weakness of the national parties handicaps the President as a leader in much the same way that it does congressional officers. But the obstacles are not quite so serious. Presidential power is concentrated in one man, as against the diffusion of the power of leadership within Congress among a score or more members of two independent houses. The President is a national figure and can claim to speak for a majority of the people of the country. The congressman is well aware that it is not the people of the country but only the voters in his own locality or state who control his fate. Yet for this very reason he is apt at times to be more impressed by the opinions and recommendations of a man who is in close touch with the American people as a whole than he is by the wishes of his congressional leaders, who, like himself, represent limited sections of the country. Again, insofar as a congressman who belongs to the same party as the President does have a sense of party loyalty, or believes that his own political future will be affected by the fate and fortunes of his party, he will tend to look to the President as the most powerful figure within his party. This is not to say that the average member of Congress may not be more kindly disposed toward his own colleagues in Congress or be on closer personal terms with them than he is with the President. But he cannot fail to be impressed by the strong institutional position which the President occupies.

Before the parliamentary revolution of 1910 the Speaker possessed sufficient power to enable him as a single person to claim the right of leadership. But the very revolt against his power in that year was based in part upon the unwillingness of his colleagues in the House to accept leadership in such an office. Moreover, he had no power over the Senate, and it is a fact there has never been any centralized leadership in House or Senate that has been able to bridge the gap between the two houses. This, too, has encouraged the President to seek to lead a Congress which is incapable of providing its own leadership.

the changing character of government encourages presidential leadership

Congress's inability to initiate policy

A third reason for the President's concern with legislation is found in the nature of the times in which we live. The world over, in democratic and nondemocratic countries alike, the increasingly technical character of problems of policy determination has compelled legislative bodies to defer more and more to the wishes and advice of the executive authority in government. This trend of the times has long been apparent in the United States. It may be seen in Congress's tendency to await the President's recommendations before it even begins the formulation of broad policy, for it recognizes that the President's proximity to the problem itself and his superior access to data and necessary information give him the right to speak first. This is not to say that Congress no longer makes any effort to inform itself about such problems or to formulate its own conclusions on the basis of the data it may gather independently. For example, tax policy is still largely originated by Congress. The Treasury Department and other administrative agencies regularly submit data and recommendations, but Congress —in particular the Ways and Means Committee of the House of Representatives —jealously guards its right to obtain its own information and to arrive at its own conclusions.

But there are many examples of the opposite situation. The formulation of our social security policy is one, for from the beginning of policy development in this field, Congress has depended upon the President to provide the information and to make recommendations. To be sure, Congress has rejected some of the executive findings, and has insisted upon altering the proposed policies, but it has recognized its own inability to make the initial study of the problem or to originate a policy.

Congress's inability to determine the details of policy

The increasing dependency of the legislature upon executive leadership which is occasioned by the character of the times may be seen in another way. It is possible to point to statute after statute where Congress has delegated vast discretionary power to the President and his assistants to fill in the details of policy because of its own inability to determine such details. An extreme example of this tendency is to be seen in the famous Lend-Lease Act adopted by Congress in 1941. As the statute came from Congress it did little more than announce a policy to the effect that the United States was prepared to aid certain foreign nations, whose defense was considered vital to our own, in their struggles against aggressors. Beyond that, Congress said little. Instead, it directed the President to determine which nations should be placed in this unusual category, what materials and assistance should be sent to them, and what sort of arrangement should be made with them for repayment. While the bill was before Congress numerous attempts were made to amend it so as to make its policy more explicit by incorporating considerably more detail in it. It was argued that Congress itself should name the nations to be aided under the program. But it did not require much argument to show the lack of wisdom in such a proposal. The world was at war, international relations were extremely unstable, and startling changes were occurring with hardly a moment's notice. It seemed clearly desirable to let the President undertake the responsibility of evaluating these changes and to exercise power to revise from time to time the list of nations to be helped. In this respect and in many others the statute gave the President vast discretionary power to formulate the detail of our lend-lease program on a day to day basis.

Yet it would be a mistake to conclude that Congress thereby abdicated its position as the supreme policy determining agency of our government, for it did lay down the broad lines of a fundamental policy of tremendous importance. As late as 1941 there was powerful isolationist sentiment both in Congress and in the country at large that completely denied the assertion that our national defense was in any way dependent upon what was happening in Europe or Asia. When a majority of the members of both houses of Congress passed the Lend-Lease Act our legislature was rejecting this argument of the isolationists and consciously selecting and approving a contrary policy.

Many factors combine, then, to make the President a powerful force in legislation. The Constitution by its own words recognizes the propriety of such activity by the President and vests in him several significant powers relating to lawmaking. The institutional absence of leadership within Congress operates to emphasize the natural potentialities for legislative leadership which exist in the President's office. And, finally, the increased use by the President of his legislative powers in modern times is merely the American manifestation of a world-wide phenomenon—a closer concern by administrators with policy determination.

informal methods by which the President influences legislation

Some of the methods by which the President influences Congress in the making of laws are expressly provided for in the Constitution: control over the sessions of Congress, the sending of messages to Congress, and the veto power. These have already been considered. There are other, less formal methods which have developed through the years from the necessities of the situation. These have found their constitutional justification in the doctrine of implied powers, or have been extraconstitutional in character.

the use of the patronage to influence policy making

Chief among these additional means of presidential influence has been the patronage power. The Constitution expressly grants the appointing power to the President, but it does not in so many words acknowledge its use as a means of giving the President greater influence over Congress. Nonetheless, its employment by the President for this purpose is as old as our government itself. This does not mean that Presidents have indulged in a crude business of purchasing votes in Congress for legislation by offering to make appointments according to the wishes of congressmen. Such a practice has been rather rare. Much more common is the less pointed use of the patronage power by the President as a means of cultivating friendly relations with members of Congress, thereby encouraging sympathetic consideration of executive proposals.

The development of the merit system in recent decades has, of course, lessened the significance of patronage as a means of controlling Congress. This has not been a disappointing development to Presidents, for the use of the patronage has always been fraught with danger to presidential desires. A congressman who has once fed at the patronage trough is apt to develop an insatiable hunger. The patronage, moreover, is limited, and it is probable that in the long run its use has been as much a liability as an asset to the President who seeks to persuade congressmen to follow his wishes in legislative matters. Nonetheless, the patronage still remains an effective means by which the President, at least upon occasion, may influence the course of congressional business. There are certain types of federal offices—district judgeships, for example—which are still commonly filled in accordance with congressional suggestions to the President. The use of the patronage in this respect is apt to be at its peak in the very first session of Congress after a new President assumes office, when there are both many offices to be filled and many new bills that the President wishes Congress to pass. A good illustration of this situation is to be seen in the famous special session of Congress in 1933 at which many of the most important New Deal measures, sponsored by President Roosevelt, were passed. In this instance the patronage power was successfully used in a somewhat novel fashion—instead of bargaining with congressmen during the session, the administration let it be understood that the patronage would not be distributed until after the session had come to a close. In this way congressmen, eager for certain appointments, were compelled to give favorable consideration to the President's legislative requests if they wished to remain on friendly terms with him.

the President's strong bargaining power

The President has other means of bargaining with congressmen. A promise of support for a congressman's pet measure, or a threat of presidential opposition to it, hope of political advancement, or fear lest presidential displeasure mean an end to a congressional career—all these are factors that may influence a congressman's attitude toward a President's legislative program. Although the national party is loosely organized and poorly controlled from the top down, many congressmen do have a feeling of party loyalty which persuades them to give favorable consideration to the President's legislative program. Congressional rejection of presidential proposals is bound to have political repercussions which may endanger the chances of the President's party in the next election. Congressmen who come from districts that are evenly balanced in party strength may find the effect of the failure of Congress and President to work together more than sufficient to bring about their defeat. On the other hand, congressmen from "safe" districts may hold committee chairmanships which will be in danger if the party majority is threatened at the next election. Thus these men, too, may think twice before opposing the President on an important issue.

the use of friendly, informal contacts

Presidents have employed various methods of keeping in touch with congressmen and the congressional scene. The formal message to Congress is frequently used to provide an official indication of presidential wishes. But no President who hopes to influence Congress can depend exclusively upon formal procedures. There must be follow-up action of an informal nature. There are many possibilities. Congressional leaders may be called to the White House for breakfast or lunch, and individual congressmen may be invited to confer with the President at the executive offices. White House agents may operate discreetly in the cloakrooms of the Capitol or in the committee rooms. The President may go on the air with a fireside chat, or make a carefully planned statement at a press conference in an attempt to rally public opinion to his position and force favorable action by Congress.

Upon assuming office President Truman startled the country by making several visits to the Capitol for informal luncheon meetings or conferences in the offices of congressmen. As a former senator he did not intend to lose the advantage he possessed in his close friendship with a great many congressmen. Members of Congress are notoriously gregarious in character. Hence a President who can persuade legislators that he is a "good fellow" or one of the crowd may gain favor with Congress. This is not easy, for the White House and the Capitol are at opposite ends of Pennsylvania Avenue in more ways than one, and a President who is by nature shy or reserved does not find the way to intimacy with congressmen an easy one. Wilson, Coolidge, and Hoover were all particularly unsuccessful in establishing close personal relations with congressmen. Other Presidents, by the sheer warmth of their personalities, their charm, or the respect they are able to command from others, may gain much influence with Congress. Of course, there is always the danger, as in the case of Harding, that a man's acceptance as a good fellow, or as "one of the gang," will cheapen his office, lessen his prestige, and even betray him into the hands of men who will use him to serve their own ulterior purposes. A President may win much by his human qualities, but he must always preserve his dignity if he wishes to retain control of the situation. No President who becomes subservient to Congress can serve the country well.

the use of a firm hand

A President naturally hopes to win his way with Congress by friendly, persuasive methods. On the other hand, he may often find it necessary to adopt tougher, more vigorous means in his dealings with the legislature. Certainly President Truman's well-intentioned efforts to preserve a friendly, informal relation with his former colleagues on Capitol Hill did not in the long run seem to win him much support for his legislative program, and he was compelled to use a firmer hand in his dealings with Congress.

What methods are available to the President when he decides to pursue a stiffer policy with Congress? An appeal to the people by carrying an issue to them over the heads of congressmen will sometimes prove effective. A public address at a well-chosen moment may result in the bringing of much pressure upon congressmen which they will be unable to ignore. In extreme instances, he may begin making threats of political reprisals against unfriendly congressmen. But a President must think twice before he takes this latter step, for the institutional arrangement is not entirely in his favor. He cannot threaten to dissolve Congress or to call a new election. Even though a regular election may be impending, if his quarrel is with members of his own party, he cannot very well ask for the election of members of the opposite party. To secure the defeat of his own party colleagues he must go into the primaries and conventions in the states and try to persuade party members to replace these men with new men who will be more loyal to him. President Roosevelt discovered, to his sorrow in 1938, that this is not easily done. Aside from the way in which party lines render presidential intervention in congressional elections difficult, it is almost impossible for the President to focus the attention of the voters on national issues. Accordingly, a President who seeks to carry an issue to the people is in something of a quandary as to how actually to proceed.

Occasionally, a President may employ an even more pointed threat in seeking action from Congress. In his first inaugural address in 1933 President Roosevelt stated that he hoped the normal balance of executive and legislative power could be maintained, but he warned Congress that if it failed to support his policies he would ask for "broad executive power to wage a war against the emergency as great as the power that would be given me if we were in fact invaded by a foreign foe." Again in September, 1942, in an address to Congress in which Roosevelt insisted that Congress accept certain recommendations pertaining to price control, he said, "I ask the Congress to take this action by the first of October. Inaction on your part by that date will leave me with an inescapable responsibility to the people of this country to see to it that the war effort is no longer imperiled by threat of economic chaos. In the event that the Congress should fail to act, and act adequately, I shall accept the responsibility, and I will act." [5a]

Congress took the step demanded by the President, thus relieving him of the necessity of carrying out his threat to take independent executive action in the matter.

[5a] 88 *Congressional Record* (September 7, 1942), 7044.

Finding the proper approach in his dealings with Congress is not an easy matter for the President. He must maintain his dignity, providing national leadership in a manner that suggests the statesman; yet he can never quite drop the role of politician, for in his relations with Congress he must be the negotiator and the manipulator if many of his requests are to find acceptance.

One thing is certain: the American people hold a President finally responsible for the development of a satisfactory legislative program during his term of office. But at the moment judgment is being passed by the voter, little attention is given to the constitutional or political difficulties that hamper the President in his attempts to influence legislative policy. Certainly in November, 1932, the American voter was holding Herbert Hoover responsible for the failure of the national government to formulate a more satisfactory policy in dealing with the serious depression through which the nation was passing. And it availed Mr. Hoover nothing to argue that Congress had failed to cooperate with him, and that for two years he had had to deal with a Democratic House of Representatives, for in the final analysis the people expect the President to provide leadership, to dominate Congress, and to take the initiative in developing the nation's legislative program. It is true that at times the voter, in inconsistent fashion, criticizes the President for the manner in which he asserts his authority over Congress; but the President must realize that, while he is expected to show proper respect for Congress and its prerogatives, he must also manage somehow to lead the way. History will remember the success or failure of his "administration" long after it has forgotten the composition and peculiarities of the Congresses with which he had to work. And so it is up to the President to get along with Congress, to dominate but not irritate, to compromise but not surrender, to lead and yet not dictate, to be a statesman and yet a politician.

traditional antagonism between President and Congress

The fact is that there has come into being a sort of permanent antagonism between President and Congress. The causes of this antagonism are varied. One is the strong, independent status that each agency enjoys under the Constitution. This inevitably results in a feeling of rivalry between the two. Each feels that it owes nothing to the other, each is impressed by its own importance.

A second cause is found in the different methods by which congressmen and Presidents are elected to office. The President is chosen in a national election and receives the support of 25 million or more voters. He thus finds it relatively easy and natural to think and act in terms of grand strategy of national policy. Congressmen, on the other hand, are chosen by their states or districts and must necessarily be sensitive to the demands of local pressure groups. The President is relatively immune to the demands of pressure groups both because of the original design of the office and because of the changes that have occurred in the electoral system. As planned by the Founding Fathers, the office was to be that of a moderator selected by a council of elder statesmen. Today, the popular election of the President has made him a tribune of the people.[6] In contrast, no member of Congress owes allegiance to the American people at large. At best, a senator may represent a large and important state. The average representative or senator reflects the homogeneous interests of the district that has elected him. The homogeneity of these districts may not be complete in every respect. As a result, the average congressman is always subject to pulls and tugs in different directions which can be traced back to conflicts that exist in his own home district; but because he owes his election only to these people at home he often escapes the need for compromise and mediation on a broad national scale which is the lot of a President. It has been said there is no institutional reason for a congressman to have a national point of view.[7]

It is fortunate for the general welfare that the President and his administrative subordinates necessarily have a good deal of sensitivity both to national interests and to technical considerations. It is also fortunate that the President and his assistants have an important part to play in the legislative process. This is not to say that the forces of localism are not entitled to a voice in national policy formation. Yet the participation in the work of policy determination by men who reflect different pressures from those to which congressmen are most sensitive is bound to result in argument and conflict. This contrast in the interests represented by President and Congress heightens the feeling of psychological rivalry that exists between them and does not make it any easier for the two to work together. The congressman's inability to resist the extreme pressure which is sometimes brought upon him by groups of his constituents at times causes him to resent the relative ease with which the President ignores such a factor in calling for enlightened *national* legislation. This resentment is apt to lead to a heightened feeling of congressional independence. It has been said: "It is traditional that those who, yielding to other pressures, fail to ratify presidential proposals should disguise their opposition as an endeavor to maintain the integrity and independence of the legislative branch of government." [8]

A third cause for antagonism between the two branches is that the President tends to favor action, whereas Congress is constantly tempted to follow a do-nothing or let-well-enough-alone policy. There are, of course, many exceptions to this, but in the last generation it is the President who has taken the initiative in suggesting positive ways of attacking the nation's problems, and it is Congress that has held back and has either rejected presidential proposals out-

---

[6] See Pendleton Herring, *Presidential Leadership* (New York: Rinehart & Company, Inc., 1940), p. 8.

[7] Roland Young, *This Is Congress* (New York: Alfred A. Knopf, Inc., 1945), p. x.

[8] O. R. Altman, "First Session of the Seventy-fifth Congress," *American Political Science Review*, XXXI (December, 1937), 1083.

right or has been persuaded to approve them only in reluctant fashion. The causes for this condition are varied and confused. But it may be said that because the President represents the nation at large, because he is not caught in the cross fire of self-centered, conflicting pressure groups as a congressman is, he is relatively free to keep his eyes fixed on the larger issues confronting the country at large. These issues, in turn, have for the last twenty years been so complex and so fraught with danger that no man serving as President, be he radical or conservative, could avoid proposing positive action of some sort in an effort to avoid the dangers. Congressmen, on the other hand, because they reflect the forces of localism and the antagonisms of conflicting groups, find it much more difficult to support courageously and enthusiastically a vigorous, orderly, and logical program of action. Professor James M. Burns, in his lively and intelligent little book, *Congress on Trial*, calls attention to the number of social scientists who are worried about "the threat of stasis." By "stasis" is meant "the failure of functional groups in the community to bridge their differences" and thus to maintain "social equilibrium" through "conscious collective action." To avoid stasis the government "must be organized to represent the whole people (or at least a majority of the voters), and not simply the parts." Here is where Congress presents the difficulty, for congressmen "who act chiefly as pleaders and promoters for special interests" cannot readily be brought together in support of a positive program for the promotion of national interests.[9]

It is only by keeping such considerations in mind that one can understand the antagonism that seems always to exist between the President and Congress. It is all too easy to talk about the need for greater cooperation between the executive and legislative branches of government, as though the petty quarrels and disagreements of small and selfish men were alone preventing the formation of satisfactory national policy. Admittedly, there must be cooperation between President and Congress if the United States is to pursue an intelligent policy in an age so beset and bedeviled by fearfully difficult and complex problems as is ours today. But we cannot further that cooperation by overlooking the real difficulties that lie in the way of its achievement.

should the United States adopt parliamentary government?

There have always been those critics of the American system of government who have taken the position that the fundamental conflict between Congress and the President can be solved only by the adoption of parliamentary government in the United States. By parliamentary government they have had in mind some arrangement approaching the British political system. In England the Prime Min-

---

[9] James M. Burns, *Congress on Trial* (New York: Harper & Brothers, 1949), pp. 128 ff.

ister and his principal assistants in the executive branch who compose the cabinet are themselves members of Parliament. They are elected to office in the first instance as members of the legislature and receive their posts in the executive branch because they are the leaders of the majority party in the House of Commons, which party is ordered by the King to form a "government." It is then the power and duty of this "government," i.e., the Prime Minister and the cabinet, to prepare a legislative program for submission to the House of Commons. Thereafter, any continuing conflict between the legislature and the executive is impossible, in theory at least, because if the House of Commons rejects any major proposal submitted to it by the government, the Prime Minister and his cabinet are expected to resign and to advise the King either to appoint new executive officers who can win the support of Parliament, or to dissolve the House of Commons and to order a new election in which the voters will presumably indicate a solution to the conflict.

the Finletter proposal for parliamentary government in the United States

One of the most stimulating proposals of recent years for fundamental reform in congressional-presidential relations is made by Thomas K. Finletter in his little book, *Can Representative Government Do the Job?* [10] It is Finletter's thesis that the present inability of the President and Congress to work together in the development of a positive, systematic program for the achievement of the twin goals of peace and prosperity for the United States represents a major threat to the national welfare. He would attack the unsatisfactory relationship between the two branches of government, first, by placing the President, senators, and representatives on a common six-year-term basis—which would mean that they would all be elected to office simultaneously; second, by creating a joint executive-legislative cabinet to prepare a legislative program for consideration by Congress; and, third, by giving the President power to dissolve both branches of the government in case of a deadlock and to order a new election. The Finletter plan would stop short of the British parliamentary system in the sense that the chief executive would remain an independent officer elected directly to his post by the voters in a national election, rather than become the leader of the majority party in Congress, having been elected to the legislature by the voters in a state or a district. Otherwise, the proposal would closely approximate the theory, if not the practice, of the British system. It is Finletter's contention that were his plan adopted, the American people would then have a national government democratically organized and possessing both the power and responsibility for vigorous, positive action in the interest of the national welfare.

---

[10] Thomas K. Finletter, *Can Representative Government Do the Job?* (New York: Harcourt, Brace Company, 1945).

*the Burns proposal for "party government" as the solution to the presiden-
tial-congressional conflict*

Burns in *Congress on Trial*, while agreeing with Finletter's diagnosis of
the weakness of our present political system, takes a quite different position concerning the best way to correct it. Burns contends that Finletter and others who
have favored reproducing the British system in the United States have not only
greatly minimized the difficulties of transplanting to a foreign land a government indigenous to one country, but have also overlooked an all-important factor in the situation, namely, the American party system, decentralized
and undisciplined as it is. It is Burns's contention that parliamentary government will not work in the United States unless it is accompanied by vigorous,
disciplined national parties. And it is his conclusion that could we establish such
a party system, it alone would produce the desired result and the parliamentary
system would not be necessary.[11] As Burns sees it, "The secret of the English
system is not simply in the cabinet. It is mainly in their party system." And conversely, the chief difficulty of the American system is not the separation of powers between an independent Congress and an independent President, but rather
in our weak party system, which has failed to bridge the gap between these two
branches of government and to provide the means of securing responsible, party
government at the national level—"meaning by party government a condition
where centralized and disciplined parties formulate national policy on key issues
and use governmental machinery to carry out that policy. The term is used in
contradistinction to presidential government, congressional government, and cabinet government, not one of which . . . can safely and effectively master the
problems arising in an era of chronic crisis." [12] Burns argues that party government would increase the leadership powers of both the President and the
officers of Congress and would compel them, through the development of some
such arrangement as a legislative-executive cabinet, to learn to work together
and to share the great power and responsibility that would come to them.

Not the least important aspect of his proposal, he argues, is that the basic
change could be brought about without the extremely difficult business of amending the Constitution.

bibliographic note

Wilfred E. Binkley's *President and Congress* (New York: Alfred A. Knopf, Inc.,
1947) is a historical analysis of the struggle for supremacy between the Pres-

---

[11] See particularly his Chapter 9, "Cabinet Government: Fact & Fiction."
[12] Burns, *Congress on Trial*, pp. 193–194.

ident and Congress. It contains a number of suggestions for improvement in the relations between the two branches of the government. Lawrence H. Chamberlain's *The President, Congress, and Legislation* (New York: Columbia University Press, 1946) analyzes the making of some ninety statutes with emphasis upon the relative roles played by the President and Congress in their enactment. Chamberlain concludes that Congress is perhaps more able to provide its own leadership than many authorities have thought to be the case. The famous question-period plan is examined by its chief sponsor, Estes Kefauver, "The Need for Better Executive-Legislative Teamwork in the National Government," an article in the *American Political Science Review*, XXXVIII (April, 1944) 317.

During the last quarter of a century a series of books has appeared which examine the existing relationship between the President and Congress and which suggest reforms in this relationship, ranging all the way from the adoption of parliamentary government to mere tinkering with the present system. In the order of their appearance the following titles may be noted: William MacDonald, *A New Constitution for a New America* (New York: B. W. Huebsch, Inc., 1921); William Y. Elliott, *The Need for Constitutional Reform* (New York: McGraw-Hill Book Company, 1935); Henry Hazlitt, *A New Constitution Now* (New York: McGraw-Hill Book Company, 1942); Thomas K. Finletter, *Can Representative Government Do the Job?* (New York: Harcourt, Brace Co. Inc., 1945); James M. Burns, *Congress on Trial* (New York: Harper & Brothers, 1949); Arthur C. Millspaugh, *Toward Efficient Democracy: The Question of Governmental Organization* (Washington: The Brookings Institution, 1949). The Finletter and Burns volumes will perhaps be of greatest interest and use to students. The point of view of several of these books is examined in the present chapter.

A recent article on this same problem is Arnold J. Zurcher's "The Presidency, Congress, and Separation of Powers: A Reappraisal," *Western Political Quarterly*, III (March, 1950), 75. The author is somewhat more sympathetic toward a continued separation of powers between President and Congress than are the authors of most of the books which have just been noted.

An interesting article describing the use of the veto power by one President is George C. Robinson's "The Veto Record of Franklin D. Roosevelt," *American Political Science Review*, XXXVI (February, 1942), 75.

government personnel:
the congressman

*N*O PUBLIC officer has been the subject of more bitter criticism in recent years than the congressman. The attacks have come from every direction and have been exceedingly varied in character. To some critics the congressman is a "dunderhead," an unintelligent, shortsighted man with little understanding of the serious problems confronting the nation. To others he is too much the "good fellow," a back-slapping, cigar-smoking individual who looks upon his seat in Congress as serving the primary purpose of giving him membership in a social club. Still others attack the congressman for his selfishness, his subservience to vicious pressure groups, and the readiness with which he places special interests above the general welfare. To the random critic the congressman is an ignoramus, a politician, a self-seeker; he loafs on the job, feeds at the public trough, puts his wife or his nephew on the public payroll, votes himself a pension or an increase in salary, holds on blindly to outmoded, inefficient procedures, and has no interest in modernizing congressional organization. In short, he is a liability rather than an asset, and the critic concludes that the nation must have more honest, respectable, and intelligent legislators, congressmen who will be less the politicians, more the statesmen, less lazy, more energetic, less easygoing, more dignified, and above all, less bumbling and ineffectual, more understanding and successful.

How much of this criticism is valid? What sort of person is the congressman actually? What kind of job has he been doing? To what extent may the shortcomings in the legislative process be laid at his feet as a person; to what extent are they the result of impersonal defects in the legislative system? What kind of person makes a good congressman, anyway? These are questions which come readily to mind and which must be answered if an understanding of Congress, its character, and its work, is to be achieved.

It may be asserted at once that much of the criticism of congressmen is exaggerated, or overlooks the extent to which all institutional arrangements are handicapped by the frailties and imperfections of the human beings who must man and operate them. It is significant that a committee on Congress set up by the American Political Science Association in 1945 concluded, ". . . we have found that our national legislature today is made up of substantial, conscientious, hard-working, well educated men and women who are better qualified for their great tasks than is sometimes supposed." [1]

Specific complaints as to the inadequacy of congressional personnel may be divided into three categories for purposes of this analysis. The first complaint concerns the congressman's lack of background and preparation for his job; the second concerns the congressman's failure to work hard in the national legislature and to give the service expected of him; the third charges that the congressman's reasons for voting the way he does are improper if not dishonest.

the background of the "average" congressman

A statistical analysis of the personnel of Congress reveals that the "average" congressman is by no means ill-prepared for the job he undertakes. He is somewhat past middle age, has served in Congress for a number of years, and has had previous political experience before coming to Congress, such as membership in his state legislature. He was born in the state he represents, has a college degree, attended a graduate school, is a lawyer by profession, and is a war veteran.[2]

age

In 1941 the average age of representatives was 52, that of senators was 58. Thirty-two members of Congress were over 70, and only four were under 30. Two men in the House were only 27 when they took their seats in 1941. One hundred and fifty-two members were over 60, whereas only fifty-nine were under 40. Moreover, the average age of congressmen is increasing and, contrary to popular belief, the congressman of the past was a younger man. For example, in the Forty-first Congress, which served just after the Civil War, the median age of the members of Congress was 44.64, but by 1923 the median age had risen to 51. This tendency has certainly not been reversed in the last twenty-five years.

---

[1] *The Reorganization of Congress,* A Report of the Committee on Congress of the American Political Science Association (Washington: Public Affairs Press, 1945), p. 86.

[2] These generalizations and the statistics that follow are based upon two sources: an article by Madge M. McKinney, "The Personnel of the Seventy-seventh Congress," *American Political Science Review,* XXXVI (February, 1942), 67; and George B. Galloway, *Congress at the Crossroads* (New York: Thomas Y. Crowell Company, 1946), Chap. 2, "How Congress Is Composed." Similar statistical information for current Congresses is published in the *Congressional Quarterly.* In general these statistics do not vary greatly from one Congress to the next.

There is thus a preponderance of older men in Congress and this fact should indicate experience, stability, and a tendency toward that conservatism which often comes with age. Youth, with its spirit of liberalism and its willingness to experiment, is underrepresented in Congress, although this is not one of the complaints usually voiced by the critics of Congress.

length of service

When the Eighty-first Congress convened in January, 1949, there were 136 new members, 24 of whom, however, had had previous service in the Seventy-ninth or earlier Congresses. Twenty-six senators had served in the upper house for ten or more years; 39 for five or more years. In the House of Representatives 140 members had served for ten or more years; 223 for five or more years. On the other hand, only two senators and 15 representatives had had more than twenty-five years of service. Thus, the average member of Congress has served in that body for some time and presumably has gained political experience from such service; but the normal span of a man's career in Congress is a definitely limited one.

previous political experience

The majority of congressmen have held public office before serving in the national legislature. One hundred and fifty-six members of the Seventy-seventh Congress had had previous service as members of state legislatures, 18 had been governors of states, 28 had held other state administrative posts, 50 had been judges, state or federal, 59 had held a city or a county office, 109 had been prosecuting attorneys.[3] Slightly more than one quarter of the members of the Senate had had previous service in the House of Representatives. It is, of course, impossible to evaluate the experience gained from the holding of these former offices, but it seems clear that the average congressman is not a political novice when he arrives in Washington.

place of birth

Three hundred and seventy-four members of the Seventy-seventh Congress were born in the states they represented; 132 were born in other states, although in many instances they had moved in their youth to the states they now represented. Only twenty-three members of Congress were foreign born. These figures demonstrate in a decisive manner the very close ties that exist between congressmen and the constituencies they represent. Apart from the fact that congressional service itself tears a man away from his native state, our national legislators are men who are provincial rather than cosmopolitan in outlook; they have their roots deep in the states from which they come.

---

[3] The same congressman may figure in more than one of these categories.

education

Congressmen are well educated. Eighty-eight per cent of the members of the Seventy-seventh Congress had gone through college; in addition, 66 per cent had had some graduate training, mostly in law schools. Again, the wisdom or knowledge that a man obtains from formal education is difficult to evaluate, but academically the congressman is well prepared for his task.

previous occupations

All studies of the former economic interests of congressmen agree upon one point: law is far and away the most important steppingstone to a career as a national legislator. Three hundred and three lawyers were serving in Congress in 1945. There were 57 former businessmen, 34 newspapermen, 26 teachers, 24 real-estate or insurance men, 18 farmers, and 12 bankers. In the Seventy-seventh Congress in 1941 only one member claimed to have been a factory worker. Twenty-six held union cards, although in some cases these were honorary or represented membership in a skilled or professional union such as the Teachers Federation.

These statistics on the business or professional interests of congressmen indicate a strong conservative influence. Since a lawyer's business is, after all, with the law, it is not strange that so many lawyers become congressmen. However, the lawyer's approach to the business of *making* laws is but one of many and is more often than not a conservative one because of the strong influence of precedent and tradition in the practice of the law. Charles A. Beard once observed that American politics has long been under bondage to lawyers. George Galloway has added that "critics of this bondage have taken the view that, while a lawyer is peculiarly fitted by training and practice to get himself elected to public office, the same qualities do not necessarily equip him to solve national problems." [4] Although the average law school training undoubtedly gives the lawyer excellent technical preparation in the field of the law, it is all too frequently true that the social and economic approaches to the problems of modern society have been ignored or but lightly treated.

Labor is decidedly underrepresented in Congress, but so too, although in less marked fashion, are many professions and business groups. It must be remembered that our national legislature is not organized with economic or social interests as the basis of representation. Lawyers are often closely identified with business interests; nonetheless, in the large number of lawyers and teachers in Congress is found a type of representative whose economic interests are reasonably general and impartial and who is usually free from personal identification with any one set of business, agricultural, or labor interests.

---

[4] Galloway, *Congress at the Crossroads*, p. 29.

military service

One hundred and ninety-five members of Congress in 1941 had had military service in wartime. This figure rose to about 250 in 1949 and seems likely to remain high indefinitely, now that some ten million men with service in the recent war have been added to the veterans of World War I. It is not easy to indicate the significance of this factor. It is a truism in politics that the war veteran has an edge over the candidate who is not a war veteran. It is also true that Congress is inclined to lend a willing ear to the suggestions and requests that originate with the Army, the Navy, and the veterans' organizations. On the other hand, it is easy to exaggerate the extent to which the war veteran in Congress is motivated by military considerations. He is subject to many other loyalties, economic, geographical, and social in character, which often serve in a particular situation as offsets to military influences on him. And yet among the facts that stand out in any analysis of congressional personnel, the presence of so many war veterans is one that cannot be ignored.

sex, religion, and race

There were only nine women in Congress in 1949. The number varies from Congress to Congress but has never exceeded ten. Thus it is obvious that women are grossly underrepresented. Whether the presence of larger numbers of women in Congress would result in any change in legislative attitudes or whether sex is even a characteristic of any significance in the analysis of congressional personnel is a controversial question. Seventy-one per cent of the members of the Seventy-seventh Congress indicated affiliations with Protestant churches, 18 per cent were Catholics, and a little more than 1 per cent were Jews. Data on the racial and national backgrounds of congressmen are not readily available. One very sizable minority in the United States which has had very little representation in Congress is the Negro. In recent years one or two Negroes, representing New York City and Chicago districts, have been found in the House of Representatives, and that is all. During the Reconstruction era a Negro, Blanche K. Bruce, actually served a full six-year term in the Senate, representing Mississippi.

is Congress a mirror of the nation?

Although the significance of much of these statistical data concerning congressional personnel is difficult to determine, it seems clear that the average congressman has a reasonably good background of training and experience for the office he fills. In this respect, attention should be given to the common assertion that members of Congress are a representative sample of the general population, or "a mirror of the nation." Certainly, more than almost any other man in public life, the congressman is a typical American. More than the state or local official he gives expression to national characteristics, at least in his collective being, and more than the judge or administrator in national government he typifies the average man and the nonprofessional approach to life and its problems. One attempt to characterize the members of Congress runs as follows:

> Elected to service in the federal legislature, these men and women come from the highways and byways of the nation, from towns big and little, and they bring with them into the marble corridors of the Capitol a deeply American cross section of intelligence and stupidity, industry and indolence, pomposity, demagoguery, and plain common sense.[5]

Some authorities believe that this "cross section" or "average man" description of the personnel of Congress has been exaggerated. For example, the Committee on Congress of the American Political Science Association points out: "If Congress were a representative sample of the people, it would be younger on the average, half of its members would be women, they would be less well educated than they are now, and the occupational distribution of the members would be different from what it now is." [6]

Nonetheless, one cannot overlook the extent to which the members of Congress offer a pretty good cross section of the American people, and it is this quality which paradoxically leads to much of the criticism that congressmen are ill-prepared and poorly qualified to meet their tasks. The average congressman, like the average American of middle age, is not an imposing individual in appearance; he is apt to be somewhat careless in his dress, easygoing and genial in manner, and a good fellow who enjoys friendly, leisurely contacts with a wide variety of persons. There is little about him that is professional or imposing. He has little of the seeming briskness or efficiency of the businessman, little of the intellectual's interest in the deeper significance of social problems, little of the technical expert's concern for the use of scientific methods in attacking these problems—although, of course, all such characterizations are apt to be more fictitious than real.

does the "average" man make a good congressman?

Insofar as the congressman is not an impressive individual is he nonetheless an adequate man for the job he fills? In other words, what are the requirements of this particular public office? What kind of man does make a good member of Congress? In seeking answers to these questions we should bear in mind that it is the legislator's peculiar function to represent the people in the determination of broad public policy. Although this task requires all of the honesty and wisdom that can possibly be brought to it, it does not call primarily for the services of the technical expert or the scholarly intellectual. The role of the legislator is not the same as the role of the judge or the role of the administrator. The func-

---

[5] "The Seventy-seventh Congress," *Fortune Magazine*, April, 1941, pp. 73, 76.
[6] *The Reorganization of Congress*, p. 85.

tions of the latter two officers do call for much specialized knowledge, for a directness and a scientific approach to a problem that are often less important in the work of legislating. To be sure, the contrasts between legislator, judge, and administrator are often exaggerated, and there is much about the work of the judge and the administrator that calls for the same human qualities that should characterize the legislator. But the fact remains that it is the legislator's job in a democracy to understand the people, to reflect their wants and interests, and to recognize that the formation of public policy is a complex, compromise operation in which technical considerations play an important but not an exclusive role.

the "scholar in politics"

To put the matter in somewhat different words, critics of Congress sometimes seem to take the position that if congressmen were "experts" or were more highly educated men, the legislative record would be far better than it is. The trouble with this position is that it ignores the congressman's social point of view and his ability to represent his constituents. To take an example, a dozen years or so ago there were two men in Congress, one in each house, who were recognized scholars and, in particular, accomplished students of legislative procedure. Both were authors, and one had written several highly regarded books on the legislative process. But neither man enjoyed an outstanding career as a congressman. Experts they were, but one man was also an isolationist and the other was an economic conservative. In the end these personal views proved to be unrepresentative of public opinion in their districts, and both men were retired from Congress by the voters after making disappointing records as "scholars in politics." Still further back, the senior Henry Cabot Lodge was another famous "scholar in politics," but his career as a United States Senator also left something to be desired. In his routine activity he was a petty politician, and in his broader dealings with matters of national welfare and international concern he held views that are now regarded by historians as having been shortsighted and mistaken.

This is not to say that the more "ordinary" a congressman, the less he is an educated man, or that the closer he comes to being the lowest common denominator of the people he represents, the better qualified he will be to serve as a legislator. Congressmen do need training, skills, and a broad understanding of the social problems with which they must deal. But it by no means follows that the college graduate, the "scholar," the "expert," the "engineer," or the "businessman" will make a good national legislator merely because he has had a better education or has been more "successful" than have his fellow men. Actually, the facts show that most of the congressmen who have served us have not been mediocre men. In spite of his everyday appearance and manner, the congressman is, more often than not, a reasonably able, well-educated, intelligent man who has won the support of his constituents and who has sufficient native talent and energy to make a success as a national legislator. Often he has been quite successful in some private occupation before going to Congress. Accordingly, there is reason to conclude that the type of individual who is now found in Congress, whatever his shortcomings and inadequacies, is not poorly suited to his job merely because by education, interests, and temperament he is classified as an amateur rather than as a professional student of government.

a day in the life of a congressman

The second criticism of congressmen is that they are lazy. Is this a valid criticism? Do our representatives fail to work hard, to use the talents they do possess in finding legislative solutions to the nation's problems? Answers to these questions are often given in the affirmative, and it must be conceded there is much damning evidence. Perhaps the proof that is most often cited is the small attendance on the floor of the House or Senate when important business is being transacted. Admittedly "absenteeism" is a problem in the halls of Congress as well as in the mine, the factory, or the office. Moreover, there are congressmen who do not take their duties seriously enough, men who carry on a private business while serving in Congress, men who are never averse to junketing about the country filling lecture engagements or "studying" public problems, and men who succumb to the pleasant, time-consuming social life of Washington that a congressman may enjoy if he wishes. There is no doubt that a seat in Congress should be a full-time job and that congressmen should be discouraged from engaging in personal enterprises for pay. One way to prevent this would be to provide substantially higher salaries for congressmen and to make provision for pensions upon retirement. The present salary is $12,500 a year plus a $2,500 nontaxable expense account. In addition each congressman has an allowance of twenty cents a mile for traveling to and from sessions, a basic $12,500 allowance for a secretarial and office force, and various other allowances, for telephone calls, stationery, and similar purposes. But many authorities think this compensation is inadequate. The National Planning Association's study of Congress makes the bold proposal that the straight salary be increased to $25,000. Even this latter figure is none too high, although because of the "political" danger that lies in voting higher salaries, Congress probably cannot be persuaded to go that far.

Granted that some congressmen spend much time on personal business pursuits, or lead a pleasant social life, there is much about outward appearances in a congressman's mode of life and daily activity that is misleading and that gives a false impression about the degree of seriousness and industry he brings to his job. Many attempts have been made to describe a day in the life of a congressman, and it must be conceded at once that there is no description that fits all members of Congress or all of the days in the life of any one legislator. Still, it is interesting and worth while to note the activities that frequently mark the congressman's day.

answering mail

The Congressman usually arrives at his office in the Senate or House Office Building at an early morning hour. The work of a congressman is by no means limited to mere attendance at the formal sessions of House or Senate which begin at noon, and his desk is always piled high with unfinished business. Mail looms very large in the congressman's life. It is impossible to generalize, for much depends upon the size of his constituency and the public interest that is being shown in legislative issues which are before Congress at the moment. In any case, the volume of a representative's or a senator's mail continues large day after day. Mail is today one of the congressman's most valuable contacts with the people back home. The yearlong sessions that have characterized the work of Congress in recent times have made it relatively difficult for the congressman to keep in close personal touch with his constituents, and the wise member answers every letter that comes into his office from back home, whether its query, complaint, or request for service is legitimate or not.

running errands for constituents

Before the morning is far advanced a steady stream of visitors begins to flow through the legislator's office. A few will be persons from home who must be courteously received. Other congressmen will drop in to discuss common problems or to seek advice. The telephone is soon ringing and the congressman may be in communication with a dozen administrative agencies of the government before the day is over. He wishes to check a matter with the Department of Agriculture before he attends a committee meeting, or he puts through a call to the War Department to make inquiry about plans for a new bridge in his district that has not yet been approved, or he gets in touch with the Civil Service Commission to find out the rating of a constituent on an examination recently taken. Many of these calls are made to provide the congressman with information needed in his work, but the majority of them are made in the process of dealing with constituents and meeting their inquiries and requests. It may be argued that such activity does much to humanize government. The administrative agency is not always in close touch with the people, and intercession by a congressman may well help to soften the harsh, impersonal character of the law or of administrative practice. Yet in performing these services the congressman is at times reduced to the level of an errand boy for his constituents, and admittedly many of his errands are of an inconsequential character hardly befitting the dignity and importance of his office. Moreover, a congressman, if he is not careful, soon finds himself making requests that he knows are unreasonable and improper. The report of the Political Science Association's committee frowns on this practice:

> . . . we hope that this government can remain or become a government of laws and not of men. Without attempting to state how much, we can at least say that some part of the services of Congressmen to their constituents consists in efforts to get special favors for them from executive agencies. These agencies depend upon the favor of Congress and are too prone to try to curry favor with individual members.[7]

The report goes on to suggest the "Congress might well formulate a Charter of Congressional Freedom from trivial errands and attempt to demarcate some of the lines between general directives to executive branches and specific interferences with administration."

meeting with pressure groups

Throughout the day, in one form or another, whether by answering mail, talking with visitors to his office, or making trips to other governmental offices, a considerable portion of a congressman's time is taken up in dealings with lobbyists or informal representatives of pressure groups. Again much of this time may seem wasted; the requests of many persons seeking to influence legislation are unreasonable or cannot possibly be met; or the congressman finds it difficult to maintain his dignity and his honesty in resisting the selfish pressures that are exerted upon him. Still, he cannot refuse to listen to such people: legislative policies are about to be determined; it is the congressman's duty to give representation to his constituents, and so he must listen patiently to requests or demands that he support this bill or oppose that one.

Moreover, the congressman has discovered by experience that many lobbyists are experts in the areas in which they operate; they can provide him with much assistance in obtaining data about legislative problems and, everything considered, constitute a valuable source of factual information. Many an able lobbyist now avoids mere argument or personal pressure in his attempts to persuade a congressman to vote a certain way, and instead seeks to win over the congressman by the weight of the data and information that he can present. Of course, a wise and honest congressman remembers always that both the supporters and the opponents of a proposed bill can usually assemble much evidence in support of their positions, that it remains his responsibility to evaluate such evidence. Nonetheless, the information presented by lobbyists is often of the type that the member of Congress would want to obtain, by one means or another, and frequently he is considerably aided in his search for an understanding of a legislative problem by his contacts with lobbyists, just as he keeps in

---

[7] *The Reorganization of Congress*, p. 66.

touch with the sentiment of his constituents by giving much time to his mail or to friendly welcomes to visitors from home.

attending committee meetings

As the day proceeds, the congressman's activity becomes more formal. At ten o'clock in the morning he may attend a meeting of one of the congressional committees of which he is a member. Not every committee meets every day, or even every week. But every senator is a member of two important committees and every representative a member of one important committee, and sooner or later in a congressional session each of these committees is certain to hold a lengthy series of hearings and executive sessions on legislative proposals. For example, members of the House Appropriations Committee will find it necessary in the early months of each year to attend meeting after meeting, first as members of a subcommittee giving preliminary consideration to one of the regular annual appropriation bills, and then as members of the full committee giving final consideration to all of these bills.

During the period when his committee is active, the congressman will find it necessary to devote much time to careful study of bills, transcripts of hearings on such bills, the language of proposed amendments, the wording of committee reports or of proposed speeches to be made on the floor of the House or the Senate when a bill is taken up for consideration. To a lesser degree the legislator will want to make a similar personal study of bills that have originally been the concern of committees of which he is not a member, for he must vote on these bills when they come to the floor. Of course, not every congressman faithfully pursues such studies, and there are many members of both houses who do shirk their duties, take life easy, and as a consequence are seldom well versed on current legislative problems. But the facts seem to indicate that more congressmen than not do engage in a considerable amount of such labor, labor that readily misses the eye of the observer who complains because congressmen are not continuously in their seats when the houses are in session.

attending sessions of House or Senate

The second formal duty of the day's work will be attendance on the floor, if the House or the Senate is in session that day. The usual hour for the opening of a session being noon, the average congressman will be present in his seat at or shortly after that hour, although he may soon leave to resume his office work or to hold interviews with visitors and lobbyists, returning to the floor from time to time to vote on amendments, listen to debate, or to make some personal contribution to the proceedings. But the volume of daily business that is carried on in a congressman's office is usually so great that it is impossible for all 531 members of Congress to take their seats at noon and remain in attendance throughout a session of House or Senate until a five or six o'clock adjournment is reached.

the congressman's staff

Lest it seem that no member of Congress can possibly engage in all of the daily activity that has been discussed up to this point, emphasis should now be given to the very valuable assistance that a congressman obtains from his secretariat. Every member of Congress is supplied with funds for the maintenance of an office staff and is usually able to obtain the services of one well-paid, full-time secretary and several stenographers or clerks. The secretary, usually a man, must be well versed in the technical aspects of legislative business as well as in the practical problems of a congressman's life in Washington if he is to serve his chief well. It is his duty to act as executive director of the congressman's office, and if he is able, shrewd, and loyal, he can be an invaluable right-hand man. Of course, if a congressman is to obtain maximum aid from his office force, he must devote a great deal of time and care to the selection of his assistants, to their training, and finally to the continuous supervision of their work.

In addition to the secretariat of the individual congressmen, similar aid is available on two higher levels—to the committees and to Congress as a whole. The standing committees all have appropriations enabling them to employ a certain number of permanent secretaries and clerks. For Congress as a whole there are the Legislative Reference Service and the Office of the Legislative Counsel. The first of these is an agency in the Library of Congress which functions as a general research organization, providing congressmen with various materials—pamphlets, digests of bills, data for use in speeches, abstracts of current literature, and studies of special problems of interest to individual congressmen or the committees. The second is a somewhat smaller agency staffed with lawyers and clerks, the chief function of which is to draft bills, at the request of congressmen or committees, so that all proposed legislation may employ proper legal language.

One of the gains achieved by the Legislative Reorganization Act of 1946 was a substantial increase in the funds available for the staffing of Congress. In particular, authority was given for large increases in the appropriations for the two Congress-wide service agencies just mentioned and for the staffs of the standing committees. But little was done to improve the staff of the individual congressman. The La Follette-Monroney Committee had recommended that every member of Congress be authorized to engage the services of a highly trained expert who would serve him as a sort of "assistant congressman." This proposal was rejected, although separate authority was later voted for senators to hire an "administrative assistant." Congressmen are in need of staff assistants who might serve them much as the "law clerk" serves the Supreme Court Justice. Such assistants might conduct research for congressmen into legislative problems, assemble data, prepare speeches, and help the legislator orient himself with respect to the large social issues of the day. The present top secretary can do a certain amount of this work, but his job as office manager and errand runner forces him to devote much of his time to the *mechanics* of the congressman's problems rather than to their *substance*. He is often able to provide his chief with shrewd political advice, but there is room for a well-paid and loyal assistant to each congressman who would devote his full time to legislative rather than to housekeeping or political problems.

The need to give Congress additional expert assistance is very pertinent to this general consideration of congressional personnel. There can be no denying Congress's tremendous need for scientific information if it is to find wise solutions to the complex legislative problems that confront the nation today. Yet it is highly desirable that the congressman himself remain a nonexpert, an amateur, a representative of ordinary citizens. Accordingly, if we are to resist the unfortunate tendency for congressmen to be dependent on nonelective administrators, lobbyists, and pressure groups for their needed information, or if we are to avoid the eventual filling of congressional seats with professional experts, the case for a more elaborate staff of expert assistants within the legislative establishment itself seems very strong.

It is true that Congress has long been able to draw upon the executive branch of the government for expert advice and help. But administrative officers frequently have a personal or a professional interest in matters before Congress, and it is desirable that Congress have independent sources to which it can also turn for help. However, the possibility that an unnecessary sense of rivalry and jealousy will develop between two such sets of experts is a very real danger. In the end Congress must depend upon the executive branch for a great deal of the expert assistance it needs, and any attempt to build its own staff facilities to a point where they parallel the executive research facilities in size or extent of interests would be a serious mistake.

why a congressman votes the way he does

The third common criticism directed against the individual congressman is that the seeming motivation of his voting on bills is often improper and unfortunate. It is argued that his reasons for his vote on an important measure are apt to be petty and selfish—that he is too much inclined to let party influences control him, or to follow the wishes of lobbyists, or to concentrate his attention on listening for a ground swell from home. Instead of showing sensitivity to the forces that he commonly does, the argument continues, the congressman who would be a statesman should make up his own mind in an honest, impartial way, moved only by considerations of the general public welfare or national concern.

the congressman's sensitivity to local pressures not entirely unfortunate

Undoubtedly this criticism is often a sound one, for at times the voting in Congress on crucial measures of great consequence to the nation is most exasperating to the observer who has the general welfare in mind. The continuous role of localism as a force in the career of the average congressman is almost impossible to exaggerate. Nonetheless, as has been seen, this is not a condition in which there is no good. In a country as large as the United States, both in area and in population, and in a country with tremendous social and economic diversities, it seems desirable that the local point of view should at some point in the governmental process receive careful consideration.

Insofar as generalization about such matters is permissible, it may be said that the presidency tends to provide an influence in the legislative process that reflects considerations truly general or national in scope, the influence of the administrative agencies upon legislation in turn often reveals an awareness of the technical side of a problem, whereas the congressman is sensitive to the local interest in the problem. Since both President and administrator play a part in the making of public policy, the nature of their influence offsets in some degree the force of provincialism which is strong in Congress. A second saving feature to the situation is that in the House and Senate the interest of district or state is offset by the different interests of 434 other districts and 47 other states.

conclusions concerning the congressman

the congressman represents "the people"

Certain conclusions concerning congressional personnel and the force of personality in the legislative process may now be made. In the first place, whatevery else may be said of him, the congressman is usually a humanist. Both in legislating and in rendering service to his constituents by intervening for them with administrative agencies, the congressman is a close friend of the people. At the same time this is one of his strongest points and the source of an undeniable weakness in him. The strong point is that the everyday needs of the people find democratic expression in the congressman's action; the weakness is seen in the congressman's lack of broad and responsible statesmanship in his outlook concerning large problems. The former is a priceless quality; the latter is at times a serious handicap to better government. The legislative process is not perfect, and Congress is in need of much modernization, but in the congressman's strong interest in human beings and in his closeness to the people, we find a condition that is not necessarily to be deplored.

the congressman does have a personality of his own

A second conclusion is that personality plays an important part in the legislative process. In other words, the congressional system allows for a good deal

of personal independence in the member of Congress. It is true that the congressman often votes the way he does because of outside forces acting upon him—
the force of party, of pressure group, and of section. But the degree to which he
is often personally in tune with some if not all of these outside forces must not
be overlooked. The congressman is a typical American—or, more correctly, a
typical product of his own state or district—but he is very much a human being, however much he may be an "average" man. Moreover, he may be a man
of the people and yet have strong personal beliefs and idiosyncrasies. How else
can one explain the striking contrasts to be seen in the two senators from the
same state, even where these two men are members of the same party? There
have been many such contrasts. A decade or so ago the two Democratic senators from New York were Royal Copeland and Robert Wagner. Wagner was a
"fighting liberal," untiring in his support of progressive legislation. Copeland
was a pronounced conservative, loyal to property interests and opposed to reform. At about the same time the two Nebraska senators were George Norris and
Edward Burke. Burke, a Democrat, was conservative; Norris, first a Republican and then an independent, was one of the leading liberals of his time. More
recently, the two Republican senators from Minnesota were Henrik Shipstead
and Joseph Ball. Ball was one of the foremost exponents of internationalism;
Shipstead was a staunch isolationist and one of the two men in the Senate to vote
against ratifying the Charter of the United Nations. Yet it might be said of
these six men that each of them was typical of the state and the people he represented.

Occasionally, a senator, or less often a representative, becomes such a
vigorous personality in the legislative arena that his role as the representative of
a particular group of people is reduced to a minimum. This is sometimes true of a
congressman who comes from a state with a small population and is, in a certain
measure, free from local forces and influences. This condition can be seen in the
work of two senators of modern times who were chairmen of the Senate Foreign
Relations Committee—Key Pitmann of Nevada and William Borah of Idaho.
Borah, particularly, was frequently called "the Nation's Senator." His political
position with the voters of Idaho was so secure that he was able to function to a
high degree as a free agent, and to leave the imprint of his own personality upon
American foreign policy. In Borah's case it becomes necessary to turn away
somewhat from the notion that legislators are typical of their constituencies,
or the inevitable product of local forces that are at work upon them, and, instead,
to recognize that political accident plays a part in the legislative process. For in
a sense it was a mere accident that Borah appeared upon the scene at a given moment and by the force of his character—with considerable help from the seniority
rule—was able to shape American foreign policy so closely to the mold of his
own peculiar ideas. And yet it must be recognized that there was some exaggeration in the idea of Borah as "the Nation's Senator." In many ways he was

typical of Idaho and the western country he represented. On many issues, such as those pertaining to mining, coinage, and monetary policies, he yielded to no congressman in his sensitivity to the interests of his own state. Moreover, even in his foreign policy and his work as chairman of the Foreign Relations Committee, his own particular brand of isolationism was certainly not alien to western thinking on this subject.

The congressman's "independence" is both a virtue and a vice. It is praiseworthy that the legislative system allows individual legislators to express their personalities, to make unique contributions to the work of Congress. Yet, as has been seen, much of this opportunity for individual expression is purchased at the price of a responsible party system in Congress. The unique, colorful, fearless, independent congressman has been much admired. Whether he has served democracy well is a more debatable issue.

much criticism should be directed at Congress, not at congressmen

A third conclusion is that much of the criticism of congressmen as individuals might more properly be directed against Congress as an institution—against its organization and its modes of procedure. Perhaps some congressmen are lacking in background and ability; perhaps they are too typical of the average man or show too much sensitivity to local pressure groups in their voting records in Congress. If so, the fault is to be found at least in part in the inadequate salaries of congressmen, in our decentralized elections, in the absence of strong, well-disciplined national political parties, and in the tradition that the congressman must be a long-time resident of the district he represents. Moreover, the average congressman's lack of a national point of view is one of the consequences of the American tradition of federalism. We cannot have our cake and eat it too. If we desire a national legislature in which national interests are dominant, we must pay the price by centralizing and unifying our institutions to a much greater extent than most Americans have been willing to do up to now.

Likewise, the criticism that the congressman does not work hard enough—or that if he does, he does not accomplish very much—is often unfair in the sense that it is the institution and not the man that is at fault. Congressional organization and procedures are complex and cumbersome; our legislative system needs to be streamlined for a modern age. There is something wrong about Congress at almost every point; there are too many committees, too many meetings of House and Senate, too much long-winded and irrelevant debate, too many checks and balances in the course of a bill through Congress, too much time devoted to inconsequential legislation, and too much emphasis upon seniority. We have too little party discipline and responsibility for legislation, too little vigorous leadership within Congress, too little freedom from the selfish demands and threats of pressure groups, too little help in the form of an adequately trained legislative secretariat, and too little recognition of merit in the filling of important congressional posts. In other words, it seems quite possible that if the present 531 members of Congress could suddenly find themselves serving in an up-to-date, scientifically organized legislature, some, at least, of the existing shortcomings which are attributed to the defects of congressional personnel would promptly disappear.

It is frequently asserted that the congressman, in spite of his genial and intensely human quality, is essentially a frustrated individual who has a chip on his shoulder. Congressional tempers are notoriously bad and antagonisms exist at almost every point along the way. But, again, this quality does not seem to be inherent in the average congressman; instead it perhaps has its origin in some of the institutional difficulties that the legislator is forever encountering. It is reasonable to suppose that the congressman often resents the extreme sensitivity he must show to local interests and pressure groups and wishes that he might acquire more stature as a national statesman; that he is disgusted by the inefficiency of congressional organization and the way in which this inefficiency forces him to waste his time in ineffectual labors; and that he regrets the absence of vigorous, intelligent leadership within Congress and shows a natural reluctance to accept leadership from a rival branch of the government. Here, too, it is quite possible that the congressman's seeming inferiority complex and much of the pettiness that is so often the consequence of such a state of mind are remediable faults that might be cured by alterations in congressional organization or procedure.

This is not to say that the general level of congressional personnel cannot be raised, but it does seem that many of the attacks upon the congressman as an individual are misdirected. It seems fair to say that in his personal—as opposed to his institutional—character, the average congressman is honest, hard working, sincere, and loyal. He has his faults, but some of the worst ones—his partiality toward particular interests, his too great anxiety to earn an extra dollar, the inefficiency of much of his work, and his antagonism towards his leaders, particularly the President, grow out of the system in which he finds himself and are not necessarily native to his own character.

bibliographic note

The *Congressional Directory* (Washington: Government Printing Office), published in several editions each year, is a useful volume giving detailed biographical material on each member of Congress. The *Biographic Directory of the American Congress* (Washington: Government Printing Office, 1928) contains a brief biography of every person who served in the Congress (and its predecessor bodies) between 1774 and 1927. The *Congressional Quarterly* referred to in an earlier bibliographic note is also an excellent source of data on the personnel of Congress.

Interesting information about the human side of congressional activity may be found in "Congressman: A Case History," *Fortune Magazine*, XXVII (April, 1943), 76–80, and in Madge M. McKinley's "The Personnel of the Seventy-seventh Congress," *American Political Science Review*, XXXVI (February, 1942), 67. Jerry Voorhis's *Confessions of a Congressman* (Garden City: Doubleday & Company, 1947) is a revealing account of the life of a congressman by an able, recent member of the House of Representatives.

part 5

---

the administration of justice

the judicial process

*I*T IS the role of the legislature to make public policy in general terms; it is the role of the court to apply that policy to specific individuals and situations. Through the enactment of statutes the legislature fixes standards of conduct which govern human affairs; through the rendering of decisions courts apply these standards in specific cases, resolve conflicts between individual and individual, between government and individual, and thereby render justice. A legislature defines embezzlement as a crime against society, or determines that an employer shall compensate a worker injured on the job. By measuring his conduct against the former statute, a court determines the guilt of a bank clerk who has pilfered funds; under the latter statute a court decides whether an injured worker is entitled to a monetary award.

Such is the theory of the legislative process, the judicial process, and the relationship between them. Moreover, this relationship is pointed to as an important illustration of one of the central principles of our political system: separation of powers. Law is made by a legislative body without regard to specific individuals or a particular situation; it is then applied to such persons and situations by an independent law enforcement branch of government of which courts are a part. In this way the individual in a free society is protected against the ancient danger of arbitrary treatment by the state where the same agency both makes and enforces law.

Unquestionably this theory has had much meaning in practice. Present-day democratic government has come a long way from the day when judges, in the absence of legislators, not only largely made the rules by which men lived but applied those rules to individuals; and also from the day when legislators through the dreaded bill of attainder not only defined crimes generally but pronounced the guilt of specific individuals. Indeed, in the last century or two the belief has been widely held that a judge's function is a strictly administrative one, completely divorced from policy making. For example, Montesquieu says in *The Spirit of the Laws,* one of the great classics of political science: "The national judges are no more than the mouth that pronounces the words of the law, mere passive beings, incapable of moderating either its force or rigour." [1] This position is echoed in the words of Chief Justice Marshall: "Courts are the mere instruments of the law, and can will nothing. . . . Judicial power is never exercised for the purpose of giving effect to the will of the Judge; always for the purpose of giving effect to the will of the Legislature; or, in other words, to the will of the law." [2]

In spite of the political wisdom of these men, and notwithstanding the fact that legislature and court are today quite separate agencies of government performing distinct functions, the exact nature of the judicial function is much more elusive than has thus far been suggested. An absolute separation between policy determination and policy administration, however attractive in theory, is difficult, if not impossible, to obtain in practice.

the nature and growth of law

A better understanding of the judicial process can be had by first examining the nature, the methods of growth, and the forms of law. Law is a most intangible term and one of the most difficult of all political concepts to explain or define. It is perhaps adequate to say that it consists of the rules by which human conduct is governed in an organized society, and, in particular, of those rules which are recognized and enforced by courts. In its origins law represents one of the most striking illustrations of man's quest for certainty in life. From the beginning man has rebelled against the mystery of the universe and has tried to mark out a way of life which can be followed in accordance with known rules. In his dealings with government and with his fellow men he has tried to formulate regulations with respect to basic human relations involving ownership of property, titles to land, making and enforcement of contracts, organization of business enterprises, employment of labor, buying and selling of goods, marriage and divorce, inheritance of estates, and commission of antisocial acts such as murder, arson, and burglary. It is man's desire to know in advance his rights and his responsibilities and to have assurance that government will enforce the regulations upon which these rights and responsibilities rest. Certainty through law is the ideal toward which man strives.

judges as makers of the common law

A careful examination of the Anglo-American tradition reveals that our law had its origins not so much in statutes enacted by legislative bodies as in customs, in church teachings and practices, and in decisions rendered by judges in the absence of legislation. In England during the centuries after the Norman Conquest

[1] Vol. I, Bk. xi, Chap. 6 (Nugent, trans.).
[2] *Osborn* v. *Bank of the United States*, 9 Wheaton 738, 866 (1824).

as conflicts arose between individuals in their daily lives, judges were called upon to referee disputes. In doing so they rendered decisions, based in part upon customary usages and in part upon their own personal wisdom, common sense, or prejudices concerning the problems of life.[3] In this way there came into being a body of judicial rulings, said to be derived from "the common custom of the realm," which became known as *common law*. Common law is thus judge-made law, whereas statute law is made by a legislature. As a result of the gradual development of the common law there came to be recognized rules, in the words of Blackstone, "that the eldest son alone is heir to his ancestor;— that property may be acquired and transferred by writing;—that a deed is of no validity unless sealed and delivered;—that wills should be construed more favorably, and deeds more strictly;—that money lent upon bond is recoverable by action of debt;—that breaking the public peace is an offense, and punishable by fine and imprisonment." [4] All of these rules preceded statutory enactments. Indeed, it is said that legislation as a basis of English law "played no highly significant part . . . until the second quarter of the nineteenth century." [5]

On the other hand, statutory law where it exists is always superior to judge-made rules of common law. When an English or American legislature has chosen to do so, it has always been able to enact a statute specifically altering the common law. It has already been noted that the adoption of the Sherman Antitrust Act by Congress in 1890 altered certain common-law rules concerning monopoly. One of the most striking changes in the common law made by modern statutes concerns the degree to which an employer is liable for injuries suffered by his workers while on the job. The common law excluded such liability where an injury resulted solely from the negligence of a fellow worker and the employer was not at fault. Today, however, in the interest of safeguarding workers against the hazards of industrial employment, statutes almost universally provide that the employer shall compensate an injured worker under such circumstances.[6]

the principle of stare decisis

At an early stage in the development of common law, the quest for certainty led to the appearance of the rule of *stare decisis* ("adhere to the decisions"). Thus the importance of precedent in the application of the law came to be recognized. Where a case had its counterpart in previous litigation, the presumption was that

---

[3] Blackstone in his famous *Commentaries on the Laws of England*, originally published in 1765, emphasized the extent to which English judges drew upon custom in evolving rules of law. Later scholars have argued that these judges frequently disregarded custom and invented new rules where by so doing, for example, the interests of the King, whose agents they were, could be advanced. See J. A. Corry, *Elements of Democratic Government* (New York: Oxford University Press, 1947), p. 320.

[4] Blackstone, *Commentaries* (Chase, 3d ed.; New York: Banks & Brothers, 1896), I, 68.

[5] Corry, *Elements of Democratic Government*, p. 321.

[6] For example, see the Federal Employers Liability Act of 1908, 45 U.S.C. §§ 51–59.

the decision in the earlier case should govern the disposition of the later one. In this way an effort was made to give the administration of justice and the growth of the law a historical continuity—as opposed to a system in which judges might try to render justice in each case anew without regard to what had gone before. By means of *stare decisis* "as cases grew in number and variety they became a storehouse of knowledge and understanding, representing the cumulative experience of the bench in resolving the tangles of human affairs." [7]

The judge in the Anglo-American system has thus had the double function of deciding the specific case at hand in a just way, and of declaring and following general rules of law. The two functions are closely related, for in the long run the rendering of justice in individual cases is furthered by the following of fixed, known rules. But in any given case, to follow a fixed rule so that there may be stability in the law may make it difficult to deal justly with the parties to the dispute; or conversely, disposing of the case fairly may necessitate departing somewhat from established law.

code law in contrast with common law

In the civil-law countries of the European continent, law is said to be found in written codes rather than in court decisions. Each case is decided by direct reference back to the written rule rather than to precedents established in earlier decisions in similar cases. Actually, there is reason to believe that the two systems are more alike in practice than they are in theory. Precedent does play a part in European courts, for judges can hardly be expected to disregard their own previous rulings. Precedent does give way to the ends of justice in Anglo-American courts, for judges are bound at times to let the human factor outweigh the force of continuity in judicial decisions.

the development of equity

One of the most significant and revealing chapters in the growth of the Anglo-American legal system is that which tells the story of the supplementary system of law known as *equity*. Through the centuries the common law had developed as a judge-made, national system of law covering most of the social and economic problems existing in English society. But gradually the common law tended to harden into a more or less permanent mold with a rather precise set of forms of action which enabled people to go to court for relief only in standard situations. This rigidity prevented the common-law courts from hearing cases which lay outside the fixed pattern. But since the English social system was still a fluid, evolving one, strong pressures arose for the establishment of judicial machinery and legal rules which would make it possible to obtain justice in situations where the common law was seemingly inadequate. Accordingly it came

---

[7] Walton H. Hamilton, "Judicial Process," *Encyclopaedia of the Social Sciences*, VIII, 450, 452–453.

about that petitions to the King for justice in cases where the regular courts were unable or unwilling to provide relief were referred increasingly to a member of the King's executive council, known as the Chancellor. Although his duties had originally been of a quite different character, his department, the Chancery, came to be recognized as a court, separate and apart from the common-law courts and possessed of jurisdiction over cases which the latter could not hear. For example, the chief common-law remedy in civil suits was an award of money damages to compensate for a wrong, and the common law could do little or nothing to prevent or abate the wrong itself. Thus if a man's neighbor threatened to cut down his valuable shade tree, he could seek no help from a common-law court until the threat had been carried out, when he might sue for damages. Equity, however, offered a form of direct relief in the writ of injunction. Faced with a threat of irreparable damage, such as the loss of his prized shade tree, a man could go to the Chancery and ask for a restraining order forbidding his neighbor to cut down the tree. Serving as a sanction to enforcement of the order was the threat of a citation for contempt of court.

The origin of rules of equity, like the origin of common-law rules, remains obscure. Since there were no precedents to follow, early equity cases were said to be decided on the basis of "natural justice." But equity, like the common law, soon began to accumulate precedents. Under the principle of *stare decisis* these rulings presently had the same vitality in equity which similar rulings had in the common law.

For many centuries courts of law and courts of equity remained separate. Different procedures were followed. For example, equity cases were tried without a jury and on appeal were tried anew both as to the facts and the law, whereas common-law cases were tried with a jury and on appeal were subject to a partial review as to questions of law only.

Equity was a force for reform in the growth of the law. Appearing at a time when the common law had seemingly lost its power to change and expand, equity provided the element of development which must be present in the legal system of a dynamic society. In more recent times this need for growth in the law has been met in good part by the modern legislature which revises traditional law and adapts it to contemporary conditions through the enactment of statutes. But at the time equity was filling the breach and keeping alive the vital force in English law, Parliament had not yet become a true lawmaking body.

By the middle of the nineteenth century the historic reasons which had brought about the existence of these two rival systems of law administered by separate courts had ceased to exist. In both England and the United States the gap between the two systems is bridged and the same courts are given jurisdiction to hear cases in both law and equity. Indeed, under Article Three of the American Constitution the federal courts had such jurisdiction from 1789 on.

Although equity is still regarded in the technical sense as a separate body of rules, it is now enforced by most courts simultaneously with law, and largely in accordance with the same procedures as are followed in law cases.[8]

ideal and reality in the administration of justice

Both the common law and equity tried to give expression to the ideal of certainty by providing, through the *leading case*, known and definite rules which could and would be followed in settling the human conflicts which occur in a civilized society. This ideal was and is one of the highest aspirations of man, but the reality has always fallen somewhat short of the ideal. How wide is the gulf between ideal and reality? To what extent do judges automatically apply fixed rules in deciding cases? Or contrariwise, to what extent do they enjoy an element of personal choice in the decisions they render?

do judges exercise discretionary power?

Lawyers, scholars, and laymen have long differed in the answers they give to those questions. At one extreme are the assertions of Montesquieu and Marshall that judges exercise no discretion at all but always decide cases in strict accordance with established rules. Other authorities have gone to the opposite extreme. For example, Professor Fred Rodell of the Law School of Yale University has argued that most

> legal principles . . . are couched in such vague, general language that they cannot possibly be guides to a specific decision on a specific matter; practically every legal principle . . . can be countered with another principle or exception which contradicts in whole or in part the first principle; scarcely ever does a court decision necessarily follow from the principle or concept which is said to dictate it; and in just about every instance, the "controlling" principle, or principles, resembles nothing so much as a loose rationalization of what a court orders done, applied after the decision is made.[9]

Jerome Frank, long one of the leading scholars of the law, and now a federal judge, says that the belief that there can be certainty in the law is a "basic myth." "Why do men seek unrealizable certainty in the law?" he asks. "Because . . . they have not yet relinquished the childish need for an authoritative father and unconsciously have tried to find in the law a substitute for those attributes of firmness, sureness, certainty and infallibility ascribed in childhood to the father." [10] Some of our greatest jurists have admitted how uncertain the law

---

[8] See Walter Wheeler Cook, "Equity," *Encyclopaedia of the Social Sciences*, V, 582.
[9] Fred Rodell, *Woe Unto You, Lawyers!* (New York: Harcourt Brace and Company, 1939), pp. 149–150.
[10] From *Law and the Modern Mind* by Jerome Frank, p. 21. Copyright, 1949, by Coward-McCann, Inc.

can be at times. Chancellor Kent made this clear over a century ago when he explained in a personal letter just how he arrived at a decision: "He first made himself 'master of the facts.' Then (he wrote) 'I saw where justice lay, and the moral sense decided the court half the time; I then sat down to search the authorities. . . . I might once in a while be embarrassed by a technical rule, but I *almost always found principles suited to my view of the case. . . .*' " [11]

Perhaps the most careful weighing of the element of certainty in the law has been made by a great judge of the New York Court of Appeals and of the United States Supreme Court, Benjamin Cardozo. In two series of lectures delivered at the Law School of Yale University in 1921 and 1923 he considered "The Nature of the Judicial Process" and "The Growth of the Law." In the very first of these lectures he stated: "I take judge-made law as one of the existing realities of life." [12] Later he said: "I was much troubled in spirit, in my first years upon the bench, to find how trackless was the ocean on which I had embarked. I sought for certainty. I was oppressed and disheartened when I found that the quest for it was futile. . . . As the years have gone by, and as I have reflected more and more upon the nature of the judicial process, I have become reconciled to the uncertainty, because I have grown to see it as inevitable." [13]

the inevitability of uncertainty

Why did Benjamin Cardozo reconcile himself to the inevitability of uncertainty in the law? Why does the judicial process necessarily involve the exercise of some measure of discretion by judges in the deciding of cases? Why cannot the law always provide a clear answer to any human problem that arises?

uncertainty in law reflects the complexity of society

Answers to these and similar questions are not difficult to provide, once a fundamental misconception is cleared away. The misconception lies in the belief that modern life can be reduced to a series of known, standard situations or problems, which can then be controlled by fixed rules. Or to put it differently, it is fallacious to believe that laws can ever be sufficiently numerous, and sufficiently detailed, to provide advance yardsticks against which to measure any human conflict that may conceivably arise in a society as complex as our own. The total body of law—statutory, judge-made, or otherwise—has become very extensive and detailed indeed. But life in our present-day industrial civilization has become so varied and intricate that no body of law, however complete, can possibly provide a specific rule for the settlement of any problem that may arise. The law can be,

[11] *Ibid.*, p. 104. Italics presumably by Frank.
[12] *The Nature of the Judicial Process* (New Haven: Yale University Press, 1921), p. 10. The excerpts quoted from this work are used by permission of the Yale University Press, publishers.
[13] *Ibid.*, p. 166.

and is, sufficiently complete to deal in a general way with all the basic, traditional problems that occur in society. But it cannot be so detailed as to make its application to any particular variant of a standard problem an automatic operation. Any attempt to make law so detailed would result in a collection of rules so technical and extensive as to be utterly unmanageable. For one thing, such a collection would be so complicated that few if any men could understand it or keep its rules in mind. Thus one of the advantages of law—that it be known in advance of its application—would be lost. Moreover, it would be so precise as to defeat the central purpose of the law—a basis for justice in resolving the tangled affairs of men. If law is to provide the means for a just solution of each case as it arises, there must be some play in the joints, some element of flexibility. Human beings are not always predictable and rational. Their affairs can become so confused and disordered that a just solution to a specific problem must often, in part at least, be an improvised and personal one.

precedents and counterprecedents.

Because of the nature of life, law in England and America is not a body of consistent, precise, scientific principles. The great maxims of the law which have evolved through the centuries have without exception come to be qualified; precedent has been offset by counterprecedent; judges have been granted a very great measure of discretion—not for the sake of making them powerful and influential public officers, but to give them that element of choice in their work necessary if the judicial process is to serve the ends of justice. Law must always be a mixture of rule and counterrule, and, for that reason, less than completely certain.

Benjamin Cardozo tells of a case which the New York Court of Appeals was called upon to decide, in which it was necessary to weigh precedent and counterprecedent very carefully. Had the law applicable to the case been completely unequivocal it might have been difficult if not impossible to render a just decision. The case was that of *Riggs* v. *Palmer,* in which the court decided that a murderer could not receive property bequeathed to him by the will of the person he had killed. Cardozo points to the conflicting legal principles which bore upon this situation:

> There was the principle of the binding force of a will. . . . That principle, pushed to the limit of its logic, seemed to uphold the title of the murderer. There was the principle that civil courts may not add to the pains and penalties of crimes. That, pushed to the limit of its logic, seemed again to uphold his title. But over against these was another principle, of greater generality, its roots deeply fastened in universal sentiments of justice, the principle that no man should profit from his own inequity or take advantage of his own wrong. The logic of this principle prevailed over the logic of the others. . . . One path was followed, another closed, because of the conviction in the judicial mind that the one selected led to justice. . . . In the

end, the principle that was thought to be the most fundamental, to represent the larger and deeper social interests, put its competitors to flight.[14]

law and changing times

The necessity of allowing an element of flexibility in the law so that individual cases may be decided justly in the light of their subtle differences is one reason why law can never be completely certain. A further reason for flexibility—and thus uncertainty—is that law must be kept adaptable to the needs of changing times. Society does not stand still but forever changes. New problems appear; old problems lose some, and occasionally all, of their importance, or their character changes to such an extent that new solutions must be found. The law of corporations must be adjusted to the enterprises utilizing atomic energy; the law of bankruptcy must be altered to ease the plight of unprofitable but socially useful enterprises; the law of communications must be adjusted to the needs of radio and television; the law of property must be broadened to include the use of the air for aviation purposes. Were law to consist of a fixed and complete body of rules for the governing of the affairs of men promulgated at any given moment, it would begin to lose its adequacy from that moment forward. Moreover, any thought that the entire body of law can be revised in formal fashion at regular intervals to take care of the problems of changing times is completely unrealistic. Social progress is erratic and uneven; change is continuous but unpredictable. Instead of keeping the law up-to-date through a series of periodic reformulations, it can be made to serve the needs of a changing society only through continuous growth.

the influence of past and present in the law

Accordingly, law at any given moment hovers between past and present. Justice Holmes has said: "A system of law at any time is the resultant of present needs and present notions of what is wise and right on the one hand, and, on the other, of rules handed down from earlier states of society and embodying needs and notions which more or less have passed away." [15] It goes without saying that the influences of past and present in the law frequently clash vigorously. At times a society is tempted to slough off the influence of the past and to make law exclusively a matter of contemporary rules for the solution of current problems. But it quickly realizes that to do so would mean dispensing with legal continuity and thus any measure of certainty beyond the limits of the fleeting moment. At other times it is tempted to emphasize the force of the past so as to take maximum advantage of man's experience and accumulated wisdom. But then it

---

[14] Cardozo, *Nature of the Judicial Process*, pp. 40–42.

[15] Oliver Wendell Holmes, Jr., *Collected Legal Papers* (New York: Harcourt, Brace and Company, 1920), p. 156. Reprinted by permission of Harcourt, Brace and Company, publishers.

realizes that this would give continuity and certainty but endanger the dynamic quality of civilization. The conflict between past and present in the law must be settled in a less sensational way than by giving one a dominant position over the other. There must always be a large measure of the past in the law of the present; but so, too, must the law of the present yield to current needs and pressures. Cardozo has said: "We shall have to feel our way here as elsewhere in the law. Somewhere between worship of the past and exaltation of the present, the path of safety will be found." [16]

the law of the legislature and the law of the court

Further attention must now be given to the suggestion that the degree of uncertainty in the law, and thus of judicial discretion, can be reduced by increasing the measure of legislative lawmaking. There are two possibilities for increased legislative control: one, that the legislature provide, initially, a detailed and precise statute for each aspect of human conduct requiring legal supervision; the other, that the legislature revise each of these statutes at regular and frequent intervals, thus keeping the law up-to-date through legislative rather than judicial change.

can code law replace common law?

There can be no doubt about the constitutional or political power of a British or an American legislature to replace judge-made law by statute law. Conceivably a legislature may enact a comprehensive series of statutes, superseding all other evidences of law, and encompassing the entire area of human problems which necessitate social control. Moreover, it may thereafter revise these statutes at regular intervals, amending them in the light of new problems and changed conditions. In short, the idea of a code of law is completely feasible. It is entirely possible for the legislature to seek to replace judge-made law with a statutory codification which endeavors to be complete, logically arranged, and concise and clear. Indeed, more than one hundred years ago a movement looking toward codification of the law began in the American states, and from 1873 on, Congress has experimented with the codification of federal law.

But there can be a wide gap between the enactment of a legislative code and the complete replacement of court law by statute law. The federal code, for instance, is little more than an attempt to rearrange existing statutes systematically under topic headings so as to bring together all related statutes dealing with the same problem or subject, regardless of the date of their enactment. There has been no attempt to incorporate in the federal code rules supplanting the decisions of federal courts and hence to make it unnecessary to refer back to such decisions in order to ascertain the law. It is true that in European *civil-law*

---

[16] Cardozo, *Nature of the Judicial Process*, p. 160.

countries, and to a limited extent in certain American states, a legal "code" replaces decision law. Civil-law countries operate upon the theory that judges, in deciding cases, refer back in each new case to the pertinent rule as stated in the code, rather than to the decision in a *leading case* under the principle of *stare decisis.*

But again reality departs somewhat from theory. It is impossible to make statutory law truly comprehensive, whether in the form of a systematic code or in the form of a series of unrelated enactments. Gaps there will inevitably be which courts must fill in by following rules of their own making in deciding disputes between men. And where the legislature itself eventually fills in such a gap, the statute can never be made so detailed and complete that no discretion remains to those who must interpret and apply it.

the law of the legislature and the law of the court are inextricably mixed

In the end what passes for law in society is an inextricable mixture of statutes, common law, and equity. There are several reasons why that is so. In the first place, when a legislature passes a statute it may be strongly influenced by common law and attempt merely to give more definite form to an essentially similar rule originally made by judges and long applied by them. Cardozo has said: "In the everyday transactions of life the average man is governed, not by statute, but by common law, or at most by statute built upon a substratum of common law, modifying, in details only, the common law foundation." [17]

In the second place, even where a statute does break with common law and states a public policy at least partially new, the influence of the common law may still be strongly felt in the administration of the policy. The statute will sooner or later be subject to judicial interpretation. In Dean Roscoe Pound's words: "It is not what the legislature desires, but what the courts regard as juridically permissible that in the end becomes law. Statutes give way before the settled habits of legal thinking which we call the common law. Judges and jurists do not hesitate to assert that there are extraconstitutional limits to legislative power which put fundamental common law dogmas beyond the reach of statutes." [18]

In the third place, even where, following the enactment of a statute, a court called upon to enforce it is motivated by no wish to reformulate the law in line with ancient doctrines of the common law, there is almost always a necessity for further growth. What happens is something like this: Years pass and the courts render hundreds and even thousands of decisions under this statute. As the years

---

[17] Benjamin N. Cardozo, *The Growth of the Law* (New Haven: Yale University Press, 1924), p. 136. The excerpts quoted from this work are used by permission of the Yale University Press, publishers.

[18] Roscoe Pound, "Law in Books and Law in Action," *American Law Review,* XLIV (January–February, 1910), 27.

go by conditions change and new problems of application arise. The courts do the best they can with the statute, interpreting it in the light of new conditions and problems, thereby adding to its meaning. As a result, the law that actually operates and controls is something more than the original statute. It is this statute plus many important court decisions clarifying and extending its meaning in the absence of any specific or further action by the legislature. These decisions supplementing the original statute become a part of the common law in its broader sense. Thus, in spite of the greatly increased number of statutes passed by legislatures in modern times, and in spite of the enactment of systematic codes of law, courts still play an important, seemingly inevitable, part in the lawmaking process.

It is clear that judge and legislator both have policy-making roles to play in a democratic society. In an admirable passage in *The Growth of the Law,* Cardozo points to the way in which statute and court decision intermesh to make possible progress in social policy:

> Justice is not to be taken by storm. She is to be wooed by slow advances. Substitute statute for decision, and you shift the center of authority, but add no quota of inspired wisdom. If legislation is to take the place of the creative action of courts, a legislative committee must stand back of us at every session, a sort of supercourt itself. . . . I do not mean to deprecate unduly the value of the statute as an instrument of reform. Legislation can eradicate a cancer, right some hoary wrong, correct some definitely established evil, which defies the feebler remedies, the distinctions and the fictions, familiar to the judicial process. Legislation, too, can sum up at times and simplify the conclusions reached by courts, and give them new validity. Even then, its relief is provisional and temporary. The cycle is unending. "Code is followed by [judicial] commentary, and commentary by [legislative] revision, and thus the task is never done." The adaptation of rule or principle to changing combinations of events demands the creative action of the judge. You may praise our work or criticize it. You may leave us with the name we have, or tag us with some other label, arbitrators or assessors. The process is here to stay.[19]

the courts as fact-finding agencies

Up to now this discussion of the judicial process has emphasized the extent to which judges have a lawmaking function. It is important to recognize that courts are also fact-finding agencies. When a trial court is called upon to decide a case —be it a civil case in which John Doe is seeking relief against Richard Roe in some private conflict between the two men, or a criminal case in which the state is prosecuting an individual who stands accused of murder—there are two major

---

[19] Cardozo, *The Growth of the Law,* pp. 133–135. Reprinted by permission of the Yale University Press, publishers.

determinations which must be made. The law applicable to the situation must be singled out and applied to the case; and the facts of the situation itself must be ascertained with as much accuracy as possible. Jerome Frank, a federal court of appeals judge, has attempted to describe this twofold operation by means of a simple formula. He has written:

> For convenience, let us symbolize a legal rule by the letter R, the facts of a case by the letter F, and the court's decision of that case by the letter D. We can then crudely schematize the conventional theory of how courts operate by saying
>
> $$R \times F = D.$$
>
> In other words, according to the conventional theory, a decision is a product of an R and an F. If, as to any lawsuit, you know the R and the F, you should, then, know what the D will be.[20]

Enough has already been said to show that the determination of the R factor in a case involves a good deal of uncertainty and necessitates the exercise of much discretion by judges. Judge Frank insists that the same thing is true of the fact-finding aspect of a case and that students of the judicial process have not paid sufficient attention to this part of the work of courts. He says: " . . . it is as unjust to apply the 'right' rule to the wrong facts as to apply the 'wrong' rule. Or, rather, no rule can be the 'right' rule, the just rule, in any specific law suit, if applied to facts that did not occur, to unreal, spurious facts." [21] Moreover, he points out that fact finding is very largely the function of trial courts, whereas courts of appeals are very largely concerned with determining the correct rules to apply in given cases. And he adds:

> Since . . . the specific applications of the rules depend on fact-finding, the upper courts, which function primarily as guardians of the rules, have far less importance in our legal system than the trial courts. In the first place, the overwhelming majority of cases are not appealed; probably 95 per cent of all cases end in the trial courts. In the second place, since, in most of the few cases that are appealed, the upper courts accept the trial court's fact-findings, the trial courts decide the fate of, say, 98 per cent of all cases.[22]

Having called attention to this distinction between the work of the trial courts and that of the appellate courts—between the fact-finding and the rule-finding aspects of the judicial process—it is Judge Frank's contention that there is at least as much uncertainty about the outcome of a case at the level of the trial court as there is at the level of the appellate court. And he argues that in-

---

[20] Jerome Frank, *Courts on Trial* (Princeton: Princeton University Press, 1950), p. 14. The excerpts quoted from this work are used by permission of the Princeton University Press, publishers.

[21] *Ibid.*, p. 33.

[22] *Ibid.*, p. 33.

creased attention should be given to trial courts with a view toward making them more satisfactory fact-finding agencies. After all, a fact is a fact. There may be good reason why the rule-making function of the courts can never be made a clear-cut, predictable operation in every case. But there is no reason why courts should not become more efficient agencies for the determination of the true facts pertaining to a case.

the jury as a fact-finding agency

Much of the fact-finding work of the trial court is centered in the jury. In theory the judge of the lower court "presides" over the trial of a case. He helps the parties to the case define the legal points at issue, he sees to it that evidence and arguments are presented in accordance with prescribed rules of procedure, he advises the jury concerning its duties, and he pronounces sentence or renders a judgment after the jury has returned its verdict. But it is the jury in which the discretionary power rests, for it is the function of the jury to pass on the conflicting evidence in a case and to determine the "true facts." In practice, it is quite clear that juries also apply a good deal of law, for in the business of deciding cases it is utterly impossible to keep law and fact entirely separate.

That juries are unpredictable agencies is clearly apparent to anyone who follows the work of courts closely. Again and again, newspaper reporters, lawyers, and other persons present in courtrooms during the course of important trials are unable to predict jury verdicts with any high degree of accuracy. In other words, the facts of a case, as well as the law, are often sufficiently confused that each of the twelve members of the jury is compelled to apply his individual judgment and wisdom to the situation as the group tries to return a fair verdict.

This uncertain aspect of jury decisions has been variously regarded as both a strong point and a weak point in the judicial process. Judge Frank sees the jury as an outmoded and unsuccessful means of determining facts in a case: "To my mind a better instrument than the usual jury trial could scarcely be imagined for achieving uncertainty, capriciousness, lack of uniformity, disregard of the [rules,] and unpredictability of decisions." And he quotes Carl Becker, the noted historian, to this effect: "Trial by jury, as a method of determining facts, is antiquated . . . and inherently absurd—so much so that no lawyer, judge, scholar, prescription-clerk, cook, or mechanic in a garage would ever think for a moment of employing that method for determining the facts in any situation that concerned him." [23]

On the other hand, the discretionary power exercised by juries has sometimes been viewed as a means of reaching just decisions because it operates as a counterforce to strict legal rules in the disposition of cases. Many years ago Judge Frank himself wrote:

---

[23] *Ibid.*, pp. 123, 124.

[The jury system] preserves the basic legal dogma in appearance and at the same time (albeit crudely and bunglingly) circumvents it in fact, to the end of permitting that pliancy and elasticity which is impossible according to the dogma but which life demands. . . . While men want the law to be father-like, aloof, stern, coldly impartial, they also want it to be flexible, understanding, humanized. The judges too emphatically announce that they are serving the first of these wants. The public takes the judges seriously, assumes that the judges will apply hard-and-fast law to human facts, and turns to the jury for relief from such dehumanized justice.[24]

And Justice Holmes, while observing that he had not found juries "specially inspired for the discovery of truth," or "freer from prejudice" than judges, noted that they "introduce into their verdict a certain amount—a very large amount, so far as I have observed—of popular prejudice, and thus keep the administration of the law in accord with the wishes and feeling of the community."[25]

the limits of judicial discretion

It is important not to exaggerate the measure of judicial discretion, of uncertainty concerning the outcome of cases. This is true whether one is thinking of the discretion which courts exercise in choosing among the principles and counterprinciples of the common law, or of the choices open to them when they apply statutes to factual situations and adapt them to changing needs. For example, Cardozo, while emphasizing judge-made law as a reality of life, was careful to delimit the discretionary power which he believed judges in fact exercise: "In countless litigations, the law is so clear that judges have no discretion. They have the right to legislate within gaps, but often there are no gaps."[26] And speaking of his experience as a member of the highest court of appeals in New York State, he reported: "Of the cases that come before the court in which I sit, a majority, I think, could not, with semblance of reason, be decided in any way but one. The law and its application alike are plain."[27] Later he said: "Nine-tenths, perhaps more, of the cases that come before a court are predetermined —predetermined in the sense that they are predestined—their fate pre-established by inevitable laws that follow them from birth to death. The range of free activity is relatively small."[28] It is doubtful whether Cardozo ten years later, as a member of the United States Supreme Court, would have estimated the range of judicial discretion so narrowly. Nonetheless, it is significant that at the

[24] From *Law and the Modern Mind* by Jerome Frank, pp. 172–175. Copyright, 1949, by Coward-McCann, Inc.

[25] Holmes, *Collected Legal Papers*, pp. 237–238.

[26] Cardozo, *Nature of the Judicial Process*, p. 129.

[27] *Ibid.*, p. 164.

[28] Cardozo, *Growth of the Law*, p. 60.

same time (1921 and 1923) that Cardozo insisted that judges must participate in policy making, he chose also to emphasize the limits within which judges legislate.

One such limit to judicial lawmaking, Cardozo pointed out, is the duty of the judge to seek out and follow the will of the legislature if he can find any expression of legislative intent. And where such an expression cannot be found, Cardozo asserted that the judge should try to follow the will of the community rather than his own personal predilections:

> When the legislature has spoken and declared one interest superior to another, the judge must subordinate his personal or subjective estimate of value to the estimate thus declared. . . . Even when the legislature has not spoken, he is to regulate his estimate of values by objective rather than subjective standards, by the thought and will of the community rather than by his own idiosyncrasies of conduct and belief.[29]

Notice has been taken of the difficulties which prevent legislatures from keeping a systematic watch over judicial interpretation and application of statutes. But here, too, it is possible to overestimate the extent of judicial freedom. Admittedly a legislature cannot through a *continuous* series of amending statutes pass judgment upon every court decision affecting the administration of an original statute. But it can keep track of the main lines of policy development by the courts and *periodically* check this process through further statutory enactments. In the long run, it would seem that a legislature has both the duty and the opportunity to keep watch over the main lines of social policy and ultimately to speak the final word as to any major issue of statute interpretation which may arise in the courts.

What conclusion should be drawn from the knowledge that the law is less than completely certain at every point, that courts necessarily exercise some measure of discretion in deciding cases, and that judges upon occasion are influenced in their search for facts and law by their own prejudices, and even intuitions?

In attempting to find answers to questions such as this one the student should remember that all human institutions and processes are imperfect. But because they fall short of man's highest ideals and aspirations it is not necessarily wise or desirable that existing arrangements be rejected. It is important that the citizen avoid an attitude of naïveté concerning law and the courts, but it does not follow that he must adopt an attitude of cynicism toward these matters. It is significant that modern students of the judicial process, such as Holmes, Cardozo, Pound, and Frankfurter, while emphasizing the element of choice and the importance of personality in the work of courts, do not reject the validity of the basic ideal of life under law. Instead, they conclude that we should put our

---

[29] *Ibid.*, pp. 94–95.

information to work in an effort to secure a better approximation of the idea. "Much will be gained," Dean Pound has written, "when courts have perceived what it is they are doing, and are thus enabled to address themselves consciously to doing it the best that they may." [30] Likewise, much will be gained when citizens perceive what it is that courts are doing and direct their energies toward seeing that the job is done as best it may.

bibliographic note

The two little volumes by Benjamin N. Cardozo, *The Nature of the Judicial Process* (New Haven: Yale University Press, 1921) and *The Growth of the Law* (New Haven: Yale University Press, 1924), originally delivered as lectures at the Yale School of Law, are perhaps the most revealing descriptions of the judicial process ever made. Oliver Wendell Holmes's *Collected Legal Papers* (New York: Harcourt, Brace and Company, 1920) and Felix Frankfurter's *Law and Politics* (New York: Harcourt, Brace and Company, 1939) are also good sources of information about the judicial process. These are, however, collections of essays and do not examine the judicial process in the systematic way that the Cardozo volumes do. Moreover, the essays by Frankfurter were written before he became a judge. A contemporary federal judge, Jerome Frank, has for many years insisted that scholars have given too much attention to the work of appellate courts and that the work of trial courts has been neglected. His *Courts on Trial* (Princeton: Princeton University Press, 1949) is a collection of scattered writings in which this point of view is asserted and in which the author tries to remedy the shortcoming by analyzing the organization and work of trial courts.

Raymond Moley and Schuyler C. Wallace have edited a volume of *The Annals* of the American Academy of Political and Social Science entitled *The Administration of Justice*, CLXVII (May, 1933), which contains articles on various aspects of the judicial process.

See also the bibliographic note to Chapter 3, "Constitutionalism and the Rule of Law."

---

[30] Roscoe Pound, "The Theory of Judicial Decision," *Harvard Law Review*, XXXVI (June, 1923), 959.

the structure and jurisdiction
of the courts

An OUTSTANDING characteristic of American courts is the high de-gree of independence which they enjoy. Insofar as this independence refers to the status of the courts as coequal branches of the government, it is firmly estab-lished in constitutional law as one of the basic illustrations of the doctrine of separation of powers. But the independence of the courts is sometimes thought of as going well beyond this. To many people a court is an agency that has little if anything to do with other agencies of government. It is viewed as a separate government, existing entirely apart from all other political machinery. At times this idea is pushed to such an extreme that the court is thought of not as part of the government, but as an independent social agency which performs a function quite different from that of government. Even judges themselves seem occa-sionally to fall into this manner of thinking and to talk as if they were not pub-lic officers; they complain about the expanding bureaucracy or the regulatory function of government as though they were themselves private citizens.

To what extent are these varying views of the independence of courts valid? Are they helpful as a means of understanding the organization and work of the courts, or do they give a misleading impression? Straightforward answers to questions of this type are not easy to give. In part, emphasis upon the independ-ence of the courts is valid and helpful; in part, it results in misunderstanding.

the independence of the courts

In the development of Anglo-American political institutions it is historically true that courts emerged more or less independently of other governmental machin-ery, even preceding legislatures in origin. Moreover, they have in a sense per-formed a function which is quite different from that of other governmental agencies.

Considered first from the standpoint of organization, the independence of the Anglo-American courts can best be seen by contrasting them with the courts of western Europe that have developed from Roman civil-law traditions. On the Continent the judiciary is but one of the many arms of the executive branch of government. In most countries a *ministry of justice* controls the organization of the courts. This ministry is one of the regular administrative agencies of government, like our own Department of State or Post Office Department, and like the Secretary of State or Postmaster General, the head of the ministry is a member of the executive cabinet. Judges in this system are a part of the civil service. That is to say, a man seeks judicial office much as he would employment in the foreign service, by meeting technical qualifications and gaining appointment at a junior level in a career service. He gains advancement by being an efficient and cooperative worker in a vast administrative bureaucracy, much as a junior attaché in the foreign service may work his way up through the ranks and ultimately receive an important assignment. When compared with its European counterpart the American court stands out as an agency of great independence. It is in no sense just another administrative department. The national government does contain a Department of Justice, whose head, the Attorney General, is a member of the President's cabinet, but the department is charged not with the *trial* but with the *apprehension* and *prosecution* of those who violate the federal laws.

The American constitutional system preserves the independence of the courts in several ways. At the federal level judges are appointed to office for life, not from a pool of civil service employees, but directly from the nation's legal profession or from its political service. Once appointed, such a judge is subject to no control by a supervisory administrative agency. Apart from a modicum of control within the judicial hierarchy itself or from the extremely remote possibility of impeachment by the legislature, he is free to fulfill his constitutional duties within the limits of his own ability and integrity. By the terms of the Constitution he is even protected against diminution of his salary throughout his period of office.

From the standpoint of function the American court is also strikingly independent. In western Europe the business of deciding cases and rendering justice is viewed as one of the many administrative activities of government. Government is expected to provide this service much as it is expected to deliver mail, build highways, or aid the needy and aged. In England and America the business of deciding cases is viewed as a unique operation. It is almost as though two governments exist to serve the people: one, made up of the legislative and executive branches, which, in a continuous, systematic way, makes law, renders a wide variety of public services, and regulates society; the other, consisting of the courts, which functions periodically, settling conflicts between private citizens when asked by them to do so, and pronouncing judgment against transgressors when asked to do so by the prosecuting arm of the government. The former government is a political one, which in a democracy means that it must be closely controlled by the people so that it will continuously represent them and their wishes. The latter government is a nonpolitical one in the sense that it is detached from and is above the conflict of social interests. It is an impartial agency which stands ready to referee conflicts among men without bias and without any direct responsibility to the citizenry.

the dependence of the courts

For all its detachment from the political scene, it is easy to exaggerate the independence of the American court. For one thing, as has already been seen, separation of powers is not a pure or isolated principle; it is offset by the counterprinciple of checks and balances. Accordingly, with regard to such matters as its structure, its jurisdiction to hear cases, the appointment and removal of its personnel, and provision of its operating funds, the American court is frequently subject to a very considerable measure of control by legislature and executive.

Moreover, in the business of deciding cases and rendering justice it is impossible for courts to preserve absolutely their aloofness from the rest of the political process or to confine their labors to the function of a referee. Inevitably the judge plays a part in lawmaking. In so doing he becomes a rival of the political branches of government and necessarily subjects himself to a measure of popular control in a democratic society.

In still another sense the judicial process is but an integrated part of the total governmental process. Although we refuse to accept the European view of the court as one of many agencies serving the people, the fact remains that it provides a necessary public service much as do the Army and Navy, the Department of State, or our post offices, police forces, and welfare departments, to mention only a few of the infinite variety of governmental agencies rendering direct services to the people. For this reason, it seems fair to hold courts to the same standards of efficiency and service which other political agencies must meet. Otherwise, undue emphasis upon judicial independence or untouchability might easily result in a failure to safeguard and promote the public interest for which courts exist.

And yet it will not do to classify the court finally as an administrative agency performing just another function of government. To settle the conflicts of men on a basis of justice was one of the first functions of government, and efforts always have been made, particularly in democratic countries, to maintain not only the efficiency of the judicial service but its integrity and impartiality as well. Hence the Anglo-American tradition of the court as an agency which exists apart from the ordinary bureaucratic machinery of government. This is a tradition which a freedom-loving people should hesitate to abandon. At the same time one who would understand government must not over-look the court as a part of a nation's political machinery.

the hierarchy of courts

A second characteristic of American courts, federal and state, is their hierarchal arrangement. The judicial hierarchy has two main levels, a lower one con-sisting of courts of original jurisdiction, and an upper one made up of courts of appellate jurisdiction. The lower level is further subdivided into courts of general jurisdiction and courts of special, or limited, jurisdiction. The upper level is subdivided into courts of intermediate appellate jurisdiction and courts of highest jurisdiction.

the function of trial courts

At the base of the hierarchal arrangement are found the trial courts with gen-eral authority to hear and decide the great mass of cases which arise in a com-plex civilization. *Insofar as it is the business of courts to settle disputes involving private persons, these are the important tribunals.* Cases are heard by these courts, facts are ascertained, law is applied, and justice is rendered, and that might well be an end to the matter. If the judges associated with the court are able students of the law and personally honest and impartial, and if the busi-ness of the court is conducted efficiently, in a sense the judicial function is fully and properly performed, and no cause for complaint would exist because of absence of opportunity to keep litigation alive through further court action.

the function of courts of appeals

But the arrangement of courts becomes truly hierarchal by the appearance, above these base-courts, of courts of appeals. Historically the appellate phase of the judicial process came into being almost immediately after courts of orig-inal jurisdiction began to function, and two factors have always operated to support the idea of appeal in the judicial process. The first of these grows out of the fact that courts not only decide cases involving specific individuals, but in so doing also state the law which governs all men. It is clearly desirable that in an organized, unified political state the law should operate uniformly on all men alike, wherever they may live within the state, and whether the law be judge-made common law or judge-interpreted statute law. If a state had but a single court, a uniform interpretation of the law would result automatically, but in-variably the pressure of legal business in modern society results in the establish-ment of a series of courts either scattered geographically throughout the state or divided along functional lines. This at once creates the possibility that law will be made or interpreted by different judges in different ways. By providing for an appeal of those cases in which the meaning of law is involved, ultimately if not directly to a single court of highest jurisdiction, an authoritative ruling as to the doubtful legal issue can be obtained and thereafter followed by all of the lower courts. *Thus, insofar as it is the business of courts to announce law to all men, the court of appeals is the important tribunal.*

The second reason for appeal grows out of the interests of the individual parties to litigation and the need to safeguard the element of justice in the decision. Judges are human and may err. A court of original jurisdiction may decide a case incorrectly and do a serious injustice to one of the parties. Thus it was early thought desirable to allow appeal to higher courts at the request of the parties to litigation so that errors might be corrected and the ends of justice served.

If the appellate process is to lead finally to a single high court of appeals which is to supply a uniform interpretation of law, the judicial arrangement must be hierarchal. It follows at once that if such an arrangement is to prove workable, some sort of winnowing-out process is necessary so that the volume of business at the appellate level may be held within manageable limits. In the Anglo-American court systems this is accomplished by limiting review to those cases in which the law at issue has not already been clearly interpreted or defined, or to those judgments of lower courts in which it can be shown that fairly substantial errors have been committed which are resulting in real injustices to the parties to the litigation. In this latter respect, however, it has been found necessary to distinguish between errors of law and errors of fact. On the theory that, unless a court of appeals tries a case anew, listening to all the witnesses and considering all the evidence, it cannot have as good a basis for evaluating facts as did the trial court, appeal has been limited in common-law cases to errors of law. Since factual issues are customarily determined in the trial court by a jury, a further reason exists for denying an opportunity to reopen the factual side of a case at the appellate level. In most cases not tried by juries, however, such as, for example, cases in equity, a broader appeal, both as to issues of fact as well as to issues of law, had been traditionally permitted. Today, there are many exceptions to the rule that a court of appeals is concerned only with disputed *legal* points, but the principle still has much vitality and does help to hold down the volume of appellate business.

the dual character of the American court system

A third, and unique, characteristic of the American judiciary is the existence, side by side on a geographical basis, of two entirely separate court systems. On one side is the federal judiciary consisting of more than a hundred courts scattered throughout the nation. On the other side are the elaborately organized judiciaries in the forty-eight states with the total number of courts running into the thousands. This dual system is, of course, a result of our federal system of government, and more specifically of the fact that both national and state governments make and enforce law. Thus it is the primary function of the state courts to enforce state law and of the federal courts to enforce federal law.

This duplication of judicial machinery is not an absolute necessity in a federal state. The judicial enforcement of national law could be assigned to local courts in each section of a country, or, conceivably, local law could be enforced by decentralized national courts. It is probably true that if state courts were to enforce national law, there would be needed at the very least one national supreme court to provide a uniform interpretation of national statutes for state courts to follow, and also to settle disputes between states, and between a state and the national government. The American Constitution does specify that there shall be one federal Supreme Court, but it has left the creation of inferior federal courts to the discretion of Congress. In its very first session in 1789 Congress exercised its discretion by establishing, in the famous Judiciary Act of that year, a system of inferior federal courts adequate to the nation's needs at the time.

federal jurisdiction under the Constitution

The maximum limits of jurisdiction for all federal courts are clearly indicated by the Constitution. Moreover, the principle of the Tenth Amendment, which reserves to the states all powers not delegated to the national government, operates just as fully with respect to the jurisdiction of courts as it does with respect to the powers of legislatures.

Article Three of the Constitution expressly sets forth federal jurisdiction in one of the most succinctly worded paragraphs of the entire document. To begin with, jurisdiction is limited to "cases" and "controversies." This has always been held to mean that the federal courts must confine their work to the settlement of bona fide disputes between opposing parties who have a true conflict of interests. The settlement of friendly, collusive, or "trumped-up" suits and the rendering of advisory opinions are beyond the power of the federal courts.

Article Three then enumerates the specific types of jurisdiction which may be exercised by federal courts. These fall roughly into two categories: one type of case which depends upon the nature of the subject matter being litigated; and a second which depends upon the nature of the parties to the litigation. In all there are nine kinds of "cases" or "controversies" which may be heard in federal courts. These are:

A. *Nature of the Subject Matter*
  1. Cases arising under the federal Constitution, or a federal statute or treaty.
  2. Cases falling within the fields of so-called admiralty and maritime law.

B. *Nature of the Parties*

3. Cases affecting ambassadors and other agents of foreign governments.
4. Controversies to which the federal government itself is a party.
5. Controversies between two or more state governments.
6. Controversies between a state government and citizens of another state.
7. Controversies between citizens of different states.
8. Controversies between citizens of the same state claiming lands under grants of different states.
9. Controversies between a state government, or citizens of a state, and a foreign government or its citizens or subjects.

This is a full statement of federal jurisdiction. Unless a case falls within one of these nine categories it cannot possibly be heard by any federal court, either in the first instance or on appeal. It does not follow from this, however, that federal courts will always have jurisdiction even in these categories. The language of Article Three clearly indicates that Congress may (a) assign some or all of this jurisdiction to the state courts on a concurrent or even an exclusive basis, and (b) distribute this total federal jurisdiction in any way it sees fit among the courts of the federal hierarchy. The only exception is that Congress may not alter the original jurisdiction of the Supreme Court to hear cases affecting ambassadors and other foreign agents and cases to which a state government is a party.

The Supreme Court is the only federal court specifically mentioned in Article Three. Moreover, its jurisdiction is exclusively appellate except as to the two types of cases just mentioned. Since the appellate jurisdiction of the Supreme Court and the number, organization, and jurisdiction of the inferior federal courts are all subject to congressional control, it is necessary to turn to federal statutes for more specific information about the federal court system. From the beginning of its history Congress has provided by law for the organization and operation of federal courts. This it has done in a series of famous "Judiciary Acts." As has been indicated, the first of these was passed in 1789 and determined the initial organization of the federal judiciary. Many of the current provisions of the federal judicial code can still be traced back to this act of 1789, but at irregular intervals since that date Congress has passed further legislation dealing with the judiciary. In the present century the Judiciary Acts of 1911, 1922, 1925, 1937, and 1939 have been of considerable importance.

federal courts and their jurisdiction under statute

the federal district court

At the bottom level of the federal judicial hierarchy is found the district court, first established by Congress in 1789. This is the federal court of general, original jurisdiction. The forty-eight states are divided into eighty-four districts, with one court for each district. For the most part the districts coincide with states, but some states have been divided into two or more districts. No district crosses state boundaries. Six additional district courts have been provided for the District of Columbia and the territories and dependencies. A district court is usually presided over by a single judge, as are most other trial courts. However, a district may have two or more judges who move around the district and hold court simultaneously in different places. The number of federal district judges was just short of two hundred in 1948, each judgeship having been authorized by Congress.

The district courts have original jurisdiction only, and it is here that the overwhelming majority of federal cases are first heard. It is here, also, that most of the ordinary litigation between private persons which falls within federal jurisdiction—such as disputes between citizens of different states, or cases arising under federal statutes—is settled. And it is here that all prosecutions under federal criminal statutes occur. Since the Constitution guarantees the right to trial by jury in both civil and criminal cases, the district court frequently sits with a jury.

the federal court of appeals

At the second, or intermediate appellate, level of the federal judiciary is found the court of appeals, established by Congress in 1891. These courts, as the name suggests, have appellate jurisdiction only. The forty-eight states are divided into ten "circuits," with one of these courts for each circuit. The District of Columbia also has a "Court of Appeals." There are about sixty federal judges assigned to these eleven courts, the usual procedure being for three judges to sit together, *en banc,* in reviewing a case. Certain kinds of cases may be appealed directly from a federal district court to the Supreme Court, but the great majority of district court judgments—in civil and criminal cases alike—if they are reviewed at all, are reviewed by a court of appeals and go no higher. Less than one case in twenty heard by the courts of appeals is reviewed by the Supreme Court. The courts of appeals do not receive any cases from the state courts on appeal, but they do review directly certain orders of administrative agencies, such as the Interstate Commerce Commission and the Federal Trade Commission, the district courts being by-passed in these instances.

the United States Supreme Court

At the top of the federal judiciary is found the United States Supreme Court, which, as we have seen, is the only federal court actually provided for in the Constitution—all of the others having been organized by acts of Congress. Even the Supreme Court is mentioned in the Constitution by name only, and depends for its actual organization upon congressional legislation. The Supreme Court is almost exclusively a court of appeals. Of the two kinds of cases over which it

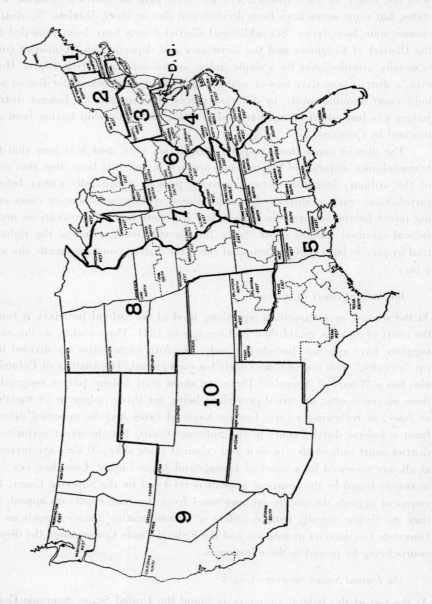

Federal Judicial Courts and Districts. Numerals designate courts of appeals areas, called "circuits." The names, such as "Oklahoma West," designate district court areas. (*Source: Administrative Office of the United States Courts.*)

has original jurisdiction, those which affect ambassadors and foreign agents almost never arise, and those to which a state is a party are not very numerous.

The present-day procedure by which some 100–150 cases annually reach the Supreme Court for review from lower tribunals is technically rather complex and will be but briefly indicated here. There are four streams in which cases flow to the Supreme Court. The first stream comes from the state courts. The Supreme Court may accept cases for review directly from these courts in a few situations, as, for example, those in which the validity of a state or a federal statute under the federal Constitution is in question. The second stream, a small one, comes from the federal district courts. For example, under the Judiciary Act of 1937, if a district court holds against the constitutionality of a federal statute in a case in which the United States is a party, the government may appeal the ruling directly to the Supreme Court. The third stream comes from the federal courts of appeals. This stream is a relatively large one, for the Supreme Court may review such circuit court decisions as it chooses, upon petition by the losing parties. The fourth stream brings to the Supreme Court an occasional case from the federal Court of Claims or the Court of Customs and Patent Appeals.

The problem of holding the business of the Supreme Court within manageable limits has long been a serious one. Following the Civil War the appellate burden of the Court increased by leaps and bounds. In the 1880's as many as fifteen hundred cases were docketed with the Court at one time, and the Court had fallen three years behind its docket. This condition led to the creation of the circuit courts of appeals, which were designed to relieve the Supreme Court of a considerable part of its burden of reviewing cases from the federal courts of original jurisdiction. For many years, however, it was very difficult to know where the line between the jurisdiction of the two courts rested, and it is said that even "the ablest lawyers could not advise with any degree of confidence." During these years Congress passed a series of statutes designed to make it possible for the Supreme Court to control the volume of its business. The so-called Judges Act of 1925 was the culminating law in the series, and it achieved the desired result by greatly expanding the area of cases reviewed by means of the writ of *certiorari* rather than by writs of *error* or *appeal*. The significance of certiorari lies in the fact that it vests in a superior court complete discretionary power to accept or reject a case for review, thus enabling it to take jurisdiction only over those cases that present issues of major importance. A few types of cases can still be carried to the Supreme Court by the technical process known as appeal. The significance of this method is that it gives one of the parties to a case opportunity to demand review of a lower court's ruling as a matter of right.

A few cases also reach the Supreme Court by means of *certificate*, a process by which a court of appeals may certify to the Supreme Court questions or propositions of law for advice or instructions for it to follow in disposing of a case. The Supreme Court may either give the instructions asked for or order the entire case sent up to it for final disposition.

the courts of appeals and the Supreme Court contrasted

The successive limiting of the appellate jurisdiction of the Supreme Court by law has resulted in a rather important contrast between the functions of the intermediate appellate courts and the high court of appeals in the federal system. By and large, the courts of appeals have become the final courts for what is known as common-law adjudication—the deciding of cases between private individuals through the application of established principles of law to the facts of disputes important primarily to the litigants. The Supreme Court has become very largely a court of public law, for its work is now confined in good part to cases which present constitutional issues or questions of statute interpretation, cases in the outcome of which the American people, as well as the litigants, have a major interest. This changing character of the work of the Supreme Court will be examined further in Chapter 23, "The Supreme Court as an Instrument of Government." But it may be noted here that the court of appeals has in good part been given final responsibility for that aspect of the judicial function that involves settling disputes between private parties, whereas the Supreme Court has responsibility at the appellate level for that part of the judicial function that involves the making of public policy.

overlapping jurisdiction of the federal and state courts

Under the dual judicial system which exists in the United States it is not always easy to draw the line between the case that may be heard in the state courts and the case that may be heard in the federal courts. In the first place, the subject matter of a case may involve both state and federal laws. In theory at least, such a case falls within the jurisdiction of both courts. This is true in several areas of criminal jurisdiction. For example, such offenses as kidnaping or automobile stealing are crimes under both state and federal law. Accordingly, depending upon who arrests him and whether he crossed a state boundary during the commission of the crime, a kidnaper or an automobile thief may be prosecuted in either a state or a federal court. Conceivably he may be prosecuted in both, for by his single action he may have committed two crimes—one against state law and one against federal law.

In the second place, Congress has by law deliberately left part of the area of federal jurisdiction as set forth in the Constitution to be exercised by state courts, either concurrently with federal courts or even exclusively. This is particularly true of cases between citizens of different states, and of cases arising under federal statutes. A moment's thought makes it clear that the number and types of cases in these two categories are potentially very extensive. There is almost no kind of human conflict known to law which cannot under certain circumstances involve citizens of different states. Likewise, federal statutes have now become so numerous and detailed that the amount of private litigation which arises under them is very great indeed. Thus to limit the work of the federal courts and to channel much of the everyday litigation between private persons into the state courts, Congress has provided that the federal district courts may take jurisdiction over civil suits between citizens of different states, or arising under federal statutes, only if the amount in controversy exceeds the sum or value of $3,000. If the amount at issue is less than that sum, state courts have what in effect is exclusive jurisdiction. [1] Nor is this all. Even if the amount in controversy exceeds $3,000, the parties to a case, though they be citizens of different states, may choose to take their dispute to a state court rather than to a federal one.

On the other hand, Congress has provided that the federal courts shall have exclusive jurisdiction over several of the areas which, potentially, under the Constitution might be shared by the states. This is true, for example, of all cases arising under federal patent or copyright statutes, of all proceedings in bankruptcy, and of all suits against ambassadors and foreign agents.

These technicalities of national and state jurisdiction illustrate one of the complexities of the federal system. It has been a real problem in statecraft to set up two rival court systems, each a complete hierarchy in itself, and at the same time to minimize jurisdictional conflicts and confusion. By the process of experimentation and frequent reorganization Congress has finally brought the federal judiciary to a point where it is reasonably well integrated with the state judiciaries. Of course, the difficulty could have been avoided by the simple expedient of not creating any federal courts with original jurisdiction. But it is doubtful whether the local judiciary in each state could have been depended upon to enforce federal law satisfactorily. It must be admitted that the federal judiciary has come finally to enjoy a reputation for honesty and efficiency in the rendering of justice which cannot be matched by many of the state judiciaries. It is probable that through the existence of federal courts the nation has fared better than would have been the case had it been entirely dependent upon state courts for the performance of the judicial function.

---

[1] There are a few exceptions. See section 41 of title 28 of the United States Code. Title 28 is entitled "Judicial Code and Judiciary" and contains all federal statutory provisions relating to the courts. Section 41 enumerates twenty-eight types of federal district court jurisdiction.

special federal courts

pressures for the creation of courts of limited jurisdiction

From the beginning of Anglo-American judicial history one of the most trouble-some problems has been the court of limited or special jurisdiction. To be sure, the main lines of judicial development have been such that the word "court" today suggests an agency that has broad jurisdiction to hear many kinds of cases. But always there has been pressure for the creation of courts of limited jurisdiction to specialize in particular areas of the law. "Multiplying of tribunals," Dean Pound has pointed out, "is a characteristic of the beginnings of judicial organization. When some new type of controversy or new kind of situation arises and presses for treatment, a new tribunal is set up to deal with it. So it was at Rome. So it was in England from the twelfth century to the sixteenth, and indeed, on the whole, down to the nineteenth century." [2] When, for example, Sir Edward Coke published his *Fourth Institute* in 1644, he described no fewer than seven-teen English courts of special jurisdiction. At the time of Blackstone's *Commentaries on the Laws of England* (1765-1769), which was widely read in America during the years before the Constitutional Convention, the English court system had been simplified somewhat but still included many special courts.

relative absence of special courts from the federal judiciary

From the beginning of judicial history there have also been counterpressures for the establishment of courts of general jurisdiction only. Among these pressures has been the desire for uniformity in the administration of law and for a straightforward judicial procedure which will not be overly confusing to the citizens of a country. One of the most significant things about the organization of federal courts by Congress since 1789 has been the almost complete absence of specialized courts in the federal system. For example, the complete merging of courts of law and courts of equity in the Constitution of 1787 and in the Judiciary Act of 1789 long preceded the same result in England and in many of our states. The state judiciaries, on the other hand, followed the English pattern more closely and have always included many courts of special jurisdiction, particularly at the petty court level.

the three special federal courts

Apart from the special territorial courts which have been established for the District of Columbia, Alaska, Hawaii, Puerto Rico, and elsewhere, there exist today only three federal courts of special jurisdiction lying outside the regular organization of district courts, courts of appeals, and the Supreme Court. These are the Customs Court, the Court of Customs and Patent Appeals, and the

---

[2] Roscoe Pound, *Organization of Courts* (Boston: Little, Brown & Company, 1940), p. 5.

Court of Claims. The special jurisdiction of these courts is fairly well indicated by their names. Such courts are sometimes referred to as "legislative" rather than "constitutional" courts, on the theory that they are authorized not by Article Three of the Constitution but by the eighteenth grant of power in Article One, which permits Congress to use all means "necessary and proper" to carry out any of its expressly granted powers, such as the power "to lay and collect . . . duties." So far as the Constitution is concerned, therefore, Congress is not required to grant the judges of a legislative court life tenure during good behavior, or to observe the provision of Article Three restricting constitutional courts to the hearing of "cases" and "controversies." Actually, however, Congress has provided that the judges of these special courts shall have life tenure, and from time to time there has been doubt whether Congress intended these special courts to be regarded as legislative or constitutional tribunals.[3] But there is no doubt about the power of Congress to create a special tribunal and to place it in the legislative court category if it so desires.

That Congress has not been completely systematic in distinguishing, both as to jurisdiction and as to constitutional status, between these courts and the general courts is seen in the case of the Court of Claims. In theory the federal government cannot be sued. In practice this government, like most others, permits itself to be sued within certain limits. In creating the Court of Claims in 1855 Congress gave its consent to such suits, but from the beginning the jurisdiction of this court to hear claims against the government has been restricted. By and large it has been limited to cases involving claims against the government growing out of contractual disputes. Until 1946 claims resulting from torts committed by federal officers could be approved only by act of Congress. Under the Legislative Reorganization Act of that year jurisdiction over such claims cases was given to the federal district courts.

the short-lived federal Commerce Court

A significant federal experiment with the special tribunal was made in 1910 when Congress created a Commerce Court and gave it jurisdiction over litigation growing out of the work of the Interstate Commerce Commission. By centralizing the handling of railroad cases in this one court Congress hoped to relieve courts of general jurisdiction of a very difficult and technical type of work. However, the Commerce Court was abolished in 1914 after a brief, stormy career, which saw one of its judges impeached and removed from office, and a number of its important rulings reversed by the Supreme Court. Its duties were transferred to the federal district courts. Had this experiment been more successful it is possible that the court of specialized jurisdiction might have come into wider use in the national government.

---

[3] See R. J. Harris, *The Judicial Power of the United States* (University: Louisiana State University Press, 1940), Chap. 4, "Legislative Courts."

the problem of specialized law enforcement

The problem of specialization in the judicial process has not been finally settled. Modern society grows ever more complex, and with this development goes inevitably the need for law, statutory and otherwise, to become more and more extensive and detailed. This raises the question whether general courts, as traditionally conceived and organized, are adequate agencies for the interpretation and application of law in a wide variety of difficult, technical fields. Can the same judge be sufficiently learned, experienced, and wise to render satisfactory decisions dealing with the infinite variations and complications of law in such fields as taxation, corporate finance, labor-management relations, security and stock exchange regulation, antitrust control, price control, many areas of crime, naturalization, suffrage and elections, and civil rights—all of which today concern the federal court of general jurisdiction?

A satisfactory answer to this question necessitates, among other things, a very careful examination of the relationship which has come to exist between court and administrative agency. Although a large number of specialized courts have not been created at the federal level, the years since 1887 have seen the establishment of a number of independent administrative commissions, among which the Interstate Commerce Commission, the Federal Trade Commission, the Securities and Exchange Commission, and the Federal Communications Commission are outstanding examples. The fact that these agencies perform quasi-judicial functions has long been recognized and approved by the Supreme Court. In part these agencies act as courts of original jurisdiction by interpreting and applying law for the first time to specific situations. When the Federal Trade Commission, for example, receives a complaint that a business concern is using unfair advertising methods in violation of federal law, and holds a hearing, and perhaps even issues a cease and desist order, it is certainly engaging in an activity that is at least quasi-judicial. Indeed, the Federal Trade Commission in a sense takes the place of the district courts, for Congress has provided that its rulings shall be reviewed on appeal by the courts of appeals. The district courts are thus completely by-passed in this area of law enforcement.[4]

The proper relation that should exist between court and administrative agency, the desirable measure of judicial supervision and review of administrative rulings, and the mechanics of such review are problems which are far from settled. But it seems clear that the need for specialized tribunals to enforce law in difficult, technical areas is being, and will continue to be, met in part by the administrative agency.

A further possibility is to preserve the courts of general jurisdiction but to allow individual judges to become specialists in different fields of the law. This

---

[4] See 28 U.S.C. § 225, and 15 U.S.C. § 45.

can be done wherever a court system is sufficiently flexible to permit the assignment of individual judges to the hearing of limited and particular types of cases. For example, in the federal district courts most cases are heard by single judges, and in the courts of appeals, by three judges. Yet the number of judges attached to each district court averages better than two, and to each court of appeals better than five. Accordingly, some opportunity to permit judges to specialize through assignment to particular types of cases does exist. Moreover, it is possible under present law to shift judges from district to district and even from one circuit to another. Even with the Supreme Court there is a limited chance for specialization. Individual justices may gain considerable influence with their colleagues in specific fields of law because of their admitted knowledge or experience in these fields. The writing of opinions can also be assigned to justices according to their known specialties.

the search for a unified court system

The American court has been notably independent not only in its external relations with the executive and legislative departments, but in its relations within the internal judicial organization. Professor Walton Hamilton has spoken of "the unorderly and almost leaderless army of judges." [5] And Felix Frankfurter and James M. Landis assert "not only were the judges rendered independent of the President and Congress; they were rendered independent of each other. Congress created a hierarchal system of courts, not of judges." [6] The average American judge, federal and state, has gone his own way subject to little direct supervision or control. This has been particularly true with respect to control of administrative matters. With respect to substantive legal matters the judge's desire to have his rulings stand up when reviewed by a higher court has perhaps led him to accept a certain measure of leadership. The Supreme Court has always had great influence upon the lower courts in the following of legal principles. But the Chief Justice has never possessed within the judicial branch any administrative authority comparable to that exercised by the President as chief of the executive branch.

As already indicated, a high degree of administrative centralization has been achieved in the courts of Roman civil-law countries through ministries of justice. Needless to say, such an arrangement tends to result in an efficient, integrated court system. But it has always been vigorously resisted in England and the United States because of the threat to the impartiality of judges and the independence of courts which it obviously offers. However, this resistance has left

---

[5] "Judicial Process," *Encyclopaedia of the Social Sciences*, VIII, 454.
[6] Felix Frankfurter and James M. Landis, *The Business of the Supreme Court*, (New York: The Macmillan Company, 1927), p. 218.

unsolved the problem of securing a systematic, integrated organization of the judiciary itself.

the federal Judicial Conference

In controlling the development of the federal judiciary Congress has from time to time taken statutory steps looking toward a more systematic court structure. Three specific changes have been made in the last quarter century which have resulted in an increased measure of unity and orderliness in the federal judiciary. In 1922 legislation was passed establishing a Judicial Conference, consisting of the Chief Justice of the United States and of the senior judge in each of the federal circuits. The Conference meets regularly each year to examine the condition of the federal courts and the state of their business. In particular it takes notice of delay in the disposition of cases in any of the ninety districts and eleven federal circuits. It may recommend to Congress the creation of new judgeships where it finds that additional manpower is needed. Actual power to order district judges to move from one district to another in order to correct lags in the handling of cases has been vested by Congress in the senior circuit judge if the move is within a circuit; and in the Chief Justice, acting with the approval of the senior circuit judges in the circuits affected, if the move is from circuit to circuit. But the Conference usually lays the groundwork for such shifts by keeping a careful watch over the business of the courts. In this way, one of the functions performed by a ministry of justice—the assignment of additional judges to courts which are falling behind in their work—is cared for without subjecting the individual court or judge to the large measure of bureaucratic control which a ministry might entail. The Conference also approves the budgetary estimates for the federal judiciary before the annual request for operating funds is submitted to Congress. Occasionally the Conference suggests to Congress statutory changes in the Judicial Code.

the Administrative Office of the United States Courts

In 1939 Congress took a second step by creating an Administrative Office of the United States Courts to act as a sort of business office in handling the housekeeping functions of the federal judiciary. At its head is a director appointed by the Supreme Court, but the Office is under the general direction of the Judicial Conference. Its two main duties are met through separate divisions: one a business administration division which supervises the work of all court clerks, provides the courts with supplies, and disburses all moneys appropriated by Congress for the maintenance of the courts; the other a division of procedural studies and statistics which keeps a constant watch over court dockets with a view to making recommendations to the Judicial Conference and to Congress, if necessary, for changes that will permit the speedier handling of cases. By the same law the circuit judges in each circuit are directed to form a judicial council to keep watch over judicial business in their areas. Under the supervision of these councils annual conferences are held in each circuit attended by all federal judges in the circuit. Members of the bar are invited to attend some of the sessions, thus affording an opportunity for judges and lawyers to discuss their common problems.

the federal codes of civil and criminal procedure

As a third measure, Congress, in 1934 and in 1940, authorized the Supreme Court to supervise the preparation of formal codes of civil and criminal procedure for use in the federal district courts. These codes, prepared and promulgated in 1938 and in 1946, now provide uniform procedures to be followed in all of the federal district courts, whereas previously, for example, civil procedure in each district court conformed to the practice of the state courts in the state where the federal court was located.

bibliographic note

There are several excellent studies of the organization of the American judiciary. Attention may be called to Charles W. Bunn's *A Brief Survey of the Jurisdiction and Practice of the Courts of the United States* (St. Paul: West Publishing Company, 4th ed., 1939); Clarence N. Callender's *American Courts: Their Organization and Procedure* (New York: McGraw-Hill Book Company, 1927); and Roscoe Pound's *Organization of Courts* (Boston: Little, Brown & Company, 1940). Raymond Moley's *Our Criminal Courts* (New York: Minton, Balch & Co., 1930) is a readable analysis of the criminal courts.

An excellent study of the history and modern program of the United States Department of Justice is Homer S. Cummings and Carl McFarland's *Federal Justice* (New York: The Macmillan Company, 1937).

Robert J. Harris's *The Judicial Power of the United States* (University: Louisiana State University Press, 1940) is a case study of the jurisdictional limits of the federal courts as determined by both Congress and the federal courts themselves. There is a good chapter on the so-called legislative courts.

the courts at work

 $\mathcal{I}$ T IS the function of the judiciary to decide cases in accordance with justice. Speed and efficiency, in particular, have always been regarded as indispensable to the administration of justice. "Justice delayed is justice denied," runs one proverb of the law which is grounded firmly in the belief that the "law's delay" is one of the most serious of all threats to the interests of litigants. Significantly, the new rules governing the procedure of federal courts emphasize the need for speed in the disposition of cases. Rule One of the *Rules of Civil Procedure*, adopted in 1938, provides: "These rules . . . shall be construed to secure the just, speedy, and inexpensive determination of every action." And Rule Two of the *Rules of Criminal Procedure*, adopted in 1946, states: "These rules are intended to provide for the just determination of every criminal proceeding. They shall be construed to secure simplicity in procedure, fairness in administration, and the elimination of unjustifiable expense and delay."

the formality of court procedure

Speed is essential to justice. Yet delay is frequently the necessary consequence of the high degree of formality which marks judicial procedure. All governmental procedures tend to become formalized. In Congress the progress of a bill is controlled by rule and convention. In the making of laws there is a good deal of informality behind the scenes, but such steps as the reference of bills to committee, the making of committee reports, debate, amendment, voting, and conference are taken in a fixed and traditional manner. Some of the President's actions are informal, but in addressing messages to Congress, issuing executive orders, appointing public officers, and conducting relations with diplomatic agents, the chief executive adheres closely to forms that are highly formal and often ceremonial.

But nowhere has the tendency toward formalism been more marked than in the work of the courts. There is little about traditional judicial procedure that

426

is improvised or informal. It is true, of course, that judges in America no longer wear wigs, that certain ancient procedures such as indictment by grand jury are not so widely followed as they once were, that specialized tribunals such as the juvenile court are dispensing with many if not all of the trappings of judicial ritual, and that administrative tribunals with simplified procedures are taking the place of courts in many areas of the law. Nonetheless, the American court remains on the whole the most formalized of governmental agencies, and its procedures the most rigidly prescribed by law and custom.

Formality in governmental procedures reflects in part man's quest for certainty, his desire to avoid the vacillating or unpredictable side of human nature in the affairs of government. History teaches that this emphasis upon form and ritual as a means of ensuring a fixed, impartial justice for all men has a wise and sound basis. In its absence judges have all too often served not as impartial dispensers of justice but as prejudiced agents of a cause, of a political party, or of a man. Yet the ritual of court procedure has a debit as well as a credit side. Whim, uncertainty, and improvisation have been eliminated from the courtroom, but at the expense of a complexity and rigidity which constantly threaten to overwhelm the human element in the administration of justice. Here we are confronted with one of the dilemmas of political organization. Its ancient and complex forms and procedures give the court a dignity and impartiality which are strong safeguards of man's traditional liberties. Yet the court is frequently so ceremonial and tortuous in its operation as to make it difficult to render individualized justice. It is not too much to say that there has developed a conflict between the desire for speed and efficiency on one hand and the preservation of form and ceremony on the other. The rise of administrative tribunals employing streamlined procedures in the deciding of cases illustrates a tendency to prefer speed and efficiency over form and ceremony. Yet the administrative tribunal is today under attack on this very point, and it is clear that the adaptation of traditional judicial procedure to the needs of a high-speed civilization is one of the most difficult problems of statecraft confronting American democracy.

trial court and appellate court procedures contrasted

In any discussion of the courts at work it is necessary to make a careful distinction between the trial court and the appellate court. Their functions are different and so are their procedures. It is the function of the trial court to hear cases for the first time and to decide them by applying known rules of law to factual situations involving specific individuals. Thus the trial court is primarily a fact-finding agency. It is the function of the appellate court to clarify the law, and, by reviewing the work of the trial court, to make certain that the ends of justice are being served. Thus the appellate court is primarily a law-finding agency.

There are three things which a trial court must do in the course of an ordinary case, whether the case be a civil or a criminal one. First, it must determine the nature of the conflict and define carefully the point or points at issue. Second, it must obtain an accurate account of the factual side of the conflict. Third, it must apply law to the issue in the light of the facts and pronounce judgment. The second of these processes is apt to be a long and laborious one, and it is with this that trial court procedure is primarily concerned. It is here that the complicated and lengthy business of listening to witnesses and receiving evidence occurs, and it is here that the services of a jury are frequently used.

When a case is carried to a higher court on appeal, the primary purpose is to secure a careful review of the way in which law has been applied to the facts of the case. To obtain a reversal in a higher court, a litigant must show that the trial court has not properly defined the legal nature of the conflict, or has committed procedural errors, or has pronounced an improper judgment in the light of the evidence. In short, the appellate court is asked to review a case whenever it is alleged that legal errors have been committed. It is not asked to check the factual side of a controversy or to try a case anew. It may send a case back to a court of first instance for a retrial, but it will not itself undertake to try such a case over again.

The trial court is concerned with the drama of human affairs, with the stuff of life. Contending attorneys argue, witnesses testify, and jurymen listen and ponder so that the facts of a controversy may be ascertained and justice rendered under law. Presiding over the trial, but in a sense detached from the proceedings, is the judge, who sees to it that proper forms are observed and customary procedures followed, and that the litigants and the jury are never at a loss for authoritative legal advice and rulings.

The appellate court presents a very different scene. Absent are the witnesses and the jury. Attorneys are confined to the secondary role of pointing to the disputed points of law by means of written brief and limited oral argument. Human drama is at a minimum; the atmosphere of the courtroom is a quiet and scholarly one. Indeed, most of the work of the appellate judge is done in his study and in the conference room. The trial judge is often limited at the end to the mere pronouncing of a *judgment* already clearly indicated by the verdict of the jury, but the appellate judge hands down a legal *decision* supported by a written *opinion*.

the trial court at work

the difference between civil and criminal cases

Trial courts hear both civil and criminal cases. In civil cases both the plaintiff and the defendant are ordinarily private persons. The state prescribes the laws which govern the civil relations of men, and it provides the machinery whereby controversies arising under the laws may be settled. So far as the merits of the dispute are concerned, the state's attitude is one of "benevolent neutrality," unless by chance it happens to be a party to the case in its own right. In the criminal case, on the other hand, the state is always the plaintiff and an accused individual the defendant. Here the state not only prescribes law governing human conduct; it seeks in a positive way to enforce the law by invoking the law's sanctions against wrongdoers.

procedure in civil cases

The procedure followed in a civil case is the product of centuries of Anglo-American judicial practice, which long had only a common-law or customary basis. Today, procedure in both the federal and the state courts is based upon statutory codes, which are, however, derived in good part from the unwritten traditions of the past. Under these codes the civil case is divided into two parts: a written or pleadings stage, and an oral or trial stage. It is the purpose of the pleadings to frame an issue which can then be tried. To begin with, the plaintiff, who presumably has suffered an injury from an unlawful act of the defendant, takes the initiative in invoking the law by asking for the aid of a court. This he does by filing with the court a *complaint* in which he states his case as he sees it. The court then notifies the defendant and directs him to submit an *answer*. In this answer the defendant sets forth the case as *he* sees it. Thereupon various counterclaims and amendments may be filed, and the court ultimately fixes a date for trial, and the case moves from the pleadings to the trial stage.

The second or trial stage consists of a series of formal steps. After a jury has been selected (unless, of course, the parties elect to waive a jury trial), the attorneys deliver their opening speeches, present the evidence for their respective parties by marshaling their own witnesses and exhibits and cross-examining those of the other side, and finally close their case by an appeal to the jury. Then the judge charges the jury to render a fair verdict in accordance with the facts established, the jury deliberates, and, if it can reach agreement (which must usually be unanimous), it returns a verdict. Finally, the judge pronounces judgment in accordance with the jury's verdict.

procedure in criminal cases

In a criminal case, either by means of a grand jury *indictment* or by an *information* filed with the court by the prosecuting attorney, the government orders the trial of an individual formally accused of a crime. Prior to this, of course, the state will already have taken the initiative by arresting the suspected lawbreaker, filing charges against him, and obtaining a court ruling that he be held for further proceedings. Following the indictment the case goes to trial, where the proceedings are quite similar to those in a civil case.

changing court procedures

Such are the main outlines of trial procedure in civil and criminal cases. Needless to say, the details are far more complicated and technical than those suggested here, and they vary considerably from one jurisdiction to another. Although the pattern of traditional English practice is still apparent in the procedure of the American court, many changes have been made, and will continue to be made, by legislative action. In general these changes simplify court procedures and adapt them to the needs of modern times. But, as has been suggested, efforts to improve judicial procedure have not been without their complications. In the late Middle Ages the law allowed the judge a good deal of discretion in conducting a criminal trial and even in determining the severity of punishment. But such star-chamber proceedings became a notorious symbol of injustice, and by the eighteenth century court procedures had become more rigidly prescribed, and crimes and their penalties more precisely defined. In our own time, in an unconscious effort to complete the circle, the humanitarian frequently argues for more informal courtroom procedure, and for the sentencing of the guilty to indeterminate periods of imprisonment so that procedure and punishment may be made to fit the individual criminal. Between these two opposing tendencies in the conduct of trials—formal, impersonal procedure and informal, personalized procedure—there can be no ultimate choice. Each has at different times seemed highly desirable. Here, as elsewhere, society must feel its way ahead in devising satisfactory and workable forms and procedures.

relations between the trial court and the state's attorney

trial courts do not seek cases

By this time it should be clear that, in general, trial courts do not act on their own initiative, nor do they function continuously or systematically as law enforcement agencies. Instead, the judicial wheels begin to turn only when specific business is brought to the courts from outside. Requests that courts bring their powers into play by hearing cases and rendering judgments come from two sources —from private citizens who bring their civil disputes to the courts for solution, and from public officers who are charged with the enforcement of law. Unless these officers, who range all the way from the President of the United States to the local policeman on the beat, take steps to enforce law, courts are powerless, by and large, to play any part in the law enforcement process. The administrative activities of governmental agencies may result in civil actions and in criminal prosecutions, either of which brings business to the courts. Civil actions may grow out of the work of almost any public agency. A highway department seeks the aid of the courts in acquiring private property for a new thoroughfare; a labor board seeks a restraining order to prevent an unlawful strike; a public service commission fixes rates that an electric power company resists as "unreasonable"; or the Post Office Department issues an order denying a magazine certain mailing privileges which is contested in the courts as bordering on censorship.

the function of the prosecuting attorney

But more often than not, the government initiates court action through a specialized legal agency staffed with public attorneys. Terminology varies considerably. At the local level such an officer may be known as the "prosecuting attorney," "county attorney," "district attorney," or "state's attorney"; at the state and federal level he is known as the "attorney general." These officers have various types of assistants. At the federal level, the Attorney General is assisted in each one of the ninety federal judicial districts by a "United States attorney" who represents the United States government in starting court action under federal law. These public attorneys—federal, state, and local—are first of all prosecuting attorneys who start criminal proceedings against persons who break the criminal law. But often it is their duty to initiate civil actions in the name of the government. Under the federal antitrust laws, for example, the Attorney General is authorized to take action against offenders either by criminal prosecution or by civil suit.

Tradition has been a powerful force in governing the work of these public attorneys. Often they go about their duties in an informal way, and the personal factor looms very large. In the states an efficient law enforcement program, particularly with respect to criminal statutes, depends very largely upon the local prosecuting attorney, who is all too frequently an incompetent lawyer further hampered by an inadequate office organization. In most states the state attorney general has relatively little power to institute proceedings for the enforcement of state law; this power is lodged instead in the local public attorney.

the Attorney General and the Department of Justice

At the federal level, the last seventy-five years have witnessed a substantial growth in the law enforcement work centered in the office of the Attorney General. Although one of the oldest members of the President's cabinet, the Attorney General was for almost a century a secretary without a department, for it was not until 1870 that Congress established the Department of Justice. Even today the work of this department is frequently misunderstood. It is not, for example, a ministry of justice in the European sense. Previous to the establishment of the Administrative Office of the United States Courts it took care of some of the housekeeping needs of the federal courts. The Attorney General also advises the President in making appointments to federal judicial posts, but otherwise the Department of Justice has no direct control of the federal court system.

Broadly speaking, the functions of the Attorney General and his staff are twofold. He acts first as legal adviser to the executive branch of the government, providing rulings or "opinions" on points of law at the request of the President or other executive officers. Second, he has the duty of prosecuting suits for the United States government and of representing the government in any litigation to which it is a party. This latter duty brings the Attorney General into close personal relations with the courts. It is probably more than coincidence that four Attorneys General—Harlan Stone, Frank Murphy, Robert Jackson, and Tom Clark—and one solicitor general[1]—Stanley Reed—have served as Supreme Court justices in recent years. Nonetheless, there is no formal connection between the Department of Justice and the federal judiciary. Indeed, their separation reflects the Anglo-American tradition that there shall be no direct tie between prosecutor and judge.

the appellate court at work: the United States Supreme Court

The way in which a court of appeals goes about its work can best be seen by examining the procedures followed by the Supreme Court of the United States. Although practice differs considerably among appellate courts, the pattern set by the Supreme Court can be recognized to a considerable extent in the work of the federal courts of appeals and the appellate courts of the states.

The Supreme Court, it will be recalled, has a small measure of original jurisdiction. It is theoretically possible, therefore, for it to sit as a trial court in both civil and criminal cases, and even to use a jury. But in practice the overwhelming majority of cases heard by the Court come to it on appeal. Those cases which it tries in the first instance are seldom of a conventional nature, and it almost never employs the traditional procedures of the trial court. So far as can be ascertained, the Supreme Court has never sat with a jury. Where it has been necessary in original cases for the Court to rule on issues of fact, it has usually assigned an attorney called a "master" or "referee" to take evidence. But even this is a rare procedure.

determination of Supreme Court procedures

The rules and procedures under which the Supreme Court operates are determined in part by the Constitution, in part by act of Congress, and in part by the Court itself. To cite an example of each, the Constitution provides that the Court may not re-examine a fact tried by a jury except in accordance with common-law rules; Congress has fixed by law the beginning of a Supreme Court term as the first Monday in October and has set six out of nine justices as a quorum; and the Court itself has prescribed the character of written briefs

---

[1] The assistant of the Attorney General who actually argues the government's cases before the Supreme Court.

which attorneys may file with it and has limited the duration of oral arguments before it. This sharing of responsibility for the Court's rules is somewhat unfortunate and has in the past prevented the Court from following completely systematic and orderly procedures. It is only fair to add, however, that Congress has shown an increasing tendency to let the Court make its own rules of procedure. Fortunately, too, the rules prescribed by the Constitution are not numerous.

a typical Supreme Court week

An examination of a typical week on its calendar gives a good picture of the Supreme Court's procedures. During its annual term, which runs from October to June, the Court convenes at noon for a public session each day from Monday through Friday. Since Monday is traditionally "decision day," all opinions and rulings which are ready for release are announced at the beginning of the session on that day. Thereafter, on Monday and during the rest of the week the Court hears oral arguments in pending cases. In spite of the fact that it has been possible since the Judiciary Act of 1925 to hold down the number of cases heard each year to 150 or less, it is still necessary to restrict oral argument to one hour for each party to a case. Actually, for a systematic presentation of the arguments, the justices depend heavily upon the written briefs submitted by the parties, and the time for oral argument is frequently consumed by specific questioning of the attorneys by the justices. Fortunate, indeed, is the attorney who is permitted to use his hour to present his oral argument without interruption. Such a policy of interruption has, to be sure, much to commend it; as Felix Frankfurter and James M. Landis point out in their study, *The Business of the Supreme Court,* "questioning, in which the whole Court freely engage, clarifies the minds of the Justices as to the issues and guides the course of argument through real difficulties." [2] Not surprisingly, since he became a member of the Court, Justice Frankfurter has been one of the leading exponents of the "Socratic method" during oral argument.

the Saturday conference of the Supreme Court

At frequent intervals during a term the Court takes two-week recesses from its public sessions to study cases already argued and to prepare opinions. Saturday of each week is set aside for a conference of the justices. At these meetings the justices discuss the cases already argued and decide how to dispose of them. By tradition the Chief Justice is the first to voice his opinion during the discussion and the last to vote when the decision is being determined. Conversely, the junior member of the Court is the last to speak and the first to vote. In this way the Chief Justice and the senior associate justices gain a slight advantage; by speaking first they can influence the direction of the discussion, and by voting

---

[2] Felix Frankfurter and James M. Landis, *The Business of the Supreme Court* (New York: The Macmillan Company, 1927), p. vii.

last they can note the tentative line-up in a divided case and, if they wish, let that be a factor in determining their own stand.

Unfortunately, little is known of what goes on in Supreme Court conferences, for there is no formal reporting of these meetings, and the justices themselves have been very discreet about preserving their confidential character. Often the discussion is lengthy and, when the justices find themselves in disagreement, frequently vigorous. It is obvious, from the length of time a case is sometimes held before a decision is handed down, that a single conference is not always enough to enable the justices to come to an agreement.

the preparation of the written opinions

Sooner or later, however, a decision is reached, and a written opinion must be drafted. If the Court is unanimous, the Chief Justice assigns the preparation of a first draft to one of the justices. If the Court is divided and the Chief Justice is with the majority, he still makes the assignment and the senior justice among the dissenters assigns the preparation of a dissenting opinion. In the event that the Chief Justice aligns himself with the dissenting group, the senior justice in the majority group makes the assignment. The justices within the majority and minority groups not infrequently differ among themselves as to the reasoning by which the group's decision or dissent is reached. When these differences are rather serious, a justice usually files a separate opinion agreeing with the result but dissociating himself from the reasoning employed by the group with which he has aligned himself. When such a separate opinion is written in support of the majority's position, it is known as a *concurring* opinion. First drafts of all opinions are circulated among the justices, and presumably a considerable measure of revision may occur at this stage. In times past, members of the Court have been more willing than they are today to compromise their views and language in the interest of preparing a single opinion which the entire Court might accept. For individual justices known for their polished and frequently pungent literary style, this watering down of original drafts to make them palatable for all the justices concurring in the result was sometimes hard to bear. Justice Holmes, one of the finest literary craftsmen ever to sit on the bench, once referred to this diluting process as "pulling out all the plums and leaving the dough." As Professor Arthur Schlesinger, Jr., points out, however, "the system did produce a greater impression of unity, even if it sacrificed individualities of style and doctrine." [3]

the value of written opinions

The written opinions, majority and dissenting, of the Supreme Court and, to a lesser degree, the opinions of the federal courts of appeals, and of the state

[3] "The Supreme Court: 1947," *Fortune Magazine*, XXXV (January, 1947), 73.

appellate courts, constitute one of our most valuable original sources of information about the governmental process. Professor Walton Hamilton has observed that the court opinion "serves the multiple purpose of helping the bench to be critical of its own intellectual processes, keeping lower courts in order, announcing legal standards for acceptable human conduct, extending the courtesy of an answer to arguments which do not prevail and affording an opportunity to justify a judgment." [4]

the significance of obiter dictum

Upon occasion the rationalization of a decision in the opinion wanders beyond the limited legal problem presented by the facts of the case at hand, and includes language that is broader than is needed for the disposition of the exact point at issue. Such language is known as *obiter dictum* ("that which is said in passing"). In theory it does not have the force of law and will not necessarily be followed in later cases under the rule of *stare decisis*. In practice the Supreme Court does not always draw a careful line between established legal principles and mere obiter dicta. Many a rule has found its way into constitutional law by this path. On the other hand, there are striking examples of the repudiation of such dicta. For example, in 1926, in *Myers* v. *United States*,[5] the Supreme Court upheld the right of the President to remove a postmaster from office without restraint by Congress. In the majority opinion, Chief Justice William Howard Taft used obiter dictum to the effect that the removal power of the President extended to the members of the independent regulatory commissions. But in 1935, in *Rathbun* v. *United States*,[6] Taft's dictum was repudiated, and it was held that Congress might by law restrict the President's power to remove from office members of the Federal Trade Commission.

the tradition of dissent

There has been much controversy concerning the dissenting opinion. Although dissents among Supreme Court justices have been at an all-time high in recent years, the tradition of dissent has always been an honored one with the Court. This is in contrast with the very sparing use of dissenting opinions by some state supreme courts.

Criticism of dissent rests on a number of grounds. Those who believe in the certainty of the law and who think that there is only *one* "correct" solution to any legal problem are, of course, critical of dissenting opinions. "Judicial dissent often is blamed," Justice Holmes has said, "as if it meant simply that one side or the other were not doing their sums right, and, if they would take more

---

[4] "Judicial Process," *Encyclopaedia of the Social Sciences*, VIII, 450, 455.
[5] *Myers* v. *United States*, 272 U.S. 52 (1926).
[6] *Rathbun* v. *United States*, 295 U.S. 602 (1935).

trouble, agreement inevitably would come." [7] As Holmes implies, this criticism is not a sound one, for it ignores the high degree of legal uncertainty in a case—particularly in the area of constitutional law—which often permits able, honest, and hard-working judges to disagree.

More sophisticated critics of the dissenting opinion hold that, although differences among justices are frequently legitimate on intellectual grounds, the desirability of giving law a seeming unity should persuade minority justices to abandon their dissenting views in favor of a unanimous stand. This, it is argued, would lead to greater public respect for courts, and would make for a more law-abiding citizenry. This position has a good deal of merit, but it would strengthen legal certainty and stability at the expense of experimentation and progress in the law. In the area of public law the degree of uncertainty is sometimes so great that there is always a chance that a dissenting position, even where held by a single justice, may prove ultimately to be sounder than the position of the majority. Accordingly, it can be argued that it is desirable that such a judge state his views openly and formally so that if indeed his judgment should prove to be the wiser, it may be recorded and stand as an invitation to future change. As Hamilton has pointed out, "the path of constitutional law has often been blazed in dissent." [8] And in his Columbia Law School lectures Charles Evans Hughes stated: "A dissent in a court of last resort is an appeal to the brooding spirit of the law, to the intelligence of a future day, when a later decision may possibly correct the error into which the dissenting judge believes the court to have been betrayed." [9] A present member of the Supreme Court, Justice William O. Douglas, has said: "When judges do not agree it is a sign that they are dealing with problems on which society itself is divided. It is the democratic way to express dissident views. Judges are to be honored rather than criticized for following that tradition, for proclaiming their articles of faith so that all may read." [10]

A striking example of the power which a dissenting opinion may have is to be seen in the handling by the Supreme Court of the issue of the compulsory flag salute. In 1940 the Court sanctioned a state requirement that school children salute the flag, rejecting the argument that the requirement violated the due process clause of the Fourteenth Amendment. Justice Harlan Stone alone dissented. Just three years later, as the result of certain changes in Court personnel, and also of a change of heart by several justices who had participated in

---

[7] Oliver Wendell Holmes, Jr., *Collected Legal Papers* (New York: Harcourt, Brace and Company, 1920), p. 180.

[8] "Judicial Process," VIII, 455.

[9] Charles Evans Hughes, *The Supreme Court of the United States* (New York: Columbia University Press, 1928), p. 68.

[10] Address delivered to the American Bar Association as reported in the *New York Times,* Sept. 9, 1948, p. 32.

the earlier case, the Stone dissenting position was sanctioned by a majority and the compulsory flag salute was declared unconstitutional. [11]

In view of the dynamic role which dissent has played in the development of constitutional law, it is no accident that dissenting opinions receive a great deal of attention. Particularly when the dissent has been registered by such distinguished justices as Holmes and Brandeis, this attention has sometimes exceeded that given to those opinions in which they speak for a Court majority. A further reason for this attention is that in the dissenting opinion a justice has a better opportunity to make an accurate and uncompromising statement of his legal and constitutional philosophy than is possible where he is speaking for a majority of the justices. As Hamilton has pointed out, "The dissent is [a justice's] own utterance, unconfused by the need of voicing the opinion of others; it is not the law, but the law as he would have it be." [12]

the reversal of decisions

Closely related to the matter of dissent is the practice by which appellate courts occasionally reverse previous decisions and alter a legal principle—in spite of the rule of *stare decisis*. Again the Supreme Court affords a good illustration of this practice. In the ten-year period from 1937 through 1946 the Court overruled thirty-two previous decisions.[13] A count made by Justice Louis Brandeis in 1932 indicates that the Court had reversed itself at least twenty-nine times previous to that year.[14]

In many of these reversals the new position of the majority closely approximates an earlier position taken by dissenting justices, thus proving the correctness of the Hughes thesis that the dissenting opinion may sometimes appeal successfully to the intelligence of a later day. Nonetheless, the reversal of earlier decisions by the Supreme Court has been viewed with alarm by many people. Outstanding among criticisms of the practice is the angry protest found in Justice Roberts's dissenting opinion in *Smith* v. *Allwright*. In that 1944 case the Supreme Court expressly reversed its earlier decision in *Grovey* v. *Townsend* and held that action by a political party excluding Negroes from participation in a primary election was *state* action subject to the prohibitory clauses of the Fourteenth and Fifteenth Amendments. [15] Justice Roberts's objections were in the following words:

---

[11] The original stand was taken in *Minersville School District* v. *Gobitis*, 310 U.S. 586 (1940); the reversal occurred in *West Virginia State Board of Education* v. *Barnette*, 319 U.S. 624 (1943).

[12] Walton Hamilton, "The Jurist's Art," in *Selected Essays on Constitutional Law* (Chicago: The Foundation Press, Inc., 1938) I, 604.

[13] C. H. Pritchett, *The Roosevelt Court* (New York: The Macmillan Company, 1948), pp. 57, 300–301.

[14] *Burnet* v. *Coronado Oil and Gas Co.*, 285 U.S. 393, 405–409 (1932).

[15] *Smith* v. *Allwright*, 321 U.S. 649 (1944) reversing *Grovey* v. *Townsend*, 295 U.S. 45 (1935).

This tendency [to overrule earlier decisions], it seems to me, indicates an intolerance for what those who have composed this court in the past have conscientiously and deliberately concluded, and involves an assumption that knowledge and wisdom reside in us which was denied to our predecessors. . . . The reason for my concern is that the instant decision, overruling that announced about nine years ago, tends to bring adjudications of this tribunal into the same class as a restricted railroad ticket, good for this day and train only. . . . It is regrettable that in an era marked by doubt and confusion, an era whose greatest need is steadfastness of thought and purpose, this court, which has been looked to as exhibiting consistency in adjudication, and a steadiness which would hold the balance even in the face of temporary ebbs and flows of opinion, should now itself become the breeder of fresh doubt and confusion in the public mind as to the stability of our institutions.

Justice Holmes likewise once warned against too frequent reversals, although his own record of dissent strongly suggests that he believed the Court had misconstrued many rules of constitutional law:

I do not expect or think it desirable that the judges should undertake to renovate the law. That is not their province. Indeed, precisely because I believe that the world would be just as well off if it lived under laws that differed from ours in many ways, and because I believe that the claim of our especial code to respect is simply that it exists, that it is the one to which we have become accustomed, and not that it represents an eternal principle, I am slow to consent to overruling a precedent, and think that our important duty is to see that the judicial duel shall be fought out in the accustomed way.[16]

Benjamin Cardozo has stated what is perhaps a reasonable and workable policy concerning the abandonment of established rules of law:

. . . the labor of judges would be increased almost to the breaking point if every past decision could be reopened in every case, and one could not lay one's own course of bricks on the secure foundation of the courses laid by others who had gone before him. . . . But I am ready to concede that the rule of adherence to precedent, though it ought not to be abandoned, ought to be in some degree relaxed. I think that when a rule, after it has been duly tested by experience, has been found to be inconsistent with the sense of justice, or with the social welfare, there should be less hesitation in frank avowal and full abandonment.[17]

Finally, it should be recognized that there are transitional periods in history when change in the law must inevitably accompany the changes which are

---

[16] Holmes, *Collected Legal Papers*, p. 239.

[17] Benjamin N. Cardozo, *The Nature of the Judicial Process* (New Haven: Yale University Press, 1921), pp. 149–150. Reprinted by permission of the Yale University Press, publishers.

occurring in society. In view of the economic and international crises which have confronted the United States during the last twenty years, it is not surprising that legislators and judges alike have been compelled to revise old laws and make new ones for the better control of social conflicts and problems. "As conditions and opinion become stable," Hamilton has written, "the law tends toward organic unity; at the impact of an advancing culture it becomes disorderly." [18]

the future of court procedure

It seems clear that court procedure must grow more flexible. Courts exist so that there may be machinery to settle human conflicts. As life in a modern industrial society has grown more complex, the tangled affairs of men have placed an increasingly difficult burden upon the courts. By and large the judiciary has been forced to meet its growing responsibilities with forms and procedures which took shape centuries ago when the volume and the complexity of litigation were quite different from what they are today. In part, the persistence of ancient judicial patterns is a fortunate thing, for the Anglo-American court is certainly one of the most satisfactory institutions ever devised for the settlement of litigation. Among the court systems known to human history ours has been unusually successful in giving a measure of reality to the ideal of "equal justice under law."

And yet the present inadequacies of traditional judicial procedure are leading to dependence upon other institutions for the prompt and efficient disposition of cases. The increasing importance of the regulatory commission has already been noted. A further illustration of this tendency is seen in the growing use of arbitration and mediation, rather than adjudication, as means of resolving conflicts. There are probably many areas of human affairs where this is a wise and sensible procedure. Arbitration has made particular headway as a means of settling business disputes. Through trade association agreements and clauses in private contracts large areas of commercial conflict are now subject to private arbitration rather than to adjudication in a public court. This development might have taken place in any case, but it has been hastened and strengthened by the delays and complexities of court procedure. [19] Arbitration is also widely used today to settle disputes between labor and management.[20]

It should not be thought that our traditional courts have resisted all pressures to modify their procedures in the light of present-day conditions and

---

[18] "Judicial Process," VIII, 454.

[19] See Wesley A. Sturges, "Arbitration, Commercial," *Encyclopaedia of the Social Sciences*, II, 151.

[20] See Carter Goodrich, "Arbitration, Industrial," *Encyclopaedia of the Social Sciences*, II, 153.

needs. For example, the small claims court found in many cities is clearly an attempt to adapt the device of arbitration to judicial procedure. Minor disputes—monetary and otherwise—are settled by a judge in an informal way, frequently without the need of lawyers to represent the parties and without undue emphasis upon finding a decision dictated by legal precedents. The juvenile court also illustrates the ability of our judicial system to abandon rigid and complex rituals where they stand in the way of the wise disposition of cases in the light of new scientific knowledge concerning human beings and their troubles. Here again lawyers are dispensed with, or their function is minimized, and procedure is simplified with the aim of obtaining a just but humane solution of the problem.

The need to adapt judicial procedures to the complexities of modern life is felt most keenly at the level of the trial court. The most serious problem at the appellate level has been to adapt procedures so as to limit both the kind and the number of cases accepted for review. In good part this problem has been solved, at least with respect to the federal judiciary. The Supreme Court has developed into a "public law" tribunal whose primary assignment is to "make law" by interpreting and applying the Constitution and federal statutes. But the further adaptation of the ancient procedures of the trial court to the changing nature of litigation in the mid-twentieth century remains one of our most pressing problems of government reorganization.

bibliographic note

Because of the use made of precedents, Anglo-American law is in good part "case law." For this reason, the reporting of court decisions has always been an important characteristic of the American and British judicial systems. This is particularly true of the decisions of appellate courts, for it is at this level that legal principles are made and refined. The trial court does not usually record its judgments in written opinions, although some of its rulings during the course of a trial may ultimately be published to serve as precedents in future cases.

The reporting system now in use in the federal courts is a remarkably complete one. To begin with, the opinions of the Supreme Court—majority, concurring, and dissenting—are published each year in a series of volumes known as the *United States Reports*. These volumes appear at the rate of about 3 a year and have now reached a total of nearly 350. Until shortly after the Civil War the volumes bore the name of the Court reporter and were privately published. Thus the citation of the *Dred Scott* case is 19 Howard 393 (the 19th volume edited by Howard, beginning at page 393), and that of *McCulloch* v. *Maryland* is 4 Wheaton 316. Since 1875, the volumes have been cited simply as *United*

States. Thus the Wagner Act cases are found in 301 U.S. 1 (the 301st volume of the *United States Reports* beginning at page 1). In addition to the *United States Reports,* which is an official publication of the federal government, two commercial editions of Supreme Court decisions are published by private concerns. One of these is known as the *Supreme Court* reporter (the citation of the Wagner Act cases is 57 Sup. Ct. 615), and the other as the *Lawyers' Edition* (the citation of the Wagner Act cases is 81 L. Ed. 893). These private series are annotated and carry additional aids which make them somewhat more useful to practicing lawyers than is the official edition.

The rulings of the lower federal courts are not available in a government-printed edition, but are published in private series by the West Publishing Company of St. Paul, Minnesota, under an agreement with the federal government. There are four separate series. The rulings of the lower federal courts from "the earliest times" to 1880 are contained in a series of thirty volumes known as the *Federal Cases.* The cases are numbered (1 to 18,313) and are arranged alphabetically rather than chronologically, since lower-court decisions were not published contemporaneously until 1880. From 1880 to 1924 lower-court cases were reported year by year in chronological fashion in a series of 300 volumes known as the *Federal Reporter.* In 1924 the *Federal Reporter* (2d series) was started and now numbers more than 170 volumes. In 1932 this series was limited to the decisions of the circuit court of appeals, and beginning in that year the miscellaneous rulings of the district courts were reported in a series known as the *Federal Supplement.*

The titles referred to in the bibliographic notes to the two preceding chapters are in most instances also concerned with the courts at work. W. F. Willoughby's *Principles of Judicial Administration* (Washington: The Brookings Institution, 1929), a companion volume to his *Principles of Legislative Organization and Administration,* is an excellent collection of essays. There are chapters on the problem of crime and law enforcement, on the work of departments of justice, on the role of the prosecuting attorney, on the organization of police departments, on court organization (federal, state, and local), and on the courts at work. The work of courts of appeals is examined in Roscoe Pound's *Appellate Procedure in Civil Cases* (Boston: Little, Brown & Company, 1941). A systematic analysis of the handling of appeals in criminal cases is found in Lester B. Orfield's *Criminal Appeals in America* (Boston: Little, Brown & Company, 1939). The Pound and Orfield volumes are part of the Judicial Administration Series, sponsored by the National Conference of Judicial Councils. Felix Frankfurter and James M. Landis's *The Business of the Supreme Court* (New York: The Macmillan Company, 1927), a classic study by two famous students of the judicial process, is somewhat misnamed. It is largely concerned with the history of the judiciary acts of Congress by which the Court's jurisdiction has gradually been brought within manageable limits.

the Supreme Court as an instrument of government

HE Supreme Court has . . . ceased to be a common law court. The stuff of its business is . . . public law and not the ordinary legal questions involved in the multitudinous lawsuits of *Doe* v. *Roe* of other courts. The construction of important federal legislation and of the Constitution is now the staple business of the Supreme Court." [1] This observation made some twenty years ago by Felix Frankfurter suggests that there are three functions which have been or are now performed by the Supreme Court: (1) adjudicating common-law or private law disputes between individuals which are of no great concern to the public; (2) construing federal statutes; and (3) testing the constitutionality of legislative and executive acts. The second and third functions are of great concern to the public and fall within Frankfurter's "public law" category.

In a nation as large and as complex as the United States there is an undeniable need for a single, great court of appeals standing at the apex of the judicial system. This need is a twofold one. First is the need for a body to act as a final arbiter in construing the Constitution and in refereeing conflicting claims of power between the states and the national government on the one hand or between the states themselves on the other, lest half a hundred semisovereign states tread upon one another's toes or encroach upon the powers of the national government. Second is the need for a single court to provide one uniform interpretation of national law. Once law of this character has been authoritatively declared and interpreted, its application to the conflicts of private individuals no longer need concern the highest court in the land.

In a sense the first of the needs for a high court could be met by the national legislature. But since Congress is often a direct opponent of the states in the

---

[1] Felix Frankfurter, "Supreme Court, United States," *Encyclopaedia of the Social Sciences,* XIV, 474.

struggle for power, there is much to be said for the settlement of disputes between the nation and the states by an independent judicial body. The second need can be met only by a court, since it is the unique function of the judiciary in a democracy to provide a final interpretation of the law. If federal laws are to mean the same thing throughout the United States, not only as to the exact language of statutes but with respect also to the judicial gloss which courts add to statutes in enforcing them, obviously one court of appeals must provide a final interpretation.

the theory and origin of judicial review

the meaning and extent of judicial review

The first of the two needs is met through the practice of judicial review, which Professor Edward S. Corwin has called "the most distinctive feature of the American Constitutional system." Judicial review may be defined as the process by which courts test the acts of other governmental agencies—legislatures particularly—for compliance with fundamental constitutional principles. It is a power which is possessed, and from time to time exercised, by all American courts, federal and state. Any federal court can declare any statute—state or federal—invalid under the federal Constitution and refuse to enforce it. Similarly, any state court can declare a federal statute invalid under the federal Constitution, or a state statute invalid under either the federal or a state constitution. The only thing that deters any particular court from exercising such power is the nature of its jurisdiction; it can invalidate a statute only in the process of deciding a case involving the statute, a case which it has authority to hear. In the end, however, it is the Supreme Court of the United States which, almost without exception, determines whether or not a state or a federal statute is in conflict with the federal Constitution.

judicial review before 1787

There has been much controversy concerning the origin of judicial review in the United States. The controversy has been encouraged by the fact that the Constitution itself is ambiguous on the point and by the knowledge that judicial review was not widely known in 1787 and certainly had not become a *normal function* of courts in any country. Some scholars have argued that before the drafting of the American Constitution judicial review had been employed in England and in the American colonies to the extent that it had come to be viewed as a normal, traditional judicial function, and that thus there was no need to make elaborate mention of it in the Constitution. But the evidence will not support this position. It is true that in 1610 Sir Edward Coke, the great English Chief Justice, in his famous opinion in *Dr. Bonham's Case* seemingly championed judicial review when he said: "And it appears in our books that in many cases the common law will controul acts of parliament and sometimes adjudge them to be utterly void: for when an act of parliament is against common right or reason, or repugnant or impossible to be performed, the common law will controul it and adjudge such act to be void." [2] But even at the time, Coke's dictum was not widely accepted in England, and with the Revolution of 1688 it was for all practical purposes repudiated in favor of the absolute *legislative supremacy* of Parliament.

In America during the colonial period, and in the decade preceding the Philadelphia convention in which independent governments were operating in the thirteen states, scattered evidences of judicial review can be found. For example, in a handful of cases decided between 1776 and 1787 several state courts seemingly invalidated acts passed by state legislatures. The most famous of these cases was *Trevett* v. *Weeden*, in which a Rhode Island court in 1786 pronounced null and void an act of the state assembly requiring paper money to be accepted as legal tender. But historians have disagreed as to whether the facts of these cases show true judicial review in operation; in any event their number is so small that they cannot support an argument that judicial review was viewed as a normal judicial function when the Philadelphia convention met in 1787.

the intention of the Constitutional Fathers as to judicial review

It is very clear that the Constitution itself does not *in so many words* authorize the Supreme Court, or any other court, to declare acts of Congress unconstitutional. What the Constitution does say in section two of Article Six is this: "This Constitution, and the laws of the United States . . . shall be the supreme law of the land; and the judges in every State shall be bound thereby, anything in the Constitution or laws of any State to the contrary notwithstanding." From this it may be argued that judicial review as to state legislation is provided for in reasonably unambiguous language. But nowhere, it must be emphasized, is there any express provision for judicial invalidation of federal legislation.

Whether the framers of the Constitution intended the Supreme Court to invalidate acts of Congress is a historical puzzle which will probably never be solved, since the debates of the Philadelphia convention throw very little light on the matter. Charles A. Beard, after a careful study of the issue, concluded that a majority of the influential delegates favored judicial review.[3] Most other historians have agreed with Beard, but it is true, as Corwin, possibly our greatest student of the American Constitution, has pointed out, that "neither party, perhaps, has quite all the truth on its side. That the Framers anticipated some sort of judicial review of acts of Congress there can be little question. But

---

[2] 8 Co. 114a; 2 Brownl. 255.

[3] Charles A. Beard, *The Supreme Court and the Constitution* (New York: The Macmillan Company, 1912), pp. 17–18.

it is equally without question that ideas generally current in 1787 were far from presaging the present vast role of the Court." [4]

Judicial review has had to find its official basis, then, not so much in the words of the Constitution or in historical usage as in rationalization and constitutional interpretation. The beginnings of what may be called the official theory supporting judicial review are to be seen in *The Federalist,* the famous papers published during the struggle over the ratification of the Constitution. In Number 78 of the papers, written by Alexander Hamilton, the following specific defense of judicial review is found:

> The interpretation of the laws is the proper and peculiar province of the courts. A constitution is, in fact, and must be regarded by the judges, as a fundamental law. It therefore belongs to them to ascertain its meaning, as well as the meaning of any particular act proceeding from the legislative body. If there should happen to be an irreconcilable variance between the two, that which has the superior obligation and validity ought, of course, to be preferred; or, in other words, the Constitution ought to be preferred to the statute, the intention of the people to the intention of their agents. [5]

judicial review established in Marbury v. *Madison*

A few years later this statement provided inspiration for the Supreme Court's own position as to judicial review. In 1803, in *Marbury* v. *Madison,* a provision of federal law was for the first time declared unconstitutional. [6] The narrow point at issue was the Court's own jurisdiction. William Marbury, who had been appointed to the office of justice of the peace in the closing days of the Adams administration, asked the Court to take original jurisdiction over his case under a provision of the Judiciary Act of 1789 and to issue a writ of mandamus ordering Madison, the new Secretary of State under Jefferson, to deliver his commission to him. The Supreme Court, speaking through Chief Justice John Marshall, found a specific conflict between Article Three of the Constitution, which limited the Court's original jurisdiction to two situations, and the act of 1789, which seemed to give it such jurisdiction in a third situation. Assuming that such a conflict between Constitution and statute existed, did it follow that the Court must invalidate the statute? Marshall believed that it did, and his argument runs something like this: *It is one of the purposes of a written constitution to define and limit the powers of the legislature. The legislature cannot be permitted to pass statutes contrary to a constitution, if the latter is to prevail as superior law.*

---

[4] "The Constitution as Instrument and as Symbol," *American Political Science Review,* XXX (December, 1936), 1078. For a position directly opposite to that of Beard, see L. B. Boudin, *Government by Judiciary* (New York: William Godwin, Inc., 1932), Vol. I, Chaps. 3–10.
[5] *The Federalist* (Henry Cabot Lodge, ed.; New York: G. P. Putnam's Sons, 1888), pp. 485–486.
[6] 1 Cranch 137 (1803).

A court cannot avoid choosing between the Constitution and a conflicting statute when both are relevant to a case which the court is asked to decide. Since the Constitution is paramount law, judges have no choice but to prefer it to the statute and to refuse to give effect to the latter. To buttress this general line of reasoning Marshall cited Article Three of the Constitution, which specifically authorizes judges to decide cases "arising under this Constitution," and Article Six, which requires them to take an oath to support the Constitution. Accordingly, the Court concluded that the provision in the act of 1789 was invalid, and that it must refuse to take jurisdiction over the case or to issue the requested writ of mandamus.

It is interesting to note that Marshall failed to cite any judicial precedents or historical evidence to support the Court's decision. The opinion consists solely of logical reasoning concerning the nature of constitutional government, and, as such, the argument is a very convincing one. Nonetheless, the fundamental point in the Chief Justice's logic—that a judge confronted with a conflict between a statute and the Constitution must necessarily uphold the Constitution and declare the statute null and void—is not unassailable.

The use of similar logic to reach an exactly opposite conclusion has never been better illustrated than by Justice Gibson of the Pennsylvania Supreme Court in a dissenting opinion in the 1825 case of *Eakin* v. *Raub.* His reasoning runs as follows: *It may be granted that a judge may be asked in a specific case to enforce a statute which he believes is in conflict with constitutional principles. Yet there is nothing in the judge's oath or in his duties of office which requires him to determine a statute's constitutionality before he proceeds to apply it. It is the business of courts to interpret and apply statutes, not to determine whether the legislature erred in passing them. If a legislature has in fact passed an unconstitutional statute, the responsibility rests exclusively with the legislators. Judges have no positive duty to correct the error; neither do they commit any unconscious wrong in giving effect to such a law.*[7]

judicial review in practice

the sparing and sporadic use of judicial review

One of the most striking things about judicial review is the sparing and sporadic use to which it has been put by the Supreme Court. Following *Marbury* v. *Madison* the power to invalidate a federal statute was not used again by the Supreme Court for more than half a century until the *Dred Scott* case in 1857.

---

[7] 12 Sergeant and Rawle 330 (1825). Gibson's dissenting opinion is reprinted in Cushman, *Leading Constitutional Decisions* (New York: Appleton-Century-Crofts, Inc., 9th ed., 1950), p. 252.

In the meantime the Court first held a state law void under the federal Constitution in *Fletcher* v. *Peck* in 1810.[8] Up to the Civil War only two federal
statutes and fewer than twenty state laws were invalidated. Not until about
1890 did the Court begin to invalidate federal or state laws with any regularity,
and even then the number of laws rejected has been far smaller than is often
supposed. To the present day the Supreme Court has invalidated provisions of
federal law in some eighty cases. In most of these cases only a part of a statute—
often a minor and unimportant part—has been annulled. Only eight or ten
statutes have been declared unconstitutional in their entirety.[9] Since 1789 Congress has passed about 30,000 public acts. [10]

The spotty character of judicial review is made further apparent by an
analysis of the constitutional clauses which have served as a basis for judicial
rulings invalidating legislation. Until about 1890 most state laws invalidated by
the Supreme Court were held to contravene one (or sometimes both) of two
clauses of the original Constitution. The first of these was the clause in section
eight of Article One, which grants to Congress the power to regulate interstate
and foreign commerce; the second was the clause in section ten of the same
article, which forbids the states to pass laws "impairing the obligation of contracts." After 1890, however, the second clause was cited less often, and a large
number of state measures were struck down on the ground that they violated the
prohibitions of the Fourteenth Amendment against state action depriving persons of life, liberty, or property without due process of law, or denying persons
the equal protection of the laws.[11] On the other hand, the Court has at no time
made more than a very sparing use of a third prohibition in the Fourteenth
Amendment forbidding the states to abridge the privileges or immunities of
citizens of the United States. Indeed, in refusing in 1873 to invalidate a state law
on this ground the Court expressly stated that it did not wish to become "the
perpetual censor" of state legislation.[12]

With respect to federal legislation the Court has seldom chosen to in-

---

[8] *Fletcher* v. *Peck*, 6 Cranch 87 (1810).

[9] It is rather difficult for technical reasons to be absolutely accurate in presenting such
statistics. See *Provisions of Federal Law Held Unconstitutional by the Supreme Court of
the United States*, prepared by W. C. Gilbert of the Legislative Reference Service, Library
of Congress (Washington: Government Printing Office, 1936), pp. 1–91, for an analysis of
cases in which federal laws have been invalidated and a further list of questionable cases.

[10] Between 1789 and 1945 Congress passed a total of 64,446 laws. Of these, 28,237 were
public acts, and 36,209 were private acts.—George B. Galloway, *Congress at the Crossroads*
(New York: Thomas Y. Crowell Company, 1946), pp. 147–149.

[11] Of 128 state laws invalidated by the federal courts before 1888, 50 involved impairment
of contracts, 50 interference with interstate commerce, and only 1 the taking of property
without due process of law.—Charles G. Haines, *The American Doctrine of Judicial Supremacy* (Berkeley: University of California Press, 2d ed., 1932), p. 401n.

[12] *Slaughter-House Cases*, 16 Wallace 36, 78 (1873).

validate a measure solely on the basis that it deprives persons of their liberty or property without due process of law, as forbidden by the Fifth Amendment. Instead, it has preferred to hold that in enacting certain laws Congress has exceeded the limits of the positive legislative powers expressly granted to it in section eight of Article One of the Constitution. But here the Court has been highly selective in its references to the specific powers said to have been exceeded. It has been relatively free about invalidating statutes based upon the commerce power, but slow to strike down laws based upon the taxing, spending, postal, and war powers. Of course, this seeming inconsistency is partly explained by the fact that Congress itself has made greater use of the commerce power as a basis for the enactment of controversial legislation. Yet it has made wide use of the other powers named, and not a few of the resulting laws have been challenged as to constitutionality. But the number of such challenges upheld by the Supreme Court has been proportionately far smaller than in the area of the commerce clause.

the Supreme Court's self-imposed limitations upon judicial review

The invalidation of legislation has been further restricted by the Supreme Court itself through a number of limitations, mostly self-imposed, designed to prevent the exercise of judicial review in all save unusual and clear-cut circumstances. These limitations may be listed as follows:

1. Judicial review is to be exercised only in the course of actual, bona fide litigation. There must be a real "case" or "controversy" involving opposing parties with conflicting interests before the Court will pass upon a statute's constitutionality. Collusive or friendly suits as a basis for the testing of a law must be rejected. Likewise the issue of constitutionality may not be passed upon in *advisory opinions* requested of the courts by the legislature.

2. Judicial review will be exercised only when absolutely necessary to the proper disposition of a case. If in deciding a case the Court can see that justice is done to the litigants without considering the issue of constitutionality, it will do so.

3. If a statute is reasonably susceptible of differing interpretations, by one of which it would be unconstitutional and by another constitutional, the latter construction will be preferred.

4. A decision declaring a law invalid will never be rendered in a doubtful case. Every possible presumption will be made in favor of a law's validity. A law will be struck down only when it is proved invalid beyond a reasonable doubt.

5. If a statute is valid upon its face, it will not be annulled because of allegedly unconstitutional motives which may have influenced the legislature to enact it.

6. If a statute is valid in part and invalid in part, only the invalid part will be annulled, provided the valid part is separable from the invalid part.

7. The constitutionality of statutes will not be passed upon in cases presenting so-called *political questions* as opposed to legal questions. Just where the line is to be drawn between the two kinds of questions the Supreme Court has never made clear. But from time to time it has refused to review the validity of legislative acts on the ground that the issue presented by the case is a political one that must be settled by the *political* (i.e., nonjudicial) branches of the government. Into this category have been placed such constitutional questions as whether or not a state has a "republican form" of government (Article Four, section four), and whether or not the federal Constitution has been properly amended (Article Five).

There has been much controversy concerning the use of these seven limitations by the Supreme Court. It has been argued that they have not been followed strictly or consistently. For example, when the Court invalidates a statute by a five-to-four vote, has it in fact given the law the benefit of the doubt? If four justices vote to uphold a law, can the majority claim that its invalidity has been proved beyond a reasonable doubt? Or again it is sometimes said that the rule concerning the political question is a mere rationalization by which the Court avoids passing upon difficult, controversial, or politically embarrassing constitutional issues. Then, too, if the rule had been followed consistently, would the Court have passed on such seemingly political questions as the proper procedure to be followed in congressional investigations, or the extent to which the President may exercise his removal power?

And yet it seems clear that these limitations have operated to restrict the scope of judicial review. The Court may at times have applied the rules opportunistically or inconsistently, but in the end the rules have served to hold the exercise of the Court's power within narrower limits than might well have prevailed without them. Justice Louis Brandeis once went so far as to refer to these limitations as "a series of rules under which [the Supreme Court] has avoided passing upon a large part of all the constitutional questions pressed upon it for decision." [13]

the element of choice in judicial review

There has been much disagreement about the *kind of power* the Supreme Court exercises when it declares a statute unconstitutional. Does it exercise an automatic power by which it does only what the logic and force of constitutional principles permit it to do? Or does it exercise a discretionary power by which the justices determine the fate of a statute either way, as they will it?

---

[13] *Ashwander* v. *TVA*, 297 U.S. 288, 346 (1936).

the theory that the Supreme Court
exercises no discretion in judicial review cases

In many cases it is apparent that the Court has not arrived automatically at a predestined decision. Such is obviously the situation when eminent lawyers are uncertain which way a decision will go, when the Court itself is sharply divided in its judgment, or when it reverses the decision of a lower court or even one of its own earlier decisions. And yet, as Felix Frankfurter has pointed out, "it would seem that multitudes of Americans seriously believe that the nine justices embody pure reason, that they are set apart from the concerns of the community, regardless of time, place, and circumstances, to become the interpreter of sacred words with meaning fixed forever and ascertainable by a process of ineluctable reasoning." [14]

Indeed, Supreme Court justices have sometimes insisted in the course of their opinions that such is the true character of judicial review. In one of the most famous of these utterances, Justice Roberts—in the majority opinion in *United States* v. *Butler,* the case in which the first Agricultural Adjustment Act was declared unconstitutional by a six-to-three vote—said:

> There should be no misunderstanding as to the function of this court. . . . It is sometimes said that the court assumes a power to overrule or control the action of the people's representatives. This is a misconception. The Constitution is the supreme law of the land ordained and established by the people. All legislation must conform to the principles it lays down. When an act of Congress is appropriately challenged in the courts as not conforming to the constitutional mandate the judicial branch of the Government has only one duty—to lay the article of the Constitution which is invoked beside the statute which is challenged and to decide whether the latter squares with the former. All the court does, or can do, is to announce its considered judgment upon the question.[15]

the "choice" theory concerning judicial review

Such testimony notwithstanding, many authorities have pointed to the very large element of choice which is usually present in a case involving the constitutionality of a controversial statute. Constitutional law would seem to be as uncertain in this respect as common and statutory law. Indeed, the language in which principles find expression in the Constitution, and against which the validity of a statute must be determined, is, if anything, even less clear than the language of a typical statute or maxim of the common law. Speaking of the due process

---

[14] Felix Frankfurter, *Law and Politics* (New York: Harcourt, Brace and Company, 1939), p. 108. The excerpts quoted from this work are used by permission of Harcourt, Brace and Company, publishers.

[15] *United States* v. *Butler,* 297 U.S. 1, 62–63 (1936).

and equal protection clauses of the Fourteenth Amendment, which have been involved in so many judicial review cases, Felix Frankfurter states:

> . . . these broad "guarantees" in favor of the individual are expressed in words so undefined, either by their intrinsic meaning, or by history, or by tradition, that they leave the individual Justice free, if indeed they do not actually compel him, to fill in the vacuum with his own controlling notions of economic, social and industrial facts with reference to which they are invoked. These judicial judgments are thus bound to be determined by the experience, the environment, the fears, the imagination of the different Justices.[16]

Almost the same thing might be said of the commerce clause, the taxing clause, the war power clauses, and the other portions of the Constitution which have been involved in judicial review cases. Some sections of the Constitution, it is true, are quite specific, but these are usually not the sections against which the Court is asked to measure the constitutionality of statutes.

the controversy over judicial review

the continuity of attacks upon judicial review

The exercise of the power of judicial review by the Supreme Court has never long been free from controversy. The storm which raged about the Court in 1936 and 1937 as the result of its anti-New Deal decisions was only the most recent of many such storms in the Court's history. During the Marshall period, when the Court was dominated by the principles of the Federalist party, the Jeffersonian party, which had continuous control of the executive and legislative branches between 1801 and 1825, criticized the Court repeatedly and bitterly for many of its decisions. During Andrew Jackson's administration, the President was so irritated by rulings of the Court that upon one occasion he is reported to have said: "John Marshall has made his decision. Now let him enforce it." A little later the decision in the *Dred Scott* case brought down upon the Court abuse and criticism so bitter and vehement that it is doubtful whether the Court could have withstood the attack without giving ground had not the Civil War intervened to dispose of the issue of slavery in a different and more far-reaching way. The decision soon after the Civil War against the legal-tender policies of the national government was so unpopular that the Court was soon persuaded to reverse itself.[17] The action of the Court in 1895 invalidating a federal income tax law by a five-to-four vote aroused an opposition that did not abate until the decision was reversed through the adoption of the Sixteenth Amendment in 1913. The conservative decisions of the Court soon after the turn of the

---

[16] Frankfurter, *Law and Politics*, p. 13.

[17] See *Hepburn* v. *Griswold*, 8 Wallace 603 (1870); *Knox* v. *Lee*, 12 Wallace 457 (1871); and *Juilliard* v. *Greenman*, 110 U.S. 421 (1884).

twentieth century were bitterly debated, provoking strong anti-Court stands by the Roosevelt third party in 1912 and the La Follette third party in 1924.

It is important to note that in this continuing controversy over judicial review all political parties have sooner or later added their voices to the chorus of criticism, for no one party has been consistently the Court's champion or critic. "Every American political party at some time has sheltered itself behind the Supreme Court and at others has found in the Court's decisions obstructions to its purposes." [18]

The critics of the Court in the instances just mentioned did not always confine their attacks to the decisions which aroused their anger. Instead, the Court itself and its exercise of the power of judicial review were brought under fire; indeed, since 1803 there has been an almost constant stream of proposals for the alteration of the Supreme Court or its powers.

controversy over judicial review in relation to the incidence of its use

It may well be asked why, in view of the sparing use which the Court has made of the power of judicial review, demands for the control or alteration of this power should have been so strong and persistent. In part the answer is provided by reference to the cases mentioned above. It is true that the Court has not often invalidated federal laws and that many of the laws actually struck down were of minor importance. Yet in a half-dozen or more instances, coming at varying intervals, the Court has rejected federal statutes of major importance, over whose enactment great political battles had been fought and in whose successful enforcement millions of persons had a strong interest.

In part the answer is found in the realization that the importance of judicial review is not to be measured solely, or even primarily, by the number of times it has been used. The very existence of this judicial power has unquestionably had a limiting influence upon Congress and the state legislatures. The knowledge that the Court has invalidated similar laws, or that it is not inclined to look kindly upon particular kinds of legislative experiments, has certainly had a deterring effect at certain periods upon legislative bodies. Particularly in its most conservative periods has the Court by its negative influence served as a powerful restraining force against the enactment of progressive social legislation. For example, in 1923 the decision in *Adkins* v. *Children's Hospital*,[19] invalidating a District of Columbia minimum-wage law for women and children, had the effect of rendering inoperative similar laws in several of the states, and for a decade discouraged both Congress and the state legislatures from further experimentation with minimum-wage standards. Or, to refer to a Supreme Court decision invalidating a state law, the 1928 ruling in *Ribnik* v. *McBride*, annulling a New Jersey statute regulating employment agencies, automatically deter-

---

[18] Frankfurter, "Supreme Court, United States," XIV, 480.
[19] *Adkins* v. *Children's Hospital*, 261 U.S. 525 (1923).

mined "the constitutionality of similar statutes in perhaps twenty other states." [20]

reform proposals

Attention may now be given to the specific proposals which have been made for change in the Supreme Court. These proposals can be grouped roughly into four categories: (1) those affecting Court personnel; (2) those affecting Court structure and jurisdiction; (3) those affecting Court procedure; and (4) those seeking to overcome the adverse effect of Court rulings.

1. CHANGES IN COURT PERSONNEL. More proposals have perhaps looked toward changes in the personnel of the Court than toward any other change. In the struggle over the Court in 1937 the specific proposal advocated by the President was that the Court be enlarged by act of Congress so that its views on the Constitution might be altered through the appointment of new justices. Although Congress rejected the proposal, it should be noted that the size of the Court had previously been changed by act of Congress several times. The Court originally consisted of six members. It was reduced to five in 1801, increased to seven in 1807, to nine in 1837, and to ten in 1863. In 1866 it was reduced to seven, and finally fixed at nine in 1869. In every one of these instances there is at least some evidence that the change was designed to influence the Court's decisions.

Impeachment is another method which has been used in an attempt to influence the Supreme Court through control of its personnel. In 1805, the Jeffersonians who controlled Congress tried to remove from the Court one of its leading Federalist justices, the irascible Samuel Chase. The Jeffersonian party succeeded in obtaining his impeachment in the House of Representatives, but in the Senate the vote for conviction fell just short of the required two thirds. This failure, plus the fact that the letter of the Constitution makes it clear that removal of an officer by impeachment is only to be made for such serious offenses as treason, bribery, or other high crime or misdemeanor, pretty well discouraged further efforts to use this method as a means of influencing or altering the Supreme Court's constitutional views.

Compulsory retirement of justices at a fixed age and the recall of judges by popular election have also been suggested. The latter proposal has not been seriously made as to Supreme Court justices but the former has been repeatedly urged. Congress has encouraged voluntary retirement of federal judges but no proposal for compulsory retirement has ever been accepted.

2. CHANGES IN COURT STRUCTURE OR JURISDICTION. Several reform proposals have been based upon Congress's undeniable power to control the structure and jurisdiction of the federal courts. Under the Constitution it is actually possible for Congress to abolish a federal court. It is true that the Constitution

---

[20] Walter F. Dodd, *Cases on Constitutional Law* (St. Paul: West Publishing Company, 2d ed., 1937), p. 97.

provides that there shall be one Supreme Court, but Congress might attempt to abolish the existing Court and replace it with another. In 1861, as part of the attack upon the Supreme Court occasioned by its decision in the *Dred Scott* case, Senator John P. Hale of New Hampshire introduced a resolution embodying just such a proposal. The resolution, of course, was not adopted. The Constitution also gives Congress authority to fix by law the classes of cases which the Supreme Court may hear. In 1868 Congress passed a law curtailing the appellate jurisdiction in such a manner as to prevent the Court from taking jurisdiction over a case which raised the issue of the constitutionality of the Reconstruction Acts.[21] But extensive use of this method of controlling the Court's rulings would not be very feasible.

3. CHANGES IN COURT PROCEDURE. The most significant proposals for altering the Court's procedures have been directed at the five-to-four decision. One line of attack has proposed that a larger majority be required for the invalidation of federal laws. It has been suggested that a two-thirds vote, or even seven out of nine, be required. Whether such a change would require a constitutional amendment, or whether it could be done by act of Congress or even a rule voluntarily adopted by the Court, is subject to argument. An alternate proposal which has several times been made is that the Constitution be amended so as to empower Congress to repass a law over an adverse decision of the Supreme Court. Senator Burton K. Wheeler of Montana made such a proposal in 1937. His proposed amendment required that a national election must intervene between the Court ruling and the repassage of the law, and also that the reenactment be by a two-thirds vote in both houses of Congress.

4. OVERCOMING COURT DECISIONS BY CONSTITUTIONAL AMENDMENT. Finally, many proposals have been made that adverse Supreme Court decisions be overcome by constitutional amendment dealing with the substance of the disputed legislative power or legislation, rather than with the mechanism of judicial review. Some of the proposed amendments would have broadened and clarified congressional power generally. Others have been limited to an approval of the specific legislative policy rejected by the Court. The Sixteenth Amendment expressly authorized a federal income tax, thus repudiating the adverse ruling of the Court on this point in *Pollock* v. *Farmers' Loan and Trust Co.* in 1895.[22] Similarly the Eleventh and Fourteenth Amendments reversed specific adverse Supreme Court rulings.

an evaluation of judicial review

It is significant that not one of the many controversies over the Supreme Court's use of its power to invalidate legislation has resulted in a serious and straight-

[21] See *Ex Parte McCardle*, 7 Wallace 506 (1869).
[22] *Pollock* v. *Farmers' Loan and Trust Co.*, 157 U.S. 429; 158 U.S. 601 (1895).

forward proposal that judicial review itself be entirely abolished. The failure of any major political party or responsible candidate for public office to advocate this particular constitutional change indicates perhaps that, no matter how unpopular the Court may be at a given moment, its power to invalidate legislative acts seems to be inviolable.

Actually, if one accepts fully the premise of democracy as the basis of American government, a strong, logical argument can be made against judicial review. The argument runs as follows: The ambiguities of our Constitution allow personal predilections to play a part in the rulings of the Court as to the validity of legislation. Such discretionary power should not be entrusted to officials who are appointed rather than elected, and who hold office for life rather than for fixed terms. Under these circumstances the interpretation of the Constitution is better entrusted to the people's chosen representatives—the President and the Congress.

Any attempt to weigh the pros and cons of judicial review must take into account the difference between invalidation of state legislation and invalidation of federal legislation. One can disagree with a Supreme Court decision annulling a specific state law, but it is difficult to see how to avoid vesting power in some such central judicial body as the Supreme Court to check the actions of forty-eight state governments for compliance with the national Constitution. On this point Justice Holmes once said: "I do not think the United States would come to an end if we [the justices of the Supreme Court] lost our power to declare an Act of Congress void. I do think the Union would be imperiled if we could not make that declaration as to the laws of the several States." [23]

But even judicial review of federal legislation has never been in serious danger, for proposals to "reform" the Court have always fallen short of an attack upon judicial review itself. In this respect it is significant that some of the great liberal scholars of the law, although often critical of particular decisions of the Supreme Court, have come to the conclusion that judicial review serves a desirable end. As Benjamin Cardozo put it a few years before he was elevated to the Supreme Court:

> The great ideals of liberty and equality are preserved against the assaults of opportunism, the expediency of the passing hour, the erosion of small encroachments, the scorn and derision of those who have no patience with general principles, by enshrining them in constitutions, and consecrating to the task of their protection a body of defenders. By conscious or subconscious influence, the presence of this restraining power, aloof in the background, but nonetheless always in reserve, tends to stabilize and rationalize the legislative judgment, to infuse it with the glow of principle, to hold the standard aloft and visible for those who must run the race and

---

[23] Oliver Wendell Holmes, Jr., *Collected Legal Papers* (New York: Harcourt, Brace and Company, 1920), pp. 295–296.

keep the faith. . . . Great maxims, if they may be violated with impunity, are honored often with lip-service, which passes easily into irreverence. The restraining power of the judiciary does not manifest its chief worth in the few cases in which the legislature has gone beyond the lines that mark the limits of discretion. Rather shall we find its chief worth in making vocal and audible the ideals that might otherwise be silenced, in giving them continuity of life and expression, in guiding and directing choice within the limits where choice ranges. This function should preserve to the courts the power that now belongs to them, if only the power is exercised with insight into social values, and with suppleness of adaptation to changing social needs.[24]

Equally impressive are the words of Felix Frankfurter—like those of Benjamin Cardozo, written before he was appointed to the Supreme Court:

The Supreme Court is indispensable to the effective workings of our federal government. If it did not exist, we should have to create it. I know of no other peaceful method for making the adjustments necessary to a society like ours—for maintaining the equilibrium between state and federal power, for settling the eternal conflicts between liberty and authority—than through a court of great traditions free from the tensions and temptations of party strife, detached from the fleeting interests of the moment. But because, inextricably, the Supreme Court is also an organ of statesmanship and the most powerful organ, it must have a seasoned understanding of affairs, the imagination to see the organic relations of society, above all, the humility not to set up its own judgment against the conscientious efforts of those whose primary duty it is to govern. . . .[25]

Although no formal alteration of judicial review has ever occurred, it is erroneous to conclude that the Supreme Court has not been affected by the storms that have raged about it. The evidence clearly indicates that its exercise of the power of judicial review has often been influenced by pressure brought to bear upon it from without. The justices have frequently been influenced by the expressions of unmistakable displeasure which their decisions in controversial constitutional cases have sometimes evoked from the American people. The conclusion to be drawn is obvious. Judicial review is a firmly established part of the American political process, and attempts to remove it are doomed to end in failure. At the same time this particular aspect of our political system is by no means beyond the influence of public opinion and popular control. Accordingly, it should be recognized that the Supreme Court is, on the whole, subject to many of the same forces and influences as are the other agencies of democratic

---

[24] Benjamin N. Cardozo, *The Nature of the Judicial Process* (New Haven: Yale University Press, 1921), pp. 92–94. Reprinted by permission of the Yale University Press, publishers.
[25] Frankfurter, *Law and Politics*, pp. 52–53.

government and that when a case presenting a great "constitutional" issue arises, the decision is bound to be at least partly political.

statute interpretation by the Supreme Court

The second great function of a public law court is the interpretation of statutes. Moreover, it is the function of a "supreme court" to provide a uniform interpretation of statutes which can be followed by all lower courts. The Supreme Court of the United States has been the final authority from which has flowed an endless series of rulings giving authoritative and definitive meaning to the great national statutes under which so many phases of our social and economic activity are regulated. The importance of this phase of the Supreme Court's work has never been sufficiently recognized. There has been a tendency to emphasize the function of judicial review and to overlook the function of statute interpretation—to give a great deal of attention to cases in which statutes are invalidated outright, and to give relatively little attention to cases in which statutes are merely construed and applied. If one is interested in the total power of the Supreme Court and the full record of its participation in the governmental process, it is a serious mistake to minimize cases of the latter type.

Since 1936 the Supreme Court has invalidated only two minor provisions of federal law.[26] State laws have been declared void far more infrequently than was true a generation ago. Yet the work of the Court continues to be most important, and at many points highly controversial. This is due in part to the fact that many great statutes, some old—such as the Sherman Antitrust Act and the Interstate Commerce Act—and some new—such as the Fair Labor Standards Act, the National Labor Relations Acts, and current tax laws—have been brought repeatedly to the Court for interpretation and application with respect to specific situations and problems. Although no single decision in which the Court merely construes one of these laws could be as significant as would a decision declaring the law unconstitutional, it should be realized that a statute can be amended in substance by the mere process of construction. When it is seen, moreover, that a single statute may and frequently does come to the Court's attention through the years in a score or more cases it becomes apparent that the cumulative imprint which the Court makes upon a statute can be very great indeed. In this respect, Charles Evans Hughes once went so far as to say: "The Court is the final interpreter of the Acts of Congress. Statutes come to the judicial test . . . with respect to their true import, and a federal statute finally means what the Court says it means. . . . Congress voluntarily leaves much to the Courts." [27]

---

[26] See *Tot* v. *United States,* 319 U.S. 463 (1943), and *United States* v. *Lovett,* 328 U.S. 303 (1946).

[27] Charles Evans Hughes, *The Supreme Court of the United States* (New York: Columbia University Press, 1928), pp. 229–232.

the work of the Supreme Court during an annual term

Much of what has already been said about the role of the Supreme Court as an instrument of government can perhaps be better understood through an examination of the pattern of the Court's work as revealed by the record of a single term. The annual term which began in October, 1947, and ended in June, 1948, may be taken as an example. During this term the Court decided cases by means of written opinions in 119 instances. It refused to consider four or five times that number of cases. The writ of certiorari was the all-important means by which the Court drew the line between those cases heard and those cases rejected. Thirty-nine cases were decided by a unanimous Court; 80 brought forth dissenting opinions. In 24 cases four justices dissented. The tendency toward multiple opinions is seen in the fact that three or more opinions were written by the justices in 30 cases.

Fewer than 25 cases fell into the category of judicial review. In 15 of these the constitutionality of state legislation was in question. Seven cases concerned the validity of federal laws. Nine of the former resulted in the invalidation of state laws. No federal law was declared invalid.

In 48 cases the major issue which the Court was called upon to decide was one of federal statute interpretation or application. For example, the antitrust laws were involved in 11 cases.

It is difficult to make a precise division of the cases into traditional categories of constitutional law, for there is considerable overlapping, and many of the cases involving statute interpretation do not in the strict sense present any issue of *constitutional* law. However, it may be said that 10 cases dealt with interstate commerce, 5 with taxation, 4 with citizenship, 4 with the power and procedure of administrative agencies, 14 with the jurisdiction or procedure of the federal courts, 13 with federal criminal law, 21 with due process of law, 6 with equal protection of the laws, 35 with civil rights. Six cases dealt with the extent of federal power, 5 with state encroachment upon federal power, and 1 with separation of powers within the federal government.

The sources of cases reaching the Supreme Court in the 1947–1948 term were as follows: 79 cases came from the lower federal courts; 40 cases came directly from state courts. No case reached the Supreme Court during the year under its original jurisdiction.

the power to govern

It is almost impossible to exaggerate the importance of the role the Supreme Court has played, and is continuing to play, in the governmental process. To be sure, it is possible to disagree violently with past decisions and to argue that the Court has usurped more power than it was intended to exercise under the Constitution. Even among the justices on the present Court there is striking disagreement as to the essential nature of the judicial process and the extent of power which judges should exercise. One group of justices is said to follow the principle of "judicial self-restraint," which in reviewing the constitutionality of laws means giving Congress and the state legislatures the widest possible latitude, and which in interpreting laws means staying close to the language of statutes and making every effort to ascertain the intention of the legislature where there is doubt. A second group is said to believe in "judicial activism," a principle which would lead to the ready invalidation of laws—particularly those that threaten civil rights—and to the use of wide judicial discretion in interpreting statutes. [28]

This explanation of the differences which separate the justices of today finds partial verification in the record of Court decisions. Both points of view concerning the Court's function are defensible intellectually, and each has a supporting basis in constitutional traditions. Yet in the final analysis the explanation is a much too simple one. It is doubtful whether any such choice of routes is available to the Court in practice. Certainly there are differing degrees of self-restraint or self-expression which the Court can show in its work of passing upon the constitutionality and meaning of statutes. But even if the justices were to show the maximum humility which the nature of their work and responsibility would allow, they would still possess and exercise a broad measure of discretionary power. In no event is there likely to occur a "twilight of the Supreme Court."

From the time of John Marshall to the present day the Supreme Court has had an important share in the power to govern. By its exercise of this power it has profoundly influenced the course of American life in at least three ways. First of all, it has helped shape the main outlines of our political system by filling in some of the details of the Constitution and by giving vitality to fundamental constitutional principles. Such has been its contribution, for example, in giving specific meaning to the vague principles of federalism and separation of powers, in determining the extent of personal rights reserved to the people, and in developing the institution of judicial review itself. This is not to say that Congress and the President have not also participated in this process of "continuous constitution making." But many of the final decisions in this process have fallen to the Court, and it seems unlikely that this work of the Court is at an end.

Secondly, the Supreme Court has labored endlessly to help provide a uniform, workable set of rules for governing those increasingly important human relations which are subject to federal control. True, through the enactment of statutes Congress has tried increasingly in modern times to satisfy the need for

---

[28] See the article by Arthur M. Schlesinger, Jr., "The Supreme Court: 1947," *Fortune*, XXXV (January, 1947), 73.

rules which make life livable in a complex society. But it has become clear, if the matter ever was in doubt, that such statutes can indicate only the main directions of public policy. It falls to the lot of administrators and judges to give detailed meaning to these initial statements of policy, and to shape them continuously to everyday needs. In this process it has been the responsibility of the Supreme Court to pass upon and to interpret virtually every major statute which has been enacted by Congress so that the lesser courts and administrative agencies might have authoritative guidance in applying law to specific situations.

Finally, more than any executive or legislative agency and more than any other court, the Supreme Court has profoundly influenced the formation of the American sense of justice, with its strong basis in law and its abiding assurance to the individual of respect for his person and his beliefs. Some sense of that spirit of fairness which the Court has done much to establish in our land is to be seen in the words of Justice Hugo Black in the Court's opinion in *Chambers* v. *Florida*, a case in which four Negroes were saved from a sentence of death pronounced by a Florida court after they had been bullied into a confession by use of "third-degree" methods:

> Under our constitutional system courts stand against any winds that blow as havens of refuge for those who might otherwise suffer because they are helpless, weak, outnumbered, or because they are non-conforming victims of prejudice and public excitement. Due process of law, preserved for all by our Constitution, commands that no such practice as that disclosed by the record in this case shall send any accused to his death. No higher duty, no more solemn responsibility, rests with this Court, than that of translating into living law and maintaining this constitutional shield deliberately planned and inscribed for the benefit of every human being subject to our Constitution—of whatever race, creed, or persuasion. [29]

bibliographic note

No agency of American government has been more written about than has the Supreme Court. The leading general history of the Court is Charles Warren's *The Supreme Court in United States History* (Boston: Little, Brown & Company, 2 Vols., 1922). The Warren volumes are written from a decidedly conservative and sympathetic point of view. A history of the Supreme Court, written from a vigorously critical point of view, is Louis B. Boudin's *Government by Judiciary* (New York: William Godwin, Inc., 2 Vols., 1932).

Many studies of the Supreme Court are particularly concerned with the

[29] *Chambers* v. *Florida*, 309 U.S. 227, 241 (1940).

operation of judicial review. Charles G. Haines's *The American Doctrine of Judicial Supremacy* (Berkeley: University of California Press, 2d ed., 1932), a systematic examination of this subject, has become a classic. Notice may be taken of the same author's *The Role of the Supreme Court in American Government and Politics, 1789–1835* (Berkeley: University of California Press, 1944), which lays emphasis upon the personal beliefs and political attitudes of the judges of the Supreme Court during the period covered by the book. Charles A. Beard's *The Supreme Court and the Constitution* (New York: The Macmillan Company, 1912) is an attempt to answer the question whether the Constitutional Convention intended the Supreme Court to exercise the power of judicial review. Charles E. Hughes's *The Supreme Court of the United States* (New York: Columbia University Press, 1928) is an important collection of lectures given at Columbia University during the interim between Mr. Hughes's two periods of service on the Court. It is a readable, highly informative study of the Court at work. In his *Congress, the Constitution, and the Supreme Court* (Boston: Little, Brown & Company, 1925) Charles Warren examines the actual operation of judicial review and concludes that it has served a useful purpose.

The controversy over the Supreme Court's invalidation of New Deal legislation and the subsequent decisions of the "Roosevelt Court" has resulted in the publication of a series of books. Attention may be called to Robert K. Carr, *The Supreme Court and Judicial Review* (New York: Rinehart & Company, 1942); Edward S. Corwin, *Court over Constitution: A Study of Judicial Review as an Instrument of Popular Government* (Princeton: Princeton University Press, 1942); Charles P. Curtis, Jr., *Lions under the Throne* (Boston: Houghton Mifflin Company, 1947); Paul A. Freund, *On Understanding the Supreme Court* (Boston: Little, Brown & Company, 1949); and C. Herman Pritchett, *The Roosevelt Court: A Study in Judicial Politics and Values, 1937–1947* (New York: The Macmillan Company, 1948). The last-named is a unique statistical analysis of the work of the Court over a ten-year period, with particular emphasis upon the extent of dissenting opinions.

Robert E. Cushman has edited a series of articles which analyze in detailed fashion the decisions of the Supreme Court during a recent ten-year period: "Ten Years of the Supreme Court: 1937–1947," *American Political Science Review,* XLI (December, 1947), 1142, and XLII (February, 1948), 32. The individual articles and authors of the series are David Fellman, "Federalism"; Oliver P. Field, "Separation and Delegation of Powers"; Vincent M. Barnett, Jr., "The Power to Regulate Commerce"; Robert J. Harris, "Due Process of Law"; Robert E. Cushman, "Civil Liberties"; C. Herman Pritchett, "The Roosevelt Court: Votes and Values." Other recent articles dealing with the work of the Supreme Court are Vincent M. Barnett, Jr., "The Supreme Court and the Capacity to Govern," *Political Science Quarterly,* LXIII (September, 1948), 342; Oliver P. Field, "Unconstitutional Legislation by Congress," *American Political*

Science Review, XXXIX (February, 1945), 54; Robert J. Harris, "The Decline of Judicial Review," *Journal of Politics*, X (February, 1948), 1.

Edward S. Corwin, one of the great students of the Supreme Court, has published a number of volumes dealing with the work of the Court and estimating its significance as an instrument of government. In addition to the titles already mentioned in previous notes, attention may be called to his *Constitutional Revolution, Ltd.* (Claremont, Calif.: Claremont Colleges, 1941); *The Twilight of the Supreme Court* (New Haven: Yale University Press, 1934); and *Court over Constitution: A Study of Judicial Review as in Instrument of Popular Government* (Princeton: Princeton University Press, 1938).

Benjamin R. Twiss's *Lawyers and the Constitution: How Laissez-Faire Came to the Supreme Court* (Princeton: Princeton University Press, 1942) is a unique study of the influence on the Court of lawyers who have argued cases before it.

government personnel: the judge

*I*N LAW also men make a difference." The personality of the judge is often a powerful force both in the shaping of the law and in its administration. Judges, whether of courts of public law or common law, do exercise an element of discretionary power in the performance of their judicial duties. Accordingly, attention must be given to the individuals who man our courts—to their backgrounds, their interests, and their attitudes—if a full understanding of the nature of the judicial process is to be gained. Many students of the law and of the courts have pointed this out. Felix Frankfurter, in a passage from which come the words at the beginning of this paragraph, has said: "The history of the Supreme Court is not the history of an abstraction, but the analysis of individuals acting as a Court who make decisions and lay down doctrines, and of other individuals, their successors, who refine, modify, and sometimes even overrule the decisions of their predecessors. . . . *In law also men make a difference.* . . . There is no inevitability in history except as men make it." [1] And elsewhere: ". . . the work of the Supreme Court is the history of relatively few personalities. . . . The fact that they were *there* and that others were not, surely made decisive differences. To understand what manner of men they were is crucial to an understanding of the Court." [2]

Judges, then, are no less human than are legislators and administrators. Like other men, moreover, the judge is the end product of a complex series of physical forces and political, economic, and moral influences which have been at work upon him throughout his life. Of the existence of many of these he may be unconscious, but they play their part nonetheless. The result is that the judge, like other men, has a point of view. Inevitably he has taken his stand in life,

---

[1] Felix Frankfurter, *Mr. Justice Holmes and the Supreme Court* (Cambridge: Harvard University Press, 1938), pp. 8–9 (italics added).

[2] Felix Frankfurter, *Law and Politics* (New York: Harcourt, Brace and Company, 1939), p. 113. Excerpts reprinted from this work are used by permission of Harcourt, Brace and Company, publishers.

and it is inconceivable that when he is called upon to exercise choice in the settlement of human conflicts he should not fall back upon his personal scheme of values as a frame of reference. Some judges have been frank and realistic enough to admit this. "There is in each of us a stream of tendency," Benjamin Cardozo has said, "whether you choose to call it philosophy or not, which gives coherence and direction to thought and action. Judges cannot escape that current any more than other mortals." And again: "The great tides and currents which engulf the rest of men, do not turn aside in their course, and pass the judges by." More specifically, he has spoken of forces "deep below consciousness," "the likes and the dislikes, the predilections and the prejudices, the complex of instincts and emotions and habits and convictions, which make the man, whether he be litigant or judge." [3]

influences upon the judge

If it be granted that law and evidence do not always compel a single outcome in a case and that the personality of the judge often plays a part in determining the result, then what are the influences to which he is subject? What forces or considerations motivate the choice he makes in those cases in which discretion must be exercised? Unfortunately, in trying to answer questions of this kind it is often difficult to obtain information about judges, particularly as to the early, formative years of their careers. Of late a few good biographies of such Supreme Court justices as Marshall, Taney, Field, Miller, Day, Taft, Holmes, and Brandeis have appeared.[4] Occasionally a judge himself, in writing about his work on a court, reveals, sometimes consciously, sometimes unconsciously, certain of the influences to which he is subject in deciding cases.[5] There are very few systematic biographies of federal or state trial court judges. However, fragments of information about these judges are available, and even though systematic data

---

[3] Benjamin N. Cardozo, *The Nature of the Judicial Process* (New Haven: Yale University Press, 1921), pp. 12, 167, 168. Reprinted by permission of the Yale University Press, publishers.

[4] Albert J. Beveridge, *The Life of John Marshall* (Boston: Houghton Mifflin Company, 1916); Carl B. Swisher, *Roger B. Taney* (New York: The Macmillan Company, 1935), and *Stephen J. Field* (Washington: The Brookings Institution, 1930); Charles Fairman, *Mr. Justice Miller and the Supreme Court* (Cambridge: Harvard University Press, 1939); Joseph E. McLean, *William Rufus Day* (Baltimore: Johns Hopkins Press, 1946); Henry F. Pringle, *The Life and Times of William Howard Taft* (New York: Rinehart & Company, 1939); Catherine D. Bowen, *Yankee from Olympus* (Boston: Little Brown & Company, 1944); Alpheus T. Mason, *Brandeis: A Free Man's Life* (New York: The Viking Press, 1946).

[5] For example, see the article by the federal judge, Joseph C. Hutcheson, "The Judgment Intuitive: The Function of the 'Hunch' in Judicial Decision," *Cornell Law Quarterly*, XIV (April, 1929), 274. The writings of such federal judges as Jerome Frank and Learned Hand have been particularly revealing concerning the motivation of judicial decisions.

are lacking, we know enough about the judicial process to be reasonably certain that the same forces which help shape appellate judges have their effect upon trial judges too.

What are the "likes," "dislikes," the "predilections" and "prejudices," the "complex of instincts," "emotions," "habits" and "convictions" that may influence a judge as he decides a case? Obviously, there is a whole host of possibilities, some simple, some tangled and complex. The judge may be a wealthy man interested in the continued sanctity of private property and the steady flow of dividends. He may be a self-made man with little patience for the man who has done less well with his opportunities. Again his own struggle to make a way in life may have given him a deep respect for the dignity and liberty of the individual as against all material considerations of wealth and power. He may be a man of limited intellectual stature and thus incapable of a sophisticated understanding of human nature and of human institutions. He may be an elderly man who has reached the age where he is likely to feel that the only good lies in the past and that modern ways are bad ways. The judge may have strong family ties or deep religious feelings which are bound to influence him in certain fields of the law. He may be a bitter partisan politically, intensely antagonistic to governmental officers of a political faith that is the opposite of his own. He may have been a successful corporation attorney who has grown contemptuous of government regulatory agencies and policies. Or he may have been a law school professor, a man of theory and broad social vision, convinced that government must play a large role in human affairs.

Obviously, there is much room for speculation and disagreement in any attempt to probe deeply into the factors that motivate a judge. Some of the judge's experiences, characteristics, and loyalties are easily discovered, and their influence upon his judicial career is not difficult to see. Among these are his age and resultant outlook on life, his legal training and experience, and his political beliefs and activities. These will now be examined. Much of the actual illustrative material will be drawn from Supreme Court experience, but many of the points noted and conclusions drawn almost certainly have validity for judges of other courts.

the advanced age and resulting conservatism of judges

Professor Cortez A. M. Ewing has prepared tables showing the average age of Supreme Court justices by decades since 1789.[6] During the first decade of the Court's existence, the age was fifty-three, whereas during the first seven years of the 1930's it was sixty-nine. The increase in average age during this period of

---

[6] Cortez A. M. Ewing, *The Judges of the Supreme Court 1789–1937* (Minneapolis: The University of Minnesota Press, 1938), pp. 63–76.

fifteen decades has been almost continuous. Ewing has also assembled figures on the ages of justices at the time of appointment. During the first forty years of the Court's history, four justices were less than forty years old at the time of appointment and twelve were under fifty. None was over sixty, and only eight were fifty or over. During the forty-year period ending with 1937, no justice was under forty-five when appointed to the Court, and only one was under fifty. On the other hand, seven were sixty or over, and twelve were fifty-five or over. By way of contrast, it may be noted that the average age of Presidents on assuming office has fallen from fifty-eight during the first forty-year period, to fifty-three during the forty-year period ending with 1937. Thus it is by no means true that all national officeholders have been increasing in age during our history.

It is usually assumed that the older a man grows the more conservative he becomes. This is the kind of generalization that has many exceptions, but it remains a fundamentally sound observation as to the nature of man. It is probably equally true that judges as a class are more conservative than legislators or administrators in their willingness to approve experimentation or to accept social progress and reform. The great English legal historian, A. V. Dicey, pointed this out nearly half a century ago in a lecture delivered at the Harvard Law School:

> The Courts or the judges, when acting as legislators, are of course influenced by the beliefs and feelings of their time, and are guided to a considerable extent by the dominant current of public opinion. . . . But whilst our . . . judges . . . are swayed by the prevailing beliefs of a particular time, they are also guided by professional opinions and ways of thinking that are, to a certain extent, independent of and possibly opposed to the general tone of public opinion. The judges . . . are men advanced in life. They are for the most part persons of a conservative disposition. They are in no way dependent . . . upon the favor of the electors. . . . They are more likely to be biassed by professional habits and feeling than by the popular sentiment of the hour. . . .
>
> It is quite possible that judicial conceptions of utility or of the public interest may sometimes rise above the ideas prevalent at a particular era. . . . In the field of commercial law Lord Mansfield carried out ideas which, though in harmony with the best opinion of the time, could hardly have been, during the era of old toryism, embodied in Acts of Parliament. . . . However, . . . we may, at any rate as regards the nineteenth century, lay it down as a rule that judge-made law has, owing to the training and age of our judges, tended at any given moment to represent the convictions of an earlier era than the ideas represented by parliamentary legislation. If a statute . . . is apt to reproduce the public opinion not so much of to-day as of yesterday, judge-made law occasionally represents the opinion of the day before yesterday. . . . The legislative action of the Courts represents in truth a peculiar cross-section of opinion, which may in more ways

than one modify the effect of that predominant opinion of the day which naturally finds expression in a representative assembly. . . .[7]

In similar vein Justice Oliver Wendell Holmes has written: "Judges commonly are elderly men, and are more likely to hate at sight any analysis to which they are not accustomed, and which disturbs repose of mind, than to fall in love with novelties." [8]

A present member of the Supreme Court, Justice Robert H. Jackson, made much the same point when he was Attorney General of the United States:

> The Court . . . is almost never a really contemporary institution. The operation of life tenure in the judicial department, as against elections at short intervals of the Congress, usually keeps the average viewpoint of the two institutions a generation apart. The judiciary is thus the check of a preceding generation on a present one; a check of conservative legal philosophy upon a dynamic people, and nearly always the check of a rejected regime on the one in being.[9]

With respect to specific legal issues, or at certain periods of time, judges may be more progressive than legislators. Dicey referred to Mansfield's great decisions in the field of commercial law—progressive decisions which carried English law forward in a way that would not have been politically possible by Act of Parliament at the time. In the United States the courts have softened the application of such harsh and bigoted laws as the so-called "blue laws" which enforce strict observance of the Sabbath and those laws enacted during the Victorian period which penalize obscenity. It has proved far easier to liberalize these laws through judicial interpretation than by legislative amendment. The evidence strongly suggests that since 1937 the Supreme Court and many of the lower federal courts have been more liberal in their handling of many social and legal issues than has Congress. But these liberal tendencies shown by the judiciary are the exception rather than the rule. In evaluating the part played by the judge in the political process, judicial conservatism may almost be taken for granted.

It would be a mistake to attribute the conservatism of judges exclusively to their advanced age. In the passage quoted above, Professor Dicey refers to such additional factors leading to judicial conservatism as the "conservative disposition" of the kind of man who becomes a judge, his freedom from responsibility to an electorate, and his "professional habits and feeling." The last of these factors is apt to be particularly important. The study of the law, emphasizing as

---

[7] A. V. Dicey, *Law and Public Opinion in England* (New York: The Macmillan Company, 1905), pp. 361–368. Used with the permission of The Macmillan Company.

[8] Oliver Wendell Holmes, Jr., *Collected Legal Papers* (New York: Harcourt, Brace and Company, 1920), p. 230.

[9] Robert H. Jackson, *The Struggle for Judicial Supremacy* (New York: Alfred A. Knopf, Inc., 1941), p. 315.

it does the origins of our legal and judicial systems in the dim past and the slow evolution of legal principles, can hardly fail to give even the most progressively minded individual a sobering respect for precedent and tradition. In many ways respect for the past is a healthy and desirable thing, but it does lead sometimes to neglect of the need for further growth in the law.

Naturally, there are exceptions to the rule that advanced age leads to legal conservatism. The most famous exceptions of modern times are found in the careers of Justice Holmes and Justice Brandeis. Both men were fairly well along in years at the time of their appointment to the Supreme Court. Yet Holmes served on the Court for twenty-nine years, retiring at ninety-one, and Brandeis for twenty-three years, retiring at eighty-two. During these long terms both men remained flexible in outlook, and avoided to the end that tendency to oppose change which advancing age brings to so many men.

the judge's political beliefs and activities

It is commonly believed that judges must be, and for the most part in fact are, above politics. If by this is meant that judges are not active participants in party politics, the tradition is reasonably valid for the federal judiciary. It is less valid for state judiciaries, in part because of the fact that many state judges are elected to office for short terms on a partisan basis. In some states political parties co-operate in supporting common candidates for judicial posts, whereas in other states the judge is too frequently enmeshed in partisan politics and required to remain a loyal and active member of a political party throughout his public career.

It is significant that Presidents have from the time of Washington made most of their appointments to the federal judiciary from their own party ranks. Professor Charles G. Haines says that Washington "exercised peculiar care" to name only supporters of the new Constitution to the Supreme Court, and that without exception these proved to be "ardent Federalists." "Thus Washington himself 'initiated the system of appointing political adherents, and political adherents only to places on the Supreme bench. That system has seldom been departed from.' " [10] Only two of the twelve men who have served as Chief Justice belonged to a different political party from the party of the Presidents who appointed them. Moreover, federal judges have frequently been selected from among the most active and loyal groups of party workers, and not from groups whose members were only nominally party men. This has been particularly true of federal district judges, whose appointment is frequently subject to the rule of

---

[10] Charles G. Haines, *American Doctrine of Judicial Supremacy* (Berkeley: University of California Press, 2d ed., 1932), pp. 345–346. Haines is quoting W. D. Coles, "Politics and the Supreme Court of the United States," *American Law Review*, XXVII (March–April, 1893), 183.

senatorial courtesy and thereby to the operation of the spoils system. Even such Supreme Court justices as McReynolds, Brandeis, Sutherland, Taft, Hughes, Black, Murphy, and Vinson were all vigorous workers in the parties of the Presidents who appointed them.

Supreme Court justices have by no means always suspended their party interests once they have gone on the bench. Frequently, a justice's decisions have been in harmony with the traditions and interests of his own party. This can be seen in the opinions of Chief Justice John Marshall in such cases as *McCulloch* v. *Maryland, Gibbons* v. *Ogden,* and *Dartmouth College* v. *Woodward,* which coincided closely with the Federalist position; in the opinions of Chief Justice Roger B. Taney, which often adhered closely to Democratic principles; and in the decisions of Chief Justice William Howard Taft, which seldom departed from a sound Republican philosophy.

party politics not a strictly accurate measurement of a judge's political bias

And yet it is possible to exaggerate the importance of *party* politics in a judge's work. More often than not the personal frame of reference which a judge uses in deciding cases is one in which the fires of pure party politics do not burn as strongly as do fires of a different kind. For example, the four famous conservative justices of the Supreme Court who so often stood together in opposition to the New Deal in the 1930's—McReynolds, Butler, Sutherland, and Van Devanter—divided evenly in their party affiliations, the first two having been Democrats, the last two Republicans. The famous team of liberal dissenting justices, Holmes and Brandeis, likewise divided politically, Holmes having been a Republican, Brandeis a Democrat. Similarly, the fact that the Supreme Court of 1948, all nine of whose members were appointed by Democratic Presidents and only one of whom was a Republican, was, up to that year, the most divided Court in American history shows that something more than differing party loyalties separates justices.

the interest of Presidents in the politics of their Supreme Court appointees

This is not to say that judges do not have loyalties of a "political" sort which influence their decisions. That Presidents have sometimes been aware of the extent to which a judge's party membership may be less important than his other political loyalties is seen in the following passage from a letter written by Theodore Roosevelt to Henry Cabot Lodge in 1906, when he was about to make an appointment to the Supreme Court:

Nothing has been so strongly borne in on me concerning lawyers on the bench as that the *nominal* politics of the man has nothing to do with his actions on the bench. His *real* politics are all-important. In Lurton's case, Taft and Day, his two former associates, are very desirous of having him on. He is right on the Negro question; he is right on the power of the federal government; he is right on the Insular business; he is right about corporations; he is right about labor. On every question that would come before the bench, he has so far shown himself to be in much closer touch with the policies in which you and I believe than even White because he has been right about corporations where White has been wrong.[11]

Further evidence that Presidents have again and again satisfied themselves that a man's "political" loyalties were sound before appointing him to the Supreme Court can be cited. Albert J. Beveridge, in his *Life of John Marshall*, reports that "doubtless the President's choice of Marshall was influenced by the fact that his 'new minister,' Marshall, did all to [his] entire satisfaction." [12] When Theodore Roosevelt named Holmes to the Court it is clear that he was seeking a justice who held definite views. In another letter to Lodge he wrote: "I should like to know that Judge Holmes was in entire sympathy with our views, that is, with your views and mine . . . before I would feel justified in appointing him. . . . I should hold myself as guilty of an irreparable wrong to the nation if I should put [in this vacancy] any man who was not absolutely sane and sound on the great national policies for which we stand in public life." [13]

A decade later, it is entirely clear that the progressive Woodrow Wilson of the "New Freedom" years consciously selected a man of liberal views in appointing Brandeis to the Court in 1916. In a letter to Senator Charles A. Culberson of Texas he wrote:

> I have tested [Brandeis] by seeking his advice upon some of the most difficult and perplexing public questions. . . . Mr. Brandeis has rendered many notable services to the city and State with which his professional life has been identified. He successfully directed the difficult campaign which resulted in obtaining cheaper gas for the city of Boston. It was chiefly under his guidance and through his efforts that legislation was secured in Massachusetts which authorized savings banks to issue insurance policies for small sums at much reduced rates. And some gentlemen who tried hard to obtain control by the Boston Elevated Railway Co. of the subways of the city for a period of 99 years can probably testify as to his ability as the people's advocate when public interests call for an effective champion.[14]

In the early 1920's the conservative Harding added four justices to the Supreme Court in a little over two years. It is no coincidence that his appointees—

---

[11] *Selections from the Correspondence of Theodore Roosevelt and Henry Cabot Lodge*, (New York: Charles Scribner's Sons, 1925), II, 228. Lurton was a Democrat. Actually he was finally passed over by Roosevelt in 1906, but was named to the Court in 1909 by Taft.

[12] Beveridge, *Life of John Marshall*, II, 553–554.

[13] Quoted by Frankfurter in *Law and Politics*, p. 67.

[14] *Senate Documents*, 64 Cong. 1 Sess., XVII (1916), 239–241.

Taft, Butler, Sanford, and Sutherland—were themselves men of conservative views. Nor was it surprising that the eight men appointed to the Court by Franklin Roosevelt were, whatever their later differences as justices, all men of pronounced liberal views—most of them having served as active and loyal New Dealers.

Of course, there have been exceptions. Not every President has been entirely consistent about his appointments to the Supreme Court. For instance, Wilson, who named such progressive justices as Brandeis and Clarke, also appointed McReynolds, who proved to be one of the most conservative justices in the entire history of the Court. Likewise, such conservative Presidents as Coolidge and Hoover have appointed to the Court such liberal justices as Stone and Cardozo.

Nor should the role played by chance in the selection of judicial personnel be overlooked. For example, not all Presidents have had the same opportunity to influence the political coloration of court decisions through the naming of judges. Some Presidents have been in a position virtually to remake the Supreme Court, whereas others have enjoyed no such opportunity. Five Presidents —Washington, Jackson, Lincoln, Taft, and Franklin Roosevelt—all appointed five or more justices, thus naming new court majorities. In each instance the Court showed the influence of these Presidents in its decisions for many years to come. On the other hand, the three Presidents who appointed no justices and the eighteen Presidents who appointed only one or two justices obviously left little or no imprint upon the Court.

It is sometimes asserted that, try as Presidents may, to influence the Court and the development of constitutional law by naming certain men as justices they have invariably failed in their efforts. The assertion is not a well-founded one. Many a President who has consciously tried to influence future decisions of the Supreme Court by the naming of certain men of known views has had very little cause for disappointment. Some justices have disappointed the Presidents who appointed them by their decisions in isolated cases. For example, reference is always made in this respect to Justice Holmes' stand against the government in the *Northern Securities* case, a stand that disappointed Theodore Roosevelt, the President who had appointed Holmes to the Court. But in the long run Holmes proved to be the kind of justice that Roosevelt hoped he would, and by means of this appointment Roosevelt certainly influenced the course of constitutional law in a conscious, positive way.

the judge's legal training and experience

Presumably any judge must be "learned in the law." In some states laymen may serve as judges of minor courts. But a knowledge of the content and techniques of the law is today regarded as indispensable for any judge serving on an important court. However, in weighing a judge's technical qualifications a distinction must be made between a judicial post which is largely concerned with public law, and one which has as its main concern common-law adjudication of private disputes. A judge of the first type perhaps has less need of a thorough knowledge of the working rules of everyday law than has a judge of the second type. For example, there is evidence that the greatest of all American judges—John Marshall—was not an outstanding craftsman in the technical intricacies of the common law. His talent as Chief Justice of the United States lay in his understanding of broad political principles and in the practical wisdom he brought to the great "constitutional" issues which confronted the Court in his day. He was not a "lawyer-judge"; rather he was a "statesman-judge."

There is a wide variation in the legal qualifications of judges. It may be taken for granted that today all judges have had formal law school training, for the time when would-be lawyers could "read" law in law offices is gone. The kind of training which future judges receive, however, will vary greatly from law school to law school. Some schools emphasize the social background of the law and prepare the judge for his role as legislator. Others concentrate largely upon cases and rules of law and pay little attention to the judicial process except in its narrowest sense.

previous experience of Supreme Court justices

After graduation from law school and admission to the bar, the lawyer who would one day become a judge finds several paths open to him. Unlike the European law graduate, he may not immediately choose a judicial career and enter the judicial civil service by way of employment in the Ministry of Justice. The men who have served on the Supreme Court illustrate the alternatives open to an American lawyer. Some justices, such as Mathews, Fuller, Butler, and Roberts, had been, before their appointment, highly successful practicing lawyers whose services were much sought after by rich corporations. Others, such as Stone, Frankfurter, Douglas, and Rutledge, had been teachers of law in great universities. Still others, such as Holmes and Cardozo, had been judges during a good part of their lives—career men who had come up through the lower courts to reach at last the goal of every lawyer's dreams. Finally, there are others, such as White, Sutherland, Black, and Burton, who had been members of Congress—practicing politicians. A great many Supreme Court justices, of course, have had varied backgrounds. When Charles Evans Hughes was appointed Chief Justice in 1930, he had been governor of New York, an associate justice of the United States Supreme Court, Republican nominee for President, Secretary of State under two Presidents, a law school lecturer, and a highly successful practicing attorney. Harlan Stone and William O. Douglas, in addition to being teachers of the law, had held important administrative posts with the federal government. At the time of his appointment as Chief Justice, Fred M.

Vinson had served in all three branches of the federal government—as a member of the House of Representatives from Kentucky, as a judge of the Court of Appeals for the District of Columbia, and as Secretary of the Treasury, in addition to filling several other administrative posts.

the narrow, legalistic background of many judges

Unquestionably one of the most serious shortcomings of many judges is their narrow legal training and experience. The result of this limited background is, as one writer puts it, that "for every Brandeis familiar with economics, for every Holmes versed in literature, for every Cardozo learned in philosophy, there are a dozen judges who regard such learning as esoteric if not irrelevant." [15]

It is at the level of the appellate court that the narrow, legalistic background of some judges is most unfortunate. Here a technical knowledge of the law gained from a career as a successful practicing attorney is only one of many resources which must be utilized in the making of wise decisions. When it comes to such problems as the making and application of antitrust policy, the regulation of management-labor relations, and the protection of civil rights, technical rules of law alone will not adequately promote the public welfare. Indeed, any court, high or low, whose judges have had training in such fields as economics and sociology as well as the law, or who have had experience as politicians, businessmen, or labor leaders, and not simply as practicing attorneys, is almost certain to benefit by this broad background of its members.

law schools and the legal profession

All formal legal systems in history have been accompanied by the development of strong legal professions. This is the inevitable result of the complex, technical character which law must take in a highly organized society. On the other hand, the tendency for professionals to monopolize the practice of law has almost always been resisted. The lawyer's very ability to help persons negotiate their way out of difficult tangles is bound to arouse a certain distrust of him as a clever agent who uses his technical knowledge to gain personal profit from the misfortunes of other people. Until 1933 the state of Indiana had a provision in its constitution establishing the right of any citizen to practice the law.

Nonetheless, the legal process from beginning to end has come to be dominated by lawyers. Lawyers are far and away the largest single profession represented in legislative bodies; they man the courts, both as judges and as counsel to the opposing parties; and they advise the lay members of society how to conduct their personal affairs in a law-abiding way. In this latter respect the lawyer

[15] Henry Steele Commager, "Constitutional History and the Higher Law," *The Constitution Reconsidered* (Conyers Read, ed.; New York: Columbia University Press, 1938), p. 243.

has made himself particularly invaluable to the businessman. When it comes to such operations as "drafting documents, . . . conveyancing a property, organizing business enterprises, securing the orderly course of credits and managing the entire paper work of commerce" the lawyer's monopoly is most evident.[16]

the education of lawyers

Because of this dominant role of the lawyer in society, education for the practice of the law and the organization and social control of the profession are matters of great importance. The present-day law school places much reliance in the "case method" of teaching law, originally introduced at the Harvard Law School by Dean Christopher Langdell in the nineteenth century. This method has tended to sharpen the minds of law students and to prepare them well for private practice. But it is necessary to remember that "in the common law system the judges are recruited from the legal profession, without . . . any special training for the function." [17] It seems clear that law schools, with a few exceptions, have given less attention than is socially desirable to the training of the future judge. It would probably be unwise to follow the European practice of distinguishing at an early point between the education of lawyers and the education of judges. But there is a need to place more emphasis in legal education upon the nature, theory, and history of law, and upon the broad social process if judges (and practicing lawyers, too, for that matter) are to be adequately prepared for their work in society.

admission to the bar

It is often said that the legal profession is overcrowded. Whether or not this is true depends upon such abstract considerations as the maximum social and economic activity of which a society is potentially capable, and upon the number of legal technicians necessary to serve a society that is operating at its full potential. In any case, admission to the profession has come to be restricted. This is probably desirable as a means of ensuring the integrity and ability of the law practitioner, even though it would not be justified as a means of letting those admitted to the bar make more money from their practice. There are two ways in which the number of lawyers is today limited. The first barrier encountered by the would-be lawyer is the difficulty of gaining admission to a law school. The second barrier is the bar examination which must be passed if one is to gain a license to practice. This examination is generally administered by a board of examiners. Although the right to practice is theoretically in the nature of a franchise granted by the state, admission to the bar is largely controlled by members of the profession itself.

---

[16] A. A. Berle, Jr., "Modern Legal Profession," *Encyclopaedia of the Social Sciences*, IX, 343.
[17] *Ibid.*, p. 340.

the work of bar associations

The bar association is a private organization of lawyers which has as its historic function the safeguarding of the integrity and social usefulness of the legal profession. It has come to engage in a number of important activities which are of great consequence to the public welfare. Among these are keeping watch over the administration of bar examinations, maintaining a lookout for improper activities by members of the profession and recommending the disbarment of lawyers guilty of unethical practices, passing upon the qualifications of candidates for judicial office, watching over the work of the courts with a view toward suggesting the removal of incompetent or dishonest judges and the reorganization of judicial structure, participating in judicial conferences, and recommending legislation to Congress, the state legislatures, and municipal councils. An example of the last-named activity is to be seen in the federal Administrative Procedures Act of 1946, the adoption of which is generally regarded as having been brought about through the efforts of the American Bar Association.

Because of the tremendous power and influence wielded by bar associations, their activities have been subject to careful scrutiny by students and commentators. Much criticism of the way in which the bar meets its responsibilities can be found. One responsible critic says: ". . . the bar has changed in character; from an organization concerned primarily with maintaining the dignity and serviceableness of a profession it has become a substantial agreement among attorneys to protect each other." [18] This judgment is probably too harsh, for bar associations have in recent years shown a strong tendency to emphasize their public-service functions. Nonetheless, the bar remains essentially a trade union of lawyers, and it is not surprising that it should be primarily concerned with protecting the economic status of its members or advancing their social interests through the tactics of the pressure group.

the selection of judges

appointment vs. election of judges

Judges are chosen in the United States in a variety of ways, most commonly, however, by one of three methods—appointment by the executive, appointment by the legislature, and election by the voters. All federal judges are appointed by the President, by and with the advice and consent of the Senate. Today about ten states follow the federal example and vest the power of appointment in the governor subject to confirmation usually by some sort of advisory body. Three use selection by the legislature. About three quarters of the states choose their judges by popular election.[19]

---

[18] Berle, "Modern Legal Profession," IX, 343. This article was written in the early 1930's.
[19] See *The Book of the States, 1948–1949* (Chicago: The Council of State Governments, 1948), pp. 497, 501.

The choice between the appointment and the election of judges has been much argued. The advantages of the appointment of judges over their election by the voters are said to be twofold. First, it is said that the good judge is one who has a thorough technical knowledge of both the substance and the procedures of the law, and that the electorate is not ordinarily prepared to weigh the varying qualifications of rival candidates for judicial offices in this respect. Second, it is argued that judges must be free to decide cases exclusively on the basis of law and justice, and that to hold a judge accountable to the voters forces him to be sensitive to other considerations, since the public view of a case is not usually based upon a thorough understanding of law, and by no means always coincides with justice.

On the other hand, a strong argument is made in favor of the election of judges on the ground that they necessarily make law in the process of deciding cases, and thereby help shape public policy. In a democracy, the argument continues, all policy-making officials should be chosen by the people.

In practice, however, it is probable that appointment has produced better results than has election. Each method has worked well at times, and badly at others. It may be said that the widespread practice of electing judges in the American states has failed to produce a state judiciary comparable in prestige and ability to that which has been obtained at the federal level through appointment. But there are exceptions. For example, the New York Court of Appeals, the members of which are elected for fourteen-year terms, is generally regarded as one of the greatest of American courts. On the other hand, the judges of the Massachusetts Supreme Judicial Court, which is often joined with the New York court for praise, are appointed by the governor for life terms.

Ingenious attempts have been made in California and in Missouri to combine the methods of appointment and election in the selection of judges and also to give the legal profession a special voice in the process. In California the governor appoints appellate judges subject to the approval of a judicial commission consisting of the chief justice, a court of appeals judge, and the attorney general. After his first term has expired, the judge may then be returned to office or rejected by the voters in a noncompetitive election. The Missouri plan is very similar except that the original appointment by the governor has to be made from a list of nominees submitted to him by the judicial commission. In both states the extension of the plan to trial judges is made dependent upon its adoption by the voters in the various judicial districts.

Some measure of popular control of judges is necessary in a democracy. But outright election of judges is probably not the answer. It is significant that in spite of the storms that have raged periodically over the federal Supreme Court, no strong or persistent demand has ever been made that its justices be elected to their high offices. But the Supreme Court has been subjected to a measure of popular control in other ways. The Court has not been insensitive to popular pressure and has in its broader policy-making function "followed the election returns."

the retirement of judges

Federal judges hold office for life "during good behavior." They are subject to impeachment and removal from office by Congress for treason, bribery, or other high crimes or misdemeanors. Indeed, nine of the twelve federal officers who have been impeached by the House of Representatives were judges. All four of the impeached officers who have been convicted by the Senate were judges. The language of the Constitution strongly suggests that Congress may provide by law for a different way of removing judges from office where the offense is failure to maintain "good behavior" rather than one of the more serious actions necessary to impeachment. Various bills have been introduced in Congress to this effect—one in 1940 proposing that when charged with misbehavior by the House of Representatives a judge be tried by a panel of circuit judges named by the Chief Justice—but none has ever been enacted into law.

The problem of the aged judge who grows increasingly reactionary, if not senile, with advancing years has been a serious one in American national government. It has been most noticeable with the Supreme Court, for unquestionably many of its justices have prolonged their periods of service beyond their years of greatest usefulness. Professor Charles Fairman has made a careful study of the matter and has assembled a long and impressive list of justices who stayed on the Supreme Court after their faculties had begun to decline, sometimes with unfortunate results.[20] For example, Justice Stephen J. Field cast the deciding vote in the controversial five-to-four income tax case at the age of seventy-eight, years after his mental faculties had begun to fail. Fairman makes this comment: "No rationalization can justify a system whereby the powers of government in a matter of such high moment are finally determined by a mind so somnolent and prepossessed as Justice Field's had become by that time." [21]

It seems clear that the solution of the problem of the aged justice cannot depend upon voluntary retirement. Well over half of the men who have served on the Supreme Court have died in office, most of them at advanced ages. Fairman concludes that "voluntary retirement, in any real sense, is very rare indeed." [22] Charles Evans Hughes, in his lectures at Columbia University in

---

[20] Charles Fairman, "The Retirement of Federal Judges," in *Selected Essays on Constitutional Law* (Chicago: The Foundation Press, Inc., 1938), I, 885; originally published in *Harvard Law Review*, LI, January, 1938), 397.
[21] Fairman, "Retirement of Federal Judges," I, 885, 910.
[22] *Ibid.*, p. 912.

1928, remarked, "It is extraordinary how reluctant aged judges are to retire
and to give up their accustomed work. They seem to be tenacious of the appearance of adequacy." [23]

If voluntary retirement is not the answer, neither is impeachment or removal from office for misbehavior a proper method of getting rid of the super-
annuated judge. Accordingly it has been proposed that the Constitution
be amended to provide for the compulsory retirement of federal judges at some
fixed age, such as seventy or seventy-five. Hughes favored seventy-five in his
1928 lectures, and then, as if to verify his own observation about the reluctance of aged judges to retire, when reappointed in 1930 he stayed on the Supreme Court until 1941, when he retired at seventy-nine. Fairman strongly favors seventy as the age at which all federal judges should be required to retire,
although he would permit the President, with the consent of the Senate, to re-
appoint the exceptional judge for an additional limited period of eight years.

As a result of the controversy in 1937 over the more drastic Roosevelt
proposals for court reform, Congress strengthened federal law to provide that a
judge who reaches seventy and has ten years of service may retire to inactive
duty (rather than resign outright) on full salary. Several justices of the Supreme
Court have "retired" since 1937 under this law, but nearly all delayed their
departures until they were well beyond seventy.

In all but a few states judges are either appointed or elected to office for
fixed terms. Even allowing for the fact that these judges may frequently serve
more than one term, state judicial careers are usually shorter than those on the
federal bench. Even so, about half a dozen states have compulsory retirement
systems for judges, seventy being the usual age.[24] Slightly more than half of
the states have laws providing for voluntary retirement on full or part salary.

what makes a great judge?

Throughout the history of the United States it is evident that courts have played
an exceedingly important role in the affairs of the nation, and that the need for
great men in the judiciary has thus been no less than the need for great men in
legislative and executive positions. Many of our public officers whom history
views with great favor have been judges. Such men as Marshall, Taney, Holmes,
Brandeis, Taft, Cardozo, and Hughes are as well known as any men of their
times, save perhaps for a few Presidents. It is true that Taft was President as
well as Chief Justice, but it is generally agreed that he will be longer remembered, and certainly more highly regarded, in his latter capacity than in his former. That Hughes was governor of New York, Republican candidate for Presi-

---

[23] Charles Evans Hughes, *The Supreme Court of the United States* (New York: Columbia
University Press, 1928), p. 75.

[24] Fairman, "Retirement of Federal Judges," I, 912.

dent, and Secretary of State is of less significance to history than the fact that he presided over the Supreme Court during one of its most fateful decades.

there is no one mold for great judges

What are the qualities that make the great judge? No one answer can be given. Obviously, much depends on the character of the times and the nature of the problems which confront a particular court at a given moment. Clearly the work of trial courts and of appellate courts is so different that the requirements necessary for greatness in the judges of these courts are in many ways dissimilar. Moreover, the personal qualities that make for greatness in the judge are many and varied, and no one judge has ever possessed all of them.

Naturally, there is no one mold to which all great judges have conformed. This is seen if we do no more than compare Justice Holmes and Justice Brandeis, two of the greatest judges in American history who served on the Supreme Court through much the same period of years and often stood together in the work of the Court. If there is a similarity among great judges, these two men who seemingly had so much in common might be expected to show it. Actually they were quite unlike one another in many ways. Holmes was a conservative man by nature, a cultured scholar little interested in the details of economics or politics. But he was a tolerant man who believed that experimentation is one of the keys to progress. Accordingly, he held that courts should not interfere with progressive legislation, however much they might believe it unwise or dangerous, unless they found it beyond all doubt in conflict with the Constitution. Brandeis was a liberal by nature, an active man of affairs much interested in business and governmental problems. Accordingly, as a judge he frequently voted to uphold liberal laws because of the intrinsic merit and social wisdom he saw in them. Holmes's opinions are very often brief essays in which he reiterates his belief, in simple but effective words, that in the main the Constitution does not prevent the people from having the kind of laws they want. Brandeis's opinions are frequently lengthy, and include much factual data marshaled to show the wisdom or necessity or reasonableness of the legislation under attack. Holmes as a judge was a philosopher whose understanding of life led him to be patient and tolerant of man's efforts toward progress. Brandeis as a judge was a reformer whose factual knowledge led him to approve much social experimentation on its merits.

qualities that make the great judge

Although no two great judges have been exactly alike, there are, nonetheless, certain qualities of the great judge which can be noted. First, more often than not the great judge has been an able craftsman in the law, thoroughly at home in its history, and a master of its maxims and procedures, at least in certain areas. This quality is perhaps less necessary for the appellate judge than it is for the trial judge. Certainly Marshall was not an outstanding legal technician. Holmes and Cardozo, on the other hand, were brilliant students of the common law, and although, as Supreme Court justices they were not often called upon to make use of their detailed technical knowledge, nevertheless their opinions frequently revealed their sense of the history and philosophy of the law.

Along with his mastery of the technical side of his trade the great judge usually shows a deep understanding of public affairs. He is aware of the direction in which history is moving and of the large issues which confront his generation. As Professor Walton Hamilton has put it, "The judge must become the statesman without ceasing to be the lawyer." [25] In other words, he must direct his energies and talents toward the solution of many of the same human problems that face the legislator and executive but he must do so, of course, within the somewhat restricted framework of the judicial process.

Third, the great judge, while understanding the times in which he lives, must be reasonably detached in his personal interests and aspirations from the political, economic, and social conflicts of life. Admittedly, courts as well as legislatures are the arenas in which conflicting groups of men contend for mastery. Moreover, the notion that any public officer, whether he be legislator or judge, can act as a completely disinterested broker or referee in resolving these conflicts is more idealistic than realistic. But it is a goal toward which we must strive in the democratic state. The man who is a zealot, a fighter for a cause, or a leader in a movement, whether in the fields of politics, of business, of labor, or even of morals, is a useful and necessary member of society, but his too strong commitments will often handicap him as a judge.

At the same time that the great judge avoids direct participation in the rough-and-tumble conflicts of life, he must have a strong human quality. His detachment from the conflicts of life must not be so great that he has little understanding of the ways of men and the foibles of human nature. It is not the business of judges to apply law cold-bloodedly or with complete disregard of the human factor in a case. Justice may be blind, but its concern is with man. Accordingly it must be based upon an understanding that all men are less than gods.

Finally, a great judge should have a personality of his own. He should have a carefully thought out legal approach to the problems which confront his court, and, if an appellate judge, he should have a literary style of some distinction. The decisions of the great judge are certain to have a lasting value. A judge can hardly be regarded as great unless he leaves an imprint upon the law. The opinion which shows neither legal ingenuity nor literary excellence is not apt to become a living force in the law.

Clearly the qualities mentioned do not exhaust the list, and they are always

---

[25] Walton Hamilton, "Judicial Process," *Encyclopaedia of the Social Sciences*, VIII, 450, 455.

found in great judges in varying combinations. One can argue that this or that great judge was lacking in one or more of the qualities mentioned: that Marshall was not a craftsman in the law; that Holmes had little interest in the details of public policy or social reform; that Taft was too much the partisan; that Brandeis was not sufficiently detached in his views; that Hughes wrote in an undistinguished style. Some of these judgments might be challenged, but even if conceded they merely prove that a judge can have a weakness and still be considered great on other counts. But the judge who fails many of the tests which have here been suggested is not likely to be one that history considers great. That Holmes, for example, did combine a number of qualities which make for greatness in the judge was never better indicated than in a comment by Archibald MacLeish: "Mr. Justice Holmes was a man of the world, who was also a philosopher, who was incidentally a lawyer. The result was that he was a very great judge. . . ." [26]

is there such a thing as *"judicial temperament"*?

It is sometimes said that a man must have "judicial temperament" if he is to be a great judge, or even a good one. By that phrase many things may be meant. Some people use it as a synonym for judicial conservatism. So interpreted, the quality has no relation to judicial greatness, for a great judge must of necessity make some sort of contribution to the progress of law, and thus his conservatism must at the very least be mixed with a measure of liberalism. More often the phrase is used to suggest an ability of the judge to disregard his personal views and to render impartial justice. This is clearly a *sine qua non* for a good judge, let alone a great one. But it does not follow from this that a judge may have no personal views at all, or that his philosophy of life should never show through in his rulings. For a trial judge in a criminal case to allow his personal dislike of labor organizers to prejudice him against a defendant would be infamous. For a Supreme Court justice to allow his economic philosophy to show through in adjusting the delicate balance between federal and state power, or in determining the degree of laissez faire encompassed by the due process clause of the Fourteenth Amendment is something else altogether. That personal views influence the interpretation of vague constitutional clauses or of ambiguous statutes may be shocking to the person who persists in believing that justice is, or should be, abstract and impartial. But if we are to talk about "judicial temperament," there must be some allowance for the fact that judges are men, and that "in law also men make a difference." In the words of Justice James C. McReynolds, ". . . while 'an overspeaking judge is no well-tuned cymbal' neither is an amorphous dummy unspotted by human emotions a becoming receptacle for judicial power." [27]

---

[26] Foreword to Frankfurter, *Law and Politics*, p. xvii.
[27] *Berger* v. *United States*, 255 U.S. 22, 43 (1921).

bibliographic note

Part 4 of W. F. Willoughby's *Principles of Judicial Administration* (Washington: The Brookings Institution, 1929) is devoted to judicial personnel. The article by Arthur Schlesinger, Jr., referred to in the text, "The Supreme Court: 1947," *Fortune*, XXXV (January, 1947), 73, is an interesting, albeit controversial, attempt to weigh the influence of personality upon the work of the Supreme Court. Wesley McCune's *The Nine Young Men* (New York: Harper & Brothers, 1947) contains brief biographies of the nine members of the Supreme Court in 1947 and attempts to estimate the significance of the personality factor in the judicial process.

In addition to the biographies of the Supreme Court justices already referred to in footnotes, attention may be called to John P. Frank's *Mr. Justice Black: The Man and His Opinions* (New York: Alfred A. Knopf, Inc., 1949); Willard L. King's *Melville Weston Fuller* (New York: The Macmillan Company, 1950); and Samuel J. Konefsky's *Chief Justice Stone and the Supreme Court* (New York: The Macmillan Company, 1945). Kenneth B. Umbreit's *Our Eleven Chief Justices: A History of the Supreme Court in Terms of Their Personalities* (New York: Harper & Brothers, 1938) contains brief biographical treatments of the first eleven Chief Justices of the United States.

Cortez A. M. Ewing's *The Judges of the Supreme Court, 1789–1937: A Study of Their Qualifications* (Minneapolis: The University of Minnesota Press, 1938) presents interesting and significant statistical information concerning the personnel of the Supreme Court over a period of a century and a half.

part 6

---

securing the blessings of liberty

liberty vs. authority

$\mathscr{T}$HE world has never had a good definition of the word 'liberty,' and the American people just now are much in need of one. We all declare for liberty, but in using the same word we do not all mean the same thing."

These words were spoken by Abraham Lincoln in 1864,[1] but they are just as valid today as they were when he uttered them nearly a century ago. Our own generation has just as great a need for a good working definition of liberty as did one which had to fight a great civil war to establish the right of millions of Americans to enjoy basic personal freedom. Unfortunately, our own generation seems to be just as far away from a satisfactory definition of liberty as was Lincoln's. Certainly, it is obvious that people do not all mean the same thing when they use the word. It begins to look as though, in part at least, the difficulty is insurmountable, and that liberty is one of those words like democracy, progress, welfare, and justice, which in the final analysis is probably not susceptible of a precise or formal definition that all men will accept as correct. And yet it should be possible to describe in meaningful fashion some of the qualities of liberty and the prerequisites to its existence in the modern world, even though the search for a universal, formal definition proves futile. In particular, it is desirable that the relationship between liberty and government should be analyzed and understood. Are liberty and authority opposing forces? Is government, whatever its form or the scope of its activities, necessarily a threat to liberty? Or may government, particularly if it be democratic in form and spirit, be a means whereby liberty is strengthened and safeguarded?

liberty under government

No tradition in America is stronger than our high regard for human freedom. Ours is a nation founded and settled chiefly by people seeking to escape de-

---

[1] Address, Sanitary Fair, Baltimore, April 18, 1864. *Complete Works of Abraham Lincoln* (John G. Nicolay and John Hay, eds.; New York: Lamb Publishing Company, 1905) X, 77.

tested restraints and to find greater liberty to live their lives as they pleased. Many of the great events in American history—the Revolutionary War, the settlement of the West, the Civil War, the coming of tens of millions of immigrants to our shores, participation in two great world wars—have had the greater liberty of the individual as their motivating force. We in America have come increasingly to believe in the importance of the individual person and in the right of every man to express his personality and to seek to realize his potentialities. To achieve these goals we believe that each man must have a large measure of liberty, of freedom from restraint.

Regard for authority has also been a strong tradition in this country— stronger than is often realized. Always in our history we have shown a willingness to accept authority while seeking liberty. The colonist, newly arrived on American shores, lost no time in establishing authority whether in the form of organized church, town government, or cooperative farm. Those who advocated revolution in 1776 claimed that life, liberty, and the pursuit of happiness were unalienable rights, but they hastened to add that it was to secure these rights that governments were instituted among men. A century later, the western pioneer, famed for his individualism, nonetheless made extensive use of authority whether for the purpose of providing protection against Indian and outlaw, or of securing the immediate development of public services—such as roads and schools—to ease the hardships and limitations of life on the frontier.

There is no denying the existence of both a historical and a philosophic conflict between authority and liberty—between the power of the state and the freedom of the individual. How can man's searching spirit find complete self-expression when there are rules of the game to be observed? Or how can law and order be maintained if each man wanders fancy free? How can liberty survive in the face of authority; how can authority prevail where there is insistence upon liberty? From the earliest political beginnings, choosing between authority and liberty has created a dilemma that has plagued the architects of government and the poets of human freedom alike. In no small degree the history of human progress is told in the story of the varying success man has enjoyed in reconciling liberty with authority, authority with liberty. It is as a chapter in this long history that the work of the American Founding Fathers is to be regarded. As Charles and Mary Beard have put it, the Fathers were confronted with this fundamental problem: "How to set up a government strong enough to serve the purposes of the Union and still not too strong for the maintenance of the liberties of the people." [2] And Abraham Lincoln merely echoed the dilemma that faced the Fathers when he asked this question: "Must a gov-

---

[2] Charles A. and Mary R. Beard, *A Basic History of the United States* (New York: New Home Library, 1944), p. 131.

ernment of necessity be too strong for the liberties of its own people, or too weak to maintain its own existence?"[3]

The Founding Fathers' solution of the dilemma must be regarded as one of the greatest achievements in the history of political institutions. Nonetheless, theirs was a triumph that can only be completely understood and appreciated when it is considered in the light of the political and social traditions in which the makers of our constitutional system lived and worked.

backgrounds of American liberty and authority

the influence of the Stoics and Christians

Scholars have suggested that for the beginnings of the present-day attitudes toward liberty and authority which prevail in the democracies of the Western world, it is necessary to go back to the philosophy of the Greek Stoics and the religion of the early Christians. In both of these groups a fundamental belief in the importance and integrity of the individual was strongly held. Both accepted a superior law, divine or natural in character, which taught that the individual should live a life of freedom as a rational being.

This attitude toward the importance of the individual meets such ready acceptance in the American mind today that we are almost inclined to take it for granted and to forget that there have been religions and philosophies which taught that the individual was of little importance. From the time of the ancient Greek and Roman civilizations to the modern totalitarian state, there have always been some men to advocate, and other men to accept, religious or philosophic beliefs that the individual is but a unit in the group and that society or the state, as against the individual members of which they consist, is of first importance. It is important to remember that philosophies which teach the importance of the individual and his right to live his life as he pleases have had no historic inevitability.

While the Stoics and the Christians advocated the cause of man, as opposed to men, they also viewed life on this earth in rational fashion and this led them to conclude that some authority, some organization in society, was necessary if chaos was not to prevail. Christianity insisted that man's soul was his own and that in expressing his innermost aspirations he was responsible only to God. But it warned against a refusal to render unto Caesar an obedience in the ordinary, everyday things of life. Similarly, Stoicism, while primarily interested in the individual, taught that social organization was inevitable and that its authority should be accepted.

---

[3] Special Session Message, July 4, 1861.—*Messages and Papers of the Presidents*, compiled by James D. Richardson (New York: Bureau of National Literature and Art, 1903), VI, 20, 23.

That the Founding Fathers came to grips with the dual problem of liberty and authority as men who were products of the Stoic-Christian traditions as to life and its meaning is self-evident. To this influence may be added two developments from the history of more recent centuries which had a profound effect upon the founders of the American political system. The first of these is seen in certain general changes that took place in Western civilization at the end of the Middle Ages; the second is more peculiarly identified with English and American political history.

the influence of four events in early modern times

Modern democracy owes much to the historical events and circumstances that combined to bring to an end the thousand years of the Dark Ages and that permitted the Western world, or parts thereof, to achieve during the last five hundred years progress of an unprecedented character. Four historical events contributed heavily to this result—one economic, one political, one religious, and one aesthetic in character. The economic event was the rise of capitalism; the political, the rise of the national state; the religious, the Reformation; and the aesthetic, the Renaissance. Any grouping of such widely diverse and nebulous events as these to prove anything about modern liberty is bound to involve serious oversimplification. Nonetheless, historians stress the fact that all of these developments involved a throwing off of restraints, an escape from the restrictive and limiting forces of the Middle Ages, a freeing of the individual so that greater personal liberty might be exercised in the major decisions and activities of life. Capitalism was a victory over feudalism, and feudalism as an economic system was so restrictive and conservative in its influence that for one thousand years man had had little incentive or opportunity for any economic enterprise of his own. During these long centuries, man did things as he had always done them, there was little inclination to experiment, and the economy stood still— stood still, unfortunately, at a level that meant a low standard of living and permitted the individual little chance to better his lot. Capitalism, on the other hand, whatever its later shortcomings were to be, did unquestionably free man from the bonds of a restrictive economic system, and open to him vast new vistas for individual enterprise.

The rise of the national state had much the same effect, whatever force the argument may have that in the long run the national state has merely provided man with a stronger and more authoritarian ruler. For at the time the national state was emerging, its political authority became centered in the king, and the king found that he had good cause to join forces with the businessman. Thus the national state fought with capitalism against the restraints of feudalism and the shortsighted pettiness and conservatism of the feudal lord.

The Reformation also increased the measure of man's freedom. Whatever the pros and cons of the religious controversy between Catholic and Protestant, the latter was seeking greater opportunity for self-expression. Likewise, the Renaissance stands in human history as one of man's greatest victories in his struggle to broaden his right to exercise his talents free from tradition and restraint.

The cumulative effect of these changes tremendously altered the status of the individual. Because of the developments of the preceding five hundred years, eighteenth-century man breathed the pure air of freedom as no man before him had done. Optimism and change were the rule of the day, and mankind seemed on the verge of achieving a nearly perfect order of things by the free and rational exercise of the individual's talents and skills. That the enormity of the problem of life and the task of organizing a more perfect society were being grossly minimized soon became only too clear, but this was in fact an Age of Reason. If it be true that in the last century and a half America has made progress in seeking a better political order of things, we owe much to this Age of Reason and the freedom that it provided.

Because events did combine at the end of the medieval period to give man more liberty, it does not follow that authority lost ground in any proportional degree. Indeed, it was perhaps because man gained greater freedom to conduct himself more rationally that he replaced the rejected authority with the new. Thus the businessman identified himself with the king and the national state and sought the help and protection of government in his individualistic enterprises. The Protestant, free at last to worship as he pleased, made haste to erect new churches to contain the religious spirit, and to establish new authoritarian dogmas which the faithful must observe. The free artist of the Renaissance soon accepted rules of form, style, and taste and found himself once more subject to limitations of convention and "school." The free man of the eighteenth century gloried in his new liberty, but reason dictated that he accept a rule of authority lest the chaos of unlimited freedom prove to be no freedom at all. Too much authority spelled despotism, but too little authority was bound to result in anarchism. Both were the enemies of liberty.

the influence of the English Bills of Rights

The second development, more closely identified with England and America, is the emergence of what may be called the principle of the Bill of Rights. Beginning in England with Magna Carta in 1215, and continuing through the Petition of Right in 1628 and the Bill of Rights in 1689, there was established in that country a definite written code of civil liberties. These were liberties belonging primarily to the individual which were guaranteed against violation by the government, for it was the state that the Englishmen of the late Middle Ages and early modern era had learned to fear as the primary threat to his liberties. Thus, Magna Carta forbade the sale of justice, provided that no man was to be imprisoned or deprived of his property save by legal judgment of his peers and in accordance with the established law of the land, and restricted the King from the commission of certain arbitrary acts. The Petition of Right forbade the billeting of soldiers in the homes of the people, restricted trial by martial law as opposed to trial by civil law, forbade the collection of taxes not authorized regularly by Parliament, and prohibited imprisonment without specific charges and an orderly trial. The Bill of Rights forbade the King to suspend laws, protected the right to petition the government without fear of punishment, prohibited a standing army in time of peace except as authorized by Parliament, provided that parliamentary elections were to be held regularly and free from influence by the King, guaranteed freedom of debate in Parliament, and proscribed excessive bail in criminal cases.[4]

Naturally enough the English colonists who came to America in the seventeenth and eighteenth centuries brought with them this idea of a specific and formal listing of personal rights upon which government should be forbidden to encroach. However, their first real opportunity to formulate such codes did not come until 1776 with the drafting of the Declaration of Independence. Thereafter, many of the new state constitutions written between 1776 and 1787 contained bills of rights, so that when the national Constitutional Convention met in Philadelphia in the latter year the principle of a formal, written bill of rights had been well established.

the influence of Locke and Rousseau

These historical events which began with the passing of the Dark Ages in Europe and which contributed so much to the freedom of man were accompanied from time to time by considerable theorizing on the part of political philosophers. In England, John Locke, particularly, was regarded as the philosopher of the great revolutionary events of the seventeenth century in that country. In France in the eighteenth century Jean Jacques Rousseau was responsible for the formulation of somewhat similar philosophic ideas. The relevant portions of the theories of these men may be set forth in simple terms as follows.[5] Originally man lived in a state of nature and was controlled in his acts by certain fundamental natural laws which he discovered but did not make. Then for varying reasons life in this state of nature became chaotic and unsatisfactory, and the establishment of governmental institutions with positive authority to preserve law and order took place. This establishment of political institutions was made by means of a *socal contract* consisting of two parts. By the first part a government was set up and the people surrendered certain *alienable* rights to that government, rights that had belonged to the individual in the state of nature. This surrender was made in return for a just and effective governmental program. By the second part the people retained certain *unalienable* rights which natural law forbade them to delegate to governmental authorities even if they had been so in-

---

[4] Robert E. Cushman, "Civil Liberties," *Encyclopaedia of the Social Sciences*, III, 509–513.
[5] Charles H. McIlwain, "Bills of Rights," *Encyclopaedia of the Social Sciences*, II, 544–546.

clined. These rights the government was forbidden to encroach upon. That such a prohibition might be more certain of observation, a formal bill of rights became part of the constitutional settlement.

Not all modern students of government are willing to accept this philosophical justification of the principle of the bill of rights. Apart from scholarly criticism of the details of the philosophies of Locke and Rousseau, such a modern political scientist as Harold J. Laski was inclined to repudiate these entire philosophies as mere rationalizations.[6] In his opinion the age-old search for personal liberty rests upon more pragmatic grounds, and the victories that have been achieved from time to time, such as Magna Carta in 1215, have been won by aggressive groups, races, or creeds seeking "a place in the sun denied to them." Laski by no means denied the significance of these victories or the value to a democratic society of these liberties so won, but he very much doubted that people fought for such liberties because of conscious considerations of philosophy or principle.

civil liberties in the Philadelphia convention

In the light of the strong English tradition of the Bill of Rights and in the light of the action of the American states in the decade before 1787, it might have been expected that the Philadelphia convention would surely include a bill of rights in the Constitution it formulated. It did not do so. The reasons for this somewhat surprising action are not entirely clear. We have seen that the Founding Fathers were seemingly convinced that the needs and problems of their times called more clearly for a strengthening of governmental authority in the United States than they did for any reaffirmation of the liberty of the individual. It has been said that constitutionalism is a means "of adjusting the perennial and confused relations of government authority and private freedom." [7] To the Fathers it certainly seemed that the confusion of their day resulted from too little centralized governmental authority, and too much decentralized freedom—at least for the several states if not the individual person. To them the adjustment called for in making a new constitutional settlement was a swing toward more political power rather than toward more personal liberty. On the other hand, it is easy to oversimplify the attitude of the Philadelphia convention on this important point of a bill of rights.

liberty safeguarded by the original Constitution

In the first place, liberty, as against authority, was not entirely ignored in the original Constitution. It is clearly stated in the Preamble that one of the fundamental purposes of the Constitution is "to secure the blessings of liberty to our-

[6] Harold J. Laski, "Liberty," *Encyclopaedia of the Social Sciences*, IX, 442–446.
[7] Charles A. Beard, *The Republic* (New York: The Viking Press, 1944), p. 178.

selves and our posterity." It is true that the Preamble has little practical meaning and it may be that this phrase was included for tactical reasons in an attempt
to appease those who felt that liberty came off second best in the Constitution.
It has also been argued that these words were placed in the Constitution to suggest freedom from foreign restraint and authority rather than liberty in the domestic sense. In any case, the words are there, and they carry weight as a noble
and inspiring statement of purpose.

Even more important is the fact, often overlooked, that the original Constitution does contain a rudimentary bill of rights. Section nine of Article One
consists of an enumeration of some eight prohibitions affecting the national government, and some of our most important civil liberties stem from these particular prohibitions. Moreover, the very next section in the same article establishes a
somewhat similar set of prohibitions against state action. One or two other scattered clauses in the original Constitution further restrict the use of governmental
power, or protect individual liberties. Still and all, the decision of the Philadelphia convention was a conscious and deliberate one to reject a formal bill of
rights, and the Fathers did not think of the sections just mentioned as serving
in any such capacity. The inclusion or exclusion of a bill of rights was certainly not one of the questions that gave the Convention great trouble or occupied much of its time. When, some five days before the adjournment of the
Convention, George Mason of Virginia proposed that a bill of rights be added
to the Constitution, every state that had delegates in attendance at that time
voted against the proposal.

separation of powers as a protection of liberty

In the second place, the character of the finished Constitution makes it clear that
its authors were by no means so obsessed with the need for strengthening authority as to be completely disinterested in the cause of liberty. In the principle of
separation of powers the Fathers thought they were making provision against
arbitrary or tyrannical exercise of power by the agencies of the national government. They were aware of the dangers inherent in a government possessing strong political power, and although the motivation for the inclusion of the
principle of separation of powers was certainly confused, that principle was intended to provide some protection for individual liberties.

Hamilton's argument against a bill of rights

The argument made by Alexander Hamilton defending the Convention's decision
to exclude a bill of rights should be noted. This argument is to be found in the
eighty-fourth paper in *The Federalist*. Hamilton argues that it is unnecessary to
protect particular civil liberties by forbidding the national government to encroach upon them when in fact that government is one of limited powers and is
granted no positive power that it might use to violate such rights. Why, he argues,

forbid Congress to interfere with a free press when the Constitution grants Congress no power to regulate the press? Hamilton himself anticipates a possible rebuttal to his argument and tries to show that the power to tax, for example, could not or would not be used in such a way as to restrict the press. His reply is certainly not an adequate one, for the exercise by Congress of its powers to tax, to raise and support an army, and to provide a postal system has upon occasion raised serious questions of possible improper interferences with the freedom of the press.

One cannot quite escape the feeling that Hamilton's logic has a tenuous quality. In any case the people to whom the argument was directed remained unconvinced. "Absurd" though it might be for them to allege that the absence of a bill of rights from the Constitution was a serious shortcoming, make the allegation they did, and the supporters of the Constitution were forced to give ground. In many of the states, ratification of the Constitution was obtained only after an understanding was clearly established that the First Congress would submit to the states amendments to the Constitution incorporating a bill of rights. This was promptly done, Congress proposing twelve amendments. Ten of these were adopted and became part of the Constitution in 1791.

the threat to civil liberties from private persons and organizations

It is commonly believed that the only threat to civil liberty is found in the authority wielded by the state. Actually, a careful reading of American history since 1789 shows that more often than not government has been a friend rather than an enemy of civil liberty. Contrary to the fears of the eighteenth century, some of the most serious interferences with civil rights have resulted from the activity of private individuals and private organizations rather than from the activity of governmental agencies or public officers. This is a statement that is difficult to prove statistically, and yet even a casual reading of history makes it clear that the lynch spirit, the hooded mob, and the night rider have always been common phenomena in this country.

In general it is correct to say that it is not government per se that offers the basic threat to civil liberty, but the people themselves. Such rights as freedom of expression, the right to vote, or equality of opportunity are in danger from time to time because one man fears that the exercise of these rights by another man will do harm to his interests. Sometimes this fear leads him to take steps as an individual to prevent the exercise of rights by the other man. More frequently, it leads him to seek action against the other man through social institutions. Admittedly, government is one of the social institutions through which one group of men may seek to encroach upon the rights of another group, and all too often such efforts are successful. But there are other nongovernmental social organizations, ranging all the way from such disreputable groups as the Ku Klux Klan to such respectable institutions as business organizations, labor unions, and even the church, through which a successful attack upon the civil rights of certain people may be, and often is, undertaken. It is here that government may become a friend and protector, rather than an enemy, of civil rights. One way it does this is by defining willful and deliberate interference with an individual's civil rights as criminal conduct to be punished accordingly. Traditionally, it is such antisocial acts as murder, arson, and burglary that have been dealt with through criminal laws. But certain types of interference with civil liberty have also long fallen into this category. Examples are to be seen in laws defining as criminal conduct lynching or interference with the right of qualified persons to vote. Virtually every state in the Union has such laws upon its statute books. Moreover, there is today widespread pressure for the extension of statutory protection of civil rights against private interference. A good example is seen in the agitation for state and federal fair employment practice laws. A half-dozen states, led by New York, have actually adopted legislation of this type, which declares that the right of a qualified worker to receive a job in private employment, without being discriminated against because of his race, color, religion, or national origin, is a basic civil right. Laws of this type also provide the means of protecting the right against employers, labor unions, or employment agencies which do discriminate against potential workers for any of the forbidden reasons.

liberty and authority reconciled

liberty dependent upon authority

The evolution of man's political institutions has been largely concerned with a search for a satisfactory equilibrium between governmental authority on one hand and individual liberty on the other. The very idea that such an equilibrium is an attainable thing suggests that there is no irreconcilable conflict between authority and liberty. Indeed, it may be argued that the most powerful motivating force leading to the creation of political authority has, throughout all history, been a desire to preserve and protect liberty. It is true that many examples can be provided of the establishment or use of political power for the sake of power alone or for the advancement and glory of a tyrant, a king, or some other autocratic ruler or ruling class. But from the time of the cave man to the civilized man of the twentieth century, it has been seen that authority can be used to foster liberty. Ancient man emerging from an animal existence soon discovered that tribal authority could protect his crops or domestic animals from marauders, and that submission to such authority guaranteed him liberty to enjoy the fruits of his labors. Without such protection his liberty was likely to become theoretical in the face of the dangers that threatened him every moment of his existence. The twentieth-century sophisticate may fret and fume as the red of the traffic light forces him to stop his car and delays him in his travels, but his irritation is only surface-deep; he knows that without traffic regulations enforced by government he might well never reach his destination at all.

The basic notion that liberty in the modern world is dependent upon authority for its continued existence and enjoyment has been very well put by Chief Justice Charles Evans Hughes, a man who in his personal politics certainly did not favor a broad or unrestrained exercise of the power of the state: "Civil liberties, as guaranteed by the Constitution, imply the existence of an organized society maintaining public order without which liberty itself would be lost in the excesses of unrestrained abuses." [8]

philosophical anarchy rejected

A certain instinctive reluctance in man to accept the idea that liberty and authority can be reconciled is both inevitable and desirable. From time to time a few free souls try to refute the argument that liberty can be enjoyed only under the protection of authority. Occasionally such persons even try to escape from the restraints of civilization to enjoy pure freedom in its fullest measure. Now and then the case for liberty without authority has been expressed philosphically in very persuasive fashion by men of considerable intellect. But the Thoreaus, with their essays on civil disobedience and their sojourns in the wilderness, have won few converts. Most men have found it easier to understand the Rousseaus who look longingly back to the days when men lived the lives of noble savages free from restraints and authority, who sigh at the realization that such a time probably never existed, and who turn with some enthusiasm to the enjoyment of life in a civilized society where a rationally conceived system of law and order guarantees to the individual a reasonable opportunity to express his personality, free from the fearful dangers and dark chaos of anarchy.

This pragmatic willingness of Western man to get on with the business of reconciling liberty and authority, although he has often faltered along the way, has been one of his outstanding characteristics since the revolutions of the seventeenth and eighteenth centuries. Here again our English inheritance has been of considerable value, for the English people seem to have shown more common sense in reconciling authority and liberty than have those of any other nation. It has been said:

> The Englishman is a psychic entity; he does not surrender his personality to any social idol—church or State or king. Yet he can compromise enough, grumbling loudly the while, to get along in society and so save his institutions from anarchy. He seems to be our most practical social animal; and

---

[8] *Cox v. New Hampshire*, 312 U.S. 569, 574 (1941).

his dual nature, facing both toward personality and toward society, makes him the very pattern for civil liberty. We inherit something of this gift.[9]

liberty is relative, not absolute

The conclusion that liberty and authority are not in any final sense irreconcilable is further strengthened when one understands the danger of the use of absolutes in this area. It cannot be repeated too often that all rights in an organized society are relative rather than absolute. Justice Oliver Wendell Holmes's famous remark that freedom of speech does not include the right falsely to shout "Fire!" in a crowded theater has been recalled so often that it is in danger of becoming hackneyed, but it remains one of the most perceptive observations ever made about the nature of freedom. Every right is exercised within limits. Freedom of the press stops short of the right to print obscenities; freedom of religion does not include the right to practice polygamy; freedom of assembly cannot justify the holding of a meeting at a time or in a place conducive to panic or disorder.

Moreover, two rights are often found to be in conflict with each other, and in resolving the conflict one or both may have to be limited through some exercise of authority. A good current example is to be seen in recent Supreme Court cases involving criticism of procedures of trial courts in newspaper articles or editorials. Freedom of the press certainly includes the right to criticize the government, but irresponsible or malicious newspaper attacks upon a court or a judge may be pushed to the point where the right of parties to litigation to enjoy a fair trial in an impartial court is endangered. When such a point is reached, the two rights must be brought into balance, and this may well mean limiting one so that the other may be preserved.

Above all it is necessary to avoid confusing liberty with unbridled license or sheer anarchy. It has been pointed out that when the Englishman and the American talk about civil liberty they have in mind "social liberty, liberty within the State, to be enjoyed by responsible members of the society".[10] Nonetheless, there has been a great deal of loose talk in America about liberty. Often people use such phrases as "laissez faire," "free enterprise," and "the American way of life" as though they meant that the use of governmental authority to curb the freedom of the individual was a violation of American traditions. Whatever else may be said of the generation of statesmen who made our constitutional system, it is clear that when they talked of liberty they did not use the word as though it were synonymous with laissez faire. In America the poet's unbridled cry, "Let freedom ring," has given way to the more restrained, "Thy liberty in law."

---

[9] Leon Whipple, *Our Ancient Liberties* (New York: The H. W. Wilson Company, 1927), p. 18. Reprinted by permission of The H. W. Wilson Company, publishers.
[10] *Ibid.*, p. 9.

And yet there is a danger at the other extreme, too. Liberty in the modern state is dependent upon authority for its existence. But a free people must be ever on guard lest this truth become a rationalization used to justify unnecessary encroachments by government upon the individual's freedom. Edmund Burke, the great English liberal, provided a good working principle for the proper balancing of liberty and authority when he said: "Liberty, too, must be limited in order to be possessed. The degree of restraint it is impossible in any case to settle precisely. But it ought to be the constant aim of every wise public counsel to find out by cautious experiments, and rational, cool endeavors, with how little, not how much, of this restraint the community can subsist. . . ." [11]

the changing character of liberty

rights may become obsolete

There is no irreconcilable conflict between liberty and authority. But it by no means follows that all liberty can be reconciled with all authority. There is authority that inevitably destroys particular liberties, and there are liberties that make the maintenance of certain forms of authority difficult. So the search for a workable equilibrium between liberty and authority is a very real and continuing problem, one that has always troubled man, and one that has ended in failure more often than in success. Establishing such a balance is a difficult task at best, but the problem has not been rendered easier by the fact that man's attitudes have been constantly changing. The relationship between authority and liberty has been a highly dynamic rather than a static one. What one generation has regarded as an absolutely indispensable liberty, another has felt might well be sacrificed to the needs of changing times and conditions. The words of the Bill of Rights make it clear that in 1790 a grand jury hearing before indictment was regarded as a right that the federal government should not tamper with. This right was not extended to the area of state government, and with the passing years the people of many states came to the conclusion that the cause of justice could be better served if the device of the grand jury were dispensed with. A somewhat similar attitude is even coming to prevail concerning trial by jury itself. When this right was won centuries ago in England men felt that a great victory had been achieved in the struggle for great security of the person. With this right guaranteed, man needed no longer fear that his government would arrest him and try him for his life or his freedom by some arbitrary star-chamber procedure. But today, at least in the United States, we can calmly consider the proposal that jury trials be abandoned and that, even in the case of serious or capital crimes, a man be tried by a judge or perhaps a panel of judges. This is not to say that such a

---

[11] *Burke's Politics* (R. J. S. Hoffman and P. Levack, eds.; New York: Alfred A. Knopf, Inc., 1949), p. 109.

change is either a desirable or an inevitable one, but only that the sum total of an individual's liberty would not necessarily be lessened were trial by jury to give way to some other mode of judicial procedure.

Conditions change; attitudes change. Because of this an almost constant revision of the governmental program is required; some problems are solved and the exercise of authority may cease; new problems arise and authority must be enlarged if they are to be dealt with. Americans believe that every man should be free to choose his own occupation in life and that government should not interfere with that right. But let our nation become involved in total war with a dangerous enemy and we conclude that government may well tell men how and where to labor. In a similar way, other crises less serious than war may persuade a people to change its thinking concerning a proper balance between liberty and authority. We may agree, then, with Laski, who said: "Liberty . . . is always changing with the conditions of time and place. . . . Liberty, in a word, has to be reconciled with the necessities of the social process; it has to find terms upon which to live with authority." [12]

are some liberties fundamental and eternal?

In the discussion of changing attitudes toward such matters as grand jury indictments or trial by jury no attempt has been made to weigh the social arguments for or against such changes. The point is that these changes do take place and one is forced to admit that they can occur without any revolutionary alteration in the political system or in the position of the individual as a member of a free society. The question may now be asked: Are there some liberties that are absolutely indispensable, liberties that would be grievously missed were they to disappear in the ever-changing course of history?

An answer to this question can be given in the affirmative without hesitation. We may conceivably do without grand jury hearings, but freedom of speech and freedom of the press are surely basic to our way of life. The right to be free from self-incrimination is by no means synonymous with justice in a system of criminal procedure, but the right of the mature and responsible citizen to vote and otherwise participate in the political process is surely indispensable in a democratic society. As the list of civil liberties is examined, some seem fundamental, some seem merely convenient or desirable in the light of particular conditions or attitudes. Drawing the line between these two types of liberty is not always an easy matter. But an analysis of the reasoning which leads us to support freedom of expression and the right to participate in the political process makes it clear why these and certain other rights are indispensable.

---

[12] Laski, "Liberty," IX, 444.

freedom of expression a fundamental liberty

As members of a free society we believe that there is a choice between good and bad, wise and unwise, ways of attacking our social problems. We believe that man is a rational being, that he can use his intelligence to discover the good or wise ways, and thereby fashion for himself an ever more satisfying existence on earth. Historically, man has found that the best way of evolving a wise social policy seems to lie in experience, in the process of trial and error. At this point, liberty enters the story. How can a people benefit by experience unless each individual has freedom of expression—freedom to discuss the lessons learned from the process of trial and error? If there were but one true, wise way of life and if we were certain we knew what that way was, we might safely curb the individual's freedom to discuss alternative ways. But at many points we are clearly not certain of ourselves, whether it be on the minor point of preserving a four-year term for the presidency, or on the major point of limiting our national sovereignty and joining a world-state. So we discuss these matters, we weigh the results of our experiments, we calmly and rationally consider proposed changes, and we let every man speak his mind on these subjects. If we do decide to accept certain changes we accept them on the basis of reasoned discussion in which all members of the society are free to participate, and not as the result of the employment of force, or dictation by one man, or even a few men.

The classic statement in support of "free trade in ideas" is found in Justice Holmes's opinion in the case of *Abrams* v. *United States,* decided in 1919:

> . . . when men have realized that time has upset many fighting faiths, they may come to believe even more than they believe the very foundations of their own conduct that the ultimate good desired is better reached by free trade in ideas—that the best test of truth is the power of the thought to get itself accepted in the competition of the market, and that truth is the only ground upon which their wishes safely can be carried out. That at any rate is the theory of our Constitution. It is an experiment, as all life is an experiment.[13]

The underlying spirit of our democratic society makes it reasonably clear that liberty of expression is indispensable. Unless individuals can freely discuss the results of past experiments or the merits of proposed changes, the search for truth is obstructed. The President's Committee on Civil Rights in *To Secure These Rights,* its report published in 1947, puts the argument for freedom of expression in the following words:

> In a free society there is faith in the ability of the people to make sound, rational judgments. But such judgments are possible only where the people have access to all relevant facts and to all prevailing interpretations of the

---

[13] *Abrams* v. *United States,* 250 U.S. 616, 630 (1919).

facts. How can such judgments be formed on a sound basis if arguments, viewpoints, or opinions are arbitrarily suppressed? How can the concept of the marketplace of thought in which truth ultimately prevails retain its validity if the thought of certain individuals is denied the right of circulation? [14]

freedom to participate in the political process also fundamental

The freedom of every citizen to participate in the political process upon a strict basis of equality with every other citizen is a further *sine qua non* of the democratic process. Each man must have access to the ballot box subject to reasonable restrictions such as those based upon age or literacy. Perhaps, as philosophers have often argued, some men are their brothers' intellectual superiors. But who is to designate the superior man? Who is to weigh his ballot more heavily on Election Day? We are seemingly compelled to live by a rule of absolute equality in the casting of votes and in the making of social decisions in a people's search for a better way of life. Freedom of speech, freedom of the press, freedom to participate in the making of decisions—these at least seem utterly fundamental and indispensable to our way of life, granted the premises which have been assumed. This is not to say that there are not other similiar liberties. For example, the President's Committee on Civil Rights lists as indispensable rights in a democratic society the two we have discussed—freedom of expression, and participation as citizens in the political process—and also the right to safety and security of the person, and the right to equality of opportunity.

fundamental rights are of value both to the individual and to society

It may be asked: Are fundamental civil liberties to be determined primarily by testing their value to *society* or their value to the *individual*? In trying to answer this question it is significant that the President's Committee on Civil Rights found both tests to be important. It says of the right to safety and security of the person:

> Where the threat of violence by private persons or mobs exists, a cruel inhibition of the sense of freedom of activity and security of the person inevitably results. Where a society permits private and arbitrary violence to be done to its members, its own integrity is inevitably corrupted. It cannot permit human beings to be imprisoned or killed in the absence of due process of law without degrading its entire fabric. [15]

Of the right to vote it says:

> Without the right to vote, the individual loses his voice in the group effort and is subjected to rule by a body from which he has been excluded. Like-

---

[14] *To Secure These Rights* (Washington: Government Printing Office, 1947), pp. 8–9.
[15] *Ibid.*, p. 6.

wise, the right of the individual to vote is important to the group itself. . . . Every time a qualified person is denied a voice in public affairs, one of the components of a potential majority is lost, and the formation of a sound public policy is endangered.[16]

And of the right to equality of opportunity it says:

Without this equality of opportunity the individual is deprived of the chance to develop his potentialities and to share the fruits of society. The group also suffers through the loss of the contributions which might have been made by persons excluded from the main channels of social and economic activity.[17]

freedom to end freedom?

Since the existence of civil liberty is of importance to society as well as to individuals, this question is raised: Should civil liberties be denied to those members of society who would use these rights to undermine and destroy the political system and the liberties it provides? The question is a perennial one, but it has received increasing attention in recent years.[18] Activity during the last two decades by communists, fascists, nazis, and other groups who have owed allegiance to, or given intellectual support to foreign doctrines alien to the American political system has given the question added meaning. These groups have frankly admitted that if they could they would remake American political institutions, patterning them after the new governmental forms that have appeared in Europe and elsewhere in recent times. Under such altered political institutions there would be little or no place for such liberties as freedom of speech and press. Moreover, members of these groups have admitted that they have only contempt for the American idea of civil liberty, even though they are perfectly willing to make use of American freedom to secure their ends. Accordingly, it is not surprising that many people have concluded that ways and means must be found to deprive these groups of their freedom of expression and activity.

argument for the suppression of antidemocrats

Persons who have arrived at this conclusion argue that by the natural law of self-preservation a nation or a society cannot permit its enemies to destroy it from within. Some liberals, they assert, are much too willing, in a world in which might seems all too prone to triumph over right, to place complete depend-

---

[16] *Ibid.*, p. 8.

[17] *Ibid.*, p. 9.

[18] See, for example, Osmond K. Fraenkel, *Our Civil Liberties* (New York: The Viking Press, 1944), Chap. 2; Archibald MacLeish, "Freedom to End Freedom," *Survey Graphic* XXVIII, (February, 1939), 117–119; Robert E. Cushman, "Civil Liberty after the War," *American Political Science Review*, XXXVIII (February, 1944), 1–20.

ence upon the ability of the American ideal of freedom to prevail against the arguments, however beguiling, in favor of alien, illiberal doctrines. And the question is asked, is it not tragic irony for a government to sanction the exercise of freedom of speech to a point where such speech seeks to tear down the very structure upon which such rights rest? Moreover, it is argued, we have always made exceptions to freedom. We have not hesitated to curb grossly im-

"Fire!"

HERBLOCK

(Reprinted with permission of Herblock and the Washington Post Co.)

moral speech because of the social harm it may do. Wherin lies the difference in curbing grossly revolutionary speech because of the political harm it may do?

argument against suppression of antidemocrats

A second school of thought cautions against the lack of wisdom in a policy that would curtail liberty so that liberty may be protected. The members of this school do not defend the doctrines that fascists or communists teach. Moreover, they agree that because of the ultimate desire of such radicals to abolish the very system that provides us with our civil liberties, these persons have sacrificed any personal right to continued possession and exercise of these liberties. But they contend with considerable logic that once the decision is made to curtail the liberties of some people because of the doctrines they are supporting, it becomes exceedingly difficult thereafter to draw any satisfactory or workable line between ideas that are entitled to be expressed and those that are too dangerous or radical to enjoy circulation. From a policy of denying freedom of expression to those who preach revolutionary changes would it not be an all too easy step to the suppression of the merely "radical" or "progressive" advocate of change in our political system—suppression of the man who advocates that our presidential form of government be replaced with parliamentary government, or that our forty-eight states be consolidated into twelve regional governments?

At this point members of the first group point out that distinctions of degree must always be made in the formation and administration of public policies. They argue that distinction between the suppression of those two advocate revolution and the protection of those who merely advocate political changes by means of constitutional amendment is not an impossible one to make.

The neutral observer seems forced to conclude that the denial of freedom of speech to those who preach revolution would constitute a precedent which might thereafter be applied in cases increasingly more innocent in character. The line between such cases would have to be drawn by political officers exercising discretionary authority, and such power would be more than ordinarily susceptible of abuse. It is no argument against the exercise of political power that it may be abused, but it is perhaps wise to avoid, if possible, powers which, because of their nature, are peculiarly subject to abuse. The power of a political officer to curtail another man's freedom of speech because of the radical character of the words he utters is just such a power.

"freedom for the thought we hate"

Reflection makes it clear that the only valid test for the existence of civil liberty in a society arises in respect to freedom for those with whom the majority finds itself in disagreement. Every man believes in freedom for those who agree with him. There is seldom much controversy over the exercise of civil liberty by those who are in the middle of the main currents of social thought and practice. "Freedom for the thought we hate" is quite a different matter. Unless we are willing to recognize and fight for such freedom, civil liberty has little meaning, logical or practical. We may agree with Justice Holmes in what he says of communism: "If in the long run the beliefs expressed in proletarian dictatorship are destined to be accepted by the dominant forces of the community, the only real meaning of free speech is that they should be given their chance and have their way." [19]

If, on the other hand, such ideas are not strong enough to become dominant, then there is no danger at all in permitting them to be freely expressed. This is

---

[19] *Gitlow* v. *New York*, 268 U.S. 652, 673 (1925).

perhaps the most practical argument in favor of taking no drastic step against those who would use freedom to end freedom. If we are so certain that these radicals are wrong in their beliefs, and if we are so certain of the merits of the American way of life and of its permanency, what cause is there to harbor fears that these people will ever make much headway with their dangerous and un-American notions? Three hundred years ago John Milton gave voice to this argument in these words:

> And though all the windes of doctrin were let loose to play upon the earth, so Truth be in the field, we do injuriously by licencing and prohibiting to misdoubt her strength. Let her and Falsehood grapple; who ever knew Truth put to the wors in a free and open encounter? [20]

The *status quo* almost always enjoys a tremendous advantage. New ideas must fight an uphill battle. "The chief danger is not that false ideas and doctrines will supplant established truth, but that established error will seek to protect itself against the truth by suppressing all dissenters."[21] Moreover, it has sometimes been argued that, paradoxically enough, civil liberty is apt to be in particular danger in a democracy for the very reason that in a democracy the majority is often so certain of the soundness of its beliefs and position that it is contemptuous of minorities. The great French observer of American political institutions, De Tocqueville, said in 1835: "I know of no country in which there is so little independence of mind and real freedom of discussion as in America." [22] One may well question the soundness of this observation. It is possible that in the European autocracies and aristocracies of De Tocqueville's day the members of a relatively small intellectual group enjoyed greater "independence of mind" and "freedom of discussion" than American intellectuals did. But when one remembers the prison of intellectual ignorance and stagnation to which the overwhelming majorities of European peoples were condemned in the early nineteenth century, De Tocqueville's comment on America seems somewhat exaggerated. Yet he was unquestionably putting his finger on a potential weakness of democratic societies. For this reason, too, the people of a free society should bend over backward in permitting great freedom of expression to the dissenter in its midst.

subversive acts may be punished

This is not to say that, where the basic idea of civil liberty is accepted for conservative and radical alike, a society is powerless to protect itself against an

---

[20] John Milton, *Areopagitica* (Hales ed.; New York: Oxford University Press, 1917), pp. 51–52.

[21] J. Allen Smith, *The Growth and Decadence of Constitutional Government* (New York: Henry Holt and Company, 1930), p. 163.

[22] Alexis de Tocqueville, *Democracy in America* (Phillips Bradley, ed.; New York: Alfred A. Knopf, Inc., 1945), I, 263.

enemy within and must stand helplessly by while its foundations are undermined or its walls pulled down. A society that accepts the historical validity of war against its international enemies cannot hesitate to use force against equally dangerous enemies within its own borders. Certain distinctions need to be kept in mind, however. We have been discussing so far the use of freedom of expression by the acknowledged enemy of existing institutions. The moment he goes beyond mere intellectual or emotional appeals for change and shows signs of organizing for physical activity or employing force or revolutionary methods, the restraining hand of the government may be vigorously applied. Freedom for radical groups to express their revolutionary ideas by word of mouth or the printed page is one thing; freedom for them to organize private armies, to wear uniforms, to engage in military training, to carry weapons, to engage in espionage, or to practice sabotage is quite a different matter. The former may easily be permitted at the same time that criminal statutes are invoked against the latter. Such a distinction is entirely reasonable.

In addition to outlawing revolutionary acts, such as those just mentioned, society may also find it necessary to draw the line between those uses of freedom of speech and press that are merely designed to give expression to new ideas, and those that are designed to incite immediate acts of violence against the established order. It does not follow that merely because a man limits himself to the use of the spoken word he cannot be restrained. If a person deliberately counsels others to violate existing laws or to commit offenses against society he may properly be punished for the mere speaking of words. Judge Learned Hand, one of the wisest of modern judges, has said: "Words are not only the keys of persuasion, but the triggers of action, and those which have no purport but to counsel the violation of law cannot by any latitude of interpretation be a part of that public opinion which is the final source of government in a democratic state." [23]

People, then, who argue that civil liberties should not be denied those who would use their freedom to undermine these very same liberties are not to be understood as opposing any and all resistance by the government against such groups. There is nothing illogical or inconsistent about a point of view that says that the radical shall have freedom to obtain circulation for his intellectual ideas but shall meet with prompt governmental resistance if he shows signs of employing more dangerous and forceful methods. The making of such a distinction has much to commend it. And yet where the attempt is made to draw a line between words that are a mere preachment of radical ideas and words that are an actual incitement to violence, the benefit of the doubt must inevitably be given to the free exercise of the rights of speech and press. Words should not be suppressed unless the way in which they incite to violence is so serious as to con-

[23] *Masses Publishing Co.* v. *Patten*, 244 Fed. 535, 540 (1917).

stitute a "clear and present danger" to established institutions. In this respect we cannot do better than to note the words of Justice Louis Brandeis:

> It is the function of speech to free men from the bondage of irrational fears. To justify suppression of free speech there must be reasonable ground to fear that serious evil will result if free speech is practiced. There must be reasonable ground to believe that the danger apprehended is imminent. There must be reasonable ground to believe that the evil to be prevented is a serious one. . . .
>
> Those who won our independence by revolution were not cowards. They did not fear political change. They did not exalt order at the cost of liberty. To courageous, self-reliant men, with confidence in the power of free and fearless reasoning applied through the processes of popular government, no danger flowing from speech can be deemed clear and present, unless the incidence of the evil apprehended is so imminent that it may befall before there is opportunity for full discussion. If there be time to expose through discussion the falsehood and the fallacies, to avert the evil by the processes of education, the remedy to be applied is more speech, not enforced silence. Only an emergency can justify repression. Such must be the rule if authority is to be reconciled with freedom.[24]

bibliographic note

The achievement of a satisfactory balance in society between authority and liberty is a problem that has always interested political scientists. Many of the publications cited in the bibliographic note to Chapter 1 contain interesting treatments of this subject. Although no attempt can be made here to list all relevant works in the history of political theory, attention may be called to two nineteenth-century British theorists whose ideas greatly influenced succeeding generations. John Stuart Mill's *On Liberty* (New York: Appleton-Century-Crofts, Inc., 1947), originally published in 1851, is a famous attempt to define the proper limits of liberty and authority. Although this work is regarded as a classic statement of the case for individual freedom, it has been said that it also contains an "inarticulate confession of the necessity for control" in society. Herbert Spencer's *The Man Versus the State* (Caldwell, Ida.: The Caxton Printers, Ltd., 1940), originally published in 1884, is a dogmatic defense of individual freedom as against all forms of authority. To Spencer, government was a necessary evil whose power and activity should be held to an absolute minimum. As he viewed the role of government, government should do no more than keep order and see to it that men kept their economic contracts. Unlike Mill, he was

---

[24] *Whitney v. California*, 274 U.S. 357, 376, 377 (1927).

against all social services, even public education. Spencer believed that if society would depend upon the operation of certain natural laws, a utopian condition would ultimately be reached in which government could largely be dispensed with.

A nineteenth-century American philosopher who was notably interested in individual liberty was Henry D. Thoreau. His essay "Resistance to Civil Government," originally published in 1849 and now available as a chapter in his *On the Duty of Civil Disobedience* (New Haven: Yale University Press, 1928), is an impassioned statement of the duty of the individual to resist unjust governmental authority. Thoreau was one of the greatest of American individualists, and he protested against the "heedless onrush of American life" toward organization, efficiency, and material success. However, like Mill, Thoreau believed in many forms of collective action, particularly in the need for social services.

In our own time many eminent philosophers and political scientists have come to grips with the problem of the role of the state in a democratic society. Among those who believe that a considerable measure of political authority can and must exist without endangering individual freedom are Bertrand Russell, *Authority and the Individual* (New York: Simon and Schuster, 1949); Harold J. Laski, *Liberty in the Modern State* (New York: The Viking Press, 1949); and Karl Mannheim, *Freedom, Power, and Democratic Planning* (New York: Oxford University Press, 1950). Albert Jay Nock's *Our Enemy, the State* (Caldwell, Ida.: The Caxton Printers, Ltd., 1946) is a vigorous statement by a rugged individualist who views even a minimum of political authority as a threat to liberty. In a recent publication by Harold Metz and C. A. H. Thompson, *Authoritarianism and the Individual* (Washington: The Brookings Institution, 1950), the conclusion is reached that "a vast expansion of the power and functions of government is tolerable only when political authority is genuinely responsible to the demands of the people." The encroachment through the centuries of authoritarian governments upon individual freedom is examined and a plea is made for court-enforced constitutional government as the means of reconciling authority and liberty.

Carl Becker's *Freedom and Responsibility in the American Way of Life* (New York: Alfred A. Knopf, Inc., 1945) is a further collection of essays by one of America's wisest and most sophisticated historians. Although sometimes cynical, Becker believed that the modern welfare state could be reconciled with the freedom of the individual.

our civil liberties:
the great freedoms

*W*HAT are our civil liberties in America?[1] We cannot go very far in seek-ing an answer to this question without discovering that the courts have played a dominant role in determining the meaning and extent of civil liberty in the United States. Indeed, there is little exaggeration, if any, in the assertion that our civil liberties today mean whatever the courts say they mean. Why is this so? Does not our federal Constitution, both in the original document and in the Bill of Rights, contain a lengthy enumeration of specific civil liberties? Why, then, do the courts play such an important role in determining the final meaning of these rights? The answer is that the Constitution here, too, often employs vague or ambiguous words and leaves much to depend upon interpretation. Moreover, there is a constant need to balance the power and the liberty aspects of the Con-stitution. We have already seen that the interpretation of the Constitution has come to be peculiarly and finally the work of the courts. When the Constitution says, as it does, that cruel and unusual punishments shall not be inflicted, that excessive bail shall not be required, that no warrants shall issue but upon prob-able cause, or that the right of the people peaceably to assemble shall not be abridged, it does not provide working rules for the governing of actual situations. When do punishments become cruel and unusual? Is the execution by shooting of a justly tried and properly sentenced murderer cruel or unusual? or by hang-

[1] The discussion in this and the next chapter largely ignores the distinction between rights protected against the national government and rights protected against the state governments. This distinction will be examined as a separate problem in Chapter 28. The purpose of this and the next chapter is to explain the meaning and extent of the several civil liberties, as such, without particular reference to the question of against whom or against what agency a liberty is protected. It may also be noted that no attempt is made in these chapters to make any technical distinctions between such terms as "rights," "liberties," "freedoms," or "privileges." Such distinctions have frequently been made in the past, but these terms have now come to be used so interchangeably that there is little to be gained by attempting to preserve such past technical differences.

ing? or by exposure to a lethal gas? Today one would be inclined to say that whipping is a cruel punishment; yet the national government made use of the whipping post for fifty years after the Constitution forbade cruel and unusual punishments. When does bail become excessive? Might $10,000 bail be reasonable in one case and excessive in another? What is the "probable cause" for which a warrant may properly be issued? When is an assembly a peaceable one? Does a noisy and unruly crowd cease to be peaceable?

The list of such questions may be extended indefinitely, but their implication is clear; the wording of the Constitution in reference to civil liberties leaves much to be clarified as the Constitution is applied in actual situations. In the final analysis there is not a single civil liberty enumerated in the Constitution that does not today depend upon a considerable body of judicial analysis and interpretation for its meaning.

legislative and executive officers also help define civil liberty

And yet it should be recalled that the interpretation of the Constitution is by no means the work of the courts alone. Executive agency and legislature also play a part in the process. For example, a demand may arise in a community for the enactment of an ordinance curbing the sale of "comic books" because of the ill effects they are said to have on children. During debate in the local council on the proposal the point may be raised that such an ordinance would perhaps violate freedom of the press. The council may conclude that the point is well taken and refrain from passing the ordinance. Or it may decide that as it understands the meaning of freedom of the press, such an ordinance would be valid and it proceeds to enact the proposal into law. If the council does enact legislation, the soundness of its judgment on the constitutional issue may ultimately be tested in the courts. But it is only after the legislature has taken the initiative in passing such legislation that the courts gain an opportunity to interpret the Constitution.

In a similar way much depends upon the activities of executive authorities. A town may have a local ordinance designed to restrict the distribution of handbills as a means of preventing unsightly litter. Let us assume that an attempt is made to start a new newspaper by an enterprising printer who at first chooses to give his paper away, causing a copy to be placed on every doorstep. An established newspaper, resenting this development, brings pressure upon local administrators to invoke the ordinance against the distribution of the new paper. The printer replies that such action would abridge his right to freedom of the press. In such a situation the administrative authorities must make a decision one way or the other. Either they must conclude that freedom of the press has nothing to do with the matter and enforce the ordinance in an attempt to protect householders against the littering of their yards and porches with unwanted literature, or they must conclude that the constitutional guarantee does protect the distribution of such a newspaper and refrain from enforcing the ordinance in that particular situation.

Where a legislature or a law enforcement officer refrains from enacting or administering a law because of constitutional doubts, the courts do not ordinarily have any opportunity to review the action, or nonaction, and the political branches have had the final word. Thus, there is frequently a complete absence of judicial activity so long as civil liberties are being respected. The aid of the courts is ordinarily invoked only where positive action by executive and legislative agents is said to interfere with civil liberty.

It is true that frequently there are court decisions already available that serve as precedents in aiding legislative or administrative officials to deal with situations in which civil rights are involved. There are, for example, Supreme Court decisions on the distribution of handbills under constitutional guarantees of freedom of the press. Even where such decisions are available, however, they are frequently ignored; the person who is restrained from distributing handbills may not be aware of the court decisions protecting his right, or for reasons which seem sufficient to him, he does not choose to contest an administrative ruling against him, and legislative and administrative action proves final.

how civil rights cases reach the courts

Fortunately, many Americans are well aware of the general character of their civil liberties as guaranteed by the Constitution and are prepared to resist a threatened or actual infringement of a civil liberty resulting from legislative or administrative action. What forms may such resistance take? A great deal depends upon the particular civil liberty in question and the nature of the interference with the liberty. The following possibilities may be noted. (1) If a person is prosecuted and convicted for violation of a law which he feels interferes with one of his liberties, he may appeal his sentence to the higher courts and ask that the law under which he has been convicted be declared unconstitutional and that his conviction be set aside. (2) In the absence of a criminal prosecution, a person who feels that governmental action is interfering with his valid liberties may invoke other remedies. He may accuse a public officer of wrongful action which has harmed him personally and seek damages or other redress through a civil action in the courts. Or in the face of threatened wrongful action he may seek judicial protection through a writ of injunction forbidding the threatened action. If a court decides that it has jurisdiction it may proceed to the consideration of the constitutional issue of civil liberty inherent in the case.

Emphasis upon court decisions in examining the subject of civil rights does not mean that the problems encountered in this field are primarily legalistic in character. The subject is a complex one that has important and difficult social, economic, and psychological implications. But often a civil rights conflict is brought into focus as a "case" which the courts are asked to decide. Thus an examination of such cases is one of the easiest and most profitable ways of studying the subject. However, one should look beyond the rule of law which a civil rights case produces and give attention to the larger social problem which the case illustrates.

the right to be free

It goes almost without saying that foremost among the individual's rights in a democratic society is the right to freedom itself. Yet our Constitution was in effect nearly eighty years before this right was written into the supreme law of the land. Moreover, during this period millions of persons in the United States were not free, being held in a bondage as cruel and complete as anything known to history. Not until 1865 did the Thirteenth Amendment bring to the Constitution an express statement that ours is a society of free men only: "Neither slavery nor involuntary servitude, except as a punishment for crime whereof the party shall have been duly convicted, shall exist within the United States or any place subject to their jurisdiction." This particular right, unlike so many others guaranteed by the Constitution, operates not only against governmental encroachment but against encroachment by private persons. Moreover, Congress is given power to protect the right "by appropriate legislation."

Since the Civil War brought an end to slavery in its historical form most of the controversies that have arisen under the Thirteenth Amendment have centered about real or alleged instances of "involuntary servitude." In general the Supreme Court has interpreted the involuntary servitude clause of the Constitution rather narrowly, refusing, for instance, to hold that any discrimination against, or segregation of, Negroes, whether by action of private persons or by the force of law, constitutes involuntary servitude.[2]

forced labor prohibited

In 1867 Congress passed an Antipeonage Act making it a federal crime to hold persons in involuntary servitude. Peonage has been defined by the Supreme Court as "a status or condition of compulsory service, based upon the indebtedness of the peon to the master." [3] Thus, attempts to force a debtor or a party to a contract to fulfill his obligations by involuntary labor are outlawed from our society. There are a few borderline exceptions, one of which affects workers in certain occupations involving the public safety. Courts have ruled that seamen may be compelled to complete terms of service to which they have agreed, and that railway workers can be prevented from ceasing work until they have brought their passengers to their destination or ensured their safety. Apart from these special situations, courts generally have considered themselves prevented

---

[2] *The Civil Rights Cases*, 109 U.S. 3 (1883) ; *Plessy* v. *Ferguson*, 163 U.S. 537 (1896).
[3] *Bailey* v. *Alabama*, 219 U.S. 219, 242 (1911).

by the Thirteenth Amendment from issuing writs compelling workers to return to or remain on the job. The Supreme Court has recently said: "The undoubted aim of the Thirteenth Amendment as implemented by the Antipeonage Act was not merely to end slavery but to maintain a system of completely free and voluntary labor throughout the United States." [4]

convictions under the federal Antipeonage Act

Where there is any suggestion that a particular individual is being forced to labor against his will the courts have become increasingly inclined in recent years to intervene under the Thirteenth Amendment. For example, in 1944 a conviction under the federal Antipeonage Act was obtained against a large plantation owner in Arkansas who "consistently terrorized both the Negro and white laborers on his plantation, threatening to kill them if they left his place, and lending color to these threats by always carrying a gun, a revolver, and a pair of brass knuckles. White men as well as black so feared him that they would slip away from his farm at night, leaving behind their possessions, including their standing crops." [5] In another recent case in a federal court, sentence was pronounced against a Georgia roadhouse keeper who forced girls, who had voluntarily accepted employment with him as waitresses, to serve as prostitutes. He had assumed that he was immune from federal prosecution because he had carefully avoided any interstate activity and thus could not be prosecuted under the Mann Act. But the Antipeonage Act was held to prohibit such wrongdoing. [6] Finally, the Supreme Court has in recent years declared Florida and Georgia labor contract statutes invalid under the Thirteenth Amendment. These laws made it criminal for a person to obtain an advance payment of wages by falsely promising to perform labor. The Court pointed out that it is perfectly permissible for a state to make the act of obtaining money under false pretenses a crime, but it felt that here these statutes had the improper effect of forcing a man to remain at labor against his will by holding forth the threat of a criminal penalty if he failed to do so. [7]

the right to equality

Second only to the right to be free is the right of every individual to enjoy equality—not equality in the possession of worldly goods or native talents, but equality as to the protection which the law provides, and equality of opportunity to enjoy the advantages, cultural and economic, offered by a free society.

---

[4] *Pollock* v. *Williams*, 322 U.S. 4, 17 (1944).

[5] Francis Biddle, "Civil Rights and the Federal Law," in *Safeguarding Civil Liberty Today* (Ithaca: Cornell University Press, 1945), p. 138.

[6] *Pierce* v. *United States*, 146 F. 2d 84 (1944).

[7] *Taylor* v. *Georgia*, 315 U.S. 25 (1941); *Pollock* v. *Williams*, 322 U.S. 4 (1944).

equality under the law

The Fourteenth Amendment of the Constitution provides: "No State shall . . . deny to any person within its jurisdiction the equal protection of the laws." The Fifth Amendment does not contain a specific equal protection clause, but it has generally been agreed that its due process of law clause serves much the same purpose in protecting individuals against a denial of the equal protection of the laws by the federal government.[8]

The courts have invariably approved the axiom that the requirement of equal protection does not prevent legislatures from classifying people for purposes of statutory regulation. It would be ludicrous, for example, to argue that a statute denying persons under fourteen years of age the right to drive an automobile subjected them to unequal treatment under law. Obviously, the classification of persons for regulatory purposes is often reasonable and necessary.

On the other hand, there are many situations in which the courts have held that a statutory classification does have the effect of denying persons the equal protection of the law. A good illustration is found in a 1948 decision of the Supreme Court holding that a California law which prohibited the issuance of commercial fishing licenses to persons ineligible for American citizenship (largely persons of Japanese descent) denied such persons equality of treatment under the law and was thus unconstitutional.[9]

"Jim Crow" legislation and equal protection of the law

Courts as well as legislatures can err in failing to see the threat to a civil right offered by a law. In upholding certain statutes providing for the classification of persons, the Supreme Court has at times been criticized for its failure to insist upon a higher degree of equality under the law. For example, "Jim Crow" laws, which establish racial segregation in such places as railroads, busses, hotels, theaters, parks, and schools, have generally been upheld by the Supreme Court on the theory that segregation does not itself involve inequality. This ruling had its origin in the case of *Plessy v. Ferguson* in 1896. In the majority opinion the Court said:

> We consider the underlying fallacy of the plaintiff's argument to consist in the assumption that the enforced separation of the two races stamps the colored race with a badge of inferiority. If this be so, it is not by reason of anything found in the act, but solely because the colored race chooses to put that construction upon it.[10]

The logic of this opinion was challenged in a ringing dissenting opinion by Justice John M. Harlan:

---

[8] See *Hirabayashi v. United States*, 320 U.S. 81, 100 (1943). For a contrary opinion see *Truax v. Corrigan*, 257 U.S. 312, 332 (1921).

[9] *Takahashi v. Fish and Game Commission*, 334 U.S. 410 (1948).

[10] *Plessy v. Ferguson*, 163 U.S. 537, 551 (1896).

Our Constitution is color-blind, and neither knows nor tolerates classes among citizens. . . .

The arbitrary separation of citizens, on the basis of race, while they are on a public highway, is a badge of servitude wholly inconsistent with the civil freedom and the equality before the law established by the Constitution. It cannot be justified upon any legal grounds. . . .

We boast of the freedom enjoyed by our people above all other peoples. But it is difficult to reconcile that boast with a state of the law which, practically, puts the brand of servitude and degradation upon a large class of our fellow citizens, our equals before the law.[11]

In its *Plessy* decision the Court did rule that segregation could be enforced only where separate accommodations were provided for Negroes equal in quality to those provided whites. This qualification to the Court's ruling upholding segregation led Justice Harlan to assert: "The thin disguise of 'equal' accommodations . . . will not mislead anyone, nor atone for the wrong this day done." In recent years the Court has become increasingly firm in insisting upon proof that this requirement of equal accommodations is being met. In 1938 the Court ruled that the state of Missouri must maintain within its own boundaries a separate graduate school of law for Negroes or permit them to attend the regular law school at the state university. An existing policy by which the state offered to pay a Negro's tuition at a law school in some other state was declared inadequate.[12] Ten years later it repeated this ruling in directing Oklahoma to provide a legal education for Negroes, and it added the requirement that the state provide such an education "as soon as it does for applicants of any other group." [13] The ruling received still further support in 1950 in two cases involving the admission of Negroes to the graduate schools of the University of Texas and the University of Oklahoma.[14] The Supreme Court has never quite abandoned the *Plessy* decision that segregation itself is not unconstitutional, but its increasingly firm insistence that separate schools must indeed be equal in quality is having the practical effect of forcing states that have in the past pursued a segregation policy to admit Negroes to their regular universities, at least at the graduate school level.

While accepting state laws segregating Negroes for the purposes mentioned above, the Supreme Court has refused to permit discrimination against Negroes in certain other respects. Among these are voting, since the Fifteenth Amendment specifically forbids such discrimination, jury service, and ownership of property.

---

[11] *Ibid.*, pp. 559, 562.

[12] *Missouri ex rel. Gaines* v. *Canada*, 305 U.S. 337 (1938).

[13] *Sipuel* v. *Board of Regents*, 332 U.S. 631 (1948); *Fisher* v. *Hurst* 333 U.S. 147 (1948).

[14] *McLaurin* v. *Oklahoma State Regents*, 339 U.S. 637 (1950); *Sweatt* v. *Painter*, 339 U.S. 629 (1950).

equality of opportunity

The President's Committee on Civil Rights chose to emphasize the right to equality in terms of equality of *opportunity* for all men "to enjoy the benefits of society and to contribute to its progress." And it added, "The opportunity of each individual to obtain useful employment, and to have access to services in the fields of education, housing, health, recreation and transportation, whether available free or at a price, must be provided with complete disregard for race, color, creed, and national origin." [15]

The committee found that there are still many areas of American life in which such equality of opportunity is not available to all persons, and it recommended prompt action to correct such inequalities. Some of these inequalities can be corrected by court action alone, such as, for example, through court orders directing public officers to maintain equal school facilities for children of all races. But much positive action is needed if full equality of opportunity is to exist; accordingly the committee recommended the enactment by Congress and the state legislatures of laws guaranteeing equality of opportunity in such fields as employment, education, and housing.

the right to property

The right to acquire and hold property is traditional to the American way of life and is inextricably entwined with our economic and political systems. The Fifth Amendment specifically forbids the national government to deprive any person of his property without due process of law or to take private property for public use without just compensation. The Fourteenth Amendment places essentially similar restrictions upon the states. Even so, the right to property, like all other rights, is a relative one. The courts have held that the language of the Fifth and Fourteenth Amendments does not preclude interference with the use of property or even the taking of private property without compensation through the valid exercise of the taxing power and the police power.

Although the right to property is basic to our way of life, it has not been customary to speak of it as a *civil liberty* any more than the right to a job, or to a living wage, or to social security is regarded as a civil liberty. And yet in recent years many persons have argued that *civil* and *political* liberties have been emphasized in the United States to the almost total exclusion of *economic* liberties.

freedom of expression: speech and press

Almost the very first words of the Bill of Rights provide: "Congress shall make no law . . . abridging the freedom of speech or of the press." The command is

---

[15] *To Secure These Rights* (Washington: Government Printing Office, 1947), p. 9.

peremptory, *Congress shall make no law* abridging freedom of speech or press. But what is freedom of speech and press? Finding a satisfactory working answer to this question is one of the most difficult problems of statecraft confronting a free people. For one thing this freedom, while indispensable in a democracy, varies in its application with changing times and conditions. As we shall see, new modes of expression have raised difficult issues concerning the right's coverage. Second, no right, however basic, better illustrates the *relativity* of freedom in the modern state. Accordingly, one should not be surprised to discover that the Supreme Court has consistently taken the view that it is not the purpose of the First Amendment to protect unbridled freedom of expression. Moreover, the Court has held that the proper limits of this freedom are to be found not by making a philosophical analysis of the words used to define it in the Constitution, but by seeking the practical meaning of the freedom in its historical context and in its application to the changing circumstances and problems of the present day. In the words of the Court: "Liberty of speech, and of the press, is . . . not an absolute right, and the State may punish its abuse. . . . Liberty, in each of its phases, has its history and connotation and, in the present instance, the inquiry is as to the historic conception of the liberty of the press and whether the statute under review violates the essential attributes of that liberty." [16]

censorship is forbidden

What, then, are the limits of permissible speech and publication? In the first place the government may not establish a system of advance censorship, or "previous restraint," to curb ideas *before* they are expressed. Punishment after the act is one thing; to seek to prevent the act is another. Curbing the utterance or publication of words by a board of censors is, then, forbidden by our Constitution. However, there may be exceptions, for the Supreme Court has said:

> . . . protection even as to previous restraint is not absolutely unlimited. But the limitation has been recognized only in exceptional cases: "When a nation is at war many things that might be said in time of peace are such a hindrance to its effort that their utterance will not be endured so long as men fight and that no Court could regard them as protected by any constitutional right." [17]

Thus it would seem that the courts would not be unwilling to allow government to establish a considerable measure of censorship of speech and press in time of war if it chose to do so. In World War II this point was not raised specifically because the government preferred to depend upon a voluntary system of cen-

---

[16] *Near* v. *Minnesota*, 283 U.S. 697, 708 (1931).
[17] *Ibid.*, p. 716.

sorship and made little or no effort to compel the American people to submit to compulsory censorship established by law.

punishment after words have been expressed

In the second place, the Constitution provides a measure of protection against punishment *after* words are uttered. Freedom of expression would have little value if it protected the individual only against previous restraint and left him to take the consequences for words actually uttered. Obviously, to have any practical value, freedom in this respect must operate both before and after the act. In general, the government may not attempt to prevent *any* words from being uttered; but once ideas have been expressed, persons may be punished under law if their remarks, spoken or printed, are in certain ways inimical to the public interest. Four areas in which such punishment has been held to be permissible will now be examined.

1. PUNISHMENT FOR LIBEL AND SLANDER. Libel and slander may be defined as words (*printed* in the case of libel, and *spoken* in the case of slander) used with a malicious intent to defame the character of an individual or to expose him to public hatred, contempt, or ridicule. For centuries English law and American law have regarded such conduct as harmful to the individual and dangerous to the public welfare and have provided civil and criminal remedies against it. In either case the aid of the courts may be invoked under the law to penalize an individual for the way in which he has expressed ideas, and it is not considered that such penalties violate the constitutional guarantee of freedom of expression.

2. PUNISHMENT FOR OBSCENITY. It has long been clear that the right to utter obscene or blasphemous words is entitled to no protection under the Constitution. Any reasonable law restraining speech or publications along these lines is apt to be upheld by the courts. Here the courts are called upon to weigh the exercise of a positive power for a general welfare purpose against the influence of a negative constitutional restraint designed to protect the liberty of the individual.

There is, in fact, no case in which the Supreme Court has invalidated a law designed to curb pornography or blasphemy. But it by no means follows that the courts will always decide such a case in favor of the statute, and it is certainly not a sufficient argument in favor of a statute to claim that it is aimed against obscenity. In recent years there has been a rising volume of protest against the curbs which have been placed upon certain types of literature alleged to be obscene. Both common law and statutory law have been invoked to penalize the publishers and distributors of various books, pamphlets, and magazines. In some instances it has seemed to many people that the restraints have been unduly harsh. It is not at all impossible that the Supreme Court will one day begin striking down laws aimed against allegedly obscene publications on the ground that freedom of the press is endangered. It is worth noting that wherever there has been a relaxing of overly strict standards of obscenity this result has been largely achieved by the courts. It is almost impossible to discover a single instance in which a legislative body has modified the terms of the many statutes aimed against obscenity as defined by Victorian standards. There are, however, a number of court decisions in which the judicial arm of the government, recognizing the force of new standards and tastes in literature, has refused to permit the application of such statutes in doubtful cases. Nineteenth-century legislation against obscenity remains on the statute books almost intact, but because of the increasing difficulty of obtaining convictions in court, law enforcement officers have become more restrained in their application of these laws.

Closely analogous to legislation curbing obscenity are laws designed to protect the public from the harmful effects of lurid publications dealing with crime and bloodshed. For example, in 1948 the Supreme Court found it necessary to pass upon the constitutionality of a New York State law which made it an offense to publish or sell periodicals or books dealing principally with crime and bloodshed and which so "massed" this material as to incite violent and depraved crimes against the person. The law was brought to the Court's attention by a case in which a bookdealer had been convicted for selling a crime-story magazine. The difficulty of balancing social needs against individual rights in the situation is illustrated by the six-to-three vote by which the Court disposed of the case. The majority ruled that the statute was invalid because it failed to define the forbidden conduct with sufficient preciseness. The decision implies that freedom of expression may be limited as a means of preventing crime, but the limitation must be held to a minimum and be carefully defined.[18]

3. CONTEMPT OF COURT AS A RESTRAINT UPON FREEDOM OF EXPRESSION. A further illustration of a valid restriction upon speech or press is to be seen in the right of judges to cite individuals for contempt of court and to impose punishment upon them for remarks or publications which are thought to impede the work of the courts. Thus, to alter somewhat Justice Holmes's famous aphorism, no man can claim the right to cry out in a courtroom that the presiding judge is dishonest. Nonetheless, the Supreme Court has grown more and more inclined in recent years to limit the use of a judge's contempt power to instances where the threat against the integrity of a court or its procedure is particularly serious. In 1941, for example, the United States Supreme Court by a five-to-four vote upset state court judgments holding Harry Bridges, the labor leader, and the Los Angeles *Times* in contempt of court because they had published statements critical of the courts' with respect to cases still pending. Although the

---

[18] *Winters* v. *New York*, 333 U.S. 507 (1948).

common law has long recognized judicial power to punish as contempt out-of-court publications tending to obstruct justice, the Supreme Court majority here felt that such action had the effect of denying Bridges and the *Times* freedom of the press.[19]

4. PUNISHMENT FOR SEDITIOUS UTTERANCES. A very important type of legitimate interference by law with freedom of expression is to be seen in the operation of laws aimed against sedition, although it is by no means sufficient to establish the constitutionality of a statute limiting freedom of expression by asserting that it is aimed at the crime of "sedition." In general, laws of this type prescribe punishment for words that are incitements to unlawful action. The first federal sedition act was passed by Congress in 1798 and contained an extreme clause providing that any speech or writing which had the intent to defame or bring into contempt or disrepute the President or Congress should constitute a misdemeanor punishable by fine or imprisonment. This clause was used in a partisan way by the Federalists against their political enemies, the Jeffersonian Republicans, and as so enforced was almost certainly unconstitutional, although it was never declared so by the Supreme Court. Some twenty-five persons were prosecuted under this act and ten of these persons were convicted. The act expired in 1801 and Jefferson pardoned those persons who had been convicted under it. Later, the government repaid the fines that it had imposed under the act.

During World War I, under the pressure of wartime needs and conditions, Congress passed an espionage act and a sedition act. Together these laws made it criminal action punishable by heavy fines and prison terms to interfere with the draft, obstruct recruiting, encourage disloyalty, incite insubordination in the armed services, obstruct the sale of United States bonds, or to "willfully utter, print, write, or publish any disloyal, profane, scurrilous, or abusive language about the form of government of the United States, or the Constitution . . . or to bring the form of government . . . or the Constitution . . . into contempt. . . ."[20] Finally, the Alien Registration Act of 1940 makes it unlawful to teach or advocate the overthrow of government by force or violence, to advocate insubordination or disloyalty in the armed services, or to organize any society or print or distribute literature for the advancement of these purposes.[21]

Throughout the years these federal statutes have been supplemented by numerous state laws aimed aganst "insurrection," "criminal syndicalism," "criminal anarchy," and similar offenses. It is easy enough to understand the desire of Congress and the state legislatures to legislate against truly disloyal or seditious conduct. The danger inherent in "fifth column" activity was made far

---

[19] *Bridges* v. *California*, 314 U.S. 252 (1941). See also *Pennekamp* v. *Florida*, 328 U.S. 331 (1946) ; and *Craig* v. *Harney*, 331 U.S. 367 (1947).

[20] 40 Stat. 217, 553.

[21] 54 Stat. 670.

too clear in World War II for anyone to minimize the harm that seditious agents can do. Nonetheless, the way in which our legislatures have worded statutes so broadly as to enable government agents to take action against dangerous persons of every conceivable sort has led inevitably to criticism. It is one thing to convict and imprison a man who urges mutiny in the armed services or assassination of public officers; it is an altogether different thing to prosecute an individual who has criticized, perhaps unfairly and irresponsibly, what he regards as bungling in the war program by civilian or military authorities. Fortunately, in the last twenty years the courts have shown an increasing reluctance to sanction extreme prosecutions under these laws. However, no one of the federal statutes in this field has ever been declared unconstitutional, nor has the Supreme Court been inclined to set aside convictions under these laws although powerful dissenting opinions have been written in some of these cases.[22] Not all of the state laws have fared quite so well, since in some instances not only have convictions been set aside but the statutes themselves have been invalidated.[23]

It is not surprising that the courts have had great difficulty in drawing an intelligent, consistent line between words that may be punished because of their threat to society and words that are protected under the constitutional guarantee of free speech. Insofar as the Supreme Court has succeeded in establishing any legal principle in dealing with this problem, it is to be seen in the so-called "clear and present danger" test. This test was first announced in 1919 by Justice Oliver Wendell Holmes in the decision of the Court in *Schenck* v. *United States* upholding the Espionage Act of 1917: "The question in every case is whether the words used are used in such circumstances and are of such a nature as to create a clear and present danger that they will bring about the substantial evils that Congress has a right to prevent. It is a question of proximity and degree." [24]

Schenck as general secretary of the Socialist party had been responsible in 1917 for the printing and distribution of some 15,000 leaflets attacking the war and urging men to resist the draft. Holmes admitted that "in many places and in ordinary times the defendants in saying all that was said in the circular would have been within their constitutional rights. But the character of every act depends upon the circumstances in which it is done." Schenck's conduct in the given circumstances seemed to Holmes to constitute a clear and present danger that Congress had power to prevent.

---

[22] See *Schenck* v. *United States*, 249 U.S. 47 (1919); *Debs* v. *United States*, 249 U.S. 211 (1919); *Abrams* v. *United States*, 250 U.S. 616 (1919); *Schaefer* v. *United States*, 251 U.S. 466 (1920). See, however, *Hartzel* v. *United States*, 322 U.S. 680 (1944).

[23] See, for example, *Gitlow* v. *New York*, 268 U.S. 652 (1925); *Gilbert* v. *Minnesota*, 254 U.S. 325 (1920); *Whitney* v. *California*, 274 U.S. 357 (1927); *Stromberg* v. *California*, 283 U.S. 359 (1931); *Herndon* v. *Lowry*, 301 U.S. 242 (1937).

[24] *Schenck* v. *United States*, 249 U.S. 47, 52 (1919).

general police power regulations as restraints upon freedom of expression

Freedom of expression may be indirectly affected by the operation of certain general statutes which do not on their face purport to control this freedom. For example, a newspaper publishing company may properly be subjected to ordinary business regulatory laws. There is no reason why such a company should not pay taxes, observe the local building code, maintain safe working conditions in its plant, or meet various labor standards concerning wages, hours, and collective bargaining. At times it may seem as though such regulations actually interfere with freedom of the press itself. The Associated Press challenged the constitutionality of the National Labor Relations Act on the ground that the act prevented it from dismissing one of its editorial employees for labor union activity and thus interfered with its freedom of the press. The Supreme Court rejected this argument, pointing out that the act did not prevent the Associated Press from dismissing an editor for incompetence or for failure to edit the news faithfully without bias or prejudice:

> The business of the Associated Press is not immune from regulation because it is an agency of the press. The publisher of a newspaper has no special immunity from the application of general laws. He has no special privilege to invade the rights and liberties of others. He must answer for libel. He may be punished for contempt of court. He is subject to the anti-trust laws. Like others he must pay equitable and nondiscriminatory taxes on his business. The regulation here in question has no relation whatever to the impartial distribution of news.[25]

On the other hand, where such a statute, seemingly general on its face, is actually intended to interfere with the free operation of a newspaper, the Supreme Court is not slow to intervene. When the Louisiana legislature placed a tax of 2 per cent on the gross receipts of newspapers having a circulation of more than 20,000 a week, the Court recognized that this tax was intended to embarrass newspapers hostile to the Huey Long machine, and the law was invalidated as an interference with freedom of the press.[26]

freedom of expression: the motion picture and the radio

The fact that freedom of expression is a relative rather than an absolute right and also that it has a changing rather than a constant meaning is illustrated by the development in recent years of two new media for the communication of ideas—the motion picture and the radio. Neither of these agencies has been able to claim the same protection under the Constitution enjoyed by speech and press. Instead, both have been subjected to rather drastic forms of government

---

[25] *Associated Press* v. *N.L.R.B.*, 301 U.S. 103, 132–133 (1937).
[26] *Grosjean* v. *American Press Co.*, 297 U.S. 233 (1936).

regulation, including even some measure of censorship. The Supreme Court long ago denied that the motion-picture industry could claim protection against state censorship under the freedom of speech and press guarantees of the Constitution. The Court took the attitude that the motion picture, like the stage, is primarily a spectacle or a mode of entertainment rather than a medium for the expression of ideas or the circulation of news.[27] A strong argument can be made to the contrary, and the Supreme Court may one day be persuaded to reverse itself on this point. But up to now the original ruling stands.

In the case of the radio, Congress has provided for a drastic measure of control of radio broadcasting by the Federal Communications Commission, including the licensing of all stations and the allocation of wave lengths. Because of the limited number of wave lengths suitable for broadcasting purposes, it was inevitable that some control over their allocation and use be established by government. It is true that the national government has not attempted to establish any systematic censorship over the content of radio programs. At the same time, the FCC is authorized to use its discretion in licensing stations by giving thought to the "public interest, convenience, or necessity." Moreover, licenses are subject to cancellation or renewal every three years. In granting such renewals the commission has necessarily given consideration to the content of radio programs and in a few instances renewals have been refused because of objectionable programs or objectionable practices. Thus although there is little evidence that the FCC has exercised any substantial supervision over the broadcasting of controversial political or social information, a limited measure of supervisory censorship undoubtedly exists. The Supreme Court has upheld this control and has stated:

> The right of free speech does not include, however, the right to use the facilities of radio without a license. The licensing system established by Congress in the Communications Act of 1934 was a proper exercise of its power over commerce. The standard it provided for the licensing of stations was the "public interest, convenience, or necessity." Denial of a station license on that ground, if valid under the Act, is not a denial of free speech.[28]

freedom of expression: picketing

A further difficult application of the guarantees of freedom of speech and press to modern conditions has arisen in connection with the right of workers to engage in peaceful picketing in the course of a labor dispute. The picket line is one of labor's traditional weapons, and one of the chief purposes of picketing has been to give publicity to the facts of a labor dispute as labor sees them so that the public may have a fair picture of the controversy. Picketing has always met

---

[27] *Mutual Film Corp.* v. *Ohio Industrial Commission*, 236 U.S. 230, 241–245 (1915).
[28] *National Broadcasting Co.* v. *United States*, 319 U.S. 190, 227 (1943).

with considerable opposition, and frequently legislation has been enacted restricting its use. The prohibitive effect of this legislation has often been heightened by the free issuance of antilabor injunctions by the courts restraining workers from certain types of conduct. Labor has not been slow to meet the challenge offered by such exercise of governmental power. Specifically, legislative and judicial attempts to curb peaceful picketing have been attacked as interferences with freedom of expression. Does the picket line, with its display of banners and placards, enjoy protection similar to that enjoyed by the newspaper or the speaker on a public platform under the First and Fourteenth Amendments? The Supreme Court was slow to answer this question with any finality, and it was not until 1940 that a definitive ruling was obtained. In that year the Court decided that "publicizing the facts of a labor dispute in a peaceful way through appropriate means, whether by pamphlet, by word of mouth or by banner, must now be regarded as within that liberty of communication which is secured to every person by the Fourteenth Amendment against abridgment by a state." [29]

The Court proceeded to lay down the broad principle that any law or administrative act or judicial ruling placing a blanket prohibition upon peaceful picketing is unconstitutional. The Court has recognized that the use of the picket line can be abused and that mass picketing, the use of violence in connection with picketing, or the use of the picket line to accomplish an unlawful objective constitutes an evil which may properly be curbed by government.

freedom of expression: the sound truck

The fact that changing times bring new means of giving public expression to words and ideas is well illustrated by the appearance of the sound truck—a device by which the human voice is amplified electrically and projected readily to all parts of a community from a movable vehicle. Many communities have tried to regulate the use of these trucks so as to prevent traffic congestion or other hazards to the public safety, and also to give reasonable protection to the right to quiet and privacy. These regulations have taken many forms: some cities forbid sound amplification altogether in certain areas or at certain times; others permit it but limit the volume of sound; still others forbid the use of sound trucks except under licenses granted by a public officer.

In 1948 in a controversial five-to-four decision the Supreme Court in-

---

[29] *Carlson* v. *California*, 310 U.S. 106, 113 (1940). See also *Thornhill* v. *Alabama*, 310 U.S. 88 (1940); *Milk Wagon Drivers' Union* v. *Meadowmoor Dairies*, 312 U.S. 287 (1941); *A.F. of L.* v. *Swing*, 312 U.S. 321 (1941). In *Giboney* v. *Empire Storage and Ice Co.*, 336 U.S. 490 (1949) and subsequent cases some observers have seen a tendency on the part of the Supreme Court to backtrack with respect to the protection of the right to picket. But it seems correct to say that the Court still recognizes the basic right as encompassed by freedom of expression.

validated an ordinance of the city of Lockport, New York, which gave the chief of police discretionary authority to grant or withhold permits for the use of sound amplification devices in public places. The majority opinion holds that the "ordinance is unconstitutional on its face, for it establishes a previous restraint on the right of free speech in violation of the . . . Fourteenth Amendment. . . . Loud-speakers are today indispensable instruments of effective public speech." [30] The dissenters protested vigorously against this ruling, and doubt was cast upon its status when, early in 1949, again by a five-to-four vote, the Court upheld a Trenton, New Jersey, ordinance which forbade the projection of "loud and raucous" sound from a moving vehicle on the city streets.[31]

freedom of assembly and petition: the right to political association

The First Amendment to the Constitution also provides that "Congress shall make no law . . . abridging . . . the right of the people peaceably to assemble, and to petition the government for a redress of grievances." In its broadest aspects this constitutional provision may be considered as guaranteeing the right of the American people to engage in political activity. They may assemble to discuss political questions, and they may organize with a view to securing political action. More specifically, they may form political parties and work to bring about the adoption of specific governmental policies, and they may form pressure groups and petition public officers in an attempt to influence the governmental program. These rights are obviously fundamental to our American democratic system, for they promote the free and open discussion of proposed public policies and bring about the ultimate determination of policies in accordance with the wishes of the majority.

These freedoms are no more absolute than is freedom of expression. The right of assembly is subject to reasonable police power restrictions designed to ensure safety and order in the conduct of meetings. The Constitution does not guarantee to a group, political or nonpolitical in character, any right to demand permission to conduct an open-air meeting on a public street or square if traffic will be disrupted or lives endangered. Similarly, it is clear that the right of a group to organize or assemble is limited in that its purpose must be lawful. There is no absolute constitutional right that protects a Black Hand society in organizing or meeting to plan a program of violence and murder.

the Jersey City case

It is not such extreme cases but rather the in-between situations that have given trouble. A political meeting is forbidden on the ground of resulting traffic con-

[30] *Saia* v. *New York*, 334 U.S. 558, 559–560, 561 (1948).
[31] *Kovacs* v. *Cooper*, 336 U.S. 77 (1949).

gestion, but the charge is made that the real motive behind the prohibition is a desire to obstruct the political movement in question. There may well be evidence suggesting that both motives have been present. How, then, is a court to rule in such a case? In the case of *Hague* v. *CIO* the Court passed upon the legality of the action of the chief of police of Jersey City in denying the right of the CIO to hold public meetings in Jersey City in public streets and parks. The chief claimed he acted on the basis of an ordinance forbidding meetings without permits and asserted that he refused the CIO a permit to prevent disorder. The justices of the Supreme Court were badly divided in their reasoning, but a majority agreed that the ordinance was unconstitutional. Justice Roberts in his opinion stated:

> Wherever the title of streets and parks may rest, they have immemorially been held in trust for the use of the public and, time out of mind, have been used for purposes of assembly, communicating thoughts between citizens, and discussing public questions. . . . The privilege . . . to use the streets and parks for communication of views on national questions may be regulated in the interest of all; it is not absolute, but relative, and must be exercised in subordination to the general comfort and convenience, and in consonance with peace and good order; but it must not, in the guise of regulation, be abridged or denied.[32]

the problem of the Communist party

A difficult problem has arisen in recent years because of the activity of radical or revolutionary groups which in varying degrees seem to advocate the overthrow of the existing order. In particular, the status of the Communist party and its members has given trouble. Ideologically, the Communist position seems to be that the overthrow of democratic capitalism by violent political revolution is inevitable and necessary. Moreover, there is evidence that American Communists have a strong loyalty to a foreign power. Does it therefore become desirable or permissible to deny the rights of organization and assembly (as well as speech and press) to the Communist party or to persons associating with it?

A number of federal statutes enacted since 1939 have been aimed at curbing Communist activity although Congress has stopped short of attempts to outlaw the party itself. In particular, the Alien Registration Act of 1940 makes it a criminal offense to knowingly or willfully advocate or teach the overthrow of the government by force or violence.[33]

The Supreme Court has not yet ruled flatly on the factual issue of whether the Communist party does advocate the violent overthrow of the existing order, or on the legal issue of whether such a party can be outlawed. However, in

---

[32] *Hague* v. *C.I.O.*, 307 U.S. 496, 515–516 (1939).
[33] 54 Stat. 670, 671.

several cases in recent years it has protected the right of Communists under the First Amendment to engage in normal political activity. For example, in *De Jonge* v. *Oregon* the Court reviewed the sentencing of De Jonge to seven years in prison by the Oregon courts for alleged violation of the Oregon criminal syndicalism statute which made it a crime to organize, preside at, or assist in conducting a meeting at which political change by violent means was advocated. De Jonge, a party member, was a speaker at a meeting held under Communist party auspices. There was no evidence that De Jonge's speech contained any advocacy of violence. Instead, the prosecution was based on the contention that merely speaking under the auspices of a party that advocated violent revolution made De Jonge subject to punishment under the act. The Court unanimously ruled that the statute as applied in this case was unconstitutional. The Court was of the opinion that it would be a denial of the rights of free speech and assembly to punish a man because of a speech delivered under allegedly improper auspices where his own remarks were unobjectionable.[34]

It seems fair to say that the Supreme Court is inclined to bend over backward in protecting the right of individuals to form political parties and to be active within them, however radical they may seem to be. It is likely that the Court will refuse to sanction any punishment of an individual for such activity and will insist upon protecting such individuals and their conduct under the free speech, press, and assembly guarantees of the Constitution unless it can be shown, first, that a particular party does in fact advocate violence and revolution and that such advocacy presents a clear and present danger to the established order; and, second, that the individual against whom the punishment is inflicted is aware of the party's advocacy of violent methods.

freedom of religion

In addition to the provisions already examined, the First Amendment states: "Congress shall make no law respecting an establishment of religion, or prohibiting the free exercise thereof. . . ."

There should also be noted the clause in the third section of Article Six of the original Constitution which provides: ". . . no religious test shall ever be required as a qualification to any office or public trust under the United States."

Freedom of religion is peculiarly an American civil liberty in its origin, for no such guarantee was to be found in the English constitutional documents from which so many of our other civil liberties were derived. By and large this freedom has been secure throughout most of our history. The Supreme Court has been called upon to decide a number of difficult cases concerning freedom of religion, but a large proportion of them have concerned the alleged violation of

---

[34] *De Jonge* v. *Oregon*, 299 U.S. 353 (1937).

the religious freedom of two rather small minorities, the Mormons and the Jehovah's Witnesses.

government and "an establishment of religion"

It is clear that our Constitution provides for a complete separation of church and state. Government in America may not regulate or restrict the practice of religion; neither may it support it. There can be no one "established" church in this country; neither may the government support all churches. At the same time our governments have certainly not been unfriendly toward religion and the church. Many public officials take oaths of office in the name of God, the sessions of Congress and other governmental bodies are usually opened with prayer,[35] and, what is more important, virtually all churches are subsidized by the government in the form of exemptions from various taxes, particularly the property tax.

The Supreme Court did not have occasion to pass upon the meaning of the "establishment of religion" clause of the First Amendment until 1947, when by a five-to-four vote it held that the use of public funds to transport pupils to a parochial school was not improper. The majority felt that this use of public funds was intended to ensure the safety of children going to and from school rather than to give support to church schools. The majority opinion did state:

> The "establishment of religion" clause of the First Amendment means at least this: Neither a state nor the Federal Government can set up a church. Neither can pass laws which aid one religion, aid all religions, or prefer one religion over another. . . . No tax in any amount, large or small, can be levied to support any religious activities or institutions, whatever they may be called, or whatever form they may adopt to teach or practice religion. Neither a state nor the Federal Government can, openly or secretly, participate in the affairs of any religious organizations or groups and vice versa.[36]

The four dissenting justices all believed that the expenditure in question did give aid to religion as well as protect the welfare of children.

A year later the Court passed upon the validity of the "released time" program and, with but one justice dissenting, found that the program violated the Constitution. There are many variations of "released time," which by 1947 was estimated to affect almost 2 million pupils in 2,200 communities. In its main outlines it provides for the "release" of children from their regular schoolwork during school hours so that they may receive religious instruction given by church authorities. The Court concluded, in invalidating the program used in Champaign, Illinois, that the facts showed "close cooperation between the

---

[35] It is interesting to note that a motion made by Benjamin Franklin in the Philadelphia convention that regular prayers be offered was rejected.

[36] *Everson* v. *Board of Education of Ewing*, 330 U.S. 1, 15, 16 (1947).

school authorities and the religious council in promoting religious education. . . . This is beyond all question a utilization of the tax-established and tax-supported public school system to aid religious groups to spread their faith." [37]

There has been much criticism of this ruling in the *Champaign* case on the ground that it insists upon an extreme separation of church and state which ignores the spiritual force which has always been a component of American life, and that if followed to its logical extreme it would require a complete secularization of public affairs wholly alien to American traditions.

government interference with religious freedom

Where the government has been accused of violating the second part of the religious freedom guarantee, i.e., "prohibiting the free exercise" of religion, the case has usually concerned some small religious group which is endeavoring to preach or practice certain beliefs that lie outside the range, admittedly wide at all times, of commonly accepted, normal religious tenets. In the middle nineteenth century the Mormons were such a group. Their insistence that the practice of polygamy was a necessary consequence of their religious beliefs was bound to clash with our firmly established social beliefs and customs as to marriage. Congress was not slow to outlaw the practice of polygamy in the territory of Utah by statute, and not surprisingly the Supreme Court unanimously upheld the constitutionality of such legislation.[38] In one of the Mormon cases the Court said:

> With man's relations to his Maker and the obligations he may think they impose, and the manner in which an expression shall be made by him of his beliefs on those subjects, no interference can be permitted, provided always the laws of society, designed to secure its peace and prosperity, and the morals of its people, are not interfered with. However free the exercise of religion may be, it must be subordinate to the criminal laws of the country, passed with reference to actions regarded by general consent as properly the subjects of punitive legislation.[39]

the Jehovah's Witnesses

In more recent times the activities of the Jehovah's Witnesses have come into conflict with the law again and again, and the Supreme Court has repeatedly been called upon to adjudicate the issue between religious freedom on one hand and the power of government on the other. Many of these cases have been extremely difficult ones, and there have been serious disagreement among the justices of the Supreme Court in many of the decisions that have been rendered. In the six-year period from 1938 through 1943 the sect was responsible for sixteen

---

[37] *McCollum* v. *Board of Education*, 333 U.S. 203, 209–210 (1948).

[38] *Reynolds* v. *United States*, 98 U.S. 145 (1879); *Davis* v. *Beason*, 133 U.S. 333 (1890).

[39] *Davis* v. *Beason*, 133 U.S. 333, 342 (1890).

major cases reaching the Supreme Court. Three of these cases resulted in five-to-four decisions, two in six-to-three decisions, and in the course of rendering decisions in these sixteen cases the Court reversed itself twice.[40]

Stated briefly, the nature of the conflict in these cases is as follows: The Jehovah's Witnesses hold several rather extreme religious beliefs which they try to put into practice in their daily lives. They discourage participation in political affairs and refuse to support war. They are opposed to the worship of images and accordingly refuse to salute the flag. Every Witness is regarded as an ordained minister and he is expected to be an active proselytizer. These "ministers" wander around the country, sometimes in sizable groups, invading towns, preaching upon street corners, and pushing their way into homes to play phonograph records, distribute literature, and solicit funds. They do not hesitate to show their dislike for other religions and in particular are bitter in their denunciation of the Catholic faith. Wherever they have found established social customs or religious traditions conflicting with their own, they have, in strongly individualistic, almost anarchistic fashion, refused to abide by such customs or respect such traditions. They are long on courage and short on tact. Inevitably, the persistent views and practices of the sect have subjected its members to prosecution for violation of law and to persecution for the flouting of custom. Particularly in small towns have their activities aroused antagonism, with the result that they have regularly found local public opinion inflamed against them and the power of local government invoked to prevent them from carrying on their business. The statute books of the average city or town contain many ordinances that can be utilized against such activity. Under such ordinances they have been charged with distributing literature or soliciting funds without a permit, engaging in disorderly conduct on the streets, parading without a license, using children to solicit funds, and with failure to salute the flag. Where ordinances have been invoked against the Witnesses convictions have frequently resulted in the local courts. The sect has been prompt to raise the cry of interference with religious freedom and has appealed many of these convictions to the Supreme Court of the United States, arguing that the First Amendment has been violated. More often than not the sect has been successful in these appeals,

---

[40] See Robert E. Cushman, "Constitutional Law in 1942–1943," *American Political Science Review*, XXXVIII (April, 1944), 266, 277; Victor Rotnem and F. G. Folsom, Jr., "Recent Restrictions upon Religious Liberty," *American Political Science Review*, XXXVI (December, 1942), 1053. Among the most important of the decisions of the Supreme Court dealing with the activities of the Jehovah's Witnesses the following may be noted: *Lovell* v. *Griffin*, 303 U.S. 444 (1938); *Schneider* v. *Irvington*, 308 U.S. 147 (1939); *Cantwell* v. *Connecticut*, 310 U.S. 296 (1940); *Minersville School District* v. *Gobitis*, 310 U.S. 586 (1940); *Cox* v. *New Hampshire*, 312 U.S. 569 (1941); *Chaplinsky* v. *New Hampshire*, 315 U.S. 568 (1942); *Jones* v. *Opelika*, 316 U.S. 584 (1942); *Murdock* v. *Pennsylvania*, 319 U.S. 105 (1943); *Martin* v. *Struthers*, 319 U.S. 141 (1943); *West Virginia State Board of Education* v. *Barnette*, 319 U.S. 624 (1943); *Taylor* v. *Mississippi*, 319 U.S. 583 (1943); *Prince* v. *Massachusetts*, 321 U.S. 158 (1944).

for the Supreme Court in a series of decisions has invalidated many of the ordinances which have been invoked against the Witnesses.

The refusal of the Jehovah's Witnesses to comply with laws providing for a compulsory flag salute has occasioned the most notable constitutional controversy involved in any of the many cases pertaining to this sect. Moreover, it has resulted in one of the most remarkable about-faces by the Supreme Court in its entire history. The problem was admittedly a borderline one of great difficulty: Was the requirement of the flag salute a device of sufficient importance in encouraging patriotism and respect for country as to outweigh an individual's prejudice against such a salute based upon religious grounds? In 1940, by an overwhelming eight-to-one majority, the Court upheld a requirement of this type, Justice Harlan Stone being the lone dissenter.[41] A year or two later, three of the justices who had made up the majority, in a move almost without precedent, announced that they were now convinced they had been wrong.[42] Shortly thereafter the Supreme Court took jurisdiction over a second flag salute case and agreed to reconsider the problem. Four of the justices who had participated in the first decision were now ready to invalidate compulsory flag salute legislation. They were joined by two new members of the Court to make up a six-to-three majority which finally outlawed legislation requiring the flag salute, as an unconstitutional interference with religious freedom.[43]

It is difficult to evaluate the importance of the decisions in the *Jehovah's Witnesses* cases. The sect is such an extreme one in the religious views it holds and its bold and persistent activities have been so obnoxious to many people whose peace has been disturbed that it has almost seemed that in protecting the sect against governmental restraints the Supreme Court was tilting with windmills. It is clear from the Court's position in these cases that it feels it is going to the limit of its powers in protecting the sect's activities. Were other equally persistent and annoying minorities to claim the same rights and descend upon towns and cities in similar fashion, the Court would almost certainly have to recognize the right of government to maintain peace and order and perhaps sanction some of the restraints that it has been inclined to outlaw as applied to the Jehovah's Witnesses. For the present such other religious minorities have not appeared or so conducted themselves. This sect is almost unique in its conduct, and accordingly the Court has perhaps been well advised to err in the direction of emphasizing religious freedom as against the authority of government. It is impossible to say that these decisions have not had a salutary effect in reaffirming the importance of religious liberty in America.

The plight of the Jehovah's Witnesses has in good part resulted from the

---

[41] *Minersville School District* v. *Gobitis,* 310 U.S. 586 (1940).

[42] *Jones* v. *Opelika,* 316 U.S. 584 (1942).

[43] *West Virginia State Board of Education* v. *Barnette,* 319 U.S. 624 (1943).

actions of private persons and organizations. The widely publicized decisions of the Supreme Court have all dealt with governmental interferences with the rights of these people, but a careful reading of the story of their struggles makes it clear that although they have often been restrained by municipal ordinances forbidding the distribution of handbills and by the unfriendly actions of local police officers, an equally serious threat to their activity has been met in the antagonistic attitudes of private persons. According to a summary prepared by two officials in the federal Department of Justice:

> Between June 12 and June 20, 1940, hundreds of attacks upon the Witnesses were reported to the Department of Justice. Several were of such violence that it was deemed advisable to have the Federal Bureau of Investigation look into them. At Kennebunk, Maine, the Kingdom Hall was burned. At Rockville, Maryland, the police assisted a mob in dispersing a Bible meeting. At Litchfield, Illinois, practically the entire town mobbed a company of some sixty Witnesses who were canvassing it, and it was necessary to call on the state troopers to protect the members of the sect. Several Witnesses were charged with riotous conspiracy at Connersville, Indiana, their attorney was mobbed, and he and several other Witnesses who had attended the arraignment were beaten and driven out of town. At Jackson, Mississippi, members of a veterans' organization, led by an individual claiming the rank of major, forcibly removed a number of Witnesses and their trailer homes from the town.[44]

freedom of political activity:
the right to citizenship and its privileges

Citizenship is the individual's badge of full membership in society. Only citizens may customarily enjoy such political rights as voting or holding public office; moreover, noncitizens are often excluded by law from certain private trades and professions. Thus the right of the mature, responsible member of society to enjoy the status of citizens is axiomatic in a democracy. Although the original Constitution speaks often of "citizens" and gives Congress express power to grant citizenship by naturalization, it nowhere defines citizenship in such a way as to establish this right on a firm basis. In 1868 the Fourteenth Amendment remedied this defect and provided in unequivocal language that all persons born in the United States and subject to its jurisdiction are automatically native citizens both of the nation and of the states where they live. Citizenship by naturalization is still subject to complete control by Congress.

Although the right to vote is today regarded as an essential characteristic of citizenship in a democratic society, neither the original Constitution nor the

---

[44] Rotnem and Folsom, "Recent Restrictions upon Religious Liberty," p. 1061. Reprinted by permission of *American Political Science Review*, publishers.

Bill of Rights gave it express recognition. Article One, section two, did provide that those who were qualified to vote for members of the more numerous branch of the legislature in each state were to be automatically qualified to vote in congressional elections. In a sense this established a federal right to vote. But it was not until 1868, with the addition of the Fourteenth Amendment, that the Constitution in effect guaranteed to male citizens over twenty-one years of age the right to vote in federal and state elections. The Fifteenth Amendment, added at the same time, forbade the states to deny any citizen the right to vote because of race, color, or previous condition of servitude, and the Nineteenth Amendment, added in 1920, forbade the states to use sex as a basis for discrimination in voting.

Perhaps no right guaranteed by the Constitution has been more consistently or flagrantly violated than the right to vote. In particular, eighty years after the adoption of the Fourteenth and Fifteenth Amendments, the Negro still finds himself barred from the ballot box in many states. In fact, securing this right to every mature American remains perhaps the greatest unsolved political problem confronting our democracy.

bibliographic note

Leon Whipple's *Our Ancient Liberties* (New York: The H. W. Wilson Company, 1927) is a neglected volume containing an inspiring statement of the basic freedoms of the American way of life. *The Story of Civil Liberty in the United States* (New York: The Vanguard Press, 1927) by the same author is almost the only attempt that has ever been made to write a history of civil liberty in the United States. Osmond K. Fraenkel's *Our Civil Liberties* (New York: The Viking Press, 1944) is perhaps the best systematic account of the various civil rights which are protected under the American Constitution. *Safeguarding Civil Liberty Today* (Ithaca: Cornell University Press, 1945) is a useful collection of essays by such authorities as Robert E. Cushman, Francis Biddle, and Max Lerner on current aspects of the problem of civil liberty. *Essential Human Rights* edited by William Draper Lewis, *The Annals* of The American Academy of Political and Social Science, CCXLIII (January, 1946) is also a useful collection of essays in this field. Robert E. Cushman's pamphlet, "Safeguarding Our Civil Liberties" (New York: Public Affairs Committee, Inc., 1943), is an excellent review of the current civil liberties scene by an outstanding authority on civil rights.

There are a number of excellent studies of freedom of speech and press. Zechariah Chafee's *Free Speech in the United States* (Cambridge: Harvard University Press, 1941) has become one of the classics of the literature on civil rights. It provides an excellent account of the threat to freedom of expression inherent in espionage and sedition statutes. Morris L. Ernst's *The First Freedom* (New York: The Macmillan Company, 1946) is a detailed examination of certain threats to freedom of expression arising out of the economic order. There is a detailed discussion of the growth of monopolies in the newspaper and radio businesses. J. Edward Gerald's *The Press and the Constitution, 1931–1937* (Minneapolis:The University of Minnesota Press, 1948) contains a good review of court cases bearing upon freedom of the press. Several of the titles mentioned in the bibliographic note to the chapter entitled "The Political Process" are also concerned with freedom of expression.

Milton R. Konvitz's *The Constitution and Civil Rights* (New York: Columbia University Press, 1947) is a systematic examination of governmental efforts, particularly at the state level, to eliminate racial and religious discrimination from American life.

our civil liberties:

criminal justice

ONE of man's most cherished civil liberties is the right to be free from un-fair arrest and imprisonment. For centuries governments have given man good cause to fear such evils. In the words of the Supreme Court:

> Tyrannical governments . . . immemorially utilized dictatorial criminal procedure and punishment to make scapegoats of the weak, or of helpless political, religious, or racial minorities and those who differed, who would not conform and who resisted tyranny. . . . The rack, the thumbscrew, the wheel, solitary confinement, protracted questioning and cross questioning, and other ingenious forms of entrapment of the helpless or unpopular . . . left their wake of mutilated bodies and shattered minds along the way to the cross, the guillotine, the stake and the hangman's noose.[1]

It is not surprising, then, that in modern times in the democratic state much emphasis should be given to the ideal of equal justice under law. Nor is it sur-prising that a very considerable portion of the American Bill of Rights should be concerned with various guarantees designed to ensure just treatment to the unfortunate individual who commits an offense against the law and finds him-self charged with a crime. This is not to say that the ideal of criminal justice should necessarily weigh the balance in the criminal's favor so as to make it particularly difficult for the state to secure a conviction against him, or to en-sure him a light sentence if he is found guilty. Instead, the meaning of civil liberty at this point must be to guarantee to every person accused of crime fair, humane treatment by means of regular, impersonal procedure in a court free from passion or prejudice.

> Freedom can exist only where the citizen is assured that his person is secure against . . . arbitrary arrest and punishment. . . . Moreover, to be free, men must be subject to discipline by society only for commission of offenses

---

[1] *Chambers* v. *Florida*, 309 U.S. 227, 236–238 (1940).

clearly defined by law and only after trial by due process of law. Where the administration of justice is discriminatory, no man can be sure of security.[2]

The ideal of a fair trial in accordance with the established "law of the land" is, among all American civil liberties, derived most directly from English practice and tradition. More than one phrase in our Bill of Rights dealing with criminal procedure has come down almost unchanged through centuries of English and American legal practice from such remote compacts as Magna Carta, the Petition of Right, or the English Bill of Rights. Thus, certain of our specific civil liberties in this field would not be recognized as desirable or necessary in many modern states that have not been influenced by English traditions, but states which nonetheless adhere to liberal, democratic ideals. Indeed, there is a tendency to question the continuing validity of certain of these rights in the United States today. Collectively, some such body of rights may be said to be indispensable to a system of justice like our own, but individually these rights may well be subject to re-examination in the light of changing concepts of criminal justice.

In examining these rights it will help to understand their meaning and importance if the successive steps in our system of criminal procedure are kept in mind. In general this procedure runs somewhat as follows: (1) A person suspected of crime is arrested and evidence against him is seized. (2) A preliminary hearing is given this person before a police magistrate or a justice of the peace. If there seem to be sufficient grounds for further proceedings, the suspect is "bound over" to the proper authorities. (3) Bail is fixed, by this device the accused in most instances being permitted to remain at liberty between the time of his arrest and his trial. (4) The accused is indicted. Specific charges are lodged against him; some, at least, of the evidence against him is indicated; and either by grand jury action or by decision of the public prosecutor, he is ordered held for trial. (5) The trial takes place and the guilt or innocence of the accused as to the offense he is alleged to have committed is determined. Two issues are of importance at this trial, a factual one concerned with the question whether the defendant actually committed the act of which he is accused, and a legal one concerned with the interpretation and application of whatever law may be relevant to the case at hand. In theory, unless the accused pleads guilty, all issues of fact in his case are passed upon by a jury, and all issues of law by a judge, who also pronounces sentence if the jury returns a verdict of guilty. (6) An opportunity to appeal from the decision of the trial court to some higher court may be provided. Such appeals are ordinarily limited to claims based upon the insufficiency of the legal case against the accused, or upon legal errors alleged to have occurred in the conduct of his trial.

To these customary steps in criminal procedure may be added the following

---

[2] *To Secure These Rights*, (Washington: Government Printing Office, 1947), p. 6.

fundamental premises which underlie the entire process: (1) An accused person is considered innocent until proved guilty. (2) The burden of the proof in a criminal case is upon the prosecution. (3) If the accused is to be convicted, his guilt must be proved beyond a reasonable doubt. (4) The final decision as to the basic issue of guilt or innocence is made by a nonprofessional jury of ordinary citizens.

freedom from unreasonable search and seizure

The Fourth Amendment to the federal Constitution provides:

The right of the people to be secure in their persons, houses, papers and effects, against unreasonable searches and seizures, shall not be violated, and no warrants shall issue, but upon probable cause, supported by oath or affirmation, and particularly describing the place to be searched, and the persons or things to be seized.

In speaking of the Fourth Amendment the Supreme Court has recently said, ". . . the forefathers, after consulting the lessons of history, designed our Constitution to place obstacles in the way of a too permeating police surveillance, which they seemed to think was a greater danger to a free people than the escape of some criminals from punishment." [3] Although the main purposes of the amendment may seem obvious on its face, it is one of the sections of the Constitution that has required considerable interpretation in its application to specific problems and situations. Moreover, although the words of the amendment are positive and straightforward, many exceptions have been made to its seeming prohibitions.

search warrant procedure

The search warrant clause was directed against "general" warrants which enabled officers of the law to engage in "fishing" expeditions in searching private homes for evidence. The "writs of assistance" of our own colonial period by which homes were searched for smuggled goods were such general warrants. Yet from the very beginning the prima-facie meaning of the clause has been departed from in that it has usually been permissible to arrest a lawbreaker at the scene of the crime without a warrant, and to seize such evidence as may be at hand, also without a warrant. Such an exception shows that this right, like so many others, has a relative rather than an absolute value. Its purpose is to protect individuals from *unreasonable* searches and seizures by governmental agents, but it is by no means intended to make the apprehension of criminals or the gathering of necessary evidence so difficult that governmental agents will be completely frustrated in their efforts to arrest and prosecute lawbreakers.

---

[3] *United States* v. *Di Re*, 332 U.S. 581, 595 (1948).

Yet the compromise character of the situation has made the pricking out of the line between what is permissible and what is not under the amendment a difficult process. In general, here, as elsewhere, the tendency has been to err in the direction of giving the benefit of the doubt to the alleged criminal. This tendency has frequently been criticized on the ground that it makes it possible for criminals to escape prosecution and conviction. Justice Oliver Wendell Holmes has replied to such a contention in these words: "We have to choose, and for my part I think it a less evil that some criminals should escape than that the government should play an ignoble part." [4]

This difficulty of drawing the line between reasonable and unreasonable searches and seizures has increased in modern times because of the technical character of our machine civilization. During the prohibition era of the twenties the process of obtaining "evidence" against bootleggers sometimes resulted in the employment of dubious methods by overzealous government agents. However, because of the ease with which evidence could quickly be removed far from the area of a crime in an automobile or other modern vehicle the Supreme Court ruled that such a vehicle could be searched without a warrant where there was probable cause to believe that a law had been violated. [5]

the problem of wire tapping

Similarly, the Court has ruled that it is permissible to tap telephone wires and obtain evidence against persons suspected of crime even though such a procedure seems very much like the outlawed "fishing expedition" in which much irrelevant evidence is sorted to discover relevant evidence. [6] This last decision was by a five-to-four vote and has been much criticized. In part it has been nullified by legislation, for, in passing the Federal Communications Act in 1934, Congress decreed: "No person not being authorized by the sender shall intercept any communication and divulge or publish the existence, contents, substance, purport, effect or meaning of such intercepted communication to any person." [7] The Supreme Court thereupon ruled that this provision of law applies to government agents as well as to private persons and that accordingly evidence obtained by wire tapping cannot legally be used in a federal criminal case against the person

---

[4] *Olmstead* v. *United States*, 277 U.S. 438, 470 (1928). The continuing difficulty of determining what kinds of search and arrest are proper under the amendment is illustrated by seven cases decided by the Supreme Court between 1947 and 1950. Three were decided by five-to-four votes, one by a five-to-three vote, one by a six-to-three vote, and one by a seven-to-two vote. *Harris* v. *United States*, 331 U.S. 145 (1947); *United States* v. *Di Re*, 332 U.S. 581 (1948); *Johnson* v. *United States*, 333 U.S. 10 (1948); *Trupiano* v. *United States*, 334 U.S. 699 (1948); *McDonald* v. *United States*, 335 U.S. 451 (1948); *Brinegar* v. *United States*, 338 U.S. 160 (1949); *United States* v. *Rabinowitz*, 339 U.S. 56 (1950).

[5] *Carroll* v. *United States*, 267 U.S. 132 (1925).

[6] *Olmstead* v. *United States*, 277 U.S. 438 (1928).

[7] 48 Stat. 1063.

whose conversations have been tapped.[8] In the words of Justice Felix Frank-furter, such evidence is outlawed because it is "fruit of the poisonous tree." To complicate matters further, the Supreme Court, three justices dissenting, later ruled that evidence obtained by unlawful wire tapping can be used in criminal prosecutions against persons other than those whose conversations have been tapped.[9]

freedom from excessive bail

The Eighth Amendment in its first clause makes the terse statement, "Excessive bail shall not be required." This provision has not been the subject of much controversy nor has it presented unusual difficulties of interpretation. It is clearly a relative right. For example, it does not prevent complete denial of bail in cases involving capital offenses. If an accused person thinks that his bail has been fixed too high, he can have the amount reviewed. Thereupon the reviewing tribunal presumably takes into account the severity of the offense, the ability of the accused to meet the amount imposed, and the possibility that he will forfeit his bail and fail to appear at his trial if he is released on bail. It is obvious that very wide discretion must be left to the courts in fixing bail; ordinarily it is quite difficult for an accused person successfully to invoke this constitutional provision in seeking any relief from the bail actually imposed in his case.

the right to indictment by a grand jury

The first clause of the Fifth Amendment provides: "No person shall be held to answer for a capital, or otherwise infamous crime, unless on a presentment or indictment of a grand jury. . . ."

The purpose of this clause, historically, has been to protect innocent persons against the indignity of being brought to trial on trumped-up charges or in the absence of sufficient evidence. It is to the grand jury as a preliminary body that a prosecuting officer presents the evidence he has collected against a person suspected of crime. If this grand jury is convinced that this evidence is sufficient to indicate that the accused person may well have committed the crime, it brings in "a true bill" or "indicts" him. The grand jury system has sometimes served to mitigate the harshness of the law in particular cases. Even though it is impressed by the evidence against a person, such a jury may refuse to indict him, believing that no good purpose will be served by his prosecution and that it is better to let him go free. In any case, unless an indictment is returned by the grand jury, it is impossible to proceed with the prosecution of a person.

---

[8] *Nardone* v. *United States*, 302 U.S. 379 (1937).

[9] *Goldstein* v. *United States*, 316 U.S. 114 (1942).

The reference in the Fifth Amendment to "capital" and "infamous" crimes limits the grand jury requirement to cases where the penalty involves death, hard labor, or a penitentiary term. The Constitution also specifically exempts members of the Army and the Navy and members of the militia "when in actual service in time of war or public danger" from the protection of this constitutional guarantee.

criticism of the grand jury system

The grand jury system has become increasingly subject to criticism in modern times, and many able students of criminal procedure advocate its abolition. In its place they would allow the public prosecuting official to file an "information" against a person, which action would be equivalent to an indictment. Actually the information is almost as old a method of determining whether to hold a person for trial as indictment by a grand jury. Those who favor increased use of the information argue that we need no longer fear capricious or tyrannical prosecutions of persons in the absence of evidence to back up the charges. They also argue that the modern prosecuting attorney, influenced by a desire to win a high proportion of the cases he prosecutes, is more apt to shy away from prosecuting any but the strongest cases than he is to go out of his way to prosecute the weak cases. The right to a grand jury hearing is one of the civil liberties of the Constitution that definitely does not restrict state governments, and in twenty-four states the grand jury indictment has been replaced in whole or in part by the information. Certainly there is nothing about the grand jury that makes it indispensable to a modern system of criminal justice.

the grand jury's investigating function

The grand jury has had a further use which, although not directly concerned with the protection of the rights of the individual, is not unrelated to the subject of civil liberties. This is the activity of the grand jury as an investigating body. The grand jury is not always dependent upon the presentation to it of charges against alleged criminals by prosecuting officials. Instead, where, as is often true in populous communities, a grand jury is in almost continuous session, it may upon its own initiative investigate charges of crime or corruption, particularly where these involve, directly or indirectly, public officials. Sometimes such an investigatory body is called "a runaway grand jury." If it discovers evidence of wrongdoing, it may issue indictments without any request having been made to it for such action. Or it may refrain from indicting specific individuals and, instead, return a presentment in which it criticizes a law enforcement program generally or in which it suggests the enactment of new laws to correct an unsatisfactory situation. Frequently, grand juries have rendered valuable public service in taking such action where police officers or prosecuting officials have been either inefficient or actually dishonest. For this reason the complete abolition of the grand jury would perhaps be unfortunate.[10]

the right of habeas corpus

One of the greatest of the rights guaranteed by the original Constitution is the right to the writ of habeas corpus. Section nine of Article One of the Constitution provides: "The privilege of the writ of habeas corpus shall not be suspended, unless when in cases of rebellion or invasion the public safety may require it."

The writ of habeas corpus is one of the famous writs, along with the writs of error, certiorari, quo warranto, mandamus, and injunction, which English and American courts have issued for centuries in sustaining their commands or in bringing matters before them.[11] The writ of habeas corpus, sometimes called "the writ of liberty," was especially designed to prevent arbitrary arrest or unlawful imprisonment without the bringing of charges against, or the granting of a trial to, the incarcerated person. Where this right is available, any person who is arrested and detained by public officers may ask the nearest court for such a writ, or such a request may be made by his lawyer or by his friends. The writ will be directed against the officers who are detaining a person and orders them to bring the person into court and show legal cause for holding him—in other words to charge formally that he has violated some specific provision of law. If such cause is not shown or if charges are not brought, the court will order the person released from custody.

suspension of the writ of habeas corpus

Much controversy has centered about the suspension of the writ of habeas corpus. The Constitution provides that the writ may be suspended only in case of rebellion or invasion, but it does not make it clear whether such suspension must be limited to those areas immediately affected by the rebellion or invasion, and it does not specify the agency of government which may order the suspension. Early in the Civil War President Lincoln assumed that the power to suspend the writ belonged to him, and he proceeded to order the writ suspended in various parts of the country, both in combat areas and in areas outside the scene of battle, without any congressional authorization. This action of the President was challenged by Chief Justice Roger B. Taney who, sitting as a circuit judge, argued in his opinion in *Ex parte Merryman* that the power to authorize suspension of the writ rested exclusively with Congress.[12] Most students of American government now agree that Taney was correct. It is worth noting that thereafter

[10] See Raymond Moley, "Grand Jury," *Encyclopaedia of the Social Sciences*, VII, 148.
[11] See Pendleton Howard, "Habeas Corpus," *Encyclopaedia of the Social Sciences*, VII, 233.
[12] Fed. Case No. 9,487 (1861).

Congress passed legislation specifically authorizing the President to suspend the writ when in his judgment such action was necessary.

As to the area in which the writ may be suspended, there is no doubt that this constitutional privilege and others may temporarily be denied civilians in an actual theater of warfare. The question as to suspension in areas outside such theaters was answered somewhat indecisively by the Supreme Court in the famous case of *Ex parte Milligan.*[13] Milligan was a civilian who had been charged with insurrection and tried by a military commission in Indiana in 1864. He was found guilty and sentenced to be hanged. He appealed to the Supreme Court, arguing that he should have been tried by a regular civilian court. In the decision in the case all nine justices agreed that the President could not upon his own authority suspend the writ of habeas corpus and set up military government in an area outside the scene of battle. Five justices felt that not even Congress could order the suspension of the writ of habeas corpus outside the actual theater of war, whereas four justices thought that Congress could so act if it wished. As a result of the decision, Milligan was set free. There has been no attempt since the Civil War by either Congress or the President to suspend the writ of habeas corpus in the United States. Congress has actually strengthened this right by a statutory enactment ordering federal law enforcement officials to take arrested persons before the nearest federal court immediately so that the accused may have a prompt hearing.

the right to trial by jury

The Constitution contains three separate provisions dealing with jury trial. Section two of Article Three of the original Constitution provides:

> The trial of all crimes, except in cases of impeachment, shall be by jury; and such trial shall be held in the State where the said crimes shall have been committed; but when not committed within any State, the trial shall be at such place or places as the Congress may by law have directed.

This provision from the original Constitution was further strengthened by the Sixth Amendment in the Bill of Rights which says:

> In all criminal prosecutions the accused shall enjoy the right to a speedy and public trial, by an impartial jury of the State and district wherein the crime shall have been committed, which district shall have been previously ascertained by law. . . .

Finally, the Seventh Amendment to the Constitution provides:

> In suits at common law, where the value in controversy shall exceed twenty dollars, the right of trial by jury shall be preserved, and no fact tried by a

---

[13] *Ex parte Milligan,* 4 Wallace 2 (1866).

jury shall be otherwise re-examined in any court of the United States, than according to the rules of the common law.

common-law jury traditions followed

It is clearly the intention of the Constitution to guarantee trial by jury in federal cases, both civil and criminal. Beyond this general intention the Constitution is largely silent concerning details except as to the question of the place of such trial. Nonetheless, it has been held that these clauses of the Constitution establish the right of jury trial in all its details largely as it existed in 1789. For example, although nothing is said about the common-law tradition of a jury of twelve members or the requirement of a unanimous verdict, the Supreme Court has ruled that these are necessary features of our federal jury system. Moreover, it has been held that jury trial does not extend as of right to equity cases or admiralty cases, since this was not traditional in 1789. Again, the courts have held that provision may be made for the trial of petty crimes without a jury.[14] And although the Constitution guarantees a jury trial in criminal cases, this does not prevent the accused from waiving the right and electing to be tried by a judge.

exclusion of Negroes from juries

There has been considerable controversy about the make-up of federal juries. Although no person has any right to demand that he shall be tried by a jury consisting in whole or even in part of persons of his own kind, whether in terms of race, color, sex, or economic or social class, the Supreme Court has now clearly established the rule that systematic exclusion of Negroes from grand or petit juries does deprive a Negro defendant of his constitutional right to the equal protection of the law.[15]

the problem of the "blue-ribbon jury"

The use of the so-called "blue-ribbon" jury raises a question that is not easily answered. As the words indicate, a blue-ribbon jury is one composed of persons who have met additional tests of qualification and fitness beyond those used for the selection of ordinary jurymen. There is no provision in federal law for the use of such special juries in the federal courts, but they are employed in certain states. New York State, for example, has had a blue-ribbon jury law since 1901. Under this law a judge may order the use of such a jury where "by reason of the intricacy of the case, a special jury is required" or "the issue to be tried has been so widely commented upon . . . that an ordinary jury cannot without delay and difficulty be obtained," or that for any other reason "the due, efficient

---

[14] *Springville* v. *Thomas*, 166 U.S. 707 (1897); *Thompson* v. *Utah*, 170 U.S. 343 (1898); *In re Debs*, 158 U.S. 564 (1895); *District of Columbia* v. *Clawans*, 300 U.S. 617 (1937).
[15] *Norris* v. *Alabama*, 294 U.S. 587 (1935); *Smith* v. *Texas*, 311 U.S. 128 (1940).

and impartial administration of justice in the particular case would be advanced
by the trial of such an issue by a special jury." It is estimated that in New York
County the operation of this law shrinks the regular jury panel from about
60,000 to about 3,000 names.

Admittedly it is desirable that the members of a jury be alert and intelligent. But if unusual provision is made for the selection of particularly competent jurors, does not this endanger the cross-sectional character of the traditional jury and perhaps threaten the constitutional rights of the defendant? The
closeness of the issue is shown by the fact that the Supreme Court has recently
twice upheld the constitutionality of the New York system by five-to-four
votes.[16] Although the majority felt that a state might reasonably employ blue-
ribbon juries as a means of making the administration of justice more efficient,
the dissenters were vigorous in their condemnation of the system. Justice Frank
Murphy asserted:

> The vice lies in the very concept of "blue ribbon" panels—the systematic
> and intentional exclusion of all but the "best" or the most learned or intelli-
> gent of general jurors. Such panels are completely at war with the demo-
> cratic theory of our jury system. . . . One is constitutionally entitled to be
> judged by a fair sampling of all one's neighbors who are qualified, not
> merely those with superior intelligence or learning.[17]

In 1946 the Supreme Court did set aside a conviction in a federal criminal
case where there was evidence that court officials had "deliberately and intention-
ally excluded from the jury lists all persons who work for a daily wage." The
fact that the motive for such exclusion was to protect wage earners from the
financial sacrifice necessitated by low jury pay did not in the Court's opinion
alter the impropriety of the result.[18]

the jury system questioned

There has been an increasing tendency in modern times to question the continuing soundness and desirability of the jury system per se. The jury system has
much to be said in its favor so far as tradition and principle go. It was the common-law intention that in criminal cases the jury would determine all issues of
fact and the judge all issues of law. There was much merit in this arrangement
whereby purely factual questions were answered by twelve "good men and true"
who represented a cross section of the ordinary nonprofessional members of
society. But it is doubtful whether the original distinction between the role of
the jury and the role of the judge has been preserved in the United States. For
one thing, the American people have departed from the common-law jury sys-

---

[16] *Fay* v. *New York*, 332 U.S. 261 (1947); *Moore* v. *New York*, 333 U.S. 565 (1948).

[17] *Moore* v. *New York*, 333 U.S. 565, 570 (1948).

[18] *Thiel* v. *Southern Pacific Co.*, 328 U.S. 217 (1946).

tem by seriously curbing the powers of the trial judge in such matters as his right to comment on the evidence, his charge to the jury, his right to set aside jury verdicts, and his power to pronounce sentence.[19] In England the judge has remained a more powerful figure in trial procedure, and for that reason the jury system is said to have operated more satisfactorily there. Dean Roscoe Pound speaks of "jury lawlessness" in America, using that phrase to describe the result that prevails where juries are allowed to decide legal issues, and to decide them in terms of nonlegal considerations. It is sometimes argued in return that the tendency of juries to decide cases in terms of common sense or elementary justice, even though they thereby ignore or violate the dictates of law, is not entirely an unfortunate thing. It is said that a too rigid adherence to the letter of the law sometimes produces unfortunate results and that upon occasion it is desirable that some agency, such as the jury, be in a position to soften the harsh, arbitrary effects of law. Nonetheless, it is clear that this "lawlessness" of juries is often carried to extremes. Accordingly the question is asked increasingly whether equal justice under law might not be better secured through a system of criminal procedure in which judges took over part or all of the function of the jury.

the right to a defense

It is axiomatic to a system of justice that the accused in criminal cases shall have a reasonable opportunity to defend himself. To give meaning to this axiom our Constitution specifically provides in the Sixth Amendment: "In all criminal prosecutions the accused shall enjoy the right . . . to be informed of the nature and cause of the accusation; to be confronted with witnesses against him; to have compulsory process for obtaining witnesses in his favor, and to have the assistance of counsel for his defense."

There has been relatively little controversy about the observance of these guarantees in federal criminal procedure. In the state courts there has been much controversy in late years concerning the right of an accused person to enjoy the assistance of counsel for his defense. In 1932 the Supreme Court ruled that the states are compelled by the Fourteenth Amendment to provide a defendant in a murder case, where the death penalty may be imposed, with the benefit of counsel if he is unable to engage an attorney himself. Thereafter, however, the Court held that this requirement did not necessarily prevail in noncapital criminal cases, with the result that it is difficult to say just what the extent of the right is today.[20]

---

[19] Roscoe Pound, "Jury," *Encyclopaedia of the Social Sciences*, VIII, 492.
[20] See particularly *Powell* v. *Alabama*, 287 U.S. 45 (1932) and *Betts* v. *Brady*, 316 U.S. 455 (1942).

freedom from self-incrimination

Nowhere is the tendency in our system of criminal justice to give the advantage to the accused person better illustrated than in this provision of the Fifth Amendment: "No person . . . shall be compelled in any criminal case to be a witness against himself. . . ."

In practical terms this means that the prosecutor in a criminal case cannot compel the accused to take the witness stand and answer questions. Instead, he must attempt to prove his case against the defendant by other and more roundabout methods. Of course, if the defendant elects to take the witness stand in his own defense, he may then be subjected to cross-examination by the prosecution.

The constitutional guarantee of freedom from self-incrimination is not limited solely to an accused person actually on trial in a criminal case. It has been interpreted to protect all persons from giving testimony in any sort of proceedings which might later be used against them in a criminal prosecution. Thus a mere witness in a routine hearing before some administrative or legislative committee may refuse to give testimony on the ground that to do so would incriminate him. However, Congress may by legislation grant immunity from prosecution because of any testimony given by a witness and where complete immunity has been so provided the witness may not refuse to testify. Again, freedom from self-incrimination has been held to outlaw *involuntary* confessions obtained by police officers from suspects through the use of "third-degree" methods. The introduction of such a confession as evidence during a trial is regarded as being equivalent to forcing the defendant to take the witness stand and testify against himself. Of course, a *voluntary* confession is admissible as evidence.

Some students of modern criminal procedure have come to question the wisdom of this constitutional guarantee of freedom from self-incrimination, and are inclined to argue that the cause of justice would be benefited rather than injured if the defendant in a criminal case were compelled to submit to a calm, reasonable questioning by prosecuting officers. Justice Benjamin N. Cardozo has said:

> Indeed, today as in the past there are students of our penal system who look upon the immunity [from self incrimination] as a mischief rather than a benefit, and who would limit its scope or destroy it altogether. No doubt there would remain the need to give protection against torture, physical or mental. . . . Justice, however, would not perish if the accused were subject to a duty to respond to orderly inquiry.[21]

Other authorities, however, argue that if our criminal procedure is to remain unchanged in other respects this immunity should be preserved. Osmond

---

[21] *Palko* v. *Connecticut*, 302 U.S. 319, 325 (1937).

K. Fraenkel, a lawyer who has long interested himself in problems of civil liberty, says: "So long as the presumption of innocence remains a part of our legal system, evidence against an accused should come from sources other than the accused himself." [22]

freedom from double jeopardy

The Fifth Amendment states: ". . . nor shall any person be subject for the same offense to be twice put in jeopardy of life or limb. . . ." Historically, this guarantee has been found in most systems of criminal justice in one form or another. The obvious purpose of such a protection is to prevent an accused person from being tried over and over again until a conviction or a verdict acceptable to the prosecution is obtained. It is closely related to the principle of *res judicata* in general law, which provides that once a disputed legal point is adjudicated, the point is not to be raised again in a similar case by the same parties. In general this guarantee means that once the accused has been acquitted in a criminal case, he cannot, for any reason, be tried again for the same offense.

As might be expected, this guarantee is subject to certain exceptions. Under our federal plan of government, an antisocial act may well violate federal and state laws, and the guarantee does not protect a person from prosecution by both governments for such an offense. This situation was a particularly serious one during the period when the Eighteenth Amendment was in effect. Although the federal and state governments by one means or another often refrain from such double prosecutions, they are not compelled to do so by the double jeopardy clause of the Fifth Amendment. Even where a person has violated federal or state law only, the possibility of a double prosecution is not completely ruled out, for a single act may violate two or more criminal statutes. In such circumstances the accused may be tried and convicted for each separate offense. Again, freedom from double jeopardy does not prevent the prosecution from bringing a man to trial a second time where, following a first trial which resulted in a finding of guilt, the accused has persuaded a higher court to set aside the original verdict because of procedural errors in the first trial.

freedom from unusual punishment

The Eighth Amendment protects accused persons from the infliction of cruel and unusual punishments. The relative quality of all civil liberties is here well illustrated, for clearly it cannot easily be determined in any final sense when punishment ceases to be legitimate and becomes cruel and unusual. Although the use of torture in executing a criminal would unquestionably be held to violate this amendment, the mere exaction of a death penalty is not per se regarded as

---

[22] Osmond K. Fraenkel, *Our Civil Liberties* (New York: The Viking Press, 1944), p. 148.

cruel and unusual. Yet what is today acceptable in this respect to society may tomorrow become repulsive. Accordingly, this is a constitutional clause that must be interpreted to harmonize with changing attitudes as to criminal justice.

the right to due process of law

Those guarantees of the Bill of Rights that offer protection against specific practices or methods in criminal procedure have now been examined. There remains, however, a more general and comprehensive provision offering protection to a person accused of crime. This is the guarantee that no person shall be deprived of his life, liberty, or property, in punishment for a crime, without due process of law. As has already been noted, there are two such guarantees in the federal Constitution: one in the Fifth Amendment, which controls federal procedure; and one in the Fourteenth Amendment, which controls state procedure. In general these two clauses guarantee to the defendant in a criminal case a fair, reasonable trial in which the ends of justice are observed. This is the *procedural* aspect of due process of law as opposed to the *substantive* aspect.

A question that immediately suggests itself with respect to procedural due process of law is what further protection, if any, this guarantee gives that is not provided by the more specific guarantees of the Bill of Rights. To begin with, since the rights guaranteed an accused person by the first ten amendments of the federal Constitution concern only possible violations by the federal government, it is clear that the due process clause of the Fourteenth Amendment may well offer a defendant in a state court protection not afforded him by the federal Bill of Rights. But to a certain extent the due process clauses also afford protection that goes beyond that provided by the other guarantees of the Bill of Rights.

The language of the due process of law clause has been traced by scholars back to Magna Carta, where it appeared in a somewhat different version as "the law of the land." This provision of Magna Carta was designed to guarantee, among other things, that criminal proceedings should take place in accordance with the provisions of law and not the arbitrary whim of the King or any other public officer. Perhaps no attempt to interpret this provision of Magna Carta has been more successful than Daniel Webster's paraphrase in his argument in the *Dartmouth College* case: "By the law of the land is most clearly intended the general law; a law which hears before it condemns; which proceeds upon inquiry, and renders judgment only after trial." From this it will be seen that due process of law is not entirely a matter of following particular procedural forms. Instead, the emphasis is upon the spirit of judicial proceedings rather than upon their form. For example, in 1923 in the case of *Moore* v. *Dempsey*, the Supreme Court set aside the judgment of an Arkansas court by which five Negroes were found guilty of murder and sentenced to death. The Supreme Court did not find that a specific procedural error had been committed by the trial court.

Rather the Court felt that a proper spirit of justice had been lacking from the proceedings as a whole and that accordingly the execution of the men would deprive them of their lives without due process of law. There was evidence that although all of the proper forms had been observed, the trial had taken place in an atmosphere of mob hysteria, and in the presence of a belief that the defendants would be lynched unless they were found guilty. The Court said in its opinion:

> The Court and neighborhood were thronged with an adverse crowd that threatened the most dangerous consequences to anyone interfering with the desired result. The counsel did not venture to demand delay or change of venue, to challenge a juryman or to ask for separate trials. He had had no preliminary consultation with the accused, called no witnesses for the defense although they could have been produced, and did not put the defendants on the stand. The trial lasted about three-quarters of an hour and in less than five minutes the jury brought in a verdict of guilty . . . there never was a chance for the petitioners to be acquitted; no juryman could have voted for an acquittal and continued to live in Phillips County. . . .[23]

Several specific rules in criminal procedure seem to stem from the due process clauses rather than from the more direct guarantees of the Bill of Rights. Among these are the rules that a conviction based on perjured testimony cannot stand, that the presiding judge must be free from gross partiality or prejudice, that a conviction cannot stand where evidence in support of an essential part of the crime charged against the accused is wholly lacking, and that criminal statutes must be sufficiently definite to enable reasonable people to know when they are violating them. In general the Supreme Court has been slow to base a reversal in a criminal case upon any one of these considerations.[24]

the right of appeal

It is ordinarily said that our American constitutional system does not guarantee a defendant in a criminal case the opportunity to appeal a verdict against him in the sense that he can, as a matter of right, request an appellate court to review the proceedings in the trial court on the chance that certain errors have been committed. The Supreme Court itself has said: "A review by an appellate court of the final judgment in a criminal case, however grave the offense of which the accused is convicted, was not at common law, and is not now a necessary element of due process of law."

If it is not a part of due process of law, there is certainly no item in the Bill

---

[23] *Moore* v. *Dempsey*, 261 U.S. 86, 89 (1923).

[24] See *Ward* v. *Texas*, 316 U.S. 547 (1942); *Lisenba* v. *California*, 314 U.S. 219 (1941); *Mooney* v. *Holohan*, 294 U.S. 103 (1935); *Mooney* v. *Smith*, 305 U.S. 598 (1938); *Fiske* v. *Kansas*, 274 U.S. 380 (1927); *Chambers* v. *Florida*, 309 U.S. 227 (1940).

of Rights which in so many words guarantees any right of appeal. And yet it would seem that in an implied sense our Constitution does guarantee a right of appeal. Insofar as an accused person may complain that he has been denied the use of one of the protective devices guaranteed by the Constitution itself, such as the assistance of legal counsel or the right of compulsory process to obtain witnesses in his favor, he can request a higher court to set aside an adverse verdict in the trial court. In other words, where the request to the higher court is based upon some alleged violation of the Constitution, appeal is available as a matter of right. Moreover, the number of such appeals can be very large in view of the great number of specific requirements as to criminal procedure contained in the Bill of Rights. It should also be noted that some sort of appeal in criminal cases has been made available as a *statutory* right by Congress and by most state legislatures.

freedom from bills of attainder

Among the clauses of the original Constitution that have a bearing upon criminal justice are two in sections nine and ten of Article One, which forbid Congress and the state legislatures to pass bills of attainder. In the words of the Supreme Court, "A bill of attainder is a legislative act, which inflicts punishment without a judicial trial." [25] In the evolution of our modern Anglo-American system of criminal procedure, one of the most vital developments was the establishment of the principle that legislative bodies should confine themselves to the definition of criminal acts by the passage of general statutes, and leave to the courts the application of these laws to specific individuals. There had been a time in English history when Parliament was known to flout the ordinary forms of law and judicial procedure by declaring particular individuals guilty of such a crime as treason and ordering them put to death. But the prohibition against such legislative action had been so well established by 1787 that relatively little use has had to be made of these constitutional clauses since that time. In those few instances where they have been invoked, the alleged bills of attainder were rather more technical than they were real attempts by a legislative body to single out particular individuals and subject them to punishment for crime. For example, shortly after the Civil War the Supreme Court held invalid a clause in the Constitution of Missouri which denied to any person who had failed to support the Union side in the recent war the right to hold public office or to become a lawyer or a minister. This was declared to be a legislative punishment and thus a bill of attainder.[26] At the same time a similar act of Congress requiring attorneys wishing to practice law before the federal courts to

---

[25] *Cummings* v. *Missouri*, 4 Wallace 277, 323 (1867).
[26] *Ibid.*

take an oath that they had been loyal to the Union was also invalidated as a bill of attainder.[27] Four justices dissented in these two cases. Again in 1946 the Court held that action by Congress in specifically providing in an appropriation act that no salary should be paid to three named federal employees because of alleged subversive activity was punitive action and thus unconstitutional as a bill of attainder.[28]

freedom from ex post facto laws

Sections nine and ten of Article One of the Constitution also prohibit ex post facto legislation on the part of Congress and the state legislatures. There is some opinion that it was the intent in these prohibitions against ex post facto laws to outlaw all types of retroactive legislation. But in one of the first great cases decided by the Supreme Court is was held that these clauses prohibit only retroactive *criminal* laws.[29] In other words, an ex post facto law is one which in any way operates to the disadvantage of a person accused of a crime which was committed before the law was passed. Such laws, like bills of attainder, had been relatively common in England during the political upheavals of the seventeenth and eighteenth centuries. Moreover, the use that may be made of such measures by a government inclined toward tyranny or dictatorship is obvious. By and large, American legislatures have carefully observed the prohibition against ex post facto laws.

In the two cases already mentioned, in which the Supreme Court held that legislative attempts following the Civil War to disqualify ex-Confederates from certain professions were bills of attainder, the majority of the justices also ruled that such action violated the ex post facto prohibition in that it prescribed punishment for an act after the act had taken place. There are other scattered cases in which state legislation has been questioned under the ex post facto clause. In none of these cases has the prohibition been used to forestall any flagrantly unfair or unreasonable mode of dealing with persons accused of crime. Nonetheless, the presence of these clauses in the Constitution outlawing bills of attainder and ex post facto laws is a salutary thing, for they serve to remind us how far we have come in the development of our system of criminal justice. It is all too easy for the American to take for granted life in a society where one is subject to punishment only for wrongful acts carefully defined by laws enacted before the wrongs are committed, and only as the result of a trial before a judicial body in which these laws are impartially and impersonally applied to the case at hand.

---

[27] *Ex parte Garland*, 4 Wallace 333 (1867).

[28] *United States* v. *Lovett*, 328 U.S. 303 (1946).

[29] *Calder* v. *Bull*, 3 Dallas 386 (1798).

limitation of the crime of treason

Throughout all history treason against the state has been regarded as one of the most heinous of crimes, and properly so. At the same time no crime has been subject to greater abuse on the part of the state, for the political use of laws against treason to reach and punish individuals regarded as dangerous to the ruling class in a country has been all too common. The men who made the American Constitution were aware of the use made of treason as a weapon against nonconforming persons during the troubled times of the preceding century or two in England. Accordingly, they determined to prevent any such arbitrary action in America. This they did by inserting a section in Article Three of the original Constitution which defines treason narrowly:

> Treason against the United States shall consist only in levying war against them, or in adhering to their enemies, giving them aid and comfort. No person shall be convicted of treason unless on the testimony of two witnesses to the same overt act, or on confession in open court.
>
> The Congress shall have power to declare the punishment of treason, but no attainder of treason shall work corruption of blood or forfeiture except during the life of the person attainted.

These clauses have well served their intended purposes, and we have had relatively few charges of treason brought against individuals. In fact, the first case involving the interpretation of the treason clauses of the Constitution did not reach the Supreme Court until 1944.[30] At the same time this constitutional restraint upon the government has had less significance than might have been expected because, although treason as a crime is narrowly defined, Congress is not prevented from broadening the criminal law against subversive activity by using other nomenclature. Thus Congress has defined such crimes as sedition, espionage, and conspiracy so as to include acts that cannot be regarded as treason, but which are made subject to heavy penalties. And yet it is fair to observe that our history has been relatively free of that tyrannical use of power to punish men for political reasons which the Founding Fathers hoped to prevent by narrowly defining the crime of treason.

criminal justice under the Constitution—an evaluation

It may now be seen that the particular civil liberties which have been examined in this chapter combine to form a constitutionally prescribed basis for our American system of criminal justice. This system, with its long evolution through

---

[30] *Cramer* v. *United States,* 325 U.S. 21 (1945). See also *Haupt* v. *United States,* 330 U.S. 631 (1947).

centuries of English and American legal history, is unquestionably one of man's greatest political achievements. Its all-abiding purpose is equal justice under law, a purpose that safeguards the integrity and security of each individual by offering him every assurance of fair, equal treatment under law should he be accused of an offense against society's rules. And yet the final character of this system of justice is not one that is beyond questioning. Two criticisms of the system may now be examined.

does criminal procedure favor the accused unduly?

Roscoe Pound, the great American legal scholar, is inclined to question whether the cause of justice has been entirely served by placing the burden of proof in criminal cases so completely upon the government and by providing so many mitigating devices which operate to the benefit of the accused person. For example, he lists the following possibilities existing at one point or another in our system of criminal procedure which permit a relaxing of the law's intent as to the treatment of an offender against society's rules: (1) The discretion which police or other law enforcement officers can use in deciding whether to arrest a suspected lawbreaker in the first place; (2) the authority of a magistrate to discharge a person upon preliminary examination; (3) the authority of the grand jury to refuse to indict a person, or the related discretion of the prosecuting attorney to refrain from bringing a case to trial; (4) the right of the jury to acquit the defendant in the face of evidence of his guilt, however strong; (5) the discretion of the trial judge or the appellate judges to grant new trials; (6) the discretion of the trial judge as to the severity of the sentence pronounced against the accused person; (7) the discretion of various authorities as to the suspension or mitigation of the sentence; (8) the authority vested in various officers to parole or pardon the convicted person.[31]

In trying to evaluate Pound's argument it is important to keep in mind the long-standing belief that it is better that nine guilty persons should go free because of the law's laxity than that one innocent person should be punished because of the law's severity. On the other hand, the concept of criminal justice does in the long run depend for its success upon the conviction of the guilty as well as on the freeing of the innocent. It is quite possible that the balance between prosecutor and accused in our system of criminal procedure could be altered in favor of the former at certain points, without endangering justice itself.

does criminal procedure clash with modern sociology?

A somewhat different criticism of our system of criminal justice is that it employs outmoded procedures which conflict with modern, scientific knowledge concerning the causes of crime and the treatment of criminals. This criticism,

---

[31] Pound, "Jury," VIII, 492.

somewhat in contrast to Pound's position, stresses the rigidity and impersonality of the criminal procedure required by the Bill of Rights. It is suggested that in our commendable desire to establish equality of treatment under law by carefully defining each and every crime and rigidly prescribing every step in criminal procedure, we do not in the end serve the cause of justice. This suggestion is based upon the premise that modern doctrines of criminology show that emphasis should be placed upon the criminal and not upon the crime; that instead of making the trial a strictly impersonal proceeding controlled by elaborately prescribed legal rules, trial procedure should be flexible so that every lawbreaker could be analyzed as an individual and judgment pronounced in terms of the strictly personal details of his own case. "Make the punishment fit the criminal and not the crime" is one of the slogans of modern criminologists.

Unquestionably the prescriptions of the Bill of Rights do at many points stand in the way of a modern system of criminal procedure. In this respect it is well to recall once more that the provisions of the Bill of Rights were in many instances designed to prevent serious abuses that had been current in the seventeenth and eighteenth centuries, when governmental authorities possessed entirely too much power and discretion to punish individuals in highly personalized fashion. In its attempt to curb such arbitrary and capricious action by political rulers the emphasis in the Bill of Rights upon impersonality and equality in criminal procedure is readily understandable.

It has been said, "Bills of rights are for the most part reactions against evils of the past rather than promises for the future." [32] It has also been observed that the American bills of rights of the constitutional period

> looked back to England, and set up rights against a King, not the rights of a citizen against his own democratic government. Some parts of the Bills were therefore obsolete when written. Other parts are made up of abstract and ambiguous moral rules and political theories. Still others were the hasty inventions of a period of danger rather than the products of careful political reasoning. They are after all only expressions of good will and faith, getting such power as they have from the current public belief in them.[33]

The difficulty which has just been examined well illustrates the truth in these observations and suggests one disadvantage that may inhere in any attempt to prescribe criminal procedures in a bill of rights. It may be argued that we in the United States have today turned our backs so completely upon the tyranny and arbitrariness of governmental practices of past centuries that we can now afford to relax somewhat the rigid prescriptions of the Bill of Rights and permit

---

[32] William Seagle, in a book review in *The Nation*, September 30, 1944, p. 388.
[33] Leon Whipple, *Our Ancient Liberties* (New York: The H. W. Wilson Company, 1927), pp. 50–51. Reprinted by permission of The H. W. Wilson Company, publishers.

more experimentation in the development of a modern, personalized system of criminal justice. Yet in replying to this argument many careful students of government point immediately to the revival of tyrannical and autocratic governments in other parts of the world. Moreover, many of the states in the American Union have recently shown by their prejudiced and unjust treatment of certain criminals that they are not ready to be freed from rigid constitutional limitations as to procedure.

It may safely be said that this dilemma—the reconciling of man's commendable desire for constitutional protection against injustice in criminal proceedings with the equally commendable desire for a scientific and flexible criminal procedure—is today one of the most important problems of constitutional development which we face.

bibliographic note

Hermann Mannheim's *Criminal Justice and Social Reconstruction* (New York: Oxford University Press, 1946) surveys recent trends of thought and action in the field of criminal justice and suggests a number of specific reforms. Roscoe Pound's *Criminal Justice in America* (New York: Henry Holt and Company, 1930) is a classic treatment of the subject of criminal justice by a noted legal scholar, who has devoted a considerable part of a long and varied career to thought and work in this field. *Crime in the United States*, edited by J. B. Shalloo, *The Annals* of The American Academy of Political and Social Science, CCXVII (September, 1941), is a useful collection of articles dealing with the problem of crime. Lester R. Orfield's *Criminal Procedure from Arrest to Appeal* (New York: New York University Press, 1947) is a detailed and somewhat technical examination of court procedures in criminal cases.

our civil liberties:

rights protected against the states

$\mathscr{S}$TATE and local governments, as well as the national government, can prove to be enemies of civil liberty. Freedom of the press may as readily be endangered by a municipal ordinance curbing house to house distribution of printed matter, or by a discriminatory state law taxing the profits of a newspaper business, as by a national law forbidding newspaper criticism of governmental policies or officials. Accordingly, if civil liberty is to have full meaning in America, protection must operate against three levels of government—national, state, and local.

the threat to civil liberty from state and local governments

There are forty-eight state governments, as compared with one national government, whose activities may offer a threat to civil liberty. Moreover, there are tens of thousands of local political units within the states—counties, cities, towns, and school districts—whose activities constantly threaten to encroach upon the freedom of the individual.

The danger inherent in the activities of state and local governments is particularly serious because of the extent to which these political units wield the police power under our Constitution. It is this power which, more than any other, brings government into close contact with the daily lives of the people. Thus it is the typical police power measure dealing with such matters as public health, safety, or morals that may encroach unduly upon the rights of the individual. The same thing is true as to criminal procedure. As has been seen, civil liberty is extensively concerned with the rights of the person accused of crime. It is the state or the city which, nine times out of ten, accuses an individual of crime, places him on trial in a court, and thereby subjects him to the risk that one of his sacred civil rights may be violated. It is true that the national government, utilizing its constitutional powers, has concerned itself in the present century to a much greater degree than ever before with prescribing law as to crime and with punishing individuals accused of crime. Yet it remains true today that punishment for crime is largely the concern of the states.

When one turns from theoretical analysis of our political system to an actual examination of the record, the hazard to civil liberty in the exercise of state power becomes all too clear. The facts show that through the years encroachments upon specific civil liberties emanating from state and local activity, as compared with federal activity, have been both more numerous and more serious. Unfortunately, local violations of civil liberties often go unchallenged and unnoticed, and accurate and complete statistics concerning such violations are not available. Nonetheless, historical accounts of civil liberty in the United States show a continuous record of violations of civil rights by the states and their subdivisions. Leon Whipple has assembled much data as to specific violations of our liberties throughout the entire history of the United States. A reading of his volume, *The Story of Civil Liberty in the United States,* reveals in striking fashion the extent to which the states have ever offered the gravest threat to freedom of speech and the press, to freedom of religion, to the judicial rights of the defendant in a criminal case, and to our other liberties.[1] This is not to suggest that the national government has an absolutely clean record in these respects. But one significant indication of the greater threat that has inhered in state activity is to be seen in the fact that the great decisions regarding civil liberty made by the United States Supreme Court have, almost without exception, been concerned with state rather than with federal violations. It is true that some authorities are in disagreement on this point. Charles Warren, a well-known historian of the Supreme Court, argues: ". . . it is a solemn fact that, even in times of comparative freedom from emergency or excitement, Congress, or one of its branches, has violated the provisions of the Bill of Rights at least ten times since the year 1867; and at least ten times has the Supreme Court saved the individual against Congressional usurpation of power."[2]

But Warren's assertion has been vigorously challenged by other scholars. Henry W. Edgerton, formerly a Cornell Law School professor, and now a federal judge, has carefully analyzed the ten cases mentioned by Warren and comes to the conclusion that these cases "give small support to the theory that Congress has attacked, and judicial supremacy defended, 'the citizen's liberty.' "[3] And an able American historian, Professor Henry Steele Commager, after examining the evidence assembled by both Warren and Edgerton, con-

---

[1] Leon Whipple, *The Story of Civil Liberty in the United States* (New York: The Vanguard Press, 1927).

[2] Charles Warren, *Congress, the Constitution, and the Supreme Court* (Boston: Little, Brown & Company, 1925), p. 150.

[3] Henry W. Edgerton, "The Incidence of Judicial Control over Congress," *Selected Essays on Constitutional Law* (Chicago: The Foundation Press, Inc., 1938), I, 793, 805.

cludes: "The fact is, of course, that there are very few instances where the Congress has threatened the integrity of the constitutional system or the guarantee of the Bill of Rights." [4]

Be that as it may, there is certainly no difficulty about putting one's finger on a great many Supreme Court decisions involving extremely serious invasions of civil liberty by agencies of state government. A number of these cases have already been examined in the preceding two chapters, cases in which such fundamental liberties as freedom of speech, freedom of the press, and freedom of religion have been gravely threatened. Moreover, there is no difficulty about finding repeated instances in which the principle of a fair and just trial for any man accused of crime has been flagrantly violated by state courts.[5] Thus, there is evidence of a definite need for protection of civil liberty against arbitrary action by state governments.

protection of civil liberty by state constitutions and courts

There is to be found in every one of the state constitutions a bill of rights, patterned, in most instances, after the federal Bill of Rights. These state bills of rights are enforceable by the state courts and are intended to provide the individual with much the same protection against adverse state action that he enjoys against the national government under the federal Constitution. Unfortunately, this intention has not always been fulfilled, for the protection afforded by state bills of rights has sometimes proved inadequate. In the first place, these state bills of rights vary, and some are less complete than others in their enumeration of the full catalogue of generally accepted liberties. For example, five states provide no protection in their constitutions against double jeopardy and three do not guarantee the right of petition.

But a far more serious inadequacy has been the failure of state governmental agencies, particularly the courts, to provide strong enforcement of state constitutional provisions protecting civil liberties. More often than not, these state bills of rights are in themselves perfectly adequate, but a bill of rights that is narrowly interpreted and grudgingly observed by the officials upon whom its implementation depends has a very limited practical value. Practically all of the famous Supreme Court cases involving violations of civil liberties by state governments originated in state courts and were appealed to the Supreme Court because state courts failed to protect the rights of the individual. Time and

---

[4] Henry Steele Commager, *Majority Rule and Minority Rights* (New York: Oxford University Press, 1943), p. 47.
[5] See, for example, *Moore* v. *Dempsey*, 261 U.S. 86 (1923); and the *Scottsboro* cases, *Powell* v. *Alabama*, 287 U.S. 45 (1932), and *Norris* v. *Alabama*, 294 U.S. 587 (1935).

time again the Supreme Court has reversed these state decisions and provided the protection asked for.[6]

early demands for federal protection

action in the First Congress

In the light of this situation it is not surprising that there has been an almost continuous demand throughout American history that civil liberties be "federalized" or "nationalized" so that comprehensive protection by the federal courts under the federal Constitution against all violations, federal or state in character, might be available. This demand originated over a century and a half ago in the First Congress under the new Constitution in 1789. It will be recalled that the federal Bill of Rights was prepared and submitted to the states by the First Congress, and was clearly intended to rectify what many people considered to be a serious defect in the original Constitution as it came from the Philadelphia convention. Among the several proposals that this Congress considered for inclusion in the Bill of Rights was the following: "No State shall infringe the equal rights of conscience, nor the freedom of speech or of the press, nor the right of trial by jury in criminal cases."

This proposal was actually approved by the House of Representatives, but the Senate rejected it. Madison, who had much to do with the adoption by Congress of the Bill of Rights, is said to have regarded this particular item as "the most valuable of the whole list" and to have regretted the failure of Congress to accept it.[7]

Barron v. Baltimore

The federal Bill of Rights was thus rather clearly intended by Congress to provide protection against agencies of the federal government only. However, the language of the first ten amendments is not always as specific on this point as it might be. Although the First Amendment does specifically provide that *Congress* shall make no law . . . ," the other amendments in the Bill of Rights are worded generally and do not mention the national government as the only government affected by the restraints in question. This vagueness of the first ten amendments was seized upon by those who sought to subject the state governments to the limitation of a federal bill of rights and became the basis of the next move in the long attempt to nationalize civil liberties. In 1833, in the famous case of *Barron v. Baltimore*, an attempt was made to persuade the Supreme Court to rule that a certain action by the city of Baltimore violated the Fifth Amendment. This, the Supreme Court, in a decision written by Chief

---

[6] See, for example, *Near v. Minnesota*, 283 U.S. 697 (1931); *Herndon v. Lowry*, 301 U.S. 242 (1937); and *Chambers v. Florida*, 309 U.S. 227 (1940).

[7] Osmond K. Fraenkel, *Our Civil Liberties* (New York: The Viking Press, 1944), p. 46.

Justice John Marshall, definitely refused to do, and it has been clear ever since that agencies of the state governments are not directly affected by the federal Bill of Rights.[8]

protection under the Fourteenth Amendment

There the matter rested until after the Civil War. Then came the Fourteenth Amendment to the Constitution, which in its first section places three separate restraints upon the state governments:

> No State shall make or enforce any law which shall abridge the privileges or immunities of citizens of the United States; nor shall any State deprive any person of life, liberty, or property, without due process of law; nor deny to any person within its jurisdiction the equal protection of the laws.

Much bitter argument has been waged over the meaning of the Fourteenth Amendment. Vigorous charges and countercharges have been made concerning the alleged distortion of its clauses. In spite of the relatively late date at which this amendment was added to the Constitution it has been impossible to determine with complete certainty its meaning at many points. In particular, there has been strong disagreement as to whether the three clauses just quoted were intended to extend the provisions of the federal Bill of Rights against the activities of state governments. Professor Carl B. Swisher, a careful student of American constitutional history, argues persuasively that such was the intention of at least some of the leading men who were active in bringing about the formulation and adoption of the amendment. On the other hand, Professor Charles Fairman, an equally careful scholar, comes to the conclusion that its framers did not intend the amendment to incorporate the Bill of Rights.[9] Whatever the intention of the framers, it fell to the lot of the Supreme Court to decide the final meaning of the amendment. This it did in one of the most amazing series of decisions in its entire history, a series that covered more than half a century, involved several false starts, and witnessed strongly divided courts and more than one reversed judgment.

protection under the Fourteenth Amendment:
the privileges or immunities clause

Let us consider first the privileges or immunities clause of the Fourteenth Amendment. It seems reasonably clear that in the phrase "No State shall make or enforce any law which shall abridge the privileges or immunities of citizens

---

[8] *Barron* v. *Baltimore*, 7 Peters 243 (1833).

[9] Carl B. Swisher, *American Constitutional Development* (Boston: Houghton Mifflin Company, 1943), pp. 330–334; Charles Fairman, "Does the Fourteenth Amendment Incorporate the Bill of Rights? The Original Understanding," *Stanford Law Review*, II (December, 1949), 5.

of the United States," the Constitution provided a basis which, without any undue distortion of the actual words, could have been used for the protection of civil liberties against state governments. It would only have been necessary for the Court to have concluded that the specific guarantees of the Bill of Rights—freedom of speech and press, the right to be free from double jeopardy, and all the rest—were "privileges or immunities" of citizens of the United States. Then a violation of one of these liberties by a state government could have been corrected by the federal courts under this clause. But such an interpretation was not to be followed. In an early series of cases the Supreme Court took the position that the several guarantees of the first eight amendments were not to be considered as privileges or immunities of citizens of the United States, although from the start some of the justices dissented from this conclusion.[10] As recently as 1935 the Supreme Court seemed to be on the verge of abandoning this position. In one case, certain of the justices actually asserted that the rights of assembly and free speech were to be regarded as privileges or immunities of citizens, but in 1940 the Court specifically repudiated this attempt to broaden the meaning of the clause, and there the matter seems to rest.[11] Thus the privileges or immunities clause remains for the most part meaningless and unused. Indeed, it has been called the "stepchild" of the Constitution, a clause "to which the Supreme Court has almost always refused to give effective meaning." [12]

protection under the Fourteenth Amendment: the due process clause

The long attempt to persuade the Supreme Court to use the due process clause of the Fourteenth Amendment to protect civil liberties against state encroachment had a more favorable outcome. The argument advanced was very similar to that used in support of a broad interpretation of the privileges or immunities clause and was to the effect that the word "liberty" in the clause "nor shall any State deprive any person of life, liberty, or property, without due process of law," should be interpreted to include the civil liberties enumerated in the Bill of Rights. So interpreted, the clause could readily be used as a basis for invalidating state action deemed to encroach upon any of these liberties. It is probably true that at the time the due process clause of the Fifth Amendment was placed in the Constitution in 1791 the word "liberty" was considered to mean only freedom from arrest or other physical restraint. But in the light of the probable purposes intended for the Fourteenth Amendment, and in the light of the broadened scope given to many other words and phrases of the Constitu-

[10] *The Slaughter-House Cases,* 16 Wallace 36 (1873) ; *Maxwell* v. *Dow,* 176 U.S. 581 (1900) ; *Twining* v. *New Jersey,* 211 U.S. 78 (1908).

[11] See *Colgate* v. *Harvey,* 296 U.S. 404 (1935) ; *Hague* v. *C.I.O.,* 307 U.S. 496 (1939) ; *Madden* v. *Kentucky,* 309 U.S. 83 (1940) ; and *Edwards* v. *California,* 314 U.S. 160 (1941).

[12] Fraenkel, *Our Civil Liberties,* p. 5.

tion through the years, the extension of the word "liberty" to include civil liberty was not impossible or unreasonable. At first, however, the Supreme Court resisted pressure for such an interpretation as vigorously as it did the pressure for expansion of the privileges or immunities clause. As recently as 1922 the Court continued to adhere to this position.[13] However, there were dissents by individual justices from this position during this period. For example, as early as 1907, Justice John M. Harlan had said in a dissenting opinion:

> I go further and hold that the privileges of free speech and of a free press, belonging to every citizen of the United States, constitute essential parts of every man's liberty, and are protected against violation by that clause of the Fourteenth Amendment forbidding a state to deprive any person of his liberty without due process of law.[14]

In 1923 the Supreme Court began to define "liberty" in the due process clause much more broadly.[15] The change came about rather slowly, and it was not until 1931 that the Court for the first time flatly invalidated a state law on the ground that it violated one of the liberties defined in the federal Bill of Rights and protected against state encroachment by the due process clause of the Fourteenth Amendment. This action was taken in the case of *Near* v. *Minnesota* in which the Court invalidated a state law on the ground that it encroached upon freedom of the press. In spite of the long controversy over such an interpretation of the Fourteenth Amendment, and in spite of the revolutionary character of the Court's change in position, it dismissed the point at issue with the bare statement: "It is no longer open to doubt that the liberty of the press, and of speech, is within the liberty safeguarded by the due process clause of the Fourteenth Amendment from invasion by state action." [16]

Thus nearly three quarters of a century after the Fourteenth Amendment became part of our Constitution its due process of law clause was utilized by the Supreme Court to protect civil liberties against state encroachment. And, as will shortly be seen, *Near* v. *Minnesota* has been followed by subsequent decisions extending such protection to several other specific civil liberties.

protection under the Fourteenth Amendment: the equal protection clause

The third clause of the Fourteenth Amendment, which specifies that no state shall "deny to any person within its jurisdiction the equal protection of the

---

[13] See *Maxwell* v. *Dow*, 176 U.S. 581 (1900) ; *Twining* v. *New Jersey*, 211 U.S. 78 (1908) ; and *Prudential Insurance Co.* v. *Cheek*, 259 U.S. 530 (1922).

[14] *Patterson* v. *Colorado*, 205 U.S. 454, 465 (1907).

[15] *Meyer* v. *Nebraska*, 262 U.S. 390 (1923) ; *Pierce* v. *Society of Sisters*, 268 U.S. 510 (1925) ; and *Gitlow* v. *New York*, 268 U.S. 652, 666 (1925).

[16] *Near* v. *Minnesota*, 283 U.S. 697, 707 (1931).

laws," was also to serve as a basis for the nationalizing of civil liberty. As has been seen, this was the first clause in the Constitution to emphasize expressly the doctrine of the equality of all men under the law. Moreover, it was definitely intended by its sponsors to prohibit any discrimination in state policies based upon considerations of race or color. It is true that the Supreme Court has, at times, seemed more interested in using this clause to strike down liberal social legislation because of alleged discrimination against property or business interests than it has in using it to prevent discrimination against racial or national groups. Nonetheless, as early as 1880 the Court used it to protect Negroes against discriminatory state legislation. In particular, the equal protection of the laws clause has been used to prevent discrimination against Negroes in respect to the right to vote, the right to be tried by juries from which members of their race have not been systematically excluded, and the right to hold property.[17] Moreover, the Court has recently invalidated California legislation discriminating against persons of Japanese descent in regard to the right to acquire agricultural land and the right to engage in commercial fishing. This legislation was held to deny such persons equal protection of the laws. But in other respects the Court has shown an unfortunate reluctance to enforce the equal protection clause against certain racial discriminations. There has been particular criticism of its numerous decisions upholding state laws requiring segregation of the races in various public places.[18]

In addition to the guarantee this clause affords against discriminations based upon race or nationality, it can and does protect the rights of individuals against other types of discrimination. For example, in 1942 the Supreme Court invalidated an Oklahoma statute providing for the sterilization of habitual criminals. There is perhaps nothing basically wrong about a public policy that prevents persons with proved biological weaknesses of a criminal character from reproducing their kind, but it is clear that government should be very certain of its case before it forcibly deprives any person of this natural power and right. The Supreme Court concluded that the Oklahoma law was an ill-considered one which drew an illogical and unscientific line between criminals who were to be sterilized and those who were not. Accordingly the law was held to deny persons affected by it their right to equal protection of the laws.[19]

---

[17] *Strauder* v. *West Virginia*, 100 U.S. 303 (1880); *Norris* v. *Alabama*, 294 U.S. 587 (1935); *Hill* v. *Texas*, 316 U.S. 400 (1942); *Nixon* v. *Herndon*, 273 U.S. 536 (1927); *Smith* v. *Allwright*, 321 U.S. 649 (1944); *Buchanan* v. *Warley*, 245 U.S. 60 (1917); *Shelley* v. *Kraemer*, 334 U.S. 1 (1948); *Hurd* v. *Hodge*, 334 U.S. 24 (1948). See John P. Frank and Robert F. Munro, "The Original Understanding of 'Equal Protection of the Laws,'" *Columbia Law Review*, L (February, 1950), p. 131.

[18] *Plessy* v. *Ferguson*, 163 U.S. 537 (1896) and subsequent cases. The alien-land law case is *Oyama* v. *California*, 332 U.S. 633 (1948); and the commercial fisheries case is *Takahashi* v. *Fish and Game Commission*, 334 U.S. 410 (1948).

[19] *Skinner* v. *Oklahoma*, 316 U.S. 535 (1942).

what civil liberties does the Fourteenth Amendment protect?

not all of the Bill of Rights encompassed by the Fourteenth Amendment

Which are the specific guarantees of the federal Bill of Rights that are now protected against violation by the states under the Fourteenth Amendment? It might have been supposed at the time of the decision in *Near* v. *Minnesota* that all of the liberties enumerated in the first eight amendments were henceforth to be safeguarded from invasion by state action. Six years after the *Near* case, the Court, speaking through Justice Benjamin N. Cardozo, noted this assumption:—"Whatever would be a violation of the original bill of rights (Amendments 1 to 8) if done by the federal government is now equally unlawful by force of the Fourteenth Amendment if done by a state"—but tersely rejected it with the words, "There is no such general rule." And the Court went on to state:

> The line of division may seem to be wavering and broken if there is a hasty catalogue of the cases on the one side and the other. Reflection and analysis will induce a different view. There emerges the perception of a rationalizing principle which gives to discrete instances a proper order and coherence. [Certain of the liberties guaranteed in the federal Bill of Rights] . . . are not of the very essence of a scheme of ordered liberty. To abolish them is not to violate a "principle of justice so rooted in the traditions and conscience of our people to be ranked as fundamental." . . . Few would be so narrow or provincial as to maintain that a fair and enlightened system of justice would be impossible without them. . . .
>
> We reach a different plane of social and moral values when we pass to the privileges and immunities that have been taken over . . . and brought within the Fourteenth Amendment by a process of absorption. . . . the process of absorption has had its source in the belief that neither liberty nor justice would exist if they were sacrificed. . . . [The question in each case must be: Is the treatment of the individual] to which the statute has subjected him a hardship so acute and shocking that our polity will not endure it? Does it violate those "fundamental principles of liberty and justice which lie at the base of all our civil and political institutions?" [20]

civil rights protected by the Fourteenth Amendment

With this philosophy of the Court in mind, the liberties which have been carried over from the Bill of Rights by the Fourteenth Amendment and protected against state encroachment may be noted. In the first place, every one of the several guarantees of the First Amendment has now been the subject of a Supreme Court decision providing protection against state interference. In numerous cases, freedom of religion, freedom of speech and press, the right of assembly, and the right of petition have been so protected and definitely included in the list

---

[20] *Palko* v. *Connecticut*, 302 U.S. 319, 325–328 (1937).

of "fundamental" rights.[21] Second, the guarantee of the Fifth Amendment that private property shall not be taken for public use without just compensation has often been invoked against state action by means of the due process clause of the Fourteenth Amendment, although this guarantee is perhaps to be regarded as dealing with a property right rather than a civil liberty.[22] Third, the guarantee of the Sixth Amendment that the accused in a criminal case shall have the assistance of counsel for his defense has been protected against state action. But although the Court so protected this guarantee in one case, later action casts some doubt upon the extent to which the Court regards this right as fundamental.[23] Fourth, the guarantee of the Fourth Amendment against unreasonable searches and seizures has been held by the Court to be protected against state action. But the value of this holding is dubious in view of the Court's attitude that the Fourteenth Amendment does not forbid the admission in a state court of evidence obtained by an unreasonable search and seizure. In other words, the unreasonable search, itself, is forbidden, but evidence obtained by such a search may nonetheless be introduced in court.[23a]

civil rights not protected by the Fourteenth Amendment

The Supreme Court has clearly indicated that a number of the specific guarantees of the federal Bill of Rights are not protected by the Fourteenth Amendment against state encroachment. These include freedom from self-incrimination, the right to a grand jury hearing before indictment, and even the right to trial by jury itself both in civil and in criminal cases.[24] As to this latter right, the Court has said: "Trial by jury may be modified by a state or abolished altogether."

doubtful rights under the Fourteenth Amendment

There are several guarantees in the Bill of Rights which the Supreme Court has not yet clearly placed in either of the categories discussed in the preceding two paragraphs. This is true of such rights as freedom from excessive bail, freedom from cruel and unusual punishment, and freedom from double jeopardy. In determining the status of one of these rights, the Court will be influenced in part by the facts of the case raising the constitutional issue. In the following words the Court has indicated the extent to which it is influenced in these cases by the exact degree of interference with fundamental rights:

---

[21] See the many cases dealing with these rights which are discussed in pp. 515–531.

[22] *C. B. & Q. R. R. Co.* v. *Chicago,* 166 U.S. 226 (1897), and subsequent cases.

[23] *Powell* v. *Alabama,* 287 U.S. 45 (1932); *Betts* v. *Brady,* 316 U.S. 455 (1942).

[23a] *Wolf* v. *Colorado,* 338 U.S. 25 (1949).

[24] *Twining* v. *New Jersey,* 211 U.S. 78 (1908); *Hurtado* v. *California,* 110 U.S. 516 (1884); *Walker* v. *Sauvinet,* 92 U.S. 90 (1876); *Maxwell* v. *Dow,* 176 U.S. 581 (1900); *Adamson* v. *California,* 332 U.S. 46 (1947).

The . . . [due process clause of the Fourteenth Amendment] formulates a concept less rigid and more fluid than those envisaged in other specific and particular provisions of the Bill of Rights. Its application is less a matter of rule. Asserted denial is to be tested by an appraisal of the totality of facts in a given case. That which may, in one setting, constitute a denial of fundamental fairness, shocking to the universal sense of justice, may, in other circumstances, and in the light of other considerations, fall short of such denial.[25]

Further doubt exists as to the length to which the nationalization of civil rights has been carried under the Fourteenth Amendment because of the divided votes by which the Supreme Court has decided many cases in this area. For example, in 1947, in *Adamson* v. *California* the Court by a five-to-four vote refused to abandon the forty-year-old holding of *Twining* v. *New Jersey* [26] that the Fourteenth Amendment does not compel the states to grant persons accused of crime freedom from self-incrimination. The majority opinion asserts: "For a state to require testimony from an accused is not necessarily a breach of a state's obligation to give a fair trial." [27] And in a separate concurring opinion Justice Felix Frankfurter, speaking with approval of the decision in the *Twining* case, says: "The notion that the Fourteenth Amendment was a covert way of imposing upon the States all the rules which it seemed important to Eighteenth Century statesmen to write into the Federal Amendments was rejected by judges who were themselves witnesses of the process by which the Fourteenth Amendment became part of the Constitution." [28]

The position of the majority in the *Adamson* case is vigorously assailed by the four dissenting justices. Justice Hugo L. Black asserts: "I would follow what I believe was the original purpose of the Fourteenth Amendment—to extend to all the people of the nation the complete protection of the Bill of Rights. To hold that this Court can determine what, if any, provisions of the Bill of Rights will be enforced, and if so to what degree, is to frustrate the great design of a written Constitution." And he virtually accuses the majority of considering "the Bill of Rights to be an outworn 18th Century 'strait jacket.' " [29]

Thus the matter stands. Where all earlier attempts failed, the due process clause of the Fourteenth Amendment finally became the instrumentality by which civil liberties gained the protection of the federal courts under the federal Constitution against state action. It was perhaps after all not so unfortunate that the Supreme Court resisted all attempts to persuade it to utilize the privileges or

---

[25] *Betts* v. *Brady*, 316 U.S. 455, 462 (1942).
[26] *Twining* v. *New Jersey*, 211 U.S. 78 (1908).
[27] *Adamson* v. *California*, 332 U.S. 46, 54 (1947).
[28] *Ibid.*, pp. 63–64.
[29] *Ibid.*, p. 89.

immunities clause of the Fourteenth Amendment to achieve this "nationalization" of civil liberties. Whereas the privileges or immunities clause, however interpreted, could offer protection only to "citizens of the United States," the
wording of the due process clause makes it possible to use it to safeguard the
liberties of all "persons." Aliens, as well as citizens, may thus breathe the pure
air of freedom under its protecting force.

review by the Supreme Court of state criminal cases

It would be a mistake to give the impression that the Supreme Court today engages in any continuous business of setting aside state laws interfering with such
rights as freedom of speech, or that it intervenes regularly in state criminal
cases. As to the latter, the Court is still properly reluctant to review the proceedings in state criminal cases, and always insists that the appellant exhaust all of
his remedies in the state courts before invoking the due process clause of the
Fourteenth Amendment as a means of securing possible help from the federal
courts. It is still true that the overwhelming majority of all state criminal cases,
even where there are serious charges of miscarriage of justice, are finally disposed of by the appellate courts of the states. Nonetheless, the possibility of
federal intervention in such cases must now always be taken into account, and
there can be little doubt that this has encouraged the states to take greater precautions in guaranteeing a fair trial to every defendant in a criminal case.

the Supreme Court and the Sacco-Vanzetti case

The attitude of the Supreme Court of the United States toward the two most
famous state criminal cases of modern times provides a good illustration of
the contrast between policy before 1931 and policy after that year. The first of
these two cases concerned Sacco and Vanzetti, two Italian anarchists who
were tried for murder in the Massachusetts courts in the nineteen twenties. The
second is the *Scottsboro* cases in which nine Negroes were tried for the crime of
rape in the Alabama courts in the nineteen thirties. Both cases were ordinary
criminal proceedings of the kind that occur in the state courts almost continuously. But in both cases there were serious charges that justice had miscarried,
and many impartial observers were impressed by these charges. In the *Sacco-
Vanzetti* case, after all efforts to obtain relief from the appellate courts and the
administrative agencies of Massachusetts had failed, an attempt was made to
persuade the Supreme Court of the United States to intervene on the ground that
the execution of the two condemned men would deprive them of their lives without due process of law contrary to the Fourteenth Amendment. Various
technicalities relating to the alleged miscarriage of justice in the case were
suggested to justices of the Supreme Court as possible grounds for holding that

the Fourteenth Amendment had been violated, but the Court rejected all of these contentions and refused even to accept jurisdiction and review the case. At that time this action was in line with the Court's traditions in this situation and it would have been rather unusual had the Court intervened. Thus Sacco and Vanzetti went to their deaths without benefit of any examination or review of their case by a federal court.

the Supreme Court and the Scottsboro cases

By the time of the *Scottsboro* cases the traditions had changed, and the Supreme Court twice intervened in this case to set aside verdicts of guilty and to order the state of Alabama to grant the men new trials. It is true that in neither instance did the Supreme Court intervene on the broad basis of a general and fundamental miscarriage of justice in the Alabama courts. Instead, in one instance the intervention was based on the specific allegation that Alabama had failed to provide the accused men with adequate legal counsel for their defense, and in the other instance that the state had systematically excluded Negroes from the juries in the case.[30] Nonetheless, in the end the Court twice compelled the state of Alabama to reconsider criminal proceedings that had shocked the sense of justice of impartial observers all over the nation. The defendants were finally given a fair trial, much less severe sentences were pronounced, and no Negro was ever executed for the crime—an outcome that had seemed imminent when the Supreme Court first intervened. This is not to minimize the importance of the technical grounds upon which the Court actually intervened in the case, or to say that in any state criminal case where there has been a shocking failure of justice the Supreme Court will always find some such ground upon which to intervene in order to correct the basic injustice in the state proceedings. And yet it seems unlikely that ever again will any state criminal case, which receives as much national attention as did the *Sacco-Vanzetti* case or the *Scottsboro* cases and in which serious charges of injustice are widely made, be finally disposed of without some sort of review by the United States Supreme Court.

criticism of the nationalization of civil liberty protection

In view of the seeming salutary effect of the increasing use of the Fourteenth Amendment by the Supreme Court to protect civil liberties, against violations by state governments, it is perhaps surprising that this development has not been unanimously approved. But some people have claimed to see in this supervision of state legislative policy and criminal procedure by the federal courts a further and dangerous tendency toward political centralization in the United States.

---

[30] *Powell* v. *Alabama,* 287 U.S. 45 (1932); *Norris* v. *Alabama,* 294 U.S. 587 (1935).

Writing at a time when the Supreme Court was first showing signs that a change in constitutional interpretation in this area was impending, such a respected scholar as Charles Warren deplored the new tendency. His position is quite typical of the critics of this development. He vigorously objects to the resulting interference with states' rights, refers to "the progress we have made away from the principles of government believed in by the framers of the Constitution," and asks, with obvious rhetorical intent, the following question: "In the change of conditions from the year 1868, is the 'liberty' of the citizen to be freed from State restraint, by National interposition, of greater or less importance than the 'liberty' of the State to control its own affairs and to regulate its own welfare and good order, under its own State Constitution as construed by its own State Courts?" [31]

Somewhat the same criticism has been heard from certain Supreme Court justices themselves. In some of the civil rights cases that have divided the nine justices, the argument has been heard that the Court must not usurp the power or the responsibility of the states to run their criminal courts in their own way, short only of flagrantly unjust results. Justice Frankfurter has said in a civil rights case, "Great tolerance toward a State's conduct is demanded of this Court." [32]

It is true that the new constitutional development to be seen in the decisions in the *Near* case and its successors marks a considerable shift in the balance of federal and state power and a substantial increase in centralized government. To be sure, it is more a matter of increased centralization in the operation of a curb upon governmental power than it is centralization of governmental power itself. But the result is much the same, for even though the transfer of power is from state court to federal court, rather than from state legislature to Congress, federal power is thereby enhanced. In other words, this change reveals that our recent constitutional development has been marked not only by increased centralization in the use of the "power" aspects of the Constitution but also by increased centralization in the implementation of its restraining or prohibitory aspects.

In answer to the criticism advanced by Mr. Warren it may properly be argued that the change in constitutional interpretation to which he objects has come about very slowly and only as the result of powerful and prolonged pressure from the American people. The fact is undeniable that the people in almost all periods of our history have had greater respect for and confidence in the federal Constitution and federal courts than they have had in state constitutions and state courts. It is not surprising, then, that there should have been a persistent demand that the federal courts protect civil liberties against state encroachment.

[31] Charles Warren, "The New 'Liberty' under the Fourteenth Amendment," in *Selected Essays on Constitutional Law* (Chicago: The Foundation Press, Inc., 1938), II, 237, 265.
[32] *Louisiana ex rel. Francis* v. *Resweber*, 329 U.S. 459, 470 (1947).

Certainly, the Supreme Court did not invite the change. Instead, it resisted it over a long period of years in the face of growing popular pressure for it, and even now shows no desire to make extensive use of its power. Again and again in its recent decisions the Court has indicated that it has no intention of opening the floodgates to the torrent of appeals that might be made from any and every criminal case in the state courts or from the application of run-of-the-mill police power laws where some person fancies that his rights are being encroached upon. It seems fair to say that the Court has made a modest though effective use of its new power and that the effect upon the state of our civil liberties, bearing in mind the merits of local self-government, has been highly salutary.

bibliographic note

A number of legal scholars have given attention to the problem of federal protection of civil rights against encroachment by state governments and private persons. Although written nearly half a century ago, Horace E. Flack's *The Adoption of the Fourteenth Amendment* (Baltimore: The Johns Hopkins Press, 1908) provides a useful examination of the motives and intentions that lay behind the adoption of the Fourteenth Amendment. John H. Leek's article, "Due Process: Fifth and Fourteenth Amendments," *Political Science Quarterly*, LX (June, 1945), 188, is a good brief review of the process by which the "nationalization" of certain civil rights has been achieved under the Fourteenth Amendment. In two recent articles in the *Stanford Law Review* (II [December, 1949], 5, 140), "Does the Fourteenth Amendment Incorporate the Bill of Rights? The Original Understanding" by Charles Fairman, and "Does the Fourteenth Amendment Incorporate the Bill of Rights? The Judicial Interpretation" by Stanley Morrison, the conclusion is reached that the Fourteenth Amendment was not intended to serve as a means of protecting against state encroachment all of the liberties enumerated in the Bill of Rights. On the other hand, an article by John P. Frank and Robert F. Munro entitled, "The Original Understanding of 'Equal Protection of the Laws,'" *Columbia Law Review*, L (February, 1950), 131, reaches the conclusion that the equal protection clause of the Fourteenth Amendment was intended to serve as a broad basis for the protection of certain personal rights, particularly against racial discrimination.

federal protection of civil rights

HAT is the state of our civil liberties in America? To this question the President's Committee on Civil Rights replied: "The record is neither as black as our detractors paint it, nor as white as people of good will would like it to be." [1] And it added: "There is a great deal [in the record]; enough, we believe to warrant our conviction that no nation in history has ever offered more hope of the final realization of the ultimate ideal of freedom and equality than has ours. In no other nation have so many people come as close to this ideal as in America." But it was also forced to observe: "From our work as a Committee, we have learned much that has shocked us, and much that has made us feel ashamed." And again:

> The pervasive gap between our aims and what we actually do is creating a kind of moral dry rot which eats away at the emotional and rational bases of democratic beliefs. There are times when the difference between what we preach about civil rights and what we practice is shockingly illustrated by individual outrages. There are times when the whole structure of our ideology is made ridiculous by individual instances. And there are certain continuing, quiet, omnipresent practices which do irreparable damage to our beliefs. [2]

Clearly the condition of civil liberty in America today leaves much to be desired. From the facts of the Supreme Court cases that have been examined, it is evident that inequality, injustice, suppression, opportunity denied, and even persecution are all too common. Of course, one must avoid the standard of perfectionism and maintain a relative point of view. Conditions might be worse. Compared with the absence of freedom in many foreign lands, compared even with the inadequacies of our own past history, the present high state of our civil liberties is without precedent. But the struggle for liberty is never ending, can

---

[1] *To Secure These Rights* (Washington: Government Printing Office, 1947), p. 13.
[2] *Ibid.*, pp. 17, 10, 139–140.

never result in total victory. The room for improvement is much too obvious, much too extensive, to justify any relaxation in the constant battle for liberty. What is wrong? From what directions come the threats to our liberty? What can be done to meet these threats?

The chief threats seem to be two in number. One is from organized government—federal, state, and local; the other is from private individuals and groups of individuals. Everyone is familiar with the first threat; the second has not been sufficiently recognized. Let us consider them in order.

the threat to civil liberty from government: wartime violations

The threat from government cannot be minimized. It was this threat particularly that the guarantees of the Constitution were designed to meet. Moreover, to a high degree this design has been fulfilled in practice. In the field of federal government perhaps the most serious threat to freedom is that which has emanated from governmental activity *in wartime.*

governmental threats of the Civil War period

The American Civil War was the first war following the adoption of our present Constitution that presented any serious question of the violation of civil liberties by the government. Curiously enough, virtually all of the acts of government during the Civil War period which were alleged to endanger civil liberties were acts of the executive or military agencies under the leadership of President Lincoln. Congress passed absolutely no laws restricting freedom of speech, of the press, or of assembly. No espionage or sedition laws were enacted.[3] Congress did pass two measures strengthening the law dealing with treason and increasing the penalty for conspiracy against the government, but these measures were not vigorously enforced. Instead, most of the governmental activity that was said to threaten civil liberty was undertaken by the President, at first, at least, upon his own responsibility. In September, 1862, Lincoln issued an executive proclamation, without any specific legislative authorization, under which persons who discouraged men from enlisting, who resisted the draft, or who engaged in other disloyal practices were subjected to martial law, and provided for their trial by military commission. Moreover, the privilege of the writ of habeas corpus was suspended. The record reveals that in pursuance of this policy thousands of persons were tried by military tribunals and many were imprisoned. Likewise, newspapers in many of the largest cities of the country were suppressed by means of military orders.

Lincoln himself was well aware of the threat to freedom inherent in his

---

[3] Robert E. Cushman, "Civil Liberty after the War," *American Political Science Review,* XXXVIII (February, 1944), 1, 5.

policies, but in defense of his acts he offered the old rationalization of the end justifying the means. He wrote in a letter:

> Was it possible to lose the nation and yet preserve the Constitution? By general law, life and limb must be protected, yet often a limb must be amputated to save a life; but a life is never wisely given to save a limb. I felt that measures otherwise unconstitutional might become lawful by becoming indispensable to the preservation of the Constitution through the preservation of the nation. Right or wrong. I assume this ground, and now avow it.[4]

One can agree completely with the wisdom and expediency of Lincoln's policy; yet it is well to remember that every public officer who encroaches upon civil liberty undoubtedly justifies his action in his own mind by some similar reasoning. The sad truth of the matter is that war is not a happy time for those who worship freedom above authority. War necessitates a greatly increased exercise of governmental powers, and inevitably certain liberties of the individual must give way. Indeed, in time of war the nation does not hesitate to ask of the individual that he make the supreme sacrifice and give his life, if necessary, in the nation's service.

the record of World War I

World War I witnessed even more serious threats to civil liberty from government in the United States. This time state governments joined the national government in activities which threatened the individual's freedom. Congress and the state legislatures vied with each other in passing espionage, sedition, and similar laws that seriously restricted freedom of speech and press and other liberties. According to a summary prepared by Professor Robert E. Cushman, nearly five thousand persons were prosecuted under these laws, and nearly two thousand were convicted and sent to prison, some for terms of as much as thirty years.[5] Moreover, this lessening of civil liberty occurred even though at no time during that war was there any immediate danger to the safety of our institutions, such as had existed during the Civil War.

But the picture can be painted too darkly. It is true that in both the Civil War and World War I governmental policy at times became somewhat hysterical, and individuals found their rights curtailed in ways which were not always necessary to the successful pursuance of the war program. Yet in neither war was there any general censorship of speech or press. The regular governmental processes were for the most part preserved, and there was ample opportunity for criticism of the government in the halls of Congress, in the press, and on the

---

[4] *Complete Works of Abraham Lincoln* (John G. Nicolay and John Hay, eds.; New York: Lamb Publishing Co., 1905), x, 66.
[5] Cushman, "Civil Liberty after the War," p. 6.

street corner. In World War I persons accused of endangering the safety of the nation were given open trials in the regular courts. If the prison sentences meted out were often unduly severe in the light of the offenses committed, the President took the edge off the harsh program by granting pardons soon after the war was over.

the record of World War II

The record in World War II was on the whole better than that in the first, showing that, even in a period of modern "total" warfare, interference with the individual's liberties can be kept at a minimum. In this war many factors contributed to the more satisfactory record. The state governments wisely refrained from attempting to curb subversive conduct and for the most part left the problem to be dealt with uniformly by the national government. It is true that Congress, in the Alien Registration Act of 1940 and in certain other statutes, showed a tendency to legislate in such drastic terms with respect to subversive conduct as to raise serious questions about the preservation of civil liberties. Fortunately, the administrative agencies of the national government, particularly the Department of Justice, pursued very moderate policies in enforcing these laws. As a result, there was an almost complete absence of the excesses of the earlier war, when thousands of prosecutions were brought in doubtful or harmless cases.[6]

The record was not perfect. There was a certain amount of unfortunate "Red baiting" within governmental agencies, some extremists in the government urged that naturalized German-Americans be deprived of their citizenship, and the government did not succeed in preventing discrimination against Negroes and other minority groups either in the armed services or in defense industries. Here, too, however, the record was certainly no worse than it had been in previous wars, and in certain respects notable improvements were made. For example, the President issued an executive order forbidding racial discrimination in the government services and in private industries with which the government had defense contracts. A Fair Employment Practices Commission was set up by executive order to enforce the President's policy, and although its achievements were limited, it represented a step in the right direction.

evacuation of the Japanese-Americans from the West Coast

Perhaps the most serious governmental threat to civil liberty in World War II resulted from the drastic treatment meted out to more than one hundred thousand persons of Japanese descent who were living in West Coast areas at the start of the war. Indeed, this episode has been called "our worst wartime mistake," and a scholarly volume on the subject bears the title *Americans*

---

[6] Robert E. Cushman, "Civil Liberties," *American Political Science Review*, XXXVII (February, 1943), 49.

Betrayed.[7] The large majority of the persons affected were native-born Americans, and their complete loyalty to this country was above suspicion. Nonetheless, the presence of so many persons of Japanese descent in an area that might very well have been subject to invasion after the Pearl Harbor disaster seemed to the military authorities to constitute a real hazard. Accordingly, utilizing authority conferred upon it by act of Congress and presidential order, the Army issued a series of restrictions which severely curtailed the freedom of these people. A curfew order compelling all persons of Japanese ancestry in the West Coast area to remain in their homes from 8 P.M. to 6 A.M. was followed by later orders excluding them from this area altogether and compelling them to reside, at least temporarily, in relocation centers while loyal individuals were winnowed out and allowed to take up residence in other parts of the country.

The Supreme Court upheld the constitutionality of the curfew policy and the order of exclusion from the Pacific area.[8] But the Court was obviously reluctant to sanction such an extreme invasion of the liberty of American citizens. In the decision on the exclusion program Justice Black said: "Compulsory exclusion of large groups of citizens from their homes, except under circumstances of direst emergency and peril, is inconsistent with our basic governmental institutions. But when under conditions of modern warfare our shores are threatened by hostile forces, the power to protect must be commensurate with the threatened danger."[9] Three justices dissented from this decision.

The Court drew the line at the detention camp program, holding that such an extreme measure as applied to persons of unquestioned loyalty was unconstitutional, even though the program had been administered with considerable fairness and intelligence by a War Relocation Authority. The Court felt that the Army and the WRA had exceeded the authority granted to them by statute and executive order, and that accordingly it was their action that was improper and not that of Congress or the President.[10]

the threat to civil liberty from government: peacetime violations

Although the threat to civil liberty offered by government has been most serious in time of war, the peacetime record is far from clean. Large numbers of American citizens are still being denied the right to vote by state laws and regulations in direct violation of the letter and spirit of the constitutional provi-

---

[7] Eugene V. Rostow, "Our Worst Wartime Mistake," *Harper's Magazine*, XCCI (September, 1945), 193; Morton Grodzins, *Americans Betrayed* (Chicago: The University of Chicago Press, 1949).

[8] *Hirabayashi* v. *United States*, 320 U.S. 81 (1943); *Korematsu* v. *United States*, 323 U.S. 214 (1944).

[9] *Korematsu* v. *United States*, 323 U.S. 214, 219–220 (1944).

[10] *Ex parte Endo*, 323 U.S. 283 (1944).

sions guaranteeing this great freedom. Throughout the states criminal justice still has its weak moments. There are still too many cases in which accused persons are subjected to arbitrary arrest and imprisonment. Moreover, still too common is the situation in which local ordinances are invoked against minority groups in such a way as to interfere with religious freedom or freedom of speech and press.

the civil rights of government employees

These illustrations by no means exhaust the list of peacetime government practices which threaten civil liberty. For example, increasing concern has recently been shown about the way in which the rights of government employees are sometimes curtailed. Various state and federal restrictive regulations can be cited which endanger the freedom of speech of certain types of government workers and their right to engage in political activity. The Hatch Act of 1940, which forbids most of the employees in the executive branch of the federal government to take "any active part in political management or in political campaigns," is an instance of this type of restriction. The penalty is dismissal from the federal service and a ban on re-employment. However, this legislation has its good side as well, for it is intended, at least in part, to protect government employees from making forced contributions to political parties or from other unwilling involvements in politics. Indeed, the members of the Supreme Court divided four-to-three on the issue of the constitutionality of the Hatch Act's ban on political activity. The majority upheld the ban as a reasonable means of promoting the efficiency of the public service. But in a dissenting opinion Justice Black says: "I think the Constitution prohibits legislation which prevents millions of citizens from contributing their arguments, complaints, and suggestions to the political debates which are the essence of our democracy . . ." [11]

An even more serious threat to the civil rights of government employees is that offered by the "loyalty" tests which have been developed since the close of World War II. Chief among these is the one to which more than two million federal employees (or applicants for federal jobs) were subjected under an executive order issued by President Truman in 1947. This federal test was designed to weed out of the federal service all individuals, where "on all the evidence, reasonable grounds exist for the belief that the person involved is disloyal to the Government of the United States." Early in 1949 the administering of the test had been largely completed, and on the whole it appeared to have been fairly conducted. Nonetheless, it was argued that the test set a dangerous procedural precedent in that persons accused of disloyalty were not told the source of the accusations against them nor allowed to confront their accusers,

---

[11] *United Public Workers of America* v. *Mitchell*, 330 U.S. 75, 111 (1947). See also *Oklahoma* v. *United States Civil Service Commission*, 330 U.S. 127 (1947).

and were thereby denied the traditional opportunity available to accused persons to make an adequate defense. Likewise the test was attacked on the ground that insofar as the disloyalty of a person was determined by his membership in allegedly subversive organizations, it made use of the standard of guilt by association as opposed to the Anglo-American traditional standard of personal guilt. It was also argued that such a test tends inevitably to have an intimidating effect upon public employees in that they gain the impression that they should avoid any conduct—and even thought—which may be regarded as radical or controversial.

the House Un-American Activities Committee

In the minds of many people the most serious threat to civil liberty offered by the federal government since 1939 is to be found in the work of the House Un-American Activities Committee. This committee was given the assignment of making a special investigation of subversive activity in the United States with a view to recommending new legislation to Congress. However, it was made a permanent House committee in 1945 and it has seemed more interested in maintaining a continuing check on subversive activity through the holding of sensational hearings than it has in recommending the enactment of remedial laws. The committee's critics have argued that it has used unfair procedural methods in the treatment of its witnesses and other persons affected by its hearings, and also that it offers a serious threat to freedom of thought and expression by emphasizing loyalty or conformity to a set of narrowly defined, conservative principles of "Americanism." The committee's friends have tended to minimize the procedural shortcomings of the committee's work, and to argue that since we are living in revolutionary times we must necessarily try to evaluate the threat of subversive activity in our land and take steps to protect the established order against such activity. Moreover, it is argued that the committee has unearthed enough serious information verifying the existence of subversive activity to outweigh its seeming concern at times with activities regarded by many people as harmless.

the Smith and McCarran Acts

Another disturbing threat to freedom of thought and political activity is found by many people in the Smith Act and the McCarran Act. The former, passed by Congress in 1940 (and also known as the Alien Registration Act), makes it a federal crime knowingly or willfully to advocate or teach the overthrow of government by force or violence, or to help organize or join a group or society that so advocates the overthrow of government.[12] In 1949 eleven top leaders of the Communist party were convicted in a federal court for violation of the act. In August, 1950, the Court of Appeals of the Second Circuit affirmed this conviction

---

[12] 54 Stat. 670.

and also upheld the constitutionality of the Smith Act.[13] The Supreme Court has agreed to review the case.

The McCarran Act (also known as the Internal Security Act) was passed by Congress late in 1950 over President Truman's veto. The act is a long and complex one, and it is difficult to tell which of its provisions may prove most significant as the law is interpreted and enforced. Although portions of the act apply to all "totalitarians," it is aimed primarily at Communists. It requires all Communist and Communist-front organizations, and the individual members of such groups, to register with the federal government. A Subversive Activities Control Board is created to decide what organizations are Communist or Communist fronts. In addition to the registration requirement, all members of such organizations are forbidden to receive passports or to work for the government or in any defense plant. The act also provides for the internment of Communists in time of emergency and it places severe immigration and naturalization restrictions upon Communists.

Those who defend the Smith and McCarran Acts say that they either are limited to the outlawing of conduct that clearly and presently endangers the well-being of the American state, or merely require American Communists to identify themselves so that the people may better evaluate their propaganda. Those opposed to these laws assert that they contain many vague passages that may serve as instruments of suppression in the hands of irresponsible administrators, and that, however limited their scope may prove to be, they create an atmosphere of thought control which cannot help do damage to the American traditions of free expression and political activity. The opponents of these laws also argue that the real current threat to American democracy is an external one offered by the Soviet Union and that to meet this threat we must use the traditional methods of diplomacy and military preparedness. The danger that the Communist party of the United States will corrupt the American people through propaganda is said to be so slight as not to warrant the curtailment of political thought and activity which the two Acts are bringing about.

the threat to civil liberty from private sources

It is much more difficult to prepare a balance sheet showing the contemporary state of civil liberty, so far as interferences by private persons and organizations are concerned, than it is to enumerate governmental encroachments upon civil rights. All too frequently the first type of interference escapes notice altogether, or at least is not widely publicized. On the other hand, what government does is out in the open, and in a democratic society governmental threats to civil liberty are usually quickly recognized and promptly become the subject of public debate and controversy. A newspaper publisher may quietly go about

---

[13] *United States* v. *Dennis*, 183 F. 2d 201 (1950).

the business of suppressing competition, thus endangering freedom of the press, without attracting much notice. But let a city council enact an ordinance that threatens free and open circulation of newspapers, say by restraining their sale on public streets, and a hue and cry is certain to go up immediately that a fundamental civil liberty is being encroached upon.

private encroachments upon the rights of racial minorities

Perhaps the most widespread and serious denial of liberty in the United States today is to be seen in the discriminatory treatment of Negroes and other racial minorities. Admittedly, these minorities have suffered much, so far as loss of fundamental freedoms is concerned, at the hands of government. The Negro has frequently been kept from the ballot box on Election Day by law. There are still seventeen states which through the operation of segregation laws exclude the Negro from the main streams of society. But for every Negro who is kept from voting by means of legal restraints there is at least one other Negro who is prevented from voting through acts of intimidation by private persons. And it is a clearly established fact that in the thirty-one states that have no segregation laws the Negro is still far from free to associate with other men in places of business, the labor union, the church, the theater, the school, or wherever men gather.

the private threat to freedom of the press

A second illustration of the nongovernmental threat to civil rights may be seen in the present state of freedom of the press in the United States. It seems fair to assert that the threat to this fundamental freedom which results from private action is at least as great as the threat from government. We have been slow to recognize the truth of this assertion because of the extent to which discussions of freedom of the press have almost always emphasized possible or alleged encroachments by governmental agencies. Where there has been recognition of the danger to a free press inherent in private activity, attention has usually been concentrated upon the restraining influence of large advertisers or upon institutional groups within the community that can bring pressure to bear upon newspaper policy by threatened boycotts. Only in recent years has the threat to freedom that exists within the press itself received sufficient attention. It is significant that when the staid *Atlantic Monthly* ran a contest in 1944 for the best discussion of freedom of the press, the prize-winning essay stressed just this point. In this essay, "For a Free Press," Mr. Robert Lasch argues that the modern economic development of the newspaper business is undermining freedom of the press. In particular, he deplores the alarming decline in the number of newspapers in the country, a decline which, unlike European experience, has not been the result of government control. From 1920 to 1942 the number of daily papers in America fell off by more than 10 per cent. In 1942 more than one thousand cities were dependent for their printed news upon one local paper. Lasch points to the great social power wielded by the remaining newspaper publishers, refers to their identification with conservative economic and political groups, and regrets the passing of the day when each important economic faction or political group within a community had a paper of its own.[14]

Mr. Lasch's conclusions find support in the views of the late William Allen White, perhaps the most respected newspaperman of modern times in the United States. In an article which he published in 1938 he also emphasizes the extent to which a newspaper in a modern American city has become a "big business" enterprise. He talks about "the sense of property that goes thrilling down the line" in a newspaper office, flatly repudiates the notion that it is "the advertising department that controls the news," and states as his opinion the belief that newspapers have done neither a fair nor an able job of reporting news in such a field as labor relations.[15]

These views of individual newspapermen were corroborated in 1947 by the report of the Commission on Freedom of the Press. This commission consisted of thirteen eminent private citizens who were asked by *Time* Magazine to make an impartial study of freedom of the press in the United States. The commission found that the threat to a free press inherent in governmental activity or regulation was far outweighed by the threat existing within the press itself. This latter threat was said to be most apparent in the monopolistic tendencies which have become increasingly strong in the business of communicating information to the mass of the people by newspaper, motion picture, and radio.[16]

strengthening our civil liberties: (1) less reliance upon the Bill of Rights as enforced by the courts

What can be done about the inadequacies in the present state of our civil liberties? Three suggestions have been offered in recent years. The first of these is a somewhat surprising one to the effect that we will do well to place less reliance upon federal and state bills of rights as enforced by the courts. Two arguments have been offered in support of this suggestion.

a bill of rights not an automatic safeguard of liberty

In the first place, it is asserted that worship of a bill of rights can blind a nation to the fact that liberty cannot rest solely upon constitutional language but depends also upon the spirit and traditions of the people. The truth of this

---

[14] Robert Lasch, "For a Free Press," *Atlantic Monthly*, CLXXIV (July, 1944), 39–44.

[15] William Allen White, "How Free Is Our Press?" *The Nation*, CXLVI (June 18, 1938), 693–695.

[16] Commission on Freedom of the Press, *A Free and Responsible Press* (Chicago: The University of Chicago Press, 1947).

assertion is to be seen in the fact that almost any person can be persuaded to accept the ideal of civil liberty in the abstract sense, but the same person will often be found opposing a particular civil liberty in a practical situation. The assertion is not new. It was in part the argument that Hamilton employed against the inclusion of a bill of rights in the Constitution when he said:

> . . . its security [of such liberties as freedom of the press] whatever fine declarations may be inserted in any constitution respecting it, must altogether depend upon public opinion, and on the general spirit of the people and of the government. And here, after all, . . . must we seek for the only solid basis of all our rights.[17]

This is not to say that we would be better off without a bill of rights or courts to enforce it. Admittedly such an enumeration of civil liberties serves an all-important purpose in putting our highest aspirations in noble and inspiring language and in keeping these aspirations constantly in view. A bill of rights and court decisions enforcing it provide a starting point in the struggle to foster and protect liberty. They have an educational and stimulative effect in making for that "general spirit" upon which the preservation of liberty must depend. The difficulty arises when people believe that a bill of rights provides an automatic safeguard of liberty.

inadequacy of court enforcement of a bill of rights

In the second place, it is pointed out that court enforcement of a bill of rights cannot possibly provide a means of correcting all of the day to day violations of such a bill. To begin with, it seems likely that only a small percentage of the total infractions of American bills of rights have ever been brought to the attention of the courts. Persons wronged are often unaware of their legal or constitutional rights, and even where such awareness exists they are often disinclined to go to court about their rights. It takes money, persistence, and often a considerable measure of courage to fight back against the violators of civil liberty, particularly where, as is so often the case, the victim is a person with little standing in the community, and the oppressor is a person with a good deal of standing.

Even where the assistance of the courts is invoked and a favorable decision is obtained, all too frequently the individual who has thereby vindicated his rights enjoys but a momentary benefit. Moreover, the gain is by no means generalized to affect all persons similarly situated the country over. The Supreme Court may rule against a particular state policy denying Negroes the right to vote. And yet other states, and indeed in some instances, the same state, continue to follow similar if not identical policies. Admittedly, a series of such decisions issuing from the Supreme Court of the United States over a period of years begins finally to take effect, and a resulting improvement in the state of civil

---

[17] *The Federalist*, No. 84.

liberty throughout the land can be seen. But it is clear that the beneficial effect of such a decision is too often confined to the individuals and localities immediately concerned.

Professor Henry Steele Commager has put the argument against dependence upon favorable court decisions for the protection of our civil liberties in a somewhat different way.[18] He admits that many recent decisions, such as those in the Jehovah's Witnesses cases, have resulted in distinct short-term gains for the cause of liberty, but he argues that in the long run liberty will be secure only when the people and their legislators have been sufficiently educated to the advantages of liberty to prevent the enactment of laws endangering individual rights. He says:

> The tendency to decide issues of personal liberty in the judicial arena alone has the effect of lulling the people into apathy towards issues that are fundamentally their concern, with the comforting notion that the courts will take care of personal and minority rights. It effectively removes these issues from the arena of public discussion and thus deprives democracy of the inestimable benefit of experimentation.[19]

And he quotes with approval from Justice Felix Frankfurter's opinion in the first *Flag Salute* case:

> . . . to the legislature no less than to courts is committed the guardianship of deeply-cherished liberties. . . . Where all the effective means of inducing political changes are left free from interference, education in the abandonment of foolish legislation is itself a training in liberty. To fight out the wise use of legislative authority in the forum of public opinion and before legislative assemblies rather than to transfer such a contest to the judicial arena, serves to vindicate the self-confidence of a free people.[20]

It is difficult to refute the logic of the Frankfurter-Commager argument. However, most people will probably conclude that these men are somewhat idealistic in their vision of a society in which both the people and their legislators have learned by experience to avoid any action that would endanger civil liberty. The average man will probably persist in a belief that, even in such an intelligent society, legislatures would continue to make mistakes that could best be corrected by immediate court decisions protecting individual rights rather than by waiting for the slower corrective process to set in in the legislative arena itself. Moreover, there is probably no such final antipathy between these two modes of correction, or no need to choose between them, as Frankfurter and Commager imply. And yet it must be admitted that in warning us that legislative

---

[18] Henry Steele Commager, *Majority Rule and Minority Rights* (New York: Oxford University Press, 1943). See particularly pp. 65–83.

[19] *Ibid.*, p. 73.

[20] *Minersville School District* v. *Gobitis*, 310 U.S. 586, 600 (1940).

correction is fully as important as judicial correction, these men are making an important point. Admittedly we are at times too much inclined to look exclusively to the Bill of Rights as enforced by the courts for the protection of our civil liberties. We need to remember that "nine men in Washington cannot hold a nation to ideals which it is determined to betray." [21]

strengthening our civil liberties: (2) the need for an economic bill of rights

A second suggestion that is frequently made for improving the state of our civil liberties is that we should supplement our political Bill of Rights with an economic bill of rights. Those who advocate this change argue that many existing conflicts within our society can be traced to the precariousness of man's economic security, to the individual's feeling that he must compete with his neighbor for his share of the goods and services that society offers. Undoubtedly, many present-day interferences with freedom of speech and press, with religious freedom, with the right to vote, and even with the procedural right to a fair trial, grow out of economic conflicts such as those between management and labor, white man and Negro, and capitalist and collectivist.

Accordingly, it is argued that if government would guarantee to every man certain basic economic rights, many conflicts between individuals, seemingly social rather than economic in nature, would disappear. Among the economic rights for which such a guarantee is sought are usually listed the right to a job, the right to a home, to food and clothing; the right to an education and to membership in the arts and professions solely on the basis of one's skills and learning; and the right to protection against the hazards of life over which one has little personal control—unemployment, accidental injury, sickness, and old age.

It seems clear that if a bill of rights is to be effective it must be coupled with a practical attempt to understand the conflicts of our present society, and to soften economic and social antagonisms wherever possible. Charles A. Beard spoke of the importance of the "economic underwriting of our Constitution." [22] As he saw it, no mere political arrangement of things can ever be expected to succeed unless it is given a chance to work out in an economic environment that is reasonably compatible with the main purposes of the political experiment.

What constitutes a favorable economic milieu for the protection of civil liberty is not easily determined. The rather steady improvement in the state of our own civil liberties would seem to indicate that we in the United States are not on the wrong track in the search for a satisfactory economic system. And yet we have not finally made all civil rights secure for all men. The point to

---

[21] Thomas Reed Powell, quoted in Zechariah Chafee, *Free Speech in the United States* (Cambridge: Harvard University Press, 1948), p. xiv.

[22] Charles A. Beard, *The Republic* (New York: The Viking Press, 1944), Chap. 19.

be made here is that it is probably futile to seek a more satisfactory legal or constitutional definition of civil liberties or more adequate political or judicial protection of those liberties without at the same time seeking to alleviate the economic conflicts out of which the violations of liberty so often come. One observer is perhaps pointing the way in the following words:

> So long as labor permits itself to make unreasonable and violent demands upon the property group, it will provide an excuse for the invasion of the workers' rights. So long as the property classes are greedy for excessive profits and resist labor's need for economic independence, just so long will labor be provoked to invade the rights of property. . . . nothing would go further to diminish infractions of the Bill of Rights than for the class struggle to be mitigated by a series of compromises that would assure each group that it may safely permit the other to talk, write and assemble to its heart's content.[23]

What is here said about the conflict between labor and property is equally valid as applied to our other social conflicts, whether those involving race against race, religious group against religious group, or one political faction against another. We must give attention to the causes of these conflicts if we would make civil liberty more secure.

There are some who see in the affording of any such series of social benefits a force that might weaken a people by the protection it would give to the less able members of society and by the way it might discourage the ambition and competitive spirit of society's ablest members. Admittedly, such unfortunate results might be encountered if the power of government were employed to force all men into a position of complete economic equality. But no such extreme policy need result from an attempt to establish certain basic, minimum economic rights for all persons, and above all to guarantee equality of economic *opportunity*. Whether guaranteeing such rights would so satisfy each person that, even though he might well desire to advance his own interests beyond this minimum level, he would respect the rights of every other man and have less incentive to encroach upon those rights, is by no means an assured result. But the logic of the argument carries much weight, and in the age-old struggle for freedom the formulation of an economic bill of rights would seem to be as promising a step as was the formulation of a political bill of rights nearly two centuries ago.

It is in connection with such an economic bill of rights that the right of private property should receive attention. Our Constitution does specifically recognize and afford protection to the right of property; yet this right is not customarily regarded as a "civil right" in the traditional sense. The possession of private property is, however, one of the most significant aspects of American life,

---

[23] Ralph M. Blagden, "The Bill of Rights in 1939," *The Christian Science Monitor*, April 1, 1939, pp. 6, 12.

it is a goal toward which nearly every man aspires, and much of the individual's sense of economic security depends upon the possession of property. Accordingly, the right to a job and the right to property seem closely related to each other and might properly be given much the same status in the American constitutional system.

strengthening our civil liberties: (3) government's responsibility to protect our rights

A third suggestion for the enhancement of American civil liberty is that the federal government should play a more positive role in protecting civil liberty. Indeed, this is the central recommendation of the President's Committee on Civil Rights. In its report, *To Secure These Rights,* the committee asserts: "The National Government of the United States must take the lead in safeguarding the civil rights of all Americans." [24] Moreover, it calls for the enactment of much new federal legislation designed to protect specific rights. The committee offers several arguments in support of its position. In particular, it stresses these three: (1) Many of the most serious interferences with civil rights result from the activity of state and local public officers and of private individuals. Action by the federal government is needed to end these interferences: "The very fact that . . . outrages continue to occur, coupled with the fact that the states have been unable to eliminate them, points clearly to the strong need for federal safeguards." [25] (2) "It is a sound policy to use the idealism and prestige of our whole people to check the wayward tendencies of a part of them." [26] In the committee's opinion, there have always been a deeper understanding of freedom and democracy and a higher regard for civil rights in our nation at large than have existed in many states and communities. (3) The American record of civil rights has a growing international importance. Civil rights offenses, particularly those committed against members of racial and religious minorities, can do us great harm and endanger the success of our foreign policies, by prejudicing people in foreign countries against us. Accordingly the national government cannot safely disregard the civil rights problem nor wait for the slowest state or the most backward community to put its house in order.

The President's Committee on Civil Rights anticipates certain objections to its recommendation of federal action and endeavors to answer them. It points out that the national government has traditionally been viewed as the enemy of civil liberty and that the Bill of Rights is designed to protect liberty against this government. But there is no reason, the committee asserts, why the national government cannot also be a friend and protector of civil liberty:

[24] *To Secure These Rights,* p. 99.
[25] *Ibid.,* p. 100.
[26] *Ibid.*

There is no essential conflict between freedom and government. Bills of rights restrain government from abridging individual civil liberties, while government itself by sound legislative policies protects citizens against the aggressions of others seeking to push their freedoms too far. Thus in the words of the Declaration of Independence: "Man is endowed by his Creator with certain unalienable rights. Among these are life, liberty, and the pursuit of happiness. To secure these rights, *governments are instituted among men.*" [27]

Secondly, the committee considers the objection that civil rights violations have their origins in prejudice and intolerance and consequently cannot be prevented by government action. This objection merely repeats the old argument: "You cannot change human nature by passing laws; you cannot legislate morality." While agreeing that efforts should be made through education and other voluntary means to eliminate intolerance and prejudice, the committee insists that human *conduct* can be controlled by law: "It may be impossible to overcome prejudice by law, but many of the evil discriminatory practices which are the visible manifestations of prejudice can be brought to an end through proper government controls." [28] It is perhaps a fair analogy to point out that although laws against murder have obviously not succeeded in eliminating all murderous hatreds and drives from men, there is no doubt that they have succeeded in preventing many potential murderers from putting their hatreds and drives into practice.

The opponents of governmental efforts to protect civil rights through laws also refer to the practical difficulties of administering such laws and warn that they will prove to be as unenforceable as were the prohibition laws, or that it will take a standing army to back them up in certain sections of the country. Admittedly, civil rights laws—particularly those carrying criminal sanctions—are not always easy to enforce. But the difficulties can be exaggerated. For example, the record of the Civil Rights Section of the federal Department of Justice shows that civil rights laws carrying criminal sanctions can be enforced, at least to the extent that they are responsible for the improvement in the civil rights situation. The work of this agency is clearly one of the forces responsible for the drastic decline in lynchings and the increase in Negro voting during the last decade or so.

The recent experience of New York State under its Fair Employment Practices Act demonstrates that racial and religious discrimination in employment can be ameliorated by a law under which, although it provides criminal sanctions, it has never been necessary to take offenders to court. Through such methods as negotiation and conciliation, much has been accomplished by the administrative commission charged with the enforcement of the act, which has

---

[27] *Ibid.*, p. 5.
[28] *Ibid.*, p. 103.

Government Sanctions to Safeguard Civil Rights. (*Source: The Report of the President's Committee on Civil Rights,* To Secure These Rights. *Government Printing Office, 1947.*)

not needed to use even the cease and desist order that the law authorizes it to issue when confronted with recalcitrant offenders.

Actually the choice in seeking to protect civil rights is not between law and no law. Much intolerance and discrimination are themselves encouraged or even produced by law. This is particularly true of the many states in which Negroes are denied the right of first-class citizenship through segregation laws. Thus, it is not true that those who advocate protection of civil rights through legislation are necessarily trying to force people to abandon private voluntary practices—to interfere with "folkways." Those who are opposed to civil rights laws on the ground one cannot legislate morality overlook·the fact that we have been legislating immorality.

constitutional difficulties in the way of federal protection of civil rights

There are constitutional difficulties in the way of a federal program for the protection of civil rights. Nowhere in the Constitution—least of all in the Bill of Rights—is any express power granted to the central government to take positive steps toward general protection of civil liberty in the United States. Moreover, if this silence of the Constitution is not enough to give one pause, certain adverse decisions of the Supreme Court offer a further barrier to federal action in support of civil rights. Following the Civil War, in the one great attempt in American history that Congress has made to throw the weight of the national government behind the rights of the individual, seven civil rights laws were passed. These laws were based largely on the power granted to Congress in the three Civil War amendments to the Constitution. Almost immediately, however, this legislation was attacked as to constitutionality, and in a series of decisions the Supreme Court declared important aspects of the program null and void, largely on the ground that the national government was overreaching its proper powers in undertaking to protect civil rights.

adverse court decisions

The fate of the Civil Rights Act of 1875 illustrates the constitutional difficulties encountered by the program. This act was designed to outlaw racial segregation from American life. Specifically it forbade race discrimination by private persons in the operation of "inns, public conveyances on land or water, theatres, and other places of public amusement." This prohibition was declared unconstitutional by the Supreme Court in 1883 in the *Civil Rights Cases*. In its decision the Court asserted that the Fourteenth Amendment did not authorize Congress to protect civil rights against encroachment *by private persons*.[29]

---

[29] *Civil Rights Cases*, 109 U.S. 3 (1883).

In spite of the silence of the Constitution and in spite of the adverse decisions of the Supreme Court, the Report of the President's Committee on Civil Rights hopefully concludes that the way is open to the development of a national program in defense of our rights. With respect to the hostile court decisions, it points out that there are other Supreme Court cases in which federal civil rights legislation of varying types has been upheld. For example, the Thirteenth Amendment, which forbids slavery and involuntary servitude, is so worded as to protect persons against slavery which results from coercion by private persons as well as slavery which is based on law. Accordingly, the Supreme Court showed no hesitation in upholding the constitutionality of the federal Antipeonage Act, which makes it a federal crime for one person to force another into involuntary servitude. Similarly, the Supreme Court has held that the Constitution establishes a right to vote which is protected against private as well as governmental interference, and that Congress may by law protect the right against both kinds of interference.[30]

In fact, the President's Committee on Civil Rights notes the existence of some eleven specific constitutional bases upon which a federal civil rights program might be built. No one of the eleven separate bases noted in the Report is regarded as sufficiently broad or express to support a comprehensive civil rights program, but "collectively . . . they provide an encouraging basis for action." [31]

a program of action

The Report of the President's Committee on Civil Rights is not limited to a philosophic consideration of the nature of civil liberty or of the importance of safeguarding our rights. A comprehensive program of action is set forth with specific recommendations under six headings. These recommendations may be summarized briefly as follows:

better machinery

(1) To strengthen the machinery for the protection of civil rights, the committee urges that the Civil Rights Section of the Department of Justice, established in 1939, be raised to the status of a division headed by an assistant attorney general and be given ample manpower and resources to make possible more effective enforcement of federal civil rights legislation. A permanent advisory committee, similar to the President's Council of Economic Advisers, attached to the Executive Office of the President, is also recommended. This body would keep a close watch over the state of civil liberty in America and through periodic reports advise the President of the need for further action. To provide a parallel body in the legislative department, the Report urges the creation of a joint

---

[30] *Ex parte Yarbrough*, 110 U.S. 651 (1884).
[31] *To Secure These Rights*, p. 107.

House-Senate committee on civil rights to receive and consider presidential messages concerning this subject. Finally, the state governments are encouraged to establish similar enforcement machinery at the state and local levels.

new legislation

(2) To strengthen the right to safety and security of the person, the committee recommends the adoption of new federal legislation which would include amendments to existing federal civil rights laws designed to correct recognized weaknesses and to bring them up-to-date, an antilynching act, and a law establishing a procedure for the settlement of claims for property and business losses resulting from the wartime evacuation of the Japanese-Americans from the West Coast area.

(3) To strengthen the right to citizenship and its privileges, the Report recommends action by both Congress and the states to end the poll tax as a voting prerequisite. Other federal laws are urged which would protect the right of qualified voters to participate in federal and state primaries and elections against certain types of interference; establish local self-government in the District of Columbia, and give District residents representation in Congress and the right to vote in presidential elections; modify the federal naturalization system to permit the granting of citizenship without regard to the race, color, or national origin of applicants; and eliminate racial and religious discrimination and segregation from all branches of the armed services. Arizona and New Mexico are urged to grant the suffrage to their Indian citizens, and California and certain other states are urged to repeal their alien land laws and other legislation discriminating against aliens who are now ineligible for national citizenship because of race or national origin.

(4) To strengthen the right to freedom of conscience and expression, the committee recommends the enactment of federal and state laws which would require the disclosure of pertinent factual information by organizations seeking to influence public opinion. Action is also urged by Congress and the President to clarify the loyalty obligations of federal employees, and to establish standards and procedures by which the civil rights of public workers may be scrupulously observed by the government.

toward equality of opportunity

(5) To strengthen the right to equality of opportunity, a long series of federal and state laws is recommended. Among these are federal and state fair employment practice laws, state fair educational and fair health practice laws, a federal law forbidding racial segregation in interstate commerce, and state laws guaranteeing equality of access to places of public accommodation without regard to race or religion. Moreover, the committee urges Congress to enact a series of

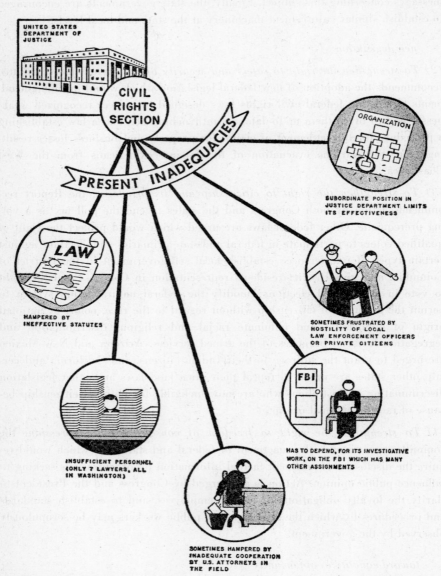

Our Federal Civil Rights Machinery Needs Strengthening. (*Source: The Report of the President's Committee on Civil Rights*, To Secure These Rights. *Government Printing Office, 1947.*)

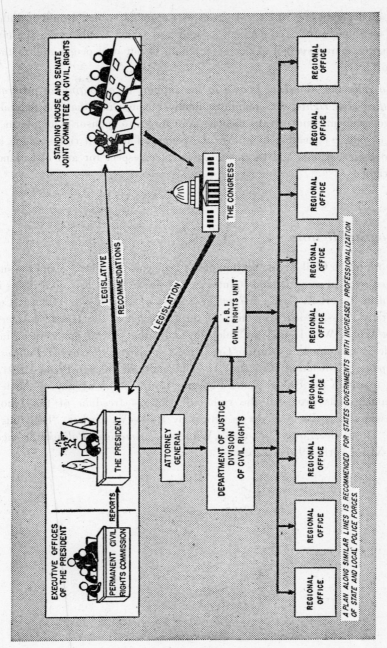

Recommendation by the President's Committee for Stronger Civil Rights Enforcement Machinery. (*Source: The Report of the President's Committee on Civil Rights,* To Secure These Rights, *Government Printing Office, 1947.*)

model civil rights laws for the District of Columbia, which would include the above measures and certain others as well and which would make the city of Washington a true symbol of democracy both to our own people and to the entire world.

(6) To rally the American people to the support of a continuing program to strengthen civil rights, the committee finally recommends that the federal and state governments and private agencies join forces to sponsor a long-term campaign of public education to inform the people of the civil rights which are a part of their heritage and to encourage greater respect for and observance of these rights.

bibliographic note

The work of the Civil Rights Section of the Department of Justice and the success it has enjoyed in using federal statutes as a means of protecting civil rights is examined in Robert K. Carr's *Federal Protection of Civil Rights* (Ithaca: Cornell University Press, 1948). The story of the treatment of the Japanese-Americans during World War II and the role played by the federal government in this episode is examined in Morton Grodzins's *Americans Betrayed: Politics and the Japanese Evacuation* (Chicago: The University of Chicago Press, 1949). The extent to which the United States Supreme Court, as an agency of the federal government, has protected the right to religious freedom of the Jehovah's Witnesses sect is discussed in an article by Hollis W. Barber, "Religious Liberty v. The Police Power: Jehovah's Witnesses," *American Political Science Review*, XLI (April, 1947), 226.

part 7

---

the implementation of policy

processes of administration

$\mathcal{B}$Y "processes of administration" is meant the combinations of decisions and actions by means of which government does the things that the people want done. If the business of constitutional government is said to be conducted in accordance with law, then administration is the phase of governmental activity that is concerned chiefly with law enforcement. As we have seen, the process of lawmaking centers in the legislature. Similarly, the processes of law enforcement are centered in the executive branch of the government. The relationship between lawmaking and law enforcement may be visualized as two distinct but overlapping spheres. The work of Congress is not confined to the formulation of policy, and the work of the executive branch is not limited to the execution of policy; the activities of each spill over into the area of the other. In this chapter, however, we are concerned principally with the nature of the activities that take place within the sphere of administration. The central idea of the discussion has been well stated by Professor John M. Gaus: ". . . administration is intermingled with the entire process of government, and with the environment in which the people affected by the government exist." [1]

the environment of administration

the role of technology

Technology—the application of scientific knowledge for practically useful purposes—is a relatively recent but crucial force in American life. In 1800, the mechanical power available to each citizen averaged about one twelfth of one horsepower. In 1900, the average for each person was about one fifth of one horsepower. In 1950, the share of each of us was over ten horsepower, or the equivalent of the labor of three hundred men. The increase is a rough indicator

---

[1] John M. Gaus, *Reflections on Public Administration* (University: University of Alabama Press, 1947), p. 125. Students of government are heavily indebted to Professor Gaus for his valuable work in developing this theory of public administration.

of the acceleration of technological developments since the establishment of our government. Observe that the amount of horsepower available doubled in the nineteenth century; but it increased fiftyfold in the first half of the twentieth century. The tempo of technological developments is also illustrated by the fact that our first million inventions were recorded in the Patent Office during our first 120 years, and the second million, in the 20 years following. Since every newly established fact can be used in conjunction with every other established fact, we may assume that the acceleration will continue.

Within the memory of mature adults and as a result of technological developments, incredible changes have taken place in American society. In this period, radio, automobile, and moving pictures have been invented, mass produced, and mass distributed. Deprived of their use, the average family today feels that life has lost much of its richness. In this period, also, man flew successfully for the first time. Thereafter commercial aviation was established as a safe and convenient method of transport, and military aircraft carried destructive warfare to cities and civilian populations. Television grew from a novelty to a major industry. Atomic energy was successfully released, to provide men with a new and terrifying weapon and with potential industrial and medical uses that have yet to be explored.

The rising tempo of social change makes increasingly difficult the task of understanding and assimilating change.

> Whereas at the beginning of this period (300 years ago) the rate of new discovery and invention was such that the digestion of major change extended over the better part of a century, it has steadily increased until the process of digestion must now be accomplished within a decade. This is something new in history. The better part of a century is a long human lifetime, and within this span, adjustment, both personal and social, is comparatively easy. When the time available for the digestion of a change is reduced to a single generation, then, though individual adjustment is more of a problem, social adjustment is still not too difficult. But once the rate of major change has overtaken the rate of social reproduction, and is down to a half or a third of a generation, a new and formidable problem is introduced. The individual himself is asked to recast his ideas and his attitude once or even twice within the space of his active working life.[2]

specialization in society

Under the impact of technology, our society becomes increasingly specialized. A small radio tube depends upon complex fabrication processes in the tube factory, in which each workman has a relatively minor task to perform on the assembly line. But before fabrication begins, coal, copper, and tungsten are mined, processed, and delivered, with other materials and parts, to the factory.

---

[2] Thorstein Veblen, quoted in Gaus, *Reflections on Public Administration*, p. 22.

If the supply of plastic, rubber, or other materials is cut off, the assembly line slows down or stops, until the essential component is once more available. The tube cannot be completed until the separate parts and processes are fitted together in their designed relationship. Just as these specialties are interdependent, so are the various parts of an industrial society. A dislocation of one group or process has ramifications that may extend throughout the entire country. The balances in such a society are so delicate that they are easily disturbed by shock, which is transmitted rapidly throughout the country.

Specialization has affected us as individuals. Our occupations, most of which were unknown a century ago, are highly specialized. There are fewer and fewer occupations for the unskilled. The trend is from unskilled jobs to the skilled, and from the skilled to those requiring engineering knowledge and techniques. The machines used in manufacturing are precise, complex, and delicate. Employers prefer the young and flexible worker to the experienced middle-aged. Science shortens a man's working life, but progressively lengthens his total life span, and the problem of security in old age becomes more serious.

The sharp rise in the productivity of farms, made possible by machines and scientific husbandry, has produced another kind of specialization. Because fewer and fewer people are needed to raise the food that we require, masses of farm people have moved to the cities. In 1800, when most commodities were produced with simple hand tools, 85 per cent of our people lived on farms; by 1950 more than 85 per cent did not. This fundamental change in the characteristic of our society is made possible by the perfection and wide use of tractors, combine harvesters, cotton pickers, and other labor replacement machines.

mobility of population

Americans are a highly mobile people. We move easily from job to job and from community to community. About one third of us live in huge metropolitan areas, comprising many separate cities and towns. Within these areas transportation facilities are highly developed, and it is not uncommon for a man to travel twenty or thirty miles from home to place of work. Often we live in one community and work in another. Because of the circumstances of work and residence, families do not develop easily a sense of identity with a community in whose affairs they become active participants. Families move from one community to another without much sense of loss.

We are also moving westward. Although the frontier areas of vast unsettled lands have disappeared, the social and economic attractions of the West continue to draw millions of people from the eastern half of the United States. This shift means constant readjustment of social and political organizations and relationships. California and Washington gain additional representation in Congress; New York and other eastern states lose representatives. The area that ten years ago was the center of a business is no longer the center, and the manufacturing and sales organizations must shift accordingly. States and communities that lose population and wealth find it difficult to maintain satisfactory services for their citizens. States and communities that receive large increases of population find that their highways, schools, or health facilities are no longer adequate. A society whose center of population moves steadily must adapt itself continuously to new conditions.

coercions of industrial society

The nature of our society limits greatly the power of any individual to control his own destiny. His life and fortune are in large degree in the hands of individuals and groups whom he never sees face to face. The forces that coerce him and his family are impersonal, indirect, and indeterminate. He may lose his wages for weeks because a strike hundreds of miles distant closes down the plant where he works. He may lose his job because of an economic catastrophe over which neither he nor his employer has any control. His pattern of life may be disrupted and broken by a war whose causes will be debated by historians a century hence. His business may cease to be profitable because of the invention of new materials or new processes; he may see the work of a lifetime disappear because he cannot find the money to re-equip his plant. A whole community may be undermined by a single technological development that strikes at the material basis of its life.

Technology is the most radical factor in society. Change is the inevitable result of technological developments. For some, change provides new opportunities; for others, it creates new insecurities. A one-hour television show may require the completion of 250 different jobs and the work of 150 people. But while it is on the air, thousands of people are at home who might otherwise be in a motion-picture theater. The petroleum industry considers the diesel engine a boon, but to the coal industry the popularity of the diesel means shrinking coal markets. A skilled worker fights the adoption by his plant of a machine or process that makes his skills less valuable. The pattern underlying these relationships is clear. First, technology produces change; second, change creates insecurity; and, third, insecurity leads to demands for control.

control through cooperative action

In a technological society, the central problem is how to control the forces that knock us about. When our own efforts prove futile, we seek greater effectiveness by associating with other individuals who share our purposes. Property owners form a volunteer fire company which they equip and maintain. The employees in a plant participate in a health insurance plan under which all the members share the cost of expensive illnesses of individuals. The employer, in order to reduce absenteeism and labor turnover, sets up medical facilities in his factory and shares the cost with his employees. The community, with the aid of state and federal governments, provides clinical and hospital facilities for tuberculosis or polio victims. The cooperative associations that we form may be either public or private. We may join with other individuals who share our purposes and needs in a private organization, such as the Blue Cross health services, or the bar or medical associations, or a labor union. Such organizations are of major significance in our lives, but they do not meet all of our needs. When they become inadequate, we turn to government. The history of our attempts to deal with social problems indicates that there is a movement from private to public organizations.

the role of government

Attempts to control social forces by means of government are divided among local, state, federal, and international governmental organizations. Under our political traditions, some activities, such as the provision of education, are local concerns. Others, such as the conduct of war, are national concerns. In the past, we have been reluctant to vest any significant control functions in an international agency. But these historic allocations of governmental functions are subject to increasing pressure in our industrial society. Pressure tends to move an activity from the area of local government to that of state government; from state government to national government; and, in the matter of atomic energy control, from national to international government.

There are many illustrations of this tendency to shift problems to successively higher levels of government. In 1700, we considered education a private rather than a public function. Today, publicly supported schools are the rule, and although private schools exist side by side with public schools, they are exceptions to the general practice. As public agencies began to provide educational facilities, it was assumed that the function was the province of local communities. But as standards of quality were raised, and as the service became more expensive, it became difficult for many communities to provide satisfactory schools. At this point, a state interest was recognized and state aid was extended to local communities, with preference given to the poorer areas. Wide variations in the ability of states to support public schools has become increasingly apparent, and a national interest emerges when, as in World War II, rather widespread illiteracy was found among our people. We have now come to the point of considering federal aid to education. Another example of this process is provided by public welfare activities. At first, assistance to the poor was thought to be a matter of private charity. Then the towns were expected to care for their own unfortunates. During the depression of the 1930's, towns and cities lacked the resources to care for the unemployed, and state assistance became necessary. Soon the resources of state governments were exhausted, and the federal government assumed responsibility for ameliorating the effects of the depression. The regulation of railroad rates is another illustration. The states first took responsibility for regulation of rates when farmers and other shippers complained of excessive and discriminatory charges. State control became ineffective when local lines were merged with national systems. Then those who relied upon the railroads for transportation insisted that the federal government take over the control function.

Although there appears to be a tendency to shift more and more activities to the federal government, the trend is not unopposed. In general, we prefer to solve our problems without the aid of government; and when we need the help of government, we prefer to get it from local or state governments rather than from the national government. The fact is that we have no means of determining readily what activities should be handled privately, or locally, and what governmentally, or nationally. Although the role of government has unquestionably expanded in response to our wishes, each significant enlargement has been resisted and attacked. Felix Frankfurter believes that this conflict results from an inadequacy of our political theory.

> The paradox of both distrusting and burdening government reveals the lack
> of a conscious philosophy of politics. It betrays some unresolved inner con
> flict about the interaction of government and society. I suspect that it im
> plies an uncritical continuance of past assumptions about government and
> society. We have not adjusted our thinking about government to the over
> whelming facts of modern life, and so carry over old mental habits, tradi
> tional schoolbook platitudes and campaign slogans as to the role, the pur
> poses, and the methods of government.[3]

In the absence of an adequate formula, we have dealt with problems as they arose, generally with little advance planning, and often without weighing relevant experience.

the search for the public interest

Governmental activity is undertaken in the "public interest." We turn to a public agency because, in conflicts between private interests, the public need is neglected. If competing groups perceive, understand, and admit a larger interest than their own, the problem may be solved without government intervention. But the structure of our society is such that it is generally difficult for us to grasp the full significance of an issue about which there is intense and conflicting opinion. Our society is so fragmented as a result of the impact of technology that it is extraordinarily difficult to know in a particular situation just what the "public interest" is. All of the processes of government are handicapped in their search for the "public interest" by the elusiveness of the "public." John Dewey has described some of the difficulties:

---

[3] Felix Frankfurter, *The Public and Its Government* (New Haven: Yale University Press, 1930), pp. 4–5.

Political apathy . . . ensues from inability to identify one's self with definite issues. These are hard to find and locate in the vast complexities of current life. : . . The old principles do not fit contemporary life as it is lived, however well they may have expressed the vital interests of the times in which they arose. Thousands feel their hollowness even if they cannot make their feeling articulate. The confusion which has resulted from the size and ramifications of social activities has rendered men skeptical of the efficiency of political action. Who is sufficient unto these things? Men feel that they are caught in the sweep of forces too vast to understand or master. Thought is brought to a standstill and action paralyzed. Even the specialist finds it difficult to trace the chain of "cause and effect"; and even he operates only after the event, looking backward, while meantime social activities have moved on to effect a new state of affairs.

. . . The ramification of the issues before the public is so wide and intricate, the technical matters involved are so specialized, the details are so many and so shifting, that the public cannot for any length of time identify and hold itself. It is not that there is no public, no large body of persons having a common interest in the consequences of social transactions. There is too much public, a public too diffused and scattered and too intricate in composition. And there are too many publics, for conjoint actions which have indirect, serious, and enduring consequences are multitudinous beyond comparison, and each of them crosses the others and generates its own group of persons especially affected with little to hold these different publics together in an integrated whole.[4]

The elusiveness of the public affects all of the processes of government. The central task is to perceive and define a national interest among the particular interests of amorphous publics. Group demands must be adjusted to produce a reasonably well-balanced and harmonious relationship that will be satisfactory to the general public. The search for the "public interest" requires all of the energy, patience, and wisdom that we can command. We have noted elsewhere the contributions of the political, legislative, and judicial processes to the solution of these problems. The work of these public agencies is channeled into the actual enforcement of law, which is the characteristic activity of the executive branch.

forms of administrative action

Out of our experience with problems of law enforcement have developed several forms of administrative action. Each form of action is a tool that is designed for a

---

[4] John Dewey, *The Public and Its Problems* (Chicago: Gateway Books, 1946), pp.134–135, 137. Reprinted by permission of Gateway Books, publishers.

particular kind of job. Also, each form of action is associated with a characteristic "administrative process" that is different from that of other forms. When Congress enacts a law, it determines which of the available forms of action is to be used in administering the new legislation. In making this decision, the legislature considers the objectives of the law and the nature of the social problem with which it is concerned.

A form of administrative action that is effective for one law may be poorly suited to another. For example, it is the policy of the United States to seek an adequate standard of living for all of its people. Social security and minimum-wage laws help accomplish this purpose. Although these laws have a common objective, different processes are used in their administration. The social security program provides payments to retired workers and their dependents, for whom the payments help maintain an adequate standard of living. The central administrative problem with respect to this legislation is the collection of social security taxes from employers and employees, the determination of eligibility for benefits, and the payment of benefits to eligible persons. We forbid an employer to pay less than a minimum wage of seventy-five cents an hour to his workers, who could not maintain a satisfactory standard of living on a smaller wage. The central administrative problem in minimum-wage legislation is to ascertain whether an employer is paying less than the legal minimum and to take steps necessary to get violators to comply with the law. Here the problem and the solution are different from the problem and the solution in social security legislation.

noncoercive administrative action

Some forms of administrative action are less coercive than others. Administration of laws providing social services is not based primarily upon authority to compel cooperation by means of penalties. For example, the public school system is a familiar example of a remarkably successful service enterprise. In school administration, the emphasis is upon the qualifications of teachers, on the curriculum and methods of instruction, and on the provision of adequate buildings and other facilities. The Post Office Department is another example of a governmental activity that has service as its primary purpose. In the administration of postal laws, the major effort is upon orderly transportation and delivery of mail and the management of property used for this purpose. Another type of service is provided by such agencies as the Weather Bureau and the Bureau of Standards, which conduct research and publish results that are useful to us.

The line between coercive and noncoercive administrative actions is often indistinct. Even service activities are not completely devoid of compulsory elements. Service agencies insist that their employees meet set standards of performance and conduct. Attendance of children at school normally is required by law, and parents may be penalized for their child's truancy. It is a crime to use the mails to defraud or for the transmission of objectionable matter, and violations may be punished by heavy fines or imprisonment. Coercion may be indirect but not less effective for that reason, as the federal government's soil conservation program shows. We do not deny a farmer the right to use soil-depleting methods; but if he chooses to follow an approved program of soil conservation, he is eligible for direct subsidy payments. There may even be compulsory elements in the work of a research agency such as the Bureau of Standards. This agency is noted for its development of quality standards for manufactured products. There are no laws compelling manufacturers to meet the specifications fixed by the Bureau of Standards. But the results of the bureau's work are widely publicized, and most government and many private purchasing agents buy only commodities that meet federal specifications. Manufacturers whose products are not up to standard are at a competitive disadvantage.

Badly needed improvements in the quality of our food supply have resulted from the cooperation of government and industry in the development of standards.

> The technical experts of the government have aided the industries in studies of factors that lead to deterioration of the product. With the elimination of these factors much of the incentive to adulteration has been removed, and at the same time the industry has gained public confidence. This change has brought about a system of voluntary policing of these industries by the manufacturers themselves in cooperation with the federal authorities.[5]

control by inspection

The development of standards may be coupled with inspection by government employees to determine whether or not the standards are being followed. The Bureau of Mines of the Department of the Interior attempts to reduce accidents in the mining industry. It investigates the causes of accidents and devises equipment and practices that reduce the risks of workers in a dangerous but essential occupation. It has a staff of inspectors who visit mines periodically to investigate safety conditions. The manager of a mine is informed of any dangerous situations that are discovered and corrective measures are suggested. The bureau has no authority to compel mine operators to comply with its suggestions, but much can be accomplished by competent and persuasive inspectors. Here, too, there are elements of coercion. If there is an explosion in a mine whose management has neglected to take precautions recommended by an inspector, there is certain to be adverse publicity and public concern. More important, the miners' unions may be reluctant to sign contracts with operators who neglect safety fac-

---

[5] Dr. Gaylord W. Anderson, "Regulation in Public Health," in George A. Graham and Henry Reining, Jr., eds., *Regulatory Administration* (New York: John Wiley & Sons, Inc., 1943), p. 74. This is a useful collection of essays about administrative problems and processes in such activities as police, public health, labor, public-utility, and railroad regulation.

tors. Improvements in working conditions often mean as much to striking miners as wage increases. There is an identity of interest among miners, mine operators, and the Bureau of Mines that helps make the bureau's work successful.

The food industry provides an illustration of inspection coupled with direct penalties. Interstate shipment of meat is now restricted by federal law to meat slaughtered and processed under the supervision of federal inspectors. A processor whose plant does not meet federal standards of sanitation may sell his meat legally only in local markets. Since the bulk of the meat consumed in America passes through a few packing centers, such as Chicago and Kansas City, federal control by inspection is highly effective.

control through licensing

Licensing is one of the oldest and most effective types of administrative control. The procedures in licensing are simple and clear-cut. The individual desiring to engage in the regulated activity applies for a license. The government investigates his application and determines whether the issuance of a license would be in the public interest. If the decision is favorable, the license is issued and the individual may engage in the activity subject to regulations that may subsequently be imposed. If the decision is unfavorable, he may not enter the activity without risking the penalties, usually fine and imprisonment, provided by law. A license may be granted outright or with the understanding that stipulated conditions be met; it may be revoked for failure to comply with the conditions or with other governmental regulations.

Professions and occupations are usually controlled by means of licenses. Persons engaging in law, medicine, barbering, the sale of liquor, and other activities involving possible danger to public health, safety, or morals are licensed. The Civil Aeronautics Administration licenses aircraft and aviators; men and planes that do not meet standards of safe performance are not permitted to carry passengers. The Federal Communications Commissions licenses and assigns wave lengths to broadcasting stations. The Atomic Energy Commission licenses the manufacture of atomic energy materials. Securities that have not been "registered" (that is, licensed) by the Securities and Exchange Commission may not be sold in interstate commerce. In all of these examples of government control, licensing has proved to be an invaluable administrative tool.

administrative rule making and adjudication

When the legislature is unable to find sufficiently exact solutions for urgent problems, it may delegate to an administrative agency rule making or adjudicative powers. In discussions of constitutional theory, these powers are often termed "quasi-legislative" and "quasi-judicial." The rule-making power is legislative in character. Rules and orders issued in the exercise of a rule-making power have the force of laws enacted by Congress. An adjudicative power is a power to investigate and decide disputes to which a private citizen is a party; decisions in these cases have the force of judicial determinations. Normally, an agency that is granted rule-making powers is also given powers of adjudication. The combination is found, for example, in the independent regulatory commissions. Other agencies, such as the Court of Claims and the United States Court of Customs and Patent Appeals, exercise only adjudicative powers and are essentially administrative courts.

The rule-making power may be used to compel an individual to refrain from acts that the agency deems contrary to law. For example, when the Interstate Commerce Commission believes that the rates charged by a railroad are unreasonable or discriminatory, it may determine what will be just and reasonable and order the railroad to "cease and desist" from charges that are contrary to the new schedule.[6]

An agency may issue rules of general applicability. The grant of authority to the Securities and Exchange Commission is typical: the commission . . . shall have power to make such rules and regulations as may be necessary for the execution of the functions vested in . . . [it]." These rules define proper conduct for groups of individuals, rather than single out an offender, as is the case with the "cease and desist" order. The authority to issue rules of general applicability was first granted in 1790, but it did not come into general use until the emergencies of World War I and the depression of the 1930's. So numerous are the delegations of rule-making power that the volume of published rules and regulations now greatly exceeds that of acts of Congress. The formulation of rules often follows a process similar to the legislative process. There are investigations, hearings, conferences, and discussions of proposed regulations prior to promulgation. Also, the legality of rules is subject to review by the courts, as are acts of Congress.

The procedures followed in administrative adjudication are similar to those of the courts. The parties to a dispute are given notice of hearings to be held and are told of the points to be covered. They may be represented by counsel and have the opportunity of presenting evidence and arguments in support of their positions. A careful record is made of the testimony and of the evidence submitted at the hearing. The decision of the agency is confined to the case as shown by this formal record. And the decisions are subject to review by the courts to determine whether the powers of the agency have been exceeded or the rights of citizens improperly determined.[7]

informal methods of law enforcement

Whatever formal processes of law enforcement are used, the vast majority of cases arising between citizens and government are settled informally. The formal

---

[6] 49 U.S.C. §1004, 54 Stat. 899.

[7] Administrative Procedures Act, 5 U.S.C. §1001, 60 Stat. 237.

processes of administration are significant chiefly because they are available if their use ultimately becomes necessary. Normally, however, an investigation by administrative officials, conferences with the citizen interested in the case, and a preliminary decision by the agency suffice to settle the matter. Both the government and the citizen are reluctant to resort to expensive procedures or litigation until all other means of reaching a satisfactory agreement have failed.

The public's attitude toward the law is an important factor in administration. As we know from our experiences with prohibition and with price control and rationing in World War II, compliance with law rests upon widespread acceptance of its purposes and methods. It is difficult to enforce a law that does not have the support of most of the people who are affected by it. Conversely, administrative problems are eased when the law is generally accepted. In many primitive communities the relations between individuals and groups are regulated by means of customs that are accepted by all. Violators are punished by the whole community, and there is no need for officials with "authority" to enforce custom. In an industrial society, also, social pressure based upon custom is essential to law enforcement. For this reason, administrative officials devote much of their time and energy to winning public support for their activities.

processes of administrative management

The forms of administrative action discussed above are used by the government in direct action on behalf or in restraint of citizens. Another type of administrative process is used to maintain the organizations that administer law. These "housekeeping" activities are preliminary to the action that affects the citizen, but if they are not satisfactorily performed, the main action suffers. Their nature may be seen in a simple and familiar form of cooperative action. Let us suppose that we wish to move a boulder that cannot be handled by one individual. The first step is to find men willing and able to do the job, and to arrange for them to work. Next, needed equipment is provided. Then a work plan is devised that gives each worker specific tasks. The boulder is moved—the action toward which everything else pointed. To complete the job, the men are paid for their work and the equipment is returned to its proper place.

Administration depends upon similar activities. Someone takes charge of the job. The general requirements of organization and personnel are determined. Men and women with needed skills are brought into the organization. Office supplies and other necessary equipment are bought and paid for. There are activities involving organization, personnel, finance, and, with respect to each of these, planning. The operations which these functions entail constitute a type of administrative process.

aspects of policy and administration

Many students of government are perplexed by the relation of policy to administration. In any governmental activity, an observer may see a policy element—the
making of decisions about what is to be done—and an administrative element
—the actions by which the thing decided is accomplished. On first impression
these elements seem reasonably distinct, but on closer scrutiny they appear to
merge. Are policy and administration distinct and separable? Are they simply
different aspects of the intricate processes of government? Is it Congress *alone*
that formulates policy, and the executive *alone* that administers policy? Or do
both branches both make and execute policy?

belief in the separability of policy and administration

The idea that policy can and should be divorced from administration is often accepted as fundamental principle. This point of view is said to have originated in
an essay by Woodrow Wilson in 1887, in which he stated:

> Every particular application of general law is an act of administration. The
> assessment and raising of taxes, for instance, the hanging of a criminal, the
> transportation and delivery of the mails, the equipment and recruiting of
> the army and navy, *etc.*, are all obviously acts of administration; but the
> general laws which direct these things to be done are as obviously outside
> and above administration. The broad plans of governmental action are not
> administrative; the detailed execution of such plans is administrative.[8]

Wilson did not intend to say that there is a sharp distinction between policy
and administration, but several factors led to this interpretation of his statement.
First, separation of powers seems to support the idea that policy and administration are separate. The characteristic function of Congress is the formulation of
policy; the characteristic function of the executive is the administration of policy.
Second, the idea of the separation of policy and administration was congenial to
the drive for civil service reform, which focused attention upon the deficiencies
of administrative personnel selected solely for political reasons. Political influence, so the argument ran, should be confined to policy, and competence alone
should govern the selection of men whose work was administration. Third, belief that a science of administration could be established reinforced the idea that
policy and administration were separable. A science of administration should
apply to all kinds of administrative activity, irrespective of the type of organization or of differences in policy.

---

[8] Woodrow Wilson, "The Study of Administration," *Political Science Quarterly*, II, No. 2
(June, 1887), 212.

policy and administration are interrelated

More recently, we have come to recognize that policy making and policy execution are closely interrelated. Policy and administration do not take place in self-contained and separate compartments. The processes of policy making and administration intermingle at many points, so that it is frequently difficult to say that *this* is policy and that *that* is administration. There are, in fact, striking similarities between policy making and policy execution. First, both have a common objective: to adjust social conflicts or to provide services in accordance with the public interest. Second, they rely on essentially the same methods. There is investigation, to define the problem. There is discussion and deliberation, to formulate the most satisfactory solution to the problem. There is persuasion, to win the consent and support of those whose interests are affected by the solution. Third, both policy and administration are tentative in the sense that review and revision of the decisions made and the actions taken are continuous. Finally, both are political in the sense that they are subject to the influence of politics and politicians.

policy decisions in administrative processes

Policy decisions are made in administrative processes at many points, and by many people. First, the formulation of policy by Congress is not isolated from questions of administration. When Congress decides that a new activity should be undertaken, it also determines how the activity is to be administered. A new agency may be created, or an existing agency may be given a new responsibility. Congress also determines which of the various forms of administrative action are to be used in enforcing the new law. Decisions on matters of this kind are decisions about administration. In this sense, debates over the European Recovery Program or over the control of atomic energy were as much concerned with administration as with policy. Congressional determinations of policy are a part of administration in another sense. As we know, the President advises Congress about pending legislation, as do the departments and agencies of the executive branch. This advice is an outgrowth of administrative experience. Moreover, Congressional committees advise administrative officials about the policy matters that arise in the course of law enforcement. This practice is so pervasive that some careful students of the subject have concluded that in terms of actual supervision, executive departments and agencies receive more guidance from Congress and its committees than they receive from the President.

Second, the President makes policy decisions on matters for which he is responsible. His policy role is paramount in military and foreign affairs. As head of the executive branch, he directs the work of administrative agencies. Limitations of time and energy mean that some agencies receive little presidential attention; but the President does attend personally to departmental and agency questions affecting national interests. In some instances, the President makes the decisions himself after consultations with administrative officials; in other cases, he approves of decisions that have already been made.

Third, the courts are concerned with policy and administration. Judges have little interest in noncoercive administrative action, but they supervise rather closely the work of administrative agencies that exercise licensing, rule-making, and adjudicatory powers. Although only a small percentage of administrative decisions are reviewed by the courts, these decisions usually concern matters of broad policy and hence are a major factor in the subsequent activity of the agency. The courts also review the procedures used by administrative agencies when it appears that statutory or constitutional requirements have not been followed.

Finally, the people responsible for the administration of governmental activities make policy with respect to questions that arise in the course of their work. These decisions are particularly significant in agencies that exercise rule-making or adjudicatory powers, but they are inevitable in all law enforcement agencies. Pendleton Herring has described the conditions under which these decisions are made by administrative personnel:

> Upon the shoulders of the bureaucrat has been placed in large part the burden of reconciling group differences and making effective and workable the economic and social compromises arrived at through the legislative process. Thus Congress passes a statute setting forth a general principle. The details must be filled in by supplemental regulation. The bureaucrat is left to decide as to the conditions that necessitate the law's application. He is in a better position than the legislators to perform these duties. His daily occupation brings him into direct contact with the situation the law is intended to meet. He knows what can be enforced and he can better envisage the limits of legislative fiats. This increase in administrative discretion, while making possible the more understanding application of rules to concrete situations, nevertheless places a heavy duty on the administrator. The words of the statute delimit his scope, but within the margin of his discretion he must write his interpretation of state purpose.[9]

The policy decisions made by administrative personnel are of varying degrees of significance. If they concern an entire department, or several departments, the decision may be made by the highest departmental officials or by the President. If the question is of interest to a small unit within a department, the decision is made by the persons responsible for the unit's work. Questions of intermediate significance are disposed of at appropriate points within the organization by officials with the knowledge and judgment that their disposition requires.

---

[9] From *Public Administration and the Public Interest*, by E. P. Herring, p. 7. Copyright, 1936. Courtesy of McGraw-Hill Book Co.

the merging of policy and administrative questions

Dean Paul Appleby, in commenting upon the relation between policy and administration, has said:

> Executives do not sit at two different desks, treating policy at one and administration at the other. Even intellectually, they more often deal with whole problems than they deal with them as exclusively problems of policy or problems of administration. . . . It is believed that the relationship exists even at the Congressional level. . . . A cabinet member similarly considers what to do and how to do it as one problem; his instructions about program goals have to be tied closely to, and are limited by, administrative directions designed to insure attainment of goals. The reports he listens to or reads are both administrative reports and program reports of achievement, shortcomings and difficulties. He receives administrative and policy recommendations alike. Some may be more strictly administrative, some more strictly pertaining to policy, but without program considerations there is no sense at all in administration, and without administration nothing would happen with respect to policy. The functions of policy-making cannot actually be vested exclusively at any one point or level in the government. Wherever there is action affecting the public, there is policy-making.[10]

Instead of a separation of policy and administration, Dean Appleby prefers to speak of a "tentative delegation of power" under which officials regularly exercise "only those powers felt to be necessary to their respective general responsibilities, delegating everything else, and reserving the right to review anything done under delegation." Congress, for example, acts under such a delegation from the public; the public reserves the right to elect a new Congress if it wishes to withdraw the delegation. Similarly, the President, the head of a department, the head of a bureau, or other administrative officials decide "policy" questions that they believe to be major, and delegate to others the tasks of "administration." From the standpoint of a department head, for example, the questions that he refers to the President or decides himself are policy questions; those that he passes on to his subordinates are administrative questions. But "certain aspects of administration and certain aspects of policy require treatment together at the level of Congress; certain aspects of administration and policy must be treated at the level of the President; certain aspects of both must be treated at the level of a Department head—and so on down the administrative hierarchy."[11]

In short, the view taken here is that policy and administration are so intricately related that those who exercise the powers of government inevitably

---

[10] Paul H. Appleby, *Policy and Administration* (University: University of Alabama Press, 1949), pp. 19–20. Reprinted by permission of the University of Alabama Press, publishers.
[11] *Ibid.*, p. 21.

make *and* execute policy. The theme of this discussion—that administration is intermingled with the entire process of government—is nowhere better illustrated than in the area of policy and administration. As Dean Appleby has said:

> . . . the whole governmental context is important to legislation, to administration, to policy-making, and to court decisions. By "context" it is intended to suggest that courts can be judged and their decision-making understood only in the light of what is done by Congress and by administrators; that administration can be judged and its policy-making understood only in the light of what is done by courts and Congress and the administrative hierarchy itself; that Congressional policy-making similarly can be understood only in the light of what is done by courts and by administrators; that the three branches can be understood only in the light of popular political activities.[12]

politics and administration

The theory that policy and administration can and should be separated has a counterpart in the belief that administration can and should be insulated from political influence. If we accept the theory that policy and administration are in fact intertwined, doubt is cast on the wisdom of trying to separate administration and politics. If policy decisions are made only by Congress, we can control policy development through the electoral process. But if administrators are important policy makers, how can we be certain that their decisions are in line with the desires of the people? What is the desirable relationship between those who wield political power and those who administer our nation's laws?

political influence is inevitable

Political influence in administration is inevitable, for two reasons. First, the vital character of the work of administrative agencies invites political pressure. When our personal interest is intense, it is normal and human for us to reinforce our arguments for favorable treatment with whatever political influence we can muster. Second, there are means to make it effective. Our constitutional system establishes in the executive branch the channels through which political influence flows. The President is a political leader, is elected by the people, and is head of the executive establishment. Members of Congress are also popularly elected and they are also politicians. They exercise, as a legislative body and as individuals, enormous influence in administrative agencies. The heads of departments and agencies are usually appointed by the President with the approval of the Senate. Sometimes these officials are politicians and sometimes they are not. But at all times they are acutely aware of political factors that are important to

---

[12] *Ibid.*, pp. 10–11.

the President or to the members of Congress to whom they look for support. The heads of departments and agencies normally select their principal assistants; the assistants generally are not political figures, but they must be sensitive to the political factors that concern their chief. The extension of the civil service to the higher positions in the executive branch has reduced, but not eliminated, the points of political pressure.

congressional influence in administration

Since administrative agencies derive their authority and their financial support from legislative enactments, it is natural for Congress and congressmen to take a lively interest in administration. First, Congress, chiefly by means of standing and special committees, tries to keep itself informed about the work of executive agencies. This knowledge is essential to wise appropriations and to intelligent changes in laws that fail to achieve congressional purposes. Second, administrators, if for no other reason than to keep in the good graces of powerful congressional committees, frequently seek the advice of congressmen on questions relating to the work of their organizations.

> But Congressmen go much farther than this. The advice they give the administrator and the complaints they address to him are not always concerned with matters of general policy, nor are they always compatible with anyone's conception of the general public interest. The trouble lies in the fact that the Congressman is more than a representative of the general public; he is a representative of his particular constituency and all of the special interests within it. He not only speaks for groups of people who have a common interest; he is Washington agent for individuals and business firms located in his constituency and having business to transact with the federal government.[13]

the pressure of special interests

Special interest groups, such as the American Farm Bureau Federation, the National Association of Manufacturers, and the American Federation of Labor, influence the administration of laws that affect their welfare. Their interest in legislation is well known, but they are no less active in the executive branch. Since many of these groups can claim hundreds of thousands of members, the leaders are not slow to express their points of view to congressmen, to administrative officials, and even to the President. Frequently a congressional committee can be interested and can be persuaded to make to the administrative agency a recommendation that is satisfactory to the group. This recommendation may or may not be in the general public interest, but its adoption by a congressional

---

[13] Charles S. Hyneman, *Bureaucracy in a Democracy* (New York: Harper & Brothers, 1950), p. 160.

committee is almost certain to move the agency in the direction of the group's objective.

"Representatives" maintained in Washington by the big national organizations carry on several functions. First, they answer specific inquiries concerning administrative and legislative matters and they keep their clients generally informed about what to expect from government. Second, they try to create a favorable attitude toward their clients by cultivating friendly relationships with administrators, congressmen, and newspaper and radio reporters. Horrendous accounts of the difficulties encountered by citizens in dealing with their government frequently can be traced to a story told by a "national representative." More often than not, however, they prefer to work quietly and on terms of friendship with government officials. Finally, when their clients have business with the government, the representatives see that the business is presented to the proper official and do what they can to effect its speedy and favorable dispatch.

The number of these representatives of interest groups has increased with the expansion of governmental activities. The representatives undoubtedly perform a useful function in helping the citizen to find his way among the maze of government agencies with which he wishes to conduct business. Agency officials find them a valuable source of information about practices that affect administrative problems and about the attitudes of their organizations toward government policy. When the operations of national representatives are confined to this sphere, there can be little criticism of their practices. Some of them, however, sell "personal friendship" with important personages to gullible clients, to whom they give the impression that all problems will be solved by a sufficiently large retainer fee. An investigation generally reduces these friendships to no more than casual acquaintance, evidenced, perhaps, by an autographed picture supplied by an official as a courtesy. It is surprising how many otherwise shrewd Americans conclude from such evidence that the lobbyist has access to the highest places, and that responsible officials actually dispense public business as a personal favor. Occasionally, however, a government administrator may make a special interest group a vehicle for his own rise to power. An official who identifies his personal interests with such a group is not a safe repository of a public trust.

Some administrative agencies channel the views of interest groups into the administrative process by means of advisory committees. These groups advise administrative officials concerning agency policy, legislative proposals that are being formulated, or administrative difficulties and deficiencies that should be corrected. Occasionally they are helpful in finding personnel for vacancies within the agency. They may be used by administrators to organize support for agency activities. Wisely used, advisory committees are valuable in giving an administrative agency the reaction of the governed to its program. But the development is not without danger.

> It daily sharpens the need for administrative authorities who are skillful in consultation, vigilant in arranging representation that is reasonably comprehensive, sympathetic but wary, above all independent. Only by careful use of advisory boards will the danger of compromising administration at its core be avoided.[14]

political parties

Political parties have not been given a role in administration comparable to that of the special interest groups. For the most part, party influence is confined to key officials appointed by the President. Our reluctance to go further is in part a result of the general acceptance of the merit principle in the appointment of administrative personnel. Most of us consider party interest, "patronage," or "politics" irrelevant to the choice of officials. Also, we are suspicious of decisions that "politicians" have helped to make. This attitude is prevalent among government administrators, who prefer to deal directly with special interest groups rather than with them indirectly through the political middleman. As a result, the administrative processes are shielded from the political parties on which so much of the process of government now depends. Party leaders must conceal their efforts to exert legitimate influence in administration. That this result is conducive to the most effective and most democratic administration is by no means clear. Why should a group representing a narrow interest be more competent to speak on behalf of the public than a political party? In the future we are likely to see the development of a recognized and closer relationship between the administrative and political party processes.

administration as synthesis

Synthesis is defined in *Webster's Collegiate Dictionary* (1949) as "1. Composition or combination of parts, elements, etc., so as to form a whole . . . ." Administration is a process for synthesizing the specialized skills, occupations, and interests that comprise our industrial society. Technological developments fragment social unity without strengthening the devices for synthesis; but without synthesis, the multiplication of specialties in society rapidly produces chaos.

reconciling the judgments of experts

The growth of specialties that characterizes our society has also taken place in government. At the end of the last century, not more than one thirtieth of the jobs in the federal government required technical, scientific, or professional

---

[14] Arthur W. Macmahon, "Advisory Boards," *Encyclopaedia of the Social Sciences*, II, 609–612.

training; today, about one third of the jobs require such training. But the significance of the work of government specialists is not adequately reflected by the numbers employed. Experts move into influential, if not dominant, positions as the government expands scientific research, imposes controls on the economy, or manufactures atomic weapons.

There are several troublesome consequences of this trend, of which the most serious is the lack of reliable and accepted devices for reconciling the conflicting judgments of experts. It is unfortunately true that experts differ even with respect to problems about which scientifically precise information is available. For example, in the field of national defense there are many such problems. Should we or should we not spend hundreds of millions of dollars to develop a hydrogen bomb? Would this money be more wisely spent to manufacture atomic weapons that have now been perfected? How much of our appropriations for national defense should go to the Army and how much to the Navy and the Air Force? The naval air specialist recommends that we construct large numbers of planes that can operate from the decks of carriers. The Army air specialist tells us that the submarine and the atomic bomb have made the carrier obsolete, and that we should rely on land-based bombers that can fly nonstop halfway around the world. Which is right? Although the experts disagree, decisions must be made; the debate cannot go on endlessly without endangering national security.

Usually the disagreements between experts are resolved by men who are not themselves experts. In the English government it is said that the "expert is on tap, not on top." He is there to give advice when it is needed; but he *advises*; he does not make decisions. The expert in our government has a similar role. The President and Congress, for example, after hearing the arguments of their advisers, decide how our money for national defense is to be spent. Many of these questions are so involved that the average person cannot pretend to have adequate judgment about them; for this reason, they may not contain "political" questions in the normal sense of that term. But there are social implications about which the expert's judgment is unreliable. Within government departments, administrative officials supplement the specialist's knowledge with understanding of the social and political factors. An expert who prepares himself to handle these factors normally cannot keep abreast of developments in his field of knowledge. We may say, then, that the administrator is a generalist who seeks a workable integration of the views of the political specialist and the technical expert. Brooks Adams has said of this relationship:

Administration is the capacity of coordinating many and often conflicting, social energies in a single organism, so adroitly that they shall operate as a unity. This presupposes the power of recognizing a series of relations between numerous special social interests, with all of which no single man can be intimately acquainted. Probably no highly specialized class can be strong in this intellectual quality because of the intellectual isolation incident to specialization; and yet administration or generalization is not only the faculty upon which social stability rests, but is, possibly, the highest faculty of the human mind.[15]

disunity in structure, unity in operation

Administration synthesizes in yet another way. The framers of the Constitution devised a government in which the power of officials was counterbalanced by the power of other officials. This arrangement was achieved by means of separation of powers, checks and balances, and the federal system. The President checks Congress, Congress checks the President, and each checks the courts. The national government and the governments of the separate states check each other. This lack of unity disperses authority for action and throws upon some group the burden of unifying governmental operations. As Woodrow Wilson said:

> [The government] is modified by its environment, necessitated by its tasks, shaped to its functions by the sheer pressure of life. No living thing can have its organs offset against each other as checks, and live. On the contrary, its life is dependent upon their quick cooperation, their ready response to the commands of instinct or intelligence, their amicable community of purpose. Government is not a body of blind forces; it is a body of men, with highly differentiated functions, no doubt, in our modern day of specialization, but with a common task and purpose. Their cooperation is indispensable, and their warfare fatal. There can be no successful government without leadership or without the intimate, almost instinctive, coordination of the organs of life and action.[16]

The task of unifying governmental operations falls most heavily upon the executive branch and, especially, upon the President. Administration is pre-eminently the government in action. When the Department of Agriculture or the Securities and Exchange Commission acts on behalf of or in restraint of a citizen or corporation, it is the *government* that acts, not the legislature, the judiciary, or the executive. For this reason, the responsible officials must consider all aspects of the enforcement problem. What does the statute require or permit? What have congressional committees said in elaboration of the statute? What is the attitude of the courts? How does the congressman or the senator whose constituent is affected feel about the problem? Should an interested pressure group be consulted? Or political party leaders? Is there a political factor of interest to the President? Is there another executive agency that is interested in the problem or that contemplates action under a related law? Is the problem one

---

[15] Brooks Adams, *The Theory of Social Revolutions* (New York: The Macmillan Company, 1913), pp. 207–208.
[16] Woodrow Wilson, *Constitutional Government in the United States* (New York: Columbia University Press, 1921), p. 56.

in which state or local governments are interested? What action would most nearly satisfy the purposes of all of the governments—federal, state, and local? Administrative officials constantly have such questions before them as they direct the work of their organizations. They—and, indeed, the American people—look to the presidency for the leadership required for the effective functioning of the American government.

Writing before World War I, Brooks Adams observed: "We have extended the range of applied science until we daily use infinite forces, and those forces must, apparently, disrupt our society, unless we can raise the laws and institutions which hold society together to an energy and efficiency commensurate to them." [17] Since Adams wrote, two world wars, a world economic catastrophe, and marvelous technological developments have speeded the disruption of our society. In some countries, the resulting social convulsions have taken the form of violent revolutions. In other countries, such as Great Britain and the United States, governmental institutions have been able to assimilate change sufficiently to maintain a relatively stable society. Whether we shall be able to do so in the future is largely a matter of—to use Adams's term—administrative efficiency. Robert Frost has said: "Yes, revolutions are the only salves. But they're one thing that should be done by halves." [18] Administration is a process through which society has its revolutions by halves.

bibliographic note

Sources for further reading about the theory and practice of public administration range from technical publications to popular fiction. Not along ago, the Journal of the American Society for Public Administration, *Public Administration Review*, recommended a novel as a "tremendously important book which every serious student of public management ought to read and reread many times."—IV, No. 4 (Autumn, 1944), 372. The novel, John Hersey's *A Bell for Adano* (New York: Alfred A. Knopf, Inc., 1944), shows clearly the ways in which administration influences, and is influenced by, human beings and their physical and social environment. This obvious but often neglected idea may be followed also in case studies such as Alexander H. Leighton, *The Governing of Men* (Princeton: Princeton University Press, 1945), concerned with administrative problems in one of the relocation camps to which Japanese-Americans were transferred from the Pacific Coast in the early days of World War II; and

---

[17] Adams, *The Theory of Social Revolutions*, p. 28.
[18] From *A Witness Tree* by Robert Frost, Copyright, 1942, by Robert Frost. Used by permission of Henry Holt and Company, Inc.

Henry L. Stimson and McGeorge Bundy, *On Active Service in Peace and War* (New York: Harper & Brothers, 1947), the autobiography of a great American whose long life was spent in the service of humanity. For a brief but inclusive statement of the principal characteristics of our industrial society, see John M. Gaus, "American Society and Public Administration," in *Frontiers of Public Administration* (Chicago: The University of Chicago Press, 1936); in the same volume, "Responsibility of Public Administration," by the same author is also worthy of close attention. Books about technological development in society are Roger Burlingame, *Backgrounds of Power* (New York: Charles Scribner's Sons, 1949), and his *Engines of Democracy* (New York: Charles Scribner's Sons, 1940). These volumes show the results of the application of science in industry and in society. Excellent studies of the same problem are Lewis Mumford's *Technics and Civilization* (New York: Harcourt, Brace and Company, 1934) and *The Culture of Cities* (New York: Harcourt, Brace and Company, 1938). The necessity for effective government in technological society is described in John B. Martin, "The Blast in Centralia No. 5," *Harper's Magazine, CXCVI*, No. 1,174 (March, 1948), 193–220.

The brief discussion of forms of administrative action in this chapter may be supplemented by a more advanced text, such as Leonard D. White, *Introduction to the Study of Public Administration* (New York: The Macmillan Company, 3d ed., 1948). Ernst Freund laid the foundation for subsequent work on this subject with his *Administrative Powers over Persons and Property* (Chicago: The University of Chicago Press, 1928), a monument to the prodigious scholarship of the author and a standard reference on the subject. Although adequate solutions are yet to be found, an enormous amount of attention has been given to problems arising out of the creation and expansion of regulatory agencies vested with rule-making and adjudicatory powers. A persuasive argument for these authorities is made by James M. Landis, *The Administrative Process* (New Haven: Yale University Press, 1938), and by Walter Gellhorn, *Federal Administrative Proceedings* (Baltimore: The Johns Hopkins Press, 1941). There is an abundance of critical literature, of which Gordon Hewart, *The New Despotism* (New York: Cosmopolitan Book Corp., 1929), concerned with the problem in Great Britain, is illustrative. There are important studies by official groups in both England and the United States. *Report of Committee on Ministers' Powers*, Cmd. 4,060 (London: His Majesty's Stationery Office, 1932), is the work of a group of distinguished scholars and officials. The report of the special committee appointed by the United States Attorney General, and headed by Dean Acheson, is exhaustive: "Administrative Procedures in Government Agencies," *Senate Document* No. 8, 77 Cong., I Sess (1941). This report explains the causes of the increasing reliance upon administrative regulatory techniques and the weaknesses and strengths of current practices and institutions, and proposes constructive remedies for the principal difficulties. Congress attempted to safeguard the abuse of power by administrative agencies by passing the Administrative Procedure Act of 1946. This legislation is discussed from varying points of view in *The Federal Administrative Procedure Act and the Federal Agencies* (George Warren, ed.; New York: New York University Law School, 1947). For cogent critical discussion of this law, see Frederick F. Blachley and Miriam E. Oatman, "Sabotage of the Administrative Process," *Public Administration Review*, VI, No. 3 (Summer, 1946), 213–227, and Julius Cohen, "Legislative Injustice and Supremacy 'of Law,'" *Nebraska Law Review*, XXVI (March, 1947), 323–345. John Dickinson, *Administrative Justice and the Supremacy of Law* (Cambridge: Harvard University Press, 1927), treats comprehensively the subject of judicial review of administrative determinations; a less intensive analysis is J. Roland Pennock, *Administration and the Rule of Law* (New York: Rinehart & Company, 1941). The independent regulatory commissions in the federal government are discussed with impressive scholarship in Robert E. Cushman, *The Independent Regulatory Commissions* (New York: Oxford University Press, 1941). Other helpful discussions are by Charles S. Hyneman, *Bureaucracy in a Democracy* (New York: Harper & Brothers, 1950), and by James W. Fessler, in *Elements of Public Administration* (Fritz Morstein Marx, ed.; New York: Prentice-Hall, Inc., 1946).

Literature about the relation of policy and administration is increasing in volume and in quality. For excerpts from numerous sources, see Chapter 3 of a book of readings edited by Albert Lepawsky, *Administration* (New York: Alfred A. Knopf, Inc., 1949). Woodrow Wilson's essay, *"The Study of Administration,"* cited in the text of this chapter, might be followed by Frank J. Goodnow, *Politics and Administration* (New York: The Macmillan Company, 1900), which adopts the view that policy and administration are distinct and separable. Pendleton Herring, *Public Administration and the Public Interest* (New York: McGraw-Hill Book Company, 1936), shows the influence of pressure groups on policy formulation by administrative agencies. For discussions of the interrelations of policy, politics, and administration, see John M. Gaus, *Reflections on Public Administration* (University: University of Alabama Press, 1947); Paul M. Appleby, *Policy and Administration* (University: University of Alabama Press, 1949), and his *Big Democracy* (New York: Alfred A. Knopf, Inc, 1945); and Charles S. Hyneman, *Bureaucracy in a Democracy*, cited above. These four books are distinguished examples of recent writing in the field of American government.

John M. Gaus, *Reflections on Public Administration*, is a perceptive essay elucidating the conception of *administration as synthesis*. Brooks Adams, *The Theory of Social Revolutions* (New York: The Macmillan Company, 1913), is an early and brilliant discussion of the need for generalists as well as specialists in a modern industrial society. The same theme is well discussed in Appleby, *Big Democracy*, cited above. There are excellent chapters in *Dynamic Administration*, a collection of Mary Parker Follett's papers edited by Henry C. Metcalf and L. Urwick (New York: The Macmillan Company, 1940), and in Chester I. Barnard, *Organization and Management* (Cambridge: Harvard University Press, 1948), particularly "The Nature of Leadership" and "Education for Executives." The literature dealing with the role of the expert in society is not extensive. John Dewey, *The Public and Its Problems* (Chicago: Gateway Books, 1946), is concerned with this subject and is a "must" for students of political science. Several worth-while articles have appeared in the English journal *Public Administration*: Charles Christie, "Democracy and the Expert," XI, No. 4 (October, 1933), 351–368; F. L. C. Floud, "Sphere of the Specialist in Public Administration," I (April, 1923), 117–126; J. R. H. Roberts and A. S. M. MacGregor, "The Professional Expert and Administrative Control," VII, No. 3 (July, 1929), 247–259; and L. A. C. Herbert "The Expert in Civil Service," and F. H. Smith and Arthur Collins, "The Expert in the Local Government Service," XXII, No. 1 (Spring, 1944), 23–30; 30–46. Fritz Morstein Marx, "The Lawyer's Role in Public Administration," *Yale Law Journal*, LV, 498–526 (April, 1946), is an excellent discussion of a difficult problem. A provocative examination of the strengths and weaknesses of the professional soldier in World War I is Liddell Hart, *The War in Outline* (New York: The Modern Library, 1936); the ideas advanced have application in civil as well as military organizations.

the presidency:

responsibilities and powers

THE balancing of power and restraint that is so characteristic of American democracy is nowhere better illustrated than in the presidency. The American chief executive is entrusted with functions that in England are shared by the King and the Prime Minister and in France by the President and the Premier. Our President is, in fact, the most powerful official produced by a democratic society. He has attained this distinction gradually; the presidency as we know it has developed over a period of 160 years. In this time America has been threatened periodically by wars and depressions, and national survival has required the vigorous use of all the powers that Presidents have been able to command. More significantly, the challenge of danger has been met, aside from the Civil War, without penalizing dissent and without rule by violence. Over the years our Presidents have increased their own powers and have also fortified the protections against despotism. The President's power is still limited by the Constitution as interpreted by Congress and the judiciary, and the right to criticize his conduct is supported by political traditions that Presidents have helped to strengthen.

the nature of the presidency

The presidency—the office as distinguished from the occupant—is the product of many forces. It is uniquely subject to the influence of personality. A President gives to the office the imprint of his own character and achievements and thereby changes it for his successors. Conversely, a man frequently has been transformed by the challenge and the responsibility of the office. This relationship is so close that it is futile to discuss the presidency except in terms of the interaction of man and institution. Secondly, all aspects of government, including the executive, are conditioned by influences that affect society generally. The presidency has responded to changing social needs, so that it is one thing in one generation and something quite different in the next. Finally, the presidency has been shaped by the judgments and conceptions of the framers as embodied in the Constitution. The constitutional provisions concerning the presidency are in this sense an outgrowth of early American governmental experience.

colonists suspicious of executive power

Colonial experiences led to a distrust of executive power. The colonists brought to this country attitudes that were influenced by the struggle in England between King and Parliament. Although opinion in America was divided, there is no doubt that a large number of men came to the conclusion that, as a matter of principle, the executive should be subordinate to the legislature. Attempts to control the expenditures of government centered attention on the taxing power, which gradually became the prerogative of the legislatures. When this point was established, the legislatures had a weapon that could be used to defeat the policies of the governors. In disputes over matters of finance, delegates to the colonial legislatures generally could be counted upon to oppose the governor when his proposals appeared to be detrimental to the interests of their fellow colonists. As war approached, England imposed onerous restrictions that were bitterly resented. Thus, at the outbreak of the Revolution, the view was widely held that executive power was selfish, arbitrary, and a threat to liberty.

the revolutionary executives were weak

Executive officials were given minimal powers in the governments that were established to carry on the war against England. The state constitutions provided brief terms for the governors, sharply limited their powers, and generally subordinated them to the legislatures. The thirteen states were joined, under the Articles of Confederation, in what Benjamin Franklin termed a "league of friendship." The league was fatally defective in that it denied to the national government the essential powers of taxation and of regulation of commerce. The executive was equally defective. During the early years of the Revolution, Congress relied upon standing committees to carry on public affairs when it was not in session; but neither the committees nor the rudimentary executives that later evolved from them were adequate to the needs of war.[1] There was ample opportunity for thoughtful men to observe these governments in action, to relate their experiences to the ideas that had grown up before the Revolution, and to formulate new proposals that seemed more appropriate to the needs of the country.

discussions in the Constitutional Convention

The framers of the Constitution did not resolve easily the conflicting elements of their experience. The dangers inherent in executive power unrestrained by

---

[1] Jennings B. Sanders, *Evolution of Executive Departments of the Continental Congress, 1774–1789* (Chapel Hill: University of North Carolina Press, 1935).

law were generally understood. But, in retrospect, it was also clear that the legislative-dominated governments of the Revolutionary period failed in important respects. An American victory had not been by any means a foregone conclusion, and on occasion after occasion weaknesses of the Confederation government jeopardized success. This government also had great difficulty in the reconstruction period. To be sure, the central government was at best the junior in a cooperative activity in which the states had the controlling voice. But the state governments had been unable to take an active part in reconstruction; in fact, they were hard pressed merely to maintan order. In Massachusetts, for example, it had been necessary to use troops to suppress Shays' Rebellion. This experience argued for stronger government and independent executives, an idea that found support in writings of Montesquieu and Locke which members of the convention had studied carefully.

Discussions of the nature of the executive occupied the members throughout the Constitutional Convention. The problem was two-sided: to create an executive whose position and authority would energize the government; and to surround him with sufficient safeguards so that dictatorship would be unlikely. One group of delegates shared the view of Roger Sherman, who considered "the Executive magistracy as nothing more than an institution for carrying the will of the Legislature into effect" and thought that the executive "ought to be appointed by and accountable to the Legislature only, which was the depository of the supreme will of society." [2] For a time this group was attracted to the idea of a plural executive, possibly three men, on the general grounds that it would be less dangerous to liberty. Finally, however, a majority was won over to the view that the executive should be a single individual, with wide authority, and independent of Congress. Because the minority view was based upon deep conviction, in the end it was necessary to compromise on the method of electing the President and in the choice of language defining his powers and duties. The compromise is embodied in Article Two and related provisions of the Constitution.

Article Two is ambiguous

"The executive power shall be vested in a President of the United States." This short opening statement is characteristic of the entire article, which goes on to declare: "the President shall be Commander-in-Chief of the Army and Navy"; "he shall nominate, and, by and with the advice and consent of the Senate, shall appoint ambassadors, other public ministers and consuls, judges of the Supreme Court, and all other officers of the United States whose appointments are not herein otherwise provided for, and which shall be established

---

[2] Max Farrand, *The Records of The Federal Convention* (New Haven: Yale University Press, 1911), I, 65.

by law"; "he may require the opinion, in writing, of the principal officer in each of the executive departments"; "he shall receive ambassadors and other public ministers"; and "he shall from time to time give to the Congress information of the state of the Union, and recommend to their consideration such measures as he shall judge necessary and expedient." Thus are stated some of the executive powers and duties of the President. The article is brief—about half the length of Article One, which describes the organization and powers of Congress. The statement of the powers of Congress contains about thirteen hundred words; about four hundred are used to define the President's powers.

The generality and ambiguity of these provisions is striking. Does the opening clause mean simply that the chief executive is to have the title "President of the United States"? Or does it grant to the President a broad and undefined "executive power"? If it confers power, what specific acts are thereby authorized? Is it significant that Article One states that "all legislative powers herein granted shall be vested in a Congress of the United States," whereas the term "herein granted" does not appear in Article Two? Are there executive powers that are not given to the President? What, specifically, can or must the President do as commander-in-chief? Are his powers in this capacity in addition to those contained in the grant of "executive power"? Or does the commander-in-chief clause define more precisely the nature of executive power referred to in the opening statement of the article?

The Constitution does not provide precise answers to these and related questions. Article Two enumerates the President's major responsibilities and confers general powers that he may use in meeting his responsibilities. The enumerated powers, however, are merely nuclei about which are clustered other powers that may be termed implied, informal, or extraconstitutional. These latter powers have come into existence, in response to need, by legislative enactment, judicial interpretation, and custom.

a task for superman?

In a thoughtful book about the Constitution, Herbert W. Horwill wrote: "No one can read the descriptions of the everyday routines of the White House . . . without being convinced that his task is one for a superman." [3] What does a President do in a normal week? Many of his actions are "off the record" and never come to public attention; but others are reported in detail by newspapers and radio. Examination of these reports provides useful insights into the nature of the presidency.

For example, early in 1950 the following activities of Harry S. Truman were noted by the press: [4] On Sunday he participated in ceremonies commemo-

---

[3] H. W. Horwill, *The Usages of the American Constitution* (London: Oxford University Press, 1925), p. 85.

[4] Washington *Post*, week of February 12, 1950.

'rating the birth of Abraham Lincoln. Two days later he spoke before a Conference on Law Enforcement Problems. On Thursday night the President delivered a major political speech in the presence of fifty-three hundred Democrats who had come to Washington to hear their party leaders and to raise money to finance their party activities. These appearances were photographed for the newsreels and broadcast by radio and television for millions of listeners throughout the United States and several foreign countries—a fact that unquestionably added significance to the occasions.

The President discussed veterans' benefits with Democratic leaders of Congress and later sent to Congress a message urging passage of legislation dealing with the problem. He designated an acting chairman of the Atomic Energy Commission and, presumably, continued to search for a suitable replacement for the retiring chairman. He made decisions concerning negotiations for settlement of a dispute between the United Mine Workers of America and the coal mine operators. (In spite of his efforts, which seemed inadequate to some citizens and excessive to others, the strike continued, railroad schedules were curtailed, and factories and schools were closed by an acute coal shortage.) Also, he received an award for his efforts in extending civil rights to minority groups and he approved loans totaling $6.5 million to help twenty-eight states and Puerto Rico build low-cost public housing.

During the week the President had appointments with a list of people that included, in this order, the president of the Baldwin Piano Company; the president of the National Maritime Union; the Secretary of Labor and the president of the National Association of Manufacturers; a senator and two residents of West Virginia; a former congressman from the President's home district; the recently resigned chairman of the Atomic Energy Commission; a Texas senator, the mayor of Houston, and the president of the Houston Press Club; the Federal Housing Administrator; the Secretary of Defense; the mayor of Los Angeles; the United States ambassador to Finland; the Secretary of State; the members of the Democratic National Committee; the Cuban ambassador; the Director of the Budget; the national officers of the Disabled Veterans of America; a former attorney general of Texas and a member of Congress from Texas; the governor of Montana and a Montana senator; the mayor of St. Louis; and he and Mrs. Truman received at the White House several hundred Democratic party leaders.

The President met with his cabinet and, later, held his weekly meeting with the White House corps of newspaper reporters, columnists, and radio commentators. At the press conference he was taken to task because he had given an exclusive interview to a *New York Times* columnist, and he was queried on such widely divergent subjects as the coal strike, the relations between the United States and the Soviet Union, his attitude on a statement by a senator that there were fifty-seven members of the Communist party employed in the Depart-

ment of State, his plans for campaigning during the coming congressional elections, and his authority to remove from office the general counsel of the National Labor Relations Board.

Although relatively few of these activities are mentioned specifically in
the Constitution, most of them can be traced to words or phrases found in Article
Two. Moreover, they may be grouped under one or another of the President's
main areas of responsibility—national leader, chief executive, chief of foreign
relations, or commander-in-chief.

the President as national leader

Capacity for leadership is an essential quality of American Presidents. Without
some ability to influence others, a man is not likely to win the nomination or to
be elected to office; with outstanding leadership qualities a President may achieve
great things for his country and a place in history for himself. In operation,
checks and balances and other features of our constitutional and political system mean that the President shares authority with people whose cooperation
must be won if his administration is to function smoothly. He cannot escape
this burden, since it is generally the President who is blamed for an impasse between Congress and the executive. He must, therefore, devote a major part of
his time and energy to conferences with members of Congress, party leaders,
presidents of business and labor organizations, and other key figures of public
and private life. In an earlier and simpler time, it was possible for a President
either to choose a course of positive leadership or to leave this role to others. A
President no longer has that choice; the demands of the times are such that
he must use constantly whatever talents of leadership he possesses. Louis
Brownlow, who has known personally every President since Theodore Roosevelt, writes: "In a word, the Presidency has become the symbol in which the
American people see made one their purpose, their plans, and their aspirations;
the President has become the supreme servant who is expected to take the lead
in realizing that purpose, those plans and aspirations." [5]

What qualities does this role require of our President? The President should understand the forces that operate within society and should perceive correctly the direction in which civilization is moving. Rapid change is a
prime characteristic of modern society. Since men are fearful of change, even
when they are unhappy with the present, it is part of a President's job to help
cushion the disruptions incident to change. He must be willing to strike out
against currents that run strongly against a position that seems to him to be required by high principles, even at the cost of popularity or office. A great President is more than a mirror that reflects the views of the majority; an important

---

[5] Louis Brownlow, *The President and the Presidency* (Chicago: Public Administration
Service, 1949), p. 19.

part of his job is to help create a majority view that will support the policies and objectives of his administration.

For these tasks the President needs enormous reserves of vitality and zest. His attitude should convey a sense of concern about the problems of human beings and a desire to take positive steps to help overcome their difficulties. In emergencies, he should appear to the people as a confident, fighting, democratic leader, with a vigorous program worthy of their support. A President should have a liking for the management of opinion and for the rough-and-tumble of political campaigns. Politics in a democracy is a continuing battle to win the support of public opinion, and the President must not shun the offensive on issues of fundamental importance. He must be aware of difficulties but not become preoccupied with them. He cannot be oversensitive to criticism; there will be opposition in any case, and it may be especially biting when he acts most courageously. There are times when a touch of the "Damn the torpedoes! Full speed ahead!" spirit is desirable. Perspective and a sense of humor will help shield him from the corrosive attacks that all Presidents must endure. Finally, the President must be able to convey to his executive subordinates and to the people the essential qualities of sympathy, courage, and optimism.

chief of state

As chief of state, the President symbolizes to Americans and to the rest of the world the power and glory of the United States government. He and his wife lend color and drama to public ceremonies; they provide the theatricals that help to relieve, at least momentarily, the cares and routines that press upon men. The President personifies the government and thereby gives the ordinary person a livelier sense of its meaning.

This role does not give any substantive powers of great significance, but it does require the expenditure of precious energy. The President and his wife must entertain prominent citizens, important political leaders, and diplomats and visiting dignitaries from other countries. In the year 1939, for example, there were at the White House 323 house guests, 4,729 dinner guests, and about 23,000 people for teas and receptions.[6] Events and activities that are considered routine in a normal household take on great significance when they concern the President or his family. The press keeps a close watch on the White House, reporting in detail the fact that the President has decided to take a walk every day, or to drive in the country; that he swims every afternoon; that he did or did not go to church Sunday. All of the ordinary difficulties and pleasures of family life are magnified when they occur in the "first family" and the slightest deviation from the conventional is seized upon as a subject for gossip, or, by the opposition, as a political weapon. The President must buy the first

---

[6] Eleanor Roosevelt, *This I Remember* (New York: Harper & Brothers, 1949), p. 95.

Christmas seal and the first veteran's poppy. He must have his picture taken throwing out the first baseball of the season, even though he throws awkwardly. He is expected to do all of these things because, in the minds of the people, he and his wife are, to use Bagehot's phrase, "the head of the pageant of life."

public opinion

The President as leader of public opinion performs an educational and a political function. He has a major responsibility to arouse public interest in the big issues of the times, and to help provide information necessary for understanding and intelligent decision. In general, the mass media give more adequate coverage to crime and sports news than to public affairs; and information released through the special interest groups tends to be one-sided. A carefully prepared and well-timed major address by the President can help millions of citizens to understand a current problem and the alternative solutions. The significance of this function is illustrated by Franklin D. Roosevelt's statements about the threat of totalitarian government, which undoubtedly were a major factor in the formation of American public opinion with respect to Germany, Italy, and Japan.

From the political point of view, the President must take an active part in the formation of opinion because, if he does not, his administration cannot be successful. Many of his key proposals inevitably are controversial and arouse congressional opposition that must be overcome. Woodrow Wilson believed that the President can override Congress only if he "has the nation behind him and Congress has not. He has no means of compelling Congress except through public opinion." [7] Franklin Roosevelt was masterful in his use of the "fireside chat" to enlist public support for controversial legislation. But, as Coolidge observed, the President cannot appeal to the public too often or "after a while he will get no response." [8] The President must maintain general public confidence in his leadership and his program; if he does, Congress will feel the pressure of public opinion and view his proposals in a cooperative spirit.

The President influences opinion principally by making public statements. A major presidential address is normally front-page news and is heard by millions of people over radio and television. Many messages to Congress attract wide interest. Informal statements are also effective. These may come in the form of brief messages of felicitations on important anniversaries, published letters to individuals, or interviews with the press. Woodrow Wilson was one of the first Presidents to see the possibility of the press conference. Harding was

---

[7] Woodrow Wilson, *Constitutional Government in the United States* (New York: Columbia University Press, 1921), p. 70.
[8] W. E. Binkley, *The Powers of the President* (Garden City: Doubleday & Company, 1937), p. 245.

unable to handle the press successfully, and it was not until the election of Franklin Roosevelt that the President's press conference was fully utilized as a method of reaching the public. There is always the danger that an opposition reporter will catch the President off guard and elicit a statement that may later prove to be embarrassing; but this danger is avoidable if the President is carefully briefed by his advisers and if he refuses to be drawn into casual comment about controversial matters.

political leader

First and foremost, the President is a political leader. The growth of the party system changed drastically the Founding Fathers' conception of the government and, especially, of the presidency.[9] When a candidate for the presidential office receives the nomination, he becomes, and after election continues to be, the head of his party. He cannot be elected and he cannot do his job without his party's support. The position of leader of the Democratic or Republican parties is in a sense symbolic. These parties are in reality loosely knit coalitions of state and local factions that cannot be directed from a central point—by the President or by anyone else. For this reason, the President must use all of the political acumen that he and his advisers can command if he is to weld the factions into a responsible party organization. If he is a strong vote getter, the state and local bosses may feel indebted to him for helping them to stay in power. As often as not, the bosses boast of their achievement in electing a President who would have been defeated without their support. During the first months of a new administration, the President may hold his party in line by the strategic disposition of jobs, but "the effectiveness of patronage as a means of control is limited by the number of jobs and by the gratitude of the job holders."[10]

These relationships are inherent in our governmental system. In order to be an effective leader, the President must "resort to secret and unseen influences, to private interviews, and private arrangements. . . ."[11] It is not realistic or fair to expect the President to ignore the interests of his party. His first loyalty is to the nation, but there are many occasions when there is no conflict between the interests of nation and party, and it is quite proper for him to act in a partisan manner. By such action he builds up support that can be used later for important national projects.

chief legislator

The President has become the chief legislator in the sense that the executive is a principal source of stimulation and guidance in the formulation of public

---

[9] See Chapters 9, 12, and 18.

[10] Pendleton Herring, *Presidential Leadership* (New York: Rinehart & Company, 1940), p. 70.

[11] *Ibid.*, p. 46.

policy.[12] His role as a congressional leader is supported by the power to veto acts of Congress, by the fact that Congress has not developed within itself a cohesive leadership, and by the expectations of the people. Because the framers did not anticipate this development and provide for it in the Constitution, the President as chief legislator must rely heavily on his effectiveness in mobilizing public opinion and party support.

The general plan of the Constitution, especially the separation of legislative and executive branches, is an obstacle to sustained legislative leadership. The President is chosen by a national electorate for a four-year term; members of the House of Representatives are elected by local districts for two-year terms; and senators are elected for six-year terms. As a result of these differences in terms of office, the presidency and Congress can be controlled by different political parties. Even when stalemates occur, as they do occasionally, the President and members of Congress must serve out their respective terms. There is no constitutional method for the President to dissolve Congress and call a new election; and Congress cannot, short of impeachment, bring about a change in the presidency. In this respect our system differs fundamentally from that of England, France, and other nations with "parliamentary" or "cabinet" governments, in which members of the legislature must follow the executive's leadership on policy matters or be prepared to face an immediate election and possible defeat.

The lack of a disciplined party organization is another factor that limits the President's effectiveness as chief legislator. Members of Congress trace their strength back to local political groups rather than to a central party organization, and naturally they are concerned with the effect of proposed legislation upon their constituents. But because of this concern, it is generally difficult, and frequently impossible, for the party in nominal control of Congress to maintain a continuing majority in support of controversial measures. Thus, as a result of the nature of representation and of the party organization, Congress normally takes a negative attitude toward the national questions which have a first claim upon the President's time and energy.

In spite of these difficulties, most of our Presidents have been able to provide a satisfactory degree of legislative leadership. An attractive legislative program helps a candidate and his party to win elections. Also, Congress is so large and unwieldy that it cannot easily initiate proposals; it works best when considering and revising the proposals of others. It is not reasonable, either, to expect a congressman to become expert on more than a few of the wide range of matters which Congress considers. For these reasons, Congress has turned increasingly to the President and the executive agencies for suggestions about pending problems and for preliminary drafts of bills.

---

[12] See Chapter 18 for a detailed discussion of the problem of presidential leadership in Congress.

the President as chief executive

The management and direction of the executive branch is one of the President's principal jobs. Without effective execution, the wisest policies cannot accomplish all that was intended or possible. But from the standpoint of a President, the problems of administration are bound to be less pressing than the demands of congressional relations, foreign affairs, or party politics. Soon after his election, Franklin Roosevelt stated: "The Presidency is not merely an administrative office. That is the least part òf it. It is more than an engineering job, efficient or inefficient. It is pre-eminently a place of moral leadership." [13] This view would undoubtedly represent the judgment of most of our Presidents. Certainly a President should not sacrifice his position as national leader simply to ensure a tidy operation of the executive establishment.

the enforcement of law

Law enforcement is a major responsibility that does not require the President's continuing and active attention. He is charged by the Constitution to "take care that the laws be faithfully executed," that is, faithfully executed by others. The executive departments and agencies carry, under presidential supervision, the day by day burdens of enforcement. Provisions of law that impose fines or imprisonment for convicted violations are enforced by the Department of Justice and the federal courts. Since the majority of our citizens comply voluntarily with the law when they know what it requires, relatively few cases actually go to trial. Most enforcement activities of federal departments are educational in the sense that they are intended to inform the people how the law affects their conduct. Thus law enforcement methods include speeches by officials, published articles, letters, and conferences as well as police surveillance, indictment, and trial.

The President's enforcement responsibilities have been enlarged by the congressional practice of "delegating legislative power." Because of the complexity of legislative problems, Congress often passes laws that state in general terms the underlying policies and procedures, and gives to the President or other executive officials the task of filling in statutory details by the issuance of rules and regulations. Rules, orders, and regulations issued under congressional authority have the force of law. The President may also issue orders under authority derived directly from the Constitution. From the standpoint of their effect, presidential orders fall into two general categories: those that relate to the internal administration of the executive branch, such as civil service rules or executive orders providing for the reorganization of a department; and those that affect people outside the government. The first group of orders consists of instructions to the President's subordinate officials concerning the discharge of

---

[13] Binkley, *Powers of the President*, p. 262.

their duties; hence they are a part of the machinery for presidential supervision of the executive branch. The second group of orders normally supplements acts of Congress; in this sense they are legislative rather than executive in character. Rules and regulations issued by executive departments are also concerned with internal administration or with the activities of private citizens. Since 1936, rules, orders, and regulations of the executive branch, including the executive orders issued by the President, have been published in the *Federal Register* and the *Code of Federal Regulations*. Since they are in effect law, their publication is as essential as that of acts of Congress.

The practice of delegating legislative power to the executive has created two important problems—one constitutional, and one administrative. The constitutional problem, simply stated, is this: in view of the principle of the separation of powers, under what conditions may legislative powers be delegated to and exercised by the executive? In 1934, a statute giving broad powers to the President was declared unconstitutional on the grounds that Congress had not provided sufficient "standards" to guide executive action.[14] In the absence of satisfactory guides or standards, it can be argued that Congress has *abdicated*, rather than *delegated*, its function of making basic policy. But the practical difficulty of anticipating in detail the application of a complex law requires that Congress leave to enforcement officials the task of specifying what is allowed and what is forbidden. If Congress settles the major issues, it seems both reasonable and proper that the executive be permitted to decide matters of detail. The balance between the two branches is maintained by the Supreme Court, which determines whether a particular delegation violates the Constitution.

An administrative problem is created when Congress delegates legislative power directly to administrative officials in executive departments rather than to the President. In this form of delegation, Congress takes the view that the administration of the law is subject to congressional, rather than to presidential, supervision. The effect of this legislation is to weaken the President's control over the executive branch and to make it difficult for him to discharge his constitutional obligation to "take care that the laws be faithfully executed." In practice, the President must rely on departmental officials to exercise many of his powers; but it is desirable that the President be able to control a subordinate whose actions are contrary to presidential policy. The President does not have this control when the subordinate is legally responsible to Congress.

appointment and removal of officials

The quality of the President's appointments sets the tone of his administration. Able subordinates who are devoted to his service rather than to self can relieve him of many of the cares of office and release energies for matters worthy of

---

[14] *Panama Refining Co. v. Ryan*, 293 U.S. 388 (1934).

his attention. Dishonest, careless, or stupid assistants can disgrace their chief and do great damage to their country. The President's responsibility in this respect is not as burdensome as it was before the adoption of the civil service system, when, according to President Taft, "even the humblest churchman or janitor felt a throb of personal interest in the political life of the President." [15] The extension of the merit system to rank-and-file positions means that the vast majority of these jobs will be filled, without effort on the President's part, by loyal and capable employees.[16] He continues, however, to have an active part in the selection of thousands of executive officials, judges, and diplomatic officers.

The Constitution, in Article Two, section two, describes the appointment power in the following terms:

> . . . And he shall nominate, and, by and with the advice and consent of the Senate, shall appoint ambassadors, other public ministers and consuls, judges of the Supreme Court and all other officers of the United States whose appointments are not herein otherwise provided for, and which shall be established by law; but the Congress may by law vest the appointment of such inferior officers as they think proper in the President alone, in the courts of law, or in the heads of departments.

The appointment of officials under this provision involves three steps. First, the President submits a nomination to the Senate. The nomination is referred to a committee, which may hold a hearing to satisfy itself that the nominee is qualified for office. Second, the committee reports the nomination, generally with a recommendation, to the Senate, and the members vote on the question of confirmation of the nomination. Finally, if the vote is favorable, the President makes the appointment and issues a commission to the official. If the Senate disapproves the nomination, the President normally submits another name. Occasionally, however, he waits until Congress adjourns and then gives an "interim" or "recess appointment" to his original choice. As an alternative, he may resubmit the original nomination to the Senate.

The Senate's attitude toward confirmation depends upon the position being filled. There is a growing disposition for members of the opposition party to be critical of the President's nominees and to vote against their confirmation. But approval is almost always given when the nomination is for a cabinet post and is rarely withheld for other top positions in the executive branch. The President is given freedom of choice in the selection of these officials because they are considered his personal advisers and assistants. Rejection of one of these nominations usually indicates either that the Senate considers the nominee unworthy of an important trust, or that it has lost confidence in the President. Approval is

---

[15] William Howard Taft, *The Presidency* (New York: Charles Scribner's Sons, 1916), p. 52.
[16] See Chapter 33, "Government Personnel: The Civil Servant."

also perfunctory for commissioned officers in the armed services, the public health service, and the career foreign service. These organizations are highly professional, and Congress has complete confidence in their systems for determining advancement of personnel. With respect to nominations of postmasters, districts court judges, and other officials who are appointed by and with the advice and consent of the Senate, friction is avoided by the practice known as "senatorial courtesy." It has been customary since George Washington's day for the President to consult in advance of nomination the senators in whose states the official will serve, if they are members of his political party. If the President fails to consult them, the senators may ask their colleagues to vote against confirmation; under "senatorial courtesy" the senators will usually comply, thereby defeating the nomination. Moreover, senators who have not been consulted by the President in accordance with custom may vote against confirmation of the President's nominees for top executive posts. If the senators in whose state the official will serve do not belong to the President's party, the state party chairman, rather than the senators, is usually consulted before an appointment is made.

The volume of nominations is so great that neither the President nor the Senate has time to investigate the qualifications of the nominees for subordinate positions. In the decade 1933–1942, 100,328 nominations were submitted to the Senate. A little more than half of these were commissioned officers in the armed services, and a third were postmasters.[17] Between January 3 and May 31, 1949, the President transmitted to the Senate 42,505 nominations.[18] Although he does not attempt to pass upon the qualifications of these nominees, the President is required to sign their commissions. President Taft considered this ". . . the greatest manual duty the President has to perform. . . . A substantial part of each day is taken up with signatures." [19]

The President's power to remove officials, like the appointive power, depends upon the nature of the office. It is established that he may remove, without prior consultation with the Senate, any member of his cabinet or any personal assistant or adviser. Politically, however, the President may consider it wise to consult key senators if the official is popular "on the Hill" or has strong political backing elsewhere. An entirely different question is presented when the President seeks to discharge an official who is outside his immediate entourage. If the official was appointed by and with the advice and consent of the Senate, must the Senate also consent to his removal? In 1926 the Supreme Court upheld President Wilson's removal, without senatorial consultations, of a first-class post-

---

[17] Arthur W. Macmahon, "Senatorial Confirmation," *Public Administration Review*, III, No. 4 (August, 1943), 281.

[18] *Congressional Record*, XCV, Part 18, Daily Digest, June 1, 1949, D348.

[19] Taft, *The Presidency*, p. 35.

master whose nomination had been submitted to the Senate for approval.[20] Since an act of Congress stipulated that the Senate must consent to this removal, the decision seemed to mean that Congress could not compel the President to secure the Senate's consent to the removal of officials whose nominations it had confirmed.

The question came before the Supreme Court again in 1935. This time the official removed by the President was a member of the Federal Trade Commission, one of the "independent regulatory commissions." The President thought that his views and those of the official, W. E. Humphrey, were incompatible, and he requested the latter to resign; when Humphrey refused to do so, the President removed him, in the face of a statutory provision that apparently limited removal to cases involving "inefficiency, neglect of duty, or malfeasance in office." In upholding this provision the Court stated that its decision in the *Myers* case was limited to "an executive officer restricted to the performance of executive functions." A different question is presented when the official in question is a member of the Federal Trade Commission, which "acts in part quasi-legislatively and in part quasi-judicially."

> The authority of Congress in creating quasi-legislative or quasi-judicial agencies, to require them to act in discharge of their duties independently of executive control cannot well be doubted; and that authority includes, as an appropriate incident, power to fix the period during which they shall continue in office, and to forbid their removal except for cause in the meantime. For it is quite evident that one who holds his office only during the pleasure of another, cannot be depended upon to maintain an attitude of independence against the latter's will.[21]

As a result of the *Myers* and *Rathbun* cases, it is difficult to state precisely the extent of this presidential power. Clearly the Court was on solid ground in distinguishing between the duties of a postmaster and those of a member of a regulatory commission. But the Secretary of Agriculture is an "executive" officer; and Congress has delegated to him powers that are essentially like those exercised by the regulatory commissions. Presumably these powers are "quasi-legislative and quasi-judicial." But certainly it does not follow that Congress could protect the "independence" of their exercise by limiting the President's power to remove from office the Secretary of Agriculture. About the only thing that can be said clearly as to those officials appointed by the President with the consent of the Senate is that Congress may not restrict the removal of department heads or officers with strictly routine duties and that it may restrict removal of the members of the independent regulatory commissions.

---

[20] *Myers* v. *United States,* 272 U.S. 52 (1926).
[21] *Humphrey's Executor* (Rathbun) v. *United States,* 295 U.S. 629 (1935).

the pardoning power

The Constitution vests in the President the power to "grant pardons and reprieves." Historically, this power was inherent in the King as the dispenser of mercy, and the grant of a pardon was considered an act of grace. Today, however, the pardon has lost its personal character and has become an established part of our machinery for the administration of justice.

A pardon is a grant to an individual absolving him from all or a part of the legal consequences of the crime that he committed. A reprieve merely suspends the penalties of the law. If a pardon is granted to a group of people whose offenses are political in character, it may be called a "grant of amnesty." Under the pardoning power the President may grant a full pardon, a pardon to terminate sentence and restore civil rights, a pardon to restore civil rights, a conditional pardon, amnesty, amnesty on condition, reprieve, commutation of sentence, commutation on condition, and remission of fines and forfeitures.[22]

Applications for pardons are handled by the Department of Justice, which normally disposes of about half of the applications without referring them to the President. The five hundred or more cases involving the pardoning power that come to the President's desk each year provide another illustration of the fact that relatively minor aspects of the office require a substantial amount of time during the course of a presidential term.

the President as chief of foreign affairs

Under the impact of war and depression the President's responsibilities have acquired an international dimension. The framers of the Constitution intended that the chief executive should be the principal officer concerned with the conduct of foreign affairs, but it is only in the last generation that the President has become an international figure of the first magnitude. His international stature came with the maturing of the United States as a world power and with the abandonment of the policy of isolationism. More fundamentally, the change is the result of forces created by the application of scientific discovery to fields such as manufacturing, transportation, and communication. Technology is propelling civilization in the direction of the interdependency of men, communities, and nations. Although the President can do little or nothing to reverse this trend, it is his responsibility to see that the interests of the United States are not adversely affected.

Today a President who fails as an international leader cannot be said to have discharged satisfactorily the duties of his office. In World War II President Roosevelt achieved a just fame for his part in the defeat of the Axis powers.

---

[22] W. H. Humbert, *The Pardoning Power of the President* (Washington: American Council on Public Affairs, 1941), p. 22.

After victory, the task became one of holding together a coalition of governments friendly to the interests and objectives of the United States and of building up the strength of international cooperation through the United Nations and its related organizations. In the struggle between communist and anticommunist ways of life, the President is expected to express our philosophy, aspirations, and policies in terms that reassure and encourage our friends. He is expected, also, to find effective solutions to problems that weaken the anticommunist coalition and the United Nations. The Truman administration's program to aid recovery in postwar Europe and the economic and military alliance of the North Atlantic nations were notable examples of effective international leadership. The full import of the President's position as an international leader was made manifest when, in June, 1950, the communist forces of North Korea invaded the Republic of Korea. Within a matter of days this act was condemned by the Security Council of the United Nations, and the President, to enforce the Council's orders, sent into battle units of the American Army, Navy, and Air Force. The President's decision was followed by similar action upon the part of Great Britian, France, the Netherlands, and other members of the United Nations; and there was hope that the United Nations might evolve into an effective agency for collective security. If the incident had this result, the forthright action of the American President would be reckoned the major contributing factor.

nature and allocation of power over foreign affairs

The powers of the national government in the field of foreign affairs are complete, inherent, and exclusive. In order to be effective, our government must possess power equal to that of the foreign governments, including totalitarian dictatorships, with which it has relations. This power is inherent in the sense that it *"owes its existence to the fact that the American People are a sovereign entity at international law."* [23] The constitutional powers of the government are not limited, in this field, to those specifically enumerated or implied therefrom: "The powers to declare and wage war, to conclude peace, to make treaties, to maintain diplomatic relations with other sovereignties, if they had never been mentioned in the Constitution, would have vested in the Federal government as necessary concomitants of nationality."[24] Finally, the national power is exclusive in the sense that it is not limited by powers that have been reserved to the states.[25]

Although authority over foreign affairs is practically unlimited, it is divided, within the government, among several agencies. The Constitution dis-

---

[23] Edward S. Corwin, *The President: Office and Powers* (New York: New York University Press, 1940) p. 202. Italics are Corwin's.

[24] Justice Sutherland's opinion, *United States* v. *Curtiss-Wright Export Corp.*, 299 U.S. 318 (1936).

[25] *Missouri* v. *Holland*, 252 U.S. 416 (1920).

tributes responsibility for external relations among the President, the Senate, and Congress as a whole. This distribution has meant that the President must secure the participation of the House and Senate in the formulation of objectives and foreign policies. Unless there is a disposition toward mutual cooperation, conflicts over particular policies and actions are to be expected, and the great potential power of the federal government will not be realized. Moreover, responsibility for foreign affairs within the executive branch is shared by several departments and agencies. The Departments of State, Treasury, Commerce, and Defense, and the Economic Cooperation Administration have major interests, and a total of forty-six agencies are involved in some degree. It is a major presidential task to maintain congressional support and to unify the policies and administration of these executive agencies.

communication with foreign governments

Under the Constitution the President is the sole channel of communication between the United States and foreign governments. In Article Two, section three, he is directed to "receive ambassadors and other public ministers," that is, the representatives sent by foreign governments to this country. In section two of the same article his powers include the appointment, "by and with the advice and consent of the Senate" of the "ambassadors, other public ministers, and consuls" who represent the United States abroad. In establishing the Department of State, Congress directed the Secretary to "perform and execute such duties as shall from time to time be enjoined on or entrusted to him by the President of the United States, agreeable to the Constitution, relative to correspondences, commissions or instructions to or with public ministers or consuls, from the United States, or to negotiations with public ministers from foreign states or princes. . . ." [26] The effect of the constitutional and statutory provisions is that only the President or his agents in the diplomatic service communicate officially with other governments on behalf of the United States. Conversely, communications from foreign governments to the United States are directed to the President or his representatives. On rare occasions an emissary of a foreign government may address the Congress in person, as did Winston Churchill and Madam Chiang Kai-shek during World War II; but these are personal rather than official appearances.

In recent years the development of intercontinental communication systems has greatly enlarged the opportunities for personal relationships between the President and other chiefs of state. Winston Churchill has testified that his frequent conversations with President Roosevelt during World War II helped immensely to create mutual sympathy and confidence. Messages by transatlantic cable helped pave the way for face to face conferences of the chiefs of state and

---

[26] 1 Stat. 28, Act of July 27, 1799.

their military and diplomatic aides at which were made decisions of the most basic character. Of this exchange of messages Churchill wrote:

> I sent my cables to the American Embassy in London, which was in direct touch with the President at the White House through special coding machines. The speed with which answers were received and things settled was aided by clock-time. Any message which I prepared in the evening, night, or even up to two o'clock in the morning, would reach the President before he went to bed, and very often his answer would come back to me when I woke the next morning. In all, I sent him nine hundred and fifty messages and received about eight hundred in reply.[27]

The people of Great Britain were heartened by President Roosevelt's speeches heard via radio; and surely Winston Churchill's words of encouragement to his people made a deep impression when they were broadcast in America. Personal messages and conferences have supplemented, rather than replaced, the traditional communications transmitted by diplomatic representatives.

By receiving an ambassador, the President *recognizes* the emissary's government, that is, he signifies that the government is accepted by the United States as an equal in the family of nations. Henceforth diplomatic intercourse may be carried on between the two governments, and treaties and other agreements of mutual benefit may be negotiated. Thus the accrediting of diplomatic representatives, an act that was perhaps intended to be largely ceremonial, has become a potent instrument in the day to day conduct of foreign relations. By recognition the President may strengthen a newly established government at a time when its future is uncertain. Washington thus aided the French Republic by receiving its ambassador; recognition of the independent government of Cuba preceded war with Spain. The power is equally significant when it is not used. President Wilson's refusal to recognize the Huerta regime in Mexico in 1915, and the aid extended to resistance elements, helped bring about the overthrow of that government. The U.S.S.R. was recognized by President Roosevelt in 1933, but the refusal of his predecessors to do so was resented by Soviet leaders and for years was a troublesome factor in American-Soviet relations.

The power to receive an ambassador implies the right to dismiss him—to request his recall. An ambassador whose personal behavior is offensive to this country may be dismissed without disrupting relations between his government and the United States. More significantly, if the President wishes to express this government's unalterable opposition to the policies of another government, he may dismiss its entire corps of diplomatic personnel stationed in the United States. Almost certainly the recall of the American ambassador and his staff would follow, after which direct negotiations could not be carried on be-

---

[27] Winston S. Churchill, *Their Finest Hour* (Boston: Houghton Mifflin Company, 1949), p. 23. Reprinted by permission of Houghton Mifflin Company, publishers.

tween the two governments. When this point is reached, history shows that armed hostilities are not unlikely. Since the power of receiving and dismissing the representatives of foreign governments is vested in the President alone, he may take these actions on his own initiative and without previous consultation with the Senate or Congress, even though the actions may make a declaration of war inevitable.

the making of international agreements

American foreign policy today is based on the principle that our national interests can be advanced most surely by cooperation and agreement with the foreign governments concerned with the same matters. This principle in application means that the United States is a party to an increasing number of international agreements and is a member of international organizations covering practically every field of human activity. The commitment to international cooperation has been made only in the last twenty-five years and is in sharp contrast to the essentially negative and isolationist policies that were followed in the first 150 years of our history. Although the principle on which our foreign policies is based has changed radically, there has been no change in the methods available for effecting the new policy of cooperation. Our government relies today, as it has in the past, upon treaties and executive agreements.

In section two of Article Two the Constitution gives to the President the "power, by and with the advice and consent of the Senate, to make treaties, provided two-thirds of the Senators present concur." The making of a treaty requires three steps: negotiation, approval by the Senate, and ratification.

Negotiation—the process of discussing and reaching an agreement about the contents of a proposed treaty—is the sole concern of the President and his subordinates in the executive branch. It is likely that the framers of the Constitution intended the President to consult with the Senate during the negotiation of treaties. Washington, on one of the early occasions involving the negotiation of a treaty, sought in person the Senate's advice. The result, however, was not encouraging, and since that time Presidents have considered the negotiation of treaties an executive prerogative, a view that has been supported by the Supreme Court.[28] In practice, treaties are negotiated by officials of the Department of State or by special delegates appointed by the President. Usually the Secretary of State consults informally the congressional committees on foreign affairs, and these consultations undoubtedly achieve in some degree the objectives that the framers sought in providing for Senate participation in treaty making. The President is almost certain to see that Senate leaders are informed of the progress of negotiations if the treaty is one that will require the appropriation of money or the enactment of other legislation.

---

[28] *United States* v. *Curtiss-Wright Export Corp.*, 299 U.S. 304, 319 (1936).

Before ratification a treaty must be submitted to the Senate and receive the approval of two thirds of the members present. A treaty that does not receive the Senate's approval cannot be ratified by the President. The requirement of a two-thirds majority for approval means in effect that each opponent has two votes compared with the single vote of each of the treaty's supporters. This provision, therefore, gives the Senate ample opportunity to review the policies underlying the treaty, to defeat the treaty if it disagrees with those policies, or to vote amendments that may make the treaty acceptable to the necessary majority. If a pending treaty is amended by the Senate, the President must secure the acceptance of the amended treaty by the other governments.

Ratification, the final step in the making of a treaty, is executed by the President. After ratification, a treaty becomes a contract between the United States and the foreign governments who are parties to it. Moreover, Article Six of the Constitution states: "This Constitution and the laws of the United States which shall be made in pursuance thereof, and *all treaties made, or which shall be made, under the authority of the United States,* shall be the supreme law of the land." [29] The provision means that the constitutions and powers of the states do not limit the treaty-making power of the national government and that, when the rights of private citizens are in question, the treaty may be enforced in court like any other law.

If the President wishes to avoid the risk of Senate disapproval under the two-thirds rule, he may, within limits, make commitments to foreign governments through the means of *executive agreements*. The circumstances and matters that permit the use of an executive agreement as an alternative to a treaty cannot be precisely defined. The Constitution, in fact, does not provide explicitly for such agreements; but their legality is established by precedents that go back to 1790, when the Second Congress authorized the Postmaster General to enter into international postal conventions. Moreover, the Supreme Court repeatedly has given its approval to agreements, and they, as well as treaties, are enforceable through the courts. There are two kinds of executive agreements: those that are made by the President without any participation by Congress; and those that are authorized by, or receive the subsequent approval of, a majority of both houses of Congress. Since commitments for cooperation with other nations usually require the expenditure of money, and therefore a congressional appropriation, executive agreements made solely by the President are of decreasing significance in the field of foreign policy.

Prior or subsequent congressional approval of an executive agreement may take one of three forms. First, the President or his subordinate executive officials may be authorized by statute to enter into agreements for the purpose of effecting policies stated by Congress, without provision for approval of the agreements

---

[29] Italics added.

by either the House or the Senate. Examples of these statutes include the 1790 postal conventions law, the Trade Agreements Act of 1934, and the wartime Lend-Lease Act, under which war supplies were sent to our allies in World War II. Second, Congress may incorporate in a statute or a joint resolution an executive agreement that has been promulgated by the President. Several agreements made after World War II were of this type, including those providing for our participation in the World Bank and in the United Nations Relief and Rehabilitation Administration. Third, the President may submit an agreement to Congress for its "approval," just as a treaty is submitted to the Senate. This procedure is seldom used.

In view of the emphasis on cooperative foreign policies, there is a question as to whether our treaty and executive agreement procedures are adequate. The supporters of international cooperation criticize the two-thirds rule of the treaty procedure on the grounds that it encourages irresponsibility in foreign affairs. Unless a treaty is harmless, there are certain to be some senators who cannot accept it on its merits. Other senators will oppose it because its defeat would embarrass the President and his party. Since, under the two-thirds rule, each negative vote is the equivalent of two affirmatives, the senators in opposition generally can come within a few votes of defeating a major treaty. Thus, "the two-thirds requirement actually draws into our foreign policy decisions the most irresponsible type of partisanship by making any controversy on the merits a tempting chance for an easy political kill." [30] To avoid this outcome, Presidents and their Secretaries of State are under pressure to weaken the contents of treaties or to avoid the Senate hurdle by the use of executive agreements.

The principal difficulty with the executive agreement coupled with a congressional enactment is that it raises the issue of executive circumvention of the Senate. Senators who approve the substance of an agreement may oppose its sanction by Congress on the grounds that it should have been negotiated as a treaty and submitted for approval to the Senate. When this opposition joins those who question the merits of the agreement and the partisan critics, the outcome is bound to be uncertain. Moreover, this method of making international commitments is not explicitly authorized by the Constitution, whereas the treaty procedure is embodied in the constitutional document. For this reason alone, an executive agreement of major significance is bound to raise troublesome questions of legality.

The treaty procedure is defended by some who lack enthusiasm for the present trend in American foreign policies and by others who believe that the procedure itself is basically sound. Simply from the standpoint of the number of treaties rejected by the Senate, the two-thirds requirement would not seem to be of major significance. Of the treaties rejected "a change in the constitutional

---

[30] John S. Dickey, "Our Treaty Procedures Versus Our Foreign Policies," *Foreign Affairs*, XXV, No. 3 (April, 1947), 364.

requirement to a simple majority in the Senate would have altered the ultimate fate of but seven cases, eight-tenths of one per cent of the 787 treaties before the Senate."[31] From this point of view, the solution to the difficulty lies in closer cooperation between the Senate, the President, and the Department of State.

the President as commander in chief

The ultimate responsibility of the President in the event of war is to preserve the United States of America. This objective sustained Lincoln in the bleakness of the Civil War and Wilson and Roosevelt during World Wars I and II. When a nation is threatened with destruction, its most cherished beliefs and traditions are subordinated to the objective of survival. Thus it is a fundamental of American government that the President is duty bound to meet attack by attack and force with force, as effectively as he can in light of the known circumstances and the resources available to him. No man can shoulder a greater responsibility.

the national war power

The government of the United States may take whatever action is necessary to wage war successfully unless such action is specifically forbidden by the Constitution. As is the case in the field of foreign affairs, this power is as great as that possessed by any other government. It is inherent in the sense that it is derived from our status as an independent national state and not from the Constitution. Within the government, the war power is shared by the President and Congress. In the words of Article Two, section two, the President is "Commander-in-Chief of the Army and Navy, and of the militia of the several States when called into the actual service of the United States." This provision establishes civilian control over the military and gives to the President the powers of a military commander. He is limited, however, by powers entrusted to Congress. Only Congress can declare war and, subject to the right of presidential veto, it has the authority to appropriate money for the maintenance of the armed services and to conscript men for military duty.[32] These provisions do not limit the war power itself, but simply regulate the exercise of specific powers.

the impact of total war

The President's role as commander in chief was transformed by the advent of "total war." First, there is no longer the preliminary of diplomatic negotiation leading to a formal declaration of war and then to combat. As we know from the Japanese attack on Pearl Harbor in 1941, we must expect a surprise assault directed to inflict the maximum destruction with the initial blow. The probability

---

[31] Royden J. Dangerfield, *In Defense of the Senate* (Norman: The University of Oklahoma Press, 1933), p. 312.

[32] The war powers of Congress are enumerated in Article One, section eight.

of war coming without warning means that, until permanent peace is assured, the armed services must be maintained at fighting strength. Second, it appears that the only threat to the United States comes from the U.S.S.R. and other communist-dominated governments. These governments resort to deception whenever it is to their advantage to do so, and they have developed the techniques of subversion as a principal means of attack upon nations they wish to destroy. In planning its defense the President must take into account the probable use of deception and subversion against the United States. Finally, it becomes impossible in total war to distinguish between civil and military affairs. World War II was fought with economic and psychological weapons as well as with military machines, and it is to be expected that in any future war the belligerents will attempt to strangle the enemy's economy and demoralize his civilian population. Total war cannot be carried on without the imposition of controls over labor, industrial materials and facilities, food, transportation, and other basic factors of the economy. The rationing of food and gasoline becomes essential to the continued operation of the civilian economy and the maintenance of military supplies.

The pervasive character of total war can be seen clearly in the field of labor relations. In World War II, the United States could not permit strikes to interrupt essential production of military supplies. Less than a week after the declaration of war, President Roosevelt asked leaders of labor and management to forgo strikes and lockouts for the duration and to submit unresolved labor disputes to a government agency for settlement. This principle was accepted by labor and management, and the National War Labor Board was created for the purpose of deciding labor disputes. The board was established by executive order issued by Mr. Roosevelt as President and commander in chief, and the orders issued by the board carried the full weight of his war powers. Whenever war production was seriously disrupted by a dispute which the board was unable to resolve, the President ordered the Army or the Navy to seize and operate the plant. Under this procedure bituminous coal mines were taken over by the government and operated under its direction and even the mail-order firm of Montgomery Ward & Co., Inc., was seized by the President's order.[33]

the national security organization

The changing character of diplomacy and war has caused a major reorganization of the presidency insofar as national security is concerned. A workable solution

---

[33] The National War Labor Board was established by Executive Order No. 9,017, *Federal Register* VII (January 12, 1942), 237. See *The United States at War* (Washington: Bureau of the Budget, 1946), for an account of wartime labor relations. A federal district court ruled that the government lacked the power to seize Montgomery Ward & Co., Inc., 58 F. Supp. 408 (1945), but was overruled on appeal by the circuit court of appeals, 150 F. 2d 369 (1945). The Supreme Court did not pass upon the issue of whether the government could seize, under its war powers, a business such as a mail-order house. See 326 U.S. 690 (1946).

to the organization problem must provide for satisfactory relationships among the agencies concerned with the administration of civil, military, foreign, and domestic affairs. Earlier it was observed that the conduct of foreign relations is intimately associated with planning for the nation's military defense. There must be also continuing cooperation among land, sea, and air forces, on matters ranging from weapon design and procurement of supplies to combat. During World War II this collaboration, difficult at best, was impaired by the fact that there were separate Departments of War and Navy, each headed by a Secretary whose immediate superior was the commander in chief, and each with a strong tradition of independence from the other. After careful study of the lessons of World War II and of the probable character of hostilities of the future, Congress established the present national defense organization.[34]

Under the present law, the Secretary of Defense is the President's principal assistant in matters involving the armed services. As head of the Department of Defense, he is a member of the President's cabinet, in which he represents the Departments of the Army, Navy, and Air Force. Both the President and the Secretary of Defense are served by the Joint Chiefs of Staff, which consists of a chairman appointed by the President with the consent of the Senate, the Chief of Naval Operations, and the Chiefs of Staff of the Army and the Air Force. This group is responsible for the preparation of plans for any military operations that may become necessary, for reviewing the personnel and material requirements of the armed services, and for the establishment of unified commands in combat areas when they are needed.

In the overlapping areas of foreign and military policies the President has the guidance of the National Security Council, of which he is chairman. Other members are the Vice-President, the Secretaries of State and of Defense, the chairman of the National Security Resources Board, and officials of other executive departments and boards whom the President may appoint to the council with the Senate's approval. The council is directed to "advise the President with respect to the integration of domestic, foreign, and military policies relating to national security," to "assess and appraise the objectives, commitments, and risks of the United States in relation to our actual and potential military power, in the interest of national security." [35]

As commander in chief, the President must see that plans are made for national mobilization in case of war. The objective of mobilization planning is to enable the nation to meet an attack quickly and strongly and to set into im-

---

[34] The National Security Act, 50 U.S.C. §401, 61 Stat. 495, was passed in July, 1947; it created the National Defense Establishment. In August, 1949, the name was changed to the Department of Defense and the authority of the Secretary of Defense was strengthened. 5 U.S.C., Supp. III, §171, 63 Stat. 579.

[35] 50 U.S.C. §402, 61 Stat. 496, 497. The National Security Council was transferred to the Executive Office of the President by Reorganization Plan IV, *Federal Register*, XI (August 19, 1949), 5227.

mediate operation the complex machinery necessary for war production on a vast scale. Congress established the National Security Resources Board to advise the President on matters related to military, industrial, and civilian mobilization.[36] The membership of the board is appointed by the President and at the present time comprises a chairman and the Secretaries of State, Treasury, Defense, Interior, Agriculture, Commerce, and Labor.[37] The task of this group is to develop plans that may be put into operation in the event of war for the utilization of manpower, raw materials, industrial facilities; for economic stabilization; and for the unification of government agencies concerned with production, procurement, distribution, or transportation of military or civilian supplies. The plans of the board must be current in the sense that they take into account recent events such as developments in foreign affairs, the discovery of new weapons, or changes in industrial processes.

the President as military commander

The President as commander in chief is responsible for, and should make, the decisions on fundamental strategy for the conduct of war. It is proper and desirable that he act always upon full advice from his military staff; but in a war for survival the nation cannot afford to have broad principles, in which military and political questions are intertwined, decided by professional military officers. On the other hand, the President should not intervene in the execution of strategy or make decisions about the conduct of particular military campaigns. Henry L. Stimson, who served as Secretary of War for seven years under two Presidents, has provided, in his appraisal of the war leadership of Franklin D. Roosevelt, a valuable statement of the role of the President as a military commander:

> His vision over the broad reaches of events during the crises of war has always been vigorous and quick and clear and guided by a very strong faith in the future of our country and of freedom, democracy and humanitarianism throughout the world. Furthermore, on matters of military grand strategy, he has nearly always been sound and he has followed substantially throughout with great fidelity the views of his military and naval advisers. . . . His role has not at all been merely a negative one. He has pushed for decisions of sound strategy and carried them through . . . [and] his relations to his military advisers and commanders were admirably correct. In the execution of their duties he gave them freedom, backed them up, and held them responsible. In all these particulars he seems to me to have been our greatest war President.[38]

---

[36] 50 U.S.C. §404, 61 Stat. 499. The NSRB was also transferred to the Executive Office of the President by Reorganization Plan IV.

[37] Executive Orders 9,905 (*Federal Register* XII, 7613) and 9,931 (*Federal Register* XIII, 763).

[38] Henry L. Stimson and McGeorge Bundy, *On Active Service in Peace and War* (New York: Harper & Brothers, 1947), pp. 665–667. Reprinted by permission of Harper & Brothers, publishers.

Acting in accordance with this philosophy and method, a President has the opportunity to affect significantly the conduct and outcome of a war. The possibilities were illustrated in World War II by the following presidential decisions.

The first great strategic question of World War II was whether the United States should concentrate its resources in Europe and later turn to the Pacific, or launch an immediate, all-out attack on Japan. Which offered the greater threat to national security, Japan or Germany? Americans living on the West Coast and in Hawaii were more fearful of the Japanese than they were of the Nazis; another view was that if the Nazis should organize the industrial resources of captive Europe, they would be virtually invincible. The pattern of the war was set when the President decided that our resources would be concentrated first to defeat Germany, and then Japan.

The second great strategic decision was made within two weeks after the declaration of war in 1941, when President Roosevelt and Prime Minister Churchill decided, at a White House conference, that America and Great Britan would fight as a unified team. Henceforth military operations were planned and carried out in concert. This decision greatly enhanced the military power of each nation, hastened victory, and reduced the cost in lives and resources.

Another question of basic strategy was decided by the President's order to ship military supplies to Russia when it appeared that she would go down before the Nazi armies. When the decision was made, the United States did not have sufficient quantities of equipment to supply her own forces. Moreover, military experts predicted that the Russians would be smashed quickly and that military supplies sent to them would not get there in time, would be lost in hopeless fighting, or would be captured by the enemy. The risks were great, but the recovery of the Russian armies after the initial Nazi onslaught and their magnificent contributions to the Allied victory proved the correctness of the presidential decision.

A different type of problem was presented in the question of what should be done in the field of atomic research. In the fall of 1941 we were not at war; but to many, war seemed inevitable and imminent. Moreover, it was clear that, if war came, we would find ourselves at some point fighting the Germans. Also, it was known that as early as 1938 German scientists had successfully experimented with atomic fission, and that these experiments were being continued. Had the Germans developed atomic weapons that could be used on the field of battle? If not, how close were they to such weapons? Since there was no assurance that an atomic bomb was feasible, would it be better to devote our resources to the refinement of traditional weapons of known effectiveness? How could the enormous expenditures required for the atomic projects be justified to Congress without divulging secret information to the enemy? These were troublesome questions. But, if atomic weapons were to be used in battle, it was vital that the United States have such weapons before they were available to a potential enemy. The President threw the full weight of his office behind the atomic research projects; and, although the war in Europe was won without the atomic bomb, its use brought the Japanese war to a quick conclusion.

martial law and civil disorder

When ordered to do so by the President, the military forces of the United States may be used to suppress domestic disorders that disrupt the normal processes of government. The use of this power in its most drastic form means establishment of "martial law" and replacement of civil law and civilian courts by military law enforced by military tribunals. Establishment of martial law suspends the writ of habeas corpus, the right to which is protected by Article One, section nine, of the Constitution, except when rebellion or invasion requires the suspension of the writ. Thus martial law has been declared only in time of war. During the Civil War Lincoln adopted the view that the entire country was in the theater of military operations; the privilege of habeas corpus was suspended for people suspected of disloyalty to the Union; and military tribunals tried these persons, even though they lived hundreds of miles from any area in which battle was likely to be joined. Although the trials later were declared illegal by the Supreme Court, the victims were effectively incarcerated until the end of the war.[39]

The problem of defining the war theater arose again in World War II. Immediately after the Japanese attack on Pearl Harbor, military government was instituted in Hawaii. Martial law was declared and civilians were tried before tribunals set up under a military program that took over all government and suspended civil law and courts. When this procedure was questioned before the Supreme Court, the Court said that, in authorizing martial law, Congress had not intended to authorize the supplanting of courts by military tribunals; and it ordered the release of civilians sentenced by the military courts.[40] In another case, however, the Court upheld an equally drastic war measure. In the spring and summer of 1942, over 70,000 American citizens and some 30,000 aliens of Japanese ancestry were removed from their homes on the West Coast by military authorities and placed in internment camps in the interior. The evacuation was supported as a military measure essential to national defense; it was carried out under authority of an executive order issued by the President and later it was endorsed by Congress. In the evacuation, no effort was made to distinguish the loyal citizens from the disloyal. None of the group was charged with any crime and there was no evidence, then or later, that any of them had attempted any act of sabotage. As a group their offense was that they were descended from Japanese ancestors. In upholding the evacuation order the Supreme Court said:

---

[39] *Ex parte Milligan*, 4 Wallace 2 (1866).
[40] *Duncan* v. *Kahanamoku*, 327 U.S. 304 (1946).

Compulsory exclusion of large groups of citizens from their homes, except under circumstances of direct emergency and peril, is inconsistent with our basic governmental institutions. But when under conditions of modern warfare our shores are threatened by hostile forces, the power to protect must be commensurate with the threatened danger. . . . [Korematsu] was excluded because we are at war with the Japanese Empire, because the properly constituted military authorities feared an invasion of our West Coast and felt constrained to take proper security measures, because they decided that the military urgency of the situation demanded that all citizens of Japanese ancestry be segregated from the West Coast temporarily, and finally, because Congress, reposing its confidence in this time of war in our military leaders—as inevitably it must—determined that they should have the power to do just this. There was evidence of disloyalty on the part of some, the military authorities considered that the need for action was great, and time was short. We cannot—by availing ourselves of the calm perspective of hindsight—now say that at that time these actions were unjustified.[41]

Since in modern warfare the belligerents' civilian population is considered a legitimate target for bombing attacks and sabotage, it is clear that in a future war the whole of the United States may be in the area of military operations. If so, the precedents would seem to permit the President to take whatever action seemed to him necessary for the nation's defense, in view of the circumstances then confronting it, including the segregation and internment of potentially disloyal citizens and the establishment of martial law.

The armed forces of the United States may also be used to suppress peacetime domestic disturbances. Section four of Article Four of the Constitution directs the national government to protect each state, "on application of the legislature, or of the executive (when the legislature cannot be convened), against domestic violence." An act of Congress authorizes the President to use land and naval forces of the federal government or state militia in discharging this obligation.[42] Congress also has provided for the use of troops when the enforcement of laws of the United States by ordinary judicial proceedings is in the President's judgment impracticable. Congress lists as the causes of enforcement difficulty "unlawful obstructions, combinations, or assemblages of persons, or rebellion."[43] Before troops are used under either of these provisions, the President must issue a proclamation commanding the "insurgents to disperse and retire peaceably to their respective abodes."[44] *The issuance of*

---

[41] Justice Hugo Black's opinion for the Court, *Korematsu* v. *United States*, 323 U.S. 219, 223 (1944). For an analysis and criticism of the evacuation policy, see Morton Grodzins, *Americans Betrayed* (Chicago: The University of Chicago Press, 1949).

[42] 50 U.S.C. §201.

[43] 50 U.S.C. §202.

[44] 50 U.S.C. §204, 12 Stat. 282.

this proclamation does not establish martial law. The military forces do not replace civilian agencies but merely assist them to maintain their authority and normal operations.

Since the Whisky Insurrection in 1794 there have been many instances of domestic disorder that required the intervention of federal troops. Most of the early occasions resulted from the enforcement of unpopular revenue measures. Beginning with the great railroad strike in 1877, industrial disputes have been the most important single cause of serious disturbances. Throughout our history, Presidents have been reluctant to use armed force to quell domestic disorders, and on the whole they have been meticulous in observing constitutional and legal procedures and in respecting the rights of the states. Most significantly, no President has declared martial law as a means of suppressing a peacetime domestic disturbance.[45]

emergencies and the presidency

The problem of coping with temporary emergencies is particularly perplexing in a constitutional government. The essence of constitutionalism is that the governors are restrained by law in their choice of political objectives and methods; they are limited as to ends and as to means. These legal restraints are designed for the normal needs of society rather than for the sudden emergencies that on occasion confront all governments. Some emergencies spend themselves, but others cannot be dissipated without prompt governmental intervention. A constitutional government normally does not act quickly. The distribution of power among various government departments and officials, and the consequent necessity for consultation and cooperation on matters of principle, produces deliberation rather than speed. This characteristic of constitutional government is accentuated by special features of the United States system, for example, by the existence of independent states, the nature of the party system, and the judiciary's right to determine finally the constitutionality of legislative and executive acts. The nation's achievements since the adoption of the Constitution show that these arrangements are adequate for long-run problems. Have we been equally successful in dealing with the emergencies of war, insurrection, and economic catastrophe?

three examples of emergency action

A study of American crises shows that the impact of the emergency has been felt first by the President and that he has been chiefly responsible for subsequent ameliorative action. At the oubreak of the Civil War, for example, it was essential

---

[45] Bennett M. Rich, *The Presidents and Civil Disorder* (Washington: The Brookings Institution, 1941), p. 209.

to expand the federal army as rapidly as possible. The normal legal procedure was for Congress to authorize the expansion; but Congress was not in session and, because of difficulties of communication, could not be convened for several weeks. President Lincoln ordered a drastic increase in the size of the Army, an illegal act that he considered justified by the nation's plight.

In 1940 President Roosevelt gave to Great Britain fifty "overage" destroyers of the United States Navy, in exchange for rights to certain naval bases. The transfer was made without the knowledge of Congress and without specific legal authorization. In the opinion of some legal experts, in fact, this disposition of government property was actually contrary to law. The President's action, questionable from the legal standpoint, was in his judgment necessary because of Great Britain's desperate military situation. In requesting the assistance, the Prime Minister wrote: ". . . If we cannot get a substantial reinforcement the whole fate of the war may be decided by this minor and easily remediable factor." [46] There was reason to believe that the transfer of destroyers might forestall a Nazi invasion of Great Britain intended to knock her out of the war. The President's act was perhaps decisive in another sense; in the Prime Minister's judgment it "brought the United States definitely nearer to us and to the war, and it was the first of a long succession of increasingly unneutral acts in the Atlantic which were of the utmost service to us. It marked the passage of the United States from being neutral to being non-belligerent." [47]

An economic crisis may call for emergency executive action. The President's authority in suppressing domestic disturbances growing out of industrial disputes has already been noted. A more dramatic illustration occurred in 1933, when the economic life of the nation was paralyzed by a depression of unprecedented severity. Banks were closing, businesses were failing, and unemployment was increasing throughout the United States and the world. American business was panic-stricken. In his inaugural Franklin D. Roosevelt discussed the situation in the following terms:

> I am prepared under my constitutional duty to recommend the measures that a stricken nation in the midst of a stricken world may require. These measures or such other measures as Congress may build out of its experience and wisdom, I shall seek within my constitutional authority to bring to speedy adoption.

> But in the event that the Congress shall fail to take one of these two courses, and in the event that the national emergency is still critical, I shall not evade the clear course of duty that will then confront me. I shall ask the Congress for the one remaining instrument to meet the crisis—broad execu-

---

[46] Churchill, *Their Finest Hour*, p. 402. Cable message to President Roosevelt.
[47] *Ibid.*, p. 404.

tive power to wage a war against the emergency, as great as the power that would be given to me if we were in fact invaded by a foreign foe.[48]

Action followed: the banks were closed for four days under a statute passed during World War I, and an embargo was placed on the export of gold. A special session of Congress was called by the President, and legislation recommended by him was quickly passed. The members of both parties in Congress accepted his suggestions with little debate, and for about three months Roosevelt's legislative leadership achieved successes unequaled by any President before or since.

requisites of effective emergency action

The presidency has become the focal point in emergencies because, of the three branches of government, it satisfies most completely the requisites of effective action—leadership, initiative, energy, knowledge, and power. The President is always "in session." He may summon on short notice his principal aides and consult with them about the steps to be taken. Their consultations are private and, if secrecy is advisable, the nature of the decisions need not be divulged to the public. The responsibility for decision rests with the President; hence it is not necessary to prolong discussions in order to reach a compromise among the views of men whose agreement to a course of action must be secured. Since the presidency is at the center of a network of information and intelligence agencies, last-minute developments can be related quickly to the President and plans altered in accordance with changing circumstances.

A totalitarian dictatorship may have all of these advantages, plus the additional advantage that it is not hampered by a commitment to a constitutional system. If the purpose of presidential emergency action is the preservation of constitutional government, there must be a return to normal procedures at the termination of the emergency. If the government does not revert to constitutional practices, the dictatorship established for a limited time and purpose is likely to become permanent and absolute.

If three conditions are met, the requisites of effective action may be provided within the confines of our constitutional system. First, the period of the emergency must be relatively short. Second, the President cannot have the final authority to determine the need for emergency powers. And third, the power must be legitimate in the sense that it is derived from constitutional and statutory sources, rather than acquired by illegal usurpation. Since men are not always able to determine the duration of war or other catastrophes, the first of these conditions cannot be controlled by constitutional means. The second and third conditions, however, are met in the American constitutional system.

---

[48] "First Inaugural Address of Franklin D. Roosevelt," *Senate Document* No. 1, 73 Cong., Spec. Sess., p. 4.

the sources of emergency power

The government's emergency powers are derived either from the Constitution directly or from congressional enactments in pursuance of the Constitution. The general scope of these powers may be indicated by four points of constitutional theory. First, an emergency does not create new power or increase, or remove restrictions from the use of, existing powers. Second, an emergency may permit the use of powers that may not be used in the absence of an emergency. Third, the government's powers must be great enough to permit it to deal effectively with the emergency as it presents itself. And fourth, the Supreme Court is reluctant to invalidate an emergency action of Congress or the President unless it was plainly excessive at the time it was taken.

The response of the United States government to emergencies has been effective in part because the Constitution does not define precisely the powers of the President. The vagueness of the Constitution gives a President confronted by an emergency a large measure of freedom of action. Because of this fact, the nature and use of emergency powers depend more upon the personal conceptions of the individual in the presidential office than upon the constitutional document. In general, the views of Presidents on this point fall into one of two groups. The conception that is most appropriate in a war or similar crisis was described by Theodore Roosevelt in the following terms:

> My view was that every executive officer in high position, was a steward of the people bound actively and affirmatively to do all he could for the people, and not to content himself with the negative merit of keeping his talents undamaged in a napkin. I declined to adopt the view that what was imperatively necessary for the Nation could not be done by the President unless he could find some specific authorization to do it. My belief was that it was not only his right but his duty to do anything that the needs of the Nation demanded unless such action was forbidden by the Constitution or by the laws. . . . I did not usurp power, but I did greatly broaden the use of executive power. In other words, I acted for the public welfare, I acted for the common well-being of all our people, whenever and in whatever manner was necessary, unless prevented by direct constitutional or legislative prohibition.[49]

Another conception of the nature of the presidential office was expressed by William Howard Taft:

> The true view of the Executive functions is, as I conceive it, that the President can exercise no power which cannot be fairly and reasonably traced to some specific grant of power or justly implied and included within such express grant as proper and necessary to its exercise. Such specific grant

---

[49] *Theodore Roosevelt: An Autobiography* (New York: The Macmillan Company, 1913), p. 389. Used with the permission of The Macmillan Company, publishers.

must be either in the Federal Constitution or in an act of Congress passed in pursuance thereof. There is no undefined residuum of power which he can exercise because it seems to him to be in the public interest.[50]

The enactments of Congress are a major source of power for presidential use in emergencies. Since Congress seldom repeals outright a statute dealing with military or economic crises, the number of delegations of authority to the President has gradually increased. Statutes passed during World War I, for example, were available for use from 1939 to 1941, before the entry of the United States into World War II. In this period there were approximately 250 different statutes delegating discretionary authority to the President or other executive officials. Of these, about 150 were concerned with the military services, the remaining 100 dealing with various aspects of the economy. Under this authority the President was able to lay essential foundations for military and industrial preparedness and to give assistance to the nations that were to become our allies in World War II. Many of these statutory powers are also available for use during economic crises and peacetime domestic disturbances. Today a President who conceives of himself as a "steward" can probably find some authority for almost any act that he may deem appropriate in an emergency.

safeguards

There are three major safeguards against presidential abuse of emergency powers. First, since so many of the powers are derived from statutes, Congress may withdraw the authority. Although Congress has been slow to repeal statutory delegations of power, it undoubtedly would act quickly if a President began to use them for personal aggrandizement. We have been fortunate in the Presidents who have held office during crises; they have been uneasy under their responsibilities and have given up emergency power voluntarily as soon as it was safe to do so.

Congress's normal antagonism toward the executive provides a second safeguard. Even in the critical phases of a war, members of Congress are reluctant to forgo opportunities to embarrass the President and are quick to point out his serious mistakes. Legislation concerned with the armed services is generally voted without searching debate. But proposals not directly related to military affairs, such as those dealing with the mobilization of industry and agriculture, labor relations, or rationing, are viewed with skepticism and even suspicion. When legislation on these subjects is enacted, Congress usually follows its administration carefully, frequently through the device of investigating committees. These committees are able to review with reasonable objectivity executive actions taken in the heat of an emergency, and careful study often leads to

---

[50] William Howard Taft, *Our Chief Magistrate and His Powers* (New York: Columbia University Press, 1916), p. 139.

desirable change. The effectiveness of these congressional safeguards depends ultimately upon the alertness and intelligence of Congress itself.

Finally, the Supreme Court is available to check the abuse of emergency powers. The Court's general philosophy gives to the President considerable freedom in combating a serious emergency. But it does not hesitate to declare invalid an action that in its judgment is contrary to the basic principles of our constitutional system. Two examples of such invalidation—the establishment of martial law in the Civil War, and in Hawaii during World War II—have already been noted.

succession to the presidency

An emergency arises in the presidency when a President dies in office or is incapacitated by illness. In order to preserve stability within society, there must be an accepted and orderly procedure for devolving power when it is necessary to replace the chief of state. The absence of such a procedure inevitably invites struggles for power, political crises, and even revolution. Have we arranged succession to the presidency so that the nation is assured of continuing leadership?

Seven Presidents have died in office, of whom three were assassinated. No man can carry the burdens of the presidency for an extended period without injury to his health. The volume of work, the variety of problems, and, above all, the dreadful responsibility of making decisions that are vital to a great nation tax to the utmost a man's physical endurance. President Truman described this burden before a group of Federal employees:

> I have been thinking every week that perhaps the next week will not be quite so hectic as the week just passed, but the coming week is always a little more hectic. This is one place where you never lack for action and there is always a crisis just around the corner, and I have to do something about it. But the next day that crisis is passed, and it's just like yesterday's newspaper. That's the way we must face those things.[51]

The pressures become intense during a major emergency such as war. It is significant that of the three great war Presidents, Abraham Lincoln was assassinated; Woodrow Wilson collapsed in office, was disabled for many weeks, and never regained his health; and Franklin Roosevelt died of a cerebral hemorrhage shortly before the end of World War II and at the beginning of his fourth term.

The Constitution, in Article Two, section one, states that the Vice-President shall succeed to the presidency upon the removal, death, resignation, or inability of the President to discharge his duties, and authorizes Congress to provide by law for the succession in the event that the Vice-President is unable to carry on the office. Two questions arise under these provisions: Who determines

---

[51] New York *Times*, February 10, 1946.

whether the President is unable to discharge his duties? Who succeeds the Vice-President in the event that both the President and the Vice-President die, resign, or are removed?

Two cases have arisen in the history of the country in which Presidents have been incapacitated for extended periods. President Garfield was unable to discharge the duties of his office for several weeks after he was shot, and President Wilson was disabled for several months following his collapse in September, 1919. On both of these occasions there were extended discussions about the steps that should be taken. It was suggested that the Vice-President decide the issue of "inability," that it be decided jointly by the Vice-President and Congress, and that it be decided by Congress alone. In each case it was the President's family and intimate associates who determined the issue of disability and determined it contrary to the apparent fact. The constitutional uncertainties have not yet been resolved by establishment of a clear-cut procedure.

Congress has passed three different acts governing succession to the presidency in the event of the death, removal, or incapacity of the Vice-President. In 1792 it stipulated that the order of succession should be the President pro tempore of the Senate, and then the Speaker of the House of Representatives. In 1886 a new law provided that cabinet officers who were otherwise qualified under the Constitution should succeed in the order of the creation of their departments. The issue that developed in the discussion of these acts was whether the Vice-President should be succeeded by an elected or an appointed official. Under the existing law, passed in 1948, the Speaker of the House of Representatives acts as President upon the death, removal, or resignation of both the President and the Vice-President.[52] Next in the line of succession are the President pro tempore of the Senate, the Secretary of State, the Secretary of the Treasury, the Secretary of Defense, the Attorney General, the Postmaster General, the Secretary of the Interior, the Secretary of Agriculture, the Secretary of Commerce, and the Secretary of Labor. The law requires the Speaker of the House or the President pro tempore to resign from Congress before taking office as President.

bibliographic note

Of writing by Presidents, for Presidents, and about Presidents there is no end. The voluminous literature on this subject includes presidential messages to Congress and to other groups, diaries such as those of John Quincy Adams and James K. Polk, recollections of cabinet members and other intimates of Presidents, and studies of scholars. There are several excellent volumes surveying

---

[52] 62 Stat. 672 at 677, Act of June 25, 1948.

the presidency in its more general aspects; these studies frequently deal also with one or another of the specialized functions of the office. All of the following are worthy of careful reading: W. E. Binkley, *The Powers of the President* (New York: Doubleday & Company, 1937), which traces the historical development of the office and includes a useful bibliography; Louis Brownlow, *The President and the Presidency* (Chicago: Public Administration Service, 1949), concerned primarily with the adequacy of the office in view of the demands made upon the President; Edward S. Corwin, *The President: Office and Powers* (New York: New York University Press, 1st ed., 1940), an authoritative study of the constitutional development of the office by a great scholar which includes also an abundance of interesting information in footnotes; Pendleton Herring, *Presidential Leadership* (New York: Rinehart & Company, 1940), which examines the relations between President, party, and Congress; Harold J. Laski, *The American Presidency* (New York: Harper & Brothers, 1940), an interpretation of the office by a leading British political scientist; and George Fort Milton, *The Use of Presidential Power* (Boston: Little, Brown & Company, 1944), a highly readable book with the theme that the "office is rich with examples of the way great leaders, confronted with great crises, can keep the nation whole." An entire issue (Vol. XI, No. I, February, 1949) of the *Journal of Politics*, published by the Southern Political Science Association, deals with the "presidency in transition" and includes a number of excellent articles.

A number of memoirs have appeared recently that are a rich source of information about the presidency under Franklin D. Roosevelt. They include James F. Byrnes, *Speaking Frankly* (New York: Harper & Brothers, 1947); Cordell Hull, *The Memoirs of Cordell Hull* (New York: The Macmillan Company, 1948); Frances Perkins, *The Roosevelt I Knew* (New York: The Viking Press, 1946); Robert Sherwood, *Roosevelt and Hopkins* (New York: Harper & Brothers, 1947); Edward R. Stettinius and Walter Johnson, *Roosevelt and the Russians* (New York: Doubleday & Company, 1949); and Henry L. Stimson and McGeorge Bundy, *On Active Service in Peace and War* (New York: Harper & Brothers, 1947). All of these volumes are based upon the recollections and private papers of people who served in the President's cabinet.

Also useful in understanding the role of the President are Calvin Coolidge, *The Autobiography of Calvin Coolidge* (New York: Cosmopolitan Book Corp. 1929); H. F. Pringle, *Theodore Roosevelt: A Biography* (New York: Harcourt, Brace and Company, 1931) and his *Life and Times of William Howard Taft* (New York: Rinehart & Company, 2 vols., 1939); William Howard Taft, *Our Chief Magistrate and His Powers* (New York: Columbia University Press, 1916); Ray Stannard Baker, *Woodrow Wilson: Life and Letters* (New York: Doubleday & Company, 8 vols., 1927–1939); and Charles Seymour, *The Intimate Papers of Colonel House* (Boston: Houghton Mifflin Company, 1926). Although written before he became President, two books by Woodrow Wilson help to throw light on his use of the office: *Congressional Government* (Boston: Houghton Mifflin Company, 1885) and *Constitutional Government in the United States,* originally delivered as lectures at Columbia University in 1907 (New York: Columbia University Press, 1921).

Authoritative accounts of the origins of the presidency may be found in W. E. Binkley, *The Powers of the President;* E. S. Corwin, *The President: Office and Powers;* James Hart, *The American Presidency in Action, 1789* (New York: The Macmillan Company, 1948); Jennings B. Sanders, *Evolution of Executive Departments of the Continental Congress, 1774–1789* (Chapel Hill: University of North Carolina Press, 1935); Charles C. Thach, Jr., "The Creation of the Presidency," *Johns Hopkins University Studies in History and Political Science,* Series 40, No. 4 (Baltimore: The Johns Hopkins Press, 1922); and Leonard D. White, *The Federalists* (New York: The Macmillan Company, 1948).

All of the general studies and memoirs cited at the beginning of this note help to illumine the President's role as national leader. The contributions of a chief of state to the morale of a democratic society are discussed in a stimulating fashion by Walter Bagehot, *The English Constitution* (London: Oxford University Press, 1928, World's Classics edition), pp. 30–50. The bibiographic note to Chapter 18 lists references dealing with presidential leadership in legislative matters. The history of presidential relations with the press is traced in an exceptionally comprehensive study by James E. Pollard, *The President and the Press* (New York: The Macmillan Company, 1947).

Professor Corwin's *The President: Office and Powers* is an excellent reference on the President as chief executive. Chapter 4, pp. 111–153, discusses the President's law enforcement duties, and Chapter 3, pp. 64–110, is concerned with his powers of appointment and removal. A book-length discussion of the pardoning power is W. H. Humbert, *The Pardoning Power of the President* (Washington: American Council on Public Affairs, 1941). Two systematic but rather out-of-date studies of presidential legislative power are John P. Comer, *Legislative Functions of National Administrative Authorities* (New York: Columbia Universtity Press, 1927), and James Hart, "The Ordinance Making Powers of the President," *Johns Hopkins University Studies in History and Political Science,* Series 43, No. 3 (Baltimore: The Johns Hopkins Press, 1922). Charles S. Hyneman, *Bureaucracy in a Democracy* (New York: Harper & Brothers, 1950), discusses at many points the responsibilities of President and Congress for supervision and control of law enforcement agencies. Professor Hyneman emphasizes the practical limits of presidential supervision and the democratic values of congressional control; his view is somewhat different from that taken in this chapter.

Numerous references to studies of the President's role as chief of foreign relations and commander in chief are given in the bibliographic notes to Chapters 45–49. The memoirs of Byrnes, Hull, Colonel House, Stettinius, and Stimson, and Sherwood's *Roosevelt and Hopkins,* all cited in this note, and Winston Churchill's memoirs, one volume of which has been cited in this chapter, will be considered interesting and significant by the careful student. A good but somewhat out-of-date study is Howard White, *Executive Influence in Determining Military Policy in the United States* (Urbana: University of Illinois, 1925). The author examines the constitutional provisions affecting the power to determine military policy, discusses at length the precedents set in the period 1789–1797, and traces presidential influence in military affairs from 1797 to 1923. The volume also contains a useful bibliography. Elias Huzar, *The Purse and the Sword* (Ithaca: Cornell University Press, 1950), is an excellent study of congressional control of the army by means of appropriations. The *American Political Science Review,* XLIII, No. 3 (June, 1949), contains four useful articles on national defense policy and organization: John D. Millett, "National Security in American Public Affairs," pp. 524–534; Sidney W. Souers, "Policy Formulation for National Security," pp. 534–543; William Frye, "The National Military Establishment," 543–555; and Ralph J. Watkins, "Economic Mobilization," pp. 555–563.

The use of presidential power to suppress domestic disorders is treated comprehensively in Bennett M. Rich, *The Presidents and Civil Disorder* (Washington: The Brookings Institution, 1941). For discussions of problems pertaining to martial law see, in addition to sources cited in footnotes of this chapter, E. S. Corwin, *The President: Office and Powers,* pp. 176–184; and Charles Fairman's rewarding article, "The President as Commander-in-Chief," in *Journal of Politics,* XI, no. 1 (February, 1949), 145–170.

Additional reading concerning succession to the presidency might include Corwin, *The President: Office and Powers,* pp. 51–58, as well as the information incorporated in footnotes, pp. 236–256; Everett S. Brown and Ruth C. Silva, "Presidential Succession and Inability," *Journal of Politics,* XI, No. 1 (February, 1949), 236–256; and J. E. Kallenbach, "The New Presidential Succession Act," *American Political Science Review,* XLI, No. 5 (October, 1947), 931–941.

Further study of the impact of crises upon democratic institutions should start with Frederick M. Watkins's remarkably competent discussion, "The Problem of Constitutional Dictatorship," in *Public Policy* (C. J. Friedrich and E. S. Mason, eds.; Cambridge: Harvard University Press, 1940) pp. 324-379. Clinton L. Rossiter, *Constitutional Dictatorship,* Princeton: Princeton University Press, 1948), elaborates ideas set forth by Professor Watkins and analyzes crisis government in the United States, Great Britain, and the French and German republics; this is an invaluable piece of scholarship. A short discussion is Albert L. Sturm, "Emergencies and the Presidency," *Journal of Politics,* XI,

No. 1 (February, 1949), 121–144. The scope of presidential emergency powers and the problems created by their existence are discussed, with respect to 1939– 1941, in Louis W. Koenig, *The Presidency and the Crisis* (New York: King's Crown Press, 1944). For a list of emergency war powers, see Appendix A and B of Koenig's book; Appendix I of Herring, *Presidential Leadership;* "Executive Powers under National Emergency," *Senate Document* No. 133, 76 Cong., 2 Sess.; and Title 50 of the *United States Code.*

the presidency:

organization and staff

*O*NE individual cannot discharge unaided the array of responsibilities that comprise the presidency of the United States. Each of the major categories of work—national leader, chief executive, chief of foreign affairs, and commander in chief—is a full-time job. In terms of the amount of work to be done, a case can be made for having four Presidents, rather than one. The volume of work has increased rapidly. Abraham Lincoln handled White House problems with the help of two or three correspondence clerks. Grover Cleveland answered his own telephone and wrote most of his papers in longhand. President Taft thought it remarkable that the volume of business in his day required the assistance of twenty-five clerks and stenographers. From McKinley's administration until the close of Herbert Hoover's term, one man, Ira Smith, was able to take care of all the mail that came to the White House. Coolidge used to sit on the corner of Smith's desk while Smith slit the envelopes and passed him his letters. Before Smith retired in 1948, after fifty-one years of service, he had a staff of fifty clerks to help him with the mail. For twelve years under Franklin D. Roosevelt, an average of 5,000 letters were delivered to the White House each day, and as many as 175,000 letters on a single day. The number of letters to President Roosevelt dropped during World War II, but about 4,000 now come to President Truman each week. Today the White House Office includes approximately 300 employees; the Executive Office of the President, about 1,000 persons. Moreover, the whole executive branch of the government is in a sense part of the presidential staff. But since the President as chief executive is responsible for the management of this vast organization, his burdens are measurably increased by its existence.

management of the executive branch

political significance of presidential management

Presidential management of the executive branch is one of the principal ways we have of keeping the bureaucracy within the limits of the democratic process.

661

To state the matter concisely, a law passed by Congress and signed by the President is an expression of the will of the people. But, as Jefferson observed in 1789, "The execution of the laws is more important than the making of them." If a law is not enforced with congressional objectives constantly in view, if the provisions of the law are ignored or distorted, the public's purposes will be thwarted. The most effective way the public has of expressing its pleasure or displeasure with the actions of government is by its choice of Presidents and members of Congress. Congressmen, by enacting and amending legislation, appropriating money, and investigating administration, exert great influence over the execution of policy. By the Constitution and by necessity, the continuing supervision of administration is an executive rather than a legislative function. Congressional controls must be coupled with effective presidential management of the executive branch if the administration of policy is to be kept responsive to public opinion.

The constitutional provisions supporting the President's managerial authority are brief. Under Article Two, the "executive power" is vested in him; he shares with the Senate the power to appoint and remove officials; he is named "Commander-in-Chief of the Army and Navy"; he is authorized to "require the opinion, in writing, of the principal officer in each of the executive departments, upon any subject relating to the duties of their respective offices"; and he is charged to "take care that the laws be faithfully executed." These provisions give to the President the task of directing and controlling administrative agencies, in accordance with laws enacted by Congress.

responsibility for executive organization

Congress determines, with respect to the executive branch, the number of administrative units, the nature of their activities, and the title and authority of their chief officials. The authority of Congress to decide these matters is based on custom rather than on explicit constitutional provision. Some members of the Constitutional Convention believed that, since the President was obligated to ensure the faithful execution of laws, he should have the power to determine the nature of the executive organization; other members felt that the power was essentially legislative in character and that it should be exercised jointly by Congress and the President. Although the issue was not resolved by the Constitution, precedents of the First Congress established the authority of Congress to create executive departments and to define their duties. Congress is not in a position, however, to supervise closely the work of some eighteen hundred administrative units that comprise the executive establishment. Its essential and most significant contributions are made in formulating policy and in determining the general character of the administrative organization.

The problem of effective organization of the executive branch is not solved by the legislative creation of new agencies or the assignment of new activities to existing agencies. Over a period of time, these enactments lead to difficulty, for two reasons. First, the number of agencies is increased beyond the limits of effective presidential direction or wise congressional supervision. The President can spend only a few hours each week with the chief officials of major departments and perhaps not more than one hour during a year with officials of less important agencies. Similarly, congressional appropriation committees try to become well informed about the problems of the more costly organizations and of necessity have little time for agencies whose annual appropriations are relatively small. Second, in the assignment of new activities the big departments inevitably acquire responsibility for such diverse and unrelated programs that they have difficulty maintaining desirable unity. When a department becomes too complex, its personnel, the President, Congress, and the public are baffled by its problems. These difficulties lead to periodic drives to "reorganize" the executive branch.

Although final authority to reorganize rests with Congress, the reorganization process requires the collaboration of Congress and the President. The principle underlying this process is that the President should have freedom to shape the organization of the executive branch as long as Congress does not object to particular proposals. The principle is embodied in the Reorganization Act of 1949, the latest in a series of laws going back to 1932.[1] Under the 1949 act, the President may submit to Congress proposals to reorganize or abolish existing agencies, to create new agencies, or to abolish all or a part of the functions of existing agencies. Any reorganization plan proposed under this authority becomes effective unless it is vetoed by a majority of the entire membership of either of the two houses of Congress. The authority under the act expires April 1, 1953.

Presidential reorganization plans generally have followed the recommendations of groups created to study the organizational problems of the government. President Taft's Commission on Economy and Efficiency was the first group of this kind. Franklin D. Roosevelt appointed The President's Committee on Administrative Management in 1936 and subsequently submitted to Congress several proposals incorporating the committee's recommendations. In July, 1947, Congress created the Commission of the Organization of the Executive Branch of the Government. Former President Hoover served as chairman of this commission, which comprised four members appointed by the President, four appointed by the President pro tempore of the Senate, and four appointed by the Speaker of the House of Representatives. The Hoover Commission's study was carried on by several hundred people over a period of two years and cost approximately three million dollars. It resulted in recommendations dealing with most of the major problems of federal administration; the commission's pro-

---

[1] Reorganization Act of 1949, 5 U.S.C. §133z, 63 Stat. 203.

posals for strengthening presidential organization and staff are noted in this chapter.

There is much to be said for the approach to executive reorganization illustrated by the act of 1949. The procedure protects a basic congressional interest in the quality of law enforcement agencies. By giving each house of Congress an opportunity to veto a reorganization plan, the procedure prevents the President from destroying an activity or an agency that Congress wishes to maintain. Moreover, the possibility of a congressional veto should deter a President from instituting ill-considered proposals that would do more harm than good. On the negative side, the experience with the Hoover Commission's recommendations suggests that the process may be unduly cumbersome. To take a single point, approximately a hundred different bills have been introduced in Congress to effectuate the commission's proposals. It is difficult to see how Congress within a reasonable period of time can give intelligent consideration to these measures. It is true that the number of bills is a result of the fact that the executive branch was the subject of an intensive scrutiny that produced sweeping recommendations for change. Perhaps the remedy to the difficulty lies in continuous study and reconsideration over a period of years rather than the periodic, intensive approach represented by the President's Committee on Administrative Management and the Commission on the Organization of the Executive Branch of the Government.

importance of presidential management

The essence of the President's managerial task is to weave together the activities of different agencies responsible for related aspects of the same problem. This task is inescapable because there is no way to assign functions among departments so that *all* aspects of a single problem come within the jurisdiction of a single agency. The intelligent assignment of jobs to departments eases the President's managerial load, but it does not, and cannot, eliminate it.

Government's characteristic activity is the adjustment of conflicting interests that are inevitably present in any society. The significance of this activity can be seen clearly when violence replaces negotiation and discussion in the settlement of labor disputes. On such occasions the police force has the job of restoring and maintaining order. It is desirable that conflicting interests be reconciled before they result in violence. For this reason we have come to accept government regulation of the employer-employee relationship by laws dealing with collective bargaining, minimum wages, and other conditions of work. Similar problems exist in other fields; in a highly organized industrial society there are many groups whose immediate welfare can be advanced only at the expense of other groups.

It is paradoxical that the job of maintaining a balance among these groups falls upon a government that is itself characterized by diversity and conflict. The propensity for division within the government is a result of the architecture of the Constitution—for example, of such features as separation of powers, checks and balances, federalism, and the geographical structure of political power. This divisive tendency carries down into the executive branch, where conflicts between departments and their components and inconsistent policies are taken as a matter of course. For example, the Army Corps of Engineers is concerned primarily with local flood control; the Bureau of Reclamation of the Department of the Interior is interested in irrigation. There are many instances in which these two agencies, pursuing legitimate interests, have worked at cross-purposes in the development of the same river, "the Corps working up the river, meeting the Bureau coming down." Further, the Federal Security Agency, the Federal Power Commission, the Department of Agriculture, and the Tennessee Valley Authority have by law been given responsibilities for various phases of river development and control and compete in some degree with each other and with the Corps of Engineers and the Department of the Interior in carrying out their projects. Relationships between departments in other fields of activity are comparable to those in the field of water development. The President must do his best to curtail the wasted effort and unsatisfactory performance that these conflicts produce.

The President's achievements as general manager affect Congress's ability to formulate wise decisions on questions of public policy. Congress has come to count heavily on suggestions from the executive branch. Because of the necessity for dividing governmental activities among many departments and agencies, there is no easy method of bringing to focus the knowledge and judgment of executive officials. Government actions that later prove to be serious mistakes often can be avoided by weighing carefully the judgments of officials who know most about the problem. It is up to the President, with whatever help he is able to muster, to see to it that the proper officials are consulted, that the various factors of the problem are carefully analyzed, and that alternatives of action are considered before decisions are made or advice is given to Congress. This process may require conferences with many people and much hard work; but without such investigation and discussion there can be no assurance that the maximum intelligence and best informed judgment go into the formulation and administration of public policy.

magnitude of the managerial job

The President's job as manager of the federal government is determined by the size and complexity of the government itself. In its final report the Hoover Commission stated:

As a result of depression, war, new needs for defense, and our greater responsibilities abroad, the Federal Government has become the largest enterprise on earth. In less than 20 years its civil employment has increased from 570,000 to over 2,000,000. Its bureaus, sections and units have increased fourfold to over 1,800. Annual expenditures have soared from $3 billion to over $42 billion. . . . Only 10 per cent of the over 2,000,000 Federal employees are located in Washington; the balance are in the field service. In September, 1948 more Federal civilian employees were working outside the continental limits of the United States than in the city of Washington.[2]

The number of departments and agencies that report directly to the President and require his supervision is a measure of the size of his managerial job. The number varies from 65 to 85, depending upon the inclusion of certain agencies whose relationships to the President are not clear. The President is directly responsible for agencies ranging in importance from the Department of Defense to the Combined Tin Committee. If the President devoted one hour each week to conferences with the heads of agencies whose work he is supposed to direct, he would need to spend ten hours each day of the week on such conferences. This schedule would not leave any time for his duties as legislative and political leader, chief of state, commander in chief, or the other major functions of the presidency. If one takes into account also the incredible variety of subjects about which the President is expected to have some judgment, it is clear that the demands made upon him as supervisor of the executive establishment are impossible.

lack of continuity in the presidency a factor

The management aspects of the presidency are complicated by the tradition of frequent change in the office. A business organization such as the General Electric Company or the General Motors Corporation does not place a man in its top managerial position until he has had a wide range of experience in its affairs. Moreover, a corporation expects to retain the services of a successful president for a long period of years. The general assumption is that effective direction of complex affairs requires continuity of experience and personnel and that it is wasteful to change the top management officials frequently as a matter of principle.

This degree of continuity cannot be provided within the presidency. A President is unable to acquire much relevant experience before assuming office. Whatever executive experience he had before becoming President cannot prepare him adequately for the responsibilities that he must assume immediately upon taking the oath of office. If his experience should be as legislator or judge, he may find that the work habits acquired in those positions hinder rather than help him. When he begins to gain some understanding of his tasks, the opposition party and press declare that it is time for a change. If he is lucky and does a

---

[2] Commission on Organization of the Executive Branch of the Government, *Concluding Report* (Washington: Government Printing Office, 1949), pp. 3–4.

reasonably good job, he can perhaps count upon a second term. Beyond that, he must overcome the tradition against a third term, an obstacle that is substantial but not insurmountable. If he is still alive after leaving office, he may have an audience as an elder statesman or as a columnist. It is also significant that, with a change in the presidency, there is a change in the key White House assistants and most of the cabinet members. Thus every few years the officials responsible for the management of the federal government are replaced by new and less experienced men.

To describe this difficulty is not to suggest that it would be better to continue a President in office indefinitely. In the first place, of course, it is essential that the voters be able to change the occupant of the White House if they do not like the way things are going. Second, the job of being President of the United States is literally man-killing, and it is highly important to maintain freshness and vigor in the affairs of government. But the fact that change is the rule makes considerably more difficult the task of providing the President with suitable organization and staff.

why not an assistant President?

The executive branch is managed by the President without the help of an assistant President. Although the number of presidential assistants has increased over the years, none of them has become the President's alter ego, authorized by law to act on the President's behalf. To be sure, a President may give a man in whom he has deep confidence assignments of the most delicate and urgent character, and, as a later discussion of personal advisers shows, a person of great competence may acquire under these circumstances the cloak of an "assistant President." But his authority has its source in friendship and is not carried over into succeeding administrations. The question of what makes a satisfactory assistant is complex and highly personal, and a President quite naturally prefers to work with a staff of his own choosing rather than with one selected by his predecessors.

Similarly, the usefulness of the Vice-President is limited by his ability to work easily with his chief; but other factors are perhaps more significant in his case. First, the Constitution makes him the presiding officer of the Senate. If this is not itself a full-time job, it at least makes it difficult for the Vice-President to accept any other high position with fixed responsibilities. From time to time Presidents have attempted to utilize the services of Vice-Presidents, but with uneven success. During World War II Henry Wallace served as the head of two major war agencies and on occasion met with President Roosevelt's cabinet. But this experimentation, which probably would not have taken place during normal times, did not lead to any lasting change in the relations between President and Vice-President. Vice-President Barkley has been useful to the President in the field of executive-legislative relations, but there is no evidence that he has relieved the President of any important managerial functions. Second, a candidate for the vice-presidency is not selected for his ability to serve the President or for his promise as a possible successor to the office. He is chosen for political reasons: to reward an "elder statesman"; to placate a party faction; or to sidetrack a rival candidate for the presidency. As a result, election as Vice-President traditionally relegates a man to obscurity. Finally, the Constitution does not give to the Vice-President the position or powers of an assistant President. Heads of departments and agencies are not willing to accept the decisions of the Vice-President on matters they consider important to themselves or their organizations. For these reasons, the vice-presidency has not attracted able and vigorous men of the type that could render substantial service as a member of the President's working team.

Obstacles to the development of an assistant President were overcome during the later stages of World War II. President Roosevelt found that the military and diplomatic phases of the war required all of his attention, and that essential "home front" activities sagged because of lack of presidential attention. In May, 1943, he established the Office of War Mobilization and appointed James F. Byrnes Director of War Mobilization. Byrnes was authorized to direct and unify the activities of federal departments and agencies concerned with the civilian side of the war, such as war production, civilian manpower, and transportation. Since one of the difficulties was the frequent disagreements among these agencies over matters of policy, Byrnes was directed to "resolve and determine all controversies between such agencies or departments." [3] The director and staff of the Office of War Mobilization were given space in the White House, and Byrnes made final decisions on many matters that normally would have gone to the President. Although this experiment was reasonably successful, it is unlikely that a President would undertake it in peacetime, or that the heads of departments and agencies would accept the "assistant President's" decision as final judgments of the President himself.

over-all organization of the executive branch

the hierarchic pattern

In general outline, the structure of the executive branch of the government resembles that of the Army and that of large business and religious organizations. This outline is most frequently presented as a triangle or pyramid, with the President and his staff at the apex and the departments and agencies at the base. In theory, the President's authority extends downward to the executives responsible for departmental actions, and these executives, in turn, are responsible to the President. Presidential control over activities at the base of the triangle is

---

[3] Executive Order No. 9,347, *Federal Register*, VIII (May 26, 1943), 7207.

exercised through the departmental and agency executives. This pattern of organization is technically known as a "hierarchy." The relationships within the hierarchy were described by Tolstoy as follows:

> Men always combine together for the performance of common action in such relations that the more directly they take part in the action, the less they command, and the greater their numbers; and the less direct the part they take in the common action, the more they command, and the fewer they are in number; passing in that way from the lower strata up to a single man at the top, who takes least direct share in the action, and devotes his energy more than all the rest to giving commands. This is the relation of persons in command to those whom they command, and it constitutes the essence of the conception of what is called power.[4]

components of the hierarchy: departments and agencies

The major governmental activities are administered by departments or agencies. The term "department" by statute and common usage designates an organization whose chief executive has the title of Secretary and is a member of the President's cabinet. Currently, this group includes the Departments of State, Defense, Treasury, Justice, Post Office, Interior, Agriculture, Commerce, and Labor. One exception to this usage should be noted. The Department of Defense includes three "departments," Army, Navy, and Air Force, each headed by a "secretary." These departments, however, are represented in the cabinet by the Secretary of Defense, rather than by their own top officials. For a number of years there has been great interest in the creation of a new department concerned with health, education, and welfare activities. The President's Committee on Administrative Management recommended in 1937 the establishment of a Department of Social Welfare; and the Hoover Commission in 1949 favored a Department of Social Security and Education. Although the President's Reorganization Plan No. 27 (1950) would have created a Department of Health, Education, and Security, the House of Representatives vetoed the proposal. The nine executive departments employ about 1.7 million persons, or roughly 80 per cent of all the civilian employees of the federal government.

The term "agency" is applied to administrative organizations that are included in the executive branch but are not represented in the President's cabinet. There are approximately seventy such organizations in the executive branch, excluding the General Accounting Office, the Government Printing Office, and the Library of Congress, which are congressional rather than executive agencies. The seventy agencies can be divided into two groups, according to whether or not the President is expected to supervise them. Eight of the agencies, the independent regulatory commissions, are for important purposes outside the President's

---

[4] Leo Tolstoy, *War and Peace* (New York: The Modern Library, 1931), p. 1119.

authority.[5] Although these commissions are a part of the executive branch, they are "independent" in the sense that the President is not expected to influence their formulation of policy. Thus the independent regulatory commissions fall within the hierarchic pattern but are outside the line of command that extends downward from the President. The second group of agencies is subject to presidential direction and control, and includes such important establishments as the Veterans Administration, which has about 200,000 employees and spent in 1949 more than $5 billion, and the Atomic Energy Commission, which is responsible for research in medical and industrial uses of atomic energy and for the development and manufacture of atomic weapons.

The officials responsible for the administration of departmental and agency affairs comprise the core of the President's staff. To use business terminology, they are "operating vice-presidents." In terms of complexity, variety, and magnitude, the responsibilities of the heads of organizations such as the Department of Agriculture or the Atomic Energy Commission are second only to those of the President of the United States.

components of the hierarchy: the Executive Office of the President

The President's principal help, aside from that provided by the cabinet officers, comes from the Executive Office of the President, which was established in 1939. In this office, the three agencies that give the most aid to the President are the White House Office; the Bureau of the Budget, established as a part of the Treasury Department by the Budgeting and Accounting Act of 1921 but transferred to the Executive Office by executive order in 1939; and the Council of Economic Advisers, created by the Employment Act of 1946. Each of these agencies is discussed later in this chapter. The work of the National Security Council and the National Securities Resources Board, which were transferred to the Executive Office of the President in 1949, was discussed in Chapter thirty-one.

proposed changes in the over-all organization

The reports of the President's Committee on Administrative Management (1937) and the Commission on Organization of the Executive Branch of the Government (1949) are unusually significant in the development of federal administration. One of the major accomplishments of the 1937 report was its successful advocacy of an Executive Office of the President. The Hoover Commission's appraisal of the current status of the Executive Office, and proposals for improvements, are discussed in sections below dealing with the various constituent

---

[5] The independent regulatory commissions are: Civil Aeronautics Board, Interstate Commerce Commission, Federal Communications Commission, Federal Power Commission, Federal Trade Commission, National Labor Relations Board, Federal Reserve Board, and Securities and Exchange Commission. The Maritime Commission was abolished as an independent agency and its functions transferred to the Commerce Department by reorganization plan No. 21, effective May 24, 1950.

agencies of that office. The two reports were in general agreement about major defects in the organization of the executive branch.

First, the President is expected to supervise directly too many people. The 1937 report declared:

> . . . in equipment for administrative management our Executive Office is not fully abreast of the trends of our American times, either in business or in government. Where, for example, can there be found an executive in any way comparable upon whom so much petty work is thrown? Or who is forced to see so many persons on unrelated matters and to make so many decisions on the basis of what may be, because of the very press of work, incomplete information? How is it humanly possible to know fully the affairs and problems of over 100 separate major agencies, to say nothing of being responsible for their general direction and coordination?[6]

Former President Hoover, speaking in support of the 1949 recommendations, stated: "The executive agencies have grown up like a series of 'lean-tos' all around the President's power. . . . Therefore, the whole mechanism is a series of accretions from 160 years of congressional and administrative action with no effective plan." [7] The Hoover Commission proposed a regrouping of federal activities so that the President would be the chief of an administrative staff composed of not more than thirty departments and agencies. If carried through, this proposal would reduce to a manageable size the number of officials reporting directly to the President.

Second, too many agencies have been established by Congress outside the President's jurisdiction. The Hoover Commission concluded that there are in all about thirty-seven bureaus or commissions that are presumed to have authority independent of the President. Eight of these are independent regulatory commissions, like the Interstate Commerce Commission. "In the congressional setup over the years there has been great encroachment into executive authority. . . . No doubt [the independent agencies] usually would comply with the direction of the President, but they don't have to, at least in their own view." [8] Both President Roosevelt's Committee on Administrative Management and the Hoover Commission concluded that the President should have a greater degree of control over the independent agencies but differed as to desirable remedies.

The Hoover Commission asked for the repeal of legislation giving independent authority to the heads of departments and agencies normally responsible to the President, and for the transfer to executive departments of the executive functions of independent regulatory commissions. Under this recommendation

---

[6] President's Committee on Administrative Management, *Administrative Management in the Government of the United States* (Washington: Government Printing Office, 1937), p. 3.
[7] Transcript of interview with Herbert Hoover, June 3, 1949, *U.S. News & World Report,* an independent weekly magazine on national and international affairs, published at Washington.
[8] *Ibid.*

the commissions would retain their independent status with respect to their legislative functions; but an activity such as the construction, operation, and sale of ships by the Maritime Commission would be given to an executive department.

Third, Congress has made the President's managerial task more difficult by laying down statutory instructions about the way in which the powers of subordinate officials must be exercised. Much of this legislation is concerned with the manner in which departments and agencies handle their routine fiscal, purchasing, and personnel affairs, and it is the source of much "red tape." For example, there are 199 statutes affecting personnel management in the Department of Agriculture. The repeal of this legislation, as recommended by the Hoover Commission, would give administrative officials the flexibility needed in the management of large organizations.

Fourth, the Hoover Commission concluded that the executive branch was poorly organized for the maintenance of buildings, the management of records, and the purchase and distribution of supplies. It proposed the centralization of these functions, a recommendation that was carried out by the creation of the General Services Administration.[9] The President now has an agency whose primary concern is the efficient management of these "housekeeping" services.

These and related proposals of the Hoover Commission are noncontroversial in the sense that Presidents and departmental and agency officials of both political parties have attested to their basic soundness. But there is a wide gap between "acceptance in principle" and a completed installation. Considerable progress has been made in effecting the commission's recommendations, within limits set by the authority of the President and officials of the executive branch. As noted elsewhere, the effectuation of some of the most important proposals depends upon enactment of legislation. Much of the pending legislation would increase the power of executive officials at the expense of Congress; hence it is problematical that there will be equal progress in the future.

the President's cabinet

The President's cabinet is composed of the heads of the executive departments. Before the creation of agencies and commissions, the President saw at a cabinet meeting all of the officials immediately responsible for the administration of the activities entrusted to the executive branch. Today, however, approximately sixty-five agencies under some degree of presidential supervision are not represented at cabinet meetings. None of the independent regulatory commissions participates in these sessions, nor, for example, does the Veterans Administration, the Tennessee Valley Authority, or the Atomic Energy Commission.

---

[9] 41 U.S.C. §211, 63 Stat. 379.

nature of the cabinet

A member of the cabinet serves in two capacities. His first responsibility is the management of the department over which he presides. His second and perhaps more significant role is that of adviser to the President.

Although the Constitution does not provide for a cabinet in so many words, the Founding Fathers clearly contemplated that the President would look to the heads of departments for advice and counsel. When Congress debated the question of the establishment of departments in 1789, the point was made that the President should be relatively free to choose departmental heads in whom he had confidence, and to remove them when he became dissatisfied, without the concurrence of the Senate. Confidence between the President and the principal departmental officers was thought to be essential to the successful administration of the executive branch.

The President's cabinet is not really a cabinet in the sense in which that term is used in a parliamentary system like Great Britain's. Cabinet members do not share with the President collective responsibility for the administration's policies and decisions on major questions. The President is not even bound to consult the cabinet, and he often makes significant decisions without this consultation. During the Civil War President Lincoln met infrequently with his cabinet, apparently did not insist that members make a point of being present, and on occasion did not attend himself. Theodore Roosevelt and Woodrow Wilson both regarded their cabinet members as a group of administrators rather than as policy advisers concerned with the broad strategy of affairs. Wilson did not read his war message to the cabinet because he did not want to subject its language to review and discussion.

During the early years of his presidency, Franklin Roosevelt considered a cabinet meeting an opportunity to hear the views of the members about pending issues of presidential concern, but as the years went on the meetings deteriorated. Frances Perkins, for twelve years President Roosevelt's Secretary of Labor, has said: "Roosevelt's cabinet administration came to be like most previous ones—a direct relationship between a particular cabinet officer and the President in regard to his special field, with little or no participation or even information from other cabinet members. Certainly almost no 'cabinet agreements' were reached." [10] Henry Stimson characterized the sessions during World War II as "no earthly good" and he thought that "Mr. Roosevelt's own view of Cabinet meetings was not wholly different." [11] President Roosevelt seems, in fact, to have come to the conclusion that cabinet members were not especially helpful. Harold Smith, Director of the Budget from 1939 until Roosevelt's death, re-

---

[10] Frances Perkins, *The Roosevelt I Knew* (New York: The Viking Press, 1946), p. 377.

[11] Henry L. Stimson and McGeorge Bundy, *On Active Service in Peace and War* (New York: Harper & Brothers, 1947), p. 561.

ported: "Roosevelt saw the Cabinet officers not as members of his own staff but as theater commanders, each with his own special area, interests, problems and demands. You couldn't expect any of them to see the picture whole, as the President had to do." [12] During his first year or two in office, Harry S. Truman tried to regularize cabinet meetings, to conduct discussions in accordance with agenda previously submitted to the members, and, at least occasionally, to have a record made of the points covered and agreed to. Testimony of his cabinet as to the effectiveness of these devices is not yet available, but it will not be surprising to find that the innovations did not make a great difference in the value of the cabinet sessions.

selection of cabinet members

A President weighs many factors in selecting a cabinet member. He must consider groups and individuals whose support contributed significantly to his election. If his party is badly split, or if there is a national crisis, he may wish to appoint one or two representatives of an opposing faction or party. Lincoln selected two of his rivals for the nomination, and Franklin Roosevelt brought into his war cabinet two prominent Republicans to head the War and Navy Departments. Such appointments help to solidify party and nation. Since the President must work closely and, presumably, for four years with his cabinet, the question of compatibility is important. Woodrow Wilson sought, in general, men who shared his ideas and philosophy; the result was an able and congenial group with relatively little political prestige or influence. Normally, the cabinet includes one or two men whose position with Congress is especially strong; one, frequently the Postmaster General, who is adept in the management of party affairs; and representatives of important religious groups and geographical areas. A President is not compelled to choose party leaders or men who are widely known and respected for their competence or for their views on public affairs. It is not traditional, either, to appoint as head of a department a man who is an expert in the activities for which he will be responsible. In some cases, it is enough that key pressure groups do not object to an appointment. The Secretary of Labor, for example, must be acceptable to both the CIO and the AFL.

cabinet members are spokesmen of departments

Whatever the reasons leading to their selection, cabinet members soon become the spokesmen of the departments that they direct. This is a natural development in view of the fact that they do not share a collective responsibility. William Redfield, Secretary of Commerce under Wilson, explained that differences within the cabinet, which was usually harmonious, resulted in part from the fact that the members had "varying temperaments and training" and differing points of

---

[12] Robert E. Sherwood, *Roosevelt and Hopkins* (New York: Harper & Brothers, 1948), p. 159.

view and experience: "Each Secretary also inherited certain traditional antagonisms. They were there before he arrived and he took them over on assuming
office, often without knowing it. They had their roots in departmental traditions and in the overzealous loyalties of subordinates."[13]

Many former cabinet members have testified that it is customary to take up
with the President personally departmental affairs of major importance. To
Henry Stimson, for example, cabinet meetings "were useful principally as a way
of getting into the White House to have a word with the President in private
after the meetings were over. . . ." [14] In practice this means that a carefully
prepared memorandum is handed quietly to the President, perhaps before or
after cabinet meetings, with a few words of explanation. If possible, discussion
in which other interested members might participate is avoided, at least until
the President has given a preliminary reaction. Occasionally, a Secretary can obtain the President's hasty approval of a proposal that would be considered by
other department heads to be highly controversial and even unwise. Thus Secretary of Commerce Wallace secured President Truman's approval of a draft of a
speech on foreign affairs that ran counter to the policies then being followed by
the Secretary of State. In this case the incident led to the offending cabinet member's resignation, an action that is not normally the cost of this method of conducting business.

cabinet unimportant as a unifying force

For a number of reasons, the cabinet does not operate as a unifying force in the
affairs of the executive branch of the government. The President personally must
make decisions on the great problems of the day, in the light of whatever judgment and information are available. When disagreements concerning interdepartmental matters arise among members of the cabinet, the cabinet itself does
not resolve them. The President may prefer to ignore the difficulty, but if he cannot, he must intervene and resolve the issue himself. Even though he has the right
to remove a member of the cabinet, in fact he finds it highly desirable politically
to preserve the appearance of peace in his official family.

Many of the disputes between government officials reported in the press occur because the President is preoccupied with other matters. A department head
may take advantage of a busy President and of his colleagues to advance the interests of his own department or to sabotage a presidential policy. Members of
the cabinet sometimes develop "forgetfulness as a fine art":

Half of a President's suggestions, which theoretically carry the weight of
orders, can be safely forgotten by a Cabinet member. And if the President
asks about a suggestion a second time, he can be told that it is being inves·

---

[13] W. C. Redfield, *With Congress and Cabinet* (New York: Doubleday & Company, 1924),
pp. 68–69.
[14] Stimson and Bundy, *On Active Service*, p. 561.

tigated. If he asks a third time, a wise Cabinet officer will give him at least a part of what he suggests. But only occasionally, except about the most important matters, do Presidents ever get around to asking three times.[15]

Needless to say, tactics of this sort do not make any easier the President's task of giving direction to the activity of the executive branch, nor do they enhance the cabinet member's value as a member of the President's staff.

strengthening the cabinet

More effective utilization of the cabinet must take place within a framework of delicate relationships. Although they were intended to describe the British cabinet, Winston Churchill's observations apply also to our own system:

> In any sphere of action there can be no comparison between the positions of number one and number two, three, or four. The duties and problems of all persons other than number one are quite different and in many ways more difficult. It is always a misfortune when number two or three has to initiate a dominant plan or policy. He has to consider not only the merits of the policy, but the mind of his chief; not only what to advise, but what it is proper for him in his station to advise; not only what to do, but how to get it agreed, and how to get it done. Moreover, number two or three will have to reckon with numbers four, five, and six, or maybe some bright outsider, number twenty. Ambition, not so much for vulgar ends, but for fame, glints in every mind. There are always several points of view which may be right, and many which are plausible. . . . At the top there are great simplifications. An accepted leader has only to be sure of what it is best to do, or at least to have made up his mind about it. The loyalties which centre upon number one are enormous. If he trips, he must be sustained. If he makes mistakes, they must be covered. If he sleeps, he must not be wantonly disturbed. If he is not good, he must be pole-axed. But this last extreme process cannot be carried out every day; and certainly not in the days just after he has been chosen.[16]

There have been many suggestions for strengthening the cabinet. In general, these proposals emphasize either the problem of legislative-executive relations or the problem of presidential management of the executive branch.

One suggestion for dealing with the first problem is the substitution of a legislative-executive council for the present cabinet. The President would select his principal advisers from among congressional leaders of his own party. To this core of legislative leaders might be added departmental and agency officials especially competent to deal with problems being discussed by the cabinet. Pro-

---

[15] Jonathan Daniels, *Frontier on the Potomac* (New York: The Macmillan Company, 1946), p. 31.
[16] Winston S. Churchill, *Their Finest Hour* (Boston: Houghton Mifflin Company, 1949), p. 15. Reprinted by permission of Houghton Mifflin Company, publishers.

fessor Edward S. Corwin believes that this type of cabinet would achieve three things: (1) "Without necessarily abolishing bed-chamber Presidential advisers, it would guarantee their subordination to politically responsible advisers." (2) ". . . it promises to mitigate the often senseless and always detrimental antagonisms of President and Congress"; and (3) in crises it would reduce the necessity for presidential action of an extralegal character by making readily available the national lawmaking power. [17]

A second proposal for improved executive-legislative relations is that members of the cabinet attend sessions of Congress from time to time to participate in discussions about which they have knowledge and to answer questions put to them by members of Congress. There is probably no very good reason why department and agency heads should not be subjected to a legislative "question period" and there are supporting precedents. Secretary of Foreign Affairs John Jay apparently attended a session of Congress in 1787 and explained pending matters in which he was interested. In May, 1950, Secretary of State Dean Acheson reported the results of an international conference, from which he had just returned, to an "informal joint session" of Congress and then submitted to questioning from the floor by senators and representatives "rather as a British minister confronts the House of Commons." [18] Agency heads, who now spend a great deal of time testifying before congressional committees, would find it advantageous on occasion to present their viewpoints to the whole Congress. The principal difficulty with this proposal is that the most significant deliberations take place in congressional committees and not before the entire membership of Congress. Also, as a "visitor" and presidential representative, a cabinet member undoubtedly would find it advisable to treat with restraint even the most virulent and irresponsible attacks of opposition congressmen. For this reason alone, the question period probably would not achieve the quality of a similar session of the House of Commons. Nevertheless, as a supplement to committee hearings, the suggestion is undoubtedly promising enough to warrant a fair trial.

Modification of the present cabinet practice along these lines would not convert our "presidential system" into the "parliamentary" form of government.[19] The President would not have the power to dissolve Congress in the event of an impasse; he would not be shorn of any of his constitutional powers or duties; and it is unlikely that the instruments for party discipline would be strengthened. The legislative-executive council might be valuable chiefly in legalizing consultations between the President and congressional leaders. Although these

---

[17] Edward S. Corwin, "Wanted: A New Type of Cabinet," *New York Times Magazine,* October 10, 1948, p. 67. A similar cabinet is proposed in Charles S. Hyneman, *Bureaucracy in a Democracy* (New York: Harper & Brothers, 1950).

[18] New York *Times,* June 1, 1950.

[19] On this point see the discussion in Chapter 18, "The President and Congress: Legislative Leadership."

conferences now take place, they are generally at the President's invitation, and he is not bound to consult the legislators, as presumably he would be under the council arrangement.

Other suggestions for improving the cabinet are intended to make it a more effective device for management of the executive branch. In this connection it is interesting to note that neither President Roosevelt's Committee on Administrative Management nor the Hoover Commission dealt directly with the problem of the cabinet. Both of these groups recommended that the number of people reporting to the President be reduced, and that many of the agencies outside the cabinet be transferred to executive departments with related functions. This recommendation strikes at one of the deficiencies of the present cabinet structure (that it does not include major governmental agencies), but it would not of itself make the cabinet a more effective managerial device.

It has also been suggested that the cabinet be enlarged to include the heads of important agencies that are not now represented. If the Hoover Commission suggestions are carried through, this cabinet would comprise thirty or more members. In a group of this size a President probably would be unwise to discuss confidential matters. In the government, most of the "leaks" of confidential information to the press occur at the top, a fact that is appreciated equally by government officials and political reporters.[20] Moreover, a cabinet made up of these officials would be too large to carry on effective study and discussion of difficult problems. These matters, however, might be referred to a number of standing committees assigned to broad areas of public policy, such as foreign affairs, fiscal policy, agriculture, and labor relations. Each of the committees could be headed by a presidential assistant, who would specialize in the subject matter assigned to his committee. He would bring to the committee the President's general point of view, but he would not make decisions for the President. He would see that the committee had before it relevant information and judgments from departments and agencies not represented in its membership, and, on matters involving legislation, that congressional leaders were informed and consulted.

Reconstruction of the cabinet along these lines might achieve two things: the heads of the most important executive agencies would be brought into the deliberations of the cabinet; and smaller groups of officials who know most about pressing problems would be able to make constructive recommendations for the President's consideration. Suggestions of this type recognize that there is little possibility of changing radically the President's relationship with his cab-

---

[20] Apparently this was true even during World War II. When Roosevelt began to invite "outsiders" to cabinet meetings, "a strange reserve came over meetings. Less and less were confidential or important matters discussed. There had been a good many leaks. What a cabinet officer said in meeting might meet his eye in the public press the next morning, and that did not encourage him to further frank expressions of opinion."—Perkins, *The Roosevelt I Knew*, p. 377.

inet. But a great deal might be done within the present framework to make the cabinet a more effective tool of presidential management.

Finally, the cabinet's effectiveness as a bridge between Congress and the executive could be increased by more appointments of party leaders to cabinet positions. A cabinet member's position is a blend of administrative and political elements. As the head of a large organization he must be a good administrator; at a minimum, the President should be able to assume that the affairs of the department will be administered with intelligence, competence, and fidelity.

> But it is just as important—perhaps even more important—that he be a good politician, in the broadest sense of the word. The department head's primary responsibility to the public, to the chief executive, and to his subordinates is for active political leadership. . . . The department head, however, has no obligation to continue in office for a fixed period. The measure of his success is how much he contributes, rather than how long he lasts. He is politically expendable. It is his function to take risks, to expose himself to hostile fire, and to withdraw or be carried off the field when he has performed his mission. The department head who always plays it safe, and who lets his chief run interference for him rather than get into the interference himself, is operating on the wrong level. He should apply to the nearest post office for an announcement of the next civil service examinations and get a job that really suits him.[21]

the White House Office

the White House staff a recent development •

The White House staff has developed rapidly since the end of the last century. Before McKinley's administration, Presidents had "personal" or "private" secretaries to help with correspondence, but they were not recognized as officials of the government. This arrangement was consistent with the theory that all "official" matters were referred to appropriate departments for action and that the correspondence of the President was "personal." [22]

McKinley was the first President to have an official secretary, and Calvin Coolidge found that he could keep two busy, one to handle relations with Congress and the other to specialize on patronage and party affairs. Since 1928 there have been three presidential secretaries, one each to handle relations with press and radio, relations with Congress, and questions involving the heads of administrative departments and agencies.

---

[21] George A. Graham, "Essentials of Responsibility" in Fritz Morstein Marx (ed.), *Elements of Public Administration*, p. 515. Copyright 1946 by Prentice-Hall, Inc.

[22] Presidents still think of their "papers" as personal property to be taken with them when they leave the White House or otherwise disposed of as they direct.

the career staff

The key permanent official is the executive clerk who, with his assistant, provides essential continuity in White House Office procedures. Until recently, Rudolph Forster and Maurice Latta, respectively the executive and assistant clerks, had served Presidents from McKinley to Truman. Their job is to see that state papers are properly signed, recorded, and distributed; that the correspondence that comes to the White House is handled in an orderly way; and that the large staff of clerks, stenographers, and telephone operators who attend to necessary but routine operations of the White House Office are properly supervised.

The President's military aides normally are career men chosen by the President to advise him on military affairs as well as to carry out the social duties that formerly constituted their major assignments.

the President's personal staff

The President's personal staff includes the three "secretaries," an "assistant to the President," a "special counsel," six "administrative assistants," and the stenographers who type his letters, speeches, and other papers. These assistants are chosen by a President and usually are not reappointed by his successor.

THE ANONYMOUS SIX.   In 1937 the President's Committee on Administrative Management declared, "The President needs help" and it recommended that he be given not more than six administrative assistants, men who it said should have "high competence, great physical vigor and a passion for anonymity." Jonathan Daniels, who served as an administrative assistant to President Roosevelt for several years, stated "neither that the men nor their tasks were often so romantic as they sounded." He also characterized their work as "doing the President's chores and running his errands." [23] Although these assistants in theory do not have the power of decision, their intimacy with the President in fact gives them positions of great influence. They, and the other personal assistants to the President, "have the power of contact which is sometimes difficult to maintain in big government. They work with the force of friendship which presumably has no other concern. And sometimes because of it they can, if they wish, play litle Presidents themselves outside the room." [24]

PERSONAL ADVISERS TO THE PRESIDENT.   The needs of a President are too varied to be met satisfactorily by a small group of assistants with fixed assignments. For this reason it is not unusual for a President to rely on personal advisers who may or may not hold regular or official posts. This practice goes back at least as far as Andrew Jackson's famous "kitchen cabinet"—a group of personal friends whom he consulted and relied upon more heavily than he did the members of his cabinet. Woodrow Wilson called upon Colonel House to carry

[23] Daniels, *Frontier on the Potomac*, p. 45.
[24] *Ibid.*, p. 43.

out missions that he considered too vital to entrust to government officials. And during Franklin Roosevelt's administration, especially during the war years, Harry Hopkins exercised enormous influence as the President's personal and confidential assistant. The range of Hopkins's activities was practically as wide as the affairs of the government: he picked men for top administrative posts in war agencies; he straightened out tangles that impeded the war operations of the United States; and he conducted face to face negotiations with Prime Minister Winston Churchill and with Marshal Stalin. Perhaps his greatest service was performed after his health forced his resignation as a public official.

> The extraordinary fact was that the second most important individual in the United States Government during the most critical period of the world's greatest war had no legitimate official position nor even any desk of his own except a card table in his bedroom. However, the bedroom was in the White House.[25]

There can be little doubt that men like House and Hopkins perform an essential function. They are both intimates of the President and, ideally, experts in public affairs; but perhaps their most significant contributions are made as intimates. Franklin Roosevelt testified on this point to Wendell Willkie, who questioned the propriety of the President's use of Hopkins:

> Someday you may well be sitting here where I am now as President of the United States. And when you are, you'll be looking at that door over there and knowing that practically everybody who walks through it wants something out of you. You'll learn what a lonely job this is, and you'll discover the need for somebody like Harry Hopkins who asks for nothing except to serve you.[26]

The President needs to discuss with a sympathetic person ideas and plans that are still in an amorphous state and to gain some respite from the cares of office by talking over trivial matters that interest him or by chatting about men and affairs, with the confidence that his remarks will not go beyond the room. This assistant must have constant access to the President's mind if he is to anticipate his point of view on matters that are not of first importance and that should therefore, be settled by someone other than the President. Also, he should have access to all of the information available to the President. His knowledge of the President's attitude, and of the facts upon which decisions must be based, and his lack of the prejudice that goes with any position entailing responsibility for a single department or agency make him especially useful in settling differences that develop between government officials.

---

[25] Sherwood, *Roosevelt and Hopkins,* p. 212. Reprinted by permission of Harper & Brothers, publishers.
[26] *Ibid.,* p. 3.

the Bureau of the Budget

The Bureau of the Budget is the largest and is generally considered the most important of the agencies whose primary task is to help the President manage the executive branch. The Hoover Commission said of the Bureau of the Budget: "It is a misconception to think of this office merely as an agency for the collection and compilation of estimates in the annual preparation of the budget document. . . . It is the President's main reliance as an instrumentality for the improvement of management and the attainment of economy and efficiency throughout the Executive branch." [27]

The Bureau of the Budget did not acquire its present significance until it was transferred in 1939 from the Treasury Department to the Executive Office of the President. In terms of employees, this development is indicated by an increase from 40 in 1939 to approximately 500 in 1949. The bureau is headed by the Director of the Budget, who is appointed by the President without Senate confirmation.

budgeting

The focus of the bureau's activity is the formulation and execution of the federal budget, which today is accepted as a major responsibility of the chief executive.[28] Before the passage of the Budgeting and Accounting Act of 1921, departments and agencies presented estimates of their financial requirements directly to Congress. There was no general budget for the executive branch until an employee of the appropriations committee assembled the separate budgets submitted by the several departments. Under this system even the most experienced legislators had difficulty in determining the relative needs of competing departments.

The President was under an even greater handicap. He could not supervise and control departments that received money from Congress to carry on activities that he thought should not be undertaken at all. He lacked the most useful of managerial tools, that of fiscal control. Yet, under the Constitution, he was held responsible for the operations of all of the executive establishment.

The Budget and Accounting Act requires all executive agencies to submit budget estimates first to the President and then, with his approval, to Congress. It also provides that the Bureau of the Budget "shall have authority to assemble, correlate, revise, reduce, or increase the estimates." The act gives the President the authority that he needs in order to control the expenditures of the executive branch and it provides a group of specialists to help him use this authority intelligently. By reducing or eliminating funds requested to carry out

---

[27] Commission on Organization of the Executive Branch of the Government, *General Management of the Executive Branch* (Washington: Government Printing Office, 1949), p. 25.

[28] See Chapter 43 for a detailed treatment of "Budgeting and Expenditures."

programs which the President does not support, the bureau helps to keep departmental programs within bounds set by the President. Congress can, of course, override the decisions made on these matters.

improving organization and management

Another duty of the Bureau of the Budget is to help improve the organization and management of the executive branch, which it does in two ways. In the first place, the bureau provides technical assistance in preparing plans for the reorganization of the executive branch of the government. This phase of its work is especially important when the President is given authority by Congress to carry out extensive structural changes, as he was in 1939, 1945, and 1949. Much of the technical work of carrying out the recommendations of the Commission on the Organization of the Executive Branch is being handled by the staff of the Bureau of the Budget.

In the second place, the bureau stimulates and assists executive departments and agencies to improve their internal organization and operating procedures. The executive establishment is so vast that it cannot be directed and controlled solely from the Executive Office of the President. Long-run improvements in organization and operations depend in large part upon the ability of each department to search out and correct its weaknesses. The staff of the Bureau of the Budget is useful in making departments sensitive to opportunities for improvement, and in informing all agencies of the best methods in use throughout the government.

These activities are ancillary to the main function of the Bureau of the Budget, but they result in greater efficiency of operations, which means ultimately that citizens get more service for each dollar spent. In the long run, therefore, efforts to budget wisely and to improve organization and management have the same objective.

clearing house for legislative proposals

The Bureau of the Budget also helps the President to control legislative requests made by executive departments and agencies. Before the establishment of this control, it was possible for a department to obtain passage of legislation that later required expenditures to which the President objected. Today a staff originally assembled in the interests of better financial control is useful in other ways. With information provided by the Bureau of the Budget the President is able to state to legislative leaders whether a particular bill has his support, whether he is indifferent about it, or whether it is contrary to his program. In the process of compiling information the bureau's staff points out conflicts in proposals from different departments and in other ways prevents competing or ill-advised proposals from being submitted to Congress as "administration bills." Congress finds it useful to know that legislative proposals with a single subject but emanating from different departments have at least been considered side by side and that an effort has been made to review them from an overall point of view.

Moreover, the bureau is able to keep the President informed about bills pending in Congress and those that have been passed. The bureau's staff surveys interested departments and agencies to find out how they would be affected by a bill that has been passed and on which the President must act. If the consensus is against the bill, the President is informed of that fact and probably provided with a draft of a veto message. The President, of course, consults legislative leaders as well as executive officials. If the advice of the legislators conflicts with that of the executive departments, he finds it easier to make up his own mind because of the background of information assembled by the Bureau of the Budget.

the Council of Economic Advisers

The Employment Act of 1946 requires the President to send to Congress soon after the opening of each regular session an economic report, and it created the Council of Economic Advisers to help prepare the report. The President's Economic Report in general describes the economic state of the nation, discusses trends in employment and production, and appraises federal economic programs. It also recommends actions necessary to maintain the objectives stated in the act— maximum employment, production, and purchasing power. The council is composed of three members appointed by the President, by and with the advice and consent of the Senate. [29]

The council meets with the President from time to time during the year and with the President and cabinet at a regular quarterly meeting. There are indications that the council is succeeding in bringing together the best economic thinking within the government and that the President has come to rely upon its advice on matters of economic policy. [30]

It is worth noting that the Council of Economic Advisers in a sense replaced the National Resources Planning Board, which Congress abolished in 1942. At that time there was strong suspicion of activities of the board touching upon economic planning, many congressmen doubting the propriety of any government agency concerning itself with "planning," which seemed alien to democratic institutions. The fact that Congress was willing to establish the Council of Economic Advisers in the Executive Office is an indication of more general acceptance by the public of the role of government in economic affairs.

---

[29] 15 U.S.C §1021, 60 Stat. 23. See Chapter 42, "Government Planning," for a discussion of the role of the Council in economic planning.

[30] Ralph E. Flanders, "Administering the Employment Act—the First Year," *Public Administration Review*, VII, No. 4 (Autumn, 1947), 221–227.

The Hoover Commission recommended that the council be replaced by the Office of the Economic Adviser to the President. It pointed out that the council is a new agency, and that "no one can judge its strength or weakness with confidence at this early stage. . . ." It objected, however, to the requirement of Senate confirmation of the members of the council. In its view, the Economic Report is the President's responsibility, and the members of the Council of Economic Advisers should be comparable to the Director of the Budget with respect to their relation to Congress and the President. The commission declared that "to put a full-time board at the head of a staff agency is to run the risk of inviting public disagreement among its members and of transplanting within the President's Office the disagreements on policy issues that grow up in the executive departments or in the Congress." [31] The issue here is whether the members of the Council of Economic Advisers are exclusively a part of the President's staff or whether they are also agents of Congress with respect to the Employment Act of 1946. Until the role of economic planning becomes more firmly established, it is likely that the Senate will wish to retain its check over the members of the Council.

need for an office of personnel

The federal government, as the employer of over two million people, is faced with intricate personnel problems. The next chapter discusses the general problem of government personnel, but at this point it is desirable to observe the President's need for staff assistance in handling his personnel responsibilities.

The President, as general manager of the executive branch, is responsible for seeing that these problems are solved satisfactorily. The Civil Service Commission is the government agency immediately responsible for recruitment and other aspects of personnel management, but the commission was deliberately placed beyond the President's control. As a result, the President is not in a position to handle effectively questions relating to the morale, efficiency, and quality of federal employees.

In 1939 the President's Committee on Administrative Management recommended that the Civil Service Commission be replaced by a personnel agency in the Executive Office of the President. This recommendation was not accepted by Congress, chiefly on the grounds that it would permit the President to undermine the merit system, whose protection was considered the principal function and greatest contribution of the Civil Service Commission. Instead, there was established in the Executive Office a Liaison Officer for Personnel Management to keep the President informed and advised about problems of federal personnel, and to maintain a close relationship with the Civil Service Commission. This of-

---

[31] *General Management of the Executive Branch*, pp. 16–17.

ficer undoubtedly has helped to improve relationships between the White House, the Civil Service Commission, and the Bureau of the Budget on questions affecting the federal civil service. But a single individual cannot accomplish the variety of objectives which the Committee on Administrative Management had in mind when it recommended the transfer of the Civil Service Commission to the Executive Office of the President.

The Commission on Organization of the Executive Branch also recommended that Congress establish an Office of Personnel in the Executive Office. It proposed that the chairman of the Civil Service Commission serve as director of this Office of Personnel. He "should function as the principal staff adviser to the President in connection with problems related to the career service of the Federal Government"; should keep "in close touch with the work of the various offices of personnel within the departments and agencies"; and should "advise the President as to steps which need to be taken to put the Government in a position where it will be looked upon as one of the most progressive employers in the Nation." [32]

can the executive branch be efficient?

Critics of the executive branch commonly point out examples of wasteful expenditures which the President is presumed to condone. Dismay is expressed over the "fact" that government is not as efficient as business and usually some variation on the "more business in government and less government in business" solution is offered. During a political campaign legislators join in the chorus, and promise that their party will improve the administration of government if it is given control. What is meant by the term "efficiency" and is the executive branch "efficient?"

two tests of efficiency

The efficiency of the executive branch should be measured by two tests. First, does the executive branch contribute maximum wisdom to policy formulation by Congress and the President? Are relevant information, experience, and judgment made available quickly and easily and when they are needed? Is the information drawn from all parts of the organization that are in a position to be helpful? Is it presented in coherent form, so that it may be appraised by the President or Congress with little chance for misunderstanding or misinterpretation? Second, is policy administered faithfully and vigorously, with maximum achievements and minimum costs in terms of expenditure of men, money, and materials? Can the organization act quickly, with full knowledge of the policy and of the circumstances in which the action must take place? Are the people

---

[32] *General Management of the Executive Branch,* pp. 23–24.

satisfied with the services provided by the government? With the way in which they are treated by government employees? Are the government employees satisfied with their jobs? Do they try to serve the public with dispatch and courtesy?

Administrative efficiency viewed in these terms is a social rather than a bookkeeping concept. It cannot be determined by the amounts spent for governmental services. It should be measured by the satisfaction which the American people derive from the activities of their government. Its internal aspects can be measured in part by the morale of government workers. This is not to say that the costs of governmental services are unimportant or that economy of operations is not a legitimate objective. Economy is simply one element of governmental efficiency, and its importance may vary from time to time. When the nation is at war, for example, or when it is attempting to relieve unemployment, economy is of secondary importance. On the general nature of efficiency, the Hoover Commission said: "While we recognize that efficiency in itself is no guarantee of democratic government, the sobering fact remains that the highest aims and ideals of democracy can be thwarted through excessive administrative costs and through waste, disunity, apathy, irresponsibility and other by-products of inefficient government." [33]

obstacles to reorganization

Major changes in the organization of the executive branch of the government would increase its efficiency, and there is general agreement on the major defects and remedies; nevertheless, it is often virtually impossible to get congressional consent to specific proposals. Two causes of this state of affairs may be cited:

First, Congress tends to suspect that a President who seeks reorganization of the executive branch is selfishly interested in increasing his own power. President Hoover's sweeping reorganization plan was rejected by Congress; charges of dictatorship greeted President Roosevelt's support of the recommendations of the Committee on Administrative Management; and some of President Truman's proposals have been rejected for this reason.

Second, the bureaus and the pressure groups that work with them develop vested interests in the existing organization and procedures which lead them to oppose reorganization proposals. Herbert Hoover's comments on this point are illuminating:

Q. What is the principal obstacle in reorganizing the Government?
A. The barriers are that everybody wants to reorganize everybody else in the United States, but he wants to be let alone himself.
Q. That is, the bureaus?

---

[33] *Concluding Report,* p. 3.

A. Not only the bureaus but all their affiliated associations throughout the country. Every one of these bureaus has the backing of some sort of citizens' association whose interests lie in promoting it.

Q. Friends or relatives, or those they do favors for?

A. No, not that. For example, we have the bankers who are naturally interested in the conduct of various financial concerns of the Government. Those agencies in some cases are able to command the propaganda activities of the American Bankers Association. There are the Army Engineers, with efficient citizens' organizations advocating flood control projects. The Reclamation Bureau has citizens' associations. The Forest Service has active citizens' associations. All they have to do is to turn on these associations when changes are prepared.

Q. You mean that they can bring pressure to bear on Congress?

A. We have a vivid example of it: One Senator alone received 2,000 telegrams of protest on the suspicion that we might suggest consolidating the construction agencies of the Government into one place, which would mean transferring the flood control and river and harbor construction from the War Department.[34]

Congressional suspicion of a strong executive and pressure group activity undoubtedly go far to explain the fact that Presidents are more interested in reorganization than Congress is.

relativity of efficiency

There is much speculation about efficiency in government as compared with efficiency in business. Any discussion of this question is certain to be inconclusive, for several reasons. First, many of the functions of government are undertaken because they are beyond the capacity of private enterprise. How, for example, can the efficiency of the government's conduct of foreign affairs be compared with the way in which the General Motors Corporation handles its export trade? To take another case: Was World War II waged efficiently? Was too much money spent for planes, tanks, ships? Were too many men inducted into the armed services? Certainly costly mistakes were made; would any of them have been avoided by a private organization? Second, the objectives of government and business are different. A government agency tries to administer the laws entrusted to it so that the President, Congress, and the public will be satisfied. The immediate objective for a business is to make money for the owners. Although the size of the annual profits makes it relatively easy to measure the success of the business, the business by this fact is not more efficient than a government agency. Third, some government agencies are efficient and some inefficient, just as some businesses are efficient and some inefficient. The Tennessee Valley Authority's record in dam construction might well be envied by a

---

[34] Hoover Interview, June 3, 1949, *U. S. News & World Report,* an independent weekly magazine on national and international affairs; published at Washington.

private construction company or by the Army Corps of Engineers, which, it might be noted, contracts with private firms for the construction of dams. There is a tendency to compare an inefficient government agency with a highly efficient business and to draw general conclusions therefrom about the relative merits of public and private organizations. Fourth, the general public knows more about the inefficiencies of government than it knows about the mistakes of business. A frustrating experience with a department store that repeats and compounds its original mistake in filling an order is not likely to be deemed newsworthy. A similarly frustrating incident in a government agency may become the principal item on a "news" broadcast by Fulton Lewis, Jr.

There is speculation, also, about the relative efficiency of constitutional government and dictatorships. Perhaps the most revealing evidence on this point comes from World War II. In reviewing this evidence Luther Gulick has said:

> The administrative advantages claimed for dictatorship in time of war are based on two approaches. The first insists that dictatorship is free of democracy's delays, divided counsels, inertia, and conflicts between entrenched interest groups, and is not limited by the low mentality and disabilities of the "average man." The second claim to superiority is more positive. It asserts that dictatorships, resting on a single "leader" and a small, highly integrated elite, alone have the ability to make adequate and far-seeing plans; to integrate and coordinate the economy; to act with vigor, intelligence, and dispatch; to interrelate military, political and economic strategy; to master timing and surprise, protected by complete control over secrecy of action; and to develop fanatic national unity and enthusiasm. . . .

> Neither Germany nor Japan freed themselves from the weaknesses listed, nor achieved the positive virtues claimed. In both categories, Great Britain, Canada, and the United States showed fewer weaknesses and greater strengths than did the three Axis governments.[35]

Drawing upon the evidence of the strategic bombing survey on Germany and Japan,[36] Gulick lists the following as examples of demonstrated superiority of democracy over dictatorships. First, "Both Germany and Japan, though they selected the dates to start the fighting and were successful beyond their dreams at first, completely misjudged the eventual developments and military requirements. The action of the totalitarian leaders was irresponsible and disastrous in the nth degree." Second, in Germany and Japan the ablest administrators were displaced or ignored, while "in the democracies, the outpouring of skilled and

[35] Luther Gulick, *Administrative Reflections from World War II* (University: University of Alabama Press, 1948), pp. 122–123. Reprinted by permission of the University of Alabama Press, publishers.

[36] *The Effects of Strategic Bombing on the German War Economy* (Washington: Government Printing Office, 1945); and *The Effects of Strategic Bombing on the Japanese War Economy* (Washington: Government Printing Office, 1946).

able manpower from business, from the universities, from the professions, into government was extraordinary and extremely effective." Third, "As to the speed of military and industrial mobilization, and the magnitude of the effort realized in relation to the available resources, the record of the democracies is notably better than the record of the dictatorships." Fourth, "The democracies clearly outdid the dictatorships in the use of technology and science." And finally, Gulick concludes, "the greatest superiority of the free peoples . . . arose from two things: the superiority of their broad plans and their elasticity, their quickness to change in the face of need." The debates and consultations that delay the formulation of broad plans in a democracy also produce wiser plans. Moreover, the experience of men directly involved in the action is communicated freely to the persons in command, so that plans are changed quickly in response to experience.

This appraisal of the comparative success of democracy and dictatorship was concluded by Gulick's observation: "I want you to grasp the central fact which this war experience drives home: that good administration and democracy are not incompatible. They are inseparable allies; neither can exist long or survive without the other." [37]

bibliographic note

The magnitude of the President's job is a common theme in the general studies of the presidency and in the memoirs cited in the preceding bibliographic note. Louis Brownlow, *The President and the Presidency* (Chicago: Public Administration Service, 1949), is a short but revealing discussion written by an expert in governmental administration who is also fully aware of the political functions of the office. A useful short essay is Don K. Price, "The Presidency: Its Burden and Its Promise," in *The Strengthening of American Political Institutions* (Ithaca: Cornell University Press, 1949), p. 79. For incisive comment about political control of administrative agencies and the problem of reconciling legislative and presidential interests in administrative organization, see Charles S. Hyneman, *Bureaucracy in a Democracy* (New York: Harper & Brothers, 1950). The bibliographic notes in Professor Hyneman's book contain many valuable references for further reading about problems discussed in this chapter. Louis C. Hatch, *A History of the Vice Presidency of the United States*, edited and revised by Earl Shoup (New York: The American Historical Society, Inc., 1934), is a systematic study of the role of the Vice-President and of the relation of that office to the presidency.

A good place to begin further study about the theory of organization is

[37] Gulick, *Administrative Reflections from World War II*, pp. 124–129.

one of the standard public administration texts: Leonard D. White, *Introduction to the Study of Public Administration* (New York: The Macmillan Company, 1948), pp. 25–39; John D. Millett, "Working Concepts of Organization," in *Elements of Public Administration* (Fritz Morstein Marx, ed.; New York: Prentice-Hall, Inc., 1943), pp. 140–157; Herbert A. Simon, Donald W. Smithburg, and Victor A. Thompson, *Public Administration* (New York: Alfred A. Knopf, Inc., 1950), Chap. 4–8. An essay by John M. Gaus, "A Theory of Organization," in *Frontiers of Public Administration* (Chicago: The University of Chicago Press, 1936), is an excellent brief statement. For a more technical statement of organizational theory and practice, see Luther Gulick and L. Urwick, eds., *Papers on the Science of Administration* (New York: Institute of Public Administration, 1937). Albert Lepawsky, ed., *Administration* (New York: Alfred A. Knopf, Inc., 1949), Pt. 2, provides a useful collection of readings on the subject.

Some students of organization tend to forget that human beings do not often conform to organizational patterns that are "ideal" from the theoretical and impersonal point of view. There is, however, a growing literature on the subject of human factors in organization, a field in which the following were pioneer studies: Elton Mayo, *The Human Problems of an Industrial Civilization* (New York: The Macmillan Company, 1933); T. N. Whitehead, *Leadership in a Free Society* (Cambridge: Harvard University Press, 1936); and F. J. Roethlisberger and W. J. Dickson, *Management and the Worker* (Cambridge: Harvard University Press, 1939). These volumes report aspects of a carefully controlled series of experiments at the Hawthorne plant of the Western Electric Company. Earlier Mary Parker Follett emphasized many of the same principles; see a collection of her papers edited by Henry C. Metcalf and L. Urwick, *Dynamic Administration* (New York: The Macmillan Company, 1940). Significant research is being carried on in this field by the Survey Research Center of the University of Michigan, but the results have not been published in readily available form. A valuable annotated bibliography from the social sciences is Alfred de Grazia, *Human Relations in Public Administration* (Chicago: Public Administration Service, 1949). James Gould Cozzens, *Guard of Honor* (New York: Harcourt, Brace and Company, 1948), is a Pulitzer Prize novel that can be read with profit by students interested in the way an organization actually functions.

A standard history of the executive branch is Lloyd M. Short, *The Development of National Administrative Organization in the United States* (Baltimore: The Johns Hopkins Press, 1923). Schuyler Wallace, *Federal Departmentalization* (New York: Columbia University Press, 1941), analyzes theories and principles that have influenced the departmental structure of the federal government. Three departmental studies of value are John M. Gaus and Leon O. Wolcott, *Public Administration and the United States Department of Agriculture*

(Chicago: Public Administration Service, 1940) ; Charles H. Pritchett, *The Tennessee Valley Authority* (Chapel Hill: University of North Carolina Press, 1943) ; and Graham H. Stuart, *The Department of State* (New York: The Macmillan Company, 1949).

The basic study of the presidential cabinet is Henry B. Learned, *The President's Cabinet* (New Haven: Yale University Press, 1912) ; a useful volume is Mary L. Hinsdale, *A History of the President's Cabinet* (Ann Arbor: George Wahr, 1911). In addition to the memoirs cited in the preceding bibliographic note, of which those of Frances Perkins and Henry L. Stimson are notable, the following throw light on the problems of the President and his cabinet: Gideon Welles, *Diary of Gideon Welles* (Boston: Houghton Mifflin Company, 3 vols., 1911) ; W. C. Redfield, *With Congress and Cabinet* (New York: Doubleday & Company, 1924) ; and David F. Houston, *Eight Years with Wilson's Cabinet* (New York: Doubleday & Company, 1926). Burton J. Hendrick, *Lincoln's War Cabinet* (Boston: Little, Brown & Company, 1946), is a case study in President-cabinet relations that were remarkable for tension and conflict. For a discussion of the respective merits of the presidential and parliamentary systems see the articles by Don K. Price and Harold J. Laski, *Public Administration Review*, III No. 4 (Autumn, 1943) 317–334, and IV, No. 4 (Autumn, 1944), 347–359, 360–363. On strengthening the cabinet, see E. S. Corwin, *The President: Office and Powers* (New York: New York University Press, 1940), pp. 297–308; "Wanted: A New Type of Cabinet," by the same author in *New York Times Magazine*, October 10, 1948; Charles S. Hyneman, *Bureaucracy in a Democracy*, pp. 557–576; and the references given in the bibliographic note to Chapter 18.

There are a number of excellent discussions of the Executive Office of the President and its components. The statement of the President's Committee on Administrative Management in *Administrative Management in the Government of the United States* (Washington: Government Printing Office, 1937) is a starting point. A readable treatment is by Harold D. Smith, Director of the Budget from 1939 to 1946, *The Management of Your Government* (New York: McGraw-Hill Book Company, 1945). Clinton L. Rossiter, "The Constitutional Significance of the Executive Office of the President," *American Political Science Review*, XLIII, No. 6 (December, 1949), 1206–1217, contains several interesting observations. For a stimulating article about possible future development of the Executive Office of the President, see Arthur W. Macmahon, "The Future Organizational Pattern of the Executive Branch," *American Political Science Review*, XXXVIII, No. 6 (December, 1944), 1179–1191. Two articles of special interest in a symposium on federal reorganization are Wayne Coy, "Basic Problems," *American Political Science Review*, XL, No. 6 (December, 1946), 1124–1137, and Don K. Price, "Staffing the Presidency," pp. 1154–1168 of the same issue. Articles tracing the development of the Bureau of the Budget are

Fritz Morstein Marx, "The Bureau of the Budget: Its Evolution and Present Role," *American Political Science Review*, XXXIX, No. 4 (August, 1945), 653–684, and No. 5 (October, 1945), 869–898; and Norman M. Pearson, "The Bureau of the Budget: From Routine Business to General Staff," *Public Administration Review*, III, No. 2 (Spring, 1943), 126–149.

For an excellent critical study of the Office of War Mobilization in World War II, see Herman Miles Somers, *Presidential Agency OWMR* (Cambridge: Harvard University Press, 1950).

The Commission on Organization of the Executive Branch of the Government, popularly known as the Hoover Commission, assembled a wealth of information about the organization and activities of the major departments and agencies. In addition to reports to Congress, studies of individual agencies by "task forces" have been published. *General Management of the Executive Branch*, a report submitted to Congress in February, 1949, deals with the problem of organization and staffing of the presidency; the *Concluding Report*, dated May, 1949, states the general theory underlying the commission's recommendations and summarizes its proposals. The commission reports have been put in convenient form in *The Hoover Commission Report* (New York: McGraw-Hill Book Company, 1949), but the task force reports and minority views of members of the commission, unfortunately, are not included in the volume. "Progress on Hoover Commission Recommendations" is reported by the Committee on Expenditures in the Executive Departments, *Senate Report* No. 1,158, 81 Cong. 1 Sess. Bradley D. Nash and Cornelius Lynde, *A Hook in Leviathan* (New York: The Macmillan Company, 1950), show the objectives underlying the commission's work and provide useful interpretive comment upon its principal recommendations. A symposium on the Hoover Commission is Louis W. Koenig, ed., *American Political Science Review*, XLIII, No. 5 (October, 1949), 933–1000.

The approach of the Hoover Commission to the problem of executive reorganization was quite similar to that of the President's Committee on Administrative Management, whose *Report with Special Studies* (Washington: Government Printing Office, 1937) was a valuable addition to the literature of public administration.

See Lewis Meriam and Laurence F. Schmeckebier, *Reorganization of the National Government* (Washington: The Brookings Institution, 1939), for a critical evaluation of the President's Committee on Administrative Management and for a history of attempted reorganization during Herbert Hoover's administration.

An excellent and entertaining description of personal relationships within the presidential staff is Jonathan Daniels, *Frontier on the Potomac* (New York: The Macmillan Company, 1946). The memoirs of cabinet members are also recommended for this purpose.

For additional reading on the subject of efficiency in a democratic government, see Marshall E. Dimock, "Administrative Efficiency within a Democratic Polity," in *New Horizons in Public Administration* (University: University of Alabama Press, 1945); the same author's "The Criteria and Objectives of Public Administration" in *Frontiers of Public Administration*; Luther Gulick, "Science, Values and Public Administration" in *Papers on the Science of Administration*; Gulick's *Administrative Reflections from World War II*, quoted in this chapter; Chapter 15 of Arthur C. Millspaugh, *Democracy, Efficiency, Stability* (Washington: The Brookings Institution, 1942); and Paul M. Appleby, *Big Democracy* (New York: Alfred A. Knopf, Inc., 1945).

government personnel:

the civil servant

*I*F ANY group of Americans is criticized more persistently and with more enthusiasm than the politicians, it must be the federal civil servants. More often than not, the civil servant is called a "bureaucrat," a term used to express reproach and contempt. The "bureaucrat" imposes "bureaucratic" controls upon our private lives; he asks meaningless questions and from the answers compiles incomprehensible statistics; he cannot himself answer simple inquiries in plain, straightforward English; he takes refuge in "rules and regulations" and avoids decisions whenever possible by referring the problem to another bureaucrat; and, to add insult to injury, he is paid for his incompetence by the taxpayers whose lives he makes miserable. So goes the popular impression of the civil servant. What is he really like? How does he get his job? How much is he paid? How does he like his work? What are his weaknesses?

The two million federal civil servants have the same characteristics, are perplexed by the same problems, and enjoy the same pleasures as the American public generally. The men and women who ride the streetcars and busses in Washington are much like the people seen in any other large city. In Washington a larger proportion of the crowds work for government; but from appearance and behavior it is not possible to tell which individuals work for banks or department stores and which are federal employees. The buildings in which government employees work perhaps are not notable architectural achievements; but they are not more depressing than office buildings in New York or Chicago. If some federal workers persistently avoid undue exertion on the job, they are not without their counterparts among businessmen, laborers, or college students. The efficiency of other workers is impaired by worry over domestic problems or by illness; but emotional and physical disturbances are not peculiar to government employees, and there is no evidence that they occur more frequently or are of greater severity among civil servants.

The civil servant engages in most of the occupations found in private life.

The federal government, for example, employs doctors, lawyers, engineers of all kinds, chemists, botanists, physicists, economists, sociologists, political scientists, historians, aerial photographers, social workers, teachers, nurses, and dentists. Thousands of clerks, stenographers, messengers, telephone operators, janitors, and skilled and unskilled laborers are also required to carry on the affairs of the government. An employee who works in any of these capacities uses the same skills and equipment that he would use in a private occupation. The doctor or lawyer must have the same educational preparation and experience, the stenographer must know how to take shorthand notes and to use a typewriter, and the shipyard worker or airplane mechanic must have the knowledge that enables him to perform his tasks satisfactorily, whether he works for government or for business.

No one has bothered to make the statistical analysis that would be required to describe the "typical civil servant." It would be interesting, but not necessarily useful, to know more about this mythical man. But to find him among two million people would be an expensive undertaking, and, as likely as not, he would be the post-office employee who delivers mail in your home town. It is possible, however, to describe the "typical government executive." Recently a directory was compiled of approximately sixteen hundred people who occupy top administrative positions in the federal government in Washington. The list included cabinet officers and other executives whose appointments normally are political in character, but the majority of the persons were career officials. Generally speaking, the "typical executive" is "52 years old, married and has two children. In addition to being a college graduate, he holds a law degree from Harvard. As a legal resident of New York he represents one of the most concentrated population areas of the country. He is a veteran, having served in either World War I or World War II as an officer. Fourteen years of his life have been spent in the Federal Service. For athletic relaxation his favorite pastime is golf, and he enjoys fishing, football, and baseball. During his leisure time he favors gardening and photography." [1]

Some will be distressed, and others reassured, by the fact that only 1 per cent of the sixteen hundred top federal executives are women. Of the entire group, 93 per cent are married and 38 per cent have two or more children. About one fourth graduated from Harvard, Columbia, Princeton, Yale, Massachusetts Institute of Technology, and Cornell; and about one tenth from the universities of Chicago, Ohio State, Indiana, Illinois, Michigan, and Northwestern. Only 17 per cent of the sixteen hundred had no college degree; and more than half hold graduate or professional degrees beyond the baccalaureate level. These included 136 masters' degrees and 185 doctorates in arts or science. Apart from

---

[1] Jerome M. Rosow, ed., *American Men in Government* (Washington: Public Affairs Press, 1949), p. xix. The information that follows is also from this source.

Army, Navy, and Air Force officers, almost 39 per cent have rendered military service in addition to their federal employment. The group reported an interest in sixty different hobbies, ranging from flying to mushroom hunting and mammalian taxonomy.

the selection of civil servants

The vast majority of federal workers get their jobs under the provisions of a merit system. When the Civil Service Act was passed in 1883, about 10 per cent of the employees in the executive branch were brought into the merit system. Through the years the system has been extended to more and more positions, so that today over 90 per cent of all federal employees are under civil service. Moreover, a few agencies that do not come within the Civil Service Act, principally the Tennessee Valley Authority, the Federal Bureau of Investigation, the Public Health Service, the Foreign Service of the Department of State, and the Army, Navy, and Air Force service personnel have their own merit systems.

merit as the criterion for selection

Selection on the basis of merit is important to every American citizen. The quality of the services performed by the government is determined by the quality of the civil service. Mediocre personnel cannot be expected to give first-class service, any more than water can be expected to run uphill. On this point Professor John Gaus has said:

> . . . the sole, the basic criterion for selecting officials and judging their public acts is their ability to accomplish the public purpose. To select them for any reason other than their equipment for that purpose, to select them, for example, because they are jobless, or former soldiers, or because they helped win an election, is to select them for a private and distorting, not a public and fulfilling, reason. It is to destroy utterly the very reason for their existence . . . always, at the center is the question: is the John Jones who is serving as Health Inspector, or Director of the Water Department, competent to perform his task, in terms of general education, innate abilities, experience, and training in the field?[2]

spoils system as an alternative to merit

The spoils system, under which the party winning an election replaces government employees with its own members, is the principal alternative to the merit system for the selection of government employees. The spoils system is supported by party leaders, who see in it wider opportunities for patronage; it has also been espoused on the grounds that it tended to strengthen political democ-

---

[2] John M. Gaus, Leonard D. White, Marshall E. Dimock, *The Frontiers of Public Administration* (Chicago: The University of Chicago Press, 1936), pp. 111–112.

racy. A classic statement of this point of view is found in Andrew Jackson's first annual message to Congress.

> There are, perhaps, few men who can for any great length of time enjoy office and power without being more or less under the influence of feelings unfavorable to the faithful discharge of their public duties. Their integrity may be proof against improper considerations immediately addressed to themselves, but they are apt to acquire a habit of looking with indifference upon the public interests and of tolerating conduct from which an unpracticed man would revolt. Office is considered as a species of property, and government rather as a means of promoting individual interests than as an instrument created solely for the service of the people. Corruption in some and in others a perversion of correct feelings and principles divert government from its legitimate ends and make it an engine for the support of the few at the expense of the many. The duties of all public officers are, or at least admit of being made, so plain and simple that men of intelligence may readily qualify themselves for their performance; and I cannot but believe that more is lost by the long continuance of men in office than is generally gained by their experience.[3]

Jackson asked ". . . whether the efficiency of the Government would not be promoted and official industry and integrity better served by a general extension of the law which limits appointments to four years. . . . The proposed limitation . . . would, by promoting that rotation which constitutes a leading principle of the republican creed, give healthful action to the system." [4]

Although Jackson's desire to eliminate arrogance and selfishness among government officials was commendable and his advocacy of rotation as a remedy was plausible, acceptance of his proposal resulted in a decline in the competence and integrity of the government service. By the outbreak of the Civil War the spoils system was deeply entrenched, and the quality of government personnel continued at a low level through most of the nineteenth century. Gifford Pinchot, who devoted his life to the conservation of the nation's natural resources, wrote amusingly of the conditions in the Forest Service before the adoption of merit as the criterion for selection of personnel.

> Since jobs on the Forest Reserves were for distribution to politicians, Commissioner Binger Hermann of the General Land Office was careful to get his while the getting was good. The average appointee was plenty bad enough, but Binger's personal appointments were horrible. My notes made in the West at the time describe them. . . .

---

[3] James D. Richardson, comp., *Messages and Papers of the Presidents* (Washington: Bureau of National Literature and Art, 1903), II, 448–449.

[4] *Ibid.* The law referred to was the Tenure of Office Act of 1820, which limited to four years the terms of certain Federal officials.

One of Binger's brothers-in-law was "an old man absolutely worthless in his position." Another brother-in-law was "ignorant. General report makes him incompetent, and in league with the sheepmen," who were running their herds, legally or illegally, on the Forest Reserves. A third brother-in-law, "an ideally unfit man. Utterly useless in every way," was a Special Agent to report on the Grand Canyon Forest Reserve. . . . A son-in-law was a Special Agent. Since my notes make no comment on him, we might hope for the best, except that he was on duty in his and Binger's home town of Roseburg, Oregon, where there were neither forests nor public lands. . . .

Senator Bliss had a relative on the force. He came from New Jersey, had once been a preacher, and had compiled two little volumes on the trees and shrubs of Northeastern America, all of which would naturally qualify him to take charge of a Forest Reserve in California, where he was stationed. He was a timid little man, as unable to deal with Sierra Nevada mountaineers as he was to travel the mountains. His explorations went as far as the stage went, and stopped right there. When I saw him he wore a white lawn tie and a shawl around his shoulders.

Influential members of House and Senate shared the loot. Joe Cannon of Illinois had a man named Buntain, "an invalid, incapable and ineffective." He was given charge of Reserves in Arizona and New Mexico. Buntain was in the last stages of consumption. Another of Uncle Joe Cannon's men was a one-lunger with one leg. When Buntain resigned, another of Uncle Joe's men took his place. This man "made the Forest Reserve a sort of private benevolence, recommending the appointment of many consumptives who had gone to Santa Fe for their health."

Superintendent Glendenning had two Supervisors on the Bitterroot Reserve. One of them conducted a saloon and although it was notorious that he never was on his Reserve but once during the time he held office, his service reports showed that he regularly "patrolled out and looked over the Reserve." As a fact he walked out with scrupulous regularity from the interior of his saloon to the front porch thereof and from that observation point "looked over" his Reserve, which was in plain view from there.

The reports of the other Supervisor, which were "models in form and elegant chirography, showed the Supervisor most zealous in patrolling his territory 'with saddle horse and pack horse,' for which he was allowed $1.00 a day each when in actual use. What he actually used them for was delivering beef for a butcher," for which he was paid $2.50 per day.

. . . Ranger Anderson of Kooskia, later of Stites, Idaho, was a veterinarian, and while he was in the Service regularly drawing $60 per month he did not leave his business and never saw the Reserve. . . . Ranger Malcom

Glendenning, a son of the Superintendent, pulled down $60 a month from Uncle Sam without interfering with his duties as a bookkeeper for Charles Sweeney at a salary of $125 a month. . . .[5]

recruitment of civil servants

Recruitment of federal workers—the process of finding suitable candidates for job opportunities—is a responsibility of the Civil Service Commission. The magnitude of this task is indicated by the fact that the government hires about 500,000 persons each year. If the quality of the civil service is to be improved steadily, it is apparent that there must be an active and imaginative program for interesting competent people in these appointments.

The Civil Service Commission's general approach to recruitment is one of relative passivity. It does not exert itself to *find* the best qualified people for the positions that it fills. More often than not, the commission is content to discover the most competent among the candidates who present themselves. Above all, it seeks to prevent the employment by executive departments and agencies of the patently unfit. This essentially negative philosophy is an outgrowth of the commission's origin and of the American tradition of equality of opportunity. When the commission was established, the central problem was to combat the evils of the spoils system. This was a police function to prevent the departments and agencies from selecting personnel for political or other extraneous reasons. This reform objective was proper in the early years of the commission, but today the problem is quite different.

Suppose, for example, that the Department of Agriculture has a vacancy for a man with successful administrative experience, a broad scientific background, and substantial experience in handling problems of soil erosion. A satisfactory person is not available among the existing departmental employees. How would such a man be found? The Civil Service Commission normally would advertise the vacancy, if it did not have at the time any persons to suggest. Announcements would be displayed in post offices, newspapers and periodicals, and employment offices. Since the position calls for a scientist, the commission might also advertise through one or another of the professional journals. Through this kind of publicity, the commission would hope to call the vacancy to the attention of several good men, and it would endeavor to ascertain which of those interested seemed the most competent. In other words, everyone who had the necessary educational and experience qualifications would have an "equal opportunity" to get the job. In general, the commission has not been willing to conduct careful investigations of a limited number of candidates and to offer the position to the best of the group. If this process were followed—and it is the one normally used in filling important positions in business and educa-

---

[5] Condensed from *Breaking New Ground* by Gifford Pinchot, pp. 162–166. Copyright, 1947, by Harcourt, Brace and Company, Inc.

tional institutions—the commission might be charged with favoritism. In terms of civil service recruitment, "equality of opportunity" means "all must have equal knowledge of job opportunities" and "all who apply must be considered."

A recent study of the problems of federal employment shows the ineffectiveness of these methods of attracting applicants. A group of 730 civil servants in six different departments, with salaries in excess of $4,900, were asked a number of questions about their employment. One question was to state the source of information that led these people to government service. One fourth of the group said that they learned of job opportunities through friends, and another fourth, through government employees. About 16 per cent got their information from a member of a college faculty. About 10 per cent read posted announcements in newspapers or professional publications.[6]

A survey of a group of college seniors made in 1948 showed a similar situation. "Less than 7 per cent felt that they were well informed about job opportunities" in the federal government, and "25 per cent stated that they were completely uninformed." Of those with some knowledge of job possibilities in government, only 5 per cent got their information from civil service announcements, and a large number attributed their information to "relatives or friends who work for the government." [7]

These studies reinforce other evidence and support the observation that the federal government "too often fails to get the right man for the job or the right job for the man." A part of the difficulty arises out of the Civil Service Commission's attitude toward recruitment; but it is only fair to the commission to note that active recruitment programs cannot be carried out by a central personnel agency for jobs that are in some degree peculiar to employing organizations. Experience during World War II indicated that this type of recruitment can be handled by the departments more effectively than by the Civil Service Commission, and with little danger to the merit principle. The Hoover Commission recommended that the Civil Service Commission turn over to the major departments and agencies recruitment for "all high-level administrative, professional, and technical positions," "all positions peculiar to the agency," and any other positions which, in the commission's judgment, can be filled more effectively by the agencies.[8]

examination of candidates

The Civil Service Commission uses examinations to screen the qualified applicants from the unqualified. A great deal of progress has been made in examin-

---

[6] Frances T. Cahn, *Federal Employees in War and Peace* (Washington: The Brookings Institution, 1949), p. 193.

[7] Commission on Organization of the Executive Branch of the Government, *Task Force Report on Federal Personnel* (Washington: Government Printing Office, 1949), p. 13.

[8] Commission on Organization of the Executive Branch of the Government, *Personnel Management* (Washington: Government Printing Office, 1949), p. 17.

ing techniques, and there is considerable reason to believe that the men and women who do best on the examinations now being used have the qualities needed on the jobs that are being filled. Written examinations are most useful for positions that involve relatively simple duties. Competence in typing, short-hand, and manual dexterity can be tested quite satisfactorily. Knowledge of statistics, chemistry, and other subjects can also be appraised. But it is much more difficult to discover by an examination whether a man is a good researcher; and as yet no satisfactory tests have been devised for selecting people for high administrative positions. Appraisal of a candidate's qualifications for an executive post must take into account previous experience on similar jobs, general training and background, personality, judgment, character, and other factors that are not susceptible of measurement by written examinations. In cases where intangible qualities are essential, a personal interview is considered desirable. A skillfully conducted interview can reveal much about the candidate that could not be discovered in a written examination. But here again there are limitations. The interview generally does not last long, and during it the candidate is under great strain. A potentially strong person may make a bad impression for this reason, whereas a less competent candidate with more poise may get the job. Moreover, if the interviewer is so minded, a candidate with strong political backing may be given a high enough rating on the "oral examination" to ensure his appointment, even though his performance on the written examination was not satisfactory.

certification of successful candidates

After the examination has been given and the papers of each person have been corrected, the candidates are ranked according to their grades. The Civil Service Commission then compiles a list or "register" of persons who passed the examination and are eligible for appointment. In this process, adjustments are made for men and women whose veterans' status entitles them to additional points. When a government agency has a vacancy to fill, it asks the Civil Service Commission for the names of candidates available for appointment. Agency officials then select from the persons certified by the commission the one who seems to meet their requirements most fully.

the compensation of civil servants

It is not enough to find the right man for the job by vigorous recruitment; the right man frequently must be persuaded to accept appointment. And, if he is chosen wisely and develops as expected, the government should retain his services. Compensation is one of the most important factors in the recruitment and retention of able people. Since government competes with business for the best personnel, it cannot get its share of the competent unless its pay scales are some-what comparable to those of private employers.

compensation in lower brackets

Earnings of federal employees in the lower pay brackets compare favorably with those of privately employed persons. A college graduate who enters the federal service without previous experience or graduate study receives $3,100 a year. This is about as much as he could expect from private industry and is as much as or more than most colleges pay inexperienced instructors with two or three years of graduate study.

The compensation of the lower brackets is not relatively as favorable as it was before World War II. Real wages in private employment have increased over 58 per cent since 1939. If adjustments are made for increases in the cost of living, government employees, as well as teachers and other salaried persons, actually receive less real income today than they did before 1939. Thus additional increases in the lower brackets are needed if the government is to maintain the competitive position that it had ten years ago.

salaries in top federal positions unfavorable

The salaries paid at the top bracket are so low that the federal government cannot retain its best executives in competition with industry. In the spring of 1949 there were about fifty vacancies in top administrative positions of the federal government. The vacancies comprised one fourth of all the positions in these categories. It is no exaggeration to say that the work of the United States government was greatly handicapped, and its security perhaps imperiled, by the President's inability to persuade competent men to accept these positions. For six months there was a vacancy in the chairmanship of the Atomic Energy Commission, and the National Securities Resources Board was without a chairman for many months. A director of the budget, chairmen of the Securities and Exchange Commission, the Federal Communications Commission, and the Federal Trade Commission, an undersecretary of state, and many other key officials resigned from their positions because they felt that they could not refuse opportunities to increase their salaries that were offered by private organizations. The top officials of the government are expected to maintain a standard of living that cannot be supported on the salaries that government pays. In addition to these expenses, there are, of course, the normal costs of maintaining families and educating children. The Hoover Commission *Task Force Report on Federal Personnel* stated that 107 individuals who left the government in 1945 obtained average increases over their government pay of 92 per cent.[9]

Even before World War II, top federal officials received substantially less

---

[9] *Task Force Report on Federal Personnel,* p. 31.

than their equals in private enterprise. Their position has worsened steadily in recent years. The pay increases voted by Congress during that war were relatively small for men in the higher brackets. A prewar maximum salary of $2,600 by 1949 had been increased to $3,725, or by 43 per cent. A prewar maximum salary of $9,000 was raised in 1948 to $10,330, or by about 14 per cent. Congress in 1949 increased substantially the salaries of about 225 officials, including cabinet officers, heads of agencies, and some of the principal departmental officials. The salary of a cabinet officer was raised from $15,000 to $22,500, and that of undersecretaries from $10,000 to $17,500.[10] These increases will help to attract and keep men in key administrative positions in the government. But even with the increases, the men filling these posts receive considerably less than they could get in private industry.

The salaries are less adequate for civil servants in other administrative, technical, and professional positions. For 25 of these positions Congress has set a maximum salary of $14,000; a maximum of $13,000 for 75 positions; and a maximum of $12,000 for 300 positions. Other salaries formerly limited to $10,330 now pay up to $11,000.[11] A maximum of $18,000 would not be too high for government employees who are qualified for the best professorial chairs in the nation's great universities, for successful legal or medical practice, or for top research positions with a large industry.

effect on promotional opportunities

The failure to increase salaries at the top severely limits the opportunities for advancement in the federal service. Recently the salaries at various age and service levels in government were compared with those of two large private companies. These studies show that "Federal employees are better compensated and progress more rapidly up to age 35, but receive progressively less compensation, on an average, thereafter." Also, "Federal employees fare somewhat better during the first 15 to 20 years of service, but worse during the remainder of their careers." [12] This salary structure operates against the government service in two ways. First, it discourages college graduates from looking to the government for a career. Second, it tends to push out of the government career executives whose experience and competence are badly neded.

benefits other than compensation

Aside from compensation, there are benefits in the public service that make it more attractive than industry. In the first place, government service has fewer of the risks that go with responsible positions in industry. Aside from the heads of departments and agencies and their aides, a competent civil servant who does his

---

[10] 5 U.S.C. §3, 63 Stat. 880.

[11] Classification Act of 1949, 5. U.S.C. §1071, 63 Stat. 954.

[12] *Task Force Report on Federal Personnel*, p. 33.

job well and avoids subversive political activity has a position that is reasonably secure for life. He is not protected, of course, if the agency in which he works, or his job, is abolished. But even in these cases he enjoys a priority that normally means he will be appointed to another position within a relatively short period of time.

The federal service also provides liberal vacation, sick-leave, and retirement benefits. After a year of service, an employee has approximately a month's vacation with pay each year. Also, he is entitled to two weeks of sick leave if it becomes necessary for him to be absent from his job because of illness. An employee who makes the federal government service his lifework may also count upon a reasonably adequate pension upon retirement. The benefits have been liberalized from time to time, and the government shares with the employee the cost of the annuity.

the problem of inertia

The civil servant is often visualized as a dullard who follows the letter of his regulations in minute detail, resisting all change that might disrupt his precious routines. In the cartoonist's hands he becomes a wizened little man, obviously incapable of survival in the world of businessmen, with his meager powers strangled by reams of "red tape." This characterization is exaggerated, to be sure, but it does contain a hard core of truth. The lines laid down in a department to guide the conduct of its affairs tend eventually to become deep ruts from which it becomes increasingly difficult to turn. This tendency, it should be added quickly, is not confined to government; it is present in any organization whose size requires orderly procedures, and it becomes more pronounced as the organization grows older. Institutions, like men, become more conservative as they age. The fact of survival confirms the value of the old habits. Moreover, established routines give a sense of confidence to the men whose work they control. Innovation may have the charm of the unknown; but the unknown is also a potential threat. All of us unconsciously fear and resist change in accustomed ways of doing things. Are civil servants more susceptible to this human trait than others?

the effect of security upon the civil servant

The security that has been noted as characteristic of the civil service is not wholly advantageous. There can be little doubt that many of mankind's notable triumphs have been achieved under the stress of insecurity. To recognize this truth is not to suggest that a man does his best work under constant threat of unemployment or when adequate support for his family is in jeopardy. For every masterpiece produced by a starving artist, a potential masterpiece may be lost because the artist starved. But when life becomes too certain, predictable, or comfortable, most of us succumb to varying degrees of laziness. The civil servant is virtually assured of continuing employment. And in too many government agencies advancement in salary and in responsibility is given for "years of service" rather than as a reward for unusual performance. These two features of the civil service—permanent tenure and advancement by seniority—undoubtedly encourage intellectual sluggishness. How can it be overcome? Somewhere between the extremes of anxiety and security is an area in which we all do our best work. The government has not been completely successful in delineating this area for its civil servants. The problem, however, is not unique to government; one of the persistent personnel questions in industrial, educational, religious, and military organizations is how to provide incentives without undermining essential security.

the criticism of civil servants

The American custom of criticizing public servants is thought by some to be a desirable antidote to the deadening effect of the security that civil servants enjoy. Certainly it is irritating to have one's every act censored, as the partner of a nagging spouse knows. But is unmerited criticism helpful? Do the motives of the critic affect the result?

Americans criticize government officials for many reasons. When, Sir William Beveridge visited the United States in 1942, he said: "In Britain we are not afraid of our Government because we know our Government is a democracy and we can control it. You, I think, still retain something of the mental outlook of the men 150 years ago who felt that government was tyranny." [13] Unfortunately there is considerable truth in this observation. Our tendency to think of government as an enemy rather than a servant undoubtedly helps to explain the paradox noted by students of American society, namely, that we Americans distrust government, yet steadily heap more tasks upon it. Some of our scorn for civil servants is perhaps due to the fact that ours is essentially a business culture; in most communities it is the businessman whose advice is sought, rather than the teacher, the postmaster, or the head of the employment office. Many bitter attacks on officials can be explained by a desire for publicity: a charge of "incredible mismanagement" of important public affairs is certain to make the front page of most newspapers. Still other critics are in honest disagreement with officials' actions and would like to see them changed.

Criticism affects different people in different ways, and it is difficult to come to a firm conclusion about its effect upon the government employee. On the favorable side, it may be noted that some officials of the Tennessee Valley Authority believe that the continuous and searching criticism of that agency by Congress, the press, and the public has been a major factor in keeping it alert and

---

[13] John J. Corson, "To Get Better Men for a Better Government," *New York Times Magazine*, March 27, 1949, p. 49.

vigorous. Sooner or later, as operations become routinized and personnel older, a deadening lethargy overtakes an organization and its employees lose verve and the sense of adventure. Even destructive and unfair critics may stimulate a civil servant to re-examine his activities and in this way may help to maintain desirable freshness of ideas. Perhaps criticism is most effective when it disturbs most deeply.

Some individuals, however, are deeply hurt by criticism that they consider undeserved, and no doubt a number of able men leave government positions because they see no point in exhausting their energies for inadequate salaries and an ungrateful public. The career of James Forrestal is perhaps a case in point. Forrestal left a successful Wall Street business to work for the United States government. He served as one of President Roosevelt's administrative assistants and later became Secretary of the Navy and then the first Secretary of Defense. His arduous duties during the war led to an illness diagnosed as "operational fatigue" and characterized by nervous exhaustion and depression. He took his own life while a patient in the Naval Hospital at Bethesda, Maryland. Close observers of Forrestal's career believe that irresponsible criticism of his policies by newspaper columnists and radio commentators accentuated the mental exhaustion that led to his death. In an editorial entitled "The Tragedy of James Forrestal," the Washington *Post* commented:

> An inner conviction seems to have seized James Forrestal that his career had been a failure. It produced a despairing and all-encompassing anxiety in a man who had hitherto appeared to the world as an earthy man lacking altogether in any neurosis. . . . Then there was something in the nature of a last straw. He who had appeared to be indifferent to what was said about him felt a new torment in the talebearing and false witness of persons in his vicinity. It was all too much to bear for a man worn out by exertion and fearfully troubled in spirit.[14]

Criticism may accentuate the natural timidity of men and women for whom the security of government service was a chief attraction. Since advancement may depend upon avoiding trouble, the cautious civil servant soon adopts the rule, "Never stick out your neck." Although employees of this type are not likely to rise to top executive positions, they may set the tone of an important activity. Moreover, they represent a waste of human resources. Too many promising young civil servants become unimaginative public officials, content to carry out faithfully the orders that someone else issues. Astute observers believe that this atrophy is caused in part by the abuse that civil servants receive at the hands of pressure groups, press, and members of Congress.

Undeserved criticism of civil servants may also make it more difficult for the government to attract competent young people. This is the view of Robert Lovett,

---

[14] Washington *Post*, April 23, 1949.

a Wall Street banker who served with distinction in a number of government posts, as Under Secretary of State, and most recently as Deputy Secretary of Defense. He has said that "some able men avoid government service, and discourage their sons from entering the career service, because they fear that no matter how blameless he is, he may be used as a target to get headlines by some sensation-seeking politician." [15]

On balance, it is doubtful that criticism as such is an adequate counteractive to the inertia of the civil service. But it is also clear that there is no way in a democratic society to curtail public criticism of public servants. Constructive criticism is helpful and essential, and destructive criticism cannot be avoided. The consumer has a right to complain about his purchase, its producer, or the salesman who sold it. For this reason, an official of the United States government needs both a sense of humor and the common sense not to take himself too seriously.

the spur of politics

The civil servant is under continuous pressure from political officers whose programs for change conflict with tradition. The President and the department and agency heads feel directly the attitudes and desires of Congress and the voters. As wise politicians, they try to respond. They are not unduly concerned if response means that departmental policies or procedures of long standing have to be overturned. On the other hand, the body of permanent career servants represents stability. They provide the continuity of experience which makes it possible to administer the public's business. A civil servant respects tradition, and its disruption seems to him something to be avoided. Without established procedures his life would be chaotic; and it must be said that, within limits, he is right. Hence the relationships between a newly appointed department head and the permanent staff typify the continuous struggle in life between change and stability.

The underlying theory of the civil service is that permanent employees do not engage actively in party politics and that, if they have strong political beliefs, they do not act upon them insofar as their official duties are concerned. Under this doctrine of "political neutrality," the civil servant is expected to carry out faithfully the policy instructions of his superiors. Because of this neutrality, it is not necessary for a party recently come to power to replace the rank-and-file government employees with men of their own party and choice. In fact, however, the relationship is not quite this clear-cut. Men who spend a lifetime on a particular job cannot help acquiring the attitude that they know more about the work and what ought to be done than a department head whose tenure terminates with the President's. For this reason, many department heads find that

---

[15] Quoted by Corson, "To Get Better Men for a Better Government," p. 44.

their subordinates are not as responsive to new ideas and policies as they should like them to be. In unusual cases, indeed, subordinate officers of a department may sabotage policies that have the support of the department head, the President, and the general public.

Viewed in these terms, the relationships between civil servants and policy officers pose a basic issue. If the civil servants do not respond to political changes in society, our government will cease to be democratic. On this subject Dean Paul Appleby of Syracuse University has said: "(1) It is essential that there be sufficiently direct political control to ensure responsiveness to changed national policies and national needs. (2) It is imperative to maintain and safeguard the career service to assure administrative continuity and technical and managerial competence." [16] Dean Appleby, who served for eleven years on the staff of the Secretary of Agriculture and later held other top government administrative posts, suggests that the solution of the problem may lie in giving the department head greater freedom in appointments, and in closer relationships between political leaders and executive officials:

> No incoming secretary, unaided, may be expected to be able to crack the shell of tradition in his department. He therefore needs complete freedom in selecting a few staff aides, the number varying with the size, nature, and complexity of the department. . . . Next, I believe there should be recognition of a right to name up to perhaps a dozen persons in any one bureau and up to a total of perhaps thirty in an entire department—these in addition to his personal staff. . . . These appointments, however, should all be subject to the approval of the Civil Service Commission and to the understanding that they would be used only as and when the need for greater political and administrative responsiveness might develop in unanticipated places. [17]

Dean Appleby believes that it is possible for a department to designate a large number of jobs that require only simple qualifications and that could be filled as well as not by people recommended by party leaders. In any such cases, however, "the responsible administrators—not the politicians—must select the specific people who are employed." The Department of Agriculture could well have made "a little more conscious and organized search for persons with political prestige, administrative understanding, and desirable policy attitudes to fill a number of places which, as it was, were filled on the basis of straight, nonpolitical selection."

Administrators can often find throughout the country men of real political standing who possess all the other desired qualifications as well. These men

---

[16] Paul Appleby, *Big Democracy* (New York: Alfred A. Knopf, Inc., 1945), p. 146. Reprinted by permission of Alfred A. Knopf, Inc., publishers.
[17] *Ibid.*, p. 148.

could be used to fill a somewhat larger percentage of the fairly important, non-Civil Service positions than is now the case. Political leaders would accept such selections with enthusiasm and would moreover be drawn closer in communication and understanding by them. The process must not be carried to the point of giving undue emphasis to party politics, of neglecting technical and specialized qualifications, or of undermining administrative responsibility, but it can contribute to total effectiveness.[18]

Although one need not accept Dean Appleby's solution, there can be little doubt that he is concerned with a real problem. Progressive extension of the career service to important executive positions has created opportunities for competent men and women and thereby has strengthened government personnel. At the same time, it has become more difficult for department heads and other responsible officers to inject new ideas and new policies. The need now is for some compromise of the patronage and merit systems that will preserve the values of the career service and maximize the responsiveness of the civil servant to democratic influences. In effect, Dean Appleby's suggestion is that we reintroduce, in a limited and controlled way, the "rotation in office" principle espoused by Andrew Jackson. This suggestion has the merit of recognizing that a department head's functions are at least as political as they are administrative. Consequently, a secretary might be expected to discharge both responsibilities more successfully if he were allowed to appoint a considerable number of competent politicians to important administrative posts. The requirement that the Civil Service Commission approve such appointments might prevent them from degenerating into the old-fashioned spoils system.

the question of loyalty

Under the Constitution a man cannot become President of the United States until he takes the oath of office: "I do solemnly swear (or affirm) that I will faithfully execute the office of President of the United States, and will to the best of my ability preserve, protect, and defend the Constitution of the United States." Congressmen, judges, and other officials of the government are also "sworn in." It is not unusual, therefore, or beyond the contemplation of the Constitution, that public officials be required to declare their fundamental loyalty to the government. The question of loyalty is of special significance, however, when civil war or subversion threatens, or attack by a foreign power seems imminent.

background of the loyalty program

Since 1939, employees of the government have been treated as a special group with respect to the question of political loyalty. The Hatch Act of that year

---

[18] *Ibid.*, p. 154.

makes it unlawful to pay from federal funds any person who is a member of a political organization or party that advocates the overthrow of the United States government.[19] A year later Congress passed the Alien Registration Act, which makes it a penal offense for any person to advocate knowingly the overthrow by force and violence of any government in the United States, or to help to organize any group or society, or hold membership in any group or society, advocating the overthrow of the government.[20] In the same year the Civil Service Commission adopted a policy of not certifying for employment the name of any member of the Communist party, the German-American Bund, or any other communist or Nazi organization. In 1941 Congress made the first grant of funds, which has been renewed periodically, to the Federal Bureau of Investigation to finance investigation of civil servants alleged to be "members of subversive organizations or to advocate the overthrow of the Federal Government." In 1942 the War and Navy Departments were authorized by statute to dismiss summarily employees considered by the departments to be "bad security risks," and this authority was given to the Department of State in 1946. After the end of World War II, there was widespread concern in Congress and elsewhere that members of the Communist party might advance to important positions in the federal government, from which they could work for the interests of the Soviet Union. On March 21, 1947, after a study made by a presidential committee, President Truman issued an executive order with a twofold objective: to afford (1) "maximum protection . . . [to] the United States against infiltration of disloyal persons into the ranks of its employees," and (2) "equal protection from unfounded accusations of disloyalty . . . [to] the loyal employees of the Government." [21]

A major problem in a loyalty program is to define satisfactorily what is meant by "disloyalty." Under the President's Loyalty Order an employee may be separated from the federal service if, "on all the evidence, reasonable grounds exist for belief that the person involved is disloyal to the Government of the United States." The activities to be considered in the evidence are (1) sabotage and espionage; (2) treason or sedition or advocacy thereof; (3) advocacy of revolution or force to alter the constitutional form of government of the United States; (4) intentional, unauthorized disclosure of confidential documents under circumstances indicating disloyalty; (5) acting so as to serve the interests of another government in preference to the interests of the United States; and (6) "membership in, affiliation with, or sympathetic association with any foreign or domestic organization, association . . . designated by the Attorney General as totalitarian, fascist, communist, or subversive. . . ."

---

[19] 18 U.S.C. §61i, 53 Stat. 1147.
[20] 18 U.S.C. §10, 54 Stat. 671.
[21] *Executive Order* 9,835, *Federal Register*, XII (March 21, 1947), 1935.

procedures for testing loyalty

Briefly stated, the procedures established to test the loyalty of government employees involve these steps: (1) The Federal Bureau of Investigation investigates fully any employee about whom there is "derogatory information." (2) If the results of the investigation indicate that there is reason to suspect the employee's loyalty, the FBI makes a report to the department or agency in which he is employed. (3) A departmental loyalty committee investigates the case; if the judgment of the committee is adverse, the employee is provided with a statement of charges that is as detailed as security will permit. (4) At the hearing the testimony and evidence of the employee are taken; he may have the advice of counsel if he so desires; and he is supplied with a transcript of the proceedings. (5) If, after this hearing, the departmental loyalty committee concludes that there are reasonable grounds for believing that the employee is "disloyal" or a "bad security risk," he is suspended. (6) A suspended employee has the right to appeal to the head of the department or agency. (7) If the department or agency head upholds the decision of the loyalty committee, the employee may appeal to the central loyalty review board, established for that purpose by the President.

Although this procedure provides a "hearing" and "appeals," it does not give to suspect employees the protections normally provided under American law to persons accused of crime. At the initial hearing the employee is given an opportunity to make a statement in his own defense. The hearings are held before agency officials, but they are not open to the public nor is the record of the hearing made public. The agency that investigated the employee is not required to reveal the source of the information that led to charges of disloyalty. The employee need not be told the names of his accusers, and he is not given an opportunity to confront or to cross-examine them. He may not be informed of the exact nature of the charges against him if, for "security reasons," specific charges appear unwise. Finally, there is no requirement that his disloyalty be established beyond a reasonable doubt.

The Loyalty Review Board is composed of twenty-three respected citizens from both political parties. The board has tried to prevent abuse of the loyalty procedures and has said that it will not permit the program to become a witch hunt. It will not consider advocacy of a change in the form of government or economic system disloyal unless "that advocacy is coupled with the advocacy or approval, either singly or in concert with others, of the use of unconstitutional means to effect such change."

effect of program on morale

This statement of policy by the Loyalty Review Board is reassuring in view of the effect of the program on the morale of civil servants. It has been said often, and probably with considerable truth, that the rank-and-file civil servant is apt to be a person who is himself insecure and who finds the security of the government service one of its attractions. As observed previously, men and women who spend years working in large organizations tend to become overly cautious, to avoid rather than to seek responsibility. Government service seems to provide a favorable environment for the growth of these attitudes in people who have a propensity for them. It is this segment of the civil service that is particularly affected by the threat of abrupt dismissal.

For this group, fear of dismissal from a secure position is a corrosive thing. Individuals begin to avoid their colleagues, who *may* be suspected of disloyalty. They seek out secluded spots where they can lunch alone. They avoid the associations that are a part of the working mechanisms of a bureaucracy. As feelings of insecurity grow, the volume and quality of work drop. For this reason, if for no other, it is important that the loyalty program be administered as openly as possible and with all possible fairness.

For example, administrative disloyalty should not be identified with political disloyalty; criticism of the agency head or the President, with subversive activity. Every man at times likes to complain about his boss. Some people unwisely become preoccupied with the pleasures of idle complaint and indulge in commentary that would itself be grounds for dismissal in a business organization. Such people should be disciplined or discharged for incompetence and irresponsibility and not dismissed as bad security risks or disloyal Americans. Since the tenure of the civil servant is surrounded with many safeguards, there is a real danger that disloyalty procedures will be used for other purposes. This matter is terribly serious, since a person dismissed from the government for disloyalty can scarcely expect to find employment in private business. Even people cleared by the Loyalty Review Board find it difficult to re-establish themselves in their old jobs and virtually impossible to find private employment of comparable attractiveness.

There is also the danger that the loyalty program will discourage from public service the bold, imaginative, but unconventional person who is badly needed. These persons value intellectual independence and freedom of inquiry and expression. If government employment means that they must surrender these basic values or risk accusations of disloyalty, the government will undoubtedly lose their services. The result in a field such as scientific research might be disastrous to the nation.

results of the loyalty program

In April, 1950, Seth W. Richardson, chairman of the Loyalty Review Board told a Senate subcommittee the results of the loyalty program. During the three years that the program had been in existence, approximately 3,000,000 files were reviewed, and the FBI conducted full investigations in 10,000 cases. This prodigious search produced "not one single case" of espionage anywhere in the ranks of federal employees. The board approved the discharge of 182 persons about whose loyalty there was reasonable doubt, and it restored to their federal positions 125 persons whose dismissal had been recommended by departmental or agency loyalty committees. Undoubtedly other employees left the government voluntarily rather than submit to investigations, and still others had not appealed departmental orders for dismissal to the Loyalty Review Board.[22]

The program has not been completely effective. There are undoubtedly persons on the federal payroll who are not sympathetic to constitutional government; probably some of these would be actively disloyal if given a favorable opportunity. But the results of the loyalty program at the present indicate that the vast majority of the civil servants are loyal Americans.

opportunities for the civil servant

Recently a group of 3,448 seniors in 94 colleges and universities were asked to compare the relative advantages of private and federal employment. The attitudes of these students toward the government are indicated in the following table:

RANKING OF GOVERNMENT IN RELATION TO PRIVATE INDUSTRY BY
3,448 COLLEGE SENIORS

		% WHO CONSIDER GOV'T		
Relative Importance	*Factors*	*Better*	*Worse*	*Same or Don't Know*
1	Salary	9.7	56.3	34.0
2	Opportunities for promotion	12.4	48.6	39.0
3	Security of job	74.4	6.7	18.9
4	Interesting associations and work	18.5	20.4	61.1
5	Opportunities for personal development	11.3	39.5	49.2
6	Opportunities for public service	60.8	5.9	33.3
7	Prestige and recognition	18.9	36.5	44.6
8	Calibre of associates	16.0	18.3	65.7
9	Incentives to improve efficiency	9.5	51.6	38.9
10	Leave, retirement, and health benefits	52.0	2.6	45.4

Source: Commission on Organization of the Executive Branch of the Government, *Task Force Report on Federal Personnel* (Washington: Government Printing Office, 1949), p. 7.

Of the group, one in four expressed a positive interest in government service, and only one in five of those completing professional, scientific, or technical educations indicated a willingness to accept federal employment. Since about one third of all federal jobs now require professional, scientific, or technical competence, this attitude is a serious obstacle to the continued improvement of

[22] New York *Times*, April 16, 1950.

the career service. In spite of the limitations of the civil service, with which we have thus far been principally concerned, the federal government does offer rich opportunities for outstanding young men and women. In concluding our study of the civil servant, it is appropriate to say something of the nature of these opportunities.

the opportunity for interesting work

One of the attractions of government service is the magnitude of the problems that officials are called upon to solve. In terms of complexity and interest, these opportunities in government cannot be matched in business. It was not unusual for businessmen to find, after service in the government during World War II, that their old jobs were relatively simple and dull. One man commented that he "was called upon to decide more complex policy questions each day while in the public service during the war than confront him in a year in private business." [23] Another, whose government job involved responsibility for the nation's export policy, returned to the vice-presidency of one of America's great corporations, where he had to content himself with determining the quantity of his firm's product to be exported monthly to specific foreign countries.

A young college graduate without previous experience does not, of course, move immediately into a position with responsibilities of great magnitude. It is also fair to note that a civil servant may receive his first job under a chief who gives him too many assignments involving petty details or routine procedural matters. Although the situation is improving, it is still not easy to transfer quickly from one agency to another. Nevertheless, the best young government employees are given important assignments early in their careers and even routine assignments are likely to be more significant, in terms of peoples' lives and money, than would be the case in private employment.

opportunities for promotion

That there are opportunities for rapid advancement in the federal civil service is illustrated by the careers of two young officials who were appointed in 1950 to high executive positions.

The Assistant Secretary of State for Administration was thirty-five years of age at the time of his appointment. He received an A.B. degree from the University of Maryland in 1937, and then served for three years as an assistant to the president of that institution. He entered the Army in 1941 and left in 1945 with the rank of colonel. During the war he was assigned as a staff member to several of the major international conferences between President Roosevelt and other chiefs of state. From 1945 to 1946 he was personnel director for the "Colonial Williamsburg" organization. In 1946 he went to the Department of

---

[23] Corson, "To Get Better Men for a Better Government," p. 46.

State as director of the Office of Departmental Administration, at a salary of $8,750. From 1947 he was director of the Executive Secretariat and his salary was $10,330, the maximum for civil servants at that time. In July, 1950, he was appointed Assistant Secretary of State, at a salary of $15,000.

Another example is that of the Assistant Director of the Bureau of the Budget, who was also thirty-five at the time of his appointment in 1950. He received his B.A. degree from McPherson College (Kansas) in 1935, an M.A. from the University of Kansas the following year, and a Ph.D., with a specialty in public administration, from the University of Minnesota in 1939. He entered the Bureau of the Budget in 1939 as one of the first staff members recruited for work in the field of administrative management, at a salary of $2,600. He served as administrative analyst until 1943, when his title was changed to that of budget examiner; and as budget examiner until 1946. During the period 1943–1946 he was in charge of the staff assigned to budgeting and management functions in the civilian war agencies, at a peak salary of $7,175. From 1946 to 1947 he was assistant to the Director of the Budget and in 1947 became Assistant Director responsible for the bureau's legislative clearance functions; his salary was increased to $9,975. When he became Assistant Director in 1950, his salary was increased to $16,000. As Assistant Director of the Budget, he is second in command of the President's most useful staff agency and works closely with cabinet officers and other presidential advisers.

Although both of these officials are college graduates, many civil servants who have little more than high school educations reach the top ranks of the executive branch. The Postmaster General selected by President Truman in 1948 provides an illustration of the fact that a competent person may overcome the handicap of not having had a college education. He attended the public schools at Oconee and the Shelbyville Normal School in Illinois. He was certified as a first-grade teacher, but in 1908 entered the Post Office Department as a letter carrier; he soon became a clerk in the Shelbyville post office, where he continued until 1911. From 1911 to 1915 he served as postal supervisor in Muskogee, Oklahoma. From 1915 to 1932 he was a postal inspector; in 1932 his salary as inspector in charge at Chattanooga, Tennessee, was $4,300. In 1933 he was in charge of the inspection division and the following year he became deputy second assistant postmaster general, at a salary of $6,500. In 1934 he was raised to $7,000. From 1935 to 1942 he was deputy first assistant and his salary was $7,500. From 1943 to 1945 he was chief post office inspector and his salary was $8,250. In 1946 he was appointed first assistant postmaster general, and his salary was raised to $9,800 and to $10,000 the following year. When he became Postmaster General in 1948, the position carried a salary of $15,000; it has since been raised to $22,500. As Postmaster General, he is responsible for one of the world's largest businesses, with more than half a million employees and a revenue of $1.3 billion a year.

The careers of W. A. Jump, who started in the Department of Agriculture as a messenger after completing his first year of high school, and Daniel W. Bell, who started in the Treasury as an "expert counter" after completing the second year of high school, might also be mentioned. Mr. Jump became the most influential career servant in the Department of Agriculture, and Mr. Bell was appointed acting Director of the Budget in 1934 and refused to accept appointment as Director. From 1940 to 1946 he was Under Secretary of Treasury; he left the government in 1946 to become president of the American Security and Trust Co.

But the opportunity for public service, rather than personal advancement, should be the primary appeal of a career in public affairs. When, in November, 1948, ill-health forced Mr. Jump to retire, he said:

> . . . there is no finer place in America than the Department of Agriculture in which to grow up and spend a lifetime, as I have done. I feel that I have been most fortunate in having had that privilege.

> Not a week passes, even after all these years, that I am not stimulated by some new and fresh evidence of the spirit of true public service that is the strong foundation of the Department of Agriculture. Somehow, and in some way, the fact that from the beginning the Department has existed for the sole purpose of making life in America a better, richer and fuller experience, has resulted in an honest, vigorous and intensely realistic public service concept on the part of the staff of the Department, high and low, that is truly remarkable. This makes the Department a most stimulating and inspiring place in which to work. A member of the Department of Agriculture does not have the feeling that he is just helping to turn the wheels that make a large organization work; he feels he is a partner in a great enterprise. That has been my experience for 42 years. I know it is the experience of countless others in the Department who could not be tempted to work anywhere else.[24]

In a society where a satisfactory life depends upon cooperation rather than individual action, government's work, which now ranges from postage stamps to atomic energy, is increasingly significant to all of us. If public affairs do not attract the competent of each generation, if the civil servant actually becomes the inhibited and unimaginative creature of the cartoons, the quality of American life will deteriorate. A people discontented with the life that society makes possible may be expected to turn to new forms of cooperation that promise greater fulfillment. It is not too much to say that upon the civil servant ultimately rests the future of American democracy.

---

[24] W. A. Jump to the Secretary of Agriculture, printed in *Public Administration Review*, IX, No. 1 (Winter, 1949), 64.

bibliographic note

Arthur W. Macmahon and John D. Millett, *Federal Administrators* (New York: Columbia University Press, 1939), present many short biographies of supervisory administrative personnel and analyze the method of their selection, their educational qualifications, experience, and governmental careers. More recent but less valuable is Jerome Rosow, ed., *American Men in Government* (Washington: Public Affairs Press, 1949), which contains biographical data about approximately fifteen hundred top-level political and career executives in the federal government. The United States Civil Service Commission publishes each year the *Official Register of the United States,* which gives the names and salaries of persons in top governmental positions. Short biographical statements about State Department personnel are available in the *Register of the Department of State,* April, 1950 (Washington: Government Printing Office, 1950).

The challenges and rewards of public service are portrayed in biographies such as Harvey W. Wiley, *An Autobiography* (Indianapolis: The Bobbs-Merrill Company, 1930); Henry L. Stimson and McGeorge Bundy, *On Active Service in Peace and War* (New York: Harper & Brothers, 1947); Gifford Pinchot, *Breaking New Ground,* (New York: Harcourt, Brace and Company, 1947); Viscount Haldane, *Richard Burden Haldane: Autobiography* (London: Hodder & Stoughton, Ltd., 1929); and Cosmos Parkinson, *The Colonial Office from Within* (London: Faber & Faber, Ltd., 1947). For a list of other relevant biographies, see Leonard D. White, *Introduction to the Study of Public Administration* (New York: The Macmillan Company, 3d ed., 1948), p. 334, n. 2.

Leonard D. White's book also includes an excellent series of chapters dealing with all phases of public personnel management. Professor White writes with authority acquired from close participation in the affairs of the United States Civil Service Commission over a long period of time. More intensive examination is provided by William E. Mosher and J. Donald Kingsley, *Public Personnel Administration* (New York: Harper & Brothers, 3d ed., 1941). In 1933 the Social Science Research Council appointed the Commission of Inquiry on Public Service Personnel. As a result of investigations by this commission and of its sponsorship of study by others, there are several excellent volumes that are still useful (although, unfortunately, out-of-date in some respects) including *Minutes of Evidence* (New York: McGraw-Hill Book Company, 1935); the commission report, entitled *Better Government Personnel* (New York: McGraw-Hill Book Company, 1935); and five monographs published in *Problems of the American Public Service* (New York: McGraw-Hill Book Company, 1935). The President's Committee on Administrative Management, *Report with Special Studies* (Washington: Government Printing Office, 1937), includes a monograph by Floyd W. Reeves and Paul T. David, "Personnel Administration in the Federal Service," that is worthy of attention. The *Task Force Report on Federal Personnel, Personnel Management,* and pp. 23–25 of *General Management of the Executive Branch,* published by the Commission on Organization of the Executive Branch of the Government, (Washington: Government Printing Office, 1949) are of current interest.

A study of personnel problems from the standpoint of the supervisor, rather than from that of the Civil Service Commission, is Lewis Meriam, *Public Personnel Problems* (Washington: The Brookings Institution, 1938). Sterling D. Spero, *Government as Employer* (New York: Remsen Press, 1948), deals with labor unions among government employees, collective bargaining, strikes, the closed shop, and other phases of employer-employee relationships. Frances T. Cahn, *Federal Employees in War and Peace* (Washington: The Brookings Institution, 1949), is a useful factual study of civil service practices.

Two interesting discussions of the Civil Service Commission are John McDiarmid, "The Changing Role of the U.S. Civil Service Commission," *American Political Science Review*, XL, No. 6 (December, 1946), 1067–1096, and Charles S. Hyneman, *Bureaucracy in a Democracy* (New York: Harper & Brothers, 1950), pp. 383–417. There is a useful *History of the Federal Civil Service, 1789 to the Present,* by the Civil Service Commission (Washington: Government Printing Office, 1941).

The civil service principle was not the invention of America. For descriptions of the systems of other countries see *Civil Service Abroad*, Commission of Inquiry on Public Service Personnel (New York: McGraw-Hill Book Company, 1935), including Leonard D. White, "The British Civil Service," Walter R. Sharp, "Public Personnel Management in France," and Fritz Morstein Marx, "Civil Service in Germany"; Robert M. Dawson, *The Civil Service of Canada* (London: Oxford University Press, 1929); Hiram M. Stout, *Public Service in Great Britain* (Chapel Hill: University of North Carolina Press, 1938); E. N. Gladden, *The Civil Service: Its Problems and Future* (London: Staples Press, Ltd., 1945), and J. Donald Kingsley, *Representative Bureaucracy* (Yellow Springs, Ohio: Antioch Press, 1944).

The Civil Service Assembly, an organization dedicated to the extension of the merit principle in the public service, has published several studies of high caliber, of which the following are of general interest: *Recruiting Applicants for the Public Service* (Chicago: Civil Service Assembly, 1942); *Placement and Probation in the Public Service* (Chicago: Civil Service Assembly, 1946); and *Employee Training in the Public Service* (Chicago: Civil Service Assembly, 1941).

Luther Gulick, one of the foremost authorities in the field of public administration, edited an issue of *The Annals* of the American Academy of Political and Social Science, Vol. CLXXXIX (January, 1937), entitled "Improved Personnel in Government Service."

An excellent symposium concerned with the personnel needs of government and the. education of prospective civil servants is Joseph E. McLean, ed., *The Public Service and University Education* (Princeton: Princeton University Press, 1949).

For further reading on the subject of the problem of inertia, see John M. Gaus, "The Responsibility of Public Administration," in *Frontiers of Public Administration* (Chicago: The University of Chicago Press, 1936); Marshall E. Dimock, "Bureaucracy Self-Examined," *Public Administration Review* IV, No. 3 (Summer, 1944), 197–207; Ludwig von Mises, *Bureaucracy* (New Haven: Yale University Press, 1944); J. M. Juran, *Bureaucracy* (New York: Harper & Brothers, 1944); "Responsibility," Chapter 3 of Monograph 7 by Carl J. Friedrich, in *Problems of the American Public Service*, cited above; Charles S. Hyneman, "The Problems of Inefficiency and Red Tape" in *Bureaucracy in a Democracy*; and Paul M. Appleby, *Big Democracy* (New York: Alfred A. Knopf, Inc., 1945).

A vigorous case against the present loyalty program is made by Thurman Arnold in *The Strengthening of American Political Institutions* (Ithaca: Cornell University Press, 1949), p. 53; in the same volume, p. 74, Arthur E. Sutherland calls attention to the conditions that gave rise to the program. Robert E. Cushman, "The Purge of Federal Employees Accused of Disloyalty," *Public Administration Review*, III, No. 4 (Autumn, 1943), 297, is a careful analysis of the development of the program, as is Roger S. Abbott, "The Federal Loyalty Program," *American Political Science Review*, XLII, No. 3 (June, 1948), 486–499.

part 8

---

promoting the general welfare

government and economic life

HE most striking fact about the government of the United States in mid-twentieth century is the breadth and scope of its activities. A mere listing of all of these activities would itself require a book. They range from eradication of plant pests to international warfare; from control of food and drugs to regulation of railroad rates; from construction of flood control and power dams to construction of battleships; from sale of postage stamps to sale of atomic energy; from protection of migratory birds to support of widows and orphans; from education of Indian children to stimulation of basic scientific research; and from provision of old-age pensions to promotion and maintenance of a healthy, vigorous economy.

The program of the national government is so vast today that it entails "normal" expenditures of more than $40 billion each year, the services of about 2.1 million civilian employees and at least as many members of the armed services, and the operation of 1,800 departments, agencies, bureaus, commissions, corporations, sections, and units. It now costs more to pay the interest on the national debt than it did to finance the total cost of the federal government in 1933. The federal government today is four times larger in terms of agencies and employees, and twelve times larger in terms of expenditures, than it was twenty years ago. In concluding its survey of national governmental activities, the Hoover Commission reported:

> It is almost impossible to comprehend the . . . problems of the Federal Government unless one has some concept of its hugeness and complexity. The sheer size, complexity, and geographical dispersion . . . almost stagger the imagination. As a result of depression, war, new needs for defense, and our greater responsibilities abroad, the Federal Government has become the largest enterprise on earth.[1]

---

[1] The Commission on Organization of the Executive Branch of the Government, *Concluding Report* (Washington: Government Printing Office, 1949), pp. 3–4.

two broad purposes of governmental activity

As Chapters 1 and 2 have emphasized, activities of government have in general two purposes. One purpose is to help people to meet needs that they cannot meet satisfactorily themselves or through organizations other than government. The other purpose is to regulate conflicting group and individual interests so that people may live together peaceably in a highly complex and interdependent society.

The attitude of a businessman, farmer, or laborer toward a government activity depends in large part on whether he is being served or regulated. For example, a farmer may resist government regulation of his dairy, but the people who buy his products support the regulation because it protects them from milk of low quality or dangerously high bacterial content. A manufacturer may object to government inspection and control of working conditions in his plant because it increases his costs, whereas his employees consider these regulations essential for their safety. Workers object to government restrictions on their right to strike, but the consumer may support these restrictions as essential to the continued operation of railroads, electric plants, or other essential industries.

It is characteristic that individuals and groups oppose vigorously government regulation of their activities, and support vigorously government activities that directly benefit them. This fact was illustrated with startling clarity in a 1934 dispatch in the Paris edition of the New York *Herald-Tribune*:

> White Sulphur Springs, W. Va., Oct. 31—The Convention of the Investment Bankers Association, meeting here, offered today its full assistance to President Roosevelt in his recovery program.
>
> A resolution was passed in which it was stated that the members of the association would stand behind the President *in all measures which were not calculated to infringe on their own interests*. The bankers offered Roosevelt their *whole-hearted support in particular in all his efforts on their behalf*.[2]

A businessman may resist government regulation of prices or the establishment of rules of fair competition for the buying and selling of goods, but he may favor regulation to establish minimum prices for the goods he sells. Farmers may oppose expansion of governmental services generally but normally favor continuation of direct government aids in the form of agricultural research, cash benefits, and the advice of government agricultural experts. Similarly, workers oppose the imposition of ceilings on wages as a device for keeping prices down but favor government regulation of prices to keep down the cost of living. Occasionally, an industry may seek government regulation of

---

[2] As quoted by Paul M. Appleby in *Big Democracy* (New York: Alfred A. Knopf, Inc., 1945), p. 6.

conditions that otherwise would be too chaotic for satisfactory business operation; the radio industry is an example of this rather unusual attitude.

causes of governmental expansion

the factor of "bigness" in the economy

An industrial society has a tendency to concentrate and centralize economic and political power. It is difficult to say whether this tendency is inevitable and uncontrollable, or whether it is merely the result of particular policies and conditions in the societies in which the development has been observed. In America, certainly, the expanding power of government has no more than matched the growth of economic power.

Bigness in economic enterprise is encouraged by competition and by technological advances. The foundation of modern industrial structures was laid with the invention of the steam engine and the discovery that the cost of manufacturing complex machines could be reduced greatly by the mass production of interchangeable parts. Thereafter, manufacturing became a matter of machine tools and assembly lines rather than the skilled use of handtools. The nineteenth century saw the competitive drive for profits lead to the widespread adoption of mass production methods based upon new inventions and the specialization of labor. Large-scale production in turn stimulated new inventions. Big producing units were able to increase output, reduce costs, sell goods at lower prices, and still make higher profits.

> The cumulative forces of machine industry . . . made a steady growth in the volume and velocity of mass production the outstanding feature of American economy, with correlative influences on American slants of thought, modes of living, manners, and aesthetic expression. Year by year new mechanical inventions encroached on the area occupied by hand workers: ingenuity gave a pneumatic drill to the miner underground, electric appliances to the woman in the kitchen, a tractor to the farmer, and a radio to the child. At length the day arrived when in all the land save in out-of-the-way places, there could be found none but machine-made objects, duplicated by the ton, impersonal, standardized according to patterns adapted to fingers of steel, and circulated by publicity drives.[3]

Gradually the corporation replaced simple proprietorships, which seldom could command sufficient capital to finance a large-scale enterprise, as the dominant form of business organization. The growth in the number of corporations was accompanied by an increasing concentration of wealth in a relatively few organizations. Berle and Means reported in 1932 that 200 of the largest

---

[3] Charles A. and Mary R. Beard, *The Rise of American Civilization* (New York: The Macmillan Company, 1930), II, 713–714.

corporations controlled half of all corporate wealth (other than banking) and exercised control over business generally through trade associations, informal agreements, interlocking directorates, and other devices.[4] The Federal Trade Commission estimated that in 1947, the 113 largest manufacturing corporations owned 46 per cent of the net capital assets in manufacturing.[5] Justice Brandeis in 1933, describing the corporation as "the modern Frankenstein which States have created by their corporation laws," declared:

> Through size, corporations, once merely an efficient tool employed by individuals in the conduct of private business, have become an institution—an institution . . . which has brought such concentration of economic power that so-called private corporations are sometimes able to dominate the State. The typical business corporation of the last century, owned by a small group of individuals, managed by their owners, and limited in size by their personal wealth, is being supplanted by huge concerns in which the lives of tens or hundreds of thousands of employees and the property of tens or hundreds of thousands of investors are subjected, through the corporate mechanism, to the control of a few men. Ownership has been separated from control; and this separation has removed many of the checks which formerly operated to curb the misuse of wealth and power. And as ownership of the shares is becoming continually more dispersed, the power which formerly accompanied ownership is becoming increasingly concentrated in the hands of a few. The changes thereby wrought in the lives of the workers, of the owners and of the general public, are so fundamental and far-reaching as to lead . . . scholars to compare the evolving "corporate system" with the feudal system; and to lead other men of insight and experience to assert that this "master institution of civilized life" is committing it to the rule of a plutocracy.[6]

The growth of machine industry and corporate power had its counterpart in the development of the labor movement. The individual worker was no match for his corporate employer in bargaining over wages, hours, and other conditions of employment. Labor organizations grew in size, power, and militancy as the number of industrial wage earners increased. Workers resorted to collective effort to obtain more favorable working conditions; the strike was the ultimate weapon. During the 1920's, when industrial activity was at a high level, there was a general disposition on the part of employers to share the system's benefits with their employees. During the depression years, 1929–1933, labor organizations were relatively weak and were not a major influence in the determina-

---

[4] A. A. Berle, Jr. and Gardiner Means, *The Modern Corporation and Private Property* (New York: The Macmillan Company, 1932).

[5] *Report of the Federal Trade Commission on the Concentration of Productive Facilities: 1947* (Washington: Government Printing Office, 1949).

[6] From the dissenting opinion in *Liggett* v. *Lee*, 288 U. S. 517, 565 (1933).

tion of economic policy.[7] But in the next ten years there was a tremendous resurgence in the power of labor, and by 1942 from eight to ten million workers in major industries had been brought into collective bargaining units. Partially as a result of government manpower policies followed during World War II, labor unions continued to grow in size and power. By 1950 approximately 15 million workers belonged to unions, and Congress had found it desirable to enact legislation to curtail their power.

The trend in agriculture has been somewhat different from that in business and labor. First, there has been a gradual decline in the number of Americans who earn their living by agricultural pursuits. In 1900 about 35 per cent of the gainfully employed were occupied in agriculture; in 1950, only 12.5 per cent were so employed. Second, agriculture as a commercial enterprise is increasingly in the hands of a relatively small percentage of producers. In normal times, about 60 per cent of the farmers produce only 10 to 15 per cent of the volume of crops distributed commercially. The trend toward huge commercial farms of thousands of acres and worth millions of dollars has been inevitably accelerated by the perfection of laborsaving devices such as the power combine and the mechanical cotton picker. There has been a long-time decline in the relative importance of agriculture in the economy, and several millions of farmers have come to look to the government to ease the pressures and effects of uncontrolled competition.

the factor of democratic influences

It is of considerable significance that the opportunities of American citizens to participate in governmental processes expanded as their ability to control economic forces and institutions declined. Gradual extension of the right to vote, the development of vigorous political parties and pressure groups, the popular election of senators, and, in effect, of the President, all resulted in the strengthening of popular government. These developments in governmental procedures and institutions created a more direct relationship between the individual citizen and the government officials who determine public policy. When the problem of coping with unfriendly or unfairly competitive interests became too great, the individual had an opportunity to present his case before public officials whose continuation in office depended upon the satisfaction of the electorate. By joining other individuals with common problems and objectives, a citizen might magnify his power sufficiently to bring the government in on his side. It was not an accident that the growth and concentration of power in the economy, the strengthening of democratic institutions, and the expansion of governmental activities were parallel developments.

Activities of the government are undertaken in response to the wishes and

---

[7] Gardiner C. Means, "Economic Institutions," *American Journal of Sociology*, XLVII, No. 6 (May, 1942), 944.

needs of the American people. The government does not maintain these activities merely for the sake of spending money, of regulating people's lives, or of giving civil servants something to do. The government acts always in response to pressures created by the misfortunes or dissatisfactions of groups of citizens. Since democracies generally take action gradually, the government's response to these needs is slow rather than rapid, reluctant rather than eager, and piecemeal rather than planned. Demands from individuals and groups for governmental services outstrip society's ability to plan, organize, and finance the desired activities.

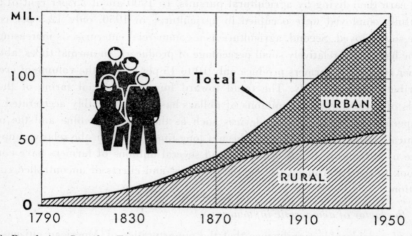

U.S. Population Growth. Total population of the United States increased from 4 million when the first census was taken in 1790, to 150 million in 1950. For 80 years after 1790, most of our people lived in rural areas. From 1870 to 1930, urban population gained rapidly. In this period, the increase in total population was 12 to 17 million each decade. The rate of increase in the total population slowed down during the 1930's but picked up sharply during and following the years of World War II. Urban population has increased in recent years at a more rapid rate than the rural—by 15 per cent from 1940 to 1948, compared with 6 per cent for the rural. (*Source: U.S. Department of Agriculture,* Agricultural Outlook Charts—1950, *p. 5.*)

The powers of government must be exercised in ways that are acceptable to the American people as a whole. This principle means, in practice as well as in theory, that any policy decision of national significance must have the support of a legislative majority. The President on occasion may set a course of national action without the guidance of legislation, but before the action is very far advanced it is generally necessary to obtain legislative approval in the form of appropriations of funds. Because of the crucial effect of legislative opinion, political parties and pressure groups work continuously to impress upon congressmen their views of what should and should not be done. In short, the effective response of government to the needs of the people is a result of the interplay of views of officials in the three branches of government with those of business, agriculture, and labor interests as expressed through political parties and pressure groups.

The role of the communications industries should be noted in any assessment of democratic influence in the determination of what government does and does not do. Without freedom of speech and press, democratic institutions would be impossible. As Professor Charles S. Hyneman has so well stated:

> The right to vote would be a mockery if people did not have ways and means of learning what is going on in the world, of finding what their interests are, of observing where other people stand in relation to their interests. There is no hope for democratic government unless there are facilities for communication which carry fact and opinion throughout the population; which make knowledge and supposition, desires and preferences, beliefs and prejudices, common property of all the nation.[8]

The communications industries undoubtedly have met the quantitative aspects of this need. Millions of newspapers are published each day; radio programs almost blanket the nation; books and periodicals are mass-produced and distributed, without government censorship; motion pictures are available in every community of any size; television is rapidly becoming a major industry; and transcontinental communication by telephone and telegraph is a matter of daily routine. These facilities have linked remote areas with the political and social capitals of the nation; their importance as a unifying force can scarcely be overestimated.

There is, however, question about the quality of the information transmitted through these diverse channels. Since the normal desire of a publisher or a producer is to reach the widest possible audience, the product is pitched at the "mass mind." The "Hooper rating" is watched much more closely than the intellectual quality and integrity of the presentation. The average newspaper reports crime, scandal, and sports much more adequately than it does public affairs; the soap operas occupy far more time on the radio than do discussions of pending issues of national importance. There can be little doubt that these deficiencies of the mass media affect public opinion about governmental problems.

Recently another aspect of the communications industries was closely studied. Most major newspapers, radio and television stations, and motion-picture companies are controlled by large combinations of interests. The ability of citizens to know and to understand is heavily dependent upon newspapers and radio stations operated for profit. The study concluded that the American press under corporate control obstructs the presentation of diverse opinions on important public issues, frequently distorts news, and treats public affairs inadequately.

---

[8] Charles S. Hyneman, *Bureaucracy in a Democracy* (New York: Harper & Brothers, 1950), p. 13.

Metropolitan newspapers, it was said, generally represent the attitudes of large-scale business in discussions of problems affecting government and the economy.[9]

the nature of the economy

The nature of the system on which Americans rely for the satisfaction of material needs has escaped precise definition. Economists, who presumably know more about these matters than anyone else, are unable to agree on a theory that explains adequately the "normal" behavior of the economic system. When an aberration occurs, such as a depression, the problem becomes even more difficult. What caused the disturbance? What is its probable course? What if anything can be done to ameliorate its effects? These questions are of more than theoretical concern, since the phenomenon which the economist terms a "disequilibrium" means unemployment for millions of voters. But the specialists cannot agree on a diagnosis, and disputes about therapy are intense, prolonged, and inconclusive. Since politics and economics are thus intertwined, an understanding of at least the broad outlines of the economic system is essential for the student of government.

traditional theory: competition, universal law, and freedom

Competition is the mainspring of an economy. The element of competition is not peculiar to our system; it occurs throughout life and in all societies.

> It is manifest in a struggle between germ cells for a chance at life; plants for sunlight and growth; bats and beavers and elephants, for food and mates; and kind against kind and like against like, for a foothold on the earth. . . . It appears in every social order in which men have lived; in the conflicts of tribes for unhappy hunting grounds; of holy men, for the glory of saying the most prayers; of barons, for castles on the Rhine; of merchant adventurers, for the spoils of the East; and of capitalists, to bag the largest profits and to establish the biggest and best foundations.[10]

In theory, competition is a great stimulus. Under its spur, the individual develops his latent capacities to the utmost; he exploits every opportunity that presents itself or that he creates; and his efforts are rewarded by independence and security. In an imperfect world, not everyone can be happy; resources are limited and demands insatiable. The value of each man's services is fixed in the market place, in competition with other men performing like services. Those who plan most carefully and work the hardest receive the largest share of the available wealth.

---

[9] Commission on Freedom of the Press, *A Free and Responsible Press* (Chicago: The University of Chicago Press, 1947).

[10] Walton Hamilton, "Competition," *Encyclopaedia of the Social Sciences.* IV. 142.

Competition also has a negative aspect. Men of imperfect character may be tempted to match shrewdness with cunning, and hard work with graft. The desire for independence and security may lead to avarice; bargaining in the market place may give way to theft; the deserving may be robbed rather than rewarded for their efforts. These distortions of the ideal are known in every social order. How can the theory and the reality be reconciled in the economic order?

Classical economic theory took an optimistic view of the universe. Men were rational and could be expected to temper selfishness with enlightenment. Thought was dominated by the conceptions of Newtonian physics: the elements of the universe were counterpoised; each element followed its own course; it was held within the system by other elements, also pursuing individual courses; all moved in accordance with natural laws that harmonized their diversity. Applied to the field of economics, this pattern of thought led to the assumption that conflicts between individuals were harmonized by a law of the universe, that the maximum wealth for society would be produced by each individual striving for selfish gain. Since the primary objective of society was to produce wealth, competition between individuals should not be discouraged by government interference.

Freedom from restraint imposed by others is a third element in this theory of the nature of the economy. The importance of this idea was emphasized by the French physiocrats in the eighteenth century, who urged upon government a "laissez-faire" policy. The physiocrats spoke on behalf of an emerging capitalism stifled by the rigidities and controls of the mercantile and guild systems. They protested governmental grants of special privilege in the form of monopolies that restricted trade and commerce to relatively few persons.

The doctrine of laissez faire received its classic statement in Adam Smith's *Wealth of Nations*, published in 1776. Smith opposed all governmental activities that restricted free enterprise, but he favored governmental activities to promote the general welfare.[11] The enforcement of contracts by which men, materials, and facilities are organized in the production system, the maintenance of patent rights, and the provision of a stable money system were regarded as essential to a laissez-faire economy. Although Adam Smith attacked tariff restrictions imposed by government, in the nineteenth century the tariff became a major instrument for the promotion of trade.

This idea of freedom was given a new twist by Herbert Spencer, who applied certain Darwinian conceptions to the field of economic behavior. To Spencer, the "survival of the fittest" was a universal law, applicable to society as well as to the biological world. Those too weak to survive in the competition for the means of existence perished, and their elimination hastened the march of progress. This view tended to emphasize the negative aspects of competition; it

---

[11] Jacob Viner found twenty-six instances in which Smith advocated government interference to protect the public interest. See his "Adam Smith and Laissez-Faire," in *Adam Smith 1776–1926* (Chicago: The University of Chicago Press, 1928), pp. 134–155.

substituted jungle behavior for enlightened self-interest. In the competitive struggle for the means of existence, it was "every man for himself and the Devil take the hindmost." Any effort on the part of government to take care of the poor and distressed was contrary to law and an obstacle to progress.

traditional theory: prices, profits, and "supply and demand"

Today the most commonly accepted theory of the American economic system is a modification of eighteenth century laissez-faire philosophy. Men enter into the production and distribution of goods and services in order to acquire wealth. The price that consumers are willing to pay in the market place determines what is to be produced, and how much. If the demand exceeds the supply, consumers compete with each other for the available goods. As the price of the article goes up, manufacturers increase its production. When demand slackens, the price also falls. A falling price means less profit, and with falling profits, the producer turns to other goods for which the consumer is willing to pay a satisfactory price. In short, the free play of consumer demand in the market place determines the price or value of an article; and price automatically and continuously adjusts supply to demand.

The theory, and the role which it permits government, was clearly stated in the middle of the depression of the thirties by a representative of the Chase National Bank:

> In general, it is not the function of government under the capitalist system to produce or perform economic services. The actual direction of industry, the decision whether more wheat shall be planted and less corn, or more shoes shall be produced and less hats, is not made by the State, or by collective society, but is left to the choice of independent producers. These independent producers make their decisions with reference to the state of the market. The up-and-down movements of prices and wages determine whether more or less of a given thing shall be produced. . . . Under this system of free, private enterprise, with free movement of labor and capital from industry to industry, the tendency is for an automatic balance to be maintained and for goods and services to be supplied in right proportions. A social order is created, a social cooperation is worked out, largely unconscious and largely automatic under the play of the impersonal forces of market prices and wages. . . . The ability to understand the highly intricate economic life of today, the ability to see through it and to see the different parts in relation to one another, to coordinate wants and efforts, to distribute resources properly among conflicting claimants— this ability does not exist.[12]

---

[12] Quoted in Charles A. and Mary R. Beard, *America in Midpassage* (New York: The Macmillan Company, 1939), II, 871.

Thus any effort to use economic theory effectively "in the actual regulation of economic life," in the way of social planning and control, "is an impossibility." As the Beards summarized this view, "individuals, government, and society stood in the presence of an unconscious, largely automatic, self-adjusting system, akin to the mechanism of nature."

admixture of private and public enterprise

The American economic system is a combination of private and public enterprise, of monopoly and free competition. Most of the nation's business is private in character; it is financed by private capital rather than by public funds; and it is controlled by the judgments of private individuals rather than by the decisions of government officials. The balance between privately and publicly controlled enterprise is not firmly fixed; it shifts, in response to national or world conditions, first in one direction and then in the other. It is therefore difficult, if not actually impossible, to state reliably the proportion of the economy for which government is responsible. But by such simple tests as the percentage of national income represented by government expenditures, or the ratio of government offices to the grocery, hardware, and department stores, service establishments, and manufacturing plants in an American city, or the amount of the average individual's income that goes into private channels and the amount that is paid in taxes, it appears that the activities of government seldom account for more than one fourth of the national economy.

It is also difficult to ascertain to what extent free competition is a characteristic of the economy. Within the private sector of the economy, there are both competition and monopoly. Some industries, such as the manufacture and sale of clothing, are highly competitive. In some industries, such as the manufacture of aluminum, competition is practically eliminated by agreements among a few huge units that control the activity. In other industries, such as the manufacture of automobiles, a relatively few firms compete with each other for the bulk of the business.

There is relatively little competition in businesses conducted by government. Municipal governments own and operate electric-power, water-supply, and transportation systems without competition. One of the most familiar and most essential of businesses—the postal service—is a vast monopolistic enterprise. The government carries on other businesses in collaboration with private agencies. Government-owned hydroelectric plants manufacture and sell power to privately owned "public-utility" companies, which distribute it to consumers at a profit. Under this arrangement, the government maintains a monopoly over production, and the private organization is granted a monopoly over distribution. Important phases of the atomic energy industry have been turned over to private companies, licensed and directed, with respect to this aspect of their business, by the

United States Atomic Energy Commission, which also owns and operates manufacturing plants. In the field of education, however, government dominates but does not preclude competition; public and private institutions function side by side in some communities, and educational institutions operated for private profit are not unknown.

The economy is also "mixed" in the sense that the government supports directly many "private" businesses. It is unlikely, for example, that the aviation industry could have reached its present state of development without government air mail contracts and government purchases of combat and transport planes. Although there has been a merchant marine since the first days of the republic, this industry cannot operate today without direct government subsidy. Newspaper and periodical publishers, advertising agencies, and, indeed, almost all forms of business, receive an invaluable subsidy in the form of below-cost mail rates. The system of unemployment compensation and old-age pensions relieves industry of the necessity of taking care of its labor force. Agriculture is protected against price fluctuations by a complex system of privileges and subsidies. The automobile industry owes its success to the patent system and to highways and bridges constructed at public expense. A rapidly growing motor freight business is able to compete with railroads in part because license fees do not begin to pay for the use of highways and city streets.

Government support of the economy is not of recent origin. The delegates to the Constitutional Convention in 1787 believed that the powers of the national government should be strengthened and used to promote economic welfare. Under the leadership of Alexander Hamilton, Washington's administration took steps to promote trade, to protect struggling American industry from foreign competition, and to establish a stable currency and banking system without which business could not flourish. Before the Civil War, several states, including Massachusetts, New Jersey, Pennsylvania, and Virginia, chartered corporations in order to promote industries whose operations were considered to be in the public interest. To stimulate "internal improvements," the legislatures of Pennsylvania and Virginia authorized the purchase of stock of private corporations by the state government.

changes wrought by the depression of the thirties

In the 1930's traditional economic theory was tested against the unpleasant realities of a great depression. By 1933, the unemployed numbered 13 million and national production had dropped 38 per cent from the 1929 peak. People were unable to buy the goods and services they needed because they had no jobs; manufacturing plants closed down because the demand for their products had dried up. The reactions of distressed Americans were sometimes dramatic and direct. Farmers, generally considered the bulwark of conservative individualism, destroyed milk on the way to market in the hope that their action would push prices up; and they forcibly prevented foreclosures on farm mortgages. Businessmen who preached and believed in "free enterprise" used all their influence to obtain higher tariffs, government subsidies for exports, and legislation to prevent price cutting. Labor unions whose philosophy about the role of government had been as conservative as that of business, turned to government for unemployment compensation and for other types of relief for the unemployed. It is unlikely that these and other demands represented a rational and deliberate rejection of laissez-faire philosophy. Rather, agriculture, business, and labor groups looked to the government for the solution of urgent practical problems, without much consideration of any conflict between their needs and their economic beliefs.

There was, however, a growing disposition to question some of the more extreme assumptions of laissez-faire doctrine. For one thing, civilized people are reluctant to accept the inevitability of suffering; their normal reaction is to try to do something about it. The distress of millions could not be explained by the doctrine of the "survival of the fittest":

> One of the early effects of the depression was to arouse the social conscience and to fortify the feeling of humanitarianism and the concept of social justice. Increasingly, individuals and organizations, many of which had hitherto been deemed conservative, proclaimed their intellectual dissatisfaction and moral indignation over the fact that the depression had been permitted to occur and over the suffering that it had brought.[13]

This tendency was strengthened by a Senate investigation conducted in 1933, which shed considerable light on the working of the financial system. In instance after instance, it was shown that the "value" of stock was determined by careful manipulation by human beings rather than by the automatic play of the market. By rumor, false information, and misleading newspaper publicity, the market price of the stock of a weak or failing company was skyrocketed; the principal owners of the enterprise would quietly dispose of their holdings, often at an enormous profit; and in the inevitable drop in the "value" of the stock, gullible speculators who wished to take advantage of a "hot tip on a good thing" were wiped out.

On the whole, the impression reigned that

> . . . "legitimate members of the banking fraternity" had nothing to do with such manipulations, in fact discountenanced them as injurious to sound business. But after the Senate committee started its inquiry, innocence gave way to knowledge and a sense of double outrage developed—over personal losses incurred at the game and the prestidigitation practiced at the expense of simple, if greedy, players.[14]

---

[13] Arthur C. Millspaugh, *Democracy, Efficiency, Stability* (Washington: The Brookings Institution, 1942), p. 230.

[14] Beard and Beard, *America in Midpassage*, I, 161.

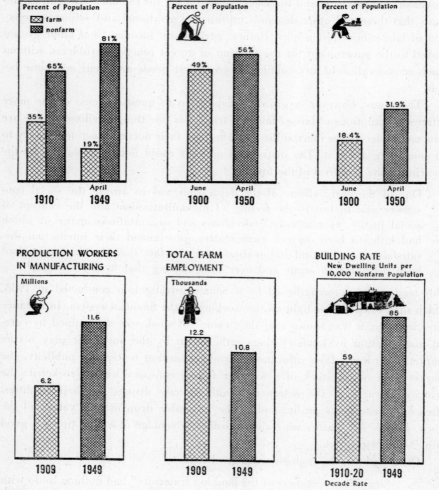

A Half Century of Economic Growth. Average weekly earnings given are in 1935–39 dollars. (*Source:* Monthly Labor Review, *LXXI, No. 1, July, 1950, 38–39.*)

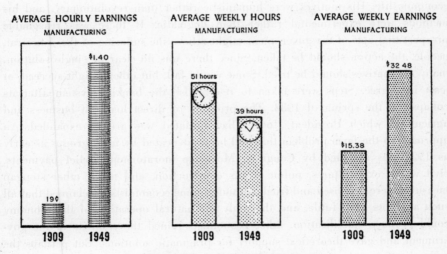

Changes in Dietary Habits
PER CAPITA

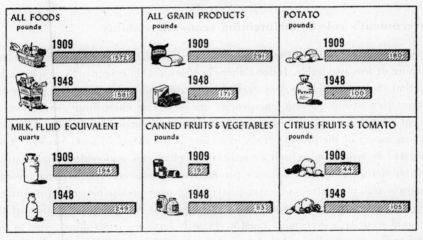

A Half Century of Economic Growth (*continued*). Average weekly earnings are given in 1935–39 dollars.

The inauguration of President Franklin D. Roosevelt coincided with the bottom of the depression. From what is now known about this period, it is clear that Roosevelt did not have any new theory about the relation of government to economic life. His motives were humanistic rather than revolutionary, and his methods were experimental rather than dogmatic. If there was reasonable prospect that acts of the government might relieve the suffering of the American people, the action should be taken. Since there was no clear or single solution, many alternatives should be tried. Some would fail, but others might succeed, at least in degree. Steps were taken to re-establish the banking system after its collapse in the spring of 1933. The program of direct loans to business and agriculture which President Hoover had initiated was greatly expanded. An approach to the farm problem that had been advocated by farm groups as early as 1922 was accepted by Congress. Mortgage moratoriums, relief payments, civil works expenditures, public works construction, and many other stopgap measures were proposed and tried. Although some economists proclaimed that all such attempts were futile, and that only the natural operation of the economy could produce stablilization, other economists joined the councils of the government and gave theoretical support for pragmatic solutions. But perhaps the most significant development of this period was popular acceptance of government's responsibility for the nation's economic welfare.

government's role in maintaining economic stability

In mid-twentieth century the periodic recurrence of emergencies must be taken as more or less inevitable. Indeed, there is considerable evidence to support a belief that the present era is one marked by continuous crisis. Whether this be the correct view or not, present emergencies are inevitably compelling government to accept a large responsibility for the maintenance of economic stability. The most serious aspect of the present crisis in society is the threat of war. Modern "total warfare" is economic as well as military in character and makes almost unbelievable demands upon a nation's productive mechanism. The national defense program today requires an exceedingly close partnership between government and the economy, and because of its responsibility for the preservation of the national security, government must necessarily have the controlling voice in this partnership. It may be said that one of the crucial issues facing our democratic society today is how to give government the control over the economy necessary if our national defense is to be adequate and at the same time to preserve the American tradition of individual initiative and private enterprise.

The American economy also continues to be marked by fluctuations between prosperity and depression. Indeed, it would appear that all societies, whether capitalist, socialist, communist, or any other type, continue to face the threat of ups and downs in the business cycle. Moreover, it is now clear the depressions tend to be world-wide in character. The American economy is certain to be affected, directly or indirectly, by developments in other economies, and conversely, the condition of the American economy is bound to affect the economic well-being of the rest of the world. With so much depending, both in America and in foreign countries, upon the maintenance of prosperity and the avoidance of the kind of severe depression that swept through the world during the 1930's, government's responsibility for establishing and preserving economic stability takes on an unprecedented urgency and significance. It seems reasonably clear that public opinion will no longer tolerate severe economic depressions, and that no administration that may be in office in time of economic crisis will be able to resist the political pressure upon the government to act. The pressure for such action will find support in economic principles, for whatever their disagreements concerning the details of their theories, many economists now believe that it is possible for government to take positive steps to prevent an extended period of depression and to ameliorate the effects of temporary business recessions.

There is nothing new about government's concern for the protection of the nation's security against foreign enemies or even for relieving the hardships caused by economic depressions. However, in times past, this concern did not necessarily lead government to take positive steps to secure a high level of economic production. For one thing, people were less certain that such action was government's responsibility or that government could accomplish beneficial results if it did act. Wars and depressions of the past were also more often successfully localized than are those of today. They did not spread so readily or so inevitably from one end of the world to the other. Many people were so insulated in their ways of life that they were able successfully to escape the full brunt of these crises. It seems unlikely that such will ever again be true. For better or worse, modern man has created a way of life that is closely coordinated politically and highly integrated economically. Our complex mechanical civilization will not allow us to ignore our neighbor's plight or to escape the consequences of his misfortunes. The mushrooming cloud of the atomic bomb is but a symbol of the interdependence of society and the rapidity with which economic shock or military dissension speeds rapidly from one sector of society to another. Whatever may have been the possibility in times past of successfully following a laissez-faire philosophy with respect to the relationship between government and the economy in the United States, it is clear that the political realities of the modern world and the facts of economic life now compel government to accept primary responsibility for the satisfactory operation of the economy.

characteristics of government's concern for the economy

government control of the economy begins at state and local levels

It is difficult to find an aspect of the regulatory or promotional activities of government concerning economic activity that did not originate at the state or local level. The national government has seldom been responsible for the first efforts to control a hitherto unregulated economic enterprise. An exception may be seen in the case of a totally new form of enterprise, such as the production and use of atomic energy, which emerges so suddenly and upon such a broad scale that national control is immediately necessary. But in times past, when economic enterprise was conducted almost exclusively upon a local scale, it was only natural that the first pressure for government activity either to promote or to regulate this enterprise should first have been felt at the local level. So long as businesses remained relatively small and produced goods and services for local markets, local units of government were able to devise and administer regulatory policies with a considerable degree of success. But as business enterprise expanded beyond the political boundaries of single communities, local government controls became less effective and the pressure for regulation soon spread to the states. It is difficult to date these successive periods in American history with complete accuracy, for conditions varied from one enterprise to another and from one section of the country to another. It would not be wholly erroneous, however, to say that in the period up to the Civil War such government regulation or promotion of the economy as existed was primarily local. Thereafter, until the close of the nineteenth century, the state governments assumed increasing responsibility for the satisfactory handling of economic problems.

This period in which government regulation of the economy was centered in the states was destined to be a relatively brief one. By the end of the nineteenth century the center of such activity was definitely shifting to the national government. This shift, as was true of the earlier shift from local to state government, came about gradually and was achieved only as a reluctant national government was persuaded step by step to accept the new responsibility. But the shift, like the earlier one, could not be permanently resisted. As transportation facilities improved, business enterprise burst through state boundaries, and goods were soon being sold and consumed thousands of miles away from the places where they had been produced. Many businesses hitherto local or state-wide in scope now expanded and entered regional or national markets. The corporate form of business enterprise was perfected and eased the transition from locally owned and managed establishments to the great national concerns of today owned by hundreds of thousands of security holders and operated by a managerial class ordinarily quite distinct from the owner or capitalist class. The state inevitably found the regulation of these new forms of business enterprise increasingly difficult, and around the turn of the century demands began to be made that Congress undertake to establish necessary national controls. However, it is important to remember that federal controls were set up only as local and state controls proved ineffective or inadequate. Moreover, although federal regulatory statutes and programs are today apt to be the best-known and most spectacular aspects of government regulation of the economy, it must also be remembered that local and state governments still carry on vast programs of business regulation. To give but one example at this point, it is still true that the organization of the business *corporation* is largely determined and controlled by state laws.

public economic policies have developed in an unplanned way

Governmental policies concerning economic enterprise in the United States have not developed according to a carefully conceived plan or systematic philosophy. Instead they have been evolved through a trial-and-error process and reflect the traditional experimental approach which has prevailed in almost all phases of American social development. As Professors Merle Fainsod and Lincoln Gordon have pointed out, government control of the economy "has represented a series of empirical adjustments to felt abuses. It has been initiated by particular groups to deal with specific evils as they arose, rather than inspired by any general philosophy of governmental control." [15]

Regulation of economic enterprise has certainly not been established as the result of any evil master-plan to destroy capitalism or free enterprise. As often as not, the immediate motivation behind a particular line of government control has been a desire to protect the free-enterprise system against forces or conditions threatening to destroy it from within. For example, the whole policy of antitrust regulation by government is certainly designed to protect small competitive enterprises against the threat of monopoly—to save the free-enterprise system against an evil force arising in its own midst. Moreover, the pressure for such a policy has come largely from businessmen themselves.

The result of this unplanned development of government control of the economy is that the existing relationship between business and the government is not a logical or systematic one. It cannot be analyzed, explained, or evaluated from the point of view of any one scheme of values or politico-economic philosophy. In part, this result is unfortunate, for it means that the "American way" lacks logic and contains many inconsistencies within itself. But in part, the result is fortunate, for it reflects the pragmatic character of American institutions, a quality that undoubtedly helps to explain the successful history of our nation. In other words, the relationship between business and government in the United States has been a highly flexible one. It has not been necessary to adjust every

---

[15] Merle Fainsod and Lincoln Gordon, *Government and the American Economy* (New York: W. W. Norton & Company, 1948), p. 226.

phase of the relationship to the dictates of some orderly, comprehensive philosophy. Instead, it has been possible to adjust the solutions of particular problems to "felt abuses" and "specific evils."

the evolution from legislative to administrative control of the economy

Government regulation and promotion of the economy have taken many different forms in the United States and still do. As has already been seen, there has been a progression from local to state to national control, and yet local and state governments are still actively enforcing many controls. Similarly, the executive, legislative, and judicial branches of government have all had important roles to play in formulating and administering controls, and still do. At the same time, American history has been marked by a significant development away from the role played by legislatures and toward the role played by administrative agencies. Thus, before 1860 most government control of the economy in the United States was the work of city councils and state legislatures, with very little assistance from executive agencies. Occasionally a legislature established an administrative body to assist it by investigating a certain phase of the economy and reporting its findings to the legislature. But these administrative activities were the exception and not the rule.

After the Civil War the economy became increasingly industrialized, and the work of legislatures increased by leaps and bounds. Legislatures soon found themselves unable to cope with the burden of regulatory activity. Led by Massachusetts in 1869, the states began to establish commissions to administer the regulatory statutes enacted by the legislatures. At first the powers granted such commissions were few, tentative, and largely advisory in character. But it was only a question of time before these powers were increased and became regulatory in character. In particular, the Granger movement, which took shape after 1870, led to the granting of power to administrative commissions to fix and control the rates charged by such public-utility enterprises as railroads and grain warehouses for the services rendered by them to the public.

The first federal regulatory agency, the Interstate Commerce Commission, was established by Congress in 1887. Professors Fainsod and Gordon see this step as symbolizing the beginning of a new era in government regulation of business—an era marked by increasing federal participation in the program of control and by increasing use of administrative bodies as the agencies of control:

> It marked the end of a century of expansion in the course of which a continent was occupied, industry became national in scope, and government helped to create new engines of wealth and power that threatened to evade all effective control. It stood at the threshold of a new era when to an increasing degree the consequences of the first period of industrial development and exploitation began to be critically appraised, and when the result

ing uneasiness crystallized in the creation of new instruments of national power to control and direct policy in important sectors of the economy.[16]

the role of the courts in the control of the economy

The courts have always played an important part in the control of the economy by government. Indeed, the courts were actively engaged in regulating and promoting economic enterprise in England and America even before legislatures or administrative agencies. An important function of the common-law court in England was to settle litigation growing out of business conflicts between private persons, particularly those having to do with contractual obligations. Long ago, business found it impossible to prosper without assistance from the government, and it was the court that became the first instrument of such assistance. Moreover, these early court rulings illustrate the fine line that often separates government promotion of business from government regulation of business. A court decision settling a contractual dispute between private parties inevitably *promoted* the interests of the winning party and *regulated* the interests of the losing party.

As early as 1824 in the case of *Gibbons* v. *Ogden*, the Supreme Court of the United States rendered a decision which profoundly affected the course of government control of the economy. When this decision is closely examined it is discovered that its effect was to promote the interests of one private person while regulating and curtailing the interests of another, to promote one form of government control of the economy while curbing another, and to promote the public interest at the same time that the interest of one of the parties to the litigation was being advanced. Specifically the Court canceled a private monopoly in the operation of steamboats in New York—New Jersey waters that had been granted by the New York legislature, and upheld the license of a competing concern obtained from the national government. The Court ruled that the federal commerce power established the prior right of Congress to control such navigation, and it upheld a federal statute providing for the free issuance of licenses to coastal vessels while invalidating a state law granting a monopoly to such a vessel. It has been said that this ruling marked the beginning of a federal antitrust policy.[17]

Control of the economy through the courts illustrated from the beginning the way in which a system of government regulation can reflect the public interest or be dominated by selfish private interests. In general, American courts have been conservative bodies that have often used constitutional and legal formulas in seeming disregard of the public interest as means of protecting business interests against an extension of legislative or administrative controls opposed by these interests.

---

[16] *Ibid.*, p. 236.
[17] *Gibbons* v. *Ogden*, 9 Wheaton 1 (1824).

The federal courts have made particular use of the commerce clause of Article One of the Constitution and of the due process of law clauses of the Fifth and Fourteenth Amendments as means of reviewing the validity of legislative and administrative controls of the economy. During the nineteenth century, when state and local controls were more numerous than federal controls, conservative courts used the commerce clause to invalidate state controls by asserting that they encroached improperly upon power delegated by the Constitution to the federal government. In the present century, as the center of control shifted from the states to the central government, conservative courts reversed this reasoning and held that federal use of the commerce power had become so broad as to involve encroachment upon powers reserved to the states by the Constitution—in particular, the power to regulate intrastate commerce. At times it seemed that the courts had succeeded in creating a twilight zone in which neither the states nor the federal government could act effectively.

The Fifth and Fourteenth Amendments forbade the national government and the states respectively from depriving any "person" of liberty or property without due process of law. Beginning in the last decade of the nineteenth century, lawyers, acting on behalf of businessmen, succeeded in persuading courts to define "person" to include corporations and to interpret "due process of law" to invalidate progressive regulatory legislation. For example, maximum railroad rates established by statute or by administrative regulation were frequently invalidated by the courts on the ground that they were fixed so low as to prevent the railroads from earning a fair profit and thus to deprive them of their property in unreasonable or arbitrary fashion—that is, without due process of law.

Through narrow interpretations of the commerce and due process clauses of the Constitution and of statutes enacted under them, the courts obstructed government regulation of the economy in the half century following 1885. One branch of the government set itself up in opposition to the two other branches, and for many years the development of an orderly, progressive program of government control of the economy was rendered difficult if not impossible. In the middle 1930's came a fundamental reversal in judicial policy, and the federal Supreme Court reinterpreted the commerce and due process clauses so as to bring virtually to an end their use as barriers to state and federal regulation of economic enterprise. Indeed, in recent years the courts have viewed positive government efforts to regulate the economy with somewhat more favor than have legislatures and executive agencies. This has been particularly true of the federal courts.

An examination of American history makes it apparent that the pattern of relations between the government and the economy has not been fixed and unalterable. Private economic interests in the field of business, agriculture, and labor have frequently changed their minds concerning government intervention in private enterprise, and these changes have promptly been reflected in changing pressures upon government, and in changing government policies. Severe economic depressions, natural disasters such as floods, earthquakes, and fires, and, above all, wars, have likewise created irresistible pressures upon government to promote and regulate economic activity in the public interest. The result has been the bringing of the American economy to its present state of development, one that remains essentially private in character, but which depends upon an increasing measure of government activity and control to safeguard and promote the public interest and to fulfill our national destiny.

In the chapters that follow, the range of federal government activity will be examined, in part from the point of view of the three great interest groups in the economy—business, agriculture, and labor; in part from the point of view of social needs, such as social security, medical care, education, and housing; and in part from the point of view of the problems government faces in meeting social pressures for increased service and regulation, such as the problems of planning, and budgeting.

bibliographic note

There are a number of very useful economic histories of the United States. One of the best for introductory courses is Thomas C. Cochran and William Miller's *The Age of Enterprise* (New York: The Macmillan Company, 1943). A. A. Berle, Jr., and Gardiner Means, in *The Modern Corporation and Private Property* (New York: The Macmillan Company, 1932), have made the classic analysis of the separation of ownership and control in corporate industrial enterprise and the resulting changes in our concept of private property. Robert Brady, *Business as a System of Power* (New York: Columbia University Press, 1943), analyzes the political and economic power exercised by corporations organized in trade associations and other business groups. The contemporary economic setting of corporate enterprise and the activities of its managers are outlined in Robert A. Gordon, *Business Leadership in the Large Corporation* (Washington: The Brookings Institution, 1945). A. D. H. Kaplan emphasizes the role of small-scale business in the American economy in *Small Business: Its Place and Its Problems* (New York: McGraw-Hill Book Company, 1948). In *The Folklore of Capitalism* (New Haven: Yale University Press, 1937), Thurman Arnold lucidly and wittily exposes the virtues and absurdities of the gospels of American capitalism. In "Business Organized as Power: The New Imperium in Imperio," *American Political Science Review*, XLIV, No. 2 (June, 1950), 323–342, Alpheus T. Mason discusses the efforts of some business spokesmen to allocate to business the task of formulating and administering welfare programs and (on p. 342) poses the question: How much social power can a free society permit individuals and groups to annex and hold without depriving government of the authority essential for maintaining order and security?

The impact of economic and social developments on American political institutions has been discussed in a variety of works. In *The Web of Government* (New York: The Macmillan Company, 1947), Robert M. MacIver provides a contemporary theoretical analysis of the functions of the modern state. See especially pp. 314–359. In *Public Administration and the Public Interest* (New York: McGraw-Hill Book Company, 1936), E. Pendleton Herring emphasizes the difficulty of determining the public interest in a society which is organized in private interest groups. One of the most recent analyses is found in Thomas I. Cook, "The Functions of Modern Government," *The Western Political Quarterly*, I, No. 1 (March, 1948), 16–28.

government promotion of business

*A*LL groups in the economy have a vital stake in the general condition of economic life. Businessmen, wage earners, and farmers hope to share in the expansion of the economy. Government attempts to promote an environment in which businessmen, labor, and farmers can achieve steady economic growth. It tries to build up natural resources, to open up the channels of competition, and to stimulate expanding employment opportunities. Above all it seeks to eliminate poverty in American life and to provide protective measures against human insecurity.

structure of American business enterprise

trends in business population

Generally the trend in the number of business firms in operation has been upward. Between 1900 and 1950 the number of business firms in operation more than doubled. In 1900, an estimated 1.7 million firms were in operation, compared to nearly 4 million in 1949. Manufacturing and construction firms, and enterprises in finance, insurance, and real estate account for approximately 25 per cent of all firms in the latter year. Firms in the wholesale and retail trade and in the service industries account for approximately 70 per cent.[1]

Large business enterprises are almost always organized as corporations. On the other hand, smaller firms are often unincorporated and take the form of simple proprietorships or partnerships. It is estimated that between four and five hundred thousand firms are organized as corporations today and that 3.5 million firms are unincorporated. Numerically the small, owner-operated business remains the dominant business type in the United States. In economic terms, however, the corporation has become, in Veblen's phrase, "the master institution of civilized life."

---

[1] U. S. Department of Commerce, *Survey of Current Business*, May, 1948, p. 15.

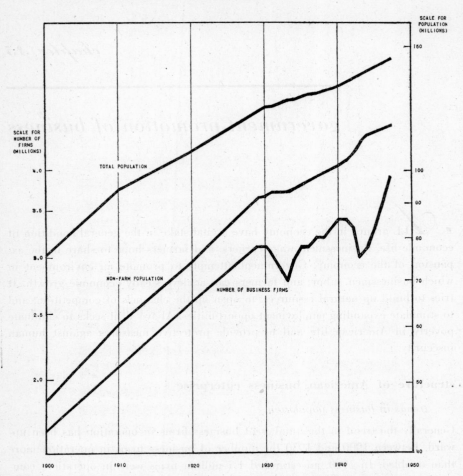

Business Population Compared with Human Population, 1900–1948. Ratio scale: equal vertical distances represent equal percentages. (*Source:* Business Size and the Public Interest, *November, 1947, p. 6. Reprinted with permission of the National Association of Manufacturers.*)

concept of the national income

National income is the net product or net return realized from the economic activity of all individuals, firms, and institutions. It includes wages and salaries paid by private business and by governments, interest payments, incomes of unincorporated businesses, corporation profits, and rents.

Today about 85 per cent of national income is derived from business activities of all kinds. The remaining 15 per cent is composed principally of payments made by governments to individuals and business firms for wages and salaries, for veterans' pensions, and for social security and other benefits.

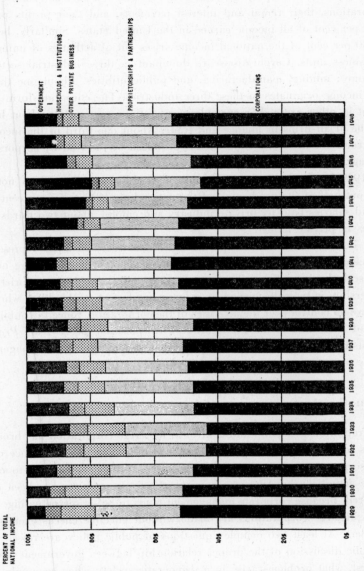

Origin of National Income, 1929–1948. (*Source:* Business Size and the Public Interest, *November, 1949, p. 9. Reprinted with permission of the National Association of Manufacturers.*)

the corporate share of national income

Income originating in corporate business in the form of wages and salaries paid by corporations, their rental and interest payments, and their profits provide about 50 per cent of all income earned in the United States. Similarly, between 25 and 30 per cent of the national income arises out of activities of unincorporated business units. Corporations are dominant in three industrial sectors of the economy: mining, manufacturing, and public utilities. About one third of national income originates in these three industries. The corporate form is less important in other areas. For example, corporations account for about half of the income of all firms in finance and trade. About one third of the income in the construction and service industries is produced or received by corporations. Only in agriculture does the corporation play a negligible role.

In 1949 Professor Sumner Slichter estimated that corporations not only direct about half of the production of the nation but also pay 75 per cent of all wages and salaries paid by private industry and employ about two thirds of all employees in private industry.[2]

The dominance of the corporation in American business represents a marked change from a free enterprise economy composed of a large number of small-scale business firms. The corporation, unlike the single proprietorship or partnership, is typically owned by a large number of stockholders who ordinarily have no control over the activities of the corporation. Since the publication in 1932 of Berle and Means's *The Modern Corporation and Private Property*, economists have noted the development of a professional group of managers who effectively control corporate enterprise.

issues in the American economy

The separation of ownership and control in the large corporation has broad implications for the nature of the American economy. For example, since ownership of corporate stock in fact gives the owner little or no power to control corporate activities, the American concept of private property has been drastically altered. Because corporate management tends to be self-perpetuating, policy decisions in large corporations are made without effective checks exercised by stockholders. At least two complex questions of public policy are raised which color public discussion of the proper relationship between government and business. First, what problems arise in a democratic society when economic power is concentrated in a few hands? Second, does the separation of ownership and control in the modern corporation challenge the validity of the principle of individual initiative in industrial enterprise? Does it suggest that the importance of the profit motive in American business is exaggerated?

---

[2] Sumner Slichter, "The Businessman in a Laboristic Economy," *Fortune*, XL (September, 1949), 112.

Broadly speaking, the emergence of the corporation as the dominant institution of modern industrial society has raised doubts about the classic economic doctrine of free enterprise, and has created a feeling of uneasiness and insecurity in some businessmen. The concentration of productive facilities among a few large manufacturing corporations in a single industry has radically reduced the control which the individual has over economic activity. The farmer and the small businessman have little or no control over the market prices of the goods which they buy and sell. On the other hand, the control of prices and production in many industries has been concentrated in the hands of a relatively small number of giant corporations. It is difficult to avoid the conclusion that, for better or worse, enormous power has been concentrated in private hands in the large corporations.

In general businessmen have taken two positions with respect to the structure of the American economy. The small businessman tends to accept the desirability of an economy of small-scale businesses operating in a truly competitive manner. He wants to return to a small business economy by having the government enforce the antitrust laws vigorously. The big businessman generally admits that corporations do exercise great power, but he urges, first, that the businessman be regarded as a trustee acting on behalf of society, and, second, that the businessman be relied upon to exercise his trusteeship in the public interest without governmental attempts to hold him accountable.

government aids business by providing a favorable economic environment

The most significant point about the relations of government and business in the United States is that government promotes business by providing favorable conditions for business organization and operation which do not exist naturally. Government has developed institutions which provide a stable legal order within which business operates: the legal establishment and protection of private property, provision of legal forms of business enterprise and rules for bankruptcy, the grant of patent rights, and the maintenance of a monetary system.

governmental protection of private property and the obligations of contract

In the promotion of business enterprise, the most fundamental government-supported institution is the right to own and dispose of private property. The protection of private property rights forms the basis of a private enterprise system. The primary way in which government protects private property is the enforcement of contracts entered into by individuals and business enterprises with respect to private property. Through the legal establishment of the rights of property and their enforcement through the law of contracts, private economic relationships become more certain, more definite, and more secure. An economy in which the basic decisions are made by private individuals and firms can exist only to the extent that individuals and firms are given rights over the use of their property.

Justice Benjamin N. Cardozo has said that "ownership . . . is only a bundle of rights and privileges invested with a single name." [3] The bundle of rights which government accords private property involves several things. First of all, the owner has the power to prevent others from using his property and the power to use the property as he desires. Reciprocally, others are obliged to respect the rights of ownership in property. The government is inextricably involved in the private property system, for property rights cannot exist without the enforcement of such rights by government.

Business cannot exist in a private enterprise system unless contracts and property rights are enforceable. Almost all business transactions in such a system are based on contracts concerning the use and disposition of private property. The individual who buys food at the corner grocery store, the businessman who deposits money in the bank, the doctor who treats a patient, the employer who hires workers—all enter into contracts. Although governmental action to protect private property rights is essentially promotional in character, it also carries with it a degree of control or regulation as distinguished from promotion of business enterprise. For the power to protect property and enforce contracts carries with it, at least potentially, the power to establish limits to private contracts. In recent years, government has been called upon to limit the rights of employers, for example, to contract freely with labor with respect to wages, hours, and working conditions. Conflicts of policy today over property rights concern the desirability or undesirability of further governmental limitations on the use of private property and freedom of contract.

governmental provision of legal forms of business enterprise

One of the most obvious and most important ways in which government promotes business enterprise is the establishment by law of organizational forms for business enterprise. The three major forms legally established by government include the individual proprietorship, the partnership, and the corporation. These forms have distinctive characteristics and different rights, obligations, and privileges.

The individual proprietorship is based on the personal right to engage in business. In operating an individual enterprise, the proprietor is personally liable for the debts and obligations incurred in the course of the business. He is

---

[3] *Steward Machine Co.* v. *Davis,* 301 U.S. 548, 581 (1937).

responsible for debts not merely to the extent of his investment but to the full extent of his personal financial resources. The proprietor may also employ other individuals to serve as his agents subject to a complex set of legal restrictions. Upon the death of the proprietor, the business is terminated.

The partnership permits two or more individuals to combine their resources to carry on a business enterprise. In the partnership, each partner is fully liable for the debts and obligations of the enterprise. Like the individual proprietorship, the partnership establishes no limitation of personal liability and is dissolved upon the death of a partner.

The third organizational form for business enterprise is the corporation. It was developed largely in response to the need for a form of enterprise adapted to large-scale production made possible by machine technology and the development of a national transportation system and national markets. Large-scale production required large investments, a technical management to operate the enterprise, and, because of the large investments required, a life for the enterprise that would be separate and apart from the life of individual stockholders or managers. Gradually laws of business organization were modified by government during the nineteenth century to encourage the adoption of the corporation as a means of organizing productive activity.

advantages of the corporation over individual proprietorships and partnerships

Three characteristics distinguish the corporation from other forms of business enterprise: limited liability of investors, extension of the life of the corporation as an entity for a more or less indefinite period, and greater ease of separation of management from ownership. These characteristics give to the corporation marked advantages over the individual proprietorship and the partnership. Since shareholders as owners of corporations are not liable personally for the debts of the corporation, it is easier for the corporation to raise the relatively large sums required to finance corporate enterprise. Shareholders have the government-granted privilege of limiting their personal liability merely to the extent of their actual investment rather than to the full extent of their financial resources.

By giving the corporation the form of an artificial entity with indefinite life, government relieves the corporation of the risk of dissolution brought on by the death of an investor or a manager. Moreover, the corporation, under the law, may select managers and technical staff more freely without regard to their financial holdings in the enterprise. Since the owners enjoy the privilege of limited liability, the corporation finds it easier to delegate managerial responsibilities to an employed staff of managers.

The widespread use of the corporation, particularly in mining, manufacturing, and public utilities, testifies to the importance of limited liability, indefinite life, and the ease of separation of management from ownership. By providing laws of incorporation granting such privileges, government has promoted the development of business corporations and has made possible the emergence of the corporation as the dominant economic institution of modern industrial society.

evolution of governmental policy of incorporation

In the American political system, the states rather than the federal government exercise the responsibility of granting charters of incorporation to business enterprises. There is no general federal law of incorporation. State legislatures were originally averse to granting charters. They usually restricted such grants to companies engaged in constructing "internal improvements" such as canals, roads, and bridges. A charter was considered originally as a special privilege to be conferred only upon showing that a public purpose would thereby be fulfilled. With some exceptions, the privileges of incorporation were rather rigidly restricted, and incorporation was regarded by the state legislatures as a way of regulating industrial activity.[4]

After 1840, the legislative practice of granting charters by special legislative acts was gradually replaced by general statutes on business incorporation. States attempted to attract corporate enterprises by offering competing advantages and privileges of incorporation, with the result that the charter ceased to be an instrument for the public regulation of industry. However, as the traffic in charters became more widespread and as states minimized the requirements for obtaining charters, the demand for re-establishing some restriction on corporations increased. In particular the federal government has imposed some restrictions on those corporations which operate in interstate commerce. For example, the Securities and Exchange Commission has restricted the use of proxies in voting at stockholders' meetings and the manner in which proxies are solicited. The commission has also restricted the trading by directors and officers in the securities of their own corporation.

Federal incorporation of companies in interstate commerce was recommended as early as 1904 by James R. Garfield, then Federal Commissioner of Corporations, and in 1910 by President Taft and more recently by Senator Joseph C. O'Mahoney and the Temporary National Economic Committee. It is argued that federal incorporation would end state competition for charters and would provide uniform and more vigorous rules of incorporation as well as more effective administration.

The history of governmental policies of incorporation indicates the difficulty of drawing a clear-cut distinction between governmental promotion and governmental regulation of business enterprise. Although the grant of corporate char-

---

[4] For a brief statement of the development of the law of incorporation, see Justice Louis Brandeis's dissenting opinion in *Liggett Co.* v. *Lee* (*The Florida Chain Store Tax* Case), 288 U.S. 517 (1933).

ters has been significant primarily as a device for promoting business, it was developed originally as a method of regulating industry. Conceivably it could be used again as a means of imposing controls and restrictions on corporate business.

governmental rules for bankruptcy

In addition to promoting business by providing conditions favorable to business organization and operation, government aids business by providing an easy way out when business enterprises fail. By establishing rules of bankruptcy and business reorganization, government supplies a procedure for winding up the affairs of a financially insolvent business. Under the rules of bankruptcy a businessman can discontinue his business, make financial settlements with his creditors, and start another business without carrying over the financial obligations of the business which has failed.

Before the adoption of the federal Constitution, each state fixed its own rules of bankruptcy. Partly because of the great variety of bankruptcy provisions in the states and the uncertainty of economic conditions in the period following the Revolutionary War, creditors and property owners turned to the Constitutional Convention for the protection of property. Thus Article One, section eight, of the Constitution authorized Congress "to establish uniform laws on the subject of bankruptcies throughout the United States."

Bankruptcy proceedings under federal law are carried on in the federal district courts. They may be instituted by a debtor who voluntarily wishes to enter into bankruptcy, or by key creditors, who are permitted under certain circumstances to force a debtor into bankruptcy. In the case of involuntary proceedings, the courts appoint referees in bankruptcy who handle the assets and business of the debtors. Eventually the assets of the insolvent person or business are sold, the creditors receive proportionate shares of the proceeds, and the bankrupt person or firm receives a discharge which legally wipes out his debts. When it is desirable to maintain a bankrupt business as a going concern, the courts may in certain circumstances order a receivership to reorganize the business and to put it on a more solvent financial footing. During periods of deep economic depression, bankruptcy laws have been subjected to attack. For example, during the 1930's, the depression dramatically threatened the solvency of many businesses, and debtors demanded amendment of the bankruptcy law to permit them to remain in business. Several states enacted debt moratory laws relating to farm mortgages. Federal legislation in 1933 and 1934 permitted farmers to stave off insolvency and provided for the reorganization of insolvent railroads. The Reconstruction Finance Corporation made extensive loans to banks, railroads, and industries to help avoid bankruptcy. The Chandler Act of 1938 generally revised federal bankruptcy law and authorized the Securities and Exchange Commission to make its investigating facilities and technical expertness available to the federal courts and to advise the courts in matters involving corporate reorganization.

The Chandler Act marks a new development in bankruptcy law. Before 1938, bankruptcy proceedings were regarded as private controversies between debtors and creditors in which the public interest was preserved by establishing standard bankruptcy proceedings and a forum for the settlement of controversies. The Chandler Act recognizes that the public interest in business enterprise extends also to the preservation, through corporate reorganization, of businesses that have a social usefulness even though they appear to be failing from the point of view of the standards of private enterprise. Perhaps the best illustration of a business whose continuance is vital to the public welfare is the railroad. Government has attempted to maintain the railroad as the major unit in the national system of transportation in the face of serious financial problems in the industry. Government aid in the form of provisions for corporate reorganization and loans can be considered as an alternative to government ownership and operation of essential enterprises.

granting patent-rights

Another important governmental tool for the promotion of business is the grant of patent rights. The Constitution in Article One, section eight, authorized Congress: "To promote the progress of science and useful arts, by securing for limited times to authors and inventors the exclusive right to their respective writings and discoveries." The grant of a patent or a copyright confers a temporary monopoly in the use of an invention or a piece of writing. A patent may represent very substantial property values and affect profoundly manufacturing processes and the distribution of income. Patents must be justified on the ground that they stimulate inventions which contribute to the general welfare of society.

The national patent system, which Congress established in 1790, was intended to stimulate invention by rewarding its discovery with a monopoly of its use for a limited period. Since 1790 patent policy has liberalized the issuance of patents and has enlarged the patent protection afforded business enterprise. In 1802 the Patent Office was created as a distinct bureau in the Department of State. After several organizational changes, the Patent Office was placed in 1925 in the Department of Commerce.

The Patent Office investigates all new applications for patents. The application must present patentable subject matter.[4a] For example, it must deal with an art, a manufacture, a machine, an ornamental design, or a botanical plant.

[4a] In *The Great Atlantic and Pacific Tea Company* v. *Supermarket Equipment Corporation,* decided December 4, 1950, the Supreme Court suggested that mere gadgets are not patentable. This decision may mark a change toward a more restrictive grant of patent rights.

Almost any new or novel tangible thing is patentable. In addition the application must include a detailed specification of the invention and must show that the invention is useful and will work. Decisions of the Patent Office may be appealed first to the Board of Appeals in the Patent Office and then to the Court of Customs and Patent Appeals or to a federal district court. A few patent cases are also appealed to the Supreme Court.

A number of patent problems remain unsolved today:

1. Under the statute, a patent is granted for seventeen years, but some protection is afforded as soon as an application is filed. Thus the seventeen-year period may in effect be extended by the period during which the patent application is pending. Usually the cases of long pendency involve the more important inventions. Businessmen have complained that patent pendency may withhold an improved device or process from general use for more than seventeen years and may produce uncertainties and obstructions in business enterprise.

2. The large volume of patent applications raises questions about the merit of granting patent monopolies to so many inventions. Some observers believe that the stimulation of invention through the patent system has been offset by the issuance of unwarranted patents and that the standards of patentability should be made more stringent.

3. There are instances in which patents have been purchased in order to suppress their utilization in manufacturing. Corporations have occasionally tried to "fence in" the use of patent rights. For example, by corporate ownership of necessary secondary patents, they may try to stop the owner of a fundamental patent from using his patent to the fullest extent. Or companies may, through research, improve their products and take out new patents on the improved products in order to extend the period of patent monopoly.

4. Perhaps the most serious abuse of the patent grant grows out of schemes of corporations to pool or interchange patents. Such agreements have been important factors in increasing the concentration of control in industry and the growth of industrial monopolies.

governmental provision of a monetary system

The American economic system is organized primarily in terms of the exchange of goods and services. Buying and selling of goods and services are made possible in modern industrial society by a number of governmental or government-regulated institutions. These include money, which serves as a medium of exchange, and the deposit banking system. By providing and regulating money and by regulating private banking institutions, the government helps to supply or to control the tools necessary to carry on economic activities.

The most elementary task of government in the monetary field is the supplying of money. Government establishes either gold or silver coins as standards of value and guarantees their uniform metallic content and weight. The federal Constitution, in Article One, sections eight and ten, gives to Congress the exclusive authority to coin money, to regulate its value, and to punish counterfeiting. Gradually the monetary powers of the federal government have been expanded through judicial interpretation to make possible a wide variety of monetary functions. For example, Congress may charter a bank;[5] make paper bills, so-called "greenbacks" not backed by gold or silver, legal tender in the payment of debts;[6] and cheapen the value of the dollar so that it buys more.[7]

cheap vs. dear money

Governments have on a great many occasions manipulated the value of money for specific purposes. During the three decades following the Civil War, one of the major political controversies centered around conflicting arguments of "cheap" vs. "dear" money. In a period of declining farm prices but increasing industrial prices, farmers organized into political action groups and political parties to campaign for printing more paper money and for cheapening the value of the dollar. Farmers and debtor classes generally hoped that a cheap dollar would ease the burden of private debt and would help to boost prices. It was also hoped that cheaper dollars would stimulate other countries to purchase more surplus American goods.

On the other hand, prosperous businessmen and creditors were anxious to protect their property values by maintaining the stability of money. Advocates of stable or dear money favored the first and second Banks of the United States, urged the retirement of greenbacks after the Civil War, successfully opposed the restoration of the silver standard toward the end of the nineteenth century, and decisively defeated the presidential candidacy of William Jennings Bryan. Bryan had campaigned on a platform to restore silver coinage at the rate of sixteen ounces of silver to one ounce of gold at a time when sixteen ounces of silver were worth less than one ounce of gold. Silver coinage at the 16:1 ratio would have meant a reduction in the value of the dollar and probably an increase in prices. Bryan's defeat was a victory for the advocates of sound or dear money, and not until the depression of the thirties were effective demands again made for manipulating currency values to relieve debt burdens or to increase prices.

The important point about the controversy between cheap and dear money in American economic development is that the government has power to ma-

---

[5] *McCulloch* v. *Maryland*, 4 Wheaton 316 (1819).

[6] *Hepburn* v. *Griswold*, 8 Wallace 603 (1870); *Knox* v. *Lee*, 12 Wallace 457 (1871); *Juilliard* v. *Greenman*, 110 U.S. 421 (1884).

[7] *Norman* v. *Baltimore and Ohio Railroad Co.*, 294 U.S. 240 (1935); *Perry* v. *United States*, 294 U.S. 330 (1935).

nipulate money values either in the direction of relieving debtors or in the direction of aiding creditor groups by maintaining monetary stability. Creditor and debtor groups have clashed politically to gain control of monetary policy. The political struggles over monetary policy have been vigorous and hard-fought because the stakes have been high.

From 1900 to 1933 the currency system was based on gold, which meant that any lawful money could be redeemed in gold, that individuals could freely trade in gold, and that the government and the banks kept gold reserves to back up all other money. The economic collapse of 1929 caused many people to withdraw their bank deposits in gold. As bank reserves declined, banking stability was further endangered, and on June 5, 1933, Congress, by joint resolution, abrogated the gold standard. The gold content of the dollar was reduced to about 59 per cent of what it had been, and the government bought all gold produced in the United States, or imported into it, at $35 an ounce. The coinage of gold ceased, and all gold bullion was stored.

Today the Bureau of the Mint in the Department of the Treasury directs the coinage of money and storing the nation's gold and silver stocks. The Bureau of the Public Debt and the Bureau of Engraving and Printing, also in the Department of the Treasury, print and supervise the issuance of paper money.

governmental control of banking

The deposit banking system is a major element in the American monetary system. In the nineteenth century, conflicts between advocates of cheap vs. dear money illustrate the attempts of various interests to use governmental power to protect or to improve their economic positions. During the present century, monetary conflicts have been more concerned with banking policy as a technique for controlling the availability of bank credit for private investment.

Banks and other financial institutions hold a strategic position in the nation's economy. They make loans to business enterprises, purchase securities of industrial corporations, and hold a very large proportion of all outstanding obligations of federal, state, and local governments. In serving as a source of credit, banks act as trustees for depositors who deposit their savings. Banks make it possible to pool the savings of individuals and to make those savings available to business enterprises and to other individuals in the form of loans and credit. The interest rate established on bank loans can be manipulated up or down to encourage or discourage private investment.

Because of the broad public interest in the stability and safety of private banking operations, government has regulated banking practices. Banking is peculiarly a business affected with the public interest, and government has been inevitably concerned with the soundness of banks and their practices. States have attempted to control banks organized under state law by supervising their original organization, by establishing regulations relating to the maintenance of reserves and the investment of assets, and by examining periodically their financial condition. The federal government exercises some control over banks through the Comptroller of the Currency, the Federal Reserve Board, and the Federal Deposit Insurance Corporation.

Because of the deep public interest in banking activities, government controls the organization and the number of banks which operate in a community; it also passes on the character and ability of persons who want to establish banks. In the states, banking departments generally control the chartering of new state banks, whereas the Comptroller of the Currency in the Department of the Treasury controls the chartering of national banks organized under federal law. The Comptroller of the Currency examines national banks at least twice each year and requires regular reports on their financial condition.

operation of the Federal Reserve System

When the Federal Reserve System was established in 1913, the federal government for the first time was able to control the volume of bank credit available for private investment and the terms on which it was available. The system consists of a board of governors, twelve federal reserve banks, and member banks. All national banks must have membership in the system, and state banks may join voluntarily. The Federal Reserve banks are not commercial banks serving the public. The principal function of the system is to maintain monetary and credit conditions which are favorable to sound business activity. Its activities influence financial stability through controls exerted over the credit policies of banks.

insurance of bank deposits

Bank failures have been common in American economic development and the social cost of these failures in terms of property loss and human suffering has been high. In order to insure individuals against the loss of deposits through bank failures, the Federal Deposit Insurance Corporation was established in 1933. All member banks of the Federal Reserve System are automatically insured, and nonmember banks may apply for insurance. Since 1950, individual deposits in insured banks are protected in full against loss up to $10,000. The insurance scheme is financed by annual assessments on the deposit of insured banks. Although state and federal interest in banks has taken the form of regulations concerning their organization and operation, the principal effect of governmental control has been to promote the stability of the banking system and, consequently, the stability of the economy in general. By developing sound financial practices in banks, both federal and state governments have helped to create conditions favorable to business enterprise.

current issues in banking policy

Since banks are strategic institutions in a private enterprise economy, several issues with respect to banking policy arise. First, should the number of banks be increased or decreased? A weeding out of smaller banks might provide greater financial stability. However, it might also concentrate economic power dangerously in a few hands. Second, to what extent should large banks be permitted to maintain branches? Does branch banking lead to monopoly in banking which deprives local areas of control over their own economic development? Third, should all banks be subject to federal regulation or should the dual system of national and state banks be maintained? Fourth, do governmental controls unduly restrict the managerial freedom and initiative in private banks? And fifth, can our present network of governmental controls over banking be effective in preventing economic depressions or in mitigating their worst effects?

direct governmental aids to business

The most characteristic feature in the relation between government and business during the nineteenth century was the governmental policy of aiding business directly. Despite the growth of governmental regulation of business since 1887, the government has continued to promote the interest of the business community by protecting industry and encouraging international trade through tariffs, by granting subsidies and other forms of direct financial assistance to business enterprises, and by providing important services to business.

tariff policy

The federal government protects American industry from foreign competition through tariffs on imports. Protective tariffs have constituted one of the most sought-after forms of government aid. Advocates of tariffs have justified them as devices for protecting infant industries, for maintaining the standard of living of American workers, and for promoting economic self-sufficiency and national defense.

A protective tariff is a tax on imported goods which is sufficiently high to prevent goods manufactured in foreign countries at lower prices from competing with products manufactured in the United States. Since protective tariffs offer such direct aid to protected industries, the competition of industries for protective tariffs has been great. American political history is filled with tales of the logrolling efforts of specific industries to gain economic advantage by securing protective tariffs. In the past, American tariff policy has had two conflicting purposes: to raise revenue for government operations, and to protect American business. Since the Civil War the revenue-producing tariff has gradually given way to the protective tariff. Article One, section eight of the Constitution clearly gives Congress the right to levy duties for revenue purposes. The constitutionality of protective tariffs, although seriously questioned during the nullification controversy in Jackson's administration, was not settled until 1928, when the Supreme Court upheld the power of Congress to enact protective tariffs. In the course of its decision, the Court said: "The fact that Congress declares that one of its motives in fixing the rates of duty is so to fix them that they shall encourage the industries of this country in competition with producers in other countries in the sale of goods in this country, cannot invalidate a revenue act so framed." [8]

Modern tariff administration begins in 1916 with the creation of the United States Tariff Commission. In general, the commission investigates the administration of tariff laws and tariff relations with foreign countries and prepares surveys of industries. It acquires basic factual information on the import trade and investigates charges of unfair acts in importing articles into the United States. It conducts special investigations at the request of the President and Congress.

In recent years tariff reform has been considered an important factor in achieving more harmonious international relations. As the United States exported more goods to foreign countries than it imported, there have been increasing demands that it reduce tariff barriers in order to make possible more imports from foreign countries. Since 1934 the principal feature of American tariff policy has been the reciprocal trade agreement. The Trade Agreements Act of 1934 authorized the President to negotiate trade agreements with foreign countries in which the United States could reduce existing import duties up to 50 per cent in exchange for corresponding reductions on duties paid by American exporters to foreign countries. Under the 1934 act, the chief duty of the Tariff Commission is to assist the State Department and the President in negotiating reciprocal trade agreements. Since the end of World War II additional efforts have been made to rehabilitate the economies of the western European democracies by encouraging foreign trade. In the long run, it is argued, the United States will have to buy more foreign goods in order to maintain the present level of exports. It is argued also that free trade among nations, unhampered by tariff walls, will lead to international understanding and peace.

governmental subsidies

American government has a long tradition of aiding business through direct money subsidies or grants to specific industries. The American merchant marine has benefited from a variety of governmental aids, including preferential tax treatment and subsidies for carrying mail. Dissatisfaction with the opera-

---

[8] *J. W. Hampton, Jr., and Co.* v. *United States,* 276 U.S. 394, 413 (1928).

tion of the mail subsidy program led to its abandonment in 1936 in favor of direct subsidies to shippers for the construction and operation of ships. The Merchant Marine Act of 1936 created the United States Maritime Commission, and declared the policy of the United States to foster the development and encourage the maintenance of an efficient merchant fleet capable of serving as a naval and military auxiliary in time of war or national emergency. Today the Commerce Department may refray the cost of construction of ships and then sell the ships to private operators engaged in interstate commerce at a price equal to the cost of constructing the ships in a foreign shipyard. A similar subsidy is designed to permit American ships to compete with foreign ships engaged in foreign commerce.

The railroads have been one of the most favored beneficiaries of government aid. Before 1850, railway lobbies concentrated their efforts on obtaining state and local rather than federal aid. In several states, the railroads successfully captured control of state legislatures. Between 1850 and 1871, federal land grants to railways became common, and in the 1860's, over 100 million acres of public lands were given to railroads. The abuses and scandals involved in railroad land grants led the House of Representatives in 1870 to resolve that "the policy of granting subsidies in public lands to railroad and other corporations ought to be discontinued." In 1940 it was estimated that federal and state land grants to railroads totaled 183 million acres.[9]

Governmental aid has been extended to other forms of transportation. The states and the federal government actively promoted canal building in the period before the Civil War, and since 1910 millions of dollars in public funds have been spent for river and harbor improvements and for the construction of shipping terminals and lighthouses. Through the construction of roads and highways, government has aided the motor carrier industry. Direct aid has been extended to the air transport industry since 1926 through mail contracts to air carriers. In addition Congress has authorized a federal grant-in-aid, matched by local funds, for the construction of additional airport facilities, and has provided for the operation of the Federal Airways System, consisting of beam lights, radio communications, weather-reporting services, control stations, and other devices designed to facilitate safe flying.

Another government aid is the postal subsidy to the publishing business. By granting below-cost postal rates for mailing newspapers and periodicals, the federal government gives publishers a tremendous economic advantage. The Postmaster General recently estimated the postal subsidy at $200 million annually.

Governmental subsidy programs have been rationalized on the ground that the people generally benefit in the long run through the maintenance of healthy conditions in essential industries. For example, aids to the merchant marine and

---

[9] Federal Coordinator of Transportation, *Public Aids to Transportation* (Washington: Government Printing Office, 1940), I, 13.

civil aviation industries are based largely on the need to maintain adequate transport facilities for purposes for national defense. Since good transportation is vital to the national economy, business activity and the public in general have benefited from improved transportation facilities developed with direct governmental aid.

governmental services to business

In his *Report on Manufactures*, Alexander Hamilton strongly recommended the establishment of a board in the federal government to promote agriculture, manufactures, and commerce. And in 1825, a resolution was introduced in the House to create a Home Department to promote the interest of agriculture, commerce, and manufactures. Between 1880 and 1900 frequent proposals were submitted to Congress for the creation of a department of commerce. A Department of Commerce and Labor was eventually established in 1903, and the transfer of labor functions to a Department of Labor in 1913 marked the beginning of the modern development of the Department of Commerce as an agency for the fostering, promoting, and developing of foreign and domestic commerce and manufacturing.

Through the Department of Commerce the federal government encourages business activity by providing several types of valuable services:

1. It furnishes technical, scientific, and engineering information to businessmen in general and makes a special effort to help small businessmen operate their enterprises successfully.

2. It prepares statistical reports on current activity in the retail, wholesale, and service trades and on the output and inventories of many manufactured commodities.

3. It makes studies of the level of economic activity in the nation and analyzes current business developments. Such studies help businessmen to solve day to day problems and to plan future business operations.

4. Through the National Bureau of Standards, it carries on research programs on safety problems in manufacturing and construction and develops national codes and specifications that are universally used as a basis for the intelligent purchase of commodities.

Through the activities of the Department of Commerce, business enterprises of all types can receive assistance in handling their individual problems and can study reports on the nation's economic activity in order to plan their own operations more intelligently.

government credit facilities for business

Acting primarily through the Reconstruction Finance Corporation, the federal government has served as moneylender to American business enterprise. Congress has authorized the RFC to aid in financing agriculture, commerce, and industry, to encourage small business, and to assist in promoting maximum employment and production. Within these broad policy limits, the RFC may purchase the obligations of, or make loans to, any business enterprise or financial institution operating under state or federal law, or to any public agency or government. In the past over 90 per cent of all RFC loans have been made to business enterprises. Loans are not made unless the applicant can show that financial assistance is not obtainable from private lending sources on reasonable terms. The RFC cannot compete with private sources of credit.

A recent addition to the lending activities of the RFC is the participation in the making of loans not exceeding $100,000 to small business enterprises. The extension of credit facilities to relatively smaller businesses was largely a logical development from the work of the Smaller War Plants Corporation established by Congress in 1942 to secure the more productive participation of small contractors in the war production program.

Many businessmen have regarded governmental promotion of business enterprise as a mixed blessing. For one thing, governmental programs of assistance and promotion have often been accompanied by regulation of business enterprises. Furthermore, governmental promotion of business enterprise has stimulated demands for governmental programs to assist other interest groups in the economy, including farmers and workers.

bibliographic note

The historical development of public policies for the promotion of business is presented clearly in Merle Fainsod and Lincoln Gordon, *Government and the American Economy* (New York: W. W. Norton & Company, rev. ed. 1948). An important textbook which stresses the role of government in establishing a framework for economic activity is Leverett Lyons, Myron Watkins, and Victor Abramson, *Government and Economic Life* (Washington: The Brookings Institution, 2 vols., 1939). The functions of government corporations in promoting economic enterprise are analyzed by Marshall E. Dimock in "Government Corporations: A Focus of Policy and Administration," *American Political Science Review*, XLIII, Nos. 5 and 6 (October, December, 1949), 899–921, 1145–1164. The role of pressure groups in stimulating government promotion of business is outlined in Donald C. Blaisdell, *Economic Power and Political Pressures* (Temporary National Economic Committee, *Monograph* No. 26; Washington: Government Printing Office, 1941) and in E. Pendleton Herring, *Group Representation before Congress* (Baltimore: The Johns Hopkins Press, 1929).

For case illustrations of the process of government promotion of business, see E. E. Schattschneider, *Politics, Pressures, and the Tariff* (New York: Prentice-Hall, Inc., 1935); Paul M. Zeis, *American Shipping Policy* (Princeton: Princeton University Press, 1938); and Federal Coordinator of Transportation, *Public Aids to Transportation* (Washington: Government Printing Office, 4 vols. 1938–1940).

government regulation of business

EGULATION of business by government is based essentially on the same case made for governmental promotion of business. Regulation is regarded as desirable or necessary in order to promote the larger interests of the community. Regulation in the public interest takes two principal forms in the United States, depending on the economic character of business enterprise. If an enterprise is regarded as an ordinary enterprise subject to forces of competition, regulation takes the form of maintaining competitive conditions in order to prevent the development of monopoly and the concentration of economic power which accompanies monopoly. On the other hand, if the enterprise is regarded as a legal or natural monopoly or as an industry in which competition produces results harmful to the public interest, regulation of prices and services is substituted for competition as the appropriate force for stimulating efficient operation in the public interest.

antitrust policy

American tradition has placed a high value on individual enterprise and initiative in business. Confidence in an economy of small-scale businesses which compete rigorously with one another rests on several grounds. Politically, individual enterprise was identified with democratic ideas of equality of economic opportunity and diffusion of economic power widely among the people. Growth of monopoly in industry was said to undermine the democratic concept of limited power. In economic terms, individual enterprise rested on the belief that competition among small enterprises in the buying and selling of goods in the market place would foster efficient operation and bring about reductions in the prices paid by the consumer. In broad social terms, individual enterprise was regarded as a source of strength in the community and the nation because it developed self-reliance and independence.

The problem of antimonopoly policy is to destroy monopolies in ordinary retail, wholesale, and service trades and in manufacturing, mining, construction, and financial enterprises and to maintain truly competitive conditions in business enterprise generally. The destruction of monopolies and the maintenance of competition became public problems because of the rapid development of large-scale industries, especially after the Civil War. As business corporations became larger and wealthier and less competitive, small businessmen and farmers organized politically to obtain governmental protection against monopolistic practices and the loss of initiative and independence in business enterprise. The problem has become more intense as large corporations grew in size, bought up smaller businesses, and acquired greater power to affect economic conditions and to achieve political control of government.

In order to come to grips with monopoly control in business, Americans have relied on governmental action, first, to check restraints of trade, and, second, to prohibit unfair monopolistic practices.

the Sherman Act

The Sherman Act was passed by Congress in 1890 with the purpose of keeping American business competitive and free. It outlawed contracts and combinations of businesses in restraint of trade. It was passed after attempts by states to limit the spread of monopoly had failed because of the inability to control business activities extending across state boundaries.

The Sherman Act was regarded as a basic charter of freedom for American business. However, the statute itself was vague, and difficulties in administration and enforcement developed immediately. Although the statute outlawed every contract, combination, or conspiracy in restraint of trade, it established no standards for identifying monopolistic practices in restraint of trade. Consequently, the courts inherited the task of defining monopolistic practices. The legal history of the Sherman Act provides sufficient evidence that the courts have generally been reluctant to include in the definition of prohibited practices such collusive behavior as outright mergers of companies.

Congress apparently believed that the Sherman Act would be self-enforcing, for it provided meager funds for the enforcement of the act. For many years the Antitrust Division in the Department of Justice attempted to enforce the act with only a handful of lawyers and small appropriations. Perhaps the chief obstacle to successful enforcement of the antimonopoly policy of the act was the difficulty of reversing the increasing trend toward concentration of control in a small number of very large corporations.

Modern devices of monopoly have become more subtle and harder to detect. Outright purchase of firms and mergers have been replaced by such schemes as agreements among corporations to establish identical prices or to follow the leadership of a particular manufacturer in setting prices. Such collusion is hard to prove since price agreements or agreements to divide markets are not arrived at openly.

the operations of the Antitrust Division

The Antitrust Division of the Department of Justice depends largely on complaints from small businessmen for information about alleged monopolistic practices. Complaints are screened and the most serious ones are investigated further by the Federal Bureau of Investigation. Cases are selected for legal suit depending on the degree of proof of violation of the Sherman Act and the importance of the case to the whole economy. The trial of a case is very costly and time consuming, and proof of violation is difficult to obtain.

If a violation is flagrant and willful, a criminal prosecution may be instituted with the object of punishing the violator with a fine or a prison sentence or both. In cases of less flagrant and willful violations, the Antitrust Division may institute a civil suit to seek an injunction in a federal court to enjoin the corporation and its officers from engaging in the prohibited practices. In uncontested civil cases, the corporation charged with violation may negotiate with the division for a consent decree to settle the case out of court. Both injunctions and consent decrees may require specific future action on the part of the offending corporation to eliminate the unlawful practices and to restore conduct of a lawful nature.

A civil suit is also instituted in order to break up and dissolve a monopolistic company. Dissolutions have been rare. They have been accomplished only when concentration has been obviously complete, as in the case of the Standard Oil Company in 1911.

Penalties in criminal and civil proceedings have been rather light. No businessmen have ever been sent to prison for violating the Sherman Act. The average fine in criminal cases has been approximately $2,300. Larger sums have actually been collected in cases settled out of court. The sentences imposed on violators may be so lenient that they encourage rather than deter violations. After minor fines were recently assessed against one of the largest American corporations, an official of the Justice Department complained:

> The present feeling, which seems to prevail in the business community, is that you need not be alarmed if you are caught in a violation of the antitrust laws because in so far as past transactions are concerned, you can pay a fine which is merely a license fee and which may be charged off as the cost of doing illegal business.

> Frequently the amount which is to be gained by such law violations is very large when compared with the amount which would be lost by fines if the violator is caught.

If this feeling of indifference to the penal provisions of the Sherman Act is allowed to prevail in the business world, there seems little possibility of using criminal sanctions of the anti-trust law as effectively as the Congress intended.[1]

The Sherman Act has been enforced rather fitfully. Before 1914 it was applied primarily against labor unions rather than against monopolistic businesses. After several adverse court decisions in the 1920's, industry enjoyed a virtual moratorium from antitrust suits. The traditional antimonopoly policy was abandoned from 1933 to 1935 during the life of the National Industrial Recovery Act but was revived again in 1938 with the appointment of Thurman Arnold to head the Antitrust Division. With the exception of the World War II interim, the period since 1938 has been marked by increasingly vigorous prosecution of companies engaging in monopolistic practices. More cases were instituted in the 1940's than in the entire previous fifty-year history of the Sherman Act. For example, in the twelve months ending on June 30, 1949, 57 cases were instituted and 42 cases were successfully completed by the Antitrust Division, and on November 1, 1949, 126 cases were pending in the courts.

results of antitrust policy

Antitrust policy has not curbed the trend toward bigness in industry and has not achieved marked success in outlawing monopolistic practices. In addition to ambiguities in the meaning of the statute and weaknesses in enforcement, two basic difficulties have contributed to the relative failure of antitrust policy. First, the legal concept of what constitutes a monopoly has lagged far behind the economic development of monopolies. Second, there is some doubt whether Americans are prepared to pay the cost of breaking up monopolies. Vigorous enforcement of the Sherman Act would probably require a frontal assault on the whole structure of modern corporate enterprise. Giant corporations would have to be replaced by smaller competitive enterprises. In the face of general unwillingness or inability to undertake such a planned assault on corporate enterprise, the faith of many Americans in antitrust laws has become rather sentimental and unreal.

Many suggestions have been made to strengthen the Sherman Act. These include proposals to increase appropriations for enforcement purposes, to utilize the prison sentence to achieve greater compliance, to plug various loopholes in the statutes, and to define more precisely by statute monopolistic practices. Senator Joseph C. O'Mahoney has proposed compulsory federal charters for corporations doing a nation-wide business. Charters would be revoked to control monopolistic practices.

In the long run the major problem of antitrust policy is the clarification of

---

[1] New York *Herald Tribune*, November 13, 1948.

public opinion. Unless American citizens develop stronger support for an antitrust policy, we are destined to continue to apply antitrust laws to corporations
without substantially changing the basic structure of modern enterprise. Can we
continue to depend on traditional enforcement devices to bring about truly competitive conditions? Will the failure to check the trend toward concentration of
control lead to demands for more effective governmental regulation and even
outright government ownership and operation of basic manufacturing industries?

the regulation of trade practices

In addition to checking restraints of trade and monopolistic practices under the
Sherman Act, the federal government has attempted to maintain competition in
ordinary business activities by regulating trade practices. The Clayton Act and
the Federal Trade Commission Act supplement the Sherman Act in several ways.
Although the Sherman Act is concerned mostly with the prohibition of
monopoly and restraint of trade, the supplementary statutes are designed to prevent certain specific practices on the ground that they are unfair or destroy competition. The Sherman Act would break up combinations in restraint of trade;
the Clayton and Federal Trade Commission Acts would prevent practices leading to restraint of trade from arising. The Clayton Act condemned certain practices as unlawful and in restraint of trade; the Federal Trade Commission Act
created the Federal Trade Commission to enforce both the Clayton and the
Federal Trade Commission Acts and to develop, through judicial enforcement,
a law of unfair competition in which specific practices deemed to be unfair would
be outlawed.

The Federal Trade Commission, as established in 1914, is an independent
regulatory commission of five members appointed by the President with the consent of the Senate. It tries to prevent certain deceptive practices, price discriminations, interlocking directorates, exclusive dealing arrangements, and corporate stock acquisitions.

the operation of the Federal Trade Commission

Cases of unfair competition arise primarily from complaints from businessmen.
The FTC makes its own investigations of complaints. When the evidence of violation is reasonably conclusive or when an offending company desires to avoid
formal hearings before the commission on the charges, the company may agree
to a stipulation. Under a stipulation, the offending company agrees to discontinue the unfair practices. If the case is not settled by stipulation, it is formally
heard before a trial examiner of the FTC and later in oral argument before the
commission. If the commission determines that the company has engaged in
unfair practices, it may issue an order to the company to cease and desist from
the unfair practices. Cease and desist orders are enforceable in the United States

circuit courts of appeal. A company may appeal to such a court an order to cease and desist.

The FTC has devoted most of its time to the prevention of false and misleading advertising practices, which are relatively trivial offenses. Seventy per cent of its proceedings for orders to cease and desist have involved false and misleading advertising and other deceptive practices. Only 30 per cent have dealt with discriminations and anticompetitive practices, and the bulk of these cases have involved small corporations of little consequence to the economy.[2]

The FTC has endeavored to encourage compliance with its regulations through the use of the conference on trade practices. When a particular unfair practice is widespread, it may call a conference of members of the industry to draw up rules of fair-trade practices. Companies are asked to sign an agreement to abide by the rules, and a committee of the industry helps to keep member companies in line. Since there is no statutory basis for conferences on trade practices and rules of fair-trade practices, the work of such conferences is informal and conciliatory.

The FTC has done its most significant work in economic investigation. The initiative for most investigations has come from Congress. The FTC has collected data on the propaganda activities of the National Electric Light Association and other groups attempting to discredit governmental regulation of electric utilities. It studied price-fixing agreements in the tobacco industry, the merger trend in business enterprise, the concentration of productive facilities in manufacturing, the operation of the basing point system, and chain stores. These investigations have produced significant reports dealing with economic activity but have not been related directly to the commission's responsibility of preventing unfair trade practices.

appraisal of the Federal Trade Commission

The FTC was intended to provide a commission of trained experts, free from partisan political influence, to prevent the development of monopolistic and restrictive practices: "By continuous, expert attention, it was expected to adopt and apply the general terms of the statutes to current business practices, to make their enforcement more effective, and to build up a body of precedents to govern business conduct."[3]

The Hoover Commission's task force was highly critical of the FTC. In January, 1949, it reported:

Measured by these hopes, the Commission's record has been disappointing. The reasons have been various. The Commission has been hampered by in-

---

[2] See The Commission on Organization of the Executive Branch of the Government, *Task Force Report on Regulatory Commissions* (Washington: Government Printing Office, 1949), Appendix N, pp. 119–133.

[3] *Ibid.*, p. 119.

adequate funds, hostile court rulings, mediocre appointments. Its operations, programs, and administrative methods have often been inadequate,
and its procedures cumbersome. It has largely become absorbed in petty
matters rather than basic problems.[4]

Antitrust policy has had a difficult course to maintain. Several statutes have
been enacted which conflict with the basic antitrust objective of preventing
monopolistic and unfair practices. The Webb-Pomerene Export Act exempts export associations from the provisions of the Sherman Act on the assumption that
export associations would stimulate foreign trade. The Reed-Bulwinkle Act of
1948 permits railroads to cooperate in matters affecting railroad rates without
fear of antitrust action. The Miller-Tydings Act of 1938 amended the Sherman
Act by making it possible for states to permit manufacturers to set fixed prices
for so-called "fair-traded items."

the future of antimonopoly policy

Neither enforcement of the Sherman Act by the Antitrust Division against
monopolistic businesses nor the attempts of the FTC to prevent monopolistic and
unfair practices have halted the trend toward concentration of economic power
in American society. After more than sixty years of antitrust enforcement, manufacturing corporations are larger rather than smaller, and economic power is
more highly concentrated. The free enterprise system exists only to the extent
that competition remains vital and vigorous. The relative failure of antitrust
policy to reverse the trend toward concentration of control and monopoly raises
doubts whether the American people are fully committed to the principles of a
free enterprise economy. Do we really want competition, or are we willing to
permit more and more power to be concentrated in fewer and fewer corporations? If competition cannot be restored and monopolistic corporations broken
up, should the government impose regulations on corporate activity? Should
governmental regulation be substituted for competition as the stimulant for
efficient operation, reasonable prices, and democratic control?

public-utility regulation

Antitrust policy is founded on the concept that competition should prevail in
most of the economy. Public-utility regulation is founded on the concept that
certain enterprises are natural monopolies in which competition should be
eliminated. These enterprises are called public utilities. They include industries
which provide such essential public services as gas and electricity, street railways,
all forms of transportation, and water systems. Monopoly in providing utility

---

[4] *Ibid.*

services is regarded as socially desirable. For example, it would be wasteful and inconvenient to have two sets of street railways on one street or two sets of telephone lines serving the same area. Since monopoly in providing utility services is desirable, government has regulated public-utility companies instead of maintaining competition in the provision of utility services.

There is no simple formula or definition which indicates whether any particular industry or business is a public utility. In the last sixty or seventy years, the public-utility concept has been broadened to include many industries. Historically and legally, a public utility was "a business affected with the public interest." Narrowly construed, such a description meant that the business required the use of public property for operation, or that the business was a "natural monopoly." In addition, a public utility normally must continue to serve the public until it is permitted to discontinue service. It must meet acceptable standards of service and deal equitably with its consumers, and its rates must be reasonable and not excessive. In return for enjoying monopoly privileges in supplying certain services to the community, the utility company is subject to governmental regulation of its rates, services, and business practices.

Most public utilities fall into one of three business areas: power, transportation, and communication. The major regulatory problems and policies in each of these areas are outlined briefly in the following section.

regulation of the power industry

Power industries include electric and gas companies of all types, but the electric power industry, which is the most important, will be emphasized here. The states and the federal government regulate the electric utilities. State regulation is confined to the intrastate operations of electric companies, whereas federal regulation covers their interstate operations. In the United States about 80 per cent of the electric industry is privately owned but is regulated by government, and about 20 per cent is publicly owned and operated.

In an industrial society, electric power is a crucial factor in economic development. Young and aggressive, the electric power industry has posed difficult problems of public regulation:

1. The government grants permission to engage in the operation of public utilities. It grants a franchise or a "certificate of public convenience and necessity," which is a legal permit to engage in a business. Since a franchise or certificate may be an important economic privilege, governments have been subjected to great pressure from utility interests seeking it. Before franchises or certificates of convenience and necessity are granted, the regulatory body is supposed to determine whether the proposed service is needed, whether an existing company can provide the service, and whether the grant would be in the public interest.

2. In order to regulate utility operations, regulatory bodies must establish

uniform accounting rules to be followed by utility companies. In the accounting field, a number of serious problems have arisen. What accounting procedures shall be followed for depreciating the value of utility property? If the company's reserve for depreciation is larger than is justified, the utility is able to pass higher rates on to the consumer. Depreciation accounting has especially troubled the state regulatory commissions because of their relative lack of experienced accounting staffs. As a result, most state public-utility commissions have not been able to enforce accounting standards adequately.

3. The regulatory bodies must approve and enforce standards of services supplied by public utilities. They must investigate consumer complaints about the quality of service and determine when a service can be abandoned or extended. Regulation of rates would be incomplete without tying rates to a standard of service.

4. Another duty of the regulatory body is to control the financial structure of electric utilities. Some states have authority to approve or disapprove the issuance of stocks and bonds by utilities and to regulate their financial transactions. The purposes of financial regulation are to protect investors and consumers against manipulation and to prevent companies from engaging in practices not in the public interest. Most regulatory bodies also have jurisdiction over the merger of two or more companies and over the structure and operations of holding companies.

5. In order to establish reasonable electric rates, regulatory bodies must make a valuation, or an appraisal in money terms, of the property and assets of the company. Under judicial interpretations of governmental authority to regulate public utilities, rates will not be accepted by the courts as reasonable unless they permit a "fair return on fair value" to the company. That is, the company must be able to set rates which permit it to earn a reasonable profit on its investment. The problem of fair value or valuation has been so troublesome in utility regulation that little study has been made of the problem of "fair return." The determination of the value of the properties and investments of an electric company has become essentially a legal procedure involving conflicts, delays, and uncertainties. Judicial decisions on valuation have been vague and contradictory, and the courts must bear much of the responsibility for the lack of regulatory progress in this industry.

6. The primary object of regulation is to establish reasonable rates. The setting of rates is the end product of the regulatory process which includes the grant of a franchise to operate, the establishment of uniform accounting standards, the enforcement of standards of service, the supervision of financial practices, and the valuation of utility property. The effectiveness of utility regulation can be measured in terms of the reasonableness of rates and in terms of the performance of the regulatory body in establishing an objective basis for rate regulation.

appraisal of state public-utility regulation

Public-utility regulation in the states is normally handled by a state public-utility commission of three or more members appointed by the governor with some legislative consent. New York and Wisconsin established the first state utility commissions in 1907. The commissions were intended to provide an expert forum, free from political interference and influence. They developed during the years 1900–1914, when reformers were outraged by fraud and corruption in American public life and by ugly disclosures by the "muckrakers" of the evil machinations of political party bosses and machines, especially in urban areas. Although the state commissions were supposed to keep regulation out of politics, they have rarely succeeded in doing so. It may be doubted whether freedom from politics is a sound objective for the operation of a government agency concerned so vitally with the public interest.

On the whole, state regulation of electric utilities has been disappointing. Appointments of commissioners have frequently been made on the basis of partisan political considerations, and in some states appointments have been dictated by the major utility companies. The commissions' staffs have been small and rarely expert enough to deal with the highly-paid staffs of the electric utilities. Given the lack of adequate staff and the absence of strong leadership from commissioners, most state agencies have not followed aggressive programs of research and investigation to formulate standards of service and to establish rates which would keep the companies efficient and serve the public interest. Most commissions have relied heavily on information supplied by the utilities and have depended on formal hearings rather than on independent investigations to clarify the issues in a specific controversy. Instead of carrying on vigorous administrative programs, most state commissions have become rather passive and more like courts in their behavior.

State regulatory experience raises several questions about governmental regulation of electric and other utilities. Is the conventional mechanism of the independent commission adequate? Can the underlying policy of providing fair return on fair value be accepted any more as logical and realistic? Should we frankly acknowledge the political character of the regulatory process? Is the alternative to ineffective public regulation more public ownership?

federal regulation of electric power

The federal government regulates electric utilities doing an interstate business in three ways:

1.   The Federal Power Commission regulates the wholesale rates of electric power transmitted across state lines. In addition it controls the development of hydroelectric power. The FPC has taken the initiative in working out clearer

concepts of valuation and fair return and has encouraged the development of better accounting practices in the electric-utility industry.

2. Under the Public Utility Holding Company Act of 1935, the Securities and Exchange Commission is able to attack the tendency of utilities to escape state regulation by extending their operations into other states. The purpose of the act is to prevent the abuses practiced by many large utility companies in the late 1920's and early 1930's by limiting mergers and combinations of gas and electric utilities engaged in interstate commerce.

3. Although government ownership and operation of electric utilities is not regulation in the conventional sense, government ownership has had important regulatory consequences. Activities of such public power developments as the Tennessee Valley Authority, Bonneville Dam, Grand Coulee Dam, and the Rural Electrification Administration have probably been more effective than the regulatory commissions in stimulating the privately owned utilities to improve service and efficiency and reduce rates without impairing their earnings position.

regulation of transportation

Economic development depends to a considerable degree on adequate transportation. For this reason, all governments in the United States have been concerned with the development and use of transport facilities, from the street railway and the taxicab to airplanes and ocean ships. The various forms of transportation have been regarded as particularly appropriate recipients of direct governmental aid. Part of the price for such aid has been government regulation to ensure the protection and promotion of the public interest in providing adequate transport facilities at reasonable rates.

Procedurally, public utilities in transportation are regulated in substantially the same way as electric utilities. Therefore this discussion will emphasize problems and policies of particular importance at the federal level.

the lack of a national transportation policy

Federal regulation of transportation by a number of regulatory commissions has been piecemeal rather than comprehensive. Problems in each form of transportation have been considered as they intensified and became critical. The federal government has not been guided by any overriding principles or policies. As a result, Congress has adopted inconsistent regulatory policies.

A rather bewildering array of federal agencies regulates the various types of transportation. The Interstate Commerce Commission, the oldest federal regulatory commission, has the broadest jurisdiction, covering railroads, motor carriers, inland water carriers, and pipelines (other than water or gas). The Federal Power Commission regulates natural gas pipelines; the Civil Aeronautics Board, aviation; and the Maritime Board of the Department of Commerce, shipping.

These agencies were established at different times to deal with specific regulatory problems without reference to a national transportation policy and without any attempt to develop general standards and procedures for regulating privately owned transport facilities.

Federal regulation of transportation is the product of more than sixty years of experimentation. From 1887 to 1920, federal regulation was intended to protect the public against the abusive exercise of monopolistic practices by the railroads. In 1920, however, the Interstate Commerce Commission was empowered to take a more constructive approach to transportation matters to guide railroad development in order to meet the nation's needs. Some control was also extended over inland water carriers. Interstate motor carriers were added to ICC jurisdiction in 1935, and controls over domestic water transportation were expanded in 1940. The United States Maritime Commission, the predecessor of the Maritime Board, was established in 1936 with jurisdiction over ocean shipping, and the Civil Aeronautics Board was created in 1938 to administer controls over the civil aviation industry.

regulatory problems in transportation

A number of problems encountered in federal regulation of transportation should be noted:

1. The right to operate transport enterprises is controlled by government agencies. Since 1920, the ICC has controlled the construction and abandonment of interstate railroads. Because by 1920 railroad expansion was largely completed, the ICC has been concerned more with the abandonment of obsolete lines than with the construction of new ones. The ICC's control of the right to engage in business has been more important for motor carriers and inland water carriers because of the rapid development of highway and water transportation since 1935. However, important segments of motor and water transportation are exempt from ICC control in this respect. No person may engage in or abandon the business of air transportation without authorization from the Civil Aeronautics Board. While the CAB's jurisdiction extends only to air transportation, the ICC must administer its control over several forms of transportation and must maintain safe, adequate, economical, and efficient conditions in rail, motor, and water transportation without unjust discrimination and destructive competition among the competing forms.

2. The core of transport regulation lies in the regulation of rates and the prevention of discriminatory rates. Public criticism of discriminatory rates among individual shippers and communities supplied the original stimulus for railroad regulation. In fact, rate discrimination remains one of the principal regulatory problems. Perhaps the most important type of discrimination has been preferential rates for particular geographical areas. The southern states have

long fought territorial discrimination as prejudicial to the economic development of the South.

3. Rate regulation is used to stabilize competition among the various forms of transportation. The control of rates helps to allocate traffic among the competing forms and helps to maintain their solvency. The ICC sets minimum as well as maximum rates in order to prevent destructive competition. As in the case of electric-utility regulation, the technical problems of establishing the cost of operation of transport facilities are considerable. Railroads and pipelines, which are now privately financed, must be able to pay their own way. In contrast, motor, water, and air carriers use public facilities or receive public subsidies and therefore do not need to set rates high enough to cover all costs of operation. Because some forms of transportation receive governmental assistance and others do not, the establishment of fair competitive rates for the different forms is difficult to accomplish. Traffic may, in fact, be allocated among the different forms of transportation more in accordance with the amount of government aid received rather than according to the real cost of the transport service.

4. Another major regulatory problem is the coordination of all transport services into a national transportation system. The independence of the various regulatory agencies has been an obstacle to the achievement of interagency coordination. The various transportation mediums which receive preferential treatment from an agency resist efforts to coordinate transportation policies.

In 1949 the Brookings Institution recommended to the Hoover Commission the consolidation of federal transportation agencies into a single Department of Transportation. A single executive department, it argued, would focus responsibility for developing a national transportation program. The Hoover Commission rejected this proposal and proposed instead that some of the functions of the ICC, the Maritime Commission, and the CAB be transferred to the Department of Commerce.[5] The Brookings Institution and the Hoover Commission agree, however, that the diffusion of transport functions among separate agencies is wasteful and inconsistent. The coordination of transport regulation remains a major problem of the federal government.

regulation of communications

The communications industry includes telephone, telegraph, radio broadcasting (including television), and cable. State public-utility commissions generally have jurisdiction over intrastate telephone services, whereas the Federal Com-

---

[5] The Commission on Organization of the Executive Branch of the Government, *The Independent Regulatory Commissions* (Washington: Government Printing Office, 1949), pp. 11–15. For a detailed statement of the recommendation of the Brookings Institution, see Charles Dearing and Wilfred Owen, *National Transportation Policy* (Washington: The Brookings Institution, 1949).

munications Commission exercises control over interstate communication in the telephone, telegraph, cable, and radio industries. Regulation of communications is relatively recent and encounters difficulties because of the newness of the communications industry and the rapidity of technological advancement. Since regulatory problems in telephone and telegraphic communication are similar to those in the electrical and transportation utilities, this discussion will focus on broadcasting.

Regulation of broadcasting is distinguished from other forms of government regulation because it was established at the request of the broadcasters themselves in order to overcome electrical chaos on the air. The Federal Communications Commission is authorized to regulate broadcasting in the "public interest, convenience, or necessity." The problems in radio broadcasting arise from the application of this mandate.

Because of the shortage of frequencies on the air, the FCC must ration scarce frequencies to qualified persons. A broadcaster must first obtain a license from the FCC, which is valid for only three years. Upon the expiration of his license, the broadcaster must apply for its renewal. Frequently the FCC is confronted by competing applications for a single frequency. It has established some guiding principles to govern its decisions in such cases. The most important factor in considering renewal applications is the program performance of the broadcaster. Broadcasters have disputed the authority of the FCC to consider their past performance on the grounds that such action constitutes censorship of the air, which is forbidden by the Communications Act of 1934 and also violates the freedom of speech guaranteed to broadcasters under the First Amendment. In general the Supreme Court has upheld the authority of the FCC to consider program performance although, as of 1950, the issue had not yet been conclusively settled.

Faced with the opposition of a highly organized and powerful industry, the FCC has been rather timid in developing radio regulation. On two occasions the FCC sought to promote the public interest aggressively. In 1938 it completed an investigation of chain broadcasting and ordered the separation of the two networks of the National Broadcasting Company. In 1946 it issued the controversial "Blue Book," which stated the policies the commission would use in evaluating applications for renewal. Since 1946, however, these policies have not been widely used to revoke or to refuse renewal of licenses.

The FCC is faced with a number of difficult problems. Can or should it apply its standards of program performance more vigorously? Does it have a responsibility for improving radio programing in the interests of the listening public? Will it be able to make radio broadcasting available to underserved areas in the southern and western sections of the United States? Is it in the public interest to prevent common ownership of newspaper and radio facilities in a community in order to maintain competition in the communications industry? Is the control exercised by the three major networks excessive and should it be lessened? What type of color television should be authorized?

governmental regulation of securities

In order to protect investors in corporate business, government has endeavored to regulate both the issuance of securities and the operation of securities markets. Regulation developed in response to demands from investors and consumers for protection against shady, manipulative, or deceptive practices in the sale of corporate securities and in the financial administration of corporations.

States attempted to regulate securities as early as 1911, but state regulation was not effective, chiefly because states had no authority to control interstate transactions. The stock market crash and the lurid and shocking disclosures of fraud and dishonesty revealed by the Senate investigation of stock exchange practices in the early 1930's led to the enactment of a group of securities statutes and the creation of the Securities and Exchange Commission.

The principal objective of the Securities Act of 1933 is to compel disclosure of all pertinent information about new security issues. It applies only to securities which are publicly offered for sale and sold through the mails or in interstate commerce. The statute was based on the theory that investors would be protected if they were in a position to know the significant facts about a security issue. Governmental securities, securities offered privately, and securities of banks, railroads, and cooperatives are exempt from regulation. Regulation is based on the filing of a detailed registration statement with the SEC. In addition, a digest of the registration statement must be made available to persons to whom securities are offered for sale. No securities may be offered to the public until twenty days after the filing of the registration statement. SEC examines the statement and may refuse registration if the statement is false, incomplete, or inaccurate.

The Securities Exchange Act of 1934 governs securities after issuance. Its purpose is to prevent manipulation in the securities market. All securities traded on the national securities exchanges must be registered with the Securities and Exchange Commission. The commission may restrict borrowing by members of exchanges and stock brokers and prohibit manipulative practices. After the reform of the New York Stock Exchange following the Whitney scandal in 1937, the commission has encouraged stock exchange leaders to adopt self-policing practices to safeguard the investing public.

What is the proper scope of federal securities regulation? In requiring disclosure of pertinent information, the SEC seeks to prevent the sale of fraudulent securities and misstatements of fact about securities by sellers. Should the SEC also pass on the financial soundness or probable safety of securities? There is general agreement that the securities legislation does not call upon the government to guarantee the soundness of securities issues. However, critics have claimed that "the Commission was so bent upon protecting the public that in practice there was a tendency on the part of zealous administrators to prevent the flotation of securities whose ultimate soundness might be in doubt." [6]

influence of the courts on regulation

The courts have deeply affected the course of governmental regulation of business. The modern development of regulation was accompanied by vigorous judicial efforts so to interpret key sections of the Constitution as to invalidate attempts to regulate business enterprises. Relying on interpretations of the due process clauses of the Fifth and Fourteenth Amendments and the commerce clause, the courts, in the period from 1885 to 1937, were able to restrict or declare void many governmental regulatory efforts. For decades the courts refused to apply the sanctions of the Sherman Act to giant corporations with monopolistic market control. Through the vague requirement of "fair return on fair value," the courts were able to hamstring effective utility regulation. By restricting the meaning of "commerce" in the commerce clause, the expansion of federal controls was halted.

Since 1937, however, the Supreme Court has reinterpreted several constitutional clauses to permit more governmental regulation. One observer has noted that "the commerce clause as now interpreted by the Court tends to place in legislatures, and not in courts, the primary duty of meeting commercial problems arising out of modern-day industrialization and technological advance." [7]

defects in the operation of independent regulatory commissions

With few exceptions, independent regulatory commissions have not achieved notable administrative success. Their main shortcomings have been cited by the Hoover Commission: [8]

1. Appointments of commissioners "are sometimes below desirable standards because of the inadequate salaries offered, or the failure of the Executive to appreciate the importance of the positions."

2. The commissions have had to undertake purely executive functions which interfere with the performance of their regulatory functions.

3. Internal organization of the commission is not satisfactory. Administra-

[6] Willard Atkins, George Edwards, and Harold Moulton, *The Regulation of the Security Markets* (Washington: The Brookings Institution, 1946), p. 95.

[7] Vincent M. Barnett, Jr., "The Power to Regulate Commerce," *American Political Science Review*, XLI (December, 1947), 1170, 1181.

[8] *The Independent Regulatory Commissions*, pp. 3–4.

tive direction is not centralized. "No one has responsibility for planning and guiding the general program of commission activity."

4. "Unnecessary red tape has crept into their procedures causing useless delay and expense."

5. "Coordination between these commissions and the general program of the executive departments is often loose and casual and sometimes non-existent."

The analysis of the Hoover Commission leaves open the question of the authority and responsibility of the President in the various regulatory fields. Can a national policy be achieved so long as the commissions remain relatively independent of the President and the executive branch of the government? Are independent commissions, in fact, responsible to the Congress, as intended by the enabling statutes, or are they irresponsible agencies?

the meaning of American regulatory experience

There has been a world-wide trend toward increasing governmental regulation of economic life. This trend has not been reversed under conservative governments either in the United States or elsewhere. Regulation of business in the United States did not begin with the New Deal, although regulation was expanded greatly during Roosevelt's administration. Nor is regulation a function exclusively of the highest level of government. Because of the American federal system of government, it was natural that state and local governments should pioneer in the development of regulation.

The growth of governmental regulation may be viewed as an attempt to adopt governmental institutions and practices to changes in our social and economic structure. Regulation has changed and expanded in response to the growing concentration of economic control, the enlargement of markets for manufactured goods, and the extension of transportation facilities. It has also grown in response to changes in ideas about the proper role of government in American society. The drive for social justice during the period from 1900 to 1914 and the slow development today of the idea that no individual should be permitted to fall below a minimum level of existence illustrate the change in ideas about the role of government.

Governmental regulation and the growth of public powers have been inevitable results of the rise of industrialism and the spread of democratic ideas. Regulation by administrative agencies is also a modern reaction to the inadequacy of regulation by legislatures and by the courts. Regulation has always encountered strong opposition in the United States and must face the challenge of opposition in the future. This fact suggests that effective regulation requires both widespread public support and strong political leadership. A regulatory commission is unlikely to maintain its authority without a good measure of both. In the last analysis regulation cannot be effective unless it overcomes the apathy of the public.

Finally, governmental regulation can be regarded as an effort to adapt modern enterprise to changing economic and political conditions. Regulation is designed to protect the public against the excesses of arbitrary economic power which develop in a highly industrialized society. Although regulation transfers from business enterprise to government the authority to make or control certain business decisions, it still leaves unregulated and unfettered a very broad area of private decision making.

The alternatives to government regulation of business are reasonably clear. One alternative lies in the uncontrolled centralization of more power in giant corporations. The other lies in the development of government ownership.

bibliographic note

There are several important general analyses of problems of government regulation of business. Robert E. Cushman emphasizes the legislative history of the development of federal regulatory commissions in *The Independent Regulatory Commissions* (New York: Oxford University Press, 1941). John M. Clark devotes his *Social Control of Business* (New York: McGraw-Hill Book Company, 2d ed., 1939) to a broad-gauged philosophical and economic study of regulatory problems. Perhaps the two most important books which describe the political and economic environment in which government regulation operates are Pendleton Herring's *Public Administration and the Public Interest* (New York: McGraw-Hill Book Company, 1936), and Jerome Frank's *If Men Were Angels* (New York: Harper & Brothers, 1942). The findings and recommendations of the Hoover Commission and its task force on regulatory commissions can be found in two publications of the Commission on Organization of the Executive Branch of the Government: *Report to the Congress on Regulatory Commissions* (Washington: Government Printing Office, 1949), and *The Task Force Report on Regulatory Commissions* (Washington: Government Printing Office, 1949), Appendix N. A rather favorable appraisal of the Hoover Commission's views is contained in C. Herman Pritchett, "The Regulatory Agencies Revisited," *American Political Science Review*, XLIII, No. 5 (October, 1949), 978–989. George A. Graham and Henry Reining, Jr., eds., *Regulatory Administration* (New York: John Wiley & Sons, 1943), have collected essays on different types of regulatory functions of government. The record of the largest American business corporations in complying with government regulations is analyzed provocatively in Edwin H. Sutherland's *White Collar Crime* (New York: The Dryden Press, 1949).

The use of the charter of incorporation as a governmental device for controlling and promoting corporate business has been the subject of a number of important works in the past few years. The experience of Pennsylvania is set forth in *Economic Policy and Democratic Thought* (Cambridge: Harvard University Press, 1948), by Louis Hartz. Oscar and Mary F. Handlin record the experience of Massachusetts in *Commonwealth; a Study of the Role of Government in the American Economy* (New York: New York University Press, 1947), and John W. Cadman, Jr., analyzes New Jersey's efforts to control corporate enterprise in *The Corporation in New Jersey* (Cambridge: Harvard University Press, 1949). For a study of state participation in corporate enterprise, see the article by Carter Goodrich, "The Virginia System of Mixed Enterprise: A Study of State Planning of Internal Improvements," *Political Science Quarterly*, LXIV, No. 3 (September, 1949), 355–387.

Students of government regulation have until recently been preoccupied with legal problems of regulation. The classic analysis of judicial interpretation of the commerce clause of the Constitution is found in Edward S. Corwin, *The Commerce Power and States' Rights* (Princeton: Princeton University Press, 1936). An excellent summary of the state of constitutional law on federal government regulation is contained in Vincent M. Barnett, Jr., "The Power to Regulate Commerce," *American Political Science Review*, XLI, No. 6 (December, 1947), 1170–1181. In *The Administrative Process* (New Haven: Yale University Press, 1938), James M. Landis analyzes the role of administrative adjudication in the regulatory process, while Walter Gellhorn, in his *Federal Administrative Proceedings* (Baltimore: The Johns Hopkins Press, 1944), sets forth the role of fair procedures in safeguarding the rights of private parties appearing before government regulatory agencies.

The literature of antimonopoly policy is enormous, and only a handful of items can be mentioned here. There is an excellent historical treatment of antimonopoly policy in Merle Fainsod and Lincoln Gordon, *Government and the American Economy*, (New York: W. W. Norton and Co., 1948, revised edition), pp. 432–620. A recent textbook which emphasizes antimonopoly problems is Vernon A. Mund, *Government and Business* (New York: Harper & Brothers, 1950). The hearings and reports of the Temporary National Economic Committee are summarized by David Lynch in *The Concentration of Economic Power* (New York: Columbia University Press, 1946). One of the most urbane and thoughtful appraisals of traditional American antimonopoly policy has been written by J. K. Galbraith in "Monopoly and the Concentration of Economic Power," in Howard S. Ellis, ed., *A Survey of Contemporary Economics* (Philadelphia: The Blakiston Company, 1949), pp. 115–128. In *Meat and Man* (New York: The Viking Press, 1950), Lewis Corey studies the relationship between monopoly, unionism, and food policy in the meat-packing industry. In "Giantism and Basing Points," *Yale Law Journal*, LVIII, No. 2 (February, 1949), 383, and in "The Politics of Basing Point Legislation," *Law and Contemporary Problems*, XV, No. 2 (Spring, 1950), 272–310, Earl G. Latham demonstrates clearly the impossibility of separating politics and economics in analyzing the monopoly problem. A convenient summary of congressional action in the antitrust field is contained in the House Select Committee on Small Business, *Congress and the Monopoly Problem: Fifty Years of Antitrust Development 1900–1950* (Washington: Government Printing Office, 1950, Committee Print). The proceedings of the most recent congressional investigation of the monopoly problem can be found in the House Committee on the Judiciary, [Celler] Subcommittee on Study of Monopoly Power, *Hearings on Study of Monopoly Power*, Serial No. 14 Pt 1, 2–A, 2–B, 3, 4–A, and 4–B, 81 Cong., 1 and 2 Sess. (Washington: Government Printing Office, 1949–1950).

Proposals for improving public-utility regulation are outlined by John Bauer in *Transforming Public Utility Regulation* (New York: Harper & Brothers, 1950). In *National Transportation Policy* (Washington: The Brookings Institution, 1949), Charles L. Dearing and Wilfred Owen argue the case for consolidating federal regulation of transportation in a single department. Edward T. McCormick presents a full-scale description and analysis of federal regulation of the securities market in *Understanding the Securities Act and the S.E.C.* (New York: American Book Company, 1948).

government and agriculture

$\mathscr{T}$HE condition of agriculture and farmers has been a persistent and major issue of American politics. In recent years agricultural problems have become more complex and perhaps more difficult to solve. They concern city as well as rural families because city dwellers are dependent upon the farmer for the food they require.

the agricultural problem

The agricultural problem is to build a stable and prosperous agricultural system which will produce adequate food supplies at reasonable prices and provide a decent standard of living for farmers. It consists of four major elements:

1. Farm income and economic security
2. The organization of American agriculture
3. Disadvantaged farm groups
4. The management of soil resources

farm income and economic security

Inadequate farm income has always been the chief complaint of American agriculture. The income received by many farm families from farming generally has been too low to support a reasonable standard of living. Measured in terms of hourly wages, farmers and farm workers have never earned as much as the industrial worker has earned. Farmers have been dependent on foreign markets to take up the surplus of farm production, but foreign trade has fluctuated widely over the years and has been highly uncertain in many periods of the nation's history.

Since 1860 farm production has expanded during the four wars in which the United States has been involved. During war periods, prices for agricultural commodities rose rather sharply because of increased demand. A reduction in demand accompanied by declining prices has customarily followed a war period. The resulting fluctuation in farm prices has been a major source of farm discon-

787

tent and insecurity. Agricultural development has also been affected profoundly by technological advances. Such inventions as reapers, harvesters, gang plows, tractors, and cotton pickers have enormously increased the productivity of farms. By utilizing new types of farm machinery, farmers have at times been able to produce more food than consumers were able to buy. As a result, surplus production has been a chronic factor leading to unstable farm prices and lower farm income.

Increases in farm productivity have also created problems in the marketing of agricultural commodities. Farmers have frequently been at the mercy of those who controlled the storage and transportation facilities of the country, including grain elevators, railroad cars, and warehouses.

Farmers have demanded governmental assistance to overcome the inadequacy of farm income. They have demanded and received aid in the form of loans, crop insurance, and money payments in return for some governmental control of agricultural production and the marketing of farm produce.

the structure of American agriculture

The typical agriculture unit is the family farm, frequently regarded as uneconomic and obsolete in the face of technological advances. However, it has persisted as the key farm unit by successfully demanding governmental aid to enable it to buy and use farm machinery.

Farms in the United States vary tremendously in productivity and in financial stability. A small proportion of farms produce the bulk of all agricultural commodities. In addition, thousands of persons who work on farms do not own farms. They include sharecroppers, migrant workers, and farm tenants whose income is frequently wholly inadequate to support a satisfactory standard of living. In the United States today there are more very large farms than fifty years ago. Agriculture has not escaped the trend toward concentration of production in the largest producing units.

Because of the wide variety of agricultural units and the great disparities in productivity, the government has been forced, through pressure from organized agricultural groups, to undertake different programs to help different groups and to preserve the family farm. How efficient is the family farm? Should the public continue to support its maintenance by governmental aid and regulation?

disadvantaged farm groups

About half of American farms make no significant contribution to food production and are not important commercially. This suggests that, from an economic point of view, too many people are engaged in farming. Farm population has been declining since 1916, yet many families are unable to earn a decent income from farming. The bottom half of American farms are frequently characterized by acute distress. They lack economic security and suffer from grossly inadequate social institutions, including schools, health services, recreation facilities, and housing. These groups are made up of run-down farms on farmed-out land operated by men unable to afford farm machinery, and small units incapable of producing commodities economically because of poor management or poor land or because of lack of capital.

The family farm has been specifically excluded from the benefits of modern social legislation. The establishment of minimum wages or maximum hours have not been applied to agriculture; old age insurance had covered agricultural employment only since 1951. How can rural poverty be eliminated? Should the government endeavor to improve the position of these disadvantaged farm groups, or should we recognize the fact of excess farm population and attempt instead to shift families on uneconomic farm units to urban communities?

the management of soil resources

Agriculture in the United States has been based on the free and full ownership of land by individuals. With the exception of Canada, the United States is the only large nation in which individual ownership of land carries no responsibility to the government. The institution of free and full ownership raises certain difficulties in connection with the utilization of land and the conservation of soil. Private ownership of land with complete power over its use and disposition permits the destruction of land and resources in which society has an interest. As the supply of abundant fertile land dwindled, farmers themselves could no longer afford to engage in practices which destroyed the fertility of the soil.

Government has spent large sums of money to improve and maintain privately owned land. It has spent money to induce farmers to engage in soil-conserving practices. Although soil conservation principles have been well known for a century, most farmers were slow to apply them for several reasons. Farm management on the family farm is not specialized. Farming is much more complex than most city dwellers imagine, and the number of variables, such as the weather and uncertain prices, is very great. The farmer is tied down closely to routine operations and he tends to become absorbed in them. Moreover, the farmer is working all the time and has little time to consider new ideas and to experiment.

The problem of managing soil resources extends far beyond the adoption of conservation practices by individual farmers to include the management of all basic raw materials. In the field of soil protection, the Soil Conservation Service in the Department of Agriculture estimates that at present we are losing land at an annual cost to the nation of one billion dollars. Scarcities in oil and lumber already have placed a heavy burden on the economy. What can the government do to encourage better land use and conservation practices? What policies should be followed in the areas of flood control, irrigation of arid sections of the West and the South, the development of hydroelectric power, the development of new fertilizers, and the use of public lands in the West for cattle ranges?

agriculture and the national economy

The agricultural problem of the United States is, above all, merely one aspect of the national problem of developing and maintaining economic stability. The disposition of excess agricultural population would be relieved if the national economy were able to absorb more industrial workers and more persons generally into urban life. Agricultural surpluses might be decreased substantially if the purchasing power of Americans could be increased to permit them to afford more balanced diets with higher nutritive content. Agricultural maladjustments would be reduced if business fluctuations were avoided.

The following sections analyze the structure of American agriculture, the long-range objectives of agricultural policy, and current governmental programs and activities in agriculture.

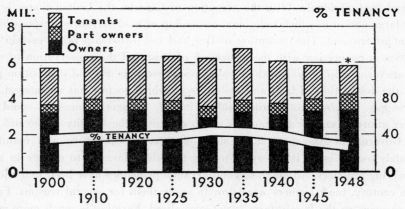

*ROUGH ESTIMATE DERIVED BY APPLYING PERCENTAGE GROUPINGS AS SHOWN IN 1948 ENUMERATIVE SAMPLE SURVEY TO CENSUS NUMBER OF FARMS IN 1945

Farm Owners and Tenants. A recent nationwide survey shows that the proportion of tenant farms has continued to decline sharply. For 1948 only 27.4 per cent of all farms were tenant-operated, the lowest since 1900. Part-owner farms, contrariwise, have continued upward since 1900, but the rate has become more rapid since the war. The trend for full-owner farms likewise has continued upward. The proportion of land under lease has declined at a slow rate, owing to the increase in land leased by part owners. The average size of farm has continued to increase, from 195 acres in 1945 to 204 acres in 1948. Mechanization and improved techniques of farming have caused part of these changes and have meant an increase in gross production per worker. The increase in part-time farming near population centers has helped to increase the proportion of owner-operated farms. Also, relatively high farm incomes have made it easier for many operators to buy farms. In addition, the veterans' on-farm training program has contributed particularly to the increase in part owners, (*Source: U.S. Department of Agriculture*, Agricultural Outlook Charts—1950, *p. 32.*)

the structure of American agriculture

The agricultural problem can be understood best in the context of the structure of agriculture. Structure includes the following factors: number and size of farms, farm population and ownership, farm income and production, and farm organizations.

number and size of farms

There are approximately 6 million farms of all types in the United States with an average size of about 200 acres. About 30 per cent are part-time units or may be considered as farms only nominally. An example of a nominal farm is a country estate which carries on some farming as a side line. About half of all farms may be classified as medium or small commercial family farms which produce commodities for the market. About 100,000, or less than 2 per cent, are large-scale, highly industrialized farms operated as industrial enterprises rather than family farms. In many cases the operator of a small farm may work at another occupation as much as a hundred days or more every year.

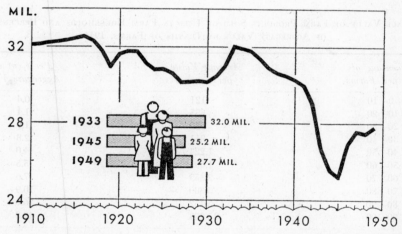

Farm Population, 1910–1949. From 1916 to 1930, the number of persons living on farms decreased each year except during the recession years of the early 1920's and during 1925. In the depression of the early 1930's, farm population rose rapidly, totaling 32.0 million in 1933. The principal reason for this increase was a cutting down of migration away from farms. After 1933, the number of persons on farms decreased yearly through 1945. During World War II the rate of decrease grew as large numbers of people left farms for the cities or went into the armed forces. By 1945 only 25.2 million persons lived on farms. After World War II, farm population increased substantially for two years, but since then the changes have been slight. Farm population appears to have leveled off about half-way between its prewar size and the wartime low. (*Source: U.S. Department of Agriculture,* Agricultural Outlook Charts—1950, *p. 30.*)

farm population and ownership

The number of people living on farms has declined markedly since 1910. In 1949, farm population was estimated to be 27.8 million, and nonfarm population, 119.7 million. For every ten farms, approximately six are fully owned by the operator, one is partly owned, and three are operated by tenants. The proportion of tenant farms has been declining since 1935. The increase in part-time farming near population centers has probably increased the number of owner-operated farms. Also, relatively high farm incomes in the 1940's made it easier for many operators to buy farms.

farm income and production

The bulk of farm production and the major share of farm income is accounted for by a small proportion of farms. As the following table shows, nearly half of all farm products are produced by the top 10 per cent of farms, whereas the bottom half of all farms produce only 10 per cent of the product. In dollar terms, 40 per cent of all farms produced less than $900 worth of commodities in 1944, and only 40 per cent produced more than $2,000 worth of commodities.

AVERAGE VALUE OF FARM PRODUCTS SOLD OR USED IN FARM HOUSEHOLDS AND PERCENTAGE OF AGGREGATE VALUE BY TENTHS OF FARMS, 1944.

Percentage of Classified Farms	Average Value per Farm $	Per Cent of Aggregate Value
0– 10	121	0.4
10– 20	355	1.1
20– 30	580	1.9
30– 40	861	2.8
40– 50	1,224	4.0
50– 60	1,695	5.5
60– 70	2,355	7.6
70– 80	3,380	10.9
80– 90	5,152	16.6
90–100	15,223	49.2

Source: House Committee on Agriculture, *Hearings on Long-Range Agricultural Policy*, 80 Cong., 1 Sess. (Washington: Government Printing Office, 1948), Pt. 1, p. 108.

Over 50 per cent of all farm families and individuals not living in families had money incomes below $2,000 in 1948, and 30 per cent had money incomes below $1,000. Farm families typically receive less income than nonfarm families, although they are normally able to supplement their cash income with goods and services. The relatively lower economic status of farm families and individuals is sharply revealed in the following table:

DISTRIBUTION OF FAMILIES AND INDIVIDUALS BY TOTAL MONEY INCOME, FOR THE UNITED STATES, URBAN AND RURAL, 1948

Total Money Income	Total Urban	Rural, nonfarm	Rural, farm
Per Cent	100.0	100.0	100.0
Under $500	6.6	8.4	17.0
$500 to $999	7.4	8.7	13.8
$1,000 to $1,499	6.9	8.2	12.7
$1,500 to $1,999	6.8	8.7	10.3
$2,000 to $2,499	9.8	11.6	9.9
$2,500 to $2,999	9.3	10.4	8.3
$3,000 to $3,499	11.1	10.7	7.9
$3,500 to $3,999	8.7	8.0	4.9
$4,000 to $4,499	7.5	6.6	3.2
$4,500 to $4,999	5.3	4.2	2.2
$5,000 to $5,999	8.1	6.0	3.3
$6,000 to $9,999	9.8	6.6	4.2
$10,000 and over	2.7	1.9	2.2
Median income	$3,142	$2,717	$1,814

Source: Compiled from U. S. Department of Commerce, *Current Population Reports: Consumer Income*, Series P–60, No. 6, p. 15.

In 1950 a congressional committee reported that "in certain areas of the country the main cause of continuing agricultural poverty appears to be that too many people, using outmoded methods, are trying to make a living exclusively from agriculture." [1] Rural poverty is responsible for poor housing and inadequate health and educational facilities. For example, about half of all children of school age live in rural areas which receive only 10 to 12 per cent of the nation's annual income. Consequently the burden of rural education is disproportionately heavy. Even though rural regions contribute a higher proportion of their incomes to support schools than do wealthier urban areas, the urban children have about a two-to-one advantage in educational opportunity over rural children. [2]

The problem of low-income Negro farm families is a special aspect of rural poverty. Over 80 per cent of Negro farm families receive less than $2,000 annually, as against 44 per cent of white farm families. Rapid mechanization of cotton cultivation is also displacing the Negro cotton farmer.

Although farm population is nearly 20 per cent of total population, per-

[1] Joint Committee on the Economic Report, *Low-Income Families and Economic Stability* (Report of the Subcommittee on Low-Income Families, *Senate Document*, No. 146, 81 Cong., 2 Sess.; Washington: Government Printing Office, 1950), p. 4.
[2] C. C. Taylor, ed., *Rural Life in the United States* (New York: Alfred A. Knopf, Inc., 1949), Chap. 6.

sonal income received from agricultural activities accounted for only approximately 10 per cent of all personal income received in 1949.[3]

farm political organizations

Farmers have not hesitated to organize politically to press for favorable governmental action. The three major farm organizations are the National Grange, the American Farm Bureau Federation, and the National Farmers Union. The Grange and the Farm Bureau have attracted primarily the medium and the large-scale farmer, whereas the Farmers Union is composed mostly of small farmers and tenant farmers, especially in the West.

The strength of farm organizations is derived from the American system of legislative representation by geographical area. Although farm population has continued to decline, representation in many state legislatures has continued to be predominantly agricultural. Because each state has two senators in the United States Senate, agricultural states have been able to secure and maintain representation out of proportion to their population. At the same time, urban areas have been underrepresented in most state legislatures and in Congress. Legislatures controlled by farm interests have resisted attempts to reapportion representation. The overrepresentation of agriculture has given the farm groups a tremendous political advantage which neither their population nor their economic significance warrants.

The strength of farm organizations comes from their strong local organizations. Local community interest is maintained by tying local farm organizations into specific governmental programs at the local and state level. For example, farm organizations at the grass roots are concerned directly with state or federal regulation of milk marketing, and committees of farmers consider soil conservation questions and problems of crop control.

Both the Grange and the Farm Bureau aggressively promote the welfare of the more prosperous farmers. Their leaders have worked closely and often intimately with government officials and legislators in drafting legislative policy in agriculture and participated in the development of agricultural adjustment programs in the 1930's. They have generally opposed governmental programs to aid the disadvantaged classes in agriculture. Although they regularly adopt annual resolutions calling for reductions in governmental expenditures, the demand for economy has not been extended to the curtailment of agricultural aid.

The Farmers Union has pressed for governmental programs to rehabilitate low-income farmers, to provide relief for poor farm families, to combat tenancy, and to help sharecroppers and migrant workers. It has urged revision of farm aid programs to give more direct help to the small family farms. More broadly, the Union has pursued a vigorous antimonopoly policy and has fostered the de-

---

[3] See *The Economic Report of the President*, January, 1950 (Washington: Government Printing Office, 1950), Table C-5, p. 153.

velopment of cooperative organizations to serve farmers. It has favored a close political alliance with organized labor.

Farm pressure groups want government to help the farmers they represent. All want a larger share of the national income in order to improve living standards. The interests and economic conditions of the relatively prosperous commercial farmers in the Grange and the Farm Bureau diverge sharply from those of the small farmers and tenants who belong to the Farmers Union. The Grange and the Farm Bureau are concerned almost exclusively with economic measures to increase farm income, whereas the Union in addition supports a variety of social legislation to improve the status of the disadvantaged classes. The farmers in the Union are least able to withstand the impact of a depression. Therefore, the Union is more clearly aware of the fact that the welfare of its members depends heavily on general economic stability throughout the country.

long-range objectives of agricultural policy

Because so many factors in agriculture are beyond individual control, it is natural for farmers to petition government for assistance. Individually farms are unable to cope with problems of excessive production, low prices, and substandard living conditions. Since 1921 farmers have turned more and more to the state and federal governments for direct aid, particularly to improve farm prices. Farmers have been successful in making the welfare of agriculture a major problem of public policy.

Governmental agricultural programs can be understood best as a group of activities undertaken to achieve certain goals or objectives. There are four principal long-range objectives of agriculture policy:

1. The maintenance of economic stability for farmers
2. The conservation of agricultural resources
3. The assurance of a continuous and abundant supply of farm products for all Americans
4. The elimination of rural poverty

The major goal of agricultural policy is to improve the economic position of farmers by assuring them a more stable income and high farm prices. The objectives can be summarized as a fair share of the national income for farm families and a fair exchange value for farm products. Agricultural policy has been largely shaped by the belief that agriculture has never had a fair share of the national income or has never achieved equality of income with industry and labor. Farmers did not share in the general prosperity of the 1920's, and since that time they have carried on a political fight for increasing and stabilizing farm income.

The fight for agricultural equality has been directed toward the achievement of a fair exchange value or "parity price" for farm products. Parity price may be defined as that level of farm prices which will give farmers purchasing power to buy the things they need. The theory of parity for agriculture is that the price of the things the farmer sells should give him a purchasing power equivalent to the cost of the articles he buys. Parity has customarily been based on the relation between agricultural and nonagricultural prices in the period from 1909 to 1914. In this period farm production and industrial production were well balanced, and the farmer obtained a fair exchange value for farm products.

The second objective of agricultural policy is to provide for the conservation and wise use of agricultural resources. Much land in the United States has been ruined or damaged by erosion. Many farms have been worn out through destruction of the soil, overgrazing by cattle, or wasteful practices in cutting timber. The depletion of soil and forests has led to floods, shortages in timber, and reductions in soil fertility. The misuse of land is probably rooted in the abundance of land and in unrestricted private ownership of land. Many families were permitted to settle on poor land or on plots too small to be operated economically. Many acres of grass and trees were mistakenly opened up to farming. Land speculation encouraged wasteful management of soil resources. Farming practices developed in periods in which land was abundant and cheap and have been carried over into periods of scarcity of land and much higher land values. Incentive to conserve land developed only after cheap and abundant land was exhausted. In agricultural policy, conservation is closely linked to the objective of farm economic security. Government assists farmers in earning a fair share of the national income partly in return for the adoption of soil-conserving practices.

The third objective of agricultural policy is to achieve abundant and continuous production in order to assure adequate supplies of food and fiber for consumers. A corollary objective is the expansion of domestic consumption of food, not only quantitatively but also in terms of providing better-balanced diets of higher nutritive content. Securing abundant food production is closely related to general economic conditions. If family incomes can be increased, food consumption will rise and farmers will be able to sell more commodities at favorable prices.

A fourth objective of agricultural policy is the elimination of rural poverty and the rehabilitation of the disadvantaged farm groups. Not only does the government hope to raise farm income above the poverty line for all farmers, but it hopes to encourage the stability of farm homes by encouraging farm ownership or by improving the status of farm tenants. It hopes to develop satisfactory rural institutions capable of providing adequate social services.

the formulation of agricultural policy

Farmers have been the most important formulators of the objectives of agricultural policy. Working through farm organizations, they have made their political demands known and have successfully put pressures on legislatures to secure the adoption of their proposals. It would be difficult to exaggerate the influence of the farm organizations, particularly the American Farm Bureau Federation, on agricultural policy.

The United States Department of Agriculture, which was established in 1862, has developed numerous programs to help farmers become more efficient and more prosperous. In its decades of dealing directly with farmers the department has come to represent farmers and their interests in the executive branch of the federal government. Farmers also find spokesmen for agricultural interests in the legislatures. By working closely with the agricultural committees in the Congress, farm organizations are able to make known their proposals and ideas for agricultural policy and can develop rather potent political support for them. They are aided immeasurably by urban underrepresentation in the legislatures. Farmers are a minority group, but they have learned to organize their minority strength and to use it to improve their welfare.

governmental programs to achieve objectives of agricultural policy

Efforts to achieve the long-range objectives of agricultural policy have led government to adopt and carry out a bewildering array of activities which call for local farmer participation in federal programs, federal-state cooperation, and governmental controls over the production and marketing of farm produce.

control of agricultural production

Many schemes have been adopted to stabilize farm production and farm prices at profitable levels in order to promote the economic security of farmers. Various methods have been used to limit the supply of agricultural commodities and to promote efficiency on the farm for the purpose of helping the farmer receive a fair share of the national income and a fair exchange value for farm products.

The ever-normal granary program is designed to help the farmer adjust his production to consumer needs and to sell his produce at favorable prices. The Agricultural Adjustment Administration of the United States Department of Agriculture, under the Agricultural Adjustment Act of 1938, operates the ever-normal granary program on the theory that the farmer should try to adjust his production of staple crops to probable demand in order to avoid surpluses which lead to low prices. If harvests are heavy or if consumer demand declines, the farmer stores his seasonal surpluses until they are needed. In this way, farm marketing can be more orderly and profitable to the farmer, low prices and gluts on the market will be avoided, and the annual supply of food and feeds can be stabilized. For example, prices need not rise after a serious drought or crop failure so long as stored surpluses of farm products can be directed into the market.

Stabilization of farm production and marketing is accomplished in several ways by the AAA:

1. The basic scheme is the establishment of national acreage allotments for staple, storable commodities, including cotton, wheat, corn, tobacco, rice, and peanuts. Acreage allotments are based on crop and market information and represent careful computations, in advance of the planting season, of the probable demand for any given crop. The national acreage allotment is broken down by crop into state, county, and individual farm allotments, so that each farmer can make his own plans for planting. Within the counties, local committees of farmers determine the allotments for individual farmers. In working out individual allotments, local committees consider the past performance of a farm, its size, the degree of soil erosion, its conservation practices, and other factors.

2. Farmers who cooperate in acreage allotment programs are eligible to receive benefit payments. The acreage controls are voluntary; there is no penalty for overplanting except that the benefit payment for staying within the allotment is correspondingly reduced or forfeited. The benefit payments are based on the parity formula in order to raise farm prices to more favorable levels. The payments serve as an incentive to induce farmers to adjust their production to probable requirements for domestic consumption, exports, and reserves and to adopt soil-conserving practices.

3. Commodity loans are important factors in stabilizing farm prices and production. Farmers depend on selling their crops for their income. Most farmers must sell their crops immediately after harvesting because they need the money or cannot afford to store them. To avoid oversupplying the market and to give the farmer an opportunity to store his crops until such time as he can sell them at a favorable price, the AAA program provides loans on the security of his stored commodities. Commodity loans give farmers an immediate cash income and at the same time protect them from the price-depressing effects of surplus production. The loans are made through the Commodity Credit Corporation in the Department of Agriculture. The effect of the loan is to put a floor under the price of the stored commodities and to permit farmers to market their staple commodities in an orderly way. It also contributes to the ever-normal granary by storing surpluses in good crop years for use in poor crop years, and by preventing drastic fluctuations in farm prices in periods of surplus or short production.

4. When supplies of staple commodities become excessive, marketing quotas may be established. To prevent the flooding of markets with farm commodities and the resulting breakdown of farm prices, the Agricultural Adjustment Act of 1938 establishes marketing quotas to regulate the supply in the market channels of cotton, corn, wheat, tobacco, rice, and peanuts. Supplies

must rise to a certain level well above the normal supplies before a marketing quota may be established. When supplies reach these excessive levels, farmers are asked to vote in a referendum on the approval of the quota. A two-thirds vote of approval is required to make the quota effective. When a national marketing quota becomes effective, it is allocated among individual producers so that it gives to each producer his equitable share in marketing the crop. If a producer markets more than his share, he must pay a penalty.

In addition to marketing quotas, marketing agreements may be arranged for certain perishable commodities in order to prevent excessive production and marketing. Fruit and vegetable agreements may regulate the grade and size of produce and their shipment. Perhaps the most common agreements are those which regulate the marketing of milk in metropolitan areas. Milk marketing agreements set up minimum prices which milk distributors must pay producers. The Department of Agriculture also supervises trading in agricultural commodities on the commodity exchanges. Producers of perishable commodities and of cattle and hogs are protected against unfair and fraudulent practices and market irregularities. Several statutes establish and enforce quality standards or grades for such commodities as cotton, tobacco, and various grains. The Department of Agriculture also supplies current market information to help keep farmers up-to-date about market conditions and to enable them to plan their production and marketing more intelligently. Marketing quotas and agreements, regulation of commodity exchanges, establishment of quality standards, and current market information help to systematize the marketing of farm produce and to maintain an even, orderly flow of produce to the markets.

5.   Government provides crop insurance in varying degrees for wheat, cotton, flax, corn, and tobacco to protect farmers against losses from unavoidable damage caused by insects, plant disease, bad weather, or accidents. Under the Federal Crop Insurance Act of 1938, producers of these commodities are certain that they will have some income every year, no matter what crop conditions may be. Crop insurance is particularly important for farmers in areas where climatic risks are substantial.

6.   Since the early 1940's, the most important government program to stabilize farm prices and income is an elaborate system of price support which places a floor under agricultural prices. The plan is administered through a commodity loan program in which the Commodity Credit Corporation purchases commodities whose excess production would otherwise bring about a decline in prices. The over-all purpose of the program is to keep farm prices from falling below a certain minimum level. It was applied before the end of World War II as some farm prices dropped to or below the support levels.

Three groups of commodities were included in the price support program in 1950: (1) the so-called basic commodities, that is, cotton, wheat, corn, tobacco, rice, and peanuts; (2) commodities added by the Steagall Amendment of 1944,[4] including hogs, eggs, chickens, turkeys, milk, soybeans, potatoes, and other crops; and (3) a miscellaneous group of less important commodities. The prices are tied to the parity formula. In the late 1940's, many commodites were supported by prices equivalent to 90 per cent or more of the parity. During periods when expansion of production is required, price support is useful as a guide for farm production. Floors under prices lessen the risk undertaken by farmers and encourage the production of needed crops. In periods when consumer demand declines, price support programs force the government to buy and store large quantities of commodities in order to maintain the price.

Since the end of World War II, some details of the price support plan have been changed, but the basic program has remained unchanged. In 1948 the Department of Agriculture was required by law to support the prices of nineteen major agricultural commodities. In 1950, price supports still dominated American agricultural adjustment policy although the opposition to price supports had increased. On the one hand, some observers take the position that mandatory high price supports are economically unsound, cause unsettled market conditions, and lead to unfavorable public reaction. On the other hand, farmers have been characteristically haunted by fears of unsalable farm surpluses and low farm prices and hesitate to renounce governmental aid. During 1949 and 1950, the price support program forced the Department of Agriculture to accumulate huge stocks of wheat, corn, cotton, eggs, and other storable commodities. There were indications that the program would force the government to place agricultural activities under more crop controls and market quotas.

7.   Through an elaborate and diversified agricultural credit system, the government makes loans to farmers on favorable terms and helps to finance improvements in the farm, the purchase of farm machinery, and almost every other type of farm activity. For purposes of agricultural credit, the United States is divided into twelve districts. Under the supervision of the Farm Credit Administration in the Department of Agriculture, each district includes four types of banks or lending agencies. These institutions make farm mortage loans, short-term loans to finance crop and livestock production, emergency crop and feed loans, loans for farmers' cooperatives to finance capital improvements or every-day operations, and welfare loans to rehabilitate disadvantaged groups.

conservation and use of land

Several governmental programs have the objective of conserving agricultural resources and improving land management and land use. One of the most important is the benefit payment program of the AAA under which the farmer receives payments for shifting his land from soil-depleting to soil-conserving crops and uses, and for improving his productivity. More specific programs have been

---

[4] Section 4(a) of the "Act to Extend the Life and Increase the Credit Resources of the Commodity Credit Corporation," July 1, 1941, as amended, 55 Stat. 498.

worked out for such sections of the country as the dust bowl of the Middle West and the range-lands in the great plains and Rocky Mountain areas.

The Soil Conservation Service of the Department of Agriculture administers the federal soil conservation program and cooperates with state agricultural agencies in soil-conserving work. It utilizes several methods to teach farmers how to make better and more productive use of soil without depleting its fertility. It maintains erosion control demonstrations in various agricultural regions to show the best methods for handling problems of erosion. It helps to analyze the erosion problems of individual farms and advises farmers on cropping, fertilization, grazing, and other practices. Through the establishment of soil conservation districts under state law, the Soil Conservation Service works with states to organize communities for cooperative action in combating soil erosion. A soil conservation district maintains an inventory of existing erosion conditions and prevailing land-use practices and enters into agreements with farmers to help them develop individual soil conservation plans. A district may also provide farmers with technical assistance and loans.

Under the Bankhead-Jones Act, the Soil Conservation Service purchases submarginal, cutover lands which can no longer support adequate living standards for farmers. It develops such lands in cooperation with state and local governments. The program of land purchase and utilization has probably gone further in the great plains because of the serious problem of wind erosion in that area.

Much of the western and southwestern sections of the United States is arid and semiarid. Irregular rainfall is a constant hazard to agriculture. The Soil Conservation Service works with the western states in developing water facilities, while the Reclamation Service in the Department of Interior provides water for irrigation purposes in several arid regions of the West. The Forest Service in the Department of Agriculture helps to develop the nation's forest resources by teaching forest-conserving practices and by studying improved methods of forest cultivation and management. Flood control projects of the state and federal governments reduce hazards of floods to the soil and help to provide a cheap source of electricity to operate electrical appliances on farms. The Soil Conservation Service has stimulated the cultivation of grasslands to prevent overstocking and overgrazing of cattle, to restore the protective cover to land, and to reduce the erosion caused by wind and rain.

agricultural education and research

One of the oldest objectives of the Department of Agriculture, is the provision of educational and research programs to promote agricultural development. By cooperating closely with states under federal grant-in-aid programs, the federal government has been instrumental in organizing schools of agriculture in the land-grant colleges and agricultural experiment stations. Under the Smith-Lever

Act of 1914, Congress established a cooperative federal-state scheme of the Agricultural Extension Service manned by county agricultural agents. County agents are usually selected by state agricultural extension offices or by the state agricultural colleges, and in the past their appointments have been influenced by the American Farm Bureau Federation. They are local representatives of the Department of Agriculture and are a source of advice and assistance to individual farmers. Many of the federal agricultural programs rely heavily on county agents to interpret them to farmers and to win the farmers' acceptance and understanding. The Agricultural Extension Service carries the major responsibility for organizing educational, demonstrational, and technical service programs and is the principal medium for reaching the farm people.

Within the Department of Agriculture, the Agricultural Research Administration carries on vast research projects. Laboratories conduct investigations to eradicate and control animal and plant diseases, to improve the production and breeding of domestic animals, to develop improved practices in the manufacturing of dairy products, and to control insects injurious to man. Special laboratories study plants to reduce the hazards of crop production and to improve the yield and quality of crops. The physical and chemical properties of soils are examined to make the earth more productive. Engineering phases of agriculture, such as the use of electricity on the farm and the proper design and construction of farm buildings, are under continuous study.

Programs of research and education are aimed primarily at the family farm and are intended to give the family farmer the information and skill he requires to carry on farming successfully. With few exceptions, the government has almost taken the functions of research and experiment out of the hands of the individual farmer. The research function, which in manufacturing industries is carried on by private corporations, has been transferred to government. The farmer can confidently rely on governmental agencies to make available current information about the probable supply of and demand for agricultural commodities, the weather, price developments, and improved methods of cultivation.

expansion of consumption of agricultural products

Part of the farm problem is on the farm, but part of it lies in the cities and towns and in foreign countries. Several governmental programs have the objective of expanding the outlets for agricultural commodities. These programs take three general forms: (1) expansion of domestic food consumption; (2) expansion of food exports to foreign countries; and (3) development of new uses for farm products.

The domestic consumption of food needs to be expanded to put abundant food production to use. The most important governmental programs to expand consumption are those which seek to maintain high levels of employment at reasonable wages to give wage earners the purchasing power to buy more and better food and provide more nutritious and better-balanced diets for their families. If consumers' income is high, farmers are able to sell larger quantities of agricultural commodities at reasonable prices.

During the depression of the 1930's, state and federal agencies purchased food directly from farmers and processors for distribution through relief agencies. Direct purchase and distribution of surplus foods are possible so long as the costs of distribution are not excessive. The food and cotton stamp plans developed in 1939 by the United States Department of Agriculture represented a new approach to the problem of agricultural surpluses. Low-income families were given food stamps which were exchanged for surplus foods in grocery stores. The stamps were issued by the department through relief and welfare agencies to families certified as being eligible for relief. Merchants obtained cash for their stamps from local banks or from food wholesalers, and the stamps were redeemed by the Treasury Department.

Several other programs help to provide needy families with surplus farm products or to improve health and nutritional standards. Under the school lunch program, financed by federal grants-in-aid, free lunches are supplied needy and undernourished school children. Several cities use federal funds to operate low-cost milk programs to enable low-income families to obtain milk at a reduced price.

Foreign markets are a major outlet for abundant food production. In the years immediately following World War II, the United States helped to relieve the world shortage of food by shipping large quantities abroad. Under the Marshall Plan, the Economic Cooperation Administration has been instrumental in financing the shipment of agricultural products to distressed areas in western Europe and elsewhere. Foreign trade is also promoted by international agreements covering such commodities as wheat, cotton, and sugar.

The Department of Agriculture undertakes research programs in order to develop industrial uses for farm commodities and to discover profitable uses for wastage in farm production. Through research and investigation, the government hopes to counteract the effects of technological change that have deprived farmers of many markets. For example, many industrial uses have been found for soybeans, and the industrial use of cottonseed oil accounts for the increased demand for cotton. Corn is being developed as a source of alcohol. Four regional research laboratories are operated by the Department of Agriculture to expand the industrial utilization of farm products, and the Forest Products Laboratory at Madison, Wisconsin, develops new uses for wood products.

social rehabilitation of farm families

Many governmental programs assist not only the commercial farms whose production is important to the nation but also those farm families who produce negligible amounts of food and whose incomes are insufficient to support a rea-

sonable standard of living. These programs aim to develop rural institutions of
education, health, and recreation, to improve farm homes, to provide them with
electricity, to re-establish farm families on land more suited to farming, to enable tenants to purchase farms, and to assist migrant farm families. The objective of these programs is the full development of rural human resources.

The Farmers Home Administration in the Department of Agriculture succeeded the Farm Security Administration as the administrator of most farm
rehabilitation programs. Its work is based on the assumption that the underprivileged groups in agriculture must be given help to make them effective farm
units and to increase their income. Small farmers, tenant farmers, and sharecroppers are given loans to assist them to become farm owners, to improve farm
operations, to purchase seed, feed, and farm machinery, to build or improve water facilities, and for other purposes. The loan programs are based primarily on
concepts of welfare rather than on economics, although the government expects the loans to be repaid.

There is no question that rural poverty is disastrous to the nation and leads
to a tremendous waste of human resources. Obviously the public interest requires
government to undertake measures to relieve distress and poverty on the farm.
However, it may be questioned whether the settlement of more farmers on productive farm units is the best solution to the problem of rural poverty.

We know that 50 per cent of the farms produce only 10 per cent of farm
products. Rural poverty takes its toll from these unproductive units. Since agriculture today cannot provide a reasonable living standard for at least half of
the farm families, the conclusion cannot be avoided that too many people are
trying and failing to make a living out of farming. The long-range objective
of eliminating rural poverty can probably be achieved only by reducing the overpopulation on farms. Much can be done to improve health and nutritional standards and school facilities in rural areas. Nevertheless, the fact remains that many
farms are not effective economic units. Moreover, if the government succeeded
in making them efficient producing units, the problem of marketing agricultural
surpluses would be aggravated. The solution seems to lie, first, in locating more
farms close to industrial centers to enable farm families to supplement their
income substantially through industrial employment, and second, in moving families off the farms. The second proposal can be accomplished only by maintaining
and expanding outlets for employment in the cities and towns.

unresolved problems in agriculture

By 1949 the familiar duality of want and plenty existing side by side began to
reappear. During World War II, the primary problem was to overcome food
shortages by expanding production. Since the war, however, surpluses have begun
to accumulate. The Department of Agriculture has had to purchase huge quan-

tities of storable commodities in order to maintain farm prices at satisfactory levels. Price supports and commodity loans have helped to maintain a high level of farm prices but have also tended to stimulate overproduction by guaranteeing a good price for many agricultural commodities. And as technology improves, increased productivity also contributes to the building up of farm surpluses.

Programs designed to shore up agricultural prices through price supports have several disadvantages. First, they tend to freeze agricultural activities into the pattern of 1914 and to discourage flexible adaptation to changing conditions of supply and demand. Second, unless they are tied to restrictive crop controls, price supports encourage farmers to produce more food than consumers in the United States and abroad are willing and able to buy. Third, they do not significantly help low-income farmers. The major agricultural problem of the future is to develop programs which will give farmers a fair share of the national income without the disadvantages of the price support program as administered in 1950.

Rural poverty grows out of overpopulation on farms. Too many farm families fail to eke out a satisfactory or even a minimal existence from farming. Although the extension of social security measures and the improvement of rural health, educational, and recreational facilities would substantially improve rural living, it would not necessarily help farm families at the bottom of the income scale. The gradual transfer to nonfarm areas and occupations appears to be the long-run solution for rehabilitating these families.

The 1950 census provides a basis for reapportioning legislative representation in the Congress and in the states. If urban areas gain representation in proportion to their population, the political strength of agricultural interests will decline somewhat. On the other hand, if presidential and congressional elections remain close in the years ahead, the Republican and Democratic parties will compete for the farmers' vote. As strategically placed voters, farmers may still be able to keep most of their political strength. In any case, the chairmen and key members of congressional agricultural committees are likely to continue to support farm interests.

bibliographic note

The economic history of American agriculture is presented clearly in United States Department of Agriculture, *Farmers in a Changing World,* Yearbook of Agriculture, 1940 (Washington: Government Printing Office, 1940). Agricultural developments for the period 1860–1897 are covered by Fred A. Shannon's *The Farmer's Last Frontier* (New York: Rinehart & Company, 1945). For incisive comments on American agricultural policy, see Theodore W. Schultz, *Ag-*

riculture in an Unstable Economy (New York: McGraw-Hill Book Company, 1945) ; American Farm Economic Association, *Readings in Agricultural Policy* (Philadelphia: The Blakiston Company, 1949) ; Charles M. Hardin, "Reflections on Agricultural Policy Formulation in the United States," *American Political Science Review*, XLII, No. 5 (October, 1948), 881–905; and House Committee on Agriculture, *Hearings on Long-Range Agricultural Policy*, 80 Cong., 1 Sess. (Washington: Government Printing Office, 1948). There is a convenient summary of problems of agricultural policy in Walter W. Wilcox, *Alternative Policies for American Agriculture* (Public Affairs Bulletin No. 67, Legislative Reference Service, Library of Congress; Washington: Government Printing Office, 1949).

The best study of the administration of federal agricultural programs has been made by John M. Gaus and Leon Wolcott in *Public Administration and the United States Department of Agriculture* (Chicago: Public Administration Service, 1941). *Our Landed Heritage* (Princeton: Princeton University Press, 1942), by Roy M. Robbins, is a history of public land policies from 1776 to 1936. The special problems of migrant farm workers are dramatized by Carey McWilliams in *Ill Fares the Land* (Boston: Little, Brown & Company, 1942). One of the classic government reports of the New Deal period is Natural Resources Committee, *Report of the President's Committee on Farm Tenancy* (Washington: Government Printing Office, 1937).

There have been few studies of the political activities of farm organizations. In *The Farm Bureau Movement* (Baltimore: The Waverly Press, 1948), O. M. Kile presents the official history of the American Farm Bureau Federation since 1920. Robert and Rosalind Engler describe the political activities of the National Farmers Union in their pamphlet, "The Farmers Union in Washington" (Washington: 1948). A general picture of the politics of organized agriculture can be found in Wesley McCune, *The Farm Bloc* (New York: Doubleday & Company, 1943). *The Wallaces of Iowa* (Boston: Houghton Mifflin Company, 1947), written by Russell Lord, is the biography of America's most famous agricultural family.

government and labor

HE public's interest in labor policy has become vitally important in modern industrial society. Proposals to change public policies relating to the promotion or regulation of labor always arouse widespread interest. The identification of the public interest in labor affairs as expressed in legislation and public administration remains one of the most controversial tasks of public policy today.

what is the labor problem?

It is easier to mark out what employers and employees want in the field of labor policy than to identify the public's interest. The employer wants an adequate number of disciplined and effective workers to enable him to earn a profit on his investment. The employee wants a job which pays fair wages, provides reasonable working conditions, and offers some security of employment. In its simplest form, the public interest in labor is to find ways to harmonize the aspirations of employers and employees in order to promote and maintain general economic progress for the benefit of all and at the same time provide security for those who work.

From the point of view of the public, the labor problem has four major aspects:

1. The maintenance of continued production of goods and services at high levels
2. The improvement of living standards
3. The protection of workers against hazardous and discriminatory working conditions
4. The peaceful settlement of disputes between workers and management

The public interest in maintaining an adequate supply of goods and services is obvious. Production of needed commodities and services is essential to the maintenance of modern industrial society in the United States. The average man's expectations of improving his economic status depend for their fulfillment largely upon our capacity as a nation to achieve maximum levels of production which in turn provide employment for those willing and able to work.

In a democratic society, persistent goals of public policy include the development of greater equality of opportunity for all citizens and the refusal to permit individual citizens to fall below a certain minimum level of existence. These goals can be met in part through policies and programs designed to im-

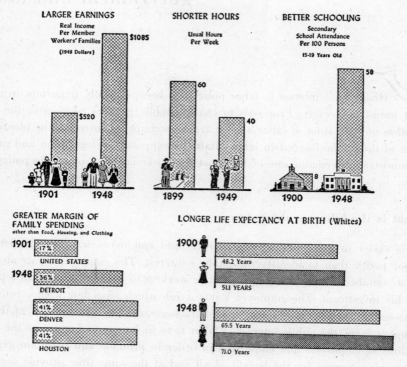

A Half Century of Change in Living Standards. (*Source:* Monthly Labor Review, *LXXI, No. 1, July, 1950, 27.*)

prove the standard of living of workers. For example, the share of the worker in the product of his labor has been tripled since 1900. Government can promote the public interest in the improvement of living standards by preventing unemployment and by establishing minimum wages.

Since a democratic society is based on the belief in the essential dignity of man, one of the problems of public labor policy is to prevent the exploitation of workers by employers. In the past such exploitation has been the inevitable result of the weaker economic position of the worker. Exploitation has taken the form of long working hours under unsafe or unhealthful conditions at very low wages. Sometimes particular groups of workers, such as women, children, and Negroes, have been discriminated against in one way or another.

The definition of labor problems from the public's point of view has come to include the protection of the workers' right to organize into unions to promote their common interest. One of the most controversial areas of labor policy concerns the specific conditions under which the right of workers to form unions and to seek to improve their status may be legally exercised.

Because of the public interest in maintaining high levels of production, furthering general economic progress, and improving living standards, the government has come to play an important role in contributing toward the peaceful cooperation of employers and employees. There is today little or no dispute about the right of the government to help workers and management to resolve conflicts which curtail production and employment. However, there is considerable controversy about the proper methods to be used by government and whether the government's role should be more than merely advisory. Should the government compel workers and management to submit their disputes to arbitration? Should the courts have the power to force unions to end a strike or desist from certain antiemployer tactics? Should work stoppages be tolerated in industries like electric power where uninterrupted production is essential to public welfare?

The public interest in labor policy illustrates two important aspects of the role of government in promoting the general welfare. First, government both promotes and regulates labor. The interests of labor are furthered by protective labor legislation covering such matters as child labor, hours of work, minimum wages, and workmen's compensation. It is assumed that the elimination of child labor and the improvement in working conditions benefit the general public as well as particular workers. In other matters, the public interest and the interests of labor may not be identical, or may even be held to be opposed. In such cases, governmental action is more likely to take the form of regulation. For example, the public's interest in maintaining essential production and services may be used to justify the application of a court injunction directing a union to stop a strike. Or a labor union may be regulated by prohibiting its members from engaging in certain practices held to be unfair to employers.

Second, the resolution of labor problems inevitably involves attempts to harmonize the conflicting claims of labor, management, and the public. The determination of the best way to resolve such conflicting claims has not been easy. Attempts by the government to control the private rights of workers and employers are met by cries that individual liberties are being destroyed by the collective action of the government. One of the consequences of the conflict between individual rights and the public interest has been a shifting of the balance between the two. Employers today accept or abide by public policies which their fathers and grandfathers opposed as confiscatory.

the setting of the labor problem

The determination of the public interest in labor policy does not remain fixed. Rather it varies, depending on such matters as the structure of industry and labor, the strength of employer and labor groups, public sympathies, and cultural traditions. Some of these factors are discussed in the following paragraphs.

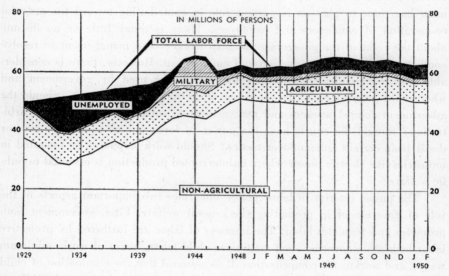

The Employment Picture. (*Source: The New York* Times, *March 12, 1950.*)

the labor force[1]

In 1949 the total labor force of the country, including all persons fourteen years of age and over, employed or seeking work, ranged from 61 million to 65 million. During the year about 1 million workers had been added to the labor force. The monthly average labor force during the year was 63.6 million, including 1.5 million persons in the armed forces and a civilian labor force of 62.1 million. Approximately 50.7 million persons were employed in nonagricultural fields, including nearly 8 million proprietors, self-employed persons, and do-

---

[1] All the statistics on the labor force are taken from *The Economic Report of the President,* January, 1950 (Washington: Government Printing Office, 1950), Tables C–9 and C–10, pp. 157–158.

mestic servants; and about 43 million wage and salary workers. Wage and salary workers were divided among various industry groups as follows:

NUMBER OF WAGE AND SALARY WORKERS IN NONAGRICULTURAL
ESTABLISHMENTS, IN 1949

Type of Employment	No. of employees in millions	Per Cent
Total wage and salary workers	42.9	100.0
Manufacturing	14.2	33.0
Trade	9.4	21.9
Government	5.8	13.5
Service	4.8	11.1
Transportation and public utilities	4.0	9.3
Contract construction	2.2	5.1
Finance	1.8	4.2
Mining	0.9	2.1

labor organizations

In 1950, about one of every four workers was a member of some union. In manufacturing industries, about two thirds of the workers were directly affected by union agreements with management. Workers in the United States began to organize on an extremely limited scale in the early days of the republic. Workingmen's parties appeared in the 1820's and 1830's to combat monetary inflation and improve factory conditions and standards of living. National unions of craft workers began to appear about 1850. Several unsuccessful attempts were made between 1866 and 1890 to form a national labor organization representing all organized workers. National labor groups either collapsed during periods of economic depression or literally fell in battle with industrial leaders. Much of the hostility between labor and management today can be traced to the warfare waged against organized labor from the 1870's to 1940.

Modern labor organization is essentially a product of the past fifty years. In 1900, about 833,000 workers (roughly 5 per cent of all wage and salary workers) belonged to 99 national unions. Union membership increased to nearly 5 million (roughly 18 per cent of all wage and salary workers) and 133 international unions by 1920. However, membership slumped to 3.4 million by 1925, and in 1935 less than 10 per cent of all wage and salary workers belonged to unions. The great stimulus in union growth came after 1935, when the CIO began its organization drive. Since 1933 union membership has increased fivefold from 3 million to 15 million.

The bulk of organized labor is split between the American Federation of Labor and the Congress of Industrial Organizations. The AFL was founded in the 1880's and led by Samuel Gompers as president until 1924. Gompers was

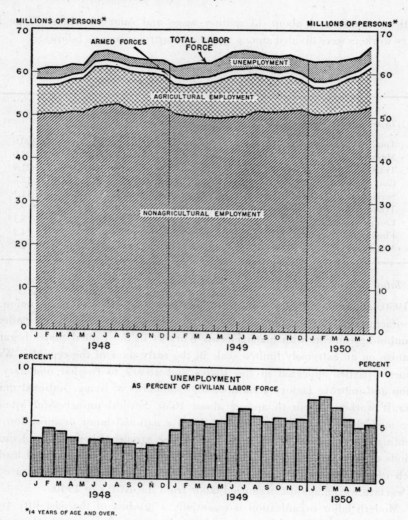

MILLIONS OF PERSONS*

ARMED FORCES   TOTAL LABOR FORCE

UNEMPLOYMENT

AGRICULTURAL EMPLOYMENT

NONAGRICULTURAL EMPLOYMENT

J F M A M J J A S O N D J F M A M J J A S O N D J F M A M J
1948   1949   1950

PERCENT

UNEMPLOYMENT
AS PERCENT OF CIVILIAN LABOR FORCE

J F M A M J J A S O N D J F M A M J J A S O N D J F M A M J
1948   1949   1950

*14 YEARS OF AGE AND OVER.

Labor Force.   Civilian employment reached an all-time high of 61.5 million in June, 1950. Nonagricultural employment was 2.5 million higher than in June, 1949, while agricultural employment was 650 thousand lower. Unemployment reached, in February, 1950, a postwar peak of 4.7 million or 7.6 per cent of the civilian labor force. By June, it was reduced to 3.4 million, or 5.2 per cent of the civilian labor force. (*Source:* The Midyear Economic Report of the President, *transmitted to the Congress, July, 1950. House document No. 644, 81 Cong., 2 Sess., 1950.*)

succeeded by William Green, who was still president in 1950. It has been estimated that until 1935 four out of five union members belonged to AFL unions.

The AFL is a federation of independent, autonomous unions. Each member union has its own traditions and internal government and works out its own policies and programs. The Federation is dominated by its largest affiliated unions, including the International Brotherhood of Teamsters, Chauffeurs, Stablemen and Helpers; the United Brotherhood of Carpenters and Joiners of America; the International Alliance of Hotel and Restaurant Employees; the International

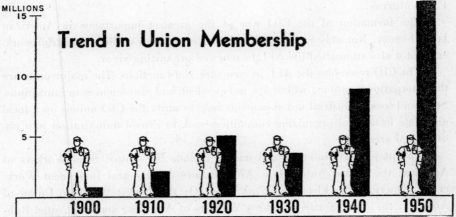

MILLIONS

Trend in Union Membership

Graph based on union reports. (*Source:* Monthly Labor Review, *LXXI, No. 1, July, 1950,* 113.)

Brotherhood of Electrical Workers; the International Hod Carriers' Union, Building and Common Laborers' Union of America; and the International Ladies' Garment Workers' Union. As the names of these unions indicate, the AFL is strongest in building construction, trucking, ladies' garment industries, and the service trades.

The national headquarters of the AFL has several important functions.

1. It settles disputes among affiliated unions and determines which union has the right to control certain jobs.

2. It provides a central informational and research service for all affiliated unions and compiles statistical data on wages and other relevant matters.

3. It maintains a lobby to influence the enactment or defeat of proposed labor legislation and works for the defeat of legislators and other political candidates who have opposed measures supported by the Federation.

4. Through various educational programs, it tries to make members more aware of social and economic problems and to teach them basic facts about economic conditions.

5. It conducts campaigns to increase union membership and particularly

to organize nonunion workers. Organizers are sent into unorganized communities to work directly with local union representatives.

    6. It directly controls local and state federations of AFL unions.

The Congress of Industrial Organizations was organized first as the Committee for Industrial Organization within the AFL in 1935. Its original purpose was to bring unorganized workers in the mass production industries into the AFL. Within two years, the Committee succeeded in unionizing more than 3 million workers. The success of the CIO led to its suspension from the AFL in 1936 and its expulsion in 1938. Since 1940 the CIO has been led by Philip Murray.

The formation of the CIO was of the greatest importance in American labor history. Not only was the CIO able to organize 6 million industrial workers, but it also stimulated the AFL to renewed organizing vigor.

The CIO resembles the AFL in structure and functions. The major units are the international unions, which are independent and autonomous organizations. State and local industrial union councils help to unify the CIO unions on a local and state basis, and organizing committees seek to extend unionization into unorganized areas.

The major CIO international unions include the United Steel Workers of America; the United Automobile, Aircraft, and Agricultural Implement Workers of America; the Electrical Workers—CIO; the Textile Workers' Union of America; the Amalgamated Clothing Workers of America; and the United Rubber Workers of America. The CIO strongholds are in steel, automobile, rubber tire, electrical, men's clothing, and textile industries.

The CIO exercises more control over its member unions than does the AFL. Such control was probably inevitable in a new organization struggling for its survival. More recently, however, there have been signs of a growing independence of action on the part of the major CIO international unions, and most observers have noted a decline in the prestige and power of the national CIO leaders.

About 450,000 railroad workers are organized into four railroad brotherhoods which are not affiliated with either the AFL or the CIO. These unions have existed for more than fifty years and have become stable organizations with rather conservative political views. They are recognized as very effective lobbyists before Congress and state legislatures. They cooperate with the CIO and the AFL on matters of common interest.

Some unions in addition to the railway brotherhoods are unaffiliated with any national organization. The two major independent unions are the International Association of Machinists and the United Mine Workers of America.

The split between the CIO and the AFL has never been overcome, although numerous attempts to merge the two organizations have been made. By 1950 some of the features that formerly had sharply distinguished the CIO from its

International Unions in the United States

BY SIZE OF MEMBERSHIP AND NUMBER OF LOCALS, 1949

(*Source:* Monthly Labor Review, LXXI, No. 1, July, 1950, 114.)

parent organization has disappeared. The reluctance of the AFL to extend unionization on an industrial basis to the mass production industries has largely disappeared. Although there remains a tendency for some of the AFL unions to be overcautious in directing their affairs and for some of the CIO unions to give a great deal of attention to non-trade-union activities, the two labor organizations have become increasingly alike in their organization and operation. Differences between them are most apparent in the leadership in the rival organizations. In general the men who lead AFL unions are old men whereas the CIO leaders are young. Studies of union leadership indicate that young organizations (CIO) make for young leaders, for CIO leaders in 1948 were characteristically younger than corporation executives, government officials, and AFL leaders. Moreover, CIO leaders have been better educated than AFL leaders.[2]

public attitudes, sympathies, and traditions

Writing in 1928, Professor Selig Perlman, a leading student of labor history and organization, noted several characteristics of the American community which have affected the development of labor organizations.[3] These factors also help to explain the setting of the labor problem. Perlman noted first the strength of the institution of private property in the United States. The labor movement hopes to deny the employer's right to absolute control of his property. Therefore the labor movement has historically been interpreted as a campaign against the rights of private property. Because of the strength of private property in the United States, Perlman saw the union living in a hostile environment.

Second, Perlman noted the absence of a strong sense of class conciousness

---

[2] See especially C. Wright Mills, *The New Men of Power* (New York: Harcourt, Brace and Company, 1948), pp. 68–83.

[3] Selig Perlman, *A Theory of the Labor Movement* (New York: The Macmillan Company, 1928), pp. 154–233.

in the ranks of American workers, who preferred to think of themselves as temporary workers hoping to become employers soon rather than as down-trodden, exploited workers forever doomed to an inferior status. The lack of "psychological cohesiveness" among American workers undoubtedly increased the difficulties of unionization.

Third, as Perlman indicates, American workers shared a distrust of govern-mental action, although, like businessmen and farmers, they never carried this distrust to the logical conclusion of denying themselves government assistance. Nevertheless, workers were skeptical of using the government as an instrument of economic reform. And they were impressed with the apparent ease with which employers' groups were able to use governmental power against the interests of labor.

It may be questioned whether Perlman's analysis of the American labor movement of the 1920's is applicable in the 1950's. Many observers report an increasing class consciousness in the American community generally, particu-larly in the lowest-income groups. The New Deal convinced a majority of work-ers that the government can also be an effective instrument of economic reform. In addition, the balance in public policy between individual rights and the pub-lic interest has shifted since the 1920's so that individual property rights can-not be exercised so freely in the 1950's. Employers today more commonly accept unionism as part of the fabric of economic activity and have adjusted their activities and managerial policies to take account of that acceptance.

Public attitudes toward unions and labor problems are affected by a number of other factors. In times of prosperity, unionism generally flourishes (with the exception of the 1920's), whereas economic depression normally weakens union organization. Internal dissension within unions may also undermine the prestige and standing of unions. The reaction of unions to public demands for destroying the power of Communists in unions helps to condition public attitudes toward unionism. The ability and willingness of union leaders to accept a wider measure of social responsibility for their activities may influence public attitudes significantly in the future.

protection of workers against exploitation and unfair working conditions

Protective labor legislation can be classified as follows:
1. Protection of special groups in the labor force, including working chil-dren, women workers, migrants, and Negroes
2. Regulation of hours of labor
3. Regulation of wages
4. Relief and prevention of accidents, occupational diseases, and sickness through workmen's compensation laws and sickness benefits

child labor

Until 1910 children were employed in increasing numbers in agriculture; in street trades such as selling newspapers or bootblacking; in domestic service; in industrial homework including such occupations as stringing bags, sorting buttons, and sewing; and in canneries. Protection of child labor developed only gradually in the United States. In 1842 Massachusetts became the first state to limit the hours of labor of children by prohibiting more than a ten-hour day for children under twelve. From the Civil War to the end of the century, most states set some minor and ineffective limits on the employment of children in factories. Effective legislation was a product of the drive for social justice which characterized the progressive movement of 1900–1917. Today almost all states forbid the employment of children under sixteen in factories and stores. The age limit is usually higher in dangerous occupations like mining. Nightwork is ordinarily forbidden, and further restrictions are usually placed on employment of children during afterschool hours.

The federal government did not successfully regulate child labor until 1938. In 1918 the Supreme Court declared unconstitutional a federal law which prohibited the interstate transportation of goods produced by child labor.[4] The Court held that Congress might regulate the interstate transportation of goods which were harmful but could not regulate the conditions of production. A subsequent attempt to curtail the practice by imposing high taxes on the products of child labor was held unconstitutional on the grounds that the legislation was not properly a tax measure and that it regulated and prevented production.[5] A constitutional amendment to give Congress authority to regulate child labor was introduced in 1924, but only twenty-eight states have ratified its adoption. Further federal efforts to regulate child labor in the National Industrial Recovery Act of 1933 were struck down by the Court's decision declaring the NIRA unconstitutional.[6] The Fair Labor Standards (Wages and Hours) Act, passed in 1938, prohibits shipment in interstate commerce of goods produced by children under the age of sixteen in mining and manufacturing and by children under eighteen in hazardous occupations. In 1941, the Supreme Court upheld the Fair Labor Standards Act of 1938[7] and the federal government's clear-cut authority to regulate child labor in connection with products shipped in interstate commerce.

The Children's Bureau enforces the child labor provisions of the Fair Labor Standards Act. It sets standards of employment in nonmining and nonmanufac-

---

[4] *Hammer* v. *Dagenhart*, 247 U.S. 251 (1918).

[5] *Bailey* v. *Drexel Furniture Co.*, 259 U.S. 20 (1922).

[6] *Schechter* v. *United States*, 295 U.S. 495 (1935).

[7] *United States* v. *Darby*, 312 U.S. 100 (1941). This decision explicitly overrules *Hammer* v. *Dagenhart*.

turing industries in interstate commerce and inspects places where minors under sixteen years of age are employed.

women workers

Women have always been employed in industrial jobs, in office work, or in the home. They offered a relatively cheap source of labor to employers. Because women were physically weaker than men, they were subject to greater exploitation than men, and their health suffered from long hours of fatiguing work at low wages.

Early efforts to limit working hours for women were unsuccessful. The legality of state restrictions of the hours of labor of women remained unsettled until 1908, when the Supreme Court, under the impact of Louis Brandeis's celebrated brief on the deterioration of health caused by long hours of work, upheld state legislation on maximum hours for women.[8] The Court recognized that the bargaining power of women workers was weak and that legislative protection of the physical well-being of women was proper and constitutional and preserved "the strength and vigor of the race." In the next thirty years, most states adopted 48 and 44-hour maximum workweeks for women, but domestic servants and farm laborers were usually excepted.

Women workers have normally received lower wages than men and in many cases were grossly underpaid. In 1912, in order to combat the evils of low wages, Massachusetts adopted the first minimum-wage law. The Massachusetts legislation, which attempted to enforce minimum wages for women only by publishing the names of employers who failed to meet the minimum wages, was followed by other mandatory laws. An Oregon minimum-wage law was sustained by a four-to-four vote of the Supreme Court in 1917.[9] About half of the states had adopted minimum-wage laws by 1923, when the Court, in the *Adkins* case, declared unconstitutional a federal statute which established minimum wages for women in the District of Columbia.[10] Finally, in 1937, the Supreme Court overruled the *Adkins* case in upholding a State of Washington minimum-wage law.[11] Said Chief Justice Charles Evans Hughes:

> We think . . . that the decision in the *Adkins* case was a departure from the true application of the principles governing the regulations by the State of the relation of employer and employed. . . . What can be closer to the public interest than the health of women and their protection from unscrupulous and overreaching employers? And if the protection of women is a legitimate exercise of state power, how can it be said that the requirement of the payment of a minimum wage fairly fixed in order to meet the very

---

[8] *Muller* v. *Oregon*, 208 U.S. 412 (1908).
[9] *Stettler* v. *O'Hara*, 243 U.S. 629 (1917).
[10] *Adkins* v. *Children's Hospital*, 261 U.S. 525 (1923).
[11] *West Coast Hotel* v. *Parrish*, 300 U.S. 379 (1937).

necessities of existence is not an admissible means to that end? The legislature of the State was clearly entitled to consider the situation of women in employment, and the fact that their bargaining power is relatively weak, and that they are ready victims of those who would take advantage of their necessitous circumstances. The legislature was entitled to adopt measures to reduce . . . the exploiting of workers at wages so low as to be insufficient to meet the bare cost of living.[12]

migratory labor

Many persons move about the country in search of work. These migrants are employed as seasonal farm laborers and as industrial workers. Seasonal farm workers follow the crops and work at various harvesting jobs. Their housing conditions are below standard and their income is low. A few states have attempted to establish minimum housing conditions for migratory farm workers, but enforcement is difficult. These workers receive inadequate medical care, and their children need better housing and education.

Industrial migrant workers can usually be found in resort areas along the northern Atlantic coast, and in mining, lumbering, canning, construction, and Great Lakes shipping. During the depression, twenty-eight states enacted laws to prevent indigent individuals seeking work from entering those states from outside. However, in 1942, the Supreme Court held that such state legislation was "an unconstitutional barrier to interstate commerce." [13]

Negro labor

Although the Negro worker and the white worker share many problems and difficulties, Negro workers find job opportunities more restricted. Job discrimination forces many of them to work at low-paying, inferior jobs and makes them the first victims of unemployment.

From 1940 to 1944, it is estimated that more than a million Negro workers moved from farm to factory into skilled jobs. During World War II, the federal government attempted to prevent discrimination in employment on grounds of race, color, or creed, and in 1943 a Committee on Fair Employment Practices (FEPC) was established as a temporary independent agency. Despite vigorous opposition, the FEPC was fairly successful. Although it went out of existence after the war, it established a pattern for fair employment practice legislation which has been adopted in several states.

New York and New Jersey adopted fair employment practice laws in 1945, and Massachusetts and Connecticut adopted similar laws in 1946 and 1947. These laws forbid employers from discriminating against any person in terms, conditions, or privileges of employment on account of race, color, creed, or

---

[12] *Ibid.*, 397–399.
[13] *Edwards* v. *California*, 314 U.S. 160 (1942).

national origin. In addition, labor unions are prohibited from discriminating against their members for these reasons. The right of a state to prohibit discrimination by labor unions against Negroes was upheld by the Supreme Court in 1946.[14] The Court said that to claim that a prohibition of discrimination in union membership on account of race, creed, or color "violated the Fourteenth Amendment would be a distortion of the policy manifested in the amendment, which was adopted to prevent state legislation designed to perpetuate discrimination on the basis of race or color."

Since 1944 the Republican and Democratic parties have officially supported proposals to create a permanent federal FEPC. President Truman has vigorously urged the Congress to enact such legislation, but filibusters in the United States Senate have succeeded in defeating such proposals.

regulation of hours of labor

Early attempts by states to limit hours of labor were generally unsuccessful. Several states did succeed in limiting hours of labor in occupations considered to be hazardous and unhealthful. In 1898 Utah limited the working day to eight hours in mining and smelting. The Supreme Court upheld the legislation as legitimate protection of the health of the workers.[15] In 1905, however, in the famous *Lochner* case, the Court held that a New York statute limiting the hours of bakers violated the right of freedom of contract and described the legislation as "mere meddlesome interferences with the rights of the individuals." In 1913 Oregon enacted a ten-hour law for factory employment which was upheld by the Court in 1917.[16]

The federal government, under the Adamson Act of 1916, regulates the hours of labor of railroad employees engaged in interstate commerce.[17] The Interstate Commerce Commission similarly limits the number of hours worked by drivers for motor carriers in interstate commerce. The Walsh-Healy Act (Public Contracts Act) limits employment of individuals working on projects contracted for by the federal government to forty hours a week on straight time. Work beyond forty hours must be paid for at the rate of time and a half. General federal regulation of hours of individuals engaged in employment in interstate commerce was achieved by the Fair Labor Standards (Wages and Hours) Act in 1938. The act established a standard forty-hour week and provided that work beyond forty hours must be paid for at the rate of time and a half. The act was upheld as constitutional in 1941.[18]

---

[14] *Railway Mail Association* v. *Corsi*, 326 U.S. 88 (1946).

[15] *Holden* v. *Hardy*, 169 U.S. 366 (1898).

[16] *Lochner* v. *New York*, 198 U.S. 45 (1905); *Bunting* v. *Oregon*, 243 U.S. 426 (1917).

[17] The act was sustained by the Supreme Court in *Wilson* v. *New*, 243 U.S. 323 (1917).

[18] *United States* v. *Darby*, 312 U.S. 100 (1941).

regulation of wages

Except for special workers, particularly women, minimum wages for workers were not established until the enactment of the Fair Labor Standards Act in 1938. The act is based on the power of Congress to regulate interstate commerce. It applies, with certain exemptions, to workers in interstate commerce or those whose work affects interstate commerce. In the *Darby* case upholding the act, the Supreme Court said:

> The power of Congress over interstate commerce "is complete in itself, may be exercised to its utmost extent, and acknowledges no limitations other than are prescribed by the Constitution." . . . That power can neither be enlarged nor diminished by the exercise or non-exercise of state power. . . . Congress, following its own conception of public policy concerning the restrictions which may appropriately be imposed on interstate commerce, is free to exclude from the commerce articles whose use in the states for which they are destined it may conceive to be injurious to the public health, morals, or welfare, even though the state has not sought to regulate their use.[19]

The act is administered by the Wage and Hour and Public Contracts Divisions of the United States Department of Labor. It provided for a minimum of twenty-five cents an hour in 1938, thirty cents an hour from 1939 to 1945, and forty cents an hour from 1945 to 1949. In 1949, the minimum wage was raised to seventy-five cents an hour, but the number of workers covered by the act was reduced.[20]

workmen's compensation

One of the problems resulting from the development of modern industry is the prevalence of industrial accidents. As industry became more highly organized under the influence of technological improvements, the possibility of serious injuries to workers increased. The major problem of public policy has been to fix the responsibility for industrial accidents.

Until the 1880's, three principles of common law were utilized by employers to escape responsibility for industrial accidents. First, under the "fellow-servant doctrine," an employer was not responsible for injuries to a workman caused by another workman if the employer had exercised reasonable care to employ suitable workers (fellow servants) and had provided safe working places and safe machines. Second, under the rule of "assumption of risk," the employer was not responsible for injuries to a workman if he had exercised reasonable precautions to prevent such injuries. It was assumed that the worker knowingly

---

[19] *Ibid*, 114.
[20] See Public Law 393, 81 Cong., cited as "Fair Labor Standards Amendments of 1949."

undertook the risks of employment and was liable for injuries so long as the employer took reasonable safety precautions. Third, under the doctrine of "contributory negligence," the employer was absolved of responsibility for injuries if the employee had exposed himself to injury through his own negligence.

Gradually the states modified these three rules and extended the liability of the employer for industrial accidents. Under state employer-liability acts common in the period 1890–1910, an injured employee could collect damages only by means of court action, which was time consuming and expensive. The inadequacies of these statutes finally led to the development of workmen's compensation laws. New York adopted the first workmen's compensation law. Similar laws are in force in all states today.

A workmen's compensation law provides that workers receive money payments or medical benefits for injuries incurred in the course of their employment. It is based on the principle that industry must bear the original burden of compensating employees for injuries so that compensation becomes part of the cost of doing business. Workmen's compensation schemes are administered usually by state boards or commissions which exercise considerable discretion in determining whether an injury arises in the course of employment, the nature of the injury, and the allowable compensation for the injury. In order to assure employees of receiving compensation for an injury, employers are required to carry compensation insurance of some kind.

Workers in several industries are subject to occupational diseases, including poisoning from lead, mercury, and other metals; poisoning from arsenic; skin infections; industrial eczema; silicosis; and asthma. Today workers covered by state workmen's compensation laws can be compensated for such occupational diseases.

cash sickness benefits

Cash sickness benefits are designed to make payments to workers who are unable to work because of illness not connected with their employment. They are based on the theory that workers who, because of sickness, are unable to work and earn their usual wages must be protected against loss of income for limited periods. By 1950, four states—California, Rhode Island, New Jersey, and New York—had passed sickness benefit laws, and the federal government had extended similar protection to railroad workers in interstate commerce.

labor organization and collective bargaining

Until the early 1930's, the American employer was almost wholly unrestricted under law in his dealings with labor unions. He was free to deal or not to deal with them. He could refuse to recognize a union as a bargaining agent for his employees. He might discharge a worker for joining a union. A union was able to maintain itself as a going concern only by taking concerted action against employers in the form of strikes, picketing, and boycotts. Employers opposed union activity by a variety of techniques, including lockouts, strikebreaking, maintenance of supplies of weapons, private police systems, labor spies, black-listing, and company-dominated unions.

In the absence of statutes, governmental regulation of labor up to 1931 largely consisted of court rulings. The extremely restrictive doctrines applied by the courts to employer-employee relations heavily penalized organized labor. Relying on the common law, the courts assumed that employers and employees were equal in their relationship and refused to question the right of the employer to make any kind of labor contract he could. Even though the bargaining power of the individual workingman was extremely weak, the courts continued to assume that the worker was as free to influence the terms of his labor contract as was his employer.

The most common weapon in labor disputes was the court injunction. Its use in labor disputes was based on the idea that the right to carry on a business is a property right and that a strike, which interrupts a business, interferes with another's right to do business.

Labor injunctions were widely used between 1890 and 1930. They could be secured by action of federal or state courts, depending on the nature of the problem. The *Debs* case of 1895 stimulated the use of the injunction in labor disputes and aroused the bitter opposition of unions to it. Eugene V. Debs, the leader of the American Railway Union, had been enjoined from interfering with the business of several railroads which handled Pullman cars. Debs did not obey the injunction and was subsequently convicted and imprisoned for contempt.[21]

After 1895 labor unions repeatedly sought relief from "government by injunction." Labor hoped that the Clayton Act of 1914 would exempt unions from antitrust laws and curtail the use of the injunction, but the act, as interpreted by the courts, appeared to increase the number of injunction suits against labor.

promotion of labor organization

Labor opposition to prevailing antiunion policies of the local, state, and federal governments gradually produced a revision in public policy. Little by little, some courts held that workers had a right to organize for self-protection. The unequal bargaining position of workers led to persistent demands to protect the workingman's status by law. This concept emerged in the 1930's as a governmental guarantee of the right of workers to bargain collectively.

In 1932 the Norris-La Guardia Act declared that in order to protect the public interest, workers should be free to form labor unions without interference

---

[21] See *In re Debs*, 158 U.S. 564 (1895).

from the employer. It recognized that "the individual unorganized worker is commonly helpless to exercise actual liberty of contract and to protect his freedom of labor, and thereby obtain acceptable terms and conditions of employment." It declared that workers may select representatives of their own choosing to negotiate the terms and conditions of their employment.[22] The act established no agency to enforce its provisions; it merely limited the use of injunctions by federal courts against labor unions.

The governmental guarantee of the right of employees to organize unions and bargain collectively over the terms and conditions of employment was next stated in 1933 in the famous section 7(a) of the National Industrial Recovery Act, which required all NRA codes to recognize that employees have the right to organize and bargain collectively through representatives of their own choosing free from the interference, restraint, or coercion of employers. It prohibited the practice of requiring an employee or anyone seeking employment to join a company union, or to refrain from joining a labor organization of his own choosing, as a condition of employment. These provisions were nullified in 1935 when the Supreme Court declared the NIRA unconstitutional in the *Schechter* case.

Within two months after the *Schechter* decision, Congress enacted the National Labor Relations Act of 1935. Known commonly as "the Wagner Act," this act and the so-called "Little Wagner Acts" passed by a few state legislatures expanded the public policy of guaranteeing the workers' right to organize and bargain collectively. The basic concept of the act was clearly stated by Chief Justice Hughes in the decision upholding its constitutionality:

> Long ago we stated the reason for labor organizations. We said that they were organized out of the necessities of the situation; that a single employee was helpless in dealing with an employer; that he was dependent ordinarily on his daily wage for the maintenance of himself and family; that if the employer refused to pay him the wages that he thought fair, he was nevertheless unable to leave the employ and resist arbitrary and unfair treatment; that union was essential to give laborers opportunity to deal on an equality with their employer.[23]

In addition to guaranteeing workers the right to organize unions and bargain collectively with employers, the National Labor Relations Act prohibited certain practices of employers as unfair, and it established machinery to designate unions to represent employees in bargaining collectively with employers over terms of employment. A National Labor Relations Board was established to administer the act. The board was authorized to order employers to

---

[22] 47 Stat. 70.
[23] *National Labor Relations Board* v. *Jones and Laughlin Steel Corp.*, 301 U.S. 1, 33 (1937).

cease and desist from practices declared to be unfair by the act and could enforce its order by appealing to the United States circuit courts of appeals.

The two major aims of the National Labor Relations Act were to encourage collective bargaining between employers and employees, and to guarantee each worker the right to join or not to join a union. In practice the encouragement of collective bargaining predominated over freedom of association. For example, when a majority of workers in a plant selected a particular union as its bargaining agent, the rest of the workers had to accept representation by that bargaining agent. Similarly a union might succeed in persuading employers to hire or keep only union members.

Labor-Management Relations Act of 1947 (the Taft-Hartley Act)

Employer dissatisfaction with the National Labor Relations Act led to the passage of the Labor-Management Relations Act (the Taft-Hartley Act) in 1947. The Taft-Hartley Act amends the National Labor Relations Act in several significant ways. It aims to "equalize" the responsibilities of employers and employees by providing a list of unfair labor practices by workers and unions. For example, it is unfair for a union to refuse to bargain with an employer, to engage in certain types of secondary boycotts and jurisdictional strikes, or to demand excessive fees or dues. The act also prohibits the closed shop, that is, one in which union membership is a condition of employment. A union shop, that is, one in which new workers must join the union, is permitted only under certain conditions. Unions must file affidavits with the Secretary of Labor that their officers are not Communists or do not belong to any organization which advocates the violent overthrow of the government. Unions also must file copies of their constitutions, bylaws, and financial reports.

The Taft-Hartley Act presents several difficult problems of meaning which have not as yet been completely solved. Experience under the law is too limited to permit a complete evaluation. It has curbed some nonsocial acts of unions, but it has also aroused deep bitterness in union officials. The act has given employers a more advantageous position in dealing with unions. To trade-union officials, the act represents an effort to weigh the scales against labor. To employers, it represents an effort to equalize the balance between workers and themselves. One of its most significant features is its great reliance on governmental intervention in collective bargaining in order to achieve peaceful labor-management relations. Some of the most considered criticism of the act emphasizes the dangers of governmental control of such subjects of hitherto voluntary collective bargaining as the closed shop, the union shop, checkoff of dues, and employee benefits. Senator Robert Taft, in supporting its enactment, said:

> I feel that the bill makes an extraordinary reversal along the right lines
> toward equalizing the power of labor unions and employers. . . . I believe

it will deal with a majority of the serious problems which now exist between employers and employees, that it will impose upon unions a responsibility more equal to the power which they have acquired, and that it will tend to bring about industrial peace in the United States.[24]

Writing in 1949, William M. Leiserson, well-known labor economist, took a different view.

The Wagner Act puts its faith in collective bargaining; but, while the Taft-Hartley Act paid lip service to the principle of collective bargaining, its insistence on "legal rights" encouraged individual bargaining and, to an even greater extent, Government determination of the labor bargain.[25]

the settlement of labor disputes

Another major objective of public labor policy is the peaceful settlement of disputes between labor and management. The Taft-Hartley Act represents the current federal policy on the settlement of labor disputes. It seeks to avoid or settle strikes in five ways.

1. COOLING-OFF PERIODS. A party to a labor contract may negotiate a change in the contract only by giving sixty days' advance notice. During the sixty-day "cooling-off" period or until the contract expires, whichever period is longer, employees may not strike.

2. UNLAWFUL STRIKES AND BOYCOTTS. It is unlawful to strike in order to force anyone to join any organization, to force a business to cease dealing with another company, and so on. A union which engages in prohibited strikes is guilty of an unfair labor practice. Anyone injured as a result of an unlawful strike or boycott may claim damages from the union in federal court.

3. STRIKES IN VIOLATION OF CONTRACT. Employers may sue unions in court for breach of contract.

4. STRIKES CREATING A NATIONAL EMERGENCY. Strikes which affect an entire industry and imperil the national health or safety such as a railroad strike, may be subject to injunction for a maximum period of eighty days. An injunction for that period may be obtained on application by the Attorney General. The President appoints a special board which advises him within sixty days on ways to settle the dispute. If the dispute is not settled, the National Labor Relations Board polls employees on accepting the employer's final offer. If the dispute is still unsettled after eighty days, the injunction expires.

5. MEDIATION AND CONCILIATION. Major public responsibility for settling labor disputes is placed in the Federal Mediation and Conciliation Service, an

[24] *Congressional Record*, XCIII (April 23, 1947), Pt. 3, 3840.
[25] William M. Leiserson, "For a New Labor Law—A Basic Analysis," *New York Times Magazine*, February 6, 1949, p. 7.

independent agency. The Service makes its labor mediators available to assist in ironing out differences between labor and management. The Service must be called into action if a national emergency strike remains unsettled.

It will be noted that the Taft-Hartley Act has renewed the use of the injunction in labor disputes. It provides that the government may ask for a temporary injunction at the time it issues a complaint of unfair labor practices against a union or an employer. In addition the injunction is relied upon heavily to settle strikes which endanger national health and safety. The effort of the Taft-Hartley Act to distinguish between ordinary strikes and strikes creating a national emergency may lead to difficulties. The distinction is difficult to make since most important strikes endanger health and safety in some way.

maintenance of full employment

In addition to protecting workers against exploitation, promoting and regulating union organization and collective bargaining, and adjusting labor disputes, government endeavors to eliminate unemployment in order to maintain economic prosperity and continued production of goods and services. It does this in several ways.

One way of preventing unemployment is to assist persons to find jobs. Ohio established the first public employment offices in the United States in 1890. By 1916, ninety-six offices had been established in twenty-six states. World War I and World War II gave impetus to a more comprehensive governmental organization of the labor market. The United States Employment Service was established in 1918 in the Department of Labor, but the Service was reduced in 1919 to gathering facts about employment and to providing slight subsidies to state employment offices. The Wagner-Peyser Act of 1933 made federal grants available to states for the support of public employment offices. In order to qualify for grants, each state is required to conduct its employment offices in accordance with the standards and regulations of the United States Employment Service, the federal supervisory agency.

Unemployment compensation, a system of insurance which makes cash payments to unemployed individuals for limited periods, is perhaps the chief current public program to alleviate the effects of unemployment. It is discussed in detail in Chapter 39.

The most significant modern development of public policy in employment matters was the enactment of the Employment Act of 1946. The act makes the federal government responsible for coordinating and utilizing its functions, resources, and programs to create and maintain employment for persons able, willing, and seeking work, and to promote maximum employment, production, and purchasing power. The act established the Council of Economic Advisers in the Executive Office of the President to study continuously the economic situation and to prepare recommendations for the President on methods of maintaining high levels of employment, production, and purchasing power.[26]

The Employment Act represents an acceptance by the federal government of a new responsibility for promoting and maintaining national economic stability. Although the record of the Council of Economic Advisers from 1946 to 1950 was disappointing to many observers, the act nevertheless places a public obligation on the federal government to use all of its resources to prevent or overcome depressions and unemployment.

unresolved issues in labor policy

Organized labor has made great progress since 1933. Fifteen million workers organized in unions represent a tremendous growth in the influence and power of labor in the national economy. Workers today have a more equitable share of the product of their labor. And the activities of organized workers have a more profound influence on the community.

Perhaps the most important problem ahead in labor policy concerns the capacity of organized labor to accept a wider measure of social responsibility for its actions. Will labor leaders be able to devise policies which not only assist their union members but also encourage a high level of employment and national income? Will union members be able to recognize the obligations for community well-being which have been won by them through their organizing efforts?

As organized labor becomes stronger and exercises greater influence on political and economic life, it will be faced by demands for public regulation of trade-union organization and activities. Is any public regulation of trade unions desirable? Should unions be required to make a public accounting of their funds? Should the federal government find new ways to force unions to observe their agreements with management? Should unions be prohibited from discriminating against individuals by denying union membership on grounds of political belief and race? Since union membership is frequently a basic requirement for continued employment, should the public regulate internal union practices in disciplining and expelling union members?

The organized labor movement has not been free from practices which are abhorrent to many Americans. What union practices are considered antisocial or undesirable? Shall unions be permitted to prevent technological progress in such industries as the construction industry? Should certain employers be required to employ an excessive number of men in order to provide employment to union members?

As industry becomes more highly organized and as labor unions and em-

---

[26] See Chapter 42 for a fuller discussion of the Council of Economic Advisers.

ployers' groups become stronger, strikes and lockouts are more apt to imperil public health and safety. Are present methods of settling disputes adequate to protect the public interest in such instances? In the event of a strike creating a national emergency, should trade unions and employers be required to submit their disputes to arbitration whenever collective bargaining fails to produce a settlement?

More generally, should the role of government in labor affairs be expanded? Or is it better for industry and unions to "slug it out" than have the government tell them what to do? Neither labor nor management has been reluctant to demand or accept governmental assistance despite protestations against governmental meddling. Many expert observers have urged a policy of abandoning the use of governmental power in labor disputes except in cases of genuine emergencies.

bibliographic note

Selig Perlman and Philip Taft have written the best history of the American labor movement in their *History of Labor in the United States, 1896–1932* (New York: The Macmillan Company, 1935). *Organized Labor* (New York: McGraw-Hill Book Company, 1945), by Harry Millis and Royal Montgomery, is a textbook containing extensive treatments of labor history as well as labor policies of American governments and employers. *The Bending Cross* (New Brunswick: Rutgers University Press, 1949), by Ray Ginger, is the best biography of Eugene Victor Debs, one of America's greatest labor leaders. Keith Sward's *The Legend of Henry Ford* (New York: Rinehart & Company, 1948) has a fascinating and brilliant account of Ford's labor policies. *American Labor Struggles* (New York: Harcourt, Brace and Company, 1936), by Samuel Yellen, tells the story of some of the most violent incidents in labor history and reveals the high degree of hostility toward labor organization which has characterized much of American history. Selig Perlman's *A Theory of the Labor Movement* (New York: The Macmillan Company, 1928) remains one of the most penetrating and incisive analyses of the nature of the American labor movement. *The American Federation of Labor* (Washington: The Brookings Institution, 1933), by Lewis Lorwin, is still the standard history of the AFL for the period up to 1932.

The most comprehensive analysis of American labor policy since 1933 is found in Harry Millis and Emily Clark Brown, *From the Wagner Act to Taft-Hartley* (Chicago: The University of Chicago Press, 1950). Special aspects of governmental policy toward labor are covered in E. E. Witte's *The Government in Labor Disputes* (New York: McGraw-Hill Book Company, 1932) and in

The Labor Injunction (New York: The Macmillan Company, 1930), by Felix Frankfurter and Nathan Greene. The development and operation of state labor legislation are surveyed in Charles Killingsworth, *State Labor Relations Acts* (Chicago: The University of Chicago Press, 1948).

The issue of the compatibility of organized labor and a capitalist economy is provocatively analyzed by Charles Lindblom in *Unionism and Capitalism* (New Haven: Yale University Press, 1949). C. Wright Mills discusses the politics of organized labor in *The New Men of Power* (New York: Harcourt, Brace and Company, 1948). The progress made by organized labor since 1900 is highlighted in a special issue of the *Monthly Labor Review*, Vol. LXXI, No. 1 (July, 1950). The portrayal of trade unionism as the conservative movement of modern industrial society is presented in Frank Tannenbaum's *A Philosophy of Labor* (New York: Alfred A. Knopf, 1951).

government and social welfare

N ALMOST universal task of government today is the protection of individuals against the loss of income caused by factors over which individuals have no real control. The major economic hazards which everyone faces are old age, unemployment, sickness and disability, and death of the family bread-winner. The principal public issue in the field of social welfare can be stated simply: How shall society undertake to protect the individual against some of these uncertainties and common economic hazards of life?

old age

One of the most important problems facing the country is the aging of our population. The proportion of people over sixty-five years of age has been rising rather steadily. It is estimated that one half of the population was less than sixteen years of age when George Washington was President. By 1950, the average age in the United States had reached thirty years and would probably rise to thirty-five years by 1975. In 1900, only 3 million persons were sixty-five years and older compared to 11 million in 1950 and an anticipated 18 million aged persons in 1975. By 1975 the aged will be five or six times as numerous as they were in 1900.

The rise in the average age of Americans creates many problems. An older population has different buying habits and tends to be more conservative politically, less productive industrially, and more dependent than a younger population. Perhaps most important is the fact that the ability to work is impaired by advancing age. There is considerable controversy about the ability of people over sixty-five to work productively, and certainly ability to work varies greatly among aged persons. Employers tend to regard old age as a disadvantage and prefer to hire young people. As a result, aged persons face a decline in earning power and many become dependent on others for their support.

unemployment

For younger workers, the most serious economic hazard both to them and to the community in general is unemployment. During the 1930's unemployment

831

OVER 65: A RISING TIDE	PERCENT OF POPULATION
1850 .6	2.6
1860 .8 *Each symbol equals one million persons*	2.7
1870 1.1	3.0
1880 1.7	3.4
1890 2.4	3.9
1900 3	4.1
1910 3.9	4.3
1920 4.9	4.7
1930 6.6	5.4
1940 9	6.8
1950 11.3	7.7

(*Source: Adapted from Seymour Harris, "What to Do with the 18 Million Aged?"*, New York Times Magazine, *July, 10, 1949.*)

ranged from 5.1 million to 14.7 million. From 1948 to 1950, unemployment varied from 2.5 million to 4.5 million. In recent years up to 1 million more persons have come into the labor market each year looking for work than have left the labor market. In 1950, about 500,000 college graduates alone entered the labor market. Employment opportunities have also been affected by advances in industrial technology. As new plants and equipment have been added, businessmen have been able to produce more with the same number of workers. The number of jobs has not kept pace with the increase in the labor force and in productivity.

sickness and disability

Like old age and unemployment, illness not only impairs the earning capacity of individuals but in addition may exhaust the family's financial resources. Since the early 1930's, studies have documented the inability of many families to meet the costs of medical care. Sickness and disability have been recognized as important threats to the economic security of the family.

Each day about one in every twenty of the population is sick. Many communities, especially in rural areas, do not have adequate medical, dental, and nursing services and hospitals. The number of doctors in proportion to the population has actually declined since 1900.

loss of the family breadwinner

The fourth major economic hazard facing the family is the risk of losing the main breadwinner through death. In 1946, it was estimated that there were 2.7 million fatherless children under eighteen years of age, about 3.7 million widows under sixty-five years of age, and approximately 3 million widows aged sixty-five and over. Providing a minimum level of economic security for such families has become a major problem of American public welfare policy.

changing views about the government's role in welfare

Until the enactment of the Social Security Act of 1935 the United States did not have a comprehensive public program with which to attack the problem of the economic security of wage earners and their families. The Social Security Act represents a milestone in the evolution of public welfare policy. Its enactment recognized officially the responsibility of their government for assuring to all Americans a reasonable degree of economic and social security.

Welfare policies of government have been influenced by the social, economic, and political development of the United States. Until the end of the nineteenth century, some free land was available to those who claimed it. Millions of immigrants found in the United States economic opportunities which they had not had before. The rapid industrial and agricultural development of the country and the exploitation of its natural resources helped foster the optimistic conviction that every individual could achieve a fair measure of economic security for himself and his family.

The traditions of individual initiative and the concept of America as a land of opportunity affected public attitudes toward the relief of destitute individuals and families. At first, aid to the needy was considered a responsibility of the local community. Individuals requiring help over long periods were regarded as shiftless and unworthy of aid. The states entered the welfare field early in American history by providing for the institutional care of persons suffering from communicable diseases. During the nineteenth century, with the advancement of sanitary and medical sciences, some local and state public health services were established. By the middle of the nineteenth century, private relief agencies had begun to develop, but their work was concentrated in large cities. Churches undertook relief programs as a part of their religious activity. About the turn of the century, social workers like Robert A. Wood and Jane Addams developed settlement houses in underpriviliged areas of large cities to provide assistance to needy families and to develop recreational and educational programs for new immigrants.

Between 1900 and 1930 the states began to provide financial assistance to local communities to aid certain needy groups, particularly the aged, the blind, and orphaned children. By 1930 twenty states gave some aid to the blind, forty-five states assisted mothers of dependent children, and twelve states had enacted old-age pension laws. Many of these state programs were highly inadequate and ineffective.

In 1929, at the beginning of the depression of the thirties, about three fourths of all relief funds came from governmental sources and one fourth from private sources, such as churches and private welfare agencies. The public and private welfare programs were still geared mainly to the needs of a predominantly agricultural population with a high level of economic opportunity. By 1929, however, the population was no longer mainly rural and the concept of unlimited economic opportunity was shattered by the severity of the depression. The destitution arising out of mass unemployment was beyond the capacity of the states and the local governments to handle. In 1932 the federal government assumed some responsibility for public relief of the needy by making loans to the states and localities. As state and local funds became exhausted, the federal government stepped in directly to provide relief in the form of jobs on public works projects and cash grants. From 1935 to 1943 the major federal relief burden was carried by the Works Progress Administration (renamed the Work Projects Administration in 1939). The WPA made direct grants to states and localities to develop work projects of various kinds. Monthly employment on WPA projects reached a peak of 3.3 million in November, 1938. In all, 8.5 million different persons were employed at some time on WPA projects during the eight-year life of the agency, and nearly $11 billion was expended.

The depression crystallized demand for more adequate public programs to aid needy persons. In June, 1934, President Roosevelt established a Committee on Economic Security to propose legislation in this area. The committee submitted its report in January, 1935, urging that a program of economic security "must have as its primary aim the assurance of an adequate income to each human being in childhood, youth, middle age, or old age—in sickness or in health. It must provide safeguards against all of the hazards leading to destitution and dependency." After several months of hearings, Congress passed the Social Security Act, which became law on August 14, 1935. It marked the transition of welfare policy from one of private charity and public poor laws to contributory social insurance and governmental assistance to needy groups on a wide scale.

The Social Security Act is based on the concept that opportunity for the individual to secure protection for himself and his family against the economic hazards of old age, unemployment, sickness, and death is essential to the sustained welfare, freedom, and dignity of the American citizen. It recognizes that many persons are unable to provide such protection for themselves and that the government should protect the community by making sure that all persons have a minimum measure of protection against the major economic hazards of life. In 1948 an Advisory Council on Social Security, appointed to assist the Senate Committee on Finance in proposing amendments to the Social Security Act, stated:

> In the last analysis the security of the individual depends on the success of industry and agriculture in producing an increasing flow of goods and services. However the very success of the economy in making progress, while creating opportunities, also increases risks. Hence, the more progressive the economy, the greater is the need for protection against economic hazards. This protection should be made available on terms which reinforce the interest of the individual in helping himself. A properly designed social-security system will reinforce the drive of the individual toward greater production and greater efficiency, and will make for an environment conducive to the maximum of economic progress.[1]

current welfare programs

The American public welfare system is composed of the following types of programs:

1. The Social Security system established by the Social Security Act, including
   a. Social insurance for aged persons and their survivors
   b. Public assistance for three groups of needy persons: persons 65 years of age and over, the blind, and dependent children
   c. Unemployment insurance
   d. Maternal and child welfare services
2. Federal security programs for special groups, including
   a. Security measures for veterans
   b. Insurance programs for railroad workers
3. Other state and local welfare programs
4. Public health and medical services

Each of these programs is described briefly in the following sections. American public welfare measures are characterized not only by diversity but also by great variety in governmental participation. Some programs are wholly federal, wholly state, or wholly local in their financing and administration; other programs are state financed and locally administered; and still others are jointly financed by federal and state governments but administered by states. The prin-

---

[1] Advisory Council on Social Security, *Old-Age and Survivors Insurance* (Report to the Senate Committee on Finance, 80 Cong., 2 Sess., *Senate Document* No. 149; Washington: Government Printing Office, 1948), p. 1.

cipal trend has been toward centralization of financial and administrative responsibility in the larger units of government with greater financial resources.

the Social Security system

difference between social insurance and public assistance

The Social Security Act of 1935 provides for both social insurance and public assistance. The two types of social security vary in several significant respects:

1. Social insurance is financed primarily by specific contributions from employees and their employers, whereas public assistance for the needy is financed out of general taxation.

2. There is some relation between the benefits payable in social insurance programs and the individual's past earnings, whereas grants made under public assistance are based on the needs of the specific applicant.

3. Social insurance laws specify in detail the conditions under which insurance payments may be made. These conditions do not require payments to be made on the basis of need. In public assistance, the standards for determining eligibility for public assistance are not precise and the amount of assistance depends upon the applicant's need. In other words, the social insurance payments are largely predictable, and public assistance payments are not.

4. Administrators of public assistance programs exercise much more discretion in determining the eligibility of a person for assistance and the amount of assistance granted.

old-age and survivors' insurance

The Social Security Act established a federal system of old-age benefits for industrial and commercial workers. The system makes payments to eligible workers sixty-five years of age and over, to their wives if they are also over sixty-five, and to their dependent children if under eighteen years of age. It also makes monthly payments to the widows and orphans of workers covered by the insurance program. The first monthly benefits to workers over sixty-five, under the program, were made in 1942.

All workers are not eligible for old-age insurance. The 1935 security program did not cover agricultural labor, domestic service in a private house, employment by federal, state, and local governments, self-employment, and service performed for nonprofit organizations organized for religious, charitable, scientific, educational, or similar purposes. Agricultural and domestic workers were excluded originally on the ground that the task of collecting contributions from them was too difficult to solve. Some government workers, especially in the federal service, were already covered by special statutes. In 1950, about three out of five jobs were covered by the act.

The Social Security Amendments Act of 1950 extends old-age insurance to an additional 10 million persons, bringing the total to 45 million persons out of a civilian labor force of 64 million. New categories of employment eligible for old-age insurance include certain nonfarm self-employed persons, agricultural workers, domestic workers, federal civilian employees not under a retirement sys-

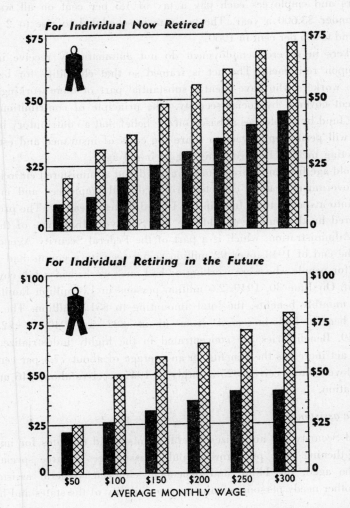

Increased Benefits under the Old Age Insurance Program. Monthly benefits: solid line represents old and crossed line represents new. Figures at the sides refer to dollar benefit payments. (*Source: The New York* Times, *June 25, 1950.*)

tem, and employees in Puerto Rico and the Virgin Islands. Farmers, physicians, lawyers, dentists, engineers, architects, ministers, certified public accountants, and persons in some other professions are excluded. Employees of state and local governments and of nonprofit organizations may be covered voluntarily if their employers elect to pay social security taxes. The new coverage provisions became effective January 1, 1951.

Under the 1950 legislation, old-age benefits are financed by a tax on the wages paid to covered employees and by a tax on the payrolls of their employers. Employers and employees each pay a tax of 1.5 per cent on all wages and salaries under $3,600 a year. The tax rate is scheduled to rise to 2 per cent in 1954 and to 2.5 per cent in 1960.

Workers in covered employment do not automatically receive insurance benefits upon retirement. The act is framed so that eligibility for benefits is limited to workers who have spent a substantial part of their working lives in employment covered by social security. The principle of contributions to the insurance fund by employees is based on the belief that a contributory insurance program will permit employees to share the costs of insurance and establish a self-respecting method for providing for their old age.

The old-age insurance program is financed and administered entirely by the federal government. Funds collected from covered employees and employers are paid into a special trust fund in the United States Treasury. The program is administered by the Bureau of Old-Age and Survivors Insurance of the Social Security Administration, which is a part of the Federal Security Agency.

By the end of 1948, over 92 million social security accounts had been established for people who were working or had once worked in a job covered by the system. On June 30, 1949, 2.6 million persons in 1.8 million families were receiving monthly benefits, the total amounting to $51.5 million. The average monthly benefit had increased from about $22 in 1940 to $25.72 in June, 1949. Beneficiaries are concentrated in the highly industrialized states. The 1950 act increases the benefits on an average of about 77.5 per cent. A retired employee who received $25 monthly in 1947 receives about $46 under the new legislation.

public assistance

The Social Security Act authorizes federal grants-in-aid to states for improving and strengthening their programs of public assistance to three special needy groups, the aged, the blind, and dependent children. General assistance or relief for other needy persons remains a responsibility of the states and localities alone.

Although the federal government contributes substantially to the financing and administration of these three public assistance programs, the administration of the programs is in the hands of the states. The federal government establishes standards for administration of public assistance, provides technical advice and consultation, and seeks to liberalize the eligibility of needy persons for aid. Since 1935 no federal funds have been available for general public assistance outside these three groups. Within federal standards, the states are free to set their own operating policies and eligibility requirements for public assistance. Consequently, public assistance varies considerably from state to state as to the average amount of payment and the number of persons receiving assistance.

The federal grants to states on a matching basis tend to encourage states to concentrate their assistance funds on the federally aided programs. Thus local governments have to carry a substantial share of the cost of general public assistance for individuals and families who are not covered by one of the federally aided programs. The Advisory Council on Social Security explained the operation of the federal program thus:

> Federal funds may be used along with State funds for an assistance payment to a man aged 65 or over, but not to his 64-year-old-wife, who may be just as much in need. Federal funds are available for assistance payments to a person handicapped by blindness but not to one incapacitated by paralysis. The Federal Government will share in the cost of aid to needy children living with certain relatives under conditions specified in the Social Security Act, but if the children are living with relatives other than those enumerated or are living with their parents under conditions other than those specified, the Federal Government assumes no share of the cost of assistance for them, regardless of how needy the children may be.[2]

In 1950 the annual cost of public assistance for the aged, the blind, and dependent children was nearly $2 billion. The federal government pays about half of all costs of old-age assistance and aid to the blind, and about 40 per cent of all costs of aid to dependent children.

In June, 1949, about 2.6 million persons, or about a fourth of all persons sixty-five years of age or over, were receiving old-age assistance. About 1.4 million children under eighteen years of age, or fewer than 3 for every 100 children in the population, were receiving aid to dependent children. About 90,000 blind persons, or about a third of all blind persons, were receiving aid to the blind. The number of persons receiving public assistance tends to be proportionately higher in the predominately agricultural states and lower in industrialized areas, where most workers are in employment covered by unemployment and old-age insurance. The average monthly payment for old-age assistance was about $44 in June, 1949, ranging from $19 in Mississippi to $71 in California. Monthly payments to dependent children and to the blind averaged about $29 and $45, respectively.

The present system of public assistance contains gaps and inequities. Dependent children receive less aid than the aged and the blind under social security legislation. Many people who do not fall within the categories of the aged, the blind, or dependent children may be in dire need of public assistance which

---

[2] Advisory Council on Social Security, *Public Assistance* (Report to the Senate Committee on Finance, 80 Cong., 2 Sess., *Senate Document* No. 204; Washington: Government Printing Office, 1948), p. 14.

cannot be granted because of the limited financial resources of the states and particularly the local units of government. Moreover, payments for old-age assistance have averaged more than payments under old-age and survivors' insurance.[3] There is a need to readjust old-age insurance and old-age assistance so that the need for old-age assistance will be reduced as the coverage of old-age insurance is expanded.

Since 1948, many proposals have been made to revise public assistance programs. These proposals generally endorse the system of federal grants-in-aid and urge the continuance of the present practice, which leaves to the states wide discretion in determining policies and standards of need. Under the 1950 amendments to the Social Security Act, federal aid to dependent children has been increased, federal grants-in-aid have been made available to states for general assistance payments to certain needy persons previously ineligible for assistance, and part of the cost of medical care for needy people is met by the federal government.

unemployment insurance

Unemployment insurance (or unemployment compensation) is a program of social insurance designed to make cash payments to workers during temporary periods of unemployment. It offers to the individual a measure of governmental protection against loss of income during periods of unemployment. Unlike the federally operated old-age insurance program, the unemployment insurance program established by the Social Security Act in 1935 is a joint enterprise of the federal and state governments.

Under the federal-state unemployment insurance system, benefits are paid, in accordance with state laws, to workers who are unemployed through no fault of their own. Benefits are financed by a federal payroll tax on employers in business and industry of eight or more workers in certain fields of employment. The Social Security Act permits employers who are paying taxes to finance a state unemployment insurance program to offset state taxes against the federal tax up to an amount equal to 90 per cent of the federal tax. If a state has passed an unemployment insurance law which meets the insurance standards of the act and if the employers' payments under state law are equal to 90 per cent or more of the rate of the federal tax, employers in the states need pay only 10 per cent of the federal tax. Out of the 10 per cent of the tax retained by the federal government, federal grants are made to states, without any matching requirement, to finance the administration of state unemployment insurance laws. The proceeds of state payroll taxes are deposited in separate accounts for each state

---

[3] In June, 1949, the average monthly payment for old-age assistance was $43.60; the average monthly payment under the old-age insurance program was $25.72. For every 100 aged persons receiving insurance payments, 147 received public assistance.

in the Unemployment Trust Fund in the United States Treasury, where they are held until requisitioned by the state for benefit payments.

In 1932 Wisconsin had been the first state to enact an unemployment insurance law. The tax-offset device of the Social Security Act provided a strong inducement to other states to enact similar laws. If states did not establish their own insurance programs, the employers in the state covered by the federal act would have to pay the entire federal payroll tax, the proceeds of which would not be used to benefit the unemployed workers of the state.

For employers to be eligible for the tax offset, the state law must fulfill the conditions set forth in the Social Security Act. Funds collected from unemployment insurance payroll taxes must be used only for payment of insurance benefits and must be paid to unemployed workers through public employment offices or other agencies designated by the Social Security Administration. States must not deny benefits to workers whose unemployment is due directly to a strike, lockout, or other labor dispute, or refusal to join a company union or to refrain from joining a legitimate labor union. The Social Security Administration has the responsibility of seeing that states meet these conditions. The federal government, through the Social Security Administration, meets all necessary and proper costs of administering state unemployment insurance laws that meet the standards noted above and certain administrative requirements, including reasonably prompt payments of benefits by the state, opportunity for a fair hearing to applicants whose claims are denied, provision of information and reports required by the Socal Security Administration, and the extension of the merit system to state administrative staffs in the unemployment insurance program.

In 1950, seven out of ten jobs in American industry were covered by unemployment insurance laws. The number of individuals in employment thus covered has increased since 1938, largely because of the increase in the active labor force in the United States. However, part of the increase is due to changes in the size of business and industrial concerns covered by state laws. Under the Federal Unemployment Tax Act, the following categories of unemployment remain outside the insurance coverage: agricultural labor; domestic service in a private home; government employment; employment in nonprofit, religious, charitable, educational, and scientific institutions; and miscellaneous services such as domestic service for college clubs. Railroad employment is covered under a separate federal system. A few states provide for broader coverage.

The benefit provisions and eligibility rules in the states vary considerably. In 1948 an unemployed aircraft worker in the State of Washington was eligible to receive $25 a week for twenty-six weeks (total, $650); whereas the same aircraft worker could receive only $20 a week for twelve weeks in Arizona (total, $240). Weekly benefit payments for unemployed workers averaged $19 for nearly eleven weeks in 1948, but the average payments by states ranged from about $23 in Utah to $11 in Kentucky. During 1949 average benefits for the country as a whole were just over $20 a week for thirteen weeks. During 1949, about 2 million workers exhausted their unemployment benefits before finding another job. In the same year, $1.7 billion in benefits were paid to more than 7 million individuals, the largest amount since payments were begun in 1937. Beneficiaries are normally concentrated in seven industrial states; California, Illinois, Massachusetts, Michigan, New Jersey, New York, and Pennsylvania.

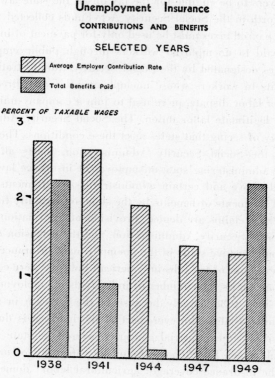

Unemployment Insurance

CONTRIBUTIONS AND BENEFITS

SELECTED YEARS

▨ Average Employer Contribution Rate

▨ Total Benefits Paid

PERCENT OF TAXABLE WAGES

(*Source:* Monthly Labor Review, *LXXI, No. 1, July, 1950, 34.*)

The federal-state system of unemployment insurance has persisted in the face of minority demands for nationalization of employment insurance. Proponents of a single national system of unemployment insurance argue that unemployment is a national problem, that it is an inappropriate area for state administration, that labor markets are not confined by state boundaries, that state plans contain too many restrictions in benefit provisions, and that the maintenance of separate systems is actuarially unsound. On the other hand, the federal-state arrangement is upheld on the grounds that the state is the proper unit to establish benefits that meet varying economic conditions in different parts of the country, that state laws ensure more adequate benefits in highly industrialized areas, and that considerable progress has already been made on a federal-state basis.

In its analysis of the unemployment insurance system in 1948, the Advisory Council on Social Security noted five major deficiencies:

1. Coverage is inadequate; only seven out of ten employees are now covered.

2. States discourage the establishment of higher benefit rates by competing in setting low contribution rates for employers.

3. Present financing, which is based on an employer's experience in maintaining stable employment, forces the contribution rate to decline when employment is high and when contributions to the unemployment insurance fund are easiest to make; and to increase when employment falls and when the need of contributions is greatest.

4. Administrative deficiencies should be overcome to speed the determination of benefit amounts for employees who have worked in more than one state and to ensure prompt payment of benefits generally.

5. Workers and citizens generally now have less influence on guiding the administration of the program and developing policy than they should have.

On April 6, 1950, President Truman wrote Congress that "our experience with unemployment insurance has revealed weaknesses as well as strengths in the existing system. While many improvements have been made in the state laws since the program began, the system is far from adequate today." He proposed that protection be extended to many workers not now covered, that nation-wide minimum levels for amounts and duration of unemployment benefits be established, that the financial soundness of the system be improved, that adequate methods be required to provide benefits for workers who move from one state to another, and that state laws for preventing or detecting fraudulent claims be revised and improved.

maternal and child welfare services

In addition to old-age insurance, public assistance, and unemployment insurance, the Social Security Act authorizes federal grants-in-aid to states for improving and strengthening their maternal and child health services, services for crippled children, and other child welfare services. These grants are administered by the Children's Bureau of the Federal Security Agency and must be matched in part by state funds. In order to qualify for federal aid, a state must meet certain conditions similar to those required under the public assistance programs. Although the federal funds are allocated among the states according to population, the Children's Bureau must also consider the resources and need for maternal and child welfare services in rural areas and in areas of special economic distress.

federal security programs for veterans and railroad workers

Two groups of persons receive special attention from the federal government—veterans and railroad workers. Veterans are considered eligible for special assistance on account of the risks to which they were subjected during wartime. Railroad workers are particularly eligible for federal assistance since they are clearly employed in occupations in interstate commerce.

security measures for veterans

It is difficult to summarize legislation dealing with the economic welfare of veterans because of the bewildering volume of legislation in their behalf and because of the great variety of benefits and assistance provided. However, four types of measures predominate: (1) money payments, including pensions, disability compensation, government insurance, and bonuses; (2) medical treatment and hospital care; (3) assistance in financing education and job training; and (4) measures to help veterans to readjust to civilian life, including reinstatement in prewar jobs, the guarantee of loans to purchase homes, farms, and business property, and special allowances to unemployed veterans. The federal program for veterans is administered mainly by the Veterans Administration, an agency employing approximately 200,000 employees. During the year ending June 30, 1950, its expenditures amounted to about $5.3 billion, or about 11 per cent of the total national budget. More than 3 million veterans received disability compensation or pensions, and more than 1.5 million received assistance through education and job training programs during the same period.

In addition, most states provide veterans' benefits of various kinds. Veterans are assisted by state officials in filing claims and obtaining business information. Some states make loans to veterans for purchasing homes and businesses, exempt veterans from property or income taxes, pay bonuses for war service, or provide special forms of public assistance for needy veterans. Both the states and the federal government also give veterans preference in government employment.

insurance programs for railroad workers

Two separate federal insurance programs provide special protection for railroad workers. The Railroad Retirement System pays benefits upon retirement, death, and permanent occupational disability. The Railroad Unemployment Insurance System provides benefits for limited periods of unemployment and for temporary disability due to illness.

The Railroad Retirement Act of 1937, as amended in 1946 and 1948, sets forth the public retirement system for railroad workers, including retirement annuities, death benefits payable to survivors, and annuities for permanent disability. The retirement system covers workers performing services in connection with transportation of passengers or property by railroads and employees of railroad and traffic associations and allied organizations. Average employment in the railroad industry for 1947 was 1.6 million. During 1948, 320,000 individuals received retirement or survivors' benefits of various types. The monthly retirement annuity averaged about $70. The retirement system is financed by equal contributions from employers and workers and is administered by the Railroad Retirement Board, an independent agency.

Unemployment and temporary disability insurance for railroad workers was established by the Railroad Unemployment Insurance Act of 1938. The coverage of the law is identical with that of the railroad retirement system. Benefits for unemployment are payable for about twenty-six weeks. Employees also receive payments during periods of temporary illness or disability including maternity. The system is financed entirely by a federal payroll tax levied on employers. Ninety per cent of the revenue is paid into a Railroad Unemployment Insurance Account and 10 per cent is deposited in a special fund to administer the system.

As of 1950, railroad workers received more protection against the loss of income and the economic hazards of employment than other American workers. In addition to receiving more liberal benefits for longer periods of time, railroad workers and their survivors have the unique protection against permanent disability whether or not the disability was incurred in the course of railroad employment. The advantageous position of railroad workers raises a question about the soundness of singling them out for preferential treatment in social security matters.

state and local welfare programs

Welfare programs operated by state and local governments are of two general types. The first type—public assistance to the aged, the blind, and dependent children—has already been described. The second type is general assistance to needy persons.

general assistance programs

General assistance to needy persons is the oldest and, until the passage of the Social Security Act in 1935, the major governmental welfare program. General assistance programs aid needy persons regardless of the cause or origin of need and are financed and administered entirely by state and local governments. States and cities establish their own terms under which relief payments are made to needy persons. In most states, some period of residence in the state is required in order to establish eligibility for general public assistance.

In June, 1949, about 1 million needy persons were receiving general assistance, or approximately 7.6 for every 1,000 in the civilian population. The average monthly payment per case was $48, ranging from $73 in New York to $11 in Mississippi. States supplied about 60 per cent of general assistance funds, and local governments paid 40 per cent. In 1949 general assistance was financed exclusively from state funds in six states, from local funds solely in fourteen states, and from state and local funds in thirty-one states.[3a]

It is difficult to evaluate the adequacy of general assistance payments because it is impossible to know whether a particular case consists of a single individual or several persons in a family. Moreover, a family receiving general public assistance might also receive aid from other public or private sources. In general, however, public assistance payments to needy persons support only a very low standard of living. Relief grants appear to be highest in the northeastern states and in the large metropolitan cities and lowest in the southeastern states and in smaller cities.

In most states, a single state agency administers the special public assistance programs. The agency may be a state board or commission or a department of public welfare. The state may share administrative responsibility with the counties. The administration of general assistance is more varied. Some states supervise local welfare agencies very closely, whereas other states maintain little or no control over local agencies. Local welfare officials may be appointed or elected.

The absence of a federal grant-in-aid for general public assistance has been criticized. It is difficult to justify the federal practice of aiding the needy aged, the blind, and dependent children while denying aid to other needy persons and families. The burden of general assistance fluctuates widely and is heaviest in periods of unemployment, when local and state financial resources are apt to be low.

public health and medical services

In the past fifty years, great progress has been made in the field of public health. Scientific research has produced new knowledge of methods of saving lives and controlling disease. Advances in medical science have proved that many deaths and sicknesses can be prevented if more adequate medical care and health facilities are available to the American people. In his report to the President in 1948 the Federal Security Administrator said:

> During the last generation, the United States steadily improved its health record, but the Nation, and the people, still suffer severe losses through sickness, disability, and death, much of which is unnecessary.

> Every year, 325,000 people die whom we have the knowledge and skills to save.

> Every year, the Nation loses 4,300,000 man-years of work through bad health.

[3a] These figures include Alaska, the District of Columbia, and Hawaii as states.

Every year, the Nation loses $27,000,000,000 in national wealth through sickness, and partial and total disability.

The record of Selective Service examinations during the war is widely known—5,000,000 men declared unfit physically or mentally for the armed forces of their country.[4]

While the Number of Physicians in the U.S. Has Increased Greatly Since 1909

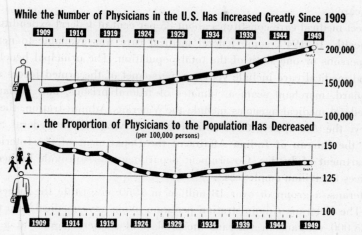

... the Proportion of Physicians to the Population Has Decreased
(per 100,000 persons)

(*Reprinted from "U.S. News & World Report," January 27, 1950, an independent weekly magazine on national and international affairs, published at Washington. Copyright 1950 United States News Publishing Corporation.*)

Since 1933, the federal government and state and local governments have expanded public facilities for protecting and safeguarding the health of the nation. Nevertheless, in 1948 there were so few physicians, dentists, nurses, and other trained workers and they were so poorly distributed that large sections of the country and millions of people were without minimum medical and health services. Although the total number of doctors is higher today than ever before, the proportion of doctors in the total population has decreased. It is estimated that fifty years ago there was 1 doctor to every 636 Americans, whereas in 1950 there was 1 to every 750. Given the increased number of older persons who need medical care, the increase in the number of families who can afford some medical care, and the medical demands of the military forces and other public agencies, the shortage of doctors is alarming. Moreover, the Federal Security Administration has estimated that the United States has only half as many acceptable hospital·beds as it needs. Even if the required hospital facilities were available today, we would be unable to staff them adequately with doctors, nurses, and other trained personnel.

---

[4] Oscar R. Ewing, *The Nation's Health—A Ten-Year Program* (Washington: Government Printing Office, 1948), p. 1.

federal medical activities

Governmental and private agencies share responsibility for improving the health of American communities. Since World War I the scope of federal activities in public health and medical services has expanded. Federal medical activities take two forms: promotion of the general health of the public, and provision of direct medical care.

Direct medical care constitutes about 85 per cent of federal expenditures for public health. In 1949, some federal medical care was available to nearly 24 million persons or one sixth of the total population. The principal beneficiaries of federal medical care include veterans, personnel of the armed forces and the Coast Guard, merchant seamen, inmates of federal prisons, and Indians. The major federal medical agencies include the Veterans Administration, the Army, the Navy, the Air Force, the Public Health Service of the Federal Security Agency, the Bureau of Indian Affairs of the Department of the Interior, and the Department of Justice. Government departments also provide limited medical services to civilian employees.

Veterans, a group of over 18 million in 1950, constitute the largest beneficiary. The Veterans Administration program alone gave medical care to more than 135,000 veterans in veterans' hospitals and soldiers' homes at a cost of nearly half a billion dollars in 1950. The great majority of veterans today are entitled to medical care on the basis of service in World Wars I and II. Three million persons, including members of the armed forces and their dependents, are entitled to receive virtually complete medical care.

Fifteen per cent of the federal medical program is devoted to general public health activities and to research. The six research bureaus of the Public Health Service are grouped together in a National Institute of Health. Four are concerned with specific diseases—cancer, heart diseases, dental diseases, and mental illnesses—and two deal with broad fields of biological and medical research. Federal grants are also made available to states to strengthen state and local mental health services and to conduct basic research to combat heart and other diseases. Promotion of general public health is accomplished primarily through federal grants to states and local governments to build hospitals, to guard against epidemics, to maintain laboratories, and to operate diagnostic clinics and disease control programs. Federal aid supports state and local public health programs and provides health services in areas which lack them. Some of the principal health programs aided by federal funds include the control of cancer, tuberculosis, mental health, and venereal disease. In addition, the Public Health Service works cooperatively with state and local health departments to develop health educational programs, to improve health instruction, and to train nurses. It helps to safeguard man's physical environment by improving sanitation in the use of food and water, by studying ways of combating air pollution, and by aiding in the establishment of industrial hygiene services in industrialized communities.

state and local medical activities

Today all states carry on a variety of public health and medical activities. State agencies typically study health problems in the states, collect vital statistics, and distribute information concerning preventable diseases. They usually give some financial aid and supervisory assistance to local health departments and maintain minimum standards of performance of work on the part of local health departments. Many states support laboratories to conduct medical research and to make diagnostic, sanitary, and related examinations. In addition states may establish minimum sanitary standards for the use and sale of food, especially milk, and administer regulations to safeguard the purity of water supplies and the disposal of human waste.

Local health agencies have expanded enormously in recent years. Not long ago local health departments limited their activities usually to sanitation, control of communicable diseases, and health information. Today health departments operate a wide variety of medical clinics and diagnostic services for venereal diseases, child health, maternity care, tuberculosis, cancer, and mental hygiene.

As in the case of the federal government, the major portion of funds for state and local medical activities goes for hospital and other institutional care for the mentally ill and the indigent sick. Hospitals for epileptics, the feebleminded, the mentally ill, and the tubercular predominate. Unfortunately most states cannot, or have been unwilling to, finance care and to provide decent facilities for patients in public institutions. Inmates in mental hospitals are subjected frequently to unspeakable cruelties and barbarisms. The mental hospitals themselves are grossly overcrowded and frequently dilapidated, and the available staffs cannot provide adequate medical or custodial care.[5]

unresolved issues in social welfare policy

the health insurance movement

Health insurance was one of the first types of social security developed by European countries. Since 1911, when the British health insurance laws were enacted, innumerable proposals have been made to establish a health insurance scheme on a contributory insurance basis in the United States. The American Medical Association has actively opposed government health insurance and has only recently ceased active opposition to voluntary health insurance schemes.

In 1938 the Technical Committee on Medical Care, which had been ap-

[5] See Albert Deutsch, *The Shame of the States* (New York: Harcourt, Brace and Company, 1948).

pointed at the request of President Roosevelt, recommended additional federal grants to states for health work. On the basis of these reports, Senator Wagner introduced a bill in Congress in 1939 to expand federal grants for health activities and to encourage states to establish compulsory health insurance laws. The bill met strong opposition from the medical profession and was defeated.

In 1948 the Federal Security Administrator proposed a compulsory prepaid federal insurance scheme for medical services to improve the nation's health. The plan specified that the insurance benefits be administered through federal-state-local cooperation, with the major emphasis on administration at the state and local levels. It was suggested that coverage by the health insurance system be identical with coverage under the old-age and survivors' insurance system. In his budget message of January 10, 1949, President Truman urged Congress to adopt a comprehensive national health program, centering in a national system of medical care insurance, accompanied by improved services and facilities for public health and medical care.

Opponents of government health insurance argue that it would socialize medical practice, that its compulsory features would have bad medical results, that it would centralize excessive authority in the federal government, that sufficient medical personnel and facilities are not available to make it effective, that it would cost too much, and that it would lower the quality of medical services. Advocates of compulsory health insurance deny the validity of these criticisms and insist that there is no other possible way of bringing adequate medical service to those American families which have earnings of less than $3,000 a year.

Given the inability of millions of families to afford adequate medical care and the aging of the population, there will be persistent demands from many groups to extend the principle of social insurance to health and disability. The health insurance movement has gained considerable momentum since the end of World War II and has aroused great public interest. One of the results of the public conflict over health insurance has been an invigoration of privately financed schemes to help individuals pay for medical care and hospitalization.

the need for protection against disabilities

The present federal social security program provides insurance against the hazards of old age and death but not against the loss of income arising out of permanent and total disability. It has been estimated that on an average day about 2 million persons are kept from gainful work because of physical disabilities which have continued for more than six months. According to the Advisory Council on Social Security:

There can be no question concerning the need for such protection. . . . The economic hardship resulting from permanent and total disability is frequently even greater than that created by old age or death. The family must not only face the loss of the breadwinner's earning but must meet the costs of medical care. As a rule, savings and other personal resources are soon exhausted. The problem of the disabled younger worker is particularly difficult since he is likely to have young children and not to have had an opportunity to acquire any significant savings.[6]

A few special programs now provide some protection against disabilities. Workmen's compensation protects workingmen against work-connected disabilities, but veterans, railroad employees, and some government employees also receive some protection. The majority of workers are left unprotected. Because of the expensive and restrictive protection offered by private life insurance companies, social insurance seems to be the only practical method of protecting individuals against the dependency resulting from permanent and total disability. In the absence of social insurance coverage, the cost of providing for the permanently and totally disabled is now met largely by public and private assistance and institutional care. A contributory social insurance scheme would reduce the cost of general assistance and public institutional care. The Social Security Amendments Act of 1950 fails to provide permanent or total disability insurance but does provide aid to permanently and totally disabled individuals over eighteen years of age who are in need.

the need for further insurance and pensions for the aged

It is estimated that only one out of every five persons now sixty-five or over is financially independent. It is generally agreed that the coverage of the social security system is still inadequate because many persons are excluded from its benefits and because benefit payments, especially old-age pensions, are too low. Although coverage of the old-age insurance scheme has now been extended to 10 million additional persons by the 1950 amendments to the Social Security Act, over 18 million persons remain ineligible for old-age insurance.

During 1949 and 1950, many large unions made successful demands upon employers to establish pension plans for workers financed entirely or primarily by employers. Union demands for private pensions raised the question whether security against old age should be provided by private or public pension schemes. If both public and private schemes continue to be developed, to what extent should one supplement the other? Should public pension plans continue to be based on the principle of contributory social insurance, or should retired persons receive a flat pension as a matter of right? Should private pension plans be financed by contributions from both employers and employees, or should employers finance pensions themselves?

---

[6] Advisory Council on Social Security, *Permanent and Total Disability* (Report to the Senate Committee on Finance, 80 Cong., 2 Sess., *Senate Document* No. 162; Washington: Government Printing Office, 1948), p. 1.

the need for improved administration of social security

With the exception of the old-age insurance program, the medical care and pension programs for soldiers and veterans, and the special welfare program for railroad workers, welfare programs in the United States are administered by state and local governments, sometimes with federal financial aid. Should the principle of federal grants to help finance public assistance to special groups and the administration of unemployment insurance be continued? Can adequate min-

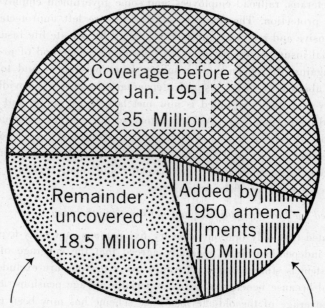

This includes farm operators, migratory workers on farms, professionals like physicians and lawyers, armed forces personnel, most government employes, workers on the nation's railroad lines.

This includes self-employed business men, some farm laborers and food processing workers, domestic servants, employees of non-profit institutions and some state and city government workers.

Coverage of Old-Age Insurance Program. (*Source: New York* Times, *June 25, 1950.*)

imum benefit provisions for unemployment insurance and public assistance to the aged, the blind, and dependent children be achieved under a cooperative federal-state plan in which the major operating decisions are made by the states? Should federal grants be made to state and local governments for general assistance?

It is likely that the pattern of federal grants to states for unemployment insurance administration and special public assistance will be continued. What can be done to improve the federal-state partnership? Should the federal government maintain closer supervision of state welfare agencies or should the states be given a greater measure of discretionary authority in the administration of federally aided programs?

The Federal Security Agency administers most federal programs in health, education, and social security. The agency has not been accorded status as a department whose head would be a member of the President's cabinet. In 1949 President Truman proposed that Congress establish a Department of Welfare, and again in 1950, he unsuccessfully urged Congress to create a Department of Health, Education, and Security. These proposals follow a number of similar proposals to strengthen federal administration of social welfare programs.

bibliographic note

The literature of social security is voluminous. Two of the more recent and more up-to-date textbooks are Eveline M. Burns, *The American Social Security System* (Boston: Houghton Mifflin Company, 1949), and Domenico Gagliardo, *American Social Insurance* (New York: Harper & Brothers, 1949). A useful collection of essays is *Readings in Social Insurance* (New York: Prentice-Hall, Inc., 1948), edited by William Haber and Wilbur J. Cohen. Interesting commentaries on the development of social welfare legislation are found in Robert E. Sherwood's *Roosevelt and Hopkins* (New York: Harper & Brothers, 1948) and Frances Perkins's *The Roosevelt I Knew* (New York: The Viking Press, 1946). The reports of the Advisory Council on Social Security to the Senate Committee on Finance are combined in *Senate Document* No. 208, *Recommendations for Social Security Legislation*, 80 Cong., 2 Sess. (Washington: Government Printing Office, 1949). American social security programs are summarized in *House Document* No. 545, *Public Social Security Programs in the United States, 1949–1950*, 81 Cong., 2 Sess. (Washington: Government Printing Office, 1950). This summary is also available in the *Monthly Labor Review*, Vol. LXX, Nos. 7–9 (January, February, March, 1950).

The role of the government in the public health field is described at length in James S. Simmons, ed., *Public Health in the World Today* (Cambridge: Harvard University Press, 1949) and in Harry S. Mustard, *Government in Public Health* (New York: The Commonwealth Fund, 1945). The frightful inadequacies of state mental health facilities and programs are underscored in *The Shame of the States* (New York: Harcourt, Brace and Company, 1948), by Albert G. Deutsch. Proposals for improving hospital care in the United States are set forth in Eli Ginzberg, *A Pattern for Hospital Care* (New York: Columbia University Press, 1949). The proposed health program of the Truman administration is outlined by Federal Security Administrator Oscar R. Ewing in *The Nation's Health—A Ten Year Program* (Washington: Government Printing Office, 1948). Recent trends in administering health programs are noted by William R. Willard of the Yale University School of Medicine in "Fifteen Years of Public Health Administration," *Public Administration Review*, X, No. 2 (Spring, 1950), 99–118.

education, housing, and consumer services

$\mathcal{P}$UBLIC education, which is now taken for granted in the United States, was once far from universally approved and accepted. It was not until the period from 1828 to 1860 that a system of public education emerged. The public education movement coincided with the movement to expand the suffrage and with the growth of cities and industries. The reformers of the 1840's and 1850's had an almost blind faith in the power of education to improve the status of the individual and to eliminate social evils. Even today "education" remains the popular remedy for almost all problems.

The principle of public education stems from the belief in the worth of the individual, which is the major premise of democratic ideology. It has grown as the concept of democracy has deepened and expanded. In order to give the individual the greatest measure of opportunity to develop himself, government undertakes today to provide schools and colleges. More specifically, public education has two related objectives: to enhance the dignity of every individual by giving him the opportunity through education to develop his intellect and his understanding; and to provide the enlightened, educated body of citizens upon which the success of democracy depends. As functions of government expand and as complex issues of public policy come to have a greater impact on individuals, the need for enlightened citizens becomes greater and our interest in public education grows stronger.

The goal of education in American society was stated in 1947 by the President's Commission on Higher Education:

> It is a commonplace of the democratic faith that education is indispensable to the maintenance and growth of freedom of thought, faith, enterprise, and association. Thus the social role of education in a democratic society is at once to insure equal liberty and equal opportunity to differing individuals and groups, and to enable the citizens to understand, appraise, and redirect forces, men, and events as these tend to strengthen or to weaken their liberties.[1]

[1] The President's Commission on Higher Education, *Higher Education for American Democracy* (Washington: Government Printing Office, 1947), I, 5.

current status of education

Each generation in the United States has received progressively more education. In 1870 nearly 7 million persons were enrolled in public schools; in 1930 the figure was over 25 million. By 1940, nearly 75 per cent of all children five to nineteen years of age were in school, compared to only 50 per cent in 1890. In 1940, most adults had had at least an elementary school education.

In 1947, half of the adults from twenty-five to twenty-nine years of age had completed secondary school compared to one sixth of the persons aged sixty-five or over. Practically all children aged six to thirteen and at least four out of five children aged fourteen to seventeen are in school today. In 1949, about 32 million persons were enrolled in educational institutions, including 22.8 million in elementary schools, 6.3 million in secondary schools, and 2.5 million in colleges and universities.

Educational status varies markedly by racial groups. In 1947, about 35 per cent of white adults had completed at least four years of high school, compared to only 13 per cent of nonwhites, including principally Negroes, Indians, Chinese, and Japanese. Similarly, only 10 per cent of white adults had less than five years of elementary schooling, compared to 30 per cent of nonwhites.

Seventeen states and the District of Columbia maintain separate school systems for white and Negro children. Generally the quality of schooling in segregated schools for Negroes is much below the educational level of schools for white children.

AVERAGE PUBLIC SCHOOL EXPENDITURES PER CHILD, 1943–1944

State	White	Negro	Per Cent Negro to White
North Carolina	$71.60	$50.07	70%
Texas	92.69	63.12	68
Florida	95.96	47.44	49
Arkansas	61.03	25.81	42
Alabama	70.20	25.65	37
Louisiana	121.32	40.25	33
South Carolina	82.43	26.85	33
Georgia	73.79	23.63	32
Mississippi	71.65	11.96	17

Source: Computed from Benjamin Fine, *Our Children are Cheated* (New York: Henry Holt and Co., 1947), pp. 152–152.

Despite vast improvements in public education, many problems remain. The National Educational Association reported in 1950 that a third of a million school children in public elementary schools are limited to half-day sessions because of overcrowding. A fifth of the school buildings in use in city school systems are fifty to eighty years old. Moreover, thousands of school children attend classes in corridors and basements of dilapidated schoolhouses. Although they lack training and qualifications, nearly 100,000 temporary or substitute teachers now teach in the public school system.

We are actually spending less of our national income today for education than we spent in 1930, when about 3 per cent of our national income was devoted to education. By 1950 the percentage was less than two.

the cost of public education

Public education is the largest single activity of state and local governments in peacetime. In 1940, $3.3 billion was spent for public and private schools and colleges, and 40 per cent of all state and local government employees worked in the nation's public school system. Of the total outlay for education, 50 per cent was devoted to elementary schools, 30 per cent to secondary schools, and

STATE AID FOR SCHOOLS, 1941, IN SELECTED STATES

State	$ Million	State Aid as Percentage of Income Received by Citizens in the State
Northern states		
New York	128	1.0
California	78	1.1
Ohio	58	1.0
Michigan	45	1.1
Pennsylvania	32	0.4
Illinois	20	0.3
Southern states		
Texas	44	1.3
North Carolina	28	2.0
Georgia	20	1.7
Louisiana	15	1.4
Alabama	15	1.5
Florida	13	1.2
South Carolina	8	1.1
Mississippi	7	1.1

Source: U. S. Census, *Federal and State Aid*, 1941, pp. 37–50; and *Survey of Current Business*, August, 1945, pp. 17–18.

20 per cent to colleges and universities. Governments provided over 80 per cent of all expenditures for education. Since the end of World War II, federal expenditures have increased tremendously to finance education for veterans and to make research grants to colleges and universities.

Local and state governments carry the main burden of financing public education. In 1941, about 11 per cent of all government expenditures were devoted to education, of which local governments contributed 88 per cent; state governments, 11 per cent; and the federal government, 1 per cent. Education accounted for about 30 per cent of local expenditures, 7 per cent of state expenditures, and less than 1 per cent of federal expenditures.[2]

Local governments rely for the most part on general property taxes for financing public education. Unfortunately, receipts from general property taxes do not rise and fall as the level of prices and incomes changes. In periods of rising prices, especially, local governments are embarrassed by inadequate tax sources. Moreover, demands on local governments by competing programs in social welfare, housing, health, and so on, have forced these units to turn to the states to meet the rising cost of public education.

The states have increased their contributions toward financing public education, and in recent years, about 30 per cent of all local educational costs have been met by state contributions. State aid for education varies widely from state to state. However, residents of southern states, which are relatively poor states, spend a larger share of their income for local education than do residents of the relatively prosperous northern states.

federal participation in education

In 1949 the Hoover Commission reported that federal funds expended for all educational purposes totaled more than $2.5 billion annually. Over $2 billion alone was spent during 1949 for the education of veterans, vocational education and rehabilitation, and related activities.[3] In 1948 the Veterans Administration paid tuition for 48 per cent of the more than 2.3 million college students. Educational benefits paid to veterans dropped sharply after June, 1950, when most veterans had exhausted their educational benefits or had completed their college courses. Federal activities related to elementary and secondary education include the study and development of school curriculums and a school lunch program to improve nutritional standards for school children. In addition the federal government is responsible for the education of children residing on federal properties, including Indians on public reservations. At the level of higher education, grants-in-aid are made to so-called land-grant colleges specializing in the teaching of agricultural and engineering subjects. Grants to colleges for scientific research are made by the military departments, the Public Health Service, the Atomic Energy Commission, and other agencies. Howard University in Washington, D.C., is maintained as an institution of higher learning for Negroes.

---

[2] For further data, see Seymour E. Harris, *How Shall We Pay for Education?* (New York: Harper & Brothers, 1948), especially Pt. 3.

[3] The Commission on Organization of the Executive Branch of the Government, *Social Security and Education—Indian Affairs* (Washington: Government Printing Office, 1949), p. 29.

Since 1946, proposals have been made to increase federal grants to states to assist them in financing the current costs of elementary and secondary schools and to make possible a better education for millions of children. The case for extending federal aid is based on the inadequacy of schools and colleges in the face of growing needs. The 1940 census revealed that more than 10 million adult Americans had had no more than four years of elementary schooling and that 2 million children aged six to fifteen did not attend any school. Moreover, in states like Georgia, Louisiana, Mississippi, and South Carolina, about one third of all adults over twenty-five years of age had not had more than four years of schooling.

Schools and educational standards continue to vary widely from state to state. The chief argument for federal aid has been the inability of several states to finance a reasonable minimum of education for children. In April, 1948, the Senate passed a bill providing federal aid for education, but the House of Representatives took no action on the measure. The bill aimed to subsidize a minimum level of expenditures of $50 a pupil in average daily attendance. In 1946–1947, one half of the states were spending at least $99 a pupil in school, whereas 10 per cent of the school children were in schools costing $50 or less a pupil. The bill would have required states receiving grants to maintain state and local support for schools at least at the 1947 level of expenditures. Aid would have been available on a flexible basis in order to equalize educational expenditures in the various states. Supporters of federal aid have split on proposals to extend federal aid to parochial schools and to states which maintain segregated schools for Negro and white children. Opponents of federal aid to education charge that federal financial assistance would lead to federal control of a function which has traditionally belonged to state and local governments.

Federal support of scientific research projects in the universities expanded tremendously during World War II and has continued at high levels. In December, 1947, the President's Commission on Higher Education urged the extension of federal support of higher education and advocated federal aid in the form of funds to provide two years of college training at public expense for all students, scholarships or grants-in-aid to worthy students, and contracts with universities for research and training projects. In 1950 Congress established the National Science Foundation to promote basic research in the physical and natural sciences and to build up the scientific resources of the nation by making grants to universities to support basic research and by awarding fellowships to qualified graduate students.[4]

---

[4] The establishment of the National Science Foundation was advocated both by the President's Scientific Research Board in 1947 and the Hoover Commission in 1949. See, especially, the President's Scientific Research Board, *Science and Public Policy: A Program for the Nation* (Washington: Government Printing Office, 1947), Vol. I.

public school administration

More American citizens participate in public school administration than in any other single governmental activity. The 115,000 school districts in the nation have a relatively autonomous status in local government, and are usually managed by locally elected school boards. These boards have broad authority to appoint the superintendent of schools, approve appointments of teachers, formulate the school budget, and determine the tax levy for school funds. Many boards also influence teaching methods and the selection of textbooks.

State boards of education exercise varying controls over public education. In most states, the boards of education establish regulations for the training, licensing, and examination of teachers, and compulsory school attendance, and may provide textbooks and other services. Standards for school buildings, length of the school term, and physical facilities may be set. In 1949 all states operated state universities or colleges of some type.

With the exception of the Veterans Administration from 1946 to 1950, the principal federal agency in the area of education has been the United States Office of Education in the Federal Security Agency. It collects statistics and facts on educational conditions, conducts research, distributes information on the organization and management of schools and methods of teaching, and furthers the cause of education. It also advises state and local school officials and university administrators on educational problems, administers grants-in-aid for vocational education and for land-grant colleges, and supervises the work of the American Printing House for the Blind, the Columbia Institution for the Deaf, and Howard University.

Despite the growth in recent years of federal financial responsibility for public education and research, there is general agreement that the basic control of public education should continue to be a state and local function. Perhaps the leading issue ahead in public education concerns the method of making federal aid available to the states without, at the same time, centralizing control of education in the federal government.

public housing

the housing problem

Governmental interest in housing grows out of gradual recognition that the general welfare and security of the nation and the living standards of its people depend in part on the provision of a decent home for every American family. How to provide adequate housing for all Americans has become the primary housing problem. Housing policies take many specific forms, ranging from financial assistance to individuals to help them build their own homes, to the elimination of slums and blighted areas and the public construction of low-rent housing. The housing problem can be clarified by noting some of the trends in American housing.

housing characteristics in America

In 1940, there were 37 million houses and apartments, over 21 million of which were located in cities and towns over 2,500 in population. They included moderately comfortable houses and expensive houses as well as hovels and slums. According to the 1940 census, about 43 per cent of these homes needed major repairs or replacement, 30 per cent had no running water, and about 45 per cent were without a private bath or shower.

In 1947, 53 per cent of nonfarm dwelling units and 65 per cent of farm homes were occupied by owners. For most Americans, 15 to 20 per cent of all their expenditures went for rent or home operation, including heat, electricity, gas, and water. Housing standards had improved during the war years. Census sample surveys revealed that by 1947 two thirds of all dwelling units had a private bath and a private flush toilet, and that 9 out of every 10 had electric lighting. One or more married couples lived as subfamilies in addition to the head of the household in 2.5 million dwellings. Negro families had considerably less desirable housing than white families. Farm dwellings were far below urban housing standards. Only 20 per cent of farm houses had both bath and toilet facilities and 67 per cent lacked running water. Regionally, housing conditions were best in the Northeast and poorest in the South.[5]

national housing policy

The federal government has been active in housing since 1932, but a firm national housing policy did not begin to emerge until 1949. From 1932 to 1949, the various federal housing programs were designed to meet a series of special or emergency situations. The first programs were stimulated by the depression of the thirties and were directed toward protecting both home owners and lending institutions against the consequences of widespread mortgage foreclosures. Subsequently programs were established to improve standards of housing construction, to revive home building by private enterprise through the insurance of private financing and improvements in the terms of mortgage credit, and through a low-rent housing program to provide decent housing for families of low income. During World War II, federal housing activity emphasized the need to provide adequate housing near essential war industries to accommodate workers and their families. Immediately after the war, an acute housing shortage developed which the government tried to overcome by additional emergency measures.

---

[5] See Joint Committee on Housing, *Final Majority Report*, Housing Study and Investigation, "Statistics of Housing," *House Report* No. 1,564, 80 Cong., 2 Sess. (Washington: Government Printing Office, 1948), Pt. 2, p. 7; and Housing and Home Finance Agency, *The Housing Situation: The Factual Background* (Washington: Government Printing Office, 1949).

Since federal housing programs were initially undertaken to meet specific emergency situations, it has been difficult to develop a comprehensive national housing policy. A preliminary step was taken in that direction in 1947, when the various federal housing agencies were regrouped in the Housing and Home Finance Agency. The emerging national housing policy is based on three assumptions. First, housing is considered to be "of sufficient importance to the economic and social welfare of the American people as a whole as to justify and require effective Federal action to help improve housing conditions." [6] Second, the primary responsibility for providing housing is regarded as resting with private enterprise. Therefore the federal government should assist private enterprise to meet the housing problem and to limit direct government construction of housing to situations beyond the scope of private enterprise. And third, local communities are recognized as having the major responsibility for planning and formulating their own housing programs.

current federal housing programs

Federal housing legislation in 1949 and 1950 has established the framework for a comprehensive national housing policy. By this policy it is hoped to realize "as soon as feasible . . . the goal of a decent home and a suitable living environment for every American family, thus contributing to the development and redevelopment of communities and to the advancement of the growth, wealth, and security of the Nation." [7] Under the Housing Acts of 1949 and 1950, five principal activities are authorized.

1. FINANCIAL AIDS TO PRIVATE HOUSING ENTERPRISE. The government aids private housing enterprise by furnishing credit to home builders, home buyers, mortgage lenders, and local communities. Although some direct loans are made to veterans, the government's principal role lies in insuring or guaranteeing private loans and in purchasing mortgages from private holders. In January, 1950, it was estimated that about a third of all new private housing construction was being financed with mortgages insured by the Federal Housing Administration, one of the constituent agencies of the Housing and Home Finance Agency. In addition, credit for home building is made available to veterans and others by purchases of government-guaranteed or insured mortgages from banks and other financial institutions. Rental and cooperative housing units are also eligible for federal financial assistance.

2. SLUM CLEARANCE AND URBAN DEVELOPMENT. Because of the high cost of removing slums and blighted areas, neither private enterprise nor local communities have been able to finance large-scale slum clearance and redevelopment projects. Since 1949 the federal government has provided loans and

---

[6] *Final Majority Report*, p. 20. The three views outlined in the text are presented in greater detail in this report.

[7] From the declaration of national housing policy of the Housing Act of 1949, section 2.

grants to local communities for acquiring, clearing, and preparing slums and other blighted areas for redevelopment by private enterprise or by public agencies. Federal financial assistance is also provided to localities to build public housing units for low-income families displaced by slum clearance projects.

3. LOW-RENT PUBLIC HOUSING. The Housing Act of 1949 continues and expands the low-rent public housing program begun in 1937. By making loans and grants to state and local housing authorities, the federal program enables communities to provide adequate housing for low-income families who otherwise would have to live in substandard housing. Federal operations, which are managed by the Public Housing Administration in the Housing and Home Finance Agency, are restricted to making loans and paying annual contributions to meet deficits. Local housing authorities construct the low-rent housing projects under contract with private builders and operate the projects. Between 1949 and 1955, 810,000 low-rent public housing units may be constructed under this program.

4. HOUSING RESEARCH. The 1949 act authorizes for the first time a housing research program. The Housing and Home Finance Agency now studies such problems as ways of reducing housing costs, the development of new and improved building materials and techniques, improved housing designs, and local zoning and building codes applicable to housing.

5. FARM HOUSING. The Department of Agriculture makes loans to farm owners to enable them to provide decent, safe, and sanitary farm dwellings and buildings for themselves and their tenants, sharecroppers, or laborers. Only those owners who are unable to secure elsewhere the credit necessary for building such housing are eligible for farm housing loans.

The housing legislation of 1949 and 1950 has been attacked as insufficient and inadequate to meet the objective of providing a decent home for every family. Some critics have urged more low-cost public housing as the major device for solving the housing problem. Other critics have questioned the desirability of public housing during boom periods of housing construction on the ground that competition between government and private enterprise for scarce building materials inflates building costs.

role of states and localities in housing

Before 1933 there were no municipal housing authorities in the United States and no state enabling legislation authorizing their creation. Although Massachusetts created a state housing agency in 1909, there was little state housing activity before 1934. The New York State Board of Housing was the only state housing agency which had authority to use federal grants when they became available in 1934. Federal grants induced many states to revise and simplify their housing laws to permit them to qualify for and take advantage of federal aid. By 1950, forty-three states had authorized the establishment of local housing authorities to build and operate federally aided low-rent housing, and nearly five hundred local housing authorities had had some experience in public housing programs.

State housing agencies perform a variety of functions. Much of their work is educational in character. They make surveys and conduct research on housing problems; administer state codes regulating hotels, rooming houses, and tenements; and maintain contacts with local housing authorities. Some states provide financial aid to local governments for housing and administer state low-rent housing projects. Local housing authorities carry the major day to day burden of clearing slums, eliminating substandard dwellings, and building low-rent housing. Under the Housing Act of 1949, local housing authorities are expanding their programs to build low-cost public housing and clear slum areas.

consumer protective services

Consumers have been notoriously weak in organizing to protect their mutual interests. The spirit of business enterprise in America has contributed to the weakness of consumer organization by stressing the importance of producer rather than consumer interests. When Americans have sought to combine to protect and promote particular policies or programs, these policies and programs have overwhelmingly concerned their status as workers, farmers, manufacturers, and professional employees. For example, the United States Department of Agriculture tends to emphasize service to the farmers as producers rather than consumers. The natural inclination of the department has been to protect the farmer from criticism by consumers regarding high farm prices. The "producer complex" has deeply affected political organization and social aspirations in America. It has contributed to the tendency of most Americans to regard themselves as members of a middle class in society and as potential, if not actual, producers of goods and services demanded by consumers.

Labor, farm, and other groups frequently join forces with consumers to promote their mutual interests. Unions may be interested in low-cost public housing programs and cooperate in a general drive for better housing for low-income groups. Farmers may share with consumer groups a desire to reduce the spread between prices received by the farmer for his products and the prices paid by consumers for food. Similarly, expansion and improvement of general governmental services in education, health, and welfare may become goals of teachers' associations and organized farmers and workers as well as general citizens' groups representing the consumer.

The most highly developed form of consumer organization is the consumer cooperative. Conceivably the consumer cooperatives could become the core of a broader, more comprehensive organization of consumers. Another significant movement designed to protect the consumer is the establishment of private organizations which test the quality and durability of products offered for sale to consumers. The best-known private research and testing groups are the Consumers Union of the United States and Consumers Research.

food and drug legislation

The most common type of governmental protection available to consumers is legislation to prevent adulteration, misbranding, and false advertising of foods and drugs. State and local governments have long regulated the sale of alcoholic beverages and narcotics. One of the traditional functions of state and local government has been the administration of sanitary regulations and the inspection of weights and measures. Beginning in Virginia in 1848, states have legislated against the adulteration of foods and drugs. State legislation and administration proved inadequate as interstate commerce in foods and drugs increased.

Federal food and drug legislation to protect the health of consumers originated in 1848. At first federal action was limited to prohibitions against the importation into the United States of adulterated drugs and medicines. Campaigns for federal regulation of the interstate sale of adulterated foods and drugs began in the 1880's. Spurred by Upton Sinclair's description in *The Jungle* of shocking practices in the slaughterhouses of Chicago, the dramatization of the injurious effects of adulterated foods by Dr. Harvey Wiley of the Department of Agriculture, and popular muckraking articles like Samuel Hopkins Adams's *The Great American Fraud*, advocates of legislation finally secured the enactment of the Pure Food and Drug Act of 1906. The act prohibited the interstate sale of adulterated and misbranded foods and drugs.

Although the 1906 legislation was reasonably comprehensive, its administration was hampered by inadequate appropriations and by the efforts of the food and drug companies to gain control of the enforcement program. The revival of popular interest in public affairs after 1929 led eventually to the expansion of federal controls in the Food, Drug, and Cosmetic Act of 1938, which increased the protection to consumers from adulteration and misbranding of foods and added heavier penalties for violations. Rules similar to those applied to foods and drugs were made applicable to cosmetics and therapeutic devices.

Under existing law, the Food and Drug Administration in the Federal Security Agency has control over the misbranding, false labeling, and adulteration of foods, drugs, cosmetics, and therapeutic devices, whereas the Federal Trade Commission has authority over misleading advertising of these products. Food and drug inspectors visit factories to inspect sanitary conditions and to examine the use of raw materials and the processing, packaging, and labeling of products to be shipped in interstate commerce. Violations are reported to the Department of Justice for enforcement action.

commodity standards

Next to food and drug legislation, the most significant type of governmental protection of consumer interests is the establishment of official standards for various commodities. The Department of Agriculture has established certain standards for food products in interstate commerce. For example, meat slaughtered in federally inspected slaughterhouses must meet certain minimum conditions of sanitation and cleanliness. Compulsory grade labeling of canned goods has lagged in the face of powerful opposition from food processors. The Office of Price Administration was prevented during World War II from tying price control of canned foods to Department of Agriculture grades. However, under the Wool Products Labeling Act of 1940, the Federal Trade Commission enforces a prohibition against the misbranding of wool products entering interstate commerce.

Commodity standards normally have been established only with the acquiescence and support of producers or distributors. Such standards advance the self-interest of consumers, producers, and distributors by assuring the consuming public that a particular industry is meeting certain minimum standards of quality.

consumer representation in government

Since the Departments of Agriculture, Commerce, and Labor are considered to represent the interests of agriculture, business, and labor, consumers have argued for more direct representation in governmental agencies. In the New Deal period, consumers were given representation on advisory boards to the National Recovery Administration and the National Bituminous Coal Commission. In 1940 a member to represent consumers was appointed to the Advisory Commission to the Council of National Defense.

Although consumer representation did make certain specific contributions toward policy formation and day to day administration, no consensus about the role of consumer representation developed. Under the impact of wartime programs, interest shifted from consumer representation in government agencies to citizen participation in administration. Both the Selective Service Administration and the Office of Price Administration relied heavily on volunteers for local administration of selective service and price and rationing controls. The experience of these agencies suggests that such untrained citizens can participate effectively in administration only if they are provided with assistance by technical experts, if their responsibilities are clearly stated, and if they are provided with efficient machinery through which to realize their purposes.

bibliographic note

The most complete study of federal activities in education is found in Hollis P. Allen, *The Federal Government and Education* (New York: McGraw-Hill Book Company, 1950), which is the study of education made for the Hoover Commission Task Force on Public Welfare. A convenient summary of federal activities is available in *Highlights in the Development of Federal Policies and Activities in Education* (*Public Affairs Bulletin* No. 30, Legislative Reference Service, Library of Congress; Washington: Government Printing Office, 1944). *The School in the American Social Order* (Boston: Houghton Mifflin Company, 1947), by Newton Edwards and Herman G. Richey, is a social history of the American public school. Problems of financing public education are highlighted in Seymour Harris's study, *How Shall We Pay for Education?* (New York: Harper & Brothers, 1948). Recently two presidential commissions have studied the need for expanding opportunities for higher education and the need for strengthening facilities of scientific research. Their reports can be found in the President's Commission on Higher Education, *Higher Education for American Democracy* (Washington: Government Printing Office, 5 vols., 1947) and the President's Scientific Research Board, *Science and Public Policy: A Program for the Nation* (Washington: Government Printing Office, 5 vols., 1947). Perhaps the most interesting book in the field of education published in recent years is A. B. Hollingshead's study, *Elmtown's Youth* (New York: John Wiley & Sons, Inc., 1949), which analyzes the relation between social behavior and class position among high school students in a small midwestern town.

One of the most informative studies of housing problems is contained in Joint Committee on Housing, *House Report* No. 1,564, *Final Majority Report*, Housing Study and Investigation, 80 Cong., 2 Sess. (Washington: Government Printing Office, 1948). *The Housing Situation: The Factual Background* (Washington: Government Printing Office, 1949) was prepared by the Housing and Home Finance Agency and contains a brief summary of housing conditions throughout the country. Short expositions of recent federal housing legislation are included in Housing and Home Finance Agency, *A Handbook of Information on Provisions of the Housing Act of 1949 and Operations under the Various Programs* (Washington: Government Printing Office, 1949) and Senate Committee on Banking and Currency, *Senate Document* No. 165, 81 Cong., 2 Sess., *Summary of Housing Act of 1950* (Washington: Government Printing Office, 1950).

The Consumer Interest (New York: Harper & Brothers, 1949), by Persia Campbell, is a study of the American economy from the consumer point of view. In *Recent Social Trends in the United States* (New York: McGraw-Hill Book Company, 2 vols., 1932), Robert S. Lynd discusses "The People as Consumers."

cooperative federalism

$\mathcal{I}$N distributing governmental powers, a nation must decide whether the central government should exercise all power to govern or whether governing powers should be divided between the central government and its major political subdivisions. Federalism is one of the ways of relating the central government to local governments. It may be defined as a division of powers between a central government and local governments by which the local governments retain some measure of independence.

centralization vs. decentralization

In the United States, discussions about methods of allocating governing responsibilities frequently turn on the issue of centralization vs. decentralization. Advocates of centralization may urge that only the federal government has the resources to carry out a particular program. Proponents of decentralization frequently argue that the concentration of authority in the federal government has become excessive and threatens the survival of local self-government, which is held to be the firm foundation of American democracy.

The process of centralization has been accompanied by an increase in governmental activities. Opposition to centralization is frequently opposition to certain functions being performed by any level of government, federal, state, or local. Public controversy over the merits of decentralization may indeed obscure more fundamental problems. For example, the Hoover Commission, in its discussion of federal-state relations, emphasized these two questions as paramount:

1. How can the American type of democracy—a democracy based on individual liberty and extensive citizen participation in and control of government—be maintained and strengthened?

2. At the same time, how shall government provide the services which people increasingly demand and which are necessary for the general welfare?[1]

---

[1] The Commission on Organization of the Executive Branch of the Government, *Overseas Administration, Federal-State Relations, Federal Research* (Washington: Government Printing Office, 1949), p. 26.

The vehemence of public debate on the issue of centralization vs. decentralization may unfortunately shift our attention away from the more basic questions outlined by the Hoover Commission. One central point needs to be kept in mind. Democratic governments are engaged in the common enterprise of providing essential services. Too often the identity of objectives among governmental units is minimized, and antagonisms, rivalries, and competition are emphasized instead. Most governmental problems cannot be solved by a single level of government acting alone. "Their solution requires cooperation and team work on the part of the States and the National Government, with understanding and support from the people at large." [2]

The history of federal-state relations indicates that the distribution of power in a federal system of government cannot be permanently fixed. As the Hoover Commission reported, "Emphasis shifts from generation to generation as the American people fashion their government to meet the needs of changing times and changing conditions." [3] The progress of urbanization and industrialization has profoundly affected the demands made by people on their governments and the capacity of governments to respond to public demands. Since the Civil War, cooperative federalism has been advanced most directly by expansion of the use of federal grants-in-aid and by new techniques in federal-state administrative relations.

federal grants-in-aid

The grant-in-aid may be defined as "a method of operation whereby funds derived from a tax levied and collected by one government are made available for expenditure and administration by another level, usually upon a matching basis, for some particular activity, and in accordance with definite and specific standards and requirements."[4] Grants-in-aid are used extensively by the federal government to support public services. In 1950, about 6 per cent of the federal expenditures took the form of grants to states for a wide variety of activities. Federal grants totaling $2.3 billion comprised about 12 per cent of all state-local expenditures in 1950.[5]

arguments supporting federal grants

The Hoover Commission cited several advantages of federal grants-in-aid:

The cooperative system based on grants-in-aid has provided needed standards of public services throughout the country in many fields—services that

---

[2] *Ibid.*, p. 26.

[3] *Ibid.*, p. 25.

[4] *Ibid.*, p. 29.

[5] *Budget of the United States Government for the Fiscal Year Ending June 30, 1951* (Washington: Government Printing Office, 1950), p. 1137.

many States would be unable to supply. It has provided for some redistribution of resources from States that have superior means to those that lack them.

The plan has developed a division of responsibility: the National Government giving financial aid and establishing broad standards—the State governments sharing the fiscal burden and maintaining primary responsibility for administration. In addition to decreasing inequalities of service, the grant-in-aid method has raised the level of all aided services, without transferring functions entirely to the National Government.

The grant-in-aid method, in fact, has added to and expanded the activities of State governments by contributing to their resources and thereby enabling them to embark upon additional or more extensive public-service programs for their own people.

It has stimulated States and localities to provide a number of public services deemed necessary and desirable in the national interest.

The cooperative method improves the administration of many State activities. National administrative standards, as in highway and welfare programs, and national advice, as in police work, have done much to increase the professional skill and effectiveness of State administrators.[6]

arguments against federal grants

In analyzing federal grants-in-aid, the Hoover Commission listed five "liabilities" of the grant-in-aid system:

Grant programs are unrelated; they are uncoordinated; and they have developed in a haphazard manner without any one agency—Federal or State —concerned with the over-all impact and the over-all effects of grants-in-aid upon the general operations of government.

The grant-in-aid method has removed large areas of discretionary power from the hands of State officials and has transferred a measurable degree of policy-making and ultimate responsibility and control for public services to the National Government.

Grants-in-aid have altered State service patterns and total State programs. Available Federal funds for matching purposes stimulate or "persuade" the States in many instances to expend large sums for an aided program while, of necessity, other needed services are neglected. The public assistance program as contrasted with the general relief program is one among many examples.

In order to provide funds for grants-in-aid, and to adjust to war and depression, the national system of taxation has been expanded until we have

---

[6] *Overseas Administration, Federal State Relations, Federal Research*, pp. 30–31.

extensive overlapping and conflicts on the part of Federal, State, and local governments. Of greater importance to State and local governments, the national need for revenue has caused the Congress in some instances to utilize productive tax sources that could be used just as effectively by State or local governments. In this manner, the circle widens. Under pressure to meet needs, Congress appropriates more for grants. In order to secure necessary revenues, the national tax base is expanded which makes it more difficult for State and local governments to secure their own revenue, and hence stimulates pressure from more and more groups for more and more grants.

Federal grants-in-aid retard and repress the initiative of the States in financing the growing needs of State and local government, because such grants frequently result in rewarding those States which avoid their responsibility and in penalizing those which accept it.[7]

Federal grants have been criticized by some as unconstitutional, but no federal-aid statute has ever been declared unconstitutional. Perhaps the most common argument against federal grants is the belief that they lead to centralization, which is regarded as dangerous. It is alleged that federal grants establish federal direction, supervision, and control of local activities and create a vast, expensive central bureaucracy. Other critics are opposed to grants because they regard them as devices permitting federal control of functions best administered by the states.

The argument that federal grants distort state budgets seems to be supported by the evidence. Some states have developed excellent highway systems with the help of federal funds, but at the same time they have been unable to finance equally important governmental activities for which no federal aid was available. Federal grants for agricultural extension and vocational training have encouraged states to develop these programs, sometimes at the expense of other educational programs. Federal grants appear to have increased the tendency for state legislatures to earmark state revenues for specific expenditures. For example, federal highway grants have probably served to rigidify state budgets by making it impossible to use state revenues from gasoline and motor vehicle taxes for purposes other than highway expenditures, however essential the other purposes might be.

All federal grants-in-aid provide for some federal supervision and control of state and local activities aided by grants. The degree of federal supervision varies greatly among grant programs. Some do not establish any but the most minimal conditions to be met by states. Other grants may require conformance to detailed administrative conditions. In 1949 a committee of the Council of State Governments reported that most state administrators believe that relations

---

[7] *Ibid.*, pp. 31–32.

with federal officials on grant-aided programs have been satisfactory. In the words of the committee: "This does not mean that federal supervision and control have been absent, but rather that the controls exercised by federal officials have been accepted by the state agencies as the expected but unwelcome accompaniment of the grants." [8] While it is apparent that the federal government has the right to insist that federal grants be used efficiently and for the purposes for which they were made, there is little agreement on the proper degree of federal supervision.

No firm conclusion can be drawn about the merits of grants-in-aid. Grant programs vary considerably in such vital matters as their impact on state budgets and the degree of federal supervision of programs aided by federal funds. As one student of federal grants said: "Federal aid is neither wholly good nor wholly bad, and a discussion of its merits and defaults without attention to the provisions and the operation of individual grants is of little merit." [9]

existing grant programs

Current federal grant-in-aid programs may be classified into the following groups:

Federal Grant-in-Aid Programs	Estimated Expenditures 1950 (in millions)	% of Total Grants
Social security	$1,193.3	53.0
Transportation (mainly highways)	490.7	22.0
Public health	203.0	9.0
Employment security (mainly unemployment insurance)	167.0	7.4
Agriculture, forestry, and wildlife	123.4	5.5
Education and general research	39.5	1.7
Veterans' services and benefits	17.4	0.8
Housing and community facilities	13.7	0.6
Total	$2,248.0	100.0

Source: Adapted from the *Budget of the United States Government for the Fiscal Year Ending June 30, 1951* (Washington: Government Printing Office, 1950), pp. 1139–1142.

1. SOCIAL SECURITY.   Grants to states for financing various programs under the Social Security Act accounted for over half of all federal grants to states in 1950. Grants for the public assistance program alone exeeded $1.1 billion. Other security programs aided by grants included maternal and child welfare services and vocational rehabilitation.[10] State public assistance programs must

---

[8] Council of State Governments, *Federal Grants-in-Aid* (Chicago: 1949), p. 47.

[9] Joseph P. Harris, "The Future of Federal Grants-in-Aid," *The Annals* of The American Academy of Political and Social Science, CCVII (January, 1940), 18.

[10] See Chapter 39, "Government and Social Welfare," for a description of these programs.

conform to certain standards to be eligible to receive federal grants. For example, state administration must be in the hands of a "single state agency," the personnel of the state agency must be employed on a merit basis, all information about applicants for public assistance must be kept confidential, and individuals whose claims for assistance are denied must be given a fair hearing before the state agency. The amount of the grant to each state is determined by a rather complicated formula. In addition, the federal government pays half of the administrative expenses of assistance programs.

2. TRANSPORTATION. The major grant-aided program in transportation is highway construction. Federal grants are now made for important through highways, for principal secondary and feeder roads (farm-to-market roads, mail routes, and school-bus routes), for highway projects within urban areas, for the elimination of railroad grade crossings, and for highways in the public lands of the United States. Federal grants may be used only for construction and in most cases must be matched dollar for dollar by state and local contributions. The total amount of federal funds is not static, and every few years Congress revises the highway-aid statutes. To be eligible for federal aid a state must have a highway department with sufficient authority and equipment to cooperate with the federal highway agency, the Public Roads Administration in the Department of Commerce. The states retain the initiative in determining what roads to build and how to maintain them, but state highway construction must be approved in advance by the Public Roads Administration.

The second major grant-aided program in transportation is the airport program begun in 1946 to help states and cities build public airports. With certain exceptions, federal aid must be matched dollar for dollar by state and local governments. The Civil Aeronautics Administration of the Department of Commerce is authorized to deal directly with cities and other local governments as well as with states that wish to build public airports, but more than half of the states now require their local subdivisions to submit airport construction plans to them for approval prior to construction. Under the Federal Airport Act of 1946,[11] the federal government may establish detailed rules and regulations for airport construction. Federal rules issued under the act have been criticized by state and local governments as so detailed as to amount to federal control. The states have also opposed the federal practice of dealing directly with political subdivisions in the states and have urged that the airport program be revised after the pattern of the highway program.

3. PUBLIC HEALTH. Over $200 million was granted to states and private institutions in 1950 for various public health projects, including hospital construction, the national school lunch program, medical research, disease control, and control of water pollution. The Department of Agriculture administers

---

[11] 60 Stat. 170.

school lunch grants, and the Public Health Service in the Federal Security Agency directs other grant programs. The school lunch program makes grants to states, through state departments of education, to assist schools in supplying food for consumption by school children and to provide equipment necessary for school lunch programs. The funds are allocated to states on the basis of relative need and school population. Through 1950, federal funds were matched dollar for dollar, but after 1950, the federal share was reduced to one dollar as against three dollars contributed by state and local governments.

Grants for hospital construction were made available by the Hospital Survey and Construction Act (Hill-Burton Act) of 1946.[12] States are aided first by grants to make surveys of hospital needs and to make plans for construction of public and other nonprofit hospitals. Second, federal funds may be made available to meet one third of the cost of construction projects approved by the Surgeon General of the United States, the director of the Public Health Service. The Surgeon General is authorized to establish general standards of construction and equipment and to prescribe the number of hospital beds of various types needed to provide adequate hospital service. In order to receive grants, states may not discriminate against persons on grounds of race, creed, or color, except that segregated hospitals may be constructed, provided that their facilities and services are equal to those in other public hospitals. An unusual feature of the hospital program is the provision that an applicant may appeal the Surgeon General's denial of his request for a grant to a United States court of appeals.

The Public Health Service also makes grants to states for general health services, for prevention and control of venereal diseases and tuberculosis, for medical research in heart and cancer diseases, and for the elimination or reduction of water pollution. These grants are allocated to states on the basis of population, the existence of special health problems, and the financial needs of the states. The existence of special health problems is the most important factor in the allocation of funds by the Surgeon General. The states must contribute one dollar for every two dollars of federal funds for general public health service and the control of venereal diseases, whereas federal grants for tuberculosis control must be matched dollar for dollar.

4. EMPLOYMENT SECURITY. Two grant programs are designed to help people find employment and protect individuals from the risk of unemployment. Federal grants are made to states to cover the administrative costs of operating the public employment offices and the unemployment insurance system.[13]

5. AGRICULTURE, FORESTRY, AND WILDLIFE. The Department of Agriculture makes grants to states for the operation of state agricultural experiment sta-

[12] 60 Stat. 1040.
[13] See Chapter 39, "Government and Social Welfare."

tions. The purpose of these grants is to advance agricultural research, distribute practical information about agriculture, and improve the marketing of agricultural commodities. Through the Extension Service, the Department of Agriculture helps states finance cooperative agricultural extension work, which is administered through state agricultural colleges. The grants for agricultural extension help pay the salaries of county agents who are employed jointly by the federal, state, and local governments. Federal grants are also made to assist states in maintaining forest-fire prevention programs, to assist farmers in their forestry work, and to promote wildlife conservation projects administered by state fish and game authorities. These grants are made under a wide variety of matching provisions and conditions of eligibility.

6. EDUCATION AND GENERAL RESEARCH. The United States Office of Education in the Federal Security Agency makes payments to states to support state agricultural and mechanical colleges. The colleges were established originally with the help of the federal land grants under the Morrill Act of 1862 and are known as land-grant colleges. The grants are used for the training of teachers and for the teaching of specified subjects, including agriculture, engineering, English, mathematics, economics, and physical and natural sciences. No matching by states is required. Additional grants are made to states to promote vocational education in agriculture, home economics, trades and industry, and other occupations. Small funds are granted to the American Printing House for the Blind to promote the education of the blind.

7. VETERANS' SERVICES AND BENEFITS. Three types of grants are made to states for the benefit of veterans. The Veterans Administration makes grants to states which maintain state homes for disabled veterans. The grants are made on the basis of $500 for every disabled veteran cared for in a state home and must be matched by the states. Since the end of World War II, grants are also made to states for supervision of business establishments participating in training programs for veterans and for the administration of veterans' unemployment benefits.

8. HOUSING AND COMMUNITY FACILITIES. Under housing legislation enacted after World War II, federal grants are made for low-rent housing programs of state and local governments and for veterans' housing programs.[14]

federal-state administrative relations

The pattern of distribution of powers between the federal government and the states has been altered by new developments in administrative relations. Joint or complementary federal and state administration varies considerably from program to program but has probably been developed most highly in the agricul-

---

[14] See Chapter 40, "Education, Housing, and Consumer Services."

tural field. The emerging pattern of federal-state agricultural relations suggests some of the ways in which American federalism is subject to continuing changes.

Agricultural activities of government are conducted by the United States Department of Agriculture, state departments of agriculture, land-grant colleges and experiment stations, county agents, various county and local committees of farmers, and even new governing units, the soil conservation districts. The development of the agricultural agencies has been accompanied by conflicts, the resolution of which has led to new intergovernmental relations. The major issue, "in the broadest terms, is over who shall set the policies, devise the programs, expand the funds, and guide the administration of the manifold public activities relating to agriculture." [15]

Since 1933, federal agricultural programs have recognized a need to establish agricultural agencies close to the farm people affected directly by governmental agricultural activities. County and local committees of various types were established by federal programs in soil conservation, extension work, rural electrification, farm credit, and farm security. The distribution of authority to make political decisions to local committees and to the states has had the effect of dividing governmental powers in agriculture among the three levels of government. Some agricultural matters are regarded as requiring unified national action and are controlled by the federal government. Others requiring varying degrees of adaptation to local or state conditions are subject to local and state determination. In allocating power to federal, state, and local agencies, Congress has not followed a consistent formula, but has dealt with each governmental program separately. In making these decisions, the following criteria have been relevant:

1. How essential is a high degree of national unity of action? Clearly it is vital in matters of national defense, international diplomacy and international trade. Is it essential in pest control? in conservation of our natural resources? in stabilization of production? in minimum wage controls?

2. Does the national government have the means wherewith to establish unity of action? Clearly it has such means in foreign trade and international relations generally. But what means has it at its disposal to prevent the wasteful use of resources by six million farmers?

3. Granted that general unity of action is needed, must the action be identical or nearly so in all parts of the nation? or can a fairly wide measure of latitude be permitted in forms of action designed to achieve certain general ends? The answer might well be one way if the activity were cotton grading and another if it were prevention of forest fires.

---

[15] John D. Black, "Federal-State-Local Relations in Agriculture" (Report of the Agriculture Committee on National Policy, mimeo., January 7, 1949), p. 1. Excerpts from this pamphlet reprinted here are used by permission of the author.

4.   Does the activity call for a high degree of adaptation to state and local conditions and circumstances?

5.   Are state and local units of government in a better position than national to secure cooperation of the public or compliance by those affected?

6.   Do state and local units of government have the financial and/or personnel resources needed to carry out the program?[16]

The principal protagonists in agricultural administration have been the Department of Agriculture and the land-grant colleges. In 1938 the two groups concluded the Mount Weather Agreement, which provided that the department was to continue federal administration of agricultural programs but was to cooperate with the land-grant colleges in setting up state and county land-use planning committees in all states and counties. The state extension services, manned by county agents, were to take responsibility for setting up the committees, consisting of farmers, governmental representatives, and the county agent. A state land-use planning committee was to coordinate the work of the county committees. Although some progress was made under the Mount Weather Agreement, the county planning committees never wholly reached their objectives. They nevertheless have served as a pattern or goal for agricultural administration in other programs.

Although agricultural activities have been administered jointly by federal, state, and local agencies, a firm pattern of administration has not developed. The desirability of national unity of action as against flexible adaptation to local conditions has never been easy to establish except in international agricultural affairs. Several legislative proposals in recent years have suggested ways of expanding the use of local and state committees acting under some federal supervision, but congressional approval of these proposals has been extremely difficult to secure. Intergovernmental relations in agriculture will continue to be in a state of flux for several years. Nevertheless, a tradition of federal-state-local joint operation has developed which will be difficult to change.

The federal government and the states now cooperate in a number of other functional areas. The National Guard is financed by the federal government, but the states are required to provide armories and other facilities; they also retain certain powers and duties. In peacetime, the National Guard is a state military force under the command of the state governor. In time of military emergency, the National Guard becomes an integral part of the Army of the United States.

Under the Interstate Commerce Act, the Interstate Commerce Commission regulates interstate busses and trucks. The act provides, however, that when a motor carrier serves no more than three states, a joint board representing the states and the ICC must be established to make the initial determination in

---

[16] *Ibid.*, pp. 6–7.

certain types of cases. The requirement of the act of formalized, compulsory collaboration between state and federal regulatory agencies was a new departure in administration. Unfortunately, it has not worked well.

Informal federal-state relations take many forms. Perhaps the most common is informal cooperation on police matters. The Federal Bureau of Investigation assists in the training of state and local police officers, and its fingerprint files and other facilities are developed with the aid of local police officials. The Alcoholic Tax Unit of the Bureau of Internal Revenue in the Department of the Treasury has considerable contact with state officials charged with the enforcement of state liquor control laws.

World War II stimulated other cooperative governmental efforts. The Selective Service System and the wartime price and rationing boards of the Office of Price Administration depended heavily on the assistance of the states and local communities in furnishing office space, encouraging citizens to volunteer for work, and in providing police protection.

interstate cooperation

The distribution of governmental power has been affected to some extent by joint action taken by two or more states. State action has taken four forms:

1. Interstate compacts and agreements
2. Uniform state laws
3. Reciprocal or contingent legislation
4. Interstate administrative cooperation

Interstate compacts are agreements between two or more states. Thirty-seven compacts were concluded between 1934 and 1947. They have been utilized to settle boundary disputes and jurisdictional conflicts, to construct interstate public works, to conserve natural resources, to prevent water pollution, to regulate interstate water resources, to develop Atlantic marine fisheries, and to supervise parolees and probationers. The compacts have ranged from mere definitions of policy to pacts establishing elaborate administrative machinery. The best-known example of the latter type is the compact between New York and New Jersey establishing the Port of New York Authority. In recent years, supporters of strong state government have urged the widespread use of interstate compacts as a means of creating governmental agencies capable of administering interstate programs of a continuing nature. The number of interstate compacts has not increased rapidly, and only a few of them deal with important problems.

The need for uniformity of action among states provided the impetus for the movement to develop uniform state laws. Since the organization of the National Conference of Commissioners on Uniform State Laws in 1892, uniformity of state legislation in certain fields has been held out as a desirable alternative to federal legislation. By 1950, nearly a hundred model state laws had been drafted and certain of them have been adopted in some states. Several federal agencies, such as the Department of Justice and the Federal Security Agency, have encouraged the adoption of uniform state laws. Reciprocal or contingent state laws have also brought about some interstate cooperation in limited fields. Thus, a state may agree to accept the administrative actions of another state if that state agrees to accept the administrative actions of the first state. For example, New York State and California may agree to accept each other's reports of state bank and insurance examiners as to the solvency of banks and insurance companies. In this way, California benefits from examinations made by New York and vice versa.

Interstate administrative cooperation takes many forms. States may adopt regulations and procedures to govern interstate dealings, or they may agree to a uniform interpretation of related statutes. They may agree to negotiate or arbitrate interstate differences. Through interstate conferences and associations of state officials, they exchange information and reports.

Techniques of interstate cooperation have not been developed as much as federal grants and federal-state cooperative arrangements. Although "Federalism without Washington" [17] has long been urged to combat centralization of governmental powers in the federal government, the results of interstate cooperation have been only marginal, with two or three major exceptions. Either the great issues of the day have been beyond the capacity of states to handle on a cooperative basis or the states have not had sufficient initiative to overcome the obstacles to the adoption of cooperative schemes.

localization of federal activities

The character of the federal government tends to obscure the fact that the great bulk of federal activities are administered in local communities by local persons. The overwhelming majority of employees of the Post Office, for example, live in the cities, towns, and rural communities which they serve. Nearly nine out of every ten federal employees live and work in communities outside Washington, D.C. These employees staff local Veterans Administration hospitals, maintain the dams and flood control projects of the Tennessee Valley Authority and other federal agencies, keep the voluminous records of the old-age insurance program in working order, track down violators of kidnaping, counterfeiting, and other federal laws, and operate the camps and other installations of the armed forces.

---

[17] The phrase is used by the Council of State Governments in its report to the Hoover Commission entitled "Federal-State Relations" to describe interstate cooperation.

alternatives to federalism

Certain critics of the American federal system of government have proposed the elimination of the states as a level of government and the substitution of a smaller number of governments embracing the area of several states. These areas, known as regions, would presumably exercise more authority than the present state governments. Opponents of the extension of federal power have suggested that regional governments would be able to handle many of the tasks now beyond the capacities of individual states. Although regional governments have appealed to some observers as an alternative to the centralization of govmental activities at the federal level, proposals to replace states with a smaller number of regional governments have not gained much support.

issues ahead

Perhaps the major unresolved problem of American federalism is whether the states can improve their capacity to undertake governmental functions. Are the states suitable units for the administration of activities covering health, education, unemployment insurance, labor conditions, railroad rates, and electric power? Can the states contribute effectively to the maintenance of economic stability and full employment? How valid is the view that federalism "presents the spectacle of forty-nine governments seeking to deal with issues for many of which they are inappropriate as instrumentalities whether in the area they cover or in the authority they may invoke?" [18]

A popular view regards the centralization of governmental power in the federal government as destructive of our liberties and freedoms. Opponents of federal action frequently assert that it will result in extravagance, waste, inefficiency, and dictatorship, and, above all, will restrict the freedom of the individual to control his own destiny. These views raise questions that require a great deal of thought. Is it clear that the states can, in fact, undertake more functions and perform them adequately and efficiently? Is local government necessarily more responsible to the will of the people than the federal government? Are local governments capable of overcoming public apathy on political issues? If it is true that great issues are needed to overcome political apathy and encourage citizen participation in government, can the state and local governments match the democratic capacity of the federal government to focus public attention on national issues?

In analyzing federal-state relations, the Council of State Governments made this report to the Hoover Commission:

---

[18] Harold Laski, "The Obsolescence of Federalism," *New Republic*, XCVIII (May 3, 1939), 367–369.

There is no panacea for these difficulties. In these problems, as in others, some of the uncertainty and inefficiency is the price paid for flexibility. . . . The obvious, large need is for some process of over-all planning of National-State programs. But whenever a need for over-all planning appears, it is closely accompanied by the need for techniques that permit flexibility, initiative, and discretion. These are required at both the National and State levels. The price of forgetting them would be a Nation frozen into administrative rigidities. The reward for encouraging them may be an enlarged possibility for cooperative success.[19]

The demands made upon government by people do not remain static. The tremendous increase in government functions at all levels is conclusive testimony to the changing character of government. It is essential to a democracy that its government be flexible and adaptable to changing conditions and changing demands for public services. The issues of federalism today are political rather than legal. Federalism will remain a major characteristic of American government so long as it remains flexible. Constant readjustment to economic and social changes is essential to its survival. The process of readjustment presents some of the most difficult political problems facing a democratic government.

bibliographic note

Two books which review and interpret trends in the changing relations between the federal and state governments are George C. S. Benson, *The New Centralization* (New York: Rinehart & Company, 1941), and Jane Perry Clark, *The Rise of a New Federalism* (New York: Columbia University Press, 1938). Questions about the ability of the states to play a vital role in the American political system are raised by Harold Laski in "The Obsolescence of Federalism," *New Republic*, XCVIII (May 3, 1939), 367–369. More current views of the capacity of states to assume more significant roles in American politics are outlined by Roy V. Peel in *State Government Today* (Albuquerque: University of New Mexico Press, 1948) and by W. Brooke Graves in "What Is Happening to Our Federal System," *State Government*, XXII, No. 11 (November, 1949), 255–259.

Grants-in-aid have dominated discussions of federal-state relations for several years. The views of the Council of State Governments are presented in Council of State Governments, *Federal Grants-in-Aid* (Chicago: 1949). An older but valuable study is the report of the National Resources Committee on *Regional Factors in National Planning* (Washington: Government Printing Office, 1935). Critical questions about the grant-in-aid techniques are posed by Jo-

---

[19] "Federal-State Relations," *Senate Document* No. 81, 81 Cong., 1 Sess., p. 60.

seph P. Harris in "The Future of Federal Grant-in-Aids," *The Annals* of the American Academy of Political and Social Science, CCVII (January, 1940), 15–26.

Federal-state-local relations today are analyzed by the Council of State Governments in its report to the Hoover Commission, reprinted as *Senate Document* No. 81, 81 Cong. 1 Sess., *Federal-State Relations* (Washington: Government Printing Office, 1949). The Hoover Commission's findings and proposals are presented in Commission on Organization of the Executive Branch of the Government, *Overseas Administration, Federal-State Relations, Federal Research* (Washington: Government Printing Office, 1949). Intergovernmental relations in agricultural policy and administration are analyzed by John D. Black in "Federal-State-Local Relations in Agriculture" (Report of the Agriculture Committee on National Policy, mimeo., January 7, 1949).

government planning

*P*LANNING is not easy to define because it means different things to different people and has become a "bad" concept for some persons. Some critics of expanding governmental activity interpret planning by government to mean central direction of economic activity. These critics of planning assert that governmental control of the economy is socialism and will destroy our traditional democratic liberties along with our free enterprise economy. Planning is therefore conceived as the opponent of free enterprise.

In this chapter planning is defined in less controversial terms as *organized foresight*. It is the process of deliberate formulation of policies to achieve stated goals or objectives. It involves the intelligent study and consideration of problems and the attempt to achieve their solution. Interpreted as organized foresight, planning is applicable to almost every area of human activity, including private as well as public affairs. It describes not only new activities and functions of government but also many activities accepted long ago as reasonable and essential.

Defined as organized foresight, planning is an essential part of any program of action. The careful consideration of programs and actions designed to achieve certain goals is an inevitable part of the process of government. Thus planning must be accepted as inevitable, essential, and desirable. Just as a business corporation must organize itself and make plans necessary for its successful operation, so must governments develop plans of action for reaching desired objectives. Although many conflicts surround important issues of public policy, especially those relating to the expansion of the scope of governmental activity, there ought to be no conflict about the need for the government to plan carefully to achieve whatever objectives are determined by the majority of citizens to be in the public interest.

results of the failure to plan carefully

The desirability and inevitability of planning can be illustrated best by reference to what happens when governments fail to plan adequately. The reports of the Hoover Commission document many situations in which the failure to make adequate plans has resulted in duplicating and competing agencies, waste of funds and personnel, and failure to achieve the objectives of legislation. For example, two large federal agencies, the Army Corps of Engineers and the Bureau of Reclamation in the Department of the Interior, are both concerned with the development of rivers. The Corps of Engineers is interested mainly in flood control, whereas the Bureau of Reclamation is interested primarily in providing water for irrigating arid areas. The Hoover Commission reported:

> With differing purposes they work on the same rivers, the Corps working up the river, meeting the Bureau coming down. There have been repeated instances where each competes with the other to begin construction on the same project. The result has been hasty planning, lack of sufficient basic data, duplicating cost of surveying and estimating, failure to consider the entire needs of the area, and the creation of strong and opposing local pressures each seeking special benefits. The end result has been needless delay, confusion, and gross waste of the taxpayers' money.[1]

Similarly, federal programs in the management of public lands and the administration of forest areas have developed conflicting policies with respect to the use of government-owned land. Farmers, ranchers, and logging operators who desire to use public lands must frequently negotiate with two or more agencies whose policies and programs are inconsistent. In the field of hospital construction, the Hoover Commission found that four large federal agencies "compete with each other in the building of hospitals without regard to the others' needs, unused bed capacity, or best utilization of scarce professional manpower."[2] In its examination of the activities of the federal independent regulatory commissions, the Hoover Commission found that these agencies were so preoccupied with the adjudication of particular cases that they neglected to plan their activities to make the best use of their funds and personnel to achieve the goals for which they were established. With respect to federal transportation programs, the separate activities of the Interstate Commerce Commission, the Civil Aeronautics Board, and the Department of Commerce are not coordinated to produce a unified national transportation policy. Consequently different and inconsistent regulatory policies are applied to ships, airlines, trucks, and railroads.

Piecemeal development of legislation has been perhaps the major obstacle to effective planning of federal activities. In health and welfare administration, for example, various public assistance and social insurance programs were developed at different times and have not been welded into a coordinated federal

---

[1] The Commission on Organization of the Executive Branch of the Government, *Concluding Report* (Washington: Government Printing Office, 1949), pp. 27–29.
[2] *Ibid.*, p. 31.

welfare program. The results are frequently incongruous and unsatisfactory. Some individuals and families are favored recipients of governmental financial assistance, while other needy persons may be ineligible for such assistance. Although social insurance is declared to be the cornerstone of federal welfare policy, insurance benefits have been too low to support a minimum level of satisfactory existence. Poor planning or the lack of planning leads to wasted effort and money and, even more important, failure to carry out public policies efficiently. Planning cannot guarantee successful programs, but programs cannot succeed unless they are planned carefully. Moreover, the results of poor planning indicate that there is no real choice between planning or not planning.

the role of Congress in planning

The need for careful planning of governmental programs will increase rather than decrease. Governmental programs today have a very significant impact on the economy. Many programs affect directly millions of individual citizens. Problems of economic stability, mobilization for national defense, regulation of business, and conduct of foreign relations cannot be solved satisfactorily without careful planning, not only by administrative agencies but also by legislatures. Administrative agencies can plan, but in a democracy the legislature must decide basic policy issues. Some of the principal questions about planning appear to be shifting from the administrative agencies to legislatures. Executive-legislative relations are becoming crucial to the development and carrying out of plans and programs in the most difficult areas of public policy. Is Congress capable of fulfilling its basic role of formulating policy objectives and reviewing the programs of administrative agencies? Can Congress in its present form of organization be an effective factor in the planning process? Is more effective party cohesion needed to keep parties in the Congress responsible for their policy decisions? Plans are meant to be placed in operation. The capacity of our legislative institutions to participate effectively in and to control the planning process may become the key to successful planning in a democracy.

principal types of governmental planning

Although the planning process is essential in all governmental activities, it is especially important in programs requiring the cooperation of two or more agencies or many professional groups like architects, engineers, lawyers, and agricultural experts, or the compromise of differences among various economic interests. The most significant types of governmental planning include city planning, conservation of natural resources, river valley development, planning for war mobilization and national security, economic stabilization, and administrative planning. Each of these types is discussed briefly in the following sections.

city planning

City planning may be defined as a municipal effort to plan the physical layout of the city and to develop its economic resources. A city planning agency tries to guide and influence the future development of the city by planning the physical location of streets and highways, by zoning the city into areas designated for various business, industrial, and residential uses, and by determining the need for and location of public auditoriums and civic centers, schools, sewage disposal systems, and public parks and playgrounds. The objectives of physical planning may be to beautify the city, to provide adequate recreational areas for children and adults, to eliminate traffic congestion, and to regulate the location and construction of homes and factories. Planning of the physical environment of the city requires the combined efforts of many professional experts. Highway and construction engineers, lawyers, landscape and building architects, analysts of population trends, economists, and others must work together to provide a physical plan to guide the future growth of the city.

Since the depression of the thirties, city planning agencies have become more concerned than before with the economic problems of urban communities. Greater attention is now devoted to public housing activities and to the improvement of economic conditions. Efforts are made to attract desirable industries in order to build up employment and to increase the income levels of city residents.

metropolitan planning

The rapid growth of cities and urban populations after the Civil War produced not only large cities but metropolitan areas which included outlying districts as well as the central city. The development of a number of contiguous municipalities in a metropolitan area created problems which no single municipality was able to solve. Gradually techniques were devised to permit some collaboration among municipalities or between a central city and its suburbs leading to the development of programs of mutual interest, such as a metropolitan park or highway system.

One of the most important political inventions was the development of the interstate compact by the states of New York and New Jersey to create the Port of New York Authority. The Port of New York Authority is a governmental agency established by the legislatures of New York and New Jersey to deal with common problems of transportation affecting New York City and communities in northern New Jersey. Neither the cities in northern New Jersey nor New York City itself was able to control the heavy interstate traffic in the New York metropolitan area or to finance the construction of adequate bridges, tunnels, highways, airports, and terminals. The Port Authority was granted power to borrow funds by selling securities in order to finance the construction of transportation projects in the metropolitan area. Perhaps its most famous projects include the Holland and Lincoln Tunnels under the Hudson River and the George Washington Bridge over the Hudson River connecting Manhattan and northern New Jersey cities, and the Triborough Bridge, which connects the boroughs of Manhattan, the Bronx, and Queens in New York City.

The 1950 census of population emphasizes the movement of people from cities to outlying suburban areas as a major population trend. The large-scale development of suburban communities near cities like Chicago, Detroit, Los Angeles, and New York has extended the limits of metropolitan areas and has created many difficult problems. The suburban residents use city facilities, create traffic congestion, but pay no city taxes. The central cities are losing tax revenues to nearby suburban communities, whereas the latter must invest large sums of money to build schools and provide such services as police and fire protection, sewage disposal, and water supply. Despite much experimentation, American cities have not yet solved the financial and political problems created by the movement of wealthier citizens to suburbs outside the taxing jurisdiction of the central city.

conservation of natural resources

Another type of planning is the development and conservation of physical resources, including land, water, minerals, and plants.[3] Planning involving natural resources has two objectives. The first objective is broad and general: to conserve and utilize the physical resources of the nation to attain a prosperous economy. It consists basically of applying human ingenuity, intelligence, and foresight to maintain an abundant supply of physical resources in order to promote economic development. The second objective is to produce certain specific benefits in the public interest. These include the development of hydroelectric power and its transmission and distribution, the improvement of navigation on inland rivers and lakes, the prevention and control of floods, irrigation of arid lands in the West and Southwest, soil and forest conservation, preservation of fish and wildlife, the construction of recreational facilities, and the management of scarce materials important to national security. Perhaps the newest program in natural resources is the atomic energy program, which produces fissionable materials for the manufacture of weapons and for the peacetime use of atomic power.

During the 1930's the role of deliberate formulation of public policies to conserve natural resources was undertaken by the National Resources Planning

---

[3] For further discussion, see Chapter 37, "Government and Agriculture."

Board, which functioned until 1943. It was given the task of collecting and analyzing basic data relating to natural resources and cooperating with and encouraging state and local planning agencies. The need for a clearinghouse for planning data and for federal-state-local cooperation was apparent for, by 1937, forty-seven state planning boards were studying the best use of state and local natural resources. The function of these various planning agencies was characterized as substituting the results of careful scientific study for uninformed judgment as the basis for the formulation of governmental plans.[4] Some of the reports of the National Resources Planning Board have become minor classics in the literature of politics and government in the United States.

A large number of federal agencies operate natural resource programs today. Land, water, and mineral programs are administered mainly by the Departments of Agriculture and the Interior. The Atomic Energy Commission is responsible for the development of atomic energy. Flood control work is dominated by the Army Corps of Engineers. No single agency provides a central point of clearance and supervision of conservation policies and programs. In 1949, the Hoover Commission recommended that federal organization be simplified by bringing all forestry and land management activities into the Department of Agriculture and by unifying the development of all subsoil and water resources in the Department of the Interior.

Planning for the wise use and development of natural resources is one of the most difficult types of governmental planning. There is widespread agreement that the welfare of the people depends heavily upon the natural resources they have at their disposal. However, there is no consensus with respect to the best methods to develop and, at the same time, to conserve natural resources. Conservation programs are likely to remain a source of conflict between the federal government and the states and will continue to bring into play powerful economic interests seeking to promote their own welfare.

river valley development

The physical and economic development of river valleys is one of the most dramatic and significant types of governmental planning. The development of a river valley has a wide variety of purposes. Some groups may be interested mainly in advancing navigation on the river. Other groups may be concerned with the improvement of agriculture in the river basin and with programs of flood control, irrigation, soil conservation, production of fertilizers, and land drainage. Still other groups have interests ranging from the generation of electric power to the building up of recreational areas for fishing, camping, and swimming.

---

[4] The President's Committee on Administrative Management, *Administrative Management in the Government of the United States* (Washington: Government Printing Office, 1937), p. 28.

These varied and sometimes conflicting purposes must be put together in a single plan of development which will enhance the status of the river valley and its residents.

what the Tennessee Valley Authority does

The Tennessee Valley Authority is the outstanding example of governmental planning for river valley development. Since it was established in 1933 as an independent federal agency, the TVA has helped the people of the Tennessee Valley[5] to achieve better control of their natural resources and to improve their economic status. The TVA contributes to the growth of the river valley by constructing and operating an elaborate system of dams in order to control the flow of water, to prevent floods, to generate hydroelectric power, and to create rec-

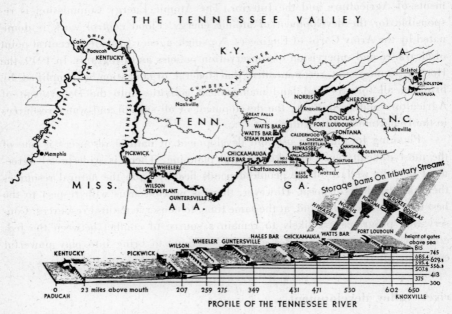

Since 1933, the Tennessee River has been transformed by TVA from a destructive stream in flood time to a water system productive the year-round. (*Source: Annual Report of the Tennessee Valley Authority, 1948.*)

reational areas. The Authority also operates chemical plants at Muscle Shoals to experiment with improved fertilizers to enrich the soil and to supply materials needed for national defense. The TVA staff also makes available to farmers the knowledge and methods they need to use their land and forests more effectively.

The Tennessee Valley is an area of more than 40,000 square miles through which flows the Tennessee River. The river is now navigable for 630 miles from

---

[5] Including parts of Tennessee, Kentucky, Virginia, North Carolina, Georgia, Alabama, and Mississippi.

Knoxville to Paducah, where it connects with the inland waterway system of the country. Twenty-seven major dams and reservoirs control the river system. About 16 billion kilowatt-hours of electricity are generated at the major dams and transmitted to homes, farms, and factories. The availability of cheap hydroelectric power enables the people of the valley to make better use of their resources and helps to promote the growth of industry and employment. The expansion of power facilities has mutiplied the farm use of electricity fiftyfold since 1933. With power-drawn machinery, fertilizer, and improved soil conservation practices, farmers are able to diversify their farm operations and increase their incomes substantially.

The harnessing of the power of the river has yielded many indirect benefits. Reservoirs are used for boating, swimming, and fishing, and safe areas have been set aside for fish and wildfowl. Water pollution has been reduced, and malaria has nearly disappeared along the river.

TVA activities have improved the standard of living in the valley and have been a stimulus to economic expansion. New manufacturing plants have opened up new employment opportunities, and the valley has improved its economic position more than the country as a whole. Average per capita income in the valley rose from $148 in 1933 to $797 in 1947, whereas the average income for the United States increased from $368 to $1,323 in the same period. Per capita income in the region remains about 40 per cent below the national average, although there has been considerable improvement in the relative position of the region.

The electric power activities of TVA have aroused considerable controversy. Much of the power generated at TVA dams is sold to more than 140 municipal and cooperative power systems which serve more than a million consumers. In 1949 TVA estimated that it earned a return of 5 per cent on the average net investment in power facilities. The act establishing the TVA directs the Authority to set rates as low as possible but sufficient to meet all costs. TVA adopted the practice of reducing rates drastically in order to stimulate greater consumption. The success of the TVA policy has encouraged privately owned utilities to follow similar pricing policies. In 1949 the average kilowatt-hour price of electricity was 1.54 cents in the TVA area compared to 2.98 cents for the United States. Consumers in the valley paid an average of $42.50 annually for 2,762 kilowatts compared to an average of $48.43 in the United States for the annual average consumption of 1,625 kilowatts.

Critics of TVA argue that neither its electric rates nor those of the municipal and cooperative systems who buy power from it include all of the costs which private utilities must pay. The major problem is the difficulty of allocating costs of the TVA program to complex activities of flood control and navigation as well as the generation, transmission, and distribution of electric power. Certain joint costs must be assigned to these various operations, and the determination of the assignment of costs will probably remain controversial for many years.

The Tennessee Valley Authority is managed by a board of three men and a general manager, who supervise about 15,000 employees. The board is responsible to the President and to the Congress. It has tried to avoid conflicts with other federal and state departments and agencies by working out agreements for joint action, especially in the fields of agriculture and land use.

more TVA's?

The success of the TVA in promoting the economic growth of the Tennessee Valley has led to demands for the creation of similar multipurpose agencies in other regions, including the Missouri Valley, the Columbia Valley, and the Arkansas Valley. Supporters of the valley authority assert that a single agency with comprehensive powers can operate more effectively than a series of separate agencies with particular interests. In 1949 the Hoover Commission concluded:

> Experience has shown that parcelling out river development responsibilities . . . produces endless confusion and conflict. A plan for the development of a river basin cannot be devised by adding together the special studies and the separate recommendations of unifunctional agencies concerned respectively with navigation, flood control, irrigation, land drainage, pollution abatement, power development, domestic and industrial water supply, fishing, and recreation. These varied and sometimes conflicting purposes must be put together and integrated in a single plan of development.[6]

There are two alternatives to the valley authority as the agent for river valley development. One is to assign all responsibilities to one department like the Department of the Interior. The other is to coordinate the efforts of several departments. The latter has been followed in the Missouri Valley where the Army Corps of Engineers is given authority over flood control, the Secretary of Agriculture controls soil erosion, and the Bureau of Reclamation in the Department of the Interior is responsible for irrigation and the sale of electric power. The possibility for successful coordination of these three agencies in the development of the Missouri Valley is not strong. Prolonged conflict between the Army Engineers and the Bureau of Reclamation led the Hoover Commission Task Force on natural resources to despair of success in reconciling conflicting viewpoints and policies.

planning for national security

During wartime, the federal government exercises comprehensive controls over the economy and the labor market. Programs to control and speed war produc-

---

[6] The Commission on Organization of the Executive Branch of the Government, *Department of the Interior* (Washington: Government Printing Office, 1949), pp. 28–29.

tion, to allocate scarce materials and supplies, to direct manpower to factories and plants, and to stabilize prices must be put into operation quickly. Planning for a war emergency has become a major function of the federal government.

Since 1947 considerable progress has been made in the preparation of mobilization plans for national security. The National Security Act of 1947 created the National Security Council and the National Security Resources Board to assist the President to discharge his broad responsibility for national security. The council's mission is to advise the President on the integration of domestic, foreign, and military policies relating to national security.

The principal burden of preparing plans for mobilizing the civilian economy for purposes of national security has been assigned to the National Security Resources Board. Under the National Security Act, the members of the board are designated by the President with the proviso that the chairman "be appointed from civilian life" with the approval of the Senate. The board advises the President concerning the coordination of military, industrial, and civilian mobilization, including

1. policies concerning industrial and civilian mobilization in order to assure the most effective mobilization and maximum utilization of the Nation's manpower in the event of war;

2. programs for the effective use in time of war of the Nation's natural and industrial resources for military and civilian needs, for the maintenance and stabilization of the civilian economy in time of war, and for the adjustment of such economy to war needs and conditions;

3. policies for unifying, in time of war, the activities of Federal agencies and departments engaged in or concerned with production, procurement, distribution, or transportation of military or civilian supplies, materials, and products;

4. the relationship between potential supplies of, and potential requirements for, manpower, resources, and productive facilities in time of war;

5. policies for establishing adequate reserves of strategic and critical material, and for the conservation of these resources;

6. the strategic relocation of industries, services, government, and economic activities, the continuous operation of which is essential to the Nation's security.[7]

The President has designated the Secretaries of the Treasury, Defense, Interior, Agriculture, Commerce, Labor, and State as members of the National Security Resources Board. The board itself is organized in a number of divisions concerned with industrial, material, and human resources. From 1948 on, the board has concentrated on the preparation of an industrial mobilization blue-

---

[7] National Security Act of 1947, 61 Stat. 495.

print. Any plan for the mobilization of the economy for national security is under constant revision. As Hanson Baldwin has suggested:

> No economic mobilization plan is ever finished; so vast is the statistical labor involved, so intangible some of the factors that influence it that it can never be completely up to date. Any such plan is, at best, a vast compilation of statistics, estimates, "questimates," and projects subject to change without notice.[8]

As a part of its plans for economic mobilization in case of war, the board has also drafted legislative proposals to authorize the President to mobilize the war economy. The proposed omnibus legislation would include sections on coordination of executive agencies, production facilities, loans, priorities and allocations, economic stabilization, authority to requisition materials and facilities, plant seizure, import and export control, censorship of communications, renegotiation of contracts, manpower controls, settlement of wartime labor disputes, and excess profits taxes.

As a result of the Defense Production Act of 1950, the board has been largely superseded in responsibility for mobilizing the economy for defense by the Office of Defense Mobilization, headed by Charles E. Wilson. The director of this office has been called an "assistant President" because of his broad responsibilities for directing the production of goods and maintaining economic stability. The two major civilian agencies under the Office of Defense Mobilization are the Defense Production Administration, which establishes production priorities and requirements, and the Economic Stabilization Agency, which administers price and wage regulations.

planning for economic stability

After the end of World War II, there was considerable fear of a business depression and widespread unemployment. Demands were made that government assume a direct responsibility for avoiding depressions and for stabilizing the economy. In response to these demands, Congress enacted the Employment Act of 1946, which declares:

> It is the continuing policy and responsibility of the Federal Government to use all practicable means consistent with its needs and obligations and other essential considerations of national policy, with the assistance and cooperation of industry, agriculture, labor, and State and local governments, to coordinate and utilize all its plans, functions, and resources for the purpose of

---

[8] Hanson W. Baldwin, "New Plans Now Unite Strategy and Industry," New York *Times*, September 26, 1948.

creating and maintaining, in a manner calculated to foster and promote free competitive enterprise and the general welfare, conditions under which there will be afforded useful employment opportunities, including self-employment, for those able, willing, and seeking to work, and to promote maximum employment, production, and purchasing power.[8a]

The essential purpose of the Employment Act is to promote economic stability as measured by maximum employment, production, and purchasing power. The acceptance of this responsibility by the federal government was considered a step forward by many who believed that the acid test of democratic society may be its ability to prevent depressions and to provide suitable employment for those able and willing to work.

Council of Economic Advisers

In general the Employment Act directs the government to use all means at its disposal consistent with the maintenance of free competitive enterprise to maintain economic stability. The principal machinery created by the act is the Council of Economic Advisers, composed of three members appointed by the President and confirmed by the Senate. The council exercises three related functions: it interprets data concerning economic trends; it appraises all federal programs to determine the extent to which they are contributing to the promotion of maximum employment, production, and purchasing power; it recommends to the President "national economic policies to foster and promote free competitive enterprise, to avoid economic fluctuations or to diminish the effects thereof, and to maintain employment, production, and purchasing power." In carrying out these functions, the council is required by statute to make an annual economic report to the President. The President in turn is directed to submit to Congress every January an economic report which sets forth current levels and foreseeable trends of employment, production, and purchasing power and which makes recommendations for achieving greater economic stability. In addition to these annual reports, the council prepares a quarterly economic review for the President, and the President submits a midyear economic report to Congress.

The annual report of the President is referred to the Joint Committee on the Economic Report, which consists of seven senators and seven representatives. This committee is authorized to make a continuing study of matters relating to the Economic Report and to report to Congress its findings and recommendations.

One of the most difficult tasks facing the Council of Economic Advisers is the development of satisfactory methods for diagnosing economic situations. The council must have access to appropriate and adequate information, and it must outline foreseeable economic trends in production, employment, and pur-

---

[8a] 60 Stat. 23.

chasing power. The council has made systematic use of advisory committees of consumers, businessmen, labor representatives, and farm spokesmen and has met regularly with other economists to review economic conditions.

The council has not attempted to make a detailed review and appraisal of government programs affecting economic stability. Rather, it tends to emphasize is advisory role and its task of making the techniques and results of economic analysis available to those who formulate national policy.

Congress intended that the council remain a small agency with a highly competent staff. During 1949 and 1950, the council's staff averaged about thirty-eight employees. The first three annual reports of the council to the President were notable primarily for their statements about the council's approach to the problems of economic stability and its interpretation of the political philosophy behind the Employment Act. In dissociating itself from advocates of a "planned economy," the council stated "that our free economy can be directed along a fairly regular course without imposing upon it intervention so extreme as to weaken private enterprise or destroy basic freedom of choice." [9] In its interpretation of "free competitive enterprise," the council appears to look less to positive government action and more to the enlightened actions of businessmen to maintain a reasonable degree of competition. It seems to rely more on the "social responsibility" of businessmen in supporting programs of stabilization than on legislation in order to adjust the relations of business and government.

One of the most important questions about any program for economic stabilization is the ability of Congress to act wisely and quickly in the face of economic crisis. In this respect, the performance of the Joint Committee on the Economic Report is scarcely reassuring. The committee does not have enough time to study the President's report and to formulate findings and recommendations with respect to it. The relations of the committee to the policy committees of the major parties, the appropriations committees, and the substantive committees of the House and the Senate have not been clarified. Perhaps the greatest obstacle facing the Congress in promoting economic stability continues to be the inability of either major party in the Congress to formulate moderately clear economic policies which are supported by most members of the party. In the absence of accepted party policies, congressional action on the Economic Report tends to be highly partisan in the worst sense of the term. There appears to be little question that a legislative program of economic stability cannot be achieved unless American political parties play a more forceful role in crystallizing public opinion about economic policies.

The Council of Economic Advisers has faced the prospect of effective congressional action hopefully and optimistically. Nevertheless the council has observed:

---

[9] Council of Economic Advisers, *Third Annual Report to the President* (Washington: Government Printing Office, December, 1948), p. 12.

Early experience under the Employment Act of 1946 has brought into sharp focus the practical difficulties which lie between the initiation of a national economic policy and the adoption of that policy by the Congress. Our American democracy will yield only slowly to the need for the deliberate formulation and integration of national policies in the interest of sustained prosperity.[10]

The council has continued to regard both the Employment Act of 1946 and its legislative and administrative machinery as adequate to achieve the goal of economic stability:

The Council of Economic Advisers in the Executive Office of the President furnishes professional staffing to enable the President to have national economic issues studied on an integrated basis above but not oblivious to the play of legitimate group interests. It facilitates his task of declaring leadership in proposing annually to the Congress an economic policy conceived in the continuing interest of the whole people. The Joint Committee on the Economic Report in the Congress facilitates in a similar way the study of the policies embodied in all particular legislative proposals to see whether they comport with a comprehensive and internally consistent national economic policy.[11]

Despite the council's faith in the adequacy of the act, in its system of reports, in the willingness of businessmen to exercise social responsibility in order to attain economic stability, and in the ability of Congress to legislate wisely and speedily, it is not yet clear that the act and the Council of Economic Advisers represent important forward steps in the development of government planning. One of the most serious tests of a democracy is likely to be its capacity for maintaining economic stability and preventing depressions. It is not yet certain that Congress will carry out its share of the task of planning for economic stability.

administrative planning

Governmental activities are not self-operating. Agencies and departments must be established to administer programs, policies must be clarified, and employees must be hired. All administrative activities in government involve a number of common problems. The work of the agency must be assigned to various sections or divisions or bureaus, and the separate programs of the agency must be geared into a general program consistent with legislative policy. Administrative planning is the task of devising appropriate organizational arrangements, techniques, and methods to carry out the program of individual agencies and of the government as a whole.

[10] *Ibid.*, p. 33.
[11] *Ibid.*, p. 33.

In general the function of planning is to prepare for taking action. Planning first places emphasis on clarifying the objectives of the government or the agency and the programs which government seeks to operate. When objectives and programs of work have been formulated, the process of performance must be planned to carry out the program and achieve the stated objectives. As one student of American government has suggested, planning affects all administrative activities:

> The more carefully the plans are prepared, the less waste will appear in accomplishment. The more comprehensive the plans, the less day to day improvisation will be necessary and the fewer crises will occur. The more adequate our plans, the surer we will be of accomplishing our purpose.[12]

One type of administrative planning deals with the organization of the structure of the government. It analyzes the total activity of government and tries to devise a government-wide administrative structure which will make for democratic, efficient, and effective operation and which will help to achieve the government's goals. A second type of administrative planning deals with the policies and programs of government agencies rather than with the structural arrangement of agencies in the government. It endeavors to attain the purpose of administrative activity by clarifying the objectives of the agency and by developing programs appropriate to the agency's objectives.

the Hoover Commission

Modern efforts to revise the administrative structure of the federal government date from President Taft's Commission on Economy and Efficiency of 1910. One of the most important studies of federal reorganization was published by the President's Committee on Administrative Management in 1937. The most recent attempt to propose a reorganization of federal agencies was made by the Commission on Organization of the Executive Branch of the Government (the Hoover Commission) in 1949. Under the chairmanship of Herbert Hoover, elaborate studies were made of almost every federal administrative activity by a series of study groups known as "task forces." Most of the reports of the task forces as well as all the reports of the commission itself have been published. A large number of unpublished studies made by members of various task forces are available in the National Archives.

Reorganization Act of 1949

The Hoover Commission recommended a regrouping of federal agencies to eliminate wasted effort, to clarify governmental goals, and to improve operation of

---

[12] John D. Millett, "Planning and Administration," in Fritz Morstein Marx, ed., *Elements of Public Administration* (New York: Prentice-Hall, Inc., 1946), p. 123.

the government. In order to carry out the recommendations of the Hoover Commission with respect to government-wide organization, Congress enacted the Reorganization Act of 1949.[13] The act authorizes the President to submit reorganization plans to the Congress. All plans become effective sixty days after presentation to the Congress unless they are disapproved by a majority of the full membership of either the House of Representatives or the Senate. The President submitted twenty-one reorganization plans in March, 1950, and six additional plans in May, 1950. The President's reorganization plans are studied by the Committees on Expenditures in the Executive Departments in the House and Senate. If a committee disapproves a plan, it introduces a resolution of disapproval which is voted upon by the House or the Senate, as the case may be. Following this procedure, the Congress has approved or has failed to disapprove a majority of the reorganization plans submitted in 1950.

Reorganization plan No. 15 of 1950 illustrates the way in which government-wide organization can be improved. This plan transfers functions relating to public works in Alaska and the Virgin Islands from the General Services Administration to the Department of the Interior. It consolidates the government's programs relating to Alaska and the Virgin Islands in a single agency "so that Federal policies and programs for promoting the general welfare of the people of these possessions may be properly coordinated. The plan, through centralization of such functions in a single agency, is intended to reduce duplication of effort and facilitate administration." [14] This plan became effective in May, 1950, since no action was taken in the House or in the Senate to disapprove it.

A more far-reaching reorganization was achieved by reorganization plan No. 21 of 1950, which abolished the Maritime Commission and transferred its functions to the Department of Commerce. Within the Commerce Department, the post of Under Secretary for Transportation was established to be responsible to the Secretary of Commerce for the administration of all transportation programs of the department. The Maritime Commission's regulatory functions covering rates, services, practices, and subsidies were transferred to a Maritime Board, and the remaining functions of the commission were assigned to a Maritime Administration. Both the Maritime Board and the Maritime Administration are under the general direction of the Under Secretary of Commerce for Transportation. Proponents of the plan believe that it will materially improve the efficiency of governmental maritime programs. Opposition to it was based on the contention that it might tend to concentrate transportation functions in the Department of Commerce and thus destroy the individual regulatory commissions now operating transportation programs. The Senate rejected a resolution to disapprove the plan, and it became effective in May, 1950.

---

[13] 63 Stat. 203.

[14] "Reorganization Plans of 1950," *Senate Document* No. 1,774, 81 Cong., 2 Sess. (Washington: Government Printing Office, 1950), p. 11.

Reorganization plans frequently raise important political issues. Should the President be in a position to influence the work of an independent regulatory commission? Will raising the Federal Security Agency to departmental status and the Federal Security Administrator to membership in the President's cabinet help to bring about a compulsory health insurance scheme? Will the abolition of the post of the General Counsel of the National Labor Relations Board destroy the effectiveness of the Taft-Hartley Act? These and other political issues were involved in a number of the reorganization plans of 1950, several of which were defeated by the Congress.

administrative planning of policies and programs

The planning of policies and programs is a universal function in administrative activity. All activities need to be related to some policy or objective and organized into a program of action. Planning of this type should occur in small offices, in major bureaus, in the offices of the secretary of a department, and in the Executive Office of the President and the White House Staff.

Several federal agencies of central direction or advice have already been noted. The National Security Council is a top-level cabinet committee which coordinates military and civilian activities in the interests of national security. The National Security Resources Board is virtually a part of the President's staff and carries the responsibility for developing plans for civilian war mobilization. The Council of Economic Advisers in the Executive Office of the President advises the President on economic trends and on the economic aspects of federal policies and programs. These and other agencies close to the President help to clarify problems of governmental policy and may help to resolve interagency conflicts of programs.

Administrative planning of programs is particularly important in the management of a large department. Because governmental functions have developed in a piecemeal fashion and have been assigned rather haphazardly to particular departments, the departments have generally not become effective centers of planning and administrative control. The average federal department tends to be a loose federation of bureaus, which in turn may be federations of smaller divisions. In the past, few department heads have had the time or were able to coordinate the activities of the bureaus to achieve a departmental program. For example, the Post Office Department has usually been managed by Assistant Postmasters General without much supervision from the Postmaster General. The Bureau of Mines, the Geological Survey, the Bureau of Reclamation, and other bureaus in the Department of the Interior have traditionally been directed by bureau chiefs subject only to a minimum of direction and control by the Secretary of the Interior.

Better departmental planning and control of programs is needed in the federal government. Two important administrative functions which have been developed to provide better direction of departmental affairs and to plan work programs to achieve departmental objectives are program planning and budgeting.

The *program planning* function is a relatively recent development in American government. A few departments, such as the Department of the Interior and the Department of Commerce, now have small staffs attached to the Office of the Secretary of the Department. These staffs review and appraise the programs of the various bureaus and divisions in the department and keep the secretary informed of important developments. They are free to undertake special assignments for the secretary and to assist him in planning the activities of the various bureaus so that departmental goals may be reached.

Program planning is as difficult as it is essential. Officials in the bureaus may have a rather narrow vision with respect to the department's program. Bureaus may develop vested interests in the bureau program and resist central direction from the secretary. Some bureau chiefs maintain close relations with particular congressmen or congressional committees who will protect their relatively autonomous status. Bureau officials may develop close ties with special interest groups who resist any change in the bureau's status out of fear that their influence on bureau policies and programs will decline.

Not only are the obstacles to departmental program planning considerable; there are also difficulties in finding the men capable of carrying on planning responsibilities. John Millett has described the attributes which a member of a program planning staff should have:

> He must be imaginative, broad-visioned, willing to explore new and unusual conceptions, free from prejudice about basic goals. He must be objective, thorough, flexible. He should be willing to canvass alternatives and forecast probable results without extravagant optimism or pessimism. He must have technical competence in his field of work. He must not be afraid of details. He must have a mind which quickly perceives interrelationships between various programs of action, and fits pieces together into a harmonious whole. He must be able to get along well with others throughout the organization.[15]

Another major tool of administrative planning is *budgeting*. The budget process consists basically of translating the work programs of a department or agency into dollars. Technically, the budget is a financial statement of the money requirements of a proposed program of work. If the department head develops the budgeting process carefully, he is able to use it as an important device of central direction. He is able to require the various departmental units to state

---

[15] Millett, "Planning and Administration," pp. 134–135.

900 promoting the general welfare

and justify their policies and programs in the course of building up estimates of their financial requirements. In this way, the budget of a department can become an extremely effective tool of planning.[16]

bibliographic note

Pros and cons of planning are cogently set forth in a number of significant books. The case for planning has been argued by Karl Mannheim in *Freedom, Power, and Democratic Planning* (New York: Oxford University Press, 1950), and by Barbara Wootton in *Plan or No Plan* (New York: Rinehart & Company, 1935) and in *Freedom under Planning* (Chapel Hill: University of North Carolina Press, 1945). The case against planning as authoritarian and antidemocratic is argued by Walter Lippmann in *The Good Society* (Boston: Little, Brown & Company, 1937). The piecemeal development of planning in American political institutions is surveyed by John M. Gaus in "The Planning Process in Government," in *Problems of the Postwar Government* (New York: McGraw-Hill Book Company, 1945), edited by T. C. T. McCormick. The organization of planning by city governments is described in Robert A. Walker, *The Planning Function in Urban Government* (Chicago: The University of Chicago Press, 1941). Appraisals of American planning experience are found in Charles E. Merriam, "The National Resources Planning Board: A Chapter in American Planning Experience," *American Political Science Review*, XXXVIII, No. 6 (December, 1944), 1075–1088; and in John D. Millett, *The Process and Organization of Government Planning* (New York: Columbia University Press, 1947).

The Tennessee Valley Authority, our most successful experiment in regional planning, is described by C. Herman Pritchett in *The Tennessee Valley Authority* (Chapel Hill: University of North Carolina Press, 1943). The former chairman of the TVA, David Lilienthal, has recorded his conviction that planning can be democratic in *TVA: Democracy on the March* (New York: Harper & Brothers, 1944). The impact of the TVA on state and local government in the South is analyzed by Joseph M. Ray in "The Influence of the Tennessee Valley Authority on Government in the South," *American Political Science Review*, XLIII, No. 5 (October, 1949), 922–32.

In *Breaking New Ground* (New York: Harcourt, Brace and Company, 1947), Gifford Pinchot tells the story of his crusade for conservation of natural resources. The role of government in conserving water resources is developed from several points of view in "Government and Water Resources," edited by James W. Fesler, *American Political Science Review*, XLIV, No. 3 (September, 1950), 575–649. The proposals of the Hoover Commission for safeguarding our

---

[16] For a fuller discussion of budgeting, see Chapter 43.

natural resources are found in Commission on Organization of the Executive Branch of the Government, *Department of the Interior* (Washington: Government Printing Office, 1949). See also the commission's *Task Force Report on Natural Resources* (Washington: Government Printing Office, 1949).

Problems of planning for national security and mobilization for war are outlined in F. M. Marx, ed., "National Defense and Democratic Society: A Symposium," *American Political Science Review*, XLIII, No. 3 (June, 1949), 524–563. The unification of the armed forces is analyzed by Elias Huzar in "Reorganization for National Security," *Journal of Politics*, XII, No. 1 (February, 1950), 128–153. How to mobilize the nation economically for national security is discussed in *Senate Document* No. 204, 81 Cong., 2 Sess., *Mobilization Planning and the National Security (1950–1960)*, prepared by William Y. Elliott as consultant to the Legislative Reference Service of the Library of Congress (Washington: Government Printing Office, 1950).

The official views of the Council of Economic Advisers on maintaining economic stability are set forth in its *Annual Report to the President* (Washington: Government Printing Office, 1946–1950). Some of the administrative problems of planning for full employment are analyzed in F. M. Marx, ed., "Maintaining High Level Production and Employment: A Symposium," *American Political Science Review*, XXXIX, No. 6 (December, 1945), 1119–1179. For a critical appraisal of the work of the Council of Economic Advisers, see the provocative article by Paul J. Strayer, "The Council of Economic Advisers: Political Economy on Trial," *Papers and Proceedings, American Economic Review*, XL, No. 2 (May, 1950), 114–154. *Congress Makes a Law* (New York: Columbia University Press, 1950), by Stephen Kemp Bailey, is a detailed study of the techniques and processes behind the enactment of the Employment Act of 1946.

The proposals of the Hoover Commission for the reorganization of the executive branch of the federal government are summarized in Commission on Organization of the Executive Branch of the Government, *Concluding Report* (Washington: Government Printing Office, 1949). Administrative reorganizations effected since the publication of the reports of the Hoover Commission are summarized in *Summary of Reorganization Progress during the Eighty-first Congress* (Washington: Government Printing Office, August 1, 1950, House Committee Print) and in *Senate Report* No. 2,581, 81 Cong., 2 Sess., *Action on Hoover Commission Reports* (Washington: Government Printing Office, October 12, 1950). The machinery set up by the Reorganization Act of 1949 is described by Ferrel Heady in "The Reorganization Act of 1949," *Public Administration Review*, IX, No. 3 (Spring, 1949), 165–174.

budgeting and expenditures

$\mathcal{T}$HE tremendous expansion in federal functions and expenditures since the outbreak of World War I has profoundly complicated the process by which the national government plans and administers its fiscal program. Total governmental expenditures rose from approximately $2.5 billion in 1913 to more than $13 billion in 1932 and to $105 billion in the peak year of 1945. From 1945 to 1950 total governmental expenditures have approached $60 billion a year. The outbreak of the Korean War in June, 1950, increased federal spending to about $47 billion during the year ending June 30, 1951.

What are the major problems which must be faced in order to understand government expenditures? Four problems stand out as critical.

1. For what purposes and activities does government spend money?

2. Who determines the amounts of money to be spent? What are the relative roles of legislatures and chief executives in determining the financial needs of the government?

3. How are expenditures accounted for? Who controls the manner in which funds are spent?

4. What are the economic effects of government spending? How does government spending affect individuals and society generally?

Each of these problems is discussed in the following sections.

government expenditures today

the level of government expenditures

In 1913 the federal government made about 29 per cent of all governmental expenditures, whereas state and local governments accounted for about 71 per cent. By 1932, federal expenditures equaled about 37 per cent of the total. During the period of World War II, federal expenditures accounted for 75 to 95 per cent of total governmental expenditures. Since 1946, federal expenditures have accounted for about two thirds of all governmental expenditures.

why have government expenditures increased?

Several factors account for the vast expansion of governmental functions and costs in the United States. The most important reason is that the cost of national defense has risen dramatically. Periods of war and preparation for war have required phenomenally large expenditures, not only for military personnel and equipment but also for mobilization of the civilian economy. War-induced costs, including interest on the public debt, pensions, contributions, and medical care for veterans, help to account for much of the increase in government spending at the federal level.

Second, the conventional governmental functions of maintaining roads and highways and providing for public education have expanded greatly to meet the requirements of an industrialized and urbanized society. Heavier expenditures for highways and education explain in considerable measure the increase of the cost of government at state and local levels. In particular, the grant of federal funds to the states for highway construction on a matching basis, except for the depression period of the thirties, has encouraged states to increase their highway expenditures.

Third, the growth of cities and the concentration of population in urban areas have created demands for public services. Such costly services as police and fire protection, inspection of food, the promotion of public health and sanitation, traffic control, high-speed transportation, and organized recreation are the inevitable products of urbanization.

Fourth, public demands made upon government during depression periods result in the assumption of new governmental functions. Depression-born functions tend to become accepted governmental functions and are not usually abolished at the end of the depression period. Generally, depression periods do not themselves produce new public demands upon government; rather, existing public demands become crystallized under the stress of economic and social collapse. Depressions have historically served as vehicles for expanding governmental activities related to social and economic welfare. For example, relief and social security measures and various programs designed to promote, encourage, and regulate industry, agriculture, and labor were formulated and established as permanent features of American political institutions during the thirties.

federal expenditures

In 1950 over 70 per cent of federal expenditures was devoted to four war-related programs: national defense, veterans' services and benefits, international affairs and finance, and interest on the public debt.

In 1950, about a third of all federal expenditures was devoted to the national defense program, which is the largest single item in the federal budget. The United States maintained active defense forces numbering approximately

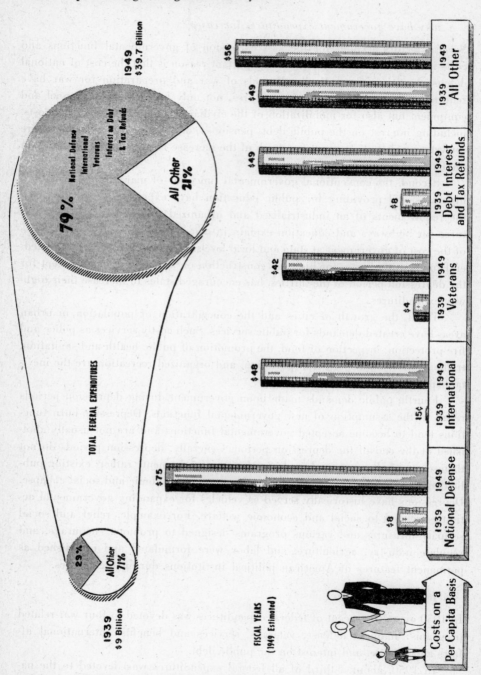

Changes in Major Government Programs 1939–1949 Compared. (*Source: U.S. Bureau of the Budget, 1950.*)

1.5 million men and women and paid for the part-time training of nearly 1 million members of the reserve forces and the National Guard. More than 800,-000 civilian workers, or roughly 40 per cent of all federal employees, were required to operate and maintain military equipment and facilities. Expenditures for personnel and maintenance alone amounted to over $9 billion. An additional $4 billion was expended for new ships, planes, guns, ammunition, and other equipment and strategic materials.

FEDERAL EXPENDITURES, 1948–1950
(IN BILLIONS OF DOLLARS)

Program	1948	1949	1950
Total Expenditures	33.8	40.1	40.2
National defense expenditures	11.0	11.9	13.5
Veterans' services and benefits	6.6	6.7	6.5
International affairs and finance	4.8	6.5	6.0
Interest on the public debt	5.2	5.4	5.7
Subtotal: four programs	27.5	30.4	31.7
Four programs as percentage of total expenditures	81.4%	75.9%	78.7%

Source: U. S. Bureau of the Budget.

Veterans' services and benefits accounted for $6.9 billion of federal expenditures in 1950. This represents the cost of services and benefits available to 18 million veterans and their families. More than 2.2 million veterans, including over 650,000 college students, received some education or training benefits costing about $3 billion. Some 3 million veterans or their families received pension and compensation payments at a cost of $2 billion. During 1950, an average daily load of 134,000 veterans were cared for in hospitals and homes at a cost of nearly $500 million, while over 400,000 veterans received medical or dental examinations and treatments at a cost of $100 million. Over $200 million was spent for construction of veterans' hospitals.

The European Recovery Program accounted for about two thirds of the $6 billion spent for international affairs and finance programs in 1950. The costs of government and relief in occupied areas were more than $800 million. Somewhat more than $1 billion covered the cost of conducting foreign affairs, maintaining diplomatic operations abroad, and paying for Philippine war damage and war claims.

In 1950 about 13 per cent of all federal expenditures, or $5.7 billion, was set aside for payment of interest on the public debt.

In 1950 all other federal government programs cost approximately $11.6 billion or from 25 to 30 per cent of all expenditures. Within this group the major expenditures were made for the following programs:

1. Grants-in-aid to states for public assistance to over 4 million aged persons, blind persons, and dependent children—$1.1 billion.

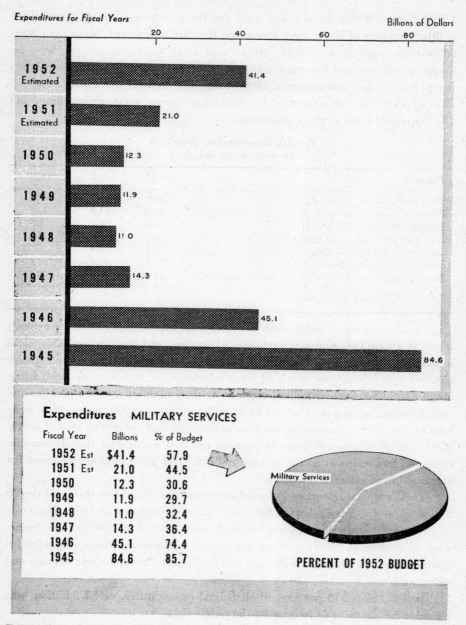

Expenditures for Fiscal Years

Billions of Dollars

	20	40	60	80

1952 Estimated — 41.4

1951 Estimated — 21.0

1950 — 12.3

1949 — 11.9

1948 — 11.0

1947 — 14.3

1946 — 45.1

1945 — 84.6

Expenditures   MILITARY SERVICES

Fiscal Year	Billions	% of Budget
1952 Est	$41.4	57.9
1951 Est	21.0	44.5
1950	12.3	30.6
1949	11.9	29.7
1948	11.0	32.4
1947	14.3	36.4
1946	45.1	74.4
1945	84.6	85.7

Military Services

PERCENT OF 1952 BUDGET

Federal Expenditures: Military Services. (*Source: U. S. Bureau of the Budget*, The Federal Budget in Brief Fiscal Year, 1952, *p. 11.*)

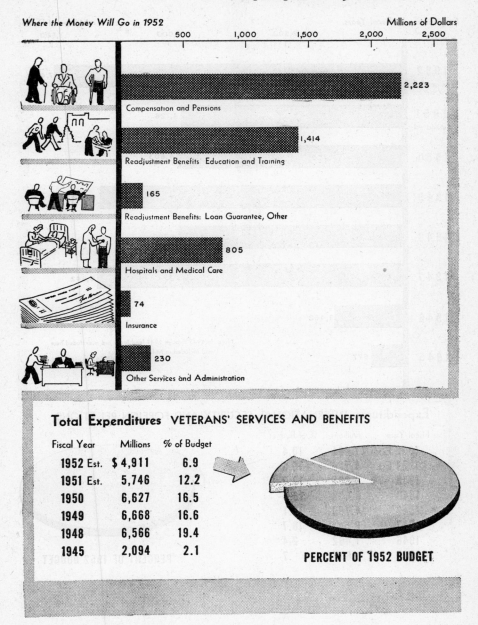

Where the Money Will Go in 1952 — Millions of Dollars

Category	Millions of Dollars
Compensation and Pensions	2,223
Readjustment Benefits: Education and Training	1,414
Readjustment Benefits: Loan Guarantee, Other	165
Hospitals and Medical Care	805
Insurance	74
Other Services and Administration	230

Total Expenditures VETERANS' SERVICES AND BENEFITS

Fiscal Year	Millions	% of Budget
1952 Est.	$4,911	6.9
1951 Est.	5,746	12.2
1950	6,627	16.5
1949	6,668	16.6
1948	6,566	19.4
1945	2,094	2.1

PERCENT OF 1952 BUDGET

Federal Expenditures: Veterans' Services and Benefits. (*Source: U. S. Bureau of the Budget, The Federal Budget in Brief Fiscal Year, 1952, p. 31.*)

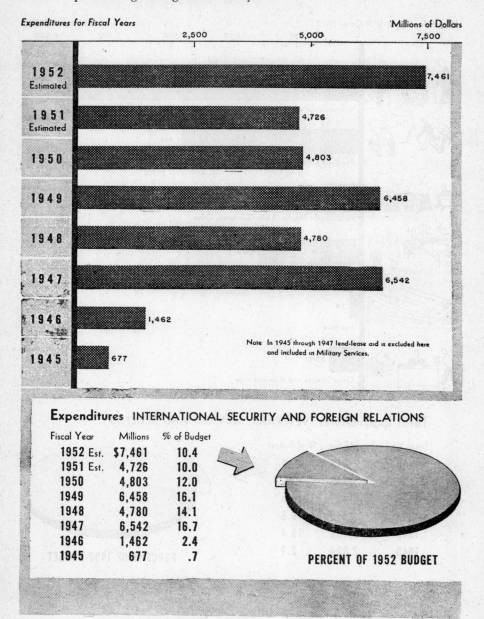

Expenditures for Fiscal Years   Millions of Dollars

Fiscal Year	Millions (bar value)
1952 Estimated	7,461
1951 Estimated	4,726
1950	4,803
1949	6,458
1948	4,780
1947	6,542
1946	1,462
1945	677

Note In 1945 through 1947 lend-lease aid is excluded here and included in Military Services.

Expenditures INTERNATIONAL SECURITY AND FOREIGN RELATIONS

Fiscal Year	Millions	% of Budget
1952 Est.	$7,461	10.4
1951 Est.	4,726	10.0
1950	4,803	12.0
1949	6,458	16.1
1948	4,780	14.1
1947	6,542	16.7
1946	1,462	2.4
1945	677	.7

PERCENT OF 1952 BUDGET

Federal Expenditures: National Security and Foreign Affairs. (*Source: U. S. Bureau of the Budget*, The Budget in Brief Fiscal Year, 1952, *p. 13.*)

PERCENTAGE OF NATIONAL INCOME

Percent

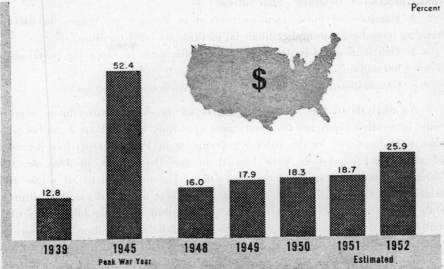

52.4						25.9
12.8		16.0	17.9	18.3	18.7	
1939	**1945** Peak War Year	**1948**	**1949**	**1950**	**1951**	**1952** Estimated

PER CAPITA

Dollars

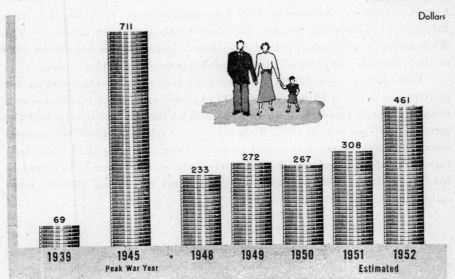

	711					
			272	267	308	461
		233				
69						
1939	**1945** Peak War Year	**1948**	**1949**	**1950**	**1951**	**1952** Estimated

Federal Budget Expenditures. (*Source: U. S. Bureau of the Budget,* The Federal Budget in Brief Fiscal Year, 1952, *p.* 37.)

2. Price support programs of the Commodity Credit Corporations in the Department of Agriculture—$1.5 billion.

3. Purchase of government-guaranteed or insured mortgages on private housing from banks and other financial institutions—$940 million.

4. Deficit incurred by the Post Office Department in supplying postal services—$500 million.

5. Grants-in-aid to states for highway construction—$350 million.

An analysis of the 1950 expenditures of the federal government reveals some interesting sidelights on government spending. First, about 2 million persons were employed by the federal government in 1950. Seventy-five per cent of all federal employees were located in the Department of Defense, the Veterans Administration, and the Post Office. The total cost of all wages and salaries was about $6.7 billion or about 15 per cent of all federal expenditures. Only a little over 200,000, or about 10 per cent of these employees, are normally located in Washington, D.C. Second, about $2.4 billion, or approximately 6 per cent of all federal expenditures, was paid to the states in the form of grants-in-aid. These payments represented about 12 per cent of all state-local revenues.

Third, some of the most controversial federal programs frequently do not account for major federal expenditures. For example, the regulatory functions of such agencies as the Federal Trade Commission, the National Labor Relations Board, and the Federal Power Commission total less than $50 million. Their complete elimination would have little effect on total federal expenditures. Fourth, federal expenditures in 1950 amounted to about $280 for each man, woman, and child in the country, compared to about $69 per capita in 1939. While the per capita cost of federal expenditures increased four times from 1939 to 1950, total income received by all persons increased about three times.

Fifth, federal expenditures were about 18 per cent of the national income in 1950, compared to 13 per cent in 1939. An interesting point is that non-war-related programs represented about 5 per cent of the national income in 1950, compared to 9 per cent in 1939. We actually spent relatively less of the national income in 1950 for non-war-related programs than we did in 1939. And sixth, expenditure figures indicate that relatively little economy can be achieved in federal expenditures without affecting the conduct of national defense, international affairs, and veterans' programs.

state and local expenditures

In 1930 state and local governments spent less than $8 billion for all state and local programs and activities. During the early 1940's, state-local expenditures ranged from $8 billion to $10 billion, roughly. After 1945, these expenditures rose sharply, reaching $20 billion by 1950.

Except for the larger cities, figures on the cost of local government are not readily available. The most striking fact about the expenditures of local governments is their decline in relation to those of the state and federal governments, despite increases in local operating costs. Since 1948, total local expenditures have fallen somewhat below total state expenditures for the first time.

Increases in state-local expenditures are due in part to expenditures for new construction, which in 1950 were seven times as large as in 1945. Since 1945, other expenditures have about doubled. The number of employees of state and local governments was about 4.2 million in 1950. Wages and salaries paid to employees, including public school teachers, accounted for about half of all state-local expenditures. Although two thirds of all government employees are employed by state and local governments, the total state-local expenditures are only one third of total government expenditures in the United States.

budgeting for expenditures

A budget is a carefully prepared statement of the revenues anticipated by government and an estimate of proposed expenditures. Revenues and expenditures for the coming year are usually explained or justified in some detail and are compared with the revenues and expenditures of the current year and previous years. The budgeting process is central to governmental operation because the planning of revenues and expenditures involves the clarification of basic policy issues on which governmental programs hinge.

federal budget procedure

The budget system of the federal government is based on the Budget and Accounting Act of 1921, which makes the President responsible for the preparation of the budget for submission to Congress. The act recognizes the need for executive direction and leadership in preparing for the consideration of Congress a program of revenues and expenditures. Under the direction of the President, federal departments and agencies are required to translate their programs into financial terms so that the various programs can be balanced with each other and within the revenue resources of the government.

The expenditures which the department proposes to make are called "estimates." Each department builds up its budget estimates in terms of the program of work to be accomplished by the department. The work program must indicate in detail the financial requirements of all programs, including the number of employees required to do the necessary work, the cost of needed supplies, equipment, office space, telephones, and so forth. The department's budget can be an accurate estimate of its financial requirements only if its programs have been carefully planned and coordinated. The departmental estimates should not exceed a maximum or ceiling figure established by the President and should conform to the general policy directions established by the President.

The budget estimates of each department are submitted first to the Bureau of the Budget in the Executive Office of the President for review and analysis. Budget examiners in the Bureau of the Budget, who have already familiarized themselves with each department's activities and programs, analyze the estimates closely for accuracy, consistency of policy, and effective planning of programs. Preliminary study of the estimates is followed by hearings conducted by the Bureau of the Budget for the departments and agencies. The hearings give opportunity for extended discussion of questionable estimates and for clarification of departmental programs and policies. After each hearing, budget examiners prepare their recommendations on the budget for discussion with the Director of the Bureau and his principal advisers. The Director and his committee, acting for the President, determine how much money to request for each department in the President's budget. The estimates are then delivered to the President for his consideration and action.

After the President makes the final determination of how much money is required for each agency, the Bureau of the Budget prepares the final budget, which is transmitted to Congress by the President, together with his budget message explaining and justifying the requested appropriations.

The President's budget is referred to the Appropriations Committee of the House of Representatives. Acting through nine subcommittees, the Appropriations Committee reviews the estimates and holds hearings to permit the agency officials to explain and justify the proposed expenditures. Other interested citizens may also be called to testify before the committee. The subcommittees are assisted in their examination and analysis of budgetary estimates by a professional staff of analysts subject to the direction of the committee. The questioning of federal officials by committee members may be penetrating and close and frequently has been hostile. The published hearings on appropriations bills constitute one of the most important sources of information about the operation of the federal government. Following hearings, the committee determines how much money to appropriate to each agency and submits its proposed appropriation bill to the House. After the House acts on the bill, it is transmitted to the Senate, which follows a similar procedure. When the appropriations bill is enacted, it is returned to the President, who has the power to veto the act as a whole but not specific items in it.

In 1950 the House Appropriations Committee for the first time prepared a so-called omnibus appropriations bill which included about 75 per cent of all proposed appropriations. Previous practice of preparing separate appropriations bills for single agencies or groups of agencies made it difficult for congressmen to know the total amount of funds appropriated until the final appropriation bill was passed.

timetable for the federal budget

1. In May and June the Bureau of the Budget prepares for the President a forecast of economic trends and government expenditures for the next five years. On the basis of the bureau's studies, the President then establishes budget ceilings for each agency, and the bureau issues to the agencies directions for the preparation of estimates.

2. In September the agency submits its estimates, which are reviewed in the Bureau of the Budget until December, when the formal budget document is prepared.

3. In January the President submits his budget to the Congress, and from January to June the Congress considers the President's budget and eventually enacts the appropriations statutes. The funds voted by Congress are made available to the agency for operations for the year beginning on July 1.

The form of the appropriation act is very important to the agencies. The appropriation may be made in one lump sum, or divided into a small number of specific categories, or allocated in detail to specific activities or functions. The greater the itemization of appropriation, the greater the influence of the legislature over the executive agencies. The theory behind the detailed itemization of appropriations has been the desirability of maintaining legislative control over the spending of public funds. However, in practice the legislative itemization of appropriations has reduced the responsibility of the executive agencies for the execution of the laws and has placed undue limitations on the expenditure of funds. A legislature cannot prescribe with accuracy the detailed allocation of funds months and sometimes over a year in advance of their actual expenditure. Moreover, itemization tends to encourage the legislature to consider the details of executive activities rather than the broad policies and standards which should guide the executive departments.

Appropriations for the older federal agencies are divided into a number of subappropriations for specified activities. Some progress has been made in recent years in reducing the number of subappropriations, but Congress is still rather reluctant to give up this type of itemization for fear of weakening its power. During World War II the trend toward lump-sum appropriations was accelerated. In the case of national defense appropriations, billions of dollars were granted to the military departments with scarcely any debate or discussion on the floor of Congress.

problems in the federal budget process

Although the federal budget process has improved substantially since 1921, many problems of budgeting have not yet been satisfactorily resolved. A few of these problems are worth noting.

1. How satisfactory are the budget estimates prepared by the departments

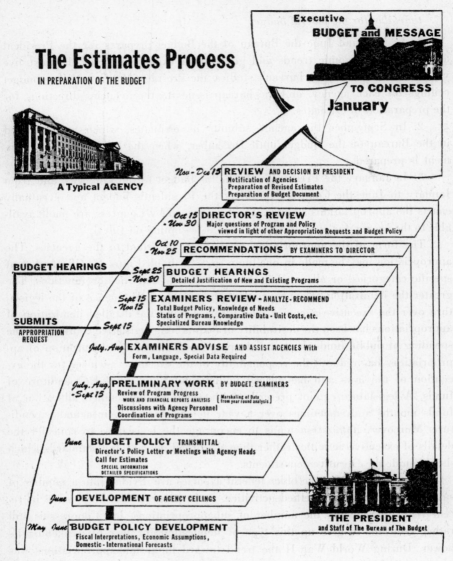

The Estimates Process
IN PREPARATION OF THE BUDGET

Executive BUDGET and MESSAGE TO CONGRESS January

A Typical AGENCY

Nov - Dec 15 **REVIEW** AND DECISION BY PRESIDENT
Notification of Agencies
Preparation of Revised Estimates
Preparation of Budget Document

Oct 15 - Nov 30 **DIRECTOR'S REVIEW**
Major questions of Program and Policy
viewed in light of other Appropriation Requests and Budget Policy

Oct 10 - Nov 25 **RECOMMENDATIONS** BY EXAMINERS TO DIRECTOR

BUDGET HEARINGS

Sept 25 - Nov 20 **BUDGET HEARINGS**
Detailed Justification of New and Existing Programs

Sept 15 - Nov 15 **EXAMINERS REVIEW** - ANALYZE - RECOMMEND
Total Budget Policy, Knowledge of Needs
Status of Programs, Comparative Data - Unit Costs, etc.
Specialized Bureau Knowledge

SUBMITS
APPROPRIATION REQUEST

Sept 15

July, Aug **EXAMINERS ADVISE** AND ASSIST AGENCIES With
Form, Language, Special Data Required

July, Aug - Sept 15 **PRELIMINARY WORK** BY BUDGET EXAMINERS
Review of Program Progress
WORK AND FINANCIAL REPORTS ANALYSIS [Marshaling of Data from year round analysis]
Discussions with Agency Personnel
Coordination of Programs

June **BUDGET POLICY** TRANSMITTAL
Director's Policy Letter or Meetings with Agency Heads
Call for Estimates
SPECIAL INFORMATION
DETAILED SPECIFICATIONS

June **DEVELOPMENT** OF AGENCY CEILINGS

May June **BUDGET POLICY DEVELOPMENT**
Fiscal Interpretations, Economic Assumptions,
Domestic - International Forecasts

THE PRESIDENT
and Staff of The Bureau of The Budget

(*Source:* U.S. Bureau of the Budget, 1949.)

and agencies? Some observers believe that the departments are the major weak spot in the budget process. When a department is effectively managed, when its programs are carefully planned and coordinated, it is able to estimate its financial requirements with reasonable accuracy and to justify its proposed expenditures. If a department, however, tends to be a loose federation of bureaus with inadequate departmental planning of work programs, the budget estimates are apt to be inadequate and not properly justified.

2. Are the President's budget and the budget message useful documents? The budget submitted to Congress frequently exceeds 1,600 closely printed pages. The Hoover Commission criticized the budget as "an inadequate budget document, poorly organized and improperly designed to serve its major purpose, which is to present an understandable and workable financial plan for the expenditures of the Government." [1] One critic describes the President's budget message and the budget document as among "the more conspicuous failures of American democracy." He adds:

> As instruments for the announcement of the policies of the Administration, the message exhausts itself through discussions in terms of accounting terminology and the document explains little or nothing in terms of program objectives and then only to the most diligent searcher. As devices for the information of the Congress, the message is almost completely deficient in explaining either what has happened or what the Administration proposes to do, and the document, except for certain summary tabulations, relates its compendious statistics neither to program nor activity. [2]

Since 1949, improvements have been made in the budget document and in the President's message. Both documents relate federal expenditures more directly to government programs and provide intelligible information to the citizen about the federal government. The Bureau of the Budget now supplements the budget document with a short explanatory pamphlet, "The Federal Budget in Brief," which explains with the help of graphic charts the purposes of proposed government expenditures.

3. What can be done to make congressional control of the spending process more effective and democratic? The legislative handling of appropriations bills has not been as effective as it should be. In a democracy, it is clear that the legislature should make the final determinations of how much money the government needs, how it should be raised, and what the money should be spent for. In dealing with estimates of proposed expenditures, many congressmen tend to stress local and state rather than national interests. They appear to be relatively unable to deal with issues and problems which are national in scope. By virtue of the seniority system, southern Democrats and midwest Republicans frequently dominate the appropriations committees and give them a somewhat unrepresentative character. Conflict has been characteristic in executive-legislative budget relations, and congressional bitterness and misunderstanding sometime seem to prevail over careful consideration and evaluation of the President's budget.

---

[1] The Commission on Organization of the Executive Branch of the Government, *Budgeting and Accounting* (Washington: Government Printing Office, 1949), p. 7.
[2] Rowland Egger, "The Division of Estimates of the Bureau of the Budget," staff report prepared for Task Force on Budgeting and Accounting, The Commission on Organization of the Executive Branch of the Government, mimeo., p. 36.

It was not until 1950 that Congress made efforts to consider the budget as a whole.

There is disagreement over the extent to which Congress should control the purse strings. Many observers now urge that Congress abandon efforts to specify in detail the amounts to be spent for particular activities and concentrate instead on resolving some of the fundamental issues of policy raised by the President's budget. Perhaps the major problem is the need to develop closer working arrangements between the executive and the legislature during the period that the budget is being prepared and approved. The President should invite congressional leaders to participate systematically in the formulation of the preliminary budget. Similarly, Congress needs to consult the President in studying the estimates and preparing appropriations bills.

Several proposals may help to give Congress more intelligent and responsible control of the purse strings. A Joint Committee on the Budget might emphasize major policies and programs in studying the estimates and be in a better position to keep Congress informed of the long-range implications of current programs. Adoption of the budget through a single act would permit legislators to gain a more comprehensive view of governmental programs and to exercise better control over them. A presidential item veto would permit the President to veto a single provision in an appropriation bill without rejecting the entire bill.

In the long run it may not be possible to bring about substantial improvement in the politics of budgeting unless the President and a majority of legislators in the President's political party can agree on major policies to be supported by the party. One student of government writes:

> To a marked degree each member of Congress is his own party when estimates are up for review, and only hopeless Congressional minorities preserve the semblance of unity and responsibility. While the disintegration of party responsibility in the face of fiscal legislation is only one manifestation of the pathological condition of party government generally in the United States, it is the most important single symptom of party impotence. As long as Presidents and their parties win the majority of elections on the hustings and lose the majority of decisions in the Congress, so long will the President's "program" be a polite and meaningless phrase, and so long will responsibility and answerability in fiscal and administrative affairs continue to be a fraud and an evasion.[3]

Whatever the solution to alleged congressional failures in providing the money for government, the authority to grant and to withhold money remains the most effective means of directing and controlling administrative activities. It is crucial to a democracy that legislative control be exercised responsibly and in the public interest.

---

[3] *Ibid.*, pp. 74–75.

accounting for expenditures

After government expenditures are estimated or budgeted by the executive and authorized by the legislature, it is necessary to account for the way they are spent. This process is known as "auditing." There are two kinds of audits. The first is properly made by executive agencies before funds are actually spent. This is known as the "preaudit." It enables the administrator to ensure that the sum to be paid has been calculated accurately and that the necessary funds are available. The second type of audit, the "postaudit," is properly made by an agent of the legislature after the funds are spent. This audit enables the legislature to be informed of any unauthorized or irregular expenditures, and is therefore an important means of securing responsible government. The federal auditing process is described briefly in the following section.

the general accounting office

The Budget and Accounting Act of 1921 set up the General Accounting Office (GAO) as an independent office to control government expenditures on behalf of Congress. The GAO is directed by the Comptoller General, who is appointed for a fifteen-year term and can be removed only for specific cause by a joint resolution of Congress. The principal functions of the GAO can be summarized briefly.

1. It prescribes the accounting systems which are followed by the various departments and agencies.

2. It reviews specific expenditures made by the administrative agencies to determine whether such expenditures have been authorized by law. This review of expenditures is known as "settling the accounts." As described by the Hoover Commission, "it means freight carloads of vouchers from all over the United States hauled to Washington for individual examination in the General Accounting Office. The Office now labors under a deluge of paper work of all kinds which requires about 10,000 people to examine." [4] And it has been said that the auditing and settling of millions of claims and vouchers, has involved the GAO in "legal hairsplitting over what was fitting and proper down to the minutest detail." [5]

3. It makes comprehensive postaudits of the financial practices of administrative agencies and reports to Congress instances of misuse or illegal use of funds.

In 1937 the President's Committee on Administrative Management recom-

---

[4] *Budgeting and Accounting*, pp. 41–42.
[5] The Commission on Organization of the Executive Branch of the Government, *Task Force Report on Fiscal, Budgeting, and Accounting Activities* (Washington: Government Printing Office, 1949), p. 81.

mended that the authority of the Comptroller General to settle accounts be transferred to the Department of the Treasury and that a General Auditing Office be established in place of the GAO to make postaudits of government expenditures and to report to Congress. This committee argued that the settlement of accounts is an executive task which should not be confused with the right and duty of Congress to make an independent review and audit of federal spending. It believed that the President cannot be held fully accountable for the activities of the executive branch so long as the Comptroller General determines the validity and reasonableness of expenditures before payment is made. The President's Committee on Administrative Management was concerned primarily with improving management practices by centering administrative responsibility in the President. It desired to strengthen the overhead management of administrative activities by providing an administrative preaudit in place of the settlement of accounts by the Comptroller General.

The task force studying budgeting and accounting problems for the Hoover Commission made a similar proposal in 1949. The Hoover Commission rejected the recommendations of its task force and instead straddled the issue. It recommended that the GAO continue to settle administrative accounts but that it abandon the practice of reviewing all expenditure vouchers in Washington.

The controversy about the proper location of the authority to settle accounts frequently turns on a difference of approach to the problems of accounting for government expenditures. Those who support the retention of the authority to settle accounts in the GAO are concerned about the need for preventing fraud and corruption in government spending. Those who would transfer the power to the executive branch are impressed by the importance of accounting controls as a means to effective executive management of administrative agencies.

some economic effects of government spending

government spending and promotion of economic stability

The depression of the thirties dramatized the responsibility of government to promote economic welfare in general and to provide and promote employment in periods of economic collapse. Out of the experience of the thirties, several economic theories have been developed dealing with the effect of government expenditures on the promotion of employment and consumer purchasing power. More specifically, the Employment Act of 1946 affirms the responsibility of the federal government to maintain employment opportunities and to promote maximum employment, production, and purchasing power.[6] The Council of Economic Advisers has interpreted this act as "frank recognition that the government ac-

---

[6] For further discussion, see Chapter 42, "Government Planning."

cepts a complementary role in areas where, or in times when, private enterprise fails to provide adequate productive use of the Nation's resources." [7]

Government expenditures may be planned for periods of economic depression to offset deficiencies in private spending. Such government expenditures, commonly called *compensatory spending*, or *pump priming*, may be used in a limited fashion to offset continued declines in national income and employment levels. Compensatory spending may also be used more ambitiously to attempt to achieve and retain a high level of income and employment. Whatever the goal may be, compensatory spending substitutes government spending for private spending in order to maintain national income at the desired level.

In periods of recession and depression in the business cycle, current demand for goods falls, producers cut costs as much as possible, and consumers reduce their expenditures. New investments decline, and banks are unable to find borrowers for their loans. In a compensatory spending program, the government undertakes to offset the income which has been removed from the economic system by injecting government funds into the economy at strategic points. The greater the decline of private spending, the more public expenditures must be made.

Government compensatory expenditures exceed current revenues and are therefore deficit expenditures. A balanced budget, that is, a budget in which current expenditures are met out of current revenues, is impossible if a policy of compensatory spending during a depression is followed. Since compensatory expenditures cannot be met out of current tax revenues, the government must borrow the necessary funds.

Decisions on ways of spending government funds become crucial in programs of compensatory spending. The general objective is to spend public money in such a way as to put the funds into the hands of people who will use the money to buy the things they need for immediate use. The shoring up of private spending for consumer goods is expected to lead to expanded production to meet consumer demands. In practice one of the greatest difficulties in a compensatory spending program is to locate with reasonable certainty the points at which public funds should be injected into the economy.

As purchasing power, consumption, and employment reach higher levels, the government must determine when and how much public spending may be tapered off. As the goal of full employment is approached, taxation must be increased in order to obtain sufficient surplus revenues to retire some of the debt created by the compensatory spending policy.

Compensatory spending may affect the confidence of the business community, which, in turn, may seriously affect the outcome of the spending pro-

---

[7] Council of Economic Advisers, *Second Annual Report to the President* (Washington: Government Printing Office, December, 1947), p. 25.

gram. Government expenditures during periods of depression entail borrowing and an unbalanced budget. Deficit spending may create doubts in the minds of some businessmen about the ability of the government to meet its financial obligations and to carry its increased debt burden. Fears that government may compete with private business may offset some of the effects of public spending to promote employment.

The experience of the United States with deficit spending from 1933 to 1938 has been the subject of considerable economic analysis. In general, economists agree that public spending prevented national income from falling further than it did in the middle thirties. Pump priming by the federal government seemingly prevented further decreases in levels of employment and income and offset decreases in private spending, even though it did not generate economic recovery. Some economists trace the relative failure of pump priming to generate economic recovery during the depression of the thirties to mistakes in pump-priming policy rather than to any inherent unsoundness in a compensatory spending program.

expenditures for public works

One of the common forms of pump priming is the construction of public works projects. The term "public works" implies public construction which is relatively durable and immobile, that is, fixed on the site of construction. The idea of a public work usually suggests a construction project of considerable magnitude.[8] The expenditures for public works are ordinarily made in lump sums even though the completed project will be used for an indefinite period in the future.

The effects of public works projects are felt most directly by the construction industry. The experience of the Public Works Administration reveals that about twice as much is spent for materials as for labor in the construction of dams, bridges, highways, and public buildings.[9] Public works projects also require skilled workers who may not be on relief rolls. The experience of the Public Works Administration also indicates the undesirability of forcing contractors who undertake public works projects to hire a stated percentage of workers from relief rolls. The importance of these facts is that some of the funds expended for public works are not immediately respent. On the other hand, the construction industry is in a strategic economic position; the stimulation of construction does generate spending in other areas of the economy. In addition, public works provide socially useful capital improvements and help to maintain wages at prevailing rates.

----

[8] See National Resources Planning Board, *The Economic Effects of the Federal Public Works Expenditures 1933–1938* (Washington: Government Printing Office, 1940), p. 2.
[9] Public Works Administration, *America Builds: The Record of PWA* (Washington: Government Printing Office, 1939), pp. 19, 26.

Economists who have studied spending for public works emphasize the importance of spending public funds for capital improvements which do not compete with private investment. Highway construction, for example, is noncompetitive, whereas construction of public power systems may be competitive. However, the need for the development of river valleys, for flood control projects, for urban housing, and for slum clearance and other projects may be so urgent that the possibility of competition between public and private investment in such fields may not be critical.

Selection of projects and the timing of construction are crucial in public works planning. It is essential that the government have available a continuing program of public works which can be increased or decreased in accordance with swings in employment and economic activity. In addition to providing some work relief and generating economic recovery, the projects should be socially useful and desirable. To some extent, the construction of capital improvements like highways and school buildings can be postponed until depression periods. During a depression, the public works construction will cost less and still have important income-producing effects.

In 1944 Congress undertook to help the state and local governments develop postwar plans for public works projects. Under Title V of the War Mobilization and Reconversion Act of 1944, from 1944 to 1947 the Bureau of Community Facilities of the Federal Works Agency distributed about $60 million to more than 7,000 state and local governmental jurisdictions as repayable loans to aid in the preparation of drawings and specifications for public works. To be eligible for federal loans, the governments were required to show evidence that the work projects conformed to some over-all state, local, or regional plan approved by the appropriate government.

The Hoover Commission, in its 1949 report on the Department of the Interior, urged a realignment of functions in the department in part to provide for Congress "an over-all view of the major construction activities of the Government" and to provide a "center for planning and action of Federal construction to be coordinated with the ebb and flow of employment." The commission stated:

> In times of great employment in private construction, the Government should reduce its work (except for emergency needs) so as not to inflate costs and should save its construction for times of unemployment. . . . At the present time there is a short supply of construction labor and materials. They are urgently needed for national defense, for housing, and for current construction in private industry. In these circumstances the [federal] agencies . . . should carry on the minimum nonpostponable work, should undertake no new projects, but should have blueprints ready for use when unemployment creates a need.[10]

---

[10] The Commission on Organization of the Executive Branch of the Government, *Department of the Interior* (Washington: Government Printing Office, 1949), p. 18.

There has been increasing recognition in recent years that public works provide only one of many approaches to the problem of combating unemployment and economic depression. According to Robert Moses, chief consultant in public works to the Hoover Commission, "Public works admittedly can take care of only a fraction of the depression-employment problems, but it is an exceedingly important fraction. It is a marginal area in which men out of work will stew around helplessly unless the Government is ready to meet their problems."[11]

the impact of government spending on economic stability

Recurrence of booms and busts suggests that alternating periods of prosperity and depression are inherent in an economy of private enterprise. In the light of past experience it is fair to conclude that such an economy cannot by itself stabilize economic conditions at a relatively high level of production and employment. It seems inevitable that governmental powers be used to bail society out of periods of economic collapse and unemployment. Viewed in this way, compensatory fiscal policy is designed to create conditions under which an economy of private enterprise can survive. This view implies that high levels of public debt and taxation as well as a strong federal government are inevitable in order to maintain the current basic pattern of American economic institutions. As Robert Moses has said:

> Even among persons familiar with public finance, there are few who realize the tremendous obligations which the Federal Government must assume to stimulate employment, promote recovery, and prime the pump of private enterprise in times of recession and depression. The obligations are quite inescapable and it must be assumed that they will recur from time to time in the economic cycle. The advance planning and promotion of public works for such periods should be recognized as a continued responsibility of the Federal Government, working in cooperation with States and municipalities. It is senseless to proceed on the theory that every major slump in business and employment is an unexpected Divine visitation not to be anticipated and to be dealt with only on the basis of ineffective, wasteful, and hastily improvised emergency measures.[12]

bibliographic note

The best brief summary of the federal budget is contained in *The Federal Budget in Brief,* a well-illustrated pamphlet prepared by the Bureau of the Budget. Accounts of current budgetary practices and problems are presented

---

[11] The Commission on Organization of the Executive Branch of the Government, *Task Force Report on Public Works* (Washington: Government Printing Office, 1949), p. 5.

[12] *Ibid.,* p. 4.

in Commission on Organization of the Executive Branch of the Government, *Budgeting and Accounting* (Washington: Government Printing Office, 1949) and *The Task Force Report on Fiscal, Budgeting, and Accounting Activities* (Washington: Government Printing Office, 1949). A summary of efforts to improve federal budgetary procedures is available in George B. Galloway, *Reform of the Federal Budget Process* (*Public Affairs Bulletin* No. 80, Legislative Reference Service, Library of Congress; Washington: Government Printing Office, 1950). The historical development of the Bureau of the Budget is traced in F. M. Marx, "The Bureau of the Budget: Its Evolution and Present Role," *American Political Science Review*, XXXIX, Nos. 4 and 5 (August, October, 1945), 653–684, 869–898. The significance of budgeting as a tool of management and political control is suggested by Harold D. Smith in "The Budget as an Instrument of Legislative Control and Executive Management," *Public Administration Review*, IV, No. 3 (Summer, 1944), 181–189. The functions of the Comptroller General in accounting for federal spending are covered by Harvey Mansfield's *The Comptroller General* (New Haven: Yale University Press, 1939). The most useful and stimulating account of Congressional control over appropriations is Elias Huzar's *The Purse and the Sword* (Ithaca: Cornell University Press, 1950).

Pump-priming efforts during the 1930's are evaluated in *The Economic Effects of Federal Public Works Expenditures, 1933–1938* (Washington: Government Printing Office, 1940), a study made by the National Resources Planning Board. The importance of public works planning today as a counterdepression activity is analyzed in Commission on Organization of the Executive Branch of the Government, *Task Force Report on Public Works* (Washington: Government Printing Office, 1949).

raising the money

$\mathscr{I}$N THE past twenty years, it has become commonplace to characterize the United States government as the world's biggest business. By January, 1950, total governmental expenditures in the United States were about $60 billion compared to less than $20 billion in 1940 and about $10 billion in 1930.

The dominant financial problem of the government is to raise the money needed to finance governmental programs and activities. Fortunately the increasing need of governments for revenues has been accompanied by increases in the national income. In 1950 the national income, that is, the net return from the economic activities of all persons and businesses,[1] reached a peak of about $225 billion, as compared with $81 billion in 1940 and $75 billion in 1930.

ROUGH ESTIMATES OF GOVERNMENTAL EXPENDITURES AND NATIONAL INCOME
BY DECADE, 1930–1950

YEAR	GOVERNMENTAL EXPENDITURES (IN BILLIONS)		NATIONAL INCOME (IN BILLIONS)		*Governmental Expenditures as % of National Income*
	In current dollars	*In 1940 dollars*	*In current dollars*	*In 1940 dollars*	
1930	10	8	75	62	13
1940	20	20	81	81	24
1950	60	35	225	132	27

Source: *Statistical Abstract of the United States*, 1948; *The Economic Report of the President*, January, 1950; and U.S. Bureau of the Budget.

Despite the enormous increases in governmental expenditures in recent years, the proportion of the national income represented by governmental expenditures has only doubled since 1930. Nonetheless, a large share of the national

---

[1] For further discussion, see Chapter 34, "Government and Economic Life."

income is channeled through governments. By making contracts with private businesses for the purchase of equipment and supplies, by financing the construction of buildings and housing, by making benefit payments to veterans and other groups, and by paying salaries and wages to their employees, governments affect directly the incomes and economic activity of millions of Americans. Even more important, the volume of federal expenditures and the taxes levied to finance expenditures have an immediate as well as a long-range impact on the entire national economy and the distribution of income among individuals.

sources of government revenues

Public funds to finance governmental activities are derived from five sources: taxes, administrative revenues, commercial revenues, grants and gifts, and loans. Each of these sources will be described briefly.

taxes

Over 90 per cent of all government revenues, excluding loans, are derived from taxes. In the years 1947–1951, federal tax receipts ranged roughly from $37 billion to $44.5 billion annually, while state and local governments collected taxes amounting to from $12 billion to $15 billion annually.

administrative revenues

Administrative revenues include such items as fees, licenses, fines and penalties, and special assessments. Relatively unimportant in financing federal activities, nevertheless they account for about 5 to 10 per cent of all state and local governmental receipts. They take several typical forms. For example, corporations usually pay a state fee for the privilege of incorporation. Owners of passenger vehicles must register their cars in their state of residence and buy a motor vehicle license and a driver's license as well. Individuals must pay fees in order to practice certain professions or vocations. An American who travels abroad must first obtain a passport from the State Department and pay a fee on its issuance. A home owner may have to pay a fee to a local government for connecting his house with the sewage system. If a motorist violates a traffic ordinance, he is subject to fines payable to a local or a state government. One of the obvious characteristics of administrative revenues is that they are payable to a government at the point where the individual comes into direct contact with some administrative agency of the government. The amount paid for a license or other privilege may bear little relation to the benefit which the license confers.

Most economists have condemned the fee system. Fees have proved to be an inflexible source of funds. They cannot be adjusted to economic changes. The tendency to earmark administrative revenues for the use of the agencies which collect the fees makes it difficult to allocate revenues objectively to various governmental programs according to their relative importance. However, little has been done to modify or abolish the fee system because it is relatively unimportant as a source of public revenues.

commercial revenues

Commercial revenues include funds received by governments in direct payment for government services and commodities. They are illustrated by such items as moneys paid to the post offices for postage and other postal services; tuition and fees paid to public schools and colleges; the profits earned by state-owned retail liquor stores, and municipal gas, water, electric, and other utilities; and tolls paid on public highways, bridges, and ferries.

Government-operated business enterprises have grown in importance as a source of revenue. Considerations of revenue do not always determine whether or not the government operates a particular business enterprise. For example, the question of public versus private operation of retail liquor stores may be determined primarily by considerations of public welfare. Similarly, municipal ownership of electric utilities may be based on the desire of a local government to provide a service which private industry has not provided or to provide goods and services more cheaply. On the other hand, many communities, especially in the South, operate business enterprises because they are profitable. The earnings of municipal utilities may be used to help finance public schools or the local highway system.

On the whole, federal business enterprises have been used to influence the operation of private business or to provide essential services rather than to raise revenue. For example, the Rural Electrification Administration helps to finance cooperatives to build and operate electric facilities in rural areas where private companies consider extension of their service unprofitable. One of the oldest federal commercial enterprises is the Panama Railroad Company, which operates railroad facilities in the Panama Canal Zone. The Inland Waterways Corporation operates barges on rivers to stimulate competition among private water carriers.

State enterprises were relatively unimportant before 1932. The increase in state enterprises since 1932 is primarily a result of the introduction of alcoholic beverage monopoly systems. By 1942 sixteen states had created state liquor monopolies which earned a net income of $84 million or about 90 per cent of revenues from all state enterprises. The balance of state commercial revenues comes from the operation of toll bridges on state highways, ferries, port facilities, and other projects. Municipal commercial revenues are derived largely from the operation of water supply systems, transit systems, electric light and power plants, gas plants, and aviation and port facilities.

grants and gifts

Although some donations are made to the federal government, grants and gifts are insignificant as a source of federal revenue. Grants, however, have become important in financing state and local activities. Today roughly 10 per cent of all state-local revenues are derived from federal grants-in-aid,[2] especially for social security programs and highway construction.

loans

When government expenditures exceed the receipts from taxes, from administrative and commercial revenues, and from grants and gifts, a deficit is created, and governments must borrow funds to make it up. Great emergencies or crises like severe depressions or wars have caused government expenditures to skyrocket. Then deficits are created because of the inability of the government to pay all governmental costs out of current taxes and other revenues. During World War II, for example, the federal government borrowed billions of dollars from banks, businesses, and individuals to finance the cost of the war. Government borrowing increases the public debt, and interest must be paid regularly to investors in government bonds. The borrowing process is discussed in more detail in a later section in this chapter.

what is the tax problem?

A number of key questions together constitute the tax problem in the United States today. They may be listed as follows:

1. What are the objectives of taxation? Should taxes be used for purposes other than raising revenue?

2. What are the characteristics of a fair tax system? What taxes should be levied? Who should pay taxes?

3. What are the constitutional limitations on the power of government to tax? What kinds of taxes are legal? Is the power to tax adequate, inadequate, or excessive?

4. How shall the taxing power be divided among three more or less independent levels of government? Should the federal, state, and local governments tax the same individuals and corporations? Should certain areas of taxation be set aside exclusively for any level of government?

5. What kind of tax system is defensible in a democracy? What political tests must be met by a tax system?

what are the objectives of taxation?

The traditional objective of taxation, of course, is to raise revenue. Most tax measures are formulated in order to finance new or expanding governmental

---

[2] For further discussion, see Chapter 41, "Cooperative Federalism."

activities. However, the objectives of taxation may be nonfinancial as well as financial. Perhaps the oldest example of a nonfinancial tax is the protective tariff, the main purpose of which is to keep certain goods manufactured in foreign countries out of the United States. Other examples of a nonfinancial tax are the special taxes which have been placed on chain stores, on oleomargarine, and on the products of child labor. A tax was used in these instances to accomplish objectives unrelated to raising revenue.

Other nonfinancial objectives of taxation may be the alteration of the distribution of income among individuals, or the influencing of consumer buying habits and investment practices, or the curbing of inflation. Very heavy taxation of large incomes and more moderate taxation of smaller incomes tend to equalize the distribution of income among persons. Heavy taxation of a particular commodity may have the effect of discouraging consumers from buying it. The reliance on heavy taxation rather than on borrowing to finance governmental emergency activities may tax away private funds which otherwise might have been invested in a business enterprise or deposited in a bank. Heavy taxes levied on personal and corporate income in periods of rising prices will reduce the purchasing power of individuals and corporations and may help keep prices of commodities from rising.

A tax may also serve as an incentive to an employer to undertake certain desirable business practices. For example, many states will reduce the tax levied on an employer in the state unemployment insurance system if he is able to maintain stable employment in his plant. Such a tax is designed to stimulate stability of employment. Another example is the taxation of bank deposits in order to encourage spending, which in turn may stimulate full employment.

what are the characteristics of a fair tax system?

A tax system should be just and fair; it should be easily administered; and it should provide a steady source of revenue. What is a just or equitable tax system? How can tax burdens be distributed fairly and equitably? The question of fairness or justice in taxation is not easily resolved. First, the burden of taxation should be allocated equally among classes of taxpayers. One of the traditional tax principles maintains that taxes should be borne by those who benefit from public expenditures. This theory is subject to many objections. The people who benefit may frequently be those least able to pay taxes. Moreover, the theory tends to limit governmental services based on the ability of the recipients to pay for those services in proportion to benefits received. Obviously, benefits can scarcely be allocated accurately, since the entire economy and society benefit directly and indirectly from many kinds of governmental activities.

Because of the inadequacy of the benefit principle as a basis for an equitable tax system, economists have turned to the principle of ability to pay. According to this principle, persons or corporations with the greatest wealth or income should pay the highest taxes whether or not they derive any benefits from governmental activity. Taxes based on ability to pay also have the effect more or less of equalizing the distribution of wealth and income. Fairness in allocating the burden of a tax may vary, depending on the objective of the tax. Taxation as an instrument to promote full employment or to maintain a desired level of income for all individuals may require a tax rate or a tax base which has little or no relevance to ability to pay.

Ease of administration is the second criterion of a good tax system. Taxes should be readily collectible, and the costs of administration should be kept low. Possibilities of evasion or avoidance of taxes should be minimized. The administrative costs of collecting the federal income tax run about 3 per cent of the total collections.[3] Ease of administration requires also that the amount of tax be calculated simply and that the government have a way of knowing who is subject to the tax and how much he ought to pay.

The third criterion of a good tax system is its capacity to yield a steady amount of revenue. Taxes which can be relied upon to provide a dependable amount of revenue are generally to be preferred to those whose yield varies with general economic conditions. Especially in times of declining prices and business depression, it is important to have steady tax yields, for it is in these periods that the costs of public assistance rise substantially.

are there constitutional limitations on the power to tax?

Under Article One of the Constitution, Congress has power to lay and collect taxes and pay debts, provided three conditions are met:

1. All duties and excise taxes must be levied uniformly throughout the United States.

2. Direct taxes must be apportioned among the states according to population.

3. No tax can be levied on articles exported from any state.

Under these constitutional provisions, only one federal tax is expressly forbidden, a tax on exports. The requirement that all duties and excises be uniform means that individuals and businesses, wherever located, are subject to the same tax rates on taxable items.

For a considerable period in American history there was uncertainty about the intent and effect of the constitutional provision that direct taxes be apportioned among the states in proportion to the population. The income tax illustrates the difficulty of distinguishing between direct and indirect taxes. The income tax was first levied by the federal government during the Civil War and was later sustained by the Supreme Court.[4] That income tax was repealed

---

[3] In 1945, the Bureau of Internal Revenue expended $145 million to collect $43.7 billion, or about 3.3 per cent.

[4] *Springer* v. *United States*, 102 U.S. 586 (1880).

but another income tax law was enacted in 1894. This time the Supreme Court ruled in a five-to-four decision that a tax on incomes derived from property was a direct tax and, therefore, must be apportioned according to population.[5] In order to overcome the Supreme Court's decision and permit a uniform federal income tax, the Sixteenth Amendment was enacted in 1913. It gives Congress power "to lay and collect taxes on incomes, from whatever source derived, without apportionment among the several states, and without regard to any census or enumeration."

Under the Constitution the power to tax may be used for nonrevenue purposes. Generally, if Congress has power to regulate a matter, it may do so by enacting an excise tax.[6] For example, Congress has placed a prohibitively large tax on sawed-off shotguns, with the express purpose of curtailing business dealings in firearms.[7] In other cases, the Supreme Court has invalidated regulation by taxation when it considered federal regulation to be unconstitutional. Thus the attempt of Congress to regulate child labor by taxing the profits of companies employing child labor was declared unconstitutional on the ground that Congress was regulating a matter reserved to the states.[8] With the broadening of the meaning of the interstate commerce clause of the Constitution, there are today no important limitations on the power of the federal government to tax for nonrevenue purposes.[9]

Another major constitutional issue is the right of one government in our federal system to levy a tax on an activity of another government. In the famous case of *McCulloch* v. *Maryland*,[10] the Supreme Court under Chief Justice John Marshall declared that a state may not tax an instrumentality of the federal government. In this case the Court invalidated a Maryland tax falling on a branch of the United States Bank located in Maryland. Shortly after the Civil War the Supreme Court held that Congress could not tax an instrumentality of state government, and the term "instrumentality" was interpreted to include the salary of a state judge.[11] In 1895 the immunity of state instrumentalities from federal taxation was extended to cover the income from state and municipal bonds.[12] The Supreme Court in 1916 and 1920 continued to maintain that income received

---

[5] *Pollock* v. *Farmers' Loan and Trust Co.*, 157 U.S. 429 and 158 U.S. 601 (1895).

[6] *Mulford* v. *Smith*, 307 U.S. 38 (1939).

[7] *Sonzinsky* v. *United States*, 300 U.S. 506 (1937). See also *McCray* v. *United States*, 195 U.S. 27 (1904), upholding the authority of Congress to place a prohibitive tax on colored oleomargarine.

[8] *Bailey* v. *Drexel Furniture Co.*, 259 U.S. 20 (1922).

[9] An excellent brief discussion of the use of the taxing power for regulatory purposes is found in the note to the *Bailey* case in Robert E. Cushman's, *Leading Constitutional Decisions* (New York: Appleton-Century-Crofts, Inc., 9th ed., 1950), pp. 383–386.

[10] *McCulloch* v. *Maryland*, 4 Wheaton 316 (1819).

[11] *Collector* v. *Day*, 11 Wallace 113 (1870).

[12] *Pollock* v. *Farmers' Loan and Trust Co.*, 157 U.S. 429 and 158 U.S. 601 (1895).

by persons or corporations from state and municipal bonds was not taxable by the federal government.[13]

From 1920 to 1937, the principle of intergovernmental tax exemption was carried even further. For example, a federal excise tax on motorcycles was declared inapplicable to the sale of motorcycles to a municipality.[14] Similarly, Oklahoma was prevented from collecting a tax levied on lessees of mines or oil wells on restricted Indian lands on the theory that such lands were federal instrumentalities.[15] And as late as 1937 the Court reaffirmed the doctrine that a state could not tax the salary of a federal employee.[16]

Since 1937 intergovernmental tax immunities have been whittled down considerably, and earlier cases establishing immunity have been overruled. Taxes on lessees of government lands are now constitutional;[17] state taxes affecting contractors doing work for the federal government have been upheld on the theory that such taxation is, at most, only an indirect and remote burden on the federal government.[18] In 1939 the Supreme Court reversed earlier decisions and held that a state might levy a nondiscriminatory tax on the income of federal employees.[19] The state tax was upheld on the grounds that Congress had not specifically exempted federal salaries from state income taxation and that the tax imposed no significant economic burden on the federal government.

Under the doctrine of federal supremacy, the legal issues involving *state taxation of federal instrumentalities* is fairly well settled. Congress may expressly permit states to tax a federal instrumentality; conversely, it may expressly forbid such taxation. The area of controversy is now limited primarily to instances in which Congress has not expressed itself with respect to immunity from state and local taxation. If a state or local tax on a federal instrumentality is considered burdensome upon government, the Court will probably invalidate the tax. Gradual changes in constitutional interpretation in the tax field illustrate both the flexibility and uncertainty of the language of the Constitution and the wide measure of discretionary authority possessed by the Supreme Court.

Federal taxation of state instrumentalities is still somewhat confused. Perhaps the most important rule used by the Supreme Court to resolve the issue is that a state's immunity from federal taxation does not extend to instances in which the state enters "an ordinary private business," [20] for example, the

---

[13] *Brushaber* v. *Union Pacific Railroad Co.*, 240 U.S. 1 (1916) ; *Evans* v. *Gore* 253 U.S. 245 (1920).

[14] *Indian Motorcycle Co.* v. *United States*, 283 U.S. 570 (1931).

[15] *Gillespie* v. *Oklahoma*, 257 U.S. 501 (1922).

[16] *New York ex rel. Rogers* v. *Graves*, 299 U.S. 401 (1937).

[17] *Helvering* v. *Mountain Producers Corp.*, 303 U.S. 376 (1938).

[18] *James* v. *Dravo Contracting Co.*, 302 U.S. 134 (1937) ; *Silas Mason Co.* v. *Tax Commission*, 302 U.S. 186 (1937).

[19] *Graves* v. *New York ex rel. O'Keefe*, 306 U.S. 466 (1939).

[20] *South Carolina* v. *United States*, 199 U.S. 437 (1905).

liquor business. The determination of what is an ordinary private business has been troublesome. A waterworks was declared to be a regular governmental function, and a college football contest and the bottling and sale of mineral waters private businesses subject to federal taxation.[21]

how to divide tax revenues among federal, state, and local governments

As the need for government revenues increases, governments tend to compete with each other in developing new tax sources. How to divide tax revenues among federal, state, and local governments—three more or less independent levels of government—is becoming an urgent problem of public policy. Several alternative solutions are apparent. The federal government conceivably might lay and collect all taxes and apportion tax revenues to the state and local governments. Or each government might rely on certain taxes which could not be levied by any other level of government. For example, the federal government might be the only government to levy corporate and individual income taxes; the states might have exclusive rights to levy sales and excise taxes; and so forth. These and similar proposals have been made from time to time and have always encountered strong opposition. More progress has been made in distributing tax revenue through grants-in-aid than by assigning definite sources of tax revenues to each level of government.

what kind of taxation is politically defensible in a democracy?

A good tax system must not only be fair and just, easy to administer, capable of yielding a steady, dependable revenue, and legal; it must also be politically defensible according to democratic ideas. The belief that every individual has a stake in his government usually requires that all individuals pay some taxes, no matter how small, to support governmental activities. A tax system should avoid engendering a feeling of distrust and disrespect for the government. Tax laws must be enforced so that the taxpayer who pays his taxes is not penalized by the failure of the government to see that other taxpayers do likewise. In a democracy it is important that a tax system promote good citizenship by developing in individuals a keen interest in public affairs and governmental programs.

In the final analysis, questions about the politics of taxation are related directly to the aims and activities of government. Should the government try to distribute income more evenly? Should it try to promote and maintain general economic prosperity? Should it have responsibility for improving the standard of living of all Americans? If a democracy answers such questions affirmatively, it is politically defensible for it to utilize the tax system to achieve the objectives

---

[21] David Fellman, "Ten Years of the Supreme Court: 1937–1947, I. Federalism," *American Political Science Review*, XLI (December, 1947), 1142–1160. The taxation of the sale of mineral waters is considered in *New York and Saratoga Springs Commission* v. *United States*, 326 U.S. 572 (1946).

of equalization of income, economic stabilization, and improved standards of living.

the current tax system

the income tax

Federal taxes on the income of individuals and corporations have become increasingly important since the adoption of the Sixteenth Amendment in 1913. More than half of the states tax incomes, but at rates considerably lower than federal tax rates. A few cities, including Philadelphia, Washington, Toledo, and St. Louis, tax the incomes or wages of people working within their municipal boundaries.

The most efficient method of collecting income taxes is to collect them at the source, that is, at the point at which the income is paid to the individual. Despite successful British experience and some American experimentation, the federal government did not develop a technique for collection at the source until the withholding tax was authorized in 1943. Under the Current Tax Payments Act of 1943, employers withhold tax payments from the employee's salary or wage and transfer the amount withheld to the federal government. At the close of the income period they furnish to the employee a statement of taxes withheld. Employees then file an annual income tax report and their account is settled. If the total amount of taxes withheld exceeds the tax payable to the government, the excess payment of taxes is refunded. If the withholding tax is less than the amount of tax due, an additional payment must be made to the government.

One of the most difficult aspects of personal income taxation is the determination of "net income." In order to relate the income tax to ability to pay, individuals with incomes are permitted certain exemptions for dependents and certain deductions, including business expenses. Net income is arrived at only after the subtraction from gross income of allowable exemptions and deductions. Ability to pay may also be affected by the selection of the income period for tax purposes. Under the federal law, the income period may be any twelve-month period consistent with a taxpayer's accounting system.

Income taxes are based on ability to pay and are therefore considered equitable. They are rather easily administered when tax payments are withheld from wages and salaries. Moreover, they are a reasonably reliable source of income even though income tax revenues rise in periods of prosperity and decline in periods of depression.

general and selective sales (excise) taxes

A sales or excise tax is a tax imposed on the sale or use of goods. Some taxes are imposed on buyers or sellers based on the dollar amount of sales. Other sales taxes may be imposed on businesses for "the privilege of doing business" and are calculated on the volume of sales. Sales taxes may be general or selective. A selective sales tax is known usually as an excise tax. A general sales tax may be applied to sales of commodities at retail or at all levels of distribution.

A selective sales or excise tax, as the term suggests, is applied to a specific commodity or group of commodities. The most common excise taxes are federal and state taxes on gasoline, cigarettes, and liquor. Other common excise taxes include those on luxury items such as furs, jewelry, and cosmetics; sporting goods; tickets to theatrical amusements; luggage; and automobiles. Excise taxes have also been imposed by various governments from time to time on such items as the use of the telephone and telegraph, electric energy, safe deposit boxes, transfers of stocks and bonds, playing cards, and bowling alleys. Excise taxes may either specify the amount of the tax in dollars and cents or establish an ad valorem rate, that is, a tax based on a fixed percentage of the sales price of a taxable commodity.

General or retail sales taxes were adopted by many states during the economic depression of the 1930's to offset the loss of revenue from property and, to a lesser extent, from income taxes. In 1949, about one fourth of state and local tax revenues and nearly one fifth of federal tax revenues were derived from general and selective sales or excise taxes. Some states, like New Jersey, finance a major portion of their activities from taxes on gasoline, liquor, tobacco, and horse racing.

Sales taxes are not necessarily based on ability to pay. When they are levied on essential food items, they fall most heavily on low-income families and are not as equitable as income taxes. When the tax is collected by the seller of the taxable commodity, it is administered without any special difficulty. Sales taxes have proved to be very steady sources of revenue because the demand for such major taxable commodities as liquor, gasoline, and tobacco is rather stable and does not fall substantially in periods of economic depression.

property taxes

Taxes on property are the most important source of revenue for local governments. There are no federal property taxes, and in the present century state property taxation has been almost abandoned. The importance of property taxation in municipal finance has increased as the states developed alternative sources of tax revenue such as income taxes, sales taxes, taxes on payrolls, and other business taxes. The property tax today accounts for about 45 per cent of state and local tax revenues.

It is difficult to justify the property tax on grounds of fairness and equity. Ownership of property does not necessarily represent ability to pay. Nor has the property tax been a steady source of revenue. Property tax receipts drop sharply in periods of economic depression and do not rise in periods of prosperity unless property assessments and tax rates are raised. The main defect of the property tax, however, has been difficulty of administration.

death and gift taxes

Death and gift taxes are taxes levied on the transfer of property. Death taxes are known as estate and inheritance taxes. The estate tax is imposed on the estate of the deceased before its transfer to the heirs and is payable by the estate. The inheritance tax is levied on the shares received by the heirs and is payable by the individual heirs. Death taxes are considered to be taxes on wealth which are justified by the social objective of reducing inequalities of income and wealth among the people generally. The federal government and nearly all states administer some form of death tax. Gift taxes are paid by the giver and are not as heavy as death taxes. They are relatively unimportant as revenue-producing taxes.

Death and gift taxes are usually related in some measure to ability to pay. Death taxes are somewhat easier to administer than gift taxes because information about gifts may not be known to the taxing government. However, the lower tax rate on gifts may act as an inducement to wealthy persons to make gifts and pay gift taxes in lieu of having heavier taxes deducted from their estates after their death. With respect to their revenue-producing qualities, there is no way of knowing what revenues from death and gift taxes will be in any future year.

business taxes

Federal and state taxes on corporate income may also be classified as business taxes. Beside the corporate income tax, the most common state business tax is the corporate franchise tax, which is usually based on the amount of capital of a corporation. Many states also levy special taxes on public utilities, banks, and insurance companies. The principal federal business tax, other than the corporate income tax, is the excess profits tax, which is used chiefly during periods of war to obtain additional revenue and to curb war profiteering.

other taxes

Since the enactment of social security legislation in 1935, employment taxes have become important. Both employers and employees who are covered by old-age insurance pay a federal tax equal (as of 1949) to 1 per cent of the employee's wages. Similarly, a federal employment or payroll tax is levied on employers to finance unemployment insurance. The payroll taxes for unemployment compensation are collected by the states but deposited in a special trust fund in the United States Treasury. Payroll taxes are set aside exclusively for social security payments. They are usually not included in statistics of tax collections or government revenues. Social security tax revenues are deposited in the federal

Treasury (in the form of United States Government securities) and are drawn on to pay unemployment and old-age benefits. The old-age insurance scheme has been worked out on an actuarial basis, and future claims for old-age benefits can be predicted with reasonable accuracy. On the other hand, unemployment insurance cannot be worked out actuarially. Unlike old-age experience, there is no average pattern of unemployment experience. Hence in periods of acute and protracted economic depression, the unemployment insurance fund may be inadequate to meet all claims. Under the plan, benefit payments are made only as long as the reserve funds are adequate. Because of the relatively high level of employment since 1941, the adequacy of the unemployment insurance fund has not been subjected to a real test.

Social security payroll taxes are levied principally upon workers' income and fall most heavily on the low-paid workers. On the other hand, payroll taxes on employees are rather directly related to benefits received and help to achieve the desired goal of public welfare to prevent the dependence of the aged and unemployed.

One of the most controversial taxes is the poll tax, which is a fixed levy upon persons. Where it is used, it is administered in almost all instances by local governments. In several southern states, failure to pay the tax disqualifies the citizen from voting.

current tax revenues

Federal tax revenues averaged nearly $4 billion in the 1920's and 1930's. In the decade of the 1940's, tax revenues rose sharply to help finance the cost of World War II and postwar commitments. From 1944 to 1948, more than $40 billion was collected annually in taxes, not including social security taxes. After 1948, tax revenues dropped somewhat, but in 1951 they were once more increasing, and seemed headed to the highest level in our history.

STATE AND LOCAL TAX RECEIPTS IN SELECTED YEARS
(IN MILLIONS)

Source	1930	1940	1945	1950 (est.)
Total tax receipts	$6,672	$8,059	$9,448	$15,201
Property taxes	4,883	4,547	4,791	6,748
General and selective sales taxes	500	1,705	2,110	3,891
Corporate and individual income taxes	208	413	831	1,310
Other taxes	1,081	1,394	1,716	3,252

Source: U.S. Bureau of the Budget.

State and local tax revenues combined have increased from over $6 billion in 1930, to $8 billion in 1940, and to $15 billion in 1950. Property tax revenues in 1950 accounted for about 45 per cent of state-local tax receipts as compared to nearly 75 per cent in 1930 and over 55 per cent in 1940. Receipts from state and local sales and excise taxes and income taxes have risen markedly.

federal–state–local tax relations

One of the most difficult and troublesome problems of modern American government is the allocation of adequate tax sources among all levels of government. Rapid increases in governmental costs since 1900 have forced all governments to search for new and more productive methods of raising money for public expenditures. As a result, duplication and waste have developed in the administration of taxes. For example, income taxes and sales or excise taxes are levied by all levels of government. Since local governments are constitutionally creatures of the state governments, they have been unable to combat the tendency of states to take over certain revenue sources. Although states have developed schemes for sharing state-collected taxes with local governments, cities continue to complain about the inadequacy of state financial assistance.

Many state governors urge that the federal government give up certain excise taxes, such as gasoline and liquor taxes, for the exclusive use of the states. State officials in the more industrialized states frequently complain that the federal government takes social security payroll taxes away from the industrial states in order to finance benefit payments in poorer states. For example, New Jersey officials frequently allege that "New Jersey money" is being used to finance public assistance programs in Arkansas and Mississippi. Many states advocate the earmarking of certain taxes for their exclusive use as a way to halt the centralization of governmental activities at the federal level.

Although American governments can help to simplify tax systems by patching up rough spots, it may be doubted whether any fundamental simplification can be achieved without a drastic overhauling. Moreover, basic reform of the tax system probably cannot be accomplished without reallocating government functions among the three levels of government. It is not surprising, therefore, that the most favored methods of tax adjustment today are those which do not call for a drastic realignment of government jurisdictions, but which are adapted to the present pattern of federal–state–local relations. They include the sharing of taxes, grants-in-aid, and greater uniformity of tax practices among governments. Although these devices have resolved some of the financial problems of governments, they have tended to centralize governmental functions, first, at the state level and, secondly, at the national level. Opponents of centralization have argued that it is essentially antidemocratic and inefficient, whereas others have argued that it is an inevitable corollary of the underwriting by government of a minimum standard of living for all Americans.

borrowing and the public debt

When tax receipts and other governmental revenues are not sufficient to cover government expenditures, the government must borrow funds from banks, corporations, government agencies, and individuals, and the public debt increases. When receipts exceed expenditures, surplus funds can be used to pay off some of the public debt.

the federal public debt

The federal government has been forced to borrow funds during periods of crisis, particularly those related to economic depression and war. Expenditures exceeded revenues by approximately $23 billion in the war years 1917–19. From 1920 to 1930, the federal government maintained a surplus and was able to retire some of the public debt. By 1930, the public debt had been reduced from about $25 billion to $16 billion. Since 1930, however, the federal government has incurred a deficit annually except for 1947 and 1948. From 1931 to 1940, the deficit was caused by high emergency relief expenditures. Since 1940, the federal deficit has been due to the enormous cost of fighting World War II and maintaining national and international security. Despite high wartime tax rates, over half of the costs of World War II were covered by borrowing.

BUDGET RECEIPTS AND EXPENDITURES AND PUBLIC DEBT
SELECTED FISCAL YEARS, 1915–1950
(IN BILLIONS OF DOLLARS)

Fiscal Year	Total Budget Receipts	Total Budget Expenditures	Surplus or Deficit	Public Debt at End of Year
1915	0.7	0.7	— 0.06	1.2
1919	5.1	18.4	—13.4	25.4
1925	3.6	2.9	+ 0.7	20.5
1930	4.1	3.3	+ 0.7	16.2
1935	3.7	6.5	— 2.8	28.7
1940	5.3	9.2	— 3.9	43.0
1945	44.8	98.7	—53.9	258.7
1948	42.2	33.8	+ 8.4	252.3
1950	37.0	40.2	— 3.1	257.4

Source: U.S. Bureau of the Budget, *The Federal Budget in Brief, Fiscal Year 1952*, p. 44.

Interest must be paid on loans borrowed by the government, and interest payments have become a regular governmental expenditure. In 1939, interest on the public debt amounted to nearly $1 billion. Since 1948 over $5 billion has been paid out annually as interest on the public debt.

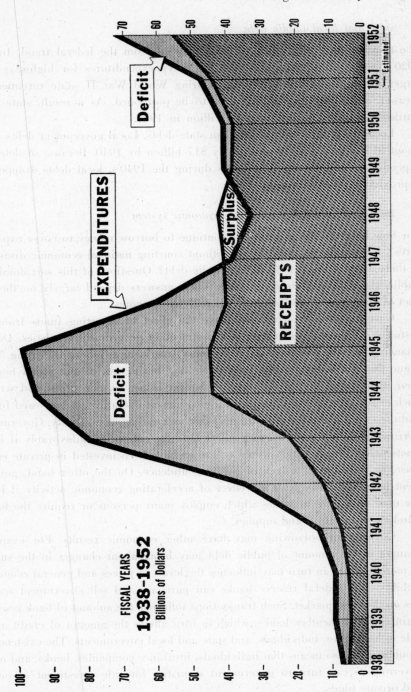

Federal Budget Receipts and Expenditures. Receipts for 1952 exclude new tax proposals.
(*Source: U. S. Bureau of the Budget, January, 1951.*)

state and local public debt

The trend of state debts has varied somewhat from the federal trend. In the 1920's, state debts rose as a result of heavy expenditures for highways and larger grants to local governments. During World War II, state revenues increased, and many expenditures had to be postponed. As a result, state debt burdens decreased to less than $3 billion in 1947.

Local debts are much larger than state debts. Local government debts were about $15 billion in 1930 and nearly $17 billion by 1940. Because of deferred expenditures and increased revenues during the 1940's, local debts dropped to approximately $14 billion by 1947.

impact of public debt upon the economic system

For how long can the government continue to borrow money to cover expenditures? How high can the debt go without courting national economic disaster? Is there any economic limit to the public debt? Questions of this sort dominate public discussions of debt problems. Their answers depend largely on the impact of government borrowing on the national economy.

Government borrowing may have the effect of diverting funds from investment in business enterprise to investment in government securities. Deficit financing has long been considered by some Americans as inherently wrong. They argue that governments, like individuals and businesses, cannot spend beyond their means, and that an unbalanced budget is per se, dangerous and wrong. Such critics may lack confidence in a government operating on borrowed funds, and their very lack of confidence may discourage economic activity. Government borrowing, in other words, may affect business enterprise unfavorably if it attracts private funds which would otherwise have been invested in private enterprise, or if it creates a lack of public confidence. On the other hand, government borrowing may have the effect of accelerating economic activity if loans are used to finance activities which employ many persons or require the heavy purchase of materials and supplies.

Government borrowing may have other economic results. For example, changes in the amount of public debt may bring about changes in the supply of money, which in turn may influence the levels of prices and general economic stability. The federal reserve banks can purchase and sell government securities on the open market. Such transactions influence the amount of bank reserves maintained by member banks, which in turn affects the amount of credit available to businesses, individuals, and state and local governments. The existence of a public debt also means that individuals, insurance companies, banks, and other governments can turn to government securities for safe investment of public and private funds.

Although economists do not agree in appraising the economic impact of public debts and deficit spending, they do agree that the common analogy of public debt and private household budgeting is misleading. Most economists appear to agree that the size of the public debt is not as significant economically as the timing of public borrowing, the purposes for which funds are borrowed, and the economic situation prevailing at the time. The burden of the public debt must be considered in terms of the level of national income. A public debt may be manageable during times of prosperity when the national income is high but excessively burdensome and dangerous in periods of depression and declining national income.

issues ahead in tax and debt policy

reducing the public debt

Both major political parties agree that the public debt should be curtailed and the federal budget balanced. They disagree on the methods with which to achieve these results. The Democratic party generally favors a modest increase in taxation to build up a surplus which can be applied to debt reduction. The Republican party tends to favor reduction of expenditures as the major technique to balance the budget. It is clear that the public debt cannot be reduced unless budget surpluses are provided. Should the emphasis be placed on cutting back expenditures or on increasing taxes? Opinions on these matters are related to views about the desirability of specific governmental expenditures.

how much government activity can we afford?

All government activities are financed basically out of taxes. If funds are borrowed, the interest payments must also be financed out of taxes or out of new loans on which interest must be paid. What level of expenditures can we afford? What proportion of our national income can we afford to devote to governmental expenditures? Can a democracy afford *not* to spend money for improved education, health, and welfare facilities? What successful demands for government expenditures will be made by our aging population? What government expenditures are essential to our economic growth and to the maintenance of employment opportunities for all those able, willing, and seeking to work?

reducing intergovernmental conflicts

Can a national plan be devised for allocating tax sources among the three levels of government? Should grants-in-aid be extended or curtailed? Should states exercise more supervision of the financial practices of local governments? If we must accept the present framework of intergovernmental taxation as basically unchangeable, can anything be done to reduce tax conflicts among governments? Should the federal government collect taxes from state-operated business enterprises? These are some of the issues ahead in intergovernmental tax relations.

bibliographic note

Three standard textbooks on public finance, written from differing points of view are Philip E. Taylor, *The Economics of Public Finance* (New York: The Macmillan Company, 1949), William J. Shultz and C. Lowell Harriss, *American Public Finance* (New York: Prentice-Hall, Inc., 1949), and Harold Groves, *Financing Government* (New York: Henry Holt and Company, 1949). The effect of tax policies on economic conditions is dealt with by Alvin H. Hansen in *Fiscal Policy and Business Cycles* (New York: W. W. Norton & Company, 1941). The position of the Committee for Economic Development, a businessman's organization, on tax policy is outlined in *Taxes and the Budget* (New York: Committee for Economic Development, 1947), prepared by the Research and Policy Committee of the CED. The story behind the tax proposals of the Treasury Department during World War II is told by Randolph Paul in *Taxation for Prosperity* (Indianapolis: The Bobbs-Merill Company, 1947). Proposals for reforming the federal tax system are presented in Henry Simon, *Federal Tax Reform* (Chicago: The University of Chicago Press, 1950). Legal problems in intergovernmental taxation are summarized in David Fellman, "Ten Years of the Supreme Court: 1937-1947, I. Federalism," *American Political Science Review*, XLI, No. 6 (December, 1947), 1142–1160.

---

national security and foreign policy

the nature of foreign policy

OR better or worse, the relative immunity of the United States from the entanglements of international politics has been irretrievably lost. Crucial, intimate, and complex relationships between the American people and the rest of the world are inescapable. Until 1939, foreign relations for the most part affected only a minority of the population and were the special concern of a few government experts and small private groups. It is obvious today, however, that foreign relations touch all the significant phases of our national life. American foreign policy, as now conceived, imposes on every citizen a personal stake in the conduct of foreign affairs. The whole population will both underwrite and be affected by major decisions. This deep involvement in international politics has come almost overnight. For nearly 150 years, historical accident, geographical position, and a relatively balanced power situation among the nations virtually guaranteed America's desire for peace, profitable trade, and the opportunity to carry on a unique political experiment unharassed by more than minimum foreign influences or responsibilities. World War II was the culmination of a set of forces which have now reversed this situation. New problems, conflicts, interests, and responsibilities have been thrust upon the United States. This has not been a matter of deliberate choice, and there is little in the American past to serve as a guide.

It would be difficult to overestimate the significance of American foreign policy in the second half of the twentieth century. A dynamic and largely unknown outer world has been brought to the American doorstep. Conditions in the remotest parts of the earth are likely to affect directly or indirectly national security. Similarly, the power and aims of the United States have greater impact than ever before. Although to some nations American power is a guarantee of peace, to others it appears to be a threat; but few can escape the ultimate consequences of action or inaction by the United States. The responsibilities and implications of this new international position are indeed far-reaching. There is an old Biblical saying: "Where there is no vision, the people perish." It is not too much to say that the health and security of American society depend greatly upon its ability to evaluate its international interests and aims, and to develop appropriate means to protect or achieve them.

the nature of foreign policy

Some idea of the range of political phenomena included in the process of foreign policy making can be derived from an analysis of what the term "foreign policy" means. It is desirable at the outset to differentiate between "foreign policy" and "foreign relations." The latter refers to those actual contacts between nations which grow out of the capacity of men to trade, travel, seek advantage, and invent instruments of power which transcend national frontiers. Basically, foreign policy regulates, defines, and limits such contacts for the sake of national aims.

what are national interests and objectives?

This may appear to be an obvious question with obvious answers. Actually, complex matters of national needs, motivations, and values are involved. What does a nation want with respect to its foreign relations? Why does it want it? How does it determine what it wants? How does it justify its wants? Is there a difference between what a nation wants and what it ought to have? Does a nation always want precisely what it says? These questions are of utmost significance.

nations have certain needs

A nation is a society of men politically organized for common purposes. Therefore it has certain wants or needs, which may be called henceforth "national interests." The term really has two meanings. One includes the interests of the total population, for example, protection against outside attack. The other includes the interests of but a segment of the total population which the latter agrees, tacitly or otherwise, shall be espoused by the government, as in the case of those business groups who wish to sell their goods abroad at a fair profit. National interests fall within one of these categories and may fall within both. Thus certain types of foreign trade may indirectly benefit the whole society even though the direct rewards go only to a few members. This is an important distinction. Some national needs are more basic than others. Furthermore, the nation has limited resources with which to support the attempt to protect both kinds of interests. National interests in general have two sources, related to each other. Some are based upon such functional necessities as the society's capacity for survival and continued operation. A strong defense establishment is not a matter of choice; it is a necessity. So is the importation of several strategic metals without which industrial production would be seriously menaced. Some national interests, however, are based upon values or preferences held by the society. These are choices and beliefs conditioned by the nation's culture and historical experience. It can be said, for example, that the United States has a national interest in the spread of genuinely democratic government throughout the world. Or, to take another example, although foreign trade is a functional necessity for the United States, the basis of that trade is a matter of preference: cash rather than barter, multilateral rather than bilateral, and minimum interference with competitive prices.

national objectives grow out of national interests

National interests move nations to seek certain objectives. Broadly speaking these are security from external threats, economic welfare or advantage, power or prestige, and moral or ideological influence. These are common to all nations. Nonetheless, nations differ in the relative importance they assign to such objectives and in the intensity with which they pursue them at particular times and under particular circumstances. Now all national objectives cannot be neatly labeled "security" or "economic." They are likely to be mixed and to shade off into one another. Economic objectives are nearly always related to security, and the search for power and the search for prestige are related to each other and to security. Security is the dominant national objective because the modern nation-state would hardly survive if it did not provide minimum protection for its citizens.

differences among national objectives

National objectives may be *long term* or *short term*. The distinction is between aspirations and hopes on the one hand, and immediate, required objectives on the other. A long-term objective of the United States is a balanced world economy. A short-term objective is the economic recovery of western Europe. The former must be pursued continuously over time. It represents an interest whose satisfaction must be awaited patiently. The latter must be accomplished in a comparatively short period and is an urgent necessity. At times immediate short-term decisions may appear to run counter to long-term objectives. The United States desires ultimate permanent peace as a fundamental condition of security, but meanwhile it must make decisions involving calculated risks of open conflict.

Not all national objectives are of equal importance. Priorities must be set among different goals. If a nation needs all the allies it can acquire in a hostile world, it may have to modify its aim to see democratic governments established everywhere and "wink" at undesirable regimes.

Therefore national objectives—consisting of goals and the values with which they are associated—tend to be inconstant, reflect shifting emphasis, and

are subject to varying interpretation from time to time. All in all, they comprise
a sort of directional frame of reference for long-range planning and day
to day decisions in foreign policy. They are a guide rather than a blueprint.

objectives differ from means to achieve them

A nation must evaluate its interests and then devise specific programs to safeguard them. Determining objectives and developing techniques are dual aspects
of the foreign-policy-making process. Techniques can best be described as diplomatic tactics and strategies employed by a nation to realize its own aims and
to prevent or reduce the effectiveness of undesirable actions by other nations.
Ability to carry out its foreign policy will depend, basically, on a nation's power
position. National power means capacity to persuade or coerce. Its main forms
are military, economic, political, and ideological. Power position rests upon geographical location and the nature of frontiers; numbers, skills, and health of
the population; material resources and technology; political and economic institutions; and the morale, values, and beliefs of the people.

the importance of national power

To stress the power element in diplomacy is not to suggest that foreign policy
is carried on solely by what have been termed "power politics." Not all foreign
relations involve the use of naked power or power conflict. Much international
business is transacted by negotiation and compromise. But even here some kind
of power will be manifest, a reality in the minds of diplomats though perhaps
not overtly stressed. Often a nation can achieve its ends by persuading other nations that their self-interest lies in a particular course of action. Beyond this,
some sort of pressure is usually necessary.

Successful implementation of foreign policy objectives not only requires
power; a nation must decide how it is to be used (if at all), must mobilize it
in appropriate form, and must apply it effectively. The choice of techniques
will therefore depend upon the extent and kinds of power available, upon what
is appropriate given the end in view, and upon the capacity of other nations
to offer countermeasures. Nations generally use techniques which come naturally to them. Some objectives may be unattainable either because power is lacking or because it cannot be mobilized and applied effectively. Also, a policy objective may be undermined for want of proper implementation.

These points can be illustrated by the case of the United States, which has
at present the overwhelming preponderance of economic power in the world.
This power—technology, dollars, resources, and skilled labor supply—exists.
It is mobilized so that America can give or lend goods, dollars, or industrial
know-how. Because this society is business-oriented, the use of this kind of power
is a natural foreign policy technique. It is an appropriate technique because the
world badly needs American economic aid and because rivals cannot compete

in offering such aid. It should be noted, however, that economic power cannot directly serve American foreign policy in eastern Europe since the opportunity to exert it there is almost totally absent as compared to western Europe.

techniques have their own effects

The use of particular techniques sometimes creates the need for further action and decision. For example, America is attempting to check Soviet expansion by providing military aid to nations under direct Communist pressure. In the case of Greece, the United States was soon deeply involved in the domestic politics of this country far beyond what was initially foreseen. Ineffective or inappropriate techniques may ultimately present new foreign policy problems and compel the use of undesired methods. Failure of the United States to support fully the old League of Nations after World War I helped to necessitate eventual participation in the European power conflict on less favorable terms. Again, the pouring of some $2 billion of aid into China from 1938 to 1948 was either insufficient or misconceived and contributed to the exceedingly difficult decisions America had to face with respect to China after 1949.

Techniques are interrelated. Obviously there is potential conflict between helping to reconstruct weak nations economically and making their armies stronger. Can both be done at the same time? If so, is not coordination necessary so that one does not obstruct the other? On the other hand, what are the domestic effects in the United States of maintaining a $45 billion annual military budget while at the same time draining the economy in order to aid world recovery?

national objectives and techniques must be specifically formulated

Thus far ends and means have been discussed as broad, general categories of phenomena. Needless to say, national objectives and techniques do not have an independent existence. They must be expressed through appropriate government agencies which more or less constantly formulate and interpret them. As will be described in detail in later chapters, the choice of techniques and the formulation of objectives are the result of interaction among various government agencies and between government and public opinion. The following list suggests the typical ways foreign policy is defined: a press conference statement by the President, his State of the Union address, or a special message to Congress; a treaty or other mode of international agreement whether concerning trade or a defeated enemy; instructions to the American commander in an occupied area; congressional legislation such as the Greek-Turkish Aid Bill of 1947 or the Foreign Assistance Act of 1948; by diplomatic conference of foreign ministers; a statement by the Secretary of State or the European Cooperation Administrator; and the policy stands taken by American representatives in the United Nations Security Council and General Assembly.

stages in the development of foreign policy

The process of formulating and executing foreign policy requires more than a simple coordination of national ends and means. World-wide social forces and political conditions, the behavior of other nations, future developments and necessities, and adjustment to situations are never completely under control. An adequate foreign policy must therefore rest upon the successful performance of certain functions: (1) collection of data by diplomatic and intelligence agencies; (2) evaluation of this data by foreign office analysts and policy makers; (3) estimation of national interests, and the calculated risks involved in achieving them; (4) the rendering of a decision or statement of policy; (5) implementation; (6) "selling" the policy at home and abroad, including a clear explanation of what the policy is intended to accomplish; and (7) re-evaluation of the policy or decision in the light of operational results and new conditions. No matter what its form of government, every nation must perform these functions in estimating and protecting its interests.

error and uncertainty in foreign policy

Weaknesses in foreign policy can usually be traced to the ineffectiveness with which one or more of the above functional requirements are fulfilled. Policies are made by fallible human beings working with complex problems, subject to many variable influences, and liable to error in their calculations. Policies are only partly the result of completely rational responses to clear-cut problems. Opportunism and accident loom large. A nation may know what it wants but be compelled to "feel its way," or it may not know; in other words, there is lack of agreement among policy makers.

Moreover, national motives may be ambiguous and may be misinterpreted. Nation X says it is seeking security. Its policy is defensive. Nation Y says X is really thirsting for power and its policy is aggressive. This is not just an academic distinction. It is also unfortunately obvious from history that nations do not always accurately estimate their true interests or the risks attached to various policies. Since appearances and realities are not always identical, the tendency to overestimate or underestimate national power in relation to objectives is forceful indeed. Throughout the years men have died or suffered unnecessarily because of mistaken calculations and impossible goals. Policy making is not an automatic, cut-and-dried process. Nor is it entirely haphazard and uncontrollable. It is both; the more one than the other, depending on whether the problems dealt with are routine and technical or delicately diplomatic and strategic.

additional factors which complicate foreign policy

Population, technology, resources, morale, and geographical position are, as noted, among the ingredients of national strength which support foreign policy objectives. But there are other factors which are partly tangible and partly not.

These factors help determine how a society uses its strength. Thus one must try to estimate how a given society—in this case the United States—behaves collectively, particularly in the face of certain situations. No society behaves as an entity all the time. There are many behavior patterns, individual and group, being carried on simultaneously. Yet collective behavior is perhaps the most important from the point of view of foreign policy. How a society reacts to international pressure, its capacity for organizing itself for a national enterprise, its methods of coming to collective decisions, its treatment of the problem of leadership—these are some of the factors which help to determine how raw elements of power will be used, or whether they will be used at all. This is an era of foreign relations in which the way a nation thinks, how accurately it appraises itself and the world in which it exists, may be more significant than its weapons or its official policy statements. If foreign policy consists, as defined, of the application of means to ends, then it becomes relevant to inquire into the broad social forces which make public decisions more or less rational. Such inquiry necessitates an awareness of the level on which political issues are discussed in the United States, the processes of social thinking, the modes of communication and education, and the barriers to a mature approach to the problems which affect every one of us. If America now stands in a unique position of responsibility and leadership and if mankind has developed weapons which will render any mistakes of statesmanship fatal to the fabric of civilization, then some clue as to how the American people *will behave and should behave* must be sought in the total complex of conditions and factors which make American society what it is or what it is becoming.

some aspects of American society which are relevant to foreign policy

national characteristics

Two basic cultural traits shared by most Americans, individualism and materialism, have a bearing on the collective behavior of the United States and how it views the world. Individualism consists of certain beliefs and activities: independence, equality, competition, faith in individual effort and its ultimate triumph, a system of personal rewards, and pursuit of personal success. Relative emphasis is on aggressive, competitive, individual action and voluntary, temporary, individualistic cooperation rather than on habitual cooperation which completely submerges individual desires in a larger social need. Society exists for the individual not vice versa.

Materialism means that success in the United States is measured primarily in monetary terms, and good living is defined in terms of material possessions. Quantity is more important than quality. Progress rests on productive achievement. Fabulous mass production and natural wealth have inclined Americans to be optimistic, impatient with obstacles, experimental, boastful, generous, efficiency-minded and skilled mechanically. It has been said that Americans are "contemptuous of ideas but amorous of devices," which suggests that America is fundamentally a nation of doers rather than thinkers. No technological problem has remained unsolved for long. Given a little time, anything is possible.

In view of the heavily materialistic nature of American culture, can the United States give the world something more than economic aid at a critical period in history? Can it, in short, provide moral and spiritual strength as well? There is some evidence that other nations have judged America to be deficient on this score. Individualism and materialism together make the United States very self-reliant and somewhat critical of those who are not or cannot be the same. Perhaps this self-reliance also indicates that America's enthusiasm for international cooperation is basically lukewarm. Is there a feeling that the United States can take care of itself no matter what happens to others? Finally, if national unity is now a primary necessity, how is it affected by the strong tradition of individualism? Short of total war, can the American people be brought together in a genuinely collaborative security program? There is at least a question as to whether the United States can continue to rely so much on haphazard and piecemeal cooperation when it is under constant diplomatic pressure.

a society in transition

American society is in a state of dynamic change. Any society undergoes change, but the rate and direction of social change are of special significance in the case of the United States because of their conjuncture with a critical international situation. Basic changes in society bring in their wake conflict and uncertainty. The United States has been the last great Western nation to be faced with sufficiently serious social, economic, and political crises to necessitate a re-evaluation of institutions. Most of the issues and problems arising from what might be called general social insecurity are unresolved in this country. Thus the nature of private property is unsettled. The role of the government in economic life has changed greatly and is still doing so. However, a basic ideological conflict remains unresolved. Given the necessity for some sort of social approach to critical problems, which of the two different types of regulatory agencies shall be charged with the major responsibility—public or private, government or business? It is regarded as one of the strengths of American society that political action has never been completely dominated by either conservative or radical views and techniques. Elements of both have been incorporated in a kind of fluid middle position. The difficulty is that America is now being compelled to make decisions and judgments on these same social issues in countries where the middle course is not always possible. Shall we support planned economy in Great Britain? France? Iran? China? Japan? It is open to question whether the United States is prepared to make fully objective decisions in view of the fact that so far its people have not, cannot, or do not need to come to a clear-cut reckoning on the great problems of property, social reform, and the scope of public authority.

economic maladjustments

The United States has been largely transformed from a rural agricultural society to an urban industrial society. The transition is not yet fully complete. Not only is there a strain between two ways of life and between two elements of the population, but specific foreign policy issues are affected. Agriculture must be subsidized, protected, or given special consideration. Prices of cotton, corn, tobacco, wheat, and peanuts have been government supported at parity regardless of the fact that they are thus overvalued on the world market and placed in a weakened competitive position. Theoretically, the more industrialized America becomes, the more dependent it should be on outside sources for agricultural needs. But the price of social adjustment of this kind is heavy. As agricultural groups continue to be hard hit by maladjustment, the pressure for certain government policies will continue. No administration can ignore it. There is nothing wrong with this, per se. What must be said is that a society severely subject to the conflict or imbalance brought about by technological change will not have maximum freedom to make foreign policy decisions on their merits.

Changing balances between consumption and investment, employment and unemployment, profit and social welfare, small and large business enterprises, labor and management affect the whole national economy. Out of these delicate, changing balances have arisen grave problems concerning which there is disagreement among experts and laymen alike. Nevertheless, the United States is moving toward a modified capitalism. One of several reasons for this modification is the growing contradiction between the insistence upon individual and corporate competition on the one hand, and the decline of opportunity and assured markets on the other. No policy—economic or otherwise—can be supported in the field of foreign relations unless it recognizes the need for expanding the outlets for capital and labor. The Foreign Assistance Act of 1948 decreed that most of the goods shipped to nations receiving aid be carried in American ships despite the fact that freight rates on foreign ships were as much as 50 per cent lower. Furthermore, no goods for the recovery program could be purchased outside the United States if surpluses existed in this country, even though prices elsewhere might be lower.

ideological contradictions

Social, economic, and political equality are strong features of the American ideology. Yet our actual practices continue to be marked by widespread general discrimination against racial and religious minorities. In addition, there is mounting evidence that class distinctions are becoming more rigid. A growing discrepancy between professed beliefs and social reality is caused by both developments. Class differences, prejudice, and discrimination weaken and divide the nation. They violate the letter and spirit of the Constitution. They also put the United States in an awkward position in its rivalry with the Soviet Union for the support and friendship of hordes of human beings who differ from Americans in color, mode of worship, and way of life. In the United Nations, the United States has been periodically embarrassed by the fact that domestic social practice does not entirely conform to the values which the nation says it stands for.

diversity in the United States -

Some thirty nationality groups—German, Italian, Spanish, Austrian, Swedish, Irish, French, and so on—are found in the population of the United States. There are approximately 256 religious denominations. Hundreds of pressure groups operate in Washington. Ranging from the American Medical Association to the Zollverein, there are thousands of societies organized for one purpose or another. Within the continental United States are overlapping yet distinct regional, urban, rural, and racial cultures. The economy actually embraces several economies: agriculture, mining, manufacturing, and service industries. A population of this size, variety, and distribution forms a unique "public opinion" base for foreign policy. America is a number of things. It does not always present a consistent face to the world. The crosscurrents of American life are reflected in our international relations. It has been noted, for instance, that at one moment the nation is the soul of altruism, and at another it appears in the role of a sharp Yankee trader.

ideological factors

American beliefs and attitudes concerning human behavior and politics

Especially significant in the analysis of foreign policy is ideology, the core of ideas or values which most Americans consciously or unconsciously accept. For one thing, there seems to be a conviction that there is something unique in the American political system, something good for all humanity. Democracy is valid everywhere if only people have the will to practice it or can be left alone to do so. Freedom is a cure-all, almost an end in itself. Another type of conviction is expressed in the distrust of government: public authority is a necessary evil. It is better to err on the side of too little rather than too much. Authority personified by government is inherently bad. Totalitarianism is more than a domestic form of government abroad; it is a violation of moral principle.

Distrust of political authority has sometimes hampered policy makers and has helped to encourage discontinuity of administrative personnel. Government service is not widely recognized as a topflight social career. Often salaries are lower than in positions of similar responsibility in private life. Finally, it will be a slow and difficult process to equip the American government with the means to wage propaganda warfare against its enemies because such power is regarded as too dangerous to be entrusted to government agencies.

Flowing from this fear of an all-powerful government are the beliefs in constitutional limitations on public power, in protection of individual liberties including private property, in consent of the governed by their choice of representatives in unfettered elections, in a multiparty system, in the rule of law, in majority rule, and in free expression of political ideas, with the accompanying privilege of changing the form of the government or its personnel. Holding this political ideology together is the belief in the equality of, and respect for, the individual personality both legally and spiritually. Rightful obligations must be honored. There is, finally, a faith in the rational nature of men, in the ability of men of good will to compromise and to settle their differences reasonably and peacefully. These values are analyzed in detail elsewhere in this volume, but their special relevance to the American approach to foreign relations must be noted here.

some general values underlying American foreign policy

The key statements of recent Presidents and Secretaries of State express what might be called the value framework of American foreign policy. Such values are criteria which American policy makers apply to the analysis of specific foreign policy problems and have their basis in the ideology outlined above.

One value is a desire for stable government in every nation in the world, government resting solidly not only on democratic principles but also on firm popular support and custom. Violence, even in the interests of the majority, leads to abuse of power and neglect of essential liberties. The emphasis is on evolutionary rather than revolutionary change. Individual welfare depends on a network of relationships involving reciprocal rights and duties. No progress or prosperity is possible unless orderly government preserves these relationships, unless business enterprise and other forms of social endeavor can look into the future with assurance.

Another value concerns economic activity. The American government has usually viewed it as an end in itself rather than as an instrument of state policy. Economic enterprise grows out of individual necessity, and the task of government is to create an environment in which individual economic purposes can be carried out.

Third, there is consistent and conscious reference to "justice and morality." Individual will as well as the powers of society must be subject to moral restraints. Even the law may embody injustice. Hence there must be an appeal to higher principles of authority above the acts of men and governments. These rules have developed from reason, spiritual inspiration, and the accumulated experience of humanity. They appear to impose certain minimum limits on human behavior below which no action can remain unchallenged save at a price of undermining the Greco-Roman-Christian tradition that is one of the pillars of Western civilization.

Other values can be listed without extended comment: (1) the United States seeks no territorial expansion or purely selfish advantage over other nations; (2) it believes in the eventual return of sovereign rights and self-government to all peoples who have been deprived of them by force; (3) it will approve no territorial change unless freely accepted by the peoples concerned; (4) all peoples prepared for self-government should be permitted to choose their own form of government without interference from any foreign source; (5) defeated enemies should be helped to establish peaceful democratic governments; (6) the United States refuses to recognize any government imposed upon any nation by the force of any foreign power; (7) all states members of the family of nations should have equal access to the trade and raw materials of the world; (8) full economic collaboration between all nations is required to raise the living standards of all peoples and to banish fear and want, which produce political upheaval; (9) the United States will strive to promote freedom of worship and freedom of expression throughout the peace-loving areas of the world; (10) the preservation of peace requires an organization composed of all peace-loving states which are willing to prevent aggression and maintain peace by force if necessary.

types of American thinking about foreign policy and relations

Certain persistent trends in public thinking are both revealing and significant. For one thing, foreign relations have been either tolerated as a necessary evil or distrusted. The obvious accomplishments of the American way of life have bred a vigorous self-reliance. America does not need to entangle itself in contacts with outsiders. By and large, such contacts offer greater rewards to other nations than to the United States and require large risks for small gain. Linked to this is a military optimism based on the fact that since 1815 the nation has never been defeated in war. Superiority attitudes and chauvinism have sometimes colored popular thinking. Past wars with greatly inferior enemies (Spain and Mexico) and American relations with nations to the south have provided justification for both. The crude tourist selling a bigger and better America abroad has often been a more effective representative of the United States than regular diplomats. Another tendency has been to divide all foreigners into oppressors and oppressed, or into the masses and their corrupt governors. Sympathy has been indiscriminately extended to the oppressed regardless of who they were, what they believed in, and whether or not they shared American interests or ideals.

Apathy, provincialism, and caprice have also characterized public thinking. Attention to foreign policy issues has usually been called forth by "crises" or threats, for interpreting which the average person has little background. Newspapers admittedly stress the sensational aspects of foreign news. Objectivity and acceptance of foreign policy problems as a normal feature of politics have been minimized. In some respects, America is a most provincial nation, using caricatures like "John Bull" as a basis of judgment about other nations. Despite the most highly developed educational system in the world, the American people have been guilty of the most startling lack of awareness of what kind of world lies beyond their shores. A combination of this apathy and ignorance has produced a "fad" type of thinking. A good illustration of this is the trend of public attitudes toward the Soviet Union from 1917 to 1948. There are distinct phases, depending upon what was happening in the United States. During the early period of postwar isolation and prosperity, the Soviet experiment was something to be ignored and distrusted. As we entered the depression period, 1929 to 1933, the Russian five-year plans were regarded with more respect, since capitalism was obviously working badly. From 1933 to 1939 the Soviet Union was simply a nation with unique political institutions but which was desirous of peace. The 1939 pact between Germany and Russia brought disillusionment and criticism in the United States, but this was wiped out and Russia was welcomed as an ally after the valiant battle of Stalingrad turned the Germans back. Disillusionment set in again after 1945, when it became clear that Russia did not share American war aims and also took a quite different view of the world. The conclusion is that fashions in American attitudes toward Russia changed abruptly and were not founded on a realistic appraisal of what Russia was and what she was after. The same kind of thinking occurred with respect to Germany and Japan: underestimation and overestimation of their power and their foreign policy aims. Naturally attitudes change when conditions change, but in these cases it is the rapidity and degree of change, its direction, and its resulting miscalculations which are noteworthy.

A strong moral flavor pervading American judgments has tended to frame foreign policy issues in terms of right or wrong, black or white. International issues and the behavior of nations can seldom be reduced to such clear-cut evaluations. Misapplication of standards of right and wrong may actually obscure a rational appraisal of foreign policy issues. Much public apathy can be explained in terms of a reaction to the nasty game of world politics. Americans have believed—and still believe—that their government has been fair and just in its dealings with other nations. The record bears them out. Whether they have a realistic understanding of international relations is another question.

Thinking about foreign policy has often centered around clichés and stereotypes: "power politics," "peace offensive," "Red," "aggression," "secret diplomacy," "appeasement," "cheap foreign labor," and so on. Over a period of time, these words and phrases have become so imprecise that much of the reality behind them is lost. Appeasement, for example, really means international blackmail and the sacrifice of valuable objectives for ones less valuable. It refers specifically to the process whereby Hitler pointed a gun at the rest of the Western world from 1934 to 1939 and said, "Satisfy me or else," a process which culminated in the Munich Pact, which was supposed to have bought "peace in our time." Now the word is being applied to the rivalry of the United States and the Soviet Union. The future peace depends essentially upon the reconciliation of Soviet and American power, yet legitimate proposals to this end may be labeled "appeasement." If all diplomatic concessions are prejudged as appeasement, the cause of peace is lost. But there is a fundamental difference between making reluctant concessions from weakness with nothing received and making willing concessions from strength in return for substantial concessions. The latter is hardly appeasement.

The intention of the preceding remarks has not been to ridicule American public thinking. The point is that the chief thought patterns concerning foreign relations were formed when the position of the United States in the world was quite different and when the ability of the whole society to evaluate its international interests and responsibilities properly was not crucial. There is not, as yet, abundant evidence to indicate that the types of thinking noted briefly above have been completely replaced by others more appropriate.

foreign policy and domestic politics

significance of the relationship

Despite the lessons of the past ten years, there is still a tendency to ignore or gloss over the intimate relationship between foreign policy and domestic politics. One reason is that, historically, the impact upon the rest of the world of what was going on in the United States was either unclear or unimportant. By the same token, events outside the United States had little direct effect internally. Actually, the two areas of policy are, and have always been, different aspects of the same thing: the use of the political arm of American society to accomplish national purposes. Since foreign policy and foreign relations now affect the whole society, they are no longer in a compartment by themselves but are joined with domestic policy as a part of the total political process of securing national welfare through government action. The relationship is therefore reciprocal. A brief analysis of the various types of connecting links will amplify the causal relationship between foreign and domestic policy.

bonds with the rest of the world

Trade, travel, the need for certain scarce raw materials, cultural ties with the Western world, and Americanized minorities who never completely lose their interest in countries of their origin comprise bonds of the obvious sort. In an age of fantastic weapons, space takes on a new aspect, and bases outside the continental United States are necessary. Given modern communications, the United States cannot insulate itself against the flow of ideas. The triumph of a certain set of ideas abroad might impose almost as great a strain upon American institutions as a direct military attack.

the rivalry of foreign and domestic policies for political attention

In recent years, Congress and the President have been compelled to give priority to foreign or domestic problems, depending on the time and circumstances. It was considered necessary for reasons having to do with domestic conditions that the United States withdraw its support of the important London Economic Conference of 1933. There seems little doubt that this action contributed to the failure to stabilize international currencies and trade, which in turn later diminished the market for American goods. On the other hand, from 1947 to 1949 requirements of foreign policy were placed ahead of pressing domestic problems. Here too there seems little doubt that the time, energy, and resources expended in setting up the European Recovery Program, the Greek-Turkish Aid Program, and a huge military establishment deprived urgent domestic legislative needs of adequate attention. In each case the national interest was being served, and in each case the relative emphasis on one of the two areas of public policy caused repercussions in the other.

the same political machinery must develop both foreign and domestic policy

As is shown elsewhere in this volume, policy making in general in the United States has become more and more complex, depending upon more agencies and consuming more time than ever before. Accordingly, the day has passed when a small group in the inner recesses of the State Department has a monopoly on foreign policy decisions. The governing officials who are gaining a larger voice in these decisions are the same ones who tend to dominate the legislative process for domestic policy decisions. Therefore there are stronger links between the two than ever before.

the nation-state faces two ways

The state internally performs legitimate and necessary functions demanded by its citizens. Theoretically, there is no limit to these demands, but two sets of consequences follow from the state's internal service and regulatory functions. Since the state faces outward and since its behavior affects other states, the measure of power necessary internally to provide security for its citizens may menace other states and create ill will which makes achievement of foreign policy aims difficult. Thus the existence of a strong American military power, although reassuring to the American people, adds an element of insecurity to international relations. Secondly, the greater the degree of state regulation of domestic life, the greater the degree of control over foreign affairs which may be required. As national domestic planning increases, so may the necessity for foreign policy planning, lest the purposes of the former be thwarted. For example, grain prices could not be maintained by government purchase and subsidy if unrestricted imports from abroad were allowed. Relations between governments are in turn becoming more significant because as state control grows, nothing in the realm of foreign affairs is completely unimportant.

influence of domestic insecurity

General social insecurity heightens sensitivity toward domestic problems and may lead to a relative neglect of foreign policy interests. Or it may cause fears to be focused on a particular foreign country. It is no coincidence that Soviet communism either lurks behind or enters into the discussion of domestic economic policy in the United States. Tensions and insecurity do not provide a sound basis for settling political problems. Foreign threats distort domestic issues, and domestic difficulties may distort foreign policy. The ability of the United States to accomplish its foreign policy objectives in the next twenty years will depend greatly on whether the course of domestic politics is comparatively stable or unstable. If there is an inflationary period, if production lags because of strikes, if there is continued "witch hunting," if there is widespread distrust among Americans, if selfish pressure groups put their interests ahead of the interests of the whole country, and if there are unnecessary conflicts or delays in Congress, then the United States will be proportionately weakened in its international dealings.

bibliographic note

A careful reading of *Strengthening the Forces of Freedom* (Department of State *Publication* No. 3,852, General Foreign Policy Series 28; Washington: Government Printing Office, 1950), containing selected speeches and policy statements of Secretary of State Dean Acheson from February, 1949, to April, 1950, will reveal the ideological foundations and overtones of current American foreign policy. The best analysis of some major social factors which condition American public attitudes and opinions on foreign relations generally, including chapters on national character and social class, is to be found in G. A. Almond, *The American People and Foreign Policy* (New York: Harcourt, Brace and Company, 1950). *American Foreign Policy* (New York: Rinehart & Company, 1948), pp. 401–402, 406–409, by L. H. Chamberlain and R. C. Snyder, contains brief notes by the editors on general principles and beliefs related to American foreign policy. Chapter 1 of Kurt London, *How Foreign Policy Is Made* (New York: D. Van Nostrand Company, 1949), is a general discussion of the meaning of foreign policy and some of the basic factors which influence it. A good, concise statement of the signifiance of foreign affairs and an analysis of the sources of foreign policy appear in Chapters 1 and 2 of J. L. McCamy, *The Administration of American Foreign Affairs* (New York: Alfred A. Knopf, Inc., 1950). Certain aspects of America's new world position and new lines of foreign policy are given provocative treatment in Leland Stowe, *Target: You* (New York: Alfred A. Knopf, Inc., 1949). Chaps. 2, 3, 6–11. Percy Bidwell's "Ideals in American Foreign Policy," *International Affairs*, XX (October, 1946), 479–487, comments on the changing emphasis in foreign policy thinking with reference to the conflict between idealism and realism. Robert Cushman reviews a very important aspect of contemporary American foreign relations in "The Repercussions of Foreign Affairs on the American Tradition of Civil Liberty," *Proceedings of the American Philosophical Society*, October 25, 1948. The general significance of the assumptions underlying foreign policy is discussed in a very useful article by Laurence Sears, "American Foreign Policy and Its Consequences," *The American Scholar*, XVIII, No. 4 (Autumn, 1949), 470–484, which critically analyzes those assumptions thought to determine America's present policy.

the new international position
of the United States

*A*MERICAN foreign policy is in transition. General trends and specific policies are responding to change. Different American interests are emerging, new objectives have been established, and new techniques are being put into practice. What are the main elements in the new international position of the United States?

the new distribution of national power

the bipolar focus of world politics

The United States is one of two great superpowers in the world today, the other being the Soviet Union. In terms of power these two nations are in a class by themselves. The fact that they are the only nations now capable of waging modern warfare on a global scale is one of the reasons for saying that we live in a bipolar world. The remaining national power units are usually thought of as being attracted to or influenced by one of these two major powers. Great Britain, although retaining considerable power and influence, is no longer in the same class with America and Russia. Former great powers, France, Germany, Italy, and Japan, seem destined to achieve little more than subordinate rank in the immediate future.

The great powers are now world powers in the precise sense of the word. Their power can be exerted in both the Eastern and the Western Hemisphere. Coupled with this is the fact that Europe, the Mediterranean basin, the Middle East, and the Far East (chiefly China, Japan, and the islands of the Pacific) have become "outer" security zones for these two big powers. What each does or tries to do in these areas is of prime importance to the other. The new distribution of power has forced the United States to think in terms of global strategy and its effect upon national objectives. There is not now, as there was from 1815 to 1914, a sufficient number of independent nations whose power and interrelationships might preserve a stable balance to the advantage of the United States. During that earlier period Europe, for example, suffered internal conflicts which prevented any one European state from challenging the United States in the Western Hemisphere.

Two consequences of the new bipolar distribution of power must be noted. First, there is no effective mediation possible with the world's power centered in two countries. It is far easier to have compromise and mediation when there are six or seven great powers. No nation, or even a group of nations, has sufficient power or leadership to be a balancing force. Nearly all serious international disputes are direct or indirect disputes between Russia and America. Second, the areas lying between the two powers tend to gravitate one way or the other because the effective means to make war are so concentrated.

the power of the United States

National power is relative to national objectives and to the power of other states. It is comprised partly of the allies a country may attract. National power may be actual or potential. It must be evaluated, mobilized, and used wisely. The way in which national power is used may in turn affect national aims. In a sense, then, the American power position is constantly shifting. It is difficult to draw up a balance sheet which will be valid for a long period. Changing power relationships are one of the fluid aspects of the international situation in which United States foreign policy must operate.

the military position

The military power position of the United States cannot be analyzed by merely adding up men, tanks, ships, planes, and weapons. Nor is it enough to note that the military budget for 1950–1951 was approximately $45 billion, though this is a very significant figure in itself. Military power is related to economics. Military strength must be viewed in the light of national solvency. Since American military power is comprised primarily of highly technical weapons operated by skilled personnel, the productive skills and methods supporting the military establishment are really the key elements. Furthermore, the commitments and purposes to which military power might be applied must be considered. The United States was able to put on a spectacular impromptu show with the Berlin Air Lift in 1948–1949 in order to remain in Berlin and to sustain the population in the American and British zones. Here power was adequate. Whether we could have defended western Europe against a land attack is doubtful. To the military power of the United States must be added the strength of the members of the Atlantic Alliance. Some of these nations add to American power in terms of strategic position or materials. Others have constituted a drain on American resources because they have been too weak to defend themselves alone. Finally, *having* military power is one thing; *using* it is another. The United States could probably have landed a division or two to participate in the Chinese Civil War in 1948, but as a practical measure the American people would not have supported it despite the fact that there was tacit public approval for more extensive military planning and preparedness than at any previous time in our history.

For the time being, the United States is, on almost any criterion—except number of men under arms—the strongest military power in the world.[1] Temporarily America has a real technological advantage in the perfection and production of atomic bombs, guided missiles, long-range planes, and biological weapons. This provides an important strategic advantage. Superiority in naval and air forces is clear. Military operations from strategic places like Greece, Turkey, North Africa, Japan, certain Pacific islands, western Germany, and Greenland can be controlled or influenced for offensive or defensive purposes. A security pact binds the Western Hemisphere to defend itself against outside attack. Potential enemies are weaker in resources and industrial development; moreover, they are temporarily landlocked except for submarines.

This is a general picture and is in no sense unchangeable. Invention and the development of new techniques can alter it. So can the behavior of other nations. The important points to be made on the basis of the foregoing analysis are clear despite elements of uncertainty. The United States is capable of placing more emphasis on military techniques in its foreign policy than at any previous time in its history. In the absence of general international security, the over-all military strength of the United States assumes major significance. Preoccupation with military preparedness may itself create conditions with which our foreign policy will have to reckon, and it may cause neglect of other devices through which American objectives might be achieved. The growing military power of the United States—whether employed or not—adds an ingredient to the present international situation which differentiates it from the period after World War I, when the withdrawal of the United States altered the power balance which the victory of the Allies had established.

the economic position

As remarked earlier, the economic strength of the United States is imposing. It probably constitutes the most effective American diplomatic weapon. Professor Jacob Viner of Princeton University has aptly remarked: "Since the beginning of nation-wide boundaries there probably has never been so great a proportionate concentration of the world's goods and of the world's capacity to produce them within the limits of any single country." [2] Broadly speaking, all this rests

---

[1] In January, 1951, the United States had 2,300,000 men in its armed services.
[2] L. H. Chamberlain, R. C. Snyder, *American Foreign Policy* (New York: Rinehart and Company, 1948), p. 739.

upon a large, vigorous population with general mechanical aptitudes and technical abilities; upon industrial facilities—transportation, manufacturing, and agricultural; upon abundant natural resources, especially iron ore, oil, coal, uranium, and cotton, plus the access and purchasing power necessary to bring in supplies of others from outside the United States; and upon a technology capable of efficiently mobilizing skills and resources. The accomplishments of the American economy are well known. From the point of view of foreign relations, suffice it to say that this economy supported a four-year war effort, sent upward of $25 billion in loans and goods to friends and allies, and is now underwriting European recovery to the tune of $5 billion annually.

It would be a mistake to assume, however, that the United States enjoys a position of economic invulnerability. Weaknesses are evident and on the whole somewhat serious. Our merchant marine is costly and inadequate. Recently such books at Fairfield Osborne's *Our Plundered Planet* and William Vogt's *The Road to Survival* have suggested that the wanton wastage of our soil resources is becoming a threat to national strength. There are mineral shortages, particularly in copper, lead, zinc, and cobalt. In the case of fourteen other minerals, among them manganese, mercury, tungsten, tin, and antimony, there is either no national supply or only a five-year reserve. In 1947 the Armed Forces released a list of some fifty-three strategic minerals for which there are no synthetics, no substitutes, and insufficient sources of supply.

Other difficulties are more deep-seated. Temporarily at least, production of new weapons is not rapid and economical. Items like durable paints and specialized fuels have become bottlenecks. A general decline in the *rate* of industrial growth and exploitation of new sources of raw materials has set in. We lack scientific personnel. There was a total increase during the whole war period of only 35,000 professional scientists. Apparently there are less than adequate teaching and laboratory facilities for the training of 600,000 students annually. In 1948, two years after the Atomic Energy Act had been passed, one phase of the Atomic Energy Commission's program was stalled because only 25 per cent of the required staff could be found.

The American economy is somewhat delicately balanced and is potentially vulnerable to foreign pressures. Reasonably full employment is required. Inflation and recessions produce almost intolerable strains, given the nature of the social order. Considerable damage might conceivably be done both from within and without. Subversive activities—strikes and sabotage—applied at key points might paralyze production, as tugboat, coal, railroad, and automobile strikes have amply demonstrated. Such strategic materials as tin from Bolivia or bauxite from the Guianas conceivably might be cut off. A disorganization of the world's grain market could cause hardships among large sections of our agricultural population. Control of foreign trade abroad could cut off markets for American exports which would in turn have an effect on other purely domestic business. The general spread of economic chaos in the world would certainly contribute to inflation and recession in the United States.

A long-term diversion of economic resources to war production would certainly influence the nature of consumption, introduce new inflationary pressures, and, unless well managed, might create political problems. Overemphasis on arms and vast expenditures on maintenance rather than on development would waste national resources on a scale which can be ill afforded. Much depends on the success with which the American people are able to maintain a reasonably balanced, expanding, and adaptable economy. Weaker enemies, without putting a foot inside the boundaries of the United States, could make this task infinitely more difficult by imposing tensions and problems on us which would drain our economic strength.

the political strengths and weaknesses of the United States

Thus far the obvious elements of power, the economic and the military, have been discussed. Beyond purely economic or military techniques, though these are foundation stones, are those broadly classed as political. To borrow a worn phrase from Dale Carnegie, political power rests upon the ability of the United States to "win friends and influence people" internationally. Partly this is a matter of ideas, prestige, and moral persuasion. America has some objectives and needs which for a number of reasons cannot be attained solely by economic or military means.

It will suffice if several general points indicating the political strengths and weaknesses of the United States in the present world situation—factors which add to or detract from our ability to persuade others either by example or by diplomatic pressure—are mentioned. One source of strength is American internal stability. Despite crises and economic ups and downs it is probably true that over the past twenty-five years, American society has been less unstable than any other major society. This stability has been accompanied by obvious productive achievements which have made possible an unparalleled standard of living. Neither of the two great wars produced the direct effects on everyday living in the United States that were produced in England, Europe, the Mediterranean, and large areas of the Far East. To a world in which mere existence has become a desperate and jaded business, America appears to have fabulous wealth and strength. That America has been richly endowed by nature and that its relative achievements have not been entirely due to inherent virtues are irrelevant. The point is that if the appearance of success, certainty, and vigor constitutes one of the qualities of leadership, America has a potential, if only partially realized, source of political strength.

Whether the United States can or will ultimately use all its available means and techniques is open to question. The fact that it has the material resources to support a wider range of foreign policy techniques than any other nation is of enormous political significance. For example, it is only the United States which can at the moment supply the technological skills and capital necessary for the industrialization of backward areas.

A nation's political strength also lies in its capacity to attract allies for both peacetime and wartime objectives. During the years 1945 to 1949 the United States showed considerable ability to win support for its views on major policy matters among the middle-sized and small states of the world. There are several causes for this. The great military and economic power of the country acted as a magnet. In an age of uncertain peace, nations incapable of completely defending themselves must look for support where they can qualify for it without losing more freedom than it is worth. In its United Nations policy, the United States has made a deliberate effort to throw its weight behind the causes of smaller powers—Iran, Syria, Lebanon, and Greece. The American tactic of building majority support in a manner calculated to provide reasonable justice and security for all states in the United Nations has undoubtedly enhanced our political attractiveness.

It is of immense importance that the United States came to a position of international leadership with a relatively clean record of international dealings. America has had no traditional enemies and is not prominently marked by the world as an exploiter of humanity. Not that America has made no mistakes, made no "manifest destiny" claims, or made no attempts to let its power weigh too heavily in its foreign relations (particularly with Latin American countries until 1930). Yet America had no grand imperialistic aims far beyond its frontiers. If largely an unknown quantity, it has been known at least as a well-meaning country whose word could be largely trusted. The other countries with international influence after World War I—particularly Russia and Great Britain—had extended their rule to various parts of the world at one time or another, with the result that distrust and hostility arose against them. The case is not black or white, but America's relative lack of an unfortunate diplomatic past is a factor of consequence. In some areas, as in the Near East and in China, the United States had in 1945 a substantial reservoir of good will.

Finally, the political power position of the United States has been given support by the blunders of the Soviet Union. It appears clear that in many of the United Nations agencies Great Britain and the United States have been thrown together by the persistent perverseness of Soviet diplomacy when they might otherwise not have had a common interest. The unreasonable nature of some Soviet charges and the grossness of some Soviet techniques have helped to create useful political influence for the United States. Even nations like Australia and Belgium, anxious to play the role of mediator, have on occasion been forced to the American side in exasperation or fear.

The weaknesses of the American political power position are just as important as its strengths. First might be mentioned uncertainty concerning American aims and intentions. This is more a general feeling than anything else and involves several factors. It is apparently still a suspicion in some quarters that the United States may one day withdraw from its present degree of participation and leadership in world affairs, reverting to some form of isolationism. American power is not always trusted, not so much because of possible aspirations to conquest and dominion, but because of doubts as to whether it will be used wisely. Many foreign statesmen have noted ruefully that despite great technological skills and great material power, the American government has not always shown an awareness of the limitations of these things, an awareness of the more subtle aspects of human relations. The chasm of fear and distrust between the United States and the Soviet Union causes fear among two groups of nations: those who think America will blunder into war, and those who are afraid that America may soften its "containment" policy. American strength, good health, and prosperity are resented because they are viewed through the eyes of people short of food and fuel, through the eyes of governments who wonder if the price of American aid means going along with American views with which they disagree or which they resent. There seems little doubt that Communist propaganda, especially in Europe, has helped some to believe in the imperialistic nature of the present American foreign policy.

Fundamentally, all this would seem to result from a failure to state American aims clearly, from a failure properly to coordinate word and deed, from inexperience, and from having to make too many adjustments in a short time. In the period after World War II the meager talents and experience America brought to its new problems were stretched thin. By-passing the United Nations with a program of $300 million aid to Greece and Turkey in March, 1947 (the Truman Doctrine) is a case in point. The political position has been further embarrassed by tacit approval given to such regimes as Franco's Spain and Peron's Argentina, although the United States is on record as unalterably opposed to many of their methods. One reason for this tolerant attitude is an unwillingness to sacrifice possible military associates or alienate areas of strategic importance. Hence while military strategy logically dictates a certain policy, the American political position is weakened because of the appearance of inconsistency.

coalition warfare and its aftermath

No proper understanding of the new conditions underlying American foreign policy is possible without the realization that the United States fought a war in alliance with nations—chiefly France, Great Britain, China, and the Soviet Union—whose war aims were not identical. True, they all wanted the military defeat of the enemy. But military defeat is more than an end in itself. It is a means to an end, namely the political conditions to follow victory. The declarations embodying the war and peace aims of the victorious allies in World War II —the Atlantic Charter (1941), the United Nations Declaration (1942), the Moscow Declaration (1943), and the Crimea Declaration (1944)—were all *general* in their language. It was almost inevitable that when the time came to implement these agreed aspirations, disagreements would arise. There were disagreements over the meaning of words. There were disagreements over how to carry out peace aims in concrete situations. And there were disagreements over how changed conditions were to affect earlier intentions. War and peace aims proposed under one set of circumstances had to be carried out under another. Germany and Japan were defeated. Out of the defeat arose two giants, America and Russia, who soon became very suspicious of one another. Assumptions made by the policy makers of the Allies at the beginning of the conflict turned out to be largely false, partly because war changes the world in which it is fought and breeds its own special problems.

A gigantic military campaign which covered almost the entire continent of Europe, the Mediterranean, the Middle East, and the Far East, which brought the movement of alien armies over local communities, and which shattered social life everywhere was bound to create conditions which would be politically significant once peace was restored. The war ended with Russian troops in complete control of all eastern Europe (except Austria and Greece) and part of the Far East, Manchuria. Western troops controlled North Africa, Greece, Italy, Japan, the insular Pacific, and western Europe including part of Germany. In view of the fact that no formal peace treaty yet embraces most of these territories, the distribution of military forces on the last day of the war was of immense importance. It provided the basis of a new power situation which could have been altered only if the original lines of attack had been different or if a formal peace agreement had resulted in troop withdrawal.

A further complication is the fact that the war had an unequal effect upon the different allies. The Russians endured a more severe physical punishment. They suffered a costly land invasion from the West for the third time within the memory of many. Russia and America were bound to take different views of the postwar situation in Europe. To Russia, the defeat of Germany signified an opportunity to strike a blow for future security. There is always a tendency after coalition victories for the members to take individual measures once the common effort has succeeded, especially if the coalition is formed primarily by the accident of having been attacked by the same enemy.

The United Nations was established and began functioning before the war really ended and before the new power situation could be formally recognized by treaty. As a result, nearly every practical issue which confronted the new organization after 1945 was characterized by a direct or an indirect maneuvering for position among the victorious nations. Since the United Nations Organization was not originally designed to handle the problem of peacemaking after World

War II, every question arising from the ending of the war (such as the issue of the blockade of Berlin by the Russians) which was taken under consideration by the organization in some respect hindered the task of building a new world order. Furthermore, the failure to make formal peace also affected the occupation of the former enemy states of Germany and Japan. Instead of being a common effort of the victors to carry out the disarmament and rehabilitation of the defeated nations in terms of agreed aims, occupation tended steadily to become both a means of achieving individual national aims and an opportunity to fit the former enemies into the distrust and power struggle among the Allies. The point is that occupation policies for Germany and Japan would have been quite different had there been general agreement between Russia and the Western nations.

From the standpoint of the United States, occupation has turned out to be of longer duration and more expensive than was contemplated. More important, one of the new conditions underlying American foreign policy is the extent to which America has been forced to become involved in the domestic politics of occupied countries. This development has brought with it some of the most troublesome problems American statesmen have had to face. For example, should occupation policy aim at general stability or should extensive political and social reforms, possibly accompanied by disorders of various kinds, be undertaken? If these two aims are to be compromised, what relative weight should be attached to each? Again, should Japan be strengthened militarily as a buttress against Communist China and the Soviet Union in the Far East? If so, what are the risks of the rebirth of the very aggressiveness which involved the United States in war with Japan? Occupation, therefore, especially in view of the Russian-American conflict, is not just a matter of policing a nation while it goes about its business. It is an exercise in government, in the enforcement of certain crucial decisions by military and political force. For such a task America was badly prepared. The United States had had little previous experience and was by tradition unsympathetic to the activities required for ruling others. Mistakes were inevitable, and it was not unnatural that American occupation forces at times appeared to vacillate between the role of the naïve candy-bearing liberator and the role of the conqueror who brings with him his own habits which belie his official pronouncements and often confuse or irritate the local populace. In the early period of occupation, policy was further handicapped by the desire for a quick return of the regular draft army, with subsequent replacement by younger, more inexperienced troops. Successful occupation requires special skills, training, patience, single-mindedness of purpose. It also requires understanding of the culture, institutions, and behavior of the defeated enemy. On top of it all, the United States was faced with the task of rebuilding crumbled economies in Germany and Japan, as well as repairing war-imposed damages to the social systems in both countries. The way in which the United States adjusted to these difficulties has left its imprint on the attitudes the Japanese and western Germans have toward the American people and their foreign policy.

the international environment in which American foreign policy must operate

Nothing could be more basic to an understanding of the new factors which condition the operation of American foreign policy than some awareness of the major social forces and situations prevailing outside the United States—particularly in critical areas such as western Europe, the Middle East, the Far East, and Latin America. Most of the world's population is living through a period of social change.

This is an age of dynamic social forces. War and technological developments have altered ways of living. Outmoded institutions and intolerable living conditions are being rebelled against. New loyalties and beliefs, or, in some cases, no loyalties or beliefs at all, are replacing old ones. Social habits which kept the lives of men stable and, on the whole, nonviolent for most of the previous century are no longer controlling. A quick glance around the world in 1951 revealed open warfare or civil disorders in Greece, Palestine, India, Malaya, Indonesia, South Africa, Indo-China, Korea, and China. Western Europe, Germany, Italy, and Japan were somewhat quiescent but could hardly be regarded as fundamentally stable. All these areas—key areas in the sense of being geographically and strategically between the United States and the Soviet Union and also in the sense of being torn between two rival systems—have certain conditions in common. In nearly all of them, the populations are large, growing larger, and very poor. By far the most numerous class is the peasant–small farmer group unable to eke out more than a bare living. This class does not own the land it tills; consequently there is an animosity between landowners and peasants. In few of these areas has industrialization proceeded far enough to absorb the growing population in productive labor. There is no democratic tradition. Political institutions are old and no longer operate effectively. Rule is by class minority—a small clique which clings to power by force, by exploitation, by the apathy and weakness of the masses, and by aid from abroad. Economic unbalance and an uncertain social structure are the rule. Stability, needed reforms, and economic reconstruction are extremely difficult to attain and appear to be many years away. In one degree or another these areas are moving from feudalism to some form of socialism. Because of the absence of a sizable, free, and effective middle class and large capital resources, the transition would seem to be feasible only through an extension of government control. Greece, for example, into which millions of American dollars have been poured since 1947 is a country where the activities of left-wing and right-wing armed bands, the disorganization of the population, and the fall of one government after another are related to the lack of land, houses, and jobs among the masses.

Such developments must be accepted as among the facts of international life in the mid-twentieth century. The rise of the Chinese peasant to political awareness and power, the decline of the Chinese family system, and increasing overpopulation in China are all related to the question of what American policy toward that country should be and can be. Changes in the relationship between ruler and ruled in the in-between world will continue because of the irresistible forces of social change. Two problems result. One problem is what American foreign policy should be toward social revolution. Can the United States draw a distinction between Soviet-inspired communist movements and the local social revolution which the former tries to exploit? The way any society governs itself is the result of a cluster of factors: its historical experience, its economic organization, its social values, its ideas, its adaptation to local needs. Can or should the United States be tolerant of the development of "socialization" even though it runs counter to the American view of what is appropriate? Will the United States be able to pick its true friends out of the shifting power struggle or will it support those who stand to lose by political changes on the ground that they are also against communism?

The second problem concerns the potential conflict between a desirable policy toward social change in, say, Greece and strategic interests there. Instability, which usually accompanies political realignment, may make it more difficult to prevent a strengthening of local communist forces or it may expose Greek frontiers to encroachments from Greece's Soviet-guided neighbors. On the other hand, to "sit on the lid" of social change, so to speak, may require an increase in military and monetary aid to Greece and may result in the latter being less and less effective as time goes by.

ideology and foreign policy

Another factor which complicates and conditions the position of the United States in the world is the increasingly significant role of ideas in foreign relations. By this time it is clear that a crucial element in the Russian-American conflict stems from the difference in political, economic, and social beliefs which influence and guide the international conduct of the two nations. Ideological cleavages are by no means new, but it is probably true that today they are more serious because they are a cause of international tension. Earlier ideological conflicts —the Protestant Reformation or the attempt to defend monarchy by the Holy Alliance—occurred when the most powerful nations were at least united by Christian beliefs, and they were primarily struggles between ruling groups and governments, not struggles between great masses of people. They appear to have been political conflicts over power and empire. Today such struggles directly affect and stimulate whole populations. Political issues now have a broad social and economic base. As the masses have increased their political power, their beliefs and attitudes have become more important. The attitude of men toward the social situation in which they live is important because group organization and mass communications have made possible and necessary the recognition of different economic and social interests. Appeals can be made to these interests. Technology and the unequal distribution of the fruits of labor have tended to create differences and dissatisfactions.

But modern ideologies are more than emotional appeals to real or alleged interests. They are embodied in and supported by national power. A totalitarian state can be held together both by an appeal to national solidarity and by some kinds of class interest. One consequence of this is that an ideology is not simply a disembodied set of ideas floating around as intellectual currency. It is a program of social and political action backed by the power of one nation or group of nations. One nation is pitted against another not only because of all the reasons which set group against group—conflicts of interest, and the like— but because the peculiar form of economic and social organization of one is a menace to the other.

Ideologies are a weapon of international politics. Foreign policy objectives may be specific or general. Russia directs a fairly specific appeal to those who will help her foster the cause of world proletarian revolution. The United States, insofar as it uses definite ideological techniques, tries to build maximum good will abroad. An active national ideology also serves to mobilize a society beforehand against real or imagined external enemies. There is no better way to curb dissent then to stress a threat by outside groups to domestic institutions and safety. The concentration in the United States on the "American way" as one of the stakes in World War II suggests that ideological appeals may also materialize after a threat emerges.

Another purpose of ideological techniques is to weaken potential enemies by sowing dissent internally or trying to drive a wedge between allies. Under modern conditions, making war or the undertaking of effective political action in time of crisis (especially in democratic nations) requires a high degree of cooperation and morale, a solid agreement that the group's beliefs and ways of doing things are worth dying for if necessary. An ideological fifth column—highly organized local minorities who respond favorably to beliefs propounded by a government other than the one under which they dwell—can be an efficient dissolver of morale. The German Nazis skillfully and successfully split French opinion before, during, and after the fall of France in 1940, a fact which helped make it impossible for the French nation to see and to pursue effectively its national interest.

Ideas are more than weapons of foreign policy. They are, as indicated, a

prolific source of national conflict. They are at once the cause of fear and distrust and a reason why states commit themselves to policies based upon an erroneous appraisal of the policies of other states. The United States suspects
Russian actions because of their professed revolutionary, communistic designs,
and there are good grounds for doing so. However, such actions may also be
misinterpreted because they are viewed in terms of American values and beliefs.
Similarly, American actions may be misinterpreted by the Soviet Union because
Soviet leaders interpret the world in terms of a particular set of ideas and beliefs.
At any rate, it appears clear that the Russian-American impasse consists in part
of a mutual distrust of ideas. Neither feels it could live in a world dominated by
the other's system of political and social thought. Basically this would seem to
indicate that neither is willing to entrust its international interests to a political
process substantially different from the process which serves it well at home.
From the point of view of Russia, the spread of the Western democratic ideology,
with its emphasis on individual rights, representation, multiparty practice, and
majority rule, would not only violate Soviet beliefs about how politics should
operate but would open the door to anti-Russian policies and to antiproletarian
activities by the "decadent" bourgeoisie in countries dominated by this ideology.
On the other hand, the spread of the Moscow brand of communist governmental
technique, with its emphasis on one party, minority rule, unchallenged power
of officials, and socialized economic life, would confront the United States with
totalitarian regimes on every side whose appetites for further political encroachment would be expected to be insatiable.

the impact of technology

Technology is another basic factor underlying American foreign policy in the
new international situation. It is an overworked truism to say that technology
has knit the world together. There are other important considerations. Scientific
progress has weakened traditional sea power, opened up new elements of sea
power, increased the mobility of land troops, infused new vitality into air power,
and made available atomic bombs, guided missiles, germicidal and other weapons. The changed power situation (described above) and technology have given
the United States a new geographical position. Land masses have been rearranged
by the airplane, and now the Arctic and Antarctic are areas of strategic importance. They are bases which must not fall into the hands of a possible enemy.
America can no longer rely on one major military arm as she did for many years
on her navy. There is a new time factor: *potential* power is not sufficient. Experts
are agreed that if there is another Pearl Harbor no breathing spell will follow it.
Therefore it is necessary that the United States rest its military strength on a
core of what Hanson Baldwin, military editor of the New York *Times*, calls

"readiness potential" [3]—an offensive striking power ready for action at a moment's notice.

The implications of these propositions affect foreign policy. Complete military security is impossible. Only relative security is feasible. This means an element of calculated risk has been introduced. Unless scientific progress ceases entirely, the development of new weapons will continue to change military tactics and strategy. The face of war will be altered in the laboratory. Since war is not an end in itself but a means to an end, the effect of new inventions on the length and outcome of war is important. It may well be that at a time when technology and political tension have focused attention on military planning and techniques, the use of the new weapons has become more and more costly. If military security is only relative, if immediate readiness is necessary, if new time-space-power factors have been created, and if military strength is dependent on a totality of the ingredients comprising the over-all position of the United States, then coordination and adaptation must become the order of the day.

Planning is required. To some extent the totality of war must be preserved in peacetime. In part this is decreed by technology since the nature of the American military machine is not such that it can be assembled overnight. Furthermore, security planning must take place in terms of indefinite conditions. No one can be entirely certain what commitment our military establishment will be forced ultimately to undertake. In the meantime, supplies of strategic materials must be guaranteed, advance bases must be secured, research in new weapons must be financed and guided, and some thought must be given to civilian protection against scientific warfare which may be brought to American shores. These necessities involve more than military decisions. They have political implications because they affect our relations with the rest of the world.

These considerations can be summarized and pointed up in the following way. The United Nations at the moment cannot prevent war between the two great powers. There is no international agency which can guarantee security. One of the factors influencing foreign policy is the necessity for the United States to rely on self-help and the help of potential allies insofar as security must rest upon military strength. Technology not only decrees military planning but imposes a certain condition on military planning: the relationship between kinds of armed forces and the relationship between armed forces and the tasks which they must perform must be explored. Once the appropriate nature of an armed force is determined, it must be kept in constant readiness. Two questions emerge: Can the United States pursue the kind of military policy which

---

[3] Hanson Baldwin, *The Price of Power* (New York: Harper & Brothers, 1948), Chap. 16.

technology necessitates without costly pressures on her domestic institutions? Assuming that military strength is *one* of the important elements in diplomatic effectiveness and in minimizing the possibilities of aggression against America, can that strength be maintained without yielding to the very forces which we are trying to resist? The monetary burden of a technological military establishment is one aspect: How much of a drain can the economy stand? There is a related question: Will our devotion to the new weapons symbolized by the atomic bomb actually interfere with the employment of other techniques in alleviating the present crisis? Can military techniques (preparedness) be operated simultaneously with other techniques (economic or political) under modern technological conditions?

the nature of the transition affecting American foreign policy

It is difficult to exaggerate the revolution through which American foreign policy is passing. In some areas—western Europe and the Middle East—American participation is new; interests have to be carefully defined and proper means chosen. In other areas—China and the whole Far East—the presence of the United States is not new; but old policies must be revised and fresh appraisals of our position made. Other adjustments include membership in the United Nations, Russian-American tension, and problems directly related to the last war. Moreover, change has become an independent causal factor in itself, for the great number and variety of problems have heavily taxed the policy-making resources of the nation.

No more impressive proof of this can be offered than to list briefly the foreign policy problems facing Congress and the administration in early 1949. All of them, of course, revolved about the "cold war" against the Soviet Union, the policy of "containing" Russian national power and Soviet communism within its current frontiers and area of influence: (1) a $15 billion military budget; (2) $5 billion needed for the second year of the Marshall Plan; (3) the opportunity to join the new International Trade Organization; (4) the fate of the fourteen-year-old Reciprocal Trade Program, center of the American government's liberal commercial policy; (5) the probable need for more military aid to Greece, where the internal situation seemed to be growing less and less stable; (6) a proposed military alliance—involving military lend-lease—binding the United States, Great Britain, France, Belgium, the Netherlands, and Luxembourg; (7) a costly air lift into Berlin ($350,000 a day); (8) the problem —and how to get out of it without losing face—of organizing western Germany if no agreement on all of Germany was forthcoming; (9) the problem of whether to establish normal diplomatic relations with Franco's Spain—a policy offensive to France and Great Britain but favored by some military leaders; (10) the Communist victory in China; (11) the lack of a peace treaty for

Japan and the implementation of a new policy of not liquidating Japan's industrial monopolies; (12) a wave of revolutions in Latin America, particularly in Costa Rica, which tested the Rio Pact of 1947; and (13) the problem of how to bring to an end the fighting between Israel and the Arab world in Palestine and what course to follow toward the new state.

Several conclusions are indicated. First, the major lines of American foreign policy are global. Second, most problems involve conflict with Russia. Third, policy decisions are not required solely in Washington, but in Germany, in Japan, at United Nations headquarters, and in meetings of foreign ministers. Fourth, all these problems are interrelated. None can be approached without considering the others. To a certain extent, the necessity for establishing priorities is inherent in them all.

Another factor is the rapidity with which these issues are presented to American policy makers for action. The Palestine crisis unfolded so quickly from November 29, 1947, to March, 1948, that a kind of hasty, fumbling "holding action" had to be devised until the situation could be clarified. The United States suffered a blow in prestige when it felt it necessary to turn its back on a resolution to partition Palestine between the Jews and Arabs passed by the General Assembly of the United Nations on November 29, 1947, after taking the lead in pressing for its adoption. Under the circumstances it is difficult if not impossible for key policy makers to have a complete grasp of all questions. On paper the list of problems looks like an orderly program of things requiring attention. In practice, various issues have to be juggled simultaneously by officials who can not be everywhere—before congressional committees, talking to the British ambassador, attending sessions of the United Nations, or briefing the President.

Withal, American foreign policy is becoming positive and anticipatory. Policy is gradually being planned and the required studies are being made. America has declared it will use its power. The reorientation of American policy toward planned security—meaning not only relative safety from attack but the preservation of a world environment most conducive to the advancement of American interests—is not confined to military planning. Through the United Nations and by unilateral action the United States is trying to internationalize the prevention of aggression, is refusing to withdraw from the liquidation of a great conflict as it did once before, is willing to stand guard over former enemies for many years if necessary, is leading the campaign to remove economic causes of conflict and to rebuild a stable world economy, is trying to encourage the growth of free political institutions. American policy is becoming positive in the sense that a conscious effort is being made to mobilize resources behind objectives in a world in which nearly everything of importance is important to America.

bibliographic note

A brief, highly suggestive statement of the impact of the present international environment on American foreign policy problems can be found in the first two chapters of G. A. Almond, *The American People and Foreign Policy* (New York: Harcourt, Brace and Company, 1950). *The Price of Power* (New York: Harper & Brothers, 1948), by Hanson Baldwin, military analyst of the New York *Times*, is an adequate, though somewhat dated, analysis of the economic, political, and military power of the United States and the new strategic position imposed by technology and the bipolar distribution of power. Chapters 1–4 of Nathaniel Peffer, *America's Place in the World* (New York: The Viking Press, 1945), constitute an excellent long essay on how America lost its immunity from world politics and what kinds of choices confronted her after World War II. A brief examination of the present world power pattern and the factors which shape it is to be found in Joseph Roucek and associates, *Introduction to Political Science* (New York: Thomas Y. Crowell Company, 1950), Chap. 21. S. F. Bemis, an outstanding diplomatic historian, discusses the United States and the balance of power in historical perspective in "The Shifting Strategy of American Defense and Diplomacy," *Virginia Quarterly Review*, XXIV (July, 1948), 321–325. W. G. Carleton discusses the role of ideology in foreign policy in "Ideology or Balance of Power," *The Yale Review*, XXXVI, No. 4 (June, 1947), 590–602. Two thought-provoking articles by Raymond Fosdick, "We are Living in Two Centuries," *New York Times Magazine*, November 24, 1946, and "We Must Not Be Afraid of Change," *New York Times Magazine*, April 3, 1949, explore the effects of the discrepancy between eighteenth-century thinking and twentieth-century reality and of social change on international politics and foreign policy. A very useful analysis of some implications of the ideological conflict between Russia and America is contained in G. T. Robinson, "The Ideological Combat," *Foreign Affairs*, XXVII (July, 1949), 525–539.

the role of the President and Congress in foreign affairs

*I*N THE two previous chapters, a brief analysis was made of some of the more important general factors which currently influence the making of foreign policy decisions. Attention will now be focused on the policy-making process itself—the agencies and practices by which the American people decide their course in world affairs. Certain aspects of American government, discussed more comprehensively elsewhere in this volume, will be analyzed in terms of their particular application to foreign policy. Some of the agencies and practices which comprise the total foreign-policy-making process are devoted exclusively to foreign policy issues, for example, the Department of State. Others have a dual role in the sense that the same agency deals with both domestic and foreign policy issues. It has been suggested that something of a revolution has taken place with respect to the role of the United States in the world and with respect to the role of foreign policy in national affairs. American political institutions have a new and different set of burdens. Therefore a significant question should be kept in mind: Are procedures and processes which serve tolerably well to evolve and administer domestic policy adequate and appropriate for new problems and responsibilities in foreign policy?

the Constitution and foreign affairs

the written Constitution

On the whole the constitutional provisions regarding foreign affairs are rather ill-defined. The most important ones referring to foreign policy or relations may be listed briefly: (1) the President appoints (with the consent of the Senate) ambassadors, ministers, consuls; the President alone receives diplomatic representatives from abroad; (2) the President negotiates treaties which must be approved by two thirds of the Senate; (3) the President is commander in chief of the armed forces, which must be financed by Congress every two years; (4)

Congress has the power to declare war, pass uniform naturalization laws, control foreign trade and immigration; (5) no money can be expended except that made available by "lawful appropriation"—action by both houses and signature by the President; (6) treaties are part of the supreme law of the land; (7) the individual states *cannot* declare war, make treaties, enter alliances or confederations, maintain troops, or levy import or export duties except by permission of Congress; (8) foreign ambassadors and public ministers are subject to the original jurisdiction of the Supreme Court; (9) no member of Congress can hold office under the United States. It will be noted that in addition to being rather scant, these provisions reflect the restricted nature of foreign relations in the early days of the republic, namely matters of war, peace, and trade.

custom, legislation, and judicial interpretation

Clearly the imposing structure of the foreign relations power as it has grown through the years has had more underpinning than that provided by the written Constitution. Congressional statutes, custom and usage, and judicial interpretation have all spelled out the above provisions. Thus, usage has decreed that Congress can, if it wishes, refuse to pass supplementary legislation for a treaty despite the fact that the "supreme law of the land" proviso would seem to make treaties self-operating. Again, presidential agents and executive agreements are not directly sanctioned in the written Constitution. Originally it was intended that the "advice and consent" of the Senate in the treaty-making process should reflect the late eighteenth-century practice of genuine collaboration between a small upper chamber and the executive. In practice, of course, nothing of the kind has developed, the actual drafting of a treaty being solely in the President's hands. Custom and Supreme Court decisions have combined to make the President a towering figure in respect to foreign relations.

the foreign relations power of the federal government

Power to conduct foreign relations (using the term in the broadest sense) is centralized in the federal government. The treaty power is an express power, and if a treaty is valid, federal action to implement it can be justified under the necessary and proper clause.[1] State laws and state action give way before a treaty or other federal action with respect to foreign affairs. Indeed it seems to be true that the federal power, if embodied in a legitimate international agreement, can reach into the area covered by the powers reserved to the states under the Tenth Amendment. Furthermore, the foreign relations power stems not only from the Constitution, which lays down certain conditions for its exercise, but also inheres in the United States as a sovereign nation.[2] It is highly significant

---

[1] *Missouri v. Holland*, 252 U.S. 416 (1920).

[2] *U.S. v. Curtiss-Wright Export Corp. et al.*, 299 U.S. 304 (1936); *The Chinese Exclusion Cases*, 130 U.S. 581 (1889).

that the foreign relations power and the domestic power under the Constitution are quite different. Congress and the President, together or separately, can do things in the field of foreign policy which they cannot do in the field of domestic legislation. Private rights can be taken away without the due process ordinarily guaranteed by the Constitution. Thus some American citizens were denied claims against the Russian Insurance Company as a result of the 1942 decision in *United States* v. *Pink*.[3] Civil rights can be minimized or denied by government operations abroad.

the separation of powers and the foreign relations power

The separation of powers, a fundamental characteristic of our political system, has a profound effect on the formulation of foreign policy. Cooperation between the President and Congress is necessary for foreign policy appropriations, war making, treaties, and diplomatic appointments. A few words in the Constitution produce the thorny problem of how to assure proper coordination of presidential and congressional power so that policy making does not break down completely or limp badly. Congress may refuse to appropriate funds, may refuse sanction for appointments and, according to the Supreme Court, may pass statutes which override previous treaties.[4] At the same time, it has been generally decided that policy questions are for the political (nonjudicial) branch of the government to settle, and that the President and the Congress working together can do almost anything.[5] As long as each of these two branches of the federal government is within its rightful constitutional functions, powers to regulate foreign affairs may be delegated in legislation and treaties without limit on the type of power granted. This is again a departure from the practice in purely domestic legislation, where the type of power granted as well as the method of delegation is subject to close check by the courts.

some limitations on the foreign relations power

There are checks on the federal power to regulate foreign affairs. No treaty can amend the Constitution. Neither can the character of the American governmental system be changed through an international agreement. Presumably the balance of power established in the Constitution cannot be modified. Correct as these points are, two facts must be remembered. No treaty or important act of the President concerning foreign relations has ever been declared unconstitutional. The most effective checks on the federal power have been political not legal. The several states do not have substantial rights against the federal foreign relations power, but for political reasons (expressed particularly in the Senate) caution

[3] *United States* v. *Pink*, 315 U.S. 203 (1942).
[4] *The Chinese Exclusion* cases.
[5] It seems to be generally agreed that this is the meaning of the Supreme Court's decision in *United States* v. *Curtiss-Wright Export Corp.*

is exercised in pushing too far into the "police powers" controlled by the states. Indirectly the states can embarrass the nation's foreign policy by mishandling minority problems. Examples are the treatment of the Mexicans in the Southwest, the Negro in the South, and the Orientals on the Pacific Coast.

broad nature of the foreign relations power

It is clear that a very broad interpretation has been given the power of the national government to regulate our foreign relations. This is in contrast to the more restricted interpretation affecting domestic matters. In the *Curtiss-Wright* case the Supreme Court declared: "Not only . . . is the federal power over external affairs in origin and essential character different from that over internal affairs, but participation in the exercise of the power is significantly limited." Again, ". . . congressional legislation which is to be made effective through negotiation and inquiry within the international field must often accord to the President a degree of discretion and freedom from statutory restriction which would not be admissible were domestic affairs alone involved." Two assumptions underlie this opinion. One is that a fundamental restriction on the foreign relations power would impair the right of a united people to perform the necessary functions of statehood, a right they have independently of any constitution. The second is that there is no inconsistency between a broad interpretation of the foreign relations aspect of the federal power and a narrower interpretation of the domestic aspect.

It is possible that this doctrine may in the end add to the federal government's power in the domestic sphere. The federal power over foreign affairs is virtually unlimited, and so long as the purpose is legitimate the means can be found. Now when this is joined with the recognition insisted upon in an earlier chapter that there is no real separation between foreign and domestic policy it is clear that via treaties, United Nations agreements, and such policies as the European Recovery Program the way is at least open for necessary actions which might be forbidden were they applicable to the sphere of domestic policy alone. In 1950, the American government spent approximately $23 billion on economic and military means to stop world-wide spread of communism. Continued heavy expenditures for foreign policy purposes may require economic planning in peacetime. It seems safe to predict that, as adjustment to the new international situation becomes more specific and far-reaching, some adversely affected domestic interests will petition the Supreme Court for redress. Unless previous rulings are upset such interests probably cannot expect adequate redress. To repeat, these rulings were made at a time when the foreign relations of the United States were relatively simple and were overshadowed by domestic considerations. The basic changes noted in the two preceding chapters have broadened almost automatically the constitutional power with respect to a vital sphere of government in the United States.

the role of the President

The President is the key figure in the making of foreign policy and in the conduct of foreign relations generally. This statement has to be explored at some length if all the qualifications and subtleties are to be seen clearly. Perhaps it would be well to emphasize the fact that much of what is said here really applies to "the presidency"—the whole executive or administrative branch of the government as it relates to foreign policy. Insofar as this vast structure is organized around the person of the President and insofar as he dominates it, the study of how foreign policy operates in the United States becomes at once more interesting and more difficult. Personality and politics are intertwined.

Institutionally speaking, the presidency is the accumulated result of the mutual impact of constitutional provisions, political necessities, accident, and individual personalities. It is of more than casual interest to note that there is an entire generation in this country whose principal awareness of the office of President centers in the late Franklin D. Roosevelt. So many are the myths which already enshroud his memory, so partisan are the arguments over what he did or did not do that many people have gained an erroneous impression of what the true functions and powers of the President are. The tactics, customs, and conditions which finally produced the present office were evidenced during the first administration of George Washington. If Franklin D. Roosevelt was able to behave as a man of power it was because the traditions of the presidency were well enough formed to enable him to do so.

the powers of the President

The powers of the President, exercised by him directly or by those responsible to him, are imposing.

1.   He alone negotiates treaties. He controls every phase of the treaty process except where the Senate must give two-thirds approval. He can withdraw a treaty from the Senate, and he can refuse to exchange ratifications or proclaim a treaty to which the Senate has given approval. Acting through the State Department, he can denounce a treaty—an act which can have political significance as in the case of the 1911 commercial treaty with Japan which was terminated by the United States in July, 1939.

2.   The President's power to send and receive diplomatic representatives creates an important political weapon: recognition of foreign governments or states. Refusing to recognize a new government is one way the United States has of expressing disapproval. Nonrecognition may go further than that and result in some form of sanction, such as disruption of trade. Actually, recognition is tantamount to saying that a new regime or new state is admitted to the rights and duties shared by other members of the international community. Once this was a purely legal and factual matter. Now the element of approval or disap-

proval has become paramount. The implications of recognizing Russia in 1933 and the new state of Israel in 1948 were far-reaching indeed. In essence it meant the United States was accepting them, would do business with them, and might even help them despite the fact that in each case there had been actions harmful to American interests.

3.   Special statutes confer powers on the President. There are roughly one hundred statutes which give emergency powers to the President and which relate to foreign affairs in one respect or another. For example, the President can prevent the export of arms from the United States under certain conditions. More well-known statutes which confer extensive powers are the Reciprocal Trade Agreements Act (1934), the Bank Conservation Act (1933), the Silver Purchase Act (1934), the Gold Reserve Act (1934), the Commodity Credit Act (1947), and the Greek-Turkish Aid Bill (1947).

4.   The President can declare policy. This means that what the President says about foreign policy is listened to because he is President. In fact, some of our most important policies have been formulated by presidential declarations: Washington's doctrine of "no entangling alliances"; the Monroe Doctrine; the Good-Neighbor policy of Franklin Roosevelt; the Truman Doctrine of 1947. Such declarations may simply codify existing thought and practice, they may constitute "trial balloons," or they may indicate new directions in policy. They may be announced in a message to Congress, in a radio broadcast or public address, in a letter, or in a press conference. They are accepted as official by the nation and the world. By this method a persistent and skillful President can mold public opinion. So sensitive is the line of communication between the President and the public on occasion that even offhand remarks of the former are seized upon and analyzed. Early in 1949 President Truman informally remarked at a private luncheon in Washington that there were "some men in the Kremlin" who wanted to end the conflict between the United States and Russia. These words became headlines immediately, though no one was able to determine precisely what the President meant.

5.   Special agents have become an important presidential device in foreign affairs. Two kinds may be noted. One holds no official position in the federal government. Outstanding examples are Colonel House, who served and influenced Woodrow Wilson during World War I, and Harry Hopkins, who served and influenced Franklin D. Roosevelt during World War II. Men like House and Hopkins have exercised tremendous power. This fact has led to great suspicion and criticism, for, elected or formally approved by no one, they were in a position to alter the destiny of the whole country. Such men also rendered immeasurable service without any real reward, a fact less recognized by the sometimes puzzled public. Special agents of this type are responsible only to the President and are his personal agents. Nonetheless, their activities

become presidential activities and can therefore be held to account. The necessity for personal agents is admirably summed up by Robert E. Sherwood in his brilliant study, *Roosevelt and Hopkins*: "Roosevelt deliberately educated Hopkins in the arts and sciences of politics and of war and then gave him immense powers of decision for no reason other than that he liked him, trusted him, and needed him." [6] The other type of special agent is someone already holding office who is employed on a particular mission. In 1940 Franklin D. Roosevelt sent Under Secretary of State Sumner Welles to Europe to investigate confidentially the possibilities of bringing World War II to a quick conclusion.

Presidential agents can do nearly everything regular diplomats can do: negotiate agreements, talk confidentially with heads of state, collect information, attend conferences, or open diplomatic relations. Often they can do more. The chief significance of the special agent is that he has the status of the regular diplomat but, from the President's point of view, none of the liabilities. Ambassadors and ministers are often political appointees, and for one reason or another the President may wish to circumvent them. Information may be more readily accessible to a purely personal emissary of the chief executive. The special agent can concentrate on one task instead of being burdened with duties which normally confront the head of a mission. The man can be picked for the job, and full effect can be given to the advantages of specialization and flexibility.

6.   Through his position as commander in chief and by authority of several statutes, the President can, within certain limits, use the armed forces of the United States as an instrument of foreign policy. The President cannot declare war and there is a presumption that he ought not deliberately to create a state of war. Short of this the President can take steps which may make it difficult for Congress to avoid a declaration of war. The slavery policy of Abraham Lincoln, the arming of merchant ships by Woodrow Wilson in 1917, and the "shoot on sight" order of Franklin D. Roosevelt in 1941 are examples. Needless to say, acts or policies of the President outside his prerogatives as commander in chief may lead to the same result. The refusal to accede to Japanese demands in November, 1941, probably sealed the issue of war with Japan. As the chief executive the President is responsible for the protection of American lives and property and for carrying out statutes and treaties. On some eighty occasions the President has used armed forces for these purposes. In addition to constitutional responsibilities, the President as head of state can take measures in defense of international law. This point has relevance in connection with the United Nations Charter. On paper at least, the President could on his own responsibility involve the United States in an armed clash in defense of the Charter. From a legal point of view, this would not be war in the sense that there are two parties equally entitled to use force and consequently having

---

[6] Robert E. Sherwood, *Roosevelt and Hopkins* (New York: Harper & Brothers, 1947), p. 1.

legally recognized rights and duties as belligerents. Rather this would be the use of force as a defense or police action authorized by international law.

7. A final power at the disposal of the President is the power to negotiate so-called executive agreements, entered into through presidential action, since 1800. Distinguishing characteristics of these agreements are as follows: the two-thirds approval of the Senate is not necessary; the agreements are just as binding as regular treaties; they cover all the subjects that regular treaties cover; and they can be entered into by the President with or without congressional authorization. The "pure" executive agreement is distinguished from other types of executive agreement in that it does not require formal congressional approval before or after negotiation. To all intents and purposes, and in a legal sense, treaties and executive agreements have the same status in both domestic and international law.[7] The constitutionality of executive agreements rests upon custom and usage and the fact that the treaty power is not exclusive.[8]

Important steps in foreign policy have been taken by executive agreement: purchasing Louisiana; establishing a Permanent Joint Defense Board with Canada; joining the International Labor Organization; trading overage destroyers for bases in 1941; giving up American government property in Panama; and laying some important lines of postwar policy at Yalta (1943), Moscow (1944), and Potsdam (1945). By 1939, out of a total of 2,000 international engagements to which the United States has been party, 1,182 were entered into by executive agreements. Nevertheless, in major decisions of foreign policy, such as peace settlements or joining the United Nations, regular treaty procedure is used.

Executive agreements have, then, become firmly entrenched. As between the two basic types mentioned previously, the choice depends on several factors. Congressional authorization (regular legislative action of both houses) for executive agreements is retained in cases where supplementary legislation is necessary or where Congress has had an historic vested interest: tariffs, immigration, air commerce, extradition, and postal matters. The significance of congressional cooperation lies primarily in the fact that Congress is hardly likely to pass domestic legislation which conflicts with an executive agreement it has already approved. Apart from cases where appropriations or enabling legislation is needed to implement an executive agreement, the President seems limited only by political considerations in what he can do. The Supreme Court has held that so long as the President is within his proper functions, an executive agreement is valid. Until now no satisfactory method of determining whether a subject should be handled by regular treaty procedure, by congressionally authorized executive agreements, or by "pure" executive agreement has been devised.

---

[7] *United States* v. *Belmont*, 301 U.S. 324 (1937) where the phrase "equal dignity" is used.
[8] W. M. McClure, *International Executive Agreements* (New York: Columbia University Press, 1941), pp. 368–370.

sources of the President's power

The extensive powers of the President and his pre-eminent position in foreign affairs rest upon a number of different factors. To begin with, the conduct of foreign relations is an executive function. A single responsible agent is required. In addition, the President has "general executive powers" which stem from the Constitution and which give him the techniques required to carry out his prescribed tasks. Custom and usage have contributed to the growth of presidential powers, especially in the case of special agents and executive agreement. Things are done, tacitly approved, or at least not disapproved, and finally become accepted practice. To this sort of phenomena has been added the authority of Supreme Court decisions. Another source is the fact that in both domestic law and international law the President is the only one who can communicate with foreign governments. The nation must speak with one voice. Executive powers conferred by the Constitution are fortified by the prerogatives which surround the head of the state. The accumulation of information also places the President in a favored position. Diplomatic information and reports are confidential to the chief executive or his assistants. Without such data no agency could handle foreign affairs competently.

Obviously the President is in an ideal position to take the initiative in foreign policy. He is the truly national figure in the federal government. The public looks to him for leadership. He has a poise and a remoteness which appear to raise him above other political figures. He is able to speak out when the occasion demands. He has become the head of an administrative structure which gives him many potent weapons in highly specialized policy making. The essence of presidential leadership in foreign policy is that the chief executive can provide political or emotional certainty, and can be a symbol of unity. Professor Edward S. Corwin of Princeton University has thus described the position of the President: "By virtue of being a single individual and always Johnny-on-the-spot, by virtue of the constantly recurrent pressure of crises that would not admit of delay, by virtue of certain theories of executive power . . . [the] President has come to claim and has often been able to make the claim good, a quite indefinite prerogative in the sphere of foreign relations." [9]

the President's power as distinguished from his influence

There is an important distinction to be made between the President's power and his influence. Not everything the President can accomplish is based on his legal power. As noted, the Supreme Court has recognized the capacity of the President to bring the nation into actual, if not legally recognized, war. Congress has the power to make final peace terms, but decisions of the President acting

---

[9] Edward S. Corwin, *Total War and the Constitution* (New York: Alfred A. Knopf, Inc., 1947), p. 157.

as commander in chief, in effect, give him that power. Now it is also true that the President cannot always exercise his clear legal powers. Power is a subtle thing in this respect. Though it exists on paper, it must be generated and put into effect. In the American political system much can be done if conditions are right; little if they are not. Cooperation and the approval of key persons are required. During the months preceding the presidential election of 1948, when it was thought that President Truman would be overwhelmingly defeated, he was virtually powerless in the field of foreign policy. The real distinction here is between legal power and generated political power.

factors which condition the exercise of presidential power

If presidential powers are not absolutely defined and if the President's ability to get certain things done is not entirely a legal matter, what factors may influence a given situation or a given administration? Crises—foreign and domestic—have been responsible for a steady increase in the area of effective presidential activity. The periods between 1861 and 1867, between 1898 and 1902, between 1914 and 1918, and between 1938 and 1948 were characterized by conditions which required and accommodated strong leadership on the part of the chief executive; they were also punctuated with wars. Indecision is politically and psychologically intolerable in time of crisis. Emergencies justify temporary measures which later become permanent or become a precedent for later repetition. The personality of the President is another factor. Vigorous, imaginative men like Washington, Jefferson, Jackson, Lincoln, Theodore Roosevelt, Woodrow Wilson, and Franklin Roosevelt were able to accomplish much through sheer personal magnetism and the effect they had on the people whose acquiescence was important. On the other hand, Warren Harding seems to have been an attractive but not a strong person. Leadership in foreign policy from 1921 to 1923 was therefore exercised by Senator William E. Borah and Secretary of State Charles Evans Hughes. The view the President takes of his office is important. Presidents Harding, Coolidge, and Hoover, whatever their competence, all (for different reasons probably) took a restricted view of the presidency. Whether because of crisis or because it satisfies a personal ambition, his powers and functions must be broadly conceived if a President is to give full range to the possibilities inherent in his office, especially in view of the fact that there is no complete blueprint of permissible action in the field of foreign policy. One of the observable phenomena in Franklin Roosevelt's four terms was the change in the way he looked at his function as the primary architect of foreign policy: the 1944 version was much broader than the 1933 version. Of utmost significance is the "climate of opinion." Those times when presidential initiative has been most vigorous have usually been times when public opinion either asked for it or would accept it. By and large, a President may lead or follow public opinion, but in any case he dare not be too far from it. Again, the President's policies may be aided or opposed, depending on more narrow political circumstances. A hostile Congress or a hostile Senate may check a President even when public opinion is favorable. Congress may hamper both strong and weak Presidents. The effectiveness of political animosities in checking presidential leadership will depend on what the nature of the policy is. If foreign policy is in a declaratory stage (1937–1944) they matter less. When the time for implementation is reached, the situation is different. Finally, the techniques available to the President are relevant. There is little doubt that new modes of communications have stepped up the immediate participation of the President. For example, the transatlantic telephone conversations between Churchill and Roosevelt after 1940 may yet mark a new era in diplomatic intercourse. Thus a combination of factors will condition the effective exercise of presidential control of foreign relations. Here nonconstitutional limitations are found. They may appear in public apathy, in political opposition in Congress, in a lack of techniques, or in the weaknesses of the man himself. It is to be noted that only some of the factors are within his control.

difficulties and dilemmas of presidential leadership

As remarked elsewhere in this volume, the President is a lonely official and it is therefore natural for him to need and have trusted advisers or agents. The President also must protect himself against misinformation, uncertainty, various pressures and blocks which are thrown up in his way. He has to get his job done despite these handicaps, none of which he can ignore, and some of which he cannot change. He has loyalties he cannot renounce. In him conflicting forces must be resolved. There may be individuals in his own official family who oppose him, but upon whom no direct assault is possible. His advisers may not give him policy recommendations in a form he can use. He may not trust some of the influential people in the State Department. Meanwhile decisions have to be made quickly, and he will be held responsible by the nation as a whole.

The alternatives facing the President in these and other difficulties are fairly clear. He may first try to get Congress and key figures in the government to cooperate with him. This, if possible at all, is often a slow process, and may depend upon conditions beyond the President's immediate control. He may try to anticipate his needs by gaining previous authorization of power. He may use special emissaries. He may create new agencies. Much will depend on the President's immediate advisers—who they are, whether he chose them well, whether he listens to *all* or *some* of them, whether they can "reach" him when it is crucial to do so. Much will depend also on the "instincts" of the President, the subtle awareness of the trends, the needs, the possibilities, and the limits and scope of his position.

Hence there is a problem of leadership embracing control of the elements necessary to formulate and execute a sound foreign policy, and there is a problem of political power, the process of carving needed power from an undefined mass and applying it without its getting beyond necessary control. Viewed in these terms, the President's role in foreign policy implies much more than merely a recitation of powers and functions.

Congress and foreign policy

Until 1940 the direction of foreign affairs was largely dominated by the presidency. His pre-eminent position developed over a period of 150 years. Foreign policy crises usually demonstrated that the office of chief executive had powers and techniques adequate for the problems the nation had to face. On the other hand, the role of Congress in the formulation of foreign policy has changed considerably within the past ten years. Before this time, there was no compelling reason for Congress to develop special capacities for large-scale leadership and activity in the field of foreign policy. Therefore Congress has been undergoing an adjustment to a new position and to new responsibilities. Such an adjustment has highlighted some congressional handicaps which have greatly affected the content of American foreign policy and the process by which it is formulated.

the powers of Congress

At first glance, it would appear that the prescribed constitutional functions of Congress with respect to foreign relations consist primarily of possible negative checks or democratic controls on the President's actions. Congress (the Senate) can reject a treaty or amend it; Congress (again the Senate) may reject appointments; Congress can deny supplementary legislation or appropriations; jurisdiction over war, immigration, and tariffs rests solely with Congress. Congress can delegate power in the latter fields to the chief executive. Clearly Congress can thwart the President, though it cannot act on its own inititative, and it cannot negotiate a treaty or deal with a foreign country. But it would be a mistake to assume that Congress has only negative powers. It has some positive powers which provide an opportunity to influence the substance of policy. Congressmen can use floor debate as a means of gaining support for policy ideas or to embarrass the administration. Investigating committees, such as the Nye Committee (to probe the role of the munitions industry in America's entry into World War I) of the mid-thirties, which generated pacifist sentiment and helped establish a neutrality program designed to insulate America from the warlike trends of international politics, may probe foreign policy questions. Both houses can pass resolutions on international relations and foreign policy. Legally they do not bind the President, but there have been times when the President has had to give them heed.

the Senate and its foreign relations committee

The Senate is the most powerful congressional agency with respect to foreign relations, for not only does it share in the legislation (appropriations) which both houses must approve, but it alone approves treaties (by a two-thirds vote) and presidential appointments. The important treaty power and the intention of the Founding Fathers to create a special role for the Senate in foreign policy have combined to give the upper chamber a unique position. The Senate Foreign Relations Committee is the key committee in this area of public policy. The President and this committee are joined as policy makers. Insofar as foreign policy has been carried out by treaties, the Senate's voice has been influential indeed. Originally the Senate was apparently conceived as a kind of executive council which would work closely and personally with the President, especially in the field of foreign relations. Partly because the Senate did not wish to subject one of its most respected committees to undue executive pressure, close collaboration between the President and the Foreign Relations Committee never developed. In the absence of a clear definition of the Senate's role, the latter has jealously guarded its powers and has steadfastly clung to the notion that it was a coordinate, not a subordinate, agency. On the whole, the Senate has not had sufficient power to enforce its own interpretation of its role. Its actual functions have been, until recently, negative and sometimes obstructionist.

the significance of the chairman

The towering influence of the Foreign Relations Committee has owed much to the stature and ability of its chairmen. Some of the great figures in the Senate have held this post: Sherman, Sumner, Lodge, Borah, Pittman, and Vandenberg. It is not too much to say that in the period 1945–1949, the effectiveness of this committee resulted from the personal effort of Senator Arthur H. Vandenberg. The relationship between the committee and the President or the State Department has varied widely. Some chairmen, like Pittman and Connally, have often acted as administration spokesmen. Some, like Sumner, Lodge, and Borah, have taken a vigorously independent line and have regarded themselves as separate voices in matters of foreign policy. A third variation is seen in the behavior of Senator Vandenberg, who, while maintaining a scrupulous independence of mind on critical questions, was also a most important liaison between Congress on the one hand and the President and Secretary of State on the other.

the work of the Senate foreign relations committee

With respect to treaties, the committee can accept them, modify them by majority vote, prevent their reaching the Senate floor, or report them with no recommendation or nominal approval. The committee's views on a treaty are almost conclusive. In the case of 350 treaties, 90 per cent of the committee's recommendations were accepted. The *Curtiss-Wright* case, cited above, laid down the dictum that only the President can negotiate treaties, but the committee indirectly negotiates through its power to make changes. Some idea of the magnitude of the committee's task under present conditions can be gained from an analysis of its work in the Eightieth Congress. The full committee held sixty-one open-session meetings and ninety-two meetings in executive session; printed records of hearings ran to thirty-seven hundred pages. Hearings were held on the Foreign Assistance Act of 1948, during which time one hundred nongovernmental witnesses appeared before the committee. Through June 20, 1948, seventy-four Senate bills and twenty-five House bills were submitted to the committee. Thirty-one laws were enacted. The total number of nominations handled by the committee was 112—9 for the Department of State, 35 ambassadors and 14 ministers, and 47 appointments to the United Nations agencies. Senator Elbert Thomas served as representative of the United States government at the meetings of the International Labor Organization. Senators Smith, Lodge, Barkley, Hatch, and Hickenlooper served on an investigatory committee which studied the operation of the United States Information Service in Europe.

the Senate and House committee compared

The Senate Foreign Relations Committee is more influential than its House counterpart for reasons which in some cases go beyond the exclusive functions of the former: (1) the Senate has more prestige and is regarded as the traditional guardian of Congress's foreign relations power; (2) outstanding senior party leaders more often dominate the Senate and many serve on its committee, whereas the House Committee on Foreign Affairs usually has not attracted House leaders; (3) the Senate committee has been more independent in its relationship with the executive branch; (4) the Senate committee has more important functions and commands greater respect in its own legislative chamber; (5) proportionately more members of the Senate (25 per cent) serve on its committee, whereas 6 per cent of the House members serve on its Foreign Affairs Committee; (6) the House committee has had to rely heavily on the press for its information; (7) representatives probably have less all-around freedom in policy matters because of the necessity of standing for election every two years; (8) the House committee may have to choose between a critical Senate and a vigorous President; (9) House rules make it more difficult for an individual to aspire to leadership in matters of foreign policy; and (10) the Committee on Foreign Affairs has not been important enough to attract outstanding legislators.

the general position of the House of Representatives

Being a junior partner in one half of a less than equal relationship between President and Congress in foreign relations has bred some apathy and a sense of perfunctory clerical functioning in the House of Representatives. Beginning in 1943, however, the House has demanded, and has been able to assume, a larger

role. The over-all change in the role of Congress has benefited the House relatively more than the Senate. Furthermore, the House has taken an active part
in developing an executive agreement procedure which has circumvented the
regular treaty process. In May, 1945, the proposed Kefauver-Schwabe constitutional amendment to subject treaties to approval by majority of membership of
both houses was debated for two days in the House of Representatives and was
approved by a vote of 288 to 88. The arguments advanced in favor of the resolution emphasized the "half" role of the House and the undesirability of appropriating money for agreements in which the House had no voice; further, the House
helped to declare war, but was barred from helping to make peace. It seems unlikely that the Senate will yield to House pretensions with respect to the
treaty procedure. Circumstances have conspired to give the House the additional
influence it has sporadically requested. But on balance the House is less well
equipped for Congress's new role than the Senate.

types of congressional influence on foreign policy

The following are random examples of types of congressional influence on foreign policy. They will, however, suggest the basis of revived congressional power,
influence, and interest in foreign policy. In March, 1948, the House Ways and
Means Committee, by a vote of 15 to 7, agreed to a resolution on proposed
American membership in the International Trade Organization—a body which
was more or less the brain child of American diplomats and which had a charter
embodying the essential principles of American trade policy. The resolution
took note of the danger that the leadership of the State Department in initiating
the proposal, coupled with prolonged negotiations (February, 1947—January,
1948), might lead to a moral obligation to join, and said further, ". . . any
action . . . prior to the consideration by Congress of the International Trade
Organization shall not, insofar as the Ways and Means Committee of the House
of Representatives is concerned, be construed as a commitment by the United
States. . . ." At about the same time the Appropriations Committee of the House
slashed funds requested for the first year of the Marshall Plan (later restored
by the Senate) for the Foreign Service and for the Voice of America, the
latter an effective means of telling the world about the United States and its aims
abroad. This committee also gratuitously added to the administration budget
requests for special funds for the purpose of sending military aid to China—an
important modification of our China policy which was not then desired by the
State Department.

The Senate Foreign Relations Committee, under the leadership of Arthur
Vandenberg, more or less provided the original impetus for the American offer
to participate in a twenty-five-year demilitarization pact for Germany and Japan,
and for the "get tough with Russia" emphasis which colored our foreign policy
after the early weeks of 1946. Later the committee, again at Senator Vanden-

berg's urging, partially retrieved a diplomatic blunder by writing into the Greek and Turkish Aid Bill (The Truman Doctrine, March, 1947) an amendment which all but gave the United Nations the privilege of requesting cessation of such aid if it was felt to defeat the purposes of that organization.

Over President Truman's known objections, the Senate Foreign Relations Committee in December, 1945, overruled the Democratic Chairman Tom Connally and passed a resolution insisting that 100,000 Jews be admitted to Palestine and that a Jewish state be established there; the resolution had a wide and excellent press coverage. In the spring of 1948, the Rules Committee of the House of Representatives reported out a resolution to the effect that American membership in the World Health Organization should not in any way imply the official adoption of a favorable attitude toward socialized medicine in the United States. Even with some of its influence reduced by special agreement in the Eighty-first Congress, the Rules Committee remains a powerful agency with hitherto no direct contact with foreign affairs, as such. One hundred and twenty-five congressmen visited Europe in the summer of 1947; at firsthand they saw the conditions which necessitated an immediate implementation of Secretary of State Marshall's famous offer to Europe at Harvard in June of that year. It seems clear that this unprecedented, on-the-spot investigation facilitated a favorable vote on the Foreign Assistance Act of 1948.

Approving presidential nominations may appear to be merely routine; in most cases it is. Recently, however, the Senate Foreign Relations Committee, in holding hearings on appointments to high posts in the State Department, has gone beyond ascertaining technical qualifications and has inquired into the nominee's views on policy. When Dean Acheson became Secretary of State in January, 1949, the committee subjected him to very pointed examination and he was forced to explain at length that he had never been "pro-Russian" and that he contemplated making no change from the existing "hard" policy. American policy toward Argentina was criticized in 1946 when the Senate Foreign Relations Committee, approving Spruille Braden as Assistant Secretary of State for Latin America after a bitter hearing, let it be known that it disapproved the attempt to make the Argentine regime conform to hemisphere standards of democratic behavior.

significant effects of the committee system on foreign policy making

Professor Lawrence Chamberlain of Columbia University has concluded: "No other government in the world compares with that of the United States in the importance and power of its legislative committees. In no phase of the government's operation does committee action play a more crucial role than in foreign affairs." [10]

---

[10] L. H. Chamberlain, R. C. Snyder, *American Foreign Policy* (New York: Rinehart and Company, 1948), p. 115.

The effects of the committee system must be indicated briefly: (a) foreign policy, using the term broadly, is discussed bill by bill with no real examination of interrelationships; (b) there is no coordination in the House of Representatives between the Appropriations and Foreign Affairs Committees; (c) minority and negative views are overrepresented; (d) small deficiency subcommittees of the Appropriations Committee with no experience in foreign affairs make important decisions on the basis of a "certified accountant's" approach, a concern for details of expenditure rather than for larger objectives so that round figures tend to replace critical thinking; (e) Congress's attack on foreign policy problems is fragmented among many (in both houses) committees: Ways and Means, Finance, Rules, Armed Services, Appropriations, Banking and Currency, Foreign Relations, Agriculture, Judiciary; (f) there are rivalries between committees in the House and between Senate and House committees; (g) there are rivalries between committee chairmen (even within the same party) exemplified by the disagreement between Representative Taber (House Appropriations Committee) and Senator Vandenberg (Senate Foreign Relations Committee) during the debate over the European Recovery Program.

The Legislative Reorganization Act of 1946 reduced the number of committees and in consequence somewhat increased the amount of work done by subcommittees—a process which further fragments Congress's consideration of foreign policy problems; the Senate Foreign Relations Committee operated with twenty-two subcommittees during the Eightieth Congress. But the La Follette-Monroney Act did provide an expert staff for the Senate Foreign Relations Committee and the work of that committee has been noticeably enhanced thereby.

The results of the foregoing are worth noting. At present the House Committee on Foreign Affairs seems to have been pushed aside in favor of other committees in taking up foreign policy issues. Furthermore, from 1945 to 1947, $16.7 billion was appropriated for foreign aid purposes; at a time when policy toward Russia was stiffening, $1.8 billion went to her or to her satellites. During this period of gigantic appropriations, congressional committees did not undertake a systematic analysis of America's total objectives, total resources, and desirable techniques; yet the decisions of, say, a deficiency subcommittee on appropriations affected both techniques and objectives of American foreign policy. Finally, our legislative process cannot produce full-dress debates on foreign policy such as are staged in Britain's House of Commons; committees do the real legislating, and floor debate is largely for purposes of gracing the record. Two points, however, are significant. One concerns the obvious need for coordination between the Appropriations Committee and the Committee on Foreign Affairs in the House of Representatives. Secondly, Congress's enlarged role, expressed through its traditional methods and organization, offers potential opportunity for the process of policy formation to become sprawling and decentralized.

toward a new role for Congress

Congress's role in foreign policy has not been well defined. Generally speaking, it has played second fiddle to the executive. While carrying on a kind of guerrilla warfare, and while never openly admitting such a state of affairs, Congress has in fact allowed foreign policy operations to go largely by default—either because it had no convenient techniques or because it was badly constituted to share executive functions. Revolts have occurred. Franklin D. Roosevelt felt one of some proportion on the question of presidential control of neutrality policy in the period 1937–1940, a fact which had considerable effect upon the content of policy. Brisk though the rivalry between President and Congress has been, the latter has nearly always aspired to a greater role than it could feasibly fulfill.

Is there a well-defined automatic role for Congress? For some time at least, the answer would seem to be in the negative. Leadership which can direct the peculiar talents of Congress in policy making is spasmodic and can easily be shattered. Congress does not act as an organic whole, with the result that more than one of its component agencies may speak for it. The President still retains the position of initiative; foreign relations are primarily executive in formulation and operation, though increasingly legislative in content. Now more than ever before Congress is confronted by the temptation to entangle itself in details rather than to master broad lines of policy.

There is evidence that Congress is rapidly assuming a much more important role, becoming more of a coordinate equal with the President. Recent examples of joint policy making perhaps portend that Congress may more and more help to decide policy as well as implement it or set its outer limits. Before a new role for Congress can be adequately defined, it must be determined what Congress can do efficiently in foreign relations and what its capacities and incapacities in this specialized branch of policy making are. Congress can provide what may be the only public debate on certain foreign policy issues; it does not always do so, but the opportunity is there. Investigation and hearings may help to correct executive errors; the Vandenberg amendment to the Greek-Turkish Aid Bill (1947) is an example of this. For obvious reasons, congressional subcommittees may be the only force potent enough to prod administrative agencies making and executing foreign policy. Although many of the things said about the Voice of America broadcasts during the budget hearing in 1948 were ill-advised and showed slight comprehension of the issues involved, it seems likely that the end result was, on the whole, a better foreign information program. To paraphrase an old saying about generals and wars, it is probably true that foreign policy is too important to be left to experts alone; in many ways only Congress, despite its handicaps, can blow the crude, fresh air of a different level of public thinking into the channels of expert policy making.

On the other hand, Congress is not too well set up to take a "total" view of an issue. This grows out of the general incapacity of a large body to handle detailed policy making. The present committee system appears to be the heart of congressional disabilities—in fact, the disabilities are the same as they are in the field of domestic legislation, intensified by the lack of experience and information.

the President, Congress, and foreign policy

The enlarged role of Congress and the increase in the number and significance of international agreements to which the United States is a party have highlighted the effect of the constitutional separation of powers upon the formation of foreign policy. Contrary to the situation before World War II, nearly all the major aspects of American foreign policy now require some sort of cooperation between the executive and legislative branches. The always present possibility of deadlock between the two has aroused concern over whether the United States can act promptly and effectively when necessary. This concern has focused on treaties and agreements, but the problem is much broader. Congressional appropriations are as important to foreign policy as agreements or treaties and require action by both houses, plus the signature of the President.

making international agreements

There are several alternate ways in which the United States enters into agreements with other states. One is the regular treaty procedure, including negotiation by the President and approval by two thirds of the Senate. Another consists of a "pure" executive agreement requiring no action by Congress and brought into being solely by presidential action. Yet another is an executive agreement negotiated by the President but requiring some sort of congressional authorization in the form of a statute or a joint resolution. There is no settled practice regarding the appropriateness or desirability of each of these various methods. The choice among them appears to depend on the subject matter to be covered, on whether a congressional power is involved, on whether the House of Representatives has demanded a voice, on how much time is available for debate, or on the extent to which the President can risk congressional disapproval.

the problem of the two-thirds rule

Some students of American political institutions are concerned over the possibility that the two-thirds rule has outlived its usefulness. Others note the apparent contradiction between the greater participation of the House of Representatives in foreign affairs and the exclusive veto of the Senate with respect to formal treaties. Still others feel that the critical issue is the danger that presidential power may be overextended through executive agreements.

American statesmen began to express increasing anxiety after 1943 lest the two-thirds provision in the Constitution again thwart American participation in an international organization as a means of creating durable world peace. The lessons of Woodrow Wilson's defeat on the old League of Nations and the rejection of membership in the World Court in 1935 were recalled and studied. The result was that the United States joined the United Nations in 1945 without substantial obstruction from the two-thirds procedure.

Nevertheless it may be queried whether it is safe or wise to allow significant foreign policy matters to be conditioned by a rule whose original justification has long since disappeared. There appears to be no sound reason to grant a special power to the states of the Union as such. The Senate is no longer a small body and it does not function in close personal collaboration with the President, as intended in 1787. It is a large body, separated from the chief executive by partisanship, custom, and rules of procedure. Instead of preserving secrecy, protecting regional interests, and stimulating continuous respected consultations with the executive branch, the rule has in practice opened the door for minority policy making in the Senate. True, 80 per cent of all treaties have been approved without far-reaching changes, and only sixty treaties have been completely rejected.[11] True also, only twelve treaties failed to gain the requisite two-thirds majority from 1860 to 1933, and of these only two were of great importance. Not the number of treaties rejected, but the effect of possible rejection is significant. Some treaties are never submitted, and unwanted modifications on others are accepted in order to avert failure in the final vote.[12] Moreover, the defeat of the Versailles Treaty probably counterbalances a good many perfunctory approvals of less vital treaties. The point is that there lurks over any treaty the possibility that seventeen votes[13] from states representing only one twelfth of the total population may defeat it. In addition to all this, Senate procedure tends to magnify the influence of the individual senator and to weaken party cohesion.

Evidence suggests that the general public is not unaware of these difficulties. Opinion polls regularly report 60–65 per cent in favor of changing treaty procedure to require a simple majority of both houses of Congress for approval. A constitutional amendment would seem to be the most clear-cut way to avoid some of the dangers mentioned above. The argument for it is that deliberate evasion of the two-thirds rule is undesirable and risky. Yet despite the attempt by the House of Representatives to introduce a constitutional amendment, the Senate Judiciary Committee has refused to report out such a proposal for ac-

---

[11] D. F. Fleming, "The Role of the Senate in Treaty-making," *American Political Science Review*, XXVIII (August, 1934), 583.

[12] Voting on amendments to treaties in the Senate is by simple majority.

[13] Assuming that the two-thirds rule applies to the senators present and that a quorum could be 49, 17 would be one more than one third, enough to defeat a proposed treaty.

tion. It is unlikely, therefore, that any basic change in the Constitution will be forthcoming.

methods of avoiding the difficulties of the two-thirds rule

One way of minimizing the chances of a treaty veto in the Senate is an advance pledge. The Vandenberg Resolution of June 11, 1948, calling on the United States to negotiate regional security pacts within the United Nations, paved the way for the Atlantic Alliance Treaty consummated in 1949. A somewhat different device is illustrated by the so-called Green-Sayre Formula of 1943, which paved the way for American participation in the United Nations Relief and Rehabilitation Administration (UNRRA). In return for being able to suggest textual changes in the proposed executive agreement, the Senate Foreign Relations Committee agreed to a joint resolution of both houses instead of the regular treaty procedure. This result was reached after consultation among the leading members of the Senate committee, Secretary of State Cordell Hull, Assistant Secretary of State Francis Sayre, and the Republican and Democratic leaders of both houses. Another method is illustrated by the passage by Congress of a statute—such as the Reciprocal Trade Agreements Act of 1934—which permits the President to enter into agreements on certain matters.

the problem of collaboration between the President and Congress

The fact that serious deadlocks may develop between the President and Congress creates a special problem in foreign policy making. Successful employment of devices to prevent minority veto of international agreements depends greatly on the general relationship existing at any given time between the two branches of the federal government. But the necessity for close cooperation goes far beyond international agreements. The combined effect of constitutional provisions and the present nature of American foreign policy is to create a situation in which such cooperation is required for all major policies, whether embodied in agreements or not.

The fact that the executive and legislative branches have separate and unique contributions to make to the process of foreign policy formation is sometimes overlooked in the bad feelings which develop. Congress feels that the executive does not know the value of money. The executive view is that Congress approaches policy making primarily in monetary terms. Executive agencies feel that Congress often overrepresents minority opinion and interests. Congress is not always assured that these agencies represent anything but their own bureaucratic viewpoint. Congress resents being consulted after policy is decided. On the executive side, there is resentment of congressional attempts to usurp administrative functions. Congress is sensitive about being deliberately courted simply because it holds the purse strings. Executive officials become impatient because congressional committees have to be coddled and briefed at every turn.

An automatically favorable legislative response to executive leadership in foreign policy might be dangerous indeed. Yet foreign policy decisions sometimes have to be made quickly. A balance must be established between "rubber-stamping" by Congress and weak presidential leadership, between undemocratic action and fatal delays imposed by the use of the checks in the political process.

types of liaison between President and Congress

Personal relations between the president and congressional leaders are only one aspect of liaison. More important, perhaps, is the relationship between the State Department and various congressional committees. Unless the Secretary of State is a respected figure like Cordell Hull or unless an experienced Under Secretary of State devotes himself exclusively to bringing about some meeting of minds between the legislator and the expert, too much may be left to chance.

> Almost any representative of the State Department approaching the brae of the Capitol these days is a hostile object to the average Congressman. The legislator not only identifies him as an agent of the executive branch of the government . . . but as a symbol of all the headaches and frustration involved in foreign affairs today. Nor is that all. The State Department representative, usually a little too well dressed and too well-educated to be popular on the Hill, is often unconsciously treated not as a representative of his own government, but as an advocate of foreign governments.[14]

Several methods for improving the relationship between Congress and the executive agencies which make foreign policy have been suggested. Benjamin Cohen, former counsellor in the State Department, urges that at least one high policy position in the department be filled by a man of wide public and political experience in activities which Congress would respect.[15] The Secretary might make periodic reports in person to Congress, as did Cordell Hull when he returned from the Moscow Conference of 1943. It has been proposed also that the Secretary be required to appear on the floor of Congress for direct public questioning. Such proposals point up the fact that the Department of State is the only executive department not compelled by law to make scheduled reports to Congress. Public release of information which might jeopardize the nation's diplomacy poses a problem. Yet ways must be found to give congressional leaders the information they need. Recently more use has been made of the practice of having administrative officials testify before the Senate Foreign Relations Committee in closed session.

Some experts have thought it advisable to set up a cabinet committee to handle foreign policy questions. The committee might be composed of the Pres-

---

[14] William L. Langer, "The Mechanism of American Foreign Policy," *International Affairs*, July, 1948, pp. 327–328.

[15] "The Evolving Role of Congress in Foreign Affairs," *Proceedings of the American Philosophical Society*, XCII, No. 4 (October 25, 1948), 215.

ident, the Secretary of State, the Defense Secretary, a representative from the Joint Chiefs of Staff, the majority and minority leaders of Congress, and the chairmen of the key congressional committees. This "foreign affairs steering committee" might actually function as a coordinating body or it might thrash out main lines of policy and make general recommendations. Aside from the fact that merely bringing officials together is no guarantee of genuine group effort, there is fear that a body of this type might tend to become omnipotent and overshadow regular agencies. Another way of bringing Congress more directly into the formulation and execution of foreign policy is the appointment of congressmen—especially those on committees dealing with foreign affairs—to serve on American delegations to the United Nations and other diplomatic conferences. From 1945 on, there has not been an important international conference or foreign ministers' meeting which some member of Congress has not attended.[16] It would be untrue to say that the service of Senator Vandenberg at the Peace Conference of 1946 (from which the treaties with five Axis satellites emerged) or the presence of Representatives Charles Eaton and Sol Bloom at the San Francisco Conference of 1945 automatically produced a favorable reception of foreign policy plans in Congress. Nonetheless, they have certainly helped, despite the fact that the House has not been as well represented at these meetings as the Senate. The really important result is that more members of Congress understand the difficulties of international policy making than ever before.

Probably the most significant strides toward establishing harmonious relationship between the executive and legislative branches have been achieved under the so-called bipartisan foreign policy analyzed in the next chapter.

bibliographic note

Selected readings and editorial comment on the constitutional basis of American foreign policy and the role and powers of the President and Congress in policy formation are to be found in Chapters 1–5 of L. H. Chamberlain and R. C. Snyder, *American Foreign Policy* (New York: Rinehart & Company, 1948). E. S. Corwin, *Total War and the Constitution* (New York: Alfred A. Knopf, Inc., 1947), is an authoritative discussion by a distinguished scholar of the impact of war on the distribution of powers in the Constitution. The best over-all presentation of the part played by Congress in the foreign policy process, including an extended analysis of the problem of the necessary cooperation between President and Congress, is R. A. Dahl, *Congress and Foreign Policy* (New York:

---

[16] The International Trade Conferences of Geneva (1947) and Havana (1948) should probably be listed as exceptions.

Harcourt, Brace and Company, 1950). Chapter 7 in J. L. McCamy, *The Administration of American Foreign Affairs* (New York: Alfred A. Knopf, Inc., 1950), outlines the general position of the President with respect to foreign affairs. J. G. Rogers inquires into the powers of the President and Congress through nine wars and one hundred military operations covering the period 1789 to 1945 in *World Policing and the Constitution* (Boston: World Peace Foundation, 1945). Some of the effects of presidential-congressional relations on foreign policy are discussed by B. Bolles in "President, Congress and Foreign Policy," *American Perspective*, March, 1949. A noted authority on national legislative procedure, J. P. Chamberlain, briefly reviews the effects upon Congress of new developments in American foreign policy in "The Place of Congress in the New Foreign Policy," *Columbia Journal of International Affairs*, Winter, 1949. A detailed and illuminating case history of Congress's role in foreign policy is presented in R. Fangmeier, "Atlantic Pact Hearings," *American Perspective*, June, 1949. Wallace McClure, "The Presidency and World Affairs," *Journal of Politics*, XI, No. 1 (February, 1949), 206–217, examines the problem of staffing the presidency for greatly increased burdens in the realm of foreign affairs.

the role of parties, public opinion, and pressure groups in foreign affairs

$\mathscr{P}$ARTIES as such play only a minor role in the formation of foreign policy. The nature of the effect parties have had on foreign policy has been due to the primacy of domestic affairs from 1815 to 1939, the rivalry between the President and Congress, personal political conflicts, and unique wartime situations. Foreign policy issues have been of direct prominence in few national elections. Elections do, however, affect foreign policy in important ways. They may compel a President to be less than frank with the general public, and he may sincerely make campaign promises which circumstances will not let him keep. President Franklin D. Roosevelt was in somewhat this position in 1940. The risk was great that he would have been denounced as a warmonger seeking re-election if he revealed all he knew or if he attempted openly to lead public opinion. Furthermore, there is always a temptation for the President to create, by shrewd statecraft, the illusion that he and his party are indispensable. On the other hand, pre-election paralysis in making foreign policy decisions is possible, and there may be a period of suspended activity between Election Day and inauguration if the presidency changes hands. Nevertheless, despite alternate Democratic and Republican control of the national government, consistent lines of policy have developed. The real disagreements over foreign policy have not been partisan, but regional, economic, and ideological.

the problem of party politics and foreign policy

Foreign policy is weakened if it becomes a "political football." It is weakened because crucial questions of national security are no longer decided on their merits. Things are said or done for effect only. Support for policy becomes precarious. Irresponsible criticism weakens the nation's prestige and handicaps the officials who formulate policy. In addition, when Congress and the presidency are controlled by different parties, the conflict between the executive and legislative branches may be aggravated.

The foreign policy problem created by the operation of the American party system is twofold. First, national unity in a time of crisis is an obvious necessity. Yet unity must not be allowed to snuff out healthy opposition and argument in the policy-making process. Second, opposition and argument should not be carried to the point where needless uncertainty is injected into foreign policy. Uncertainty in American aims and objectives makes it more difficult for other nations to deal with the United States. Former Secretary of State James F. Byrnes had this problem in mind when he said: "Twice in a generation doubt as to American foreign policy has led other nations to miscalculate the consequences of their actions. Twice in our generation that doubt as to American foreign policy has not brought peace but war." [1]

evolution of the bipartisan approach

Real two-party cooperation began slowly in 1943 with the Green-Sayre Formula and with the nonpartisan Fulbright (House) and Connally (Senate) resolutions approving in principle American membership in an international organization. On August 16, 1944, Secretary Hull met with John Foster Dulles, foreign affairs adviser to Republican presidential candidate Thomas Dewey. They agreed that the future peace was "a nonpartisan topic." Mr. Dewey suppressed whatever desire he had to make campaign capital out of foreign policy issues. In the spring of 1945, the United States was represented by a bipartisan delegation at the San Francisco Conference. During a period in which the Democrats dominated the presidency, Republicans attended the Mexico City Conference of 1945, the first meeting of the Council of Foreign Ministers in September, 1945, the Moscow Conference of 1946, and sessions of the United Nations General Assembly. Foreign policy was not an issue in the 1948 campaign. Blair Bolles has written: "A large portion of the record of the United States in international relations since it accepted in 1945 a position of leadership in peacetime world affairs is the fruit of the bipartisan system." [2]

Bipartisanship had its origin in the desire to avoid a repetition of Wilson's plight, this time with respect to the United Nations Charter. It was given impetus by the need to minimize foreign policy issues during the presidential campaigns of 1944 and 1948. It developed during the period 1942 to 1948, when the Democrats were continuously in control of the presidency and the Republicans were intermittently in control of Congress. If the new approach continues in spite of the disappearance of the original need, it is because there is a conviction that patriotism and national unity require it and because the President never knows when he may have to seek support outside his own party.

---

[1] Address at the American Club, Paris, France, October 3, 1946.
[2] "Bipartisanship in American Foreign Policy," *Foreign Policy Reports*, January 1, 1949.

the nature of the bipartisan approach as evidenced by its evolution

In the development of this attempt to put foreign policy above party politics, the emphasis has been placed on harmony and continuity. Three types of interparty cooperation have been employed: consultation with Republican leaders *before* purely executive moves in foreign policy; request for Republican support *before* legislative programs were submitted to Congress; and the appointment of prominent Republicans, congressional leaders and otherwise, to serve on international delegations. These types of cooperation have not covered all the major phases of American foreign policy. It has been directly and indirectly indicated by the leaders of both parties that bipartisanship did not apply to foreign trade policy; foreign policy issues concerning China, Germany, Japan, Latin America, and Palestine; and the admission of war refugees into the United States. Republicans have refrained from open opposition on these issues, but their silence is a kind of threat that the usual bipartisan roles cannot be expected to operate. The new approach did not entirely prevent partisan appeals on foreign policy issues in the presidential campaign of 1948. Nor did it prevent delays and changes in the European Recovery Program. Contrary to the wishes of the Democratic administration, the Economic Cooperation Administration was established as a separate agency outside the Department of State; China was included in the projected aid; and it was decided that 50 per cent of all goods shipped under the program must be carried in American vessels.

Not all important party leaders have been included in the bipartisan system. Senators Vandenberg and Connally, Representatives Bloom and Eaton, John Foster Dulles, and presidential candidate Thomas Dewey have comprised the basic membership. In the Eightieth Congress, Senators Taft, Gurney, Brooks, Wherry, and Representatives Taber, Knutson, and Mundt—all influential—did not regard themselves as bound by it. A particularly bitter personal argument emphasized this incomplete coverage when Republican Representative Taber, Chairman of the House Appropriations Committee and Senator Vandenberg disagreed over the former's right to make alterations in the amounts requested for ERP.

There is no substantial agreement on what the term "bipartisan" means. Is it a new permanent practice in the policy-making process? Or is it a makeshift device to minimize certain difficulties in specific situations? Though he was obviously piqued at being left out of the launching of the Truman Doctrine in March, 1947, Senator Vandenberg said he thought two-party cooperation did apply to "most contemporary principles" of foreign policy. Lack of clarity as to the meaning of the bipartisan foreign policy and serious departures from it notwithstanding, the public had come to accept it as "good and right" by 1951. There was at least a significant coincidence between a deliberate effort to keep capricious party conflict or maneuvering out of foreign policy and the fact that at no time from 1943 to 1949 could it be said that the chief executive really lacked support for the major developments in foreign policy.

evaluation of the bipartisan foreign policy

To quote Benjamin Cohen: "The purpose of bipartisan collaboration in foreign policy is not and should not be to circumvent democratic control of foreign policy, but to promote effective democratic participation in shaping that policy. Its purpose is not to eliminate public discussion or criticism, but rather to render our foreign policy less vulnerable to criticism in democratic debate." [3] After some years of the bipartisan system, however, some observers have questioned whether part of the price for rendering our foreign policy less vulnerable to partisan criticism has not in fact been a reduction of public debate and a blunting of critical analysis. Has decision making been pushed into deeper obscurity? Does this approach mean that anyone who disagrees with present foreign policy is disloyal? During critical months of 1946, Prime Minister Clement Attlee of Great Britain permitted a full-dress debate on his government's policy in Germany. Does bipartisanship render this impossible in the United States? Containment of Soviet ambitions, a key objective of American policy, was decided upon early in 1946 without any thorough debate in Congress or anywhere else. In September, 1948, Senator Vandenberg indicated he was unwillingly silenced on the Palestine question. Putting American foreign policy beyond controversy seems to be logical and desirable, but much depends upon whether debate has been discreetly hidden or whether it has been suppressed. Moreover, should the President be held responsible for decisions or suggestions he feels obliged to accept during the "infighting" of two-party cooperation? If this is the price of support for presidential policies, should not the opposition party in some way be held accountable?

Does bipartisanship result in a policy based on the lowest common denominator of agreement? Satisfaction is taken in the fact that the vote in the Senate on the United Nations Charter was 89 to 2. Would 90 to 1 have been even more satisfactory? Did this vote indicate more unity among the people as a whole than might have eventually been induced behind a 65-to-26 vote? Would a stronger Charter have been desirable at the risk of a smaller majority? Did the techniques of interparty cooperation produce the nearly unanimous support or was it merely a reflection of an already established disposition toward unity? Was disagreement suppressed and kept quiet or was there no disagreement? Another question is whether the necessity of always consulting the biparty coalition does not reduce the flexibility and boldness which should now characterize executive action in foreign policy. In October, 1948, word leaked out that Presi-

---

[3] "The Evolving Role of Congress in Foreign Affairs," *Proceedings of the American Philosophical Society*, XCII, No. 4 (October 25, 1948), 215.

dent Truman had thought of sending Chief Justice Fred Vinson on a special "mission to Moscow" to try to break the log jam in Russian-American relations. The proposal was quashed, chiefly, it was revealed, by the key figures in the bipartisan system. Regardless of the merits of Mr. Truman's scheme, it is a fact of considerable consequence if he was prevented from using legitimate presidential powers.

When all is said and done, the peculiarities of the American party system probably made some sort of bipartisan approach to foreign policy making inevitable. It is a way of imposing some minimum control on political leaders who might use their party position in or out of Congress to obstruct foreign policy. Bipartisanship is also an admission that the opposition cannot be compelled to "put up or else" under the American system. Key political figures cannot be forced to obey their party's platform or its legislative leaders. Therefore bipartisanship in foreign policy is a method of bridging the gap between the President and Congress and between the two major parties by uniting certain leaders on some issues.

public opinion and foreign policy

No country pays greater tribute to the importance of public opinion as the ultimate foundation of governmental policy than the United States. Public opinion does have an impact on American foreign policy. According to democratic theory it should have.

"Public opinion" is a loose term. A brief definition to serve the present discussion is in order. "General public" means the entire unorganized adult population. At any particular time, the adult population as a whole will have certain opinions on specific aspects of foreign policy or will manifest a "mood," such as apathy or excitement or resentment toward foreign relations generally. Mass opinions or moods constitute but one of several elements in the climate of opinion within which foreign policy decisions are made. Quite different from this general public opinion are the views of smaller, more highly organized "publics" consisting of segments of the population which share a common interest in various foreign policy issues, which are more vocal, and which have some means of making their views felt. Examples of smaller publics would be national labor unions, the Foreign Trade Association, the League of Women Voters, the American Legion, or even a congressman's constituency. Another element in the climate of opinion is comprised of elites or effective opinion groups—the business and professional leaders, men respected by government officials, men whose personal contacts and social prestige enable them to influence policy. Finally, another kind of public is made up of writers and commentators like Walter Lippmann, Hanson Baldwin, and Drew Pearson, together with newspapers in both their editorial and news presentation capacities.

It is to be noted that mass opinion is probably the least effective so far as a direct, positive influence on policy is concerned. This is not to say that mass moods or attitudes are not significant. They have an important bearing, as will be seen. By and large, however, the unorganized public is not the source to which policy makers go for advice and guidance. The State Department keeps its finger on the public pulse, but organized groups, elites, experts, and influential private citizens have the power and knowledge which government officials must respect.

the impact of public opinion on foreign policy

Public opinion, as broadly defined, is a force in the formulation and execution of American foreign policy for several reasons. To begin with, under modern conditions, particularly in the United States, most government policies require some sort of support or acquiescence by the population. Support or cooperation may be necessary from the people as a whole, or from particular groups. Foreign policy decisions, especially those concerning war and peace, have come to affect more and more people. Since 1800 there has been a steady increase in the number of people who must be reckoned with politically. There are more voters and more individuals whose social status gives them power. Widespread distrust of government and diplomacy continually stimulates the active interest of segments of the general public.

The American policy maker is peculiarly sensitive to public opinion. At times he is actually fear-ridden. So various are the modes of public reaction that he never knows where to expect an attack. But he does know that public disapproval, in subtle ways, results in direct or indirect pressure upon him. Whether the public really holds the opinions policy makers think it does, or whether the public really would have reacted to a given decision as predicted, is irrelevant. The point is that policy makers behave as though these things were beyond dispute. But the fear of adverse public reaction is also based on experience. Broad matters of policy have to be developed carefully lest a rash of newspaper editorials, radio comment, and protests to influential congressmen and congressional committees embarrass policy-making officials. Foreign embassies follow trends in American public opinion too, and the State Department often lives in dread of having the ground cut from under its position in international negotiations.

public opinion is basically a negative and permissive factor

Public pressure has been known to force executive action in foreign policy. The entrance of the United States into the Spanish-American War of 1898 is one example. Perhaps the most striking case was the Pact of Paris (1929), an attempt to outlaw international war. This pact would have received a cold response from the State Department were it not for a consistent, irresistible public demand which swept it through the Senate by a vote of 85 to 1.

For the most part, however, public opinion constitutes a negative check on foreign policy. The government's policy can never be far behind or far ahead of public feeling. There are four ways in which the general public limits the content and direction of foreign policy. First, policy is influenced by the political attitudes or values of most of the American people. If enough Americans believe that Communism is not just the form of government of a suspected Great Power but is a moral evil which a Christian nation like the United States must destroy, this fact will limit severely the diplomatic alternatives among which policy makers may choose. Second, public support must be solicited for major lines of policy. This may take time. Therefore, the tempo with which a reorientation of policy may take place is restricted. It took the American public nearly six years to begin to swing solidly behind a policy first urged by President Roosevelt in 1935. The pacifism which dominated American thinking from 1921 to 1941 set limitations within which Secretaries Frank Kellogg, Henry L. Stimson, and Cordell Hull labored to save peace, and to stop the march of aggression by Japan, Italy, and Germany. Third, powerful group interests may force or check government action. Cotton and scrap iron interests would hardly have approved an extensive embargo against Japan from 1936 to 1941, the only move which would have appreciably reduced Japanese warmaking capacity. Fourth, public opinion exerts influence on the techniques which the government can use in implementing policy. Aid to Great Britain in 1945 had to be in the form of a loan, despite the fact that many government experts favored an outright gift. During 1947 and 1948, when the Palestine issue was unsettled, general public opinion strongly favored a Jewish state but strongly opposed the use of American military power to enforce such a policy.

connecting links between public opinion and policy makers

Public opinion and policy-making agencies are connected by several channels which comprise a two-way communication system. Nongovernmental experts, representing an informed public, may advise the President through a special commission such as the Finletter Air Policy Commission. Congressioal hearings and the personal contacts of individual senators and representatives with various citizens comprise another channel. The President's news conference is another. The Division of Public Liaison in the State Department daily analyzes all sources of public thinking and prepares special studies for the Secretary. Private organizations like the Council on Foreign Relations may focus the views of the "effective opinion" group. Letters are written to the White House and State Department by the general public. A very significant medium consists of the special columns, the editorials, and the news presentation of the newspapers.

We do not entirely lack for methods of mutually informing the government and the public what the other is thinking. Nor are opportunities lacking for the public to play a constructive part. Failure and inefficiency arise from the following: selfish pressure groups which work counter to the interests of the larger public; obscure processes of policy making; apathy and insufficient information; rules of procedure in Congress which enhance minority views; issues not being clearly focused; and lack of cooperation between President and Congress. Communication between the public and the policy maker through the mediums mentioned above is two way. One part of the circuit carries public attitudes, interests, and needs to the men who make decisions; the other carries information, requests for support, justifications, and "feelers" from the policy maker to the public.

weaknesses of public opinion in the field of foreign policy

What kind of thinking is being done about the most critical foreign policy issues of our day? It is not a matter of whether the public is right or wrong, at best a question susceptible of little more than a tentative answer. The crucial point is whether the citizens of the United States are ready, willing, and able to do constructive thinking. What are some of the relevant facts? Recent analyses of public opinion are revealing. The public lacks information. It is apathetic. Thirty per cent of the people have no knowledge of four out of five issues. Thirty per cent do not know the chief elements of conflict between the United States and the Soviet Union. There is little awareness of specific issues; most people have "generalized feelings" toward foreign policy. Attitudes are uncritical and there is no capacity to *interpret* facts. The British loan, the Marshall Plan, proposals to turn over the atomic bomb to an international agency are regarded as gratuitous concessions to others, not as moves to protect the self-interest of the United States. Isolationism appears to be dead, but enthusiasm for international cooperation diminishes when tested in terms of concrete examples. Seventy-five per cent of those polled think that the United Nations is a good idea, but only 36 per cent favor action in that organization on the basis of simple majority vote. The degree of international responsibility the American people will accept is not yet clear. It is also obvious that for the most part people do not see *relationships*; 75 per cent say that they oppose sacrificing a balanced budget to foreign aid, yet admit that economic conditions abroad affect the nation's economy. Inconsistencies crop up; 63 per cent favor turning the Greek and Turkish aid programs over to the United Nations while the same percentage are favorable to the Truman Doctrine.[4]

It is often said that the root difficulty with faulty public opinion is a "lack of information." There is some truth in this; yet there are reasons why information in itself is not an answer. Recent studies have confirmed this fact. Most peo-

[4] This analysis is based upon L. S. Cottrell and Sylvia Eberhart, *American Opinion on World Affairs in the Atomic Age* (Princeton: Princeton University Press, 1948), pp. 38–60.

ple lack a meaningful context within which to think about factual data. Public opinion polls have turned up the interesting point that many people think that the Russian-American conflict is nonideological—a phenomenon which would only arise from a serious misinterpretation of Russian behavior. A sizable portion of the population are chronic "know-nothings" despite concerted information campaigns. People tend to select information which is congenial to their prior attitudes. Tests have also proved that individuals interpret the same facts differently. Even when people are rational and informed, new data do not automatically change attitudes.

Perhaps a more serious difficulty is summed up in these powerful words of Charles Ferguson:

> Our present adulterated democracies continue to leave all important decisions to policy-makers and big-wigs. This practice of acting always from the top prevails not merely in government but in industry, education, charity, journalism—through the course of what we call democratic society. The result is bound to be a progressive decay of function among citizens, an oppressive conviction of uselessness. . . . In spite of all the news that is forced upon us, however, it would seem that the more we know the less we can do. We become victims of a kind of political somnambulism, moving vaguely about at the mercy of events. Our consciousness often seems to be a consciousness of images rather than realities.[5]

There is good reason to suggest that great numbers of the American people have defaulted their rightful role in foreign affairs. Many seem to feel that foreign policy is a technical subject to be "left to those who know." Others feel that their opinions do not matter. Still others are confused as to what their relationship to policy making is or should be. All this tends to leave the major public influence in hands of articulate minorities and powerful individuals.

what should be the role of the public in making foreign policy?

It is clear that in a democracy, policy determination should be subject to control by the people. And yet the general public cannot be a policy maker in the same sense that the State Department or a congressional committee can, for example, in the formulation of long range plans. The public can, however, make a choice on basic issues such as joining the United Nations or entering into an Atlantic Alliance. A choice may be one of approval or disapproval, or it may be between one course of action and another. Fateful decisions must be made in the next decade, among them, the decision whether to export American technology to backward areas. Three conditions are present which make a popular opinion on this feasible. Mass communications enable the people to keep abreast of developments in the United States and abroad; the issue can be stated simply; and the public opinion polls may offer a method of arriving at a consensus.

[5] Charles Ferguson, "End as a Pawn?" *Saturday Review of Literature*, August 21, 1948, p. 6.

The public has a further role of checking undesirable government action after larger decisions have been made. In 1945, the United Nations was probably oversold to the American people. This very fact has exercised a desirable check on some policy makers who have felt that on occasion our membership has been a diplomatic handicap. During the tense period of Russian-American relations in 1947–1948, the obvious unwillingness to use troops where a "shooting war" might result was partly due to the restraining hand of public sentiment. Within the governmental machinery itself effective criticism and opposition seldom develop on the scale needed. Such criticism must continue to come from private citizens. Perhaps the gravest danger facing the republic in the field of foreign policy is that flexibility of approach and fresh thinking will disappear. This could happen if no effort were made to improve the nature of popular opinion on its particular level in the policy-making process, if the public could not "get through" to the experts, or if some opinion groups who control mass communications became stereotyped and limited in their analysis of foreign affairs.

the problem of secrecy in foreign affairs

An attempt to assess the proper role of the public in foreign policy raises an important issue that involves the President, Congress, and the public. It also involves international commitments and executive declarations of policy. It grows specifically out of President Roosevelt's leadership during the difficult period when America was moving toward World War II. There appears to be general agreement that Roosevelt, "when confronted by an apathetic public and a critical foreign menace, felt compelled to deceive the people into an awareness of their peril." [6] The democratic dilemma posed is this: In a time of crisis to what extent can leaders take the people into their confidence and listen to their wishes? Some political scientists plead for a literal democratic foreign policy with all the risks. They would choose an absence of deception and possible harm to the nation rather than deception and national preservation. These experts say the fact that Roosevelt was largely correct is irrelevant. They hold that the responsibility of the leader is that he follow the will of the people, not that he follow his own convictions as to what national security requires. They believe that to withhold information from the electorate, on the ground that the electorate is incapable of making a correct decision, sets up a vicious circle in which the very conditions necessary for adequately preparing the public are lacking.

In refutation, it can be suggested that a "town meeting" type of democracy in foreign affairs is not necessary. The government rarely solicits consent *before* policy is formulated. What really happens is that an "upper limit" is set on the President's freedom of action by what is best termed the "resultant of public opinion forces." It has been suggested that, in general, the really crucial

---

[6] Thomas A. Bailey, *The Man in the Street* (New York: The Macmillan Company, 1948), p. 11.

point in the foreign policy process is reached when major courses of action are adopted.

A democratic foreign policy requires that, at the point of adoption, decisions should emerge from the prevailing climate of majority opinion and be determined by agencies, notably Congress, through which this opinion is represented. Open lines of communication between the public and the policy makers, congressional response to majority trends of opinion, elimination of error and confusion by the reduction of the number of individuals and agencies qualified to speak authoritatively, clear identification of those who make decisions, an effective party system, and good relations between President and Congress, are all vital.

All this must be made compatible with the need for quick decisions and minimum secrecy. Day to day responses to a changing international situation, especially if war is imminent, are not compatible with leisurely debate and referendum. With respect to secrecy, a distinction between a policy decision and the international negotiation of a decision is pertinent. The public needs and should have the information appropriate to basic decisions. The carrying out of policy is a matter for technicians, and often secrecy in diplomatic intercourse is necessary. On most of the major problems of recent years sufficient information has been available to the general public. Whether it was properly distributed and used is another point. As the ability of the public to interpret correctly the trend of international events and to foresee the implications of their choices increases, the necessity for disingenuous deception by the nation's leaders will diminish.

pressure groups and foreign policy

America is, par excellence, a nation of groups. The population is subdivided into all kinds: economic, political, racial, social, religious. Their purposes in the field of foreign policy naturally vary widely. It is an oversimplification to divide them into good and bad, selfish and unselfish. Each case must be judged on its merits. Groups are, of course, related to political parties and public opinion. They may work through the major parties or parallel to them. They may represent one segment of the public, or they may represent the unorganized populace. The reason for treating groups separately is that in a complex political process the "bystanders" seldom achieve anything. The "partisans" are always organized; that is why they succeed.[7]

major types of groups interested in foreign policy

A review of the organizations which testify on major policy legislation such as lend-lease, the British loan, and the European Recovery Program provides an

---

[7] Harold Sprout, "Pressure Groups and Foreign Policies," *The Annals* of The American Academy of Political and Social Sciences, CLXXIX (May, 1935), 114–115.

excellent roster of the group structure which impinges on foreign relations. Economic groups include: the National Association of Manufacturers, the Chamber of Commerce of the United States, the American Farm Bureau Federation, the CIO and AFL, the American Tariff League, the American Paper Institute, the United States Steel Corporation, the American Mining Congress, the National Dairy Union, and so on. Some fifty economic groups opposed the Reciprocal Trade Agreements Act alone. Important social groups include the American Legion, the Daughters of the American Revolution, the Navy League, the American Veterans Committee, the National Federation of Womens Clubs. The Federal Council of Churches of Christ and the Roman Catholic Church illustrate powerful religious groups. Professional groups which exert significant influence on foreign policy are the League of Women Voters, the United Nations Association, the Foreign Policy Association, the Brookings Institution, and the Council on Foreign Relations. Groups representing national minorities are exemplified by the Zionist Organization and the American Polish Association. Last but not least should be mentioned "government" pressure groups. These range from Army, Navy, and Air Force partisans to administrative personnel who speak for a certain policy. The Treasury, for example, had a comprehensive policy for occupied Germany in 1945.

specific influences exerted by pressure groups

Such groups, of which only a small number have been listed, have many motives: profit, protection, the privilege of social regulation, advancing the national welfare. Some are interested in the larger questions of war and peace; some speak only when an obscure action touches them. Their techniques are familiar, and they operate on all levels of the political process: public opinion, Congress (individuals and committees), administrative agencies, even the President himself. In general the role or impact of groups is threefold. First, they affect policy directly and on details. This is especially true of the tariff. Farm groups were listened to on some of the provisions of the Foreign Assistance Act of 1948, as were steel and shipping interests. From 1922 on, oil companies certainly had an influence on American policy in the Near East. Until recently foreign policy served the business interests in this area. The Zionist Organization was a key factor in the change which brought the American government around to support the establishment of the new state of Israel.

Second, groups operate in the field of public opinion. They do not create opinion. They clarify issues. They crystallize attitudes and make them vocal. In this way they influence policy indirectly. About ninety groups helped the State Department inform the public about the provisions of the United Nations Charter in 1945. The League of Women Voters is credited with mobilizing considerable effective support for the British loan in 1945. Before 1941, groups like the

Committee to Defend America by Aiding the Allies eventually succeeded in their efforts to combat isolationism because their arguments found favorable soil after Munich.

The third impact of groups arises from their serving the government in various technical capacities. Thus The Brookings Institution helped to draw up the legislation establishing the European Cooperation Administration. Again, the Harriman Committee, which produced valuable prelegislation studies on the European Recovery Program, was composed of leaders from finance, industry, and labor.

increasing importance of group influence on foreign policy

Group influence on foreign policy is increasing. More foreign policy is legislated. The relationship between foreign policy and domestic politics is closer than ever before. There are, so to speak, more "handles" on foreign policy which can be grasped by interested groups. Decisions are more far-reaching. One piece of foreign policy legislation, such as the Economic Cooperation Act of 1948, may affect all economic groups. The broader foreign policy issues become, the more they will attract approval and disapproval. The problems which now face us are so different, so complex that they constitute an open invitation to all and sundry to plead their special interests. It is also true that formulating and executing a global foreign policy program tax the government's facilities. Most of the technicians in our society are employed in private activities, mostly of an organized variety. It is not unusual now for the policy maker to farm out his tasks, or portions of them, to specialized groups such as atomic physicists, on a contract basis.

the new role for labor

Labor's present activities in foreign relations illustrate the growing contribution and influence of private groups. Under the Foreign Assistance Act of 1948 the employment of two labor advisers by the European Cooperation Administration is required. Representatives of labor attended the International Trade Organization Conference at Havana in 1948. Labor attachés are assigned to important American embassies. The AFL influenced policy in Germany when it successfully argued for postponing the dismantling of a few German plants "to provide time for the gradual re-employment of thousands of workers whose jobs would have been affected." Secretary of State George C. Marshall went so far as to suggest in the summer of 1948 that Clinton Golden of the CIO be appointed Ambassador to France. That the United States should rely more and more on the advice and service of labor representatives in numerous diplomatic enterprises abroad is natural in view of the fact that trade unionists and liberal socialists are so important in the governments of western and southern Europe.

Labor brings a point of view to foreign policy which differs in emphasis from some official pronouncements: "American unions tend to support a foreign policy which stresses Western cooperation rather than mere containment of Russia." [8]

group interest vs. national interest in foreign policy

Not all pressure groups educate the public on the broader issues. Not all perform diplomatic or other technical services. Some represent particularized minority views and the desire for private gain. Public policy must always be partially pieced together with minority demands. Time and many informal methods are available in domestic legislation for redrawing the line between the general interest and the lesser interests. But in the new era of foreign policy it is questionable whether such activity can be accepted as normal and legitimate, as it is on domestic policy. The need for coherent national policy with as few vulnerable spots as possible may lead to a revolution in the role of pressure groups. Should a group have the power to demand that the resources of the nation be pledged to the pursuit of its private aims abroad?

bibliographic note

The American People and Foreign Policy (New York: Harcourt, Brace and Company, 1950), by G. A. Almond, is an excellent social science analysis of the nature and sources of American public attitudes and reactions toward foreign policy and relations. It includes an appraisal of the role of elites in the formation of opinion and their impact upon policy making; it also sets forth the "foreign policy consensus" which undergirds official programs and activities. L. H. Chamberlain and R. C. Snyder, *American Foreign Policy* (New York: Rinehart & Company, 1948), Chaps. 12–14, present a wide selection of readings on the role and influence of public opinion, parties, and pressure groups. An informative discussion of the competence of the American electorate with respect to foreign policy problems and also the interrelationships between parties and pressure groups and the legislation of foreign policy programs are to be found in R. A. Dahl, *Congress and Foreign Policy* (New York: Harcourt, Brace and Company, 1950), Chaps. 3, 5, 6. *Public Opinion and Foreign Policy* (New York: Harper & Brothers, 1949), by Lester Markel and others, is a conventional study by recognized experts of public opinion as an instrumentality of American foreign policy both at home and abroad. E. E. Schattschneider, *Politics, Pressures, and the Tariff* (New York: Prentice-Hall, Inc., 1935), is a classic study demonstrating certain kinds of influence by pressure groups on economic foreign policy. The historical development of the bipartisan approach to foreign policy, what it has

---

[8] *Foreign Policy Bulletin*, November 26, 1948. Comment by Blair Bolles.

meant in practice, and some of the attendant problems are competently discussed by B. Bolles in "Bipartisanship in American Foreign Policy," *Foreign Policy Reports*, January 1, 1949. A stimulating argument pro and con over the merits of bipartisanship in foreign policy matters is carried on by Willmoore Kendall and others in "Is the Bipartisan Policy Democratic?" *American Perspective*, IV, No. 2 (Spring, 1950), 146–181. Various writers discuss the proper role of the general public in the making of foreign policy decisions in a symposium, "Can Foreign Policy Be Democratic?" *American Perspective*, September, 1948.

the formulation and execution of foreign policy by administrative agencies

$\mathscr{A}$ T THE heart of the foreign-policy-making process are the career officials and experts who formulate programs for the President, Congress, and the people to act upon, who execute decisions, and who carry on the day to day business of foreign affairs. The process which embraces the role and influence of these various technicians is difficult to analyze. With respect to any significant foreign policy decision, it is almost impossible for the outsider to know who did what, when, and how.

If one could examine a complete and appropriately labeled chart of the executive branch of the federal government, he would be struck by the multiplicity of agencies concerned with foreign relations—fifty-eight to be exact. For example, the following are involved in just the European Recovery Program: Departments of State, Commerce, Treasury, Interior, and Agriculture; the Export-Import Bank; the Tariff Commission; the national military establishment; the Federal Reserve Board; the Office of Defense Transportation; the Maritime Commission; and the Economic Cooperation Administration. This fragmentation is partly due to the new international position of the United States. It is also due to the fact that as the dividing line between foreign and domestic affairs has become increasingly blurred, most regular civilian agencies have become concerned with some aspect of foreign policy. Older agencies dealing with foreign affairs have expanded. New agencies such as ECA have been created. Other agencies which formerly had domestic functions have now moved into the foreign-policy-making process.

The way the United States administers its foreign affairs is largely the result of the impact of the specific problems which confronted the nation from 1938 to 1950. Essentially, policy making rests upon the proper mobilization of officials who have the necessary time, knowledge, and power to act. During a transition period when new problems arise, it is not always clear who these men are, or ought to be. Improvisation, hesitation, and duplication often result. A significant factor which complicates adjustment to new situations is change itself. Change alters problems even before all their implications can be analyzed. Change imposes a high rate of obsolescence on policy-making techniques. Thus, United Nations affairs revolved at first around the building of the new organization. Later it became a question of what policies and tactics to pursue once the organization was in operation. This necessitated an alteration in the State Department's administrative setup. Adjustments of this type exemplify a continuing phenomenon.

the Department of State

The Department of State, a key policy-making agency, is in many respects unique among government departments. It has been perhaps more tradition-bound than any other. It has kept more to itself, has jealously guarded its functions, and has generally resisted attempts to change its ways. But beginning about 1940, the rapid involvement of the United States in international affairs faced the department with tasks and decisions far wider in scope than had ever been the case before. Customary methods and ideas were strained to the utmost. Throughout the period 1941 to 1943, both its organization and its policies were condemned as "stuffy" and inefficient. Congressmen and other critics called for a thorough reorganization. Criticisms and changes were bound to come because the State Department was equipped primarily to observe world politics rather than to participate in them and to declare policy only in limited, well-defined situations.

functions of the State Department

The statute of 1789 which established the State Department says less about its specific duties than about its relation to the President. It says, in part: "The Secretary of State shall perform those duties as shall from time to time be enjoined or entrusted to him by the President . . . respecting foreign affairs . . . and he shall conduct the business of the Department in such manner as the President shall direct." This indicates that the basic function of the department is to be the chief agency under the President for the formulation and execution of foreign policy. Hence the department is the means through which the President discharges the responsibilities placed upon him by the Constitution. It acts in his name. One thing the department must do is to know at all times the exact nature of the international problems facing the United States and to have that information available for the President or other executive officials. The department also represents the United States in negotiations with other nations. This includes exploratory discussions, the drawing up of agreements, and regular diplomatic representation abroad. Finally, an important function is to explain American actions and objectives to the people of the world.

enlarged tasks of the State Department

The present nature of American foreign relations is revealed in the rather un-characteristic functions which the department has absorbed or developed. In the first place, economic matters have become more numerous and more important. The responsibilities of those in charge of economic foreign policy now include a broader trade policy as embodied in the Havana Charter and the International Trade Organization; the transformation of the economies of backward areas such as Liberia; the solution of international food shortages and fluctuating grain prices; the negotiation of bilateral air transport treaties; and the promotion of international full employment and economic stability.

Political policies specially designed for areas and peoples toward whom America was once indifferent have been devised and put into operation. Occupied territories such as western Germany, Japan, Korea, and Austria, as well as the Middle East, Greece, Turkey, Indonesia, and North Africa, are cases in point. A major area, previously treated in negative fashion, is western Europe, where the United States is fostering economic and political integration.

Reflecting the need for complete and accurate information about all countries and what is happening to them is the department's permanent intelligence program established on a separate basis to do the kind of work formerly left entirely in the hands of the Armed Forces and the Foreign Service. A special set of agencies has been created to improve the relationship between the department and the general public. An extensive foreign information program to explain America to the world by short-wave radio has been put into operation. Of great consequence in the enlarged role of the State Department is the fact that it must now staff, and make policy for, the American delegations to a vast number of international agencies which the United States has joined since 1945.

the organization of the State Department

Personnel and budget figures demonstrate how rapidly the State Department has grown in a short time. In 1790, the department had a Secretary and eight clerks. In 1920, the staff totaled 631; in 1938, 963; in 1943, 2,755; and in 1946 had grown to 10,000. By 1948 the number had tapered off to 6,450 including 1,000 in the foreign information program and 500 in intelligence work. Moreover, in 1948 the department used half of its employees in management, care of communications and records, and visas and passports. For the fiscal year 1948, the total budget, including the Foreign Service, was $147 million—five times what it was in 1943.

the policy-making team at the top

The Secretary of State has the chief responsibility for the formulation and execution of foreign policy. But the Secretary does not make policy alone. Even if this were desirable, it would be impossible, for the job of running the department is too big. In reality, the Secretary directs a team of top officials who make the decisions in consultation with him. Assisting the Secretary are the Counselor, the Under Secretary, two Deputy Under Secretaries, an Ambassador at Large, and several special advisers who report directly to him. The Counselor advises the Secretary on current and long-range programs. He also heads the important new Policy Planning Staff, which, as its name implies, concentrates on the over-all strategy of American foreign policy. The primary purpose of this group is to provide a continuous study of broader policy issues by officials and advisers who are free of ordinary departmental duties. The Under Secretary, the second in command, frequently acts for the Secretary in the latter's absence. Mainly, however, he assigns the major policy-making tasks in the department, coordinates the various units working on these tasks, and sees that reports and recommendations are made to the Secretary in finished form. Assisting the Under Secretary are two deputies. One of these devotes himself solely to policy matters. He is primarily concerned with the carrying out of decisions which are made at the top, although his advice is important when such decisions are orginally made. The other Deputy Under Secretary handles the administration of the department's personnel and organization. An Ambassador at Large is also an important aide to the Secretary. This official, free of day to day responsibilities in the department, is a kind of roving trouble shooter for the Secretary, advises him on specific matters, and sometimes takes his place at international conferences.

Directed by the Secretary, a team of high-level officials runs the Department of State. Clearly the three tasks performed by this general staff are policy planning, policy execution, and departmental administration.

operating organization

The actual work of the department is carried on by ten major units, each headed by an Assistant Secretary of State or an official of equivalent rank. These officials might be termed field commanders. They report directly to the top staff and meet daily with it. The daily meetings of the Assistant Secretaries, the Secretary himself, the Counselor, and the two Under Secretaries in charge of policy formation consititute one of the important ways in which coordination is achieved between those who make policy and those who carry it out. Five of the ten major units, which are called bureaus, are "functional" in nature: Economic Affairs, Legal Affairs, Intelligence, Public Affairs, and Congressional Relations. These bureaus are functional because they primarily advise and consult rather than engage in operations. The "operating" bureaus are European Affairs, Inter-American Affairs, United Nations Affairs, Far Eastern Affairs, and Near Eastern, South Asian, and African Affairs.

Thus within the jurisdiction of each Assistant Secretary is a special area or aspect of foreign policy. The functions of the Assistant Secretary are to make recommendations to the top officials on problems in his charge, see to it that decisions are carried out, and coordinate the work of his bureau with related work being done by other bureaus. The work of a given bureau is subdivided into offices. For example, the Assistant Secretary for Far Eastern Affairs has under him three offices: Chinese Affairs, Northeast Asian Affairs, Philippine and Southeast Asian Affairs. Each office has a staff of subject matter (economists, geographers, intelligence, and so on) and regional experts. It is at the office level that communications from Foreign Service officers in the field are received, orders are sent, information is collected, and general day to day business is transacted.

two criteria for organizing the State Department's work

It will be noted that two different bases of organization are present in the State Department—regional or geographical, and topical or functional. The Bureau of Economic Affairs represents the latter because its work is not confined to any particular country or region. The Bureau of European Affairs represents the former because it is concerned with all aspects, including the economic, of American relations with the continent of Europe. In terms of historical development, the geographical principle has been traditional and was the only basis of organization until the late 1930's. Foreign policy problems are now global and technical as well as regional; therefore the functional principle operates side by side with the other.

Something of a dilemma arises. Professor Arthur Macmahon of Columbia University has put the matter succinctly:

> The making of international policy is not simple. A factory layout may be judged in terms of physical output but the product of the State Department, in a word, is outlook, not output; and the outlook that becomes the international policy of the United States must be fabricated by viewing matters from various angles and in the light of special bodies of information, both about countries and regions as geographical complexes and also about global processes.[1]

The problem is one of coordination. Regional or country experts and subject matter specialists must be brought together where needed. The problem cannot be resolved by adopting one basis of organization or the other. Difficulties arise because those in, say, the Bureau of United Nations Affairs do not always trust and respect the judgment of the men in charge of geographical divisions and desks.

A second aspect of the organizational dilemma has been put in the form of a question by Blair Bolles: "Would the United States fare better with control over foreign affairs centralized in a strong State Department or dispersed

---

[1] Arthur Macmahon, "International Policy and Governmental Structure," *Proceedings of the American Philosophical Society*, XCII, No. 4 (October 25, 1948), 221.

throughout many bureaus in Washington?"[2] Obviously the conflict is between consistency in policy and efficiency in administration. Centering everything in the department would make for a monolithic policy and for the elimination of situations where two or more agencies might be working at cross purposes. On the other hand, such an arrangement would involve costly duplication of staff and effort. The present practice is a compromise, a compromise which often finds the department with responsibility for, but not in complete control of, all the elements in the policy-making process. Once again, a problem of coordination presents itself. Outside agencies perform two types of service for the department: carrying out of policy—the Economic Cooperation Administration, for example; and technical assistance. Overseeing policy execution by another agency is sometimes difficult for the department to do by "remote control" and may result in policy making by those not properly equipped or responsible. But so many government units execute bits of American foreign policy that they cannot all be clustered under one roof.[3] It has been pointed out that the Department of State must use extensively the technical knowledge gathered by other agencies, but since these agencies tend to serve special groups in the population,[4] the department must retain for its own experts the right to define the true national interest. Foreign policy must be reckoned in terms of "the long run and indirect advantages."[5]

policy making in the State Department

It is difficult and risky to generalize about the ways decisions are reached in the department. The brief sketch of organization suggests that there are several levels of policy making, probably six in all, ranging from the "country desk" to the Secretary. A number of factors determine where the decision is made: nature and importance of the issues, the personalities involved, the number and intensity of other issues pending. If two points of view on a proposed policy develop, this will also determine who makes the final decision. Every policy has several stages: (a) the problem arises—it may come from a diplomatic representative in the field, from a departmental committee, from the Secretary, from Congress, or from the President in the form of advice or a request; (b) research follows, involving the gathering of all relevant information—a process which may involve more than one departmental agency; (c) proposals are then in order, being prepared in the form of action papers circulated to key officials; (d) clearance is then necessary to avoid inconsistency, cross-purposes, and postannounce-

---

[2] Blair Bolles, "Reorganization of the State Department," *Foreign Policy Reports*, August 15, 1947, p. 141.

[3] Macmahon, "International Policy and Governmental Structure," p. 222.

[4] The Departments of Commerce and Agriculture and agencies like the Maritime Commission rightfully become identified with economic interests in order to serve them.

[5] Macmahon, "International Policy and Governmental Structure," p. 221.

ment sniping; finally (e) the policy is placed in operation, at which time a new set of officials may become involved. There are occasions when all of these steps are performed in and by one departmental office, and there are occasions when the circuitous route of a policy can hardly be traced. The location of decision making is really of basic significance for who decides may affect what is decided. Absence of coordination and interoffice splits are then relevant. There is seldom complete solidarity on critical issues. In recent years it has been well known that serious splits developed over Palestine, China, Latin America, and policy toward the Soviet Union. Cliques have their alliances with Congress and the military and sometimes with opinion groups. Interested vocal and influential groups in the department can often carry the day for their cause. Big issues will be decided at the top, by the Secretary and his immediate staff. If issues require long technical investigation, the influence of subordinate experts will proportionately increase. Routine, day to day matters are handled by divisions and desks.

the role of the Secretary of State

In many ways the Secretary of State has come to be regarded as the chief spokesman of foreign policy. Tradition, the technical nature of diplomacy, and capable, respected appointees have all combined to bring this about. But the office is political. Few Secretaries have been international lawyers or otherwise qualified by diplomatic experience. Until recently the office has been filled by men whose prestige has been second only to that of the President or who have had extensive political experience. The duties of the Secretary are threefold: he serves the chief executive, he formulates policy, and he is responsible for the operation of the department. That individual Secretaries have left a deep impression upon various phases of our foreign policy is undeniable. One need only to recall Hay's Open-Door Notes, the Lansing-Ishii Agreement, the Kellogg Pact, the Stimson Doctrine, the Hull Trade Program, and the Marshall Plan. Of course it has not been true that in each case the policy was due to the Secretary alone. Yet, for the most part, a particular Secretary's interests, experience, and predilections have often been controlling. Aside from policies which may bear the Secretary's name, his influence may be preponderant in arriving at important decisions. George C. Marshall, America's great wartime Chief of Staff and Secretary of State from 1947 to 1949, evidently insisted successfully that the United States should not become deeply and irrevocably involved in the Chinese Civil War which resulted in the collapse of the Chiang Kai-shek regime in 1949. Such a policy gave America a freer hand in a situation it could not control anyway. This was a difficult course to make acceptable in the United States in these years.

Basically, the role of the Secretary depends on what kind of man he is, on the character of the President, and, as always, on the time and circumstances of his tour of duty. If the Secretary is too weak, his decisions must be made by someone else. If he is too strong, the President or Congress may oppose him. He must be greatly skilled in the art he practices for his country. If the President is weak, passive, or uninterested in foreign affairs, the Secretary will probably be outstanding—by contrast if for no other reason. He will have virtually unlimited control of policy. If both the President and the Secretary are strong, there may be animosity and clash, as there was between Woodrow Wilson and William Jennings Bryan. If the President is strong and the Secretary is sometimes retiring, the latter may be circumvented, which was the case once or twice between President Franklin D. Roosevelt and Cordell Hull. Circumstances are important, too. In untroubled times the Secretary can master his task and take more responsibility. But every Secretary after 1941 suffered because the job really became too big for one man to handle. It has now become a staff position of large proportions. The changes under discussion in these chapters have in some respects altered the qualities desirable in a Secretary. He needs to be a man of sound political judgment and patience. He must also be flexible of mind and cosmopolitan in knowledge and at the same time have competence as an administrator. His role will always be difficult because he must please so many people. He is not always certain what he can do. He will tend to be blamed in any case.

the external relations of the Department of State

One of the most significant things to be said about the State Department at the present time is that it has declined in relative importance. It no longer stands alone in foreign policy formation. It shares this function with other governmental agencies: ECA, the Departments of Commerce, Agriculture, Treasury; the military establishment, and various commissions. Furthermore, Congress has a much larger role than formerly. Presidential advisers have become another rival. Hence many agencies are interlocked. Added to this is the apparent lack of an agreed over-all foreign policy within which everyone is working. The State Department may find itself opposed by another agency. In 1948 the Maritime Commission complained bitterly to Congress over the State Department's transfer of ships to countries whose merchant marines were devastated by the war. As a result of the fact that the State Department is not in complete control of policy making, foresightedness, which is essential to sound statecraft, is difficult indeed. It is, in fact, almost impossible for the State Department to know in advance what it can do with respect to a given problem.

the President and the State Department

Some Presidents—among them Franklin D. Roosevelt—have been accused of being their own Secretaries of State. Critics argue that when the President "usurps" the Secretary's functions, the prestige of the department suffers and men of stature will refuse the secretaryship lest they become mere "stooges." A convincing argument is that if the President constantly circumvents the department, this news soon gets abroad, and the department's effectiveness even in minor negotiations is undermined. Yet the President is the one who is responsible by law for the conduct of foreign relations. His Secretary of State may be a choice forced on him by political necessity, a man who may not view the world as he does, a man who may knowingly or unknowingly thwart his aims. Since the State Department does not make independent reports to Congress, it is legally responsible to it only indirectly *through* the President. Henry L. Stimson's testimony that President Hoover "abstained from giving . . . any instructions whatever" when the Secretary went to the London Naval Conference of 1930, and that "there was no time when he (the President) intervened with any instruction to us as to what we should or should not do," [6] may exemplify a desirable relationship. It is not, however, necessarily normal or required by law.

Congress and the State Department

Relations with the national legislature have been less than satisfactory in recent years. Congress has tended to be more and more critical of the department. The 1948 report of the House Appropriations Committee called attention to "great duplication of effort" and declared that "the present structure is wasteful, costly, and inefficient." [7] A most persistent complaint is that the department does not keep Congress informed. A corollary has been that the department has not always kept abreast of the feelings and developments in Congress which might affect foreign policy plans. In February, 1949, the chairman of the Senate Foreign Relations Committee, Senator Connally, announced that no one had yet seen a copy of the proposed Atlantic Alliance and that his committee would have no part of an agreement which would automatically involve the United States in war if certain nations were attacked. His blast disturbed the confidence of western European countries who perhaps thought that the State Department had promised them too much. Allegations that the department "has been shot through and through with Communists" have been another source of distrust and irritation.[8] Withal, Congress has never taken the time to offer constructive suggestions as to how the department might be improved. Meanwhile, vagaries of congressional opinion are a constant source of uncertainty in foreign policy planning.

interdepartmental committees handling foreign policy problems

One of the major problems in international policy formation is how to achieve coordination among the many executive agencies which are now operating in that field. Professor Arthur Macmahon has suggested that there are three choices:

---

[6] Before the Senate Committee on Foreign Relations, 71 Cong., 2 Sess., May 12, 1930.

[7] Quoted by Macmahon, "International Policy and Governmental Structure," p. 219.

[8] *Congressional Record*, XCIII (March 13, 1947), Pt 2, 2105.

(1) interagency committees; (2) "the State Department may be given a mandate to act as guide and arbiter with wide directive or at least veto power in any matter of foreign policy"; and (3) the President may become the unifying focus.[9] The first has become standard practice almost by default. The presidential staff has not been equipped to carry out the third choice.[10] As far as the second is concerned, the tendency has been away from giving the State Department large integrative powers.[11]

According to the Hoover Commission, there were some thirty interdepartmental committees or groups dealing with foreign affairs early in 1947.[12] It has been estimated that in two thirds of these committees, a representative of the State Department sits as chairman.[13] Some of the typical examples of this type of agency are the Intelligence Advisory Committee, the Advisory Committee on Occupied Areas Affairs, the Executive Committee on the Regulation of Armaments, the National Munitions Control Board, the National Advisory Council on International Monetary and Financial Problems, the Air Coordinating Committee, and Interdepartmental Committee on International Social Policy. Important policy decisions come from such groups. The fact that they are steadily appearing and disappearing is due, of course, to changing needs.

the Foreign Service

The Foreign Service is many things rolled into one. It is a projection of the United States abroad. It talks to foreign governments and peoples on the spot. It executes policy. It is a delicate set of antennae. It stands by the American citizen when he ventures into other lands. The average citizen's opinion about the Foreign Service tends to revolve about two extremes. On the one hand, the diplomat is regarded with some suspicion. He is a man who is in an exclusive club, who has been graduated from the best schools, who dresses in striped trousers, who is a "cooky pusher," and who goes abroad to "lie" for his country. On the other hand, the diplomat may be regarded with envy as one who goes to interesting, exotic places, who has the prestige of the American government behind him, who dwells in a constant whirl of social activity, all the while making critical decisions, handling important papers, and generally leading an exciting life. Both views contain only partial truths. Yet nothing is more important than to

---

[9] Macmahon, "International Policy and Governmental Structure," p. 225.

[10] The Hoover Commission has recommended "cabinet-level committees" to advise the President on both the domestic and the foreign aspects of matters affecting foreign affairs and involving more than one department or agency. "Report on General Management of the Executive Boards," New York *Times*, February 8, 1949, p. 18.

[11] See Chapter 47 on congressional distrust.

[12] From the "Report on General Management of the Executive Boards," New York *Times*, February 8, 1949, p. 18.

[13] Macmahon, "International Policy and Governmental Structure," p. 226.

understand what it is that the diplomatic arm of our government really does.

The conduct of business between governments is an ancient art. The art is diplomacy, which consists largely of the ability to communicate with foreign officials, to plead skillfully for one's own government, to accommodate wherever possible the desires of other governments, and to prevent disputes or conflicts leading to a breakdown of diplomatic relations. Hugh Gibson, an experienced diplomat, has written:

> The mystery and hocus-pocus of diplomacy are largely existent only in the minds of a mystery-loving public. In reality, diplomacy is a laborious business, singularly free from glamour and mystery. . . . Practical ends cannot be achieved by anything but hard, patient work, preferably by people who know the game. Diplomacy is a grim business. . . . The unfailing courtesy which should characterize it is not based, as is so generally assumed, on a spineless desire to make yourself agreeable to foreigners and give everything away. It is a reciprocal recognition that the current negotiation is a mere incident in a continuing relationship: that both parties to any controversy will have an unending series of matters to be settled in the future and that agreement will be favored by maintenance of good temper and good feeling.[14]

the organization of the Foreign Service

The Foreign Service is in the State Department, but in some respects not of it— which is another way of saying that it is almost a separate branch of the government. Actually, the Foreign Service performs tasks for forty-five federal agencies and almost 90 per cent of its reports go outside the Department of State. As might be expected, the Service is feeling the effects of the changes of the past decade. Its personnel is growing much larger, now totaling 13,000. During World War II the Auxiliary Service and the special foreign representative programs of other departments, such as Agriculture and Commerce, diluted the old organization. More recently, the increase of staff offices, technical experts (economists, labor attachés, cultural relations, and intelligence technicians), and other subordinate personnel have altered not only the size but the constituency of the personnel. At present 6,000 aliens serve American diplomatic establishments abroad. There are about 1,300 regular Foreign Service officers including about 165 reserve officers—a new additon which makes it possible to appoint specialized personnel at any appropriate salary and rank for a period of four years without the usual examinations.

Generally speaking, the Foreign Service is trying to recruit and develop a different and a better type of personnel. Candidates are being drawn from a broader educational cross section of the country. Qualities of personality, char-

---

[14] Hugh Gibson, *The Road to Foreign Policy* (New York: Doubleday & Company, 1944), pp. 31–32.

acter, and imagination are now more evenly weighed with specific factual knowledge and language proficiency. It is probably harder to get into the regular Foreign Service now than it has been before. A better in-service training (at the new Foreign Service Institute) is being given. Under the new legislation of 1946 promotions must come regularly. The door is open for mustering out those who are not going to move to the top. Salaries are higher. An officer may move, on the average, from $3,300 to $13,500 in twenty-seven years. Tax-exempt allowances for cost of living, entertainment and travel expenses have been increased. An effort is being made to base promotions upon regular efficiency ratings. Officers are not as likely to "wither on the vine" indefinitely in some out-of-the-way post, for three years of every fifteen must be spent in the United States working in the State Department, getting further training, or serving in some outside government agency. Retirement benefits are larger and more certain. Every officer receives sixty days' leave each year, and he must take a "home" leave at least every two years.

the Foreign Service Act of 1946

The present organization and future improvement of the Foreign Service rests upon the act of 1946, the most comprehensive congressional legislation ever passed on the subject of foreign representation. It grew out of increasing criticism in Congress and is an attempt to refurbish, democratize, and adapt the Service to new conditions. Certain principles are preserved intact. The Service is independent, with its own system of prescribed duties, pay, retirement plans, and so on. It administers itself and recruits primarily by initial appointment. So far as rank is concerned, there are eight grades: ambassador, minister, minister resident, chargé d'affaires, diplomatic agents, counselor of embassy, secretary of legation, and consul. There are six salary classes below that of chief of mission, ranging from $3,300 to $13,500; chiefs of missions receive from $15,000 to $25,000, depending on the importance of the post. One criticism has been that our top diplomatic officials could not afford to remain at their posts, and that they were much underpaid compared to similar British and French officials. This has been partially met; for example, the salary for the head of the London mission is $25,000 plus $25,000 for allowances. Foreign Service reserve officers are paid on the same scale as regular officers. The staff officers and employees, who comprise the third branch, are paid according to twenty-two salary classes ranging from $720 to $10,000.

the diplomatic mission

The average American diplomatic mission abroad, an embassy or legation, depending on the size and importance of the country, is equipped to handle the four phases of diplomacy: representation, reporting, protection, and negotiation. A large mission has an ambassador or minister and three secretaries as well as a sizable staff. Most heads of missions are now career men who have spent a professional lifetime in the Service; only 20 per cent of them are "political" appointees in the old sense. New and interesting functions in the Foreign Service are revealed by the nature of the embassy staff.

The Paris embassy, for example, in 1946 had twenty-nine officers and thirty clerical assistants, among whom were twenty labor, military, agricultural, and cultural attachés; it also had a director of public relations and two political officers, the latter spending most of their time at the French Foreign Ministry. It is no longer true that embassy officials are completely tied down with paper work. More often than not they are in the "field," performing some specialized duty, such as observing left-wing political movements or investigating local production methods, or compiling intelligence reports.

Consular offices are maintained in most of the major communities of foreign countries and constitute a kind of branch of the central mission, which is located only in the capital. The consul is concerned with cases arising from the activities of individual American citizens abroad, whereas those attached to the embassy are dealing with American foreign policy and relations in a national sense. For American citizens who pass through, or have business in, the foreign community where the consul resides, he performs several services. He is a business adviser, justice of the peace, veterans' counselor, commissioner of immigration, property custodian, welfare superintendent, and policy officer. He also has to be, if necessary, the "eyes" and "ears" of the United States.

Foreign Service functions and foreign policy

The immediate influence of the Foreign Service upon the foreign policy process is significant and rather obvious. A sound foreign policy must be based on the most accurate kind of information about another nation and its policies. Assumptions about the behavior of other states must rest upon analyses submitted by the expert observers of each embassy. How effective are the Communists in the French labor movement? What production gains have been made in the Netherlands as a result of ERP funds? How strong is the domestic opposition to Franco in Spain? What is the real influence of the Arab League? How stable is India? How great is the popular support for the Communist party in China? Foreign Service officers indirectly make policy by the answers they give to such questions.

The period ahead is apt to be one of no-peace, no-war, a period of political and economic struggle. Foreign Service personnel will be America's first line of security. Every scrap of information will have to be evaluated in terms of the objectives and interests of the United States. Particularly in those areas under heavy Soviet or Communist pressure, the Foreign Service officer may be the only listening post. Upon his estimates will rest our calculation of the objectives and strength of those who may be working against American interests.

No matter how soundly conceived, a foreign policy must be announced to other governments and put into operation. In this respect the Foreign Service officer acts as an administrator. The skill with which he is able to carry out the intentions of American foreign policy may be crucial. If this is an ideological struggle, a clash between alien cultures, and if there are large segments of the world's population who are watching both American and Soviet behavior before deciding where their sympathies lie, the insight and imagination with which our diplomats represent the spirit and content of American aims and beliefs will be important indeed.

the organization of national security

National security under modern conditions is a continuing problem. It is a primary function of government which touches most other aspects of government itself and modern life in general. Security depends on what Professor Edward Mead Earle has called "grand strategy": ". . . the highest type of strategy is that which so directs and integrates the policies and armaments of the nation that the resort to war is either rendered unnecessary or is undertaken with the maximum chances of victory." Modern strategy is, then, an intermingling of the political and the military, and is a responsibility of statesmanship in time of peace as well as war. The question then becomes: How can the total strength of the nation be mobilized and utilized continuously for the preservation of interests against all enemies without altering the form of government and having the mobilization actually interfere with the realization of objectives? For one thing, the proper relationship between civilian and military experts must be decided, and all the agencies concerned with security must be brought together to determine national policy. Formerly the President, the Secretaries of War, Navy, and State, along with the General Staff, could administer informally the whole field of security and no formal mechanism of coordination was required. Pearl Harbor was a cruel reminder that this was no longer a safe method of planning for national security.

the National Security Act of 1947

Accordingly, section 2 of the 1947 National Security Act declares that the new approach to security shall be:

> to provide for the establishment of integrated policies and procedures for the departments, agencies, and functions of the Government relating to the national security; to provide three military departments for the operation and administration of the Army, the Navy (including Naval Aviation and the Marine Corps) and the Air Force . . . ; to provide for their authoritative coordination and unified direction under civilian control but not to

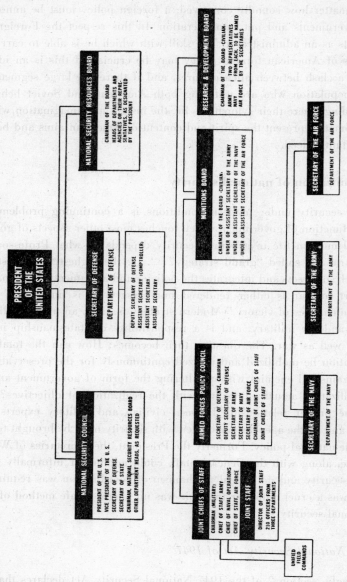

The Organization of National Security. (*Reprinted from "U.S. News & World Report," August 19, 1949, an independent weekly magazine on national and international affairs, published at Washington. Copyright 1949 United States News Publishing Corporation.*)

merge them; to provide for the effective strategic direction of the armed forces and for their operation under unified control and for their integration into an efficient team of land, naval, and air forces.[15]

The national security organization provided for under the act is designed to plan maximum security at minimum cost, given the nation's resources and political liberties.

Further suppositions of the act are as follows: (1) the primary objective of the United States is peace, but it must be ready to mobilize all its resources at a moment's notice; (2) there is to be clear civilian dominance in foreign policy and over the military organization; (3) the maximum return on every dollar spent for military purposes must be sought; (4) readiness for war is to be the fundamental objective of the national military establishment; (5) duplication among the armed forces must be avoided, but a healthy competitive spirit is to be encouraged.

Structural bases of the new organization bear out the foregoing analysis. Nothing better demonstrates the total nature of military security, the necessity for security planning, and the relation between military policy and foreign policy.

the Secretary of Defense and the Department of Defense

The Secretary of Defense directs and controls the Department of Defense, a grouping of agencies which both implement and influence the formation of foreign policy. The Secretary himself is a presidential adviser, serves on the National Security Council, rates next to the Secretary of State in cabinet prestige, and has charge of the military power of the United States.

The *Joint Chiefs of Staff* within the department, consisting of representatives from the subordinate departments of the Army, Navy, and Air Force, coordinate all military planning. This group constitutes what might be called the "shooting-war high command" and is concerned with defensive and offensive plans for actual war. Through its chairman it advises the Secretary, the President, the National Security Council and all other Defense officials working on the military side of problems having both political and military implications. The *Office of Foreign Military Affairs* coordinates within the Department of Defense all politico-military problems and policies except occupation and military assistance to friends of the United States, which are supervised by special assistants to the Secretary.

A *Research and Development Board* directs the search for new weapons. It administers a $500 million annual research program on such weapons as guided missiles, radar, new submarines, bombing planes, and so forth. *The Munitions Board* has the responsibility for supervising and coordinating the actual manu-

---

[15] 61 Stat. 495.

facture of weapons. It surveys American industry, thus providing a complete inventory of the tools and capabilities of all important plants, recommends new production facilities, and studies plant dispersal in case of atomic attack.

the National Security Council

This body is really a five-man supercabinet—the "cold-war high command." It is perhaps the outstanding feature of the 1947 act, next to the grouping of the separate armed services under a single secretary. The permanent members of the council are the President, the Vice-President, the Secretary of State, the Secretary of Defense, and the Chief of the National Security Resources Board. Its staff committee, which really does much of the work, consists of specialists from the Policy Planning Committee of the State Department, from the Central Intelligence Agency, from the Army, Navy, and Air Forces, and from the Security Resources Board. *The Central Intelligence Agency*, an extremely important part of the new security organization, functions under the council, planning, developing, and coordinating all foreign intelligence activity. Its work centers in the discovery of how strong the enemy is and what he is up to. The agency uses undercover operators abroad and a highly skilled research staff in Washington. Charged with responsibility for assessing and appraising American objectives, commitments, and risks in the light of an actual and potential military power, the Security Council has other possible functions. It may make foreign policy decisions or lay the foundation for them in the form of "policy papers." It may anticipate security problems and initiate studies of its own. It may define long-term American political objectives.

the National Security Resources Board

How strong is America? To answer this question in terms of men and machines is the purpose of the National Security Resources Board. It must coordinate future strategic needs with supporting plans for industrial mobilization and it must constantly warn the military planners of the limitations imposed by available materials.

the nature of the armed forces

The military budget is the final regulator of the size and nature of the military establishment. While the exact size, disposition, and geographical location of the armed forces are now secret, certain facts did emerge from the President's message to Congress on the national budget for the fiscal year 1951–1952.[16] The proposed military expenditures anticipated an eventual active armed force of 3.5 million men, with 2 million more available from the National Guard and

---

[16] Reprinted in full in the New York *Times,* January 16, 1951. Figures are approximate and subject to change by Congress.

Army, Naval, and Air Force Reserves. Included in military planning were: 84 air wings; reactivation of fleet units to bring the number of ships in service to 1100; new Marine divisions; expanded training facilities for the Army; and an annual production capacity for tanks and planes of 35,000 and 50,000 respectively. Important items in this budget were $1.3 billion for stockpiling strategic materials and $1 billion for weapon research and development. (It should be noted that it was estimated that upwards of $2 billion would be expended on atomic weapons quite apart from the military budget.) These figures represented a great increase in the size and cost of the military establishment over the previous year and were necessitated both by American participation in the United Nations police action in Korea and by the possibility of larger scale warfare to come. The total proposed military budget for 1952 was $42 billion or 58 cents of every budget dollar.

security planning—a summary

The whole national security organization is designed to defend the nation against sudden armed attack. It integrates domestic, foreign, and military policies. It gathers reliable intelligence and brings it together where it is most needed. It coordinates military planning with national resources and capabilities, this process being one in which resources are translated into strategic plans, and from plans into military requirements.

Accomplishments under the National Security Act of 1947 listed by the Secretary of Defense in 1949 suggest the main trends in American security planning—trends which are likely to continue unless the international situation changes greatly. (1) Long-range and short-range strategic plans have been formulated by the Joint Chiefs of Staff. (2) The military establishment rests upon an integrated budget. (3) The roles and missions of the Army, Navy, and Air Force have been coordinated. (4) "A fair margin of superiority in practically every technical area of weapon development" has been maintained. (5) A thoroughgoing study of the problem of civil defense has been made. (6) Unified commands have been established in all overseas theaters. (7) The Military Liaison Committee to the Atomic Energy Commission has been reorganized so that there is a civilian chairman and two members designated by each of the military departments.

the role of the military in foreign policy

The military is inevitably involved in the formation of foreign policy. The civilian expert and the military expert are joined in the same process. This is true because security is the basic objective of foreign policy, because political decisions have military implications, and because military decisions have political implications. Therefore it is not a matter of whether the military shall have *a* voice, or *no* voice, but what *kind* of voice.

A proper division of labor must be based upon the fact that the making of foreign policy is a political decision from which the military ought to be excluded, except possibly where the military must be relied upon for implementation. Generally speaking, the military ought to advise on the feasibility—not the desirability—of a given policy from the point of view of the force ultimately necessary to back it up. In July, 1948, it was General Lucius Clay in Germany who apparently decided, without informing the State Department, to counter the Russian blockade of Berlin. This was a political decision made by a military official. It was the wrong way to make the decision and resulted in strategy determining policy, rather than the other way around.

The problem is, then, to bring together two kinds of technicians—civilian and military—the former having supremacy under the American system. This coordination, now the function of the National Security Council, does not work automatically. In a larger sense, the problem is one of achieving a socially controlled and directed military power applied to agreed objectives, a problem which involves all phases of government: public opinion, the role of Congress, executive leadership and administration.

the United Nations—an arm of foreign policy

The United Nations is a cornerstone of American foreign policy. United States membership has led to both substantive and procedural problems. Six years of participation have seen the United States pursuing several types of policies. A systematic attempt has been made to protect the interests of small powers, notably Syria, Lebanon, Greece, and Iran. From the beginning, the Security Council has been employed as a means to check Soviet objectives. As a matter of fact, the whole organization has become an important arena of the cold war. The United States has tried to make American aims clear, and it has also thrown a spotlight on Soviet intentions in an effort to mobilize world opinion against them. In February, 1949, the Economic and Social Council brought charges that the Soviet Union was enslaving millions of laborers. The United States was able to make political capital out of the fact that the Soviet delegate had no basically effective answer to the charge. America has also argued for more broadly based membership in the United Nations, for a modification of the veto, for a strengthening of the Charter, and for improvement of rules of procedure which would make the organization more effective. In general, the United States has sought a more liberal interpretation of the Charter and the application of majority rule. The American delegation took the lead in making the General Assembly into a genuine world public forum with extensive powers of persuasion.

Problems of coordination arise. One, of course, relates to the consistency between the content of our policies in the United Nations and the content of our policies followed unilaterally, or in the Council of Foreign Ministers, or in the Atlantic Community. Obvious strains have been evident between, say, the Truman Doctrine, which is a unilateral policy, and the United Nations approach, which is a "community of interest" approach. There is a conflict between a desire or need to support friendly western European nations and the general principle of colonial trusteeship required by the Charter, as there is between a desire to have countries pursue certain policies internally as a bulwark against communism and the principle of sovereign independence of all nations embedded in the Charter.

The United Nations has become in a broad sense a policy-making process in itself, and this fact presents another problem of coordination. Participation in the various agencies of the United Nations actually constitutes an extension of the policy-making process analyzed in these chapters. American representatives in the various United Nations agencies and public opinion within the United Nations constitute another force in the shaping of American policy. Often on-the-spot decisions are made. Specific phases of American policy in regard to the international control of atomic energy have been hammered out in the many sessions of the United Nations Atomic Energy Commission. It was once thought that modern communications, together with multilateral negotiation in the United Nations, would eliminate the old practice of diplomats' either taking serious risks within their instructions or having to wait for new instructions. On the contrary, the problem is more acute than ever. Several times the American representative during the heated debates in the Security Council has literally made policy on his feet. At other times, Washington agencies have made decisions apparently without being fully aware of the trend of our policy in one of the United Nations bodies: President Truman's announcement that the United States had taken over the former Japanese-mandated islands on November 7, 1946, was apparently unexpected by John Foster Dulles, the American representative on the Trusteeship Council. This episode represents a triple coordination problem: the Navy Department favored exclusive American trusteeship; the Dependent Areas group in the State Department favored complete United Nations trusteeship; and Mr. Dulles, though representing the United States, had no voice in the final decision. Finally, even as policy makers may have a foreign policy issue thrust upon them by domestic pressure groups or by members of Congress, so now unwelcome problems may arise from cases brought by some member of the United Nations. It is doubtful whether the conflict between the Indonesian Republic and the Netherlands would have been singled out for special consideration late in 1948 if the United States had had its way.

There are some eighty-eight agencies in the United Nations from the Security Council and the General Assembly on down. Many discussions, programs, and policies progress simultaneously. The multiplicity of agencies from Washington which feed instructions to the American United Nations delegations complicates matters further. It is clear that transition and adjustment in domestic procedures and processes have diminished the flexibility of American diplomacy in the United Nations.

The number of forces, persons, and agencies involved in the formation of foreign policy is imposing. The processes involved—the bringing together of opportunity, knowledge, and power to decide—are several and complex. The possible lines of growth a given policy may take are many. Consequently, serious problems grow out of America's new position in the world, and serious problems grow out of the way America adjusts to that position. The two sets of problems interact.

Aside from the overwhelming importance of change, one dominant theme which stands out in the foregoing analysis is the necessity for coordination: between President and Congress, among congressional committees, between Congress and the State Department, among party leaders, between the general public and its representatives, within the State Department, between foreign policy and military policy, and between the State Department and other agencies. This suggests that the institutional organization of foreign policy formation will remain fluid for some time to come.

No adjustments in the field of foreign policy will be perfect. They will all take time. Unfortunately they cannot be judged solely on the basis of whether they do a specific job or result in necessary decisions. The American political process does not permit all conceivable short cuts, nor does it permit putting ends before means. Furthermore, any process of policy making may produce error. Thus it would appear that judgment of present methods of conducting foreign relations ought to be based on three criteria: Are they within American traditions? Do they permit the nation to mobilize effectively its strengths and talents behind basic objectives? Do they offer minimum chances for error?

bibliographic note

A more detailed analysis of the experience and ideas upon which the recommendations of the distinguished and influential Hoover Commission were based is to be found in *The Organization of the Government for the Conduct of Foreign Affairs*, Task Force Report on Foreign Affairs, prepared by H. H. Bundy and J. G. Rogers (Washington: Government Printing Office, 1949). Commission on Organization of the Executive Branch of the Government, *Foreign Affairs: A Report to Congress* (Washington: Government Printing Office, February, 1949), Chaps. 7 and 8, contains the recommendations of the Hoover Commission for the more efficient conduct of foreign affairs (including the role of the national defense establishment) which became the basis for the reorganization of the State Department in 1949. Indispensable sources of information are Department of State, *Department of State Bulletin* (published weekly) and the *American Foreign Service Journal* (published monthly). Chapters 7–11 in L. H. Chamberlain and R. C. Snyder, *American Foreign Policy* (New York: Rinehart & Company, 1948), provide readings and original essays by the editors on the State Department, Foreign Service, the role of the military and other agencies concerned with foreign policy. J. R. Childs, *The American Foreign Service* (New York: Henry Holt and Company, 1948), presents an accurate, readable treatment of the duties and functions of American diplomatic personnel, including basic changes made by the Foreign Service Act of 1946. The best critical analysis and description of the administrative agencies which formulate and execute America foreign policy is J. L. McCamy's *The Administration of American Foreign Affairs* (New York: Alfred A. Knopf, Inc., 1950), particularly Chapters 3–6 and 8–13. Graham H. Stuart, *The Department of State* (New York: The Macmillan Company, 1949), is a thorough and scholarly historical survey of the State Department from its establishment to the present day, including a reliable, convenient summary of the changes in State Department organization and procedure since 1939. A suggestive comment on the Hoover Commission proposals on foreign affairs appears in Part V of a symposium printed in the *American Political Science Review*, XLIII (October, 1949), 966–978, by D. S. Cheever and H. F. Haviland.

the Constitution of
the United States of America*

[Preamble]

WE the People of the United States, in Order to form a more perfect Union, establish Justice, insure domestic Tranquility, provide for the common defence, promote the general Welfare, and secure the Blessings of Liberty to ourselves and our Posterity, do ordain and establish this Constitution for the United States of America.

ARTICLE I.

Section. 1.

[Legislative Powers]

All legislative Powers herein granted shall be vested in a Congress of the United States, which shall consist of a Senate and House of Representatives.

Section. 2.

[House of Representatives, How Constituted, Power of Impeachment]

The House of Representatives shall be composed of Members chosen every second Year by the People of the several States, and the Electors in each State shall have [the] Qualifications requisite for Electors of the most numerous Branch of the State Legislature.

No Person shall be a Representative who shall not have attained to the Age of twenty five Years, and been seven Years a Citizen of the United States, and who shall not when elected, be an Inhabitant of that State in which he shall be chosen.

Representatives and direct Taxes shall be apportioned among the several States which may be included within this Union, according to their respective Numbers, which shall be determined by adding to the whole Number of free Persons, including those bound to Service for a Term of Years, and excluding Indians not taxed, three fifths of all other Persons.[1] The actual Enumeration shall be made within three Years after the first Meeting

---

*This text of the Constitution is that of the literal print as found in the U. S. Constitution Sesquicentennial Commission's *History of the Formation of the Union under the Constitution*. Footnotes and material enclosed in brackets have been supplied by the editor of *The Constitution of the United States* (Library of Congress ed.: Washington: Government Printing Office, 1950), from which this version of the Constitution is taken.

[1] Modified by Amendment XIV, Section 2.

of the Congress of the United States, and within every subsequent Term of ten Years, in such Manner as they shall by Law direct. The Number of Representatives shall not exceed one for every thirty Thousand, but each State shall have at Least one Representative; and until such enumeration shall be made, the State of New Hampshire shall be entitled to chuse three, Massachusetts eight, Rhode-Island and Providence Plantations one, Connecticut five, New-York six, New Jersey four, Pennsylvania eight, Delaware one, Maryland six, Virginia ten, North Carolina five, South Carolina five, and Georgia three.

When vacancies happen in the Representation from any State, the Executive Authority thereof shall issue Writs of Election to fill such Vacancies.

The House of Representatives shall chuse their Speaker and other Officers; and shall have the sole Power of Impeachment.

Section. 3.

[*The Senate, How Constituted, Impeachment Trials*]

The Senate of the United States shall be composed of two Senators from each State, chosen by the Legislature thereof, for six Years; and each Senator shall have one Vote.

Immediately after they shall be assembled in Consequence of the first Election, they shall be divided as equally as may be into three Classes. The Seats of the Senators of the first Class shall be vacated at the Expiration of the second Year, of the second Class at the Expiration of the fourth Year, and of the third Class at the Expiration of the sixth Year, so that one third may be chosen every second Year; and if Vacancies happen by Resignation, or otherwise, during the Recess of the Legislature of any State, the Executive thereof may make temporary Appointments until the next Meeting of the Legislature, which shall then fill such Vacancies.[2]

No Person shall be a Senator who shall not have attained to the Age of thirty Years, and been nine Years a Citizen of the United States, and who shall not, when elected, be an Inhabitant of that State for which he shall be chosen.

The Vice President of the United States shall be President of the Senate, but shall have no Vote, unless they be equally divided.

The Senate shall chuse their other Officers, and also a President pro tempore, in the Absence of the Vice President, or when he shall exercise the Office of President of the United States.

The Senate shall have the sole Power to try all Impeachments. When sitting for that Purpose, they shall be on Oath or Affirmation. When the President of the United States [is tried] the Chief Justice shall preside: And no Person shall be convicted without the Concurrence of two thirds of the Members present.

Judgment in Cases of Impeachment shall not extend further than to removal from Office, and disqualification to hold and enjoy any Office of honor, Trust or Profit under the United States: but the Party convicted shall nevertheless be liable and subject to Indictment, Trial, Judgment and Punishment, according to Law.

Section. 4.

[*Election of Senators and Representatives*]

The Times, Places and Manner of holding Elections for Senators and Representatives, shall be prescribed in each State by the Legislature thereof; but the Congress may at any time by Law make or alter such Regulations, except as to the Places of chusing Senators.

The Congress shall assemble at least once in every Year, and such Meeting shall be on the first Monday in December, unless they shall by Law appoint a different Day.[3]

---

[2] Provisions changed by Amendment XVII.

[3] Provision changed by Amendment XX, Section 2.

Section. 5.

[*Quorum, Journals, Meetings, Adjournments*]

Each House shall be the Judge of the Elections, Returns and Qualifications of its own Members, and a Majority of each shall constitute a Quorum to do Business; but a smaller Number may adjourn from day to day, and may be authorized to compel the Attendance of absent Members, in such Manner, and under such Penalties as each House may provide.

Each House may determine the Rules of its Proceedings, punish its Members for disorderly Behaviour, and, with the Concurrence of two thirds, expel a Member.

Each House shall keep a Journal of its Proceedings, and from time to time publish the same, excepting such Parts as may in their Judgment require Secrecy; and the Yeas and Nays of the Members of either House on any question shall, at the Desire of one fifth of those Present, be entered on the Journal.

Neither House, during the Session of Congress, shall, without the Consent of the other, adjourn for more than three days, nor to any other Place than that in which the two Houses shall be sitting.

Section. 6.

[*Compensation, Privileges, Disabilities*]

The Senators and Representatives shall receive a Compensation for their Services, to be ascertained by Law, and paid out of the Treasury of the United States. They shall in all Cases, except Treason, Felony and Breach of the Peace, be privileged from Arrest during their Attendance at the Session of their respective Houses, and in going to and returning from the same; and for any Speech or Debate in either House, they shall not be questioned in any other Place.

No Senator or Representative shall, during the Time for which he was elected, be appointed to any civil Office under the Authority of the United States, which shall have been created, or the Emoluments whereof shall have been encreased during such time; and no Person holding any Office under the United States, shall be a Member of either House during his Continuance in Office.

Section. 7.

[*Procedure in Passing Bills and Resolutions*]

All Bills for raising Revenue shall originate in the House of Representatives; but the Senate may propose or concur with Amendments as on other Bills.

Every Bill which shall have passed the House of Representatives and the Senate, shall, before it become a Law, be presented to the President of the United States; If he approve he shall sign it, but if not he shall return it, with his Objections to that House in which it shall have originated, who shall enter the Objections at large on their Journal, and proceed to reconsider it. If after such Reconsideration two thirds of that House shall agree to pass the Bill, it shall be sent, together with the Objections, to the other House, by which it shall likewise be reconsidered, and if approved by two thirds of that House, it shall become a Law. But in all such Cases the Votes of both Houses shall be determined by yeas and Nays, and the Names of the Persons voting for and against the Bill shall be entered on the Journal of each House respectively. If any Bill shall not be returned by the President within ten Days (Sundays excepted) after it shall have been presented to him, the Same shall be a Law, in like Manner as if he had signed it, unless the Congress by their Adjournment prevent its Return, in which Case it shall not be a Law.

Every Order, Resolution, or Vote to which the Concurrence of the Senate and House of Representatives may be necessary (except on a question of Adjournment) shall be presented to the President of the United States; and before the Same shall take Effect, shall be approved by him, or being disapproved by him, shall be repassed by two thirds of the

Senate and House of Representatives, according to the Rules and Limitations prescribed in the Case of a Bill.

Section. 8.

[Powers of Congress]

The Congress shall have the Power To lay and collect Taxes, Duties, Imposts and Excises, to pay the Debts and provide for the common Defence and general Welfare of the United States; but all Duties, Imposts and Excises shall be uniform throughout the United States;

To borrow Money on the credit of the United States;

To regulate Commerce with foreign Nations and among the several States, and with the Indian Tribes;

To establish an uniform Rule of Naturalization, and uniform Laws on the subject of Bankruptcies throughout the United States;

To coin Money, regulate the Value thereof, and of foreign Coin, and fix the Standard of Weights and Measures;

To provide for the Punishment of counterfeiting the Securities and current Coin of the United States;

To establish Post Offices and post Roads;

To promote the Progress of Science and useful Arts, by securing for limited Times to Authors and Inventors the exclusive Right to their respective Writings and Discoveries;

To constitute Tribunals inferior to the supreme Court;

To define and punish Piracies and Felonies committed on the high Seas, and Offences against the Law of Nations;

To declare War, grant Letters of Marque and Reprisal, and make Rules concerning Captures on Land and Water;

To raise and support Armies, but no Appropriation of Money to that Use shall be for a longer Term than two Years;

To provide and maintain a Navy;

To make Rules for the Government and Regulation of the land and naval Forces;

To provide for calling forth the Militia to execute the Laws of the Union, suppress Insurrections and repel Invasions;

To provide for organizing, arming, and disciplining, the Militia, and for governing such Part of them as may be employed in the Service of the United States, reserving to the States respectively, the Appointment of the Officers, and the Authority of training the Militia according to the discipline prescribed by Congress;

To exercise exclusive Legislation in all Cases whatsoever, over such District (not exceeding ten Miles square) as may, by Cession of particular States, and the Acceptance of Congress, become the Seat of the Government of the United States, and to exercise like Authority over all Places purchased by the Consent of the Legislature of the State in which the Same shall be, for the Erection of Forts, Magazines, Arsenals, dock-Yards, and other needful Buildings;—And

To make all Laws which shall be necessary and proper for carrying into Execution the foregoing Powers, and all other Powers vested by this Constitution in the Government of the United States. or in any Deparmetnt or Officer thereof.

Section. 9.

[Limitations upon Powers of Congress]

The Migration or Importation of such Persons as any of the States now existing shall think proper to admit, shall not be prohibited by the Congress prior to the Year one thousand eight hundred and eight, but a Tax or duty may be imposed on such Importation, not exceeding ten dollars for each Person.

The Privilege of the Writ of Habeas Corpus shall not be suspended, unless when in Cases of Rebellion or Invasion the public Safety may require it.

No Bill of Attainder or ex post facto Law shall be passed.

No Capitation, or other direct, Tax shall be laid, unless in Proportion to the Census or Enumeration herein before directed to be taken.

No Tax or Duty shall be laid on Articles exported from any State.

No Preference shall be given by any Regulation of Commerce or Revenue to the Ports of one State over those of another: nor shall Vessels bound to, or from, one State, be obliged to enter, clear, or pay Duties in another.

No Money shall be drawn from the Treasury, but in Consequence of Appropriations made by Law; and a regular Statement and Account of the Receipts and Expenditures of all public Money shall be published from time to time.

No Title of Nobility shall be granted by the United States: And no Person holding any Office of Profit or Trust under them, shall, without the Consent of the Congress, accept of any present, Emolument, Office, or Title, of any kind whatever, from any King, Prince, or foreign State.

Section. 10.

[Restrictions upon Powers of States]

No State shall enter into any Treaty, Alliance, or Confederation; grant Letters of Marque and Reprisal; coin Money; emit Bills of Credit; make any Thing but gold and silver Coin a Tender in Payment of Debts; pass any Bill of Attainder, ex post facto Law, or Law impairing the Obligation of Contracts, or grant any Title of Nobility.

No State shall, without the Consent of [the] Congress, lay any Imposts or Duties on Imports or Exports, except what may be absolutely necessary for executing it's inspection Laws: and the net Produce of all Duties and Imposts, laid by any State on Imports or Exports, shall be for the Use of the Treasury of the United States; and all such Laws shall be subject to the Revision and Controul of [the] Congress.

No State shall, without the Consent of Congress, lay any Duty of Tonnage, keep Troops, or Ships of War in time of Peace, enter into any Agreement or Compact with another State, or with a foreign Power, or engage in War, unless actually invaded, or in such imminent Danger as will not admit of delay.

ARTICLE. II.

Section. 1.

[Executive Power, Election, Qualifications of the President]

The executive Power shall be vested in a President of the United States of America. He shall hold his Office during the Term of four Years, and, together with the Vice President, chosen for the same Term, be elected, as follows:

Each State shall appoint, in such Manner as the Legislature thereof may direct, a Number of Electors, equal to the whole Number of Senators and Representatives to which the State may be entitled in the Congress: but no Senator or Representative, or Person holding an Office of Trust or Profit under the United States, shall be appointed an Elector.

The Electors shall meet in their respective States, and vote by Ballot for two Persons, of whom one at least shall not be an Inhabitant of the same State with themselves. And they shall make a List of all the Persons voted for, and of the Number of Votes for each; which List they shall sign and certify, and transmit sealed to the Seat of the Government of the United States, directed to the President of the Senate. The President of the Senate shall, in the Presence of the Senate and House of Representatives, open all the Certificates, and the Votes shall then be counted. The Person having the greatest Number of Votes shall be the President, if such Number be a Majority of the whole Number of Electors appointed; and if there be more than one who have such Majority, and have an equal Number of Votes, then the House of Representatives shall immediately chuse by Ballot one of them for President; and if no Person have a Majority, then from the five highest on the List the said House shall in like Manner chuse the President. But in chusing the President, the Votes shall be taken by States, the Representation from each State having one Vote; A quorum for this Purpose shall consist of a Member or Members from two thirds of the States, and a Majority of all the States shall be necessary to a Choice. In every Case, after the Choice of the President, the Person having the greatest Number of Votes of the Electors shall be the Vice President. But if there should remain two or more who have equal Votes, the Senate shall chuse from them by Ballot the Vice President.[4]

The Congress may determine the Time of chusing the Electors, and the Day on which they shall give their Votes; which Day shall be the same throughout the United States.

No Person except a natural born Citizen, or a Citizen of the United States, at the time of the Adoption of this Constitution, shall be eligible to the Office of President; neither shall any Person be eligible to that Office who shall not have attained to the Age of thirty five Years, and been fourteen Years a Resident within the United States.

In Case of the Removal of the President from Office, or of his Death, Resignation, or Inability to discharge the Powers and Duties of the said Office, the Same shall devolve on the Vice President, and the Congress may by Law provide for the Case of Removal, Death, Resignation or Inability, both of the President and Vice President, declaring what Officer shall then act as President, and such Officer shall act accordingly, until the Disability be removed, or a President shall be elected.

The President shall, at stated Times, receive for his Services, a Compensation, which shall neither be encreased nor diminished during the Period for which he shall have been elected, and he shall not receive within that Period any other Emolument from the United States, or any of them.

Before he enter on the Execution of his Office, he shall take the following Oath or Affirmation:—"I do solemnly swear (or affirm) that I will faithfully execute the Office of President of the United States, and will to the best of my Ability, preserve, protect and defend the Constitution of the United States."

Section. 2.

[*Powers of the President*]

The President shall be Commander in Chief of the Army and Navy of the United States, and of the Militia of the several States, when called into the actual Service of the United States; he may require the Opinion, in writing, of the principal Officer in each of the executive Departments, upon any Subject relating to the Duties of their respective Offices, and he shall have Power to grant Reprieves and Pardons for Offences against the United States, except in Cases of Impeachment.

He shall have Power, by and with the Advice and Consent of the Senate, to make Treaties, provided two thirds of the Senators present concur; and he shall nominate, and by and with the Advice and Consent of the Senate, shall appoint Ambassadors, other public Ministers and Consuls, Judges of the supreme Court, and all other Officers of the United States, whose Appointments are not herein otherwise provided for, and which shall be established by Law: but the Congress may by Law vest the Appointment of such inferior Officers, as they think proper in the President alone, in the Courts of Law, or in the Heads of Departments.

The President shall have Power to fill up all Vacancies that may happen during the Recess of the Senate, by granting Commissions which shall expire at the End of their next Session.

---

[4] Provisions superseded by Amendment XII.

Section. 3.

[*Powers and Duties of the President*]

He shall from time to time give to the Congress Information of the State of the Union, and recommend to their Consideration such Measures as he shall judge necessary and expedient; he may, on extraordinary Occasions, convene both Houses, or either of them, and in Case of Disagreement between them, with Respect to the Time of Adjournment, he may adjourn them to such Time as he shall think proper; he shall receive Ambassadors and other public Ministers; he shall take Care that the Laws be faithfully executed, and shall Commission all the Officers of the United States.

Section. 4.

[*Impeachment*]

The President, Vice President and all civil Officers of the United States, shall be removed from Office on Impeachment for, and Conviction of, Treason, Bribery, or other high Crimes and Misdemeanors.

ARTICLE. III.

Section. 1.

[*Judicial Power, Tenure of Office*]

The judicial Power of the United States, shall be vested in one supreme Court, and in such inferior Courts as the Congress may from time to time ordain and establish. The Judges, both of the supreme and inferior Courts, shall hold their Offices during good Behaviour, and shall, at stated Times, receive for their Services, a Compensation, which shall not be diminished during their Continuance in Office.

Section. 2.

[*Jurisdiction*]

The judicial Power shall extend to all Cases, in Law and Equity, arising under this Constitution, the Laws of the United States, and Treaties made, or which shall be made, under their Authority;—to all Cases affecting Ambassadors, other public Ministers and Consuls;—to all Cases of admiralty and maritime Jurisdiction;—to Controversies to which the United States shall be a Party;—to Controversies between two or more States;—between a State and Citizens of another State;— between Citizens of different States,—between Citizens of the same State claiming Lands under Grants of different States, and between a State, or the Citizens thereof, and foreign States, Citizens or Subjects.[5]

In all Cases affecting Ambassadors, other public Ministers and Consuls, and those in which a State shall be Party, the supreme Court shall have original Jurisdiction. In all the other Cases before mentioned, the supreme Court shall have appellate Jurisdiction, both as to Law and Fact, with such Exceptions, and under such Regulations as the Congress shall make.

The Trial of all Crimes, except in Cases of Impeachment, shall be by Jury; and such Trial shall be held in the State where the said Crimes shall have been committed; but when not committed within any State, the Trial shall be at such Place or Places as the Congress may by Law have directed.

---

[5] Clause changed by Amendment XI.

Section. 3.

[*Treason, Proof and Punishment*]

Treason against the United States, shall consist only in levying War against them, or in adhering to their Enemies, giving them Aid and Comfort. No Person shall be convicted of Treason unless on the Testimony of two Witnesses to the same overt Act, or on Confession in open Court.

The Congress shall have Power to declare the Punishment of Treason, but no Attainder of Treason shall work Corruption of Blood, or Forfeiture except during the Life of the Person attainted.

ARTICLE. IV.

Section. 1.

[*Faith and Credit among States*]

Full Faith and Credit shall be given in each State to the public Acts, Records, and judicial Proceedings of every other State. And the Congress may by general Laws prescribe the Manner in which such Acts, Records and Proceedings shall be proved, and the Effect thereof.

Section. 2.

[*Privileges and Immunities, Fugitives*]

The Citizens of each State shall be entitled to all Privileges and Immunities of Citizens in the several States.

A Person charged in any State with Treason, Felony, or other Crime, who shall flee from Justice, and be found in another State, shall on Demand of the executive Authority of the State from which he fled, be delivered up, to be removed to the State having Jurisdiction of the Crime.

No Person held to Service or Labour in one State, under the Laws thereof, escaping into another, shall, in Consequence of any Law or Regulation therein, be discharged from such Service or Labour, but shall be delivered up on Claim of the Party to whom such Service or Labour may be due.

Section. 3.

[*Admission of New States*]

New States may be admitted by the Congress into this Union; but no new State shall be formed or erected within the Jurisdiction of any other State; nor any State be formed by the Junction of two or more States, or Parts of States, without the Consent of the Legislatures of the States concerned as well as of the Congress.

The Congress shall have Power to dispose of and make all needful Rules and Regulations respecting the Territory or other Property belonging to the United States; and nothing in this Constitution shall be so construed as to Prejudice any Claims of the United States, or of any particular State.

Section. 4.

[*Guarantee of Republican Government*]

The United States shall guarantee to every State in this Union a Republican Form of Government, and shall protect each of them against Invasion; and on Application of the Legislature, or of the Executive (when the Legislature cannot be convened) against domestic Violence.

ARTICLE. V.

[*Amendment of the Constitution*]

The Congress, whenever two thirds of both Houses shall deem it necessary, shall propose Amendments to this Constitution, or, on the Application of the Legislatures of two thirds of the several States, shall call a Convention for proposing Amendments, which, in either Case, shall be valid to all Intents and Purposes, as Part of this Constitution, when ratified by the Legislatures of three fourths of the several States, or by Conventions in three fourths thereof, as the one or the other Mode of Ratification may be proposed by the Congress; Provided that no Amendment which may be made prior to the Year One thousand eight hundred and eight shall in any Manner affect the first and fourth Clauses in the Ninth Section of the first Article; and that no State, without its Consent, shall be deprived of its equal Suffrage in the Senate.

ARTICLE. VI.

[*Debts, Supremacy, Oath*]

All Debts contracted and Engagements entered into, before the Adoption of this Constitution, shall be as valid against the United States under this Constitution, as under the Confederation.

This Constitution, and the Laws of the United States which shall be made in Pursuance thereof; and all Treaties made, or which shall be made, under the Authority of the United States, shall be the supreme Law of the Land; and the Judges in every State shall be bound thereby, any Thing in the Constitution or Laws of any State to the Contrary notwithstanding.

The Senators and Representatives before mentioned, and the Members of the several State Legislatures, and all executive and judicial Officers, both of the United States and of the several States, shall be bound by Oath or Affirmation, to support this Constitution; but no religious Test shall ever be required as a Qualification to any Office or public Trust under the United States.

ARTICLE. VII.

[*Ratification and Establishment*]

The Ratification of the Conventions of nine States, shall be sufficient for the Establishment of this Constitution between the States so ratifying the Same.

done in Convention by the Unanimous Consent of the States present the Seventeenth Day of September in the Year of our Lord one thousand seven hundred and Eighty seven and of the Independence of the United States of America the Twelfth[6] In witness whereof We have hereunto subscribed our Names,

GEORGE WASHINGTON—President
and deputy from Virginia

New Hampshire { JOHN LANGDON
NICHOLAS GILMAN }

Massachusetts { NATHANIEL GORHAM
RUFUS KING

---

[6] The Constitution was submitted on September 17, 1787, by the Constitutional Convention, was ratified by the conventions of several states at various dates up to May 29, 1790, and became effective on March 4, 1789.

Connecticut	{ WM SAML JOHNSON { ROGER SHERMAN
New York . . .	ALEXANDER HAMILTON
New Jersey	{ WIL: LIVINGSTON { DAVID BREARLEY. { WM PATERSON. { JONA: DAYTON
Pensylvania	{ B FRANKLIN { THOMAS MIFFLIN { ROBT MORRIS { GEO. CLYMER { THOS. FITZSIMONS { JARED INGERSOLL { JAMES WILSON { GOUV MORRIS
Delaware	{ GEO: READ { GUNNING BEDFORD jun { JOHN DICKINSON { RICHARD BASSETT { JACO: BROOM
Maryland	{ JAMES MCHENRY { DAN OF ST THOS. JENIFER { DANL CARROLL
Virginia	{ JOHN BLAIR— { JAMES MADISON JR.
North Carolina	{ WM BLOUNT { RICHD DOBBS SPAIGHT. { HU WILLIAMSON
South Carolina	{ J. RUTLEDGE { CHARLES COTESWORTH PINCKNEY { CHARLES PINCKNEY { PIERCE BUTLER
Georgia	{ WILLIAM FEW { ABR BALDWIN

Amendments to the Constitution 1791–1933

[AMENDMENT I]

[*Freedom of Religion, of Speech, and of the Press*]

Congress shall make no law respecting an establishment of religion, or prohibiting the free exercise thereof; or abridging the freedom of speech, or of the press; or the right of the people peaceably to assemble, and to petition the Government for a redress of grievances.

[Amendment II]

[*Right to Keep and Bear Arms*]

A well regulated Militia being necessary to the security of a free State, the right of the people to keep and bear Arms, shall not be infringed.

[Amendment III]

[*Quartering of Soldiers*]

No Soldier shall, in time of peace be quartered in any house, without the consent of the Owner, nor in time of war, but in a manner to be prescribed by law.

[Amendment IV]

[*Security from Unwarrantable Search and Seizure*]

The right of the people to be secure in their persons, houses, papers, and effects, against unreasonable searches and seizures, shall not be violated, and no Warrants shall issue, but upon probable cause, supported by Oath or affirmation, and particularly describing the place to be searched, and the persons or things to be seized.

[Amendment V]

[*Rights of Accused in Criminal Proceedings*]

No person shall be held to answer for a capital, or otherwise infamous crime, unless on a presentment or indictment of a Grand Jury, except in cases arising in the land or naval forces, or in the Militia, when in actual service in time of War or public danger; nor shall any person be subject for the same offense to be twice put in jeopardy of life or limb; nor shall be compelled in any criminal case to be a witness against himself, nor be deprived of life, liberty, or property, without due process of law; nor shall private property be taken for public use, without just compensation.

[Amendment VI]

[*Right to Speedy Trial, Witnesses, etc.*]

In all criminal prosecutions, the accused shall enjoy the right to a speedy and public trial, by an impartial jury of the State and district wherein the crime shall have been committed, which district shall have been previously ascertained by law, and to be informed of the nature and cause of the accusation; to be confronted with the witnesses against him; to have compulsory process for obtaining witnesses in his favor, and to have the Assistance of Counsel for his defence.

[Amendment VII]

[*Trial by Jury in Civil Cases*]

In Suits at common law, where the value in controversy shall exceed twenty dollars, the right of trial by jury shall be preserved, and no fact tried by a jury, shall be otherwise reexamined in any Court of the United States, than according to the rules of the common law.

[Amendment VIII]

[*Bails, Fines, Punishments*]

Excessive bail shall not be required, nor excessive fines imposed, nor cruel and unusual punishments inflicted.

[AMENDMENT IX]

[Reservation of Rights of the People]

The enumeration in the Constitution, of certain rights, shall not be construed to deny or disparage others retained by the people.

[AMENDMENT X]

[Powers Reserved to States or People]

The powers not delegated to the United States by the Constitution, nor prohibited by it to the States, are reserved to the States respectively, or to the people.[7]

[AMENDMENT XI]

[Restriction of Judicial Power]

The Judicial power of the United States shall not be construed to extend to any suit in law or equity, commenced or prosecuted against one of the United States by Citizens of another State, or by Citizens or Subjects of any Foreign State.[8]

[AMENDMENT XII]

[Election of President and Vice-President]

The Electors shall meet in their respective states, and vote by ballot for President and Vice-President, one of whom, at least, shall not be an inhabitant of the same state with themselves; they shall name in their ballots the person voted for as President, and in distinct ballots the person voted for as Vice-President and they shall make distinct lists of all persons voted for as President, and of all persons voted for as Vice-President, and of the number of votes for each, which lists they shall sign and certify, and transmit sealed to the seat of the government of the United States, directed to the President of the Senate;— The President of the Senate shall, in the presence of the Senate and House of Representatives, open all the certificates and the votes shall then be counted;—The person having the greatest number of votes for President, shall be the President, if such number be a majority of the whole number of Electors appointed; and if no person have such majority, then from the persons having the highest numbers not exceeding three on the list of those voted for as President, the House of Representatives shall choose immediately, by ballot, the President. But in choosing the President, the votes shall be taken by states, the representation from each state having one vote; a quorum for this purpose shall consist of a member or members from two-thirds of the states, and a majority of all the states shall be necessary to a choice. And if the House of Representatives shall not choose a President whenever the right of choice shall devolve upon them, before the fourth day of March next following, then the Vice-President shall act as President, as in the case of the death or other constitutional disability of the President.—The person having the greatest number of votes as Vice-President, shall be the Vice-President, if such number be a majority of the whole number of Electors appointed, and if no person have a majority, then from the two highest numbers on the list, the Senate shall choose the Vice-President; a quorum for the purpose shall consist of two-thirds of the whole number of Senators, and a majority of the whole number shall be necessary to a choice. But no person constitutionally ineligible to the office of President shall be eligible to that of Vice-President of the United States.[9]

---

[7] The first ten amendments were all proposed by Congress on September 25, 1789; ratified and adoption certified on December 15, 1791.

[8] Proposed by Congress on March 4, 1794; declared ratified on January 8, 1798.

[9] Proposed by Congress on December 9, 1803; declared ratified on September 25, 1804; supplemented by Amendment XX.

[Amendment XIII]

Section 1.

[*Abolition of Slavery*]

Neither slavery nor involuntary servitude, except as a punishment for crime whereof the party shall have been duly convicted, shall exist within the United States, or any place subject to their jurisdiction.

Section 2.

[*Power to Enforce This Article*]

Congress shall have power to enforce this article by appropriate legislation.[10]

[Amendment XIV]

Section 1.

[*Citizenship Rights Not to Be Abridged by States*]

All persons born or naturalized in the United States, and subject to the jurisdiction thereof, are citizens of the United States and of the State wherein they reside. No State shall make or enforce any law which shall abridge the privileges or immunities of citizens of the United States; nor shall any State deprive any person of life, liberty, or property, without due process of law; nor deny to any person within its jurisdiction the equal protection of the laws.

Section 2.

[*Apportionment of Representatives in Congress*]

Representatives shall be apportioned among the several States according to their respective numbers, counting the whole number of persons in each State, excluding Indians not taxed. But when the right to vote at any election for the choice of electors for President and Vice-President of the United States, Representatives in Congress, the Executive and Judicial officers of a State, or the members of the Legislature thereof, is denied to any of the male inhabitants of such State, being twenty-one years of age, and citizens of the United States, or in any way abridged, except for participation in rebellion, or other crime, the basis of representation therein shall be reduced in the proportion which the number of such male citizens shall bear to the whole number of male citizens twenty-one years of age in such State.

Section 3.

[*Persons Disqualified from Holding Office*]

No person shall be a Senator or Representative in Congress, or elector of President and Vice-President, or hold any office, civil or military, under the United States, or under any State, who, having previously taken an oath, as a member of Congress, or as an officer of the United States, or as a member of any State legislature, or as an executive or judicial officer of any State, to support the Constitution of the United States, shall have engaged in insurrection or rebellion against the same, or given aid or comfort to the enemies thereof. But Congress may by a vote of two-thirds of each House, remove such disability.

Section 4.

[*What Public Debts Are Valid*]

The validity of the public debt of the United States, authorized by law, including debts incurred for payment of pensions and bounties for services in suppressing insurrection or

---

[10] Proposed by Congress on January 31, 1865; declared ratified on December 18, 1865.

rebellion, shall not be questioned. But neither the United States nor any State shall assume or pay any debt or obligation incurred in aid of insurrection or rebellion against the United States, or any claim for the loss or emancipation of any slave; but all such debts, obligations and claims shall be held illegal and void.

Section 5.
[*Power to Enforce This Article*]

The Congress shall have power to enforce, by appropriate legislation, the provisions of this article.[11]

[AMENDMENT XV]

Section 1.
[*Negro Suffrage*]

The right of citizens of the United States to vote shall not be denied or abridged by the United States or by any State on account of race, color, or previous condition of servitude.

Section 2.
[*Power to Enforce This Article*]

The Congress shall have power to enforce this article by appropriate legislation.[12]

[AMENDMENT XVI]

[*Authorizing Income Taxes*]

The Congress shall have power to lay and collect taxes on incomes, from whatever source derived, without apportionment among the several States, and without regard to any census or enumeration.[13]

[AMENDMENT XVII]

[*Popular Election of Senators*]

The Senate of the United States shall be composed of two Senators from each State, elected by the people thereof, for six years; and each Senator shall have one vote. The electors in each State shall have the qualifications requisite for electors of the most numerous branch of the State legislatures.

When vacancies happen in the representation of any State in the Senate, the executive authority of such State shall issue writs of election to fill such vacancies: *Provided*, That the legislature of any State may empower the executive thereof to make temporary appointments until the people fill the vacancies by election as the legislature may direct.

This amendment shall not be so construed as to affect the election or term of any Senator chosen before it becomes valid as part of the Constitution.[14]

[AMENDMENT XVIII]

Section 1.
[*National Liquor Prohibition*]

After one year from the ratification of this article the manufacture, sale, or transportation of intoxicating liquors within, the importation thereof into, or the exportation thereof

---

[11] Proposed by Congress on June 13, 1866; declared ratified on July 28, 1868.
[12] Proposed by Congress on February 26, 1869; declared ratified on March 30, 1870.
[13] Proposed by Congress on July 12, 1909; declared ratified on February 25, 1913.
[14] Proposed by Congress on May 13, 1912; declared ratified on May 31, 1913.

from the United States and all territory subject to the jurisdiction thereof for beverage purposes is hereby prohibited.

Section 2.
[*Power to Enforce This Article*]

The Congress and the several States shall have concurrent power to enforce this article by appropriate legislation.

Section 3.
[*Ratification within Seven Years*]

This article shall be inoperative unless it shall have been ratified as an amendment to the Constitution by the legislatures of the several States, as provided in the Constitution, within seven years from the date of the submission hereof to the States by the Congress.[15]

[AMENDMENT XIX]
[*Woman Suffrage*]

The right of citizens of the United States to vote shall not be denied or abridged by the United States or by any State on account of sex.

Congress shall have power to enforce this article by appropriate legislation.[16]

[AMENDMENT XX]
Section 1.
[*Terms of Office*]

The terms of the President and Vice President shall end at noon on the 20th day of January, and the terms of Senators and Representatives at noon on the 3d day of January, of the years in which such terms would have ended if this article had not been ratified; and the terms of their successors shall then begin.

Section 2.
[*Time of Convening Congress*]

The Congress shall assemble at least once in every year, and such meeting shall begin at noon on the 3d day of January, unless they shall by law appoint a different day.

Section 3.
[*Death of President Elect*]

If, at the time fixed for the beginning of the term of the President, the President elect shall have died, the Vice President elect shall become President. If a President shall not have been chosen before the time fixed for the beginning of his term, or if the President elect shall have failed to qualify, then the Vice President elect shall act as President until a President shall have qualified; and the Congress may by law provide for the case wherein neither a President elect nor a Vice President elect shall have qualified, declaring who shall then act as President, or the manner in which one who is to act shall be selected, and such person shall act accordingly until a President or Vice President shall have qualified.

---

[15] Proposed by Congress on December 18, 1917; declared ratified on January 29, 1919. Repealed by Amendment XXI.

[16] Proposed by Congress on June 4, 1919; declared ratified on August 26, 1920.

Section 4.

[*Election of the President*]

The Congress may by law provide for the case of the death of any of the persons from whom the House of Representatives may choose a President whenever the right of choice shall have devolved upon them, and for the case of the death of any of the persons from whom the Senate may choose a Vice President whenever the right of choice shall have devolved upon them.

Section 5.

Sections 1 and 2 shall take effect on the 15th day of October following the ratification of this article.

Section 6.

This article shall be inoperative unless it shall have been ratified as an amendment to the Constitution by the legislatures of three-fourths of the several States within seven years from the date of its submission.[17]

[AMENDMENT XXI]

Section 1.

[*National Liquor Prohibition Repealed*]

The eighteenth article of amendment to the Constitution of the United States is hereby repealed.

Section 2.

[*Transportation of Liquor into "Dry" States*]

The transportation or importation into any States, Territory, or possession of the United States for delivery or use therein of intoxicating liquors, in violation of the laws thereof, is hereby prohibited.

Section 3.

This article shall be inoperative unless it shall have been ratified as an amendment to the Constitution by conventions in the several States, as provided in the Constitution, within seven years from the date of the submission hereof to the States by the Congress.[18]

[AMENDMENT XXII]

Section 1.

No person shall be elected to the office of the President more than twice, and no person who has held the office of President, or acted as President for more than two years of a term to which some other person was elected President shall be elected to the office of the President more than once. But this Article shall not apply to any person holding the office of President when this Article was proposed by the Congress, and shall not prevent any person who may be holding the office of President, or acting as President, during the term within which this Article becomes operative from holding the office of President, or acting as President during the remainder of such term.

Section 2.

This Article shall be inoperative unless it shall have been ratified as an amendment to the Constitution by the legislatures of three-fourths of the several States within seven years from the date of its submission to the States by the Congress.[19]

---

[17] Proposed by Congress on March 2, 1932; declared ratified on February 6, 1933.

[18] Proposed by Congress on February 20, 1933; declared ratified on December 5, 1933.

[19] Proposed by Congress on March 21, 1947; declared ratified on February 26, 1951.

Charter of
the United Nations

$\mathscr{W}$e the peoples of the United Nations determined to save succeeding generations from the scourge of war, which twice in our lifetime has brought untold sorrow to mankind, and to reaffirm faith in fundamental human rights, in the dignity and worth of the human person, in the equal rights of men and women and of nations large and small, and to establish conditions under which justice and respect for the obligations arising from treaties and other sources of international law can be maintained, and to promote social progress and better standards of life in larger freedom, *and for these ends* to practice tolerance and live together in peace with one another as good neighbors, and to unite our strength to maintain international peace and security, and to ensure, by the acceptance of principles and the institution of methods, that armed force shall not be used, save in the common interest, and to employ international machinery for the promotion of the economic and social advancement of all peoples, *have resolved to combine our efforts to accomplish these aims.*

Accordingly, our respective Governments, through representatives assembled in the city of San Francisco, who have exhibited their full powers found to be in good and due form, have agreed to the present Charter of the United Nations and do hereby establish an international organization to be known as the United Nations.

CHAPTER I

PURPOSES AND PRINCIPLES

Article 1

The Purposes of the United Nations are:

1. To maintain international peace and security, and to that end: to take effective collective measures for the prevention and removal of threats to the peace, and for the suppression of acts of aggression or other breaches of the peace, and to bring about by peaceful means, and in conformity with the principles of justice and international law, adjustment or settlement of international disputes or situations which might lead to breach of the peace;

2. To develop friendly relations among nations based on respect for the principle of equal rights and self-determination of peoples, and to take other appropriate measures to strengthen universal peace;

3. To achieve international cooperation in solving international problems of an economic, social, cultural, or humanitarian character, and in promoting and encouraging respect for human rights and for fundamental freedoms for all without distinction as to race, sex, language, or religion; and

4. To be a center for harmonizing the actions of nations in the attainment of these common ends.

Article 2

The Organization and its Members, in pursuit of the Purposes stated in Article 1, shall act in accordance with the following Principles.

1. The Organization is based on the principle of the sovereign equality of all its Members.

2. All Members, in order to ensure to all of them the rights and benefits resulting from membership, shall fulfil in good faith the obligations assumed by them in accordance with the present Charter.

3. All Members shall settle their international disputes by peaceful means in such a manner that international peace and security, and justice, are not endangered.

4. All Members shall refrain in their international relations from the threat or use of force against the territorial integrity or political independence of any state, or in any other manner inconsistent with the Purposes of the United Nations.

5. All Members shall give the United Nations every assistance in any action it takes in accordance with the present Charter, and shall refrain from giving assistance to any state against which the United Nations is taking preventive or enforcement action.

6. The Organization shall ensure that states which are not Members of the United Nations act in accordance with these Principles so far as may be necessary for the maintenance of international peace and security.

7. Nothing contained in the present Charter shall authorize the United Nations to intervene in matters which are essentially within the domestic jurisdiction of any state or shall require the Members to submit such matters to settlement under the present Charter; but this principle shall not prejudice the application of enforcement measures under Chapter VII.

CHAPTER II

MEMBERSHIP

Article 3

The original Members of the United Nations shall be the states which, having participated in the United Nations Conference on International Organization at San Francisco, or having previously signed the Declaration by United Nations of January 1, 1942, sign the present Charter and ratify it in accordance with Article 110.

Article 4

1. Membership in the United Nations is open to all other peace-loving states which accept the obligations contained in the present Charter and, in the judgment of the Organization, are able and willing to carry out these obligations.

2. The admission of any such state to membership in the United Nations will be effected by a decision of the General Assembly upon the recommendation of the Security Council.

Article 5

A Member of the United Nations against which preventive or enforcement action has been taken by the Security Council may be suspended from the exercise of the rights and privileges of membership by the General Assembly upon the recommendation of the Security Council. The exercise of these rights and privilges may be restored by the Security Council.

Article 6

A Member of the United Nations which has persistently violated the Principles contained in the present Charter may be expelled from the Organization by the General Assembly upon the recommendation of the Security Council.

CHAPTER III

ORGANS

Article 7

1. There are established as the principal organs of the United Nations: a General Assembly, a Security Council, an Economic and Social Council, a Trusteeship Council, an International Court of Justice, and a Secretariat.

2. Such subsidiary organs as may be found necessary may be established in accordance with the present Charter.

Article 8

The United Nations shall place no restrictions on the eligibility of men and women to participate in any capacity and under conditions of equality in its principal and subsidiary organs.

CHAPTER IV

THE GENERAL ASSEMBLY

COMPOSITION

Article 9

1. The General Assembly shall consist of all the Members of the United Nations.
2. Each Member shall have not more than five representatives in the General Assembly.

FUNCTIONS AND POWERS

Article 10

The General Assembly may discuss any questions or any matters within the scope of the present Charter or relating to the powers and functions of any organs provided for in the present Charter, and, except as provided in Article 12, may make recommendations to the Members of the United Nations or to the Security Council or to both on any such questions or matters.

Article 11

1. The General Assembly may consider the general principles of cooperation in the maintenance of international peace and security, including the principles governing disarmament and the regulation of armaments, and may make recommendations with regard to such principles to the Members or to the Security Council or to both.

2. The General Assembly may discuss any questions relating to the maintenance of international peace and security brought before it by any Member of the United Nations, or by the Security Council, or by a state which is not a Member of the United Nations in accordance with Article 35, paragraph 2, and, except as provided in Article 12, may make recommendations with regard to any such questions to the state or states concerned or to the Security Council or to both. Any such question on which action is necessary shall be referred to the Security Council by the General Assembly either before or after discussion.

3. The General Assembly may call the attention of the Security Council to situations which are likely to endanger international peace and security.

4. The powers of the General Assembly set forth in this Article shall not limit the general scope of Article 10.

Article 12

1. While the Security Council is exercising in respect of any dispute or situation the functions assigned to it in the present Charter, the General Assembly shall not make any recommendation with regard to that dispute or situation unless the Security Council so requests.

2.   The Secretary-General, with the consent of the Security Council, shall notify the General Assembly at each session of any matters relative to the maintenance of international peace and security which are being dealt with by the Security Council and shall similarly notify the General Assembly, or the Members of the United Nations if the General Assembly is not in session, immediately the Security Council ceases to deal with such matters.

Article 13

1.   The General Assembly shall initiate studies and make recommendations for the purpose of:
   a.   promoting international cooperation in the political field and encouraging the progressive development of international law and its codification;
   b.   promoting international cooperation in the economic, social, cultural, educational, and health fields, and assisting in the realization of human rights and fundamental freedoms for all without distinction as to race, sex, language, or religion.
2.   The further responsibilities, functions, and powers of the General Assembly with respect to matters mentioned in paragraph 1 (b) above are set forth in Chapters IX and X.

Article 14

Subject to the provisions of Article 12, the General Assembly may recommend measures for the peaceful adjustment of any situation, regardless of origin, which it deems likely to impair the general welfare or friendly relations among nations, including situations resulting from a violation of the provisions of the present Charter setting forth the Purposes and Principles of the United Nations.

Article 15

1.   The General Assembly shall receive and consider annual and special reports from the Security Council; these reports shall include an account of the measures that the Security Council has decided upon or taken to maintain international peace and security.
2.   The General Assembly shall receive and consider reports from the other organs of the United Nations.

Article 16

The General Assembly shall perform such functions with respect to the international trusteeship system as are assigned to it under Chapters XII and XIII, including the approval of the trusteeship agreements for areas not designated as strategic.

Article 17

1.   The General Assembly shall consider and approve the budget of the Organization.
2.   The expenses of the Organization shall be borne by the Members as apportioned by the General Assembly.
3.   The General Assembly shall consider and approve any financial and budgetary arrangements with specialized agencies referred to in Article 57 and shall examine the administrative budgets of such specialized agencies with a view to making recommendations to the agencies concerned.

VOTING

Article 18

1.   Each member of the General Assembly shall have one vote.
2.   Decisions of the General Assembly on important questions shall be made by a two-thirds majority of the members present and voting.   These questions shall include: recommendations with respect to the maintenance of international peace and security, the election of the non-permanent members of the Security Council, the election of the members of the Economic and Social Council, the election of members of the Trusteeship

Council in accordance with paragraph 1 (c) of Article 86, the admission of new Members to the United Nations, the suspension of the rights and privileges of membership, the expulsion of Members, questions relating to the operation of the trusteeship system, and budgetary questions.

3. Decisions on other questions, including the determination of additional categories of questions to be decided by a two-thirds majority, shall be made by a majority of the members present and voting.

Article 19

A Member of the United Nations which is in arrears in the payment of its financial contributions to the Organization shall have no vote in the General Assembly if the amount of its arrears equals or exceeds the amount of the contributions due from it for the preceding two full years. The General Assembly may, nevertheless, permit such a Member to vote if it is satisfied that the failure to pay is due to conditions beyond the control of the Member.

PROCEDURE

Article 20

The General Assembly shall meet in regular annual sessions and in such special sessions as occasion may require. Special sessions shall be convoked by the Secretary-General at the request of the Security Council or of a majority of the Members of the United Nations.

Article 21

The General Assembly shall adopt its own rules of procedure. It shall elect its President for each session.

Article 22

The General Assembly may establish such subsidiary organs as it deems necessary for the performance of its functions.

CHAPTER V

THE SECURITY COUNCIL

COMPOSITION

Article 23

1. The Security Council shall consist of eleven Members of the United Nations. The Republic of China, France, the Union of Soviet Socialist Republics, the United Kingdom of Great Britain and Northern Ireland, and the United States of America shall be permanent members of the Security Council. The General Assembly shall elect six other Members of the United Nations to be non-permanent members of the Security Council, due regard being specially paid, in the first instance to the contribution of Members of the United Nations to the maintenance of international peace and security and to the other purposes of the Organization, and also to equitable geographical distribution.

2. The non-permanent members of the Security Council shall be elected for a term of two years. In the first election of the non-permanent members, however, three shall be chosen for a term of one year. A retiring member shall not be eligible for immediate re-election.

3. Each member of the Security Council shall have one representative.

FUNCTIONS AND POWERS

Article 24

1. In order to ensure prompt and effective action by the United Nations, its Members confer on the Security Council primary responsibility for the maintenance of international

peace and security, and agree that in carrying out its duties under this responsibility the Security Council acts on their behalf.

2. In discharging these duties the Security Council shall act in accordance with the Purposes and Principles of the United Nations.   The Specific powers granted to the Security Council for the discharge of these duties are laid down in Chapters VI, VII, VIII, and XII.

3. The Security Council shall submit annual and, when necessary, special reports to the General Assembly for its consideration.

Article 25

The Members of the United Nations agree to accept and carry out the decisions of the Security Council in accordance with the present Charter.

Article 26

In order to promote the establishment and maintenance of international peace and security with the least diversion for armaments of the world's human and economic resources, the Security Council shall be responsible for formulating, with the assistance of the Military Staff Committee referred to in Article 47, plans to be submitted to the Members of the United Nations for the establishment of a system for the regulation of armaments.

VOTING

Article 27

1. Each member of the Security Council shall have one vote.

2. Decisions of the Security Council on procedural matters shall be made by an affirmative vote of seven members.

3. Decisions of the Security Council on all other matters shall be made by an affirmative vote of seven members including the concurring votes of the permanent members; provided that, in decisions under Chapter VI, and under paragraph 3 of Article 52, a party to a dispute shall abstain from voting.

PROCEDURE

Article 28

1. The Security Council shall be so organized as to be able to function continuously. Each member of the Security Council shall for this purpose be represented at all times at the seat of the Organization.

2. The Security Council shall hold periodic meetings at which each of its members may, if it so desires, be represented by a member of the government or by some other specially designated representative.

3. The Security Council may hold meetings at such places other than the seat of the Organization as in its judgment will best facilitate its work.

Article 29

The Security Council may establish such subsidiary organs as it deems necessary for the performance of its functions.

Article 30

The Security Council shall adopt its own rules of procedure, including the method of selecting its President.

Article 31

Any Member of the United Nations which is not a member of the Security Council may participate, without vote, in the discussion of any question brought before the Security Council whenever the latter considers that the interests of that Member are specially affected.

Article 32

Any Member of the United Nations which is not a member of the Security Council or any state which is not a Member of the United Nations, if it is a party to a dispute under consideration by the Security Council, shall be invited to participate, without vote, in the discussion relating to the dispute. The Security Council shall lay down such conditions as it deems just for the participation of a state which is not a Member of the United Nations.

CHAPTER VI
PACIFIC SETTLEMENT OF DISPUTES
Article 33

1. The parties to any dispute, the continuance of which is likely to endanger the maintenance of international peace and security, shall, first of all, seek a solution by negotiation, enquiry, mediation, conciliation, arbitration, judicial settlement, resort to regional agencies or arrangements, or other peaceful means of their own choice.

2. The Security Council shall, when it deems necessary, call upon the parties to settle their dispute by such means.

Article 34

The Security Council may investigate any dispute, or any situation which might lead to international friction or give rise to a dispute, in order to determine whether the continuance of the dispute or situation is likely to endanger the maintenance of international peace and security.

Article 35

1. Any Member of the United Nations may bring any dispute, or any situation of the nature referred to in Article 34, to the attention of the Security Council or of the General Assembly.

2. A state which is not a member of the United Nations may bring to the attention of the Security Council or of the General Assembly any dispute to which it is a party if it accepts in advance, for the purposes of the dispute, the obligations of pacific settlement provided in the present Charter.

3. The proceedings of the General Assembly in respect of matters brought to its attention under this Article will be subject to the provisions of Articles 11 and 12.

Article 36

1. The Security Council may, at any stage of a dispute of the nature referred to in Article 33 or of a situation of like nature, recommend appropriate procedures or methods of adjustment.

2. The Security Council should take into consideration any procedures for the settlement of the dispute which have already been adopted by the parties.

3. In making recommendations under this Article the Security Council should also take into consideration that legal disputes should as a general rule be referred by the parties to the International Court of Justice in accordance with the provisions of the Statute of the Court.

Article 37

1. Should the parties to a dispute of the nature referred to in Article 33 fail to settle it by the means indicated in that Article, they shall refer it to the Security Council.

2. If the Security Council deems that the continuance of the dispute is in fact likely to endanger the maintenance of international peace and security, it shall decide whether to take action under Article 36 or to recommend such terms of settlement as it may consider appropriate.

Article 38

Without prejudice to the provisions of Articles 33 to 37, the Security Council may, if all the parties to any dispute so request, make recommendations to the parties with a view to a pacific settlement of the dispute.

CHAPTER VII

ACTION WITH RESPECT TO THREATS TO THE PEACE, BREACHES OF THE PEACE, AND ACTS OF AGGRESSION

Article 39

The Security Council shall determine the existence of any threat to the peace, breach of the peace, or act of aggression and shall make recommendations, or decide what measures shall be taken in accordance with Articles 41 and 42, to maintain or restore international peace and security.

Article 40

In order to prevent an aggravation of the situation, the Security Council may, before making the recommendations or deciding upon the measures provided for in Article 39, call upon the parties concerned to comply with such provisional measures as it deems necessary or desirable. Such provisional measures shall be without prejudice to the rights, claims, or position of the parties concerned. The Security Council shall duly take account of failure to comply with such provisional measures.

Article 41

The Security Council may decide what measures not involving the use of armed force are to be employed to give effect to its decisions, and it may call upon the Members of the United Nations to apply such measures. These may include complete or partial interruption of economic relations and of rail, sea, air, postal, telegraphic, radio, and other means of communication, and the severance of diplomatic relations.

Article 42

Should the Security Council consider that measures provided for in Article 41 would be inadequate or have proved to be inadequate, it may take such action by air, sea, or land forces as may be necessary to maintain or restore international peace and security. Such action may include demonstrations, blockade, and other operations by air, sea, or land forces of Members of the United Nations.

Article 43

1. All Members of the United Nations, in order to contribute to the maintenance of international peace and security, undertake to make available to the Security Council, on its call and in accordance with a special agreement or agreements, armed forces, assistance, and facilities, including rights of passage, necessary for the purpose of maintaining international peace and security.

2. Such agreement or agreements shall govern the numbers and types of forces, their degree of readiness and general location, and the nature of the facilities and assistance to be provided.

3. The agreement or agreements shall be negotiated as soon as possible on the initiative of the Security Council. They shall be concluded between the Security Council and Members or between the Security Council and groups of Members and shall be subject to ratification by the signatory states in accordance with their respective constitutional processes.

Article 44

When the Security Council has decided to use force it shall, before calling upon a Member not represented on it to provide armed forces in fulfillment of the obligations assumed under Article 43, invite that Member, if the Member so desires, to participate in the decisions of the Security Council concerning the employment of contingents of that Member's armed forces.

Article 45

In order to enable the United Nations to take urgent military measures, Members shall hold immediately available national air-force contingents for combined international enforcement action. The strength and degree of readiness of these contingents and plans for their combined action shall be determined, within the limits laid down in the special agreement or agreements referred to in Article 43, by the Security Council with the assistance of the Military Staff Committee.

Article 46

Plans for the application of armed force shall be made by the Security Council with the assistance of the Military Staff Committee.

Article 47

1. There shall be established a Military Staff Committee to advise and assist the Security Council on all questions relating to the Security Council's military requirements for the maintenance of international peace and security, the employment and command of forces placed at its disposal, the regulation of armaments, and possible disarmament.

2. The Military Staff Committee shall consist of the Chiefs of Staff of the permanent members of the Security Council or their representatives. Any Member of the United Nations not permanently represented on the Committee shall be invited by the Committee to be associated with it when the efficient discharge of the Committee's responsibilities requires the participation of that Member in its work.

3. The Military Staff Committee shall be responsible under the Security Council for the strategic direction of any armed forces placed at the disposal of the Security Council. Questions relating to the command of such forces shall be worked out subsequently.

4. The Military Staff Committee, with the authorization of the Security Council and after consultation with appropriate regional agencies, may establish regional sub-committees.

Article 48

1. The action required to carry out the decisions of the Security Council for the maintenance of international peace and security shall be taken by all the Members of the United Nations or by some of them, as the Security Council may determine.

2. Such decisions shall be carried out by the Members of the United Nations directly and through their action in the appropriate international agencies of which they are members.

Article 49

The Members of the United Nations shall join in affording mutual assistance in carrying out the measures decided upon by the Security Council.

Article 50

If preventive or enforcement measures against any state are taken by the Security Council, any other state, whether a Member of the United Nations or not, which finds itself confronted with special economic problems arising from the carrying out of those measures shall have the right to consult the Security Council with regard to a solution of those problems.

Article 51

Nothing in the present Charter shall impair the inherent right of individual or collective self-defense if an armed attack occurs against a Member of the United Nations, until the Security Council has taken the measures necessary to maintain international peace and security. Measures taken by Members in the exercise of this right of self-defense shall be immediately reported to the Security Council and shall not in any way affect the authority and responsibility of the Security Council under the present Charter to take at any time such action as it deems necessary in order to maintain or restore international peace and security.

CHAPTER VIII

REGIONAL ARRANGEMENTS

Article 52

1. Nothing in the present Charter precludes the existence of regional arrangements or agencies for dealing with such matters relating to the maintenance of international peace and security as are appropriate for regional action, provided that such arrangements or agencies and their activities are consistent with the Purposes and Principles of the United Nations.

2. The Members of the United Nations entering into such arrangements or constituting such agencies shall make every effort to achieve pacific settlement of local disputes through such regional arrangements or by such regional agencies before referring them to the Security Council.

3. The Security Council shall encourage the development of pacific settlement of local disputes through such regional arrangements or by such regional agencies either on the initiative of the states concerned or by reference from the Security Council.

4. This Article in no way impairs the application of Articles 34 and 35.

Article 53

1. The Security Council shall, where appropriate, utilize such regional arrangements or agencies for enforcement action under its authority. But no enforcement action shall be taken under regional arrangements or by regional agencies without the authorization of the Security Council, with the exception of measures against any enemy state, as defined in paragraph 2 of this Article, provided for pursuant to Article 107 or in regional arrangements directed against renewal of aggressive policy on the part of any such state, until such time as the Organization may, on request of the Governments concerned, be charged with the responsibility for preventing further aggression by such a state.

2. The term enemy state as used in paragraph 1 of this Article applies to any state which during the Second World War has been an enemy of any signatory of the present Charter.

Article 54

The Security Council shall at all times be kept fully informed of activities undertaken or in contemplation under regional arrangements or by regional agencies for the maintenance of international peace and security.

CHAPTER IX

INTERNATIONAL ECONOMIC AND SOCIAL COOPERATION

Article 55

With a view to the creation of conditions of stability and well-being which are necessary for peaceful and friendly relations among nations based on respect for the principle of equal rights and self-determination of peoples, the United Nations shall promote:

a. higher standards of living, full employment, and conditions of economic and social progress and development;

b. solutions of international economic, social, health, and related problems; and international cultural and educational cooperation; and

c. universal respect for, and observance of, human rights and fundamental freedoms for all without distinction as to race, sex, language, or religion.

Article 56

All Members pledge themselves to take joint and separate action in cooperation with the Organization for the achievement of the purposes set forth in Article 55.

Article 57

1. The various specialized agencies, established by intergovernmental agreement and having wide international responsibilities, as defined in their basic instruments, in economic, social, cultural, educational, health, and related fields, shall be brought into relationship with the United Nations in accordance with the provisions of Article 63.

2. Such agencies thus brought into relationship with the United Nations are hereinafter referred to as specialized agencies.

Article 58

The Organization shall make recommendations for the coordination of the policies and activities of the specialized agencies.

Article 59

The Organization shall, where appropriate, initiate negotiations among the states concerned for the creation of any new specialized agencies required for the accomplishment of the purposes set forth in Article 55.

Article 60

Responsibility for the discharge of the functions of the Organization set forth in this Chapter shall be vested in the General Assembly and, under the authority of the General Assembly, in the Economic and Social Council, which shall have for this purpose the powers set forth in Chapter X.

CHAPTER X

THE ECONOMIC AND SOCIAL COUNCIL

COMPOSITION

Article 61

1. The Economic and Social Council shall consist of eighteen Members of the United Nations elected by the General Assembly.

2. Subject to the provisions of paragraph 3, six members of the Economic and Social Council shall be elected each year for a term of three years. A retiring member shall be eligible for immediate re-election.

3. At the first election, eighteen members of the Economic and Social Council shall be chosen. The term of office of six members so chosen shall expire at the end of one year, and of six other members at the end of two years, in accordance with arrangements made by the General Assembly.

4. Each member of the Economic and Social Council shall have one representative.

FUNCTIONS AND POWERS

Article 62

1. The Economic and Social Council may make or initiate studies and reports with respect to international economic, social, cultural, educational, health, and related matters and may make recommendations with respect to any such matters to the General Assembly, to the Members of the United Nations, and to the specialized agencies concerned.

2. It may make recommendations for the purpose of promoting respect for, and observance of, human rights and fundamental freedoms for all.

3. It may prepare draft conventions for submission to the General Assembly, with respect to matters falling within its competence.

4. It may call, in accordance with the rules prescribed by the United Nations, international conferences on matters falling within its competence.

Article 63

1. The Economic and Social Council may enter into agreements with any of the agencies referred to in Article 57, defining the terms on which the agency concerned shall be brought into relationship with the United Nations. Such agreements shall be subject to approval by the General Assembly.

2. It may coordinate the activities of the specialized agencies through consultation with and recommendations to such agencies and through recommendations to the General Assembly and to the Members of the United Nations.

Article 64

1. The Economic and Social Council may take appropriate steps to obtain regular reports from the specialized agencies. It may make arrangements with the Members of the United Nations and with the specialized agencies to obtain reports on the steps taken to give effect to its own recommendations and to recommendations on matters falling within its competence made by the General Assembly.

2. It may communicate its observations on these reports to the General Assembly.

Article 65

The Economic and Social Council may furnish information to the Security Council and shall assist the Security Council upon its request.

Article 66

1. The Economic and Social Council shall perform such functions as fall within its competence in connection with the carrying out of the recommendations of the General Assembly.

2. It may, with the approval of the General Assembly, perform services at the request of Members of the United Nations and at the request of specialized agencies.

3. It shall perform such other functions as are specified elsewhere in the present Charter or as may be assigned to it by the General Assembly.

Voting

Article 67

1. Each member of the Economic and Social Council shall have one vote.

2. Decisions of the Economic and Social Council shall be made by a majority of the members present and voting.

Procedure

Article 68

The Economic and Social Council shall set up commissions in economic and social fields and for the promotion of human rights, and such other commissions as may be required for the performance of its functions.

Article 69

The Economic and Social Council shall invite any Member of the United Nations to participate, without vote, in its deliberations on any matter of particular concern to that Member.

Article 70

The Economic and Social Council may make arrangements for representatives of the specialized agencies to participate, without vote, in its deliberations and in those of the commissions established by it, and for its representatives to participate in the deliberations of the specialized agencies.

Article 71

The Economic and Social Council may make suitable arrangements for consultation with non-governmental organizations which are concerned with matters within its competence. Such arrangements may be made with international organizations and, where appropriate, with national organizations after consultation with the Member of the United Nations concerned.

Article 72

1. The Economic and Social Council shall adopt its own rules of procedure, including the method of selecting its President.

2. The Economic and Social Council shall meet as required in accordance with its rules, which shall include provision for the convening of meetings on the request of a majority of its members.

CHAPTER XI

DECLARATION REGARDING NON-SELF-GOVERNING TERRITORIES

Article 73

Members of the United Nations which have or assume responsibilities for the administration of territories whose peoples have not yet attained a full measure of self-government recognize the principle that the interests of the inhabitants of these territories are paramount, and accept as a sacred trust the obligation to promote to the utmost, within the system of international peace and security established by the present Charter, the well-being of the inhabitants of these territories, and, to this end:

a. to ensure, with due respect for the culture of the peoples concerned, their political, economic, social, and educational advancement, their just treatment, and their protection against abuses;

b. to develop self-government, to take due account of the political aspirations of the peoples, and to assist them in the progressive development of their free political institutions, according to the particular circumstances of each territory and its peoples and their varying stages of advancement;

c. to further international peace and security;

d. to promote constructive measures of development, to encourage research, and to cooperate with one another and, when and where appropriate, with specialized international bodies with a view to the practical achievement of the social, economic, and scientific purposes set forth in this Article; and

e. to transmit regularly to the Secretary-General for information purposes, subject to such limitation as security and constitutional considerations may require, statistical and other information of a technical nature relating to economic, social, and educational conditions in the territories for which they are respectively responsible other than those territories to which Chapters XII and XIII apply.

Article 74

Members of the United Nations also agree that their policy in respect of the territories to which this Chapter applies, no less than in respect of their metropolitan areas, must be based on the general principle of good-neighborliness, due account being taken of the interests and well-being of the rest of the world, in social, economic, and commercial matters.

CHAPTER XII

INTERNATIONAL TRUSTEESHIP SYSTEM

Article 75

The United Nations shall establish under its authority an international trusteeship system for the administration and supervision of such territories as may be placed thereunder by subsequent individual agreements. These territories are hereinafter referred to as trust territories.

Article 76

The basic objectives of the trusteeship system, in accordance with the Purposes of the United Nations laid down in Article 1 of the present Charter, shall be:

a. to further international peace and security;

b. to promote the political, economic, social, and educational advancement of the inhabitants of the trust territories, and their progressive development towards self-government or independence as may be appropriate to the particular circumstances of each territory and its peoples and the freely expressed wishes of the peoples concerned, and as may be provided by the terms of each trusteeship agreement;

c. to encourage respect for human rights and for fundamental freedoms for all without distinction as to race, sex, language, or religion, and to encourage recognition of the interdependence of the peoples of the world; and

d. to ensure equal treatment in social, economic, and commercial matters for all Members of the United Nations and their nationals, and also equal treatment for the latter in the administration of justice, without prejudice to the attainment of the foregoing objectives and subject to the provisions of Article 80.

Article 77

1. The trusteeship system shall apply to such territories in the following categories as may be placed thereunder by means of trusteeship agreements:

a. territories now held under mandate;

b. territories which may be detached from enemy states as a result of the Second World War; and

c. territories voluntarily placed under the system by states responsible for their administration.

2. It will be a matter for subsequent agreement as to which territories in the foregoing categories will be brought under the trusteeship system and upon what terms.

Article 78

The trusteeship system shall not apply to territories which have become Members of the United Nations, relationship among which shall be based on respect for the principle of sovereign equality.

Article 79

The terms of trusteeship for each territory to be placed under the trusteeship system, including any alteration or amendment, shall be agreed upon by the states directly concerned, including the mandatory power in the case of territories held under mandate by a Member of the United Nations, and shall be approved as provided for in Articles 83 and 85.

Article 80

1. Except as may be agreed upon in individual trusteeship agreements, made under Articles 77, 79, and 81, placing each territory under the trusteeship system, and until such agreements have been concluded, nothing in this Chapter shall be construed in or of itself to alter in any manner the rights whatsoever of any states or any peoples or the

terms of existing international instruments to which Members of the United Nations may respectively be parties.

2. Paragraph 1 of this Article shall not be interpreted as giving grounds for delay or postponement of the negotiation and conclusion of agreements for placing mandated and other territories under the trusteeship system as provided for in Article 77.

Article 81

The trusteeship agreement shall in each case include the terms under which the trust territory will be administered and designate the authority which will exercise the administration of the trust territory. Such authority, hereinafter called the administering authority, may be one or more states or the Organization itself.

Article 82

There may be designated, in any trusteeship agreement, a strategic area or areas which may include part or all of the trust territory to which the agreement applies, without prejudice to any special agreement or agreements made under Article 43.

Article 83

1. All functions of the United Nations relating to strategic areas, including the approval of the terms of the trusteeship agreements and of their alteration or amendment, shall be exercised by the Security Council.

2. The basic objectives set forth in Article 76 shall be applicable to the people of each strategic area.

3. The Security Council shall, subject to the provisions of the trusteeship agreements and without prejudice to security considerations, avail itself of the assistance of the Trusteeship Council to perform those functions of the United Nations under the trusteeship system relating to political, economic, social, and educational matters in the strategic areas.

Article 84

It shall be the duty of the administering authority to ensure that the trust territory shall play its part in the maintenance of international peace and security. To this end the administering authority may make use of volunteer forces, facilities, and assistance from the trust territory in carrying out the obligations towards the Security Council undertaken in this regard by the administering authority, as well as for local defense and the maintenance of law and order within the trust territory.

Article 85

1. The functions of the United Nations with regard to trusteeship agreements for all areas not designated as strategic, including the approval of the terms of the trusteeship agreements and of their alteration or amendment, shall be exercised by the General Assembly.

2. The Trusteeship Council, operating under the authority of the General Assembly, shall assist the General Assembly in carrying out these functions.

CHAPTER XIII

THE TRUSTEESHIP COUNCIL

COMPOSITION

Article 86

1. The Trusteeship Council shall consist of the following Members of the United Nations:

   a. those Members administering trust territories;

b. such of those Members mentioned by name in Article 23 as are not administering trust territories; and

c. as many other Members elected for three-year terms by the General Assembly as may be necessary to ensure that the total number of members of the Trusteeship Council is equally divided between those Members of the United Nations which administer trust territories and those which do not.

2. Each member of the Trusteeship Council shall designate one specially qualified person to represent it therein.

FUNCTIONS AND POWERS

Article 87

The General Assembly and, under its authority, the Trusteeship Council, in carrying out their functions, may:

a. consider reports submitted by the administering authority;

b. except petitions and examine them in consultation with the administering authority;

c. provide for periodic visits to the respective trust territories at times agreed upon with the administering authority; and

d. take these and other actions in conformity with the terms of the trusteeship agreements.

Article 88

The Trusteeship Council shall formulate a questionnaire on the political, economic, social, and educational advancement of the inhabitants of each trust territory, and the administering authority for each trust territory within the competence of the General Assembly shall make an annual report to the General Assembly upon the basis of such questionnaire.

VOTING

Article 89

1. Each member of the Trusteeship Council shall have one vote.

2. Decisions of the Trusteeship Council shall be made by a majority of the members present and voting.

PROCEDURE

Article 90

1. The Trusteeship Council shall adopt its own rules of procedure, including the method of selecting its President.

2. The Trusteeship Council shall meet as required in accordance with its rules, which shall include provision for the convening of meetings on the request of a majority of its members.

Article 91

The Trusteeship Council shall, when appropriate, avail itself of the assistance of the Economic and Social Council and of the specialized agencies in regard to matters with which they are respectively concerned.

CHAPTER XIV

THE INTERNATIONAL COURT OF JUSTICE

Article 92

The International Court of Justice shall be the principal judicial organ of the United Nations. It shall function in accordance with the annexed Statute, which is based upon the Statute of the Permanent Court of International Justice and forms an integral part of the present Charter.

Article 93

1. All Members of the United Nations are *ipso facto* parties to the Statute of the International Court of Justice.

2. A state which is not a Member of the United Nations may become a party to the Statute of the International Court of Justice on conditions to be determined in each case by the General Assembly upon the recommendation of the Security Council.

Article 94

1. Each Member of the United Nations undertakes to comply with the decision of the International Court of Justice in any case to which it is a party.

2. If any party to a case fails to perform the obligations incumbent upon it under a judgment rendered by the Court, the other party may have recourse to the Security Council, which may, if it deems necessary, make recommendations or decide upon measures to be taken to give effect to the judgment.

Article 95

Nothing in the present Charter shall prevent Members of the United Nations from entrusting the solution of their differences to other tribunals by virtue of agreements already in existence or which may be concluded in the future.

Article 96

1. The General Assembly or the Security Council may request the International Court of Justice to give an advisory opinion on any legal question.

2. Other organs of the United Nations and specialized agencies, which may at any time be so authorized by the General Assembly, may also request advisory opinions of the Court on legal questions arising within the scope of their activities.

CHAPTER XV

THE SECRETARIAT

Article 97

The Secretariat shall comprise a Secretary-General and such staff as the Organization may require. The Secretary-General shall be appointed by the General Assembly upon the recommendation of the Security Council. He shall be the chief administrative officer of the Organization.

Article 98

The Secretary-General shall act in that capacity in all meetings of the General Assembly, of the Security Council, of the Economic and Social Council, and of the Trusteeship Council, and shall perform such other functions as are entrusted to him by these organs. The Secretary-General shall make an annual report to the General Assembly on the work of the Organization.

Article 99

The Secretary-General may bring to the attention of the Security Council any matter which in his opinion may threaten the maintenance of international peace and security.

Article 100

1. In the performance of their duties the Secretary-General and the staff shall not seek or receive instructions from any government or from any other authority external to the Organization. They shall refrain from any action which might reflect on their position as international officials responsible only to the Organization.

2. Each Member of the United Nations undertakes to respect the exclusively international character of the responsibilities of the Secretary-General and the staff and not to seek to influence them in the discharge of their responsibilities.

Article 101

1. The staff shall be appointed by the Secretary-General under regulations established by the General Assembly.

2. Appropriate staffs shall be permanently assigned to the Economic and Social Council, the Trusteeship Council, and, as required, to other organs of the United Nations. These staffs shall form a part of the Secretariat.

3. The paramount consideration in the employment of the staff and in the determination of the conditions of service shall be the necessity of securing the highest standards of efficiency, competence, and integrity. Due regard shall be paid to the importance of recruiting the staff on as wide a geographical basis as possible.

CHAPTER XVI
MISCELLANEOUS PROVISIONS

Article 102

1. Every treaty and every international agreement entered into by any Member of the United Nations after the present Charter comes into force shall as soon as possible be registered with the Secretariat and published by it.

2. No party to any such treaty or international agreement which has not been registered in accordance with the provisions of paragraph 1 of this Article may invoke that treaty or agreement before any organ of the United Nations.

Article 103

In the event of a conflict between the obligations of the Members of the United Nations under the present Charter and their obligations under any other international agreement, their obligations under the present Charter shall prevail.

Article 104

The Organization shall enjoy in the territory of each of its Members such legal capacity as may be necessary for the exercise of its functions and the fulfillment of its purposes.

Article 105

1. The Organization shall enjoy in the territory of each of its Members such privileges and immunities as are necessary for the fulfillment of its purposes.

2. Representatives of the Members of the United Nations and officials of the Organization shall similarly enjoy such privileges and immunities as are necessary for the independent exercise of their functions in connection with the Organization.

3. The General Assembly may make recommendations with a view to determining the details of the application of paragraphs 1 and 2 of this Article or may propose conventions to the Members of the United Nations for this purpose.

CHAPTER XVII
TRANSITIONAL SECURITY ARRANGEMENTS

Article 106

Pending the coming into force of such special agreements referred to in Article 43 as in the opinion of the Security Council enable it to begin the exercise of its responsibilities under Article 42, the parties to the Four-Nation Declaration, signed at Moscow, October 30, 1943, and France, shall, in accordance with the provisions of paragraph 5 of that

Declaration, consult with one another and as occasion requires with other Members of the United Nations with a view to such joint action on behalf of the Organization as may be necessary for the purpose of maintaining international peace and security.

Article 107

Nothing in the present Charter shall invalidate or preclude action, in relation to any state which during the Second World War has been an enemy of any signatory to the present Charter, taken or authorized as a result of that war by the Governments having responsibility for such action.

CHAPTER XVIII

AMENDMENTS

Article 108

Amendments to the present Charter shall come into force for all Members of the United Nations when they have been adopted by a vote of two thirds of the members of the General Assembly and ratified in accordance with their respective constitutional processes by two thirds of the Members of the United Nations, including all the permanent members of the Security Council.

Article 109

1.   A General Conference of the Members of the United Nations for the purpose of reviewing the present Charter may be held at a date and place to be fixed by a two-thirds vote of the members of the General Assembly and by a vote of any seven members of the Security Council. Each Member of the United Nations shall have one vote in the conference.

2.   Any alteration of the present Charter recommended by a two-thirds vote of the conference shall take effect when ratified in accordance with their respective constitutional processes by two thirds of the Members of the United Nations including all the permanent members of the Security Council.

3.   If such a conference has not been held before the tenth annual session of the General Assembly following the coming into force of the present Charter, the proposal to call such a conference shall be placed on the agenda of that session of the General Assembly, and the conference shall be held if so decided by a majority vote of the members of the General Assembly and by a vote of any seven members of the Security Council.

CHAPTER XIX

RATIFICATION AND SIGNATURE

Article 110

1.   The present Charter shall be ratified by the signatory states in accordance with their respective constitutional processes.

2.   The ratifications shall be deposited with the Government of the United States of America, which shall notify all the signatory states of each deposit as well as the Secretary-General of the Organization when he has been appointed.

3.   The present Charter shall come into force upon the deposit of ratifications by the Republic of China, France, the Union of Soviet Socialist Republics, the United Kingdom of Great Britain and Northern Ireland, and the United States of America, and by a majority of the other signatory states. A protocol of the ratifications deposited shall thereupon be drawn up by the Government of the United States of America which shall communicate copies thereof to all the signatory states.

4.   The states signatory to the present Charter which ratify it after it has come into force will become original Members of the United Nations on the date of the deposit of their respective ratifications.

Article 111

The present Charter, of which the Chinese, French, Russian, English, and Spanish texts are equally authentic, shall remain deposited in the archives of the Government of the United States of America. Duly certified copies thereof shall be transmitted by that Government to the Governments of the other signatory states.

In faith whereof the representatives of the Governments of the United Nations have signed the present Charter.

Done at the city of San Francisco the twenty-sixth day of June, one thousand nine hundred and forty-five.